The *Muwatta* of Imam Muhammad

The *Muwatta* of Imam Malik ibn Anas
in the narration of
Imam Muhammad ibn al-Hasan ash-Shaybani

Turath Publishing
1425/2004

Published by: Turath Publishing
79 Mitcham Road
Tooting
London SW19 9PD
+44-20-8767-3666
www.turathpublishing.com

By: Muḥammad ibn al-Ḥasan ash-Shaybānī
Translated by: Mohammed Abdurrahman and Abdassamad Clarke
Dr. Asadullah Yate *(The science of invalidation (jarḥ) and authentication (taᶜdīl))*
General editor: Yaḥyā Batha
Editors: Mufti Zubair Ismail Bayat, Shaykh Sulaiman Gani *(Rijāl)*, Abdassamad Clarke, Uthman Ibrahim-Morisson, Safira Batha
Indexes: Muḥammad Ansa

British Library Cataloguing in Publication Data
ash-Shaybānī, Muḥammad ibn al-Ḥasan
Muwaṭṭa᾿ of Imām Muḥammad, The
I. Title

ISBN 0-9547380-0-4

Typeset by: Bookwright.
bookwright@bogvaerker.dk
www.bogvaerker.dk
Printed by: Mega Print, Istanbul, Turkey.
ahmet@mega.com.tr

Distributors: for UK and Europe
Azhar Academy
Cooks Road
London E15 2PW
+44-20-8534 9191
sales@azharacademy.com
www.azharacademy.com

Distributors for South Africa: Darul – Ihsan research and education centre
www.direct.za.org
info@direct.za.org
+27-835 939599

Distributors for America and Canada: Whitethread Press
http//whitethreadpress.com
ar@whitethreadpress.com
+1-(805) 968 4666

Distributors for Saudi Arabia: Ta-Ha Publishing Ltd.
1 Wynne Rd.
London SW9 0BB, UK
info@taha.co.uk
Tel: +44-207 737 7266

KEY TO TRANSLITERATION

ا	alif
ب	bā
ت	tā
ث	thā
ج	jīm
ح	ḥā
خ	khā
د	dāl
ذ	dhāl
ر	rā
ز	zā
س	sīn
ش	shīn
ص	ṣād
ض	ḍād
ط	ṭā
ظ	ẓā
ع	ᶜayn (indicated with a ᶜ)
غ	ghayn
ف	fā
ق	qāf
ك	kāf
ل	lām
م	mīm
ن	nūn
ه	hā
و	waw
ي	yā
ء	hamzah (indicated with a ᵓ)

Longer vowels are indicated by a stroke over the letter, e.g. ā, ī, ū and Ā, Ī, Ū.

SUMMARY TABLE OF CONTENTS

TABLE OF CONTENTS

THE MUWAṬṬAʾ

1. The Prayer

3. *Zakāh*

4. Fasting

5. Ḥajj

7. Divorce

14. Sales: Trading and Deferred Sales

THE SCIENCE OF THE INVALIDATION (JARḤ) AND AUTHENTICATION (TAʿDĪL) OF ḤADĪTH AND ITS ROLE IN THEIR PROTECTION AND PRESERVATION ...

INTRODUCTION

Shaykh ᶜAbd al-Ḥayy al-Laknawī (from *at-Taᶜlīq al-mumajjad)*

The introduction enumerates a number of key topics. These are set out below.

Topic One: How the Writing of Aḥādīth Spread

In addition to the spread of aḥādīth, this topic will also touch on how the recording of the compilations began, the distinctions between them in purpose, variations in their implementations, and explanations as to their categories and classifications.

Ḥāfiẓ Ibn Ḥajar al-ᶜAsqalānī said in *Hady as-sārī,* which is the introduction to his commentary on *Ṣaḥīḥ al-Bukhārī* known as *Fatḥ al-bārī*:

> Know – may Allah teach me and you – that the traditions of the Prophet ﷺ were not recorded in collections at the time of the Prophet ﷺ nor at the times of his Companions or of the great Followers, nor were they systematically organised, for two reasons:
>
> Firstly, because initially it had been forbidden, as is firmly established in *Ṣaḥīḥ Muslim* for fear that some of it would become mixed up with and confused with the Glorious Qurʾān.
>
> Secondly, because of the depth of their capacity for memorisation and the copiously retentive nature of their intellects, and because most of them did not know how to write.
>
> Then in the later time of the Followers (*Tābiᶜūn*) traditions began to be recorded and arranged in chapters when the people of knowledge spread in the great cities, and innovations grew numerous such as the Khawārij, the Shīᶜah and those who deny the decree. The first to gather them together was ar-Rabīᶜ ibn Ṣabīḥ, Saᶜīd ibn Abī ᶜArūbah and others. They used to compile each chapter on its own, until there appeared the major figures of the third level halfway through the second century who compiled the judgements (*aḥkām*). Imām Mālik compiled the *Muwaṭṭaʾ* intending to include exclusively the strong ḥadīth of the people of the Ḥijāz, combined with the sayings of the Companions, the Followers and those after them. Abū Muḥammad

ᶜAbd al-Mālik ibn ᶜAbd al-ᶜAzīz ibn Jurayj compiled ḥadīth in Makkah, Abū ᶜAmr ᶜAbd ar-Raḥmān al-Awzāᶜī in Shām (Syria), Abū ᶜAbdullāh Sufyān ath-Thawrī in Kūfa (ᶜIrāq), Ḥammād ibn Salamah ibn Dīnār in Baṣra (ᶜIrāq), Hāshim in Wāsiṭ, Muᶜammar in the Yemen, Ibn al-Mubārak in Khurāsān and Jarīr ibn ᶜAbd al-Ḥamīd in Ray (Bukhārā). All of these people lived at the same time, and we don't know which of them was first. Then many of their contemporaries followed them, weaving on their loom, until some of their imāms thought that they should specifically single out the ḥadīth of the Prophet ﷺ. It was at the end of the second century that they began to compile the collections called *musnad*[1]. ᶜAbdullāh ibn Mūsā al-ᶜAbsī compiled a *musnad*, then Nuᶜaym ibn Ḥammād al-Khuzāᶜī who resided in Egypt compiled a *musnad*, and then later the imāms followed in their steps in doing the same. There were very few imāms among the ḥadīth memorisers who did not compile his ḥadīth in a *musnad*, such as Imām Aḥmad ibn Ḥanbal, Isḥāq ibn Rāhwayh, ᶜUthmān ibn Abī Shaybah and others. Some of them compiled them both in chapters [according to the fiqh rulings] and as *musnads*, such as Abū Shaybah. When al-Bukhārī saw these compilations and he realised that with respect to their constitution they comprised those which are ṣaḥīḥ and ḥasan as well as many which are weak, then it moved his resolve to collect only the ṣaḥīḥ ḥadīth.

Ibn al-Athīr al-Jazarī said in the introduction to his book *Jāmiᶜ al-uṣūl;*

In compiling their collections people had very different purposes. Some confined their goal to compiling ḥadīth alone so that their wordings could be memorised and rulings derived, as did ᶜUbaydullāh ibn Mūsā al-ᶜAbsī, Abū Dāwūd aṭ-Ṭayālisī and others of the earliest imāms of ḥadīth, then came Imām Aḥmad ibn Ḥanbal and those after him. They established the ḥadīth according to the chains of transmission of their narrators, and so they would mention the ḥadīth with chains of transmission [isnād] of Abū Bakr aṣ-Ṣiddīq, for example, and they would establish under that everything that was narrated from him. Then after him, they would mention the Companions one after another in this manner. Some established the ḥadīth in the places which indicate them, putting every ḥadīth in the chapter peculiar to it. If it was about the prayer then they would mention it in the chapter on prayer, and if it was about zakāh they would mention it in the chapter on zakāh, as Mālik ibn Anas had done in the *Muwaṭṭaʾ*, except that because there were a small number of ḥadīth, then there were few chapters. Those after him modelled themselves on him. When the matter reached al-Bukhārī and Muslim and the number of ḥadīth in their books were numerous, then the chapters and their sub-divisions became numerous. Those after them modelled themselves on them. This type is simpler for searching and study than the former in two ways:

Firstly, a person may know the meaning for which he seeks the ḥadīth even if he doesn't know its narrator, nor who he might be in the *musnad*. In fact, he might not need to know the narrator at all.

Secondly, if the ḥadīth is narrated in the book on the prayer, the one who investigates it knows that this ḥadīth is the proof of that judgement on the prayer, and so he does not need to think any further about it.

Some of them narrated ḥadīth containing linguistic ambiguities and confused meanings, compiling books dedicated to this in particular in which they confined themselves to explaining the ḥadīth, commenting on their unusual linguistic features, their grammatical analysis and their meanings, leaving aside mention of the rulings. This was done, for example, by Abū ᶜUbaydah al-Qāsim ibn Sallām, ᶜAbdullāh ibn Muslim ibn Qutaybah and others. Some added to this mention of the rulings and the views of the *fuqahāʾ*, such as Abū Sulaymān Ḥamd ibn Muḥammad al-Khattābī and others. Some narrated the unusual wordings but not the actual texts of the ḥadīth, and commented on the unusual wordings without their ḥadīth as did Abū ᶜUbayd Aḥmad ibn Muḥammad al-Harawī and others. Some concentrated on narrating ḥadīth comprising stimulation of desire and longing [for the *dīn* and the Garden] and of fear [of kufr and the Fire] and aḥādīth comprising sharīᶜah rulings, and so they recorded them and narrated their texts alone, as did Abū Muḥammad al-Ḥusayn ibn Masᶜūd al-Baghawī in the book *al-Maṣābīḥ*.

Apart from these aforementioned imāms of ḥadīth, if we were to attempt to mention their books in detail and the differing purposes and goals they had in their compilations the length of such an examination would exceed all limits.

He also said a little before that:

> Islam spread, the territories expanded and the Companions dispersed into the regions. The openings to Islam were very many. Then the great majority of the Companions died and their own companions and followers separated, and exactitude became rare. Then the people of knowledge recognised the great need for recording ḥadīth and safeguarding them by writing them down. By my life! it is fundamental because the mind is forgetful and intelligence is sometimes absent, and memory flags, but the pen remembers and does not forget. Then the matter reached the time of a group of the imāms such as ᶜAbd al-Mālik ibn Jurayj and Mālik ibn Anas and others of their contemporaries. They recorded the aḥādīth, and so it is sometimes said, "The first book composed in Islam was that of Ibn Jurayj," and some said, "the *Muwaṭṭa᾽* of Mālik", and some others said, "The first man to compile and arrange according to chapters was ar-Rabīᶜ ibn Ṣabīḥ in Baṣra."
>
> Then the recording and collecting of aḥādīth and their division into sections and books spread. There was a great deal of that and it proved to be very useful, up until the time when the two imāms Abū ᶜAbdullāh Muḥammad ibn Ismāᶜīl al-Bukhārī and Abu'l-Ḥusayn Muslim ibn Ḥajjāj an-Naysābūrī compiled their two books. They established the aḥādīth that one could categorically assert are ṣaḥīḥ and whose transmission was clearly established according to them, and they called their two books *Ṣaḥīḥ* of ḥadīth, and they both applied this name to their books. The two of them were the first to have named a book like that. They told the truth in what they said and they fulfilled what they claimed, and for that reason Allah provided them good acceptance in the east and west of the earth, on land and sea, confirmation of their statements, and compliance to listening to the two books such as is obvious and does not need explanation.
>
> The spread of this type of compilation, collection and authorship increased. People's goals increasingly diverged and their purposes became varied up until the end of the age in which the two of them lived. A group of the people of knowledge had compiled and composed collections, for example Abū ᶜĪsā at-Tirmidhī, Abū Dāwūd Sulaymān ibn al-Ashᶜath as-Sijistānī, Abū ᶜAbd ar-Raḥmān Aḥmad ibn Shuᶜayb an-Nasā᾽ī and others of the innumerable people of

knowledge. That age was the quintessence of the ages in the attainment of this knowledge, and it is the ultimate limit. After it the search decreased, eagerness was less, and these concerns declined. Similarly with every type of knowledge, craftsmanship and the dynasties, etc., because they begin little by little and continue to flourish and grow and become strong until they reach their limit and their furthest possible extent. The furthest limit of this knowledge was attained in the time of al-Bukhārī and Muslim and by those who were in their epoch, then it diminished and grew less right up until this age of ours, and it will continue to grow less and the concern for it to grow smaller.

As-Suyūṭī said in his book *al-Wasāʾil ilā maᶜrifat al-awāʾil*:

The first to collect the ḥadīth was Ibn Shihāb az-Zuhrī during the khilāfah of ᶜUmar ibn ᶜAbd al-ᶜAzīz at his command, which the Ḥāfiẓ Ibn Ḥajar mentioned in the commentary on *al-Bukhārī*. Abū Nuᶜaym narrated in the *Ḥilyat al-Awliyā*ʾ that Mālik ibn Anas said, 'The first to collect the ḥadīth was Ibn Shihāb.' Mālik said in the *Muwaṭṭa*ʾ in the narration of Muḥammad ibn al-Ḥasan, "Yaḥyā ibn Saᶜīd informed us that ᶜUmar ibn ᶜAbd al-ᶜAzīz wrote to Abū Bakr ibn Muḥammad ibn ᶜAmr ibn Ḥazm, 'Look and see what there is of the ḥadīth of the Messenger of Allah ﷺ or of his Sunnah or the ḥadīth of ᶜUmar or the like of this and write it to me, because I fear the disappearance of knowledge and the departure of the people of knowledge.'"

The first to compile the ḥadīth and arrange them in chapters were Mālik in Madīnah, Ibn Jurayj in Makkah, Rabīᶜ ibn Ṣabīḥ or Saᶜīd ibn Abī ᶜArūbah or Ḥammād ibn Salamah ibn Salamah in Baṣra, Sufyān ath-Thawrī in Kūfa, al-Awzāᶜī in Shām, Hushaym in Wāsiṭ, Muᶜammar in Yemen, Jarīr ibn ᶜAbd al-Ḥamīd in Ray, and Ibn al-Mubārak in Khurāsān. The two Ḥāfiẓs Ibn Ḥajar and al-ᶜIrāqī said, "All of these were contemporaries, and no one knows which of them was first. That was some years after one hundred and forty."

The first to record exclusively aḥādīth with chains of transmission without any which stop short at Companions or with interrupted chains of transmission at the end of the second century were ᶜUbaydullāh ibn Mūsā in Kūfa, Musaddad in Baṣra, Asad ibn Mūsā al-Umawī in Egypt and Nuᶜaym ibn Ḥammād al-Khuzāᶜī. There is

> disagreement as to who of these was the first to compile aḥādīth according to their chains of transmission. Ad-Dāraquṭnī said that it was Nuᶜaym. Al-Khaṭīb said that it was Asad ibn Mūsā. Al-Ḥākim said that it was ᶜUbaydullāh. Al-ᶜUqaylī said Yaḥyā al-Ḥammānī. Ibn ᶜAdī said, "The first to compile aḥādīth according to their chains of transmission in Kūfa was ᶜUbaydullāh. Musaddad was the first to compile aḥādīth according to their chains of transmission in Baṣra. Asad was the first to compile aḥādīth according to their chains of transmission in Egypt and he was before the two of them and the earliest of them to die." The first to compile purely ṣaḥīḥ ḥadīth was al-Bukhārī, which Ibn aṣ-Ṣalāḥ mentioned, and he used the word 'purely' cautiously, which he added over and above the *Muwaṭṭa᾽* because it is also ṣaḥīḥ, but however it also comprises aḥādīth which stop short at Companions without their ascribing them to the Prophet ﷺ and ḥadīth with interrupted chains of transmission.

In *Tanwīr al-Ḥawālik ᶜalā Muwaṭṭa᾽ Mālik*, as-Suyūṭī relates the following:

> Al-Harawī narrated in *Dhamm al-Kalām* that az-Zuhrī said, "ᶜUrwah ibn az-Zubayr informed me that ᶜUmar ibn al-Khaṭṭāb wanted to record the sunnahs and he sought the advice of the Companions of the Messenger of Allah ﷺ about that. All of them gave him their advice that they were in favour of that. But ᶜUmar stayed for a month making the duᶜā called *istikhārah* – seeking Allah's choice – because he had some doubt about it. One day he awoke and Allah had made up his mind for him, and so he said, 'I had mentioned to you, as you know, about writing down the sunnahs, but then I remembered that some of the People of the Book before you had written books alongside the Book of Allah and then they had adhered to them and had abandoned the Book of Allah. I, by Allah! will not mix the Book of Allah with anything,' and so he abandoned the idea of recording the sunnahs." Ibn Saᶜd said in *aṭ-Ṭabaqāt,* "Qabīṣah ibn ᶜUqbah informed us that Sufyān narrated to us from Muᶜammar from az-Zuhrī that he said, 'ᶜUmar wanted to write down the sunnahs and so he sought Allah's choice [by means of the *istikhārah*] for a month. Then he awoke one day and He had made up his mind for him, and he said, "I remembered people who wrote a book and then they turned to it and abandoned the Book of Allah."'" Al-Harawī

narrated by way of Yaḥyā ibn Saᶜīd from ᶜAbdullāh ibn Dīnār that he said, "Neither the Companions nor the Followers used to write down ḥadīth, but they would only transmit them verbally and learn them by memorisation except for the book of *ṣadaqāt* [*zakāh*], and some small things upon which a researcher would come after going to the utmost lengths and of which he might fear the loss. Then many people of knowledge died and Amīr al-Muʾminīn ᶜUmar ibn ᶜAbd al-ᶜAzīz told Abū Bakr al-Ḥazmī in that which he wrote to him, 'Look and see what there is of the Sunnah or ḥadīth of ᶜUmar and write it down.'" Mālik said in the *Muwaṭṭaʾ*, in the narration of Muḥammad ibn al-Ḥasan, from Yaḥyā ibn Saᶜīd that ᶜUmar ibn ᶜAbd al-ᶜAzīz wrote to Abū Bakr ibn Muḥammad ibn ᶜAmr ibn Ḥazm, "Look and see what there is of the ḥadīth of the Messenger of Allah ﷺ or of his Sunnah or the like of this and write it for me, because I fear the vanishing of knowledge and the departure of the people of knowledge." Al-Bukhārī included it as an attached ḥadīth rather than one of the ḥadīth in the text in the *Ṣaḥīḥ*. Abū Nuᶜaym narrated it in *Tārīkh Aṣbahān* – The History of Isfahan – in the wording, "ᶜUmar ibn ᶜAbd al-ᶜAzīz wrote to all corners of the world, 'Look for the ḥadīth of the Messenger of Allah ﷺ and collect them.'" Ibn ᶜAbd al-Barr narrated in *at-Tamhīd* by way of Ibn Wahb that he said, "I heard Mālik saying, 'ᶜUmar ibn ᶜAbd al-ᶜAzīz used to write to the major cities teaching them the Sunnah and fiqh, and he would write to Madīnah asking them about what was the practice and that they should teach him what they had. He would write to Abū Bakr ibn ᶜAmr ibn Ḥazm telling him that he should collect the sunnahs and send them in writing to him. Then ᶜUmar died and Ibn Ḥazm had written books but had not yet sent them to him'"

In *Tanwīr al-Ḥawālik* as-Suyūṭī further relates:

Abū Ṭālib al-Makkī said in *Qūt al-qulūb* – the Nourishment of Hearts – "These book compilations came about after 120 or 130 AH, and it is also said that the first thing that was compiled in Islam was the book of Ibn Jurayj on the traditions, and some matters on commentary on the Qurʾān. Then after that there was the book of Muᶜammar ibn Rashīd aṣ-Ṣanᶜānī in the Yemen in which he compiled scattered sunnahs and arranged them in chapters, and then after that came the *Muwaṭṭaʾ*

in Madīnah by Mālik. Then Ibn ʿUyaynah compiled a comprehensive book with some tafsīr on different readings of the Qurʾān and on diverse ḥadīth. Sufyān ath-Thawrī produced his compilation in this period, but some say that it was compiled in 160 AH."

Topic Two: An Introduction to Imām Mālik

What will teach you who Imām Mālik is? He is the imām of the imāms, the leader who holds the reins, the chief of the great ones of the Abode of the Hijrah, the leader of the people of knowledge of Fragrant Madīnah, whose majestic qualities the tongue is incapable of mentioning, and whose praiseworthy merits man falls short in remembering.

Historians and scholars of ḥadīth exerted themselves fully in their works in mentioning biographical material on him and in praising him. A group of them compiled independent treatises mentioning various things about him, such as Abū Bakr Aḥmad ibn Marwān al-Mālikī ad-Dīnūrī al-Miṣrī (died 310 AH according to *Kashf aẓ-Ẓunūn ʿan Asāmī al-Kutub wa'l-Funūn*). Then there was Abu'r-Rūḥ ʿĪsā ibn Masʿūd ash-Shāfiʿī (died 774 AH), al-Jalal as-Suyūṭī ash-Shāfiʿī al-Miṣrī who compiled a treatise he called *Tazyīn al-arāʾik bi manāqib al-Imām Mālik.* Let us briefly mention here some things about him which are made clear in *Maʿdin al-yawāqīt al-multamaʿah fī manāqib al-aʾimmah al-arbiʿah* and other books by weighty members of the ummah by way of summary, otherwise the task would require several lengthy books.

Regarding his name and his lineage, he is Mālik ibn Anas ibn Mālik ibn Abī ʿĀmir ibn ʿAmr ibn al-Ḥārith ibn Ghayman – also said to be ʿUthmān – ibn Jathīl – also said to be Khathīl – ibn ʿAmr ibn al-Ḥārith al-Aṣbaḥī al-Madanī. His lineage is from Aṣbaḥ a tribe descended from Yuʿrab ibn Qaḥṭān. His great grandfather was Abū ʿĀmir, whom adh-Dhahabī mentions in the *Tajrīd aṣ-ṣaḥābah.* He said, "He lived during the time of the Prophet ﷺ and his son Mālik narrated from ʿUthmān and others."

With regard to his birth and death, al-Yāfiʿī mentions in the *Ṭabaqāt al-fuqahāʾ* that he was born in 94 AH. Ibn Khallikān and others mention that he was born in 95 AH. Some said in 99 AH, and al-Mizzī mentions in *Tahdhīb al-kamāl* that he died in 179 AH on the morning of the 14th of Rabīʿ al-Awwal. He was borne in the womb of his mother for three years and was buried in al-Baqīʿ, where his grave is visited and blessings sought by means of it.

His shaykhs and his companions are very numerous. His shaykhs include Ibrāhīm ibn Abī ᶜAblah al-Maqdisī, Ibrāhīm ibn ᶜUqbah, Jaᶜfar ibn Muḥammad aṣ-Ṣādiq, Nāfiᶜ the mawlā of Ibn ᶜUmar, Yaḥyā ibn Saᶜīd, az-Zuhrī, ᶜAbdullāh ibn Dīnār and others.

Among his pupils were Sufyān ath-Thawrī, Saᶜīd ibn Manṣūr, ᶜAbdullāh ibn al-Mubārak, ᶜAbd ar-Raḥmān al-Awzāᶜī who was older than him, Layth ibn Saᶜd who was one of his peers, Imām ash-Shāfiᶜī Muḥammad ibn Idrīs, Muḥammad ibn al-Ḥasan ash-Shaybānī and others.

People's praise of him and of his merits is enormous. Abū ᶜUmar Ibn ᶜAbd al-Barr said in *al-Ansāb*:

> Imām Mālik ibn Anas was the Imām of the Abode of the Hijrah in which the truth was victorious and the *dīn* was established, from which the other lands were opened [to Islam] and from which came uninterrupted support. He was called the Man of Knowledge of Madīnah, and his knowledge spread far and wide to all the provinces and became famous in all the other regions. People exhausted camels in journeying to him and they travelled to him from every distant road. He was appointed to teach when he was seventeen years old, and he lived for almost ninety years staying giving fatwās and teaching people for almost seventy years. The Followers bore witness to his knowledge of fiqh and ḥadīth.

It is mentioned in *ar-Rawḍ al-fāʾiq* that he is the man of knowledge whom the Prophet ﷺ indicated in the ḥadīth which at-Tirmidhī and others narrated, "Knowledge will be cut off, and there will not remain a man of knowledge more knowledgeable than the man of knowledge of Madīnah." It is stated in another ḥadīth from Abū Hurayrah, "People will soon beat the livers of their camels [in travelling] but they will not find a man of knowledge more knowledgeable than the man of knowledge of Madīnah." Sufyān ibn ᶜUyaynah said, "They used to think that it was Mālik." ᶜAbd ar-Razzāq said, "We used to think that it was Mālik, because this title is not associated with anyone other than him, and the livers of camels were not beaten [travelling] to anyone as they were beaten for his sake."

Ibn Muṣᶜab said, "I heard Mālik saying, 'I did not give *fatwā* until seventy shaykhs bore witness that I was worthy of doing so.'" Ash-Shāfiᶜī said, "If it had not been for Mālik and Sufyān the knowledge of the Ḥijāz [Makkah and Madīnah] would have gone." A man said to ash-Shāfiᶜī,

"Have you seen anyone of those whom you met who were like Mālik?" He said, "I heard some of those who preceded us in age and in knowledge saying, 'We have never seen the like of Mālik,' so how could we have seen the like of him?" Ḥammād ibn Salamah said, "If someone said, 'Choose someone for the ummah of Muḥammad ﷺ from whom they could take knowledge,' I would think Mālik ibn Anas suitable and appropriate for that." Muḥammad ibn Rabīᶜ said, "I performed the Ḥajj with my father when I was a boy. I slept in the mosque of the Messenger of Allah ﷺ and I saw the Messenger of Allah ﷺ in my sleep as if he had just come out of his grave and he was leaning on Abū Bakr and ᶜUmar. I stood up and greeted him and he returned my greeting, and so I asked, 'Messenger of Allah, where are you going?' He said, 'I am going to establish for Mālik the straight path.' Then I woke up and my father and I went to Mālik. I found people gathered around Mālik and he had brought out for them the *Muwaṭṭaʾ*." Muḥammad ibn al-Ḥakam said, "I heard Muḥammad ibn as-Sirrī saying, 'I saw the Messenger of Allah ﷺ in my sleep and I said, "Tell me some knowledge which I can narrate from you." He said, "Ibn as-Sirrī, I have brought Mālik a treasure for him to divide among you. It is the *Muwaṭṭaʾ*. After the Book of Allah and my Sunnah, in the unanimous agreement of the Muslims there is no discourse which is more sound than the *Muwaṭṭaʾ*, so listen to it and you will benefit from it."'" Yaḥyā ibn Saᶜīd said, "Among people there is no one who is more sound in ḥadīth than Mālik, then Sufyān ath-Thawrī and Ibn ᶜUyaynah." Abū Muslim al-Khuzāᶜī said, "When Mālik wished to sit [to narrate ḥadīth] he would perform wuḍūʾ as if for the prayer, dress in the best of clothing, and comb his beard. When someone asked him about that he said, 'By that I treat the ḥadīth of the Messenger of Allah ﷺ with respect.'" Ibn al-Mubārak said, "I was with Mālik and he was narrating the ḥadīth of the Messenger of Allah ﷺ to us and a scorpion bit him sixteen times, and his colour changed and his face yellowed, but he did not interrupt his discourse. When people had left I said to him, 'Today, I saw something amazing from you!' He said, 'I was patient in order to show honour to the ḥadīth of the Messenger of Allah ﷺ.'" Muṣᶜab ibn ᶜAbdullāh said, "When Mālik mentioned the Prophet ﷺ his colour would change and he would bow over. Someone asked him about that and he answered, 'If you saw what I see, you would not think it strange.'" Ibn Khallikān mentioned, "Mālik would not ride in Madīnah even though he was weak and had become aged, saying, 'I will not ride in a city in which is buried the body of the Messenger of Allah ﷺ.'"

Topic Three: the Merits of the *Muwaṭṭaʾ*, the Reason for its Name and what it Comprises

As-Suyūṭī said in *Tanwīr al-Ḥawālik*:

Qāḍī Abū Bakr ibn al-ʿArabī said in *Sharḥ at-Tirmidhī* – the Commentary on at-Tirmidhī, "The *Muwaṭṭaʾ* is the first source and core [material], and the book of al-Bukhārī is the second source in this process. On the two of them all of the rest are built, such as Muslim and at-Tirmidhī." Ibn al-Hayyāb mentioned that Mālik narrated one hundred thousand ḥadīth, of which he collected ten thousand in the *Muwaṭṭaʾ*. Then he continued to review them against the Book and the Sunnah, and test them against the traditions and reports until he had returned to using five hundred. Ilkiyā al-Harrāsī said in his appended notes on the principle sources, "The *Muwaṭṭaʾ* of Mālik used to comprise nine thousand ḥadīth, and then he continued pruning it until he had returned to using seven hundred." Abu'l-Ḥasan ibn Fihr narrated in *Faḍāʾil Mālik* – the Merits of Mālik – from ʿAtīq ibn Yaʿqūb that he said, "Mālik composed the *Muwaṭṭaʾ* with something like ten thousand ḥadīth but he continued to examine it every year and drop some out of it until this remained." Ibn ʿAbd al-Barr narrated from ʿUmar ibn ʿAbd al-Wāḥid, the friend of al-Awzāʿī, that he said, "We read out the *Muwaṭṭaʾ* to Mālik in forty days and he said, 'A book which I have composed over forty years, you have taken in forty days. How little you comprehend what is in it.'" Abū ʿAbdullāh Muḥammad ibn Ibrāhīm al-Kinānī al-Aṣfahānī said, "I said to Abū Ḥātim ar-Rāzī, 'Why was the *Muwaṭṭaʾ* of Mālik called the *Muwaṭṭaʾ*?' He said, 'It was something which he compiled and he made it easy (*waṭṭaʾa*) for people, so that people said, "The *Muwaṭṭaʾ* – [Book] made easy – of Mālik," just as they said, "The *Jāmiʿ* – Comprehensive Compilation – of Sufyān."'" Abu'l-Ḥasan ibn Fihr said, "Aḥmad ibn Ibrāhīm ibn Firās informed us, 'I heard my father saying, "I heard ʿAlī ibn Aḥmad al-Khalanjī saying, 'I heard one of the shaykhs saying, "Mālik said, 'I showed this book of mine to seventy of the *fuqahāʾ* of Madīnah and all of them agreed with me (*wāṭaʾa*) about it and so I called it the *Muwaṭṭaʾ*.'"'"'" Ibn Fihr said, "No one used this name before Mālik, because some of those who authored books in his age called them the Comprehensive (*Jāmiʿ*),

the Compilation (*Muṣannaf*), the Composition (*Muʾallaf*)." *Muwaṭṭaʾ* means that which is made easy and is pruned and trimmed of superfluous matters. In the *Qāmūs* [dictionary] it is stated that *waṭṭaʾa hu* means that "he prepared it, he made it even and soft, and he made it easy". A man in whose vicinity a man is possessed of dignity (*muwaṭṭaʾ al-aknāf*) is easy [natured], smooth, generous and hospitable, or his companion is at ease around him, his position causing him neither harm nor to recoil; and he is *muwaṭṭaʾ al-ʿaqib*, a sulṭān who is to be followed. All of these meanings are correct with respect to this name by way of metaphor.

Ibn ʿAbd al-Barr narrated from al-Mufaḍḍal ibn Muḥammad ibn Ḥarb al-Madanī that he said, "The first person in Madīnah to compile a book in the form of the *Muwaṭṭaʾ*, mentioning what the people of Madīnah agreed about, was ʿAbd al-ʿAzīz ibn ʿAbdullāh ibn Abī Salamah al-Majishun. He composed it in discourse form without any ḥadīth. It was brought to Mālik and he examined it and said, 'How excellent is what this man has done. If I had been the one who had done it, I would have begun with the traditions, and then I would have supported that with some discourse.' Then he resolved to compile the *Muwaṭṭaʾ* which he did.

"The people of knowledge who were in Madīnah at that time compiled many *Muwaṭṭas*. Someone said to Mālik, 'You have occupied yourself in producing this book and other people share with you in that and are producing the like of it.' He said, 'Bring me what they have done.' They brought them to him and he examined them and then put them away and said, 'You must know that only that by which the face of Allah is intended is raised up.' He said, 'It was as if those books had been thrown down wells.'"

Ash-Shāfiʿī said, "There is not on the face of the earth a book – after the Book of Allah – which is more sound than the book of Mālik." Ibn Fihr narrated by way of Yūnus ibn ʿAbd al-Aʿlā from him [ash-Shāfiʿī] in one wording, "No book has appeared on Earth which is closer to the Qurʾān than the book of Mālik," and in another wording, "There is not to be found on Earth – after the Book of Allah – anything more correct than the *Muwaṭṭaʾ* of Mālik," and in another wording, "There is nothing – after the Book of Allah – which is more useful than the *Muwaṭṭaʾ*." Ḥāfiẓ Mughlaṭāwī said, "The first to compile the sound [ḥadīth] was Mālik."

Ḥāfiẓ Ibn Ḥajar said, "The book of Mālik is sound according to him and according to those who model themselves on him based upon his criteria for deriving definitive arguments by means of mursal ḥadīth [those ascribed directly to the Prophet ﷺ without mentioning the Companion or Companions from whom they were heard], and ḥadīth with interrupted chains of transmission, etc. I say that the *mursal* ḥadīth which are in it, along with the fact that they are a definitive proof without any condition according to him and according to those imāms who agree with him, are also definitive proofs according to us [Shafi'i scholars] if they are supported [by other texts and arguments]. There is no *mursal* ḥadīth in the *Muwaṭṭaʾ* without one or more supporting [texts]. The unqualified truth is that all of the *Muwaṭṭaʾ* is sound without any exception. Ibn ᶜAbd al-Barr compiled a book in which he supplied chains of transmission for those [ḥadīth] in the *Muwaṭṭaʾ* which are *mursal*, whose chains of transmission are interrupted, or are problematic. He said, 'Everything that is in it such as his saying, "It has reached me..." or his saying, "...from someone who is trustworthy in my view..." those things for which he did not give a chain of transmission are in total sixty-one ḥadīth, all of which have chains of transmission by other ways than by Mālik except for four which are unknown. First, the ḥadīth, "I forget or I am made to forget in order that I may set a Sunnah"; second, that the Messenger ﷺ was shown the life-spans of the people before or whatever Allah willed of that, and it was as if his community's life-spans were too short for them to achieve work the like of that which others achieved in long life-spans, and so Allah gave him the Night of Decree"; third, the saying of Muᶜādh, "The last thing that the Messenger of Allah ﷺ advised me when I had placed my foot in the stirrup, was that he said, 'Make your character good towards people'"; fourth, "When a cloud appears from the direction of the sea and then goes towards Shām, it will be an abundant source of rain."'"

In *Siyar an-nubalāʾ* adh-Dhahabī said in his biographical notice on Shaykh Abū Muḥammad ᶜAlī ibn Aḥmad ibn Saᶜīd ibn Ḥazm ibn Ghālib ibn Ṣāliḥ, who is better known as Ibn Ḥazm aẓ-Ẓāhirī al-Andalusī al-Qurṭubī (died Shaᶜbān 456 AH), after mentioning his meritorious qualities and some of his defects:

I myself incline towards Abū Muḥammad's love of sound ḥadīth and towards his knowledge of them, even if I do not agree with a great deal of what he says about their narrators, defects in them and some of the disagreeable cases in both the principles (*uṣūl*) and derivative rulings. I categorically declare that he made errors in more than one matter, but I do not declare him a kāfir nor do I regard him as astray, and I hope that he will be shown pardon and liberal generosity, and I submit to the extraordinary abundance of his intelligence and the vastness of his knowledge. I think that he mentioned the position of those who say that the greatest of the compilations is the *Muwaṭṭaʾ*, and he said, "On the contrary, the books which have the most right to be honoured are the two sound books of al-Bukhārī and Muslim, the *Ṣaḥīḥ* of ibn as-Sakan, the *Muntaqā* of Ibn al-Jārūd, the *Muntaqā* of Qāsim ibn Aṣbagh, and then after them the book of Abū Dāwūd, the book of an-Nasāʾī, the *Muṣannaf* of al-Qāsim ibn Aṣbagh, and the *Muṣannaf* of Jaʿfar aṭ-Ṭaḥāwī..." I say that he did not mention the *Sunan* of Ibn Mājah nor the *Jāmiʿ* of Abū ʿĪsā at-Tirmidhī because he had not seen them and they had not been introduced into al-Andalus until after his death. He said, "... and the *Musnad* of al-Bazzār, the *Musnad* of Ibn Abī Shaybah, the *Musnad* of Aḥmad ibn Ḥanbal, the *Musnad* of Isḥāq, the *Musnad* of aṭ-Ṭayālisī, the *Musnad* of al-Ḥasan ibn Sufyān, the *Musnad* of Ibn Sanjār, the *Musnad* of ʿAbdullāh ibn Muḥammad al-Masnadī, the *Musnad* of Yaʿqūb ibn Shaybah, the *Musnad* of ʿAlī ibn al-Madīnī, the *Musnad* of Ibn Abī ʿUzrah, and the other books which have taken this course in only transmitting the words of the Messenger of Allah ﷺ. Then there are the books in which there are his words and others words such as the *Muṣannaf* of ʿAbd ar-Razzāq, the *Muṣannaf* of Abū Bakr ibn Abī Shaybah, the *Muṣannaf* of Baqī ibn Mukhallad, the book of Muḥammad ibn Naṣr al-Marwazī, the larger and smaller books of Ibn al-Mundhir, then the *Muṣannaf* of Ḥammād ibn Salamah, the *Muwaṭṭaʾ* of Mālik ibn Anas, the *Muwaṭṭaʾ* of Ibn Abī Dhiʾb, the *Muwaṭṭaʾ* of Ibn Wahb, the *Muṣannaf* of Wakīʿ, the *Muṣannaf* of Muḥammad ibn Yūsuf al-Firyābī, the *Muṣannaf* of Saʿīd ibn Manṣūr, the *Masāʾil* (cases) of Aḥmad, the *Fiqh* of Abū ʿUbayd, the *Fiqh* of Abū Thawr."

I say that Ibn Ḥazm was not fair. Rather the rank of the *Muwaṭṭaʾ* is that it should be mentioned right after the two *ṣaḥīḥ* books along with the *Sunan* of Abū Dāwūd and an-Nasāʾī. However, he was disciplined and gave preference to those *musnads* which are purely devoted to the prophetic ḥadīth even if the *Muwaṭṭa'* makes a definite impression on everyone and creates awe in the hearts and that nothing is equal to it.

Topic Four

It is possible that some may imagine some contradiction between what we saw previously transmitted from ash-Shāfiᶜī, that the most sound book after the Book of Allah is the *Muwaṭṭa'*, and the position of the dominant group of the scholars of ḥadīth, that the most sound book is that of al-Bukhārī, and then after that the book of Muslim, and that the highest of the ḥadīth are those on which they both agree, then those which al-Bukhārī alone transmitted, then those which Muslim alone transmitted, then those which are transmitted according to their conditions using the narrators that they accepted, then those which are transmitted according to al-Bukhārī's conditions, then those which are transmitted according to Muslim's conditions, then the rest of the sound books according to their different ranks. Some prefer *Ṣaḥīḥ Muslim* over *Ṣaḥīḥ* al-Bukhārī, but if what they mean is from the point of view of soundness then that is incorrect. If it is from some other point of view, then it is a matter which is outside of our investigation here. Ibn al-Hamām said some things in *Fatḥ al-qadīr*, the commentary on the *Hidāyah* in this area, but they were rejected after minute investigation by notable scholars. The details of this investigation are mentioned in the commentaries on the *Alfiyyah* [of as-Suyūṭī on the sciences of *aḥādīth*] and the commentaries on the commentary on *an-Nukhbah*, and in the studies of al-Labīb on *al-Uswat al-ḥasanah bi'l-ḥabīb* and his reply to that which is in *Fatḥ al-mughīth sharḥ alfiyyah al-ḥadīth* by as-Sakhāwī, and in *Tadrīb ar-rāwī sharḥ taqrīb an-Nawawī* by as-Suyūṭī. Apart from these two it is said that the saying of ash-Shāfiᶜī was before the existence of the books of al-Bukhārī and Muslim.

Ḥāfiẓ ibn Ḥajar said in the introduction to *Fatḥ al-bārī* transmitting from Ibn Ṣalāḥ's introduction:

> As for that which we narrated from ash-Shāfiᶜī that he said, "I do not know of any book of knowledge on earth which is more correct than the book of Mālik," and some of them narrate it without this wording, "...more sound than the *Muwaṭṭa'*," then he only said that before the existence of the two books of al-Bukhārī and Muslim.

> Moreover, the book of al-Bukhārī is the more sound of the two and the one which has the greater benefit.

He also said:

> Some imāms deem it dubious to categorically regard the book of al-Bukhārī as superior to that of Mālik along with their sharing the preconditions of soundness and acting with deliberation in the matter, and in going to great lengths in seeking to do what is most proper. The fact that al-Bukhārī has more ḥadīth does not necessarily require that it should be superior in terms of soundness. The answer to that is that it is interpreted according to the preconditions of soundness, because Mālik did not regard a break in the chain of transmission as a defect and so he narrated mursal ḥadīth, ḥadīth with interrupted chains of transmission, ḥadīth expressed in the manner "it has reached me that..." within the subject matter of the book, whereas al-Bukhārī regarded an interruption in the chain of transmission as a fault and so he would not narrate such a ḥadīth except outside the main body of the text, as in appended notes and introductory text. There is no doubt, even if some people accept the ḥadīth with interrupted chains of transmission as being valid proofs, that those ḥadīth with connected chains of transmission are stronger if their narrators are equal in terms of their standing as Muslims and their qualities of memory. By that the superiority of *Ṣaḥīḥ al-Bukhārī* is evident. Know that ash-Shāfiʿī only referred categorically to the superiority of the *Muwaṭṭa'* in relation to the compilations which were to be found in his time, such as the *Jāmiʿ* of Sufyān ath-Thawrī, the *Muṣannaf* of Ḥammād ibn Salamah and others, to which it is certainly superior and about that there is no argument.

Topic Five

One of the merits of the *Muwaṭṭa'* is that it contains many of the chains of transmission which the scholars of ḥadīth judge to be the most sound.

Some disagree on that, and some say that the soundest chain of transmission is that of Muḥammad ibn Muslim ibn ʿAbdullāh Ibn Shihāb az-Zuhrī from Sālim ibn ʿAbdullāh ibn ʿUmar from his father, ʿAbdullāh ibn ʿUmar ibn al-Khaṭṭāb. This is the position of Aḥmad ibn Ḥanbal and Isḥāq ibn

Rāhwayh, which Ibn aṣ-Ṣalāḥ declared openly. Some said that the soundest is Muḥammad ibn Sīrīn from ᶜAbīdah ibn ᶜAmr as-Salmānī from ᶜAlī ibn Abī Ṭālib. This was the opinion of ᶜAlī ibn al-Madīnī and ᶜAmr ibn ᶜAlī al-Fallās. Some said that the most sound is Ibrāhīm an-Nakhaᶜī from ᶜAlqamah from ᶜAbdullāh ibn Masᶜūd. This was the position ofYaḥyā ibn Maᶜīn and an-Nasāʾī. Some preferred az-Zuhrī from Zayn al-ᶜĀbidīn ᶜAlī ibn al-Ḥusayn from his father al-Ḥusayn ibn ᶜAlī ibn Abī Ṭālib. This was what Ibn aṣ-Ṣalāḥ related as the view of Abū Bakr ibn Abī Shaybah, and al-ᶜIrāqī related as the view of ᶜAbd ar-Razzāq. Some said that the soundest chain is Mālik from Nāfiᶜ from Ibn ᶜUmar. This was the position of al-Bukhārī, and it was the way that al-ᶜIrāqī began his words, and is a matter to which people incline and to which hearts are attracted.

Based on this Abū Manṣūr ᶜAbd al-Qāhir at-Tamīmī al-Baghdādī said that the greatest chain of transmission is ash-Shāfiᶜī from Mālik from Nāfiᶜ from Ibn ᶜUmar, because none of those who narrated from Mālik were greater than ash-Shāfiᶜī. Some of them, based on that, held that the greatest of them was Aḥmad ibn Ḥanbal from ash-Shāfiᶜī from Mālik from Nāfiᶜ, because Aḥmad was the greatest of those who learnt from ash-Shāfiᶜī. This was called the Golden Chain. Ḥāfiẓ Mughlaṭāwī followed Abū Manṣūr at-Tamīmī in his mention of ash-Shāfiᶜī with the narration of Abū Ḥanīfah from Mālik, if we consider it with respect to the greatness of the narrator, and Ibn Wahb and al-Qaᶜnabī if we consider it with respect to attention to detail. Al-Balqīnī said in *Maḥāsin al-iṣṭilāḥ*, "As for Abū Ḥanīfah, even if he did narrate from Mālik as ad-Dāraquṭnī mentioned, his narration is not well known as is the narration of ash-Shāfiᶜī." Al-ᶜIrāqī said, "The narration of Abū Ḥanīfah from Mālik in that which ad-Dāraquṭnī mentioned in his *al-Gharāʾib* is not in his narration from Nāfiᶜ from Ibn ᶜUmar, and the issue is premised on that. Yes indeed, al-Khaṭīb mentioned a ḥadīth in his narration from Mālik. Ḥāfiẓ Ibn Ḥajar said, 'As for his proposing Abū Ḥanīfah as a counter argument [as a superior narrator from Mālik], it is not good, because the narration of Abū Ḥanīfah from Mālik is not established. Ad-Dāraquṭnī and then later al-Khaṭīb only narrated it because of two narrations that came to them from him with two chains of transmission about which people say critical things. Also, Abū Ḥanīfah's narration from Mālik only occurs in that which he mentioned as conversation and mutual reminding, and he did not mean narration from him as occurred in the case of ash-Shāfiᶜī who stayed with him for a long time and who himself read out the *Muwaṭṭaʾ* to him. As for his proposing Ibn Wahb and al-Qaᶜnabī, there is no doubt that ash-Shāfiᶜī is more knowledgeable than both of them. More than one person has said that Ibn Wahb was not good in conveying [ḥadīth], and so a sound transmission from the people of ḥadīth that he was more exact in transmission from Mālik is required, even though he was certainly one who stayed with him a great deal." This abridgement concluded here.

Some say that the most sound narration is that of Shuᶜbah from Qatādah from Saᶜīd ibn al-Musayyab, meaning from his shaykhs. Some say that it is that of ᶜAbd ar-Raḥmān ibn al-Qāsim from his father from ᶜĀ'ishah, which is mentioned by al-Khaṭīb from Ibn Maᶜīn. Some say that it is that of Yaḥyā ibn Abī Kathīr from Abū Salamah from Abū Hurayrah, which is said by Sulaymān ibn Dāwūd ash-Shādhakūnī. Some say that it is that of Ayyūb from Nāfiᶜ from Ibn ᶜUmar, and that was narrated by Khalf ibn Hishām al-Bazzār from Aḥmad. Some say that it is that of Shuᶜbah from ᶜAmr ibn Murrah from Murrah from Abū Mūsā al-Ashᶜarī, which is transmitted by al-Khaṭīb as the view of Wakīᶜ. Some say that it is that of Sufyān ath-Thawrī from Manṣūr from Ibrāhīm from ᶜAlqamah from ᶜAbdullāh ibn Masᶜūd, which was the view of Ibn al-Mubārak and al-ᶜIjlī. This is what is in the *Tadrīb* of as-Suyūṭī and the *Sharḥ sharḥ nukhbat al-fikr* by Mullā Akram as-Sindī. There are detailed arguments on this issue go beyond the scope of the present discourse.

Topic Six

As-Suyūṭī said in *Tanwīr al-Ḥawālik*:

> The narrators from Mālik are so many as to exceed in number those of any other of the imāms. Ḥāfiẓ Abū Bakr al-Khaṭīb dedicated a book to the narrators who narrated from Mālik in which he narrated seven less than a thousand names. Qāḍī ᶜIyāḍ mentioned that he had composed a book about his narrators in which he mentioned in excess of 1,300 names. As for the ones who narrated the *Muwaṭṭa'* from him, the Qāḍī dedicated a chapter to them in the *Madārik* in which he named, apart from the four famous ones whom we will mention, ash-Shāfiᶜī ...

Topic Seven: Narrations of the *Muwaṭṭa*ʾ

The author of *Bustān al-muḥaddithīn,* which was written in Persian by one of the notable men of Delhi, goes into much detail with respect to the standing of the *Muwaṭṭa*ʾ, the various versions of it and in introducing its author. The main point he conveys is that there are numerous versions of the *Muwaṭṭa*ʾ which exist today in the Arabic lands.

First version: Yaḥyā ibn Yaḥyā

The one which is most in demand in our countries and which is most often understood unqualifiedly as *The Muwaṭṭa*ʾ in our age is the version of Yaḥyā ibn Yaḥyā al-Maṣmūdī, who is Abū Muḥammad Yaḥyā ibn Yaḥyā ibn Kathīr ibn Waslās ibn Shamlal ibn Manqāyā al-Maṣmūdī, whose lineage is from Maṣmūdah a tribe of the Berbers. He died in 234 AH.

Second version: Ibn Wahb

The version of Ibn Wahb. Abū Muḥammad ᶜAbdullāh ibn Salamah al-Fihrī al-Miṣrī (the Egyptian). He compiled a book on the terrors of the Rising from the Dead. One day it was read out to him and fear overcame him until he fainted and died in that state. Born in Dhu'l-Qaᶜdah, 125 AH and died on Sunday the fifth of Shaᶜbān, 197 AH.

Third version: Ibn al-Qāsim

The version of Ibn al-Qāsim. He is Abū ᶜAbdullāh ᶜAbd ar-Raḥmān ibn al-Qāsim ibn Khālid al-Miṣrī. He took knowledge from many shaykhs, among them Mālik. He was a zāhid, a faqīh and he was scrupulous. He would read the Qurʾān twice every day, and he was the first to record the *madhhab* of Mālik in the *Mudawwanah* on which the *fuqahā*ʾ of the *madhhab* depend. He was born in 132 AH and died in Egypt in 191 AH.

Fourth Version: Maᶜn ibn ᶜĪsā

Maᶜn ibn ᶜĪsā, who is Abū Yaḥyā Maᶜn ibn ᶜĪsā ibn Dīnār al-Madanī al-Qazzāz (meaning the one who sold raw silk) al-Ashjaʿī i.e. he was the mawlā of al-Ashjaʿ. He was one of the great companions of Mālik, who paid the most attention to detail. He clung to his company and he was called "The staff of Mālik" because Mālik used to lean on him when he went to the mosque after he had become old. He died in Madīnah in Shawwāl 198 AH.

Fifth version: al-Qaʿnabī

The version of al-Qaʿnabī, who is Abū ʿAbd ar-Raḥmān ʿAbdullāh ibn Maslamah ibn Qa'nab al-Ḥārithī, al-Qaʿnabī by descent from his grandfather. He was born after 130 AH and died in Makkah in Shawwāl, 221 AH. Ibn Maʿīn said, "We have never seen anyone who narrated for the sake of Allah except for Wakīʿ and al-Qaʿnabī. He had numerous merits. His supplications were answered, and he was numbered among the Abdāl."

Sixth version: at-Tinnīsī

That of ʿAbdullāh ibn Yūsuf ad-Dimashqī originally at-Tinnīsī because he resided in Tinnīs one of the cities in Morocco, but as-Samʿānī mentioned it as one of the Egyptian cities. Al-Bukhārī and Abū Ḥātim regarded him as trustworthy and al-Bukhārī narrated from him a great deal in his books.

Seventh version: Ibn Bakīr al-Miṣrī

That of Yaḥyā ibn Yaḥyā ibn Bakīr Abū Zakariyyā who is better known as Ibn Bakīr al-Miṣrī. Al-Bukhārī and Muslim narrated from him through an intermediary in their two ṣaḥīḥ books, and a great number regard him as trustworthy. He died in Safar, 231 AH.

Eighth version: Saʿīd ibn ʿUfayr

That of Saʿīd ibn ʿUfayr, who is Saʿīd ibn Kathīr ibn ʿUfayr ibn Muslim al-Anṣārī. Al-Bukhārī and others narrated from him. He was born in 146 AH and died in Ramaḍān, 226 AH.

Ninth version: Abū Muṣᶜab

That of Abū Muṣᶜab az-Zuhrī, who is Aḥmad ibn Abī Bakr al-Qāsim ibn al-Ḥārith ibn Zurārah ibn Muṣᶜab ibn ᶜAbd ar-Raḥmān ibn ᶜAwf az-Zuhrī, one of the shaykhs of the people of Madīnah and one of their *qāḍīs*. The authors of the six books narrated from him except for an-Nasāʾī who narrated from him through an intermediary. He was born in 150 AH and died in 242 AH. They say that his was the last *Muwaṭṭaʾ* to be read out to Mālik.

Tenth version: Muṣᶜab az-Zubayrī

That of Muṣᶜab ibn ᶜAbdullāh az-Zubayrī.

Eleventh version: Muḥammad ibn Mubārak aṣ-Ṣūrī

That of Muḥammad ibn Mubārak aṣ-Ṣūrī.

Twelfth version: Sulaymān ibn Bard

That of Sulaymān ibn Bard.

Thirteenth version: Abū Ḥudhāfah

That of Abū Ḥudhāfah as-Sahmī Aḥmad ibn Ismāᶜīl, the last of Mālik's companions to die. He died in Baghdād, 259 AH on the day of ᶜĪd al-Fiṭr.

Fourteenth version: Suwayd ibn Saᶜīd al-Harawī

Suwayd ibn Saᶜīd Abū Muḥammad al-Harawī, from whom Muslim and Ibn Mājah and others narrated. He died in 240 AH.

Fifteenth version: Muḥammad ibn al-Ḥasan

That of Muḥammad ibn al-Ḥasan ash-Shaybānī, the pupil of Abū Ḥanīfah.

Sixteenth version: Yaḥyā ibn Yaḥyā at-Tamīmī

That of Yaḥyā ibn Yaḥyā at-Tamīmī, who is Yaḥyā ibn Yaḥyā ibn Bakīr ibn ᶜAbd ar-Raḥmān at-Tamīmī al-Ḥanẓalī an-Naysābūrī who died in 222 AH, and from whom al-Bukhārī and Muslim narrated as well as others.

As-Suyūṭī mentioned fourteen versions in *Tanwīr al-Ḥawālik*. He states in the introduction that al-Ḥāfiẓ Ṣalāḥ ad-Dīn al-ᶜAlā᾿ī said:

A great number of people narrated the *Muwaṭṭa᾿* from Mālik, and there are differences between the narrators as to the order in which ḥadīth are narrated with respect to being brought forward or placed further back, and differences of increase and decrease in number. The one in which there is the largest number is the narration of al-Qaᶜnabī. One of those with the most additional material is the narration of Abū Muṣᶜab. Ibn Ḥazm said, "In the *Muwaṭṭa᾿* of Abū Muṣᶜab there are almost one hundred ḥadīth more than in the other *Muwaṭṭas*."

Al-Ghāfiqī, i.e. Abu'l-Qāsim ᶜAbd ar-Raḥmān ibn ᶜAbdullāh ibn Muḥammad, the Māliki faqīh who died in 381 AH, said in *Musnad al-Muwaṭṭa᾿*: "This book of ours comprises 666 ḥadīth which is the sum of ḥadīth we have having chains of transmission in the *Muwaṭṭa᾿* of Mālik. That is because I examined twelve narrations of the *Muwaṭṭa᾿* of Mālik: the narrations of ᶜAbdullāh ibn Wahb, ᶜAbd ar-Raḥmān ibn al-Qāsim, ᶜAbdullāh ibn Maslamah al-Qaᶜnabī, ᶜAbdullāh ibn Yūsuf at-Tinnīsī, Maᶜn ibn ᶜĪsā, Saᶜīd ibn ᶜUfayr, Yaḥyā ibn ᶜAbdullāh ibn Bakīr, Abū Muṣᶜab Aḥmad ibn Abī Bakr az-Zuhrī, Muṣᶜab ibn ᶜAbdullāh az-Zubayrī, Muḥammad ibn al-Mubārak aṣ-Ṣūrī, Sulaymān ibn Bard, and Yaḥyā ibn Yaḥyā al-Andalusī. I took most from their narrations and I identified their differences regarding the ḥadīth and the wordings. I mention what some of them ascribed as *mursal* ḥadīth [ascribed by a Follower directly to the Prophet ﷺ without mentioning the Companion or Companions from whom it was heard], or as *mawqūf* [statements said by Companions without ascribing it to the Prophet ﷺ], but which others gave full chains of transmission for, and also what of that was *mursal* but close to having a full chain of transmission.

"'The number of Mālik's men from whom he narrated in this *Musnad* is 95. The number of men of the Companions from whom they narrated to him is 85, and of their women 23, and of the Followers 48 men all of whom were of the people of Madīnah except for six: Abu'z-Zubayr who was one of the people of Makkah, Ḥumayd aṭ-Ṭawīl and Ayyūb as-Sakhtiyānī of the people of Baṣra, ᶜAṭāᵓ ibn ᶜAbdullāh one of the people of Khurāsān, ᶜAbd al-Karīm one of the people of the Jazīrah (northwest Mesopotamia), and Ibrāhīm ibn Abī ᶜAblah one of the people of Shām." All of the above is taken from the words of al-Ghāfiqī.

I have come across two other narrations of the *Muwaṭṭaᵓ* apart from those al-Ghāfiqī mentions: first, the narration of Suwayd ibn Saᶜīd; second, the narration of Muḥammad ibn al-Ḥasan ash-Shaybānī the companion of Abū Ḥanīfah, in which there are a few ḥadīth over and above all the other *Muwaṭṭas*. For example, "Actions are only by intentions..." By that it is clear that those who ascribe its narration to the *Muwaṭṭaᵓ* are correct and that those who say it is a mistake have themselves made a mistake. I have based myself on *ash-Sharḥ al-kabīr* for these fourteen narrations....

There is in *Kashf aẓ-ẓunūn ᶜan asāmī al-kutub wa'l-funūn* that Abu'l-Qāsim Muḥammad ibn Ḥusayn ash-Shāfiᶜī said:

There are eleven well-known *Muwaṭṭas* narrated from Mālik and their meanings are close to each other. There are four of them which are widely used: the *Muwaṭṭaᵓ* of Yaḥyā ibn Yaḥyā, Ibn Bakīr, Abū Muṣᶜab az-Zuhrī and Ibn Wahb. However, the usage of any of them other than that of Yaḥyā is small, followed by the *Muwaṭṭaᵓ* of Ibn Bakīr. In the prioritising of the chapters there are differences between the different versions...

Abū Nuᶜaym narrated in the *Ḥilyat al-Awliyāᵓ* that Mālik said, "Hārūn ar-Rashīd asked my advice about hanging the *Muwaṭṭaᵓ* from the Kaᶜbah and compelling people to follow what is in it, and so I said, 'Do not do it, because the Companions of the Messenger of Allah ﷺ differed in the derivative rulings and they separated in the lands, and each one of them hit on the truth' So he said, 'May Allah guide you aright, Abū ᶜAbdullāh.'" Ibn Saᶜd narrated in the *Ṭabaqāt* that Mālik said, "When al-Manṣūr performed the Ḥajj he said to me, 'I have decided to give the order concerning this book of yours which you have composed, that it should be copied and a copy sent to

every major city of the Muslims, and that I should tell them to act by what is in it and not turn to anything other than it.' I said, 'Do not do this, because different sayings have already reached people, and they have begun to practise them as their *dīn*, so leave people and what the people of each land have chosen for themselves.'"
This is how it is found in the ᶜUqūd *al-jumān*.

Topic Eight

Al-Abhurī Abū Bakr said:

> The sum of the traditions that are in the *Muwaṭṭa᾽* from the Prophet ﷺ, the Companions and the Followers are 720 ḥadīth, of which 600 have chains of transmission, 222 are *mursal* ḥadīth [ascribed directly by a Follower to the Prophet ﷺ without mentioning the Companion or Companions from whom they were heard], and *mawqūf* reports [statements said by a Companion without ascribing them to the Prophet ﷺ] are 613. There are 285 statements of the Followers. Ibn Ḥazm said in the book *Marātib ad-diyānah,* "I counted what there is in the *Muwaṭṭa᾽* of Mālik and found there to be just over five hundred ḥadīth with chains of transmission, just over three hundred *mursal* ḥadīth, and just over seventy ḥadīth which Mālik himself had given up acting upon. In it there are weak ḥadīth which the main body of the people of knowledge consider weak."

This is how it was narrated by as-Suyūṭī.

I say that what he meant by weak is a slight weakness, as is clear from what we have seen previously, and that it is obvious to any specialist that there are no ḥadīth in it which must be dropped or which are fabricated.

Topic Nine: Those who Wrote Commentaries on the *Muwaṭṭa᾽*

...

Topic Ten: The Noble Qualities of Imām Muḥammad and his Two Shaykhs Abū Yūsuf and Abū Ḥanīfah

They are those who are intended by the epithet, the "Three Imāms" in the books of our Ḥanafī people. The first two are known as the "Two Companions" and the latter two as the "Two Shaykhs", whilst the first and the last are known as "The Two Nobles". Their biographical notices are mentioned in many treatises, such as in the introduction to the *Hidāyah*, the introduction to *al-Jāmiᶜ aṣ-ṣaghīr*, and the *Ṭabaqāt al-Ḥanafiyyah*, etc., and here we will mention what is necessary of it.

Imām Muḥammad ibn al-Ḥasan

With respect to Muḥammad, he is Abū ᶜAbdullāh Muḥammad ibn al-Ḥasan ibn Farqad ash-Shaybānī – with an ascription through the relationship of *walāʾ* (being a mawlā) to Shaybān, the well known tribe. He was Kūfan and a companion of Imām Abū Ḥanīfah. He was originally from Damascus, from a small town called Ḥarsatā. His father came to ᶜIrāq and Muḥammad was born to him in Wāsiṭ, and grew up in Kūfa. He was a pupil of Abū Ḥanīfah and heard ḥadīth from Misᶜar ibn Kidām, Sufyān ath-Thawrī, ᶜAmr ibn Dīnār, Mālik ibn Mighwal, Imām Mālik ibn Anas, al-Awzāᶜī, Rabīᶜah ibn Ṣāliḥ, Bakīr and Qāḍī Abū Yūsuf. He resided in Baghdād and narrated ḥadīth there. Imām ash-Shāfiᶜī Muḥammad ibn Idrīs narrated from him, as did Abū Sulaymān Mūsā ibn Sulaymān al-Jūzajānī, Hishām ibn ᶜUbaydullāh ar-Rāzī, Abū ᶜUbayd al-Qāsim ibn Sallām, ᶜAlī ibn Muslim aṭ–Ṭūsī, Abū Ḥafṣ al-Kabīr and Khalf ibn Ayyūb. Ar-Rashīd appointed him to of the post of *qāḍī* in ar-Riqqah where he compiled a book called *ar-Riqqiyyat*, and then he discharged him and he came to Baghdād. When Hārūn ar-Rashīd went to Ray the first time, he told him to come with him and he died in Ray in 189 AH.

It is narrated that he said, "My father died and left thirty thousand dirhams, and I spent fifteen thousand on grammar and poetry and fifteen thousand on ḥadīth and fiqh." Ash-Shāfiᶜī said, "I have not known a plump person lighter of spirit than Muḥammad ibn al-Ḥasan. I have not seen anyone more eloquent than him. I used to think when I saw him reciting the Qurʾān that it was as if the Qurʾān had been revealed in his language." He also said, "I have not seen anyone more intelligent than Muḥammad ibn al-Ḥasan." It is narrated of him that a man asked him a question which he answered. The man said to him, "The *fuqahāʾ* disagree with you." Ash-Shāfiᶜī said to him, "Have you ever seen a faqīh? By Allah! not unless you have seen Muḥammad ibn al-Ḥasan!" A man stood up before al-Muznī and asked him about the people of ᶜIrāq saying, "What do you say about Abū Ḥanīfah?" He answered, "Their chief." He asked, "Abū Yūsuf?" He answered, "The one who most follows the ḥadīth."

He asked, "Muḥammad ibn al-Ḥasan?" He answered, "The one who derives the most rulings." He asked, "Zufar?" He answered, "The one who is sharpest in analogical reasoning." It is narrated that ash-Shāfiᶜī said, "I never reasoned in argument with anyone but that the colour of his face changed, except for Muḥammad ibn al-Ḥasan. If their language were not known we would judge that they were angels: Muḥammad in fiqh, al-Kisā'ī in grammar, al-Aṣmaᶜī in his poetry." It is narrated that Aḥmad ibn Ḥanbal said, "If in any matter there is agreement between three people, then one pays no attention to the verdict of anyone who disagrees with them." Someone asked him, "Who are they?" He answered, "Abū Ḥanīfah, Abū Yūsuf and Muḥammad ibn al-Ḥasan. Abū Ḥanīfah is the one with the most insight with respect to analogical reasoning. Abū Yūsuf is the one with the most insight with respect to the traditions. Muḥammad is the one with the most insight with respect to Arabic." As-Samᶜānī narrated all of this in the *Kitāb al-ansāb*.

Abū ᶜAbdullāh adh-Dhahabī said in *Mīzān al-iᶜtidāl*:

> Muḥammad ibn al-Ḥasan ash-Shaybānī Abū ᶜAbdullāh is one of the *fuqahā᾽* whom an-Nasā᾽ī and others regarded as weak with respect to his memory. He narrated from Mālik ibn Anas and others, and he was one of the great oceans of knowledge and fiqh, and he was strong [when he narrated] from Mālik.

Ḥāfiẓ Ibn Ḥajar said in *Lisān al-mīzān*:

> He is Muḥammad ibn al-Ḥasan ibn Farqad ash-Shaybānī, by *wala'*. He was born in Wāsiṭ and grew up in Kūfa. He learnt fiqh from Abū Ḥanīfah and ḥadīth from ath-Thawrī, Misᶜar, ᶜUmar ibn Dhirr, Mālik ibn Mighwal, al-Awzāᶜī, Mālik ibn Anas, Rabīᶜah ibn Ṣāliḥ and a whole group of people. Those who narrated from him were ash-Shāfiᶜī, Abū Sulaymān al-Jūzajānī, Hishām ar-Rāzī, ᶜAlī ibn Muslim aṭ-Ṭūsī and others. He was appointed *qāḍī* in the days of ar-Rashīd. Ibn ᶜAbd al-Ḥakam said, "I heard ash-Shāfiᶜī saying, 'Muḥammad said, "I stood at Mālik's door for three years and I heard from him more than seven hundred ḥadīth."'" Ar-Rabīᶜ said, "I heard ash-Shāfiᶜī saying, 'I carried away from Muḥammad a camel-load of books.'" ᶜAbdullāh ibn ᶜAlī al-Madīnī said that his father said about Muḥammad ibn al-Ḥasan, "An utterly truthful man."

In *Tahdhīb al-asmāʾ wa'l-lughāt* al-Khaṭīb said:

> Muḥammad was born in Wāsiṭ and grew up in Kūfa. He heard ḥadīth from Abū Ḥanīfah, Misᶜar ibn Kidām, Sufyān ath-Thawrī, ᶜUmar ibn Dhirr and Mālik ibn Mighwal. He also wrote [ḥadīth] from Mālik ibn Anas, Rabīᶜah ibn Ṣāliḥ, Bakīr ibn ᶜĀmir and Abū Yūsuf. He lived in Baghdād and narrated ḥadīth there. Ash-Shāfiᶜī, al-Jūzajānī, Abū ᶜUbayd and others narrated from him. Muḥammad ibn Saᶜd, the scribe of al-Wāqidī, said, 'Muhammad's roots were in Jazīrah. His father was in the army of Shām but he moved to Wāsiṭ and Muḥammad was born to him there in 132 AH. He grew up in Kūfa. He sought out ḥadīth and heard a great deal. He sat with Abū Ḥanīfah and heard from him. He looked into theory *(raʾy)*[2] and it was the dominant element in him. He became known for it and became a leader in that field. He went to Baghdād and lived there. People repaired to him and heard both ḥadīth and theory from him. He went to ar-Raqqah when Hārūn ar-Rashīd was there and he appointed him as its *qāḍī,* but then later he removed him from office, so he went to Baghdād. When Hārūn ar-Rashīd went to ar-Ray he told him to come with him and he died there in 189 AH.

Then al-Khaṭīb narrated with a chain of transmission that ash-Shāfiᶜī said, "Muḥammad ibn al-Ḥasan said, 'I stood at Mālik's door for three years and a bit.'" He said, "He used to say that he heard orally more than seven hundred ḥadīth." When he narrated to people from Mālik they filled his house, and there were so many people that the house was too small for them. He narrated with a chain of transmission that Ismāᶜīl ibn Ḥammād ibn Abī Ḥanīfah said, "Muḥammad used to sit in the mosque of Kūfa [to teach] when he was twenty years old." With a chain of transmission there is that ash-Shāfiᶜī said, "I have never seen a stout person more intelligent than Muḥammad ibn al-Ḥasan." Also from him, "When engaged in a case, it was as if the Qurʾān was descending; he would not move a letter forward nor put one back [i.e. he narrated verbatim]." Also from him, "Muḥammad used to fill the eye and the heart." Also, "I carried away two Bactrian camel-loads of books from him." Yaḥyā ibn Maᶜīn said, "I wrote *al-Jāmiᶜ aṣ-ṣaghīr* from Muḥammad ibn al-Ḥasan." Abū ᶜUbayd said, "I have not seen anyone more knowledgeable of the Book of Allah than him." Ibrāhīm al-Ḥarbī said, "I asked Aḥmad, 'From where do you get these subtle fiqh cases?' He answered, 'From the books of Muḥammad ibn al-Ḥasan.'" With a chain of transmission from Abū Rajāʾ it is recorded that Maḥmawiyah said, "We used to count him as one of the Abdāl." He said, "I saw Muḥammad ibn al-Ḥasan in my dreams and I said, 'Abū ᶜAbdullāh! to what end have you come?' He said, 'My Lord said to me, "I did not make you a vessel of knowledge with the intention of punishing you."' I asked, 'What has become of Abū Yūsuf?' He answered, 'He is above me.' I asked, 'And Abū Ḥanīfah?' He answered, 'He is above him by many degrees.'" This abridgement [from al-Khaṭīb] is concluded.

I say that by these statements which authoritative people have made, and other comments from trustworthy people which we have left out for fear of being lengthy, the majesty of his rank and his wonderful superiority are clear. Whoever casts aspersions on him cannot have heard these words and cannot have seen the books of the authoritative critics. The fact that ash-Shāfiᶜī praised him with these well-proportioned expressions and gracious words, and the fact of his having narrated from him are proof enough. Ibn Taymiyyah in *Minhāj as-sunnah*, which he wrote in refutation of *Minhāj al-karāmah* by al-Ḥillī the shīᶜah, denied that ash-Shāfiᶜī had been his pupil. However, those who had been before him, such as an-Nawawī, al-Khaṭīb, as-Samᶜānī and others showed that this was false, and they were more knowledgeable than he was about the state of their imām.

Imām Abū Yūsuf

As for Abū Yūsuf, he is the Qāḍī Yaᶜqūb ibn Ibrāhīm ibn Ḥabīb the Kūfan, whom adh-Dhahabī mentioned among those who are memorisers of ḥadīth in his book *Tadhkirat al-ḥuffāẓ*. He said in introducing him:

> He heard Hishām ibn ᶜUrwah, Abū Isḥāq ash-Shaybānī, ᶜAṭāʾ ibn as-Sāʾib and those of their generation. Those who transmitted from him were Muḥammad ibn al-Ḥasan the faqīh, Aḥmad ibn Ḥanbal, Bishr ibn al-Walīd, Yaḥyā ibn Maᶜīn, ᶜAlī ibn al-Jaᶜd, ᶜAlī ibn Muslim aṭ-Ṭūsī and a large number of other people. He grew up in search of knowledge. His father was a poor man, and Abū Ḥanīfah paid frequent attention to him. Al-Muzani said, "Abū Yūsuf of all people is the one who most follows ḥadīth." Ibrāhīm ibn Abī Dāwūd narrated from Yaḥyā ibn Maᶜīn that he said, "There is not among the people of theory anyone who knows more ḥadīth nor is more authoritative than him." ᶜAbbās narrated from him and said, "Abū Yūsuf is a

man of ḥadīth and a man of the Sunnah." Ibn Samāᶜah said, "Abū Yūsuf used to pray two hundred rakᶜahs every day after he was appointed *qāḍī*." Aḥmad said, "He was just in his ḥadīth." He died in 182 AH. There are reports about him both in knowledge and in imāmate. I have dedicated a volume both to him and to his companion Muḥammad ibn al-Ḥasan.

As-Samᶜānī said:

> He heard Abū Isḥāq ash-Shaybānī, Sulaymān at-Taymī, Yaḥyā ibn Saᶜīd, Sulaymān al-Aᶜmash, Hishām ibn ᶜUrwah, ᶜUbaydullāh ibn ᶜUmar al-ᶜUmarī, ᶜAṭāʾ ibn as-Sāʾib, Muḥammad ibn Isḥāq, Layth ibn Saᶜd and others, and he was a pupil of Abū Ḥanīfah. Those who narrated from him include Muḥammad ibn al-Ḥasan, Bishr ibn al-Walīd al-Kindī, Aḥmad ibn Ḥanbal, Yaḥyā ibn Maᶜīn and others. He had resided in Baghdād and he was appointed chief *qāḍī*, and he was the first in Islam to be called *Qāḍī al-quḍāt* – Chief Qāḍī. Yaḥyā ibn Maᶜīn, Aḥmad and Ibn al-Madīnī did not disagree over the fact that he was trustworthy in ḥadīth. He was the first person to compose a book on the principles of fiqh according to the *madhhab* of Abū Ḥanīfah. His knowledge spread widely across the earth.

Imām Abū Ḥanīfah

As for Abū Ḥanīfah, he has beautiful virtues and magnificent qualities of character which the human intellect falls short of grasping and the tongue fails to make clear. A group of the people of knowledge of different *madhhabs* have compiled material about his virtues, and no one casts aspersions on him except for those with strong sectarian bias or who those who are obviously ignorant.

If the one who casts aspersions is a scholar of ḥadīth or a Shāfiᶜī, then we direct him towards the books on his virtues which the people of knowledge of his own *madhhab* have compiled. We show him what is hidden from him of his virtues which the eminent people of his own *madhhab* mention, such as as-Suyūṭī the author of *Tabyīḍ aṣ-ṣaḥīfah fī manāqib al-imām Abī Ḥanīfah*, Ibn Ḥajar al-Makkī the author of *al-Khayrāt al-ḥisān fī manāqib an-Nuᶜmān*, and men such as adh-Dhahabī who mentioned him in *Tadhkirat al-ḥuffāẓ* and *al-Kāshif*, and who praised him and devoted a treatise to his virtues, Ibn Khallikān who mentioned his virtues in his history, al-Yāfiᶜī the author of

Mir'āt al-jinān in which he mentioned his virtues, and al-Ḥāfiẓ Ibn Ḥajar al-ᶜAsqalānī who mentioned him in *at-Taqrīb,* and in other works and who praised him, an-Nawawī, the commentator on *Ṣaḥīḥ Muslim* who praised him in *Tahdhīb al-asmā' wa'l-lughāt,* and Imām al-Ghazali who praised him in *Iḥyā al-ᶜulūm* and others.

If the critic is a Mālikī, we will ask him to reflect on his virtues as mentioned by the people of knowledge of his own persuasion such as al-Ḥāfiẓ Ibn ᶜAbd al-Barr and others.

If he is a Ḥanbalī, we ask him to study the clear declarations of the people of his *madhhab* such as Yūsuf ibn ᶜAbd al-Hādī al-Ḥanbalī the author of *Tanwīr aṣ-ṣaḥīfah fi manāqib Abī Ḥanīfah.*

If he is one of the scholars who are *mujtahids* and raised above the need to follow others, then we would ask him to listen to what the *mujtahids* and scholars of ḥadīth have said mentioning his splendid qualities.

If he is illiterate and without a *madhhab,* then he is cattle, rather he is further astray and we reject him and regard him as liable to discretionary punishment.

It is sufficient to mention among those of his qualities in which we take pride and which distinguish him among the famous imāms, the fact that he is one of the Followers, and even if there is some disagreement about that, then it is as Ibn Nujaym al-Miṣrī said in *al-Baḥr ar-rā'iq sharḥ kanz ad-daqā'iq* concerning the unacceptability of the testimony of someone who openly curses the right-acting first generations: "Cursing means to abuse, and the right-acting first generations, as is said in the *Nihāyah,* are the Companions, the Followers and Abū Ḥanīfah." He added in the *Fatḥ al-qadīr,* "And similarly the people of knowledge. And the difference between the right-acting first generations [*salaf*] and the *khalaf* is that the right-acting first generations are the first generations, the Companions and the Followers, and the *khalaf* are those right-acting people after them, whereas the *khalf* are the wrong-acting people. That is how it is expressed in *Mukhtaṣar an-nihāyah.* The addition of Abū Ḥanīfah to the Followers [in the sentence above] is either in the sense of a particular example based on the fact of him being one of them, as is found in *Manāqib al-Kurdarī* and as declared in *al-ᶜInāyah*, or that he is not one of them, based on what Shaykh al-Islām Ibn Ḥajar declared, because he regarded him as someone of the sixth degree of those who were contemporary with the younger Followers, but not firmly established as having met any of the Companions. He mentioned this in *Taqrīb at-tahdhīb.*" However, the sound and weightiest view is that he was one of the Followers because he saw Anas ﷺ and the fact is that a simple sighting of one of the Companions is sufficient to render a man one of the Followers, just as Ibn Ḥajar affirmed elsewhere as did adh-Dhahabī, as-Suyūṭī, Ibn Ḥajar al-Makkī, Ibn al-Jawzī, ad-Dāraquṭnī, Ibn Saᶜd, al-Khaṭīb, al-Walī al-ᶜIrāqī, ᶜAlī al-Qārī, Akram as-Sindī, Abū Maᶜshar, Ḥamzah as-Sahmī, al-Yāfiᶜī, al-Jazarī, at-Tawrbishtī, as-Sirāj and other ḥadīth scholars and historians who are to be reckoned with. Therefore, whoever denies it has to reckon with their statements, and I have mentioned these in my treatise *Iqāmat al-ḥujjah* ᶜalā *anna al-ikthār fī at-taᶜabbud laysa bi bidᶜah* – Establishment of the Proof that Increasing in Acts of Worship is not an Innovation.

Adh-Dhahabī said in *Tadhkirat al-ḥuffāẓ*:

> Abū Ḥanīfah is the greatest imām, the faqīh of ᶜIrāq, an-Nuᶜmān ibn Thābit who is Zawṭā the Kūfan. He was born in 80 AH and he saw Anas ibn Mālik more than once when Anas came to visit them in Kūfa. Ibn Saᶜd narrated from Sayf ibn Jābir that Abū Ḥanīfah used to say that. He narrated from ᶜAṭā᾽, Nāfiᶜ, ᶜAbd ar-Raḥmān ibn Hurmuz al-Aᶜraj, Salamah ibn Kuhayl, Abū Jaᶜfar Muḥammad ibn ᶜAlī, Qatādah, ᶜAmr ibn Dīnār, Abū Isḥāq and a great number of other people. Those who learnt fiqh from him include Zufar ibn Hudhayl, Dāwūd aṭ-Ṭā᾽ī, Qāḍī Abū Yūsuf, Muḥammad ibn al-Ḥasan, Asad ibn ᶜAmr, al-Ḥasan ibn Ziyād, Nūḥ al-Jāmiᶜ, Abū Muṭīᶜ al-Balkhī and a number of others. He learnt fiqh from Ḥammād ibn Abī Sulaymān and others. Wakīᶜ, Yazīd ibn Hārūn, Saᶜd ibn aṣ-Ṣult, Abū ᶜĀṣim, ᶜAbd ar-Razzāq, ᶜUbaydullāh ibn Mūsā and many others narrated from him. He was an imām who was scrupulous and knowledgeable, who put his knowledge into practice and was devoted to *ᶜibādah*. He was an imām of great importance and he would not accept the gifts of the sulṭān, but on the contrary he traded and earned [for himself]. Ibn al-Mubārak said, "Abū Ḥanīfah is the person with the most fiqh." Ash-Shāfiᶜī said, "In fiqh people are dependent on Abū Ḥanīfah." Aḥmad ibn Muḥammad ibn al-Qāsim narrated from Yaḥyā ibn Maᶜīn that he said, "There is no harm in him, and he was not suspect. Yazīd ibn Hubayrah struck him [to force him to take the post of] *qāḍī*, and he refused to be *qāḍī*." Abū Dāwūd said, "Abū Ḥanīfah was an imām." Bishr ibn al-Walīd said that Abū Yūsuf said, "I was walking with Abū Ḥanīfah and one man said to another, 'This is Abū Ḥanīfah; he does not

> sleep at night.' He said, 'By Allah! Let nothing be said of me that I do not do!' Therfore, he would spend the whole night awake in prayer, supplication and humbling himself." I have, in fact, devoted a whole volume to the virtues of this Imām.

An-Nawawī mentioned in *Tahdhīb al-asmāʾ* many of his virtues in four pages, transmitting them from al-Khaṭīb and others. He mentioned that he was born in 80 AH, and died in Baghdād in 150 AH according to the sound date well known to the majority. There is one unusual narration that he died in 151 AH, and another from Makkī ibn Ibrāhīm that he died in 153 AH.

Ibn Ḥajar al-Makkī in *al-Khayrāt al-ḥisān,* mentioned his good and praiseworthy qualities in thirty-six sections, then in the thirty-seventh section he said:

> Ḥāfiẓ Ibn ᶜAbd al-Barr mentioned: "Some of the people of ḥadīth go too far in criticising Abū Ḥanīfah, and go beyond the limit in doing that because of his having given preference to analogical reasoning over traditions. Most of the people of knowledge say that if the ḥadīth is sound then theory *(raʾy)* and analogical reasoning are invalid. However, he only added reasonable interpretations to those traditions related by chains of single narrators. This had been done by others before him, and like him, others had followed him in doing that, such as Ibrāhīm an-Nakhaᶜī and the companions of ᶜAbdullāh ibn Masᶜūd ﷺ. However, he (Abū Ḥanīfah) and his companions did it more than others who are only found to have done that sparingly. Thus, when Aḥmad was asked, 'What was the reason they were angry with him?' he answered, 'Theory *(raʾy)*.' Someone asked, 'Did Mālik not speak according to theory?' He answered, 'Yes, of course, but Abū Ḥanīfah was more theoretical than him.' Someone asked, 'Should I speak about this person according to his portion and this other person according to his portion?' But Aḥmad was silent. Al-Layth ibn Saᶜd said, 'I counted seventy cases wherein Mālik spoke according to his theory in all of which he opposed the Sunnah of the Messenger of Allah ﷺ and yet we do not find anyone of the people of knowledge of the ummah more firm in narrating the ḥadīth of the Messenger of Allah ﷺ than him, but then he rejected them by a proof such as the claim of abrogation or a consensus [on that] or a weakness in the chain of

transmission. If someone were to reject them without proof then his acceptability as a witness would be void let alone his imāmate, and it would be necessary to call him a deviant, but Allah granted them safety from that defect.' It has been narrated that the Companions used their independent reasoning in exertion of the intellect to arrive at a judgement [*ijtihād*] based on theory (*raʾy*), and they gave judgements utilising analogical reasoning based on its principles, as did the Followers – but it would be lengthy to mention all of this."

That concludes the words of Ibn ᶜAbd al-Barr. [Ibn Ḥajar concluded] The upshot is that it was not only Abū Ḥanīfah who gave verdicts based on analogical reasoning, but rather most of the actions of the overwhelming majority of the people of fiqh of all the lands is based on it.

In *al-Khayrāt al-ḥisān* the thirty-eighth section states:

Abū ᶜUmar Yūsuf Ibn ᶜAbd al-Barr said, "Those who narrated from Abū Ḥanīfah and regard him as totally trustworthy and praise him are greater in number than those who speak [negatively] about him. Amongst the people of ḥadīth who speak about him, the most that they found fault with was his plunging into theory and analogical reasoning. However, we have already seen that this is not a defect." Imām ᶜAlī ibn al-Madīnī said, "As for Abū Ḥanīfah: ath-Thawrī, Ibn al-Mubārak, Ḥammād ibn Salamah, Hishām, Wakīᶜ, ᶜAbbād ibn al-ᶜAwwām and Jaᶜfar ibn ᶜAwn narrated from him. He is trustworthy and there is no harm in him. Shuᶜbah had a good opinion of him." Yaḥyā ibn Maᶜīn said, "Our people go too far with respect to Abū Ḥanīfah and his companions." Someone asked him, "Did he lie?" He answered, "No."

In the *Ṭabaqāt* of Shaykh al-Islām at-Tāj as-Subkī it is stated, "Always bear in mind that their [ḥadīth scholars'] principle is that finding fault [*jarḥ*] with a ḥadīth narrator has priority over ascribing to him acceptability of his testimony and narrations (*taᶜdīl*) without any qualification. On the contrary, the correct position is that where someone finds fault with a man whose imāmate and good standing as a narrator are established, whose praisers are many and whose fault-finders are few, and there is evidence to suggest that the reason for this attack is because of a fanatical devotion to a *madhhab* or some other reason, then one does not pursue the matter." Then he, meaning at-Tāj as-Subkī, said, after a long passage, "We have made it clear to you that the criticism of one who finds fault with narrators is rejected, even if he justifies it, if it is about someone whose acts of obedience far outweigh his disobedience, whose praisers outnumber those who criticise him, and the number who declare him faultless outnumber those who declare him faulty, and there is evidence that the attack is motivated by fanatical devotion to a *madhhab* or because of some worldly controversy. Thus, one does not turn to ath-Thawrī's words on Abū Ḥanīfah, nor Ibn Abī Dhiʾb's words – nor those of others – on Mālik, nor Ibn Maʿīn's on ash-Shāfiʿī, nor those of an-Nasāʾī on Aḥmad ibn Ṣāliḥ, etc." He said, "If we were unqualifiedly to give priority to the ascription of a fault, not one of the imāms would remain untouched, since there is no imām on whom aspersions have not been cast by detractors, and as a result of which those who perish have perished."

The thirty-ninth section [of *al-Khayrāt al-ḥisān*] refutes what al-Khaṭīb transmitted in his history from those who found fault with him:

It is known that he only meant by that to collect together what had been said about the man as is the custom of historians, and he did not mean by that to denigrate him, nor to lessen his rank. This is shown by the fact that he related the words of those who had praised him first, adding more to it and transmitting his excellent qualities. Only then did he follow that by mentioning the words of his detractors. Another thing that shows this is the fact that the majority of the chains of transmission which he mentions with respect to detraction include people about whom things are said [also in detraction] or unknown figures. It is unanimously not permitted to impugn the honour of a Muslim by such means, so how could it be possible to do that to one of the imāms of the Muslims? The fact that what al-Khaṭīb mentioned of deprecation [of Imām Abū Ḥanīfah] has sound chains of transmission from those who said it, is not reckoned of any importance, because if it is not from one of the Imām's contemporaries then the person is a *muqallid* (someone who follows another authority) of the words or writings of someone who is against him, and if the person is one of his contemporaries and peers, then similarly [it is not acceptable] since we have seen previously that the things that contemporaries and peers have said about each other are also unacceptable. The two Ḥāfiẓs, adh-Dhahabī and Ibn Ḥajar [al-ᶜAsqalānī] were unequivocal about this. They said, "...particularly if it is apparent that it is because of hostility or because of a *madhhab*, because it is clear that no one is free of malicious envy except for those whom Allah protects and preserves from it." Adh-Dhahabī said, "I don't know of any epoch that is safe from that except for the epoch of the prophets and the *ṣiddīqīn*." At-Tāj as-Subkī said, "You who are seeking to take the right way, you ought to travel the path of courtesy with respect to the imāms of the past, and you should not take into account the words that some of them uttered about others [in criticism] unless accompanied by a clear proof, and then moreover, if you are able to make a favourable interpretation of it and to hold a good opinion [of them], then take it and hold to it. If not, then turn away from what occurred between them, and beware! Again, beware of giving ear to what happened between Abū Ḥanīfah and Sufyān ath-Thawrī, or between Mālik and Ibn Abī Dhiʾb, or between an-Nasāʾī and Aḥmad ibn Ṣāliḥ, or between Aḥmad and al-Ḥārith ibn Asad al-Muḥāsibī, and so on up until the age of al-ᶜIzz ibn ᶜAbd as-Salām and at-Taqī ibn aṣ-Ṣalāḥ, because if you occupy yourself in that you will fall into ruin. These people are notable imāms, and their words have interpretations some of which we very probably do not understand, so that the only avenue open to us is to express mutual contentment with each other and to remain silent about what happened between them, just as we remain silent about what happened between the Companions."

The Sixth Section [of *al-Khayrāt al-ḥisān*] states:

It is sound, as adh-Dhahabī said, that he [Imām Abū Ḥanīfah] saw Anas ibn Mālik when he was young, and in one version 'repeatedly', and that he used to dye [his hair and beard] red. Most of the scholars of ḥadīth agree that a Follower is someone who met a Companion even if he did not keep company with him, and an-Nawawī said that this was sound, as did Ibn aṣ-Ṣalāḥ. It has come to us by some narrations that he narrated three ḥadīth from Anas, however the imāms of ḥadīth say: "They centre around someone whom the imāms of ḥadīth suspect." It is stated in the *Fatāwā* of Shaykh al-Islām Ibn

> Ḥajar that he [Imām Abū Ḥanīfah] managed to see a group of the Companions who were in Kūfa, because he was born there in 80 AH. Hence he is one of the generation of the Followers, which is not established of any of the other contemporary imāms of the capital cities such as al-Awzāᶜī in Shām, the two Ḥammāds in Baṣra, ath-Thawrī in Kūfa, Mālik in Madīnah, and al-Layth ibn Saᶜd in [Cairo] Egypt. The above is from al-Ḥāfiẓ. Thus he is one of the outstanding men amongst the Followers who are comprised by His saying, exalted is He, "...and those who have followed them in doing good: Allah is pleased with them and they are pleased with Him." (Sūrat at-Tawbah: 101)

These statements are narrated from the trustworthy [people of knowledge], and have probably not reached the ears of the ignorant people of our age, since they cast aspersions on Abū Ḥanīfah and try to bring him down from his noble rank. However, Allah refuses aught but to perfect His light whether they like it or not, "Those who do wrong will soon know the kind of reversal they will receive!" (Sūrat ash-Shuᶜarā᾿: 226)

In summary, what has become famous among them – and it is astonishing that some of them have incorporated some of it in their compositions – are the following matters:

That he used to give priority to analogical reasoning over the prophetic Sunnah, and this is a slander without doubt. Whoever has any doubt about that should study *al-Khayrāt al-ḥisān* and *al-Mīzān* and it will become clear to him that his claim will cast him into loss and ruin.

That he was very given to theory (*ra᾿y*), so that the scholars of ḥadīth for this reason called his people the people of theory, but this is not an aspersion in reality, since for people of intelligence a great deal of theory and analogical reasoning demonstrate the eminence of the man and the fullness of his intellect. However, intellect is of no use without transmitted knowledge and transmitted knowledge is of no use without intellect. It is our belief and the belief of every fair person with respect to him that if he had reached an age in which there was a great deal of narration of ḥadīth and in which the scholars of ḥadīth had been quick to disclose their perfection then there would have been little analogical reasoning in his *madhhab*, as ᶜAbd al-Wahhāb ash-Shaᶜrānī said in his *al-Mīzān,* and Mullā Muᶜīn in his book *Dirāsāt al-labīb fi'l-uswat al-ḥasanah bi'l-ḥabīb.*

It is true that he related few prophetic traditions, but this also is not in reality an aspersion, since his rank in this resembles the rank of the aṣ-Ṣiddīq. If this is an aspersion, then Abū Bakr aṣ-Ṣiddīq, really the best human being after the prophets, has been slandered, because he also related few traditions in comparison to the rest of the Companions, so Allah forbid! and again Allah forbid! that they should be treated thus.

It is also said that he was very much given to acts of worship, so much so that he was awake the entire night, which [they say] is an innovation and an error, but this is a statement which issues from negligence, the hearing of which makes my hair stand on end, and I fall into astonishment at the person who says it, because a great deal of worship according to one's capacity, such as staying awake all night, reading all of the Qur'ān in one night, performing one thousand rakᶜahs, and the like of these are narrated by sound narrations of many of the Companions and the Followers, and of those after them among the *fuqahā'* and scholars of ḥadīth, such as ᶜUthmān, ᶜUmar, Ibn ᶜUmar, Tamīm ad-Dārī, ᶜAlī, Shaddād ibn Aws ﷺ and Masrūq, al-Aswad an-Nakhaᶜī, ᶜUrwah ibn az-Zubayr, Thābit al-Banānī, Zayn al-ᶜĀbidīn ᶜAlī ibn al-Ḥusayn, Qatādah, Muḥammad ibn Wāsiᶜ, Manṣūr ibn Zādhān, ᶜAlī ibn ᶜAbdullāh Ibn ᶜAbbās, Imām ash-Shāfiᶜī, Saᶜd ibn Ibrāhīm az-Zuhrī, Shuᶜbah ibn al-Ḥajjāj, al-Khaṭīb al-Baghdādī and innumerable others, so that then [this statement] requires all of them to have been innovators, but whoever requires that is himself the greatest innovator and astray. I have gone into great detail in the matter dealing with both sides of the case in *Iqāmat al-ḥujjah.*

It is said that Sufyān ath-Thawrī, ad-Dāraquṭnī, al-Khaṭīb, adh-Dhahabī and other ḥadīth scholars found fault with him as a narrator of ḥadīth. This is a statement which issues from negligent people, because if an unqualified criticism of someone as a narrator is taken as a defect, then the one criticized must be abandoned, meaning that al-Bukhārī, Muslim, ash-Shāfiᶜī, Aḥmad, Mālik, Muḥammad ibn Isḥāq the author of *al-Maghāzī,* and others of the greatest people of meanings must also be abandoned because each one of them has been criticized as a narrator and found fault with. Indeed, even the Companions of the Messenger of Allah ﷺ are not safe from criticism of their narrations, and so does anyone say that we should accept the criticism of them as damaging? Certainly not! By Allah! no one amongst the great intellects says that about them. Even though some categories of criticism require that one abandon the person criticized, the imām is absolutely free of that according to the people who are fair and sincere, because some of the criticisms which were made of him are obscure in meaning such as the words of adh-Dhahabī in *Mīzān al-iᶜtidāl,* "Ismāᶜīl ibn Ḥammād ibn Abī Ḥanīfah, all three of them are weak."

It is established in the principles [of the science of ḥadīth] that obscure criticism is not acceptable, especially when it is about someone the acceptability of whose testimony is firmly established, the pronouncement of him as someone whose testimony is acceptable having been fully explained and whose imāmate is established. I have expanded on this issue in my treatise *al-Kalām al-mabrūr wa's-saᶜy al-mashkūr* ᶜalā *raghmi anfi man khālafa aṣ-ṣaḥīḥ wa'l-jumhūr.* Some of the criticism came from his contemporaries and it has been established that the criticism of contemporaries are not accepted about each other, particularly if they derive from party spirit or personal animosity. If that were not the case, then Ibn Maᶜīn's criticism of ash-Shāfiᶜī would be acceptable, and Aḥmad's of al-Ḥārith al-Muḥāsibī, al-Ḥārith's of Aḥmad, Mālik's of Ibn Isḥāq the person of the ḥadīth of the two *qullahs,* and of the recitation behind the imām, and the things that other people said about others. Certainly not! By Allah! we do not accept their words about them, and we pay them their portion in full. Some of the criticisms stemmed from later people who were partisan such as ad-Dāraquṭnī, Ibn ᶜAdī and others, about whom the evidence is clear that in this criticism they are aberrant. No one is free from partisanship except for those whom the Creator of strength and power protects. It is established that the like of that is not acceptable from whoever says it, and indeed it is itself the cause of a critical mark being laid against that person himself. Shaykh al-Islām Badr ad-Dīn Maḥmūd al-ᶜAynī told the truth when he said in his research on Sūrat al-Fātiḥah in *al-Bināyah sharḥ al-Hidāyah* concerning ad-Dāraquṭnī, "How does he manage to attribute weakness to Abū Ḥanīfah? He himself is deserving of being called weak because he narrated in his *Musnad* ḥadīth which have serious flaws, are defective, rejected, unusual and fabricated." When he wrote his research on renting land and dwellings in Makkah he said, "As for what Ibn al-Qaṭṭān said, 'The cause of his ascription of weakness to Abū Ḥanīfah was his own bad manners and lack of modesty with respect to him, because Imām ath-Thawrī and Ibn al-Mubārak and their likes regarded Abū Ḥanīfah as trustworthy and praised him. So what is the status of someone who ascribes weakness to him in comparison to these great men?" There are some people who are extreme in criticising narrators, criticising them without care or consideration, and designating as fabricated ḥadīth which are not fabricated. Included among them is Ibn al-Jawzī, aṣ-Ṣaghānī, al-Jūzaqānī, al-Majd al-Fayrūzabādī, Ibn Taymiyyah al-Ḥarrānī of Damascus, Abu'l-Ḥasan ibn al-Qaṭṭān and others, as I have explained at length in *al-Kalām al-mubram* and *al-Ajwibah al-fāḍilah*. Only someone who is negligent and unaware of their posititions runs to accept their statements without verifying them. Some of them, such as Ibn ᶜAdī in his *Kāmil* and adh-Dhahabī in his *Mīzān* have the habit in their compilations of mentioning everything that has been said about the man without distinguishing what is acceptable and what is ignored. Beware! and then again beware! of criticising anyone simply because of their statements, without weighing them against the criticisms of others, all of which I have mentioned in *as-Saᶜy al-mashkūr fī radd al-madhhab al-maᵓthūr*. Some criticisms are not established by narrations which are well regarded, such as the narrations of al-Khaṭīb in criticism of him, and most of those who come after him rely upon his narrations which are rejected and are themselves subject to serious criticism.

It is said that many of his pupils were fabricators and severely criticized as narrators, such as Nūḥ al-Jāmiᶜ, Ibn Muṭīᶜ al-Balkhī, and al-Ḥasan al-Luᵓluᵓī. This criticism is contrary to His saying, exalted is He, "No burden-bearer can bear another's burden." (Sūrat al-Isrāᵓ: 15) If this were a serious criticism then many of the noble people of the Ahl al-Bayt such as Jaᶜfar aṣ-Ṣādiq, Muḥammad al-Bāqir and their predecessors would thus be open to serious criticism, because many of their pupils were shi'ite rejectors [*rāfiḍah* – rejectors of the khalifates of Abū Bakr and ᶜUmar] and were liars.

They say that he narrated a great deal from weak transmitters, but this is a matter in which all the people of knowledge share, because many of the narrators of ash-Shāfiᶜī, Mālik, Aḥmad, al-Bukhārī, Muslim and those who did similar work, were weak.

They say that he had little Arabic. Some of them included this aspersion in their compilations, even though it is not considered a defect according to the people of ḥadīth and the memorisers of traditions, and even though trustworthy people have rebutted it, as in the *Tārīkh* of Ibn Khallikān after mentioning many of his virtues and after praising him a great deal. The *Tārīkh* of al-Khaṭīb contains many things about this, and concludes with reference to those things which it would have been more fitting to leave out and turn away from.

This is an Imām about whose *dīn* there is no doubt, nor about his scrupulousness, nor his powers of memorisation, and who has no defect other than having little Arabic. There is the example of Abū ᶜAmr ibn al-ᶜAlāᵓ al-Muqriᵓ an-Naḥwī who asked him about killing someone with a heavy object, as to whether it required retaliation or not, as is the usual case in his *madhhab* but contrary to ash-Shāfiᶜī. Abū ᶜAmr asked him, "What if he killed someone with the stone projectile from a balista?" And he answered, "Even if he killed him with Abā[3] Qubays!" meaning the mountain overlooking Makkah. The reasoning given is that Abū Ḥanīfah spoke according to the dialect of those who say that the six words which are declined with prepositions: *abū hu* – his father, *akhū hu* – his brother, *ḥamū hu* – his father-in-law, *hanū hu, fū hu* – his mouth, and *dhū māl* – possessor of wealth, are declined in all three states with alif [as *abā, akhā, ḥamā, hanā, fā,* and *dhā*], and they recite in that respect:

> Her father and her father's father [...*abā abā hā* – where *abā abī hā* would be expected], ...

In summary, the Imām's virtues are innumerable, and the defects cited and the criticisms made of him are unacceptable and undependable. His position is most similar in this matter to the last of the prophets of Banī Isrā᾽īl Sayyidunā ᶜĪsā, and the last of the four khulafā᾽ ᶜAlī al-Murtaḍā, in that those who love them excessively and those who hate them excessively both perish. He is like Saᶜd when the people of Kūfa complained of him to ᶜUmar about everything so much that they said, "He doesn't perform the *ṣalāh* well." But Allah showed him how to be free of what they said, and they perished because of his supplication which was always answered. They lost a great deal, as is clear to anyone who peruses the books of sound ḥadīth, the *Sunan* books and the *Musnads*. Whoever wants to study the details of his excellent qualities must refer to the books on his virtues and others, and with these discourage the attribution of imaginary defects to him. In what we have mentioned there is sufficient for those who are fair. As for people who deviate, they are rejected and it is not appropriate that they should be addressed by fair people. We have no need to praise him with false praise or with merits which are not firmly established, as a group of his excessive devotees do, saying that Khiḍr learnt from him, peace and blessings be upon our Prophet and upon him, or that when ᶜĪsā descends at the time of the Dajjāl and the Imām Mahdī, that he and the Mahdī will judge according to his *madhhab*, or that the Messenger of Allah ﷺ gave prophetic good news of him by saying, "There will be in my ummah a man who will have the honorific of Abū Ḥanīfah and whose name will be an-Nuᶜmān..." Traditions such as these are all fabricated, and the claims they make are all falsified, as ᶜAlī al-Qārī verified in *al-Mashrab al-wardī bi madhhab al-mahdī* and as-Suyūṭī in *al-Iᶜlām bi ḥukm ᶜĪsā ᶜalayhi's-salām* and Ibn Ḥajar in *al-Khayrāt al-ḥisān fi manāqib an-Nuᶜmān.*

Topic Eleven

Most people rely upon the *Muwaṭṭa*ᵓ of Mālik in the narration of Yaḥyā al-Andalusī al-Laythī al-Maṣmūdī upon which az-Zurqānī and others wrote commentaries, so that it has come about that it is referred to unqualifiedly as the *Muwaṭṭa*ᵓ, and among all the versions of the *Muwaṭṭa*ᵓ it has become the most famous in all lands, and the people of knowledge have devoted themselves to teaching it, both those in our age and many of those before us. Many of them think that the same cannot be said for the *Muwaṭṭa*ᵓ in the narration of Muḥammad ibn al-Ḥasan ash-Shaybānī, and that it is not comparable, and that it cannot be included in that description.

What I say, seeking fairness from discerning critics, is that the factors which encourage the idea that it is unreliable are all unacceptable according to the most eminent authorities. On the contrary, [in some matters] it outweighs the *Muwaṭṭa*ᵓ of Yaḥyā for reasons which are acceptable to those who have understanding. ...

We have seen before that Yaḥyā al-Andalusī was with Mālik in the year of his death and was there at his preparation for burial, whereas Muḥammad spent three years of his life in close contact with him, and it is well known that a narration which comes from long companionship is stronger than one based upon little contact. ...

With respect to Ḥanafis in particular, there is the fact that the *Muwaṭṭa*ᵓ of Yaḥyā comprises a great deal of the judgements of Mālik which are contrary to the views of Abū Ḥanīfah and his people, and that it comprises many ḥadīth which Abū Ḥanīfah and his companions did not act by because they regarded them as abrogated, or because of a consensus in favour of a different judgement, or because of an apparent weakness in the chain of transmission, or because something else outweighed [those ḥadīth], and for other reasons which appeared to them. Thus the one who considers this can become confused, and it might cause the beginner and the untaught person to cast aspersions on the one [the *fuqahā*ᵓ] or on the other [the ḥadīth]. However, it is different with the *Muwaṭṭa*ᵓ of Muḥammad because it comprises the ḥadīth which they acted upon after mention of those on which they did not act. This becomes clear to anyone who studies the matter of raising the hands [in prayer], recitation behind the imām, and other issues. This is useful to the beginner and the untaught person and for the elite and the educated person. As for the untaught person, he will be protected from forming a bad opinion. As for the educated person he will come to know by critical study of both sets of ḥadīth, the which ruling is implied as superior. You will discover in this book of mine, inshāʾAllāh, exalted is He, mention of the weightiest judgements in their places according to the different *madhhabs* without any of the partisan spirit typical of the Jāhiliyyah.

You may say that the *Muwaṭṭa*ʾ of Yaḥyā stands out as *the Muwaṭṭa*ʾ without qualification, and that this is the result of its being weightier than the other *Muwaṭṭas*, whereas the *Muwaṭṭa*ʾ of Muḥammad does not stand out in the same way. I would say therefore, that what necessarily follows is that the *Muwaṭṭa*ʾ of Yaḥyā outweighs the *Muwaṭṭas* of al-Qaʿnabī and at-Tinnīsī also, who are the most reliable in transmitting the *Muwaṭṭa*ʾ according to Ibn Maʿīn, Ibn al-Madīnī and an-Nasāʾī, and that it outweighs the *Muwaṭṭa*ʾ of Maʿn ibn ʿĪsā also, who is the most reliable transmitter of the *Muwaṭṭa*ʾ according to Abū Ḥātim as we have mentioned in the sixth useful point, but it is not so.

You may say that the *Muwaṭṭa*ʾ of Yaḥyā is the one which is famous all over the world, whereas the *Muwaṭṭa*ʾ of Muḥammad is not so. I would say that this does not necessitate in any way that it is the weightiest, because the reason for its fame, as az-Zurqānī mentioned in his commentary, is that:

> When Yaḥyā returned to al-Andalus he became the leader in fiqh there, and because of him the *madhhab* spread and innumerable people learnt fiqh from him. He was offered the post of *qāḍī* but he refused. His standing rose higher than that of *qāḍī*, and his word was accepted by the sulṭān, and he would not appoint anyone as *qāḍī* in his regions without his counsel and his choice, and he [Yaḥyā] would only appoint his companions [whom he was sure knew the fiqh], and so people turned towards him to obtain their purposes, and this is the reason for the fame of the *Muwaṭṭa*ʾ in his narration as opposed to other narrations in the west. …

You may say that Yaḥyā al-Andalusī is a trustworthy narrator, whereas Muḥammad is not. Then I would say that if you mean by that that no aspersions were ever cast on Yaḥyā as a narrator, it is false, because of what az-Zurqānī said in his biographical material on him, "A faqīh who is trustworthy [as a narrator], who has few ḥadīth, but who has some errors. He died in 234 AH." If you say that the aspersions against him do not dent his trustworthiness, then it is similar with Muḥammad, for the aspersions which are cast against him do not require us to give him up as a narrator. The response to the aspersions against him is the same as the response to the aspersions against his shaykh, according to what we have already seen in *al-Mīzān,* that he was one of the oceans of knowledge and fiqh, who was a strong narrator from Mālik. If it is established that he is weak narrating from people other than Mālik, that does not affect us here.

If you say that many of the shaykhs in the chains of transmission which Muḥammad narrated are weak, then I say that as for the chains of transmission which he narrated by way of Mālik, their shaykhs are the same ones mentioned in the *Muwaṭṭa* of Yaḥyā and of others, and one can do no harm by mentioning them [since they have the same standing in all versions of the *Muwaṭṭa*]. As for those which he narrates from others, it is not true that all of the men who narrate them are weak. On the contrary, most of the men are strong, trustworthy men, and the fact that some of them are weak does not set us back irreversibly, because this would not be the first crystal glass to be broken in Islam. Whoever claims that all of them are weak should produce his witnesses.

If you say that a large body of the scholars of ḥadīth do not count the *Muwaṭṭa*ᵓ of Muḥammad as one of the accepted *Muwaṭṭas,* and they do not rely upon it as much as they rely on the other *Muwaṭṭas,* then I say that if that is for a real reason then so be it, but if not, then saying such a thing lacks respect, for there is a substantial body of ḥadīth scholars who count it as one of the versions of the *Muwaṭṭa* and who study its narration as critically as they do the other narrations.

If you say that Yaḥyā and other narrators of the *Muwaṭṭa*ᵓ were ḥadīth scholars whereas Muḥammad was one of the people of theory and he was not a ḥadīth scholar, then I say that it is not like that, because Muḥammad has many compilations in fiqh and ḥadīth such as this book, the *Kitāb al-āthār* and others, whereas Yaḥyā is not famous for any compilation other than his *Muwaṭṭa*ᵓ, and our discussion is about them not about anyone other than these two. As for the aspersion that he is one of the people of theory, it is unacceptable to intelligent people and sound theory as we have seen already in the discussion of his shaykhs.

Topic Twelve: Enumeration of the Ḥadīth and Traditions which are in the *Muwaṭṭa*ᵓ of Imām Muḥammad...

Topic Thirteen: The Usages of Imām Muḥammad in this Book and his Scholarship

He mentions the chapter heading and mentions immediately after it a narration from Imām Mālik whether a *mawqūf* [statement said by someone without ascribing it to the Prophet ﷺ] or a *marfūʿ* [ḥadīth ascribed to the Prophet ﷺ].

He only mentions in the title the wording 'book' or 'chapter', and sometimes the wording 'chapters'. He does not use in any place the wording 'section' except in one place on which the different copies of the text differ, and so possibly it is from the people who made those copies [and not from Imām Muḥammad].

He mentions after mentioning the ḥadīth, or a number of ḥadīth an indication of what it contains of benefit: "this we adhere to," "it is the verdict we adhere to," and then after that he mentions some details, sometimes being contented with one of the above two statements. The like of this shows his choice and his *fatwā*.

As as-Sayyid Aḥmad al-Ḥamawī said in *Ḥawāshi'l-ashbāh wa'n-nadhāʾir* among the collection of concealed and confused things:

> As for the signs which show us that it is a *fatwā*, they are such as his saying, "The *fatwā* is based on it, by the *fatwā* is given, on that one depends, by that we take, on that we depend, on that is the practice of the ummah, on that the practice is based today, that is the sound position, that is the most sound, it is the obvious position, it is the most obvious, it is the chosen position in our time, the *fatwā* of our shaykhs, it is the most like [the Sunnah], and it is the most acceptable."

He draws attention to those things derived from his narration from Mālik that contradict the path he has chosen and he mentions the chain of transmission of his *madhhab* through a way other than Mālik.

He does not confine himself, in that which he narrates from someone other than Mālik, to a specific shaykh such as Abū Ḥanīfah, but on the contrary, he gives a chain of transmission from him and from others. His practice in the *Kitāb al-āthār* was to give a great many chains of transmission from him and only a few from others.

In his narration from his shaykhs he uses the expression "He informed us" only, and he does not say, "I heard," nor "he narrated to us," nor any other phrase. It is well known as the terminology of later scholars that they distinguished between "he narrated to us," and "he informed us" in that the first was particularly for those things heard in the wording of the shaykh, such as "I heard," and the second was in the case where he himself read it out to the shaykh. Some say that it is the *madhhab* of al-Awzāᶜī, ash-Shāfiᶜī, Muslim, an-Nasāʾī, and others. Another group regard them as the same thing, and that is the *madhhab* of the people of the Ḥijāz [Makkah and Madīnah], the Kūfans, Mālik, Ibn ᶜUyaynah, al-Bukhārī and others. It is like that in the commentaries on the commentary on *an-Nukhbah*. The details of this investigation can be found in my treatise *Ẓufr al-amānī*.

He mentions, after mentioning his choice, its agreement with his Shaykh when he says, "That is the verdict of Abū Ḥanīfah," except for in a few cases where he disagreed with Abū Ḥanīfah.

He often says, after mentioning Abū Ḥanīfah, "...and [the verdict] of people in general of our *fuqahāʾ*," by which he means the *fuqahāʾ* of ᶜIrāq and Kūfa. Generality (*ᶜāmmah*) is used, according to their usage, to mean "the majority". Ibn al-Hammām said in *Fatḥ al-qadīr* while examining what the main body understood, "A body of the people who know the Arabic language took the position that 'people in general' means 'the majority' but that there is a divergence of opinion on that. The shaykhs mentioned that that is what is meant in, 'That is the verdict of people in general of the shaykhs,' and the like."

Apparently he does not mean in every occurrence of this wording "the majority", but rather he means "the group (*jamāᶜah*)" and the "party (*ṭāʾifah*)", because in some of the places which he marks with it, it is not the path which the majority took.

He also clearly makes reference to the school of Ibrāhīm an-Nakhaᶜī, since he is the pivot of the way taken by the Ḥanafīs.

The scholar of ḥadīth [Shāh Walī Allāh] ad-Dihlawī, author of *Ḥujjatu'llāh al-bālighah*, and other works, said in his treatise *al-Inṣāf fī bayān sabab al-ikhtilāf*:

> By my life! it [the treatise] really is what it is called [The Fair Position in Explanation of the Reasons for Disagreement], and whoever studies it clear sightedly will no longer be lost. When the *madhhabs* of the Companions and the Followers differed on a case, then every man of knowledge chose the *madhhab* of the people of his country and their shaykhs, because he was more acquainted with what the sound views among them were and what views were unsound. So the

> *madhhab* of ᶜUmar, ᶜUthmān, Ibn ᶜUmar, Ibn ᶜAbbās, Zayd ibn Thābit, and their people such as Saᶜīd ibn al-Musayyab – because he was the one who most memorised and protected the judgements of ᶜUmar, the ḥadīth of Abū Hurayrah, Sālim, ᶜIkrimah, ᶜAṭā᾽ and their likes – had more right than others to be taken according to the people of Madīnah. The *madhhab* of ᶜAbdullāh ibn Masᶜūd and his companions, the judgements of ᶜAlī, Shurayḥ and ash-Shaᶜbī, and the *fatwās* of Ibrāhīm an-Nakhaᶜī had more right than others to be taken according to the people of Kūfa. When the people of a country agreed upon something they seized on it with determination. That is what Mālik conveys in expressions like, "The Sunnah about which there is no disagreement with us," etc. When they differed they took the position based on the strongest [of their statements] and the weightiest.

The above is abridged. He also said in this treatise:

> Mālik was the one among them who had the most knowledge of the judgements of ᶜUmar, ᶜAbdullāh ibn ᶜUmar, ᶜĀ᾽ishah, and their companions of the seven *fuqahā᾽* [of Madīnah]. Abū Ḥanīfah was the one who most clung to the *madhhab* of Ibrāhīm [an-Nakhaᶜī] so much so that he would not exceed it, except as much as Allah willed. It was very important for him to derive judgements according to his *madhhab*, and he was minutely aware of the different aspects of derivation, turning his attention to the derivative rulings with the most complete attention. If you wish to know the truth about which I speak, then extract the statements of an-Nakhaᶜī from *Kitāb al-āthār* by Muḥammad, the *Jāmiᶜ* of ᶜAbd ar-Razzāq and the *Muṣannaf* of Ibn Abī Shaybah, and then measure them against his *madhhab* and you will find that it does not differ from that way except in very few places, and those few places in which it does does, it does not depart from the position of the *fuqahā᾽* of Kūfa. The most famous of his companions was Abū Yūsuf, who was appointed to the post of chief *qāḍī* in the days of Hārūn ar-Rashīd, and who was the cause for the victory of his *madhhab*, and the fact that judgement was issued according to it in all the areas of ᶜIrāq, Khurāsān and Transoxiana. The best of them in compilation, and the most tenacious in study was Muḥammad ibn al-Ḥasan. A part

of his story is that he learnt fiqh from Abū Ḥanīfah and Abū Yūsuf, and then he went to Madīnah and read the *Muwaṭṭaʾ* to Mālik. He then fell back on his own resources and compared the *madhhab* of his companions with the *Muwaṭṭaʾ* case by case, and if it agreed with it [well and good], but if not and he saw that a party of the Companions and the Followers had taken the same position as that of his companions, then likewise [well and good]. If he found that there was a weak analogical deduction or a weak derivation of a ruling contradicted by a sound ḥadīth that the *fuqahāʾ* acted upon, and that the practice of most of the people of knowledge contradicted it, then he would give it up for one of the positions taken by the right-acting first generations which he found to be weightier than what he had. Both of them continued on the path of Ibrāhīm [an-Nakhaᶜī] as much as possible, just as Abū Ḥanīfah had done. They differed for one of two reasons only: either because their shaykh had a derivation according to the *madhhab* of Ibrāhīm [an-Nakhaᶜī] over which they contended with him, or because Ibrāhīm and his peers had different positions [narrated from them] over which they disagreed with him as to which was the weightiest. Muḥammad compiled and he gathered the theory of these three. He benefitted many people. Then the people of Abū Ḥanīfah turned towards those compilations and summarised and clarified them, derived rulings, attended to their foundations, and deduced matters from them. Then they went to Khurāsān and Transoxiana, and that became known as the *madhhab* of Abū Ḥanīfah. The *madhhab* of Abū Yūsuf and Muḥammad was only counted as one in that they were both absolute mujtahids who disagreed on only a few things in the principles (*uṣūl*) and the derivative rulings (*furūᶜ*), because of their harmoniousness in this respect, and because of their recording their *madhhab* in *al-Mabsūṭ* and *al-Jāmiᶜ al-kabīr*. (Abridged by Shaykh ᶜAbd al-Ḥayy)

He does not mention in this book nor in the *Kitāb al-āthār* the position of his companion Abū Yūsuf, neither where it agrees nor where it differs. Beware of understanding his restricting himself to mentioning his own *madhhab* and his Shaykh's *madhhab* as a case of implied opposition, i.e. his disagreeing with him, as al-Qārī understood in some of his treatises and which you will come to see in the appropriate places [in his commentary on the *Muwaṭṭaʾ*].

Likewise, beware of implying agreement based on the fact that if he had disagreed he would have mentioned it, since his habit in *al-Jāmiᶜ aṣ-ṣaghīr* and others of his compilations is the opposite of that.

He often says, "This is good," or "beautiful", or "commendable" and the like, by which he means something broader than the equivalent of being *wājib,* as well as being placed in conjunction with his saying in some places, "This is good but it is not a *wājib,*" so that it comprises the Sunnah which is firmly established (*mu᾽akkadah*) and those Sunnahs which are not firmly established. Beware of understanding it in every case where he designates it thus, as something that is recommended but not Sunnah.

With respect to some matters which are Sunnah, he says the wording, "There is no harm," as in the examination of the *tarāwīḥ* prayers and other instances, meaning essentially permissibility and nothing else, whereas among later scholars it is in the main used to indicate something which is disapproved [but is added as a rideṛ to show that it is not forbidden]. Beware of not distinguishing between the two usages and thus falling into disgrace.

He often says, "Such and such ought to be…", so do not understand by it, with respect to the usages of later scholars, that every matter he expresses thus is recommended and is not Sunnah or wājib, because this expression is used by the earliest scholars with a more universal meaning comprising the Sunnah *mu᾽akkadah* and the wājib. Thus, when al-Qudūrī says in his abridgement, "People ought to seek the new moon on the twenty-ninth day, i.e. of Shaᶜbān," Ibn al-Hamām explained it saying, "It is a wājib for them," meaning a *wājib kifāyah* [such that if some discharge it, the others are freed of the obligation].

Ibn ᶜĀbidīn ash-Shāmī said in *Radd al-muḥtār ḥāshiyah ad-durr al-mukhtār* in the book on *jihād*:

> What is well known of the later scholars is the use of "ought" in the sense of "it is recommended", and "ought not" in the sense of "disapproved" to be steered clear of, even if in the usages of the earlier scholars it signifies something more general than that, and it occurs a great deal in the Qur᾽ān, such as His saying, exalted is He, "It would not have been fitting for us to have taken any protectors apart from You." (Sūrat al-Furqan: 18) He said in *al-Miṣbāḥ,* "It 'ought to be' such and such, meaning in the sense of *wājib* or in the sense of recommendation, according to what there is in it of request."

He may mention the *madhhab* of his shaykh Mālik also, whether agreeing with him or disagreeing, and the *madhhabs* of the Companions, with or without chains of transmission.

He uses the word tradition (*athar*) without any qualification, intending by that a more general meaning comprising *marfūᶜ* [ḥadīth ascribed directly to the Prophet ﷺ through an unbroken chain of transmitters], and *mawqūf* [statements said without ascribing them to the Prophet ﷺ] which stop short at the Companions and those after them, which is the usage of the earlier scholars, whilst some of those who disagreed with them used it particularly for those which are *mawqūf* [statements said without ascribing them to the Prophet ﷺ], which is the well known usage of later fiqh scholars, as an-Nawawī realised in *al-Minhāj sharḥ ṣaḥīḥ Muslim ibn al-Ḥajjāj* and which I have explained in detail in *Ẓufr al-amānī bi sharḥ al-mukhtasar al-manṣūb īlā al-Jurjānī,* may Allah give me success in completing it as He granted me the ability to begin it.

He mentions some traditions without chains of transmission, and introduces them with the phrase, "It has reached me," and they mention, as is found in *Radd al-muḥtār* and others, that these all have chains of transmission.

Conclusion

In this book there are no fabricated ḥadīth, even though there are some weak ones most of which are only very slightly weak and are strengthened by the many paths of transmission. Some of them are extremely weak but cause no great harm because of the similar narrations with sound paths of transmission. You will discover all of this in the appropriate places [in the commentary *at-Taᶜlīq al-mumajjad*], inshāʾAllāh.

This is the end of the introduction, and I hope from Allah for a good seal to my destiny, and a good life in the *dunyā* and the next life [*ākhirah*], and praise belongs to Allah the Lord of the worlds, and blessings and peace be upon His Messenger Muḥammad and all his family and his companions.

NOTES TO THE INTRODUCTION

[1] *Musnads* are arranged according to the names of the narrators from the chains of transmission.

[2] *Raʾy* literally means 'seeing' or 'vision' as does 'theory'. It is often mistakenly translated, in my view, as 'opinion'.

[3] Ordinarily the genitive case after a preposition would be Abī Qubays.

أبواب الصلاة

1. THE PRAYER

١ باب وقوت الصلاة

1. The Times of the Prayer

١ قال محمدُ بن الحسن: أخبرنا مالكُ بنُ أنس، عن يزيدَ بن زياد مَولَى بنياهاشم، عن عبد الله بن رافعٍ مولى أمِّ سَلَمَة رضي الله عنها زوج النَّبيِّ صلى لله عليه وسلم، عن أبي هريرةَ أنه سَأَلَهُ عن وَقْتِ الصلاة فَقَالَ أبو هُريرة أنا أُخْبِرُكَ: صلِّ الظهرَ إذا كان ظلُّكَ مثْلَكَ، والعصر إذا كان ظلُّك مثلَيْكَ، والمغرب إذا غَرَبَت الشمسُ، والعشاء ما بَيْنَكَ وبَيْنَ ثُلُثِ اللَّيْلِ، فَإِنْ نِمْتَ إلى نصف اللَّيلِ فلا نامَتْ عَيْنَاكَ، وَصَلِّ الصُّبحَ بغَلَسٍ.

1. Muḥammad ibn al-Ḥasan said: "Mālik ibn Ānas informed us from Yazīd ibn Ziyād, the *mawlā* of Banū Hāshim, that ᶜAbdullāh ibn Rāfiᶜ, the *mawlā* of Umm Salamah ﵂ the wife of the Prophet ﷺ, asked Abū Hurayrah about the times of the prayer and Abū Hurayrah said, 'I will tell you: pray *Ẓuhr* when [the length of] your shadow is equal to your height, and *ᶜAṣr* when your shadow is twice your height, and *Maghrib* when the sun has set, and *ᶜIshāʾ* from then until the [passing of a] third of the night, and, should you sleep until the passing of half the night, then let your eyes not sleep, and pray *Ṣubḥ* in darkness.'"

قال محمد: هذا قولُ أبي حنيْفَةَ رَحِمَهُ اللَّهُ في وَقْتِ العَصْرِ، وكان يَرى الإسْفَارَ في الْفَجْرِ، وأمّا في قولنا فإنّا نقولُ: إذا زَادَ الظِّلُّ على المِثْلِ فصار مِثْلَ الشيء وزيادةً من حينَ زَالتِ الشَّمْسُ، فقد دخلَ وَقْتُ العَصْرِ. وأمّا أبو حنيفةَ فإنّه قال: لا يَدْخُلُ وَقْتُ العصرِ حتّى يَصِيرَ الظلُّ مثليْه.

Muḥammad said: "This was the verdict of Abū Ḥanīfah, may Allah have mercy on him, concerning the time of *ᶜAṣr*, and he used to consider the time when [the dawn] glowed clearly as *Fajr*. As for our verdict, we say that when the shadow [of an object] has grown longer than the object, and therefore has arrived at and exceeded the length of the object as the sun moves beyond its zenith, then the time of *ᶜAṣr* has arrived. As for Abū Ḥanīfah, he said that the time for *ᶜAṣr* does not arrive until the shadow [of an object] becomes twice its length."

٢ أخبرَنا مالك، أخبرني ابن شهاب الزُّهْري، عَن عُروةَ قال: حَدَّثَتْني عائشةُ رضيَ الله عَنْها، أنَّ رسولَ الله صلى الله عليه وسلم كَانَ يُصَلِّي الْعَصْرَ والشمسُ في حُجْرَتِهَا قَبْلَ أَنْ تَظْهَرَ.

2. Mālik informed us: "Ibn Shihāb az-Zuhrī informed me that ᶜUrwah said, "ᶜĀʾishah ﵂ narrated to me that the Messenger of Allah ﷺ used to pray *ᶜAṣr* when the sun was [shining] into her room, before it had [itself] become visible [i.e. because it was still high in the sky]."

٣ أخبرنا مالك قال: أخبرني ابنُ شهابٍ الزُّهْريُّ، عن أنسِ بنِ مالكٍ أنّه قال: كنّا نصلّي العصرَ ثمّ يَذْهَبُ الذاهبُ إلى قُباء فيأتيهم و الشمسُ مرتفعة.

3. Mālik informed us: "Ibn Shihāb az-Zuhrī informed me that Anas ibn Mālik said, 'We used to pray *ᶜAṣr*, then someone would leave to go to Qubā᾽, and reach them whilst the sun was still high.'"

٤ أخبرنا مالك، أخبرنا إسحاقُ بنُ عبدِ الله بن أبي طلحة، عن أنسِ بنِ مالك، قال: كنا نصلّي العصر، ثم يخرج الإنسان إلى بني عمرو بنِ عوف فيجدُهم يصلّون العصر.

4. Mālik informed us: "Isḥāq ibn ᶜAbdullāh ibn Abī Ṭalḥah informed us that Anas ibn Mālik said, 'We used to pray *ᶜAṣr*, and then someone would go out to Banū ᶜAmr ibn ᶜAwf and find them praying *ᶜAṣr*.'"

قالَ مُحَمَّدٌ: تأخيرُ العَصْرِ أَفْضَلُ عِنْدَنا مِنْ تَعْجيلِها إذا صَلَّيْتَها وَالشَّمسُ بَيْضاءُ نَقيَّةٌ لَمْ تَدْخُلْها صُفْرَةٌ، وبذلك جاءَتْ عامَّةُ الآثارِ، وهو قولُ أبي حَنيفةَ. وقَدْ قالَ بَعْضُ الفُقَهاءِ: إنَّما سُمِّيت العَصْرُ لأنَّها تُعْصَرُ وتُؤخَّر.

Muḥammad said: "Praying *ᶜAṣr* later is better, in our view, than praying it sooner, provided you pray it while the sun is white and pure, before any yellowness enters it. That is the import of the majority of narrations and is also the verdict of Abū Ḥanīfah. Indeed, some of the *fuqahā᾽* have said, 'It is called *ᶜAṣr* for no other reason than its being squeezed [*tuᶜṣar*] and delayed.'"

باب ابتداء الوضوء

2. Beginning *Wuḍū᾽*

٥ أَخْبَرَنا مَالِكٌ، أخبرنا عَمرو بنُ يَحْيى بن عُمَارة بنِ أبي حَسَنٍ المازنيُّ، عن أبيه يحيى أنَّه سَمِعَ جدَّهُ أبا حَسَنٍ يَسألُ عبدَ اللهِ بنَ زَيْد بن عَاصِمٍ وكانَ مِن أصحابِ رسول الله صلى الله عليه وسلم قال: هل تستطيعُ أن تُرِيَني كَيف كان رسول اللّه صلى الله عليه وسلم يَتوضَّأُ قال عبدُ الله بنُ زَيْد: نَعَم، فدعا بوَضُوْءٍ فَأَفْرَغَ على يَدَيْه فغَسَلَ يَدَيْه مرَّتَين، ثُمَّ مَضْمَضَ، ثُمَّ غَسَلَ وَجْهَهُ ثَلاثًا، ثُمَّ غَسَلَ يَدَيْه إلى المِرْفَقَيْن مرَّتَيْن، ثُمَّ مَسَحَ مِنْ مُقَدَّمِ رأسِه حتى ذَهَبَ بهما إلى قَفاه، ثُمَّ رَدَّهُما إلى المكان الَّذي منه بَدَأَ، ثمّ غَسَلَ رِجْلَيْه.

5. Mālik informed us: "ᶜAmr ibn Yaḥyā ibn ᶜUmārah ibn Abī Ḥasan al-Māzinī informed us from his father Yaḥyā that he heard his grandfather Abū Ḥasan ask ᶜAbdullāh ibn Zayd ibn ᶜĀṣim, one of the Companions of the Messenger of Allah ﷺ, saying, 'Could you show me how the Messenger of Allah ﷺ used to perform *wuḍū᾽*?' ᶜAbdullāh ibn Zayd said, 'Yes,' and called for water. Then he poured [some] onto his hands and washed them twice, then he rinsed his mouth, then he washed his face three times, then he washed his arms to the elbows twice each, then using his hands, he wiped his head from the front down to the back of his neck, then [re-wiped it by] bringing them back to the place he'd started from, then he washed his feet."

قال محمد: هَذَا حَسَنٌ والوُضوءُ ثَلاثاً ثلاثاً أفْضَلُ والاثنان يُجْزِيان، والواحدةُ إذا أَسْبَغَتْ تُجزئ أيضاً وهو قول أبي حنيفة.

Muḥammad said: "This is fine, though washing three times is better, even twice is enough, and so is once, so long as it is made to cover [all the required areas]. That is the verdict of Abū Ḥanīfah, may Allah have mercy on him."

٦ أخبرنا مالك، حدثنا أبو الزِّناد، عن عبد الرحمن الأعْرَج، عن أبي هريرة، قال: إذا توضَّأ أحدُكُم فلْيَجْعَلْ في أنفه، ثم ليَستَنثر.

6. Mālik informed us: "Abu'z-Zinād narrated to us from ᶜAbd ar-Raḥmān al-Aᶜraj that Abū Hurayrah said, 'When any of you performs *wuḍūʾ*, let him take [water] into his nose and then blow [it] out.'"

٧ أخبرنا مالكٌ، حدَّثنا الزُّهري، عَنْ أَبي إِدْرِيسَ الخَولانيِّ، عن أبي هريرة: أن رسول الله صلى الله عليه وسلم قَالَ: "من توضَّأ فَلْيَسْتَنثر ومن اسْتَجْمَرَ فَلْيُوتر".

7. Mālik informed us: "Az-Zuhrī narrated to us from Abū Idrīs al-Khawlānī from Abū Hurayrah that the Messenger of Allah ﷺ said, 'Whoever performs *wuḍūʾ*, let him expel whatever is in his nostrils and whoever uses stones [to remove faeces], let him use an odd number.'"

قال محمد: وبهذا نأخُذُ، ينبغي للمتوضِّئ أن يتمضمض ويَسْتَنْثِرَ، وينبغي له أيضاً أن يَسْتَجمر. والاستجمارُ: الاستنجاء، وهو قول أبي حنيفة.

Muḥammad said: "We adhere to this [report]; whoever is performing *wuḍūʾ* ought to rinse his mouth and expel whatever is in his nose and he ought also to use stones. The 'using of stones' refers to the removal of faeces. And That is the verdict of Abū Ḥanīfah."

٨ أخبرنا مالك، أخبرنا نعيم بن عبد الله المُجْمِر، أنه سمع أبا هريرة يقول: من توضَّأ فَأَحْسَنَ وَضوءَهُ ثمَّ خَرَجَ عَامداً إلى الصلاة فهو في صلاة ما كان يَعْمِدُ وأنه تُكْتَبُ له بإحدى خَطْوَتَيْه حَسَنَةٌ، وتُمحى عنه بالأخرى سيِّئة، فإنْ سَمِعَ أحدُكم الإقامةَ فلا يَسْعَ، فإنَّ أعظَمَكم أَجْراً أبعَدُكُم داراً قالوا: لِمَ يا أبا هريرة؟ قال: من أجل كَثْرة الخُطَا.

8. Mālik informed us: "Nuᶜaym ibn ᶜAbdullāh al-Mujmir informed us that he heard Abū Hurayrah say, 'Whoever performs his *wuḍūʾ* as best he can, then sets out for the prayer, is in prayer as long as he has set out for this [purpose]; a good deed is written for every one step he takes and a bad deed is erased for every other step. So, if one of you hears the *iqāmah*, let him not hurry, for the greatest of you in reward is the one whose home is farthest away.' They said, 'Why, Abū Hurayrah?' He said, 'Because of the greater number of steps.'"

٣ باب غسل اليدين في الوضوء

3. Washing the Hands when Performing *Wuḍūʾ*

٩ أخبرنا مالك، أخبرنا أبو الزِّناد، عن الأعرج، عن أبي هريرة أنَّ رسول الله صلى الله عليه وسلم قال:

"إذا استيقظ أَحَدُكُم من نومِه فَلْيَغْسِلِ يَدَه قبل أن يُدْخِلَها في وَضُوئِه ، فإنَّ أَحَدَكم لا يَدري أين باتت يَدُه .
9. Mālik informed us: "Abu'z-Zinād informed us from al-Aʿraj from Abū Hurayrah that the Messenger of Allah ﷺ said, 'When any of you wake up let him wash his hand before he inserts it in his *wuḍū’* bowl, for he has no idea where his hand spent the night.'"

قال محمد: هذا حَسَن ، وهكذا ينبغي أن يفعَلَ وليس من الأمر الواجب الذي إنْ تركه تاركٌ أثم ، وهو قول أبي حنيفة رحمه الله .
Muḥammad said: "This is good; and this is what he ought to do, though it is not one of the compulsory matters which if someone leaves he will have done a wrong action; this is the verdict of Abū Ḥanīfah, may Allah have mercy on him."

٤ باب الوضوء في الاستنجاء

4. Washing after Defecation

١٠ أخبرنا مالك، أخبرنا يحيى بنُ محمد بنِ طَحلاء ، عن عثمانَ بنِ عبد الرحمن أن أباه أخبره: أنه سمع عمرَ بنَ الخطاب رضي الله عنه يتوضّأ وضوءً لما تحت إزاره .
10. Mālik informed us: "Yaḥyā ibn Muḥammad ibn Taḥlā informed us from ʿUthmān ibn ʿAbd ar-Raḥmān that his father told him that he heard ʿUmar ibn al-Khaṭṭāb ﷺ washing that which is below the the large cloth wrapped around the lower half of the body [*izār*]."

قال محمد: وبهذا نأخذ والاستنجاء بالماء أحبُّ إلينا من غيره وهو قول أبي حنيفة رحمه الله تعالى .
Muḥammad said: "We adhere to this; and cleaning oneself with water is preferable to us than [doing] otherwise; and that is the verdict of Abū Ḥanīfah, may Allah have mercy on him."

٥ باب الوضوء من مسِّ الذَّكر

5. Performing *Wuḍū’* after Touching the Penis

١١ أخبرنا مالك، حدثنا إسماعيل بن محمد بن سعد بن أبي وقّاص، عن مصعب بن سعد قال: كنتُ أمسكُ المصحفَ على سعد فاحتككت فقال: لعلّكَ مسستَ ذَكَرَكَ، فقلتَ: نعم، قال: قم فتوضأ قال: فقُمتُ فتوضَّأتُ ثم رجعت .
11. Mālik informed us: "Ismāʿīl ibn Muḥammad ibn Saʿd ibn Abī Waqqāṣ narrated to us that Musʿab ibn Saʿd said, 'I used to wait upon Saʿd, holding the copy of the Qur’ān, and I scratched myself so he said, "Perhaps you touched your penis?" I said, "Yes." He said, "Get up and perform *wuḍū’*." So I got up and performed *wuḍū’*, then returned.'"

١٢ أخبرنا مالك، أخبرني ابن شهاب، عن سالمِ بن عبد الله ، عن أبيه أنه كان يغتسلُ ثم يتوضّأ،فقال له: أما يُجْزيك الغُسلُ من الوضوء ؟ قال: بلى ولكني أحياناً أمس ذكري فأتوضأ .

12. Mālik informed us: "Ibn Shihāb informed us from Sālim ibn ᶜAbdullāh from his father that he used to do *ghusl* and then perform *wuḍūʾ*; so he said to him, 'Doesn't doing *ghusl* preclude you from having to perform *wuḍūʾ*?' He said, 'Yes, but sometimes I touch my penis, so I perform *wuḍūʾ*.'"

قال محمد: لا وضوءَ في مسِّ الذكر وهو قول أبي حنيفة، وفي ذلك آثار كثيرة.

Muḥammad said: "There is no [need to do] *wuḍūʾ* after touching the penis; there are many narrations concerning this."

١٣ قال محمد: أخبرنا أيّوب بن عُتبة التَّيْميّ قاضي اليَمامة، عن قيس بن طلق أن أباه حدَّثه: أن رجلاً سأل رسول الله صلى الله عليه وسلم عن رجلٍ مسَّ ذَكَرَه، أيتوضأ؟ قال: هل هو إلا بَضْعة من جسدك.

13. Muḥammad said: "Ayyūb ibn ᶜUtbah at-Taymī, the qāḍī of al-Yamāmah, informed us from Qays ibn Ṭalq that his father narrated to him that a man asked the Messenger of Allah ﷺ about a man's touching his penis, 'Should he do *wuḍūʾ*?' He said, 'Is it anything but a part of your body?'"

١٤ قال محمد: أخبرنا طلحة بن عمرو المكّي، أخبرنا عطاءُ بنُ أبي رَباح، عن ابن عباس قال: في مسِّ الذكر وأنتَ في الصلاة، قال: ما أُبالي مسستُهُ أو مسست أَنْفي.

14. Muḥammad said: "Ṭalḥah ibn ᶜAmr al-Makkī informed us, 'ᶜAṭāʾ ibn Abī Rabāḥ informed us from Ibn ᶜAbbās, who said concerning touching the penis while you are in prayer, 'I don't mind whether I touch it or I touch my nose.'"

١٥ قال محمد: أخبرنا إبراهيم ابن محمد المَدَني، أخبرنا صالح مولى التَّوأمة، عن ابن عباس، قال: ليس في مسّ الذكر وضوء.

15. Muḥammad said: "Ibrāhīm ibn Muḥammad al-Madanī informed us, 'Ṣāliḥ the *mawlā* of at-Tawʾamah informed us from Ibn ᶜAbbās, who said, 'There is no doing *wuḍūʾ* after touching the penis.'"

١٦ قال محمد: أخبرنا إبراهيم بن محمد المدني، أخبرنا الحارث بن أبي ذباب، أنه سمع سعيد بن المسيِّب يقول: ليس في مسِّ الذَّكَر وضوء.

16. Muḥammad said: "Ibrāhīm ibn Muḥammad al-Madanī informed us, 'Al-Ḥārith ibn Abī Dhubāb informed us that he heard Saᶜīd ibn al-Musayyab say, 'There is no doing *wuḍūʾ* after touching the penis.'"

١٧ قال محمد: أخبرنا أبو العوّام البصري، قال: سأل رجلٌ عطاءَ بنَ أبي رباح، قال: يا أبا محمد رجل مسَّ فرجَه بعد ما توضّأ؟ قال رجل من القوم: إنَّ ابن عباس رضي الله عنهما كان يقول: إن كنتَ تَستَنْجِسُه فاقطَعْه، قال عطاء بن أبي رباح: هذا والله قول ابن عباس.

17. Muḥammad said: "Abū al-ᶜAwwām al-Baṣrī informed us, 'A man asked ᶜAṭāʾ ibn Abī Rabāḥ, "Abū Muḥammad, [what do you say concerning] a man who touches his private parts after doing *wuḍūʾ*?" A man amongst the people said, "Ibn ᶜAbbās used to say, 'If you consider it an impurity cut it off.'" ᶜAṭāʾ ibn Abī Rabāḥ said, "This, by Allah, is the verdict of Ibn ᶜAbbās.""'

١٨ قال محمد: أخبرنا أبو حنيفة رحمه الله عن حمّاد، عن إبراهيم النَّخعي، عن عليّ بن أبي طالب رضي الله عنه في مسِّ الذَّكَر، قال: ما أبالي مسستُهُ أو طرفَ أنفي.

18. Muḥammad said: "Abū Ḥanīfah informed us from Ḥammād from Ibrāhīm an-Nakhaᶜī from ᶜAlī ibn Abī Ṭālib concerning touching the penis, that he said, 'I don't mind whether I touch that or the tip of my nose.'"

١٩ قال محمد: أخبرنا أبو حنيفة، عن حمّاد، عن إبراهيم: أنّ ابنَ مسعود سئل عن الوضوء من مسِّ الذكر؟ فقال: إنْ كان نجساً فاقْطَعْه.

19. Muḥammad said: "Abū Ḥanīfah informed us from Ḥammād from Ibrāhīm that Ibn Masᶜūd was asked about doing *wuḍūʾ* after touching the penis and he said 'If it is an impurity cut it off.'"

٢٠ قال محمد: أخبرنا مُحلٌّ الضَّبِّي، عن إبراهيم النَّخَعي في مسِّ الذكر في الصلاة، قال: إنما هو بَضْعة منك.

20. Muḥammad said: "Muḥill aḍ-Ḍabbī informed us from Ibrāhīm al-Nakha'i, concerning touching the penis whilst in prayer, that he said, 'It is nothing more than one of your body parts.'"

٢١ قال محمد: أخبرنا سلاّم بن سُلَيْم الحنفي، عن منصور بن المعتمر، عن أبي قيس، عن أرقمَ بن شُرَحْبيل، قال: قلتُ: لعبد الله بن مسعود: إني أحكُّ جسدي و أنا في الصلاة فأمسُّ ذكري، فقال: إنما هو بَضْعةٌ منك.

21. Muḥammad said: "Sallām ibn Sulaym al-Ḥanafī informed us from Manṣūr ibn al-Muᶜtamir from Abū Qays from Arqam ibn Shuraḥbīl who said, 'I said to ᶜAbdullāh ibn Masᶜūd, "I scratch my body whilst in prayer and touch my penis." He said, "It is nothing more than one of your body parts."'"

٢٢ قال محمد: أخبرنا سلاّم بن سُلَيم، عن منصور بن المعتمر عن السَّدُوسيِّ، عن البراء بن قيسٍ، قال: سألتُ حذيفةَ ابن اليمان، عن الرجُلِ مسَّ ذكَرَه، فقال: إنما هو كمسِّه رأسَه.

22. Muḥammad said: "Sallām ibn Sulaym informed us from Manṣūr ibn al-Muᶜtamir from as-Sadūsī from al-Barāʾ ibn Qays who said, 'I asked Ḥudhayfah ibn al-Yamān about a man's touching his penis, and he said, "It is just like his touching his head."'"

٢٣ قال محمد: أخبرنا مسعَرُ بن كدَام، عن عمير بن سعد النَّخَعي، قال: كنتُ في مجلسٍ فيه عَمّارُ بنُ ياسر فذكر مسَّ الذَّكَر، فقال: إنما هو بَضْعةٌ منك وإنَّ لكَفِّك لموضعاً غيره.

23. Muḥammad said: "Misᶜar ibn Kidām informed us from ᶜUmayr ibn Saᶜd an-Nakhaᶜī that he said, 'I was in a sitting with ᶜAmmār ibn Yāsir and touching the penis was mentioned and he said, "It is nothing more than one of your body parts, but your hand should be elsewhere."'"

٢٤ قال محمد: أخبرنا مسْعَر بن كِدام، عن إياد بن لَقيط، عن البراء بنِ قيسٍ قال: قال حذيفةُ بنُ اليمان في مسِّ الذكر مثل أنفك.

24. Muḥammad said: "Misᶜar ibn Kidām informed us from Iyād ibn Laqīṭ

from al-Barā' ibn Qays that he said, 'Ḥudhayfah ibn al-Yamān said, concerning touching the penis, "[It is] like [touching] your nose."'"

٢٥ قال محمد: أخبرنا مِسْعَرُ بنُ كدام، حدثنا قابوس، عن أبي ظَبيان، عن عليِّ بنِ أبي طالبٍ رضي الله عنه، قال: ما أبالي إيّاه مسستُ أو أنفي أو أُذُني.

25. Muḥammad said: "Misᶜar ibn Kidām informed us, 'Qābūs narrated to us from Abū Ẓabyān from ᶜAlī ibn Abī Ṭālib, who said, "I don't mind whether I touch that or my nose or my ear."'"

٢٦ قال محمد: أخبرنا أبو كُدَيْنة يحيى بنُ المُهَلّب، عن أبي إسحاقَ الشَّيْباني، عن أبي قَيسٍ عبد الرحمن بنِ ثَرْوان، عن علقمة، عن قيس، قال جاء رجل إلى عبد الله بن مسعود، قال: إني مسستُ ذَكَري وأنا في الصلاة، فقال عبد الله: أفلا قطعتَه؟، ثم قال: وهل ذَكَرُكَ إلاّ كسائر جسدك؟

26. Muḥammad said: "Abū Kudaynah Yaḥyā ibn al-Muhallab informed us from Abū Isḥāq ash-Shaybānī from Abū Qays ᶜAbd ar-Raḥmān ibn Tharwān from ᶜAlqamah from Qays who said, 'A man came to ᶜAbdullāh ibn Masᶜūd and said, "I touched my penis whilst in prayer." ᶜAbdullāh said, "Why did you not cut it off?" Then he said, "Is your penis any different from the rest of your body?"'"

٢٧ قال محمد: أخبرنا يحيى بنُ المهلّب، عن إسماعيلَ بنِ أبي خالد، عن قيس بنِ أبي حازم، قال: جاء رجلٌ إلى سعد بن أبي وقّاص، قال: أيحلُّ لي أن أمسَّ ذَكَري وأنا في الصلاة؟ فقال: إنْ علمتَ أنَّ منك بضعة نجسة فاقطعها.

27. Muḥammad said: "Yaḥyā ibn al-Muhallab informed us from Ismāᶜīl ibn Abī Khālid from Qays ibn Abī Ḥāzim who said, 'A man came to Saᶜd ibn Abī Waqqāṣ and said, "Is it allowed for me to touch my penis whilst in prayer?" So he said, "If you know that you have an impure body part, cut it off."'"

٢٨ قال محمد: أخبرنا إسماعيلُ بنُ عيّاش، قال: حدثني جَريرُ بنُ عثمان، عن حبيب، عن عُبيد، عن أبي الدَّرداءِ أنه سُئل عن مسِّ الذكر، فقال: إنما هو بَضعَةٌ منك.

28. Muḥammad said: "Ismāᶜīl ibn ᶜAyyāsh informed us, 'Jarīr ibn ᶜUthmān narrated to me from Ḥabīb ibn ᶜUbayd from Abu'd-Dardā', that he was asked about touching the penis and said, 'It is nothing more than one of your body parts.'"

٦ باب الوضوء مما غيّرت النار

6. *Wuḍū'* after [Eating] Something which has been Altered by Fire [During Cooking]

٢٩ أخبرنا مالك، حدثنا وهب بن كَيْسان، قال: سمعتُ جابرَ بن عبد الله يقول: رأيتُ أبا بكرٍ الصِّدِّيق أكل لحماً ثم صلّى ولم يتوضّأْ.

29. Mālik informed us: "Wahb ibn Kaysān narrated [this] to us. He said, 'I heard Jābir ibn ᶜAbdullāh say, "I saw Abū Bakr aṣ-Ṣiddīq eat meat and then pray and he did not do *wuḍū'*."'"

٣٠ أخبرنا مالك، حدثنا زيدُ بنُ أسلم، عن عطاءِ بنِ يَسار، عن ابن عباس: أنَّ رسولَ الله صلى الله عليه وسلم أكل جَنْبَ شاةٍ، ثم صلَّى ولم يتوضَّأ .

30. Mālik informed us: "Zayd ibn Aslam narrated to us from ᶜAṭā᾽ ibn Yasār from Ibn ᶜAbbās that the Messenger of Allah ﷺ ate a portion of sheep and then prayed and he did not do *wuḍū᾽*.""

٣١ أخبرنا مالك، أخبرنا محمدُ بنُ المُنْكَدِر ، عن محمد بنِ إبراهيم التَّيمي، عن ربيعةَ ، عن عبدِ الله : أنه تعشَّى مع عمر بنِ الخطاب ، ثمَّ صَلَّى ولم يتوضَّأ.

31. Mālik informed us: "Muḥammad ibn al-Munkadir informed us from Muḥammad ibn Ibrāhīm at-Taymī from Rabīᶜah from ᶜAbdullāh that he took his evening meal with ᶜUmar ibn al-Khaṭṭāb and then prayed and he did not do *wuḍū᾽*."

٣٢ أخبرنا مالك، أخبرني ضَمْرَةُ بنُ سعيدٍ المازنيّ، عن أبانَ ابن عثمان: أن عثمان بنَ عفّانَ أكل لحماً وخُبزاً فتمضمضَ وغسَلَ يديه ، ثم مسحهما بوجهه، ثم صلّى ولم يتوضّأ.

32. Mālik informed us: "Ẓamrah ibn Saᶜīd al-Māzinī informed me from Abān ibn ᶜUthmān that ᶜUthmān ibn ᶜAffān ate meat and bread, then rinsed his mouth and washed his hands, wiped them over his face and prayed and he did not do *wuḍū᾽*."

٣٣ أخبرنا مالك، أخبرنا يحيى بنُ سعيد، قال: سألت عبدَ الله بنَ عامرِ بنِ ربيعة العَدَوي ، عن الرجل يتوضأ، ثم يصيب الطعام قد مسَّته النار أيتوضّأ منه؟ قال: قد رأيتُ أبي يفعلُ ذلك ، ثم لا يتوضّأ.

33. Mālik informed us: "Yaḥyā ibn Saᶜīd informed us, 'I asked ᶜAbdullāh ibn ᶜĀmir ibn Rabīᶜah al-ᶜAdawī about a man's doing *wuḍū᾽* then eating from food which fire had touched [cooked], whether he should do *wuḍū᾽* due to that? He said, "I saw my father do that and he did not then do *wuḍū᾽*."'"

٣٤ أخبرنا مالك، أخبرنا يحيى بن سعيد، عن بُشَير بن يسار مولى بني حارثة ، أن سُويد ابن نعمان أخبره: أنه خرج مع رسول الله صلى الله عليه وسلم عام خَيْبَر حتى إذا كانوا بالصَّهباء وهي أدنى خيبر صلّوا العصر، ثم دعا رسولُ الله صلى الله عليه وسلم بالأزواد ، فلم يُؤْتَ إلاّ بالسَّويق، فأمر به فثُرِّيَ لهم بالماء، فأكل رسول الله صلى الله عليه وسلم وأكلنا، ثم قام إلى المغرب، فمضمض ومضمضنا، ثم صلى ولم يتوضأ .

34. Mālik informed us: "Yaḥyā ibn Saᶜīd informed us from Bushayr ibn Yasār, the *mawlā* of Banū Ḥārithah, that Suwayd ibn Nuᶜmān told him that he went out with the Messenger of Allah ﷺ in the year of Khaybar, then when they reached aṣ-Ṣahbā', which is the nearest part of Khaybar, they prayed *ᶜAṣr*. 'Then the Messenger of Allah ﷺ called for the provisions and nothing was brought except sawīq [a meal of cooked grains], so he gave orders and it was mixed with water for them and the Messenger of Allah ﷺ ate and we ate. Then he got up for *Maghrib* and he rinsed his mouth and we rinsed our mouths; then he prayed and he did not do *wuḍū᾽*.'"

قال محمد : وبهذا نأخذ، لا وضوء مما مسّته النار ولا مما دخل ، إنما الوضوءُ مما خَرَجَ من الحدث ،

فأما ما دخل من الطعام مما مسَّته النار أو لم تمسَّسه فلا وضوءَ فيه ، وهو قول أبي حنيفة رحمه الله .

Muḥammad said: "And we adhere to this; there is no doing *wuḍūʾ* due to [eating] what fire has touched [cooked], nor from its entering [the body]. Doing *wuḍūʾ* is only necessitated by the exit [from the body] of impurities. So, as for the entry of any food which fire has touched or has not touched, there is no need to do *wuḍūʾ* as a result of it. That is the verdict of Abū Ḥanīfah, may Allah have mercy on him."

٧ باب الرجل والمرأة يتوضّآن من إناء واحد
7. A Man and Woman Doing *Wuḍūʾ* from One Pot

٣٥ أخبرنا مالك، حدّثنا نافع ، عن ابن عمر : كان الرجالُ والنساءُ يتوضَّؤون جميعاً في زمنِ رسول الله صلى الله عليه وسلم .

35. Mālik informed us: "Nāfiʿ narrated to us from Ibn ʿUmar, "Men and women used to do *wuḍūʾ* together in the time of the Messenger of Allah ﷺ."

قال محمد : لا بأس بأن تتوضَّأ المرأةُ وتغتسلُ مع الرجلِ من إناءٍ واحدٍ إن بدأتْ قبله أو بدأ قبلها ، وهو قول أبي حنيفة رحمه الله .

Muḥammad said, "There is no harm if a woman [wife] should do *wuḍūʾ* or do *ghusl* with the man from one pot whether she starts before him or he before her; and that is the verdict of Abū Ḥanīfah, may Allah have mercy on him."

٨ باب الوضوء من الرُّعاف
8. Doing *Wuḍūʾ* because of a Nosebleed

٣٦ أخبرنا مالك، حدثنا نافع، عن ابن عمر: أنه كان إذا رعفَ رَجَعَ فتوضّأ ولم يتكلَّمْ، ثم رجع فبنى على ما صلَّى .

36. Mālik informed us: "Nāfiʿ narrated to us that when Ibn ʿUmar had a nosebleed [during the prayer], he would, without speaking, leave, do *wuḍūʾ*, return and continue his prayer from where he had left off."

٣٧ أخبرنا مالك، حدثنا يزيدُ بنُ عبد الله بن قُسَيط، أنه رأى سعيد بن المسيب رَعَفَ وهو يصلِّي فأتى حُجْرة أُمِّ سلمة زوج النبيِّ صلى الله عليه وسلم فأُتِي بوَضوءٍ فتوضّأ، ثم رَجَعَ فبنى على ما قد صلى .

37. Mālik informed us: "Yazīd ibn ʿAbdullāh ibn Qusayṭ narrated to us that he saw Saʿīd ibn al-Musayyab having a nosebleed whilst he was praying, so he came to the room of Umm Salamah, the wife of the Prophet ﷺ, and a bowl [of water] was brought to him. He performed *wuḍūʾ*, then returned and continued his prayer from where he had left off."

٣٨ أخبرنا مالك، أخبرنا يحيى بن سعيد، عن سعيد بن المسيب: أنه سئل عن الذي يَرْعُفُ فيَكْثُرُ عليه الدَّمُ كيف يصلِّي؟ قال: يُومئ إيماءً برأسه في الصلاة.

38. Mālik informed us: "Yaḥyā ibn Sa'īd informed us that Sa'īd ibn al-Musayyab was asked about how someone who has a nosebleed should pray where the bleeding has become profuse. He said, 'In the prayer he should perform its movements with his head only.'"

٣٩ أخبرنا مالك، أخبرنا عبدُ الرحمن بنُ المُجَبَّر بن عبد الرحمن بن عمر بن الخطاب: أنه رأى سالم بنَ عبد الله بن عمر يُدْخِلُ إصبعه في أنفه أو إصبعيه ثم يخرجها وفيها شيء من دم فيَفْتِلُهُ ثم يصلِّي ولا يتوضَّأ.

39. Mālik informed us: "'Abd ar-Raḥmān ibn al-Mujabbar ibn 'Abd ar-Raḥmān ibn 'Umar ibn al-Khaṭṭāb informed us that he saw Sālim ibn 'Abdullāh ibn 'Umar put his finger, or two fingers, into his nose, then take them out with blood on them, pinch his nose and then pray without doing *wuḍū'*."

قال محمد: وبهذا كلِّه نأخذ، فأما الرُّعَاف فإنّ مالكَ بن أنس كان لا يأخذ بذلك، ويرى إذا رَعَفَ الرجُلُ في صلاته أن يغسل الدَّمَ ويستقبلَ الصلاة. فأما أبو حنيفةَ فإنّه يقول بما روى مالكٌ عن ابن عمر، وعن سعيد بن المسيّب إنَّه ينصرفُ فيتوضّأ، ثم يَبني على ما صلّى إنْ لم يتكلّم، وهو قولُنا. وأما إذا كثر الرُّعَاف على الرجُل فكان إنْ أَوْمَأَ برأسه إيماءً، لم يَرْعُفْ وإن سَجَدَ رَعَفَ. أَوْمَأَ برأسه إيماءً، وأجزاه، وإن كان يَرْعُفُ كل حال سجد. وأما إذا أدخل الرجُلُ إصبَعَهُ في أنفه فأخرج عليها شيئاً من دم فهذا لا وضوءَ فيه لأنه غير سائل ولا قاطر، وإنما الوضوء في الدم مما سال أو قطر، وهو قولُ أبي حنيفة.

Muḥammad said: "We conform to all of this. As for nosebleeds, Mālik ibn Anas did not adhere to that and thought that when a man got a nosebleed in his prayer, he should wash the blood [away] and begin the prayer again. As for Abū Ḥanīfah, he based his view on what Mālik narrated from Ibn 'Umar and Sa'īd ibn al-Musayyab, that he should go, do *wuḍū'*, then continue from where he had left off if he has not spoken; and that is our verdict. As for the case where the nosebleed is such that when praying with head movements only, there is no bleeding, but when prostrating it bleeds, he should use head movements only, that being sufficient to discharge the prayer. However, if he bleeds no matter what his position, then he should prostrate. And As for the instance where a finger is placed in the nose and is removed with blood on it, this does not necessitate *wuḍū'*, since it [the blood] is neither running, nor dripping. Doing *wuḍū'* becomes necessary only for that blood which runs or drips. And That is the verdict of Abū Ḥanīfah, may Allah have mercy on him."

٩ باب الغَسل من بول الصبيّ

9.Washing the Urine of a Child

٤٠ أخبرنا مالك، حدثنا الزُّهري، عن عبيد الله بن عبد الله، عن أمِّ قيس بنت مِحْصَن: أنها جاءتْ

بابنٍ لها صغيرٍ لم يأكل الطعامَ إلى رسول الله صلى الله عليه وسلم، فوضعه النبيُّ صلى الله عليه وسلم في حُجْره ، فبالَ على ثوبه فدعا بماءٍ فنضح عليه ولم يَغْسِلْه .

40. Mālik informed us: "Az-Zuhrī narrated to us from ᶜUbaydullāh ibn ᶜAbdullāh from Umm Qays bint Miḥṣan, that she brought a young son of hers, who had not yet eaten food, to the Messenger of Allah ﷺ. The Prophet ﷺ placed him in his lap and he urinated on his garment; he called for water and sprinkled it and did not wash it."

قال محمد: قد جاءت رخصةٌ في بول الغلام إذا كان لم يأكل الطعام، وأمر بغَسْلِ بول الجارية، وغَسْلُهما جميعاً أحبُّ إلينا وهو قول أبي حنيفة .

Muḥammad said: "A concession has been granted concerning the urine of a boy who has not eaten food; and an order has been given to wash the urine of a girl. And Washing both of them is preferable to us; and this is the verdict of Abū Ḥanīfah, may Allah have mercy on him."

٤١ أخبرنا مالك، أخبرنا هشامُ بنُ عروة، عن أبيه ، عن عائشة رضي الله عنها، أنها قالت: أُتي النبي صلى الله عليه وسلم بصبيٍّ فبال على ثوبه، فدعا بماء فأَتْبَعَه إيّاه .

41. Mālik informed us: "Hishām ibn ᶜUrwah informed us from his father from ᶜĀʾishah, that she said, "A baby boy was brought to the Prophet ﷺ and he urinated on his garment, so he called for water and poured it over it."

قال محمد: وبهذا نأخذ: تُتْبِعُه إيّاه غسلاً حتى تُنْقِيَهُ ، وهو قول أبي حنيفة رحمه الله.

Muḥammad said: "We accept this [report] and we follow it up with washing until clean; and this is the verdict of Abū Ḥanīfah. may Allah have mercy on him."

١٠ باب الوضوء من المذي

10. Doing *Wuḍūʾ* because of *Madhy* [Prostatic Fluid]

٤٢ أخبرنا مالك، أخبرني سالم أبو النَّضر مولى عمر بن عبيد بن معمر التَّيمي ، عن سليمان بن يَسَار، عن المقداد بنِ الأسود، أن عليَّ بنَ أبي طالبٍ رضي الله عنه أمره أنْ يسأل رسول الله صلى الله عليه وسلم عَن الرَجل إذا دنا من أهله فخرج منه المَذْيُ ماذا عليه ؟ فإن عندي ابنَته وأنا أستَحي أن أسألَهُ، فقال المقداد: فسألتُه، فقال: إذا وَجَدَ أحدُكم ذلك فلينضَح فرجه، وليتوضَّأ وُضوءَهُ للصلاة .

42. Mālik informed us: "Sālim Abu'n-Naḍr, the *mawlā* of ᶜUmar ibn ᶜUbaydullāh ibn Muᶜammar at-Taymī, informed me from Sulaymān ibn Yasār from al-Miqdād ibn al-Aswad, that ᶜAlī ibn Abī Ṭālib told him: to 'Ask the Messenger of Allah ﷺ about what a man should do who approaches his wife and madhy [prostatic fluid] issues from him; for it is his daughter with me and I shy away from asking him.' Al-Miqdād said, 'So I asked him and he said, "If one of you finds that, let him wash his private parts with water and do *wuḍūʾ* in the same way as for the prayer."'"

٤٣ أخبرنا مالك، أخبرني زيدُ بنُ أسلَمَ، عن أبيه ، عن عمر بن الخطّاب رضي الله عنه، قال: إني لأَجِدُهُ يتحدَّرُ مني مثلَ الخُرَيْزة ، فإذا وَجَدَ أحدُكم ذلك فليَغْسِلْ فَرجه وليتوضَّأْ وضوءه للصلاة.

43. Mālik informed us: "Zayd ibn Aslam informed me from his father, that ᶜUmar ibn al-Khaṭṭāb said, 'I find it falling from me like small beads, so when one of you finds that let him wash his private parts and do *wuḍūʾ* in the same way as for the prayer.'"

قال محمد: وبهذا نأخذ: يغسل موضعَ المذْيِ ويتوضأ وضوءه للصلاة، وهو قول أبي حنيفة رحمه الله.

Muḥammad said: "We accept this [report]; he should wash the site of the madhy and do *wuḍūʾ* as he does for the prayer. That is the verdict of Abū Ḥanīfah, may Allah have mercy on him."

٤٤ أخبرنا مالك، أخبرنا الصَّلْتُ بنُ زُيَيْد أنه سأل سليمانَ بنَ يسار عن بللٍ يَجِدُهُ فقال: انْضَحْ ما تحت ثوبكَ والْهَ عنه.

44. Mālik informed us: "Aṣ-Ṣalt ibn az-Zuyayd informed us that he asked Sulaymān ibn Yasār about some wetness which he sometimes experienced and he said, "Sprinkle what is under your garment [with water] and forget about it."

قال محمد: وبهذا نأخذ، إذا كثر ذلك من الإنسان، وأدخل الشيطانُ عليه في الشكّ، وهو قول أبي حنيفة رحمه الله.

Muḥammad said: "We adhere to this, should it happen a great deal to a person and shayṭān plague him with doubt concerning it; and this is the verdict of Abū Ḥanīfah, may Allah have mercy on him."

١١ باب الوضوء مما يشرب منه السباع وتلغ فيه

11. Doing *Wuḍūʾ* with Water from which Predatory Animals Drink and Lap

٤٥ أخبرنا مالك، أخبرنا يحيى بن سعيد ، عن محمد بنِ إبراهيمَ بنِ الحارث التَّيْمي، عن يحيى بنِ عبد الرحمن بن حاطب بن أبي بَلْتَعَةَ أنَّ عُمَرَ بنَ الخطاب رضي الله عنه خرج في ركبٍ فيهم عمرُو بنُ العاص، حتى وردوا حوضاً، فقال عمرُو بنُ العاص: يا صاحبَ الحوضِ هل تَرِدُ حوضَكَ السباع؟ فقال عمرُ بن الخطاب: يا صاحبَ الحوض، لا تُخبِرْنا ، فإنّا نَرِدُ على السِّباع وتَرِدُ علينا.

45. Mālik informed us: "Yaḥyā ibn Saᶜīd informed us from Muḥammad ibn Ibrāhīm ibn al-Ḥārith at-Taymī from Yaḥyā ibn ᶜAbd ar-Raḥmān ibn Ḥāṭib ibn Abī Baltaᶜah, that ᶜUmar ibn al-Khaṭṭāb rode out in a group among whom was ᶜAmr ibn al-ᶜĀṣ, until they came to a pond, whereupon ᶜAmr ibn al-ᶜĀṣ said, 'Companion of the pond, do predators come down to your pond?" whereupon ᶜUmar ibn al-Khaṭṭāb said, "Companion of the pond, don't tell us, for we come down to water after predators and they come down after us.'"

قال محمد: إذا كان الحوضُ عظيماً إنْ حُرِّكتْ منه ناحيةٌ لم تتحرَّكْ به الناحيةُ الأخرى لم يُفسدْ ذلك الماءَ ما ولغ فيه من سَبُعٍ، ولا ما وقع فيه من قَذَر إلاّ أن يَغْلبَ على ريح أو طعم، فإذا كان حَوْضاً صغيراً إنْ حُرِّكت منه ناحية تحرَّكَتْ الناحيةُ الأخرى فولغ فيه السباع أو وقع فيه القذر لا يتوضّأ منه، ألا يرى أن عمر بن الخطاب رضي الله عنه كَرِهَ أن يُخْبِرَهُ ونهاه عن ذلك، وهذا كلُّه قولُ أبي حنيفة رحمه الله.

Muḥammad said: "If the pond is very large such that when the water on one side of it is disturbed, the ripples do not reach the other side, then no predatory animal which laps from it or filth which falls in it befouls that water, unless it causes its smell or taste to change. If the pond is small such that when the water on one side of it is disturbed the ripples reach the other side, then when predators lap from it or filth falls in it, it should not be used to do *wuḍū*ʾ. It should be noted that ʿUmar ibn al-Khaṭṭāb ﷺ did not want him [the owner of the pond] to tell him about it and prohibited him from doing so; Abū Ḥanīfah's verdict is in accordance with all of this, may Allah have mercy on him."

١٢ باب الوضوء بماء البحر

12. Doing *Wuḍū*ʾ with Sea Water

٤٦ أخبرنا مالك، حدَّثنا صفوانُ بنُ سُلَيم، عن سعيد بن سلمةَ بنِ الأزرق، عن المغيرة بن أبي بُردة، عن أبي هريرة: أن رجلاً سأل رسولَ الله صلى الله عليه وسلم فقال: إنا نركبُ البَحْرَ ونحملُ معنا القليلَ من الماء، فإنْ توضّأنا به عَطِشنا، أفنتوضّأ بماء البحر؟ فقال رسول الله صلى الله عليه وسلم: هو الطَّهورُ ماؤه الحَلالُ مَيْتَتُهُ.

46. Mālik informed us: "Ṣafwān ibn Sulaym narrated to us from Saʿīd ibn Salamah ibn al-Azraq from al-Mughīrah ibn Abī Burdah from Abū Hurayrah, that a man asked the Messenger of Allah ﷺ saying, "We go to sea taking only a little water with us; so if we do *wuḍū*ʾ with it we will go thirsty. Shall we do *wuḍū*ʾ with sea water?" The Messenger of Allah ﷺ said, "Its water is pure and its dead are *ḥalāl*."

قال محمد: وبهذا نأخُذُ: ماءُ البحر طهورٌ كغيره من المياه، وهو قول أبي حنيفة رحمه الله والعامة.

Muḥammad said: "We adhere to this. Sea water is pure, just as is other water. That is the verdict of Abū Ḥanīfah, may Allah have mercy on him, and of [our *fuqahā*ʾ] in general."

١٣ باب المسح على الخُفَّين

13. Wiping over Leather Socks [*Khuff*]

٤٧ أخبرنا مالك، أخبرنا ابن شهابٍ الزُّهري، عن عبَّاد بن زياد من وُلْد المغيرة بن شعبة: أنّ النبيَّ صلى الله عليه وسلم ذَهَبَ لحاجته في غزوة تبوك، قال: فذهبتَ معه بماء، قال: فجاء النبيُّ صلى

الله عليه وسلم ، فسكبتُ عليه ، قال: فغسَلَ وجْهَهُ ثم ذهب يُخْرِجُ يديه فلم يستطع من ضيق كُمَّي جُبَّته فأخرجهما من تحت جُبَّته فغسَلَ يديه ومسَحَ برأسه ومسَحَ على الخفَّين، ثم جاء رسول الله صَلَى الله عليه وسلم وعبد الرحمَن بنُ عوف يؤمُّهم قد صلى بهم سجدة ، فصلّى معهم رسول الله صلى الله عليه وسلم ، ثم صلّى الرَّكعة التي بَقِيَت، ففزِعَ الناسُ له ثم قال لهم: قد أحسنتم .

47. Mālik informed us: "Ibn Shihāb az-Zuhrī informed us from ᶜAbbād ibn Ziyād from one of the children of al-Mughīrah ibn Shuᶜbah, that the Prophet ﷺ went to relieve himself during the expedition of Tabūk. He [al-Mughīrah] said, 'So I went with him, carrying some water.' He continued, 'Then the Prophet came ﷺ and I poured [the water] for him. He washed his face, and then he tried to bring out his arms but he could not, due to the narrowness of the sleeves of his long robe-like outer garment [*jubbah*]; so he brought them out from under his outer garment and washed his arms and wiped his head and wiped over the leather socks [*khuff*]. Then the Messenger of Allah ﷺ came and ᶜAbd ar-Raḥmān ibn ᶜAwf was leading them, having already made one prostration with them, so the Messenger of Allah ﷺ prayed with them and then prayed the remaining *rakᶜah*. So the people were alarmed at that. Then he said to them, "You have done well."'"

٤٨ أخبرنا مالكٌ: حدَّثنا سعيدُ بنُ عبد الرحمن بن رُقَيش أنه قال : رأيت أنس بنَ مالكٍ أتى قباء، فبال، ثم أتى بماء، فتوضأ، فغسَلَ وجهَهُ ويدَيْهِ إلى المرفقين ومسَحَ برأسه، ثم مسح على الخفين ، ثم صلّى .

48. Mālik informed us: "Saᶜīd ibn ᶜAbd ar-Raḥmān ibn Ruqaysh narrated [this] to us. He said, 'I saw Anas ibn Mālik come to Qubā᾽. He urinated, and then water was brought and he did *wuḍū᾽*. He washed his face and his arms to the elbows, wiped his head, wiped over his leather socks, and then prayed.'"

٤٩ أخبرنا مالك، حدّثنا نافعٌ وعبدُ الله بن دينار : أن عبد الله بن عمر قدمَ الكوفة على سعد بن أبي وقّاص وهو أميرها ، فرآه عبد الله وهو يمسَحُ على الخفَّين، فأنكر ذلك عليه، فقال له: سَلْ أباك إذا قَدمتَ عليه، فنسي عبد الله أن يسأله حتى قَدِم سعد، فقال : أسألتَ أباك؟ فقال : لا ، فسأله عبد الله، فقال : إذا أدْخَلْتَ رجليكَ في الخُفين وهما طاهرتان فامسح عليهما، قال عبد الله : وإن جاء أحد من الغائط ؟ قال: وإن جاء أحدُكُم من الغائط.

49. Mālik informed us: "Nāfiᶜ and ᶜAbdullāh ibn Dīnār narrated to us that ᶜAbdullāh ibn ᶜUmar came to Saᶜd ibn Abī Waqqāṣ at Kūfa, and he was then its governor. ᶜAbdullāh saw him wipe over leather socks and he reproved him for it, so he said to him, 'Ask your father when you see him.' But then ᶜAbdullāh forgot to ask him until Saᶜd arrived and said, 'Did you ask your father?' He said, 'No.' So ᶜAbdullāh asked him and he [ᶜUmar] said, 'If your feet were in a state of purity when you put the leather socks on, then wipe over them.' ᶜAbdullāh said, 'Even if one of us has just returned from relieving

himself?' He said, 'Even if one of you has just returned from relieving himself.'"

٥٠ أخبرنا مالك، أخبرني نافع: أن ابنَ عمر بال بالسوق ، ثم توضّأ فغسل وجهه ويديه، ومسح برأسه، ثم دُعي لجنازة حين دخل المسجد ليصلي عليه (×)، فمَسَح على خُفَّيْه ثم صلى .

50. Mālik informed us: "Nāfi[c] informed me, that Ibn [c]Umar urinated at the market and then did *wuḍū*[ɔ]. He washed his face and arms and wiped his head. Then, when he entered the mosque, he was called to someone's funeral that he might pray [the funeral prayer] for him, so he wiped over his leather socks and then prayed."

٥١ أخبرنا مالكٌ، أخبرني هشامُ بنُ عروة، عن أبيه: أنه رأى أباه يمسَحُ على الخُفَّين على ظهورهما لا يمسح بطونهما، قال: ثم يرفعُ العمامة فيمسَحُ برأسه .

51. Mālik informed us: "Hishām ibn [c]Urwah informed me from his father, that he saw his father wipe over leather socks on their upper sides, without wiping their under sides, then lift his turban and wipe his head."

قال محمد: وبهذا كلّه ، نأخذ، وهو قول أبي حنيفة، ونرى المسحَ للمقيم يوماً وليلةً وثلاثةَ أيامٍ ولياليَها للمسافر. وقال مالكُ بنُ أنس : لا يمسَحُ المقيم على الخُفَّين. وعامّةُ هذه الآثار التي روى مالك في المسح إنما هي في المقيم، ثم قال: لا يمسح المقيم على الخُفَّين.

Muḥammad said: "We adhere to all of this, and it is the verdict of Abū Ḥanīfah. We are of the opinion that wiping may be done by a resident for a day and a night and by a traveller for three days and nights. Mālik ibn Anas said that a resident should not wipe over leather socks, whereas the majority of these reports which Mālik narrated concerning wiping are concerned with none other than residents; and then he said a resident should not wipe over leather socks."

١٤ باب المسح على العِمامة والخِمار

14. Wiping over the Turban and the Headscarf

٥٢ أخبرنا مالكٌ، قال: بلغني عن جابر بن عبد الله أنه سئل عن العمامة ؟ فقال : لا، حتى يمسَّ الشعرَ الماءُ.

52. Mālik informed us: "A report reached me from Jābir ibn [c]Abdullāh, that he was asked about [wiping over] the turban and he said, 'No, not without the water touching the hair.'"

قال محمد: وبهذا نأخذ، وهو قولُ أبي حنيفة رحمه الله.

Muḥammad said: "We adhere to this; it is the verdict of Abū Ḥanīfah. may Allah be merciful to him."

٥٣ أخبرنا مالكٌ، حدَّثنا نافع قال: رأيت صفيَّة ابنةَ أبي عُبيد تتوضَّأُ وتنزِعُ خِمَارَها ، ثم تمسَحُ برأسها . قال نافع: وأنا يومئذ صغير .

53. Mālik informed us: "Nāfi[c] narrated [this] to us. He said, 'I saw Ṣafiyyah bint Abī [c]Ubayd doing *wuḍū*[ɔ], she pulled off her headscarf then wiped her head.' Nāfi[c] said, 'and I was a young boy at the time.'"

قال محمد: وبهذا نأخذ، لا يُمسَحُ على الخمار ولا العمامة ، بَلَغنا أن المسح على العمامة كان فتُرك، وهو قول أبي حنيفة والعامَّة من فقهائنا .

Muḥammad said: "We adhere to this; the headscarf should not be wiped over, nor the turban. It has been narrated to us that wiping over the turban was practised, then abandoned. This is the verdict of Abū Ḥanīfah and our *fuqahāʾ* in general."

١٥ باب الاغتسال من الجنابة

15. *Ghusl* because of Sexual Intercourse or Ejaculation [*Janābah*][1]

٥٤ أخبرنا مالكٌ، حدثنا نافع: أن ابن عمر كان إذا اغتسَلَ من الجنابة أفرغ على يده اليُمنى فغسَلَها، ثم غَسل فَرْجَه ومَضْمَضَ واستنشق، وغسل وجهه، ونضح في عينيه، ثم غسل يدَهُ اليُمنى ثم اليُسرى، ثم غَسَلَ رأسه، ثم اغتسل و أفاض الماءَ على جلده.

54. Mālik informed us: "Nāfiʿ narrated to us that when Ibn ʿUmar did *ghusl* after sexual intercourse or ejaculation, he would pour water onto his right hand and wash it, then wash his private parts, then rinse his mouth, blow water out from his nose, wash his face and sprinkle water in his eyes; he would then wash his right arm, then his left, then wash his head, then wash himself all over, pouring the water over his skin."

قال محمد: وبهذا كلّه نأخُذُ إلاّ النَّضْحَ في العينين، فإنَّ ذلك ليس بواجبٍ على الناس في الجنابة، وهو قولُ أبي حنيفة ومالك بن أنس والعامَّة.

Muḥammad said: "We adhere to all of this, except the sprinkling of water in the eyes, for that is not incumbent upon the people where sexual intercourse or ejaculation [*janābah*] is concerned; and that is the verdict of Abū Ḥanīfah,, Mālik ibn Anas and [our *fuqahāʾ*] in general."

١٦ باب الرجل تصيبه الجنابة من الليل

16. Concerning a Man who has Sexual Intercourse or Experiences Ejaculation [*Janābah*] at Night

٥٥ أخبرنا مالكٌ، أخبرنا عبدُ الله بنُ دينار ، عن ابن عُمَرَ أن عمر رضي الله عنه ذكَرَ لرسول الله صلى الله عليه وسلم أنه تُصيبُهُ الجنابةُ من الليل، قال: توضأ واغسل ذكرَك ونَمْ.

55. Mālik informed us: "ʿAbdullāh ibn Dīnār informed us from Ibn ʿUmar, that ʿUmar mentioned to the Messenger of Allah ﷺ that he had sexual intercourse or experienced ejaculation [*janābah*] at night. He said, 'Do *wuḍūʾ*, wash your penis and sleep.'"

قال محمد: وإن لم يوضَّأ ولم يغسل ذكره حتى ينام فلا بأس بذلك أيضاً.

Muḥammad said: "And were he not to do *wuḍūʾ*, nor wash his penis before he sleeps, then there is no harm in that either."

٥٦ قال محمد : أخبرنا أبو حنيفة عن أبي إسحاق السَّبيعي ، عن الأسود بن يزيد ، عن عائشة رضي الله عنها قالت : كان رسول الله صلى الله عليه وسلم يصيبُ من أهله، ثم ينام ولا يَمَسّ ماءً ، فإن استيقظ من آخر الليل عاد واغتسل.

56. Muḥammad said: "Abū Ḥanīfah informed us from Abū Isḥāq as-Sabīʿī from al-Aswad ibn Yazīd from ʿĀʾishah. She said, 'The Messenger of Allah ﷺ would make love to his wife, then sleep without touching water; then if he awoke towards the end of the night he would return [to his wife] and then do *ghusl*.'"

قال محمد : هذا الحديث أرفق بالناس وهو قول أبي حنيفة رحمه الله.

Muḥammad said: "This report is more lenient for people; this is the verdict of Abū Ḥanīfah, may Allah have mercy on him."

١٧ باب الاغتسال يوم الجُمُعة

17. Doing *Ghusl* on the Day of Jumuʿah

٥٧ أخبرنا مالك، حدَّثنا نافع، عن ابنِ عمر، أنَّ رسول الله صلى الله عليه وسلم قال: إذا أتى أحدُكم الجمعةَ فليغتسِلْ .

57. Mālik informed us: "Nāfiʿ narrated to us from Ibn ʿUmar, that the Messenger of Allah ﷺ said, 'When any of you come to Jumuʿah, let him do *ghusl*.'"

٥٨ أخبرنا مالك، حدثنا صفوان بن سُلَيم ، عن عطاء بن يسار، عن أبي سعيد الخدري: أنَّ رسول الله صلى الله عليه وسلم قال: غُسْلُ يومِ الجُمعةِ واجبٌ على كل مُحْتَلم .

58. Mālik informed us: "Ṣafwān ibn Sulaym narrated to us from ʿAṭāʾ ibn Yasār from Abū Saʿīd al-Khudrī, that the Messenger of Allah ﷺ said, 'Doing *ghusl* on the day of Jumuʿah is incumbent upon every person who has reached puberty.'"

٥٩ أخبرنا مالكٌ، حدَّثنا الزهري، عن ابنِ السَّبَّاق : أن رسول الله صلى الله عليه وسلم قال : يا معشر المسلمين ، هذا يومٌ جعله الله تعالى عيداً للمسلمين، فاغتسلوا ، ومن كان عنده طيبٌ فلا يضرُّه أن يمسَّ منه وعليكم بالسواك .

59. Mālik informed us: "Az-Zuhrī narrated to us from Ibn as-Sabbāq, that the Messenger of Allah ﷺ said, 'Community of Muslims, this is a day which Allah has made a festival for the Muslims, so do *ghusl*; and whoever has some scent, it will not harm him to put some on; and don't neglect to use the tooth stick.'"

٦٠ أخبرنا مالك، أخبرني المَقْبُرِيُّ ، عن أبي هريرة أنه قال غُسْلُ يومِ الجمعة واجبٌ على كل محتلم كغُسل الجنابة .

60. Mālik informed us: "Al-Maqburī informed me that Abū Hurayrah said, 'Doing *ghusl* of the day of Jumuʿah is incumbent upon every person who has reached puberty, just like the *ghusl* due to sexual intercourse or ejaculation [*janābah*].'"

٦١ أخبرنا مالكٌ، أخبرني نافع: أنَّ ابنَ عمر كان لا يَرُوح إلى الجمعة إلاَّ اغتسل .

61. Mālik informed us: "Nāfic informed me that Ibn cUmar would only go to Jumucah after he had done *ghusl*."

٦٢ أخبرنا مالكٌ، أخبرني الزهري، عن سالم بن عبد الله عن أبيه: أنَّ رجلاً من أصحاب رسول الله صلى الله عليه وسلم دخل المسجد يومَ الجمعة و عمرُ بنُ الخطاب يخطب الناس، فقال: أيَّة ساعة هذه؟ فقال الرجل: انقلبتُ من السُّوق فسمعتُ النداء فما زدتُ على أن توضَّأتُ ثم أقبلت، قال عمر: والوضوءَ أيضاً! وقد علمتَ أن رسول الله صلى الله عليه وسلم كان يأمر بالغُسْل.

62. Mālik informed us: "Az-Zuhrī informed me from Sālim ibn cAbdullāh from his father, that a man from the Companions of the Messenger of Allah ﷺ entered the mosque on the day of Jumucah while cUmar ibn al-Khaṭṭāb was addressing the people so he asked, 'What time is this?' The man answered, 'I was coming back from the market when I heard the call, so as soon as I had done *wuḍū'* I came.' cUmar said, 'And doing *wuḍū'* too, when you know that the Messenger of Allah ﷺ used to order *ghusl*!'"

قال محمد: الغُسْلُ أفضلُ يومَ الجمعة، وليس بواجبٍ. وفي هذا آثار كثيرة.

Muḥammad said: "It is better to do *ghusl* on the day of Jumucah. It is not obligatory and concerning this there are many reports."

٦٣ قال محمد: أخبرنا الرَّبيع بن صَبيح، عن سعيد الرَّقاشي، عن أنس بن مالك وعن الحسن البصري، كلاهما يَرْفَعُهُ إلى النبيِّ صلى الله عليه وسلم أنه قال: من توضَّأ يوم الجمعة فبها ونِعْمَتْ ومن اغتسل فالغُسْل أفضل.

63. Muḥammad said: "Ar-Rabīc ibn Ṣabīḥ informed us from Sacīd ar-Raqāshī from Anas ibn Mālik and from al-Ḥasan al-Baṣrī, both of them attributing it to the Prophet ﷺ that he said, 'Whoever does *wuḍū'* on the day of Jumucah, that is well and good; and whoever does *ghusl*, then [know that] doing *ghusl* is better.'"

٦٤ قال محمد: أخبرنا محمد بنُ أبانَ بن صالح، عن حمّاد، عن إبراهيمَ النَّخَعي، قال: سألته عن الغُسْل يوم الجمعة، والغسل من الحجامة، والغسل في العيدين؟ قال: إن اغتسلتَ فحسنٌ، وإنْ تركتَ فليسَ عليك، فقلت له: ألم يقل رسول الله صلى الله عليه وسلم: من راح إلى الجمعة فليغتسل؟ قال: بلى، ولكنْ ليس من الأمور الواجبة، وإنما وهو كقوله تعالى: ﴿وَأَشْهِدُوا إِذَا تَبَايَعْتُمْ﴾، فمن أشْهَدَ فقد أحْسَنَ، ومن ترَك فليس عليه، وكقوله تعالى: ﴿فَإِذَا قُضِيَتِ الصَّلَاةُ فَانْتَشِرُوا فِي الأَرْضِ﴾، فمن انتشر فلا بأس ومن جلس فلا بأس. قال حماد: ولقد رأيتُ إبراهيمَ النَّخَعي يأتي العيدين وما يغتسل.

64. Muḥammad said: "Muḥammad ibn Abān informed us from Ḥammād from Ibrāhīm an-Nakhacī; [Ḥammād said] I asked him about doing *ghusl* on the day of Jumucah, and doing *ghusl* after cupping[2], and doing *ghusl* on the two days of cĪd and he answered, 'If you do *ghusl*, well and good, and if you leave it, there is no blame on you.' I said to him, 'Did not the Messenger of Allah ﷺ say, "Whoever goes to Jumucah, let him do *ghusl*."' He said, 'Yes, but it is not one

of the obligatory matters; it is comparable to His saying, "Call witnesses when you trade" (Sūrat al-Baqarah: 281). So whoever brings a witness has done best, and whoever leaves it carries no blame. And [it is comparable] to His saying, "Then when the prayer is finished spread through the earth" (Sūrat al-Jumuᶜah: 10); so whoever spreads forth, there is no harm in that, and whoever remains seated, there is no harm in that.' Ḥammād said, 'and I saw Ibrāhīm an-Nakhaᶜī come to the two ᶜĪd prayers without doing *ghusl*.'"

٦٥ قال محمد: أخبرنا محمد بن أبان، عن ابن جُرَيْج، عن عطاء بن أبي رَبَاح قال: كنّا جلوساً عند عبد الله بن عباس، فحضرت الصلاةُ، أي الجمعة، فدعا بوَضوء فتوضَّأ، فقال له بعضُ أصحابه: ألا تَغْتَسِلُ؟ قال: اليومَ يومٌ باردٌ، فتوضّأ.

65. Muḥammad said: "Muḥammad ibn Abān informed us from Ibn Jurayj from ᶜAṭāᵓ ibn Abī Rabāḥ who said, "We were sitting with ᶜAbdullāh ibn ᶜAbbās and the prayer-time [for Jumuᶜah] arrived, so he called for water and did *wuḍūᵓ*. Some of his companions asked him, 'Will you not do *ghusl*?' He said, 'It is a cold day today.' So, he had done *wuḍūᵓ*."

٦٦ قال محمد: أخبرنا سَلاّم بن سُلَيْمٍ الحنفي، عن منصور، عن إبراهيم قال: كان علقمةُ بن قَيْسٍ إذا سافر لم يصلِّ الضحى ولم يغتسل يومَ الجمعة.

66. Muḥammad said: "Sallām ibn Sulaym al-Ḥanafī informed us from Manṣūr from Ibrāhīm, who said, 'ᶜAlqamah ibn Qays, when he travelled, would not pray [*ḍuḥā*[3]] during the morning nor do *ghusl* on the day of Jumuᶜah.'"

٦٧ قال محمد: أخبرنا سفيانُ الثوريّ، حدثنا منصور، عن مجاهد قال: من اغْتَسَلَ يومَ الجمعة بعد طلوع الفجر أجزاه عن غُسْلِ يومِ الجمعة.

67. Muḥammad said: "Sufyān ath-Thawrī informed us, 'Manṣūr narrated to us from Mujāhid, who said, "Whoever does *ghusl* after dawn on the day of Jumuᶜah, has done enough with respect to *ghusl* for the day of Jumuᶜah."'"

٦٨ قال محمد: أخبرنا عبّادُ بنُ العوّام، أخبرنا يحيى بنُ سعيد، عن عَمْرة، عن عائشة، قالت: كان الناسُ عُمّالَ أنفسهم، فكانوا يَرُوحون إلى الجمعة بهيآتهم، فكان يقال لهم: لواغتسلتُم.

68. Muḥammad said: "ᶜAbbād ibn al-ᶜAwwām told us, 'Yaḥyā ibn Saᶜīd informed us from ᶜAmrah from ᶜĀᵓishah, who said, 'People used to be their own workers [because they had no servants or slaves], so they would go to Jumuᶜah in the state they were in, and then it would be said to them, "If only you would do *ghusl*."'"

١٨ باب الاغتسال يومَ العيدين

18. Doing *Ghusl* on the Days of ᶜĪd

٦٩ أخبرنا مالك، حدثنا نافع: أن ابن عمر كان يغتسل قبل أن يَغْدُوَ إلى العيد.

69. Mālik informed us: "Nāfiᶜ narrated to us that Ibn ᶜUmar used to do *ghusl* before he went out to the ᶜĪd.

٧٠ أخبرنا مالك، أخبرنا نافع، عن ابن عمر: أنه كان يغتسل يوم الفطر قبل أن يغدو.
70. Mālik informed us: "Nāfi[c] narrated to us from Ibn [c]Umar, that he used to do *ghusl* on the day of al-Fiṭr before going out."

قال محمد: الغُسْلُ يومَ العيد حَسَنٌ وليس بواجب، وهو قول أبي حنيفة رحمه الله.
Muḥammad said: "Doing *ghusl* on the day of [c]Īd is good though it is not obligatory; that is the verdict of Abū Ḥanīfah, may Allah have mercy on him."

١٩ باب التيمُّم بالصَّعيد

19. *Tayammum* with Dust

٧١ أخبرنا مالك، أخبرنا نافع، أنه أقبل هو وعبد الله بن عمر من الجُرف حتى إذا كان بالمِرْبَد نزل عبدُ الله بنُ عمر فتيمم صعيداً طيباً، فمسح وجهَه ويدَيه إلى المرفقين، ثم صلى.
71. Mālik informed us: "Nāfi[c] informed us that he had come up from al-Jurf with [c]Abdullāh ibn [c]Umar. When he reached al-Mirbad, [c]Abdullāh ibn [c]Umar got down and did tayammum with pure earth and wiped his face and his arms to the elbows, and then prayed."

٧٢ أخبرنا مالك، أخبرنا عبدُ الرحمن بنُ القاسم، عن أبيه، عن عائشة رضي الله عنها أنها قالت: خرجنا مع رسول الله صلى الله عليه وسلم في بعض أسفاره حتى إذا كنّا بالبيداء أو بذات الجيش انقطع عِقدي، فأقام رسولُ الله صلى الله عليه وسلم على التماسه، وأقام الناسُ وليسوا على ماءٍ وليس معهم ماءٌ، فأتى الناس إلى أبي بكر فقالوا: ألا ترى إلى ما صَنَعت عائشة؟ أقامت برسول الله صلى الله عليه وسلم وبالناس وليسوا على ماءٍ وليس معهم ماءٌ، قالت: فجاء أبو بكرٍ رضي الله عنه ورسولُ الله صلى الله عليه وسلم واضعٌ رأسَه على فخذي قد نام، فقال: حبست رسولَ الله صلى الله عليه وسلم والناسَ وليسوا على ماءٍ وليس معهم ماءٌ، قالت: فعاتَبَني وقال ما شاءَ اللهُ أن يقول، وجعل يَطعُنُني بيده في خاصرتي، فلا يمنعُني من التحرُّك إلاّ رأسُ رسول الله صلى الله عليه وسلم على فخذي، فنام رَسول الله صلى الله عليه وسلم حتى أصبح على غير ماءٍ، فأنزل الله تعالى آية التيمُّم فتيمَّمُوا، فقال أُسَيد بن حُضَير: ما هي بأوَّل بركتكم يا آل أبي بكرٍ، قالت: وبعثنا البعير التي كنتُ عليه فوجدنا العقدَ تحته.
72. Mālik informed us: "[c]Abd ar-Raḥmān ibn al-Qāsim informed us from his father that [c]Ā᾽ishah said, 'We went out with the Messenger of Allah ﷺ on a journey and when we reached al-Baydā᾽ or Dhāt al-Jaysh, my necklace broke [and was lost]. The Messenger of Allah ﷺ halted to look for it, and the people halted, with no water nearby and no water with them. The people came to Abū Bakr and said, "Do you not see what [c]Ā᾽ishah has done; halted the Messenger of Allah ﷺ and the people, with no water nearby and no water with them?"' She said, 'Abū Bakr arrived while the Messenger of Allah ﷺ was sleeping with his head on my thigh. Abū Bakr said, "You have detained the Messenger of Allah ﷺ and the people, with no water nearby and no water with them."' She said, 'He reproved me and said whatever Allah willed him to say,

and started jabbing me in the hip with his hand; the only reason I didn't move was because I had the head of the Messenger of Allah ﷺ on my thigh. The Messenger of Allah ﷺ slept until morning and he was without water, and so Allah sent down the *āyah* of *tayammum*. They performed *tayammum* and we performed *tayammum*; hence it was that Usayd ibn Ḥuḍayr said, "It is not the first of your blessings, family of Abū Bakr.'" She said, 'We roused the camel which I had been on, and we found the necklace underneath it.'"

قال محمد: وبهذا نأخذ، والتيمُّمُ ضربتان، ضربةٌ للوجه، وضربة لليدين إلى المرفقين، وهو قول أبي حنيفة رحمه الله.

Muḥammad said: "We adhere to this. *Tayammum* requires two light blows: one for the face and one for the arms to the elbows; that is the verdict of Abū Ḥanīfah, may Allah have mercy on him."

٢٠ باب الرجل يصيب من امرأته أو يباشرها وهي حائض
20. A Man's Having Sexual Intercourse with his Wife or Lying Skin to Skin with her During her Menstrual Period

٧٣ أخبرنا مالك، أخبرنا نافع، أن عبد الله بن عمر أرسل إلى عائشة يسألُها هل يباشر الرجلُ امرأتَه وهي حائض؟ فقالت: لَتَشُدَّ إزارها على أسفلِها، ثم يباشرها إن شاء.

73. Mālik informed us: "Nāfiʿ informed us that ʿAbdullāh ibn ʿUmar sent to ʿĀʾishah asking her, 'May a man be skin to skin with his wife during her menstrual period?' She said, 'She should tie her *izār* [the large cloth wrapped around the lower half of the body] around her lower body, then he can lie skin to skin with her if he wants.'"

قال محمد: وبهذا نأخذ، لا بأس بذلك وهو قول أبي حنيفة والعامَّة من فقهائنا.

Muḥammad said: "We adhere to this; there is no harm in doing that. That is the verdict of Abū Ḥanīfah and our *fuqahāʾ* in general, may Allah have mercy on him,."

٧٤ أخبرنا مالك، أخبرني الثقة عندي، عن سالم بن عبد الله وسليمان بن يسار: أنهما سُئِلا عن الحائض هل يصيبها زوجها إذا رأت الطُّهرَ قبل أن تغتسل؟ فقالا: لا حتى تغتسل.

74. Mālik informed us: "A man I consider trustworthy informed us that Sālim ibn ʿAbdullāh and Sulaymān ibn Yasār were asked whether the husband of a woman in her period may have sexual intercourse with her once she has seen that she is clean, but before she does *ghusl*; they said, 'No, not until she does *ghusl*.'"

قال محمد: وبهذا نأخذ، لا تُباشَرُ حائضٌ عندنا حتى تحلَّ لها الصلاة أو تَجِبَ عليها، وهو قول أبي حنيفة رحمه الله.

Muḥammad said: "We adhere to this; a woman in her period should not be made love to, in our opinion, until the prayer is allowed for her or is incumbent upon her. That is the verdict of Abū Ḥanīfah, may Allah have mercy on him."

٧٥ أخبرنا مالك، أخبرنا زيد بن أسلم : أن رجلاً سأل النبي صلى الله عليه وسلم ما يحل لي من امرأتي وهي حائض؟ قال: تشدّ عليها إزارها، ثم شأنك بأعلاها.

75. Mālik informed us: "Zayd ibn Aslam informed us that a man asked the Prophet ﷺ 'What part of my wife is permissible to me while she is in her period?' He said, 'She should put on her *izār* [the large cloth wrapped around the lower half of the body], then your concern is with her upper half.'"

قال محمد: هذا قول أبي حنيفة رحمه الله، وقد جاء ما هو أرخص من هذا عن عائشة أنها قالت: يجتنب شعار الدم، وله ما سوى ذلك.

Muḥammad said: "This is the verdict of Abū Ḥanīfah, may Allah have mercy on him. Something easier than this has come from ᶜĀ᾽ishah, who said, 'He should avoid the place of blood, and he may have whatever else.'"

٢١ باب إذا التقى الختانان هل يجب الغسل؟

21. When the two Places of Circumcision Meet, is it Incumbent to do *Ghusl*?

٧٦ أخبرنا مالك، حدثنا الزُّهري، عن سعيد بن المسيب : أن عمرَ وعثمانَ وعائشةَ كانوا يقولون : إذا مسَّ الختانُ الختانَ فقد وجب الغُسْلُ .

76. Mālik informed us: "Az-Zuhrī informed us from Saᶜīd ibn al-Musayyab, that, 'ᶜUmar, ᶜUthmān and ᶜĀ᾽ishah used to say to us, "When the place of circumcision touches the place of circumcision, doing *ghusl* is obligatory."'"

٧٧ أخبرنا مالك، أخبرنا أبو النضر مولى عمر بن عبيد الله، عن أبي سلمة بن عبد الرحمن: أنه سأل عائشةَ ما يوجب الغسل؟ فقالت : أتدري ما مَثَلُكَ يا أبا سلمة ؟ مَثَلُ الفرّوجِ يسمع الدِّيَكَة تصرخ فيصرخ معها إذا جاوز الختان الختان فقد وجب الغسل.

77. Mālik informed us: "Abu'n-Naḍr, the *mawlā* of ᶜUmar ibn ᶜUbaydullāh informed us from Abū Salamah ibn ᶜAbd ar-Raḥmān, that he asked ᶜĀ᾽ishah what makes doing *ghusl* obligatory, and she said, 'Do you know what your likeness is, Abū Salamah? Like the chick: when it hears the cocks crow, it crows with them. When the place of circumcision passes the place of circumcision doing *ghusl* has become obligatory.'"

٧٨ أخبرنا مالك، أخبرنا يحيى بن سعيد ، عن عبد الله بن كعب مولى عثمانَ بن عفّان : أنّ محمودَ بن لَبيد : سأل زيدَ بنَ ثابت عن الرجلِ يُصيبُ أهلَه ثم يُكْسِل ؟ فقال زيدُ بنُ ثابت: يغتسلُ ، فقال له محمودُ بنُ لبيد: فإنَّ أُبيَّ بنَ كعبَ لا يَرى الغُسْل، فقال زيدُ بنُ ثابت: نَزَعَ قبل أن يموت .

78. Mālik informed us: "Yaḥyā ibn Saᶜīd narrated to us from ᶜAbdullāh ibn Kaᶜb, the *mawlā* of ᶜUthmān ibn ᶜAffān, that Maḥmūd ibn Labīd asked Zayd ibn Thābit about the man who has sexual intercourse with his wife and then flags [does not ejaculate]. Zayd ibn Thābit said, 'He should do *ghusl*.' So

Maḥmūd ibn Labīd said to him, 'But Ubayy ibn Kaᶜb's opinion is that there is no [obligatory] *ghusl*.' So Zayd ibn Thābit said, 'He retracted [this opinion] before he died.'"

قال محمد: وبهذا نأخذ إذا التقى الخِتانان و توارَتْ الحشفة وجب الغُسْلُ أَنْزَلَ أو لم يُنْزِل، وهو قول أبي حنيفة رحمه الله.

Muḥammad said: "We adhere to this; when the two places of circumcision meet and the head of the penis disappears, doing *ghusl* has become obligatory, whether he ejaculates or not; that is the verdict of Abū Ḥanīfah, may Allah have mercy on him."

٢٢ باب الرجل ينام هل ينقض ذلك وضوءه؟

22. A Man Sleeps; Does that Break his *Wuḍū*ʾ?

٧٩ أخبرنا مالك، أخبرنا زيدُ بنُ أسلم، قال: إذا نام أحدكم وهو مضطجع فليتوضَّأْ.

79. Mālik informed us: "Zayd ibn Aslam informed us. He said, 'If any of you sleep whilst lying down, let him do *wuḍū*ʾ.'"

٨٠ أخبرنا مالك، أخبرني نافع، عن ابن عمر: أنه كان ينام وهو قاعد فلا يتوضأ.

80. Mālik informed us: "Nāfiᶜ informed us from Ibn ᶜUmar, that he would sleep whilst sitting and then not do *wuḍū*ʾ."

قال محمد: وبقول ابن عمر في الوجهين جَميعاً نأخذ، وهو قول أبي حنيفة رحمه الله.

Muḥammad said: "We adhere to the verdict of Ibn ᶜUmar in each of the two cases; that is the verdict of Abū Ḥanīfah, may Allah have mercy on him."

٢٣ باب المرأة ترى في منامها ما يرى الرجل

23. A Woman Sees in her Sleep what a Man Sees, [i.e. She has a nocturnal emission]

٨١ أخبرنا مالك، أخبرنا ابن شهاب، عن عروة بن الزبير، أنَّ أمَّ سُلَيْم قالت لرسول الله صلّى الله عليه وسلّم: يا رسول الله، المرأة ترى في المنام مثلَ ما يرى الرجلُ أتغتسل؟ فقال رسولُ الله صلّى الله عليه وسلّم: نعم فَلْتَغْتَسِلْ، فقالت لها عائشة: أفٍّ لك، وهل ترى ذلك المرأة؟ قال: فالتفتَ إليها رسولُ الله صلّى الله عليه وسلّم فقال: تَرِبَتْ يمينُك، ومن أين يكون الشَّبَه؟!

81. Mālik informed us: "Ibn Shihāb az-Zuhrī informed us from ᶜUrwah ibn az-Zubayr, that Umm Sulaym said to the Messenger of Allah ﷺ, 'Messenger of Allah, a woman sees in her sleep what a man sees.[4] Should she do *ghusl*?' and the Messenger of Allah ﷺ said, 'Yes, let her do *ghusl*.' So ᶜĀʾishah said to her, 'Woe to you! And does a woman see that?' So the Messenger of Allah ﷺ turned to her and said, 'May your right hand be covered in dust! So from where will the resemblance come?'"[5]

قال محمد: وبهذا نأخذ وهو قول أبي حنيفة رحمه الله.

Muḥammad said: "We adhere to this; it is the verdict of Abū Ḥanīfah, may Allah have mercy on him."

٢٤ باب المستحاضة

24. A Woman with Extra-long Menstrual Bleeding

٨٢ أخبرنا مالك، حدثنا نافع، عن سليمان بن يَسَار، عن أمِّ سلمة زوجِ النبي صلّى الله عليه وسلّم: أن امرأة كانت تُهراقُ الدَّمَ على عهد رسول الله صلّى الله عليه وسلّم فاستفتتْ لها أمُّ سَلَمَة رسول الله صلّى الله عليه وسلّم فقال: لتَنْظُر اللياليَ والأيّام التي كانت تحيضُ من الشهر قبل أن يُصيبَها الذي أصابها، فلتتركْ الصلاةَ قَدْرَ ذلك من الشهر، فإذا خَلَّفَتْ ذلك فلتغتسِلْ ثم لِتَسْتَثْفِر بثوبٍ فلْتُصَلِّ.

82. Mālik informed us: "Nāfi[c] narrated to us from Sulaymān ibn Yasār from Umm Salamah, the wife of the Prophet ﷺ, that there was a woman in the time of the Prophet ﷺ, who used to have blood [continuously] flow from her. Umm Salamah asked the Prophet ﷺ about it on her behalf and he said, 'Let her look at the nights and days she used normally to bleed in the month before what happened to her happened, and so leave the prayer that much every month. When that much has passed her by, let her do *ghusl*, then truss herself with a cloth and pray.'"

قال محمد: وبهذا نأخذ وتتوضّأ لوقتِ كلِّ صلاة وتصلّي إلى الوقتِ الآخر وإن سال دمُها، وهو قول أبي حنيفة رحمه الله.

Muḥammad said: "We adhere to this. She should do *wuḍū᾽* at the time of each prayer and may pray until the time of the next one, in spite of her continuous flow of blood. It is the verdict of Abū Ḥanīfah, may Allah have mercy on him."

٨٣ أخبرنا مالك، أخبرنا سُميّ مولى أبي بكر بنِ عبد الرحمن، أن القَعْقاع بنَ حكيم وزيدَ بن أَسْلَم أرسلاه إلى سعيد بن المسيَّب يسأله عن المستحاضة كيف تغتسل؟ فقال سعيد: تغتسلُ من طُهْرٍ إلى طُهْرٍ وتتوضّأ لكل صلاةٍ فإنْ غَلَبَها الدَّمُ استثفرتْ بثوب.

83. Mālik informed us: "Sumayy, the *mawlā* of Abū Bakr ibn [c]Abd ar-Raḥmān, informed us, that al-Qa[c]qā[c] ibn Ḥakīm and Zayd ibn Aslam sent him to Sa[c]īd ibn al-Musayyab asking about a woman whose bleeding would not stop, 'How should she do *ghusl*?' Ibn al-Musayyab answered, 'She should do *ghusl* each time she becomes clean [from her period] and do *wuḍū᾽* for each prayer; and if the blood overwhelms her she should truss herself with a cloth.'"

قال محمد: تغتسلُ إذا مضتْ أيامُ أَقرائها ثم تتوضّأُ لكل صلاةٍ وتصلّي، حتى تأتيَها أيامُ أقرائها، فَتَدَعُ الصلاةَ، فإذا مضَت اغتسلتْ غُسلاً واحداً، ثم توضّأَتْ لكلِّ وقتِ صلاةٍ وتصلي، حتى يدخُلَ الوقتُ الآخر ما دامت ترى الدم، وهو قول أبي حنيفة رحمه الله والعامّة مَن فقهائنا.

Muḥammad said: "She should do *ghusl* when the days of her normal period have passed. Then she should do *wuḍūʾ* for each prayer, praying until the days of her period come to her, when she should leave the prayer. Then when they have passed she should do *ghusl* once and thereafter do *wuḍūʾ* at each prayer-time, praying until the time of the next one arrives, as long as she still sees blood. That is the verdict of Abū Ḥanīfah, may Allah have mercy on him, and our *fuqahāʾ* in general."

٨٤ أخبرنا مالك، أخبرنا هشام بن عروة، عن أبيه، قال: ليس على المستحاضة أن تغتسلَ إلاّ غُسلاً واحداً، ثم تتوضّأ بعد ذلك للصلاة.

84. Mālik informed us: "Hishām ibn ʿUrwah informed us that his father said, 'The woman whose bleeding will not stop has to do *ghusl* only once, and after that should do *wuḍūʾ* for the prayer.'"

٢٥ باب المرأة ترى الصُّفرة والكُدْرة

25. A Woman Sees Yellowness or a Brownish [Discharge]

٨٥ أخبرنا مالك، أخبرنا عَلْقَمةُ بن أبي علقمة، عن أمِّه مولاة عائشةَ زوجِ النبيِّ صلّى الله عليه وسلّم أنها قالت: كان النساءُ يبعثن إلى عائشة بالدُّرْجة فيها الكُرْسُف فيه الصُّفْرة من الحيض فتقول: لا تَعْجَلْنَ حتى ترين القَصّة البيضاء. تريد بذلكَ الطهر من الحيض.

85. Mālik informed us: "ʿAlqamah ibn Abī ʿAlqamah informed us from his mother, the *mawlāh* of ʿĀʾishah, the wife of the Prophet ﷺ, that she said, 'Women used to send to ʿĀʾishah with their boxes with cotton in them, with the yellowness of their menstrual fluid on it and she would say, "Do not hasten until you see the white swab," meaning by that their becoming clean from their periods.'"

قال محمد: وبهذا نأخذ، لا تطهرُ المرأةُ ما دامتْ ترى حمرةً أو صُفرةً أو كُدرة، حتى ترى البياض خالصاً، وهو قول أبي حنيفة رحمه الله.

Muḥammad said: "We adhere to this; a woman has not become clean whilst she still sees redness or yellowness or a brownish [discharge]; not until she sees pure white. That is the verdict of Abū Ḥanīfah, may Allah have mercy on him."

٨٦ أخبرنا مالك، أخبرنا عبد الله بن أبي بكر، عن عمّته، عن ابنة زيد بن ثابت: أنه بلغها أن نساءً كُنَّ يدعُونَ بالمصابيح من جوفِ الليل فينظرن إلى الطُّهْر، فكانت تعيب عليهن وتقول: ما كان النساءُ يَصْنَعْنَ هذا.

86. Mālik informed us: "ʿAbdullāh ibn Abī Bakr informed us from his [paternal] aunt from the daughter of Zayd ibn Thābit, that she had heard that there were some women who would call for lanterns in the middle of the night to see if they were clean, and she would reproach them for that and say, 'Women never used to do this.'"

٢٦ باب المرأة تَغْسِلُ بعضَ أعضاء الرجل وهي حائض

26. A Woman's Washing Some of a Man's Limbs whilst in her Period

٨٧ أخبرنا مالك، أخبرنا نافع: أن ابن عمر كان تغسل جواريه رجلَيْه ويُعطينَهُ الخُمرة وهنَّ حُيَّض .

87. Mālik informed us: "Nāfiʿ informed us that Ibn ʿUmar's slave-girls would wash his feet and give him his mat whilst they were in their periods."

قال محمد: لا بأس بذلك، وهو قولُ أبي حنيفة رحمه الله .

Muḥammad said: "There is no harm in that; and it is the verdict of Abū Ḥanīfah, may Allah have mercy on him."

٨٨ أخبرنا مالك ، أخبرنا هشام بن عروة، عن أبيه، عن عائشة قالت: كنتُ أُرجّل رأسَ رسول الله صلّى الله عليه وسلّم وأنا حائض .

88. Mālik informed us: "Hishām ibn ʿUrwah informed us from his father from ʿĀʾishah, who said, 'I used to comb out the Prophet's hair ﷺ whilst in my period.'"

قال محمد : لا بأس بذلك، وهو قول أبي حنيفة رحمه الله والعامَّة من فقهائنا.

Muḥammad said: "There is no harm in that; and it is the verdict of Abū Ḥanīfah, may Allah have mercy on him, and our *fuqahāʾ* in general."

٢٧ باب الرجل يغتسلُ أو يتوضّأ بسؤر المرأة

27. A Man's Doing *Ghusl* or Doing *Wuḍūʾ* with Water Left Over by a Woman

٨٩ أخبرنا مالك، حدَّثنا نافع، عن ابن عمر، أنه قال : لا بأس بأن يغتَسلَ الرجلُ بفضلِ وَضوء المرأة ما لم تكن جُنُباً أو حائضاً .

89. Mālik informed us: "Nāfiʿ narrated to us from Ibn ʿUmar, that he said, 'There is no harm in the man's doing *ghusl* with the water left over by a woman who has done *wuḍūʾ*, as long as she was not in need of *ghusl* because of sexual intercourse [*junub*] or in her period.'"

قال محمد : لا بأس بفضل وَضوء المرأة وغسلها وسؤرها وإن كانت جنباً أو حائضاً . بَلَغَنا أن النبيّ صلّى الله عليه وسلّم كان يغتسل هو وعائشة من إناء واحد ليتنازعان الغسل جميعاً، فهو فضل غسل المرأة الجنب، وهو قول أبي حنيفة رحمه الله .

Muḥammad said: "There is no harm in the water left over by a woman who has done *wuḍūʾ*, nor her [surplus] *ghusl*-water, nor water left after she drinks, even should she be in need of a *ghusl* because of sexual intercourse or in her period. It has reached us that the Prophet ﷺ would do *ghusl*, he and ʿĀʾishah, from one pot, drawing from the bath-water together, which itself is the water left over by a woman who is in need of a *ghusl* because of sexual intercourse. That is the verdict of Abū Ḥanīfah, may Allah have mercy on him."

٢٨ باب الوضوء بسؤر الهرة

28. Doing *Wuḍū'* with that from which a Cat has Drunk

٩٠ أخبرنا مالك، أخبرنا إسحاق بنُ عبد الله بن أبي طلحة أنَّ امرأته حُمَيدَةَ ابنةَ عبيد بن رفاعة، أخبرته عن خالتها كَبْشَة ابنة كعب بن مالك وكانت تحت ابن أبي قتادة : أنَّ أبا قتادة أمرها فسكَبَتْ له وضوءاً فجاءت هرَّةٌ فشربت منه، فأصغى لها الإناءَ فشربت، قالت كبشة: فرآني أنظر إليه فقال: أتعجبينَ يا ابنة أخي ؟ قالت: قلت: نعم، قال: إن رسول الله صلى الله عليه وسلم قال: إنها ليست بنَجَسٍ إنها من الطوافين عليكم و الطوّافات .

90. Mālik informed us: "Isḥāq ibn ᶜAbdullāh ibn Abī Ṭalḥah informed us that his wife, Ḥumaydah bint ᶜUbayd ibn Rifāᶜah told him from her [maternal] aunt, Kabshah bint Kaᶜb ibn Mālik, who was the wife of Ibn Abī Qatādah, that Abū Qatādah told her to pour his water for him to do *wuḍū'* and a cat came to drink from it, so he tilted the pot for it and it drank. Kabshah said, 'So, he saw me watching him and said, "Are you surprised, niece?"' She said, 'I said, "Yes." He said, "The Messenger of Allah ﷺ said, 'It is not impure; it is one of those male and female creatures that come and go around you.'"'"

قال محمد: لا بأس بأن يتوضَّأ بفضل سُؤْر الهرة، وغيرُهُ أحبُّ إلينا منه، وهو قولُ أبي حنيفة رحمه الله .

Muḥammad said: "There is no harm in doing *wuḍū'* from the water that remains after a cat has drunk from it, but to use something other than it is preferable to us. That is the verdict of Abū Ḥanīfah, may Allah have mercy on him."

٢٩ باب الأذان والتثويب

29. The Call to Prayer [*Adhān*] and its Response

٩١ أخبرنا مالك، أخبرنا ابنُ شهاب، عن عطاء بن يزيدَ الليثيِّ، عن أبي سعيد الخُدْري أن رسول الله صلّى الله عليه وسلّم قال: إذا سمعتُمُ النِّداءَ فقولوا مثلَ ما يقول المؤذِّنُ . قال مالك، بَلَغَنا أن عمر بن الخطاب رضي الله عنه جاءه المؤذِّن يُؤْذِنُهُ لصلاة الصبح فوجده نائماً فقال المؤذِّنُ : الصَّلاةُ خيرٌ من النوم، فأمره عمر أن يجعلها في نداء الصبح .

91. Mālik informed us: "Ibn Shihāb informed us from ᶜAṭā' ibn Yazīd al-Laythī from Abū Saᶜīd al-Khudrī, that the Messenger of Allah ﷺ said, 'When you hear the call, repeat the words the caller to prayer [*mu'adhdhin*] says.'"

Mālik said, "A report reached us that the caller to prayer [*mu'adhdhin*] came to ᶜUmar ibn al-Khaṭṭāb ؓ to inform him of the dawn prayer and found him sleeping. The caller to prayer said, 'Prayer is better than sleep.' So ᶜUmar ordered him to include this in the call for the dawn prayer."

٩٢ أخبرنا مالك، أخبرنا نافع، عن ابن عمر: أنه كان يكبِّر في النداء ثلاثاً ويتشهَّدُ ثلاثاً، وكان أحياناً إذا قال حيَّ على الفلاح قال على إِثْرِها حَيَّ على خير العمل .

92. Mālik informed us: "Nāfiᶜ informed us from Ibn ᶜUmar, that he would

say, *'Allāhu akbar'* in the call, three times and *'Ashhadu* – I witness ...' three times; and would sometimes, when he said *'Ḥayya ᶜala'l-falāḥ* – Come to prosperity', say after it, *'Ḥayya ᶜalā khayri'l-ᶜamal* – Come to the best work'".

قال محمد: الصلاةُ خيرٌ من النوم يكون ذلك في نداء الصبح بعد الفراغ من النداء، ولا يجب أن يُزاد في النداء ما لم يكن منه.

Muḥammad said: "*'Aṣ-ṣalātu khayru'm-mina'n-nawm* – [Prayer is better than sleep]'; the place for this is in the call at dawn, after finishing the call. It is not necessary to add to the call anything that is not part of it."

٣٠ باب المشي إلى الصلاة وفضل المساجد

30. Walking to the Prayer and the Special Merit of Mosques

٩٣ أخبرنا مالك، حدثنا علاء بنُ عبد الرحمن بن يعقوب، عن أبيه، أنه سمع أبا هريرة، قال: قال رسولُ الله صلّى الله عليه وسلّم: إذ ثُوِّبَ بالصلاة فلا تأتُوها تسعَوْن وأْتُوها وعليكم السكينة، فما أدركتُمْ فصلُّوا وما فاتَكُم فَأتمُّوا، فإنَّ أحدَكم في صلاة ما كان يَعْمدُ إلى الصلاة.

93. Mālik informed us: "ᶜAlāʾ ibn ᶜAbd ar-Raḥmān ibn Yaᶜqūb informed us from his father, that he heard Abū Hurayrah say, 'The Messenger of Allah ﷺ said, "When the prayer is announced for the second time [the *iqāmah*] do not come to it in a rush; come to it calmly. Then pray what you catch, and complete what you miss; so long as anyone intends prayer, he is in prayer."'"

قال محمد: لا تَعْجَلَنَّ بركوعٍ ولا افتتاحٍ حتى تصل إلى الصف وتقومَ فيه، وهو قولُ أبي حنيفة رحمه الله.

Muḥammad said: "Do not hasten to bow or to begin until you join the row and stand in it; that is the verdict of Abū Ḥanīfah, may Allah have mercy on him."

٩٤ أخبرنا مالك، حدَّثنا نافع: أن ابن عمر سمع الإقامة وهو بالبقيع فأسْرَعَ المشي.

94. Mālik informed us: "Nāfiᶜ narrated to us, that Ibn ᶜUmar heard the *iqāmah* whilst in Baqīᶜ and so quickened his pace."

قال محمد: وهذا لا بأس به ما لم يُجْهدْ نفسَه.

Muḥammad said: "There is no harm in this as long as one does not distress oneself."

٩٥ أخبرنا مالك، أخبرنا سُمَيٌّ أنه سمع أبا بكر يعني ابنَ عبد الرحمن يقول: من غدا أو راح إلى المسجد لا يريد غيرَه ليتعلَّمَ خيراً أو يُعَلّمه ثم رجَعَ إلى بيته الذي خرج منه كان كالمجاهد في سبيل الله رَجَع غانماً.

95. Mālik informed us: "Sumayy informed us that he heard Abū Bakr, meaning Ibn ᶜAbd ar-Raḥmān, say, 'Whoever goes out in the morning or the evening to the mosque, not intending other than that, to learn good or to teach it, then returns to the house he departed from, is like one who strives in jihād in the way of Allah, and returns with booty.'"

٣١ باب الرجل يصلّي وقد أخذ المؤذّنُ في الإِقامة

31. A Man's Praying Individually when the Caller to Prayer [*Muʾadhdhin*] has Started the Second Call to the Prayer [*Iqāmah*]

٩٦ أخبرنا مالك، أخبرنا شَريك بن عبد الله بن أبي نَمَيْر ، أنَّ أبا سلمة بنَ عبد الرحمن بن عوف قال : سَمِعَ قومٌ الإِقامةَ فقاموا يصلُّون، فخرج عليهم النبيُّ صلّى الله عليه وسلّم فقال: أصلاتان معاً؟!

96. Mālik informed us: "Sharīk ibn ʿAbdullāh ibn Abī Numayr informed us that Abū Salamah ibn ʿAbd ar-Raḥmān ibn ʿAwf, said, 'Some people heard the second call to prayer and stood up to do individual prayers, so the Prophet ﷺ came out to them and said, 'Are there two prayers at the same time?'"

قال محمد: يُكره إذا أُقيمت الصلاة أن يُصلّيَ الرجلُ تطوعاً غير ركعَتَيْ الفجر خاصة، فإنه لا بأس بأن يصلّيَهُما الرجل إنْ أخذَ المؤذّنُ في الإِقامة، وكذلك ينبغي، وهو قول أبي حنيفة رحمه الله .

Muḥammad said: "When the *iqāmah* is announced, it is disliked for a man to pray a non-obligatory prayer, the only exception being the two *rakʿahs* of *Fajr*, for there is no harm in a man's praying them even though the *muʾadhdhin* has started the *iqāmah*, on the contrary, he should do so. That is the verdict of Abū Ḥanīfah, may Allah have mercy on him."

٣٢ باب تسوية الصف

32. Straightening the Rows

٩٧ أخبرنا مالك، أخبرنا نافع، عن ابن عمر: أنَّ عمر بن الخطاب كان يأمر رِجَالاً بتسوية الصفوف، فإذا جاؤوه فأخْبَرُوه بتسويتها كبّر بعدُ.

97. Mālik informed us: "Nāfiʿ informed us from Ibn ʿUmar, that ʿUmar ibn al-Khaṭṭāb would direct some men to make the rows straight, and only when they came to him and told him that they were straight would he say *Allāhu akbar*."

٩٨ أخبرنا مالك، أخبرنا أبو سُهَيْل بن مالك وأبو النَّضر مولى عُمر بن عُبيد الله، عن مالك بن أبي عامر الأنصاري : أن عثمان بن عفّان كان يقول في خُطبته: إذا قامت الصلاةُ، فاعْدِلُوا الصفُوفَ، وحَاذُوا بالمَناكب، فإنَّ اعتدال الصفوف من تمام الصلاة . ثم لا يكبِّر حتى يأتيه رجال قد وكَّلهم بتسوية الصفوف، فيخبرونه أن قد استوتْ فيكبِّر.

98. Mālik informed us: "Abū Suhayl ibn Mālik and Abu'n-Naḍr, the *mawlā* of ʿUmar ibn ʿUbaydullāh, informed us from Mālik ibn Abī ʿĀmir al-Anṣārī, that ʿUthmān ibn ʿAffān would say in his *khuṭbah*, when the *iqāmah* for the prayer had been called, 'So level the rows, and place your shoulders together, for the levelling of the rows is essential to the perfection of prayer.' Then he would not say *Allāhu akbar* until certain men, to whom he had entrusted the straightening of the rows, came to him and told him they were straight; then only would he say *Allāhu akbar*".

قال محمد : ينبغي للقوم إذا قال المؤذّن حيّ على الفلاح أن يقوموا إلى الصلاة فيصُفّوا ويُسَوُّوا الصفوف ويحاذُوا بين المناكب، فإذا أقامَ المؤذن الصلاةَ كبَّر الإمامُ، وهو قولُ أبي حنيفةَ – رحمه الله .
Muḥammad said: "When the caller to prayer [*mu᾽adhdhin*] has said *Ḥayya ᶜala'l-falāḥ*, the people ought to stand to pray, form rows, straighten the rows and place their shoulders together. Then, when the *mu᾽adhdhin* has said *Qad qāmati'ṣ-ṣalāh*, the imām should say *Allāhu akbar*. That is the verdict of Abū Ḥanīfah, may Allah have mercy on him."

٣٣ باب افتتاح الصلاة

33. Opening the Prayer

٩٩ أخبرنا مالك، حدَّثنا الزُّهريُّ، عن سالم بن عبد الله بن عُمر أنَّ عَبْدَ اللّه بنَ عُمَر قال: كان رسُولُ الله صلّى الله عليه وسلّم إذا افْتَتح الصلاة رفع يديه حذاءَ مَنْكِبَيْه، وإذا كَبَّر للرُّكوع رفع يديه، وإذا رفع رأسه من الرُّكوع رفع يديْه، ثم قال : سمع اللّهُ لمَن حمده، ثم قَال : ربَّنا ولك الحمد .
99. Mālik informed us: "Az-Zuhrī narrated to us from Sālim ibn ᶜAbdullāh ibn ᶜUmar, that ᶜAbdullāh ibn ᶜUmar said, 'When he opened the prayer, the Messenger of Allah ﷺ would raise his hands to his shoulders; and when he said *Allāhu akbar* for bowing he would raise his hands; and when he raised his head from bowing he would raise his hands; then he would say *samiᶜa'llāhu liman ḥamidah* – [Allah listens to whoever praises Him] and then he would say *rabbanā wa laka'l-ḥamd* – [our Lord and to You belongs the praise].'"

١٠٠ أخبرَنا مالك، حدثنا نافعٌ أن عبد الله بن عمر : كان إذا ابتدأ الصلاة رفع يديه حَذْوَ مَنْكبَيْه، وإذا رفع رأسه من الركوع رفعهما دون ذلك .
100. Mālik informed us: "Nāfiᶜ narrated to us that when ᶜAbdullāh ibn ᶜUmar began the prayer, he would raise his hands to his shoulders; and when he raised his head from bowing he would raise them less than that."

١٠١ أخبرنا مالك، حدثنا وهبُ بن كَيْسان ، عن جابر بن عبد الله الأنصاري : أنهُ يُعَلِّمُهم التكبير في الصلاة، أمرنا أن نكبِّر كلما خفضنا ورفعنا.
101. Mālik informed us: "Wahb ibn Kaysān narrated to us from Jābir ibn ᶜAbdullāh al-Anṣārī, that he would teach them to say *Allāhu akbar* in the prayer, [and] 'he ordered us to say *Allāhu akbar* whenever we lowered or raised ourselves.'"

١٠٢ أخبرنا مالك، أخبرني ابن شهاب الزهريّ، عن علي بن الحسين بن علي بن أبي طالب أنه قال : كان رسول الله صلّى الله عليه وسلّم يكبِّر كلما خفض، وكلما رفع، فلم تزل تلك صلاته حتى لقي اللّهَ عزّ وجلّ.
102. Mālik informed us: "Ibn Shihāb az-Zuhrī informed me from ᶜAlī ibn Ḥusayn ibn ᶜAlī ibn Abī Ṭālib that he said, 'The Messenger of Allah ﷺ would say *Allāhu akbar* whenever he lowered himself and whenever he raised himself; and this continued to be the way he prayed until he met Allah ﷻ.'"

١٠٣ أخبرنا مالك، أخبرنا ابن شهاب، عن أبي سلمة بن عبد الرحمن بن عوف، أنَّه أخبره أنَّ أبا هريرة: كان يصلّي بهم، فكبَّر كلما خفض ورفع، ثم انصرف قال: والله إني لأشبهكم صلاةً برسول الله صلّى الله عليه وسلّم.

103. Mālik informed us: "Ibn Shihāb informed us from Abū Salamah ibn ʿAbd ar-Raḥmān ibn ʿAwf that he told him that Abū Hurayrah would pray with them and he said *Allāhu akbar* whenever he lowered or raised himself; then when he had finished he said, 'By Allah, I am the closest of you in similarity of prayer to the Messenger of Allah ﷺ.'"

١٠٤ أخبرنا مالك، أخبرني نعيم المُجْمر وأبو جعفر القارئ، أن أبا هريرة: كان يصلي بهم، فكبَّر كلما خفض وفع، قال أبو جعفر: وكان يرفع يديه حين يكبِّرُ ويفتح الصلاة.

104. Mālik informed us: "Nuʿaym al-Mujmir and Abū Jaʿfar al-Qāriʾ informed me that Abū Hurayrah used to pray with them, and he said *Allāhu akbar* whenever he lowered or raised himself. Abū Jaʿfar said, 'And he used to raise his hands when he said *Allāhu akbar* and opened the prayer.'"

قال محمد: السنَّة أن يكبِّر الرجل في صلاته كلما خفض وكلما رفع، وإذا انحطّ للسجود كبَّر، وإذا انحطّ للسجود الثاني كبَّر. فأما رفع اليدين في الصلاة فإنه يرفع اليدين حذو الأذنين في ابتداء الصلاة مرَّةً واحدة، ثم لا يرفع في شيْء من الصلاة بعد ذلك، وهذا كله قول أبي حنيفة رحمه الله تعالى وفي ذلك آثار كثيرة.

Muḥammad said: "The *Sunnah* is that a man should say *Allāhu akbar* in his prayer whenever he lowers himself and whenever he raises himself. When he goes down into prostration he should say *Allāhu akbar*; and when he goes down into the second prostration he should say *Allāhu akbar*. As for raising the hands in the prayer: he should raise his hands to his ears once only when beginning the prayer. After that he should not raise [them] at all in the prayer. All of this is the verdict of Abū Ḥanīfah, may Allah have mercy on him, and concerning this there are many narrations."

١٠٥ قال محمد: أخبرنا محمد بن أبان بن صالح، عن عاصم بن كُلَيْب الجَرْمي، عن أبيه قال: رأيت عليَّ بن أبي طالب رفع يديه في التكبيرة الأولى من الصلاة المكتوبة، ولم يرفعهما فيما سوى ذلك.

105. Muḥammad said: "Muḥammad ibn Abān ibn Ṣāliḥ informed us from ʿĀṣim ibn Kulayb al-Jarmī from his father who said, 'I saw ʿAlī ibn Abī Ṭālib raise his hands for the first saying of *Allāhu akbar* in the obligatory prayer, and not raise them apart from that.'"

١٠٦ قال محمد أخبرنا محمد بن أبان بن صالح، عن حماد عن إبراهيم النَّخَعي، قال: لا ترفع يديك في شيء من الصلاة بعد التكبيرة الأولى.

106. Muḥammad said: "Muḥammad ibn Abān ibn Ṣāliḥ informed us from Ḥammād from Ibrāhīm an-Nakhaʿī who said, 'Don't raise your hands in any part of the prayer after the first saying of *Allāhu akbar*.'"

١٠٧ قال محمد: أخبرنا يعقوب بن إبراهيم، أخبرنا حُصَين بن عبد الرحمن، قال: دخلت أنا وعمرو بن مرّة على إبراهيم النخعي، قال عمرو: حدثني علقمة بن وائل الحضرمي، عن أبيه: أنه صلى مع رسول الله، فرآه يرفع يديه إذا كبّر، وإذا ركع، وإذا رفع، قال إبراهيم: ما أدري لعلّه لم يَرَ النبي صلى الله عليه وسلم يصلي إلاّ ذلك اليوم فحفظ هذا منه، ولم يحفظه ابن مسعود وأصحابه ما سمعته من أحد منهم، إنما كانوا يرفعون أيديهم في بَدْءِ الصلاة حين يكبِّرون.

107. Muḥammad said: "Yaᶜqūb ibn Ibrāhīm informed us 'Ḥuṣayn ibn ᶜAbd ar-Raḥmān informed us, "I went with ᶜAmr ibn Murrah to visit Ibrāhīm an-Nakhaᶜī and ᶜAmr said, 'ᶜAlqamah ibn Wā᾽il al-Ḥaḍramī reported to me from his father[6], that he prayed with the Messenger of Allah ﷺ and saw him raise his hands when he said *Allāhu akbar* and when he bowed [in *rukūᶜ*] and when he raised [himself from bowing].' Ibrāhīm said, 'I do not know; perhaps he only saw the Prophet ﷺ on that day and retained this from him, but Ibn Masᶜūd and his companions did not retain it. I never heard it from any one of them; they would only raise their hands at the beginning of the prayer when they said *Allāhu akbar*.'"'"

١٠٨ قال محمد: أخبرنا محمد بن أبان بن صالح، عن عبد العزيز بن حكيم، قال: رأيت ابن عمر يرفع يديه حذاء أذنيه في أول تكبيرة افتتاح الصلاة، ولم يرفعهما فيما سوى ذلك.

Muḥammad said: "Muḥammad ibn Abān ibn Ṣāliḥ informed us from ᶜAbd al-ᶜAzīz ibn Ḥakīm, who said, 'I saw Ibn ᶜUmar raise his hands to his ears at his first saying *Allāhu akbar* in the opening of the prayer but he did not raise them at any other time.'"

١٠٩ قال محمد: أخبرنا أبو بكر بن عبد الله النَهْشَليُّ، عن عاصم بن كُلَيب الجَرْمي، عن أبيه وكان من أصحاب علي: أنَّ عليّ بن أبي طالب كرَّم الله وجهه كان يرفع يديه في التكبيرة الأولى التي يفتتح بها الصلاة، ثم لا يرفعهما في شيء من الصلاة.

109. Muḥammad said: "Abū Bakr ibn ᶜAbdullāh an-Nahshalī informed us from ᶜĀṣim ibn Kulayb al-Jarmī from his father, who was one of the companions of ᶜAlī, that ᶜAlī ibn Abī Ṭālib, may Allah honour his face, would raise his hands in the first saying of *Allāhu akbar*, the one with which he would open the prayer, then not raise them in any [other] part of the prayer."

١١٠ قال محمد: أخبرنا الثوري، حدثنا حصين، عن إبراهيم، عن ابن مسعود: أنه كان يرفع يديه إذا افتتح الصلاة.

110. Muḥammad said: "Ath-Thawrī informed us, 'Ḥuṣayn narrated to us from Ibrāhīm from Ibn Masᶜūd, that he used to raise his hands when he opened the prayer.'"

٣٤ باب القراءة في الصلاة خلف الإمام

34. Recitation in the Prayer behind the Imām

١١١ أخبرنا مالك، حدثنا الزهري، عن ابن أُكَيْمة الليثي، عن أبي هريرة: أنَّ رسول الله صلى الله

عليه وسلم انصرف من صلاة جهر فيها بالقراءة، فقال: هل قرأ معي منكم من أحد؟ فقال الرجل: أنا يا رسول، قال: فقال: إني أقول ما لي أُنازَع القرآن؟ فانتهى الناس عن القراءة مع رسول الله صلى الله عليه وسلم فيما جهر به من الصلاة حين سمعوا ذلك.

111. Mālik informed us: "Az-Zuhrī narrated to us from Ibn Ukaymah al-Laythī from Abū Hurayrah, that the Messenger of Allah ﷺ finished a prayer in which he recited aloud and said, 'Did any of you recite with me?' So one man said, 'I did Messenger of Allah.'" [Abū Hurayrah] said, "So he ﷺ said, 'I was saying to myself, "Why am I being competed with in respect to the Qur'ān?"' So the people desisted from reciting with the Messenger of Allah ﷺ in the prayers in which he recited aloud from the time when they heard that."

١١٢ أخبرنا مالك، حدثنا نافع، عن ابن عمر: أنه كان إذا سئل هل يقرأ أحد مع الإمام؟ قال: إذا صلّى أحدكم مع الإمام فحسبُه قراءة الإمام، وكان ابن عمر لا يقرأ مع الإمام.

112. Mālik informed us: "Nāfi' narrated to us from Ibn 'Umar that when asked, 'Should anyone read with the imām?' he would say, 'When one of you prays with the imām, the recitation of the imām is sufficient for him." And Ibn 'Umar never used to recite with the imām."

١١٣ أخبرنا مالك، حدثنا وهب بن كيسان أنه سمع جابر بن عبد الله يقول: من صلى ركعة لم يقرأ فيها بأمّ القرآن، فلم يصل إلاّ وراء الإمام.

113. Mālik informed us: "Wahb ibn Kaysān narrated to us that he heard Jābir ibn 'Abdullāh say, 'Whoever prayed a *rak'ah* in which he did not recite Umm al-Qur'ān [the Fātiḥah]', has not prayed, except behind the imām."

١١٤ أخبرنا مالك، أخبرني العلاء بن عبد الرحمن بن يعقوب مولى الحُرَقَة أنه سمع أبا السائب مولى هشام بن زهرة يقول: سمعت أبا هريرة يقول: سمعت رسول الله ﷺ يقول: من صلى صلاةً لم يقرأ فيها بفاتحة الكتاب فهي خِداج هي خِداج هي خِداج غير تمام. قال: قلت: يا أبا هريرة، إني أحياناً أكون وراء الإمام؟ قال: فغمز ذراعي وقال: يا فارسي، اقرأ بها في نفسك، إني سمعت رسول الله صلى الله عليه وسلم يقول: قال الله عزّ وجلّ قُسمت الصلاة بيني وبين عبدي نصفين، فنصفها لي، ونصفها لعبدي، ولعبدي ما سأل، قال رسول الله صلى الله عليه وسلم: اقرؤا، يقول العبد: الحمد لله رب العالمين، يقول الله: حمدني عبدي، يقول العبد: الرحمن الرحيم، يقول الله أثنى عليّ عبدي، يقول العبد: مالكِ يوم الدين، يقول الله مجّدني عبدي، يقول العبد: إيّاك نعبد وإياك نستعين، فهذه الآية بيني وبين عبدي، ولعبدي ما سأل، يقول العبد: اهدنا الصراط المستقيم، صراط الذين أنعمت عليهم، غير المغضوب عليهم ولا الضآلين، فهؤلاء لعبدي ولعبدي ما سأل.

114. Mālik informed us: "Al-'Alā' ibn 'Abd ar-Raḥmān ibn Ya'qūb, the *mawlā* of al-Ḥuraqah informed me that he heard Abu's-Sā'ib, the *mawlā* of Hishām ibn Zuhrah, say, 'I heard Abū Hurayrah say, "I heard the Messenger of Allah ﷺ say, 'Whoever prays a prayer in which he does not recite the Opening [Fātiḥah] of the Book, then it is defective, it is defective, it is defective, an imperfection.'"' [Abu's-Sā'ib] said, 'I said, "Abū Hurayrah, sometimes I will be behind the imām." So he squeezed my forearm and said, "O Persian,

recite it to yourself. I heard the Messenger of Allah ﷺ say, 'Allah, exalted is He, has said, "The prayer has been apportioned between me and My slave as two halves; so half of it is for Me and half of it is for My slave; and My slave shall have what he asks for."' The Messenger of Allah ﷺ said, 'Recite! The slave says, "Praise belongs to Allah Lord of all the worlds"; Allah says, "My slave praises Me." The slaves says, "The All-Merciful the Most Merciful"; Allah says, "My slave extols Me. The slave says, "King of the Day of Judgement"; Allah says, "My slave glorifies Me." The slave says, "You alone we worship and You alone we ask for help"; Allah says, this *āyah* is between Me and My slave, and My slave shall have what he asks for." The slave says, "Guide us on the Straight Path, the Path of those whom You have blessed, not of those with anger on them, nor of the misguided"; so these are for My slave and My slave shall have what he asks for.""""

قال محمد : لا قراءة خلف الإمام فيما جهر فيه ولا فيما لم يجهر، بذلك جاءت عامة الآثار . وهو قول أبي حنيفة رحمه الله .

Muḥammad said: "There should be no recitation behind the imām whether he reads aloud or not; and this is the purport of the majority of narrations and it is the verdict of Abū Ḥanīfah, may Allah have mercy on him."

١١٥ قال محمد أخبرنا عبيد الله بن عمر بن حفص بن عاصم بن عمر بن الخطاب، عن نافع، عن ابن عمر، قال: من صلى خلف الإمام كَفَتْه قراءته.

115. Muḥammad said: "ᶜUbaydullāh ibn ᶜUmar ibn Ḥafṣ ibn ᶜĀṣim ibn ᶜUmar ibn al-Khaṭṭāb informed us from Nāfiᶜ from Ibn ᶜUmar, who said, 'The imām's recitation suffices for whoever prays behind him.'"

١١٦ قال محمد : أخبرنا عبد الرحمن بن عبد الله المسعودي ، أخبرني أنس بن سيرين ، عن ابن عمر: أنه سأل عن القراءة خلف الإمام، قال: تكفيك قراءة الإمام .

116. Muḥammad said: "ᶜAbd ar-Raḥmān ibn ᶜAbdullāh al-Masᶜūdī told us, 'Anas ibn Sīrīn informed me from Ibn ᶜUmar, that he was asked about reading behind the imām. He said, 'The recitation of the imām suffices you.'"

١١٧ قال محمد : أخبرنا أبو حنيفة، قال حدثنا أبو الحسن موسى بن أبي عائشة ، عن عبد الله بن شداد بن الهاد ، عن جابر بن عبد الله، عن النبي صلى الله عليه وسلم، أنه قال: من صلى خلف الإمام فإنّ قراءة الإمام له قراءة .

117. Muḥammad said: "Abū Ḥanīfah informed us saying, 'Abu'l-Ḥasan Mūsā ibn Abī ᶜĀʾishah narrated to us from ᶜAbdullāh ibn Shaddād ibn al-Hād from Jābir ibn ᶜAbdullāh from the Prophet ﷺ, that he said, 'Whoever prays behind the imām, then the recitation of the imām is a recitation for him.'""

١١٨ قال محمد : حدثنا الشيخ أبو علي ، قال حدثنا محمود بن محمد المروزي، قال : حدثنا سهل بن العباس الترمذي، قال: أخبرنا إسماعيل بن عليَّة، عن أيوب، عن ابن الزبير، عن جابر بن عبد الله قال: قال رسول الله صلى الله عليه وسلم: من صلى خلف الإمام، فإن قراءة الإمام له قراءة.

118. Muḥammad said: "The Shaykh Abū ᶜAlī narrated to us saying, 'Maḥmūd ibn Muḥammad al-Marwazī narrated to us saying, "Sahl ibn al-ᶜAbbās at-Tirmidhī narrated to us saying, 'Ismāᶜīl ibn ᶜUlayyah informed us from Ayyūb from Ibn az-Zubayr from Jābir ibn ᶜAbdullāh, who said, 'The Messenger of Allah ﷺ said, "Whoever prays behind the imām, then the recitation of the imām is a recitation for him."'""'"

١١٩ قال محمد : أخبرنا أسامة بن زيد المدني ، حدثنا سالم بن عبد الله بن عمر، قال : كان ابن عمر لا يقرأ خلف الإمام، قال: فسألت القاسم بن محمد عن ذلك، فقال : إنْ تركتَ فقد تركه ناس يُقتدى بهم، وإن قرأت فقد قرأه ناس يُقتدى بهم. وكان القاسم ممن لا يقرأ .

Muḥammad said: "Usāmah ibn Zayd al-Madanī informed us, 'Sālim ibn ᶜAbdullāh ibn ᶜUmar narrated to us, "Ibn ᶜUmar would not recite behind the imām." So I asked al-Qāsim ibn Muḥammad about that and he said, "If you leave out reciting, then a people whose ways are followed also left it out; and if you recite, then a people whose ways are followed also recited it." And al-Qāsim was of those who used not to recite.'"

– ١٢٠ قال محمد : أخبرنا سفيان بن عيينة ، عن منصور بن المعتمر، عن أبي وائل ، قال : سأل عبد الله بن مسعود عن القراءة خلف الإمام، قال: أنصت ، فإنَّ في الصلاة شغلاً سيكفيك ذاك الإمام.

120. Muḥammad said: "Sufyān ibn ᶜUyaynah informed us from Manṣūr ibn al-Muᶜtamir from Abū Wāᵓil, who said, 'Ibn Masᶜūd was asked about reciting behind the imām. He said, "Keep silent, for the prayer requires your attention; the imām will do that for you."'"

١٢١ قال محمد : أخبرنا محمد بن أبان بن صالح القرشي، عن حماد، عن إبراهيم النخعي: عن علقمة بن قيس: أن عبد الله بن مسعود كان لا يقرأ خلف الإمام فيما جهر فيه وفيما يخافت فيه في الأُولَيَيْن، ولا في الأُخْرَيَيْن، وإذا صلَّى وحده قرأ في الأُولَيَيْن بفاتحة الكتاب وسورة، ولم يقرأ في الأُخْرَيَيْن شيئاً .

121. Muḥammad said: "Muḥammad ibn Abān ibn Ṣāliḥ al-Qurashī informed us from Ḥammād from Ibrāhīm an-Nakhaᶜī from ᶜAlqamah ibn Qays, that when behind the imām ᶜAbdullāh ibn Masᶜūd would not recite whether the imām read aloud or silently, neither in the first two [*rakᶜahs*] nor in the last two; but when he prayed alone he would read the Opening [Fatihah] of the Book and a *sūrah* in the first two [*rakᶜahs*], and would not read anything in the last two."

١٢٢ قال محمد : أخبرنا سفيان الثوري، حدَّثنا منصور، عن أبي وائل، عن عبد الله بن مسعود، قال: أنصت للقراءة ، فإن في الصلاة شغلاً، وسيكفيك الإمام.

122. Muḥammad said: "Sufyān ath-Thawrī informed us, 'Manṣūr narrated to us from Abū Wāᵓil from ᶜAbdullāh ibn Masᶜūd, who said, "Keep silent for the recitation, for the prayer requires your attention, and the imām will suffice you."'"

١٢٣ قال محمد : أخبرنا بكير بن عامر ، حدثنا إبراهيم النخعي عن علقمة بن قيس، قال : لأن أعضّ على جمرة أحب إليّ من أن أقرأ خلف الإمام.

123. Muḥammad said: "Bukayr ibn ᶜĀmir informed us, 'Ibrāhīm an-Nakhaᶜī narrated to us from ᶜAlqamah ibn Qays, who said, 'That I should bite on a burning coal is preferable to me than that I should recite behind the imām.'"

١٢٤ قال محمد : أخبرنا إسرائيل بن يونس ، حدثنا منصور ، عن إبراهيم قال: إن أول من قرأ خلف الإمام رجل اتُّهم .

124. Muḥammad said: "Isrā'īl ibn Yūnus informed us, 'Manṣūr narrated to us from Ibrāhīm, who said, 'The first of those who recited behind the imām was a man about whom there were suspicions.'"

١٢٥ قال محمد : أخبرنا إسرائيل، حدثني موسى بن أبي عائشة، عن عبد الله بن شدّاد بن الهاد قال: أمَّ رسول الله صلى الله عليه وسلم في العصر ، قال : فقرأ رجل خلفه فغمزه الذي يليه، فلما أن صلى قال: لِمَ غمزتني؟ قال: كان رسول الله صلى الله عليه وسلم قُدّامَك ، فكرهت أن تقرأ خلفه، فسمعه النبي صلى الله عليه وسلم قال : من كان له إمام فإن قراءته له قراءة.

125. Muḥammad said: "Isrā'īl informed us, 'Mūsā ibn Abī ᶜĀ'ishah narrated to me from ᶜAbdullāh ibn Shaddād ibn al-Hād, who said, 'The Messenger of Allah ﷺ led *ᶜAṣr* and a man recited behind him, so the man next to him nudged him. When he had prayed he said, "Why did you nudge me?" He said, "The Messenger of Allah ﷺ was leading you, so I was loath that you should recite behind him." Hearing this, the Prophet ﷺ said, "Whoever prays with an imām, then the imam's recitation suffices for him."'"

١٢٦ قال محمد : أخبرنا داود بن قيس الفرّاء المدني ، أخبرني بعض وُلْد سعد بن أبي وقاص أنه ذكر له أن سعداً قال: وَددْتُ أنَّ الذي يقرأ خلف الإمام في فيه جمرةٌ.

126. Muḥammad said: "Dāwūd ibn Qays al-Farrā' al-Madanī informed us that one of the sons of Saᶜd ibn Abī Waqqāṣ mentioned to him that Saᶜd said, 'I wish that he who recites behind the imām had a burning coal in his mouth.'"

١٢٧ قال محمد : أخبرنا داود بن قيس الفراء، أخبرنا محمد بن عجلان : أن عمر بن الخطاب قال : ليت في فم الذي يقرأ خلف الإمام حجراً.

127. Muḥammad said: "Dāwūd ibn Qays al-Farrā' informed us, 'Muḥammad ibn ᶜAjlān informed us that ᶜUmar ibn al-Khaṭṭāb said, 'Would that there were stones in the mouth of him who recites behind the imām.'"

١٢٨ قال محمد : أخبرنا داود بن سعد بن قيس ، حدثنا عمرو بن محمد بن زيد، عن موسى بن سعد بن زيد بن ثابت، يحدِّثه عن جدِّه أنه قال : من قرأ خلف الإمام فلا صلاة له.

128. Muḥammad said: "Dāwūd ibn Saᶜd ibn Qays informed us, 'ᶜAmr ibn Muḥammad ibn Zayd narrated to us from Mūsā ibn Saᶜd ibn Zayd ibn Thābit, reporting from his grandfather, said, 'Whoever recites behind the imām, has no prayer.'"

٣٥ باب الرجل يُسبَق ببعض الصلاة

35. A Man's being Late for Part of the Prayer

١٢٩ أخبرنا مالك، أخبرنا نافع: أن ابن عمر كان إذا فاته شيء من الصلاة مع الإمام التي يُعلن فيها بالقراءة، فإذا سلَّم قام ابن عمر، فقرأ لنفسه فيما يقضي.

129. Mālik informed us: "Nāfi[c] informed us, that when Ibn [c]Umar missed something of the prayer with the imām in which he [the imam] recited aloud, then, after he [the imām] concluded, Ibn [c]Umar would stand up and individually recite in those [*rak[c]ahs*] he had to make up."

قال محمد: وبهذا نأخذ، لأنه يقضي أول صلاته، وهو قول أبي حنيفة رحمه الله.

Muḥammad said: "We adhere to this, for he is making up the earlier part of his prayer; that is the verdict of Abū Ḥanīfah, may Allah have mercy on him."

١٣٠ أخبرنا مالك، أخبرنا نافع، عن ابن عمر أنه كان إذا جاء إلى الصلاة فوجد الناس قد رفعوا من ركعتهم سجد معهم.

130. Mālik informed us: "Nāfi[c] informed us that when Ibn [c]Umar came to the prayer and found that the people had raised their heads from bowing, he would prostrate with them."

قال محمد: بهذا نأخذ، ويسجد معهم ولا يَعتدّ بها وهو قول أبي حنيفة – رحمه الله –.

Muḥammad said: "We adhere to this; and he should prostrate with them but not count it [the *rak[c]ah* as having been performed]. This is the verdict of Abū Ḥanīfah, may Allah have mercy on him."

١٣١ أخبرنا مالك، أخبرنا نافع، عن ابن عمر: أنه كان إذا وجد الإمام قد صلّى بعض الصلاة صلّى معه ما أدرك من الصلاة، إن كان قائماً قام، وإن كان قاعداً قعد حتى يقضي الإمام صلاته، لا يخالف في شيء من الصلاة.

131. Mālik informed us: "Nāfi[c] informed us that when Ibn [c]Umar found the imām had prayed part of the prayer, he would pray with him what he caught of the prayer, standing if he stood and sitting if he sat, until the imām concluded his prayer, not doing anything different [from the imām] in any part of the prayer."

قال محمد: وبهذا نأخذ، وهو قول أبي حنيفة رحمه الله.

Muḥammad said: "We adhere to this; it is the verdict of Abū Ḥanīfah, may Allah have mercy on him."

١٣٢ أخبرنا مالك، أخبرنا ابن شهاب، عن أبي سلمة (X)، ابن عبد الرحمن، عن أبي هريرة أن رسول الله صلى الله عليه وسلم قال: من أدرك من الصلاة ركعة فقد أدرك الصلاة.

132. Mālik informed us: "Ibn Shihāb informed us from Abū Salamah ibn Salamah ibn [c]Abd ar-Raḥmān from Abū Hurayrah, that the Messenger of Allah ﷺ said, 'Whoever catches one *rak[c]ah* of the prayer has caught the prayer.'"

قال محمد: وبهذا نأخذ، وهو قول أبي حنيفة رحمه الله.

Muḥammad said: "We adhere to this; it is the verdict of Abū Ḥanīfah, may Allah have mercy on him."

١٣٣ أخبرنا مالك، أخبرنا نافع، عن ابن عمر أنه كان يقول: إذا فاتتك الركعة فاتتك السجدة .

133. Mālik informed us: "Nāfiʿ informed us that Ibn ʿUmar used to say, "If you have missed the bowing, you have missed the prostration.""

قال محمد: من سجد السجدتين مع الإمام لا يُعتدّ بهما ، فإذا سلّم الإمام قضى ركعة تامة بسجدتيها، وهو قول أبي حنيفة رحمه الله .

Muḥammad said: "Whoever [only] does the two prostrations with the imām, they are not counted. After the imām concludes he must pray a whole *rakʿah* with its two prostrations; that is the verdict of Abū Ḥanīfah, may Allah have mercy on him."

٣٦ باب الرجل يقرأ السور في الركعة الواحدة من الفريضة
36. A Man's Reciting more than one *Sūrah* in one *Rakʿah* of the Obligatory Prayer

١٣٤ أخبرنا مالك، أخبرنا نافع، عن ابن عمر: أنه كان إذا صلى وحده يقرأ في الأربع جميعاً من الظهر والعصر في كل ركعة بفاتحة الكتاب، وسورة من القرآن وكان أحياناً يقرأ بالسورتين أو الثلاث في صلاة الفريضة في الركعة الواحدة ويقرأ في الركعتين الأوليين من المغرب، كذلك بأم القرآن وسورة سورة .

134. Mālik informed us: "Nāfiʿ informed us that when Ibn ʿUmar prayed alone, he would recite in all four [rakʿahs] of Ẓuhr and ʿAṣr, in each *rakʿah*, the Opening [Fatihah] of the Book and a *sūrah* from the Qurʾān; he would sometimes recite two or three sūrahs in the obligatory prayer, in one *rakʿah*. Similarly, he would recite in the first two *rakʿahs* of Maghrib, the Umm al-Qurʾān[7] and a *sūrah* in each of the two."

قال محمد: السُّنة أن تقرأ في الفريضة في الركعتين الأوليين بفاتحة الكتاب وسورة، وفي الأخريين بفاتحة الكتاب وإن لم تقرأ فيهما أجزأك وإن سبّحت فيهما أجزأك ، وهو قول أبي حنيفة رحمه الله .

Muḥammad said: "The *Sunnah* is to recite in the first two *rakʿahs* of the obligatory prayer the Opening [Fātiḥah] of the Book and a *sūrah*, and in the last two just the Opening [Fātiḥah] of the Book. If you do not recite in the [last two] it will suffice you, and if you say 'Subḥān'Allāh' – glorious is Allah', it will suffice you. That is the verdict of Abū Ḥanīfah, may Allah have mercy on him."

٣٧ باب الجهر في القراءة في الصلاة وما يُسْتحبُّ من ذلك
37. Reciting Aloud in the Prayer and what is Encouraged of that

١٣٥ أخبرنا مالك، أخبرني عمّي أبو سهيل أن أباه أخبره أن عمر بن الخطاب كان يجهر بالقراءة في الصلاة وأنه كان يسمع قراءة عُمر بن الخطاب عند دار أبي جَهم .

135. Mālik informed us: "My [paternal] uncle, Abū Suhayl, informed me that

his father informed him that ᶜUmar ibn al-Khaṭṭāb used to recite aloud in the prayer, and that he used to hear the recitation of ᶜUmar ibn al-Khaṭṭāb at the home of Abū Jahm."

قال محمد: الجهر بالقراءة في الصلاة فيما يجهر فيه بالقراءة حسن ما لم يُجهد الرجل نفسه.

Muḥammad said: "Reciting aloud in that prayer in which the recitation is done aloud is fine as long as the man does not strain himself."

٣٨ باب آمين في الصلاة

38. Saying *Āmīn* in the Prayer

١٣٦ أخبرنا مالك، أخبرني الزهري، عن سعيد بن المسيّب وأبي سلمة بن عبد الرحمن، عن أبي هريرة أن رسول الله صلى الله عليه وسلم قال: إذا أمَّن الإمام فأمِّنوا، فإنه من وافق تأمينُه تأمينَ الملائكة غُفر له ما تقدَّم من ذنبه، قال: فقال ابن شهاب: كان النبي صلى الله عليه وسلم يقول: آمين.

136. Mālik informed us: "Az-Zuhrī informed me from Saᶜīd ibn al-Musayyab and Abū Salamah ibn ᶜAbd ar-Raḥmān from Abū Hurayrah, that the Messenger of Allah ﷺ said, 'When the imām says *āmīn*, then say *āmīn*, for he whose saying *āmīn* coincides with the angels' saying *āmīn* will be forgiven his previous wrong actions.'" [Mālik] said, "Then Ibn Shihāb said, 'The Prophet ﷺ used to say *āmīn*.'"

قال محمد: وبهذا نأخذ، ينبغي إذا فرغ الإمام من أم الكتاب أن يؤمّن الإمام ويؤمّن من خلفه، ولا يجهرون بذلك، فأما أبو حنيفة، فقال: يؤمّن من خلف الإمام، ولا يؤمن الإمام.

Muḥammad said: "We adhere to this; it is expected that when the imām has finished Umm al-Qur'ān [the Fātiḥah] the imām should say *āmīn* and those behind him should say *āmīn*. They should not say it aloud. As for Abū Ḥanīfah, he said those behind the imām should say *āmīn* and not the imām."

٣٩ باب السهو في الصلاة

39. Making Mistakes in the Prayer

١٣٧ أخبرنا مالك، أخبرنا الزهري، عن أبي سلمة بن عبد الرحمن، عن أبي هريرة قال: قال رسول الله صلى الله عليه وسلم: إن أحدكم إذا قام في الصلاة جاءه الشيطان، فَلَبَسَ عليه حتى لا يَدري كم صلّى، فإذا وجد أحدكم ذلك، فليسجد سجدتين وهو جالس.

137. Mālik informed us: "Az-Zuhrī informed us from Abū Salamah ibn ᶜAbd ar-Raḥmān that Abū Hurayrah said, 'The Messenger of Allah ﷺ said, "When one of you stands in prayer, shayṭān will come to him and confuse him until he does not know how much he has prayed. When any of you experience that, let him prostrate twice while he is sitting."'"

١٣٨ أخبرنا مالك، حدثنا داود بن الحُصَين، عن أبي سفيان مولى ابن أبي أحمد، عن أبي هريرة

قال: صلى رسول الله صلى الله عليه وسلم صلاة العصر ، فسلَّم في ركعتين، فقام ذو اليدين فقال : أقصرت الصلاة يا رسول الله أم نسيت؟ فقال: كل ذلك لم يكن، فقال: يا رسول الله قد كان بعض ذلك ، فأقبل رسول الله صلى الله عليه وسلم على الناس ، فقال: أصدق ذو اليدين؟ فقالوا : نعم. فأَتَمَّ رسول الله صلى الله عليه وسلم ما بقي عليه من الصلاةَ ثم سلَّم، ثم سجد سجدتين، وهو جالس بعد التسليم.

138. Mālik informed us: "Dāwūd ibn al-Ḥuṣayn narrated to us from Abū Sufyān, the *mawlā* of Ibn Abī Aḥmad, that Abū Hurayrah said, 'The Messenger of Allah ﷺ prayed the prayer of *ᶜAṣr* and finished after two *rakᶜahs*, so Dhu'l-Yadayn got up and said, "Has the prayer been shortened, Messenger of Allah, or have you forgotten?" He ﷺ replied, "Nothing of the kind has happened." So he said, "Messenger of Allah, something of the kind did happen." So the Messenger of Allah ﷺ turned to the people and said, "Has Dhu'l-Yadayn spoken truly?" And they said yes. So the Messenger of Allah ﷺ completed what he still had to pray, said *as-salāmu ᶜalaykum,* then prostrated twice while still seated, after saying *as-salāmu ᶜalaykum.*'"

١٣٩ أخبرنا مالك، حدثنا زيد بن أسلم، عن عطاء بن يسار أن رسول الله صلى الله عليه وسلم، قال: إذا شكَّ أحدُكم في صلاته، فلا يَدْري كم صلّى ثلاثاً أم أربعاً، فلْيَقُم ، فليصلِّ رَكْعة، ولْيَسْجُدْ سجدتين وهو جالس قَبل التسليم. فإن كانت الركعة التي صلّى خامسةً شَفَعها بهاتين السجدتين، وإن كانت رابعةً فالسجدتان ترغيمٌ للشيطان.

139. Mālik informed us: "Zayd ibn Aslam narrated to us from ᶜAṭā᾽ ibn Yasār that the Messenger of Allah ﷺ said, 'When any of you are uncertain in his prayer, not knowing whether he has prayed three or four, then let him stand up and pray another *rakᶜah* and let him prostrate twice while he is sitting, before concluding. Then if it was a fifth *rakᶜah* which he prayed, he will have done these two prostrations to repair it. If it was a fourth then the two prostrations are to abase shayṭān.'"

١٤٠ أخبرنا مالك، أخبرنا ابن شهاب، عن عبد الرحمن الأَعْرَج، عن ابن بُحَينَة أنه قال : صلّى بنا رسول الله صلى الله عليه وسلم ركعتين، ثم قام ولم يَجْلس، فقام الناسُ فلمّا قضى صلاتَه ونظرنا تسليمه كَبَّر وسجد سجدتين وهو جالس قبل التسليم ثم سَلَّم.

140. Mālik informed us: "Ibn Shihāb informed us from ᶜAbd ar-Raḥmān al-Aᶜraj that Ibn Buḥaynah said, 'The Messenger of Allah ﷺ prayed two *rakᶜahs* with us, then he stood up [for the third *rakᶜah*] without sitting and so the people stood up. Then, when he had finished his prayer and we were awaiting his saying *as-salāmu ᶜalaykum,* he said *Allāhu akbar* and prostrated twice while sitting, before saying *as-salāmu ᶜalaykum*. Then he finished.'"

١٤١ أخبرنا مالك، أخبرنا عفيف بن عمرو بن المسيب السهمي، عن عطاء بن يَسَار قال: سألت عبدَ الله بنَ عمرو بنِ العاص وكعباً عن الذي يشكّ كم صلى ثلاثاً أو أربعاً، قال: فكلاهما قالا : فليقُمْ ولْيُصَلِّ رَكْعةً أخرى قائماً ثم يسجد سجدتين إذا صلّى.

141. Mālik informed us: "ᶜAfīf ibn ᶜAmr ibn al-Musayyab as-Sahmī informed us that ᶜAṭā᾽ ibnYasār said, 'I asked ᶜAbdullāh ibn ᶜAmr ibn al-ᶜĀṣ and Kaᶜb about someone who is uncertain whether he has prayed three or four. Both of them said, "Then let him get up and pray another *rakᶜah*, standing, then prostrate twice after praying."'"

١٤٢ أخبرنا مالك، حدثنا نافع، عن ابن عمر: أنه كان إذا سئل عن النسيان، قال: يتوخّى أحدكم الذي يظن أنه نسي من صلاته.

142. Mālik informed us: "Nāfiᶜ narrated to us that when Ibn ᶜUmar was asked about forgetfulness, he would say, 'One should assume that that which he suspects he left out was simply part of his prayer that he had prayed, but had forgotten about.'"

قال محمد: وبهذا نأخذ، إذا ناء للقيام وتغيَّرتْ حالُه عن القعود وجب عليه لذلك سجدتا السهو. وكلُّ سهوٍ وجبتْ فيه سجدتان من زيادة أو نقصان فسجدتا السهو فيه بعد التسليم. ومن أدخل عليه الشيطان الشكَّ في صلاته فلم يدرِ أثلاثاً صلى أم أربعاً، فإن كان ذلك أولَ ما لقي تكلَّمَ واستقبل صلاته، وإن كان يُبتلى بذلك كثيراً مضى على أكثر ظنه ورأيه ولم يَمْضِ على اليقين، فإنه إن فعل ذلك لم ينجُ فيما يرى من السهو الذي يُدخل عليه الشيطانُ، وفي ذلك آثار كثيرة.

Muḥammad said: "We adhere to this; once he has made to stand up and his posture has altered from sitting, the two prostrations due for an error are incumbent upon him. Every error for which two prostrations are due, whether because of an excess or a deficiency, the two prostrations for that error are done after saying *as-salāmu ᶜalaykum*. Someone in whom shayṭān puts doubt concerning his prayer, he not knowing whether he has prayed three or four, then if this was the first occurrence he should speak [break off his prayer] and start afresh. If he is afflicted with such doubts often, he should continue based on what he thinks is more probable, and should not continue on the basis of that which he is sure of; for if he does that he will never escape from the erring which shayṭān puts in him; there are many narrations concerning this."

١٤٣ قال محمد: أخبرنا يحيى بن سعيد أن أنس بن مالك صلّى بهم في سفرٍ كان معه فيه فصلّى سجدتين ثم ناء للقيام، فسبّح بعض أصحابه، فرجع ثم لما قضى صلاته سجد سجدتين.
قال: لا أدري أقبل التسليم أو بعده.

143. Muḥammad said: "Yaḥyā ibn Saᶜīd informed us that Anas ibn Mālik prayed with them on a journey on which he accompanied him. He prayed two *rakᶜahs* [*sajdahs*], then went to stand up. Some of his companions said, *'subḥān'Allāh'*, so he returned [to the sitting position]. When he had finished his prayer he prostrated twice. [Yaḥyā ibn Saᶜīd] said, 'I don't know whether it was before saying, *"as-salām"* or after.'"

٤٠ باب العبث بالحصى في الصلاة وما يُكره من تسويته

40. Shuffling Gravel in the Prayer and the Reprehensibility of Levelling it

١٤٤ أخبرنا مالك، حدثنا أبو جعفر القارئ قال: رأيتُ ابن عمر إذا أراد أن يسجدَ سَوَّى الحصى تسويةً خفيفة. وقال أبو جعفر: كنت يوماً أصلي، وابن عمر ورائي، فالتفتُّ فوضع يده في قفاي فغمزني.

144. Mālik informed us: "Abū Jaᶜfar al-Qārī᾽ narrated [this] to us. He said, 'I saw Ibn ᶜUmar, when he wanted to prostrate, gently levelling the gravel.' Abū Jaᶜfar said, 'Once I was praying and Ibn ᶜUmar was behind me and I glanced aside, so he put his hand on the back of my neck and squeezed me.'"

١٤٥ أخبرنا مالك، أخبرنا مُسلم بن أبي مريم، عن علي بن عبد الرحمن المُعاوي أنه قال: رآني عبدُ الله بن عمر وأنا أعبث بالحصى في الصلاة، فلما انصرفتُ نهاني وقال: أصنع كما كان رسول الله صلى الله عليه وسلم يصنع، فقلت: كيف كان رسول الله صلى الله عليه وسلم يصنع؟ قال: كان رسولُ الله صلى الله عليه وسلم إذا جلس في الصلاة وضع كفَّه اليمنى على فخذه اليمنى، وقبض أصابعَه كلَّها، وأشار بإصبعه التي تلي الإبهام، ووضع كفَّه اليسرى على فخذه اليسرى.

145. Mālik informed us: "Muslim ibn Abī Maryam informed us that ᶜAlī ibn ᶜAbd ar-Raḥmān al-Muᶜāwī said, 'ᶜAbdullāh ibn ᶜUmar saw me ruffling the gravel while in prayer, so when I finished he rebuked me and said, "Do what the Messenger of Allah ﷺ used to do." I asked, "What did the Messenger of Allah ﷺ do?" He answered, "When the Messenger of Allah ﷺ sat in prayer, he put his right hand on his right thigh and clasped all of his fingers and pointed with the finger next to his thumb; and he put his left hand on his left thigh."'"

قال محمد: وبصنيع رسول الله صلى الله عليه وسلم يأخذ، وهو قول أبي حنيفة رحمه الله تعالى فأما تسوية الحصى فلا بأس بتسويته مرة واحدة، وتركها أفضل وهو قول أبي حنيفة رحمه الله.

Muḥammad said: "We adhere to this practice of the Messenger of Allah ﷺ and it is the verdict of Abū Ḥanīfah. As for levelling the gravel, there is no harm in levelling it once only but leaving it is better. and That is the verdict of Abū Ḥanīfah, may Allah have mercy on him."

٤١ باب التشهد في الصلاة

41. *Tashahhud* in the Prayer

١٤٦ أخبرنا مالك، حدثنا عبد الرحمن بن القاسم، عن أبيه، عن عائشة أنها كانت تتشهّد فتقول: التحياتُ الطيباتُ الصلواتُ الزاكياتُ لله، أشهد أن لا إله إلاّ اللّهُ وحده لا شريكَ له، وأشهد أن محمداً عبدُهُ ورسولُه، السلام عليك أيها النبيُّ ورحمة الله وبركاته، السلام علينا وعلى عباد الله الصالحين، السلام عليكم.

146. Mālik informed us: "ᶜAbd ar-Raḥmān ibn al-Qāsim narrated to us from his father from ᶜĀ᾽ishah, that she would say in the *tashahhud*, 'At-

taḥiyyātu'ṭ-ṭayyibātu'ṣ-ṣalawātu'z-zākiyātu lillāh. Ashhadu an lā ilāha illa'llāhu waḥdahū lā sharīka lah, wa ashhadu anna Muḥammadan ᶜabduhū wa rasūluh. As-salāmu ᶜalayka ayyuha'n-nabiyyu wa raḥmatu'llāhi wa barakātuh, as-salāmu ᶜalaynā wa ᶜalā ᶜibādi'llāhi'ṣ-ṣāliḥīn. As-salāmu ᶜalaykum.'" [Greetings[8], good words, prayers and right actions are for Allah. I witness that there is no god but Allah alone without partner and I witness that Muḥammad is His slave and messenger. Peace be upon you, O Prophet and the mercy of Allah and His blessings. Peace be upon us and upon the right-acting slaves of Allah. Peace be upon you].

١٤٧ أخبرنا مالك، عن ابن شهاب، عن عروة بن الزبير، عن عبد الرحمن بن عبد القاريّ أنه سمع عمر بن الخطاب على المنبر يعلّم الناس التشهد، ويقول: قولوا: التحيات لله، الزاكيات لله الطيبات الصلوات لله السلام عليك أيها النبي ورحمة الله وبركاته، السلام علينا وعلى عباد الله الصالحين، أشهد أن لا إله إلا الله، وأشهد أن محمداً عبدُه ورسولُه.

147. Mālik informed us from Ibn Shihāb from ᶜUrwah ibn az-Zubayr from ᶜAbd ar-Raḥmān ibn ᶜAbdin al-Qāriyy, that he heard ᶜUmar ibn al-Khaṭṭāb, on the *minbar*, teaching people *tashahhud*. He said: "Say, *'At-taḥiyyātu lillāh, az-zākiyātu lillāh*[9], *aṭ-ṭayyibātu'ṣ-ṣalawātu lillāh.*[10] *As-salāmu ᶜalayka ayyuha'n-nabiyyu wa raḥmatu'llāhi wa barakātuh, as-salāmu ᶜalaynā wa ᶜalā ᶜibādi'llāhi'ṣ-ṣāliḥīn. Ashhadu an lā ilāha illa'llāhu, wa ashhadu anna Muḥammadan ᶜabduhū wa rasūluh.'"* [Greetings are for Allah, right actions are for Allah, good words and prayers are for Allah. Peace be upon you, O Prophet and the mercy of Allah and His blessings. Peace be upon us and upon the right-acting slaves of Allah. I witness that there is no god but Allah alone without partner and I witness that Muḥammad is His slave and Messenger].

١٤٨ أخبرنا مالك، أخبرنا نافع، عن ابن عمر: أنه كان يتشهد فيقول: بسم الله، التحيات لله، والصلوات لله، والزاكيات لله، السلام عليك أيها النبي ورحمة الله وبركاته، السلام علينا وعلى عباد الله الصالحين شهدتُ أن لا إله إلا الله، وشهدت أن محمداً رسول الله. يقول هذا في الركعتين الأوليَين، ويدعو بما بدا له إذا قضى تشهُّدَه، فإذا جلس في آخر صلاته تشهد كذلك إلاَّ أنه يقدِّم التشهد ثم يدعو بما بدا له، فإذا أراد أن يسلم قال: السلام على النبي ورحمة الله وبركاته، السلام علينا وعلى عباد الله الصالحين. السلام عليكم عن يمينه، ثم يردّ على الإمام، فإن سلّم عليه أحد عن يساره ردَّ عليه.

148. Mālik informed us: "Nāfiᶜ informed us from Ibn ᶜUmar, that he would pronounce the *tashahhud*, saying, *'Bismillāh, at-taḥiyyātu lillāhi wa'ṣ-ṣalawātu lillāhi wa'z-zākiyātu lillāh. As-salāmu ᶜalayka ayyuha'n-nabiyyu wa raḥmatu'llāhi wa barakātuh, as-salāmu ᶜalaynā wa ᶜalā ᶜibādi'llāhi'ṣ-ṣāliḥīn. Shahidtu an lā ilāha illa'llāhu wa shahidtu anna Muḥammadan rasūlu'llāh.'*– [In the name of Allah, greetings are for Allah and prayers are for Allah and right actions are for Allah. Peace be upon you, O Prophet and the mercy of Allah and His

blessings. Peace be upon us and upon the right-acting slaves of Allah. I have witnessed that there is no god but Allah and I have witnessed that Muḥammad is the messenger of Allah].' He would say this in the first two *rakʿahs* and supplicate as he saw fit having finished his *tashahhud*. When he sat at the end of his prayer, he would say the *tashahhud* in the same way, except that he would bring forward saying *shahidtu*, then when he wanted to conclude he would say, '*As-salāmu ʿala'n-nabiyyi wa raḥmatu'llāhi wa bar-akātuh, as-salāmu ʿalaynā wa ʿalā ʿibādi'llāhi'ṣ-ṣāliḥīn*' [Peace be upon the Prophet and the mercy of Allah and His blessings. Peace be upon us and upon the right-acting slaves of Allah].' [Then] '*as-salāmu ʿalaykum*' to his right, then he would reply to the [salām of the] imām; then if anyone said '*as-salāmu ʿalaykum*' to him from his left he would reply to him.'"

قال محمد: التشهُّد الذي ذُكر كلُّه حسن وليس يشبه تشهُّد عبد الله بن مسعود، وعندنا تشهُّدُه لأنه رواه عن رسول الله صلى الله عليه وسلم، وعليه العامة عندنا.

Muḥammad said: "The tashahhuds mentioned are all fine, though none are like the *tashahhud* of ʿAbdullāh ibn Masʿūd. We retain his *tashahhud* because he related it from the Messenger of Allah ﷺ and [the *fuqahāʾ*] in general agree upon it where we are."

١٤٩ قال محمد أخبرنا مُحِلّ بن مُحرِز الضَّبِّي، عن شقيق بن سلمة بن وائل الأسدي، عن عبد الله بن مسعود، قال: كنا إذا صلّينا خلف رسول الله صلى الله عليه وسلم قلنا السلام على الله، فقضى رسول الله صلى الله عليه وسلم صلاتَه ذاتَ يوم ثم أقبل علينا، فقال: لا تقولوا السلام على الله فإن الله هو السلام، ولكن قولوا: التحياتُ لله والصلواتُ والطيباتُ، السلام عليك أيها النبي ورحمة الله وبركاته، السلام علينا وعلى عباد الله الصالحين، أشهد أن لا إله إلا الله وأشهد أن محمداً عبد ورسوله.

149. Muḥammad said: "Muḥill ibn Muḥriz aḍ-Ḍabbī informed us from Shaqīq ibn Salamah ibn Wāʾil al-Asadī from ʿAbdullāh ibn Masʿūd, who said, 'We used, when we prayed behind the Messenger of Allah ﷺ, to say, "peace be upon Allah" so the Messenger of Allah ﷺ concluded his prayer one day and then turned to us and said, "Don't say, 'peace be upon Allah' for Allah is Peace. Rather say, '*At-taḥiyyātu lillāhi wa'ṣ-ṣalawātu wa'ṭ-ṭayyibāt. As-salāmu ʿalayka ayyuha'n-nabiyyu wa raḥmatu'llāhi wa barakātuh, as-salāmu ʿalaynā wa ʿalā ʿibādi'llāhi'ṣ-ṣāliḥīn. Ashhadu an lā ilāha illa'llāhu wa ashhadu anna Muḥammadan ʿabduhū wa rasūluh.*' [Greetings are for Allah and prayers and good words. Peace be upon you, O Prophet and the mercy of Allah and His blessings. Peace be upon us and upon the right-acting slaves of Allah. I witness that there is no god but Allah and I witness that Muḥammad is His slave and messenger.]'"

قال محمد: وكان عبد الله بن مسعود رضي الله عنه يَكره أن يُزاد فيه حرف أو يُنقص منه حرف.

Muḥammad said: "ᶜAbdullāh ibn Masᶜūd ﷺ used to dislike that [even] a letter should be added to it, or taken from it."

٤٢ باب السنة في السجود

42. The *Sunnah* in Prostration

١٥٠ أخبرنا مالك، أخبرنا نافع، عن ابن عمر: أنه كان إذا سجد وضع كفَّيه على الذي يَضَعُ جَبهتَه عليه، قال: ورأيتُهُ في برد شديد وإنه لَيُخْرِجُ كَفَّيه من بُرْنُسه حتى يضعَهما على الحصى.

150. Mālik informed us: "Nāfiᶜ informed us from Ibn ᶜUmar, that when he prostrated, he would place his hands on the same thing on which he placed his forehead. [Nāfiᶜ] said, 'And I saw him in intense cold and he would bring his hands out from under his cloak so that he could place them on the gravel.'"

١٥١ أخبرنا مالك، أخبرنا نافع، عن ابن عمر أنه كان يقول: من وضع جبهته بالأرض فليَضَعْ كفَّيه، ثم إذا رفع جبهته فليرفع كفيه، فإن اليدين تسجدان كما يسجد الوجه.

151. Mālik informed us: "Nāfiᶜ informed us from Ibn ᶜUmar, that he used to say, 'Whoever places his forehead on the ground, let him place his hands [likewise], and then when he raises his forehead let him raise his hands, for the hands should prostrate as the face prostrates.'"

قال محمد: وبهذا نأخذ، ينبغي للرجل إذا وضع جبهته ساجداً أن يضع كفيه بحذاء أذنيه ويجمع أصابعه نحو القبلة، ولا يفتحها، فإذا رفع رأسه رفعهما مع ذلك فأما من أصابه برد يؤذي، وجعل يديه على الأرض من تحت كساء أو ثوب فلا بأس بذلك، وهو قول أبي حنيفة رحمه الله.

Muḥammad said: "We adhere to this. A man ought, when he places his forehead in prostration, to place his hands next to his ears and gather his fingers towards the *qiblah* and not spread them. Then, when he raises his head, he should raise them [his hands] therewith. As for someone who suffers when it is cold, and so puts his hands on the ground from within his cloak or garment, there is no harm in that; and it that is the verdict of Abū Ḥanīfah, may Allah have mercy on him."

٤٣ باب الجلوس في الصلاة

43. Sitting in the Prayer

١٥٢ أخبرنا مالك، حدثنا عبد الله بن دينار، عن ابن عمر: أنه صلّى إلى جنبه رجل، فلما جلس الرجل تربَّع وثنّى رجليه، فلما انصرف ابنُ عمر عاب ذلك عليه، قال الرجل: فإنك تفعله! قال إني أشتكي.

152. Mālik informed us: "ᶜAbdullāh ibn Dīnār narrated to us from Ibn ᶜUmar, that a man prayed next to him, and when the man sat, he sat cross-legged [on his buttocks] on the ground and drew his legs together. So when Ibn

ᶜUmar finished he reproached him for that. The man said, 'But you do it.' [Ibn ᶜUmar] said, 'I have an ailment.'"

١٥٣ أخبرنا مالك، حدثنا عبد الرحمن بن القاسم، عن عبد الله بن عبد الله بن عمر: أنه كان يرى أباه يتربَّع في الصلاة إذا جلس، قال: ففعلتُه وأنا يومئذ حديثُ السنّ فنهاني أبي، فقال: إنها ليست بسنَّة الصلاة، وإنما سُنَّة الصلاة أن تنصب رجلَكَ اليمنى وتثني رجلَكَ اليُسرى.

153. Mālik informed us: "ᶜAbd ar-Raḥmān ibn al-Qāsim narrated to us from ᶜAbdullāh ibn ᶜAbdullāh ibn ᶜUmar, that he used to see his father sit [with his buttocks] on the ground in the prayer. He said, 'So I did it, and I was then still in my youth. My father reproached me and said, "It is not the *Sunnah* of the prayer. The *Sunnah* of the prayer is that you keep your right foot upright and put your left foot on its side."'"

قال محمد: وبهذا نأخذ، وهو قول أبي حنيفة رحمه الله وكان مالك بن أنس يأخذ بذلك في الركعتين الأُوليين، وأما في الركعة الرابعة فإنه كان يقول: يفضي الرجل بأَلْيَتَيْه إلى الأرض، ويجعل رجليه إلى الجانب الأيمن.

Muḥammad said: "We adhere to this and it is the verdict of Abū Ḥanīfah, may Allah have mercy on him. Mālik ibn Anas used to adhere to this in the first two *rakᶜahs*, but with regard to the fourth *rakᶜah* he used to say, 'A man should rest his buttocks on the ground and put his legs on his right side.'"

١٥٤ أخبرنا مالك، أخبرنا صَدَقَة بن يَسَار، عن المغيرة بن حكيم، قال: رأيتُ ابنَ عمر يجلِسُ على عقبيه بين السجدتين في الصلاة، فذكرت له فقال: إنما فعلته منذ اشتكيت.

154. Mālik informed us: "Ṣadaqah ibn Yasār informed us from al-Mughīrah ibn Ḥakīm that he said, 'I saw Ibn ᶜUmar sitting upon his heels between the two prostrations of the prayer, and I mentioned that to him. He said, "I have only begun to do that since I have been unwell."'"

قال محمد: وبهذا نأخذ، لا ينبغي أن يجلس على عقبيه بين السجدتين، ولكنه يجلس بينهما كجلوسه في صلاته، وهوقول أبي حنيفة رحمه الله .

Muḥammad said: "We adhere to this. One ought not to sit on the heels between the two prostrations, but one ought to sit in between as one sits in the prayer [after two *rakᶜahs* and at the end of the prayer]. That is the verdict of Abū Ḥanīfah, may Allah have mercy on him."

٤٤ باب صلاة القاعد

44. A Man's Praying Sitting Down

١٥٥ أخبرنا مالك، حدثنا الزُّهري، عن السائب بن يزيد، عن المطَّلب بن أبي وَدَاعَةَ السهمي، عن حفصةَ زوج النبيِّ صلى الله عليه وسلم أنها قالت: ما رأيت النبيَّ صلى الله عليه وسلم يصلي في سُبحته قاعداً قطُّ حتى كان قبل وفاته بعام، فكان يصلِّي في سبحته قاعداً ويقرأ بالسورة ويرتِّلها حتى تكون أطولَ من أطول منها .

155. Mālik informed us: "Az-Zuhrī narrated to us from as-Sā᾿ib ibn Yazīd

from al-Muṭṭalib ibn Abī Wadāᶜah as-Sahmī from Ḥafṣah, the wife of the Prophet ﷺ. She said, 'I never saw the Prophet ﷺ praying his voluntary prayer sitting down, until a year before his death, when he would pray his voluntary prayer sitting down. He would read a *sūrah* and would utter it slowly and clearly until it seemed to be greater in length than one longer than it.'"

١٥٦ أخبرنا مالك، حدثنا إِسماعيل بنُ محمد بنِ سعد بنِ أبي وقاص، عن مولى لعبد الله بن عَمرو بن العاص، عن عبدِ الله بنِ عَمرو: أن رسول الله صلى الله عليه وسلم قال: صلاةُ أحدِكم وهو قاعد مثلُ نصف صلاته وهو قائم.

156. Mālik informed us: "Ismāᶜīl ibn Muḥammad ibn Saᶜd ibn Abī Waqqāṣ narrated to us from a *mawlā* of ᶜAbdullāh ibn ᶜAmr ibn al-ᶜĀṣ from ᶜAbdullāh ibn ᶜAmr, that the Messenger of Allah ﷺ said, 'The prayer of one of you, sitting, is equal to half his prayer standing.'"

١٥٧ أخبرنا مالك، حدثنا الزُّهري، أن عبدَ الله بنَ عمرٍو قال: لمّا قَدمنا المدينة نالنا وباءٌ من وَعْكها شديدٌ، فخرج رسول الله صلى الله عليه وسلم على الناس وهم يُصَلُّوَن في سُبْحتهم قعوداً فقال: صلاةُ القاعد على نصف صلاة القائم.

157. Mālik informed us: "Az-Zuhrī narrated to us that ᶜAbdullāh ibn ᶜAmr said, 'When we came to al-Madīnah we were afflicted by an intense fit of its fever. The Messenger of Allah ﷺ came out to people when they were praying their voluntary prayers sitting, and he said, "The reward for praying sitting is half that for praying standing."'"

١٥٨ أخبرنا مالك، حدثنا الزّهري، عن أنس بنِ مالك: أن رسول الله صلى الله عليه وسلم ركب فرساً فصُرع عنه فجُحشَ شقُّه الأيمن، فصلّى صلاةً من الصلوات وهو جالس، فصلَّينا جلوساً، فلما انصرف قال: إنما جُعلَ الإمام ليُؤتَمَّ به، إذا صلى قائماً فصلوا قياماً، وإذا ركع فاركعوا وإذا قال: سمع الله لم حمده، فقولوا: ربنا ولكَ الحمد، وإنْ صلّى قاعداً فصلوا قعوداً أجمعين.

158. Mālik informed us: "Az-Zuhrī narrated to us from Anas ibn Mālik, that the Messenger of Allah ﷺ mounted a horse and was thrown from it and his right side was injured, so he prayed one of the prayers sitting, and we also prayed sitting. When he finished he said, 'The imām is only appointed to be taken as a model. If he prays standing then pray standing. When he bows, bow. When he says, "Allah listens to whoever praises Him," then say, "Our Lord and to You is the praise." If he prays seated then all of you pray seated.'"

قال محمد: وبهذا نأخذ، صلاة الرجل قاعداً للتطوع مثل نصف صلاته قائماً، فأما ما روي من قوله: إذا صلى الإمام جالساً فصلوا جلوساً أجمعين، فقد روي ذلك وقد جاء ما قد نسخه.

Muḥammad said: "We adhere to this; a man's praying voluntary prayers seated is equal to half his prayer standing. As for what was related of his saying, 'If he prays seated then all of you pray seated,' then that has been related, and there has also been related what has abrogated it.'"

١٥٩ قال محمد : حدثنا بشر، حدثنا أحمد، أخبرنا إسرائيل بن يونس بن أبي إسحاق السَّبيعي، عن جابر بن يزيد الجُعْفي، عن عامر الشَّعبي قال : قال رسول الله صلى الله عليه وسلم: لا يؤُمَّنَّ الناسَ أحدٌ بعدي جالساً.
فأخذ الناس بهذا.

159. Muḥammad said: "Bishr narrated to us, 'Aḥmad narrated to us, "Isrā᾽īl ibn Yūnus ibn Abī Isḥāq as-Sabīᶜī informed us from Jābir ibn Yazīd al-Juᶜfī from ᶜĀmir ash-Shaᶜbī, who said, 'The Messenger of Allah ﷺ said, "Let no one lead the people after me seated."'' So the people have adhered to this."

٤٥ باب الصلاة في الثوب الواحد

45. Praying in one Garment

١٦٠ أخبرنا مالك، أخبرنا بكَيْر بن عبد الله بن الأشجّ، عن بُسْر بن سعيد، عن عبيد الله الخَوْلاني قال: كانت ميمونةُ زوجُ النبيِّ صلى الله عليه وسلم تصَلِّي في الدِّرع والخِمار، وليس عليها إزار.

160. Mālik informed us: "Bukayr ibn ᶜAbdullāh ibn al-Ashajj informed us from Busr ibn Saᶜīd from ᶜUbaydullāh al-Khawlānī that he said, 'Maymūnah, the wife of the Prophet ﷺ, used to pray in a long shift and a head-covering, with no *izār* [the large cloth wrapped around the lower half of the body] on.'"

١٦١ أخبرنا مالك، أخبرنا ابن شهاب، عن سعيد بن المسيّب، عن أبي هريرة أنَّ سائلاً سأل رسول الله صلى الله عليه وسلم عن الصلاة في ثوب واحد؟ قال: أو لكلِّكم ثوبان ؟

161. Mālik informed us: "Ibn Shihāb informed us from Saᶜīd ibn al-Musayyab from Abū Hurayrah, that someone asked the Messenger of Allah ﷺ about praying in one garment. He said, 'Do all of you have two garments?'"

١٦٢ أخبرنا مالك، أخبرنا موسى بن ميسرة، عن أبي مرّة مولى عقيل بن أبي طالب، عن أم هانئ بنت أبي طالب أنها أخبرته: أن رسولَ الله صلى الله عليه وسلم صلّى عام الفتح ثمان ركعات ملتحفاً بثوب.

162. Mālik informed us: "Mūsā ibn Maysarah informed us from Abū Murrah, the *mawlā* of ᶜAqīl ibn Abī Ṭālib, from Umm Hāni᾽, the daughter of Abū Ṭālib, that she told him that the Messenger of Allah ﷺ in the year of the Opening [of Makkah to Islam], prayed eight *rakᶜahs* wrapped in a [single] garment."

١٦٣ أخبرنا مالك، أخبرني أبو النضر أن أبا مرّة مولى عقيل أنه سَمِع أمَّ هانئ بنتَ أبي طالب تحدِّث أنها ذهبتْ إلى رسول الله صلى الله عليه وسلم عامَ الفتح فوجَدَتْه يغتسل وفاطمةُ ابنتُه تستُرُه بثوب، قال: فسلَّمت، وذلك ضحى، فقال رسول الله صلى الله عليه وسلم: مَنْ هذا ؟ فقلتُ: أنا أمُّ هانئ بنت أبي طالب، قال: مرحباً بأمِّ هانئ فلمّا فرغ من غُسله قام فصلّي ثمانيَ ركعات ملتحفاً في ثوب ثم انصرف، فقلت: يا رسول الله، زعم ابنُ أمِّي أنه قاتَلَ رجلاً أَجَرْتُه، فلان ابن هبيرة، فقال رسول الله صلى الله عليه وسلم: قد أَجَرْنا من أجرت يا أمَّ هانئ.

163. Mālik informed us: "Abu'n-Naḍr informed me that Abū Murrah, the

mawlā of ᶜAqīl, told him that he heard Umm Hāniʾ, the daughter of Abū Ṭālib, saying that she went to the Messenger of Allah ﷺ in the year of the Opening [of Makkah to Islam] and found him doing *ghusl,* his daughter Fāṭimah screening him with a sheet. She said, 'So I offered greetings; and that it was in the morning. The Messenger of Allah ﷺ asked, "Who is it?" I said, "I am Umm Hāniʾ, the daughter of Abū Ṭālib." He said, "Welcome, Umm Hāniʾ." Then when he finished his *ghusl,* he stood and prayed eight *rakᶜahs,* wrapped in a single garment, then he finished. I said, "Messenger of Allah, My mother's son claims that he is going to kill a man to whom I have given protection, So-and-so, the son of Hubayrah;" and the Messenger of Allah ﷺ said, "We give protection to whomever you give protection, Umm Hāniʾ."'"

١٦٤ أخبرنا مالك، أخبرنا محمد بن زيد التيمي، عن أمِّه أنها سألتْ أمَّ سلمة زوجَ النبي صلى الله عليه وسلم ماذا تصلي فيه المرأة؟ قالت في الخمار والدِّرع السابغ الذي يغيِّب ظهر قدميها.

164. Mālik informed us: "Muḥammad ibn Zayd at-Taymī informed me that his mother asked Umm Salamah, the wife of the Prophet ﷺ, 'In what should a woman pray?' She said, 'In a head covering and a long shift, which covers the upper side of her feet.'"

قال محمد: وبهذا كله نأخذ، فإذا صلى الرجل في ثوب واحد توشّح به توشّحاً جاز، وهو قول أبي حنيفة رحمه الله.

Muḥammad said: "We adhere to this, all of it. If a man prays in a single piece of fabric [*thawb*] with which he clothes himself in the style called *tawashshuḥ*[11], then it is valid. That is the verdict of Abū Ḥanīfah, may Allah have mercy on him."

٤٦ باب صلاة الليل

46. The Night Prayer

١٦٥ أخبرنا مالك، أخبرنا نافع، عن ابن عمر: أن رجلاً سأل رسولَ الله صلى الله عليه وسلم كيف الصلاةُ بالليل؟ قال: مَثْنَى مَثْنَى، فإذا خشي أحدُكم أن يُصْبحَ فليصلِّ رَكْعةً واحدةً تُوتِرُ له ما قد صلّى.

165. Mālik informed us: "Nāfiᶜ informed us from Ibn ᶜUmar that a man asked the Messenger of Allah ﷺ, 'How is the prayer at night?' He said, 'In twos, then when one of you fears that he is close to morning, he should pray one *rakᶜah* which will make what he has prayed uneven.'"

١٦٦ أخبرنا مالك، حدَّثنا الزُّهري، عن عروة، عن عائشة: أنَّ رسولَ الله صلى الله عليه وسلم كان يصلِّي من الليل إحدى عَشْرَة ركعة، يوتر منهن بواحدة، فإذا فرغ منها اضطجع على شقِّه الأيمن.

166. Mālik informed us: "Az-Zuhrī narrated to us from ᶜUrwah from ᶜĀʾishah, that the Messenger of Allah ﷺ would pray in the night eleven *rakᶜahs*, making

an uneven number of them by [a single] one; then when he had finished he lay down on his right side."

١٦٧ أخبرنا مالك، حدثنا عبدُ الله بنُ أبي بكر، عن أبيه ؛ عن عبد الله بن قيس بن مخرمة، عن زيد بن خالد الجُهَني قال: قلت: لأَرْمُقَنَّ صلاةَ رسول الله صلى الله عليه وسلم، قال: فتوسَّدتُ عَتَبْته أو فُسطاطَه، قال: فقام فصلّى ركعتَيْن خفيفتَنْن، ثمّ صلّى ركعَتَيْن طويلتَيْن، ثم صلّى ركعتين دونهما ثم صلّى ركعتَين دون اللّتَيْن قبلهما، ثم أوْتَر .

167. Mālik informed us: "ᶜAbdullāh ibn Abī Bakr narrated to us from his father from ᶜAbdullāh ibn Qays ibn Makhramah from Zayd ibn Khālid al-Juhanī, who said, 'I said, "I will study carefully the prayer of the Messenger of Allah ﷺ." So I rested my head on his doorstep, or the edge of his tent, and he rose and prayed two light *rakᶜahs,* then he prayed two long *rakᶜahs,* then he prayed two *rakᶜahs* less than them, then he prayed two *rakᶜahs* less than the two before them, then he prayed the *Witr.*'"

١٦٨ أخبرنا مالك، أخبرنا محمد بن المنكدر ، عن سعيد بن جبير ، عن عائشة رضي الله عنها : أن رسولَ الله صلى الله عليه وسلم قال: ما من امرئٍ تكون له صلاةٌ بالليلِ يَغْلِبُهُ عليها نومٌ إلاّ كتب الله له أجرَ صلاته وكان نومُهُ عليه صدقة .

168. Mālik informed us: "Muḥammad ibn al-Munkadir informed us from Saᶜīd ibn Jubayr from ᶜĀ'ishah that the Messenger of Allah ﷺ said, 'Any man who does the night prayer, and sleep overcomes him in it, Allah writes for him the reward of his prayer, and his sleep is a gift [*ṣadaqah*] for him.'"

١٦٩ أخبرنا مالك، حدثنا داود بن حُصَين، عن عبد الرحمن الأعرج أن عمر بن الخطاب قال : من فاته من حزبه شيء من الليل، فقرأه من حين تزول الشمس إلى صلاة الظهر فكأنَّه لم يَفُتْهُ شيء.

169. Mālik informed us: "Dāwūd ibn Ḥuṣayn narrated to us from ᶜAbd ar-Raḥmān al-Aᶜraj that ᶜUmar ibn al-Khaṭṭāb said, 'Whoever misses part of his customary recitation in the night and recites it from when the sun moves away from its zenith until the prayer of *Ẓuhr,* then it is as if he had missed nothing.'"

– ١٧٠ أخبرنا مالك، حدثنا زيد بن أسلم عن أبيه أنه قال: كان عمر بن الخطاب يصلّي كلَّ ليلة ما شاء الله أن يصلي حتى إذا كان من آخر الليل أيقظ أهله للصلاة ويتلو هذه الآية: ﴿وَأْمُرْ أَهْلَكَ بالصَّلاة وَاصطَبِرْ عَلَيْهَا، لا نَسْأَلُكَ رِزقاً، نحنُ نَرْزُقُكَ وَالعَاقِبَةُ للتَّقْوَى﴾.

170. Mālik informed us: "Zayd ibn Aslam narrated to us from his father that he said, 'ᶜUmar ibn al-Khaṭṭāb used to pray every night, as much as Allah willed him to pray, until when the end of the night came he woke his family to pray, and would read this *āyah,* "Instruct your family to do *ṣalāh,* and be constant in it. We do not ask you for provision. We provide for you. And the best end result is gained by *taqwā.*" (Sūrah Ta Ha: 131)'"

١٧١ أخبرنا مالك، أخبرنا مَخْرَمةُ بنُ سليمان الوالبي ، أخبرني كُرَيْب مولى ابن عباس أخبره أنه بات عند ميمونةَ زوجِ النبيّ صلى الله عليه وسلم وهي خالته، قال: فاضطجعتُ في عرض الوسادة

واضطجع رسولُ الله صلى الله عليه وسلم وأهلُه في طولها قال: فنام رسولُ الله صلى الله عليه وسلم حتى إذا انتصفَ الليلُ أو قبله بقليل أو بعده بقليل جلس رسول الله صلى الله عليه وسلم فمسح النومَ عن وجهه بيديه، ثم قرأ بالعشر الآيات الخواتيم من سورة آل عمران ، ثم قام إلى شَنٍّ معلَّق، فتوضّأ منه ، فأحسن وضوءه، ثم قام يصلي: قال ابنُ عباس: فقمتُ فصنعتُ مثلَ ما صنع رسولُ الله صلى الله عليه وسلم، ثم ذهبتُ فقمتُ إلى جنبه فوضع رسولُ الله صلى الله عليه وسلم يدَه اليمنى على رأسي، وأخَذ بأُذُني اليمنى بيده اليمنى؛ فَفَتَلَها ثم قال: فصلى ركعتين ثم ركعتين ثم ركعتين ست مرات ، ثم أَوتَرَ، ثم اضطجع حين جاءه المؤذِّن ، فقام فصلّى ركعتين خفيفتين، ثم خرج فصلى الصبح.

171. Mālik informed us: "Makhramah ibn Sulaymān al-Wālibī told us, 'Kurayb, the *mawlā* of Ibn ᶜAbbās, informed me that Ibn ᶜAbbās told him that he spent the night at Maymūnah's, the wife of the Prophet ﷺ, and she was his [maternal] aunt. He said, 'So I lay down, with my head on the narrow side of the pillow, and the Messenger of Allah ﷺ, and his wife, lay down with their heads on the long side of the pillow. The Messenger of Allah ﷺ slept, until, when it was midnight, or a little before or a little after, the Messenger of Allah ﷺ sat up and wiped the sleep from his face with his hands, and then read the last ten ayahs of Sūrah Āl ᶜImrān. Then he stood up to a [water-] skin hanging there, and did *wuḍūʾ* from it in a thorough manner. Then he stood praying. So I got up and did the like of what the Messenger of Allah ﷺ had done, then I went and stood at his side. The Messenger of Allah ﷺ placed his right hand on my head and took hold of my right ear with his right hand and tweaked it. And so he prayed two *rakᶜahs*, then two *rakᶜahs*, then two *rakᶜahs*, six times; then he performed the *Witr* and then lay down until the *muʾadhdhin* came, and so rose and prayed two light *rakᶜahs*, then went out and prayed the dawn prayer.'"

قال محمد: صلاةُ الليلِ عندنا مثنى مثنى، وقال أبو حنيفة: صلاة الليلِ إنْ شئتَ صلَّيتَ ركعتين، وإن شئتَ صلَّيتَ أربعاً ، وإن شئتَ ستّاً، وإن شئتَ ثمانياً، وإن شئتَ ما شئتَ بتكبيرة واحدة ، وأفضل ذلك أربعاً أربعاً. وأما الوتر فقولنا وقول أبي حنيفة فيه واحد ، والوتر ثلاث لا يُفصل بينهنَّ بتسليم .

Muḥammad said: "The night prayer in our opinion is in twos. However, Abū Ḥanīfah said, 'The night prayer is up to you, you can pray two *rakᶜahs*, or four, or six, or eight, or as much as you will with a single saying of *Allāhu akbar*, but the best form of it is in fours.' As for *Witr*, our verdict on it and that of Abū Ḥanīfah are the same: *Witr* is three, and they should not be separated by saying *as-salāmu ᶜalaykum*.'"

٤٧ بابُ الحدَثِ في الصلاة

47. Occurrences [which Undo a Person's *Wuḍūʾ*] in the Prayer

١٧٢ أخبرنا مالك، حدثنا إسماعيلُ بنُ أبي الحكيم، عن عطاء بن يسارٍ: أن رسول الله ﷺ كبَّر في

صلاة من الصلوات، ثم أشار إليهم بيده أن امْكُثوا، فانطلق رسولُ الله ﷺ، ثم رجع وعلى جلده أثر فصلّى .

172. Mālik informed us: "Ismāᶜīl ibn Abī Ḥakīm narrated to us from ᶜAṭā᾿ ibn Yasār, that the Messenger of Allah ﷺ said *Allāhu akbar* for one of the prayers, then signalled to them with his hand to, 'remain where you are'. So the Messenger of Allah ﷺ went off and then returned with the traces of water on his skin and prayed."

قال محمد: وبهذا نأخذ، من سبقه حدث في صلاة، فلا بأس أن ينصرف ولا يتكلم فيتوضأ، ثم يبني على ما صلّى، وأفضل ذلك أن يتكلم ويتوضأً ويستقبل صلاته، وهو قول أبي حنيفة ﵀ .

Muḥammad said: "We adhere to this. If anything befalls a person in a prayer that breaks his wuḍūᶜ, then there is no harm in his turning away without speaking, doing *wuḍū᾿*, and then continuing from where he had left off. However, it is better that he speak, do *wuḍū᾿* and begin his prayer afresh, and that is the verdict of Abū Ḥanīfah, may Allah have mercy on him."

٤٨ باب فضل القرآن وما يُستحبُّ من ذكر الله عز وجل

48. The Superiority of the Qur᾿ān and what is Recommended of the Remembrance of Allah ﷻ

١٧٣ أخبرنا مالك، أخبرنا عبدُ الرحمن بن عبد الله بن أبي صعصعة، عن أبيه أنه أخبره عن أبي سعيد الخُدْري أنه سمع رجلاً من الليل يقرأ: ﴿قُل هُوَ اللَّهُ أَحَدٌ﴾ يردِّدها ، فلما أصبح حدَّث النبيﷺ كأنَّ الرجل يُقَلِّلُها ، فقال النبي ﷺ: "والذي نفسي بيده إنها لَتَعْدِلُ ثُلُثَ القرآن".

173. Mālik informed us: "ᶜAbd ar-Raḥmān ibn ᶜAbdullāh ibn Abī Ṣaᶜṣaᶜah informed us from his father, that Abū Saᶜīd al-Khudrī told him that he heard a man in the night reading *Qul huwa'llāhu aḥad* repeatedly. When the morning came, he told the Prophet ﷺ [and it was] as if the man belittled it. The Prophet ﷺ said, 'By Him in Whose hand is my self, it certainly equals a third of the Qur᾿ān!'"

١٧٤ أخبرنا مالك، أخبرنا يحيى بن سعيد قال: سمعت سعيدَ بنَ المسيب يقول: قال معاذُ بن جبل : لأن أذكرَ اللهَ من بُكرة إلى الليل أحبُّ إليّ من أن أحمل على جياد الخيل من بُكرة حتى الليل.

174. Mālik informed us: "Yaḥyā ibn Saᶜīd informed us. He said, 'I heard Saᶜīd ibn al-Musayyab say, "Muᶜādh ibn Jabal said, 'That I should remember Allah from the beginning of the day until the night is more beloved to me than that I should charge upon the finest horses from the beginning of the day until the night.'"'"

قال محمد: ذكر الله حَسَنٌ على كل حال

Muḥammad said: "The remembrance of Allah is a good thing in every circumstance."

١٧٥ أخبرنا مالك، حدثنا نافع، عن ابن عمر: أن النبي ﷺ قال: إنما مثل صاحب القرآن كمثل صاحب الإبل المُعَلَّقة ، إن عاهَدَ عليها أمسكها وإن أطلقها ذَهَبَتْ.

175. Mālik informed us: "Nāfi[c] narrated to us from Ibn [c]Umar, that the Prophet ﷺ said, 'A man who knows the Qur[ɔ]ān well is like a man who has a camel whose halter he has loosened to give her ease [*mu[c]allaqah*][12]. If he takes care of it, he keeps it, and if he lets it go, it gets away.'"

٤٩ باب الرجل يُسلَّم عليه وهو يصلي

49. A Man to whom Someone Says *as-Salāmu [c]Alaykum* while He is Praying

١٧٦ أخبرنا مالك، أخبرنا نافع أن ابن عمرَ مرَّ على رجلٍ يصلِّي، فسلَّم عليه فردَّ عليه السلام، فَرَجَعَ إليه ابنُ عمرَ، فقال: إذا سُلِّم على أحدكم وهو يصلِّي فلا يتكلَّم وَلْيُشِرْ بيده.

176. Mālik informed us: "Nāfi[c] informed us that Ibn [c]Umar passed by a man who was praying and said *as-salamu [c]alaykum* to him and he returned the greeting. Ibn [c]Umar went back to him and said, 'When it is said to one of you *as salāmu [c]alaykum* while he is praying then he should not speak, and he should gesture with his hand.'"

قال محمد: وبهذا نأخذ، لا ينبغي للمصلي أن يردَّ السلام إذا سُلِّم عليه وهو في الصلاة، فإن فعل فسدتْ صلاتُه، ولا ينبغي أن يسلَّم عليه وهو يصلِّي، وهو قولُ أبي حنيفة رحمه الله.

Muḥammad said: "We adhere to this; a man should not, while praying, answer the greeting *as-salāmu [c]alaykum* when it is said to him; and should he do so his prayer will be invalid. Nor should *as-salāmu [c]alaykum* be said to him while he is praying. and that is the verdict of Abū Ḥanīfah, may Allah have mercy on him."

٥٠ باب الرجلان يصلِّيانِ جماعة

50. Two Men Praying Together [*Jamā[c]ah*]

١٧٧ أخبرنا مالك، حدثنا الزُّهري، عن عُبيد الله بن عبد الله بن عُتْبَةَ، عن أبيه قال: دخلت على عمرَ بنِ الخطاب بالهاجرَة فوجدتُه يسبِّحُ فقمتُ وراءَه فَقَرَّبَني، فجعلني بحذائه عن يمينه، فلما جاء يَرْفَاءُ تأخَّرتُ فَصَفَفْنا وراءَه.

177. Mālik informed us: "Az-Zuhrī narrated to us from [c]Ubaydullāh ibn [c]Abdullāh ibn [c]Utbah from his father. He said, 'I went in to see [c]Umar ibn al-Khaṭṭāb during the heat of midday, and found him praying [a voluntary prayer]. So I stood behind him, but he brought me closer until I was alongside him on his right. When Yarfā[ɔ] came, I stepped back and we made a row behind him.'"

١٧٨ أخبرنا مالك، أخبرنا نافع أنه قام عن يسار ابنِ عمرَ في صلاته، فجعلني عن يمينه.

178. Mālik informed us: "Nāfi[c] informed us that he stood on Ibn [c]Umar's left in his prayer. 'So he stood me on his right.'"

١٧٩ أخبرنا مالك، حدثنا إسحاقُ بنُ عبدِ الله بنِ أبي طلحة، عن أنس بن مالكٍ: أن جدّتَه دعت

رسولَ الله ﷺ لطعام، فأكل ثم قال: قوموا فَلْنُصَلِّ بكم. قال أنس: فقمتُ إلى حصير لنا قد اسودَّ من طوال ما لُبِسَ فنضحتُه بماء، فقام عليه رسولُ اللّه ﷺ قال: فصففتُ أنا واليتيم وراءه والعجوز وراءَنا، فصلى بنا ركعتين ثم انصرف.

179. Mālik informed us: "Isḥāq ibn ᶜAbdullāh ibn Abī Ṭalḥah narrated to us from Anas ibn Mālik, that his grandmother invited the Messenger of Allah ﷺ to some food. So he ate and then said, 'Stand up and let us pray with you.' Anas said, 'So I got up and went to a mat of ours, which had been down so long it had become blackened, and I sprinkled it with water, and the Messenger of Allah ﷺ stood on it.' [Anas] said, 'Then I formed a row with the orphan behind him, and the old woman behind us, and he prayed two *rakᶜahs* with us and then departed.'"

قال محمد: وبهذا كلِّه نأخذ، إذا صلّى الرجل الواحدُ مع الإمام قام عن يمين الإمام، وإذا صلّى الاثنان قاما خلفه وهو قول أبي حنيفة رحمه الله.

Muḥammad said: "We adhere to all of this; when a lone man prays with the imām he should stand on the imam's right, and when two pray [with him] they should stand behind him, and that is the verdict of Abū Ḥanīfah, may Allah have mercy on him."

٥١ بابُ الصلاة في مرابضِ الغنم

51. Praying in Sheep Pens

– ١٨٠ أخبرنا مالك، عن محمد بن عمرو بن حَلْحَلَة الدُّؤَلي، عن حُميد بن مالك بن الخيثَم، عن أبي هريرة أنّه قال: أحسِنْ إلى غَنَمك، وأطِبْ مُراحَها، وصلِّ في ناحيتها، فإنها من دوابِّ الجنة.

180. Mālik informed us from Muḥammad ibn ᶜAmr ibn Ḥalḥalah ad-Duʾalī, from Ḥumayd ibn Mālik ibn al-Khaytham, from Abū Hurayrah, that he said, "Treat your sheep well, make sound their resting place, and pray in their environs, for they are amongst the animals of the Garden."

قال محمد: وبهذا نأخذ، لا بأس بالصلاة في مُراح الغنم، وإن كان فيه أبوالُها وبعرُها ما أكلتَ لحمها فلا بأس ببولها.

Muḥammad said: "We adhere to this; there is no harm in praying in the resting place of sheep though their urine and dung be in there. Those creatures whose meat is eaten, there is no harm in their urine."[13]

٥٢ باب الصلاة عند طلوعِ الشمس وعند غروبها

52. Praying at the Rising and Setting of the Sun

– ١٨١ أخبرنا مالك، أخبرنا نافع، عن ابن عمر أن رسول الله صلى الله عليه وسلم قال: لا يتحرَّى أحدُكم فيصلِّيَ عند طلوعِ الشمسِ ولا عند غروبها.

181. Mālik informed us: "Nāfiᶜ informed us from Ibn ᶜUmar, that the Messenger

of Allah ﷺ said, "None of you should intend to pray at the rising of the sun nor at its setting."

١٨٢ أخبرنا مالك، أخبرنا زيدُ بن أسلم، عن عطاءِ بن يسار، عن عبد الله الصُّنابحي : أن رسول الله صلى الله عليه وسلم قال: إنَّ الشمسَ تطلُعُ ومعها قرن الشيطان، فإذا ارتفعتْ زائلها ، ثم إذا استوتْ قارَنَها، ثم إذا زالتْ فارقها، ثم إذا دنَتْ للغروب قارنَها، فإذا غربَتْ فارقها، قال: ونهى رسول الله صلى الله عليه وسلم عن الصلاة في تلك الساعات.

182. Mālik informed us: "Zayd ibn Aslam informed us from ᶜAṭā᾿ ibn Yasār from ᶜAbdullāh aṣ-Ṣunābiḥī that the Messenger of Allah ﷺ said, 'When the sun rises the horn of shayṭān is with it, then when it has risen the horn separates from it. Then later when it is at the zenith it is accompanied by it, but when it moves away from the zenith it separates from it. Then later when it approaches setting, it is accompanied by it and when it sets it separates from it.'" He said, "The Messenger of Allah ﷺ forbade *ṣalāh* at these times."

١٨٣ أخبرنا مالك، أخبرني عبدُ الله بنُ دينار قال: كان عبدُ الله بن عمر يقول : كان عمر بن الخطاب يقول: لا تحرّوا بصلاتكم طلوعَ الشمس ولا غروبها، فإن الشيطانَ يطلُعُ قرناه من طلوعها، ويغربان عند غروبها، وكان يضرِبُ الناس عن تلك الصلاة .

183. Mālik informed us: "ᶜAbdullāh ibn Dīnār informed me saying, 'ᶜAbdullāh ibn ᶜUmar used to say, "ᶜUmar ibn al-Khaṭṭāb used to say, 'Do not intend to do your prayer at the rising of the sun nor at its setting, because shayṭān's two horns rise with its rising and set with its setting,' and he used to strike people to prevent them doing such a prayer."'"

قال محمد: وبهذا كلِّه نأخذ، ويوم الجمعة وغيره عندنا في وذلك سواء ، وهو قول أبي حنيفة رحمه الله .

Muḥammad said: "We adhere to all of this. The day of Jumuᶜah and other days are the same to us in that respect, and that is the verdict of Abū Ḥanīfah, may Allah have mercy on him."

٥٣ بابُ الصلاة في شدّة الحرّ

53. Praying in Intense Heat

١٨٤ أخبرنا مالك، أخبرني عبدُ الله بن يزيدَ مولى الأسود بن سفيان ، عن أبي سلمةَ بنِ عبد الرحمن وعن محمد بن عبد الرحمن بنِ ثوبان، عن أبي هريرة أن رسول الله صلى الله عليه وسلم قال: إذا كان الحرُّ فأبردُوا عن الصلاة ، فإنَّ شدَّة الحرّ من فَيْحِ جَهَنّم. وذكر أن النارَ اشتكَتْ إلى ربِّها عزّ وجلّ، فإذنَ لها في كلِّ بنفَسَيْن : نَفَس في الشتاء ونَفَس في الصيف .

184. Mālik informed us: "ᶜAbdullāh ibn Yazīd, the *mawlā* of al-Aswad ibn Sufyān, informed me from Abū Salamah ibn ᶜAbd ar-Raḥmān and from Muḥammad ibn ᶜAbd ar-Raḥmān ibn Thawbān from Abū Hurayrah, that the Messenger of Allah ﷺ said, 'When the heat is great, then let it cool down before praying, for the intensity of the heat is from the vehement raging of

the heat of Jahannam;' and he mentioned that the Fire complained to its Lord ﷻ so He allowed it two breaths in each year, a breath in winter and a breath in summer."

قال محمد: وبهذا نأخذ، نُبْرِد لصلاة الظهر في الصيف ونصلي في الشتاء حين تزول الشمس وهو قول أبي حنيفة رحمه الله.

Muḥammad said: "We adhere to this. We let it cool down before doing *Ẓuhr* prayer in the summer but pray in the winter when the sun moves away from its zenith. That is the verdict of Abū Ḥanīfah, may Allah have mercy on him."

٥٤ باب الرَّجُل ينسى الصلاةَ أو تفوتُهُ عن وقتها

54. A Man who Forgets the Prayer or Misses its Time

١٨٥ أخبرنا مالك، أخبرنا ابنُ شهاب، عن سعيد بن المسيّب: أن رسولَ الله صلى الله عليه وسلم حين قَفَل من خيبر أسرى حتى إذا كان من آخر الليل عرّس، وقال لبلال: اكلأْ لنا الصبح، فنام رسولُ الله صلى الله عليه وسلم وأصحابُه، وكلأْ بلالٌ ما قُدِّر له، ثم استند إلى راحلته وهو مقابل الفجر، فغلَبَتْه عيناه، فلم يستيقظ رسولُ الله صلى الله عليه وسلم ولا بلالٌ ولا أحد من الرَّكب، حتى ضرَبَتْهم الشمس، ففزِعَ رسولُ الله صلى الله عليه وسلم، فقال: يا بلال، فقال بلال يا رسول الله أخذ بنفسي الذي أخذ بنفسك، قال: اقتادوا فبعثوا رواحلَهم، فاقتادوها شيئاً، ثم أمر رسول الله صلى الله عليه وسلم بلالاً، فأقام الصلاة فصلَّى بهم الصبح، ثم قال حين قضى الصلاة: من نسي صلاة فليصلِّها إذا ذكرها، فإن الله عز وجل يقول: ﴿أَقِمِ الصَّلَاةَ لِذِكْرِي﴾.

185. Mālik informed us: "Ibn Shihāb informed us from Saᶜīd ibn al-Musayyab, that the Messenger of Allah ﷺ headed back from Khaybar, travelling at night, until when it was towards the end of the night he made camp and said to Bilāl, 'Keep watch for the dawn for us.' So the Messenger of Allah ﷺ and his companions slept, and Bilāl kept watch as long as was decreed for him and then leaned against his camel, facing in the direction of the dawn, and sleep overcame him. Neither the Messenger of Allah ﷺ, nor Bilāl, nor anyone of the company awoke until the sun struck them. The Messenger of Allah ﷺ started and said, 'Bilāl!' and Bilāl said, 'Messenger of Allah, He Who took your self took my self.' [The Messenger of Allah] said, 'Lead on.' So they roused their mounts and led them on somewhat and then the Messenger of Allah ﷺ ordered Bilāl to announce the *iqāmah* for the prayer and he prayed the dawn prayer with them. Then he said, when he had concluded the prayer, 'Whoever forgets a prayer, let him pray it when he remembers it, for Allah says ﷻ, "and establish *ṣalāh* to remember Me." (Sūrah Ta Ha: 13)'"

قال محمد: وبهذا نأخذ، إلاّ أن يذكُرَها في الساعة التي نهى رسولُ الله ﷺ عن الصلاة فيها: حين تَطْلُعُ الشمس حتى ترتفعَ وتبيضَّ، ونصف النهار حتى تزول، حين تحمَّر الشمس حتى تغيبَ إلا عصر يومه فإنه يصلِّيها وإن احمرَّتْ الشمسُ قبل أن تغرُبَ، وهو قول أبي حنيفة رحمه الله.

Muḥammad said: "We adhere to this, except in the case when he remembers it in the time in which the Messenger of Allah ﷺ prohibited prayer – when the sun appears until it ascends and whitens, or the middle of the day until it moves away from its zenith, or when the sun reddens until it disappears – unless it be [the prayer of] *ᶜAṣr* of that same day, in which case he should pray it before the sun sets, even though it has reddened. That is the verdict of Abū Ḥanīfah, may Allah have mercy on him."

١٨٦ أخبرنا مالك، أخبرني زيد بن أسلم، عن عطاء بن يسار وعن بسر بن سعيد، وعن الأعرج يحدّثونه عن أبي هريرة: أن رسولَ الله صلى الله عليه وسلم قال: من أدركَ من الصبح ركعةً قبل أن تَطْلُعَ الشمس فقد أدركها.
ومن أدركها من العصر قبل أن تَغْرُبَ الشمس فقد أدركها.

186. Mālik informed us: "Zayd ibn Aslam informed us from ᶜAṭā᾽ ibn Yasār, and from Busr ibn Saᶜīd, and from al-Aᶜraj, all reporting from Abū Hurayrah, that the Messenger of Allah ﷺ said, 'Whoever catches one *rakᶜah* of the dawn [prayer] before the sun appears, has caught it; and whoever catches one of *ᶜAṣr* before the sun sets, has caught it.'"

٥٥ باب الصلاة في الليلة الممطرة وفضل الجماعة

55. Prayer on a Rainy Night, and the Special Merit of the Congregation [*Jamāᶜah*]

١٨٧ أخبرنا مالك، أخبرنا نافع، عن ابن عمر، أنه نادى بالصلاة في سفر في ليلة ذات برد وريح، ثم قال: ألا صلّوا في الرحال، ثم قال: إن رسول الله صلى الله عليه وسلم كان يأمر المؤذن إذا كانت ليلة باردة ذات مطر يقول: ألا صلّوا في الرحال.

187. Mālik informed us: "Nāfiᶜ informed us from Ibn ᶜUmar, that he called [the *adhān*] for the prayer on a journey, on a cold and windy night, and then said, 'Do the prayer in your dwellings.' Then he said, 'The Messenger of Allah ﷺ would, when it was a cold and rainy night, order the *mu᾽adhdhin* to say, 'Do the prayer in your dwellings.'"

قال محمد: هذا حسن وهذا رخصة والصلاة في الجماعة أفضل.

Muḥammad said: "This is fine; it is a concession but the prayer in congregation is better."

١٨٨ أخبرنا مالك، حدثنا أبو النضر، عن بُسر بن سعيد، عن زيد بن ثابت، قال: إن أفضل صلاتكم في بيوتكم إلاّ صلاة الجماعة.

188. Mālik informed us: "Abu'n-Naḍr narrated to us from Busr ibn Saᶜīd from Zayd ibn Thābit. He said, 'The prayer of most merit is [that prayed] in your homes, except the prayer in congregation.'"

قال محمد: وبهذا نأخذ وكلٌّ حسن.

Muḥammad said: "We adhere to this, and either way is good."*

١٨٩ أخبرنا مالك، حدثنا نافع، عن ابن عمر قال: قال رسول الله صلى الله عليه وسلم: فضل صلاة الجماعة على صلاة الرجل وحده بسبع وعشرين درجة.

189. Mālik informed us: "Nāfi[c] narrated to us from Ibn [c]Umar. He said, 'The Messenger of Allah said, "The superiority of the the prayer in congregation over that of a man who prays alone is twenty seven degrees."'"

٥٦ باب قصر الصلاة في السفر

56. Shortening the Prayer on Journeys

١٩٠ أخبرنا مالك، أخبرني صالح بن كَيسان، عن عروة بن الزبير، عن عائشة رضي الله عنها أنها قالت: فُرِضَتْ الصلاة ركعتين ركعتين في السفر والحضر، فزيد في صلاة الحضر وأُقِرَّت صلاةُ السفر.

190. Mālik informed us: "Ṣāliḥ ibn Kaysān informed me from [c]Urwah ibn az-Zubayr that [c]Ā᾽ishah ﵂ said, 'The prayer was made obligatory, each prayer two *rak[c]ahs*, whether travelling or resident; then the prayer of residence was added to and the prayer of travelling was confirmed as it was.'"

١٩١ أخبرنا مالك، أخبرنا نافع: أن عبد الله بن عمر رضي الله عنهما كان إذا خرج إلى خيبر قَصر الصلاة.

191. Mālik informed us: "Nāfi[c] informed us that when Ibn [c]Umar went out to Khaybar, he would shorten the prayer."

١٩٢ أخبرنا مالك، حدثنا نافع: أن عبد الله بن عمر كان إذا خرج حاجّاً أو معتمراً قصر الصلاة بذي الحُلَيْفَة.

192. Mālik informed us: "Nāfi[c] narrated to us that when Ibn [c]Umar went on Ḥajj or *[c]umrah*, he would shorten the prayer at Dhu'l-Ḥulayfah."

١٩٣ أخبرنا مالك، أخبرني ابن شهاب الزهري، عن سالم بن عبد الله: أن ابن عمر خَرَجَ إلى رِيم فقَصَرَ الصلاةَ في مَسيره ذلك.

193. Mālik informed us: "Ibn Shihāb az-Zuhrī informed me from Sālim ibn [c]Abdullāh that Ibn [c]Umar went out to Rīm and he shortened the prayer on that journey."

١٩٤ أخبرنا مالك، حدثنا نافع: أنه كان يُسافرُ مع ابنِ عُمَرَ البريدَ فلا يَقْصُرُ الصلاة.

194. Mālik informed us: "Nāfi[c] narrated to us that he used to travel with Ibn [c]Umar the distance of approximately twelve miles [*barīd*], and he would not shorten the prayer."

قال محمد: إذا خرج المسافر أتمّ الصلاة إلاّ أن يريد مسيرةَ ثلاثة أيّامٍ كوامل بسيرِ الإبلِ ومَشي الأقدام، فإذا أراد ذلك قصرَ الصلاة حين يخرج من مصره، ويجعل البيوت خلفَ ظَهره، وهو قول أبي حنيفة رحمه الله.

Muḥammad said: "When the traveller goes out, he should pray the complete prayer, unless he intends a journey of three whole days, travelling at a camel's pace or walking pace. If he intends that, he should shorten the prayer when he goes out of his city and leaves the houses behind him; that is the verdict of Abū Ḥanīfah, may Allah have mercy on him."

٥٧ باب المسافر يدخل المصْرَ أو غيرَه متى يُتِمّ الصلاةَ

57. When a Traveller who Enters a City or Somewhere else Should Complete the Prayer

١٩٥ أخبرنا مالك، حدثنا ابن شهاب، عن سالم بن عبد الله، عن ابن عمر أنه قال: أُصلِّي صلاة المسافر ما لم أُجمع مُكثاً وإن حبسني ذلك اثنتي عَشْرَة ليلة.

195. Mālik informed us: "Ibn Shihāb narrated to us from Sālim ibn ᶜAbdullāh from Ibn ᶜUmar, that he said, 'I pray as the traveller prays as long as I have not decided in advance upon a stay, even though it should detain me for twelve nights.'"

١٩٦ أخبرنا مالك، حدّثنا الزهري، عن سالم بن عبد الله، عن أبيه: أن عمر كان إذا قدم مكة صلى بهم ركعتين، ثم قال يا أهل مكة أتمّوا صلاتكم فإنّا قومٌ سَفْر.

196. Mālik informed us: "Az-Zuhrī narrated to us from Sālim ibn ᶜAbdullāh from his father, that when ᶜUmar came to Makkah, he would pray two *rakᶜahs* with them and then say, 'People of Makkah, complete your prayer for we are a people on a journey.'"

١٩٧ أخبرنا مالك، أخبرني نافع، عن ابن عمر: أنه كان يقيم بمكة عشراً فيَقْصُرُ الصلاة إلاّ أن يشهدَ الصلاة مع الناس فيصلي بصلاتهم.

197. Mālik informed us: "Nāfiᶜ informed us that Ibn ᶜUmar would reside at Makkah for ten [days], and would shorten the prayer, unless he attended the prayer with the people, when he would pray as they prayed.'"

١٩٨ أخبرنا مالك، أخبرنا هشام بن عروة، أنه سأل سالمَ بنَ عبد الله عن المسافر إذا كان لا يدري متى يخرج يقول: أَخْرُجُ اليوم، بل أَخْرُجُ غداً، بل الساعة، فكان كذلك حتى يأتي عليه ليال كثيرة أيقصر أم ما يصنع؟ قال: يقصر وإن تمادى به ذلك شهراً.

198. Mālik informed us: "Hishām ibn ᶜUrwah informed us that he asked Sālim ibn ᶜAbdullāh about the traveller who does not know when he is leaving, saying to himself, 'I will leave today, no I will leave tomorrow, no [I will leave] now,' and so on, until many nights passed him by. Should he shorten [the prayer] or what should he do? He said, 'He should shorten though he continue in that state for a month.'"

قال محمد: نرى قَصْرَ الصلاة إذا دخل المسافرُ مصْراً من الأمصار وإنْ عَزَمَ على المُقام إلاّ أنْ يعزم على المقام خمسة عشرة يوماً فصاعداً فإذا عزم على ذلك أتم الصلاة.

Muḥammad said: "We are of the opinion that the prayer should be shortened once the traveller enters a city even if he is resolved to stay, unless he is resolved to stay for fifteen or more days. Once he is resolved upon that, he should complete the prayer."

١٩٩ أخبرنا مالك، أخبرنا عطاء الخراساني قال: قال سعيد بن المسيب: من أَجْمَعَ على إقامة أربعة أيام فلْيُتمّ الصلاة .

199. Mālik informed us: "ᶜAṭā᾽ al-Khurāsānī told us [this]. He said, 'Saᶜīd ibn al-Musayyab said, "Whoever decides in advance upon a stay of four days, let him complete the prayer."'"

قال محمد: ولسنا نأخذ بهذا، يقصر المسافر حتى يُجْمع على أقامة خمسة عشر يوماً، وهو قول ابن عمر وسعيد بن جبير وسعيد بن المسيّب .

Muḥammad said: "We do not adhere to this. The traveller should shorten the prayer until he determines upon a stay of fifteen days; that is the verdict of Ibn ᶜUmar, Saᶜīd ibn Jubayr and Saᶜīd ibn al-Musayyab."

٢٠٠ أخبرنا مالك، أخبرنا نافع، عن ابن عمر: أنه كان يصلي مع الإمام أربعاً ، وإذا صلّى لنفسه صلّى ركعتين .

200. Mālik informed us: "Nāfiᶜ informed us that Ibn ᶜUmar used to pray four *rakᶜahs* with the imām, but when he prayed by himself, he prayed two *rakᶜahs*."

قال محمد: وبهذا نأخذ إذا كان الإمام مقيماً والرجل مسافراً وهو قول أبي حنيفة رحمه الله.

Muḥammad said: "We adhere to this if the imām is resident and the man is travelling. It is the verdict of Abū Ḥanīfah, may Allah have mercy on him."

٥٨ باب القراءة في الصلاة في السفر

58. The Recitation in the Prayer on a Journey

٢٠١ أخبرنا مالك، حدثنا نافع: أنَّ ابنَ عمر كان يقرأ في الصبح بالعشر السور من أول المفصَّل يردِّدهن في كل ركعة سورة.

201. Mālik informed us: "Nāfiᶜ narrated to us that when travelling, Ibn ᶜUmar used to recite in the dawn prayer, the ten sūrahs from the beginning of the *Mufaṣṣal*, repeating them, one *sūrah* in each *rakᶜah*."

قال محمد: يقرأ في الفجر في السفر ﴿والسماء ذات البروج﴾ ﴿والسماء والطارق﴾ ونحوهما .

Muḥammad said: "When travelling, '*Wa's-samā᾽i dhāti'l-burūj*', '*Wa's-samā᾽i wa'ṭ-ṭāriq*' and their like, should be read in the dawn prayer."

٥٩ باب الجمع بين الصلاتين في السفر والمطر

59. Combining two Prayers on a Journey or in Rain

٢٠٢ أخبرنا مالك، أخبرنا نافع، عن ابن عمر: أن رسول الله ﷺ كان إذا عَجِلَ به السَّيْر جَمَعَ بين المغرب والعشاء.

202. Mālik informed us: "Nāfiᶜ informed us from Ibn ᶜUmar that the Messenger of Allah ﷺ would, when travelling in a hurry, combine *Maghrib* and *ᶜIshā᾽*."

٢٠٣ أخبرنا مالك، حدثنا نافع: أن ابن عمر حين جمع بين المغرب والعشاء في السفر سار حتى غاب الشفق.

203. Mālik informed us: "Nāfi[c] narrated to us that Ibn [c]Umar, when combining *Maghrib* and *[c]Ishā[ɔ]* on a journey, would travel until the redness of the sky [of sunset] disappeared."

٢٠٤ أخبرنا مالك، أخبرنا داود بن الحصين أن عبد الرحمن بن هرمز أخبره ، قال : كان رسولُ الله يَجْمَعُ بين الظهر والعصر في سفر إلى تبوك .

204. Mālik informed us: "Dāwūd ibn al-Ḥuṣayn informed us that [c]Abd ar-Raḥmān ibn Hurmuz informed him, 'The Messenger of Allah ﷺ combined *Ẓuhr* and *[c]Aṣr* on his journey to Tabūk.'"

قال محمد : وبهذا نأخذ . والجمع بين الصلاتين أن تُؤخَّرَ الأُولى منهما، فتُصلَّى في آخر وقتها وتُعجَّل الثانية فتُصلَّى في أول وقتها . وقد بَلَغنا عن ابن عمر أنه صلّى المغرب حين أخَّر الصلاة قبل أن تغيب الشفق ، خلاف ما روى مالك .

Muḥammad said: "We adhere to this; the combining of two prayers means that the first is delayed so that it is prayed in its latest time, and the second is hastened, so that it is prayed in its first time. A report has reached us that Ibn [c]Umar, when delaying the prayer, prayed *Maghrib* before the redness in the sky disappeared. This is at variance with what Mālik narrated."

٢٠٥ أخبرنا مالك، حدثنا نافع، عن ابن عمر: أنه كان إذا جمع الأمراء بين المغرب والعشاء جمع معهم في المطر.

205. Mālik informed us: "Nāfi[c] narrated to us from Ibn [c]Umar that, when the governors combined *Maghrib* and *[c]Ishā[ɔ]*, they would combine them with them [the people] when it was raining."

قال: لسنا نأخذ بهذا، لا نجمع بين الصلاتين في وقتٍ واحدٍ إلاّ الظهر والعصر بعرَفَةَ والمغرب والعشاء بمُزدلفة، وهو قول أبي حنيفة – رحمه الله .

He said: "We do not adhere to this. We do not combine two prayers in one time, except *Ẓuhr* and *[c]Aṣr* at [c]Arafah, and *Maghrib* and *[c]Ishā[ɔ]* at Muzdalifah. That is the verdict of Abū Ḥanīfah, may Allah have mercy on him."

قال محمد : بَلَغنا عن عمر بن الخطاب أنه كتب في الآفاق ينهاهم أن يجمعوا بين الصلاتين، ويخبرهم أنَّ الجمع بين الصلاتين في وقت واحدٍ كبيرة من الكبائر. أخبرنا بذلك الثقات عن العلاء بن الحارث ، عن مكحول .

Muḥammad said: "A report of [c]Umar ibn al-Khaṭṭāb has reached us; he wrote to the outlying lands, prohibiting them from combining two prayers and telling them that combining two prayers in one time is one of the major wrong actions. We have been told this by trustworthy narrators, narrating from al-[c]Alā[ɔ] ibn al-Ḥārith, from Makḥūl."

٦٠ باب الصلاة على الدابة في السفر

60. Praying on a [Riding] Beast when Travelling

٢٠٦ أخبرنا مالك، حدثنا عبدُ الله بن دينار قال : قال عبد الله بن عمر: كان رسول الله صلى الله عليه

وسلم يصلِّي على راحلته في السفر حيثما توجَّهتْ به، قال : وكان عبد الله بن عمر يصنع ذلك .
206. Mālik informed us: "ᶜAbdullāh ibn Dīnār narrated [this] to us. He said, 'ᶜAbdullāh ibn ᶜUmar said, "The Messenger of Allah ﷺ used to pray on his mount when travelling, whatever way it faced."' [Ibn Dīnār] said, 'And ᶜAbdullāh ibn ᶜUmar used to do that.'"

٢٠٧ أخبرنا مالك، أخبرني أبو بكر بن عمر بن عبد الرحمن بن عبد الله بن عمر أن سعيداً أخبره: أنه كان مع عبد الله بن عمر رضي الله عنهما في سفر، فكنت أسيرُ معه وأتحدَّث معه، حتى إذا خشيتُ أن يطلع الفجر تخلَّفت ، فنزلتُ فأوترتُ ، ثم ركبتُ، فلحقته ، قال ابن عمر: أين كنت؟ فقلت: يا أبا عبد الرحمن ، نزلتُ فأوترتُ وخشيتُ أن أصبح، فقال: أليس لك في رسول الله صلى الله عليه وسلم أسوة حسنة؟ فقلت: بلى والله، قال: فإنَّ رسول الله صلى الله عليه وسلم كان يوتر على البعير.

207. Mālik informed us: "Abū Bakr ibn ᶜUmar ibn ᶜAbd ar-Raḥmān ibn ᶜAbdullāh ibn ᶜUmar informed me that Saᶜīd told him that he was with ᶜAbdullāh ibn ᶜUmar on a journey, 'So I was going along with him, and speaking with him, until I began to fear that the dawn would appear, so I dropped behind and got down and performed the *Witr*. Then I mounted and rejoined him. Ibn ᶜUmar asked, "Where were you?" I answered, "Abū ᶜAbd ar-Raḥmān, I got down and performed the *Witr*. I was afraid that morning was coming." He asked, "Is there not in the Messenger of Allah ﷺ a good model for you?" I answered, "Yes, by Allah." He said, "Then, the Messenger of Allah ﷺ used to perform the *Witr* while on a camel."'"

٢٠٨ أخبرنا مالك، أخبرنا يحيى بن سعيد، قال: رأيت أنس ابن مالك في سفر يصلي على حماره، وهو متوجه الى غير القبلة يركع ويسجد إيماء برأسه من غير أن يضع وجهه على شيء .
208. Mālik informed us: "Yaḥyā ibn Saᶜīd informed us, 'I saw Anas ibn Mālik on a journey praying on his donkey while facing away from the *qiblah*, bowing and prostrating by motioning with his head, without placing his face on anything.'"

٢٠٩ أخبرنا مالك، أخبرنا نافع: أن ابن عمر رضي الله عنهما لم يصلِّ مع صلاة الفريضة في السفر التَّطوعَ قبلها ولا بعدها إلامن جوف الليل فانه كان يصلي نازلاً على الأرض ، وعلى بعيره أينما توجَّه به.
209. Mālik informed us: "Nāfiᶜ told us that Ibn ᶜUmar ﷺ did not pray a voluntary prayer with the obligatory prayer, when travelling, neither before it nor after it, except in the middle of the night, when he would pray on the ground or on his camel whichever way it faced."

قال محمد: لابأس أن يصلِّي المسافر على دابته تطوعاً إيماءً حيث كان وجهه ، يجعل السجود أخفض من الركوع، فأما الوتر والمكتوبة فإنهما تصلَّيان على الأرض وبذلك جاءت الآثار.
Muḥammad said: "There is no harm in a traveller's praying on his riding beast, performing its movements in whatever direction he is facing, and

making his prostration lower than his bowing. As for *Witr*, and the obligatory prayer, they should be prayed on the ground; many narrations to this effect have come down to us."

٢١٠ قال محمد : أخبرنا أبو حنيفة عن حصين قال: كان عبد الله بن عمر يصلّي التطوّع على راحلته أينما توجّهت به فإذا كانت الفريضة أو الوتر نزل فصلّى.

210. Muḥammad said: "Abū Ḥanīfah informed us from Ḥuṣayn, who said, 'ᶜAbdullāh ibn ᶜUmar used to pray voluntary prayers on his mount, whichever way it faced, but when it was the obligatory prayer or *Witr*, he got down and prayed.'"

٢١١ قال محمد: أخبرنا عمر بن ذر الهمداني، عن مجاهد: أن ابن عمر كان لا يزيد على المكتوبة في السفر على الركعتين، لا يصلّي قبلها ولا بعدها، ويحيي الليل على ظهر البعير أينما كان وجهه، وينزل قبيل الفجر فيوتر بالأرض، فإذا أقام ليلة في منزل أحيى الليل .

211. Muḥammad said: "ᶜUmar ibn Dhirr al-Hamdānī informed us from Mujāhid, that Ibn ᶜUmar, when travelling, would not pray more than two *rakᶜahs* in the obigatory prayer, neither praying before or after it, and would pray by night on the camel's back, whichever way he was facing. He would get down a little before dawn and perform the *Witr* on the ground, and when he stayed a night in a camp he would pray the night through."

٢١٢ قال محمد، أخبرنا محمد بن أبان بن صالح، عن حماد ، بن أبي سليمان، عن مجاهد قال: صحبت عبد الله بن عمر من مكة إلى المدينة، فكان يصلّي الصلاة كلها على بعيره نحو المدينة ويومئ برأسه إيماءً، ويجعل السجود أخفض من الركوع إلا المكتوبة والوتر، فإنه كان ينزل لهما، فسألته عن ذلك فقال: كان رسول الله صلى الله عليه وسلم يفعله حيث كان وجهه يومئ برأسه، ويجعل السجود أخفض من الركوع.

212. Muḥammad said: "Muḥammad ibn Abān ibn Ṣāliḥ informed us from Ḥammād ibn Abī Sulaymān from Mujāhid, who said, 'I accompanied ᶜAbdullāh ibn ᶜUmar from Makkah to Madīnah, and he would pray every prayer on his camel facing towards Madīnah, motioning only with his head, and making his prostration lower than his bowing, except the obligatory prayer and the *Witr*, for he would dismount for these two. I asked him about that, and he said, "The Messenger of Allah ﷺ used to do it: wherever he was facing he would motion with his head, and he would make his prostration lower than his bowing."'"

٢١٣ قال محمد: أخبرنا اسماعيل بن عيّاش ، حدثني هشام بن عروة، عن أبيه أنه كان يصلّي على ظهر راحلته حيث توجّهت ولا يضع جبهته، ولكن يشير للركوع والسجود برأسه، فإذا نزل أوتر.

213. Muḥammad said: "Ismāᶜīl ibn ᶜAyyāsh informed us, 'Hishām ibn ᶜUrwah reported to me that his father used to pray on the back of his mount, wherever it faced and would not put his forehead down, but would indicate bowing and prostrating with his head. Then when he dismounted, he performed the *Witr*.'"

٢١٤ قال محمد : أخبرنا خالد بن عبد الله عن المغيرة الضَّبِّي، عن ابراهيم النَّخعي : أن ابن عمر كان يصلّي على راحلته حيث كان وجهه تطوّعاً، يومئ إيماءً ويقرأ السجدة فيومئ، وينزل للمكتوبة والوتر.

214. Muḥammad said: "Khālid ibn ᶜAbdullāh informed us from al-Mughīrah aḍ-Ḍabbī from Ibrāhīm an-Nakhaᶜī that Ibn ᶜUmar used to pray on his mount whichever way he faced, when it was a voluntary prayer, only indicating [the prostrations and bowings]. He would recite [an *āyah* requiring] prostration and would [indicate the prostration by a] movement; and he would dismount for the obligatory and *Witr* prayers."

٢١٥ قال محمد : أخبرنا الفضل بن غزوان، عن نافع، عن ابن عمر قال : كان أينما توجّهت به راحلته صلّى والتطوع، فإذا أراد أن يوتر نزل فأوتر.

215. Muḥammad said: "Al-Faḍl ibn Ghazwān informed us from Nāfiᶜ about Ibn ᶜUmar. He [Nāfiᶜ] said, 'He would, whichever way his mount faced with him, pray voluntary prayers. When he wanted to perform the *Witr* he would get down and perform the *Witr*.'"

٦١ باب الرجل يصلّي فيذكر أنّ عليه صلاة فائتة

61. A Man's Praying, then Remembering that he Must Pray a Missed Prayer

٢١٦ أخبرنا مالك، حدثنا نافع، عن ابن عمر أنه كان يقول : من نسي صلاةً من صلاته، فلم يذكر إلا وهو مع الإمام فإذا سلّم الإمام فليصلِّ صلاته التي نسي، ثم ليصلِّ بعدها الصلاة الأخرى.

216. Mālik informed us: "Nāfiᶜ narrated to us that Ibn ᶜUmar used to say, 'Whoever forgets one of his prayers, and does not remember it until he is with the imām, then when the imām concludes, let him pray his prayer which he had forgotten and then pray the later prayer after it.'"

قال محمد : وبهذا نأخذ إلا في خصلة واحدة : إذا ذكرها وهو في صلاة في آخر وقتها يخاف أن بدأ بالإولى أن يخرج وقت هذه الثانية قبل أن يصلّيها، فليبدأ بهذه الثانية حتى يفرغ منها، ثم يصلّي الأولى بعد ذلك، وهو قول أبي حنيفة وسعيد بن المسيب.

Muḥammad said: "We adhere to this, except in one instance; when he remembers it while he is praying a prayer at the end of its time and he fears that if he were to begin with the earlier prayer, the time of the second one would run out before he could pray it. In that case, let him begin with the second one, until he finishes, then pray the earlier one after that. That is the verdict of Abū Ḥanīfah and Saᶜīd ibn al-Musayyab."

٦٢ باب الرَّجل يصلِّي المكتوبة في بيته ثم يدرك الصلاة

62. A Man's Praying the Obligatory Prayer in his House and then Catching the Prayer [in the Mosque]

٢١٧ أخبرنا مالك، حدثنا زيد بن أسلم، عن رجل من بني الدِّيل يقال له بسر بن محجن، عن أبيه : أنه كان مع رسول الله صلى الله عليه وسلم، فأذِّن بالصلاة، فقام رسول الله صلى الله عليه وسلم يصلِّي، والرجل في مجلسه، فقال رسول الله صلى الله عليه وسلم: ما منعك أن تصلِّي مع الناس ؟ ألست رجلاً مسلماً؟ قال: بلى، ولكني قد كنت صلَّيت في أهلي، فقال رسول الله صلى الله عليه وسلم: إذا جئت فصلِّ مع الناس وإن كنت قد صلَّيت.

217. Mālik informed us: "Zayd ibn Aslam narrated to us from a man of Banū ad-Dīl, called Busr ibn Miḥjan from his father, that he was with the Messenger of Allah ﷺ when the prayer was called and the Messenger of Allah ﷺ got up and prayed while the man sat where he was. The Messenger of Allah ﷺ asked, 'What prevented you from praying with the people? Are you not a Muslim man?' He answered, 'Yes, but I had already prayed among my family.' So the Messenger of Allah ﷺ said, 'When you come, then pray with the people, even though you have already prayed.'"

٢١٨ أخبرنا مالك، عن نافع: أنّ ابن عمر كان يقول : من صلّى صلاة المغرب أوالصبح، ثم أدركهما فلا يعيد لهما غير ما قد صلاهما.

218. Mālik informed us from Nāfi^c that Ibn ^cUmar used to say, "Whoever prays *Maghrib* or *Ṣubḥ*, then catches them, should not pray them more than he has already prayed for them."

٢١٩ أخبرنا مالك، أخبرنا عفيف بن عمرو السّهمي، عن رجل من بني أسد أنه سأل أبا أيوب الأنصاري، فقال: إني أصلي ثم آتي المسجد فأجد الإمام يصلّي ، أفأصلي معه؟ قال : نعم، صلِّ معه، ومن فعل ذلك فله مثل سهم جمع أو سهم جمع.

219. Mālik informed us: "^cAfīf ibn ^cAmr as-Sahmī informed us from a man of Banū Asad, that he asked Abū Ayyūb al-Anṣārī, saying, 'I pray and then come to the mosque and find the imām praying. Should I pray with him?' He answered, 'Yes, pray with him and whoever does that shall have an army's share of the spoils or the equivalent of that.'"

قال محمد: وبهذا نأخذ. ونأخذ بقول ابن عمر أيضاً أن لا نعيد صلاة المغرب والصبح لأن المغرب وتر ، فلا ينبغي أن يصلي التطوع وتراً، ولا صلاة تطوع بعد الصبح، وكذلك العصر عندنا، وهي بمنزلة المغرب والصبح، وهو قول أبي حنيفة - رحمه الله - .

Muḥammad said: "We adhere to this, and we also adhere to the verdict of Ibn ^cUmar, that we should not repeat the prayers of *Maghrib* and *Ṣubḥ*; for *Maghrib* is an uneven [number of *rak^cahs*] and a voluntary prayer should not be uneven, and there should be no voluntary prayer after *Ṣubḥ*. Likewise *^cAṣr*, in our opinion, has the same ruling as *Ṣubḥ* and *Maghrib*. That is the verdict of Abū Ḥanīfah, may Allah have mercy on him."

٦٣ باب الرجل تحضره الصلاة والطعام بأيهما يبدأ

63. If a Man is Faced with the Prayer and Food, with which Should He Begin?

٢٢٠ أخبرنا مالك، أخبرنا نافع، عن ابن عمر: أنه كان يقرَّب إليه الطعام، فيسمع قراءة الإمام وهو في بيته فلا يعجل عن طعامه حتى يقضي منه حاجته.

220. Mālik informed us: "Nāfi^c informed us that food would be brought to Ibn ^cUmar, then he would hear the recitation of the imām, while still in his house, but he would not hasten from his food until he had eaten enough."

قال محمد: لا نرى بهذا بأساً، ونحب أن لا نتوخى تلك الساعة.

Muḥammad said: "We do not see any harm in this, but we prefer not to choose that time [for meals]."

٦٤ باب فضل العصر والصلاة بعد العصر

64. The Excellence of ^c*Aṣr*, and on Praying after ^c*Aṣr*

٢٢١ أخبرنا مالك، أخبرني الزهري، عن السائب بن يزيد: أنه رأى عمر بن الخطاب يضرب المنكدرة بن عبد الله في الركعتين بعد العصر.

221. Mālik informed us: "Az-Zuhrī informed me that as-Sā᾽ib ibn Yazīd saw ^cUmar ibn al-Khaṭṭāb beat al-Munkadir ibn ^cAbdullāh for [praying] two *rak^cahs* after ^c*Aṣr*."

قال محمد: وبهذا نأخذ، لاصلاة تطوُّع بعد العصر، وهو قول أبي حنيفة رحمه الله.

Muḥammad said: "We adhere to this. Voluntary prayers should not be prayed after ^c*Aṣr*. That is the verdict of Abū Ḥanīfah, may Allah have mercy on him."

٢٢٢ أخبرنا مالك، أخبرني نافع، عن ابن عمر قال: الذي يفوته العصر كأنما وتر أهله وماله.

222. Mālik informed us: "Nāfi^c informed me from Ibn ^cUmar. He said, 'He who misses ^c*Aṣr*, is as if he had suffered a great misfortune in his family and wealth.'"

٦٥ باب وقت الجمعة وما يستحب من الطيب والدهان

65. The Time of Jumu^cah and what is Encouraged of Scent and Oiling Oneself

٢٢٣ أخبرنا مالك، أخبرني عمِّي أبو سهيل بن مالك، عن أبيه قال: كنت أرى طنفسةً لعقيل بن أبي طالب يوم الجمعة تطرح إلى جدار المسجد الغربي، فإذا غشي الطنفسة كلَّها ظلُّ الجدار خرج عمر بن الخطاب إلى الصلاة يوم الجمعة، ثم نرجع فنقيل قائلة الضحاء.

223. Mālik informed us: "My uncle, Abū Suhayl ibn Mālik, informed me that his father said, 'I used to see a rug belonging to ^cAqīl ibn Abī Ṭālib put out on the day of Jumu^cah against the western wall of the mosque. Then when

the rug was covered completely by the shadow of the wall, ᶜUmar ibn al-Khaṭṭāb would come out to the prayer on the day of Jumuᶜah, and then we would go back and have our daytime rest.'"

٢٢٤ أخبرنا مالك، أخبرنا نافع: أن ابن عمر كان لا يروح إلى الجمعة إلا وهو مدَّهنٌ متطيِّب إلا أن يكون محرماً .

224. Mālik informed us: "Nāfiᶜ informed us that Ibn ᶜUmar would always leave for Jumuᶜah oiled and scented, unless he were in *iḥrām*."

٢٢٥ أخبرنا مالك، أخبرنا الزهري، عن السائب بن يزيد : أن عثمان بن عفان رضي الله عنه زاد النداء الثالث يوم الجمعة.

225. Mālik informed us: "Az-Zuhrī informed us from as-Sā'ib ibn Yazīd, that ᶜUthmān ibn ᶜAffān ﷺ added the third call to prayer on the day of Jumuᶜah."

قال محمد: وبهذا كلِّه نأخذ، والنداء الثالث الذي زيد هو النداء الأول ، وهو قول أبي حنيفة رحمه الله .

Muḥammad said: "We go according to all of this; the third call which was added means the first call. That is the verdict of Abū Ḥanīfah, may Allah have mercy on him."

٦٦ باب القراءة في صلاة الجمعة وما يستحب من الصمت

66. The Recitation in the Prayer of Jumuᶜah, and what is Encouraged of Silence

٢٢٦ أخبرنا مالك، حدَّثنا ضمرة بن سعيد المازني ، عن عبيد الله بن عبد الله بن عتبة، أنَّ الضحاك بن قيس سأل النعمان بن بشير ماذا كان يقرأ به رسول الله صلى الله عليه وسلم على إثر سورة الجمعة يوم الجمعة؟ فقال: كان يقرأ (هل أتاك حديث الغاشية).

226. Mālik informed us: "Ḍamrah ibn Saᶜīd al-Māzinī from ᶜUbaydullāh ibn ᶜAbdullāh ibn ᶜUtbah, that aḍ-Ḍaḥḥāk ibn Qays asked an-Nuᶜmān ibn Bashīr, 'What did the Messenger of Allah ﷺ used to recite after Sūrat al-Jumu'ah on the day of Jumuᶜah?' He answered, 'He used to recite *"Hal atāka ḥadīthu'l-ghāshiyah"* (Sūrah 88).'"

٢٢٧ أخبرنا مالك، حدثنا الزهري، عن ثعلبة بن أبي مالك : أنهم كانوا زمان عمر بن الخطاب يصلون يوم الجمعة حتى يخرج عمر، فإذا خرج وجلس إلى المنبر، وأذن المؤذن قال ثعلبة : جلسنا نتحدث ، فإذا سكت المؤذن وقام عمر سكتنا، فلم يتكلم أحد منا.

227. Mālik informed us: "Az-Zuhrī narrated to us from Thaᶜlabah ibn Abī Mālik, that, in the time of ᶜUmar ibn al-Khaṭṭāb, they used to pray on the day of Jumuᶜah until ᶜUmar came out. He would come out and sit on the *minbar*, and the *mu'adhdhin* would give the call. Thaᶜlabah said: 'We sat, talking. When the *mu'adhdhin* was silent and ᶜUmar stood, we became silent, none of us speaking.'"

٢٢٨ أخبرنا مالك، حدثنا الزهري، قال: خروجه يقطع الصلاة وكلامه يقطع الكلام.

228. Mālik informed us: "Az-Zuhrī narrated [this] to us. He said, 'His coming out puts an end to praying, and his speaking puts an end to speaking.'"

٢٢٩ أخبرنا مالك، أخبرنا أبو النضر ، عن مالك بن أبي عامر : أن عثمان بن عفان كان يقول في خطبته قلّما يدع ذلك إذا خطب : إذا قام الإمام فاستمعوا وأنصتوا فإن للمنصت الذي لا يسمع من الحظّ مثل ما للسامع المنصت .

229. Mālik informed us: "Abu'n-Naḍr informed us from Mālik ibn Abī ᶜĀmir, that ᶜUthmān ibn ᶜAffān used to say in his *khuṭbah*, seldom leaving it out of his *khuṭbah*, 'When the imām stands, then listen and keep quiet, for someone who keeps quiet and does not hear shall have the same share [of reward] as someone who does hear and keeps quiet.'"

٢٣٠ أخبرنا مالك، أخبرنا أبو الزِّناد ، عن الأعرج عن أبي هريرة قال : قال رسول الله صلى الله عليه وسلم: إذا قلت لصاحبك أنصت فقد لغوت والإمام يخطب.

230. Mālik informed us: "Abu'z-Zinād informed us from al-Aᶜraj from Abū Hurayrah, that he said, 'The Messenger of Allah ﷺ said, "If you say to the one next to you, 'Be quiet', then by speaking while the imām is speaking you have spoken out of turn."'"

٢٣١ أخبرنا مالك، أخبرنا عبد الرحمن بن القاسم: أن أباه القاسم بن محمد رأى في قميصه دماً والإمام على المنبر يوم الجمعة فنزع قميصه فوضعه .

231. Mālik informed us: "ᶜAbd ar-Raḥmān ibn al-Qāsim informed us that his father, al-Qāsim ibn Muḥammad, saw some blood on his shirt while the imām was on the *minbar* on the day of Jumuᶜah. He took off his shirt and placed it aside."

٦٧ باب صلاة العيدين وأمر الخطبة

67. The Prayer of ᶜĪd and its Khuṭbah

٢٣٢ أخبرنا مالك، أخبرنا الزهري، عن أبي عبيد مولى عبد الرحمن قال: شهدت العيد مع عمر بن الخطاب، فصلّى ، ثم انصرف فخطب ، فقال: إن هذين اليومين نهى رسول الله صلى الله عليه وسلم عن صيامهما يوم فطركم من صيامكم، والآخر يوم تأكلون من لحوم نسككم ، قال ثم شهدت العيد مع عثمان بن عفان، فصلى، ثم انصرف فخطب، فقال إنه قد اجتمع لكم في يومكم هذا عيدان ، فمن أحبَّ من أهل العالية أن ينتظرَ الجمعةَ فلينتظرْها ومن أحب أن يرجعَ فليرجعْ ، فقد أذنتُ له، فقال: ثم شهدتُ العيدَ مع عليٍّ وعثمانُ محصورٌ فصلّى، ثم انصرف فخطب.

232. Mālik informed us: "Az-Zuhrī informed me from Abū ᶜUbayd, the *mawlā* of ᶜAbd ar-Raḥmān, that he said, 'I attended the ᶜĪd with ᶜUmar ibn al-Khaṭṭāb, and he prayed, finished [his prayer], then gave the *khuṭbah* saying, "These are two days on which the Messenger of Allah ﷺ prohibited fasting: the day of your breaking your fast, and the other [being] the day when you eat the meat of your slaughter."' [Abū ᶜUbayd] said, 'Then I attended the ᶜĪd with ᶜUthmān ibn ᶜAffān, and he prayed, concluded, and gave the *khuṭbah*, saying,

"Two ᶜĪds have come together in this day of yours, so whoever of the dwellers of ᶜĀliyah wants to wait for Jumuᶜah, let him wait for it. Whoever wants to go back, let him go back, for I have given him leave."' He went on, 'Then I attended ᶜĪd with ᶜAlī, when ᶜUthmān was besieged, and he prayed, then concluded and gave the *khuṭbah*.'"

٢٣٣ أخبرنا مالك، أخبرنا ابن شهاب : أن النبي صلّى الله عليه وسلّم كان يصلّي يوم الفطر ويوم الأضحى قبل الخطبة، وذكر أنَّ أبا بكر وعمر كانا يصنعان ذلك.

233. Mālik informed us: "Ibn Shihāb informed us that the Prophet ﷺ used to pray on the days of Fiṭr and Aḍḥa before the *khuṭbah*. He mentioned that Abū Bakr and ᶜUmar used to do that."

قال محمد: وبهذا كله نأخذ، وإنما رخص عثمان في الجمعة لأهل العالية لأنهم ليسوا من أهل المصر وهو قولُ أبي حنيفة رحمه الله .

Muḥammad said: "We go according to all of this. ᶜUthmān was making a concession to the dwellers of ᶜĀliyah, for they were not residents of the city. That is the verdict of Abū Ḥanīfah, may Allah have mercy on him."

٦٨ باب صلاة التطوع قبل العيد أو بعده

68. Voluntary Prayers before and after the ᶜĪd

٢٣٤ أخبرنا مالك، أخبرنا نافع، عن ابن عمر: أنه كان لا يصلّي يوم الفطر قبل الصلاة ولا بعدها.

234. Mālik informed us: "Nāfiᶜ informed us that on the day of Fiṭr, Ibn ᶜUmar would neither pray before the prayer, nor after it."

٢٣٥ أخبرنا مالك، أخبرنا عبد الرحمن بن قاسم، عن أبيه : أنه كان يصلّي قبل أن يغدُوَ أربع ركعات.

235. Mālik informed us: "ᶜAbd ar-Raḥmān ibn al-Qāsim informed us from his father, that before going out, he would pray four *rakᶜahs*."

قال محمد: لا صلاةَ قبل صلاة العيد فأما بعدها فإن شئتَ صلَّيْتَ وإن شئتَ لم تصلِّ، وهو قول أبي حنيفة رحمه الله .

Muḥammad said: "There should be no praying before the prayer of the ᶜĪd. As for after it, it is up to you whether you pray or do not pray. That is the verdict of Abū Ḥanīfah, may Allah have mercy on him."

٦٩ باب القراءة في صلاة العيدين

69. The Recitation in the ᶜĪd Prayers

٢٣٦ أخبرنا مالك، حدثنا ضمرةُ بنُ سعيد المازني ، عن عبيد الله بن عبد الله بن عتبة أن عُمَرَ بن الخطاب رضي الله عنه سأل أبا واقد الليثيَّ: ماذا كان يقرأ به رسول الله صلّى الله عليه وسلّم في الأضحى والفطر؟ قال: كان يقرأ بقافٍ والقرآن المجيد ، واقتربت الساعة وانشق القمر .

236. Mālik informed us: "Ḍamrah ibn Saᶜīd al-Māzinī narrated to us from

ᶜUbaydullāh ibn ᶜAbdullāh ibn ᶜUtbah, that ᶜUmar ibn al-Khaṭṭāb ﷺ asked Abū Wāqid al-Laythī, 'What would the Messenger of Allah ﷺ recite in Aḍḥā and Fiṭr?' He said, 'He would recite *Qāf, wa'l-Qur᾽āni'l-majīd* (Sūrah 50), and *Iqtarabati's-sāᶜatu wa'nshaqqa'l-qamar.* (Sūrah 54).'"

٧٠ باب التكبير في العيدين

70. Saying *Allāhu akbar* in the ᶜĪd Prayer

٢٣٧ أخبرنا مالك، أخبرنا نافع، قال: شهدتُ الأضحى والفطرَ مع أبي هريرة فكبَّرَ في الأولى سبعَ تكبيرات قبل القراءة، وفي الآخرة بخمس تكبيرات قبل القراءة.

237. Mālik informed us: "Nāfiᶜ told us, 'I attended Aḍḥā and Fiṭr with Abū Hurayrah [as the imām], and he said *Allāhu akbar* seven times in the first [*rakᶜah*], before the recitation, and five times in the second [*rakᶜah*], before the recitation.'"

قال محمد: قد اختلف الناسُ في التكبير في العيدين، فما أخذتَ به فهو حسن وأفضل ذلك عندنا ما روي عن ابن مسعود أنه كان يكبِّر في كل عيد تسعاً: خمساً وأربعاً، فيهنَّ تكبيرة الافتتاح وتكبيرتا الركوع، ويوالي بين القراءتين، ويؤخِّرها في الأولى، ويقدِّمها في الثانية، وهو قول أبي حنيفة.

Muḥammad said: "The people have differed concerning the saying of *Allāhu akbar* in the two ᶜĪds. Whatever you choose of that is fine. The best of it, in our opinion, is what has been related from Ibn Masᶜūd, that he would pronounce *Allāhu akbar* in every ᶜĪd nine times: five and four, including in them the takbīrs for beginning the prayer, and on bowing. He would make the two recitations close to each other, placing it last in the first [*rakᶜah*] and first in the second [*rakᶜah*]. That is the verdict of Abū Ḥanīfah."

٧١ باب قيام شهر رمضان وما فيه من الفضل

71. Standing [for Prayer] in the Month of Ramaḍān

– ٢٣٨ أخبرنا مالك، أخبرنا ابن شهاب، عن عروة بن الزبير، عن عائشة رضي الله عنها: أن رسول الله صلّى الله عليه وسلّم صلّى في المسجد، فصلّى بصلاته ناس، ثم كثروا من القابلة، ثم اجتمعوا الليلة الثالثة أو الرابعة، فكثُرُوا، فلم يخرج إليهم رسولُ الله صلّى الله عليه وسلّم، فلما أصبح قال: قد رأيتُ الذي قد صنعتُم البارحة، فلم يمنَعْني أن أخرجَ إليكم إلاّ أني خشيتُ أن يُفرَضَ عليكم، وذلك في رمضان.

238. Mālik informed us: "Ibn Shihāb informed us from ᶜUrwah ibn az-Zubayr from ᶜĀ᾽ishah ﷺ that the Messenger of Allah ﷺ prayed in the mosque, and some people prayed with him. Then on the next [night] they had grown more. Then they gathered on the third or fourth night, and grew more, but the Messenger of Allah ﷺ did not go out to them. When morning came, he said, 'I saw what you did yesterday and nothing prevented me from coming

out to you, except that I was afraid it would be made obligatory upon you.' And that was in Ramaḍān."

٢٣٩ أخبرنا مالك، حدثنا سعيد المَقْبُري، عن أبي سلمة بن عبد الرحمن: أنه سأل عائشة كيف كانت صلاةُ رسول الله صلّى الله عليه وسلّم في رمضان؟ قالت: ما كان رسولُ الله صلّى الله عليه وسلّم يزيد في رمضان ولا غيره على إحدى عَشْرة ركعةً، يصلّي أربعاً، فلا تسأل عن حُسْنهنّ وطولهنّ، ثم يصلّي أربعاً فلا تَسأل عن حُسْنهنّ وطولهنّ ثم يصلي ثلاثاً، قالت: فقلت: يا رسول الله أتنام قبل أن توتر؟ فقال: يا عائشة عيناي تنامان ولا ينامُ قلبي.

239. Mālik informed us: "Saᶜīd al-Maqburī narrated to us from Abū Salamah ibn ᶜAbd ar-Raḥmān, that he asked ᶜĀʾishah, 'How was the prayer of the Messenger of Allah ﷺ in Ramaḍān?' She said, 'The Messenger of Allah ﷺ would not pray more than eleven *rakᶜahs*, neither in Ramaḍān nor any other month. He would pray four – and do not ask about their distinction and length – then he would pray four – and do not ask about their distinction and length – and then he would pray three.' She said, 'So I asked, "Messenger of Allah, do you sleep before you perform the *Witr*?" He answered, "ᶜĀʾishah, my eyes sleep but my heart does not sleep."'"

٢٤٠ أخبرنا مالك، حدثنا الزهري، عن أبي سلمة بن عبد الرحمن بن عوف، أن رسولَ الله صلّى الله عليه وسلّم كان يرغِّبُ الناس في قيام رمضان من غير أن يأمُرَ بعزيمة، فيقول: من قام رمضان إيماناً واحتساباً غُفر له ما تقدّم من ذنبه. قال ابن شهاب: فتوفي النبيُّ صلّى الله عليه وسلّم والأمر على ذلك، ثم كان الأمر في خلافة أبي بكر وصدراً من خلافة عمرَ على ذلك.

240. Mālik informed us: "Az-Zuhrī narrated to us from Abū Salamah ibn ᶜAbd ar-Raḥmān ibn ᶜAwf, that the Messenger of Allah ﷺ used to encourage people to stand for prayer in Ramaḍān, without making it an obligatory command, saying, 'Whoever stands for prayer, for the month of Ramaḍān, out of conviction and deliberation, will be forgiven whatever wrong actions he has committed.' Ibn Shihāb said, 'So the soul of the Prophet ﷺ was taken leaving the matter as it stood, and the matter remained like that during the khilāfah of Abū Bakr, and up to the beginning of the khilāfah of ᶜUmar.'"

٢٤١ أخبرنا مالك، أخبرنا ابن شهاب، عن عروة بن الزبير، عن عبد الرحمن بن عبدٍ القاريّ: أنه خرج مع عمرَ بنِ الخطاب ليلةً في رمضان، فإذا الناسُ أوزاعٌ متفرّقون، يصلّي الرجلُ فيصلّي بصلاته الرهط، فقال عمر: والله إني لأظنني لو جمعتُ هؤلاء على قارئ واحد لكان أمثل، ثم عزم فجمعهم على أبيّ بن كعب، قال: ثم خرجتُ معه ليلةً أخرى والناس يصلّون بصلاة قارئهم، فقال: نِعْمَتْ البدعةُ هذه، والتي ينامون عنها أفضلُ من التي يقومون فيها. يريد آخرَ الليل وكان الناسُ يقومون أوله.

241. Mālik informed us: "Ibn Shihāb informed us from ᶜUrwah ibn az-Zubayr from ᶜAbd ar-Raḥmān ibn ᶜAbdin al-Qāriyy, that he went out with ᶜUmar ibn al-Khaṭṭāb, one night in Ramaḍān, and found the people separated in groups; one man praying, and a few praying with him. ᶜUmar said, 'By Allah,

I believe that if I gathered these behind one reciter it would be more fitting.' Then having made up his mind, he gathered them behind Ubayy ibn Kaᶜb. I went out with him on another night, while the people were in prayer with their reciter and he said, 'What an excellent innovation this is! That during which they sleep is more meritorious than that during which they stand,' meaning the latter part of the night. The people were standing for the first part of it.'"

قال محمد: وبهذا كلّه نأخذ، لا بأسَ بالصَّلاة في شهر رمضانَ أن يصليَ الناس تطوُّعاً بإمَام، لأن المسلمينَ قد أجمعوا على ذلك ورأوْه حسناً . وقد رُوي عن النبيّ صلّى الله عليه وسلّم أنه قال: ما رآه المُؤْمِنُوْنَ حَسَنَاً فهو عند اللّه حسنٌ، وما رآهُ المسلمُونَ قَبيحاً فهو عندَ اللّه قَبيْحٌ.

Muḥammad said: "We go according to all of this; there is no harm in praying in the month of Ramaḍān, the people praying voluntarily with an imām, for the Muslims have already decided upon that and they regard it as good. It has been narrated from the Prophet ﷺ that he said, 'That which the believers regard as good is – with Allah – good. That which the Muslims regard as ugly is – with Allah – ugly.'"

٧٢ بابُ القنوتِ في الفجر

72. *Qunūt* in [the Prayer] of *Fajr*

٢٤٢ أخبرنا مالك، عن نافع قال: كان ابنُ عمرَ لا يَقْنُتُ في الصبح.

242. Mālik informed us from Nāfiᶜ, that he said, "Ibn ᶜUmar did not use to say *qunūt* in the dawn prayer."

قال محمد: وبهذا نأخذ، وهو قول أبي حنيفة رحمه الله.

Muḥammad said: "This we adhere to; it is the verdict of Abū Ḥanīfah, may Allah have mercy on him."

٧٣ باب فضلِ صلاة الفجر في الجماعة وأمر ركعتي الفجر

73. The Excellence of Praying *Fajr* in Congregation, and the Matter of the two [Voluntary] Rakᶜahs of *Fajr*

٢٤٣ أخبرنا مالك، أخبرنا ابنُ شهاب، عن أبي بَكْر بن سليْمَانَ بن أبي حَثْمة: أنَّ عُمَرَ بنَ الخطَّاب فَقَدَ سليمانَ بن أبي حثْمة في صلاة الصُبْح، وأنَّ عُمَرَ غدا إلى السُّوق وكان منزل سليمان بين السوق والمسجد، فمرَّ عمر على أم سليمَان الشِّفاء، فقال: لم أرَ سليمانَ في الصبح، فقالت: بات يصلي فغلبته عيناه، فقال عمر: لأن أشهد صلاةَ الصبح أحبُّ إليَّ من أن أقوم الليلة.

243. Mālik informed us: "Ibn Shihāb informed us from Abū Bakr ibn Sulaymān ibn Abī Ḥathmah that ᶜUmar ibn al-Khaṭṭāb missed Sulaymān ibn Abī Ḥathmah in the *Ṣubḥ* prayer. ᶜUmar went out early in the morning to the market – and the dwelling of Sulaymān was between the market and the mosque – so he passed by Sulayman's mother, ash-Shifā', and said, 'I did not see

Sulaymān in the *Ṣubḥ* prayer.' She said, 'He retired for the night, praying, and sleep overcame him.' ᶜUmar said, 'That I attend the *Ṣubḥ* prayer is preferable to me than that I stand a night in prayer.'"

٢٤٤ أخبرنا مالك، أخبرنا نافع: أن ابن عمر أخبره عن حفصة زوج النبي صلّى الله عليه وسلّم أنها أخبرته أنّ رسول الله صلّى الله عليه وسلّم كان إذا سكَتَ المؤذّنُ من صلاة الصبح وبدأ الصبح ركع ركعتين خفيفتين قبل أن تُقام الصلاة.

244. Mālik informed us: "Nāfiᶜ informed us that Ibn ᶜUmar informed him that Ḥafṣah, the wife of the Prophet ﷺ, told him that when the *muʾadhdhin* for the dawn prayer went silent and the dawn appeared, the Messenger of Allah ﷺ would pray two brief *rakᶜahs* before the prayer was held."

قال محمد: وبهذا نأخذ، الركعتان قبل صلاة الفجر يخفّفان .

Muḥammad said: "We adhere to this; the two *rakᶜahs* before the prayer of *Fajr* should be made brief."

٢٤٥ أخبرنا مالك، أخبرنا نافع، عن عبد الله بن عمر: أنه رأى رجلاً ركع ركعتي الفجر، ثم اضطجع فقال ابن عمر: ما شأنه ؟ فقال نافع: فقلت: يفصل بين صلاته، قال ابن عمر: وأيّ فصل أفضل من السلام.

245. Mālik informed us: "Nāfiᶜ informed us that Ibn ᶜUmar saw a man pray the two [voluntary] *rakᶜahs* of *Fajr* and then lie down. Ibn ᶜUmar said, 'What is he doing?'" Nāfiᶜ said, 'I said, "He is making a separation between his prayers." Ibn ᶜUmar said, "And what separation is better than saying *'as-salāmu ᶜalaykum'*?"'"

قال محمد: وبقول ابنِ عمرَ نأخذ، وهو قول أبي حنيفة رحمه الله .

Muḥammad said: "We adhere to the verdict of Ibn ᶜUmar; it is the verdict of Abū Ḥanīfah, may Allah have mercy on him."

٧٤ باب طولِ القراءةِ في الصلاة وما يُستَحَبُّ من التخفيف

74. The Length of Recitation in the Prayer, and what is Encouraged of Brevity

٢٤٦ أخبرنا مالك، حدّثنا الزُّهريّ، عن عبيْد الله بن عبد الله عن ابن عَبَّاس، عن أمّه أمّ الفَضلِ: أنّها سَمِعَتْهُ يَقْرأ ﴿والمُرْسَلاتِ﴾، فقالت: يا بنيَّ لقد ذكَّرْتَني بقِراءتكَ هذه السورةَ أنّها لآخِرُ ما سمعتُ رسول الله صلّى الله عليه وسلّم يقرأُ في المَغرب.

246. Mālik informed us: "Az-Zuhrī informed us from ᶜUbaydullāh ibn ᶜAbdullāh from Ibn ᶜAbbās from his mother, Umm al-Faḍl, that she heard him read *'wa'l-mursalāt'* (Sūrah 77) and said, 'Son, you have reminded me by your reading this *sūrah*, that it was the last one I heard the Messenger of Allah ﷺ recite in *Maghrib*.'"

٢٤٧ أخبرنا مالك، حدَّثَني الزُّهْريُّ، عَنْ محمد بن جُبَير بن مطعم، عن أبيه قال: سمعت رسول الله صلّى الله عليه وسلّم يقرأ بالطُّور في المغرب .

247. Mālik informed us: "Az-Zuhrī informed us from Muḥammad ibn Jubayr ibn Muṭᶜim from his father, that he said, 'I heard the Messenger of Allah ﷺ recite aṭ-Ṭūr (Sūrah 52) in *Maghrib*.'"

قال محمد: العامَّة على أن القراءة تُخَفَّفُ في صلاة المغرب يقْرأُ فيها بقصار المفصَّل. ونرى أن هذا كان شيئاً فتُرِك أو لعله كان يقرأ بعض السورة ثم يركَع.

Muḥammad said: "The majority are of the opinion that the recitation should be made brief in the prayer of *Maghrib*, reciting therein the short sūrahs of *al-Mufaṣṣal* [the shorter sūrahs from the last section of the Qur'ān]. It is our opinion that this was the case and then it was abandoned, or it could be that he would read part of the *sūrah* and then bow."

٢٤٨ أخبرنا مالك، أخبرنا أبو الزِّناد، عن الأعرج، عن أبي هريرة أن رسول الله صلّى الله عليه وسلّم قال: إذا صلّى أحدُكُم للناس فليخفِّفْ، فإنَّ فيهم السقيمَ والضعيفَ والكبير وإذا صلى لنفسه فليطوِّلْ ما شاء.

248. Mālik informed us: "Abu'z-Zinād informed us from al-Aᶜraj from Abū Hurayrah, that the Messenger of Allah ﷺ said, 'When one of you leads people in prayer, let him pray briefly, for the sick, the weak and the elderly are to be found among them. When he prays for himself, let him pray as long as he wills.'"

قال محمد: وبهذا نأخذ، وهو قول أبي حنيفة – رحمه الله.

Muḥammad said: "We adhere to this; it is the verdict of Abū Ḥanīfah, may Allah have mercy on him."

٧٥ بابُ صلاةِ المغربِ وترُ صلاةِ النَّهار

75. The Prayer of *Maghrib* being the *Witr* for Daytime Prayer

٢٤٩ أخبرنا مالك، حدثنا عبد الله بنُ دينار، عن ابنِ عمرَ قال: صلاةُ المغربِ وترُ صلاة النهار.

249. Mālik informed us: "ᶜAbdullāh ibn Dīnār informed us from Ibn ᶜUmar, that he said, 'The prayer of *Maghrib* is the *Witr* for daytime prayer.'"

قال محمد: وبهذا نأخذ، وينبغي لمن جعل المغرب وتر صلاة النهار كما قال ابن عمر أن يكون وتر صلاة الليل مثلها، لا يفصل بينهما بتسليم، كما لا يفصل في المغرب بتسليم وهو قول أبي حنيفة رحمه الله.

Muḥammad said: "We adhere to this. Whoever makes *Maghrib* the *Witr* of daytime prayer, as Ibn ᶜUmar said, should make the *Witr* of night-time prayer the like of it, not separating the two [the set of two *rakᶜahs* from the single *rakᶜah*] by saying *as-salāmu ᶜalaykum*, just as he doesn't divide up *Maghrib* in two by saying *as-salāmu ᶜalaykum* in between. That is the verdict of Abū Ḥanīfah, may Allah have mercy on him."

٧٦ باب الوتر

76. *Witr*

٢٥٠ أخبرنا مالك، أخبرنا زَيدُ بنُ أَسْلَمَ، عن أبي مُرَّةَ أنه سألَ أبا هريرة : كيف كان رسولُ الله صلى الله عليه وسلَّم يوتر؟ قال : فسكت ، ثم سأله، فسكت، ثُمَّ سأله فقال : إنْ شئْتَ أخبَرْتُك كَيف أصنعُ أنا، قال: أخبرني، قال: إذا صلَّيتُ العشاءَ صليتُ بعدها خمسَ ركعات ثم أنامُ فإن قمتُ من الليل صليتُ مَثْنَى مَثْنَى، فإنْ أصبحتُ أصبَحتُ على وتر.

250. Mālik informed us: "Zayd ibn Aslam informed us from Abū Murrah that he asked Abū Hurayrah how the Messenger of Allah ﷺ used to perform the *Witr* and he went silent. Then he asked him [again] and he was silent. Then he asked him [again] and he said, 'If you will, I will tell you what I do.' [Abū Murrah] said, 'Tell me.' He said, 'Once I have prayed *ᶜIshāʾ*, I pray five *rakᶜahs* after it, and then sleep. Then, should I get up in the night, I pray in pairs [of *rakᶜahs*]. Should I sleep until morning I will have prayed *Witr*.'"

٢٥١ أخبرنا مالك، أخبرنا نافعٌ، عن ابن عمر : أنَّه كان ذات ليلة بمكة والسَّماء مُتَغَيِّمَةٌ فَخَشِيَ الصُّبْحَ ، فَأَوْتَرَ بواحدة، ثم انكشف الغيمُ، فرأى عليه ليلاً، فشفع بسجدة ثم صلى سَجْدَتَين، سجْدتين، فلما خشي الصُّبحَ أَوْتَرَ بواحدة.

251. Mālik told us: "Nāfiᶜ informed us that Ibn ᶜUmar was in Makkah at night, and the sky was overcast. He was anxious that morning was coming, so he performed the *Witr* with one [*rakᶜah*]. Then the cloud drew away and he saw night over him, so he paired [that *rakᶜah*] with a prostration and then prayed pairs of *rakᶜahs*. When he was anxious that morning was coming he performed the *Witr* with one [*rakᶜah*]."

قال محمد : وبقول أبي هريرة نأخذ، لا نرى أن يشفع إلى الوتر بعد الفراغ من صلاة الوتر، ولكنه يصلي بعد وتْره ما أحَبَّ ولا ينقض وترَه، وهو قول أبي حنيفة رحمه الله .

Muḥammad said: "We adhere to the verdict of Abū Hurayrah; we do not approve of someone pairing the *Witr*, after having finished the *Witr* prayer; rather he should pray whatever he likes after his *Witr*, as opposed to undoing it. That is the verdict of Abū Ḥanīfah, may Allah have mercy on him."

٧٧ باب الوتر على الدابة

77. [Praying] *Witr* on a [Riding] Beast

٢٥٢ أخبرنا مالك، أخبرنا أبو بكر بن عمر، عن سعيد بن يسار : أن النبي ﷺ أوتر على راحلته.

252. Mālik told us: "Abū Bakr ibn ᶜUmar informed us, from Saᶜīd ibn Yasār, that the Prophet ﷺ performed *Witr* on his mount."

قال محمد : قد جاء هذا الحديث وجاء غيره فأَحَبُّ إلينا أن يصلِّي على راحلته تطوّعاً ما بدا له، فإذا بلغ الوتر نزل فأوتر على الأرض، وهو قول عمر بن الخطاب وعبد الله بن عمر ، وهو قول أبي حنيفة والعامَّة من فقهائنا .

Muḥammad said: "There has come this report, and there has come other than it; however, we prefer that a man pray mounted, by all means, as he sees fit, then when he comes to *Witr* that he dismount and pray it on the ground. And That is the verdict of ᶜUmar ibn al-Khaṭṭāb and ᶜAbdullāh ibn ᶜUmar; and it is the verdict of Abū Ḥanīfah, and of our *fuqahā᾿* in general."

٧٨ باب تأخير الوتر

78. Delaying *Witr*

٢٥٣ أخبرنا مالك، أخبرنا عبد الرحمن بن القاسم : أنه سمع عبدَ الله بن عامر بن ربيعة يقول : إني لأوتر وأنا أسمع الإقامة أو بعد الفجر. يشكّ عبد الرحمن أيَّ ذلك قال .

253. Mālik informed us: "ᶜAbd ar-Raḥmān ibn al-Qāsim informed us that he heard ᶜAbdullāh ibn ᶜĀmir ibn Rabīᶜah say, 'I perform the *Witr* while I hear the *iqāmah*, or after dawn.'" [Mālik said] "ᶜAbd ar-Raḥmān was not sure which he said."

٢٥٤ أخبرنا مالك، عن عبد الرحمن أنه سمع أباه يقول: إني لأوتر بعد الفجر.

254. Mālik informed us from ᶜAbd ar-Raḥmān, that he heard his father say, "I do the *Witr* after dawn."

٢٥٥ أخبرنا مالك، أخبرنا هشام بن عروة، عن أبيه، عن ابن مسعود أنه كان يقول : ما أبالي لو أُقيمت الصبح وأنا أوتر.

255. Mālik informed us: "Hishām ibn ᶜUrwah informed us from his father from Ibn Masᶜūd, that he used to say, 'I don't mind if the dawn prayer has begun while I am praying *Witr*.'"

٢٥٦ أخبرنا مالك، أخبرنا عبد الكريم بن أبي المخارق ، عن سعيد بن جبير عن ابن عباس: أنه رقد ، ثم استيقظ، فقال لخادمه: انظر ماذا صنع الناس، وقد ذهب بصرُه، فذهب ثم رجع، فقال: قد انصرف الناس من الصبح، فقام ابن عباس، فأوتر، ثم صلّى الصبح .

256. Mālik informed us: "ᶜAbd al-Karīm ibn Abi'l-Mukhāriq informed us, from Saᶜīd ibn Jubayr, that Ibn ᶜAbbās slept, then awoke and said to his servant, 'See what the people have done' (he had lost his sight by then). He went, then returned and said, 'People have finished praying the dawn prayer.' Ibn ᶜAbbās got up and performed the *Witr*, then prayed [the] dawn [prayer]."

– ٢٥٧ أخبرنا مالك، أخبرنا يحيى بن سعيد: أن عبادة بن الصامت كان يَؤُمُّ يوماً، فَخرج يوماً للصبح، فأقام المؤذن الصلاة، فأسكته حتى أوتر ثم صلى بهم.

257. Mālik informed us: "Yaḥyā ibn Saᶜīd informed us that ᶜUbādah ibn aṣ-Ṣāmit one day led [the *subḥ* prayer]. He came out that morning for the prayer and the *mu᾿adhdhin* began the *iqāmah*. He silenced him until he had prayed the *Witr*, and then led them in prayer."

قال محمد: أَحَبُّ إلينا أن يوتر قبل أن يطلع الفجر ولا يؤخِّرَهُ إلى طلوع الفجر، فإن طلع قبل أن يوتر فليوتر، ولا يتعمّد ذلك، وهو قول

Muḥammad said: "It is preferable to us that he perform the *Witr* before the dawn appear and not delay it until the dawn's appearance. Should it appear before he perform the *Witr*, then let him perform the *Witr*. However, he should not do that deliberately. That is the verdict of Abū Ḥanīfah, may Allah have mercy on him."

٧٩ باب السلام في الوتر

79. Saying *as-Salāmu ᶜAlaykum* in *Witr*

٢٥٨ أخبرنا مالك، أخبرنا نافع، عن ابن عمر: أنه كان يسلِّم في الوتر بين الركعتين والركعة حتى يأمر ببعض حاجته.

258. Mālik informed us: "Nāfiᶜ informed us that Ibn ᶜUmar would say *as-salāmu ᶜalaykum* in *Witr*, between the two *rakᶜahs* and the one *rakᶜah*, so that he could give the order for something he needed."

قال محمد: ولسنا نأخذ بهذا، ولكنا نأخذ بقول عبد الله ابن مسعود وابن عباس رضي الله عنهم ولا نرَى أن يسلِّم بينهما.

Muḥammad said: "We do not adhere to this; rather we adhere to the verdict of ᶜAbdullāh ibn Masᶜūd and Ibn ᶜAbbāMessenger of Allah, may Allah bless him and grant him peace ﷺ and we do not think that *as-salāmu ᶜalaykum* should be said between them."

٢٥٩ قال محمد: أخبرنا أبو حنيفة، حدثنا أبو جعفر قال: كان رسول الله صلى الله عليه وسلم يصلِّي ما بين صلاة العشاء إلى صلاة الصبح ثلاث عشرة ركعة، ثماني ركعات تطوُّعاً وثلاث ركعات الوتر، وركعتي الفجر.

259. Muḥammad said: "Abū Ḥanīfah informed us, 'Abū Jaᶜfar narrated to us, "The Messenger of Allah ﷺ used to pray between the prayers of *ᶜIshāʾ* and *Ṣubḥ* thirteen *rakᶜahs*; eight voluntary *rakᶜahs*, three *rakᶜahs* of *Witr*, and the two *rakᶜahs* of *Fajr*."'"

٢٦٠ قال محمد: أخبرنا أبو حنيفة، عن حمّاد، عن إبراهيم النَّخَعي، عن عمر بن الخطاب رضي الله عنه أنه قال: ما أُحبُّ أني تركت الوتر بثلاث وإنَّ لي حُمْرَ النَّعَم.

260. Muḥammad said: "Abū Ḥanīfah informed us from Ḥammād from Ibrāhīm an-Nakhaᶜī that ᶜUmar ibn al-Khaṭṭāb said, 'I would not readily give up praying *Witr* with three *rakᶜahs*, not even in exchange for red hided cattle .'"

٢٦١ قال محمد: أخبرنا عبد الرحمن بن عبد الله المسعودي، عن عمرو بن مُرَّة، عن أبي عبيدة قال: قال عبد الله بن مسعود: الوتر ثلاث كثلاث المغرب.

261. Muḥammad said: "ᶜAbd ar-Raḥmān ibn ᶜAbdullāh al-Masᶜūdī informed us from ᶜAmr ibn Murrah that Abū ᶜUbaydah said, 'ᶜAbdullāh ibn Masᶜūd said, "*Witr* is three, like the three of *Maghrib*."'"

٢٦٢ قال محمد: حدثنا أبو معاوية المكفوف، عن الأعمش، عن مالك بن الحارث، عن عبد الرحمن بن يزيد، عن عبد الله بن مسعود قال: الوتر ثلاث كصلاة المغرب.

262. Muḥammad said: "Abū Muᶜāwiyah al-Makfūf narrated to us from al-Aᶜmash from Mālik ibn al-Ḥārith from ᶜAbd ar-Raḥmān ibn Yazīd that ᶜAbdullāh ibn Masᶜūd said, '*Witr* is three, like the prayer of *Maghrib*.'"

٢٦٣ قال محمد : أخبرنا إسماعيل بن إبراهيم، عن ليث ، عن عطاء ، قال ابن عباس رضي الله عنهما : الوتر كصلاة المغرب .

263. Muḥammad said: "Ismāᶜīl ibn Ibrāhīm informed us from Layth from ᶜAṭā’, that Ibn ᶜAbbās said, '*Witr* is like the prayer of *Maghrib*.'"

٢٦٤ قال محمد : أخبرنا يعقوب بن إبراهيم، حدثنا حصين بن إبراهيم، عن ابن مسعود قال : ما أجزأتْ ركعةٌ واحدة قطّ .

264. Muḥammad said: "Yaᶜqūb ibn Ibrāhīm informed us, 'Ḥuṣayn ibn Ibrāhīm informed us that Ibn Masᶜūd said, 'Never did a single *rakᶜah* suffice.'"

٢٦٥ قال محمد : أخبرنا سلاّم بن سليم الحنفي، عن أبي حمزة ، عن إبراهيم النخعي، عن علقمة قال: أخبرنا عبد الله بن مسعود : أهون ما يكون الوتر ثلاث ركعات .

265. Muḥammad said: "Sallām ibn Sulaym al-Ḥanafī informed us from Abū Ḥamzah from Ibrāhīm an-Nakhaᶜī that ᶜAlqamah said, 'ᶜAbdullāh ibn Masᶜūd informed us, "The least that *Witr* can be is three *rakᶜahs*."'"

٢٦٦ قال محمد : أخبرنا سعيد بن أبي عروبة، عن قتادة ، عن زرارة بن أبي أوفى، عن سعيد بن هشام، عن عائشة: أنَّ رسول الله صلى الله عليه وسلّم كان لا يسلِّم في ركعتي الوتر.

266. Muḥammad said: "Saᶜīd ibn Abī ᶜArūbah informed us from Qatādah from Zurārah ibn Abī Awfā from Saᶜīd ibn Hishām from ᶜĀ’ishah that the Messenger of Allah used not to say *'as-salāmu ᶜalaykum'* after two *rakᶜahs* of *Witr*."

٨٠ باب سجود القرآن

80. Prostrations During Recitation of Qur’ān

٢٦٧ أخبرنا مالك، حدثنا عبدُ الله بنُ يزيدَ مولى الأسود بن سفيان، عن أبي سلمة : أن أبا هريرة قرأ بهم ﴿إذا السَّماءُ انْشَقَّتْ﴾ فسجد فيها، فلما انصرفَ حدَّثهم أن رسول الله صلى الله عليه وسلم سجد فيها .

267. Mālik informed us: "ᶜAbdullāh ibn Yazīd, the *mawlā* of al-Aswad ibn Sufyān, narrated to us from Abū Salamah that Abū Hurayrah recited with them, *'Idha's-samā’u'nshaqqat'*, (Sūrah 84) and prostrated in it. When he finished, he told them that the Messenger of Allah had prostrated in it."

قال محمد : وبهذا نأخذ، وهو قول أبي حنيفة رحمه الله وكان مالك بن أنس لا يرى فيها سجدة .

Muḥammad said: "We adhere to this, and it is the verdict of Abū Ḥanīfah, may Allah have mercy on him. Mālik ibn Anas used to hold that there is no *sajdah* in it."

٢٦٨ أخبرنا مالك، حدثنا الزهري عن عبد الرحمن الأعرج، عن أبي هريرة : أن عمر بن الخطاب قرأ بهم النجم، فسجد فيها، ثم قام فقرأ سورة أخرى .

268. Mālik informed us: "Az-Zuhrī informed us from ᶜAbd ar-Raḥmān al-Aᶜraj from Abū Hurayrah that ᶜUmar ibn al-Khaṭṭāb recited [Sūrat] an-Najm (Sūrah 53) with them and prostrated in it, then stood up and recited another *sūrah*."

قال محمد : وبهذا نأخذ، وهو قول أبي حنيفة رحمه الله وكان مالك بن أنس لا يرى فيها سجدة .

Muḥammad said: "We adhere to this; it is the verdict of Abū Ḥanīfah, may Allah have mercy on him. Mālik ibn Anas used to hold that there is no prostration in it."

٢٦٩ أخبرنا مالك، حدثنا نافع، عن رجل من أهل مصر : أن عمر قرأ سورة الحج، فسجد فيها سجدتين، وقال: إن هذه السورة فُضِّلت بسجدتين .

269. Mālik informed us: "Nāfiᶜ informed us from a man of Egypt that ᶜUmar recited [Sūrah 22] al-Ḥajj, and prostrated twice in it, and said, 'This *sūrah* has been honoured with two prostrations.'"

٢٧٠ أخبرنا مالك، أخبرنا عبد الله بن دينار، عن ابن عمر رضي الله عنهما : أنه رآه سجد في سورة الحج سجدتين.

270. Mālik informed us: "ᶜAbdullāh ibn Dīnār informed us that he saw Ibn ᶜUmar ﷺ prostrate twice in Sūrat al-Ḥajj."

قال محمد : رُوي هذا عن عمرَ وابنِ عمرَ وكان ابن عباس لا يرى في سورة الحج إلاّ سجدةً واحدة : الأولى، وبهذا نأخذ، وهو قول أبي حنيفة رحمه الله .

Muḥammad said: "This has been reported from ᶜUmar and Ibn ᶜUmar. As for Ibn ᶜAbbās, he used to consider that there is only one prostration in Sūrat al-Ḥajj, the first one. We adhere to this, and it is the verdict of Abū Ḥanīfah, may Allah have mercy on him."

٨١ باب المارّ بين يدي المصلّي

81. Someone who Passes in front of Someone Praying

٢٧١ أخبرنا مالك، حدثنا سالم أبو النضر مولى عمر : أن بسر بن سعيد أخبره أن زيد بن خالد الجهني أرسله إلى أبي جُهَيم الأنصاري يسأله ماذا سمع من رسول الله ﷺ يقول في المارِّ بين يدي المصلّي ؟ قال : قال رسول الله ﷺ : لو يَعلَمُ المارُّ بين يدي المصلّي ماذا عليه في ذلك لكان أن يقف أربعين خيراً له من أن يمرّ بين يديه، قال : لا أدري قال أربعين يوماً أو أربعين شهراً أو أربعين سنة .

271. Mālik informed us: "Sālim Abu'n-Naḍr, the *mawlā* of ᶜUmar, narrated to us that Busr ibn Saᶜīd told him that Zayd ibn Khālid al-Juhanī sent him to Abū Juhaym al-Anṣārī to ask him what it was he had heard the Messenger of Allah ﷺ say concerning those who pass in front of someone praying. He said, 'The Messenger of Allah ﷺ said, "If the one who passes in front of someone praying was aware of what he incurred in doing that, it would have been better for him to stand for forty than to pass in front of him."' [Abu'n-Naḍr] said, 'I don't know whether he said forty days, forty months or forty years.'"

٢٧٢ أخبرنا مالك، حدثنا زيد بن أسلم، عن عبد الرحمن بن أبي سعيد الخُدْري، عن أبيه أن رسول الله ﷺ قال: إذا كان أحدُكم يصلِّي فلا يدَعْ أحداً يمرُّ بين يديه فإنْ أبى فليقاتلْه فإنما هو شيطان .

272. Mālik informed us: "Zayd ibn Aslam narrated to us from ᶜAbd ar-Raḥmān ibn Abī Saᶜīd al-Khudrī from his father that the Messenger of Allah ﷺ said, 'When one of you is in prayer, let him not ignore anyone passing in front of him. Should he persist then fight him, for he can only be a shayṭān.'"

٢٧٣ أخبرنا مالك، حدثنا زيد بن أسلم، عن عطاء بن يسار، عن كعب أنه قال: لو كان يعلمُ المارُّ بين يدي المصلِّي ماذا عليه في ذلك كان أن يُخسَفَ به خيراً له .

273. Mālik informed us: "Zayd ibn Aslam narrated to us from ᶜAṭā᾽ ibn Yasār that Kaᶜb said, 'If the one who passed in front of someone praying were aware of what he incurred in doing that, it would have been better for him if the earth swallowed him up.'"

قال محمد: يُكره أنْ يَمُرَّ الرَّجُلُ بين يدي المصلي، فإن أراد أن يمرَّ بين يديه فليدارأ ما استطاع، ولا يقاتله، فإنْ قاتَلَهُ كان ما يدخل عليه في صلاته من قتاله إياه أشدَّ عليه من ممرّ هذا بين يديه، ولا نعلم أحداً روى قتاله إلاَّ ما رُوي عن أبي سعيد الخدري، وليست العامَّة عليها، ولكنها على ما وَصفتُ لك، وهو قول أبي حنيفة رحمه الله .

Muḥammad said: "It is disliked that a man pass in front of someone praying. Should he want to walk past in front of him, the one in prayer should ward him off as best he can but not fight him, for should he fight him, then the consequences of his fighting in the prayer will be sterner for him than the other's passing in front of him. We are not aware that anyone has reported fighting the one who passes, except what has been reported from Abū Saᶜīd al-Khudrī. Neither does it reflect the general opinion, which instead is what I have described for you. That is the verdict of Abū Ḥanīfah, may Allah have mercy on him."

٢٧٤ أخبرنا مالك، حدثنا الزهري، عن سالم بن عبد الله، عن ابن عمر أنه قال: لا يقطعُ الصلاةَ شيء.

274. Mālik informed us: "Az-Zuhrī narrated to us from Sālim ibn ᶜAbdullāh that Ibn ᶜUmar said, 'Nothing interrupts the prayer.'"

قال محمد: وبه نأخذ، لا يقطع الصلاةَ شيء من مارٍّ بين يدي المصلِّي، وهو قول أبي حنيفة رضي الله عنه .

Muḥammad said: "We adhere to this; nothing that passes in front of the one praying interrupts the prayer. That is the verdict of Abū Ḥanīfah, may Allah have mercy on him."

٨٢ باب ما يُستَحبّ من التطوع في المسجد عند دخوله

82. What is Encouraged of Voluntary Prayer in the Mosque upon Entering

٢٧٥ أخبرنا مالك، حدثنا عامر بن عبد الله بن الزبير، عن عمرو بن سليم الزُّرَقي، عن أبي قتادة

السُّلَمي أن رسول الله صلى الله عليه وسلّم قال: إذا دخل أحدكم المسجد فليصل ركعتين قبل أن يجلس .

275. Mālik informed us: "ᶜĀmir ibn ᶜAbdullāh ibn az-Zubayr narrated to us from ᶜUmar ibn Sulaym az-Zuraqī from Abū Qatādah as-Sulamī that the Messenger of Allah ﷺ said, 'When one of you enters the mosque, let him pray two *rakᶜahs* before he sits.'"

قال محمد: هذا تطوّع وهو حسن، وليس بواجب .

Muḥammad said: "This is voluntary and it is good, but is not obligatory."

٨٣ باب الانفتال في الصلاة

83. Turning to the Side in [Concluding] the Prayer

٢٧٦ أخبرنا مالك، أخبرني يحيى بن سعيد، عن محمد بن يحيى بن حَبّان أنه سمعه يحدث عن واسع بن حَبّان قال: كنت أصلّي في المسجد وعبد الله بن عمر مسندٌ ظهره إلى القبلة، فلما قضيتُ صلاتي انصرفتُ إليه من قِبَل شقّي الأيسر، فقال: ما منعك أن تنصَرف على يمينك؟ قلت: رأيتُك وانصرفتُ إليك، قال عبدَ الله: فإنك قد أصبتَ فإن قائلاً يقول: انصرفْ على يمينك، فإذا كنتَ تصلّي انصرف حيث أحببتَ على يمينك أو يسارك، ويقول ناس: إذا قعدتَ على حاجتك فلا تستقبل القبلةَ ولا بيتَ المقدس، قال عبد الله: لقد رقيتُ على ظهر بيتٍ لنا فرأيت رسول الله صلى الله عليه وسلّم على حاجته مستَقْبِلَ بيت المقدس.

276. Mālik informed us: "Yaḥyā ibn Saᶜīd informed me that he heard Muḥammad ibn Yaḥyā ibn Ḥabbān,relating from Wāsiᶜ ibn Ḥabbān who said, 'I was praying in the mosque, and ᶜAbdullāh ibn ᶜUmar was leaning with his back towards the *qiblah.* When I concluded my prayer, I turned towards him, on my left-hand side.' He asked, 'What prevented you from turning to your right?' I answered, 'I saw you and turned towards you.' Ibn ᶜUmar said, 'You have done right, and some people would say, "Turn to your right." So when you are praying, turn however you like; to your right or your left. And some people say, "When you sit down to relieve yourself, do not face the *qiblah* nor *Bayt al-Maqdis."'* ᶜAbdullāh said, 'Once, I went up on to the roof of a house of ours, and I saw the Messenger of Allah ﷺ relieving himself, facing *Bayt al-Maqdis.'"*

قال محمد: وبقول عبد الله بن عمر نأخذ، ينصرف الرجل إذا سلّم على أي شقّه أَحَبّ، ولا بأس أن يستقبل بالخلاء من الغائط والبول بيت المقدس، إنما يُكره أن يستقبل بذلك القبلة، وهو قول أبي حنيفة رحمه الله .

Muḥammad said: "We adhere to the verdict of ᶜAbdullāh ibn ᶜUmar; a man may turn to whichever side he likes, when saying 'as-salāmu ᶜalaykum'. And there is no harm, when going to pass faeces or urine, in facing Bayt al-Maqdis. It is the facing of the *qiblah* which is loathed when doing that. That is the verdict of Abū Ḥanīfah, may Allah have mercy on him."

٨٤ باب صلاة المغمى عليه

84. The Prayer of One who is Unconscious

٢٧٧ أخبرنا مالك، حدثنا نافع، عن ابن عمر: أنه أُغْمِيَ عليه، ثم أفاق، فلم يقضِ الصلاة .

277. Mālik informed us: "Nāfi[c] narrated to us that Ibn [c]Umar lost consciousness, then awoke, and did not make up the prayer."

قال محمد: وبهذا نأخذ إذا أُغمي عليه أكثر من يوم وليلة، وأما إذا أغمي عليه يوماً وليلة أو أقلَّ قضى صلاته .

Muḥammad said: "We adhere to this when he has been unconscious for more than a day and a night. In the case of his being unconscious for a day and a night or less, then he should make up the prayer."

٢٧٨ بَلَغَنَا عن عمّار بن ياسر: أنه أُغمي عليه أربع صلوات، ثم أفاق فقضاها ، أخبرنا بذلك أبو معشر المديني عن بعض أصحابه .

278. It has reached us that [c]Ammār ibn Yāsir was unconscious for four prayers, then he awoke, and he made them up. Abū Ma[c]shar al-Madīnī related that to us from some of his companions."

٨٥ باب صلاة المريض

85. The Prayer of the Sick

٢٧٩ أخبرنا مالك، حدثنا نافع أن ابن عمر قال: إذا لم يستطع المريض السجود أومى برأسه.

279. Mālik informed us: "Nāfi[c] narrated to us that Ibn [c]Umar said, 'When someone who is sick is unable to prostrate, he should motion with his head.'"

قال محمد: وبهذا نأخذ، ولا ينبغي له أن يسجُدَ على عود ولا شيء يرفع إليه، ويجعل سجودَه أخفضَ من ركوعه، وهو قول أبي حنيفة رحمه الله .

Muḥammad said: "We adhere to this; and it does not become him to prostrate on a stick, or anything raised up to him. He should make his prostration lower than his bowing. That is the verdict of Abū Ḥanīfah, ﷺ."

٨٦ باب النخامة في المسجد وما يُكره من ذلك

86. Spitting Phlegm in the Mosque, and what is Disapproved of that

٢٨٠ أخبرنا مالك، حدثنا نافع، عن ابن عمر رضي الله عنهما : أن رسولَ الله صلى الله عليه وسلَّم رأى بصاقاً في قبلة المسجد فحكَّه ، ثم أقبل على الناس، فقال: إذا كان أحدُكُم يصلِّي فلا يبصقْ قِبَل وجهه، فإن الله تعالى قِبَل وجهه إذا صلَّى.

280. Mālik informed us: "Nāfi[c] narrated to us from Ibn [c]Umar ﷺ that the Messenger of Allah ﷺ saw the traces of spit in the mosque in the direction of the *qiblah*, and rubbed it clean. Then he turned towards the people and said, 'When one of you is in prayer, let him not spit in front of him, for Allah, exalted is He, is in front of him when he is in prayer.'"

قال محمد: ينبغي له أن لا يبصق تلقاء وجهه ولا عن يمينه وليبصقْ تحت رجله اليسرى .
Muḥammad said: "He should not spit in front of him, nor to his right. Let him spit under his left foot."

٨٧ باب الجنب والحائض يعرقان في ثوب

87. The Sweated Garment of Someone, who has had Sexual Intercourse, or of a Woman in her Period

٢٨١ أخبرنا مالك، حدَّثنا نافع، عن ابن عمر: أنه كان يَعْرَقُ في الثوب وهو جنب، ثم يصلي فيه.
281. Mālik informed us: "Nāfi[c] narrated to us that Ibn [c]Umar used to sweat in a garment after sexual intercourse and then pray in it."

قال محمد: وبهذا نأخذ لا بأس به ما لم يُصب الثوب من المني شيء، وهو قول أبي حنيفة رحمه الله.
Muḥammad said: "We adhere to this. There is no harm in it as long as no semen has come onto the garment. That is the verdict of Abū Ḥanīfah, may Allah have mercy on him."

٨٨ باب بَدْأ أمر القبلة وما نُسخ من قبلة بيت المقدس

88. The Initial Direction of the *Qiblah*, and what was Abrogated of the *Qiblah* of the Bayt al-Maqdis

٢٨٢ أخبرنا مالك، أخبرنا عبدُ الله بن دينار، عن عبد الله بن عمر قال: بينما الناسُ في صلاة الصبح إذ أتاه رجل، فقال إنَّ رسولَ الله صلى الله عليه وسلَّم قد أُنزل عليه الليلة قرآنٌ وقد أُمر أن يستقبلَ القبلة، فاستقبَلوها، وكانت وجوهُهُم إلى الشام فاستداروا إلى الكعبة.
282. Mālik informed us: "[c]Abdullāh ibn Dīnār informed us that [c]Abdullāh ibn [c]Umar said, 'While the people were praying the dawn prayer, there came a man to them and said, "The Messenger of Allah ﷺ had some Qur[ʾ]ān revealed to him this night, and has been ordered to turn towards the *qiblah* [of Makkah]." So they turned towards it. They had been facing towards Shām, so they turned around towards the Ka[c]bah.'"

قال محمد: وبهذا نأخذ فيمن أخطأ القبلة حتى صلَّى ركعة أو ركعتين، ثم عَلِم أنه يصلِّي إلى غير القبلة فلينحرفْ إلى القبلة فيصلّي ما بقي ويَعتدّ بما مضى، وهو قول أبي حنيفةَ رحمه الله .
Muḥammad said: "We adhere to this. In the case of someone praying in the wrong direction for a *rak[c]ah* or two, who then discovers that he has been praying in the wrong direction, let him adjust himself towards the *qiblah*, pray what remains and count as done that which has passed. That is the verdict of Abū Ḥanīfah, may Allah have mercy on him."

٨٩ باب الرجل يصلي بالقوم وهو جُنُب أو على غير وضوء

89. A Man's Leading People in Prayer, while he is *Junub* [requiring *ghusl* after sexual intercourse or ejaculation] or not in a State of *Wuḍū'*

٢٨٣ أخبرنا مالك، حدثنا إسماعيلُ بنُ أبي الحكيم أن سليمان بن يسار أخبره: أن عمرَ بنَ الخطاب صلّى الصبح، ثم ركب إلى الجُرُف، ثم بعد ما طلعت الشمسُ رأى في ثوبه احتلاماً، فقال: لقد احتلمتُ، وما شَعَرتُ، ولقد سلِّط عليّ الاحتلام منذُ وُلِّيتُ أمرَ النَّاس ثم غسل ما رأى في ثوبه، ونَضَحَه، ثم اغتسل ثم قام فصلى الصبح بعد ما طلعت الشمس.

283. Mālik informed us: "Ismā'īl ibn Abī Ḥakīm narrated to us that Sulaymān ibn Yasār told him that 'Umar ibn al-Khaṭṭāb prayed the dawn prayer, and then rode to al-Juruf. Then, after the sun had risen, he found traces of semen on his garment, and said, 'I had ejaculated [in my sleep] and was unaware. I have been more disposed to sexual intercourse and ejaculation [*janābah*] since being placed in charge of the people.' Then he washed what he could see on his garment, and sprinkled it. Then he did *ghusl*, and stood and prayed the dawn prayer after the sun had risen."

قال محمد: وبهذا نأخذ، ونرى أن من علم ذلك ممن صلّى خلف عمر فعليه أن يعيدَ الصلاة كما أعادها عمر لأن الإمام إذا فسدت صلاته فسدت صلاة من خلفه، وهو قول أبي حنيفة رحمه الله.

Muḥammad said: "We adhere to this. It is our opinion that should any of those who prayed behind 'Umar have become aware of his state, then it would fall to them to repeat the prayer as 'Umar repeated it, for if the imām's prayer goes wrong, the prayer of those behind him goes wrong. That is the verdict of Abū Ḥanīfah, may Allah have mercy on him."

٩٠ باب الرجل يركع دون الصفّ أو يقرأ في ركوعه

90. A Man's Bowing behind the Row, or Reciting during his Bowing

٢٨٤ أخبرنا مالك، أخبرنا ابن شهاب، عن أبي أمامة بن سهل بن حنيف أنه قال: دخل زيد بن ثابت، فوجد الناس ركوعاً فركع ثم دبَّ حتى وصل الصف.

284. Mālik informed us: "Ibn Shihāb informed us that Abū Umāmah ibn Sahl ibn Ḥunayf said, 'Zayd ibn Thābit entered the mosque and found the people bowing; so he bowed, and then walked slowly forward until he joined the row.'"

قال محمد: هذا يُجزئ، وأحبُّ إلينا أن لا يركع حتى يصل إلى الصف، وهو قول أبي حنيفة ﷺ.

Muḥammad said: "This is valid for him, but it is preferable to us that he not bow until he joins the row. That is the verdict of Abū Ḥanīfah, may Allah have mercy on him."

٢٨٥ قال محمد، حدثنا المبارك بن فَضَالة، عن الحسن: أن أبا بكرة رضي الله عنه ركع دون الصفّ ثم مشى حتى وَصَلَ الصف، فلما قضى صلاته ذَكَر ذلك لرسول الله صلّى الله عليه وسلّم، فقال له صلّى الله عليه وسلّم: زادك اللّهُ حرصاً ولا تَعُدْ.

tafsir, hadith and the Arabic language affords the reader ample insight into the pitfalls of attempting to derive legal rulings without first being firmly grounded in the sciences of the religion.

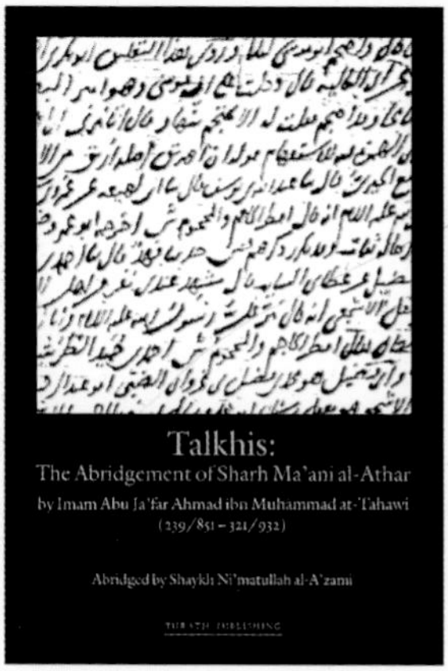

Talkhis: The Abridgement of Sharh Ma'ani al-Athar

by Imam Abu Ja'far Ahmad ibn Muhammad at-Tahawi (239/851 – 321/932) ISBN 0-9547380-6-3
Abridged by Shaykh Ni'matullah al-A'zami

This work deals exhaustively with establishing that the sources of the Hanafi madhhab, as with all of the madhhabs, conform to the Sunnah of the Prophet, and the verdicts passed by the Companions. In the process, the Imam often draws on theoretical understanding (ra'y) to buttress an argument but never as the main plank for deriving rulings. It is a dazzling display of erudition in both the demanding sciences of hadith as well as what was already in the author's age a highly sophisticated science, fiqh. Shaykh Ni'matullah has done an outstanding job in reducing the voluminous original work to a more manageable size by abridging the numerous multiplications of narrations of hadith used by the Imam in the tradition of hadith scholars, while retaining the essence of his argument. The whole work will be fully cross-referenced by Shaykh Ni'matullah.

Mukhtasar al-Quduri

by Imam Abu'l-Hasan Ahmad ibn Muhammad al-Quduri (362/973 – 428/1037) ISBN 0-9547380-7-1

Detailing about 12,500 legal questions that span the entire spectrum of fiqh, this work is an authoritative reference, not only on matters of worship, but also on financial transactions, personal relations and penal and judicial matters. Al-Mukhtasar al-Quduri is universally recognised as one of the mainstays of the Hanafi school, and forms the primary text of the renowned Hanafi work, al-Hidayah .Widely acclaimed for centuries, the Mukhtasar still forms part of the curriculum in traditional madrasahs world wide. Each general legal question is accompanied by its corresponding proof from the Qur'an and the Sunnah.

Taqlid

by Mufti Zubair Ismail Bayat ISBN 0-9547380-3-9

The author, a contemporary scholar, examines the status of taqlid or ittiba, wrongly understood as blind imitation, and investigates its validity within the context of Quran and Sunnah and the verdicts of the great ulama on this subject such as Shaykh Ibn Taymiyyah, ash-Shawkani, Shah Waliyullah and many others – showing in the process that far from being prohibited, taqlid is an essential and established tradition within Islamic jurisprudence. An essential guide to understand Taqlid and to dispel the great confusion on this subject.

Qawa'id fi Ulum al-Hadith: Principles of the Sciences of Hadith

by Shaykh Zafar Ahmad al-Uthmani at-Tahanawi (1310/1892 – 1394/ 1974) ISBN 0-0-9547380-4-7

In this remarkable work the author examines the science of hadith quoting substantially from the acknowledged masters of Jarh (critical evaluation): Jalal ad-Din as-Suyuti, Hafiz Ibn Hajar al-'Asqalani, adh-Dhahabi et al. He examines the science of isnad with a scientific thoroughness that has simply never been done before in the English language. This book will prove indispensable for any serious student of hadith. ISBN 0-0-9547380-4-7

Qawa'id fi Ulum al-Fiqh: Principles of the Sciences of Fiqh

By Shaykh Zafar Ahmad al-Uthmani at-Tahanawi (1310/1892 – 1394/ 1974) ISBN 0-9547380-5-5

In this companion volume to the above work, which is taken from the introduction to the I'la as-Sunan (Exalting the Sunnahs) and written under the direction of Shaykh Ashraf Ali at-Tahanawi, the author presents a closely wrought argument in defence of the traditional methodologies of Islamic scholarship. In the course of his detailed survey of the differences of opinion within the religion, he supplies exhaustive analyses of the arguments of, in particular, Ibn al-Qayyim al-Jawzi and Ibn Hazm. The author's rigorous scholarship in the fields of

Turath Publishing: Forthcoming Titles

Kitab al-Athar

by Imam Muhammad ibn al-Hasan ash-Shaybani
(135/752 – 189/804) ISBN 0-9547380-1-2

This compilation of traditions from the first right-acting generations of Islam, the Companions, the Followers and the Followers of the Followers and hadith of the Messenger of Allah, is understood by the ulama to have been the work of Imam Abu Hanifah. It was compiled by one of his main students, Imam Muhammad. As is his pattern with the Muwatta, he comments on each tradition and places it within the context of the fiqh rulings of his teacher, Imam Abu Hanifah. This will be an invaluable book for those interested in the early sources of Hanafi fiqh rulings, as it will also for those studying the history of the hadith and traditions.

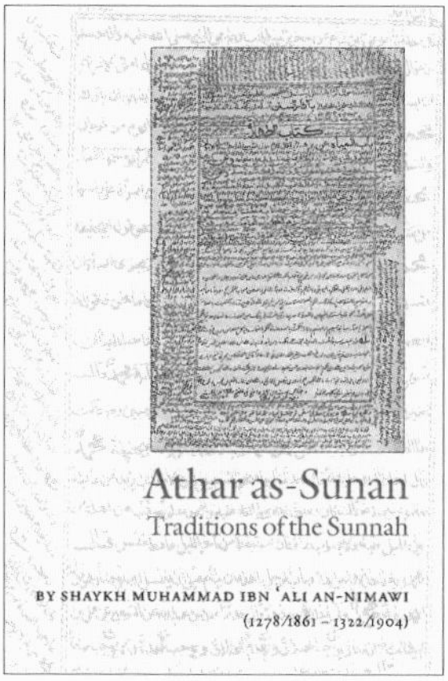

Athar as-Sunan: Traditions of the Sunnah

by Shaykh Muhammad ibn 'Ali an-Nimawi
(1278/1861 – 1322/1904) ISBN 0-9547380-2-0

In this important work the Shaykh relates fiqh judgements, particularly those of the Hanafi madhhab, to the hadith and traditions, scrutinising each for what the great scholars have said about the strength or weakness of its chain of transmission. The book was to have dealt with all of chapters of fiqh, but sadly the Shaykh only completed the book on purification and the prayer. Fascinatingly, he tackles matters that engage us all today, including practices that have become a source of controversy over the last few years and thus it will be an important reference work in everyone's library.

TURATH PUBLISHING

The Muwatta *of*
Imam Muhammad

MUHAMMAD IBN AL-HASAN
ASH-SHAYBANI
(135H -189H)

The Muwatta of Imam Muhammad

Imam Muhammad ibn al-Hasan ash-Shaybani (135/752 – 189/804)

Imam Malik composed the Muwatta over a period of forty years to represent the "well-trodden path" of the people of Madinah. Its name also means that it is the book that is "many times agreed upon" – about whose contents the people of Madinah were unanimously agreed – and that is "made easy and facilitated". Its high standing is such that people of every school of fiqh and all of the imams of hadith scholarship agree upon its authenticity. Ash-Shafi'i said, "There is not on the face of the earth – after the Book of Allah – a book which is more sahih than the book of Malik."Hafidh Ibn Hajar al-'Asqalani said: "The unqualified truth is that all of the Muwatta is sahih without any exception." Shah Wali Allah ad-Dihlawi (1114-1176 AH) said, "My breast expanded and I became certain that the Muwatta is the most sahih book to be found on the earth after the Book of Allah." ISBN 0-9547380-0-4

TURATH PUBLISHING 0044-20-8767-3666 www.turathpublishing.com info@turathpublishing.com
Distributors for UK and Europe: Azhar Academy – Islamic Dawah Academy, Cooks Road, London E15 2PW
0044-0208-5349191 / 0044-116-262-5440 info@idauk.org www.idauk.org sales@azharacademy.com www.azharacademy.com
Distributors for South Africa : Darul – Ihsan Research and Education centre 0027- 835 939599 / 0027-32 5525784 www.direct.za.org
info@direct.za.org Distributors for America and Canada: 0018 (805) 968 4666 http//whitethreadpress.com/ ar@whitethreadpress.com

285. Muḥammad said: "Al-Mubārak ibn Faḍālah narrated to us from al-Ḥasan that Abū Bakrah ☙ bowed behind the row, then walked until he joined the row. Then when he had concluded his prayer, he mentioned that to the Messenger of Allah ﷺ and he said, 'May Allah increase your eagerness, but don't do it again.'"

قال محمد: هكذا نقول: وهو يجزئ وأحبّ إلينا أن لا يُفعل.

Muḥammad said: "We say likewise. It suffices, but it is preferable to us that it not be done."

٢٨٦ أخبرنا مالك، أخبرنا نافع مولى ابن عمر، عن إبراهيم بن عبد الله بن حُنين، عن عبد الله بن حُنين، عن علي بن أبي طالب رضي الله عنه: أن رسول الله صلّى الله عليه وسلّم نهى عن لبس القَسِّيّ وعن لبس المُعَصفَر وعن تَخَتُّم الذَّهَب وعن قراءة القرآن في الركوع.

286. Mālik informed us: "Nāfiʿ, the *mawlā* of Ibn ʿUmar, informed us from Ibrāhīm ibn ʿAbdullāh ibn Ḥunayn from ʿAbdullāh ibn Ḥunayn from ʿAlī ibn Abī Ṭālib ☙ that the Messenger of Allah ﷺ prohibited wearing fabrics of mixed linen and silk (qassī) and wearing garments dyed with safflower, and wearing gold rings, and reciting [the Qurʾān] during bowing and prostration."

قال محمد: وبهذا نأخذ، تُكره القراءةُ في الركوع والسجود وهو قول أبي حنيفة رحمه الله.

Muḥammad said: "We adhere to this. Reciting during bowing and prostration is disliked. That is the verdict of Abū Ḥanīfah, may Allah have mercy on him."

٩١ باب الرجل يصلّي وهو يحمل الشيء
91. A Man's Praying while Carry ing Something

٢٨٧ أخبرنا مالك، أخبرني عامر بن عبد الله بن الزبير، عن عمرو بن سليم الزرقي، عن أبي قتادة السلمي: أن رسول الله صلّى الله عليه وسلّم كان يصلّي وهو حامل أمامةَ بنت زينب بنت رسول الله صلّى الله عليه وسلّم، ولأبي العاص بن الربيع، فإذا سجد وضعها وإذا قام حملها.

287. Mālik informed us: "ʿĀmir ibn ʿAbdullāh ibn az-Zubayr informed me from ʿAmr ibn Sulaym az-Zuraqī from Abū Qatādah as-Sulamī that the Messenger of Allah ☙ used to pray while carrying Umāmah – the daughter of Zaynab, (the daughter of the Messenger of Allah ﷺ,) and Abu'l-ʿĀṣ ibn ar-Rabīʿ – placing her down when prostrating, and carrying her when getting up."

٩٢ باب المرأة تكون بين الرجل يصلّي وبين القبلة وهي نائمة أو قائمة
92. A Woman's being Between a Man Praying and the *Qiblah*, whether she is Sleeping or Standing

٢٨٨ أخبرنا مالك، أخبرني أبو النضر مولى عمر بن عبيد الله، عن أبي سلمة بن عبد الرحمن بن عوف، عن عائشة زوج النبي صلّى الله عليه وسلّم أنها أخبرته، قالت: كنت أنام بين يدي رسول الله

صلّى الله عليه وسلّم ورِجلاَيَ في القبلة ، فإذا سجد غَمَزَني ، فقبضتُ رِجْلَيَّ ، وإذا قام بسطتُها ، والبيوتُ يومئذ ليس فيها مصابيح .

288. Mālik informed us: "Abu'n-Naḍr, the *mawlā* of ᶜUmar ibn ᶜUbaydullāh, informed us from Abū Salamah ibn ᶜAbd ar-Raḥmān ibn ᶜAwf, from ᶜĀ᾿ishah, the wife of the Prophet ﷺ, that she said to him, 'I used to sleep in front of the Messenger of Allah ﷺ with my legs in front of the *qiblah*. Then, when he prostrated, he would nudge me and I would retract my feet. When he got up I would stretch them out. In those days, there were no lanterns in the houses.'"

قال محمد : لا بأس بأن يصلِّيَ الرجل والمرأة نائمة أو قائمة أو قاعدة بين يديه أو إلى جنبه، أو تصلي إذا كانت تصلّي في غير صلاته، إنما يُكره أن تصلِّيَ إلى جنبه أو بين يديه وهما في صلاة واحدة أو يصلّيان مع إمام واحد، فإن كانت كذلك فسدت صلاته، وهو قول أبي حنيفة رحمه الله .

Muḥammad said: "There is no harm in a man's praying while the woman is sleeping, or standing, or sitting in front of him, or next to him, or while she is praying, so long as it is not the same prayer as him. It is only disliked for her to pray next to him, or in front of him, when they are in the same prayer, or praying with the same imām. If that is the case, his prayer is invalid. That is the verdict of Abū Ḥanīfah."

٩٣ باب صلاة الخوف

93. The Prayer of Fear

٢٨٩ أخبرنا مالك، حدثنا نافع، أن ابن عمر كان إذا سُئل عن صلاة الخوف، قال : يتقدّم الإمامُ وطائفةٌ من الناس فيصلّي بهم سجدةً وتكون طائفة منهم بينه وبين العدوّ ولم يصلّوا ، فإذا صلّى الذين معه سجدةً استأخروا مكان الذين لم يصلّوا ولا يسلّمون ، ويتقدّم الذين لم يصلُّوا فيصلّون معه سجدة، ثم ينصرفُ الإمامُ وقد صلّى سجدتين، ثم يقوم كلٌّ واحدة من الطائفتين فيصلون لأنفسهم سجدةً سجدةً، بعد انصراف الإمام، فيكون كلٌّ واحدة من الطائفتين قد صلَّوْا سجدتين. فإن كان خوفاً هو أشدّ من ذلك صلَّوْا رجالاً قياماً على أقدامهم أو ركباناً مستقبلي القبلة وغيرَ مستقبليها . قال نافع : ولا أُرى عبدَ الله بنَ عمرَ إلاّ حدّثه عن رسول الله صلّى الله عليه وسلّم .

289. Mālik informed us: "Nāfiᶜ narrated to us that when Ibn ᶜUmar was asked about the prayer of fear, he used to say, 'The imām goes forward with one group of people, and prays one *rakᶜah* with them, and another group of them stays between him and the enemy, not yet having prayed. Then when those with him have prayed one *rakᶜah* they take the place of those who have not prayed, without saying *as-salāmu ᶜalaykum*, and those who have not prayed go forward and pray one *rakᶜah* with him. Then the imām concludes, having prayed two *rakᶜahs*. Then everyone in the two groups stands and prays for himself, one *rakᶜah* each, after the imām has concluded, and so everyone in the two groups will have prayed two *rakᶜahs*. And if the anxiety be more intense than that, they should pray standing on their feet, or riding,

whether facing the *qiblah* or not.'" Nāfiᶜ said, "And I don't think ᶜAbdullāh ibn ᶜUmar related it from anyone other than the Messenger of Allah ﷺ."

قال محمد : وبهذا نأخذ ، وهو قول أبي حنيفة رحمه الله وكان مالك بن أنس لا يأخذ به .

Muḥammad said: "We adhere to this; it is the verdict of Abū Ḥanīfah, may Allah have mercy on him, whereas Mālik ibn Anas used not to adhere to it."

٩٤ باب وضع اليمين على اليسار في الصلاة

94. Placing the Right Hand on the Left in Prayer

٢٩٠ أخبرنا مالك، حدّثنا أبو حازم ، عن سهل بن سعد الساعدي ، قال : كان الناسُ يُؤْمَرون أن يضعَ أحدُهم يَدَه اليُمنى على ذراعه اليُسرى في الصلاة. قال أبو حازم: ولا أعلم إلاّ أنه ينمي ذلك .

290. Mālik informed us: "Abū Ḥāzim narrated to us that Sahl ibn Saᶜd as-Sāᵓidī said, 'The people used to be told that one should place the right hand on the left forearm in prayer.'" Abū Ḥāzim said, "I only think that he was accrediting that [to the Prophet ﷺ]."

قال محمد : ينبغي للمصلّي إذا قام في صلاته أن يَضَعَ باطنَ كفِّه اليُمنى على رُسْغه اليُسرى تحت السُرّة ، ويَرمي ببصره إلى موضع سجوده، وهو قول أبي حنيفة رحمه الله .

Muḥammad said: "The one praying should, once standing in his prayer, place the palm of his right hand on his left wrist, under the navel, and cast his eyes to the place where he prostrates. That is the verdict of Abū Ḥanīfah."

٩٥ باب الصلاة على النبي صلّى الله عليه وسلّم

95. Praying for Blessings on the Prophet ﷺ

٢٩١ أخبرنا مالك، حدثنا عبد الله بن أبي بكر، عن أبيه ، عن عمرو بن سليم الزرقي، أخبرني أبو حميد الساعدي قال: قالوا : يا رسول الله، كيف نصلّي عليك؟ قال: قولوا اللهمّ صلِّ على محمّد وعلى أزواجه وذرِّيَّته، كما صلَّيْتَ على إبراهيم ، وبارِكْ على محمّدٍ وعلى أزواجِه وذرِّيَّته، كما باركتَ على إبراهيم .

إنك حميد مجيد .

291. Mālik informed us: "ᶜAbdullāh ibn Abī Bakr narrated to us from his father from ᶜAmr ibn Sulaym az-Zuraqī,'Abū Ḥumayd as-Sāᵓidī informed me saying, "They asked, 'Messenger of Allah, how should we pray for you?' He answered, 'Say, "O Allah bless Muḥammad, his wives and descendants as You blessed Ibrāhīm, and continue Your blessings upon Muḥammad, his wives and descendants as You continued Your blessings upon Ibrāhīm. Truly, You are Praiseworthy, Glorious."'"'"

٢٩٢ أخبرنا مالك، أخبرنا نُعيْم بن عبد الله المُجْمر مولى عمر بن الخطاب أنّ محمد بن عبد الله بن زيد الأنصاري أخبره وهو عبد الله بن زيد الذي أُري النداءَ في النوم على عهد رسول الله صلّى الله عليه وسلّم: أن أبا مسعود أخبره، فقال: أتانا رسول الله صلّى الله عليه وسلّم، فجلس معنا في

مجلس ابن عُبادة ، فقال بشير بن سعد أبو النعمان : أمرنا الله أن نصلّي عليك يا رسول الله، فكيف نصلّي عليك ؟ قال : فصَمَت رسول الله صلّى الله عليه وسلّم حتى تمنَّيْنا أنّا لم نسألْه . قال : قولوا : اللهمّ صلِّ على محمّد وعلى آل محمد، كما صلّيت على إبراهيم وعلى آل إبراهيم، وبارك على محمد وعلى آل محمد كما باركت على إبراهيم. في العالمين إنك حميد مجيد. والسلام كما قد عُلِّمْتم .

292. Mālik informed us: "Nu^c^aym ibn ^c^Abdullāh al-Mujmir, the *mawlā* of ^c^Umar ibn al-Khaṭṭāb, informed us that Muḥammad ibn ^c^Abdullāh ibn Zayd al-Anṣārī – that is ^c^Abdullāh ibn Zayd who was shown the call [to prayer] in his sleep in the time of the Messenger of Allah ﷺ – told him, that Abū Mas^c^ūd to said to him, saying, 'The Messenger of Allah ﷺ came to us, and sat with us in the gathering of Ibn ^c^Ubādah. Bashīr ibn Sa^c^d Abu'n-Nu^c^mān said, "Allah has ordered us to pray for you, Messenger of Allah. How should we pray for you?"' [Abū Mas^c^ūd] said, 'So the Messenger of Allah ﷺ became silent, until we wished that we had not asked him, [then] he said, "Say, 'O Allah bless Muḥammad and the family of Muḥammad as You blessed Ibrāhīm and the family of Ibrāhīm. Continue Your blessings upon Muḥammad and the family of Muḥammad as You continued Your blessings upon Ibrāhīm and the family of Ibrāhīm. Among the creatures, truly, You are Praiseworthy, Glorious.' And the "salām" is as you have learnt.'""

قال محمد : كل هذا حسن .

Muḥammad said: "All of this is fine."

٩٦ باب الاستسقاء

96. Asking for Rain

٢٩٣ أخبرنا مالك، أخبرنا عبد الله بن أبي بكر بن محمد بن عمرو بن حزم أنه سمع عبّاد بن تميم المازنيّ يقول: سمعت عبدَ الله ابن زيد المازنيّ يقول : خرج رسولُ الله صلى الله عليه وسلم إلى المصلّى فاستسقى وحوّل رداءَه حين استقبل القبلة.

293. Mālik informed us: "^c^Abdullāh ibn Abī Bakr ibn Muḥammad ibn ^c^Amr ibn Ḥazm informed us that he heard ^c^Abbād ibn Tamīm al-Māzinī say, 'I heard ^c^Abdullāh ibn Zayd al-Māzinī say, "The Messenger of Allah ﷺ went out to the field of prayer, and asked for rain, and he turned his cloak inside out when he faced the *qiblah*."'"

قال محمد : أما أبو حنيفة رحمه الله فكان لا يرى في الاستسقاء صلاة ، وأما في قولنا فإن الإمام يصلي بالناس ركعتين ثم يدعو ويحوِّل رداءه، فيجعل الأيمن على الأيسر، والأيسر على الأيمن ولا يفعل ذلك أحد إلا الإمام .

Muḥammad said: "As for Abū Ḥanīfah, may Allah have mercy on him, it was not his opinion that, when asking for rain, a prayer should be prayed. As for our opinion, the imām should pray two *rak^c^ahs* with the people, then supplicate, and he should turn his cloak inside out, putting the right side on the left and the left side on the right, and none should do that except the imām."

٩٧ باب الرجل يصلي ثم يجلس في موضعه الذي صلى فيه

97. A Man's Praying, then Sitting in the Place in which he Prayed

٢٩٤ أخبرنا مالك، أخبرنا نُعيم بن عبد الله المُجْمر أنه سمع أبا هريرة يقول: قال رسول الله صلّى الله عليه وسلّم: إذا صلى أحدكم، ثم جلس في مصلاّه لم تزل الملائكة تصلّي عليه: اللهمّ صلِّ عليه، اللهمّ اغفر له، اللّهمّ ارحمه، فإن قام من مصلاّه، فجلس في المسجد ينتظر الصلاة لم يزل في صلاة حتي يصلّي.

294. Mālik informed us: "Nu^c^aym ibn ^c^Abdullāh al-Mujmir informed us that he heard Abū Hurayrah say, 'The Messenger of Allah ﷺ said, "When one of you prays, then sits where he prayed, the angels do not cease to supplicate for mercy on him, 'O Allah turn your attention to him, O Allah forgive him, O Allah have mercy on him', and should he get up from the place in which he prayed and sit in the mosque, waiting for the prayer, he does not cease to be in prayer until he prays."'"

٩٨ باب صلاة التطوع بعد الفريضة

98. Praying Voluntary Prayers after the Obligatory Prayer

٢٩٥ أخبرنا مالك، حدثنا نافع، عن ابن عمر: أن رسول الله صلّى الله عليه وسلّم يصلّي قبلَ الظهر ركعتين، وبعدها ركعتين، وبعد صلاة المغرب ركعتين في بيته، وبعد صلاة العشاءِ ركعتين، وكان لا يصلّي بعد الجمعة في المسجد حتى ينْصَرِف فَيَسْجُدَ سَجْدَتَيْن.

295. Mālik informed us: "Nāfi^c^ narrated to us from Ibn ^c^Umar that the Messenger of Allah ﷺ used to pray two *rak^c^ahs* before *Ẓuhr,* and two *rak^c^ahs* after it, and two *rak^c^ahs* after the prayer of *Maghrib,* in his house, and two *rak^c^ahs* after the prayer of *^c^Ishā^ʾ^*. He used not to pray after Jumu^c^ah, in the mosque, until he had left [and gone to his house], and then he would pray two *rak^c^ahs.*"

قال محمد: هذا تطوُّع وهو حسن، وقد بلغنا أن النبي صلّى الله عليه وسلّم كان يصلّي قبل الظهر أربعاً إذا زالت الشمس، فسأله أبو أيوبَ الأنصاريّ عن ذلك، فقال: إن أبوابَ السماء تُفتح في هذه الساعة، فأحبُّ أن يصعدَ لي فيها عمل، فقال: يا رسول الله، أ يُفْصَلُ بينهنّ بسلام؟ فقال: لا.
أخبرنا بذلك بُكير بن عامر البَجَلي عن إبراهيم والشّعبي عن أبي أيوب الأنصاري رضي الله عنه.

Muḥammad said: "This is voluntary, and it is fine; we have heard that the Prophet ﷺ used to pray, four [*rak^c^ahs*] before *Ẓuhr,* when the sun moved away from its zenith. Abū Ayyūb al-Anṣārī asked him about that, and he said, 'The doors of heaven are opened at this time, and I would like some of my striving to ascend for me during it.' [Abū Ayyūb] said, 'Messenger of Allah, are they to be divided by [saying] *"salām"*?' And he said, 'No.'" [Muḥammad said]: "Bukayr ibn ᶜĀmir al-Bajalī related that to us from Ibrāhīm and ash-Shaᶜbī, from Abū Ayyūb al-Anṣārī ﷺ."

٩٩ باب الرجل يَمَسّ القرآن وهو جنب أو على غير طهارة

99. A Man's Touching the Qurʾān while he is *Junub*, or not in a State of Purity

٢٩٦ أخبرنا مالك، أخبرنا عبدُ الله بن أبي بكر بن محمد بن عمرو بن حَزْم قال: إنَّ في الكتاب الذي كتبه رسولُ الله صلّى الله عليه وسلّم لعمرو بن حزم: لا يَمَسّ القرآن إلا طاهر.

296. Mālik informed us: "ᶜAbdullāh ibn Abī Bakr ibn Muḥammad ibn ᶜAmr ibn Ḥazm informed us, 'In the letter which the Messenger of Allah ﷺ wrote for ᶜAmr ibn Ḥazm there is: "None should touch the Qurʾān except a pure one".'"

٢٩٧ أخبرنا مالك، أخبرنا نافع، عن ابن عمر أنه كان يقول: لا يسجد الرجل ولا يقرأ القرآن إلا وهو طاهر.

297. Mālik informed us: "Nāfiᶜ informed us that Ibn ᶜUmar used to say, 'A man should not prostrate, nor read the Qurʾān, unless he is pure.'"

قال محمد: وبهذا كلّه نأخذ، وهو قول أبي حنيفة رحمه الله إلا في خصلة واحده، لا بأس بقراءة القرآن على غير طُهر إلا أن يكون جنباً.

Muḥammad said: "We adhere to all of this, and it is the verdict of Abū Ḥanīfah, may Allah have mercy on him, except in one instance; there is no harm in reciting the Qurʾān [from memory] while not in a state of purity, unless he is *junub*."

١٠٠ باب الرجل يجرّ ثوبه والمرأة تجرّ ذَيْلها فيعلق به قذر وما كُره من ذلك

100. A Man's Dragging his Garment, or a Woman's Trailing her Dress, and Filth Sticking to it, and what is Disliked of that

٢٩٨ أخبرنا مالك، أخبرني محمد بن عمارة بن عامر بن عمرو بن حزم، عن محمد بن إبراهيم بن الحارث التيمي، عن أم ولد لإبراهيم بن عبد الرحمن بن عوف أنها سألت أمَّ سلمةَ زوجَ النبي صلّى الله عليه وسلّم، فقالت: إني امرأةٌ أُطيل ذَيْلي، وأمشي في المكان القَذِر، فقالت أم سلمة: قال رسول الله صلّى الله عليه وسلّم: يطهره ما بعده.

298. Mālik informed us: "Muḥammad ibn ᶜUmārah ibn ᶜĀmir ibn ᶜAmr ibn Ḥazm informed me from Muḥammad ibn Ibrāhīm ibn al-Ḥārith at-Taymī, from a slave woman who was the mother of the children of Ibrāhīm ibn ᶜAbd ar-Raḥmān ibn ᶜAwf, that she told Umm Salamah, the wife of the Prophet ﷺ, 'I am a woman who wears long skirt-tails, and I walk in filthy places.' Umm Salamah said, 'The Messenger of Allah ﷺ said, "That which comes after it purifies it."'"

قال محمد: لا بأس بذلك ما لم يعلق بالذيل قذر، فيكون أكثر من قدر الدرهم الكبير المثقال، فإذا كان كذلك فلا يصلِّيَنَّ فيه حتى يغسله، وهو قول أبي حنيفة رحمه الله .

Muḥammad said: "There is no harm in that, as long as no filth the size of which is more than a large dirham sticks to the garment. Then when it is as much as that, it should not be prayed in until it has been washed. That is the verdict of Abū Ḥanīfah."

١٠١ باب فضل الجهاد

101. The Superiority of *Jihād*

٢٩٩ أخبرنا مالك، حدثنا أبو الزِّناد ، عن الأعرج ، عن أبي هريرة، عن رسول الله قال : مَثَلُ المجاهد في سبيل الله كَمَثَلِ الصائم القانت الذي لا يَفْتُرُ من صيامٍ ولا صلاةٍ حتى يَرْجِع .

299. Mālik informed us: "Abu'z-Zinād narrated to us from al-Aᶜraj from Abū Hurayrah, that the Messenger of Allah ﷺ said, 'The likeness of someone who wages *jihād* in the way of Allah is as the likeness of someone diligently fasting who slackens neither from fasting nor prayer, until he returns.'"

٣٠٠ أخبرنا مالك، حدثنا أبو الزناد، عن الأعرج، عن أبي هريرة قال : قال رسول الله صلّى الله عليه وسلّم: والذي نفسي بيده لَوَدِدْتُ أن أقاتلَ في سبيل الله، فأُقتل ، ثم أُحيى ، فأُقتل ثم أُحيى، فأُقتل. فكان أبو هريرة يقول ثلاثاً: أشهد للّه.

300. Mālik informed us: "Abu'z-Zinād narrated to us from al-Aᶜraj from Abū Hurayrah that the Messenger of Allah ﷺ said, 'By Him in Whose hand is my self, I wish that I could fight in the way of Allah, and be killed, then be brought back to life and killed, then be brought back to life and killed.' And Abū Hurayrah used to say three times, 'I swear by Allah'."

١٠٢ باب ما يكون من الموتِ شهادة

102. What Death is Reckoned a *Shahādah*

٣٠١ أخبرنا مالك، أخبرنا عبد الله بن عبد الله بن جابر بن عتيك، عن عتيك بن الحارث بن عتيك وهو جَدّ عبد الله بن عبد الله بن جابر أي أخبره أن جابر بن عتيك أخبره: أن رسول الله صلّى الله عليه وسلّم جاء يَعُود عَبد الله بنَ ثابت فوجده قد غُلب ، فصاح به فلم يُجبْه، فاسترجع رسولُ الله صلّى الله عليه وسلّم، وقال: غُلبنا عليك يا أبا الربيع فصاح النسوة وبَكَيْنَ، فجعل ابن عتيك يُسْكِتُهُنَّ ، فقال رسول الله صلّى الله عليه وسلّم: دَعْهُنَّ فإذا وجب فلا تَبْكِيَنَّ باكية، قالوا : وما الوجوبَ يا رسول الله؟ قال: إذا مات، قالت ابنته : والله إني كنتُ لأرجو أن تكون شهيداً، فإنك قد كنتَ قضيتَ جِهَازَك ، قال رسول الله صلّى الله عليه وسلّم: إن الله تعالى قد أوقع أجرَه على قدر نيّته، وما تعدّونَ الشهادة؟ قالوا: القتلُ في سبيل الله، قال رسول الله صلّى الله عليه وسلّم: الشهادة سَبْع سوى القتل في سبيل الله: المطعون شهيد، والغريق شهيد، وصاحب ذات الجَنْب شهيد، وصاحب الحريق شهيد، والذي يموت تحت الهدم شهيد، والمرأة تموت بجمع شهيد، والمبطون شهيد.

301. Mālik informed us: "'ᶜAbdullāh ibn ᶜAbdullāh ibn Jābir ibn ᶜAtīk informed us that ᶜAtīk ibn al-Ḥārith ibn ᶜAtīk – the grandfather of ᶜAbdullāh ibn ᶜAbdullāh ibn Jābir – told him that Jābir ibn ᶜAtīk told him that the Messenger of Allah ﷺ came to visit ᶜAbdullāh ibn Thābit and found he had lost consciousness. He called out to him but he didn't respond. The Messenger of Allah ﷺ said, 'We belong to Allah and we are returning to Him', and said, 'We have lost you, Abu'r-Rabīᶜ.' The women cried out and wept, and Ibn ᶜAtīk began silencing them, so the Messenger of Allah ﷺ said, 'Leave them, then when it is settled, let not a woman weep.' They said, 'What is settlement, Messenger of Allah?' He said, 'When he has died.' His daughter said, 'By Allah, I had been expecting you to be a *shahīd*, for you had finished preparing your outfit.' The Messenger of Allah ﷺ said, 'Allah, exalted is He, has rewarded him to the extent of his intention. And what do you count as *shahādah*?' They said, 'Being killed in the way of Allah.' The Messenger of Allah ﷺ said, 'There are seven kinds of *shahādah*, apart from being killed in the way of Allah: someone who dies of plague is a *shahīd*, the drowned person is a *shahīd*, someone who dies of pleurisy is a *shahīd*, someone who dies in a fire is a *shahīd*, someone who dies in a collapsed building is a *shahīd*, the woman who dies in childbirth is a *shahīd*, and someone who dies of stomach disease is a *shahīd*.'"

٣٠٢ أخبرنا مالك، حدثنا سُمَيّ ، عن أبي صالح ، عن أبي هريرة أن رسول الله صلّى الله عليه وسلّم قال : بينما رجلٌ يمشي وَجَد غصنَ شوكٍ على الطريق، فأخَّرَه فشكر اللهُ له فغفَر له، وقال: الشهداء خمسة : المبطون شهيد، والمطعون شهيد، والغريق، وصاحب الهَدْم ، والشهيد في سبيل الله. وقال: لو يعلمُ الناسُ ما في النداء والصفّ الأول ثم لم يجدوا إلاّ أن يَسْتَهِمُوا عليه لاسْتَهَمُوا ، ولو يعلمون ما في التهجير لاسْتَبَقُوا إليه، ولو يعلمون ما في العَتَمَة والصبح لأَتَوْهُما ولو حَبْواً .

302. Mālik informed us: "Sumayy narrated to us from Abū Ṣāliḥ from Abū Hurayrah that the Messenger of Allah ﷺ said, 'As a man was walking, he found a thorny branch on the road. He pulled it away, and Allah appreciated that and forgave him.' And he said, 'There are five *shahīds*: someone who dies of internal disease is a *shahīd*, someone who dies of plague is a *shahīd*, the drowned person, the one in a collapsed building, and the *shahīd* in the way of Allah.' And he said, 'Were the people aware of the value of the call [to prayer] and the first row, they would draw lots for it if they had to. If they were aware of the value of going early to the prayer, they would compete for it. If they were aware of the value of the *ᶜIshā᾽* prayer and the Dawn prayer, they would get there, even if it meant crawling there on their hands and knees.'"

أبواب الجنائز
2. FUNERALS

١ باب المرأة تغسل زوجها
1. A Woman's Washing her Husband's Corpse

٣٠٣ أخبرنا مالك بن أنس، أخبرنا عبد الله بن أبي بكر، أن أسماء بنت عُمَيس امرأة أبي بكر الصديق رضي الله عنه غسلت أبا بكر حين توفي، فخرجت فسألت من حضرها من المهاجرين، فقالت: إني صائمة، وإن هذا يومٌ شديد البرد فهل عليَّ من غسل؟ قالوا: لا.

303. Mālik ibn Anas informed us: "ᶜAbdullāh ibn Abī Bakr informed us that Asmā᾽ bint ᶜUmays, the wife of Abū Bakr aṣ-Ṣiddīq ✽ washed Abū Bakr when he died. Then she came out and asked those of the emigrants who were present, 'I am fasting, and it is an intensely cold day, so must I do *ghusl*?' They said, 'No.'"

قال محمد: وبهذا نأخذ، لا بأس أن تغسل المرأةُ زوجَها إذا توفي، ولا غُسل على من غَسَّلَ الميت ولا وضوء إلاَّ أن يصيبه شيء من ذلك الماء فيغسله.

Muḥammad said: "We adhere to this. There is no harm in a woman's washing her husband when he dies. There is no *ghusl* incumbent on whomever washes the dead, nor *wuḍū᾽*, unless some of that water touch him, in which case he should wash it [off]."

٢ باب ما يُكَفَّن به الميت
2. What the Dead should be Shrouded with

٣٠٤ أخبرنا مالك، أخبرنا ابن شهاب الزُّهري، عن حميد بن عبد الرحمن، عن عبد الله بن عمرو بن العاص أنه قال: الميت يُقمّص ويُؤزّر، ويُلَفُّ بالثوب الثالث، فإن لم يكن إلاَّ ثوبٌ واحد كُفِّنَ فيه.

304. Mālik informed us: "Ibn Shihāb informed us from Ḥumayd ibn ᶜAbd ar-Raḥmān that ᶜAbdullāh ibn ᶜAmr ibn al-ᶜĀṣ said, 'The deceased should be clothed in shirt and *izār* [the large cloth wrapped around the lower half of the body], and wrapped in a third covering. If only one garment can be found, he should be shrouded in that.'"

قال محمد: وبهذا نأخذ، الإزار بجعل لفافة مثل الثوب الآخر أحبُّ إلينا من أن يؤزر، ولا يعجبنا أن ينقص الميت في كفنه من ثوبين إلاَّ من ضرورة، وهو قول أبي حنيفة رحمه الله.

Muḥammad said: "We adhere to this. In addition we prefer the *izār* [the large cloth wrapped around the lower half of the body] being used as a wrapping, like the other piece of fabric, rather than that it being worn in the usual way. We dislike the deceased being shrouded in less than two garments, unless absolutely necessary. That is the verdict of Abū Ḥanīfah, may Allah have mercy on him.

٣ باب المشي بالجنائز والمشي معها

3. Walking with Funeral [Processions] and Accompanying them

٣٠٥ أخبرنا مالك، أخبرنا نافع أن أبا هريرة قال: أَسْرِعوا بجنائزكم فإنما هو خيرٌ تقدِّمونه أو شرٌّ تُلْقُونه عن رقابكم.

305. Mālik informed us: "Nāfi[c] informed us that Abū Hurayrah said, 'Move your funeral [processions] on swiftly, for it is either a good thing you are sending forward, or an evil thing you are removing from your shoulders.'"

قال محمد: وبهذا نأخذ، السرعة بها أحبُّ إلينا من الإبطاء، وهو قول أبي حنيفة رحمه الله.

Muḥammad said: "We adhere to this. We prefer prompt completion to tardiness and delay. That is the verdict of Abū Ḥanīfah, may Allah have mercy on him."

٣٠٦ أخبرنا مالك، حدثنا الزهري قال: كان رسولُ الله صلّى الله عليه وسلّم يمشي أمام الجنازة، والخلفاء هَلُمَّ جرّاً وابن عمر.

306. Mālik informed us: "Az-Zuhrī narrated to us, 'The Messenger of Allah ﷺ used to walk ahead of the funeral [procession], and [so did] the successive khulafāʾ, one after the other, and so did Ibn ʿUmar.'"

٣٠٧ أخبرنا مالك، حدثنا محمد بن المنكدر، عن ربيعة بن عبد الله بن هُدير: أنه رأى عمر بن الخطاب يقْدُمُ الناسَ أمام جنازة زينب بنت جحش.

307. Mālik informed us: "Muḥammad ibn al-Munkadir narrated to us from Rabīʿah ibn ʿAbdullāh ibn Ḥuḍayr that he saw ʿUmar ibn al-Khaṭṭāb leading the people in front of the funeral [procession] of Zaynab bint Jahsh."

قال محمد: المشي أمامها حسن، والمشي خلفها أفضل، وهو قول أبي حنيفة رحمه الله.

Muḥammad said: "Walking in front of it is fine, but walking behind it is better. That is the verdict of Abū Ḥanīfah, may Allah have mercy on him."

٤ باب الميت لا يُتْبَعُ بنارٍ بعد موته أو مِجْمَرة في جنازته

4. The Deceased's not being Followed with Fire, nor with a Brazier in his Funeral[Procession]

٣٠٨ أخبرنا مالك، أخبرنا سعيد بن أبي سعيد المقبري: أنَّ أبا هريرة نهى أن يُتْبَعَ بنارٍ بعد موته أو بمِجْمَرة في جنازته.

308. Mālik informed us: "Saʿīd ibn Abī Saʿīd al-Maqburī informed us that Abū Hurayrah forbade that he should be followed with fire after his death or with a brazier during his funeral."

قال محمد: وبهذا نأخذ وهو قول أبي حنيفة رحمه الله.

Muḥammad said: "We adhere to this; it is the verdict of Abū Ḥanīfah, may Allah have mercy on him."

٥ باب القيام للجنازة

5. Standing [out of respect] for Funeral [Processions]

٣٠٩ أخبرنا مالك، أخبرنا يحيى بن سعيد، عن واقد بن سعد بن معاذ الأنصاري، عن نافع بن جبير بن مطعم، عن معوِّذ بن الحكم، عن علي بن أبي طالب رضي الله عنه: أنّ رسول الله صلّى الله عليه وسلّم كان يقوم في الجنازة، ثم يجلس بعد.

309. Mālik informed us: "Yaḥyā ibn Saᶜīd informed us from Wāqid ibn Saᶜd ibn Muᶜādh al-Anṣārī from Nāfiᶜ ibn Jubayr ibn Muṭᶜim from Muᶜawwidh ibn al-Ḥakam from ᶜAlī ibn Abī Ṭālib ﷺ that the Messenger of Allah ﷺ used to stand for funeral [processions], then later on he used to remain seated."

قال محمد: وبهذا لا نرى القيام للجنائز، كان هذا شيئاً فتُرك، وهو قول أبي حنيفة رحمه الله.

Muḥammad said: "We adhere to this. We do not believe in standing for funeral [processions]. This was a thing practised, then abandoned. That is the verdict of Abū Ḥanīfah, may Allah have mercy on him.

٦ باب الصلاة على الميت والدعاء

6. Praying for the Dead and Supplication

٣١٠ أخبرنا مالك، حدثنا سعيد المقبري، عن أبيه أنه سأل أبا هريرة كيف يصلِّي على الجنازة، فقال: أنا لعمر الله أخبرك، أتَّبعها من أهلها، فإذا وُضعت كبَّرت، فحَمدتُ الله وصلَّيْت على نبيه، ثم قلت: اللهم، عبدُك وابنُ عبدك وابن أَمَتك، كان يشهد أن لا إله إلا أنت وأن محمّداً رسولك وأنت أعلم به، إن كان مُحسناً فَزِدْ في إحسانه، وإن كان مسيئاً فتجاوز عنه، اللّهم لا تَحْرِمْنا أجره ولا تَفْتِنَّا بعده.

310. Mālik informed us: "Saᶜīd al-Maqburī narrated to us from his father that he asked Abū Hurayrah, 'How should the funeral prayer be done?' And he said, 'By the everlasting existence of Allah! I will tell you. Follow it from the family [house], then when [the body] is placed [in the grave] you should say "*Allāhu akbar*", and praise Allah and pray for his Prophet. Then say, "O Allah, [he is] Your slave and the son of Your slave and of Your female slave. He used to witness that there is no god but You and that Muḥammad is Your Messenger, and You know best about him. If he was right acting, then increase him in goodness. If he was a wrongdoer then disregard it. O Allah, do not forbid us his reward, and do not try us after him."'"

قال محمد: وبهذا نأخذ، لا قراءة على الجنازة، وهو قول أبي حنيفة رحمه الله.

Muḥammad said: "We adhere to this. There should be no recitation [of

Qurʾān] in the funeral prayer. That is the verdict of Abū Ḥanīfah, may Allah have mercy on him."

٣١١ أخبرنا مالك، حدثنا نافع: أن ابن عمر كان إذا صلّى على جنازة سلّم حتى يُسمع من يليه .
311. Mālik informed us: "Nāfiᶜ narrated to us that when Ibn ᶜUmar prayed the funeral prayer he used to say *as-salāmu ᶜalaykum* so that the person next to him could hear [him]."

قال محمد: وبهذا نأخذ، يسلم عن يمينه ويساره، ويُسمع من يليه، وهو قول أبي حنيفة رحمه الله.
Muḥammad said: "We adhere to this. He should say *as-salāmu ᶜalaykum* to his right and his left, making it audible to the person next to him. That is the verdict of Abū Ḥanīfah, may Allah have mercy on him."

٣١٢ أخبرنا مالك، حدثنا نافع: أن ابن عمر كان يصلّي على الجنازة بعد العصر وبعد الصبح إذا صُلّيَتا لوقتهما .
312. Mālik informed us: "Nāfiᶜ narrated to us that Ibn ᶜUmar would pray the funeral prayer after the prayer of *ᶜAṣr* or *Ṣubḥ*, if they had been prayed on time."

قال محمد: وبهذا نأخذ لا بأس بالصلاة على الجنازة في تَيْنِكَ الساعتين ما لم تطلع الشمس، أو تتغيَّر الشمسُ بصُفْرة للمغيب ، وهو قول أبي حنيفة رحمه الله .
Muḥammad said: "We adhere to this. There is no harm in praying the funeral prayer in these two times, as long as the sun has not risen, or changed to yellow when setting. That is the verdict of Abū Ḥanīfah, may Allah have mercy on him.

٧ باب الصلاة على الجنازة في المسجد

7. Praying the Funeral Prayer in the Mosque

٣١٣ أخبرنا مالك، أخبرنا نافع، عن ابن عمر أنه قال: ما صُلِّيَ على عمر إلا في المسجد .
313. Mālik informed us: "Nāfiᶜ informed us that Ibn ᶜUmar said, 'ᶜUmar was prayed over in the mosque only.'"

قال محمد: لا يُصَلَّى على جنازة في المسجد، وكذلك بلغنا عن أبي هريرة . وموضع الجنازة بالمدينة خارج من المسجد وهو الموضع الذي كان النبي صلّى الله عليه وسلّم يصلّي على الجنازة فيه.
Muḥammad said: "The funeral prayer is not to be prayed in the mosque; that is how it has come to us from Abū Hurayrah. The place for funerals in Madīnah is outside the mosque, the place where the Prophet ﷺ used to pray the funeral prayer."

٨ باب يحمل الرجل الميت أو يحنِّطه أو يغسله هل ينقض ذلك وضوءه؟

8. A Man's Carrying the Deceased, or Preparing him [for Burial], or Washing him: Does that Undo his *Wuḍūʾ*?

٣١٤ أخبرنا مالك، أخبرنا نافع: أنَّ عمرَ حَنَّط ابناً لسعيد بن زيد وحَمَله ثم دخل المسجد فصلّى ولم يتوضأ.
314. Mālik informed us: "Nāfiᶜ informed us that Ibn ᶜUmar prepared a son of

Saʿīd ibn Zayd [for burial] and carried him, then went into the mosque and prayed, without performing *wuḍūʾ*."

قال محمد: وبهذا نأخذ، لا وضوء على من حمل جنازة ولا من حنَّط ميتاً أو كفَّنه أو غسله، وهو قول أبي حنيفة رحمه الله.

Muḥammad said: "We adhere to this. Performing *wuḍūʾ* is not incumbent upon someone who carries the bier, nor upon someone who prepares the dead, or shrouds him, or washes him. That is the verdict of Abū Ḥanīfah, may Allah have mercy on him."

٩ باب الرجل تدركه الصلاة على الجنازة وهو على غير وضوء

9. A Man's not having *Wuḍūʾ* when the Funeral Prayer is Held

٣١٥ أخبرنا مالك، أخبرنا نافع، عن ابن عمر أنه كان يقول: لا يصلّي الرجل على جنازة إلاَّ وهو طاهر.

315. Mālik informed us: "Nāfiʿ informed us that Ibn ʿUmar used to say, 'A man should not pray the funeral prayer, unless he is pure.'"

قال محمد: وبهذا نأخذ، لا ينبغي أن يصلي على الجنازة إلاَّ طاهر، فإن فاجأته وهو على غير طهور تيمّم، وصلّى عليها وهو قول أبي حنيفة رحمه الله.

Muḥammad said: "We adhere to this. No one should pray the funeral prayer unless he is pure. If it takes place unexpectedly, he should perform *tayammum* and pray. That is the verdict of Abū Ḥanīfah, may Allah have mercy on him."

١٠ باب الصلاة على الميت بعد ما يُدفن

10. Praying Over the Deceased after he is Buried

٣١٦ أخبرنا مالك، أخبرنا ابن شهاب، عن سعيد بن المسيّب: أن رسول الله صلّى الله عليه وسلّم نعى النجاشيَّ في اليوم الذي مات فيه، فخرج بهم إلى المصلّى، فصفَّ بهم وكبَّر عليه أربع تكبيرات.

316. Mālik informed us: "Ibn Shihāb informed us from Saʿīd ibn al-Musayyab that the Messenger of Allah ﷺ announced the death of the Negus on the day on which he died, and proceeded with them to the place of prayer, arranged them in rows, and declared *Allāhu akbar* for him four times."

٣١٧ أخبرنا مالك، أخبرنا ابن شهاب، أن أبا أُمامة بن سهل بن حُنيف، أخبره أنَّ مسكينة مَرِضت، فأُخبر رسول الله صلّى الله عليه وسلّم بمرضها، قال: وكان رسول الله صلّى الله عليه وسلّم يعود المساكين ويسأل عنهم، قال: فقال رسول الله صلّى الله عليه وسلّم: إذا ماتَتْ فآذنوني بها، قال: فأُتي بجنازتها ليلاً، فكرهوا أنْ يُؤذنوا رسولَ الله صلّى الله عليه وسلّم بالليل فلما أصبح رسول الله صلّى الله عليه وسلّم أُخبر بالذي كان من شأنها، فقال رسول الله صلّى الله عليه وسلّم: ألم آمركم أن تُؤْذِنُوْني؟ فقالوا: يا رسول الله كرهنا أن نخرجَك ليلاً أو نوقظك، قال: فخرج رسول الله صلّى الله عليه وسلّم حتى صفَّ بالناس على قبرها فصلى على قبرها فكبَّر أربع تكبيرات.

317. Mālik informed us: "Ibn Shihāb informed us that Abū Umāmah ibn Sahl ibn Ḥunayf told him that a poor woman fell sick, and the Messenger of Allah ﷺ was informed of her sickness. [Abū Umāmah] said, 'The Messenger of Allah ﷺ used to visit the the poor and ask after them.' He said, 'So the Messenger of Allah ﷺ said, "When she dies, call me."' [Abū Umāmah] said, 'She died in the night, and they were reluctant to call the Messenger of Allah ﷺ at night. When the morning came, the Messenger of Allah ﷺ was told of what had happened to her, and the Messenger of Allah ﷺ said, "Didn't I tell you to call me?" They said, "Messenger of Allah, we were reluctant to call you out at night, or wake you."' [Abū Umāmah] said, 'The Messenger of Allah ﷺ went out and arranged the people by her grave, and prayed there, declaring four times, *Allāhu akbar*.'"

قال محمد : وبهذا نأخذ التكبير على الجنازة أربع تكبيرات ولا ينبغي أن يصلِّي على جنازة قد صلِّي عليها ، وليس النبي صلّى الله عليه وسلّم في هذا كغيره ، ألا يُرى أنه صلى على النجاشي بالمدينة وقد مات بالحبشة . فصلاة رسول الله صلّى الله عليه وسلّم بركة وطهور فليست كغيرها من الصلوات، وهو قول أبي حنيفة رحمه الله .

Muḥammad said: "We adhere to this. *Allāhu akbar* should be declared four times over the dead. A funeral prayer ought not be prayed, which has already been prayed. Nor, with regard to this, is the Prophet ﷺ like anyone else. Did he not pray for the Negus in Madīnah when he had died in Abyssinia? The prayer of the Messenger of Allah ﷺ is blessing and cleansing; it is not like other prayers. That is the verdict of Abū Ḥanīfah, may Allah have mercy on him."

١١ باب ما روي أنّ الميت يعذَّب ببكاء الحيّ

11. What is Reported of the Deceased's being Punished for the Weeping of the Living

٣١٨ أخبرنا مالك، حدثنا عبد الله بن دينار، عن ابن عمر أنه قال : لا تَبْكوا على موتاكم، فإنَّ الميت يُعذَّب ببكاء أهله عليه .

318. Mālik informed us: "ᶜAbdullāh ibn Dīnār narrated to us that Ibn ᶜUmar said, 'Do not cry over your dead, for the deceased is punished for the crying of his family over him.'"

٣١٩ أخبرنا مالك، حدثنا عبد الله بن أبي بكر ، عن أبيه عن عَمْرة ابنة عبد الرحمن أنها أخبرته أنها سمعت عائشةَ رضي الله عنها زوجَ النبيّ صلّى الله عليه وسلّم و ذُكر لها أن عبد الله بن عمر يقول : إنّ الميت يُعذَّب ببكاء الحيّ، فقالت عائشة : يغفر الله لابن عمر، أمَا إنه لم يَكْذب ، ولكنه قد نسي أو أخطأ ، إنما مرَّ رسول الله صلّى الله عليه وسلّم على جنازة يُبكى عليها، فَقال: إنهم ليَبْكون عليها، وإنها لتُعذَّب في قبرها .

319. Mālik informed us: "ᶜAbdullāh ibn Abī Bakr narrated to us from his father that ᶜAmrah bint ᶜAbd ar-Raḥmān told him that she heard ᶜĀ᾿ishah ﵂

the wife of the Prophet ﷺ, when she was told that ᶜAbdullāh ibn ᶜUmar was saying that the deceased is punished for the crying of the living, so ᶜĀʾishah said, 'May Allah forgive Ibn ᶜUmar. It is not that he has lied; rather he has forgotten or misunderstood. It is just that the Messenger of Allah ﷺ passed by a funeral being cried over, and said, "They cry over her, and she is being punished in her grave."'"

قال محمد : وبقول عائشة رضي الله عنها نأخذ وهو قول أبي حنيفة رحمه الله .

Muḥammad said: "We adhere to the verdict of ᶜĀʾishah, and it is the verdict of Abū Ḥanīfah, may Allah have mercy on him."

١٢ باب القبر يُتّخذ مسجداً أو يُصلّى إليه أو يُتوسَّد

12. A Grave being Taken as a Mosque, or being Prayed to, or being Used as a Headrest

٣٢٠ أخبرنا مالك، حدثنا الزهري، عن سعيد بن المسيّب، عن أبي هريرة: أن رسول الله صلّى الله عليه وسلّم قال: قاتل اللهُ اليهودَ اتّخذوا قبورَ أنبيائهم مساجد .

320. Mālik informed us: "Az-Zuhrī narrated to us from Saᶜīd ibn al-Musayyab from Abū Hurayrah that the Messenger of Allah ﷺ said, 'May Allah fight the jews! They took the graves of their prophets as mosques.'"

٣٢١ أخبرنا مالك، قال : بلغني أنَّ عليَّ بن أبي طالب رضي الله عنه كان يتوسَّدُ عليها ويضطجع عليها . قال بشر: يعني القبور .

321. Mālik informed us: "It has reached me that ᶜAlī ibn Abī Ṭālib ﷺ used to lean on them and lie on them." Bishr said, "He meant graves."

كتاب الزكاة
3. ZAKĀH

١ باب زكاة المال
1. *Zakāh* Due on Wealth

٣٢٢ أخبرنا مالك، أخبرنا الزُّهري، عن السائب بن يزيد، أنَّ عثمان بن عفان رضي الله عنه كان يقول: هذا شهر زكاتكم، فمن كان عليه دَيْن فليؤدِّ دَيْنه حتى تحصل أموالكم فتؤدوا منها الزكاة.

322. Mālik informed us: "Az-Zuhrī informed us from as-Sā'ib ibn Yazīd that ʿUthmān ibn ʿAffān ﷺ used to say, 'This is the month of your *zakāh,* so whoever has a debt to pay, let him discharge his debt, so that you can sort out your wealth and hand over the *zakāh* from it.'"

قال محمد: وبهذا نأخذ، من كان عليه دَيْن وله مال فليدفع دَيْنه من ماله، فإن بقي بعد ذلك ما تجبُ فيه الزكاة ففيه زكاة، وتلك مائتا درهم أو عشرون مثقالاً ذهباً فصاعداً، وإن كان الذي بقي أقل من ذلك، بعد ما يَدفع من ماله الدَّيْن فليست فيه الزكاة، وهو قول أبي حنيفة رحمه الله.

Muḥammad said: "We adhere to this. Whoever has a debt to pay, and he has property, then let him pay his debt from his property. If, after that, there remains that upon which *zakāh* is incumbent, then it is incumbent; that being two hundred dirhams, or twenty mithqals of gold or more. If what remains is less than that, after paying the debt from his property, then no *zakāh* is incumbent upon it. That is the verdict of Abū Ḥanīfah, may Allah have mercy on him."

٣٢٣ أخبرنا مالك، أخبرنا يزيد بن خُصيفة أنه سأل سليمان بن يسار عن رجل له مال وعليه مثلُه من الدَّيْن أ عليه الزكاة؟ فقال: لا.

323. Mālik informed us: "Yazīd ibn Khusayfah informed us that he asked Sulaymān ibn Yasār about a man who has property and has a debt the like of it to pay, 'Is *zakāh* due on it?' And he said, 'No.'"

قال محمد: وبهذا نأخذ وهو قول أبي حنيفة رحمه الله.

Muḥammad said: "We adhere to this, and it is the verdict of Abū Ḥanīfah, may Allah have mercy on him."

٢ باب ما يجب فيه الزكاة
2. What *Zakāh* is Due Upon

٣٢٤ أخبرنا مالك، أخبرنا محمَّدُ بنُ عبد الله بنِ عبد الرحمن بنِ أبي صعصعة، عن أبيه، عن أبي

سعيد الخُدْري رضي الله عنه أنّ رسول الله ﷺ قال: ليس فيما دون خمسة أَوْسُقٍ من التمر صدقة وليس فيما دون خمسِ أواق من الوَرِق صدقة، وليس فيما دون خمس ذَوْدٍ من الإبل صدقة.

324. Mālik informed us: "Muḥammad ibn ʿAbdullāh ibn ʿAbd ar-Raḥmān ibn Abī Ṣaʿṣaʿah informed us from his father from Abū Saʿīd al-Khudrī that the Messenger of Allah ﷺ said, 'There is no *zakāh* to pay on less than five *wasqs* (three hundred *ṣāʿ*) of dates, nor is there any *zakāh* to pay on less than five *uqiyah* (two hundred dirhams) of silver, nor is there any *zakāh* to pay on less than five camels.'"

قال محمد: وبهذا نأخذ، وكان أبو حنيفة يأخذ بذلك إلاّ في خصلة واحدة، فإنه كان يقول: فيما أخرجت الأرض العُشْرُ من قليلٍ أو كثير، إن كانت تُشْرَبُ سيحاً أو تسقيها السماء، وإن كانت تُشْرَبُ بغَرب أو دالية فنصفُ عُشر، وهو قول إبراهيم النَّخَعي ومجاهد.

Muḥammad said: "We adhere to this, and Abū Ḥanīfah used to agree with it, except in one instance, for he used to say, 'One tenth [is due] upon what the earth puts forth, one tenth [is due], whether from a small or a large amount, if it is watered by streams, or rain from the heavens. If it is watered by buckets or levers, then one twentieth [is due]. That is the verdict of Ibrāhīm an-Nakhaʿī, and Mujāhid.'"

٣ باب المال متى تجب فيه الزكاة

3. When *Zakāh* Becomes Incumbent upon Wealth

٣٢٥ أخبرنا مالك، أخبرنا نافع، عن ابن عمر قال: لا تجبُ في مالٍ زكاةٌ حتى يَحولَ عليه الحَوْل.

325. Mālik informed us: "Nāfiʿ informed us that Ibn ʿUmar said, 'No *zakāh* becomes incumbent upon wealth until a whole year goes by.'"

قال محمد: وبهذا نأخذ، وهو قول أبي حنيفة رحمه الله، إلاّ أن يكتسب مالاً فيجمعه إلى مال عنده مما يُزكّى، فإذا وجبت الزكاة في الأول زكّى الثاني معه، وهو قول أبي حنيفة وإبراهيم النَّخَعي رحمهما الله تعالى.

Muḥammad said: "We adhere to this, and it is the verdict of Abū Ḥanīfah, may Allah have mercy on him, unless someone earns wealth and adds it to some wealth he has, upon which he pays *zakāh*, for when the *zakāh* becomes incumbent upon the first, he should pay the *zakāh* of the second with it. That is the verdict of Abū Ḥanīfah, and Ibrāhīm an-Nakhaʿī, may Allah, exalted is He, have mercy on them."

٤ باب الرجل يكون له الدَّيْن هل عليه فيه زكاة

4. A Man to whom a Debt is Due; Must he Pay *Zakāh* upon it?

٣٢٦ أخبرنا مالك، أخبرنا محمد بن عقبة مولى الزبير أنه سأل القاسم بن محمد عن مكاتَب له قاطعه بمال عظيم؟ قال: قلت: هل فيه زكاة؟ قال القاسم: إن أبا بكر كان لا يأخُذُ من مالٍ صدقةً

حتى يحول عليه الحول، قال القاسم: وكان أبو بكر إذا أعطى الناسَ أَعْطياتهم يسأل الرجل هل عندك من مالٍ قد وجبت فيه الزكاة؟ فإن قال: نَعَمْ، أخذ من عطائه زكاةَ ذلكَ المال، وإن قال لا، سلَّم إليه عطاءه.

326. Mālik informed us: "Muḥammad ibn ᶜUqbah, the *mawlā* of az-Zubayr, informed us that he asked al-Qāsim ibn Muḥammad about a *mukātab* slave of his [with whom he had written a contract with the slave for the purchase of his freedom], whom he had set free earlier than the contracted term for a great amount of money, 'Is *zakāh* due upon it?' Al-Qāsim said, 'Abū Bakr did not take any *zakāh* from money until a whole year went by on it.' Al-Qāsim said [also], 'Abū Bakr, before he released people's allowances to them, he would ask them, "Have you any money upon which the *zakāh* has become due?" Then if they said, "Yes," he would take the *zakāh* due on that money from their allowance, and if they said, "No," he would release their allowance to them.'"

قال محمد: وبهذا نأخذ، وهو قول أبي حنيفة رحمه الله.

Muḥammad said: "We adhere to this, and it is the verdict of Abū Ḥanīfah, may Allah have mercy on him."

٣٢٧ أخبرنا مالك، أخبرني عمر بن حسين، عن عائشة بنت قدامة بن مظعون، عن أبيها قال: كنت إذا قبضتُ عطائي من عثمان بن عفان سألني هل عندك مالٌ وَجَبَ عليك فيه الزكاة؟ فإن قلت: نَعَمْ، أخذ من عطائي زكاة ذلك المال وإلاَّ دفع إليَّ عطائي.

327. Mālik informed us: "ᶜUmar ibn Ḥusayn informed me from ᶜĀ᾽ishah bint Qudāmah ibn Maẓᶜūn that her father said, 'When I used to collect my allowance from ᶜUthmān ibn ᶜAffān, he would ask me, "Do you have money upon which the *zakāh* is due?" Then if I said, "Yes," he would take the *zakāh* due on that money from my allowance; otherwise he would pay me my allowance.'"

٥ باب زكاة الحُليّ

5. *Zakāh* Due on Jewellery

٣٢٨ أخبرنا مالك، عن عبد الرحمن بن قاسم، عن أبيه: أن عائشة كانت تلي بنات أخيها يتامى في حِجْرها، لهن حُلِيّ، فلا تُخرج من حُلِيِّهنّ الزكاة.

328. Mālik informed us from ᶜAbd ar-Raḥmān ibn al-Qāsim,from his father that ᶜĀ᾽ishah used to take care of her brother's daughters, as orphans in her custody, and they had jewellery but she would not pay out *zakāh* from their jewellery.

٣٢٩ أخبرنا مالك، حدثنا نافع: أن ابن عمر كان يُحَلِّي بناته وجواريه فلا يُخرج من حُلِيِّهنّ الزكاة.

329. Mālik informed us: "Nāfiᶜ narrated to us that Ibn ᶜUmar used to adorn his daughters and his female slaves [with jewellery] but would not pay *zakāh* on their jewellery."

قال محمد : أمّا ما كان من حُلِيّ جوهرٍ ولؤلؤٍ فليست فيه الزكاة على كل حال ، وأمّا ما كان من حُلِيٍّ ذهبٍ أو فضة ففيه الزكاة إلاّ أن يكونَ ذلكَ ليتيم أو يتيمة لم يَبْلُغا فلا تكون في مَالِهَا زكاة وهو قول أبي حنيفة رحمه الله .

Muḥammad said: "As for jewellery consisting of gems and pearls, there is no *zakāh* due on that, whatever the case, but if it is gold and silver jewellery, then *zakāh* is due upon it, unless it belongs to an orphan, boy or girl, who has not come of age, in which case there is no *zakāh* due on their money. That is the verdict of Abū Ḥanīfah, may Allah have mercy on him."

٦ باب العُشْر

6. The ᶜ*Ushr* – Tenth

٣٣٠ أخبرنا مالك، حدثنا الزُّهريّ، عن سالم بن عبد الله، عن عبد الله بن عمر : أن عمر كان يأخذ عن النَّبَط من الحنطة والزيت نصفَ العُشُر، يريد أن يكثر الحِمل إلى المدينة، ويأخذ من القِطنية العشر .

330. Mālik informed us: "Az-Zuhrī narrated to us from Sālim ibn ᶜAbdullāh from ᶜAbdullāh ibn ᶜUmar that ᶜUmar used to take from the Nabataeans a twentieth part of their corn and oil, aiming to increase their conveyance to Madīnah, while taking a tenth part of their pulses."

قال محمد : يؤخذ من أهل الذمة مما اختلفوا فيه للتجارة من قِطَنيَّةٍ أو غير قطنية نصف العشر في كل سنة، ومن أهل الحرب إذا دخلوا أرض الإسلام بأمان العشرَ من ذلك كلّه . وكذلك أمر عمر بن الخطاب زياد بن حُدَيْر وأنس بن مالك حين بعثهما على عشور الكوفة والبصرة، وهو قول أبي حنيفة رحمه الله .

Muḥammad said: "From the people of dhimmah, a twentieth should be taken out of what they trade in, whether of pulses or whatever else, every year. From people of *dār al-ḥarb* [the lands with which Muslims are at war], who enter the land of Islam under protection, a tenth [should be taken] from all that. That is how ᶜUmar ibn al-Khaṭṭāb instructed Ziyād ibn Ḥuḍayr and Anas ibn Mālik, when he put them in charge of the levies of the ᶜ*ushr* [tenth] in Kūfa and Baṣra. That is the verdict of Abū Ḥanīfah, may Allah have mercy on him."

٧ باب الجزية

7. The *Jizyah*

٣٣١ أخبرنا مالك، حدثنا الزهري : أنَّ النبيَّ صلّى الله عليه وسلّم أخذ من مجوس البحرين الجزية، وأن عمر أخذها من مجوس فارس ، وأخذها عثمان بن عفان من البربر .

331. Mālik informed us: "Az-Zuhrī narrated to us that the Prophet ﷺ took the *jizyah* from the Magians of Bahrain, and that ᶜUmar took it from the Magians of Persia, and ᶜUthmān ibn ᶜAffān took it from the Berbers."

٣٣٢ أخبرنا مالك، حدثنا نافع، عن أسلم مولى عمر: أن عُمَرَ ضَرَبَ الجزيةَ على أهل الوَرِق أربعين درهماً، وعلى أهل الذهب أربعة دنانير، ومع ذلك أرزاق المسلمين وضيافة ثلاثة أيام.

332. Mālik informed us: "Nāfiʿ narrated to us, from Aslam, the *mawlā* of ʿUmar, that ʿUmar imposed the *jizyah* as forty dirhams on the people who use silver, and four dīnārs on the people who use gold, and, in addition to that, provisions for Muslims and hospitality for three days."

٣٣٣ أخبرنا مالك، أخبرنا زيد بن أسلم، عن أبيه: أن عمر بن الخطاب رضي الله عنه كان يُؤتى بنَعَم كثيرة من نَعَم الجزية. قال مالك: أُراه تُؤخذ من أهل الجزية في جزيتهم.

333. Mālik informed us: "Zayd ibn Aslam informed us from his father that ʿUmar ibn al-Khaṭṭāb ؈ used to be brought much cattle from the cattle of the *jizyah*." Mālik said, "I see that as being taken from those subect to the *jizyah* in settlement of what is due from them."

قال محمد: السُّنَّة أن تؤخذ الجزية من المجوس من غير أن تُنكحَ نساؤهم ولا تُؤكل ذبائحهم، وكذلك بلغنا عن النبي صلى الله عليه وسلم، وضرب عمر الجزية على أهل سواد الكوفة، على المُعسر اثنا عشر درهماً وعلى الوسط أربعة وعشرين درهما، وعلى الغني ثمانية وأربعين درهماً. وأما ما ذَكَر مالك بن أنس من الإبل فإن عمر بن الخطاب لم يأخذ الإبل في جزية علمناها إلاَّ من بني تَغْلِب فإنه أضعف عليهم الصدقة، فجعل ذلك جزيتهم، فأخذ من إبلهم وبقرهم وغنمهم.

Muḥammad said: "The *Sunnah* is that the *jizyah* be taken from the Magians, even though their woman are not to be married nor their slaughtered animals eaten [by Muslims]; and that is how report has reached us from the Prophet ؈. ʿUmar imposed the *jizyah* on the population of Kūfa as twelve dirhams on those in hardship, twenty-four dirhams on the main body, and forty-eight dirhams on the rich. As for what Mālik ibn Anas spoke about of camels, we are not aware that ʿUmar ibn al-Khaṭṭāb took camels in any levy of the *jizyah*, except from Banū Taghlib, because he doubled the *zakāh* for them and made that their *jizyah*, and he took from their camels, cattle, sheep and goats."

٨ باب زكاة الرقيق والخيل والبَراذين
8. Zakāh due on Slaves, Horses and Persian Horses

٣٣٤ أخبرنا مالك، حدثنا عبد الله بن دينار، قال: سألت سعيد بن المسيب عن صَدَقَة البراذين فقال: أوَفي الخيلِ صدقة؟

334. Mālik informed us: "ʿAbdullāh ibn Dīnār narrated to us, 'I asked Saʿīd ibn al-Musayyab about the *zakāh* of Persian horses, and he said, 'Is there any *zakāh* due on horses?'"

٣٣٥ أخبرنا مالك، حدثنا عبد الله بن دينار، عن سليمان بن يسار، عن عِراك بن مالك، عن أبي هريرة قال: قال رسول الله صلى الله عليه وسلم: ليس على المسلم في عبده ولا في فرسه صدقة.

335. Mālik informed us: "ʿAbdullāh ibn Dīnār narrated to us from Sulaymān ibn Yasār from 'Irak ibn Mālik that Abū Hurayrah said, 'The Messenger of

Allah ﷻ said, "There is no *ṣadaqah* [*zakāh*] due from a Muslim upon what he has of slaves or horses.'""

قال محمد : وبهذا نأخذ ليس في الخيل صدقة سائمةً كانت أو غير سائمة . وأما في قوله أبي حنيفة رحمه الله: فإذا كانت سائمةً يُطلب نسلها ففيها الزكاة، إن شئتَ في كل فرس دينار، وإن شئت فالقيمة، ثم في كل مائتي درهم خمسةُ دراهم وهو قول إبراهيم النَّخَعي .

Muḥammad said: "We adhere to this; there is no *ṣadaqah* [*zakāh*] due upon horses, whether breeding or non-breeding. As for the verdict according to Abū Ḥanīfah, may Allah have mercy on him, if it is breeding, its offspring are highly sought, then the *zakāh* is due on it, either as a dīnār on every horse, or by value: on every two hundred dirhams, five dirhams. That is the verdict of Ibrāhīm an-Nakhaᶜī."

٣٣٦ أخبرنا مالك، حدثنا عبد الله بن أبي بكر، عن أبيه : أن عمرَ بن عبد العزيز كتب إليه أن لا يأخذ من الخيل ولا العسل صدقة .

336. Mālik informed us: "ᶜAbdullāh ibn Abī Bakr narrated to us from his father, that ᶜUmar ibn ᶜAbd al-ᶜAzīz wrote to him, saying, not to take *zakāh* from either horses or honey."

قال محمد : أما الخيل فهي على ما وصفتُ لك، وأما العسل ففيه العُشُر إذا أصبتَ منه الشيءَ الكبير خمسةَ أفراق فصاعداً، وأما أبو حنيفة فقال : في قليله وكثيره العشر ، وقد بلغنا عن النبي صلّى الله عليه وسلّم أنه جعل في العسل العشر.

Muḥammad said: "As for horses, they are as I have stated. As for honey, a tenth is due if you come by a large amount, five *faraq* [fifteen *ṣāᶜ*] or more. As for Abū Ḥanīfah, he said that a tenth is due, whether it is a large amount or a small amount. And it has reached us that the Prophet ﷺ stipulated a tenth on honey."

٣٣٧ أخبرنا مالك، حدثنا ابن شهاب، عن سليمان بن يسار : أن أهل الشام قالوا لأبي عُبَيْدَةَ بن الجرّاح : خذ من خيلنا ورقيقنا صدقة، فأبى ، ثم كتب إلى عمر بن الخطاب، فكتب إليه عمر: إنْ أحبّوا فخُذْها منهم، وارْدُدْها عليهم يعني على فقرائهم، وارزق رقيقهم.

337. Mālik informed us: "Ibn Shihāb narrated to us from Sulaymān ibn Yasār that the people of Shām said to Abū ᶜUbaydah ibn al-Jarrāḥ, 'Take *zakāh* from our horses and slaves,' and he refused. Then he wrote to ᶜUmar ibn al-Khaṭṭāb and ᶜUmar wrote to him, saying, 'If they like, take it from them and redistribute it amongst them,' – meaning, amongst their poor – 'and provide for their slaves.'"

قال محمد: القول في هذا القول الأول ، وليس في فرس المسلم صدقة ولا في عبده إلاّ صدقة الفطر .

Muḥammad said: "The verdict concerning this is the original verdict. There is no *ṣadaqah* [*zakāh*] due on the horses of a Muslim, nor on his slaves, except the *ṣadaqah* of breaking fast [*zakāt al-Fiṭr*]."

٩ باب الركاز

9. Mineral Deposits

٣٣٨ أخبرنا مالك، حدثنا ربيعة بن أبي عبد الرحمن وغيرهُ : أن رسول الله صلّى الله عليه وسلّم أَقْطَعَ لبلال بن الحارث المُزني معادنَ من معادن القَبَلية ، وهو من ناحية الفُرُع ، فتلك المعادن إلى اليوم لا يُؤخذ منها إلاّ الزكاة .

338. Mālik informed us: "Rabīᶜah ibn Abī ᶜAbd ar-Raḥmān and others narrated to us that the Messenger of Allah ﷺ set apart for Bilāl ibn al-Ḥārith al-Muzanī some of the mines of al-Qabaliyyah, which is in the direction of Furuᶜ, and, until this day, nothing is taken from those mines except *zakāh*."

قال محمد : الحديث المعروف أنَّ النبي صلّى الله عليه وسلّم قال : في الركاز الخُمُس ، قيل : يا رسول الله، وما الركاز؟ قال: المال الذي خلقه الله تعالى في الأرض يوم خَلَق السموات والأرض في هذه المعادن، ففيها الخمس . وهو قول أبي حنيفة رحمه الله تعالى والعامة من فقهائنا .

Muḥammad said: "The recognised *ḥadīth* is that the Prophet ﷺ said, 'From *rikaz* [mineral deposits] one fifth is due. Someone said, 'Messenger of Allah, what are *rikaz*?' He said, 'That wealth which Allah, exalted is He, formed in the earth, the day He formed the heavens and the earth.' So, from these mines, one fifth is due. That is the verdict of Abū Ḥanīfah, may Allah, exalted is He, have mercy on him, and the verdict of our *fuqahā᾽* in general."

١٠ باب صدقة البقر

10. The *Zakāh* due on Cows

٣٣٩ أخبرنا مالك، أخبرنا حميد بن قيس، عن طاوس : أنَّ رسول الله صلّى الله عليه وسلّم بَعَثَ معاذَ بنَ الجبل إلى اليمن، فأمره أن يأخذ من كلِّ ثلاثين بقرةً تبيعاً ومن كل أربعين مُسنَّةً ، فأُتي بها دون ذلك ، فأبى أن يأخذ منه شيئاً، وقال: لم أسمع فيه من رسول الله صلّى الله عليه وسلّم شيئاً حتى أرجع إليه، فتوفي رسول الله صلّى الله عليه وسلّم قبل أن يَقْدَمَ معاذ .

339. Mālik informed us: "Ḥumayd ibn Qays informed us from Ṭāwūs, that the Messenger of Allah ﷺ sent Muᶜādh ibn Jabal to the Yemen, ordering him to take a yearling from every thirty cows, and a two-year-old from every forty. So someone came to him with less than that, and he refused to take anything from it, saying, 'I didn't hear anything from the Messenger of Allah ﷺ concerning it. [I will] not [take anything from it] until I return to him.' And then the Messenger of Allah ﷺ died before Muᶜādh arrived."

قال محمد : وبهذا نأخذ ليس في أقلَّ من ثلاثين من البقر زكاة، فإذا كانت ثلاثين ففيها تبيعٌ أو تبيعة، والتبيع الجَذَع الحَوْلي، إلى أربعين، فإذا بلغت أربعين ففيها مُسِنَّة، وهو قول أبي حنيفة رحمه الله تعالى والعامَّة.

Muḥammad said: "We adhere to this. There is no *zakāh* due on less than thirty cows. Then if there are thirty, a yearling, male or female is due – and a yearling is one which has completed a year and begun its second year –, likewise until there are forty. When there are forty, a two-year-old is due. And That is the verdict of Abū Ḥanīfah, may Allah have mercy on him, and [our *fuqahā*ʾ] in general."

باب الكنز ١١

11. Treasure Trove

٣٤٠ أخبرنا مالك، حدثنا نافع قال: سُئل ابن عمر عن الكنز، فقال: هو المالُ الذي لا تُؤدَّى زكاتُه.

340. Mālik informed us: "Nāfiᶜ narrated to us, 'Ibn ᶜUmar was asked about treasure trove, and he said, "It is that wealth, the *zakāh* of which is not handed over."'"

٣٤١ أخبرنا مالك، حدثنا عبد الله بن دينار، عن أبي صالح، عن أبي هريرة قال: من كان له مالٌ، ولم يؤدِّ زكاته مُثِّلَ له يومَ القيامة شجاعاً أقْرَعَ، له زبيبتان يَطْلُبُهُ حتى يُمْكِنَه فيقول: أنا كنزك.

341. Mālik informed us: "ᶜAbdullāh ibn Dīnār narrated to us from Abū Ṣāliḥ that Abū Hurayrah said, 'Whoever has wealth and does not hand over its *zakāh,* then on the Day of Rising, it will be made into a hideous serpent with two carbuncles, which chases him until it corners him and says, "I am your treasure."'"

١٢ باب من تحل له الزكاة

12. To Whom Zakāh is Allowed

٣٤٢ أخبرنا مالك، حدثنا زيد بن أسلم، عن عطاء بن يسار: أنَّ رسول الله صلّى الله عليه وسلّم قال: لا تَحلُّ الصدقةُ لغنيٍّ إلاَّ لخمسة: لغازٍ في سبيل الله، أو لعاملٍ عليها، أو لغارمٍ، أو لرجل اشتراها بماله أو لرجل له جار مسكين تُصُدِّقَ على المسكين فأهدى إلى الغنيِّ.

342. Mālik informed us: "Zayd ibn Aslam narrated to us from ᶜAṭāʾ ibn Yasār that the Messenger of Allah ﷺ said, 'Ṣadaqah [*zakāh*] is not allowed for someone not in need, except in five cases: someone going forth to fight in the way of Allah, someone put in charge of collecting and distributing it, a debtor, a man who buys it with his own money, or a man who has a poor neighbour; it being given to the poor person, who gives it to someone who is not in need.'"

قال محمد: وبهذا نأخذ، والغازي في سبيل الله إذا كان له عنها غنىً يقدر بغناه على الغزو لم يُستحبّ له أن يأخذ منها شيئاً، وكذلك الغارم إن كان عنده وفاء بدَيْنه وفضل تجب فيه الزكاة لم يُستحبّ له أن يأخذ منها شيئاً، وهو قول أبي حنيفة رحمه الله.

Muḥammad said: "We adhere to this; as for someone who goes forth to fight in the way of Allah, if he can do without, being able to go forth by his own means, then it is not encouraged for him to take anything from it. Likewise the debtor, if he has the means to fulfil his debt and an amount remaining after that upon which *zakāh* is due, it is not encouraged for him to take anything from it. And That is the verdict of Abū Ḥanīfah, may Allah have mercy on him."

١٣ باب زكاة الفطر

13. *Zakāt al-Fiṭr*

٣٤٣ أخبرنا مالك، حدثنا نافع أنَّ ابنَ عمر كان يبعث بزكاة الفطر إلى الذي تجمع عنده قبل الفطر بيومين أو ثلاثة.

343. Mālik informed us: "Nāfi[c] narrated to us that Ibn [c]Umar used to send *zakāt al-fiṭr* to the one with whom it was amassed, two or three days before [[c]Īd] al-Fiṭr."

قال محمد رحمه الله: وبهذا نأخذ، يُعجبنا تعجيلُ زكاة الفطر قبل أن يخرج الرجل إلى المصلّى، وهو قول أبي حنيفة رحمه الله.

Muḥammad said, may Allah have mercy on him, "We adhere to this. It pleases us that *zakāt al-fiṭr* is paid before a man's going out to the place of prayer. That is the verdict of Abū Ḥanīfah, may Allah have mercy on him."

١٤ باب صدقة الزيتون

14. The *Zakāh* Due on Olives

٣٤٤ أخبرنا مالك، عن ابن شهاب قال: صدقة الزيتون العُشر.

344. Mālik informed us that Ibn Shihāb said, 'The *zakāh* due on olives is a tenth.'"

وقال محمد: وبهذا نأخذ إذ خرج منه خمسة أوسق فصاعداً، ولا يُلتفت في هذا إلى الزيت، إنما يُنظر في هذا إلى الزيتون، وأما في قول أبي حنيفة رحمه الله ففي قليله وكثيره.

Muḥammad said: "We adhere to this, if five wasqs or more are yielded. And the oil is not to be considered here; only the olives are considered. As for the opinion of Abū Ḥanīfah, may Allah have mercy on him, a tenth is due on a small or large yield."

أبواب الصيام
4. FASTING

١ باب الصوم لرؤية الهلال والإفطار لرؤيته
1. The Fast is Due on Sighting the New Moon, and is Broken on Sighting it

٣٤٥ أخبرنا مالك، حدثنا نافع وعبد الله بن دينار، عن ابن عمر: أن رسول الله ﷺ ذكر رمضان، فقال: لا تصوموا حتى تَرَوا الهلال، ولا تُفطروا حتى تَرَوْه، فإن غُمَّ عليكم فاقْدُروا له.

345. Mālik informed us: "Nāfi[c] and [c]Abdullāh ibn Dīnār narrated to us from Ibn [c]Umar that the Messenger of Allah ﷺ spoke about Ramaḍān. He said, 'Don't fast until you see the new moon, nor break the fast until you see it. If it is overcast, then estimate it [as thirty days].'"

قال محمد: وبهذا نأخذ، وهو قول أبي حنيفة رحمه الله.

Muḥammad said: "We adhere to this; it is the verdict of Abū Ḥanīfah, may Allah have mercy on him."

٢ باب متى يحرم الطعام على الصائم
2. When Food Becomes Forbidden for Someone Fasting

٣٤٦ أخبرنا مالك، حدثنا عبد الله بن دينار، عن ابن عمر قال: قال رسول الله صلّى الله عليه وسلّم: إنّ بلالاً ينادي بليلٍ فكُلُوا واشربوا حتى ينادي ابنُ أمّ مكتوم

346. Mālik informed us: "[c]Abdullāh ibn Dīnār narrated to us that Ibn [c]Umar said, 'The Messenger of Allah ﷺ said, "Bilāl calls the *adhān* while it is still night, so eat and drink until Ibn Umm Maktūm calls the *adhān*."'"

٣٤٧ أخبرنا مالك، حدثنا الزهري، عن سالم مثله، قال: وكان ابنُ أمٍّ مكتوم لا يُنادي حتى يُقَالَ له: قد أصبحت.

347. Mālik informed us: "Az-Zuhrī narrated to us likewise from Sālim, adding, 'And Ibn Umm Maktūm used not to call until it was said to him, "It is morning."'"

قال محمد: كان بلالٌ ينادي بليل في شهر رمضان لسحور الناس، وكان ابن أمٍّ مكتوم ينادي للصلاة بعد طلوع الفجر، فلذلك قال رسول الله صلّى الله عليه وسلّم: كلوا واشربوا حتى ينادي ابنُ أمٍّ مكتوم.

Muḥammad said: "Bilāl used to call the *adhān* at night in the month of

Ramaḍān for the people to eat their last meal, and Ibn Umm Maktūm used to call the *adhān* for the prayer after the appearance of dawn. For this reason the Messenger of Allah ﷺ said, 'Eat and drink until Ibn Umm Maktūm calls the *adhān*.'"

٣ باب من أفطر متعمداً في رمضان

3. Someone who Breaks the Fast On Purpose in Ramaḍān

٣٤٨ أخبرنا مالك، حدثنا الزُّهري، عن حُمَيد بن عبد الرحمن، عن أبي هريرة: أن رجلاً أفطر في رمضان فأمر رسول الله صلّى الله عليه وسلّم أن يكفِّر بعتق رقبة أو صيام شهرين متتابعين أو إطعام ستين مسكيناً، قال لا أجد، فأُتي رسولُ الله صلّى الله عليه وسلّم بعَرَقٍ من تمر، فقال: خذ هذا فتصدَّق به، فقال: يا رسول الله، ما أجد أحداً أحوجَ إليه مني، قال: كُلْه.

348. Mālik informed us: "Az-Zuhrī narrated to us from Ḥumayd ibn ᶜAbd ar-Raḥmān from Abū Hurayrah that a man broke the fast in Ramaḍān. So the Messenger of Allah ﷺ told him to atone for it by freeing a slave, or fasting two consecutive months, or feeding sixty of the poor. The man said, 'I cannot.' Then, the Messenger of Allah ﷺ was brought an *ᶜaraq* [30 *saᶜ*] of dates, so he said, 'Take this and give it away.' So he said, 'Messenger of Allah, I cannot find anyone in greater need of it than me.' So he said, 'Eat it.'"

قال محمد: وبهذا نأخذ إذا أفطر الرجل متعمِّداً في شهر رمضان بأكلٍ أو شربٍ أو جماع فعليه قضاءُ يومٍ مكانه، وكفّارةُ الظهار أنْ يعتقَ رقبة، فإن لم يجد فصيامُ شهرين متتابعين، فإن لم يستطع أطعم ستين مسكيناً، لكل مسكين نصف صاع من حنطة أو صاع من تمر أو شعير.

Muḥammad said: "We adhere to this. If a man breaks the fast on purpose in the month of Ramaḍān, by eating or drinking or having sexual intercourse, then he must replace it with another day and make expiation for it as *ẓihār* divorce is made expiation for, by freeing a slave, and if he does not own one, then by fasting two consecutive months, and if he cannot do that then he should feed sixty of the poor, each one of them half a *saᶜ* of corn, or dates, or barley.

٤ باب الرجل يطلع له الفجر في رمضان وهو جنب

4. A Man, who, at the Appearance of Dawn in Ramaḍān, is *Junub* [in a state requiring *ghusl* after Sexual Intercourse or Ejaculation]

٣٤٩ أخبرنا مالك، حدثنا عبد الله بن عبد الرحمن بن معمر، عن أبي يونس مولى عائشة أن رجلاً قال لرسول الله صلّى الله عليه وسلّم وهو واقف على الباب وأنا أسمع: إني أصبحتُ جُنُباً وأنا أريد الصوم، فقال رسولُ الله صلّى الله عليه وسلّم: وأنا أصبح جنباً، ثم أغتسل فأصوم، فقال الرجل: إنَّكَ لستَ مثلنا، فقد غفر الله لك ما تقدَّم من ذنبك وما تأخر، فغضب رسول الله صلّى الله عليه وسلّم وقال: والله إني لأرجو أن أكونَ أخشاكم لله عزَّ وجلّ وأعلمكم بما أتقي.

349. Mālik informed us: "ᶜAbdullāh ibn ᶜAbd ar-Raḥmān ibn Muᶜammar

narrated to us from Abū Yūnus, the *mawlā* of ᶜĀᵓishah, that a man said to the Messenger of Allah ﷺ while he was standing at the door and I could hear, 'I found myself *junub* when morning came, and I was intending to fast.' So the Messenger of Allah ﷺ said, 'I also find myself *junub* in the morning, then I do *ghusl* and I fast.' So the man said, ''But you are not like us, because Allah has "forgiven you your earlier errors and any later ones" (Sūrat al-Fatḥ).' The Messenger of Allah ﷺ was filled with anger and said, 'By Allah, I hope that I will be the most fearful of Allah ﷻ of you and the most knowledgeable of you all of what I should guard against.'''

٣٥٠ أخبرنا مالك، أخبرنا سُمَيٌّ مولى أبي بكر بن عبد الرحمن أنه سمع أبا بكر بن عبد الرحمن يقول: كنت أنا وأبي عند مروان بن الحكم وهو أمير المدينة، فذكَر أنَّ أبا هريرة قال: من أصبح جُنُباً أفطر ، فقال مروان: أقسمتُ عليك يا عبد الرحمن لتذهبَنَّ إلى أمَّيْ المؤمنين عائشة وأم سلمة فتسألهما عن ذلك، قال : فذهب عبدُ الرحمن وذهبتُ معه حتى دخلنا على عائشة، فسلَّمنا على عائشة، ثم قال عبد الرحمن: يا أمّ المؤمنين، كنا عند مروان بن الحكم، فذكر أن أبا هريرة يقول : من أصبح جُنُباً أفطر ذلك اليوم، قالت: ليس كما قال أبو هريرة يا عبد الرحمن، أترغَبُ عما كان رسول الله صلّى الله عليه وسلّم يصنع؟ قال: لا والله، قالت : فأشهدُ على رسول الله صلّى الله عليه وسلّم أنه كان يُصبح جُنُباً من جماع غير احتلام ، ثم يصوم ذلك اليوم.

قال : ثم خرجنا حتى دخلنا على أمّ سلمة فسألها عن ذلك فقالت كما قالت عائشة، فخرجنا حتى جئنا مروان، فذكر له عبد الرحمن ما قالتا، فقال : أقسمتُ عليك يا أبا محمد لتركَبَنَّ دابَّتي ، فإنها بالباب ، فلتذهبَنَّ إلى أبي هريرة، فإنه بأرضه بالعقيق ، فلتخبرَنَّهُ ذلك ، قال: فركب عبد الرحمن وركبت معه حتى أتينا أبا هريرة، فتحدث معه عبد الرحمن ساعة ثم ذكر له ذلك ، فقال أبو هريرة: لا علم لي بذلك، إنما أخبرَنيه مُخبر .

350. Mālik informed us: "Sumayy, the *mawlā* of Abū Bakr ibn ᶜAbd ar-Raḥmān, informed us that he heard Abū Bakr ibn ᶜAbd ar-Raḥmān say, 'I was with my father with Marwān ibn al-Ḥakam, while he was the governor of Madīnah, and he mentioned that Abū Hurayrah had said, "Whoever is *junub* at morning, breaks the fast." Marwān said, "I have sworn, ᶜAbd ar-Raḥmān, that you will go to Umm al-Muᵓminin, ᶜĀᵓishah, and Umm al-Muᵓminin, Umm Salamah, and ask them about it."' [Abū Bakr] said, 'So ᶜAbd ar-Raḥmān went, and I went with him, until we went in to see ᶜĀᵓishah. We greeted ᶜĀᵓishah, then ᶜAbd ar-Raḥmān said, "Umm al-Muᵓminin, we were with Marwān ibn al-Ḥakam, and he mentioned that Abū Hurayrah is saying, 'Whoever is *junub* in the morning, breaks the fast that day.'" She said, "It is not as Abū Hurayrah has said, ᶜAbd ar-Raḥmān. Do you find what the Messenger of Allah ﷺ used to do disagreeable?" He said, "By Allah, no." She said, "Then I bear witness that the Messenger of Allah ﷺ used to find himself *junub* in the morning, because of sexual intercourse, and not because of a wet-dream, and then fast that day."' [Abū Bakr] said, 'Then we left and went to see

Umm Salamah, and he asked her about that and she said as ᶜĀ᾿ishah had said. So we left, until we came to Marwān, and ᶜAbd ar-Raḥmān told him what they had said. Then [Marwān] said, "I have sworn, Abū Muḥammad, you must get on my mount, for it is [waiting] at the door, and go to Abū Hurayrah, for he is on his land at al-ᶜAqīq, and tell him."' [Abū Bakr] said, 'So ᶜAbd ar-Raḥmān rode, and I rode with him, until we came to Abū Hurayrah, and ᶜAbd ar-Raḥmān spoke with him for some time, before telling him. Abū Hurayrah said, "I have no knowledge about that. It was only that an informant told me about it."'"

قال محمد: وبهذا نأخذ، من أصبح جنباً من جماع من غير احتلام في شهر رمضان، ثم اغتسل بعد ما طلع الفجر فلا بأس بذلك، وكتاب الله تعالى يدل على ذلك، قال الله عزَّ وجلَّ: ﴿أُحلَّ لكم ليلةَ الصيام الرَّفَثُ إلى نسائكم، هنَّ لباس لكم وأنتم لباسٌ لهنَّ، علم الله أنكم كنتم تختانونَ أنفسكم، فتاب عليكم وعفا عنكم، فالآن باشروهنَّ﴾ يعني الجماع ﴿وابتغُوا ما كتب الله لكم﴾ يعني الولد ﴿وكلوا واشربوا حتى يتبين لكم الخيطُ الأبيضُ من الخيط الأسود﴾ يعني حتى يطلع الفجر فإذا كان الرجل قد رُخِّص له أن يجامع، ويبتغي الولد، ويأكل ويشرب حتى يطلع الفجر فمتى يكون الغسل إلاّ بعد طلوع الفجر. فهذا لا بأس به، وهو قول أبي حنيفة رحمه الله تعالى والعامَّة.

Muḥammad said: "We adhere to this; whoever is *junub* in the morning, because of sexual intercourse not because of a wet-dream, in the month of Ramaḍān, and then do *ghusl* after dawn has appeared, that is not disapproved; and the Book of Allah points to that. Allah, exalted is He, says, 'On the night of the fast it is lawful for you to have sexual relations with your wives. They are clothing for you and you for them. Allah knows that you have been betraying yourselves and He has turned towards you and excused you. Now you may embrace them' – meaning have sexual intercourse with them – 'and seek what Allah has written for you '– meaning children. 'Eat and drink until you can clearly discern the white thread from the black thread of the dawn' (Sūrat al-Baqarah: 186) – meaning until dawn appears. So if it has been allowed for a man to have sexual intercourse and try to have children, and eat and drink until the dawn appears, then when might the *ghusl* be done except after the appearance of dawn; so there can be no disapproval here. And This is also the verdict of Abū Ḥanīfah, may Allah have mercy on him, and of [our *fuqahā᾿*] in general."

٥ باب القُبلة للصائم

5. Someone who Kisses while Fasting

٣٥١ أخبرنا مالك، حدثنا زيد بن أسلم، عن عطاء بن يَسَار: أنَّ رجلاً قَبَّل امرأةً وهو صائم، فوجد من ذلك وَجْداً شديداً، فأرسل امرأتَه تسأل له عن ذلك، فدخلت على أمِّ سلمة زوج النبي صلّى الله عليه وسلّم، فأخبرتها أمُّ سلمة: أنَّ رسول الله صلّى الله عليه وسلّم كان يُقَبِّل وهو صائم.

فرجعتْ إليه فأخبرتْه بذلك، فزاده ذلك شرّاً فقال: إنّا لسنا مثلَ رسول الله صلّى الله عليه وسلّم، يُحلُّ الله لرسوله ما شاء، فرجعت المرأة إلى أمّ سلمة، فوجدت عندها رسول الله صلّى الله عليه وسلّم، قال رسول الله صلّى الله عليه وسلّم: ما بال هذه المرأة؟ فأخبَرَتْه أمّ سلمة، فقال: ألا أخبرتها أني أفعل ذلك ؟ قالت: قد أخبرتُها، فذهبتْ إلى زوجها، فأخبرَتْه، فزاده ذلك شرّاً، وقال: إنّا لسنا مثلَ رسول الله صلّى الله عليه وسلّم، يُحلُّ الله لرسوله ما شاء ، فغضب رسول الله صلّى الله عليه وسلّم، وقال: والله إني لأتقاكم لله، وأعلمكم بحدوده.

351. Mālik informed us: "Zayd ibn Aslam narrated to us from ᶜAṭāᵓ ibn Yasār that a man kissed his wife while he was fasting, and he became very disturbed about it. He sent his wife to ask about it for him. She went to see Umm Salamah, the wife of the Prophet ﷺ, and Umm Salamah told her that the Messenger of Allah ﷺ would kiss while fasting. So she returned to him and told him of that and it made him worse. He said, 'We are not like the Messenger of Allah ﷺ. Allah will permit for His Messenger whatever He wills.' The woman returned to Umm Salamah, and she found the Messenger of Allah ﷺ with her. The Messenger of Allah ﷺ said, 'What has happened to this woman?' And Umm Salamah told him. He said, 'Couldn't you have told her that I do that?' She said, 'I have told her, and she went to her husband and told him, and that made him worse, and he said, "We are not like the Messenger of Allah ﷺ: Allah permits for His messenger whatever He wills."' The Messenger of Allah ﷺ was filled with anger, and said, 'By Allah, I am the most wary of Allah, and the most knowledgable of you all of the limits He has set.'"

٣٥٢ أخبرنا مالك، أخبرنا أبو النضر مولى عمر بن عبيد الله: أن عائشة ابنة طلحة أخبَرَتْه أنها كانت عند عائشة رضي الله عنها زوجِ النبي صلّى الله عليه وسلّم فدخل عليها زوجُها هنالك وهو عبدُ الله ابنُ عبد الرحمن ابنِ أبي بكر ، فقالت له عائشة: ما يمنعك أن تَدْنُوَ إلى أهلك تقبّلها وتلاعبها؟ قال: أقبّلها وأنا صائم؟! قالت : نعم .

352. Mālik informed us: "Abu'n-Naḍr, the *mawlā* of ᶜUmar ibn ᶜUbaydullāh, informed us that ᶜĀᵓishah bint Ṭalḥah told him that she was with ᶜĀᵓishah ﷺ the wife of the Messenger of Allah ﷺ, and her husband came in – he being ᶜAbdullāh ibn ᶜAbd ar-Raḥmān ibn Abī Bakr – and ᶜĀᵓishah said to him, 'What is stopping you from coming up to your wife and kissing her and teasing her?' He said, 'Kiss her while I am fasting?' She said, 'Yes.'"

قال محمد: لا بأس بالقُبلة للصائم إذا ملك نفسه عن الجماع فإن خاف أن لا يملك نفسه فالكفُّ أفضل، وهو قول أبي حنيفة رحمه الله والعامّة قبلنا.

Muḥammad said: "Kissing is not disapproved of for someone fasting, if he can restrain himself from sexual intercourse; but if he is not sure he can restrain himself, then staying away is better. That is the verdict of Abū Ḥanīfah, may Allah have mercy on him and the generality of [our *fuqahāᵓ*] in general before us."

٣٥٣ أخبرنا مالك، أخبرنا نافع، عن ابن عمر: أنه كان يَنهى عن القُبلة والمباشرة للصائم.
353. Mālik informed us: "Nāfi^c informed us that Ibn ^cUmar used to prohibit kissing and intimate embraces for someone fasting."

٦ باب الحجامة للصائم

6. Cupping for Someone Fasting

٣٥٤ أخبرنا مالك، حدثنا نافع: أن ابن عمر كان يَحتجم وهو صائم ثم إنّه كان يحتجم بعد ما تغرب الشمس.
354. Mālik informed us: "Nāfi^c narrated to us that Ibn ^cUmar used to have himself cupped while he was fasting, then [later] he would have himself cupped after the sun had gone down."

٣٥٥ أخبرنا مالك، حدثنا الزُّهري: أن سعداً وابن عمر كانا يحتجمان وهما صائمان.
355. Mālik informed us: "Az-Zuhrī narrated to us that Sa^cd and Ibn ^cUmar used to have themselves cupped while they were fasting."

قال محمد: لا بأس بالحجامة للصائم، وإنما كُرهت من أجل الضعف، فإذا أُمِن ذلك فلا بأس، وهو قول أبي حنيفة رحمه الله.
Muḥammad said: "Cupping is not disapproved of for someone fasting. It is only disliked when weakness ensues, and so if he has no fear of that, there is no disapproval. That is the verdict of Abū Ḥanīfah, may Allah have mercy on him."

٣٥٦ أخبرنا مالك، أخبرنا هشام بن عروة قال: ما رأيت أبي قطُّ احتجم إلا وهو صائم.
356. Mālik informed us: "Hishām ibn ^cUrwah informed us, 'I never saw my father have himself cupped, except while he was fasting.'"

قال محمد: وبه نأخذ، وهو قول أبي حنيفة رحمه الله تعالى.
Muḥammad said: "We adhere to this. It is the verdict of Abū Ḥanīfah, may Allah have mercy on him."

٧ باب الصائم يذرعه القَيْء أو يتقيأ

7. The Fasting Person's Vomiting or Making himself Vomit

٣٥٧ أخبرنا مالك، أخبرنا نافع أن ابن عمر كان يقول: من استقاء وهو صائم فعليه القضاء، ومن ذرعه القَيْء فليس عليه شيء.
357. Mālik informed us: "Nāfi^c informed us that Ibn ^cUmar used to say, 'Whoever tries to vomit while he is fasting, must fast [a day] in place of it, and whoever is convulsed by vomiting is not required to do anything.'"

قال محمد: وبه نأخذ، وهو قول أبي حنيفة رحمه الله تعالى.
Muḥammad said: "We adhere to this, and it is the verdict of Abū Ḥanīfah, may Allah have mercy on him."

٨ باب الصوم في السفر
8. Fasting while Travelling

٣٥٨ أخبرنا مالك، أخبرنا نافع: أن ابن عمر كان لا يصوم في السفر.

358. Mālik informed us: "Nāfiʿ informed us that Ibn ʿUmar used not to fast while travelling."

٣٥٩ أخبرنا مالك، حدثنا الزهري، عن عبيد الله بن عبد الله ، عن ابن عباس رضي الله عنهما: أن رسول الله صلّى الله عليه وسلّم خرج عام فتح مكة في رمضان، فصام حتى بلغ الكُدَيد ثم أفطر فأفطر الناس معه وكان فتح مكة في رمضان، قال: وكانوا يأخذون بالأحدث فالأحدث من أمر رسول الله صلّى الله عليه وسلّم.

359. Mālik informed us: "Az-Zuhrī narrated to us from ʿUbaydullāh ibn ʿAbdullāh from Ibn ʿAbbās ﷺ that the Messenger of Allah ﷺ set out the year of the Opening of Makkah [to Islam] in Ramaḍān, and fasted until he reached al-Kadīd, then he broke the fast, so the people broke the fast with him; the Opening of Makkah [to Islam] was in Ramaḍān. [Ibn ʿAbbās] said, 'They used to adopt the most recent command of the Messenger of Allah ﷺ.'"

قال محمد: من شاء صام في السفر، ومن شاء أفطر، والصوم أفضل لمن قوي عليه ، وإنما بلغنا أن النبي صلّى الله عليه وسلّم أفطر حين سافر إلى مكة لأن الناس شَكَوْا إليه الجهد من الصوم، فأفطر لذلك، وقد بلغنا أن حمزة الأسلمي سأله عن الصوم في السفر، فقال: إن شئت فصم، وإن شئت فأفطر. فبهذا نأخذ، وهو قول أبي حنيفة رحمه الله والعامة من قبلنا.

Muḥammad said: "Whoever wants, can fast when travelling, and whoever wants, can break the fast, but fasting is better for someone who is able. And what has been narrated to us is that the Prophet ﷺ broke the fast when he travelled to Makkah because the people complained to him of the strain of fasting, and so he broke the fast for that reason. And it has been narrated to us that Ḥamzah al-Aslamī asked him about fasting when travelling, and he said, 'If you want, fast, and if you want, break [it].' So we adhere to this; and it is the verdict of Abū Ḥanīfah, may Allah have mercy on him, and the generality of [our *fuqahā*ʾ] in general before us."

٩ باب قضاء رمضان هل يُفرّق؟
9. When Making up Missed Days of Ramaḍān, Can they be Separated?

٣٦٠ أخبرنا مالك، حدثنا نافع: أن ابن عمر كان يقول : لا يفرّق قضاء رمضان.

360. Mālik informed us: "Nāfiʿ narrated to us that Ibn ʿUmar used to say, 'The days to be made up of Ramaḍān are not to be separated.'"

٣٦١ أخبرنا مالك، أخبرنا ابن شهاب: أن ابن عباس وأبا هريرة اختلفا في قضاء رمضان، قال أحدهما : يُفَرَّق بينه، وقال الآخر: لا يفرَّق بينه.

361. Mālik informed us: "Ibn Shihāb informed us that Ibn ʿAbbās and Abū Hurayrah differed concerning making up the missed days of Ramaḍān; one

of them said, 'They may be separated, and the other said, They are not to be separated.'"

قال محمد: الجمع بينه أفضل وإن فرَّقتَ وأحصيتَ العِدَّة فلا بأس بذلك، وهو قول أبي حنيفة رحمه الله والعامَّة قبلنا.

Muḥammad said: "Joining them is better, but if you separate them and keep track of the number [of days], that is not disapproved of. And That is the verdict of Abū Ḥanīfah, may Allah have mercy on him, and the generality of [our *fuqahā'*] in general before us."

١٠ باب من صام تطوعاً ثم أفطر

10. Someone who Fasts Voluntarily, and then Breaks the Fast

٣٦٢ أخبرنا مالك، حدثنا الزهري: أن عائشة وحفصة رضي الله عنهما أصبحتا صائمتين متطوِّعتين، فأُهدي لهما طعام فأفطرتا عليه، فدخل عليهما رسول الله صلّى الله عليه وسلّم، قالت عائشة: فقالت حفصة بدرتني بالكلام وكانت ابنة أبيها: يا رسول الله إني أصبحت أنا وعائشة صائمتين متطوِّعتين، فأُهدي لنا طعام فأفطرنا عليه، فقال لهما رسول الله صلّى الله عليه وسلّم: اقْضِيا يوماً مكانه.

362. Mālik informed us: "Az-Zuhrī narrated to us that ᶜĀ'ishah and Ḥafṣah ﷺ began the day fasting voluntarily, and a gift of food was left for them, so they broke the fast on it. Then the Messenger of Allah ﷺ came in. ᶜĀ'ishah said, 'So Ḥafṣah said, forestalling me in speaking, she being the daughter of her father, "Messenger of Allah, I began the day with ᶜĀ'ishah fasting voluntarily, then a gift of food was left for us, so we broke the fast on it."' And the Messenger of Allah ﷺ said to them, 'Fast another day in its place.'"

قال محمد: وبهذا نأخذ، من صام تطوُّعاً ثم أفطر فعليه القضاء، وهو قول أبي حنيفة رحمه الله والعامَّة قبلنا.

Muḥammad said: "We adhere to this. Whoever fasts voluntarily, then breaks the fast, must fast to make up for it. And that is the verdict of Abū Ḥanīfah, may Allah have mercy on him, and the generality of [our *fuqahā'*] in general before us."

١١ باب تعجيل الإفطار

11. Hastening Breaking the Fast

٣٦٣ أخبرنا مالك، حدثنا أبو حازم بن دينار، عن سهل بن سعد: أن النبي صلّى الله عليه وسلّم قال: لا يزال الناسُ بخير ما عجَّلوا الإفطار.

363. Mālik informed us: "Abū Ḥāzim Ibn Dīnār narrated to us from Sahl ibn Saᶜd that the Prophet ﷺ said, 'The people will always be in a state of well-being, as long as they hasten breaking the fast.'"

قال محمد : تعجيل الإفطار وصلاة المغرب أفضل من تأخيرهما ، وهو قول أبي حنيفة رحمه الله والعامة .

Muḥammad said: "Hastening breaking the fast and praying *Maghrib* is better than delaying them. That is the verdict of Abū Ḥanīfah, may Allah have mercy on him, and of [our *fuqahāʾ*] in general.'"

٣٦٤ أخبرنا مالك ، أخبرنا ابن شهاب ، عن حميد بن عبد الرحمن بن عوف أنه أخبره : أن عمر بن الخطاب وعثمان بن عفان كانا يصليان المغربَ حين ينظران الليلَ الأسودَ قبل أن يُفطروا ، ثم يفطران بعد الصلاة في رمضان .

364. Mālik informed us: "Ibn Shihāb informed us that Ḥumayd ibn ʿAbd ar-Raḥmān ibn ʿAwf told him that in Ramaḍān, ʿUmar ibn al-Khaṭṭāb and ʿUthmān ibn ʿAffān used to pray *Maghrib* when they could see the blackness of night [on the eastern horizon] before they broke the fast; then they would break the fast after praying."

قال محمد : وهذا كلُّه واسع ، فمن شاء أفطر قبل الصلاة ، ومن شاء أفطر بعدها ، وكلُّ ذلك لا بأس به .

Muḥammad said: "The options cover all this; whoever wants to can break the fast before praying, and whoever wants to can break fast afterwards. None of that is disapproved of."

١٢ باب الرجل يفطر قبل المساء ويظن أنه قد أمسى
12. A Man who Breaks the Fast before Evening, Thinking that Evening has Come

٣٦٥ أخبرنا مالك ، أخبرنا زيد بن أسلم : أن عمر بن الخطاب رضي الله عنه أفطر في يوم رمضان في يوم غَيْمٍ ، ورأى أنه قد أمسى أو غابت الشمس ، فجاءه رجل فقال : يا أمير المؤمنين ، قد طلعت الشمس ، قال : الخَطْب يسير وقد اجتهدنا .

365. Mālik informed us: "Zayd ibn Aslam informed us that ʿUmar ibn al-Khaṭṭāb ⚭ broke the fast on a day of Ramaḍān, an overcast day, thinking evening had come, the sun having disappeared. A man came to him and said, Amīr al-Muʾminīn, the sun has appeared.' He said, 'It is simple; we had tried our best.'"

قال محمد : من أفطر وهو يرى أن الشمس قد غابت ثم علم أنها لم تغب لم يأكل بقية يومه ولم يشرب وعليه قضاؤه ، وهو قول أبي حنيفة رحمه الله .

Muḥammad said: "Whoever breaks the fast thinking that the sun has set, and then learns that it has not set, should not eat for the rest of that day, nor drink, and he must make up that day. That is the verdict of Abū Ḥanīfah, may Allah have mercy on him."

١٣ باب الوصال في الصيام

13. Continuous Fasting

٣٦٦ أخبرنا مالك، أخبرنا نافع عن عبد الله بن عمر: أن رسول الله صلّى الله عليه وسلّم نهى عن الوصال، فقيل له: إنك تواصل، قال: إني لستُ كهيئتكم إني أُطعَم وأُسقى.

366. Mālik informed us: "Nāfi[c] informed us from [c]Abdullāh ibn [c]Umar that the Messenger of Allah ﷺ prohibited [fasting] continuously. Someone said to him, 'But you fast continuously.' He said, 'I am not the same as you; I am given food and drink.'"[14]

٣٦٧ أخبرنا مالك، أخبرني أبو الزِّناد، عن الأعرج، عن أبي هريرة: أن رسول الله صلّى الله عليه وسلّم قال: إيّاكم والوصال، إياكم والوصال، قالوا: إنك تواصل يا رسول الله؟ قال: إني لست كهيئتكم، أبيت يُطْعِمُني ربي ويَسقيني، فاكْلَفوا من الأعمال ما لكم به طاقة.

367. Mālik informed us: "Abu'z-Zinād informed us from al-A[c]raj from Abū Hurayrah that the Messenger of Allah ﷺ said, 'Beware of continuous fasting, beware of continuous fasting!' They said, 'But you fast continuously, Messenger of Allah.' He said, 'I am not quite the same as you; I spend the night and my Lord feeds me and gives me drink. So take on those tasks for which you have the capacity.'"

قال محمد: وبهذا نأخذ، الوصال مكروه، وهو أنْ يواصل الرجل بين يومين في الصوم، لا يأكل في الليل شيئاً، وهو قول أبي حنيفة رحمه الله والعامة.

Muḥammad said: "We adhere to this. A man's fasting for two days without interruption, without eating anything at night, is disliked. And that is the verdict of Abū Ḥanīfah, may Allah have mercy on him, and of [our *fuqahā'*] in general."

١٤ باب صوم يوم عرفة

14. Fasting the Day of [c]Arafah

٣٦٨ أخبرنا مالك، حدثنا سالم أبو النضر، عن عمير مولى ابن عباس، عن أمِّ الفضل ابنة الحارث: أن ناساً تمارَوْا في صوم رسول الله صلّى الله عليه وسلّم يوم عرفة، فقال بعضهم: صائم، وقال آخرون: ليس بصائم، فأرسلت أمُّ الفضل بقَدَح من لَبَن وهو واقف بعرفة فشربه.

368. Mālik informed us: "Sālim Abu'n-Naḍr narrated to us from [c]Umayr, the *mawlā* of Ibn [c]Abbās, from Umm al-Faḍl bint al-Ḥārith that some people disputed about the fasting of the Messenger of Allah ﷺ on the day of [c]Arafah, some of them saying, 'He is fasting,' and some saying, 'He is not fasting.' Umm al-Faḍl sent a bowl of milk while he was standing on [c]Arafah, and he drank it."

قال محمد: من شاء صام يوم عرفة ومن شاء أفطر، إنما صومه تطوع، فإن كان إذا صامه يُضْعِفُه ذلك عن الدعاء في ذلك اليوم فالإفطار أفضل من الصوم.

Muḥammad said: "Whoever wants to, can fast [c]Arafah, and whoever wants to, can break the fast. It is only a voluntary fast, so if in fasting it he slackens from praying on that day, then breaking the fast is more meritorious than fasting."

١٥ باب الأيام التي يكره فيها الصوم

15. The Days on which Fasting is Disapproved

٣٦٩ أخبرنا مالك، حدثنا أبو النضر مولى عمر بن عبيد الله، عن سليمان بن يسار: أنَّ رسول الله صلّى الله عليه وسلّم نهى عن صيام أيام منى.

369. Mālik informed us: "Abu'n-Naḍr, the *mawlā* of ᶜUmar ibn ᶜUbaydullāh, narrated to us from Sulaymān ibn Yasār that the Messenger of Allah ﷺ prohibited fasting the days of Minā."

٣٧٠ أخبرنا مالك، أخبرنا يزيد بن عبد الله بن الهاد، عن أبي مرَّة مولى عقيل بن أبي طالب: أن عبد الله بن عمرو بن العاص دخل على أبيه في أيّام التشريق فقرَّب له طعاماً، فقال: كُلْ، فقال عبد الله لأبيه: إني صائم، قال: كُلْ، أما علمتَ أنَّ رسول الله صلّى الله عليه وسلّم كان يأمُرُنا بالفطر في هذه الأيام.

370. Mālik informed us: "Yazīd ibn ᶜAbdullāh ibn al-Hād informed us from Abū Murrah, the *mawlā* of ᶜAqīl ibn Abī Ṭālib, that ᶜAbdullāh ibn ᶜAmr ibn al-ᶜĀṣ visited his father during the days of *Tashrīq*, and [his father] offered him food, and said, 'Eat.' ᶜAbdullāh said to his father, 'I am fasting.' And [his father] said, 'Eat, are you not aware that the Messenger of Allah ﷺ used to command breaking the fast on these days.'"

قال محمد: وبهذا نأخذ، لا ينبغي أن يُصام أيام التشريق لمُتعة ولا لغيرها، لما جاء من النهي عن صومها عن النبي صلّى الله عليه وسلّم، وهو قول أبي حنيفة رحمه الله والعامَّة من قبلنا.

وقال مالك ابن أنس يصومها المتمتع الذي لا يجد الهَدْيَ أو فاتته الأيّامُ الثلاثة قبل يوم النحر.

Muḥammad said: "We adhere to this; the days of Tashrīq ought not to be fasted, whether due to [the type of Ḥajj called] *mutᶜah*[15] or otherwise, in compliance with that prohibition on fasting them which has come from the Prophet ﷺ. That is the verdict of Abū Ḥanīfah, may Allah have mercy on him, and the generality of [our *fuqahā*ʾ] in general before us. Mālik ibn Anas gave the verdict that the person who performs [the type of Ḥajj called] *mutᶜah* who cannot find a *hady* offering and has missed three days [of fasting] before the day of slaughter, should fast them."

١٦ باب النية في الصوم من الليل

16. Making Intention to Fast in the Night

٣٧١ أخبرنا مالك، حدثنا نافع، أنَّ ابن عمر قال: لا يصومُ إلاَّ من أجمع الصيامَ قبل الفجر.

371. Mālik informed us: "Nāfiᶜ narrated to us that Ibn ᶜUmar said, 'No one is fasting unless he resolves to fast before dawn.'"

قال محمد : ومن أجمع أيضاً على الصيام قبل نصف النهار فهو صائم، وقد روى ذلك غيرُ واحد وهو قول أبي حنيفة والعامّة قبلنا .

Muḥammad said: "Whoever resolves to fast before midday is also fasting, as has been narrated by many. And That is the verdict of Abū Ḥanīfah, and the generality of [our *fuqahā᾽*] in general before us."

١٧ باب المداومة على الصيام

17. Constancy in Fasting

٣٧٢ أخبرنا مالك، حدثنا أبو النضر، عن أبي سلمة بن عبد الرحمن ، عن عائشة قالت : كان رسولُ الله صلّى الله عليه وسلّم يصوم حتى يقال لا يُفطر ، ويُفطر حتى يقال لا يصوم، وما رأيتُ رسولَ الله صلّى الله عليه وسلّم استكمل صيامَ شهرٍ قطُّ إلاّ رمضان، وما رأيته في شهرٍ أكثرَ صياماً منه في شعبان .

372. Mālik informed us: "Abu'n-Naḍr narrated to us from Abū Salamah ibn ᶜAbd ar-Raḥmān that ᶜĀ᾽ishah said, 'The Messenger of Allah ﷺ used to fast so much that it would be said, "He will not break the fast," and would break the fast so much that it would be said, "He will not fast." I never saw the Messenger of Allah ﷺ fast a complete month except Ramaḍān. I never saw him fast so much in a month as he would in Shaᶜbān.'"

١٨ باب صوم يوم عاشوراء

18. Fasting the Day of ᶜĀshūrā᾽

٣٧٣ أخبرنا مالك، أخبرنا ابن شهاب، عن حُمَيد بن عبد الرحمن بن عوف أنه سمع معاويةَ بنَ أبي سفيان عامَ حَجٍّ وهو على المنبر يقول : يا أهل المدينة، أين علماؤكم ؟ سمعت رسول الله صلّى الله عليه وسلّم يقول لهذا اليوم هذا يوم عاشوراء لم يكتب الله عليكم صيامه، أنا صائم، ومن شاء فليصم، ومن شاء فليفطر .

373. Mālik informed us: "Ibn Shihāb informed us from Ḥumayd ibn ᶜAbd ar-Raḥmān ibn ᶜAwf that he heard Muᶜāwiyah ibn Abī Sufyān, the year he made Ḥajj, whilst on the *minbar*, saying, 'People of Madīnah, where are your learned ones? I heard the Messenger of Allah ﷺ say on this day, "This is the day of ᶜĀshūrā᾽. Allah has not made its fasting obligatory for you. I am fasting and whoever wants to, let him fast, and whoever wants to, let him break the fast."'"

قال محمد : صيام يوم عاشوراء كان واجباً قبل أن يُفترض رمضان ثم نسخه شهر رمضان، فهو تطوُّعٌ من شاء صامه ومن شاء لم يصمه، وهو قول أبي حنيفة رحمه الله والعامّة قبلنا .

Muḥammad said: "Fasting the day of ᶜĀshūrā᾽ was obligatory before Ramaḍān was made obligatory, then it was overruled by the month of Ramaḍān and so it is voluntary. Whoever wants to can fast it, and whoever doesn't want to need not fast it. That is the verdict of Abū Ḥanīfah, and the generality of [our *fuqahā*ʾ] in general before us."

١٩ باب ليلة القدر

19. The Night of the Decree [*Laylat al-Qadr*]

٣٧٤ أخبرنا مالك، أخبرنا عبد الله بن دينار، عن عبد الله بن عمر أن رسول الله صلّى الله عليه وسلّم قال: تحرَّوْا ليلةَ القدر في السبع الأواخر من رمضان.

374. Mālik informed us: "ᶜAbdullāh ibn Dīnār informed us from ᶜAbdullāh ibn ᶜUmar that the Messenger of Allah ﷺ said, 'Look for the Night of the Decree [*Laylat al-Qadr*] in the last seven [nights] of Ramaḍān.'"

٣٧٥ أخبرنا مالك، حدثنا هشام بن عروة، عن أبيه : أن رسول الله صلّى الله عليه وسلّم قال : تحرَّوْا ليلةَ القدر في العشر الأواخر من رمضان.

375. Mālik informed us: "Hishām ibn ᶜUrwah narrated to us from his father that the Messenger of Allah ﷺ said, 'Look for the Night of the Decree [*Laylat al-Qadr*] in the last ten [nights] of Ramaḍān.'"

٢٠ باب الاعتكاف

20. Withdrawing [into the Mosques] for *Iᶜtikāf*

٣٧٦ أخبرنا مالك، أخبرنا ابن شهاب، عن عروة بن الزبير، عن عَمْرة بنت عبد الرحمن، عن عائشة أنها قالت: كان رسولُ الله صلّى الله عليه وسلّم إذا اعتكفَ يُدْني إليّ رأسَه فأرجِّله، وكان لا يَدْخُلُ البيتَ إلاّ لحاجة الإنسان.

376. Mālik informed us: "Ibn Shihāb informed us from ᶜUrwah ibn az-Zubayr from ᶜAmrah bint ᶜAbd ar-Raḥmān that ᶜĀʾishah said, 'The Messenger of Allah ﷺ would, when he withdrew [into the mosque for *iᶜtikāf*], hold out his head towards me, and I would loosen out his hair. He used not to enter the house except to answer the call of nature.'"

قال محمد: وبهذا نأخذ، لا يخرج الرجل إذا اعتكف إلا للغائط أو البول، وأما الطعام والشراب فيكون في مُعْتَكَفه، وهو قول أبي حنيفة رحمه الله.

Muḥammad said: "We adhere to this. A man should not go out, once he has entered *iᶜtikāf*, except to relieve himself or urinate. As for food and drink, they should be taken in his place of *iᶜtikāf*. That is the verdict of Abū Ḥanīfah, may Allah have mercy on him."

٣٧٧ أخبرنا مالك، أخبرنا يزيدُ بنُ عبد الله بنِ الهاد، عن محمد بن إبراهيم، عن أبي سلمةَ بن عبد الرحمن، عن أبي سعيد الخُدْري قال: كان رسول الله ﷺ يعتكفُ العَشْرَ الوُسَطَ من شهر رمضان، فاعتكف عاماً حتى إذا كان ليلةَ إحدى وعشرين، وهي الليلةُ التي يخرج فيها من اعتكافه قال: من كان اعتكف معي فليعتكفْ العشر الأواخر، وقد رأيتُ هذه الليلةَ، ثم أُنسيتُها، وقد رأيتُني من صُبْحَتِها أسجُدُ في ماءٍ وطين، فالتمسوها في العشر الأواخر، والتمسوها في كل وترٍ.

قال أبو سعيد: فمُطرت السماء من تلك الليلة، وكان المسجد سقفه عريشاً فوكَف المسجد.
قال أبو سعيد : فأبصرتْ عيناي رسولَ الله صلّى الله عليه وسلّم انصرف علينا، وعلى جبهته وأنفه أثرُ الماء والطِّين من صبح ليلة إحدى وعشرين.

377. Mālik informed us: "Yazīd ibn ᶜAbdullāh ibn al-Hād informed us from Muḥammad ibn Ibrāhīm from Abū Salamah Ibn ᶜAbd ar-Raḥmān that Abū Saᶜīd al-Khudrī said, 'The Messenger of Allah ﷺ used to withdraw in *iᶜtikāf* for the middle ten [nights] of Ramaḍān. He withdrew one year, up until the twenty-first night, which was the night on which he would come out of his *iᶜtikāf*, he then said, "Whoever used to do *iᶜtikāf* with me, let him do *iᶜtikāf* for the last ten [nights]. I have seen this night, then I was made to forget it, and I saw myself the morning after prostrating in water and mud. So try to find it in the last ten [nights], and try to find it on every odd [night]."' Abū Saᶜīd said, 'So it rained that night, and the mosque had a latticed roof, which leaked.' Abū Saᶜīd said, 'I saw the Messenger of Allah ﷺ with my own eyes, turn [in concluding his prayer] towards us, with the traces of water and mud on his forehead and nose, on the morning of the twenty first night.'"

٣٧٨ أخبرنا مالك، سألتُ ابنَ شهاب الزّهري عن الرجل المعتكف يذهب لحاجته تحت سقف ؟ قال: لا بأس بذلك .

378. Mālik informed us: "I asked Ibn Shihāb az-Zuhrī about a man in *iᶜtikāf* going to relieve himself under a roof [of a ruin close to the mosque]. He said, 'There is nothing wrong with that.'"

قال محمد : بهذا نأخذ، لا بأس للمعتكف إذا أراد أن يقضي الحاجة من الغائط أو البول أن يدخل البيت أو أن يمرّ تحت السقف، وهو قول أبي حنيفة رحمه الله تعالى.

Muḥammad said: "We adhere to this. It is not disapproved of for someone in *iᶜtikāf*, when he needs to relieve himself or urinate, to go into a house or under a roof [of a ruin]. That is the verdict of Abū Ḥanīfah, may Allah, exalted is He, have mercy on him."

كتاب الحج

5. ḤAJJ

١ باب المواقيت

1. The Appointed Places [for Entering *Iḥrām*]

٣٧٩ أخبرنا مالك، حدَّثنا نافع مولى عبد الله، عن عبد الله بن عمر: أنَّ رسولَ الله صلّى الله عليه وسلّم قال: يُهِلُّ أهلُ المدينة من ذي الحُلَيْفة، ويُهِلُّ أهلُ الشام من الجُحْفة، ويُهِلُّ أهلُ نجد من قَرْن. قال ابنُ عمر: ويزعُمُون أنه قال: ويُهِلُّ أهلُ اليَمَن من يَلَمْلَم.

379. Mālik informed us: "Nāfi^c, the *mawlā* of ^cAbdullāh, narrated to us from ^cAbdullāh ibn ^cUmar that the Messenger of Allah ﷺ said, 'The people of Madīnah should enter *iḥrām*[16] at Dhu'l-Ḥulayfah, the people of Shām should enter *iḥrām* at Juḥfah, and the people of Najd should enter *iḥrām* at Qarn.' Ibn ^cUmar said, 'And they say that he said, "And the people of Yemen should enter *iḥrām* at Yalamlam."'"

٣٨٠ أخبرنا مالك، أخبرنا عبد الله بن دينار، أنه قال: قال عبد الله بن عمر: أمر رسول الله صلّى الله عليه وسلّم أهلَ المدينة أن يُهلّوا من ذي الحُلَيفة وأهلَ الشام من الجُحفة، وأهل نجد من قرن. قال عبد الله بن عمر: أما هؤلاء الثلاث فسمعتهن من رسول الله صلى الله عليه وسلم وأخبرت أن رسول الله صلى الله عليه وسلم قال: وأما أهل اليمن فيهلون من يلملم.

380. Mālik informed us: "^cAbdullāh ibn Dīnār informed us that ^cAbdullāh ibn ^cUmar said, 'The Messenger of Allah ﷺ ordered the people of Madīnah to enter *iḥrām* at Dhu'l-Ḥulayfah, and the people of Shām at Juḥfah, and the people of Najd at Qarn.' ^cAbdullāh ibn ^cUmar said, 'As for these three, I heard them from the Messenger of Allah ﷺ. I have been told that the Messenger of Allah ﷺ said, "And as for the people of Yemen, they should enter *iḥrām* at Yalamlam."'"

٣٨١ أخبرنا مالك، حدثنا نافع: أن ابن عمر أحرم من الفُرُعْ.

381. Mālik informed us: "Nāfi^c narrated to us that Ibn ^cUmar entered *iḥrām* at Furu^c."

٣٨٢ أخبرنا مالك، أخبرني الثقة عندي: أن ابنَ عمر أحرم من إيلياء.

382. Mālik informed us: "I have been told by someone who I consider reliable, that Ibn ^cUmar entered *iḥrām* at Īlyā' [Bayt al-Maqdis]."

قال محمد: وبهذا نأخذ، هذه مواقيت وقَّتها رسولُ الله صلّى الله عليه وسلّم فلا ينبغي لأحد أن

يجاوزَها إذا أراد حجّاً إلاّ مُحرماً، فأمّا إحرام عبد الله بن عمر من الفُرُع وهو دون ذي الحُلَيفة إلى مكة، فإن أمامها وقت آخر وهو الجحفة وقد رُخِّص لأهل المدينة أنْ يُحرموا من الجحفة لأنها وقت من المواقيت. بلغنا عن النبي صلّى الله عليه وسلّم أنه قال: من أحب منكم أن يستمتع بثيابه إلى الجحفة فليفعل. أخبرنا بذلك أبو يوسف، عن إسحاق بن راشد، عن محمد بن علي، عن النبي صلّى الله عليه وسلّم.

Muḥammad said: "We adhere to this. These are places which were appointed by the Messenger of Allah ﷺ so no one ought to pass them, if he intends Ḥajj or ᶜ*umrah,* unless he has entered *iḥrām*. With respect to ᶜAbdullāh ibn ᶜUmar's entering *iḥrām* at Furuᶜ, which is between Dhu'l-Ḥulayfah and Makkah, there is another place appointed after Dhu'l-Ḥulayfah – that being Juḥfah. Allowance has been made for the people of Madīnah to enter *iḥrām* at Juḥfah, as it is one of the appointed places. It has reached us that the Prophet ﷺ said, 'Whoever of you wants to wear his clothes as far as Juḥfah, let him [do so].' Abū Yūsuf informed us of that from Isḥāq ibn Rāshid from Muḥammad ibn ᶜAlī from the Prophet ﷺ."

٢ باب الرجل يُحرم في دُبُر الصلاة وحيث ينبعث به بعيره

2. A Man's Entering *Iḥrām* after Praying, and wherever his Camel should Get Up with Him

٣٨٣ أخبرنا مالك، أخبرنا نافع، عن ابن عمر: أن عمرَ كان يصلّي في مسجد ذي الحُلَيفة، فإذا انبعثت به راحلته أحرم.

383. Mālik informed us: "Nāfiᶜ informed us from Ibn ᶜUmar that ᶜUmar used to pray in the mosque of Dhu'l-Ḥulayfah, then when his mount got up with him, he would enter *iḥrām*."

٣٨٤ أخبرنا مالك، أخبرنا موسى بن عُقبة، عن سالم بن عبد الله أنه سمع ابن عمر يقول: بيداؤكم هذه التي تكذبون على رسول الله صلّى الله عليه وسلّم فيها، وما أهلَّ رسولُ الله صلّى الله عليه وسلّم إلاّ من عند المسجد مسجد ذي الحُلَيفة.

384. Mālik informed us: "Mūsā ibn ᶜUqbah informed us from Sālim ibn ᶜAbdullāh that he heard Ibn ᶜUmar say, 'This plain of yours is the one concerning which you lie about the Messenger of Allah ﷺ; and the Messenger of Allah ﷺ never entered *iḥrām* other than at the mosque, the mosque of Dhu'l-Ḥulayfah.'"

قال محمد: وبهذا نأخذ يحرم الرجل إن شاء في دبر صلاته وإن شاء حين ينبعث به بعيره، وكلٌّ حَسَن وهو قول أبي حنيفة والعامة من فقهائنا.

Muḥammad said: "We adhere to this. A man can enter *iḥrām,* if he wants to, after praying, or, if he wants to, when his camel rises with him; and it is all good. It is also the verdict of Abū Ḥanīfah, and of our *fuqahā᾽* in general."

٣ باب التلبية

3. Saying *Labbayk*

٣٨٥ أخبرنا مالك، حدثنا نافع، عن عبد الله بن عمر: أنّ تلبية النبي صلّى الله عليه وسلّم: لبيك اللّهم لبيك، لبّيك لا شريك لك لبيك، إن الحمدَ والنعمة لك والملك لا شريك لك، قال: وكان عبد الله بن عمر يزيد فيها لَبَّيْكَ لبيك لبيك وسعديك والخير بيديك والرغباء إليك والعمل.

385. Mālik informed us: "Nāfi[c] narrated to us from [c]Abdullāh ibn [c]Umar that the *labbayk* of the Prophet ﷺ is, 'At Your service! O Allah, at Your service! At Your service! You have no partner. At Your service! The praise and blessing are Yours and the kingdom. You have no partner.' [Nāfi[c]] said, 'And [c]Abdullāh ibn [c]Umar used to add to it, "At Your service! At Your service! At Your service and at Your call. Good is in Your hands, and I am at Your service. Our desire is for You, and our action."'"

قال محمد: وبهذا نأخذ، التلبية هي التلبية الأولى التي رُوي عن النبي صلّى الله عليه وسلّم، وما زدتَ فحسنٌ، وهو قول أبي حنيفة والعامّة من فقهائنا.

Muḥammad said: "We adhere to this. The recognised saying of *labbayk* is that first one, which was reported from the Prophet ﷺ; and whatever you add is fine. And That is the verdict of Abū Ḥanīfah, and of our *fuqahā*ʾ in general."

٤ باب متى تُقْطع التلبية

4. When to Stop Saying *Labbayk*

٣٨٦ أخبرنا مالك، أخبرنا محمد بن أبي بكر الثقفي، أنه أخبره أنه سأل أنس بن مالك وهما غاديان إلى عَرَفَة: كيف كنتم تصنعون مع رسول الله صلّى الله عليه وسلّم في هذا اليوم؟ قال: كان يُهِلّ المُهِلّ، فلا يُنْكَرُ عليه ويكبّر المكبّر فلا ينكر عليه.

386. Mālik informed us: "Muḥammad ibn Abī Bakr ath-Thaqafī informed us that he asked Anas ibn Mālik, while they were going out to [c]Arafah, 'How did you use to do [it] with the Messenger of Allah ﷺ on this day?' He said, 'The one declaring [*labbayk*], would do so, and no fault would be found with that, and the one saying *Allāhu akbar* would do so, and no fault would be found with that.'"

٣٨٧ أخبرنا مالك، أخبرنا ابن شهاب، عن عبد الله بن عمر قال: كلُّ ذلك قد رأيتُ الناسَ يفعلونه، فأما نحن فنكبِّر.

387. Mālik informed us: "Ibn Shihāb informed us that [c]Abdullāh ibn [c]Umar said, 'I saw the people do all of that; but as for us, we say *Allāhu akbar*.'"

قال محمد: بذلك نأخذ على أن التلبية هي الواجبة في ذلك اليوم إلاّ أن التكبير لا يُنكر على حالٍ من الحالات والتلبية لا ينبغي أن تكون إلا في موضعها.

Muḥammad said: "We adhere to this, on the understanding that the saying of *labbayk* is the thing incumbent on that day, although the saying of *Allāhu akbar* is never disapproved; and the saying of *labbayk* ought not be said except in its place."

٣٨٨ أخبرنا مالك، أخبرنا نافع: أن عبد الله بن عـمر كان يَدَعُ التلبية إذا انتهى إلى الحرم حتى يطوف بالبيت والصفا والمروة، ثم يلبّي حتى يغدو من منى إلى عَرَفة، فإذا غدا ترك التلبية.

388. Mālik informed us: "Nāfiʿ informed us that ʿAbdullāh ibn ʿUmar would stop saying *labbayk* when he arrived in the Ḥaram [in Makkah], until he had gone around the house and Ṣafā and Marwah. Then he would say it until he went out from Minā to ʿArafah in the morning. Then once he had gone out he would stop saying *labbayk*."

٣٨٩ أخبرنا مالك، أخبرنا عبد الرحمن بن القاسم، عن أبيه: أن عائشة كانت تترك التلبية إذا راحت إلى الموقف.

389. Mālik informed us: "ʿAbd ar-Raḥmān ibn al-Qāsim informed us from his father that ʿĀʾishah used to stop saying *labbayk* when she went over to the standing place [at ʿArafah]."

٣٩٠ أخبرنا مالك، حدثنا علقمة بن أبي علقمة، أن أمّه أخبرته: أن عائشة كانت تنزل بعرفة بنَمِرة، ثم تحوّلتْ فنزلت في الأراك، فكانت عائشة تُهِلّ ما كانت في منزلها ومن كان معها فإذا ركبتْ وتوجّهتْ إلى الموقف تركتْ الإهلال، وكانت تقيم بمكة بعد الحج، فإذا كان قبل هلال المحرّم خرجت حتى تأتي الجُحْفة، فتقيم بها حتى ترى الهلال، فإذا رأت الهلال أهلّت بالعمرة.

390. Mālik informed us: "ʿAlqamah ibn Abī ʿAlqamah narrated to us that his mother told him that at ʿArafah ʿĀʾishah used to camp at Namirah, then she moved round and would camp at Arak. ʿĀʾishah would say the *labbayk* while she remained in her camp, and those who were with her. Then when she mounted and headed for the standing place, she stopped saying *labbayk*. She used to reside in Makkah after the Ḥajj, then, before the new moon of [the month of] Muḥarram, she would go out to Juḥfah and reside there until she saw the new moon. When she saw the new moon, she would declare *ʿumrah*."

قال محمد: من أحرم بالحجّ أو قَرَن لبّى حتى يرمي الجمرة بأول حصاة رمي يوم النحر، فعند ذلك يقطع التلبية. ومن أحرم بعمرة مفردة لبّى حتى يستلم الركن للطواف، بذلك جاءت الآثار عن ابن عباس وغيره وهو قول أبي حنيفة والعامّة من فقهائنا.

Muḥammad said: "Whoever enters *iḥrām* for Ḥajj, or pairs [Ḥajj with *ʿumrah*], should say *labbayk* until throwing the first stone at the jamrah, on the day of slaughter. On doing that he should stop saying *labbayk*. Whoever enters *iḥrām* for *ʿumrah* separately, should say *labbayk* until he reaches the Corner [of the Black Stone], before going around [the House]. With that [implication] the reports have come to us from Ibn ʿAbbās and others; and it is the verdict of Abū Ḥanīfah, and of our *fuqahāʾ* in general."

٥ باب رفع الصوت بالتلبية

5. Saying *Labbayk* with Raised Voice

٣٩١ أخبرنا مالك، أخبرنا عبد الله بن أبي بكر ، أن عبد الملك بن أبي بكر بن الحارث بن هشام أخبره، أن خلاّد بن السائب الأنصاري ثم من بني الحارث بن الخزرج أخبره، أن أباه أخبره ، أن رسول الله صلّى الله عليه وسلّم قال: أتاني جبريل عليه السلام فأمرني أن آمر أصحابي أو مَن معي أن يرفعوا أصواتهم بالإهلال بالتلبية .

391. Mālik informed us: "ᶜAbdullāh ibn Abī Bakr informed us that 'Abdul-Mālik ibn Abī Bakr ibn al-Ḥārith ibn Hishām told him that Khallād ibn as-Sāᵓib al-Anṣārī of Banū al-Ḥārith ibn al-Khazraj told him that his father told him,that the Messenger of Allah ﷺ said, 'Jibril came to me ﷺ and ordered me to order my companions' - [said the narrator] 'or those with me' – 'to raise their voices with the declaration of *labbayk*.'"

قال محمد : وبهذا نأخذ، رفع الصوت بالتلبية أفضل . وهو قول أبي حنيفة والعامّة من فقهائنا .

Muḥammad said: "We adhere to this. Raising the voice with *labbayk* is better. That is the verdict of Abū Ḥanīfah, and of our *fuqahāᵓ* in general."

٦ باب القِران بين الحج والعمرة

6. Performing Ḥajj and ᶜUmrah in One

٣٩٢ أخبرنا مالك، أخبرنا محمد بن عبد الرحمن بن نوفل الأسدي، أنَّ سليمان بن يسار أخبره: أنَّ رسول الله صلّى الله عليه وسلّم عام حجَّة الوداع كان من أصحابه من أهَلَّ بحجٍّ، ومن أهَلَّ بعمرة، ومنهم من جمع بين الحجِّ والعمرة، فحَلَّ من كان أهَلَّ بالعمرة، وأما من كان أهلَّ بالحج أو جمع بين الحج والعمرة فلم يحلّوا .

392. Mālik informed us: "Muḥammad ibn ᶜAbd ar-Raḥmān ibn Nawfal al-Asadī informed us that Sulaymān ibn Yasār told him that, of the companions of the Messenger of Allah ﷺ, in the year of his Farewell Ḥajj, there were those who entered *iḥrām* for Ḥajj, and those who entered *iḥrām* for *ᶜumrah,* and those who combined the Ḥajj and *ᶜumrah*. So those who had entered *iḥrām* for *ᶜumrah* became free of *iḥrām*; but as for those who had entered *iḥrām* for Ḥajj, or had combined the Ḥajj and *ᶜumrah,* they didn't."

قال محمد : وبهذا نأخذ، وهو قول أي حنيفة والعامة .

Muḥammad said: "We adhere to this; and it is the verdict of Abū Ḥanīfah and [our *fuqahāᵓ*] in general."

٣٩٣ أخبرنا مالك، أخبرنا نافع، أن عبد الله بن عمر خرج في الفتنة معتمراً، وقال : إنْ صُددتُ عن البيت صنعنا كما صنعنا مع رسول الله صلّى الله عليه وسلّم : قال : فخرج فأهَلَّ بالعمرة وسار، حتى إذا ظهر على ظهر البيداء التفتَ إلى أصحابه، وقال: ما أمرهما إلاّ واحد ، أُشْهِدُكم أني قد أوجبتُ الحجَّ مع العمرة، فخرج حتى إذا جاء البيت طاف به، وطاف بين الصفا والمروة سبعاً سبعاً لم يَزِدْ عليه، ورأى ذلك مُجْزياً عنه وأهدى.

393. Mālik informed us: "Nāfiᶜ informed us that ᶜAbdullāh ibn ᶜUmar set out

on *ᶜumrah* during the time of civil disturbance, and he said, 'If I am prevented from reaching the House, we shall do as we did with the Messenger of Allah ﷺ.' [Nāfiᶜ] said, 'So he set out and entered *iḥrām* for *ᶜumrah*, and continued until, when he was out on the plain, he turned to his companions and said, "There can be only one thing to do in either case: I declare to you that I have made the Ḥajj obligatory with the *ᶜumrah*." So he went forth until, when he reached the House, he went around it and went to and fro between Ṣafā and Marwah, each seven times and no more. And he considered that this acquitted him, then he slaughtered his *hady* offering.'"

٣٩٤ أخبرنا مالك، حدثنا صدقة بن يسار المكّي، قال: سمعت عبد الله بن عمر ودخلنا عليه قبلَ يومِ التروية بيومين أو ثلاثة، ودخل عليه الناس يسألونه فدخل عليه رجل من أهل اليمن ثائرَ الرأس، فقال: يا أبا عبد الرحمن إني ضَفَّرتُ رأسي، وأحرمتُ بعمرة مفردة، فماذا ترى ؟ قال ابن عمر: لو كنتُ معك حين أحرمتَ لأمرتُكَ أن تُهلَّ بهما جميعاً، فإذا قدمتَ طُفْتَ بالبيت وبالصفا والمروة وكنتَ على إحرامك، لا تحلّ من شيء حتى تحلَّ منهما جميعاً يوم النحر، وتنحَرَ هَدْيك.
وقال له ابن عمر: خُذْ ما تطاير من شعرك، واهْدِ، فقالت له امرأة في البيت وما هَدْيَه يا أبا عبد الرحمن؟ قال: هَدْيُه ثلاثاً، كل ذلك يقول هديه، قال: ثم سكت ابن عمر، حتى إذا أردنا الخروج قال: أما والله لو لم أجد إلا شاةً لكان أُرى أن أذبحها أحبَّ إليَّ من أن أصوم.

394. Mālik informed us: "Ṣadaqah ibn Yasār al-Makkī narrated to us, 'I heard ᶜAbdullāh ibn ᶜUmar, we having visited him two or three days before the day of *Tarwiyah* [8th of Dhu'l-Ḥijjah] and the people were going to see him to question him. A man from Yemen, with flaring hair, went in to see him and said, "Abū ᶜAbd ar-Raḥmān, I plaited my hair, and entered *iḥrām* explicitly for *ᶜumrah*, so what do you think?" Ibn ᶜUmar said, "Had I been with you when you entered *iḥrām*, I would have ordered you to declare them both together, then when you arrived, you would have gone around the House, and Ṣafā and Marwah, and still been in *iḥrām*, not becoming free of anything, until you had become free of them both together on the day of slaughter and then you would have slaughtered your offering." And Ibn ᶜUmar said to him, "Cut what is blowing all over of your hair, and slaughter a *hady* offering." So a woman in the house said, "And what is its due offering, Abū ᶜAbd ar-Raḥmān?" And he said three times "Its offering," each time saying, "Its offering."' [Ṣadaqah] said, 'Then Ibn ᶜUmar went silent, until when we intended to leave, he said, "I should say, by Allah, if I could find nothing but a sheep, I would consider it preferable to slaughter it than to fast."'"

قال محمد: وبهذا نأخذ، القران أفضل، كما قال عبد الله بن عمر. فإذا كانت العمرة وقد حضر الحج، فطاف لها وسعى، فليُقَصِّرْ، ثم ليُحْرِمْ بالحج، فإذا كان يوم النحر حلق وشاة تجزئه، كما قال عبد الله بن عمر، وهو قول أبي حنيفة والعامة من فقهائنا.

Muḥammad said: "We adhere to this. Performing them in one is better, as ʿAbdullāh ibn ʿUmar said. So if he is on ʿumrah, and Ḥajj has begun, and he has done the ṭawāf and saʿy for his ʿumrah, let him shorten his hair and enter iḥrām for the Ḥajj. Then on the day of slaughter he should shave, and a sheep will acquit him, as ʿAbdullāh ibn ʿUmar said. And That is the verdict of Abū Ḥanīfah and of our fuqahāʾ in general."

٣٩٥ أخبرنا مالك ، أخبرنا ابن شهاب : أن محمـد بن عبد الله بن نَوْفَل بن الحارث بن عبد المطلب حدثنا: أنه سَمِع سعد بن أبي وقّاص والضحّاك بن قيس عام حجّ معاوية بن أبي سفيان وهما يذكران التمتُّع بالعمرة إلى الحج، فقال الضحّاك بن قيس : لا يصنع ذلك إلاَّ من جَهِل أمرَ الله تعالى، فقال سعد بن أبي وقاص : بئس ما قلت، قد صنعها رسولُ الله صلّى الله عليه وسلّم، وصنعناها معه .

395. Mālik informed us: "Ibn Shihāb informed us, 'Muḥammad ibn ʿAbdullāh ibn Nawfal ibn al-Ḥārith ibn ʿAbd al-Muṭṭalib narrated to us that he heard Saʿd ibn Abī Waqqāṣ and aḍ-Ḍaḥḥāk ibn Qays, in the year Muʿāwiyah ibn Abī Sufyān performed the Ḥajj, talking about proceeding from ʿumrah to perform Ḥajj[17], and aḍ-Ḍaḥḥāk ibn Qays said, 'No one does that except someone who has no understanding of the command of Allah, exalted is He.' So Saʿd ibn Abī Waqqāṣ said, 'What an evil thing to say; the Messenger of Allah ﷺ did it, and we did it with him.'"

قال محمـد : القِران عندنا أفضل من الإفراد بالحج، وإفراد العمرة، فإذا قرن طاف بالبيت لعمرته وسعى بين الصفا والمروة وطاف بالبيت لحجته، وسعى بين الصفا والمروة، طوافان وسعيان أحبُّ إلينا من طواف واحد وسعي واحـد، ثبت ذلك بما جـاء عن علي بن أبي طالب أنه أمرَ القارن بطوافين وسعيين، وبه نأخذ، وهو قول أبي حنيفة وحمه الله والعامة من فقهائنا .

Muḥammad said: "Performing them in one is better, in our opinion, than performing Ḥajj alone, and [then] ʿumrah alone. So when performing them in one, he should go around the House, and go between Ṣafā and Marwah, for his ʿumrah, and go around the House, and go between Ṣafā and Marwah, for his Ḥajj: performing ṭawāf and saʿy, each twice, is preferable to us than once. That is affirmed by what has been reported from ʿAlī ibn Abī Ṭālib, that he ordered the person who couples Ḥajj and ʿumrah to perform ṭawāf and saʿy each twice. We go according to that, and it is the verdict of Abū Ḥanīfah, may Allah have mercy on him, and of our fuqahāʾ in general."

٣٩٦ أخبرنا مالك، أخبرنا نافع، عن عبد الله بن عمر، أن عمر بن الخطاب قال : افصلوا بين حجّكم وعُمرتكم، فإنه أتمّ لحجّ أحدكم وأتمّ لعمرته أن يعتمر في غير أشهر الحجّ .

396. Mālik informed us: "Nāfiʿ informed us from ʿAbdullāh ibn ʿUmar that ʿUmar ibn al-Khaṭṭāb said, 'Separate your Ḥajj from your ʿumrah, for that gives more weight to your Ḥajj, and it gives more weight to your ʿumrah to perform it outside the months of Ḥajj.'"

قال محمـد : يعتمر الرجل ويرجع إلى أهله ثم يحج ويرجع إلى أهله فيكون ذلك في سفرين أفضل

من القران . ولكن القران أفضل من الحج مفرداً والعمرة من مكة، ومن التمتع والحج من مكة، لأنه إذا قرن كانت عمرته وحجته من بلده وإذا تمتّع كانت حجته مكيّة ، وإذا أفرد بالحج كانت عمرته مكيّة، فالقران أفضلُ، وهو قول أبي حنيفة رحمه الله، والعامَّة من فقهائنا .

Muḥammad said: "A man can perform ᶜumrah and return to his family and then perform Ḥajj and return to his family, for doing that in two journeys is better than performing them in one. However, performing them in one is better than performing Ḥajj explicitly then ᶜumrah from Makkah, or proceeding from ᶜumrah to perform Ḥajj from Makkah, for if he performs them in one, both his ᶜumrah and his Ḥajj will be from his own land, while if he proceeds from ᶜumrah his Ḥajj will be Makkan, or if he performs Ḥajj explicitly his ᶜumrah will be Makkan. So performing them in one is better, and that is the verdict of Abū Ḥanīfah, may Allah have mercy on him, and of our *fuqahāʾ* in general."

٧ باب من أهدى هدياً وهو مقيم

7. Sending an Offering while Remaining Resident

٣٩٧ أخبرنا مالك ، حدثنا عبد الله بن أبي بكر بن محمد بن عمرو بن حزم، أن عَمْرة بنت عبد الرحمن، أخبرته أن ابن زياد بن أبي سفيان كتب إلى عائشة أنَّ ابن عباس قال: مَن أهدى هَدْياً حَرُمَ عليه ما يحرم على الحاجِّ، وقد بعثتُ بهدي، فاكْتُبي إليَّ بأمرك أو مُري صاحبَ الهدي، قالت عَمْرة: قالت عائشة : ليس كما قال ابن عباس، أنا فتلت قلائدَ هَدْي رسول الله صلّى الله عليه وسلّم بيدي ثم قَلَّدها رسولُ الله صلّى الله عليه وسلّم بيده، وبعث بها مع أبي ، ثم لم يَحْرُم على رسول الله شيء كان أحلَّه اللّهُ حتى نحر الهدي .

397. Mālik informed us: "ᶜAbdullāh ibn Abī Bakr ibn ᶜAmr ibn Ḥazm narrated to us that ᶜAmrah bint ᶜAbd ar-Raḥmān told him that Ziyād ibn Abī Sufyān wrote to ᶜĀʾishah, saying that 'Ibn ᶜAbbās had said, "Whoever sends an offering, then those things which are inviolable to someone performing Ḥajj become inviolable to him," and I have sent my offering, so write to me with your instructions or instruct the person accompanying the offering.'" ᶜAmrah said, 'So ᶜĀʾishah said, "It is not as Ibn ᶜAbbās has said. I twisted the garlands of the offering of the Messenger of Allah ﷺ with my own hand, and then the Messenger of Allah ﷺ placed them with his own hand and sent them with my father, and nothing of what Allah has permitted then became inviolable to the Messenger of Allah ﷺ until the offering was slaughtered."'"

قال محمد : وبهذا نأخذ، وإنما يحرم على الذي يتوجه مع هَدْيه يريد مكة وقد ساق بَدَنةً وقلّدها ، فهذا يكون محرماً حين يتوجه مع بدنته المقلّدة بما أراد من حج أو عُمرة. فأما إذا كان مقيماً في أهله لم يكن مُحرماً ولم يَحْرُم عليه شيء حلَّ له، وهو قول أبي حنيفة رحمه الله تعالى .

Muḥammad said: "We adhere to this; the inviolability pertains to someone who sets out with his offering, heading for Makkah and who has driven and garlanded his sacrificial animals. This person is in *iḥrām* while he is on his way with his garlanded sacrifical animals with whatever he has intended of Ḥajj or ᶜ*umrah*. As for if he is resident in his family he is not in *iḥrām* and nothing which is *ḥalāl* for him is *ḥarām* for him, and that is the verdict of Abū Ḥanīfah, may Allah, exalted is He, have mercy on him."

٨ باب تقليد البُدْن وإشعارهم

8. Garlanding and Branding Sacrifical Animals

٣٩٨ أخبرنا مالك، حدثنا نافع، عن عبد الله بن عمر: أنه كان إذا أهدى هدياً من المدينة قلّده وأشعره بذي الحُلَيفة، يقلّده قبل أن يشعره، وذلك في مكان واحد وهو موجِّهُهُ إلى القِبْلة، يقلّده بنعلين، ويُشعره من شقّه الأيسر، ثم يُساق معه حتى يُوقَف به مع الناس بعرفة، ثم يُدفَع به معهم إذا دفعوا، فإذا قَدِم منًى من غداة يوم النحر نَحَرَه قبل أنْ يحلق أو يقصِّر، وكان ينحر هديه بيده يصفُّهُنّ قياماً، ويوجِّهُنّ إلى القِبْلة ثم يأكل ويُطعم.

398. Mālik informed us: "Nāfiᶜ narrated to us from ᶜAbdullāh ibn ᶜUmar that when he used to dedicate a *hady* offering from Madīnah he would garland and brand it at Dhu'l-Ḥulayfah, garlanding it before he branded it, and doing that at the same place while making it face the *qiblah*, garlanding it with two sandals and branding it on its left side. Then he would have it driven along with him until he stood with it along with people at ᶜArafah. Then it would be moved on with him when they moved on. When he came to Minā on the morning of the day of sacrifice he would sacrifice it before shaving or shortening his hair. He would sacrifice his *hady* offering with his own hand, lining them up standing towards the *qiblah*, and then he would eat [the meat] and feed [others]."

٣٩٩ أخبرنا مالك، حدثنا نافع، أنَّ عبدَ الله بنَ عمر كان إذا وَخَزَ في سنام بَدَنَته وهو يُشعرها، قال: بسم الله والله أكبر.

399. Mālik informed us: "Nāfiᶜ narrated to us that when ᶜAbdullāh ibn ᶜUmar nicked the hump of his sacrificial animals while branding them, he used to say, '*Bismillāh wa'llāhu akbar* – In the name of Allah! Allah is greater!'"

٤٠٠ أخبرنا مالك، حدثنا نافع: أنَّ ابنَ عمر كان يشعر بَدَنَته في الشقّ الأيسر إلا أن تكون صعَاباً مقرَّنة، فإذا لم يستطع أن يَدْخل بينها أشعر من الشقّ الأيمن، وإذا أراد أن يُشعرها وجّهها إلى القِبْلة، قال: فإذا أشعرها قال: بسم الله والله أكبر. وكان يُشعرها بيده وينحرها بيده قياماً.

400. Mālik informed us: "Nāfiᶜ narrated to us that 'Ibn ᶜUmar used to brand his sacrificial animals on the left side unless they were obstinate and paired. If he was unable to get in between them, he would brand them on the right side. When he wanted to brand them he would make them face the *qiblah*.' He said, 'When he branded them he said, "In the name of Allah! Allah is

greater!" He used to brand them with his own hand and sacrifice them while they were standing with his own hand.'"

قال محمد : وبهذا نأخذ ، التقليد أفضل من الإشعار، والإشعار حسن ، والإشعار من الجانب الأيسر، إلا أن تكون صعَاباً مُقَرَّنة لا يستطيع أن يدخل بينها فليُشعرها من الجانب الأيسر و الأيمن .

Muḥammad said: "We adhere to this. Garlanding is better than branding, but branding them on the left side is good, unless they are obstinate and paired so that one is unable get in between them, in which case one should brand them on the right side."

٩ باب من تطيّب قبل أن يُحرم

9. Perfuming Oneself before Entering *Iḥrām*

٤٠١ أخبرنا مالك، حدثنا نافع، عن أسلم مولى عمر بن الخطاب: أن عمر بن الخطاب وجد ريحَ طيبٍ وهو بالشجرة ، فقال: ممن ريحُ هذا الطيب؟ فقال معاوية بن أبي سفيان : مني يا أمير المؤمنين قال: منك لَعَمْري ، قال: يا أمير المؤمنين إنَّ أمّ حبيبة طَيَّبَتْني .
قال : عزمتُ عليك لَتَرْجِعَنَّ فَلَتَغْسلَنَّه .

401. Mālik informed us: "Nāfi' narrated to us from Aslam, the *mawlā* of 'Umar ibn al-Khaṭṭāb, that 'Umar ibn al-Khaṭṭāb detected the scent of perfume while he was at ash-Shajarah, and he said, 'From whom is the scent of this perfume?' Mu'āwiyah ibn Abī Sufyān said, 'From me, Amīr al-Mu'minīn.' ['Umar] said, 'From you! by my life!' [Mu'āwiyah] said, 'Amīr al-Mu'minīn, Umm Ḥabībah put the perfume on me.' ['Umar] said, 'I insist you go back and wash it off.'"

٤٠٢ أخبرنا مالك، أخبرنا الصَّلْت بن زُبَيد، عن غير واحد من أهله: أن عمر بن الخطاب وجد ريحَ طيبٍ وهو بالشجرة وإلى جنبه كَثير بن الصلت، فقال : ممّن ريحُ هذا الطّيب؟ قال كثير: منّي، لبَّدتُ رأسي وأردت أن أحلق ، قال عمر: فاذهب إلى شَرَبَة ، فادلكْ منها رأسك حتى تنقّيَه . ففعل كثير بن الصلت .

402. Mālik informed us: "Aṣ-Ṣalt ibn Zubayd informed us from more than one of his family that 'Umar ibn al-Khaṭṭāb detected the scent of perfume while he was at ash-Shajarah, and at his side was Kathīr ibn aṣ-Ṣalt. So he said, 'From whom is the scent of this perfume?' Kathīr said, 'From me: I tucked my hair into a bun, and I was meaning to shave.' 'Umar said, 'Then go to a [palm-] trough and rinse out your hair until you have cleaned it.' And so Kathīr ibn aṣ-Ṣalt did [that]."

قال محمد : وبهذا نأخذ، لا أرى أن يتطيّب المحرم حين يريد الإحرام إلا أن يتطيّب، ثم يغتسل بعد ذلك . وأما أبو حنيفة فإنه كان لا يرى به بأساً .

Muḥammad said: "We adhere to this; I don't think someone who is going to enter *iḥrām* should put on perfume, unless he puts it on and then bathes afterwards. As for Abū Ḥanīfah, he used not to see any harm in it."

١٠ باب من ساق هَدْياً فعَطِبَ في الطريق أو نَذَرَ بَدَنَةً

10. Driving an Offering which then Has an Accident on the way, or Vowing to Slaughter a Camel

٤٠٣ أخبرنا مالك، حدَّثنا ابن شهاب، عن سعيد بن المسيِّب أنه كان يقول: من ساق بَدَنة تطوُّعاً، ثم عَطِبَت فنحرها فلْيَجْعَلْ قلادتَها ونعلَها في دمها، ثم يتركْها للناس يأكلونها، وليس عليه شيء، فإنْ هو أكل منها أو أمر بأكلها فعليه الغُرْم.

403. Mālik informed us: "Ibn Shihāb narrated to us that Saᶜīd ibn al-Musayyab used to say, 'Whoever drives a camel as a voluntary sacrifice which then suffers an accident and so he slaughters it, let him put its garlands and sandals in its blood and then leave it for the people to eat. Nothing more is incumbent upon him. However, should he have eaten from it, or ordered the people to do so, then the debt is due from him.'"

٤٠٤ أخبرنا مالك، أخبرنا هشام بن عروة، عن أبيه: أنَّ صاحب هَدْي رسول الله صلّى الله عليه وسلّم قال له: كيف نَصْنَعُ بما عَطِب من الهدي؟ فقال رسول الله صلّى الله عليه وسلّم: انْحَرْها وأَلْقِ قلادتَها أو نعلَها في دمها وخلِّ بين الناس وبينها يأكلونها.

404. Mālik informed us: "Hishām ibn ᶜUrwah informed us from his father that the man accompanying the *hady* offering of the Messenger of Allah ﷺ said to him, 'What shall we do with those animals of offering which suffer accidents?' So the Messenger of Allah ﷺ said, 'Slaughter them, and throw their garlands and sandals in their blood, and leave them for the people to eat.'"

٤٠٥ أخبرنا مالك، حدثنا عبد الله بن دينار، قال: كنتُ أرى ابنَ عمرَ بن الخطاب يُهدي في الحج بَدَنَتَيْن بَدَنَتَيْن، وفي العمرة بَدَنَة بَدنة، قال: رأيتُه في العمرة يَنْحَرُ بَدَنته وهي قائمةٌ في حرف دار خالد بن أسيد وكان فيها منزله، وقال: لقد رأيتُه طعن في لَبَّة بَدَنَته حتى خَرَجَتْ سِنَّة الحَربة من تحت حَنَكِها.

405. Mālik informed us: "ᶜAbdullāh ibn Dīnār narrated to us, 'I used to see Ibn ᶜUmar ibn al-Khaṭṭāb drive an offering on Ḥajj of two camels each time, and on *ᶜumrah* of one camel each time.' And he said, 'And I saw him during *ᶜumrah* slaughter his camel as it was standing at the perimeter of the house of Khālid ibn Asīd, which was where his camp was.' And he said, 'And I saw him pierce his camel's throat so that the blade of his spear came out from under its palate.'"

٤٠٦ أخبرنا مالك، أخبرنا أبو جعفر القارئ أنه رأى عبدَ الله بنَ عيّاش بن أبي ربيعة أهدى عاماً بَدَنتين، إحداهما بُخْتِيَّة.

406. Mālik informed us: "Abū Jaᶜfar al-Qārīᵓ informed us that one year he saw ᶜAbdullāh ibn ᶜAyyāsh ibn Abī Rabīᶜah drive an offering of two camels, one of them long-necked."

قال محمد: وبهذا نأخذ، كلُّ هَدْي تطوُّعٍ عَطِب في الطريق صنع كما صنع وخلَّى بينه وبين الناس يأكلونه، ولا يعجبنا أن يأكل منه إلاَّ من كان محتاجاً إليه.

Muḥammad said: "We adhere to this. Every offering undertaken voluntarily which suffers an accident on the way should be treated likewise and left for the people to eat. We dislike that anyone should eat from it except for those in need of it."

٤٠٧ أخبرنا مالك، حدثنا نافع، عن ابن عمر: كان يقول: الهدي ما قُلِّد أو أُشعر وأُوقف به بعرفة.

407. Mālik informed us: "Nāfi^c narrated to us that Ibn ^cUmar used to say, 'An offering is that which is garlanded, marked, and made to stand at ^cArafah.'"

٤٠٨ أخبرنا مالك، حدثنا نافع، عن ابن عمر: أنه قال: من نذر بَدَنَة فإنه يقلِّدها نعلاً، ويُشعِرُها، ثم يسوقها، فينحرها عند البيت أو بمنى يوم النحر ليس له مَحِلّ دون ذلك، ومن نذر جَزُوراً من الإبل أو البقر فإنه يَنْحَرُها حيث شاء.

408. Mālik informed us: "Nāfi^c narrated to us that Ibn ^cUmar said, 'Whoever vows [to offer] a camel should garland it with a sandal, mark it, and then drive it and slaughter it at the House or in Minā on the day of slaughter, he having no other place to do it. Whoever vows to slaughter a camel or a cow [but not as an offering] may do it wherever he wishes.'"

قال محمد: وهو قول ابن عمر، وقد جاء عن النبي صلّى الله عليه وسلّم وعن غيره من أصحابه أنهم رخَّصوا في نحر البَدَنة حيث شاء، وقال بعضهم: الهَدْي بمكة لأن الله تعالى يقول: ﴿هَدْياً بالغَ الكعبة﴾ ولم يقل ذلك في البَدَنة: فالبَدَنة حيث شاء إلاّ أن ينوي الحرم فلا ينحرها إلاّ فيه. وهو قول أبي حنيفة وإبراهيم النَّخَعي ومالك بن أنس.

Muḥammad said: "That is the verdict of Ibn ^cUmar. It has been narrated from the Prophet ﷺ and from others of his Companions that they made a concession for the slaughter of sacrificial animals [cows or camels] to be done wherever one wishes. One of them said, 'The *hady* offering is [to be sacrificed] in Makkah because Allah, exalted is He, says, "a sacrifice to reach the Ka^cbah" (Qur'ān 5: 95) but He does not say that about sacrificial animals, so the sacrificial animals are [to be sacrificed] wherever one wishes unless one has intended the Ḥaram, in which case they must only be sacrificed there."' And That is the verdict of Abū Ḥanīfah, Ibrāhīm an-Nakha^cī and Mālik ibn Anas."

٤٠٩ أخبرنا مالك، أخبرني عمرو بن عبيد الله الأنصاري أنه سأل سعيدَ بنَ المسيّب عن بَدَنَة جعلَتْها امرأةٌ عليها، قال: فقال سعيد: البُدْنُ من الإبل ومَحلّ البُدْن البيت العتيق إلاّ أن تكون سمَّتْ مكاناً من الأرض فلتنحرها حيث سمَّتْ، فإنْ لم تجد بَدَنة فبقرة فإن لم تكن بقرة فَعَشْرٌ من الغنم، قال: ثم سألت سالمَ بنَ عبد الله فقال: مثل ما قال سعيد بن المسيب غير أنه قال: إن لم تجد بقرة، فسبع من الغنم، قال: ثم جئتُ خارجةَ بنَ زيد بن ثابت فسألتُه، فقال مثلَ ما قال سالم، ثم جئتُ عبدَ الله بنَ محمد بن عليّ، فقال مثلَ ما قال سالم بن عبد الله.

409. Mālik informed us: "^cAmr ibn ^cUbaydullāh al-Anṣārī informed me that he asked Sa^cīd ibn al-Musayyab about the sacrifice of an animal which a woman had imposed on herself. Sa^cīd said, 'The sacrificial animals are camels and the place for them is the Ancient House unless she has named some

other place in the land, in which case she should slaughter them in the place she has designated. If she does not find a sacrificial camel, then a cow, and if she does not find a cow then ten sheep.' He [ᶜAmr] said, 'Then I asked Sālim ibn ᶜAbdullāh and he said the like of what Saᶜīd ibn al-Musayyab had said except that he said, "If she does not find a cow, then seven sheep."' He [ᶜAmr] said, 'Then I went to Khārijah ibn Zayd ibn Thābit and asked him, and he said the like of what Sālim had said. Then later I went to ᶜAbdullāh ibn Muḥammad ibn ᶜAlī and he said the like of what Sālim ibn ᶜAbdullāh had said.'"

قال محمد: البُدْنُ من الإبل والبقر، ولها أن تنحرها حيث شاءت إلاَّ أن تنوي الحرم، فلا تنحرها إلاَّ في الحرم ويكون هدياً، والبَدَنَة من الإبل والبقر تُجزئ عن سبعة ولا تجزئ عن أكثر من ذلك، وهو قول أبي حنيفة والعامَّة من فقهائنا.

Muḥammad said: "The sacrificial animals are camels or cows, and she may sacrifice them wherever she wishes unless she intended the Ḥaram, in which case she must only sacrifice in the Ḥaram and it will be a *hady* offering. The sacrificial camels and cows are adequately replaced by seven [sheep] but not [there is no need] by more than that. That is the verdict of Abū Ḥanīfah and of our *fuqahā*ʾ in general."

١١ باب الرجل يسوقُ بَدَنَة فيضطرّ إلى ركوبها

11. A Man who is Driving Sacrificial Camels and who is then Forced to Ride them

٤١٠ أخبرنا مالك، أخبرنا هشام بن عروة عن أبيه أنه قال: إذا اضطررتَ إلى بَدَنَتِك فاركَبْها ركوباً غير فادح.

410. Mālik informed us: "Hishām ibn ᶜUrwah informed us from his father that he said, 'If you are forced, then ride your sacrificial animals without overburdening them.'"

٤١١ أخبرنا مالك، أخبرنا أبو الزِّناد، عن الأعرج، عن أبي هريرة: أن النبي صلّى الله عليه وسلّم مرّ على رجل يسوق بَدَنَتَه، فقال له: اركبها، فقال: إنها بَدَنَة، فقال له بعد مرتين: اركبها ويلك.

411. Mālik informed us: "Abu'z-Zinād informed us from al-Aᶜraj from Abū Hurayrah that the Prophet ﷺ passed a man driving his sacrificial animal and said to him, 'Mount it.' He said, 'It is a sacrificial animal.' He said to him after the second time, 'Mount it, woe to you!'"

٤١٢ أخبرنا مالك، أخبرنا نافع، أن ابن عمر كان يقول: إذا نتجت البَدَنة فلْيَحْمِلْ ولدها معها حتى يُنْحر معها، فإنْ لم يجد له محملاً فلْيَحْمِلْهُ على أمِّه حتى يُنحر معها.

412. Mālik informed us: "Nāfiᶜ informed us that Ibn ᶜUmar used to say, 'If the sacrificial animal gives birth, then let its offspring be carried along with it until it is sacrificed along with her. If a form of conveyance cannot be

found for it then let it be carried on its mother until it is sacrificed along with her.'"

٤١٣ أخبرنا مالك، أخبرنا نافع: أن ابن عمر أو عمر شك محمد كان يقول: من أهدى بَدَنَة فضَلَّتْ أو ماتت، فإن كانت نذراً أبدلها، وإن كانت تطوّعاً، فإن شاء أبدلها، وإن شاء تركها.

413. Mālik informed us: "Nāfi[c] informed us that Ibn [c]Umar or [c]Umar – Muḥammad was unsure – used to say, 'Whoever commits a sacrificial animal as a *hady* offering and it strays or dies, then if it was an oath, let him sacrifice another in its place. If it was a voluntary optional act, then if he wishes he can sacrifice another in its place and if he wishes he can leave it.'"

قال محمد: وبهذا نأخذ، ومن اضطر إلى ركوب بَدَنَتِه فليركبْها فإن نقصها ذلك شيئاً تصدَّق بما نقصها وهو قول أبي حنيفة رحمه الله تعالى.

Muḥammad said: "We adhere to this. Someone who is compelled to ride his sacrificial animal should mount it, and if that depreciates it in any way, he should give *ṣadaqah* to the amount by which it has depreciated [in value]. That is the verdict of Abū Ḥanīfah, may Allah have mercy on him."

١٢ باب المحرم يقتل قَمْلَة أو نحوَها أو ينتفُ شعراً

12. A Person in *Iḥrām* who Kills a Louse or the Like or who Plucks out Hair

٤١٤ أخبرنا مالك، عن نافع قال: المُحْرِمُ لا يَصْلُحُ له أن ينتفَ من شعره شيئاً، ولا يحلقه ولا يقصره إلاّ أن يصيبه أذى من رأسه، فعليه فدية، كما أمره الله تعالى. ولا يحلُّ له أن يقلمَ أظفاره ولا يقتلَ قَمْلَةً، ولا يطرحها من رأسه إلى الأرض ولا من جسده ولا من ثوبه، ولا يقتل الصيد ولا يأمر به ولا يدل عليه.

414. Mālik informed us that Nāfi[c] said, "It is not fitting for someone in *iḥrām* to pluck out any of his hair, or shave it, or cut it, unless he is afflicted by a head ailment, in which case expiation is due from him, as Allah, exalted is He, has commanded him. It is not permitted for him to clip his nails, nor kill a louse, nor cast it to the ground from his head, or from his body, or from his garment, nor kill a hunted animal, nor order it to be hunted, nor lead [anyone] to it."

قال محمد: وبهذا نأخذ وهو قول أبي حنيفة رحمه الله تعالى.

Muḥammad said: "We adhere to this. It is the verdict of Abū Ḥanīfah, may Allah have mercy on him."

١٣ باب الحِجامة للمُحرم

13. Cupping for Someone in *Iḥrām*

٤١٥ أخبرنا مالك، أخبرنا نافع: أن ابن عمر كان يقول: لا يحتجم المحرم إلاّ أن يضطر إليه مما لا بدّ منه.

415. Mālik informed us: "Nāfi[c] informed us that Ibn [c]Umar used to say,

'Someone in *iḥrām* should not get himself cupped unless he is compelled to do so by some unavoidable necessity.'"

قال محمد : لا بأس بأن يحتجم المحرم ولكن لا يحلق شعراً. بلغنا عن النبي صلّى الله عليه وسلّم أنه احتجم وهو صائم محرم. وبهذا نأخذ، وهو قول أبي حنيفة رحمه الله والعامّة من فقهائنا.

Muḥammad said: "There is no harm in someone in *iḥrām* being cupped, but he must not cut his hair. It has reached us from the Prophet ﷺ that he was cupped while he was fasting and in *iḥrām*. We adhere to this, and it is the verdict of Abū Ḥanīfah, may Allah have mercy on him, and our *fuqahā'* in general."

١٤ باب المحرم يُغطّي وجهه

14. Someone in *Iḥrām* Covering his Face

٤١٦ أخبرنا مالك، أخبرنا عبد الله بن أبي بكر، أن عبد الله بن عامر بن ربيعة أخبره قال: رأيتُ عثمانَ بنَ عفان بالعَرْج وهو محرم في يومٍ صائف قد غطّى وَجْهَه بقطيفة أُرْجُوان ثم أتي بلحم صيد، فقال: كلوا، قالوا: ألا تأكل؟ قال: لستُ كهيأتكم، إنما صيد من أجلي.

416. Mālik informed us: "ᶜAbdullāh ibn Abī Bakr informed us that ᶜAbdullāh ibn ᶜAmr ibn Rabīᶜah informed him, 'I saw ᶜUthmān ibn ᶜAffān at al-ᶜArj while he was in *iḥrām* on a summer's day and he had covered his face with a red-striped cloth. Then someone brought him meat which had been hunted, and he said, "Eat!" They asked, "Will you not eat?" He answered, "I am not in the same position as you; it was only hunted for my sake."'"

٤١٧ أخبرنا مالك، حدثنا نافع، أن ابن عمر كان يقول: ما فوق الذّقن من الرأس فلا يخمّره المحرم.

417. Mālik informed us: "Nāfiᶜ narrated to us that Ibn ᶜUmar used to say, 'Whatever of the head is above the chin the person in *iḥrām* must not veil it.'"

قال محمد: وبقول ابن عمر نأخذ، وهو قول أبي حنيفة والعامّة من فقهائنا رحمهم الله تعالى.

Muḥammad said: "We adhere to the verdict of Ibn ᶜUmar, and that is the verdict of Abū Ḥanīfah and of our *fuqahā'* in general, may Allah have mercy on them."

١٥ باب المُحرم يغسل رأسه، أيغتسل؟

15. The Person in *Iḥrām* Washing his Head: Should he Wash it?

٤١٨ أخبرنا مالك، حدثنا نافع، أنّ ابن عمر كان لا يغسل رأسه وهو محرم إلا من الاحتلام.

418. Mālik informed us: "Nāfiᶜ narrated to us that Ibn ᶜUmar used not to wash his head while he was in *iḥrām* except in the event of a wet dream.'"

٤١٩ أخبرنا مالك، أخبرنا زيد بن أسلم، عن إبراهيم ابن عبد الله بن حنين، عن أبيه: أن عبد الله ابن عباس، والمِسْوَر بن مَخْرَمة تماريا بالأَبْواء، فقال ابن عباس: يَغْسل المُحرم رأسَه، وقال المِسْوَر: لا

فأرسله ابن عباس إلى أبي أيُّوب يسأله فوجده يغتسل بين القرنين وهو يُستر بثوب، قال: فسلَّمت
عليه فقال: من هذا؟ فقلت: أنا عبد الله بن حنين أرسلني إليك ابنُ عباس أسألُك كيف كان رسولُ
الله صلَّى الله عليه وسلَّم يغسل رأسَه وهو مُحْرِم؟ فوضع يديه على الثوب وطأطأه حتى بدا لي
رأسَه، ثم قال لإنسان يصبُّ الماءَ عليه: اصبُبْ، فصبَّ على رأسه، ثم حرَّك رأسه بيده، فأقبل بيده
وأدبر، فقال: هكذا رأيته يفعل.

419. Mālik informed us: "Zayd ibn Aslam informed us from Ibrāhīm ibn
ʿAbdullāh ibn Ḥunayn from his father that ʿAbdullāh ibn ʿAbbās and al-Miswar
ibn Makhramah had a difference of opinion at al-Abwāʾ and Ibn ʿAbbās
said, 'Someone in *iḥrām* may wash his head,' but al-Miswar said ,'No.' Ibn
ʿAbbās sent him [ʿAbdullāh ibn Ḥunayn] to Abū Ayyūb to ask him and he
found him washing between the two posts of a well, concealed by a garment.
He said, 'I greeted him and he asked, "Who is this?" I said, "ʿAbdullāh ibn
Ḥunayn. Ibn ʿAbbās sent me to ask you how did the Messenger of Allah ﷺ
use to wash his head while he was in *iḥrām*." He placed his hands on the
garment and pulled it down until his head appeared and then he said to
someone who was pouring water over him, "Pour!" And so [the water] was
poured over his head, and then he rocked his head with his hand, drawing
his hand from the front to the back and then back to the front, and he said,
"This was how I saw him doing it."'"

قال محمد: وبقول أبي أيوب نأخذ، لا نرى بأساً أن يغسلَ المحرمُ رأسَه بالماء. وهل يزيده الماء إلاّ
شعثاً ؟! وهو قول أبي حنيفة والعامة من فقهائنا.

Muḥammad said: "We take the verdict of Abū Ayyūb. We see no harm in
someone in *iḥrām* washing his head with water, for does the water increase
him in anything but being dishevelled? And That is the verdict of Abū Ḥanīfah
and of our *fuqahāʾ* in general."

٤٢٠. أخبرنا مالك، أخبرنا حميد بن قيس المكي، عن عطاء بن أبي رَباح، أن عمر بن الخطاب رضي
الله عنه قال ليعلى بن مُنيَّة وهو يصبّ على عمر ماءً وعمر يغتسل: اصبُبْ على رأسي، قال له
يعلى: أتريد أن تجعلها فيَّ؟ إن أمرتني صببتُ، قال: اصبُبْ.
فلم يَزِد الماءَ إلاّ شعثاً.

420. Mālik informed us: "Ḥumayd ibn Qays al-Makkī informed us from ʿAṭāʾ
ibn Abī Rabāḥ that ʿUmar ibn al-Khaṭṭāb ﷺ said to Yaʿlā ibn Munyah who was
pouring water over ʿUmar while he did *ghusl*, 'Pour it over my head!' Yaʿlā said
to him, 'Do you want to make me responsible? If you order me I will pour.' He
said, 'Pour, because water only increases the dishevelled state of the hair!'"

قال محمد: لا نرى بهذا بأساً، وهو قول أبي حنيفة رحمه الله والعامَة من فقهائنا رحمهم الله تعالى.

Muḥammad said: "We see no harm in this, and that is the verdict of Abū
Ḥanīfah, may Allah have mercy on him, and of our *fuqahāʾ* in general, may
Allah, exalted is He, have mercy on them."

١٦ باب ما يُكره للمحرم أن يلبس من الثياب

16. What Clothing is Disapproved for Someone in *Iḥrām*

٤٢١ أخبرنا مالك، أخبرنا نافع، عن ابن عمر : أن رجلاً سأل رسولَ الله صلّى الله عليه وسلّم ماذا يَلْبَسُ المحرمُ من الثياب؟ فقال: لا يَلْبَسُ القُمُص ولا العمائم ولا السراويلات ولا البَرَانس ولا الخفاف إلا أحد لا يجد نعلين، فيَلْبَس خُفَّيْن وليقطَعْهُما أسفلَ من الكعبين ، ولا تلبسوا من الثياب شيئاً مسّه الزَّعفران ولا الورس .

421. Mālik informed us: "Nāfi[c] informed us from Ibn [c]Umar that a man asked the Messenger of Allah ﷺ, 'What clothing may someone in *iḥrām* wear?' He answered, 'He may not wear shirts nor turbans nor trousers nor cloaks nor leather socks, except for someone who cannot find sandals, in which case let him wear two leather socks and cut them down to below the ankles. Do not wear any clothes that have been touched by saffron or yellow dye.'"

٤٢٢ أخبرنا مالك، أخبرنا عبد الله بن دينار قال: قال عبد الله بن عمر: نهى رسولُ الله صلّى الله عليه وسلّم أن يَلْبَسَ المحرمُ ثوباً مصبوغاً بزعفران أو وَرس، وقال: من لم يجد نعلين فيلبسْ خُفَّين. وليقطَعْهما أسفلَ من الكعبين.

422. Mālik informed us: "[c]Abdullāh ibn Dīnār informed us, '[c]Abdullāh ibn [c]Umar said, "The Messenger of Allah ﷺ forbade anyone in *iḥrām* wearing a garment dyed with saffron or yellow dye, and he said, 'Whoever cannot find two sandals may wear leather socks, and he should cut them down to below the ankles.'"'"

٤٢٣ أخبرنا مالك، حدثنا نافع، عن ابن عمر أنه كان يقول: لا تنتقب المرأة المحرمة ولا تلبس القُفَّازين .

423. Mālik informed us: "Nāfi[c] narrated to us from Ibn [c]Umar that he used to say, 'A woman in *iḥrām* may not wear a facial veil nor gloves.'"

٤٢٤ أخبرنا مالك، أخبرنا نافع، عن أسلم مولى عمر بن الخطاب، أنه سمع أسلم يحدّث عبدَ الله بنَ عمر أنَّ عمر بن الخطاب رأى على طلحة بن عبيد الله ثوباً مصبوغاً وهو مُحرم، فقال عمر: ما هذا الثوب المصبوغ يا طلحة؟ قال: يا أمير المؤمنين إنما هو من مَدَر ، قال إنكم أيها الرَّهْط أئمةٌ يقتدي بكم الناس ولو أنَّ رجلاً جاهلاً رأى هذا الثوب لقال : إن طلحة كان يَلْبَس الثياب المصبغة في الإحرام.

424. Mālik informed us: "Nāfi[c] informed us from Aslam, the *mawlā* of [c]Umar ibn al-Khaṭṭāb, that he heard Aslam telling [c]Abdullāh ibn [c]Umar that [c]Umar ibn al-Khaṭṭāb saw Ṭalḥah ibn [c]Ubaydullāh wearing a dyed garment while he was in *iḥrām*. [c]Umar said, 'What is this dyed garment, Ṭalḥah?' He answered, 'Amīr al-Mu[ɔ]minīn it is only from red clay without scent.' He said, 'You group of men are imāms on whom people model themselves. If an ignorant man saw this robe he would say, "Ṭalḥah used to wear dyed garments in *iḥrām*."'"

قال محمد: يُكره أن يَلْبَس المحرم المشبع بالعصفر والمصبوغ بالورس أو الزعفران، إلا أن يكون شيء من ذلك قد غسل، فذهب ريحه وصار لا ينفضُ ، فلا بأس بأن يلبسه .ولا ينبغي للمرأة أن تتنقَّب

فإن أرادت أن تغطي وجهها فلتَسْدِلْ الثوب سدلاً من فوق خمارها على وجهها، وتُجافيه عن وجهها. وهو قول أبي حنيفة والعامة من فقهائنا.

Muḥammad said: "It is disapproved of that the person in *iḥrām* should wear a garment heavily dyed with red or dyed with yellow or saffron unless it is something of that which has been washed so that its scent has gone and it becomes so that it does not give off any scent, then there is no harm in it being worn. A woman ought not to veil her face, so if she wishes to conceal her face she ought to let the upper part of her large outer garment down over her face, keeping it far from her face. That is the verdict of Abū Ḥanīfah and of our *fuqahā᾽* in general."

٤٢٥ أخبرنا مالك، حدثنا حميد بن قيس المكي، عن عطاء بن أبي رباح: أن أعرابياً جاء إلى رسول الله صلّى الله عليه وسلّم وهو بحُنَين وعلى الأعرابي قميصٌ به أثر صُفرة، فقال: يا رسول الله إني أهللتُ بعمرة، فكيف تأمرني أصنع؟ فقال: رسول الله صلّى الله عليه وسلّم: انزع قميصَك واغسل هذه الصُّفرة عنك وافعل في عمرتك مثلَ ما تفعل في حجك.

425. Mālik informed us: "Ḥumayd ibn Qays al-Makkī narrated to us from ᶜAṭā᾽ ibn Abī Rabāḥ that a desert Arab came to the Messenger of Allah ﷺ while he was at Ḥunayn, and the desert Arab was wearing a long shirt on which were the traces of yellow. He said, 'Messenger of Allah, I have entered *iḥrām* for *ᶜumrah*, so what do you command me to do?' So the Messenger of Allah ﷺ answered, 'Remove your shirt and wash off the traces of yellow, and then do on your *ᶜumrah* the like of what you do on your Ḥajj.'"

قال محمد: وبهذا نأخذ، ينزع قميصه ويغسل الصفرة التي به.

Muḥammad said: "We adhere to this. He must take off his shirt and wash out the traces of yellow in it."

١٧ باب ما رُخِّص للمُحرم أن يَقْتُلَ من الدوابّ

17. Those Creatures which Someone in *Iḥrām* is Allowed to Kill

٤٢٦ أخبرنا مالك، حدثنا نافع، عن ابن عمر: أن رسولَ الله صلّى الله عليه وسلّم قال: خمسٌ من الدواب ليس على المحرم في قتلهن جُناح الغراب والفارة والعَقْرب، والحِدَأة، والكلب العقور.

426. Mālik informed us: "Nafi narrated to us from Ibn ᶜUmar that the Messenger of Allah ﷺ said, 'There are five [kinds of] creatures for which there is no harm in the person in *iḥrām* killing: the crow, the rat or mouse, the scorpion, the kite, and the wild [rabid] dog.'"

٤٢٧ أخبرنا مالك، حدثنا عبد الله بن دينار، عن ابن عمر، أن رسول الله صلّى الله عليه وسلّم قال: خمسٌ من الدوابّ، من قَتَلَهُنَّ وهو محرم فلا جناح عليه: العقرب، والفارة، والكلب العَقُور، والغُراب، والحِدَأة.

427. Mālik informed us: "ᶜAbdullāh ibn Dīnār narrated to us from Ibn ᶜUmar

that the Messenger of Allah ﷺ said, 'There are five [kinds of] creatures that whoever kills them while in *iḥrām*, then there is no harm in it: the scorpion, the rat or mouse, the wild dog, the crow and the kite.'"

٤٢٨ أخبرنا مالك، أخبرنا ابن شهاب، عن عمر بن الخطاب : أنه أمر بقتل الحيّات في الحرم .

428. Mālik informed us: "Ibn Shihāb informed us from ᶜUmar ibn al-Khaṭṭāb that he ordered that snakes be killed within the Ḥaram."

٤٢٩ أخبرنا مالك، أخبرنا ابن شهاب قال : بلغني أن سعد بن أبي وقاص كان يقول : أَمَرَ رسول الله صلّى الله عليه وسلّم بقتل الوَزَغ .

429. Mālik informed us: "Ibn Shihāb informed us, 'It has reached me that Saᶜd ibn Abī Waqqāṣ used to say, "The Messenger of Allah ﷺ ordered that the species of white gecko lizard should be killed."'"

قال محمد : وبهذا كلّه نأخذ، وهو قول أبي حنيفة والعامة من فقهائنا .

Muḥammad said: "We adhere to this, and that is the verdict of Abū Ḥanīfah and of our *fuqahā᾽* in general."

١٨ باب الرجل يفوته حج

18. A Man who Misses the Ḥajj

٤٣٠ أخبرنا مالك، أخبرنا نافع، عن سليمان بن يسار : أنَّ هَبّار بن الأسود جاء يوم النحر، و عمر ينحر بُدْنَه، فقال : يا أمير المؤمنين أخطأنا في العدّة كنا نُرى أن هذا اليوم يوم عرفة، فقال له عمر: اذهب إلى مكة فطف بالبيت سبعاً، وبين الصفا والمروة سبعاً، أنت ومن معك وانحر هدياً إن كان معك، ثم احلقوا أو قصّروا وارجعوا فإذا كان قابلٌ فحجوا واهدوا ، فمن لم يجد فيصم ثلاثة أيام في الحج وسبعة إذا رجعتم .

430. Mālik informed us: "Nāfiᶜ informed us from Sulaymān ibn Yasār that Habbār ibn al-Aswad came on the Day of Sacrifice while ᶜUmar was sacrificing his sacrificial animals and said, 'Amīr al-Mu᾽minīn, we have made a mistake in calculation. We thought that today was the day of ᶜArafah.' ᶜUmar said to him, 'Go to Makkah and do *ṭawāf* of the House seven times, and go between Ṣafā and Marwah seven times, you and those with you, and sacrifice a *hady* offering if you have one. Then shave your heads or shorten your hair and return [home]. Then in a future year, perform the Ḥajj and sacrifice a *hady* offering. Whoever is unable should fast three days on the Ḥajj and seven when you return.'"

قال محمد : وبهذا نأخذ وهو قول أبي حنيفة والعامة من فقهائنا إلا في خصلة واحدة، لا هديَ عليهم في قابل ولا صوم. وكذلك روى الأعمش عن إبراهيم النَّخَعي عن الأسود بن يزيد قال: سألت عمر بن الخطاب عن الذي يفوته الحج؟ فقال: يحلّ بعمرة وعليه الحج من قابلٍ، ولم يذكر هدياً، ثم قال: سألت بعد ذلك زيد بن ثابت فقال: مثل ما قال عمر.

Muḥammad said: "We adhere to this and it is the verdict of Abū Ḥanīfah and of our *fuqahā᾽* in general except in one particular; they do not owe a *hady* offering the next year, nor fasting. In that sense, al-Aᶜmash narrated from Ibrāhīm an-Nakhaᶜī from al-Aswad ibn Yazīd that he said, 'I asked ᶜUmar ibn al-Khaṭṭāb about someone who missed the Ḥajj and he said, "He should become free of his *iḥrām* by doing the *ᶜumrah* and he must do the Ḥajj in a future year," but he did not mention a *hady* offering.' Then he said, 'After that I asked Zayd ibn Thābit and he said the same thing that ᶜUmar had said.'"

قال محمد: وبهذا نأخذ، وكيف يكون عليه هَدْيٌ فإن لم يجد فالصيام وهو لم يتمتَّعْ في أشهر الحجّ؟!

Muḥammad said: "We adhere to this. How can it be that he has to sacrifice a *hady* offering, or fast if unable to do so, given he did not perform Ḥajj *Tamattuᶜ* in the months of the Ḥajj?"

١٩ باب الحلَمة والقُراد ينزعه المحرم

19. Mites and Ticks which the *Muḥrim* Removes

٤٣١ أخبرنا مالك، أخبرنا نافع: أن عبد الله بن عمر كان يكره أن ينزعَ المُحرم حَلَمة أو قراداً عن بعيره.

431. Mālik informed us: "Nāfiᶜ informed us that ᶜAbdullāh ibn ᶜUmar used to dislike someone in *iḥrām* removing mites or ticks from their camel."

قال محمد: لا بأس بذلك، قولُ عمرَ بن الخطاب في هذا أعجبُ إلينا من قول ابن عمر.

Muḥammad said: "There is no harm in that. The saying of ᶜUmar ibn al-Khaṭṭāb on this matter is preferable to us than the saying of Ibn ᶜUmar."

٤٣٢ أخبرنا مالك، حدثنا عبد الله بن عمر بن حفص بن عاصم بن عمر بن الخطاب، عن محمد بن إبراهيم التيمي، عن ربيعة بن عبد الله بن الهُدَير، قال: رأيت عمر بن الخطاب رضي الله عنه يُقرِّدُ بعيره بالسُّقيا وهو مُحرم، فيجعله في طين.

432. Mālik informed us: "ᶜAbdullāh ibn ᶜUmar ibn Ḥafṣ ibn ᶜĀṣim ibn ᶜUmar ibn al-Khaṭṭāb narrated to us from Muḥammad ibn Ibrāhīm at-Taymī from Rabīᶜah ibn ᶜAbdullāh ibn al-Hudayr, that he said, 'I saw ᶜUmar ibn al-Khaṭṭāb ﷺ taking the ticks off his camel at as-Suqyā while he was in *iḥrām* and putting them in the clay.'"

قال محمد: وبهذا نأخذ، لا بأس به وهو قول أبي حنيفة والعامة من فقهائنا.

Muḥammad said: "We adhere to this: there is no harm in it, and that is the verdict of Abū Ḥanīfah and of our *fuqahā᾽* in general."

٢٠ باب لُبْس المِنْطَقة والهِمْيان للمُحرم

20. The *Muḥrim* Wearing a Money Belt or Belt

٤٣٣ أخبرنا مالك، حدثنا نافع: أن ابن عمر كان يكره لُبْسَ المنطقة للمحرم.

433. Mālik informed us: "Nāfiᶜ narrated to us that Ibn ᶜUmar used to dislike someone in *iḥrām* wearing a belt."

قال محمد: هذا أيضاً لا بأس به، قد رخَّص غيرُ واحد من الفقهاء في لُبْس الهميان للمُحرم، وقال: استوثقْ من نفقتك.

Muḥammad said: "There is also no harm in this; more than one of the *fuqahā*ʾ have granted a concession for someone in *iḥrām* to wear a money belt." He said, "Keep your money secure!"

٢١ باب المحرم يَحُكُّ جلده

21. The *Muḥrim* Scratching their Skin

٤٣٤ أخبرنا علقمة بن أبي علقمة، عن أمه قالت: سمعتُ عائشة ﷺ تُسألُ عن المُحرم، يحكّ جلده؟ فتقول: نعم فليحكّ وليشدُدْ، ولو رُبطت يداي، ثم لم أجد إلا أن أحكّ برِجْلَيّ لاحتككت.

434. [Mālik informed us:] "ᶜAlqamah ibn Abī ᶜAlqamah informed us from his mother that she said, 'I heard ᶜĀʾishah ﷺ being asked about the *muḥrim* scratching his skin and saying, "Yes, let him scratch and do it hard. Even if my hands were tied, and then I could not find any other way to scratch than with my feet, I would scratch."'"

قال محمد: وبهذا نأخذ، وهو قول أبي حنيفة رحمه الله تعالى.

Muḥammad said: "We adhere to this, and it is the verdict of Abū Ḥanīfah, may Allah, exalted is He, have mercy on him."

٢٢ باب المُحرم يتزوّج

22. The *Muḥrim* Marrying

٤٣٥ أخبرنا مالك، أخبرنا نافع، عن نُبَيْه بن وهب أخي بني عبد الدار: أن عمرَ بنَ عبيد الله أرسل إلى أبانَ بنِ عثمان و أبان أمير المدينة هما مُحرمان، فقال: إني أردتُ أن أُنكح طلحة بن عمر ابنةَ شيبةَ بنِ جبير، وأردتُ أن تحضر ذلك، فأنكر عليه أبان، وقال: إني سمعت عثمان بن عفان قال: قال: رسول الله صلى الله عليه وسلم: لا يَنْكِحُ المحرمُ ولا يَخْطُبُ ولا يُنْكِح.

435. Mālik informed us: "Nāfiᶜ informed us from Nubayh ibn Wahb the brother of Banī ᶜAbd ad-Dār that, 'ᶜUmar ibn ᶜUbaydullāh sent a message to Abān ibn ᶜUthmān – at the time when Abān was Amīr of Madīnah – when they were both in *iḥrām*, saying, "I want to marry Ṭalḥah ibn ᶜUmar to the daughter of Shaybah ibn Jubayr and I would like you to be present at that." Abān was against his doing that and said, "I heard ᶜUthmān ibn ᶜAffān saying, 'The Messenger of Allah ﷺ said, "The person in *iḥrām* does not get married, nor propose marriage nor arrange [another's] marriage."'"'"

٤٣٦ أخبرنا مالك، حدثنا نافع، أن ابن عمر كان يقول: لا يَنكحُ المُحرم ولا يَخْطُبُ على نفسه ولا على غيره.

436. Mālik informed us: "Nāfiʿ narrated to us that Ibn ʿUmar used to say, 'The person in *iḥrām* neither marries nor does he propose marriage, either on his own behalf or on behalf of anyone else.'"

٤٣٧ أخبرنا مالك، حدثنا غَطَفان بن طَريف أخبره: أن أباه طريفاً تزوّج وهو مُحرم فردّ عمر بن الخطاب نكاحَه.

437. Mālik informed us: "Ghaṭafān ibn Ṭarīf narrated to us [and] informed him[18] that his father Ṭarīf married while he was in *iḥrām* and ʿUmar ibn al-Khaṭṭāb repudiated his marriage."

قال محمد: قد جاء في هذا اختلاف، فأبطل أهل المدينة نكاح المحرم، وأجاز أهل مكة وأهل العراق نكاحه. وروى عبد الله بن عباس أنّ رسول الله صلى الله عليه وسلم تزوّجَ ميمونة بنت الحارث وهو مُحرم. فلا نعلم أحداً ينبغي أن يكون أعلمَ بتزوّج رسول الله صلى الله عليه وسلم ميمونة من ابن عباس وهو ابن أختها، فلا نرى بتزوج المحرم بأساً ولكن لا يُقَبِّل ولا يمسّ حتى يحلّ، وهو قول أبي حنيفة والعامة من فقهائنا رحمهم الله تعالى.

Muḥammad said: "A disagreement is narrated concerning this; the people of Madīnah regard the marriage of a person in *iḥrām* as invalid, but the people of Makkah and ʿIrāq regard it as valid. ʿAbdullāh ibn ʿAbbās narrated that the Messenger of Allah ﷺ married Maymūnah bint al-Ḥārith while in *iḥrām*, and we know of no one more likely to be knowledgeable about the marriage of the Messenger of Allah ﷺ to Maymūnah than Ibn ʿAbbās since he was her sister's son. So we see no harm in the marriage of someone in *iḥrām*, but he must not kiss or touch her [with caresses] until he is free of *iḥrām*, and that is the verdict of Abū Ḥanīfah and of our *fuqahāʾ* in general, may Allah, exalted is He, have mercy on them."

٢٣ باب الطواف بعد العصر وبعد الفجر
23. *Ṭawāf* after *ʿAṣr* and *Fajr*

٤٣٨ أخبرنا مالك، أخبرنا أبو الزُّبير المكّي: أنه كان يرى البيتَ يخلو بعد العصر وبعد الصبح، ما يطوف به أحد.

438. Mālik informed us: "Abu'z-Zubayr al-Makkī informed us that he used to see the House deserted after *ʿAṣr* and after the morning prayer without anyone performing *ṭawāf*."

قال محمد: إنما كان يخلو لأنهم كانوا يكرهون الصلاة تَيْنك الساعتين. والطواف لا بُدّ له من صلاة ركعتين، فلا بأس بان يطوف سبعاً ولا يصلي الركعتين حتى ترتفع الشمس وتبيضّ، كما صنع عمر بن الخطاب، أويصلي المغرب. وهو قول أبي حنيفة رحمه الله تعالى.

Muḥammad said: "It was only deserted because they used to disapprove of *ṣalāh* at those two times, and one has to perform a *ṣalāh* of two *rakʿahs* with the *ṭawāf*. There is no harm in someone performing *ṭawāf* seven times without praying the two *rakʿahs* until the sun rises and becomes white, as ʿUmar ibn al-Khaṭṭāb used to do, or pray *Maghrib*. That is the verdict of Abū Ḥanīfah, may Allah, exalted is He, have mercy on him."

٤٣٩ أخبرنا مالك، أخبرنا ابن شهاب، أنّ حميد بن عبد الرحمن أخبره، أن عبد الرحمن أخبره، : أنه طاف مع عمر بن الخطاب بعد صلاة الصبح بالكعبة فلما قضى طوافه نَظَر فلم يرَ الشمس، فركب ولم يسبّح حتى أناخ بذي طُوى فسبَّح ركعتين.

439. Mālik informed us: "Ibn Shihāb informed us that Ḥumayd ibn ᶜAbd ar-Raḥmān informed him that ᶜAbd ar-Raḥmān informed him that he performed *ṭawāf* of the Kaᶜbah with ᶜUmar ibn al-Khaṭṭāb after the *Ṣubḥ* prayer and when he finished his *ṭawāf*, he looked but could not see the sun. He mounted and did not perform the prayer until he dismounted at Dhū Ṭuwā where he performed two *rakᶜahs*."

قال محمد: وبهذا نأخذ، ينبغي أن لا يصلي ركعتي الطواف حتى تطلع الشمس وتبيضّ . وهو قول أبي حنيفة رحمه الله تعالى والعامة من فقهائنا.

Muḥammad said: "We adhere to this. One ought not to perform the two *rakᶜahs* of *ṭawāf* until the sun rises and becomes white, and that is the verdict of Abū Ḥanīfah, may Allah, exalted is He, have mercy on him, and of our *fuqahā'* in general."

٢٤ باب الحلال يذبح الصيد أويصيده: هل يأكل المحرم منه أم لا؟

24. Someone not in *Iḥrām* Slaughtering or Hunting Game: Can the *Muḥrim* Eat from it or not?

٤٤٠ أخبرنا مالك، أخبرنا ابن شهاب، عن عبيد الله بن عبد الله بن عتبة بن مسعود، عن عبد الله بن عباس، عن الصَّعْب بن جَثَّامة الليث: أنه أهدى لرسول الله صلى الله عليه وسلم حماراً وحشيّاً، وهو بالأبواء أوبودّان، فردّه رسول الله صلى الله عليه وسلم، فلما رأى ما في وجهي قال: إنا لم نَرُدَّه عليك إلا أنّا حُرُم.

440. Mālik informed us: "Ibn Shihāb informed us from ᶜUbaydullāh ibn ᶜAbdullāh ibn ᶜUtbah ibn Masᶜūd from ᶜAbdullāh ibn ᶜAbbās from aṣ-Ṣaᶜb ibn Jaththāmah al-Layth that he gave a gift to the Messenger of Allah ﷺ of [the meat of] some wild ass while he was at al-Abwā' or Waddān and the Messenger of Allah ﷺ returned it. 'When he saw the expression on my face he said, "We only returned it to you because we were in *iḥrām*."'"

٤٤١ أخبرنا مالك، أخبرنا ابن شهاب، عن سالم بن عبد الله، أنه سمع أبا هريرة يحدّث عبد الله بن عمر: أنّه مرّ به قومٌ مُحْرِمون بالرَّبَذَة فاستفتَوْه في لحم صيد وجدوا أحلّةً يأكلونه، فأفتاهم بأكله، ثم قدم على عمر بن الخطاب فسأله عن ذلك ، فقال عمر: بم أفتيتَهم ؟ قال: أفتيتُهم بأكله، قال عمر: لو أفتيتَهم بغيره لأوجعتُك .

441. Mālik informed us: "Ibn Shihāb informed us from Sālim ibn ᶜAbdullāh that he heard Abū Hurayrah telling ᶜAbdullāh ibn ᶜUmar that some people in *iḥrām* passed him at ar-Rabadhah and asked him for a judgement about

the meat of game which they found people not in *iḥrām* eating, and he gave them the judgement that they could eat it. Later he went to ᶜUmar ibn al-Khaṭṭāb and asked him about that, and ᶜUmar asked, 'What judgement did you give them?' He answered, 'I gave them the judgement that they could eat it.' ᶜUmar said, 'If you had given them any other judgement, I would have punished you painfully.'"

٤٤٢ أخبرنا مالك، أخبرنا أبو النضر مولى عمر بن عبيد الله، عن نافع مولى أبي قتادة، عن أبي قتادة: أنه كان مع رسول الله صلى الله عليه وسلم حتى إذا كان ببعض الطريق تخلّف من أصحاب له مُحرمين، وهو غير مُحرم فرأى حماراً وحشياً، فاستوى على فرسه فسأل أصحابه أن يُناولوه سوطه، فأبوا فسألهم أن يناولوه رُمحه، فأبَوْا، فأخذه ثم شدّ على الحمار فقتله، فأكل منه بعضُ أصحاب رسول الله صلى الله عليه وسلم وأبى بعضهم فلما أدركوا رسول الله وسلم سألوه عن ذلك فقال: إنما هي طُعمة أطعمَكُمُوها الله.

442. Mālik informed us: "Abu'n-Naḍr, the *mawlā* of ᶜUmar ibn ᶜUbaydullāh, informed us from Nāfiᶜ, the *mawlā* of Abū Qatādah from Abū Qatādah that he was with the Messenger of Allah ﷺ, while they were on the way, until he fell behind with some of his companions, who were in *iḥrām* although he was not in *iḥrām*, and he saw a wild ass. He mounted his horse and asked his companions to pass him his whip but they refused, and he asked them to pass him his spear but they refused, so he took it, caught the ass and killed it. Some of the Companions of the Messenger of Allah ﷺ ate from it and some of them refused to. When they caught up with the Messenger of Allah ﷺ and asked him about that, he said, 'It was only food that Allah fed you.'"

٤٤٣ أخبرنا مالك، حدثنا زيد بن أسلم، عن عطاء بن يسار: أن كعب الأحبار أقبل من الشام في رَكْب مُحرمين حتى إذا كانوا ببعض الطريق وجدوا لحم صيد فأفتاهم كعب بأكله، فلما قدموا على عمر بن الخطاب ذكروا ذلك له، فقال: من أفتاكم بهذا؟ فقالوا: كعب، قال: فإني أمّرتُه عليكم حتى تَرجعوا. ثم لما كانوا ببعض الطريق طريق مكة مرَّت بهم رِجْلٌ من جَرَاد، فأفتاهم كعب بأن يأكلوه ويأخذوه فلما قَدموا على عمر ذكروا ذلك له، فقال: ما حملك على أنْ تُفْتيَهم بهذا؟ قال: يا أمير المؤمنين والذي نفسي بيده إنْ هو إلا نَثْرة حوت ينثره في كل عام مرتين.

443. Mālik informed us: "Zayd ibn Aslam narrated to us from ᶜAṭā᾽ ibn Yasār that Kaᶜb al-Aḥbār was on his way back from Shām with a mounted party in *iḥrām* when at a certain point on the way they found some game meat and Kaᶜb gave them his judgement and they ate it. When they came to ᶜUmar ibn al-Khaṭṭāb they mentioned that to him and he asked, 'Who gave you this judgement?' They answered, 'Kaᶜb.' He said, 'Of course, I put him charge of you until you returned.' Then later when they were at a certain point on the way – the road to Makkah, – a swarm of locusts passed them, and Kaᶜb gave them the judgement that they could eat some and carry some. When they came to ᶜUmar they mentioned that to him and he said, 'What made you

give them this judgement?' He answered, 'Amīr al-Muʾminīn, by the One in Whose hand my self is! It is only a sneeze of a fish, which sneezes it twice a year [Both events occurred completely out of the blue].'"

٤٤٤ أخبرنا مالك، حدثنا زيد بن أسلم : أن رجلاً سأل عمر بن الخطاب فقال : إني أصبتُ جرادات بسَوْطي، فقال: أطْعِم قبضةً من طعام .

444. Mālik informed us: "Zayd ibn Aslam narrated to us that a man asked ᶜUmar ibn al-Khaṭṭāb saying, 'I struck some locusts with my whip [while in *iḥrām*].' He said, 'Give a portion of food.'"

٤٤٥ أخبرنا مالك، أخبرنا هشام بن عروة، عن أبيه : أن الزبير بن العوام كان يتزود صفيف الظِّباء في الإحرام .

445. Mālik informed us: "Hishām ibn ᶜUrwah informed us from his father that az-Zubayr ibn al-ᶜAwwām used to take provision from dried strips of gazelle meat while in *iḥrām*."

قال محمد : وبهذا كلِّه نأخذ، إذا صاد الحلالُ الصيدَ فذبحه فلا بأس بأن يأكل المحرم من لحمه إن كان صيد من أجله أو لم يُصَد من أجله لأن الحلال صاده وذبحه، وذلك له حلال فخرج من حال الصيد وصار لحماً فلا بأس بأن يأكل المحرم منه وأما الجراد فلا ينبغي للمحرم أن يصيده فإن فعل كفَّر ، وتمرة خير من جرادة: كذلك قال عمر بن الخطاب . وهذا كله قول أبي حنيفة والعامّة من فقهائنا رحمهم الله تعالى .

Muḥammad said: "We adhere to all of this. When someone not in *iḥrām* hunts and slaughters, there is no harm in someone in *iḥrām* eating the meat, whether the game was hunted because of him or was not hunted because of him. [This is] because it is was hunted and slaughtered by someone not in *iḥrām* and it is *ḥalāl* for him [to do so]. Therefore, it becomes distinct from the category of game and becomes merely meat, and so there is no harm in the person in *iḥrām* eating it. As for locusts, someone in *iḥrām* ought not to hunt them, and if he does so he must pay the penalty. A date is better than a locust, as ᶜUmar ibn al-Khaṭṭāb said. All of that is the verdict of Abū Ḥanīfah and of our *fuqahāʾ* in general, may Allah, exalted is He, have mercy on them."

٢٥ باب الرجل يعتمر في أشهر الحج ثم يرجع إلى أهله من غير أن يحج

25. A Man Performs *ᶜUmrah* in the Months of Ḥajj and then Returns to his People without Performing Ḥajj

٤٤٦ أخبرنا مالك، أخبرنا ابن شهاب، عن سعيد بن المسيَّب : أن عمر بن أبي سلمة المخزومي استأذن عمر بن الخطاب أن يعتمر في شوال، فأذن له، فاعتمر في شوال ثم قَفَل إلى أهله ولم يحجّ .

446. Mālik informed us: "Ibn Shihāb informed us from Saᶜīd ibn al-Musayyab that ᶜUmar ibn Abī Salamah al-Makhzūmī asked permission of ᶜUmar ibn al-Khaṭṭāb to perform *ᶜumrah* in Shawwāl and he gave him permission. So he performed *ᶜumrah* in Shawwāl and then returned to his family and did not perform the Ḥajj."

قال محمد : وبهذا نأخذ، ولا متعة عليه، وهو قول أبي حنيفة رحمه الله تعالى .

Muḥammad said: "We adhere to this, and he is not obliged to do the *mutᶜah* [form of Ḥajj]. That is the verdict of Abū Ḥanīfah, may Allah, exalted is He, have mercy on him."

٤٤٧ أخبرنا مالك، حدّثنا صدقة بن يسار المكي، عن عبد الله بن عمر أنه قال : لئنْ أعتمرَ قبل الحجّ، وأهدي أحبُّ إليَّ من أن أعتمر في ذي الحجة بعد الحج .

447. Mālik informed us: "Ṣadaqah ibn Yasār al-Makkī narrated to us from ᶜAbdullāh ibn ᶜUmar that he said, 'That I should perform *ᶜumrah* before the Ḥajj and sacrifice a *hady* offering is preferrable to me than performing *ᶜumrah* in Dhu'l-Ḥijjah after the Ḥajj.'"

قال محمد : كلٌّ هذا حسنٌ واسع إن شاء فعل وإن شاء قرن وأهدى فهو أفضل من ذلك .

Muḥammad said: "All of this is good and one has great latitude in it. If one wishes one does that, but if one wishes to pair it with Ḥajj in the same *iḥrām* and sacrifice a *hady* offering, then that is better."

٤٤٨ أخبرنا مالك، أخبرنا هشام بن عروة، عن أبيه : أنَّ النبيَّ صلى الله عليه وسلم لم يعتمر إلا ثلاثَ عُمَرٍ، إحداهنّ في شوال واثنين في ذي القعدة .

448. Mālik informed us: "Hishām ibn ᶜUrwah informed us from his father that the Prophet ﷺ only performed three *ᶜumrahs*, one of them in Shawwāl and the other two in Dhu'l-Qaᶜdah."

٢٦ باب فضل العمرة في شهر رمضان

26. The Superiority of *ᶜUmrah* in Ramaḍān

٤٤٩ أخبرنا مالك، أخبرنا سُمَيٌّ مولى أبي بكر بن عبد الرحمن، أنه سمع مولاه أبا بكر بن عبد الرحمن يقول : جاءت امرأةٌ إلى النبيّ صلى الله عليه وسلم فقالت: إني كنتُ تجهّزتُ للحجّ وأردتُه، فاعترض لي، فقال لها رسول الله صلى الله عليه وسلم: اعتمري في رمضان، فإن عُمْرة فيه كحجّة .

449. Mālik informed us: "Sumayy, the *mawlā* of Abū Bakr ibn ᶜAbd ar-Raḥmān, informed us that he heard his *mawlā* Abū Bakr ibn ᶜAbd ar-Raḥmān saying, 'A woman came to the Prophet ﷺ and said, "I had prepared for the Ḥajj and intended to do it but I was prevented." So the Messenger of Allah ﷺ said to her, "Do *ᶜumrah* in Ramaḍān because *ᶜumrah* in it is like Ḥajj."'"

٢٧ باب المتمتّع ما يجب عليه من الهَدْي

27. What *Hady* Offering is due from Someone who Performs *Tamattuᶜ* Ḥajj

٤٥٠ أخبرنا مالك، حدّثنا عبد الله بن دينار قال: سمعت ابن عمر يقول : من اعتمر في أشهر الحجّ في شوّال أو في ذي القعدة أو ذي الحِجّة ، فقد استمتع ووجب عليه الهَدْي أو الصيام إنْ لم يجد هدياً .

450. Mālik informed us: "ᶜAbdullāh ibn Dīnār narrated to us saying, 'I heard Ibn ᶜUmar saying, "Whoever performs *ᶜumrah* in the months of Ḥajj, or in Shawwāl, or in Dhu'l-Qaᶜdah, or in Dhu'l-Ḥijjah has performed *tamattuᶜ* and is due to pay a *hady* offering or fast if he cannot find a *hady* offering."

٤٥١ أخبرنا مالك، حدثنا ابن شهاب، عن عروة بن الزبير، عن عائشة ﵂ أنها كانت تقول: الصيام لمن تمتّع بالعمرة إلى الحج ممن لم يجد هدياً ما بين أن يهلّ بالحج إلى يوم عرفة فإن لم يصم صام أيّام منى.

451. Mālik informed us: "Ibn Shihāb narrated us from ᶜUrwah ibn az-Zubayr from ᶜĀ'ishah ﵂ that she used to say, 'Whoever performs *tamattuᶜ* [by performing] *ᶜumrah* [and leaving *iḥrām*] until Ḥajj, and cannot find a *hady* offering, fasts between the time he enters *iḥrām* for Ḥajj until the day of ᶜArafah. Then if he has not fasted he fasts on the days of Minā.'"

٤٥٢ أخبرنا مالك، حدثنا ابن شهاب، عن سالم بن عبد الله، عن ابن عمر مثل ذلك.

452. Mālik informed us: "Ibn Shihāb narrated to us from Sālim ibn ᶜAbdullāh from Ibn ᶜUmar the like of that."

٤٥٣ أخبرنا مالك، أخبرنا يحيى بن سعيد، أنه سمع سعيد بن المسّيب يقول: من اعتمر في أشهر الحج في شوال أو في ذي القعدة أو في ذي الحجة، ثم أقام حتى يحجّ فهو متمتّع قد وجب عليه ما استيسر من الهدي أو الصيام إن لم يجد هدياً، ومن رجع إلى أهله ثم حج فليس بمتمتّع.

453. Mālik informed us: "Yaḥyā ibn Saᶜīd informed us that he heard Saᶜīd ibn al-Musayyab saying, 'Whoever performs *ᶜumrah* in the months of Ḥajj, in Shawwāl, Dhu'l-Qaᶜdah or Dhu'l-Ḥijjah and then takes up residence [in Makkah] until he performs Ḥajj is performing *tamattuᶜ* and is obliged to sacrifice whatever is easy by way of *hady* offerings or to fast if he cannot find a *hady* offering. Someone who returns to his family and then later performs the Ḥajj is not performing *tamattuᶜ*.'"

قال محمد: وبهذا كلّه نأخذ وهو قول أبي حنيفة والعامة من فقهائنا رحمهم الله تعالى.

Muḥammad said: "We adhere to all of this, and that is the verdict of Abū Ḥanīfah and of our *fuqahā'* in general, may Allah, exalted is He, have mercy on them."

٢٨ باب الرَّمْل بالبيت

28. Walking at a Brisk Pace around the House

٤٥٤ أخبرنا مالك، حدثنا جعفر بن محمد، عن أبيه، عن جابر بن عبد الله الحَرَامي: أن رسول الله صلى الله عليه وسلم رمل من الحَجَر إلى الحَجَر.

454. Mālik informed us: "Jaᶜfar ibn Muḥammad narrated to us from his father from Jābir ibn ᶜAbdullāh al-Ḥarāmī that the Messenger of Allah ﷺ walked at a brisk pace from the Stone to the Stone."

قال محمد: وبهذا نأخذ، الرمل ثلاثة أشواط من الحجر إلى الحجر. وهو وقول أبي حنيفة والعامّة من فقهائنا رحمهم الله تعالى.

Muḥammad said: "We adhere to this. Walking at a brisk pace is for three circuits from the Stone to the Stone. That is the verdict of Abū Ḥanīfah and of our *fuqahāʾ* in general, may Allah, exalted is He, have mercy on them."

٢٩ باب المكّي وغيره يحجّ أو يعتمر هل يجب عليه الرَّمْل

29. Do the Makkans or Others who Perform the Ḥajj or ʿUmrah have to Walk at a Brisk Pace?

٤٥٥ أخبرنا مالك، أخبرنا هشام بن عروة، عن أبيه: أنه رأى عبد الله بن الزبير أحرم بعمرة من التَّنْعيم، قال: ثم رأيته يسعى حول البيت حتى طاف الأشواط الثلاثة.

455. Mālik informed us: "Hishām ibn ʿUrwah informed us from his father that he saw ʿAbdullāh ibn az-Zubayr put on the *iḥrām* for *ʿumrah* at Tanʿīm. He said, 'Then later I saw him exerting himself energetically in going around the House until he had done three circuits of the *ṭawāf*.'"

قال محمد: وبهذا نأخذ، الرمل واجب على أهل مكة وغيرهم في العمرة والحج، وهو قول أبي حنيفة والعامة من فقهائنا.

Muḥammad said: "We adhere to this. Walking at a brisk pace is necessary for the people of Makkah and others in *ʿumrah* and Ḥajj, and that is the verdict of Abū Ḥanīfah and of our *fuqahāʾ* in general."

٣٠ باب المعتمر أو المعتمرة ما يجب عليهما من التقصير والهدي

30. What is Obligatory on the Man and Woman Performing ʿUmrah with regard to Cutting the Hair and the Hady Offering

٤٥٦ أخبرنا مالك، حدثنا عبد الله بن أبي بكر، أن مولاةً لعَمْرة ابنة عبد الرحمن يقال لها رُقَيّة أخبرته: أنها كانت خرجت مع عَمْرة ابنة عبد الرحمن إلى مكة، قالت: فدخلت عَمْرة مكة يوم التروية وأنا معها. قالت: فطافت بالبيت وبين الصفا والمروة ثم دخلت صُفّة المسجد، فقالت: أمعك مِقَصّان؟ فقلت: لا، قالت: فالْتَمِسيه لي، قالت: فالتمسته حتى جئتُ به، فأخذتْ من قرون رأسها، قالت: فلما كان يوم النحر ذبحَتْ شاة.

456. Mālik informed us: "'ʿAbdullāh ibn Abī Bakr narrated to us that a female *mawlā* of ʿAmrah bint ʿAbd ar-Raḥmān called Ruqayyah informed him that she had gone with ʿAmrah bint ʿAbd ar-Raḥmān to Makkah. She said, 'So ʿAmrah entered Makkah on the day of tarwiyah [the day of providing oneself with water, i.e. the day before ʿArafah] and I went with her.' She said, 'She did *ṭawāf* around the House and did *saʿy* between Ṣafā and Marwah and then entered the roofed area of the mosque, and said, "Do you have scissors with you?" I said, "No." She said, "Find some for me."' She said, 'So I

looked until I could bring her them, and she cut some off her locks of the hair from her head. Then when it was the Day of Sacrifice she slaughtered a ewe.'"

قال محمد: وبهذا نأخذ للمعتمر والمعتمرة، ينبغي أن يقصِّر من شعره إذا طاف وسعى، فإذا كان يومُ النحر ذَبَح ما استيسر من الهدي. وهو قول أبي حنيفة والعامة من فقهائنا رحمهم الله تعالى.

Muḥammad said: "We adhere to this. The man and woman who perform *ᶜumrah* ought to cut their hair if they perform *ṭawāf* and *saᶜy*. Then when it is the Day of Sacrifice they slaughter whatever is easy by way of *hady* offerings. And That is the verdict of Abū Ḥanīfah and of our *fuqahā᾿* in general, may Allah, exalted is He, have mercy on them."

٤٥٧ أخبرنا مالك، أخبرنا جعفر بن محمد، عن أبيه: أن علياً كان يقول: ما استيسر من الهدي شاة.

457. Mālik informed us: "Jaᶜfar ibn Muḥammad informed us from his father that ᶜAlī used to say, '"That which is easy by way of a *hady* offering"[19] means a sheep or a goat.'"

٤٥٨ أخبرنا مالك، أخبرنا نافع، أن ابن عمر كان يقول: ما استيسر من الهدي بعير أو بقرة.

458. Mālik informed us: "Nāfiᶜ informed us that Ibn ᶜUmar used to say, '"That which is easy by way of a *hady* offering" means a camel or a cow.'"

قال محمد: وبقول عليٍّ نأخذ، ما استيسر من الهدي شاة. وهو قول أبي حنيفة والعامة من فقهائنا.

Muḥammad said: "We adhere to the verdict of ᶜAlī. 'That which is easy by way of a *hady* offering' means a sheep. And That is the verdict of Abū Ḥanīfah and of our *fuqahā᾿* in general."

٣١ باب دخول مكة بغير إحرام

31. Entering Makkah without *Iḥrām*

٤٥٩ أخبرنا مالك، حدثنا نافع: أنَّ ابنَ عمر اعتمر، ثم أقبل حتى إذا كان بقُديد جاءه خبر من المدينة، فرجع فدخل مكّة بغير إحرام.

459. Mālik informed us: "Nāfiᶜ narrated to us that Ibn ᶜUmar performed the *ᶜumrah* and was returning, when at Qudayd some news came to him from Madīnah and he went back and entered Makkah without *iḥrām*."

قال محمد: وبهذا نأخذ، من كان في المواقيت أو دونها إلى مكة ليس بينه وبين مكة وقت من المواقيت التي وُقِّتت فلا بأس أن يدخل مكة بغير إحرام وأما من كان خلف المواقيت أيّ وقت من المواقيت التي بينه وبين مكة فلا يدخلنّ مكّة إلا بإحرام. وهو قول أبي حنيفة رحمه الله تعالى والعامة من فقهائنا.

Muḥammad said: "We adhere to this. Whoever is at one of the boundaries of *iḥrām* (*mawāqīt*) or closer than that to Makkah without any of the boundaries of *iḥrām* which have been set up remaining between him and Makkah, then there is no harm if he enters Makkah without *iḥrām*. As for whoever is outside of the boundaries of *iḥrām* – i.e. there remains one of the boundaries of *iḥrām* between him and Makkah – then he may not enter Makkah except in *iḥrām*, and that is the verdict of Abū Ḥanīfah, may Allah, exalted is He, have mercy on him, and of our *fuqahā'* in general."

٣٢ باب فضل الحلْق وما يُجزئ من التقصير

32. The Superiority of Shaving, and what is Sufficient of Shortening the Hair

٤٦٠ أخبرنا مالك، حدثنا نافع، عن ابن عمر، أن عمر بن الخطاب قال: من ضَفَر فليحلِقْ، ولا تُشبِّهوا بالتلبيد.

460. Mālik informed us: "Nāfi^c narrated to us from Ibn ^cUmar that ^cUmar ibn al-Khaṭṭāb said, 'Someone who has plaited his hair should shave it, and do not plait your hair in such a way that it seems you have matted it.'"

٤٦١ أخبرنا مالك، حدثنا نافع، عن ابن عمر: أنَّ رسولَ الله صلى الله عليه وسلم قال: اللّهمّ ارحم المحلِّقين، قالوا: والمقصّرين يا رسول الله؟ قال: اللّهم ارحم المحلّقين، قالوا: والمقصِّرين يا رسول الله؟ قال: اللّهم ارحم المحلّقين، قالوا: والمُقصِّرين يا رسول الله؟ قال: والمُقَصِّرين.

461. Mālik informed us: "Nāfi^c narrated to us from Ibn ^cUmar that the Messenger of Allah ﷺ said, 'O Allah have mercy on those who shave.' They said, 'And the ones who shorten [their hair] Messenger of Allah?' He said, 'O Allah have mercy on those who shave.' They said, 'And the ones who shorten [their hair] Messenger of Allah?' He said, 'O Allah have mercy on those who shave.' They said, 'And the ones who shorten [their hair] Messenger of Allah?' He said, 'And the ones who shorten [their hair].'"

قال محمد: وبهذا نأخذ، من ضفر فليحلِق، والحلق أفضل من التقصير، والتقصير يُجزئ. وهو قول أبي حنيفة والعامة من فقهائنا.

Muḥammad said: "We adhere to this. Let whoever plaits his hair shave. Shaving is better than shortening the hair, but shortening the hair suffices. That is the verdict of Abū Ḥanīfah and of our *fuqahā'* in general."

٤٦٢ أخبرنا مالك، حدثنا نافع: أن ابن عمر كان إذا حلق في حج أو عمرة أخذ من لحيته ومن شاربه.

462. Mālik informed us: "Nāfi^c narrated to us that when Ibn ^cUmar shaved on Ḥajj or *^cumrah* he would take something off his beard and moustache."

قال محمد: ليس هذا بواجب، من شاء فعله. ومن شاء لم يفعله.

Muḥammad said: "This is not necessary, and whoever wishes may do so and whoever does not wish to may leave it out."

٣٣ باب المرأة تَقْدَمُ مكّة بحجّ أو بعمرة فتحيض قبل قدومها أو بعد ذلك

33. A Woman who Comes to Makkah for Ḥajj or ᶜ*Umrah*, but who Enters her Period before or after her Arrival

٤٦٣ أخبرنا مالك، حدثنا نافع، أن ابن عمر كان يقول: المرأة الحائض التي تهلّ بحجّ أو عمرة تهلّ بحجّتها أو بعمرتها إذا أرادت، ولكن لا تطوف بالبيت ولا بين الصفا والمروة حتى تَطَّهّر، وتشهد المناسك كلّها مع الناس غير أنها لا تطوف بالبيت ولا بين الصفا والمروة ولا تقرب المسجد ولا تحل حتى تطوف بالبيت وبين الصفا والمروة.

463. Mālik informed us: "Nāfiᶜ narrated to us that Ibn ᶜUmar used to say, 'The woman in her menstrual period who enters *iḥrām* for Ḥajj or ᶜ*umrah*, enters *iḥrām* for her Ḥajj or ᶜ*umrah* whenever she wishes, but she does not perform *ṭawāf* of the House nor go between Ṣafā and Marwah until she becomes pure. She observes all of the rites with the people except that she may not make *ṭawāf* of the House nor go between Ṣafā and Marwah, nor may she approach the mosque. She may not leave her *iḥrām* until she has made *ṭawāf* of the House and gone between Ṣafā and Marwah.'"

٤٦٤ أخبرنا مالك، حدثني عبد الرحمن بن القاسم، عن أبيه عن عائشة زوج رسول الله صلى الله عليه وسلم أنها قالت: قدمتُ مكّةَ و أنا حائض ولم أطف بالبيت ولا بين الصفا والمروة، فشكوتُ ذلك إلى رسول الله صلى الله عليه وسلم فقال: افعلي ما يفعلُ الحاجُّ غير أن لا تطوفي بالبيت حتى تَطّهَري.

464. Mālik informed us: "ᶜAbd ar-Raḥmān ibn al-Qāsim narrated to us from his father from ᶜĀʾishah the wife of the Messenger of Allah ﷺ that she said, 'I came to Makkah while I was in my menstrual period and I did not make *ṭawāf* of the House nor go between Ṣafā and Marwah. I complained of that to the Messenger of Allah ﷺ and he said, "Do everything that the person performing Ḥajj does except do not perform *ṭawāf* of the House until you become pure."'"

٤٦٥ أخبرنا مالك، حدثنا ابن شهاب، عن عروة بن الزبير، عن عائشة أنها قالت: خرجنا مع رسول الله صلى الله عليه وسلم عامَ حجّة الوداع، فأهللنا بعمرة، ثم قال رسول الله صلى الله عليه وسلم: من كان معه هَدْيٌ فليُهلّ بالحج والعمرة، ثم لا يحلّ حتى يحلّ منهما جميعاً، قالت: فقدمْتُ مكّةَ وأنا حائض ولم أطف بالبيت ولا بين الصفا والمروة، فشكوتُ ذلك إلى رسول الله صلى الله عليه وسلم، فقال: انقُضي رأسك وامتشطي وأهلّي بالحج ودعي العمرة، قالت: ففعلتُ، فلما قضيتُ الحج أرسلني رسول الله صلى الله عليه وسلم مع عبد الرحمن بن أبي بكر إلى التنعيم فاعتمرتُ، فقال رسول الله صلى الله عليه وسلم: هذه مكان عمرتك، وطاف الذين حَلّوْا بالبيت وبين الصفا والمروة ثم طافوا طوافاً آخر بعد أنْ رجعوا من منى. وأما الذين كانوا جمعوا الحج والعمرة فإنما طافوا طوافاً واحداً.

465. Mālik informed us: "Ibn Shihāb narrated to us from ᶜUrwah ibn az-Zubayr that ᶜĀʾishah said, 'We went out with the Messenger of Allah ﷺ in the year of the Farewell Ḥajj, and we entered into *iḥrām* for ᶜ*umrah*. Then the Messenger

of Allah ﷺ said, "Whoever has a *hady* offering with him, then let him enter *iḥrām* for Ḥajj and *ᶜumrah* and then let him not leave *iḥrām* until he leaves *iḥrām* for both of them together."' She said, 'I arrived in Makkah while I was in my menstrual period and I did not do *ṭawāf* of the House nor did I go between Ṣafā and Marwah. I complained of that to the Messenger of Allah ﷺ and he said, "Untie your plaits and comb your hair, then enter *iḥrām* for Ḥajj and leave out the *ᶜumrah*."' She said, 'So I did that. Then when I had done the Ḥajj, the Messenger of Allah ﷺ sent me with ᶜAbd ar-Raḥmān ibn Abū Bakr to Tanᶜīm, and I performed the *ᶜumrah* [having become free from the menstruation]. The Messenger of Allah ﷺ said, "This is the place of your *ᶜumrah*." The ones who had become free of *iḥrām* did *ṭawāf* of the House and then went between Ṣafā and Marwah, and then they did another *ṭawāf* after they returned from Minā. As for those who had joined Ḥajj and *ᶜumrah*, they only did one *ṭawāf*.'"

قال محمد: وبهذا نأخذ، الحائض تقضي المناسك كلّها غير أن لا تطوف ولا تسعى بين الصفا والمروة حتى تَطَهّر، فإن كانت أهلّتْ بعمرة فخافت فوت الحج فلْتُحْرم بالحج، وتقفْ بعرفة، وترفُض العمرة، فإذا فرغت من حجّها قضتْ العمرة كما قضتها عائشة، وذبحت ما استيسر من الهَدْي.

Muḥammad said: "We adhere to this. The woman in her menstrual period does all of the rites except that she does not do *ṭawāf* of the House nor does she do *saᶜy* between Ṣafā and Marwah until she has become purified. If she had entered *iḥrām* for an *ᶜumrah* and had feared missing the Ḥajj, then let her enter *iḥrām* for Ḥajj and stand on ᶜArafah, and let her leave out the *ᶜumrah*. Then when she has finished her Ḥajj, she may discharge the *ᶜumrah* as ᶜĀ᾿ishah discharged it, and let her slaughter whatever is easy by way of a *hady* offering."

بلغنا أن النبي صلى الله عليه وسلم ذبح عنها بقرة، وهذا كله قول أبي حنيفة رحمه الله إلا من جمع الحج والعمرة فإنه يطوف طوافين ويسعى سعيَيْن.

"It has reached me that the Prophet ﷺ sacrificed a cow for her. All of this is the verdict of Abū Ḥanīfah, may Allah have mercy on him, except that whoever unites Ḥajj and *ᶜumrah* performs two *ṭawāfs* and does *saᶜy* twice."

٣٤ باب المرأة تحيض في حجّها قبل أن تطوف طواف الزيارة

34. A Woman Entering her Menstrual Period during her Ḥajj before she has Performed the *Ṭawāf al-Ifāḍah* [before Leaving Makkah]

٤٦٦ أخبرنا مالك، أخبرني أبو الرجال، أن عَمْرة أخبرته: أن عائشة كانت إذا حجّتْ ومعها نساء تخاف أنْ تَحِضْنَ قَدَّمَتْهُنَّ يوم النحر فأَفَضْنَ، فإن حِضْنَ بعد ذلك لم تنتظر، تَنْفرُ بهن وهن حُيَّضٌ إذا كن قد أَفَضْنَ.

466. Mālik informed us: "Abu'r-Rijāl informed me that ᶜAmrah informed him that when ᶜĀ᾿ishah did the Ḥajj together with women whom she feared would enter into their menstrual periods, would send them on ahead on the

Day of Sacrifice so that they could do the *Ṭawāf al-Ifāḍah*. If they entered their menstrual periods after that she would not, but would leave in a group with them [to Madīnah] while they were in their menstrual periods since they had performed the *Ṭawāf al-Ifāḍah*."

٤٦٧ أخبرنا مالك، حدثنا عبد الله بن أبي بكر، أنَّ أباه أخبره عن عَمْرة ابنة عبد الرحمن عن عائشة قالت: قلت يا رسول الله صلى الله عليه وسلم: إنَّ صَفيَّة بنتَ حُيَيٍّ قد حاضت لعلها تَحْبِسُنا، قال: ألم تكن طافت معكن بالبيت؟ قلن: بلى إلاَّ أنها لم تَطف طواف الوداع، قال: فاخْرُجْن .

467. Mālik informed us: "ʿAbdullāh ibn Abī Bakr narrated to us that his father narrated to him from ʿAmrah bint ʿAbd ar-Raḥmān that ʿĀʾishah said, 'I said, "Messenger of Allah ﷺ, Ṣafiyyah bint Ḥuyayy has menstruated and perhaps she will detain us." He said, "Has she not done *ṭawāf* of the House with all of you?" They said, "Yes, of course, except that she has not done the *Farewell Ṭawāf*." He said, "So leave."'"

٤٦٨ أخبرنا مالك، حدثنا عبد الله بن أبي بكر، عن أبيه، أن أبا سلمة بن عبد الرحمن بن عوف أخبره عن أم سُلَيْم ابنة مِلْحان قالت: استفتيتُ رسول الله صلى الله عليه وسلم فيمن حاضت أو ولدت بعدما أفاضَتْ يومَ النَّحْر فأذن لها رسول الله صلى الله عليه وسلم فخَرَجَتْ.

468. Mālik informed us: "ʿAbdullāh ibn Abū Bakr narrated to us from his father that Abū Salamah ibn ʿAbd ar-Raḥmān ibn ʿAwf informed him from Umm Sulaym bint Milḥān that she said, 'I asked for a *fatwā* from the Messenger of Allah ﷺ concering someone who had her menstrual period or had given birth after having done the *Ṭawāf al-Ifāḍah* on the Day of Sacrifice. The Messenger of Allah ﷺ gave her permission, and so she departed.'"

قال محمد: وبهذا نأخذ، أيّما امرأةٍ حاضت قبل أن تطوف يوم النحر طواف الزيارة أو ولدت قبل ذلك فلا تنفرَنَّ حتى تطوف طواف الزيارة ، وإن كانت طافت طواف الزيارة ثم حاضت أو ولدت فلا بأس بأن تنفِر قبل أن تطوف طواف الصَّدَر . وهو قول أبي حنيفة رحمه الله تعالى والعامة من فقهائنا .

Muḥammad said: "We adhere to this. Any woman who enters her menstrual period before performing the *Ṭawāf al-Ifāḍah* on the Day of Sacrifice or gives birth before that, should not leave until she has performed the *Ṭawāf al-Ifāḍah*. If she had performed the *Ṭawāf al-Ifāḍah* and then later entered her menstrual period or gave birth then there is no harm in her departing before performing the *ṭawāf* of departure. That is the verdict of Abū Ḥanīfah, may Allah, exalted is He, have mercy on him, and of our *fuqahā*ʾ in general."

٣٥ باب المرأة تريد الحج أو العمرة فتلد أو تحيض قبل أن تُحرم

35. A Woman who Wants to do Ḥajj or *ʿUmrah* and then Gives Birth or Enters her Menstrual Period before Putting on *Iḥrām*

٤٦٩ أخبرنا مالك، أخبرنا عبد الرحمن بن القاسم، عن أبيه، أن أسماء بنت عُمَيْس وَلَدَتْ

محمدَ بن أبي بكر بالبَيْداء ، فذكر ذلك أبو بكر لرسول الله صلى الله عليه وسلم، فقال رسول الله صلى الله عليه وسلم: مُرْها فلتغتسل ثم لتهلّ .

469.Mālik informed us: "ᶜAbd ar-Raḥmān ibn al-Qāsim informed us from his father that Asmā' bint ᶜUmays gave birth to Muḥammad ibn Abī Bakr at al-Baydā'. Abū Bakr mentioned that to the Messenger of Allah ﷺ and the Messenger of Allah ﷺ said, 'Tell her to do *ghusl* and then enter *iḥrām*.'"

قال محمد: وبهذا نأخذ في النُّفساء والحائض جميعاً. وهو قول أبي حنيفة والعامة من فقهائنا .

Muḥammad said: "We adhere to this with respect to both women in the state immediately after having given birth and women in their menstrual periods."

٣٦ باب المستحاضة في الحجّ

36. The Woman on Ḥajj whose Bleeding Continues beyond its Normal Term

٤٧٠ أخبرنا مالك، أخبرنا أبو الزُّبَيْر المكي، أن أبا ماعز عبد الله بن سفيان أخبره: أنه كان جالساً مع عبد الله بن عمر، فجاءته امرأة تستفتيه فقالت: إني أقبلتُ أريد أن أطوف البيت حتى إذا كنتُ عند باب المسجد أهرقت ، فرجعتُ حتى ذهب ذلك عني، ثم أقبلتُ حتى إذا كنتُ عند باب المسجد أهرقت، فرجعت حتى ذهب ذلك عني، ثم رجعت إلى باب المسجد أيضاً، فقال لها ابن عمر: إنما ذلك رَكْضَة من الشيطان فاغتسلي ثم استثفري بثوبٍ ثم طوفي .

470. Mālik informed us: "Abu'z-Zubayr al-Makkī informed us that Abū Māᶜiz ᶜAbdullāh ibn Sufyān informed us that he was sitting with ᶜAbdullāh ibn ᶜUmar and a woman came to seek his *fatwā*. She said, 'I came wanting to do *ṭawāf* of the House, but when I came to the door of the mosque I started bleeding. I went back until that had left me, and then I returned but when I was at the door of the mosque I started bleeding. I went back until that had left me, and then I returned but when I was at the door of the mosque again…' Ibn ᶜUmar said to her, 'That [uncertainty] is only an impulse from *shayṭān*, so do *ghusl* and then bind [the private parts] with cloth and do *ṭawāf*.'"

قال محمد: وبهذا نأخذ، هذه المستحاضة فلتتوضأ ولتستثفر بثوب ثم تطوف وتصنع ما تصنع الطاهرة. وهو قول أبي حنيفة رحمه الله تعالى والعامة من فقهائنا.

Muḥammad said: "We adhere to this. This woman whose bleeding extends beyond her normal term must do *wuḍū'* [after having done a ghusl for the end of her menstrual period] and bind [her private parts] with cloth then do the *ṭawāf*, and do exactly the same as the woman who is not in her period does. That is the verdict of Abū Ḥanīfah, may Allah, exalted is He, have mercy on him, and of our *fuqahā'* in general."

٣٧ باب دخول مكة وما يُستحبّ من الغسل قبل الدخول

37. Entering Makkah and what *Ghusl* is Desirable before Entry

٤٧١ أخبرنا مالك، حدثنا نافع، عن ابن عمر: أنه كان إذا دنا من مكة بات بذي طُوى بين الثنيَّتَيْن حتى يصبح ثم يصلي الصبح، ثم يدخل من الثنيّة التي بأعلى مكة، ولا يدخل مكة إذا خرج حاجّاً أو معتمراً حتى يغتسل قبل أن يدخل إذا دنا من مكة بذي طُوى، ويأمر من معه فيغتسلوا قبل أن يدخلوا.

471. Mālik informed us: "Nāfi^c^ narrated to us from Ibn ^c^Umar that when he used to draw nearer to Makkah he would spend the night at Dhū Ṭuwā in between the two mountain trails until the dawn when he would pray *Ṣubḥ*. Then he would enter by the trail which is in upper Makkah. He would not enter Makkah when he went as a Ḥajj or one performing *^c^umrah,* unless he had performed *ghusl* before entering, when he had drawn close to Makkah at Dhū Ṭuwā. He would tell those people with him and they would perform *ghusl* before entering."

٤٧٢ أخبرنا مالك، أخبرنا عبد الرحمن بن القاسم: أنّ أباه القاسم كان يدخل مكة ليلاً وهو معتمر فيطوف بالبيت وبالصفا والمروة ويؤخّر الحِلاق حتى يصبح، ولكنه لا يعود إلى البيت فيطوف به حتى يحلق، وربما دخل المسجد فأوتر فيه، ثم انصرف فلم يقرب البيت.

472. Mālik informed us: "^c^Abd ar-Raḥmān ibn al-Qāsim informed us that his father al-Qāsim used to enter Makkah by night when performing *^c^umrah* and do *ṭawāf* of the House and go between Ṣafā and Marwah delaying the shaving of his head until the morning. However, he would not return to the House and perform *ṭawāf* until he had shaved. Often he would enter Makkah and perform *Witr* there and then go without having approached the House."

قال محمد: لا بأس بأن يدخل مكة إن شاء ليلاً وإن شاء نهاراً، فيطوف ويسعى. ولكنه لا يعجبنا له أن يعود في الطواف حتى يحلق أو يقصر كما فعل القاسم، فأما الغسل حين يدخل فهو حسن وليس بواجب.

Muḥammad said: "There is no harm in entering Makkah, if one wishes, by day or by night, performing *ṭawāf* and *sa^c^y,* but I dislike the idea that one goes back and repeats more *ṭawāf* until one has shaved or shortened one's hair, as al-Qāsim did. As for *ghusl* when one enters it is good, but it is not necessary."

٣٨ باب السعي بين الصفا والمروة

38. *Sa^c^y* between Ṣafā and Marwah

٤٧٣ أخبرنا مالك، أخبرنا نافع، عن عبد الله بن عمر: أنه كان إذا طاف بين الصفا والمروة بدأ بالصفا فرَقِي حتى يبدُوَ له البيت، وكان يكبّر ثلاث تكبيرات ثم يقول: لا إله إلا الله وحده لا شريك له، له المُلك وله الحمد يُحيي ويُميت، وهو على كل شيء قدير، يفعل ذلك سبع مرات فذلك إحدى وعشرون تكبيرة وسبع تهليلات، ويدعو فيما بين ذلك، ويسأل الله تعالى ثم يهبط، فيمشي حتى

إذا جاء بطنَ المسيل سعى حتى يظهر منه، ثم يمشي حتى يأتي المروة فيرقَى فيصنع عليها مثل ما صنع على الصفا، يصنع ذلك سبع مرات حتى يفرغ من سعيه.

وسمعتُه يدعو على الصفا: اللهم إنك قلتَ ادعوني أستجبْ لكم وإنك لا تُخلفُ الميعاد وإني أسألك كما هديتَني للإسلام أن لا تنزعَه مني حتى توفَّاني و أنا مسلم.

473. Mālik informed us: "Nāfiʿ informed us from ʿAbdullāh ibn ʿUmar that when he went between Ṣafā and Marwah he would begin at Ṣafā and would climb until the House would appear to him. Then he would say *Allāhu akbar* three times and say, 'There is no god but Allah alone without partner. His is the kingdom and His is the praise. He gives life and He gives death. And He has power over all things,' doing that seven times with twenty-one *Allāhu akbar* and seven *lā ilāha illa'llāh*. He would supplicate in between that and would ask Allah, exalted is He. Then he would descend and would walk until he came to the bottom of the water-course when he would exert himself [by walking faster] until he had come back up again. Then he would walk until he came to Marwah which he would ascend and do on it the like of what he had done on Ṣafā, doing that seven times until he had finished his *saʿy*."

٤٧٤ أخبرنا مالك، أخبرنا جعفر بن محمد، عن أبيه، عن جابر بن عبد الله: أن رسول الله صلى الله عليه حين هَبط من الصفا مشى حتى إذا انصبّت قدماه في بطن المَسيل سعى حتى ظهر منه، قال: وكان يُكبّر على الصفا والمروة ثلاثاً، ويهلَّل واحدة. يفعلُ ذلك ثلاث مرات.

474. Mālik informed us: "Jaʿfar ibn Muḥammad informed us from his father from Jābir ibn ʿAbdullāh that when the Messenger of Allah ﷺ came down from Ṣafā he walked until his feet went down to the bottom of the water-course, he would exert himself [by walking faster] until he had come back up again. He said, 'He would say "*Allāhu akbar*" three times and "*lā ilāha illa'llāh*" once,' doing that three times."

قال محمد: وبهذا كله نأخذ، إذا صَعد الرجل الصفا كبّر وهلَّل ودعا، ثم هبط ماشياً حتى يبلغ بطن الوادي، فيسعى فيه حتى يخرج منه، ثم يمشي مشياً على هيْنته حتى يأتي المروة فيصعد عليها، فيكبّر ويهلَّل ويدعوه، يصنع ذلك بينهما سبعاً، يسعى في بطن الوادي في كل مرة منهما وهو قول أبي حنيفة والعامة.

Muḥammad said: "We adhere to this, all of it. When a man ascends Ṣafā he says '*Allāhu akbar*', '*lā ilāha illa'llāh*' and supplicates. Then he descends walking until he reaches the bottom of the water-course in which he exerts himself [by walking faster] until he comes out of it. Then he walks with stillness and dignity until he reaches Marwah and climbs upon it, where he says '*Allāhu akbar*', '*lā ilāha illa'llāh*' and supplicates. He does that between the two seven times, exerting himself [by walking faster] in the bottom of the water-course every time in between them. That is the verdict of Abū Ḥanīfah and of our *fuqahāʾ* in general."

٣٩ باب الطواف بالبيت راكباً أو ماشياً

39. Making *Ṭawāf* of the House Mounted or Walking

٤٧٥ أخبرنا مالك، أخبرنا محمد بن عبد الرحمن بن نوفل الأسدي، عن عروة، عن زينب بنت أبي سلمة، عن أمّ سَلَمة زوج النبي صلى الله عليه وسلم أنها قالت: اشتكيتُ فذكرتُ ذلك لرسول الله صلى الله عليه وسلم، فقال: طوفي من وراء الناس و أنت راكبة، قالت: فطفتُ ورسولُ الله صلى الله عليه وسلم يصلي إلى جانب البيت، ويقرأ بالطور وكتاب مسطور.

475. Mālik informed us: "Muḥammad ibn ᶜAbd ar-Raḥmān ibn Nawfal al-Asadī informed us from ᶜUrwah from Zaynab bint Abī Salamah from Umm Salamah the wife of the Prophet ﷺ that she said, 'I had a complaint and so I mentioned that to the Messenger of Allah ﷺ and he said, "Do *ṭawāf* behind people, mounted."' She said, 'So I did *ṭawāf* while the Messenger of Allah ﷺ was doing *ṣalāh* at the side of the House reciting, "By the Mount and an Inscribed Book." (Sūrah 52: 1)'"

قال محمد: وبهذا نأخذ، لا بأس للمريض وذي العلّة أن يطوفَ بالبيت محمولاً ولا كفّارة عليه. وهو قول أبي حنيفة رحمه الله تعالى والعامة من فقهائنا.

Muḥammad said: "We adhere to this. There is no harm in a sick person and a person with a valid excuse performing the *ṭawāf* while being carried, and there is no expiation due from them. That is the verdict of Abū Ḥanīfah, may Allah, exalted is He, have mercy on him, and of our *fuqahā'* in general."

٤٧٦ أخبرنا مالك، أخبرنا عبد الله بن أبي بكر، عن ابن أبي مُلَيكة، أن عمر بن الخطاب رضي الله عنه مرّ على امرأة مجذومة تطوف بالبيت فقال: يا أَمَةَ الله، اقعدي في بيتك، ولا تؤذي الناس. فلما توفي عمر بن الخطاب أتت، فقيل لها: هَلَكَ الذي كان ينهاكِ عن الخروج، قالت: واللّه لا أُطيعه حيّاً وأعصيه مَيّتاً.

476. Mālik informed us: "ᶜAbdullāh ibn Abū Bakr informed us from Ibn Abī Mulaykah that ᶜUmar ibn al-Khaṭṭāb ﷺ passed a leprous woman doing *ṭawāf* of the House and he said, 'Slave of Allah, sit in your house and do not cause harm to people!' When ᶜUmar ibn al-Khaṭṭāb died, she came and someone said to her, 'The one who forbade you to go out has died.' She said, 'By Allah! I will not obey him while alive and then disobey him when dead.'"

٤٠ باب استلام الركن

40. Touching the Corner

٤٧٧ أخبرنا مالك، حدثنا سعيد بن أبي سعيد المَقْبَري، عن عُبَيد بن جُرَيج، أنه قال لعبد الله بن عمر: يا أبا عبد الرحمن، رأيتك تصنع أربعاً ما رأيتُ أحداً من أصحابك يصنعها! قال: فما هُنَّ يا ابن جُرَيج؟ قال: رأيتُك لا تَمَسُّ من الأركان إلاّ اليمانيَيْن، ورأيتُك تَلْبَس النِّعالَ السِّبْتية، ورأيتُكَ تصبُغُ بالصُّفْرة، ورأيتك إذا كنتَ بمكّة أهلَّ الناسُ إذا رأوْا الهلال ولم تهلِّلْ أنتَ حتى يكونَ يومُ التروية! قال عبد الله: أما الأركان فإني لم أرَ رسول الله صلى الله عليه وسلم استلم إلاّ اليمانيَيْن. وأما النعال السِّبْتية فإني رأيتُ رسول الله صلى الله عليه وسلم يلبس النعال التي ليس فيها شعر ويتوضأُ

فيها، فإني أحبُّ أن أَلْبَسَها . وأما الصُّفْرة فإني رأيتُ رسولَ الله ﷺ يصبُغُ بها فأنا أحبُّ أن أصبُعَ بها .
وأما الإهلال فإني لم أرَ رسولَ الله صلى الله عليه وسلم يُهلُّ حتى تنبعث به راحلته .

477. Mālik informed us: "Saʿīd ibn Abī Saʿīd al-Maqbarī from ʿUbayd ibn Jurayj that he said to ʿAbdullāh ibn ʿUmar, 'Abū ʿAbd ar-Raḥmān, I have seen you doing four things which I have not seen any of your companions doing.' He asked, 'What are they, Ibn Jurayj?' He said, 'I have seen you only touching the two Yemeni corners, I have seen you wearing hairless leather sandals, I have seen you dyeing with yellow dye, and I have seen you when you were in Makkah when people began calling out the *labbayk* when they saw the new moon [of Dhu'l-Ḥijjah], you did not call out the *labbayk* until the day of watering [the 8th of Dhu'l-Ḥijjah].' ʿAbdullāh said, 'As for the corners, I never saw the Messenger of Allah ﷺ touching any but the two Yemeni corners. As for hairless leather sandals, I saw the Messenger of Allah ﷺ wearing sandals upon which there was no hair and doing wuḍūʾ while wearing them, and so I love to wear them. As for the yellow dye, I saw the Messenger of Allah ﷺ dyeing with it and I love to dye with it. As for declaring the *labbayk*, I never saw the Messenger of Allah ﷺ declaring the *labbayk* until his mount rose to go with him [to Minā and then ʿArafah].'"

قال محمد: وهذا كلُّه حَسَن، ولا ينبغي أن يستلم من الأركان، إلا الركن اليماني والحَجَر ، وهما
اللذان استلمهما ابن عمر. وهو قول أبي حنيفة والعامة .

Muḥammad said: "All of this is good. One ought not to touch any corners except for the Yemeni corner and the Stone, which are the two Ibn ʿUmar touched. That is the verdict of Abū Ḥanīfah and of [our *fuqahāʾ*] in general."

٤٧٨ أخبرنا مالك، أخبرنا ابن شهاب، عن سالم بن عبد الله، أن عبد الله بن محمد بن أبي بكر
الصدِّيق رضي الله عنه أخبر عبدَ الله بن عمر، عن عائشة أنَّ رسول الله صلى الله عليه وسلم قال: ألم
تَرَي أن قومَك حين بَنَوا الكعبة اقتصروا عن قواعد إبراهيم عليه السلام؟ قالت : فقلت : يا رسول
الله، أفلا تردّها على قواعد إبراهيم؟ قالت : فقال: لولا حِدثانُ قومك بالكفر، قال : فقال عبد الله
بن عمر: لئن كانت عائشةُ سمعت هذا من رسول الله صلى الله عليه وسلم ما أرى رسولَ الله صلى الله
عليه وسلم ترك استلام الركنين اللذين يَلِيَان الحجرَ إلاَّ أن البيتَ لم يتمَّ على قواعد إبراهيم عليه
السلام .

478. Mālik informed us: "Ibn Shihāb informed us from Sālim ibn ʿAbdullāh that ʿAbdullāh ibn Muḥammad ibn Abū Bakr aṣ-Ṣiddīq ﷺ informed ʿAbdullāh ibn ʿUmar from ʿĀʾishah that the Messenger of Allah ﷺ said, 'Do you not see that when your people built the Kaʿbah, they fell short of the foundations of Ibrāhīm ﷺ?' She said, 'So I said, "Messenger of Allah, will you not return them to the foundations of Ibrāhīm?" and he said, "If it were not for the recentness of your people's kufr."' ʿAbdullāh ibn ʿUmar said, 'If it was ʿĀʾishah that heard this from the Messenger of Allah ﷺ, then I can only conclude that

the Messenger of Allah ﷺ left off touching the corners that come after the Stone because the House was not completely built on the foundations of Ibrāhīm ﷺ.'"

٤١ باب الصلاة في الكعبة ودخولها
41. Ṣalāh in the Kaʿbah and Entering it

٤٧٩ أخبرنا مالك، أخبرنا نافع، عن ابن عمر: أن رسول الله صلى الله عليه وسلم دخل الكعبة هو وأسامةُ بن زيد وبلال وعثمان بن طلحة الحجبي، فأغلقها عليه، ومكث فيها، قال عبد الله : فسألتُ بلالاً حين خرجوا ماذا صنع رسول الله صلى الله عليه وسلم؟ قال : جعل عموداً عن يساره، وعمودين عن يمينه، وثلاثة أعمدة وراءه، ثم صلّى ، وكان البيت يومئذ على ستة أعمدة .

479. Mālik informed us: Nāfiʿ informed us from Ibn ʿUmar that the Messenger of Allah ﷺ entered the Kaʿbah – he, Usāmah ibn Zayd, Bilāl and ʿUthmān ibn Ṭalḥah al-Ḥajabī – and [ʿUthmān] closed it after him, and he stayed inside for some time. ʿAbdullāh said, 'I asked Bilāl when they came out what the Messenger of Allah ﷺ had done? He said, "He put a pillar to his left and a pillar to his right and three pillars behind him and then he performed *ṣalāh*. The House in those days was [built] on six pillars."'"

قال محمد : وبهذا نأخذ الصلاة في الكعبة حسنة جميلة . وهو قول أبي حنيفة والعامة من فقهائنا .

Muḥammad said: "We adhere to this. *Ṣalāh* in the Kaʿbah is beautiful and good, and that is the verdict of Abū Ḥanīfah and of our *fuqahāʾ* in general."

٤٢ باب الحج عن الميت أو عن الشيخ الكبير
42. Ḥajj on behalf of a Dead Person or an Elderly Man

٤٨٠ أخبرنا مالك، أخبرنا ابن شهاب أن سليمان بن يسار أخبره أن عبد الله بن عباس أخبره قال : كان الفضل بن عباس رديفَ رسول الله صلى الله عليه وسلم، قال : فأتتْ امرأةٌ من خثعَم تستفتيه ، قال: فجعل الفضل ينظر إليها، وتنظر إليه، قال : فجعل رسول الله صلى الله عليه وسلم يَصرف وجه الفضل بيده إلى الشِّقّ الآخَر، فقالت : يا رسول الله، إنَّ فريضةَ الله على عباده في الحج أدركَتْ أبي شيخاً كبيراً لا يستطيع أن يثْبُتَ على الراحلة، أفأحجُّ عنه؟ قال: نعم ، وذلك في حجة الوادع .

480. Mālik informed us: "Ibn Shihāb informed us that Sulaymān ibn Yasār informed him that ʿAbdullāh ibn ʿAbbās informed him, 'Al-Faḍl ibn ʿAbbās was riding behind the Messenger of Allah ﷺ on the same camel.' He said, 'A woman from Khathʿam came to ask him for a *fatwā*.' He said, 'Al-Faḍl began looking at her and she began looking at him. So the Messenger of Allah ﷺ turned al-Faḍl's face away to the other side with his hand, and she said, "Messenger of Allah, the obligation of the Ḥajj upon the slaves of Allah reached my father as an old man unable to sit firmly on his mount. Should I do Ḥajj on his behalf?" He said, "Yes."' And that was during the Farewell Ḥajj.'"

٤٨١ أخبرنا مالك، أخبرنا أيوب السَّخْتياني، عن ابن سيرين، عن رجل أخبره، عن عبد الله بن عباس أن رجلاً أتى النبيَّ صلى الله عليه وسلم فقال: إنَّ أمّي امرأةٌ كبيرة لا نستطيع أن نحملها على بعير، وإنْ ربطناها خفنا أن تموت، أفأحجّ عنها؟ قال: نعم.

481. Mālik informed us: "Ayyūb as-Sakhtiyānī informed us from Ibn Sīrīn from a man who informed him from ʿAbdullāh ibn ʿAbbās that a man came to the Prophet ﷺ and said, 'My mother is an old woman whom we are unable to mount on a camel, and whom if we fastened we would be afraid that she would die. Should I perform the Ḥajj on her behalf?' He said, 'Yes.'"

٤٨٢ أخبرنا مالك، أخبرنا أيوب السَّخْتياني، عن ابن سيرين: أن رجلاً كان جَعَلَ عليه أن لا يبلغ أحدٌ من وَلَده الحَلَبَ فيَحلبُ فيشرب ويستقيه إلاَّ حجَّ وحجَّ به، قال: فبلغ رجلٌ من ولده الذي قال، وقد كَبِرَ الشيخ، فجاء ابنه إلى النبي صلى الله عليه وسلم فأخبره الخَبَرَ، فقال إن أبي قد كبر وهو لا يستطيع الحج أفأحج عنه؟ قال: نعم.

482. Mālik informed us: "Ayyūb as-Sakhtiyānī informed us from Ibn Sīrīn that a man had vowed that if any of his sons reached the age to milk [cattle], and did the milking, drank the milk and gave him to drink, then he would perform the Ḥajj with his son. He said, 'One of the man's sons attained to what he had stipulated.' He said, 'And the shaykh had become old. His son came to the Prophet ﷺ and told him the story, and he said, "My father has aged and is unable to perform the Ḥajj. Should I perform the Ḥajj for him?" He said, "Yes."'"

قال محمد: وبهذا نأخذ، لا بأس بالحجِّ عن الميت وعن المرأة والرجل إذا بلغا من الكبر ما لا يستطيعان أن يحجّا. وهو قول أبي حنيفة والعامة من فقهائنا رحمهم الله تعالى. وقال مالك بن أنس: لا أرَى أن يحجَّ أحدٌ عن أحدٍ.

Muḥammad said: "We adhere to this. There is no harm in doing the Ḥajj on behalf of a dead person or a man and a woman who have reached advanced old age as long as they are unable to perform the Ḥajj. That is the verdict of Abū Ḥanīfah and of our *fuqahā'* in general, may Allah, exalted is He, have mercy on them. Mālik ibn Anas said, 'I do not think that anyone may perform the Ḥajj on behalf of anyone else.'"

٤٣ باب الصلاة بمنى يوم التروية

43. The Prayer at Minā on the Day of Watering (8th Dhu'l-Ḥijjah)

٤٨٣ أخبرنا مالك، أخبرنا نافع: أن ابنَ عمر كان يصلي الظهر والعصر والمغرب والعشاء والصبح بمنى، ثم يغدُو إذا طلعت الشمس إلى عرفة.

483. Mālik informed us: "Nāfiʿ informed us that Ibn ʿUmar used to pray *Ẓuhr, ʿAṣr, Maghrib, ʿIshā'* and *Ṣubḥ* at Minā and then he would go to ʿArafah early in the morning when the sun rose."

قال محمد: هكذا السنَّة فإن عجَّل أو تأخَّر فلا بأس إن شاء الله تعالى. وهو قول أبي حنيفة رحمه الله.

Muḥammad said: "Thus is the *Sunnah*. If he hastens or delays, then there is no harm inshāʾAllāh, exalted is He. That is the verdict of Abū Ḥanīfah, may Allah have mercy on him."

٤٤ باب الغسل بعرفة يوم عرفة

44. Doing *Ghusl* at ᶜArafah on the Day of ᶜArafah

٤٨٤ أخبرنا مالك، أخبرنا نافع: أن ابن عمر كان يغتسل بعرفة يوم عرفة حين يريد أن يروح.

484. Mālik informed us: "Nāfiᶜ informed us that Ibn ᶜUmar used to do *ghusl* at ᶜArafah on the Day of ᶜArafah when he wanted to go in the afternoon [to the place of standing or the Mount of Mercy in particular]."

قال محمد: هذا حسن وليس بواجب.

Muḥammad said: "This is good, but it is not obligatory."

٤٥ باب الدَّفع من عرفة

45. Pressing on from ᶜArafah

٤٨٥ أخبرنا مالك، أخبرنا هشام بن عروة، أنَّ أباه أخبره، أنه سمع أسامة بن زيد يُحدِّث عن سَيْر رسول الله صلى الله عليه وسلم حين دَفَعَ من عَرَفَة، فقال: كان يَسير العَنَقَ حتى إذا وَجَدَ فَجْوَةً نَصَّ. قال هشام: والنصّ أرْفَعُ من العَنَق.

485. Mālik informed us: "Hishām ibn ᶜUrwah informed us that his father informed him that he heard Usāmah ibn Zayd narrating about the travelling of the Messenger of Allah ﷺ when he pressed on from ᶜArafah, and he said, 'He used to travel at a moderate and easy pace (*ᶜanaq*) until he found an opening, when he would press on urgently and quickly (*naṣṣ*).' Hishām said, 'Travelling urgently and quickly is higher than doing so at a moderate pace.'"

قال محمد: بَلَغَنا أنه قال صلى الله عليه وسلم: عليكم بالسَّكِينَة فإنَّ البِرَّ ليس بإيضاع الإبل وإيجاف الخيل. وبهذا نأخذ وهو قول أبي حنيفة رحمه الله.

Muḥammad said: "It has reached us that he ﷺ said, 'Be tranquil! Because good-natured right action (*birr*) is not to hurry camels and spur on horses.' We adhere to this, and it is the verdict of Abū Ḥanīfah, may Allah have mercy on him."

٤٦ باب بطن محسِّر

46. The Bottom of [the valley of] Muḥassir

٤٨٦ أخبرنا مالك، أخبرنا نافع: أن ابن عمر كان يُحَرِّك راحلَته في بطن محسِّر كقَدْر رمْيَة بحَجَر.

486. Mālik informed us: "Nāfi[c] informed us that Ibn [c]Umar used to urge his mount on in the bottom of Muḥassir for the distance one can throw a stone."

قال محمَّدٌ : هذا كلُّه واسعٌ إن شئتَ حرَّكتَ ، وإن شئت سرْتَ على هيْنَتِك بَلَغَنا أنَّ النبيَّ صلى الله عليه وسلم قال في السَّيرين جميعاً: عليكم بالسَّكينَة . حين أفاضَ من عَرَفَة، وحين أفاضَ من المُزدَالفَة .

Muḥammad said: "All of this is acceptable. If you wish you may urge [the mount] on, but if you wish you may travel at your normal pace. It has reached us that the Prophet ﷺ said concerning both movings on together [either pace], 'Be tranquil!' when he pressed on from [c]Arafah and when he pressed on from Muzdalifah."

٤٧ باب الصلاة بالمزدلفة

47. *Ṣalāh* at Muzdalifah

٤٨٧ أخبرنا مالك ، أخبرنا نافع: أن عبد الله بن عمر كان يصلي المغرب والعشاء بالمُزدَلفة جميعاً .

487. Mālik informed us: "Nāfi[c] informed us that [c]Abdullāh ibn [c]Umar used to pray *Maghrib* and *[c]Ishāʾ* together at Muzdalifah."

٤٨٨ أخبرنا مالك، أخبرنا ابن شهاب، عن سالم بن عبد الله، عن ابن عمر: أن رسول الله صلى الله عليه وسلم صلّى المغرب والعشاء بالمُزدَلفة جميعاً .

488. Mālik informed us: "Ibn Shihāb informed us from Sālim ibn [c]Abdullāh from Ibn [c]Umar that the Messenger of Allah ﷺ prayed *Maghrib* and *[c]Ishāʾ* together at Muzdalifah."

٤٨٩ أخبرنا مالك، أخبرنا يحيى بن سعيد، عن عدي بن ثابت الأنصاري، عن عبد الله بن يزيد الأنصاري الخَطْمي، عن أبي أيوب الأنصاري قال: صلّى رسول الله صلى الله عليه وسلم المغربَ والعشاءَ بالمُزْدَلفَة جميعا في حَجَّة الوَدَاع .

489. Mālik informed us: "Yaḥyā ibn Sa[c]īd informed us from [c]Adī ibn Thābit al-Anṣārī from [c]Abdullāh ibn Yazīd al-Anṣārī al-Khatmī from Abū Ayyūb al-Anṣārī that he said, 'The Messenger of Allah ﷺ prayed *Maghrib* and *[c]Ishāʾ* together at Muzdalifah during the Farewell Ḥajj.'"

قال محمد: وبهذا نأخذ. لا يصلي الرجلُ المغربَ حتى يأتي المُزْدَلفَة، وإن ذهب نصف الليل، فإذا أتاها أذَّن وأقام فيصلي المغرب والعشاءَ بأذان وإقامة واحدة. وهو قولَ أبي حنيفة رحمه الله والعامة من فقهائنا .

Muḥammad said: "We adhere to this. A man must not pray *Maghrib* until he reaches Muzdalifah, even if half of the night has gone. When he gets there he calls the call to prayer and the *iqāmah* and prays *Maghrib* and *[c]Ishāʾ* with one call to prayer and one *iqāmah*. That is the verdict of Abū Ḥanīfah and of our *fuqahāʾ* in general."

٤٨ باب ما يَحْرُم على الحاج بعد رمي جمرة العَقَبَة يوم النحر

48. What is Forbidden to the Person Performing Ḥajj after Stoning the Pillar at ᶜAqabah on the Day of Sacrifice

٤٩٠ أخبرنا مالك، أخبرنا نافع وعبد الله بن دينار، عن عبد الله بن عمر: أنَّ عمر بن الخطاب خطب الناس بعَرَفَة فعلَّمهم أمرَ الحجّ، وقال لهم فيما قال: ثم جئتم منًى، فمن رمى الجمرة التي عند العقبة فقد حلَّ له ما حَرُم عليه إلاَّ النِّسَاء والطيب، لا يَمَسَّ أحدٌ نساءً ولا طيباً حتى يطوف بالبيت.

490. Mālik informed us: "Nāfiᶜ and ᶜAbdullāh ibn Dīnār informed us from ᶜAbdullāh ibn ᶜUmar that ᶜUmar ibn al-Khaṭṭāb gave a *khuṭbah* to people at ᶜArafah and taught them the matters of Ḥajj. Among that which he said to them was, 'Then you come to Minā. Whoever stones the pillar which is at ᶜAqabah, then everything which was ḥarām to him becomes ḥalāl except for [intercourse with] women and scent. No one must touch women or scent until he has performed *ṭawāf* of the House.'"

٤٩١ أخبرنا مالك، حدثنا عبد الله بن دينار، أنه سمع ابن عمر يقول: قال عمر بن الخطاب رضي الله عنه: من رمى الجَمْرة ثم حلق أو قصَّر، ونحر هدياً إن كان معه حلَّ له ما حَرُم عليه في الحج إلاَّ النِّسَاء والطِّيبَ حتى يطوف بالبيت.

491. Mālik informed us: "ᶜAbdullāh ibn Dīnār narrated to us that he had heard Ibn ᶜUmar saying, 'ᶜUmar ibn al-Khaṭṭāb ﷺ said, "Whoever stones the pillar and then shaves or cuts his hair, and sacrifices a *hady* offering if he has one, everything which was ḥarām to him becomes *ḥalāl*, except for [intercourse with] women and scent until he has performed *fāwaṭ* of the House."'"

قال محمد: هذا قول عمر وابن عمر. وقد رَوَتْ عائشة خلاف ذلك قالت: طَيَّبْتُ رسول الله صلى الله عليه وسلم بيَدَيّ هاتين بعد ما حلق قبل أن يزور البيت، فأخذنا بقولها. وعليه أبو حنيفة والعامَّة من فقهائنا.

Muḥammad said: "This is the verdict of ᶜUmar and Ibn ᶜUmar. ᶜĀʾishah narrated the contrary of that. She said, 'I perfumed the Messenger of Allah ﷺ with these two hands of mine after he had shaved and before he visited the House,' and we adhere to her verdict, as did Abū Ḥanīfah and our *fuqahāʾ* in general."

٤٩٢ أخبرنا مالك، حدثنا عبد الرحمن بن القاسم، عن عائشة أنها قالت: كنت أُطَيِّب رسول الله صلى الله عليه وسلم لإحرّامه قبل أن يُحرم، ولحلِّه قبل أن يطوف بالبيت.

492. Mālik informed us: "ᶜAbd ar-Raḥmān ibn al-Qāsim narrated to us from ᶜĀʾishah that she said, 'I used to perfume the Messenger of Allah ﷺ for his entering *iḥrām* before he did so, and for his leaving the state of *iḥrām* before he did *ṭawāf* of the House.'"

قال محمد: وبهذا نأخذ في الطيب قبل زيارة البيت ونَدَعُ ما روى عمر وابن عمر رضي الله تعالى عنهما، وهو قولُ أبي حنيفة والعامَّة من فقهائنا.

Muḥammad said: "We adhere to this concerning scent before visiting the House and we leave out that which ᶜUmar and Ibn ᶜUmar narrated, may Allah, exalted is He, be pleased with both of them. That is the verdict of Abū Ḥanīfah and of our *fuqahāʾ* in general."

٤٩ باب من أيِّ موضع يُرمى الجمار

49. From which Place does One Stone the Pillars?

٤٩٣ أخبرنا مالك، قال: سألت عبد الرحمن بن القاسم: من أين كان القاسم بن محمد يرمي جَمرَةَ العَقَبة؟ قال: من حيث تَيَسَّرَ.

493. Mālik informed us: "I asked ᶜAbd ar-Raḥmān ibn al-Qāsim, 'From where did al-Qāsim ibn Muḥammad use to stone the pillar at ᶜAqabah?' He answered, 'From wherever it was easy.'"

قال محمَّد: أفضلُ ذلك أن يرمي من بطن الوادي، ومن حيث ما رمى فهو جائز وهو قول أبي حنفية والعامة.

Muḥammad said: "The best of that is that he should stone from the bottom of the valley, but from wherever he does stone it is acceptable. That is the verdict of Abū Ḥanīfah and of our *fuqahāʾ* in general."

٥٠ باب تأخير رمي الجمار من علّةٍ أو من غير علّةٍ وما يُكره من ذلك

50. Delaying Stoning the Pillar with and without Excuse, and what is Disapproved of that

٤٩٤ أخبرنا مالك، حدثنا عبد الله بن أبي بكر، أن أباه أخبره، أن أبا البَدَّاح بن عاصم بن عدي أَخْبَرَه، عن أبيه عاصم بن عديّ، عن رسول الله صلى الله عليه وسلم: أنه رخّص لرعاء الإبل في البيتوتة يَرْمُون يوم النحر، ثم يرمون من الغد، أو من بعد الغد ليَوْمين، ثم يرمون يوم النَّفر.

494. Mālik informed us: "ᶜAbdullāh ibn Abī Bakr narrated to us that his father informed him that Abu'l-Baddāḥ ibn ᶜĀṣim ibn ᶜAdī informed him from his father ᶜĀṣim ibn ᶜAdī from the Messenger of Allah ﷺ that he gave a concession for those pasturing camels not to spend the night [at Minā] and to stone on the Day of Sacrifice [10th Dhu'l-Ḥijjah], then to stone on the next day [11th Dhu'l-Ḥijjah], or [stone] for both days on the day after the next [12th Dhu'l-Ḥijjah] and then to stone on the day of departure [13th Dhu'l-Ḥijjah]."

قال محمدٌ: من جمع رَمْي يومين في يوم من علّة أو غير علّة فلا كَفّارة عليه إلاّ أنّه يُكرَه له أن يَدع ذلك من غير علّة حتى الغد. وقال أبو حنيفة: إذا تَرَكَ ذلك حتى الغد فعليه دمٌ.

Muḥammad said: "Whoever joins together two days' stoning on one day with or without excuse has no expiation due from him unless it is disapproved for him to leave that without excuse until the morning. Abū Ḥanīfah said, 'If he leaves that until the next day then he is required to sacrifice [as a penalty].'"

٥١ باب رمي الجمار راكباً

51. Stoning the Pillars Mounted

٤٩٥ أخبرنا مالك، أخبرنا عبد الرحمن بن القاسم، عن أبيه أنه قال: إن الناس كانوا إذا رمَوْا الجمار مَشَوْا ذاهبين وراجعين وأوّل من ركب مُعَاوِيَة بن أبي سُفيان.

495. Mālik informed us: "ᶜAbd ar-Raḥmān ibn al-Qāsim informed us that his father said, 'People used to walk there and back when stoning the pillars, and the first to do so mounted was Muᶜāwiyah ibn Abī Sufyān.'"

قال محمد: المَشْيُ أفضل ومَنْ ركب فلا بأسَ بذلك.

Muḥammad said: "Walking is better, but whoever does so mounted there is no harm in that."

٥٢ باب ما يقول عند الجمار والوقوف عند الجمرتين

52. What One Says at the Pillars and while Standing at the two Pillars

٤٩٦ أخبرنا مالك، أخبرنا نافع: أن ابن عمر كان يُكبّر كُلّما رَمَى الجمرة بحصاة.

496. Mālik informed us: "Nāfiᶜ informed us that Ibn ᶜUmar used to say *'Allāhu akbar'* every time he threw a pebble at the pillar.'"

قال محمد: وبهذا نأخذ.

Muḥammad said: "We adhere to this.

٤٩٧ أخبرنا مالك، أخبرنا نافع، عن ابن عمر: أنه كان عند الجمرتين الأُولَيَيْن يقف وقوفاً طويلاً، يكبّر الله ويسبّحه ويدعو الله ولا يقف عند العَقَبَة.

497. Mālik informed us: "Nāfiᶜ informed us that Ibn ᶜUmar used to stand for a long time at the first two pillars declaring *'Allāhu akbar'* and glorifying Him and supplicating Allah, but he would not stand at ᶜAqabah."

قال محمد: وبهذا نأخذ. وهو قول أبي حنيفة رحمه الله.

Muḥammad said: "We adhere to this. It is the verdict of Abū Ḥanīfah, may Allah have mercy on him."

٥٣ باب رمي الجمار قبل الزوال أو بعده

53. Stoning the Pillars before the Decline of [the sun] or after it

٤٩٨ أخبرنا مالك، أخبرنا نافع، عن ابن عمر أنه كان يقول: لا تُرمَى الجمار حتى تزول الشمس في الأيام الثلاثة التي بعد يوم النحر.

498. Mālik informed us: "Nāfiᶜ informed us that Ibn ᶜUmar used to say, 'The pillars must not be stoned until the sun has passed the meridian on the three days which are after the Day of Sacrifice.'"

قال محمد: وبهذا نأخذ.

Muḥammad said: "We adhere to this."

٥٤ باب البيتوتة وراء عقبة منى وما يُكره من ذلك

54. Spending the Night beyond the ᶜAqabah of Minā and what is Disapproved of that

٤٩٩ أخبرنا مالك، أخبرنا نافع، قال: زعموا أن عمر بن الخطاب كان يبعث رجالاً يُدْخِلُونَ الناس من وراء العقبة إلى منى. قال نافع: قال عبد الله بن عمر: قال عمر بن الخطاب رضي الله تعالى عنه: لا يَبِيْتَنَّ أحدٌ من الحاجّ ليالي منى وراء العقبة.

499. Mālik informed us: "Nāfiᶜ informed us, 'They claim that ᶜUmar ibn al-Khaṭṭāb used to send men to make people from beyond ᶜAqabah come in to Minā.' Nāfiᶜ said, 'ᶜAbdullāh ibn ᶜUmar said, "ᶜUmar ibn al-Khaṭṭāb ﷺ said, 'No one performing Ḥajj should spend the nights of Minā beyond ᶜAqabah.'"'"

قال محمد: وبهذا نأخذ. لا ينبغي لأحد من الحاجّ أن يبيت إلاّ بمنى لَيَالي الحج فإن فعل فهو مكروه ولا كَفَّارة عليه. وهو قول أبي حنيفة والعامة من فقهائنا.

Muḥammad said: "We adhere to this. No one of those performing Ḥajj ought to spend the night anywhere but at Minā during the nights of Ḥajj, and if he does it, it is disapproved but he has no expiation due from him. That is the verdict of Abū Ḥanīfah and of our *fuqahā᾽* in general."

٥٥ باب من قدّم نُسُكاً قبل نسك

55. Bringing a Rite forward before another Rite

٥٠٠ أخبرنا مالك، حدثنا ابن شهاب، عن عيسى بن طَلْحَةَ بن عُبَيْد الله أنه أخبره عن عبد الله بن عمرو بن العاص رضي الله عنه تعالى عنهما: أنّ رسول الله صلى الله عليه وسلم وَقَفَ للناس عام حَجَّة الوَدَاع يسألونه، فَجَاء رجلٌ. فقال: يا رسول الله لم أَشْعُر فنحرتُ قبل أن أرْمي، قال: ارم ولا حَرَج، وقال آخر: يا رسول الله، لم أشْعُرْ فحلقت قبل أن أذبح، قال: اذبح ولا حرج. فما سُئل رسول الله صلى الله عليه وسلم عن شيء يومئذ قُدِّمَ ولا أُخِّر إلاّ قال: افعل ولا حرج.

500. Mālik informed us: "Ibn Shihāb narrated to us from ᶜĪsā ibn Ṭalḥah ibn ᶜUbaydullāh who informed him from ᶜAbdullāh ibn ᶜAmr ibn al-ᶜĀṣ*aḥīḥ* ﷺ that the Messenger of Allah ﷺ stood for people to question him in the year of the Farewell Ḥajj. A man came and said, 'Messenger of Allah, I didn't know and so I sacrificed before stoning.' He said, 'Stone, and there is no harm.' Another said, 'Messenger of Allah, I did not know and so I shaved before sacrificing.' He said, 'Sacrifice, and there is no harm.' The Messenger of Allah ﷺ was not asked about anything that day which was brought forward or delayed but that he said, 'Do it, and there is no harm.'"

٥٠١ أخبرنا مالك، حدثنا أيوب السَّخْتيانيّ، عن سعيد بن جُبَيْر، عن ابن عباس أنه كان يقول: من نَسيَ من نُسُكه شيئاً – أو تَرَك – فَلْيُهرق دماً. قال أيوب: لا أدري أقال ترك أم نَسي؟

501. Mālik informed us: "Ayyūb as-Sakhtiyānī narrated to us from Saᶜīd ibn Jubayr that Ibn ᶜAbbās used to say, 'Whoever forgets anything of his rites –

or leaves one out – then let him shed blood [by sacrificing].' Ayyūb said, 'I do not know whether he said "leaves out" or "forgets".'"

قال محمد: وبالحديث الذي روي عن النبي صلى الله عليه وسلم نأخذ أنّه قال: لا حرج في شيء من ذلك. وقال أبو حنيفة رحمه الله: لا حرج في شيء من ذلك، ولم يرَ في شيء من ذلك كَفَّارَةً إلا في خَصلَةٍ واحدةٍ، المُتَمَتِّع والقَارِن إذا حَلَقَ قبل أن يذبح قال: عليه دمٌ، وأما نحن فلا نَرَى عليه شيئاً.

Muḥammad said: "We adhere to the *ḥadīth* narrated from the Prophet ﷺ when he said, 'There is no harm in anything of that.' Abū Ḥanīfah, may Allah have mercy on him, said, 'There is no harm in any of that,' and he did not think that in anything of that there was an expiation due except for in one case; people performing the *tamattu*ᶜ and *qirān* Ḥajj who shave before sacrificing, about which he said, 'He must sacrifice.' But as for us, we do not think that he is required to do anything."

٥٦ باب جزاء الصيد

56. Recompense for Hunting

٥٠٢ أخبرنا مالك، أخبرنا أبو الزبير، عن جابر بن عبد الله: أنَّ عمر بن الخطاب رضي الله تعالى عنه قضى في الضَّبُع بكَبش وفي الغزال بعنز، وفي الأرنب بعَنَاق وفي اليَربوع بجَفرة.

502. Mālik informed us: "Abu'z-Zubayr informed us from Jābir ibn ᶜAbdullāh that ᶜUmar ibn al-Khaṭṭāb gave the judgement that a hyena [must be compensated for] by a ram, and a gazelle by a she-goat, a rabbit by a she-kid of a year or under, and a jerboa by a ewe lamb."

قال محمد: وبهذا كله نأخذ لأن هذا أمثلة من النعم.

Muḥammad said: "We adhere to all of this because this [the latter of each pair of animals] is the like of it [the former of each pair] among pasturing animals."

٥٧ باب كفّارة الأذى

57. Compensatory Payment for an Affliction

٥٠٣ أخبرنا مالك، حدثنا عبد الكريم الجَزَريّ، عن مجاهد، عن عبد الرحمن بن أبي ليلى، عن كعب بن عُجْرَة: أنه كان مع رسول الله صلى الله عليه وسلم مُحرماً، فآذاه القُمَّل في رأسه، فأمره رسول الله صلى الله عليه وسلم أن يحلق رأسه وقال: صُمْ ثلاثةَ أيام، أو أطْعِمْ ستة مساكين مُدَّيْنِ مُدَّيْنِ أو نُسُكْ شاة أيَّ ذلك فَعَلتَ أجزأ عنك.

503. Mālik informed us: "ᶜAbd al-Karīm al-Jazarī narrated to us from Mujāhid from ᶜAbd ar-Raḥmān ibn Abī Laylā from Kaᶜb ibn ᶜUjrah that he was in *iḥrām* with the Messenger of Allah ﷺ and lice afflicted him on his head. The Messenger of Allah ﷺ told him to shave his head and said, 'Fast three days, or feed six poor people with two *mudds*[20], two *mudd*s [for each of them], or sacrifice a ewe. Whichever of those you do, will suffice you.'"

قال محمد: وبهذا نأخذ. وهو قولُ أبي حنيفة رحمه الله والعامة.
Muḥammad said: "We adhere to this, and it is the verdict of Abū Ḥanīfah and [our *fuqahā᾿*] in general."

٥٨ باب مَن قدَّم الضَّعَفَةَ من المزدلفة

58. Someone who Sends the Weak on ahead from Muzdalifah

٥٠٤ أخبرنا مالك، أخبرنا نافع، عن سالم وعُبَيد الله ابنَيْ عبد الله بن عمر: أنَّ عبد الله بنَ عمر كان يُقَدِّم صِبْيَانه من المُزْدَلفَة إلى منىً حتى يُصَلّوا الصبح بمنى.
504. Mālik informed us: "Nāfi[c] informed us from Sālim and [c]Ubaydullāh the two sons of [c]Abdullāh ibn [c]Umar that [c]Abdullāh ibn [c]Umar used to send his small children on ahead from Muzdalifah to Minā so that they could pray the morning prayer [*Ṣubḥ*] at Minā."

قال محمد: لا بأس بأن يُقَدِّم الضَّعَفَة ويُوغِر إليهم أن لا يرموا الجمرة حتى تطلع الشمس. وهو قول أبي حنيفة والعامة من فقهائنا.
Muḥammad said: "There is no harm in sending on the weak and commanding them not to stone the Jamrah until after sunrise, and this is also the verdict of Abū Ḥanīfah and our *fuqahā᾿* in general."

٥٩ باب جِلال البُدن

59. The Coverings of the Sacrificial Animals

٥٠٥ أخبرنا مالك، أخبرنا نافع: أنَّ ابنَ عمر كان لا يشقُّ جلال بُدنه، وكان لا يجلِّلها حتى يغدوَ بها من منى إلى عرفة وكان يُجَلِّلها بالحُلَل والقَبَاطي والأنماط، ثم يبعث بجِلاَلها، فيكسوها الكعبة. قال: فلما كُسِيَت الكعبة هذه الكسوة أَقْصَر منَ الجلال.
505. Mālik informed us: "Nāfi[c] informed us that Ibn [c]Umar would not tear the drapes of his sacrificial animals, and he would not drape them until he set forth with them in the morning from Minā to [c]Arafah. He used to drape them with garments, fine white Egyptian linen and coloured woollen coverlets, and then he would send their coverings and would drape the Ka[c]bah with them." He said, "Then when the Ka[c]bah was draped with this *Kiswah*[21], he ceased [sending] the coverings."

٥٠٦ أخبرنا مالك، قال سألت عبد الله بن دينار: ما كان ابن عمر يصنع بجلال بُدْنه؟ حتى أقصر عن تلك الكسوة. قال عبد الله بن دينار: كان عبد الله بن عمر يتصدَّق بها.
506. Mālik informed us: "I asked [c]Abdullāh ibn Dīnār, 'What did Ibn [c]Umar do with the coverings of his sacrificial animals when he ceased because of that *Kiswah*?' [c]Abdullāh ibn Dīnār answered, 'Ibn [c]Umar used to give them away as *ṣadaqah*.'"

قال محمد: وبهذا نأخذ. ينبغي أن يتصدق بجلال البدن وبِخُطُمِها وأن لا يعطي الجزَّار من ذلك

شيئاً ولا من لحومها. بلغنا أنَّ النبيَّ صلى الله عليه وسلم بعث مع علي بن أبي طالب رضي الله عنه بهَدْيٍ فأمر أن يتصدَّق بجلاله وبخطُمه وأن لا يعطيَ الجزّار من خُطُمه وجلاله شيئاً.

Muḥammad said: "We adhere to this. One has to give the coverings of the sacrificial animals and their halters as *ṣadaqah*, and must not give the slaughterman anything of it, nor any of their meat. It has reached us that the Prophet ﷺ sent a *hady* offering of animals along with ᶜAlī ibn Abī Ṭālib and told him to give their coverings and halters as *ṣadaqah* and not to give the slaughterman anything of their halters and coverings[22]."

٦٠ باب المُحْصَر

60. Someone who is Prevented [from Reaching the Kaᶜbah]

٥٠٧ أخبرنا مالك، أخبرنا ابن شهاب، عن سالم بن عبد الله، عن أبيه أنه قال: من أُحْصِرَ دون البيت بمرضٍ فإنه لا يَحِلُّ حتى يطوف بالبيت فهو يتداوى مما اضطر إليه ويفتدي.

507. Mālik informed us: "Ibn Shihāb informed us from Sālim ibn ᶜAbdullāh from his father that he [ᶜAbdullāh ibn ᶜUmar] said, 'Whoever is prevented from [reaching] the House because of an illness does not become free of his *iḥrām* until he does *ṭawāf* of the House, and he may treat himself with those remedies which are essential for him but he must compensate for it.'"

قال محمد: بلغنا عن عبد الله بن مسعود رضي الله عنه أنه جعل المحصر بالوجع كالمحصر بالعدو، فسئل عن رجل اعتمر فنَهَشَته حيَّة فلم يستطع المضي، فقال ابن مسعود: ليبعث بهدي ويواعد أصحابَه يوم أَمَارٍ، فإذا نَحَرَ عنه الهدي حَلَّ وكانت عليه عمرة مكان عمرته، وبهذا نأخذ، وهو قول أبي حنيفة رحمه الله والعامة من فقهائنا.

Muḥammad said: "It has reached us from ᶜAbdullāh ibn Masᶜūd that he regarded someone prevented because of pain the same as someone prevented because of enemy activity. He was asked about a man who performs *ᶜumrah* and is bitten by a snake and so is unable to continue. ᶜAbdullāh ibn Masᶜūd said, 'Let him send a *hady* offering, and make an appointment with his companions for a definite day [when they will slaughter on his behalf]. Then when sacrifice of the *hady* offering is made on his behalf he becomes free of *iḥrām*, and he remains liable to perform an *ᶜumrah* in place of his *ᶜumrah*.' And We adhere to this, and it is the verdict of Abū Ḥanīfah and our *fuqahā*ʾ in general."

٦١ باب تكفين المحرم

61. Shrouding Someone in *Iḥrām*

٥٠٨ أخبرنا مالك، أخبرنا نافع أن ابن عمر كفَّن ابنه واقدَ بن عبد الله وَ قد مات مُحرماً بالجُحفَة، وَخمَّرَ رأسه.

508. Mālik informed us: "Nāfiʿ informed us that ʿAbdullāh ibn ʿUmar shrouded his son Wāqid ibn ʿAbdullāh who had died in *iḥrām* at Juḥfah, and he covered his head."

قال محمد: وبهذا نأخذ وهو قول أبي حنيفة رحمه الله : إذا مات فقد ذهب الإحرام عنه.

Muḥammad said: "We adhere to this, and it is the verdict of Abū Ḥanīfah. When someone dies the *iḥrām* has left him."

٦٢ باب من أدرك عرفة ليلة المزدلفة
62. Someone who Reaches ʿArafah on the Night of Muzdalifah

٥٠٩ أخبرنا مالك، أخبرنا نافع، أن عبد الله بن عمر كان يقول: مَن وقف بعرفة ليلة المزدلفة قبل أن يطلع الفجر فقد أدرك الحج.

509. Mālik informed us: "Nāfiʿ informed us that ʿAbdullāh ibn ʿUmar used to say, 'Whoever stands on ʿArafah on the night of Muzdalifah before the dawn breaks has caught the Ḥajj.'"

قال محمد: وبهذا نأخذ وهو قول أبي حنيفة والعامة.

Muḥammad said: "We adhere to this and it is the verdict of Abū Ḥanīfah and the [*fuqahāʾ* in] general."

٦٣ باب من غربت له الشمس في النفر الأول وهو بمنى
63. Someone for whom the Sun Sets when He is in the First Group and He is at Minā

٥١٠ أخبرنا مالك، أخبرنا نافع، عن ابن عمر أنه كان يقول: من غرَبَت له الشمس من أوسط أيام التشريق وهو بمنى لا ينفرَنَّ حتى يرمي الجمار من الغد.

510. Mālik informed us: "Nāfiʿ informed us that ʿAbdullāh ibn ʿUmar used to say, 'For whoever the sun sets during the middle of the days of *tashrīq* while he is at Minā, must not leave until he has stoned the pillars [*jamrahs*] on the following day.'"

قال محمد: وبهذا نأخذ. وهو قول أبي حنيفة والعامة.

Muḥammad said: "We adhere to this and it is the verdict of Abū Ḥanīfah and our *fuqahāʾ* in general."

٦٤ باب من نفر ولم يحلق
64. Someone who Departs and has not Shaved his Hair

٥١١ أخبرنا مالك، أخبرنا نافع: أن عبد الله بن عمر لقي رجلاً من أهله يقال له المجَبَّر وقد أفاض ولم يحلق رأسه ولم يقصِّر، جهل ذلك، فأمره عبد الله أن يرجع فيحلق رأسه أو يقصر ثم يرجع إلى البيت، فيُفيض.

511. Mālik informed us: "Nāfiʿ informed us that ʿAbdullāh ibn ʿUmar met a

man from his family, said to be al-Mujabbar, who had performed the *Ṭawāf al-Ifāḍah* [the final *ṭawāf* which completes the Ḥajj] and had neither shaved his head nor cut his hair because of his ignorance of that. So ᶜAbdullāh ibn ᶜUmar told him to return and shave his head or cut his hair, and then return to the House and perform the *Ṭawāf al-Ifāḍah*."

قال محمد : وبهذا نأخذ .

Muḥammad said: "We adhere to this."

٦٥ باب الرجل يجامع قبل أن يُفيض

65. A Man who has Sexual Intercourse at ᶜArafah before he has done the *Ṭawāf al-Ifāḍah*

٥١٢ أخبرنا مالك، أخبرنا أبو الزبير المكيّ، عن عطاء بن أبي رباح، عن ابن عباس : أنه سئل عن رجل وقع على امرأته قبل أن يُفيض فأمره أن ينحر بَدَنة .

512. Mālik informed us: "Abu'z-Zubayr al-Makkī informed us from ᶜAṭāʾ ibn Abī Rabāḥ that Ibn ᶜAbbās was asked about a man who had intercourse with his wife before performing the *Ṭawāf al-Ifāḍah* and he told him to sacrifice an animal [cow or a camel]."

قال محمد : وبهذا نأخذ، قال رسول الله صلى الله عليه وسلم : من وقف بعرفة فقد أدرك حجَّه، فمن جامع بعد ما يقف بعرفة لم يفسُد حجُّه، ولكن عليه بَدَنة لجِمَاعه، وحجُّه تامٌّ، وإذا جامع قبل أن يطوف طواف الزيارة لا يفسد حجّه، وهو قول أبي حنيفة والعامة من فقهائنا .

Muḥammad said: "We adhere to this. The Messenger of Allah ﷺ said, 'Whoever has stood upon ᶜArafah has caught the Ḥajj.' So that whoever has intercourse after he has stood on ᶜArafah has not nullified his Ḥajj, but he owes a sacrificial [cow or camel] because of his intercourse and his Ḥajj is complete. If he has intercourse before he does the *ṭawāf* for visiting [the House] he has not nullified his Ḥajj, and that is the verdict of Abū Ḥanīfah and of our *fuqahāʾ* in general[23]."

٦٦ باب تعجيل الإهلال

66. Hastening to Begin the *Talbiyah* [*labbayk Allāhumma labbayk*]

٥١٣ أخبرنا مالك، حدثنا عبد الرحمن بن القاسم، عن أبيه، أن عمر بن الخطاب قال : يا أهل مكة، ما شأنُ الناس يأتون شُعثاً، وأنتم مُدَّهِنون، أهلُّوا إذا رأيتم الهلال .

513. Mālik informed us: "ᶜAbd ar-Raḥmān ibn al-Qāsim narrated to me from his father that ᶜUmar ibn al-Khaṭṭāb said, 'People of Makkah, what is wrong that people are coming with dishevelled hair while you still have oil on your hair. Begin the '*labbayk*' [and enter *iḥrām*] when you see the new moon."

قال محمد: تعجيل الإهلال أفضل من تأخيره إذا ملكتَ نفسَك. وهو قولُ أبي حنيفة والعامة من فقهائنا.

Muḥammad said: "Hastening the *'labbayk'* [and *iḥrām*] is better than delaying it if you can help it. That is the verdict of Abū Ḥanīfah and our *fuqahā᾽* in general."

٦٧ باب القُفُول من الحج أو العمرة

67. Returning from the Ḥajj or ᶜ*Umrah*

٥١٤ أخبرنا مالك، أخبرنا نافع، عن ابن عمر: أنَّ رسولَ الله صلى الله عليه وسلم كان إذا قفل من حجٍّ أو عُمرةٍ أو غزوةٍ يُكَبِّر على كل شَرَفٍ من الأرض ثلاث تكبيرات، ثم يقول: لا إله إلاَّ الله وحده لا شريك له، له المُلك وله الحمد يُحيي ويُميت وهو على كل شيء قدير، آيبون تائبون عابدُون ساجدُون لربِّنا حامدُون، صدَقَ الله وَعدَه ونَصَرَ عَبدَه وهَزَمَ الأحزابَ وَحدَه.

514. Mālik informed us: "Nāfiᶜ informed us from ᶜAbdullāh ibn ᶜUmar that when the Messenger of Allah ﷺ returned from Ḥajj or ᶜ*umrah* or an expedition, he used to say three *takbīrs* at every prominence in the land and then say, 'There is no god but Allah alone without partner. His is the kingdom and His is the praise. And He is has power over all things. Returning penitently, worshipping, prostrating, praising our Lord. Allah was true to His promise, and He helped His slave, and He alone defeated the confederates.'"

٦٨ باب الصَّدَر

68. Departure [from Ḥajj or ᶜ*Umrah* to Return Home]

٥١٥ أخبرنا مالك، حدثنا نافع، عن ابن عمر: أنَّ رسول الله ﷺ كان إذا صَدَرَ من الحجِّ أو العُمرَة أناخ بالبَطحَاء الذي بذي الحُلَيفة فيُصَلِّي بها ويُهَلِّل قال: فكان عبد الله بن عمر يفعل ذلك.

515. Mālik informed us: "Nāfiᶜ narrated to us from ᶜAbdullāh ibn ᶜUmar that when the Messenger of Allah ﷺ departed from the Ḥajj or ᶜ*umrah* [returning home] he used to make his camel lie down at Baṭḥā᾽ in the valley at Dhu'l-Ḥulayfah, and he would pray there, and recite 'There is no god but Allah.'" He said, "ᶜAbdullāh ibn ᶜUmar used to do that."

٥١٦ أخبرنا مالك، أخبرنا نافع، عن عبد الله بن عمر، أنَّ عمر بن الخطاب قال: لا يصدُرَنَّ أحد من الحاجِّ حتى يطوف بالبيت فإنَّ آخرَ النُّسُك الطَّوَافُ بالبيت.

516. Mālik informed us: "Nāfiᶜ informed us from ᶜAbdullāh ibn ᶜUmar that ᶜUmar ibn al-Khaṭṭāb said, 'Let no one depart from the Ḥajj [to return home] until he has done *ṭawāf* of the House, because the last rite is *ṭawāf* of the House.'"

قال محمد: وبهذا نأخذ، طوافُ الصَّدَر واجبٌ على الحاجِّ ومن تركه فعليه دم إلاَّ الحائض والنفساء فإنها تَنفِر ولا تطوف إن شاءت. وهو قول أبي حنيفة رحمه الله تعالى والعامة من فقهائنا.

Muḥammad said: "We adhere to this. The *ṭawāf* for departing [from the Ḥajj to return home] is obligatory for the person performing Ḥajj, and whoever leaves it out owes a sacrifice except for a woman in her period and a woman just after childbirth because they may leave and not perform the *ṭawāf* if they wish. That is the verdict of Abū Ḥanīfah and our *fuqahā'* in general."

٦٩ باب المرأة يُكره لها إذا حلّت من إحرامها أن تمتشطَ حتى تأخذ من شعرها

69. A Woman for whom it is Disapproved to Comb her Hair when she Becomes free from her *Iḥrām* before She has Cut some of it

٥١٧ أخبرنا مالك، حدثنا نافع، عن عبد الله بن عمر، أنه كان يقول: المرأة المُحرِمة إذا حلّت لا تَمتَشِط حتى تأخذَ من شعرِها، شعرِ رأسِها، وإن كان لها هديٌ لم تأخذ من شعرها شيئاً حتى تنحر.

517. Mālik informed us: "Nāfi' narrated to us that 'Abdullāh ibn 'Umar used to say, 'When a woman in *iḥrām* becomes free from her *iḥrām* she does not comb her hair until she has cut some of it. If she has a *hady* offering she does not cut any of her hair until it is sacrificed."

قال محمد: وبهذا نأخذ. وهو قول أبي حنيفة والعامة من فقهائنا.

Muḥammad said: "We adhere to this. It is also the verdict of Abū Ḥanīfah and our *fuqahā'* in general."

٧٠ باب النزول بالمحصَّب

70. Alighting at Muḥaṣṣab

٥١٨ أخبرنا مالك، حدثنا نافع، عن ابن عمر: أنه كان يصلّي الظهر والعصر والمغرب والعشاء بالمحصَّب، ثم يَدخُلُ من الليل فيطوف بالبيت.

518. Mālik informed us: "Nāfi' narrated to us that 'Abdullāh ibn 'Umar used to pray *Ẓuhr* and *'Aṣr, Maghrib* and *'Ishā'* at Muḥaṣṣab[24], and then he would enter [Makkah] at night and do *ṭawāf* of the House."

قال محمد: هذا حسن، ومن ترك النزول بالمحصَّب فلا شيء عليه.
وهو قول أبي حنيفة رحمه الله.

Muḥammad said: "This is good, but there is nothing against anyone who leaves out alighting at Muḥaṣṣab, and that is the verdict of Abū Ḥanīfah."

٧١ باب الرجل يحرم من مكة هل يطوف بالبيت

71. Whether or not a Man Entering *Iḥrām* from Makkah does *Ṭawāf* of the House

٥١٩ أخبرنا مالك، أخبرنا نافع، عن ابن عمر: أنه كان إذا أحرم من مكة لم يطُف بالبيت ولا بين الصفا والمروة حتى يرجع من منى ولا يسعى إلا إذا طاف حول البيت.

519. Mālik informed us: "Nāfiᶜ informed us that when ᶜAbdullāh ibn ᶜUmar entered *iḥrām* from Makkah he would not perform *ṭawāf* of the House, nor [perform *saᶜy*] between Ṣafā and Marwah until he had returned from Minā, and he would not perform *saᶜy* [between Ṣafā and Marwah] unless he had done *ṭawāf* around the House."

قال محمد : إن فعل هذا أجزاه ، وإن طاف ورمل وسعى قبل أن يخرج أجزاه ذلك ، كل ذلك حسن إلا أنّا نحبّ له أن لا يَترُكَ الرَّمل بالبيت في الأشواط الثلاثة الأُول إن عجَّل أو أخّر. وهو قول أبي حنيفة رحمه الله.

Muḥammad said: "If he does that it suffices him. If he does *ṭawāf*, walks at a brisk pace and does *saᶜy* before leaving, then that suffices him. All of that is good, except that we prefer him not to leave out the trotting at a moderate pace around the House in the first three of his *ṭawāfs* whether he does it early or defers it, and that is the verdict of Abū Ḥanīfah."

٧٢ باب المحرم يحتجم

72. A Person in *Iḥrām* being Cupped

٥٢٠ أخبرنا مالك، حدثنا يحيى بن سعيد، عن سليمان بن يسار : أنّ رسول الله صلى الله عليه وسلم احتجم فوق رأسه وهو يومئذ محرم بمكان من طريق مكة يقال له: لحَيُ جَمَل.

520. Mālik informed us: "Yaḥyā ibn Saᶜīd narrated to us from Sulaymān ibn Yasār that the Messenger of Allah ﷺ was cupped on the top of his head, and that day he was in *iḥrām,* in a place on the way to Makkah called Laḥy Jamal."

قال محمد : وبهذا نأخذ . لا بأس بأن يحتجم الرجل وهو محرم، اضطُرَّ إليه أو لم يُضطَرَّ إلا أنه لا يحلق شعراً وهو قول أبي حنيفة.

Muḥammad said: "We adhere to this. There is no harm in a man being cupped while he is in *iḥrām,* whether or not he is forced by circumstances to do it, except that he must not cut any of his hair, and that is the verdict of Abū Ḥanīfah."

٥٢١ أخبرنا مالك، أخبرنا نافع، عن ابن عمر قال: لا يحتجم المحرم إلا أن يُضطَرّ إليه.

521. Mālik informed us: "Nāfiᶜ informed us that Ibn ᶜUmar said, 'The person who is in *iḥrām* must not be cupped unless he is forced to do so by circumstances.'"

٧٣ باب دخول مكة بسلاح

73. Entering Makkah with Weapons

٥٢٢ أخبرنا مالك، أخبرنا ابن شهاب، عن أنس بن مالك : أن رسول الله ﷺ دخل مكة عام الفتح وعلى رأسه المغفر فلما نزعه جاءه رجل فقال له: ابن خَطَل متعلّق بأستار الكعبة، قال: اقتلوه.

522. Mālik informed us: "Ibn Shihāb informed us from Anas ibn Mālik that the Messenger of Allah ﷺ entered Makkah on the year of the Opening [of

Makkah to Islam], and on his head there was a protective head-covering of chain mail[25]. When he took it off, a man came to him and said to him, 'Ibn Khaṭal is clinging to the covers of the Kaᶜbah.' He said, 'Kill him.'"

قال محمد: إِن النبي صلى الله عليه وسلم دخل مكة حين فتحها غيرَ مُحرم ولذلك دخل وعلى رأسه المغفَر، وقد بلَغَنا أنه حين أحرم من حُنَين قال: هذه العُمرة لدخولنا مكة بغير إِحرام يعني يوم الفَتح، فَكذلك الأمر عندنا: من دخل مكة بغير إِحرام فلا بدّ له من أن يخرج فَيُهلَّ بعمرة أو بحجة لدخوله مكة بغير إِحرام. وهو قول أبي خنيفة رحمه الله والعامة من فقهائنا.

Muḥammad said: "The Prophet ﷺ entered Makkah when he opened it [to Islam] without being in *iḥrām,* and for that reason he entered with a head-covering of chain mail on his head. It has reached us that when he put on the *iḥrām* at Ḥunayn he said, 'This *ᶜumrah* is for our entering Makkah without *iḥrām,*' meaning in the Year of the Opening. That is the way the matter is with us. Whoever enters Makkah without *iḥrām* must leave and announce the *'labbayk'* for *ᶜumrah* or Ḥajj, and that is the verdict of Abū Ḥanīfah and our *fuqahāʾ* in general."

كتاب النكاح
6. MARRIAGE

١ باب الرجل تكون عنده نسوة كيف يَقْسِمُ بينهنَّ
1. How a Man who has a Number of Wives should Apportion [his Time] between Them

٥٢٣ أخبرنا مالك، حدثنا عبد الله بن أبي بكر ، عن عبد الملك بن أبي بكر بن الحارث بن هشام، عن أبيه : أن النبي صلى الله عليه وسلم حين بنى بأمِّ سلمة قال لها حين أصبحتْ عنده : ليس بكِ على أهلك هوان ، إن شئت سبَّعْتُ عندكِ وسبَّعتُ عندهنَّ ، وإن شئت ثلَّثتُ عندكِ ودُرت ، قالتَ : ثلِّثْ.

523. Mālik informed us: "ʿAbdullāh ibn Abī Bakr narrated to us from ʿAbd al-Mālik ibn Abī Bakr ibn al-Ḥārith ibn Hishām that when the Prophet ﷺ first went to see Umm Salamah [on their wedding], he said to her, when she had spent the night with him, 'It is not that you are held in low esteem by your husband. If you wish I will spend seven [nights] with you, and then seven [nights] with [each of] them [the other wives]. If you wish, I will spend three [nights] with you and then visit the others in turn.' She said, 'Make it three.'"

قال محمد : وبهذا نأخذ ينبغي أن سبَّع عندها أن يُسبِّع عندهن لا يزيد لها عليهن شيئاً وإن ثلَّث عندها أن يُثلِّث عندهن، وهو قول أبو حنيفة والعامة من فقهائنا .

Muḥammad said: "We adhere to this. He ought, if he spends seven [nights] with her, to spend seven nights with [each of] them [the other wives], and not give her any extra over them, and if he spends three [nights] with her, to spend three nights with [each of] them. That is the verdict of Abū Ḥanīfah and our *fuqahāʾ* in general."

٢ باب أدنى ما يتزوج الرجل عليه المرأة
2. The Least [Dowry] for which a Woman Ought to be Married

٥٢٤ أخبرنا مالك، حدثنا حُميد الطويل عن أنس بن مالك : أن عبد الرحمن بن عوف جاءَ إلى النبي صلى الله عليه وسلم وعليه أَثَر صُفْرة فأخبره أنَّه تزوَّج امرأة من الأنصار، قال: كم سُقْتَ إليها؟ قال: وزن نَوَاة من ذهب، قال : أَوْلِم ولو بشاة .

524. Mālik informed us: "Ḥumayd aṭ-Ṭawīl narrated to us from Anas ibn Mālik that ʿAbd ar-Raḥmān ibn ʿAwf came to the Prophet ﷺ with the traces

of yellow[26] on him and told him that he had married a woman from the Anṣār. He asked, 'How much did you send her [as dowry]?' He answered, 'The weight of a datestone in gold.' He told him, 'Give a wedding feast even if only with a sheep.'"

قال محمد : وبهذا نأخذ . أدنى المهر عَشَرة دراهم ما تُقطع فيه اليد . وهو قول أبي حنيفة والعامة من فقهائنا .

Muḥammad said: "We adhere to this. The least possible dowry is ten dirhams, which is that for [the theft of] which the hand would be cut. It is also the verdict of Abū Ḥanīfah and our *fuqahā'* in general."

٣ باب لا يجمع الرجل بين المرأة وعمّتها في النكاح

3. A Man Must not Unite a Woman and her Paternal Aunt in Marriage

٥٢٥ أخبرنا مالك، حدثنا أبو الزِّناد ، عن عبد الرحمن الأعرج، عن أبي هريرة أن النبي صلى الله عليه وسلم قال: لا يَجْمَعُ الرجلُ بين المَرأة وعمَّتها ولا بين المرأة وخالتها .

525. Mālik informed us: "Abu'z-Zinād narrated to us from ʿAbd ar-Raḥmān al-Aʿraj from Abū Hurayrah that the Messenger of Allah ﷺ said, 'A man must not unite [in marriage] a woman and her paternal aunt, nor a woman and her maternal aunt.'"

قال محمد : وبهذا نأخذ وهو قول أبي حنيفة والعامة من فقهائنا .

Muḥammad said: "We adhere to this, and it is the verdict of Abū Ḥanīfah and our *fuqahā'* in general."

٥٢٦ أخبرنا مالك، أخبرنا يحيى بن سعيد أنه سمع سعيد بن المسيِّب ينهى أن تُنْكح المرأة على خالتها أو على عمَّتها وأنْ يطأ الرجلُ وليدةً في بطنها جنينٌ لغيره .

526. Mālik informed us: "Yaḥyā ibn Saʿīd informed us that he heard Saʿīd ibn al-Musayyab forbidding a woman to be taken in marriage along with her maternal aunt or her paternal aunt, or that a man should have sexual intercourse with a female slave in whose womb is another's child."

قال محمد : وبهذا نأخذ وهو قول أبي حنيفة والعامة من فقهائنا رحمهم الله تعالى .

Muḥammad said: "We adhere to this, and it is the verdict of Abū Ḥanīfah and our *fuqahā'* in general."

٤ باب الرجل يخطب على خِطبة أخيه

4. A Man Proposing to Someone to whom his Brother [in Islam] has already Proposed

٥٢٧ أخبرنا مالك، أخبرنا يحيى بن سعيد، عن محمد بن يحيى بن حبان ، عن عبد الرحمن بن هرمز الأعرج، عن أبي هريرة: أن رسول الله صلى الله عليه وسلم قال : لا يخطبُ أحدُكم على خِطبة أخيه .

527. Mālik informed us: "Yaḥyā ibn Saᶜīd informed us from Muḥammad ibn Yaḥyā ibn Ḥabbān from ᶜAbd ar-Raḥmān ibn Hurmuz al-Aᶜraj from Abū Hurayrah that the Messenger of Allah ﷺ said, 'Let none of you propose to someone to whom his brother [in Islam] has already proposed.'"

قال محمد: وبهذا نأخذ وهو قول أبي حنيفة والعامة من فقهائنا رحمهم الله.

Muḥammad said: "We adhere to this, and it is the verdict of Abū Ḥanīfah and our *fuqahā᾽* in general."

٥ باب الثيب أحقّ بنفسها من وليّها

5. A Woman who is no longer a Virgin Having More Right Concerning herself than her Guardian

٥٢٨ أخبرنا مالك، أخبرنا عبد الرحمن بن القاسم، عن أبيه، عن عبد الرحمن ومُجَمِّع ابنَيْ يزيد بن جَارِيَة الأنصاري، عن خَنْسَاء ابنة خِذام: أنّ أباها زوّجها وهي ثيِّب، فكرهت ذلك، فجاءَت رسول الله صلى فَرَدّ نكاحه.

528. Mālik informed us: "ᶜAbd ar-Raḥmān ibn al-Qāsim informed us from his father from ᶜAbd ar-Raḥmān and Mujammiᶜ, the two sons of Yazīd ibn Jāriyah al-Anṣārī, from Khansā᾽ bint Khidām that her father committed her in marriage when she was no longer a virgin, and she disliked it. So she went to the Messenger of Allah ﷺ and he revoked her marriage."

قال محمد: لا ينبغي أن تُنْكَح الثَّيِّب، ولا البِكْر إذا بَلَغَتْ إلا بإذنهما فأما إذْن البكر فَصَمْتُها، وأما إذْن الثَّيِّب فرضاها بلسانها، زوّجها والدُها أو غيره. وهو قول أبي حنيفة والعامة من فقهائنا.

Muḥammad said: "A woman who is no longer a virgin and a virgin who has attained puberty, may only be married with their consent. The consent of the virgin is her silence. The consent of the previously married woman is her good pleasure expressed by her tongue whether it is her father or someone else who arranges for her marriage. That is the verdict of Abū Ḥanīfah and our *fuqahā᾽* in general."

٦ باب الرجل يكون عنده أكثر من أربع نسوة فيريد أن يتزوّج

6. A Man Having more than four Wives and Wishing to Marry [again]

٥٢٩ أخبرنا مالك، أخبرنا ابن شهاب، قال: بلغنا أن رسول الله صلى الله عليه وسلم قال لرجل من ثقيف وكان عنده عشر نسوة حين أسلم الثقفي، فقال له: أمسكْ منهن أربعاً، وفارقْ سائرَهُنّ.

529. Mālik informed us: "Ibn Shihāb informed us, 'It has reached us that the Messenger of Allah ﷺ spoke to a man from Thaqīf – and he had ten wives – when the Thaqafī accepted Islam, and said to him, "Retain four of them, and separate from the rest of them."'"

قال محمد: وبهذا نأخذ . يختار منهن أربعاً أيّتهنّ شاء، ويفارق ما بقي، وأما أبو حنيفة فقال: نكاح الأربعة الأُوَل جائز، ونكاحُ من بَقِي منهنّ باطل وهو قول إبراهيم النَّخَعي .

Muḥammad said: "We adhere to this. He must choose four of them, whichever of them he wishes, and separate from the remainder. As for Abū Ḥanīfah, he said, 'The marriages of the first four are valid, and the marriages of the remainder are invalid, and that is the verdict of Ibrāhīm an-Nakhaᶜī.'"

٥٣٠ أخبرنا مالك، حدثنا رَبيعَة بن أبي عبد الرحمن، أن الوليد سأل القاسم وعُرْوَةَ وكانت عنده أربع نسوة فأراد أن يَبِتَّ واحدَة ويتزوج أُخرى، فقال: نعم، فارق امرأتك ثلاثاً وتزوّج. فقال القاسم في مجالس مختلفة .

530. Mālik informed us: "Rabīᶜah ibn ᶜAbd ar-Raḥmān told us that al-Walīd – and he had four wives – asked al-Qāsim and ᶜUrwah because he wanted to sever [relations] absolutely from one and marry another, and so the two of them said, 'Yes, divorce your wife three times and marry.'" Al-Qāsim said, "[The three divorces must take place] on separate occasions."

قال محمد: لا يُعجبنا أن يتزوج خامسة وإن بَتَّ طلاق إحداهن حتى تنقضي عدَّتُها. لا يعجبنا أن يكون ماؤه في رَحِمِ خمس نِسْوَة حرائر. وهو قول أبي حنيفة رحمه الله والعامة من فقهائنا رحمهم الله .

Muḥammad said: "We dislike the notion that he should marry a fifth, even if he made an absolute divorce from one of them, until her *ᶜiddah* is completed. We dislike the notion that his sperm should lie [simultaneously] in the wombs of five free women, and that is the verdict of Abū Ḥanīfah and our *fuqahā᾽* in general."

٧ باب ما يوجب الصَّدَاق

7. What Makes the Dowry Obligatory

٥٣١ أخبرنا مالك، أخبرنا ابن شهاب عن زيد بن ثابت قال: إذا دخل الرجل بامرأته وأُرخِيَتْ الستور فقد وجب الصَّدَاق .

531. Mālik informed us: "Ibn Shihāb informed us that Zayd ibn Thābit said, 'When a man goes to his wife and the veils are let down over the two of them [so that they are alone together], then the dowry is obligatory.'"

قال محمد: وبهذا نأخذ، وهو قول أبي حنيفة والعامة من فقهائنا. وقال مالك بن أنس: إن طلّقها بعد ذلك لم يكن لها إلا نصف المهر إلا أن يطول مُكْثُها ويتلذّذ منها فيجب الصداق .

Muḥammad said: "We adhere to this, and it is the verdict of Abū Ḥanīfah and our *fuqahā᾽* in general. Mālik ibn Anas said, 'If he divorces her after that she has only a half of the dowry, unless she remains some time and he has his pleasure with her, in which case the [full] dowry is obligatory.'"

٨ باب نكاح الشِّغار

8. *Shighār* Marriage

٥٣٢ أخبرنا مالك، أخبرنا نافع، عن ابن عمر: أنّ رسول الله صلى الله عليه وسلم نهى عن الشغار. والشغار أن يُنكح الرجل ابنته على أن يُنكحه الآخر ابنته ليس بينهما صداق.

532. Mālik informed us: "Nāfiᶜ informed us from ᶜAbdullāh ibn ᶜUmar that the Messenger of Allah ﷺ forbade *shighār*, and *shighār* is that a man marry off his daughter on the condition that the other marry him his daughter without the payment of dowries."[27]

قال محمد: وبهذا نأخذ. لا يكون الصَّداق نكاح امرأة فإذا تزوجها على أن يكون صَدَاقها أن يزوّجه ابنته فالنكاح جائز ولها صداق مثلها من نسائها، ولا وَكْس ولا شطط. وهو قول أبي حنيفة والعامة من فقهائنا.

Muḥammad said: "We adhere to this. The dowry cannot be [in the form of] marriage to [another] woman. If he does marry her off on the condition that her dowry should be that the other person marry his daughter to him, then the marriage is valid but she receives the dowry which would normally be due to a woman of her standing, neither less nor more. It is also the verdict of Abū Ḥanīfah and our *fuqahā'* in general."

٩ باب نكاح السرّ

9. Secret Marriage

٥٣٣ أخبرنا مالك، عن أبي الزبير: أن عمر أُتيَ برجلٍ في نكاح لم يَشهد عليه إلا رجل وامرأة، فقال عمر: هذا نكاح السِّرّ ولا نُجيزه ولو كنتُ تَقَدَّمْتُ فيه لَرَجَمْتُ.

533. Mālik informed us from Abu'z-Zubayr that ᶜUmar was brought a man for whose marriage the only witnesses had been one man and one woman, and ᶜUmar said, "This is a marriage [conducted] in secret, and we do not regard it as valid. If I had been the first [to be involved] in it, you would have been stoned."

قال محمد: وبهذا نأخذ، لأنّ النكاح لا يجوزُ في أقلّ من شاهدَيْن وإنما شهد على هذا الذي ردّه عمر رجل وامرأة، فهذا نكاح السِّرِّ لأن الشهادة لم تكمل ولو كملت الشهادة برجلين أو رجل وامرأتين كان نكاحاً جائزاً وإن كان سرّاً، وإنما يَفْسُد نكاح السِّرِّ أن يكون بغير شهودٍ، فأما إذا كملت فيه الشهادة فهو نكاح العَلانية وإن كانوا أسرّوه.

Muḥammad said: "We adhere to this, because marriage is not valid with less than two witnesses, and in this [marriage] that ᶜUmar rejected, the only witnesses, were a man and a woman, and so this is a marriage conducted in secret, because the witnessing was not complete. If the witnessing had been complete by being two men or a man and two women, then it would have been a valid, public marriage, even if they had kept it secret."

٥٣٤ قال محمد : أخبرنا محمد بن أَبَان ، عن حمّاد ، عن إبراهيم أنَّ عمر بن الخطاب أجاز شهادةَ رجلٍ وامرأتين في النكاح والفُرْقَة .

534. Muḥammad said, "Muḥammad ibn Abān informed us from Ḥammād from Ibrāhīm that ᶜUmar ibn al-Khaṭṭāb regarded the witnessing of a man and two women as being valid for marriage and divorce."

قال محمد : وبهذا نأخذ، وهو قول أبي حنيفة رحمه الله .

Muḥammad said: "We adhere to this, and it is the verdict of Abū Ḥanīfah."

١٠ باب الرجل يجمع بين المرأة وابنتها وبين المرأة وأختها في ملك اليمين

10. A Man Uniting [Sexually] a Woman and her Daughter, or a Woman and her Sister who are under his Ownership

٥٣٥ أخبرنا مالك، حدثنا الزُّهْرِيّ، عن عُبَيْد الله بن عبد الله بن عُتْبَةَ ، عن أبيه : أنَّ عمر سُئل عن المرأة وابنتها مما مَلَكَت اليمين أَتُوْطَأ إحداهما بعد الأُخرى؟ قال: لا أُحبُّ أنْ أُجيزَهما جميعاً ونهاه .

535. Mālik informed us: "Az-Zuhrī narrated to us from ᶜUbaydullāh ibn ᶜAbdullāh ibn ᶜUtbah from his father that ᶜUmar was asked about a woman and her daughter under ownership, as to whether intercourse could be had with one of them after the other, and he said, 'I dislike the notion of making them both valid together,' and he forbade him."

٥٣٦ أخبرنا مالك، عن الزُّهْرِيّ، عن قَبِيصَة بن ذُؤَيْب : أنَّ رجلاً سأل عثمان عن الأُخْتَيْن مما مَلَكَت اليمين هل يُجمع بينهما؟ فقال: أحلَّتهما آية وحرَّمتهما آية ، ما كنت لأصْنَع ذلك، ثم خرج فَلَقِي رجلاً من أصحاب النبي صلى الله عليه وسلم، فسأله عن ذلك؟ فقال: لو كان لي من الأمر شيء، ثم أُتيتُ بأحد فعل ذلك جعلتُه نكالاً . قال ابن شهاب : أُرَاه عليّاً رضي الله تعالى عنه .

536. Mālik informed us: "Az-Zuhrī informed us from Qabīṣah ibn Dhuʾayb that a man asked ᶜUthmān about two sisters he owned whether he could unite them [having intercourse with one after the other], and he said, 'One *āyah* makes both of them permissible and one *āyah* makes both of them impermissible, so I would not do it.' Then he went out, and he met a man who was one of the companions of the Messenger of Allah ﷺ and asked him about it. He said, 'If I had any authority and then someone who did that was brought to me, I would have ordered an exemplary punishment.'" Ibn Shihāb said, "I think it was ᶜAlī."

قال محمدٌ: وبهذا كله نأخذ لا ينبغي أن يُجمع بين المرأة وبين ابنتها، ولا بين المرأة وأختها في ملك اليمين. قال عمّار بن ياسر : ما حرَّم الله تعالى من الحرائر شيئاً إلاَّ وقد حرَّم من الإماء مثلَه إلاَّ أن يجمعهن رجل. يعني بذلك أنه يجمع ما شاء من الإماء، ولا يحلُّ له فوقَ أربعِ حرائرَ. وهو قولُ أبي حنيفة رحمه الله تعالى .

Muḥammad said: "We adhere to this. One ought not to unite a woman and her daughter, nor a woman and her sister who are under one's ownership [by having intercourse with them]. ᶜAmmār ibn Yāsir said, 'Whatever Allah forbids with respect to free women, He forbids the like of it with respect to slave women, except that a man collects them,' meaning by that that he collects as many slave women as he wants, but it is not permissible for him to have more than four free women [as wives], and that is the verdict of Abū Ḥanīfah."

١١ باب الرجل ينكح المرأة ولا يصل إليها لعلّة بالمرأة أو بالرجل

11. A Man who Marries a Woman and does not Unite [sexually] with her because of some Defect in the Woman or in the Man

٥٣٧ أخبرنا مالك، أخبرنا ابن شهاب، عن سعيد بن المسيّب أنّه كان يقول: مَنْ تزوّج امرأةً فلم يستطع أن يمسها فإنّه يُضْرَب له أجل سَنَة فإن مَسَّها وإلاَّ فُرِّقَ بينهما.

537. Mālik informed us: "Ibn Shihāb informed us that Saʿīd ibn al-Musayyab used to say, 'Someone who marries a woman and is unable to have intercourse with her, then the period of a year is set for him. If he has intercourse with her [then the marriage is valid], and if not then they are separated.'"

قال محمدُ: وبهذا نأخذ، وهو قولُ أبي حنيفة رحمه الله إن مضت سنة ولم يمسّها خُيِّرَت فإن اختارَتْه فهي زوجته، ولا خيار لها بعد ذلك أبداً. وإن اختارَت نفسها فهي تطليقة بائنة، وإن قال إني قد مَسستُها السَنَة إن كانت ثيِّباً فالقول قوله مع يمينه، وإن كانت بكراً نظَرَ إليها النِّساء، فإن قلن هي بكْرٌ خُيِّرت بعدَ ما تُحلَّفُ بالله ما مَسَّها وإن قلن هي ثيِّب، فالقول قوله مع يمينه لقد مَسَسْتُها وهو قول أبي حنيفة والعامة من فقهائنا.

Muḥammad said: "We adhere to this, and it is the verdict of Abū Ḥanīfah. If a year passes and he has not had intercourse with her, then she is given the choice. If she chooses him, then she is his wife, and she never again has a choice after that. If she chooses herself [her freedom] then she is irrevocably divorced. He may say, 'I had intercourse with her during the year.' In that case, if she had been previously married, his word is accepted if accompanied by his oath. If she was a virgin, then the women examine her, and if they say, 'She is [still] a virgin,' she is given the choice after having been required to swear an oath by Allah that he did not have intercourse with her. If they said, 'She is no longer a virgin,' then his word is accepted when accompanied by his oath that he definitely had intercourse with her. That and it is the verdict of Abū Ḥanīfah and our *fuqahā᾽* in general."

٥٣٨ أخبرنا مالك، أخبرنا مُجَبَّر، عن سعيد بن المسيَّب أنَّه قال: أيُّما رجلٍ تزوّج امرأةً وبه جُنُون أو ضُرٌّ فإنها تُخَيَّر إن شاءَت قَرَّت وإن شاءَت فارَقَتْ.

538. Mālik informed us: "Mujabbar informed us that Saʿīd ibn al-Musayyab said, 'If a man marries a woman while he has some mental trouble or [physical] affliction, then she is given the choice; if she wishes, she settles [in the marriage], and if she wishes, she divorces.'"

قال محمد: إذا كان أمراً لا يُحْتَملُ خُيِّرَتْ، فإن شاءت قَرَّت وإن شاءَت فارقَتْ، وإلاَّ لا خيار لها إلاَّ في العِنِّين والمَجْبُوب.

Muḥammad said: "If the matter is intolerable, she is given the choice, and if she wishes, she settles [in the marriage], and if she wishes, she divorces. If not, she has no choice except in cases of impotence and castration."

١٢ باب البكر تُستأمر في نفسها

12. A Virgin who is Consulted concerning Herself

٥٣٩ أخبرنا مالك، أخبرنا عبد الله بن الفَضْل، عن نافع بن جُبَيْر، عن ابن عباس: أنَّ رسول الله صلى الله عليه وسلم قال: الأيِّم أَحَقُّ بنفسها من وَليِّها، والبكْر تُسْتَأمر في نفسها، وإذنها صُماتُها.

539. Mālik informed us: "ᶜAbdullāh ibn al-Faḍl informed us from Nāfiᶜ ibn Jubayr from Ibn ᶜAbbās that the Messenger of Allah ﷺ said, 'The unmarried woman who is not a virgin has more right over herself than does her guardian, and the virgin is consulted concerning herself, and her consent is her silence."

قال محمد: وبهذا نأخذ وهو قول أبي حنيفة، وذات الأب وغير الأب في ذلك سواء.

Muḥammad said: "We adhere to this, and it is the verdict of Abū Ḥanīfah. The woman who has a father and the one without a father are in the same situation."

٥٤٠ أخبرنا مالك، أخبرنا قَيْس بن الربيع الأسَدي، عن عبد الكريم الجَزَري، عن سعيد بن المسيَّب قال: قال رسول الله صلى الله عليه وسلم: تُسْتَأذَن الأبْكار في أنفسهنَّ ذَوَاتَ الأب وغير الأب.

540. Mālik informed us: "Qays ibn ar-Rabīᶜ al-Asadī informed us from ᶜAbd al-Karīm al-Jazarī that Saᶜīd ibn al-Musayyab said, 'The Messenger of Allah ﷺ said, "Virgins are asked their consent concerning themselves, those with fathers and those without fathers."'"

قال محمد: فبهذا نأخذ.

Muḥammad said: "We adhere to this."

١٣ باب النكاح بغير وليّ

13. Marriage without a Guardian

٥٤١ أخبرنا مالك، أخبرنا رجل، عن سعيد بن المسيَّب قال: قال عمر بن الخطاب: لا يصلح لامرأةٍ أن تُنْكَح إلا بإذن وليِّها أو ذي الرأي من أهلها أو السلطان.

541. Mālik informed us: "A man informed us that Saᶜīd ibn al-Musayyab said, 'ᶜUmar ibn al-Khaṭṭāb said, "It is not right for a woman to be married unless with the permission of her guardian, or a member of her family of sound judgement, or the ruler[28]."'"

قال محمدٌ: لا نكاح إلا بوَليّ، فإن تشاجَرَت هي والوليّ فالسُّلطان وليّ مَنْ لا وَليّ له. فأمّا أبو حنيفة فقال: إذا وضعت نفسها في كفاءة ولم تُقَصِّر في نفسها في صَدَاق، فالنكاح جائز، ومن

حُجَّته قول عمر في هذا الحديث: أو ذي الرَّأي من أهلها. إنه ليس بوَلِيّ، وقد أجاز نكاحه لأنّه إنما أراد أن لا تُقَصِّر بنفسها فإذا فعلت هي ذلك جاز.

Muḥammad said, "There is no marriage without a guardian. If she and the guardian have fallen out, then the ruler is the guardian of anyone who has no guardian. As for Abū Ḥanīfah, he said, 'If she places herself in a position of equality [in terms of rank, dīn, lineage, etc. with respect to her husband-to-be] and does not neglect her dowry, then the marriage is permissible.' A part of his argument was the saying of ᶜUmar in this ḥadīth, 'or a member of her family of sound judgement' in that this is not a guardian and yet the marriage is permissible; the main point then, is that she does not neglect her dowry. Therefore, if she does that [represents herself] it is permissible."

١٤ باب الرجل يتزوج المرأة ولا يفرض لها صداقاً

14. A Man who Marries a Woman and does not Appoint a Dowry for her

٥٤٢ أخبرنا مالك، حدّثنا نافع، أنّ بنتاً لعُبَيْد الله بن عمر وأُمها ابنة زيد بن الخطاب كانت تحت ابن لعبد الله بن عمر فمات، ولم يُسَمِّ لها صَدَاقاً، فقامت أمها تطلُبُ صَدَاقها؟ فقال ابن عمر: ليس لها صَدَاق ولو كان لها صَدَاق لَم نُمْسكه ولم نَظلمها.
وأبت أن تقبل ذلك فجعلوا بينهم زيد بن ثَابت فقَضَى أن لا صَدَاق لها، ولها الميراث.

542. Mālik informed us: "Nāfiᶜ narrated to us that a daughter of ᶜUbaydullāh ibn ᶜUmar whose mother was a daughter of Zayd ibn al-Khaṭṭāb, was married to a son of ᶜAbdullāh ibn ᶜUmar, and he died without specifying what her dowry should be. Her mother undertook to ask for her dowry, but Ibn ᶜUmar said, 'She has no dowry. If she did have a dowry we would not touch it and we would not wrong her,' but she refused to accept that. Then they appointed Zayd ibn Thābit [to arbitrate] between them, and he gave the judgement that she was not due any dowry but that she should inherit."

قال محمد: ولسنا نأخذ بهذا.

Muḥammad said, "We do not take this position."

٥٤٣ أخبرنا أبو حنيفة، عن حمَّاد، عن إبراهيم النَّخَعيّ: أن رجلاً تزوّج امرأة ولم يفْرض لها صَدَاقاً، فمات قبل أن يدخل بها، فقال عبد الله بن مسعود: لها صَدَاق مثلها من نسائها، لا وَكْسَ ولا شَطَطَ، فلما قضى قال فإن يكن صواباً فمن الله وإن يكن خطأً فَمنّي ومن الشيطان، والله ورسوله بريئان، فقال رجل من جلسائه: بَلَغنا أنه مَعْقل بن سنان الأشجعي، وكان من أصحاب رسول الله صلى الله عليه وسلم، قَضَيْتَ والذي يُحْلَفُ به بقضاء رسول الله صلى الله عليه وسلم في بِرْوَعَ بنت وَاشق الأشْجَعيّة، قال: ففرح عبد الله فَرْحَة ما فرح قبلها مثلها لموافقة قوله قولَ رسول الله صلى الله عليه وسلم. قَال مسْرُوق ابن الأجْدَع: لا يكون ميراث حتى يكون قبله صَدَاق.

543. Abū Ḥanīfah informed us from Ḥammād from Ibrāhīm an-Nakhaᶜī that a man married a woman and did not appoint any dowry for her. He died

before he could consummate the marriage. ᶜAbdullāh ibn Masᶜūd said, "She should have the dowry of any woman like her, no less and no more." When he passed judgement he said, "If it is right it is from Allah, and if it is a mistake it is from me and from shayṭān, and Allah and His Messenger are free of it." A man from his gathering said – and it has reached us that it was Maᶜqil ibn Sinān al-Ashjaᶜī, and he was one of the Companions of the Messenger of Allah ﷺ "You have given judgement – by the One by Whom oaths are sworn! – according to the judgement of the Messenger of Allah ﷺ in [the case of] Birawᶜ the daughter of Wāshiq al-Ashjaᶜiyyah." So ᶜAbdullāh rejoiced with such joy as he had never before shown because of the agreement of his verdict with the verdict of the Messenger of Allah ﷺ. Masrūq ibn al-Ajdaᶜ said, "There cannot be an inheritance unless there has previously been a dowry."

قال محمد : وبهذا نأخذ . وهو قول أبي حنيفة والعامة من فقهائنا .

Muḥammad said, "We adhere to this, and it is the verdict of Abū Ḥanīfah and our *fuqahā'* in general."

١٥ باب المرأة تزوّج في عدّتها

15. A Woman Marrying during her *ᶜiddah*

٥٤٤ أخبرنا مالك، أخبرنا ابن شهاب، عن سعيد بن المسيَّب وسليمان بن يَسَار، أنهما حَدَّثا: أنّ ابنة طَلْحة بن عُبَيْد الله كانت تحت رُشَيْد الثَّقفيّ، فطلّقها، فنكحت في عدَّتها أبا سعيد بنَ مُنَبِّه أو أبا الجُلاس بن مُنيَة فضربها عمر، وضرب زوجَها بالمخْفَقَة ضَرَبات ، وفَرَّقَ بينهما، وقال عمر: أيّما امرأة نكحت في عدّتها وإن كان زوجُها الذي تزوّجها لم يدخل بها فُرِّق بينهما، واعتدَّتْ بقية عدَّتها من الأول، ثم كان خاطباً من الخُطّاب، وإن كان قد دخل بها فُرِّق بينهما، ثم اعتدَّت بقية عدَّتها من الآخر ثم لم ينكحها أبداً. قال سعيد بن المسيَّب: ولها مهرها بما استحلّ من فرجها .

544. Mālik informed us: "Ibn Shihāb informed us from Saᶜīd ibn al-Musayyab and Sulaymān ibn Yasār that, 'They narrated that the daughter of Ṭalḥah ibn ᶜUbaydullāh was married to Rushayd ath-Thaqafī and he divorced her. During her *ᶜiddah* she married Saᶜīd ibn Munabbih or Abu'l-Julās ibn Munayyah, and so ᶜUmar struck her and he struck her husband with a stick a number of times, and he separated them. ᶜUmar said, "If a woman marries in her *ᶜiddah*, then if the husband who marries her has not consummated the marriage with her they are separated, and she then completes what remains of her *ᶜiddah* from the first [husband]. Then he [the second husband] is one of her suitors. If he had consummated the marriage with her, they are separated and she completes what remains of her *ᶜiddah* from the first, and then she performs an *ᶜiddah* from the second, and then he may never marry her."'" Saᶜīd ibn al-Musayyab said, "She has her dowry because he regarded her private parts as permissible [to him]."

قال محمد : بلغنا أن عمر بن الخطاب رجع عن هذا القول إلى قول علي بن أبي طالب رضي الله تعالى عنه

Muḥammad said, "It has reached us that ᶜUmar ibn al-Khaṭṭāb recanted this position in favour of the position of ᶜAlī ibn Abī Ṭālib."

٥٤٥ أخبرنا الحسن بن عُمَارة، عن الحَكَم بن عُيَيْنَة، عن مجاهد قال : رجع عمر بن الخطاب في التي تتزوَّج في عدَّتها إلى قول علي بن أبي طالب، وذلك أن عمر قال : إذا دخل بها فُرِّق بينَهُما ولم يجتمعا أَبَداً، وأَخَذ صَدَاقها، فجعل في بيت المال فقام علي كرَّم الله وجهه : لها صَدَاقها بما استحلَّ من فرجها، فإذا انقضتْ عِدَّتُها من الأول تَزَوَّجَها الآخر إن شاءَ. فرجع عمر إلى قول علي بن أبي طالب رضي الله عنهما .

545. Al-Ḥasan ibn ᶜUmārah informed us from al-Ḥakam ibn ᶜUyaynah that Mujāhid said, "ᶜUmar ibn al-Khaṭṭāb recanted concerning the woman who married during her *ᶜiddah* in favour of the position of ᶜAlī. That was that ᶜUmar [originally] said, 'If he has consummated the marriage then they are separated and may not reunite ever,' and he took her dowry and it was put in the bayt al-māl. ᶜAlī said, 'She has her dowry because he regarded her private parts as permissible [to him]. Then when her *ᶜiddah* from the first [husband] is over, the other may marry her if he wishes.' ᶜUmar recanted his position in favour of that of ᶜAlī."

قال محمد : وبهذا نأخذ . وهو قول أبي حنيفة والعامة من فقهائنا .

Muḥammad said, "We adhere to this, and it is the verdict of Abū Ḥanīfah and our *fuqahā᾿* in general."

٥٤٦ أخبرنا يزيد بن عبد الله بن الهاد، عن محمد بن إبراهيم ، عن سليمان بن يسار، عن عبد الله بن أبي أمية : أنَّ امرأةً هلك عنها زوجها، فاعتدَّت أربعة أشهر وعشراً، ثم تزوَّجَتْ حين حلَّت فمكثت عند زوجها أربعة أشهر ونصفاً، ثم ولدتْ ولداً تامّاً ، فجاء زوجُها إلى عمر بن الخطاب فدعا عمرُ نساءً من نساء أهل الجاهلية قدَمَاء ، فسألهنَّ عن ذلك، فقالت المرأة منهن: أنا أخبرك ، أما هذه المرأة هَلَكَ زوجها حين حملت، فأهريقت الدماء فَحَشَفَ ولدُها في بطنها ، فلما أصابها زوجُها الذي نكحته وأصاب الولدَ الماءُ تحرَّك الولد في بطنها، وكَبِر فصدَّقها عمر بذلك وفرَّق بينهما ، وقال عمر: أمَا إنه لم يبلغني عنهما إلاّ خيراً ، وألحق الولدَ بالأوَّل .

546. Yazīd ibn ᶜAbdullāh ibn al-Hād informed us from Muḥammad ibn Ibrāhīm from Sulaymān ibn Yasār from ᶜAbdullāh ibn Abī Umayyah that a woman's husband died, and she completed the *ᶜiddah* of four months and ten [days]. When she was permitted she married and spent four and a half months with her husband and then gave birth to a fully formed boy. Her husband went to ᶜUmar ibn al-Khaṭṭāb, and ᶜUmar called on the older women from the women of the time of *Jāhiliyyah*. He asked them about that, and one of them said, "I will tell you. This woman's husband died while she had conceived and so the blood was spilled [pseudo-menstrual bleeding] and the child became withdrawn within her womb. Then when her husband who married her

made love to her, and his fluid touched the child, the child moved in her womb and grew." ʿUmar affirmed her in that and separated them. ʿUmar said, "Nothing has reached me about you two but good," and he attached the child's [parentage] to the former.

قال محمدٌ: وبهذا نأخذ، الولد وَلَدُ الأوَّل، لأنها جاءت به عند الآخر لأقلٍّ من ستة أشهر، فلا تلد المرأة ولداً تامًّا لأقلٍّ من ستَّة أشهر، فهو ابن الأول، ويفرَّق بينهما وبين الآخر، ولها المهر بما استَحَلَّ من فرجها: الأقلُّ مما سُمِّي لها ومن مهر مثلها. وهو قول أبي حنيفة والعامة من فقهائنا.

Muḥammad said, "We adhere to this. The child is the child of the former because she gave birth to him [while married to] the latter after less than six months [of marriage], and women do not give birth to fully formed children in less than six months, and so he is the child of the former. She is separated from the latter husband, but she has her dowry because he had regarded her private parts as permissible [to him], [the amount being] that which he named for her or the dowry of someone like her, whichever is the lesser. It is the verdict of Abū Ḥanīfah and our *fuqahā*ʾ in general."

١٦ باب العزل

16. Coitus Interruptus

٥٤٧ أخبرنا مالك، أخبرنا سالم أبو النَّضر، عن عامر بن سعد بن أبي وقَّاص، عن أبيه أنه كان يَعْزِل.

547. Mālik informed us: "Sālim Abu'n-Naḍr informed us from ʿĀmir ibn Saʿd ibn Abī Waqqāṣ that his father used to practise coitus interruptus."

٥٤٨ أخبرنا مالك، أخبرنا سالم أبو النضر، عن عبد الرحمن بن أفْلَح مولى أبي أيّوب الأنصاري عن أم ولد أبي أيوب: أن أبا أيوب كان يَعْزِل.

548. Mālik informed us: "Sālim Abu'n-Naḍr informed us from ʿAbd ar-Raḥmān ibn Aflaḥ the *mawlā* of Abū Ayyūb al-Anṣārī from an *umm walad*[29] of Abū Ayyūb that Abū Ayyūb used to practise coitus interruptus.

٥٤٩ أخبرنا مالك، أخبرنا ضَمْرَة بن سعيد المازني، عن الحجَّاج بن عَمرو بن غَزيَّة: أنَّه كان جالساً عند زيد بن ثابت، فجاءَه ابن قَهْد رجل من أهل اليمن، فقال: يا أبا سعيد، إن عندي جَواريَ، ليس نسائي اللاتي كُنَّ بأعجبَ إليَّ منهنَّ، وليس كلُّهن يُعْجِبُني أن تَحمل منّي، أفَأعْزِلُ؟ قال: قال: أفته يا حجّاج، قال: قلت: غفر اللّهُ لك، إنما نَجْلِسُ إليكَ لنتعلم منك، قال. أَفْتِه، قال: قلت: هو حَرْثُكَ إن شئتَ عطَّشْتَهُ وإنْ شئتَ سقيتَه، قال: وقد كنت أسْمع ذلك من زيد، فقال زيد: صَدَقَ.

549. Mālik informed us: "Ḍamrah ibn Saʿīd al-Māzinī informed us from al-Ḥajjāj ibn ʿAmr ibn Ghaziyyah that he had been sitting with Zayd ibn Thābit when Ibn Qahd had come to him – a man from the people of Yemen – and he said, 'Abū Saʿīd, I have slave girls, and the wives I have are not more pleasing to me than they are, but not every one of them would please me if she became pregnant by me. Should I perform coitus interruptus?' He said, 'Give him the *fatwā*, Ḥajjāj.' He said, 'May Allah forgive you! we only

sit with you to learn from you.' He said, 'Give him the *fatwā*.'" He said, "I said, 'It is your fertile-field: if you wish make it thirsty and if you wish give it to drink.'" He said, "I had heard that from Zayd. Zayd said, 'He told the truth.'"

قال محمد: وبهذا نأخذ لا نرى بالعزل بأساً عن الأَمَة ، وأمّا الحُرَّة فلا ينبغي أن يَعزل عنها إلاّ بإذن، وإذا كانت الأَمَة زوجة الرجل فلا ينبغي أن يَعزلَ عنها إلاّ بإذن مولاها. وهو قول أبي حَنيفة رحمه الله.

Muḥammad said, "We adhere to this. We see no harm in practising coitus interruptus with a slave woman. As for a free woman one ought not to practise coitus interruptus without her permission. If the slave woman is the man's wife, he ought not to practise coitus interruptus without the permission of her owner. That is the position of Abū Ḥanīfah."

٥٥٠ أخبرنا مالك، أخبرنا ابن شهاب، عن سالم بن عبد الله، عن عبد الله بن عمر، أنَّ عمر بن الخطاب قال: ما بالُ رجال يَعْزِلُون عن ولائدهم ؟ لا تأتيني وليدة فيعترف سيِّدُها أنه قد ألَمَّ بها إلاَّ ألحقتُ به ولدها فاعتزلوا بعدُ أو اتركوا.

550. Mālik informed us: "Ibn Shihāb informed us from Sālim ibn ᶜAbdullāh from ᶜAbdullāh ibn ᶜUmar that ᶜUmar ibn al-Khaṭṭāb said, 'What is wrong with men who practise coitus interruptus with their female slaves? If a female slave comes to me and her owner acknowledges that he had intercourse with her I will attribute [the paternity of] the child to him. So practise coitus interruptus then or leave it."

قال محمد: إنَّما صنع هذا عمرُ رضي الله عنه على التهديد للناس أنْ يُضَيِّعُوا ولائدَهم، وهم يطؤونهنَّ. قد بلغنا أنَّ زيد بن ثابت وطئ جاريةً له، فجاءت بولد، فنفاه، وأن عمر بن الخَطاب وطئ جارية له فحملت، فقال: اللّهم لا تَلْحقْ بآل عمر من ليس منهم، فجاءت بغلام أسود، فأقرَّت أنَّه من الراعي، فانتفى منه عمر. وكان أبو حنيفة يقول إذا حصَّنها ولم يَدَعْها تخرج ، فجاءَت بولدٍ لم يسعه فيما بينه وبين ربه عزَّ وجلّ ينتفي منه، فبهذا نأخذ.

Muḥammad said, "ᶜUmar only did this in order to put fear into people so that they would not waste their slave women while they had sexual intercourse with them. It has reached us that Zayd ibn Thābit had sexual intercourse with a slave woman of his and she gave birth to a child and he repudiated it. Also, that ᶜUmar ibn al-Khaṭṭāb had sexual intercourse with a slave woman who then became pregnant. He said, 'O Allah, do not connect someone in lineage to the family of ᶜUmar who is not of them,' and then she gave birth to a black child. She affirmed that he was [the child] of a shepherd, so ᶜUmar repudiated it. And Abū Ḥanīfah used to say, 'If he jealously cares for and guards her and does not abandon her just to go out and about, and she gives birth to a child, it is not permitted to him in that which is between him and his Lord to repudiate it.' We adhere to this."

٥٥١ أخبرنا مالك، حدَّثنا نافع، عن صفية بنت أبي عبيد، قالت: قال عمر بن الخطّاب: ما بال رجالٍ

يطؤون ولائدهم ثم يَدَعُونَهُنَّ فَيَخْرُجْنَ ؟! والله لا تأتيني وليْدَةٌ فيعترف سيِّدُهَا أنْ قد وَطِئَها إلاَّ الْحقتُ به وَلَدَها فأرسلوهُنَّ بعدُ أَو أَمْسِكُوهُنَّ .

551. Mālik informed us: "Nāfiʿ narrated to us that Ṣafiyyah bint Abī ʿUbayd said, "ʿUmar ibn al-Khaṭṭāb said, "What is wrong with men who have sexual intercourse with their slave women and then abandon them so that they go out and about. By Allah! If a slave woman comes to me and her master acknowledges that he has had sexual intercourse with her then I will attribute [the paternity of] the child to him. So then, set them free or retain them."

كتاب الطلاق

7. DIVORCE

١ باب طلاق السنة

1. Divorce of the *Sunnah*

٥٥٢ أخبرنا مالك، حدثنا عبد الله بن دينار، قال: سمعت ابن عمر يقرأ: ﴿يَا أَيُّهَا النَّبِيُّ إِذَا طَلَّقْتُمُ النِّسَاءَ فَطَلِّقُوهُنَّ لِقُبُلِ عِدَّتِهِنَّ﴾.

552. Mālik informed us: "ᶜAbdullāh ibn Dīnār narrated to us saying, 'I heard Ibn ᶜUmar reciting, "O Prophet! When any of you divorce women, divorce them at the beginning of their period of purity."'"[30]

قال محمد: طلاق السُّنَّة أن يُطَلِّقَها لِقُبُل عدَّتها طاهراً من غير جماع حين تطهر من حيضها قبل أن يجامعها. وهو قول أبي حنيفة والعامَّة من فقهائنا.

Muḥammad said: "The divorce of the Sunnah is that a man divorce his wife at the beginning of their period of purity in a state of purity, after her period of menstruation and without [having had] sexual intercourse with her. at a time when she is in a state of purity before having sexual intercourse That is the position of Abū Ḥanīfah and of our *fuqahā*ʾ in general."

٥٥٣ أخبرنا مالك، أخبرنا نافع، عن عبد الله بن عُمَر أنَّه طَلَّقَ امرأته وهي حائضٌ في عَهْد رَسُول اللَّه صلَّى اللَّهُ عليه وسَلَّم، فسألَ عُمرُ عن ذلك رسول الله صلَّى اللَّهُ عَلَيه وَسَلَّم، فَقالَ: مُرْه فَلْيُرَاجِعْهَا، ثُمَّ يُمْسِكْهَا حَتَّى تَطْهُرَ ثُمَّ تَحِيض، ثُمَّ تَطْهُرَ، ثُمَّ إِنْ شَاءَ أَمْسَكَهَا بَعْدُ، وإن شاء طَلَّقَهَا قَبْلَ أَنْ يَمَسَّهَا فَتِلْكَ العِدَّةُ الَّتي أَمَرَ اللَّهُ أَنْ تُطَلَّقَ لَهَا النِّسَاءُ.

553. Mālik informed us: "Nāfiᶜ informed us that ᶜAbdullāh ibn ᶜUmar divorced his wife while she was in her period of menstruation during the life of the Messenger of Allah ﷺ. ᶜUmar asked the Messenger of Allah ﷺ about that, and he answered, 'Tell him to take her back and then he should retain her until she becomes pure [from menstruation], then let her enter her period of menstruation again, and then later become pure again. If he wishes then let him retain her, and if he wishes then let him divorce her before touching her [in sexual intercourse]. That is the *ᶜiddah* (period of purity) in which Allah commands women should be divorced.'"

قال محمد: وبهذا نأخُذ.

Muḥammad said: "We adhere to this."

٢ باب طلاق الحُرَّة تحت العبد

2. Divorce of a Free Woman Married to a Slave

٥٥٤ أخبرنا مالك، حدثنا الزهري، عن سعيد بن المسيَّب أنَّ نُفَيْعاً مكاتَب أمِّ سلمة كانت تحته امرأة حرَّة، فطلَّقها تطليقتين، فاستفتى عثمان بن عفّان: فقال : حَرُمت عليك .

554. Mālik informed us: "Az-Zuhrī narrated to us from Saʿīd ibn al-Musayyab that Nufayᶜ, the slave who wrote a contract with Umm Salamah to buy his freedom, was married to a free woman whom he divorced twice. Then he sought a ruling from ᶜUthmān ibn ᶜAffān who said, 'She is forbidden to you.'"

٥٥٥ أخبرنا مالك، حدثنا أبو الزِّناد ، عن سليمان بن يسار : أنَّ نُفَيْعاً كان عبداً لأمِّ سلمةَ أو مكاتباً ، وكانت تحته امرأة حرَّة، فطلَّقها تطليقتين، فأمره أزواج النبي صلى الله عليه وسلم أن يأتي عثمان فيسأله عن ذلك، فلقيه عند الدَّرَج وهو آخذ بيد زيد بن ثابت، فسأله فابتدراه جميعاً فقالا: حَرُمتْ عليك، حَرُمتْ عليك .

555. Mālik informed us: "Abu'z-Zinād narrated to us from Sulaymān ibn Yasār that Nufayᶜ had been a slave of Umm Salamah or a slave who had written a contract to purchase his freedom, and he had been married to a free woman whom he divorced twice. The wives of the Prophet ﷺ told him to go to ᶜUthmān ibn ᶜAffān and ask him about that. He met him at ad-Daraj[31], where he found him holding the hand of Zayd ibn Thābit, and so he asked him. They both hastened to answer him and said together, 'She is forbidden to you, she is forbidden to you.'"

٥٥٦ أخبرنا مالك، أخبرنا نافع، عن ابن عمر قال : إذا طلَّق العبد امرأتَه اثنتين فقد حَرُمَتْ حتى تَنْكِحَ زوجاً غيره، حرَّةً كانت أو أمةً، وعدَّة الحرَّة ثلاثة قروء وعدَّة الأمة حيضتان .

556. Mālik informed us: "Nāfiᶜ informed us that Ibn ᶜUmar said, 'When a slave divorces his wife twice she is forbidden to him until she marries a husband other than him, whether she is free or a slave. The *ᶜiddah* of the free woman is three periods of purity, and the *ᶜiddah* of the slave woman is two menstrual periods.'"

قال محمد : قد اختلف الناس في هذا، فأما ما عليه فقهاؤنا فإنهم يقولون : الطلاق بالنساء والعدَّة بهنَّ لأنَّ الله عزَّ وجلّ قال : ﴿ فطلِّقُوهُنَّ لعدَّتهنَّ ﴾ فإنما الطلاق للعدَّة فإذا كانت الحرَّة وزوجها عَبد فعدَّتها ثلاثة قروء وطلاقها ثلاثة تطليقاتَ للعَدَّة كما قال الله تبارَك وتعالى، وإذا كان الحرّ تحته الأمة فعَدَّتها حيضتان، وطلاقها للعدَّة تطليقتان، كما قال الله عزَّ وجلّ.

Muḥammad said: "People differ on this. As for the position our *fuqahā*ʾ take, they say, 'Divorce depends upon the [status of the] woman and the *ᶜiddah*, is according to them because Allah ﷻ says, "Divorce them during their period of purity (*ᶜiddah*)."' So divorce is only [by the expiration of the] *ᶜiddah*. If she is a free woman and her husband is a slave then her *ᶜiddah* is three periods of purity, and her [full] divorce is three divorces with the *ᶜiddah*, as Allah,

Blessed is He and exalted is He, says. If there is a free man married to a slave woman then her *ᶜiddah* is two menstrual periods and her [full] divorce is two divorces with [their] *ᶜiddah*, as Allah ﷻ says."

٥٥٧ قال محمد : أخبرنا إبراهيم بن يزيد المكّي قال : سمعت عطاء بن أبي رباح يقول: قال علي بن أبي طالب: الطلاق بالنساء والعدَّة بهنَّ. وهو قول عبد الله بن مسعود وأبي حنيفة والعامة من فقهائنا.

557. Muḥammad said: "Ibrāhīm ibn Yazīd al-Makkī told us saying, 'I heard ᶜAṭāʾ ibn Abī Rabāḥ saying, "ᶜAlī ibn Abī Ṭālib ؓ said, 'Divorce depends upon the [status of the] woman and the *ᶜiddah* is determined by that.'"' And that is the position of Ibn Masᶜūd, Abū Ḥanīfah and of our *fuqahāʾ* in general."

٣ باب ما يُكره للمطلَّقة المبتوتة والمتوفى عنها من المبيت في غير بيتها

3. What is Disapproved of for an Irrevocably Divorced Woman and a Widowed Woman Concerning their Spending the Night in Someone else's House

٥٥٨ أخبرنا مالك، حدثنا نافع، أن ابن عمر كان يقول: لا تبيت المبتوتة ولا المتوفَّى عنها إلاَّ في بيت زوجها.

558. Mālik informed us: "Nāfiᶜ narrated to us that Ibn ᶜUmar used to say, 'The irrevocably divorced woman and the widowed woman must only spend the night in their husbands' houses.'"

قال محمد: وبهذا نأخذ. أما المتوفَّى عنها فإنها تَخرج بالنهار في حوائجها، ولا تبيتُ إلاَّ في بيتها، وأمَّا المُطَلَّقَةُ مبتوتةً كانت أو غير مبتوتةٍ فلا تخرج ليلاً ولا نهاراً ما دامت في عِدَّتها. وهو قولُ أبي حنيفة والعامة من فقهائنا.

Muḥammad said: "We adhere to this. As for the widowed woman she may go out in the daytime for her necessities but must always spend the night in her own house. As for the woman who is divorced, whether or not it is irrevocably, she must not go out whether by night or by day as long as she is in her *ᶜiddah*. It is also the verdict of Abū Ḥanīfah and our *fuqahāʾ* in general."

٤ باب الرجل يأذن لعبده في التزويج هل يجوز طلاق المولى عليه؟

4. Whether a Man who Permits his Slave to Marry is Permitted to Make him Divorce

٥٥٩ أخبرنا مالك، أخبرنا نافع، عن ابن عمر أنه كان يقول: من أذن لعبده في أن ينكح فإنه لا يجوز لامرأته طلاقٌ إلا أن يطلّقها العبد، فأما أن يأخذ الرجل أمةَ غلامه، أو أمةَ وليدته فلا جُنَاحَ عليه.

559. Mālik informed us: "Nāfiᶜ informed us that ᶜAbdullāh ibn ᶜUmar used to say, 'Whoever gives his slave permission to marry, then his wife cannot be subject to divorce unless the slave divorces her. As for the man taking the

slave-girl of his slave or the slave-girl of his slave-woman, there is no wrong action against him.'"

قال محمد: وبهذا نأخذ. وهو قول أبي حنيفة والعامة من فقهائنا.

Muḥammad said: "We adhere to this, and it is the verdict of Abū Ḥanīfah and our *fuqahāʾ* in general."

٥٦٠. أخبرنا مالك، أخبرنا نافع، عن ابن عمر: أن عبداً لبعض ثقيف جاء إلى عمر بن الخطاب، فقال: إن سيدي أنكحني جاريته فلانة وكان عمر يعرف الجارية وهو يطأها فأرسل عمر إلى الرجل، فقال: ما فعلت جاريتك؟ قال: هي عندي، قال: هل تطأها؟ فأشار إلى بعض من كان عنده، فقال: لا، فقال عمر: أما والله لو اعترفتَ لجعلتُك نكالاً.

560. Mālik informed us: "Nāfiʿ informed us from Ibn ʿUmar that a slave of one the members of [the tribe of] Thaqīf came to ʿUmar ibn al-Khaṭṭāb and said, 'My master married me to his slave-girl so-and-so' – and ʿUmar used to know the slave-girl – 'and then he had sexual intercourse with her.' So ʿUmar sent for the man, asking, 'What has your slave-girl so-and-so done?' He answered, 'She is with me.' He asked, 'Are you having sexual relations with her?' One of the people who was with ʿUmar made a sign and so he answered, 'No.' ʿUmar said, 'By Allah! If you had acknowledged it, I would have made an example of you.'"

قال محمد: وبهذا نأخذ. لا ينبغي إذا زوج الرجلُ جاريتَه عبدَه أن يطأها لأن الطلاقَ والفرقةَ بيد العبد إذا زوجها مولاه، وليس لمولاه أن يُفرق بينهما بعد أن زوجها فإن وطئها يُندَم إليه في ذلك، فإن عاد أدبه الإمام على قدر ما يرى من الحبس والضرب، ولا يبلغ بذلك أربعين سوطاً.

Muḥammad said: "We adhere to this. When a man marries his slave-girl to his slave he may not have sexual relations with her, because divorce and separation are in the slave's hand when the master marries him [to her], and it is not allowed for the master to separate them after marrying her off. If he has sexual relations [with her] he is reprimanded, and if he does it again the imām should punish him, according to the degree he thinks fit, with imprisonment and beating, but it must not reach forty lashes."

٦ باب المرأة تختلع من زوجها بأكثر مما أعطاها أو أقل
5. A Woman Acquiring a Divorce from her Husband in return for Compensating him with either more or less than He gave her

٥٦١ أخبرنا مالك، أخبرنا نافع: أن مولاة لصفية اختلعت من زوجها بكل شيء لها. فلم يُنكره ابن عمر.

561. Mālik informed us: "Nāfiʿ informed us that a freed slave-woman (*mawlāh*) belonging to Ṣafiyyah gained her divorce from her husband by compensating him with everything [she owned], and Ibn ʿUmar did not reject it."

قال محمد: ما اختلعت به امرأة من زوجها فهو جائز في القضاء وما تحب له أن يأخذ أكثر مما أعطاها

وإن جاء النشوز من قِبَلها. فأما إذا جاء النشوز من قبله لم نحب له أن يأخذ منها قليلاً ولا كثيراً، وإن أخذ فهو جائز في القضاء وهو مكروه له فيما بينه وبين الله تعالى. وهو قول أبي حنيفة رحمه الله.

Muḥammad said: "Whatever a woman compensates her husband with for his divorcing her is acceptable judicially, but we do not like him to take more than he gave her even if the unkind and injurious treatment is hers. As for the unkind and injurious treatment being his, we do not like him to take from her either a little or a lot, but if he does take it, it is acceptable judicially, but it is disapproved of for him in that which is between him and his Lord, and that is the verdict of Abū Ḥanīfah.

٦ باب الخلع كم يكون من الطلاق

6. How many Divorces a Woman's Divorcing her Husband through Compensation counts for

٥٦٢ أخبرنا مالك، أخبرنا هشام بن عروة، عن أبيه، عن جُمهان مولى الأسلميين، عن أم بكر الأسلمية: أنها اختلعت من زوجها عبد الله بن أسيد ثم أتيا عثمان بن عفان في ذلك، فقال: هي تطليقة إلا أن تكون سمت شيئاً فهو على ما سمت.

562. Mālik informed us: "Hishām ibn ʿUrwah informed us from his father from Jumhān the *mawlā*[32] of the tribe of Aslam from Umm Bakr of Aslam that she got her divorce from her husband ʿAbdullāh ibn Usayd by compensating him, and then later they both went to ʿUthmān ibn ʿAffān concerning that. He said, 'She is divorced unless she named something [some terms], for then it is according to what [terms] she named.'"

قال محمدٌ: وبهذا نأخذ الخلع تطليقة بائنة إلا سمى ثلاثاً، أو نواها فيكون ثلاثاً.

Muḥammad said: "We adhere to this. Divorce achieved by the woman compensating her husband is final[33], unless he named the divorce as three [divorces] or intended it, so that then it is three."

٧ باب الرجل يقول إذا نكحت فلانة فهي طالق

7. A Man Saying, "If I marry so-and-so then she is divorced."

٥٦٣ أخبرنا مالك، أخبرنا مجبر، عن عبد الله بن عمر أنه كان يقول: إذا قال الرجل: إذا نكحت فلانة فهي طالق، فهي طالق، فهي كذلك إذا نكحها، وإذا كان طلقها واحدةً أو اثنتين أو ثلاثاً فهو كما قال.

563. Mālik informed us: "Mujabbar informed us from ʿAbdullāh that he used to say, 'If a man says, "If I marry so-and-so then she is divorced," then she is so if he marries her. If he had divorced her once, twice or thrice, then it is as he says.'"

قال محمدٌ: وبهذا نأخذ. وهو قول أبي حنيفة رحمه الله.

Muḥammad said: "We adhere to this, and it is the verdict of Abū Ḥanīfah."

٥٦٤ أخبرنا مالك، عن سعيد بن عمرو بن سليم الزرقي، عن القاسم بن محمد: أن رجلاً سأل عمر
بن الخطاب ۞، فقال: إن قُلت إن تزوجت فلانة فهي عليَّ كظهر أمي، قال: إن تزوجتها فلا تقربها
حتى تُكفِّر.

564. Mālik informed us from Saʿīd ibn ʿAmr ibn Sulaym az-Zuraqī from
al-Qāsim ibn Muḥammad that a man asked ʿUmar ibn al-Khaṭṭāb saying, "I
said, 'If I marry so-and-so then she is to me as my mother's back.'" He said,
"If you marry her then do not approach her until you have done the expiation."[34]

قال محمد: وبهذا نأخُذُ. وهو قول أبي حنيفة يكون مظاهراً منها إذا تزوجها فلا يقربها حتى يُكفِّر.

Muḥammad said: "We adhere to this, and it is the verdict of Abū Ḥanīfah
that he has performed *ẓihār* from the moment he marries her so that he
should not approach her until he has performed the expiation."

٨ باب المرأة يطلقها زوجها تطليقة أو تطليقتين فتتزوج زوجاً ثم يتزوجها الأول

8. A Woman whose Husband Divorces her once or twice, and who then Marries a [new] Husband and then the former Husband Remarries her

٥٦٥ أخبرنا مالك، أخبرنا الزهري، عن سليمان بن يسار وسعيد بن المسيب، عن أبي هريرة أنه
استفتى عمر بن الخطاب في رجل طلق امرأته تطليقة أو تطليقتين وتركها حتى تحل، ثم تنكح زوجاً
غيره، فيموت أو يطلقها فيتزوجها زوجها الأول على كم هي؟ قال عمر: هي على ما بقي من
طلاقها.

565. Mālik informed us: "Az-Zuhrī informed us from Sulaymān ibn Yasār
and Saʿīd ibn al-Musayyab that Abū Hurayrah sought a *fatwā* from ʿUmar
ibn al-Khaṭṭāb concerning a man who had divorced his wife once or twice
and had then left her until she had become free to remarry. She had then
married another husband who had died or who had divorced her, and so she
had remarried the former husband. How many divorces remain? ʿUmar said,
"She has whatever remains of her divorces."[35]

قال محمد: وبهذا نأخذ. فأما أبو حنيفة، فقال: إذا عادت إلى الأول بعد ما دخل بها الآخر عادت
على طلاق جديد ثلاث تطليقات مستقبلات. وفي أصل ابن الصواف: وهو قول ابن عباس وابن
عمر رضي الله عنهم.

Muḥammad said: "We adhere to this. As for Abū Ḥanīfah, he said, 'If she
returns to the former husband after the later one had consummated the
marriage then she returns to a new start, three future divorces [remain to
her].' Also, in the original of Ibn aṣ-Ṣawāf, 'that is the position of Ibn ʿAbbās
and Ibn ʿUmar ۞.'"

٩ باب الرجل يجعل أمر امرأته بيدها أو غيرها

9. A Man who Surrenders the Power [of divorce] to the Woman or to Someone else

٥٦٦ أخبرنا مالك، أخبرنا سعيد بن سليمان بن زيد بن ثابت، عن خارجة بن زيد ، عن زيد بن ثابت: أنه كان جالساً عنده ، فأتاه بعض بني أبي عتيق وعيناه تدمعان ، فال له: ما شأنك؟ فقال: ملَّكت امرأتي أمرها بيدها ففارتني، فقال له: ما حملك على ذلك؟ قال : القدر ، قال له زيد بن ثابت ارتجعها إن شئت فإنما هي واحدة وأنت أملكُ بها.

566. Mālik informed us: "Sa^cīd ibn Sulaymān ibn Zayd ibn Thābit informed us from Khārijah ibn Zayd from Zayd ibn Thābit that he was sitting with him and someone from Banī Abī ^cAtīq came to him, his eyes flowing with tears, and he asked him, 'What is wrong with you?' He answered, 'I gave my wife command over her own affair and so she divorced me.' So he said to him, 'What made you do that?' He answered, 'The Decree.' Zayd ibn Thābit said to him, 'Take her back if you wish because it is only one [divorce], and you have authority over her once more.'"

قال محمد: هذا عندنا على ما نوى الزوج فإن نوى واحدة فواحدة بائنة وهو خاطب من الخطُّاب وإن نوى ثلاثاً فثلاث، وهو قول أبي حنيفة والعامة من فقهائنا, وقال عثمان بن عفان وعلي بن أبي طالب رضي الله عنهما: القضاء ما قضت.

Muḥammad said: "This with us is according to what the husband intends, so that if he intends a single divorce then it is a single divorce which takes effect immediately and he becomes one among the suitors. If he intended three divorces then it is three and that is the verdict of Abū Ḥanīfah and our *fuqahā᾽* in general. ^cAlī ibn Abī Ṭālib and ^cUthmān ibn ^cAffān said, 'The judgement is whatever she decides.'"

٥٦٧ أخبرنا مالك، أخبرنا عبد الرحمن بن القاسم، عن أبيه ، عن عائشة : ﵂ أنها خطبت على عبد الرحمن بن أبي بكر ﵁ قريبة بنت أبي أمية فزوجته ثم إنهم عتبوا على عبد الرحمن بن أبي بكر. وقالوا: ما زوجنا إلا عائشة فأرسلت إلى عبد الرحمن فذكرت له ذلك ، فجعل عبد الرحمن أمر قريبةَ بيدها، فاختارته. وقالت : ما كنت لأختار عليك أحداً، فقرت تحته، فلم يكن ذلك طلاقاً.

567. Mālik informed us: "^cAbd ar-Raḥmān ibn al-Qāsim informed us from his father from ^cĀ᾽ishah ﵂ that she conveyed the proposal of marriage for ^cAbd ar-Raḥmān ibn Abī Bakr ﵁ to Quraybah bint Abī Umayyah and so she was married to him. Then later they found fault with ^cAbd ar-Raḥmān ibn Abī Bakr and they said, 'We only married her [to him because of] ^cĀ᾽ishah.' So she sent for ^cAbd ar-Raḥmān and mentioned that to him, and ^cAbd ar-Raḥmān put Quraybah's affairs in her own hands and she chose to stay with him, saying, 'I wouldn't choose anyone over you.' So she was established in her marriage to him, and there was no divorce."

٥٦٨ أخبرنا مالك، أخبرنا عبد الرحمن بن القاسم، عن أبيه، عن عائشة: أنّها زوَّجت حفصة بنت

عبد الرحمن بن أبي بكر المنذر بن الزبير، وعبدُ الرحمن غائبٌ بالشّام، فلما قَدِمَ عبدُ الرَّحمن قال: ومثلي يُصنع به هذا ويُفْتَات عليه ببناته؟ فكلمت عائشةُ المُنْذِرَ بْنَ الزُّبَيْرِ، فقال: فإن ذلك في يد عبد الرحمن، فقال عبد الرحمن: ما لي رغبة عنه ولكن مثلي ليس يُفْتَات عليه ببناته، وما كنت لأَرُدّ أمراً قَضَيْتِه، فَقَرَّتْ امرأته تحته ولم يكن ذلك طلاقاً.

568. Mālik informed us: "ᶜAbd ar-Raḥmān ibn al-Qāsim informed us from his father from ᶜĀʾishah that she married Ḥafṣah bint ᶜAbd ar-Raḥmān ibn Abī Bakr to al-Mundhir ibn az-Zubayr when ᶜAbd ar-Raḥmān ibn Abī Bakr was in Shām. When ᶜAbd ar-Raḥmān returned he said, 'Is someone like me treated like this and things arranged concerning his daughters without his command?' So ᶜĀʾishah spoke to al-Mundhir and he said, 'It is in the hands of ᶜAbd ar-Raḥmān.' ᶜAbd ar-Raḥmān said, 'I do not wish to shun him, but someone like me should not have matters arranged concerning his daughters without his command. I would not reverse a matter that you decided.' So his wife stayed with him, and there was no divorce."

٥٦٩ أخبرنا مالكٌ، أخبرنا نافعٌ عن ابن عمر، أنه كان يقولُ: إذا ملّك الرجلُ امرأته أمرهَا فالقضاءُ ما قَضَتْ إلا أنْ يُنكر عليها، فيقول: لم أُرِدْ إلا تطليقة واحدةْ فَيُحَلَّفُ على ذلك، ويكون أملَكَ بها في عدّتها.

569. Mālik informed us: "Nāfiᶜ informed us that ᶜAbdullāh ibn ᶜUmar used to say, 'If a man gives power over herself to his wife, then the judgement is whatever she decides, unless he denies her that and he says, "I only meant a single divorce." He is made to swear an oath to that. Then he will resume his authority over her during her *ᶜiddah*.'"[36]

٥٧٠ أخبرنا مالك، أخبرنا يحيى بن سعيد، عن سعيد بن المسيّب أنه قال: إذا مَلَّك الرجلُ امرأته أمرَها فلم تُفارقْه وَقَرّتْ عنده فليس ذلك بطلاق.

570. Mālik informed us: "Yaḥyā ibn Saᶜīd informed us that Saᶜīd ibn al-Musayyab said, 'When a man gives his wife power over her affairs and she does not divorce from him and remains with him, then that is not counted as a divorce.'"

قال محمد: وبهذا نأخذ. إذا اختارت زوجها فليس ذلك بطلاق وإن اختارت نفسها فهو على ما نوى الزوج، فإن نوى واحدة فهي واحدة بائنة. وإن نوى ثلاثاً فثلاث. وهو قول أبي حنيفة والعامة من فقهائنا.

Muḥammad said: "We adhere to this. If she chooses [to stay with] her husband then that is not a divorce. If she chooses go her own way [and to be divorced] then that is according to what the husband intended. If he intended a single divorce then it is a single divorce which takes effect immediately. If it was a triple divorce then it is a triple divorce. That is the position of Abū Ḥanīfah and of our *fuqahāʾ* in general."

١٠ باب الرجل يكون تحته أمة فيطلّقها ثم يشتريها

10. A Man who is Married to a Slave-woman whom He Divorces and Subsequently Purchases

٥٧١ أخبرنا مالك، أخبرنا الزهري، عن أبي عبد الرحمن، عن زيد بن ثابت: أنه سئل عن رجل كانت تحته وليدة، فَأَبَتَّ طلاقها، ثم اشتراها، أيحلّ أن يمسَّها؟ فقال: لا يحلّ له حتى تنكح زوجاً غيره.

571. Mālik informed us: "Az-Zuhrī informed us from Abū ʿAbd ar-Raḥmān that Zayd ibn Thābit was asked about a man who was married to a slave-woman whom he divorced irrevocably and whom he subsequently purchased, 'Is it *ḥalāl* for him to have sexual relations with her?' and he answered, 'She is not *ḥalāl* for him until she marries a husband other than him.[37]'"

قال محمد: وبهذا نأخذ. وهو قول أبي حنيفة والعامة من فقهائنا.

Muḥammad said, "We adhere to this, and it is the verdict of Abū Ḥanīfah and our *fuqahāʾ* in general."

١١ باب الأمة تكون تحت العبد فَتُعْتَق

11. A Slave-woman who is Married to a Slave, and who is subsequently Set free

٥٧٢ أخبرنا ملك، أخبرنا نافع، عن ابن عمر: أنه كان يقول في الأمة تحت العبد فَتُعْتَقُ: إن الخيار لها ما لم يمسَّها.

572. Mālik informed us: "Nāfiʿ informed us that Ibn ʿUmar used to say concerning a slave woman married to a slave and then she is set free, that she has the choice [whether to separate from him] as long as he has not had sexual relations with her."

٥٧٣ أخبرنا مالك، أخبرنا ابن شهاب، عن عروة بن الزبير: أن زَبراء مولاةً لبني عدي بن كعب أخبرته أنها كانت تحت عبد، وكانت أمة فأُعْتِقَتْ، فأرسلت إليها حفصة وقالت: إني مخبرتُك خبراً، وما أحبّ أن تصنعي شيئاً، إنّ أمرَكِ بيدكِ ما لم يمسّكِ، فإذا مَسَّكِ فليس لكِ من أمرك شيئاً، قالَتْ: وفارَقْتُه.

573. Mālik informed us: "Ibn Shihāb informed us from ʿUrwah ibn az-Zubayr that Zabrāʾ, the *mawlāh* of Banī ʿAdī ibn Kaʿb, told him that she had been married to a slave and she herself was a slave, but that then she was set free. Ḥafṣah sent for her and said, 'I am going to tell you something, but I hope that you do not do anything; your affair is in your hands as long as he does not have sexual relations with you. If he has sexual relations with you then you have no control over your affair.' She said, 'So I divorced him.'"

قال محمد: إذا علمت أنّ لها خياراً، فأمْرُها بيدها ما دامت في مجلسها ما لم تَقُمْ منه أو تأخذ في عمل آخر أو يمسُّها، فإذا كان شيء من هذا بطل خيارها، فأما إن مسّها وَ لم تعلم بالعتق أو علمت به ولم تعلم أن لها الخيار فإن ذلك لا يبطل خيارَها. وهو قول أبي حنيفة والعامة من فقهائنا.

Muḥammad said: "When she learns that she has the choice, then her affair is in her hands as long as she is in that gathering and has not yet stood up from it, or undertakes some other work or he has sexual relations with her. Then if any of these happen, her choice no longer exists. If he has sexual relations with her and he did not know of her being set free, or she knew of it but did not know that she had the choice, then that does not invalidate her choice and that is the position of Abū Ḥanīfah and of our *fuqahā'* in general."

١٢ باب طلاق المريض

12. A Sick Person's Divorce

٥٧٤ أخبرنا مالك، أخبرنا الزهري، عن طلحة بن عبد الله بن عوف طلّق امرأته وهو مريض فورّثها عثمان منه بعد ما انقضت عدّتها.

574. Mālik informed us: "Az-Zuhrī informed us from Ṭalḥah ibn ᶜAbdullāh ibn ᶜAwf that ᶜAbd ar-Raḥmān ibn ᶜAwf divorced his wife while he was [terminally] ill, and ᶜUthmān ibn ᶜAffān let her inherit after her *ᶜiddah* had come to an end."

٥٧٥ أخبرنا مالك، أخبرنا عبد الله بن الفضل ، عن الأعرج ، عن عثمان بن عفان: أنه ورّث نساء ابن مُكْمل منه، كان طلّق نساءه وهو مريض.

575. Mālik informed us: "ᶜAbdullāh ibn al-Faḍl informed us from al-Aᶜraj that ᶜUthmān made the wives of Ibn Mukmil his heirs, and yet he had divorced his wives while he was [terminally] ill."

قال محمدٌ: يَرِثْنَه ما دُمْنَ في العدّة فإذا انقضت العدّةُ قبل أن يموت فلا ميراث لهنّ وكذلك ذكر هُشَيْم بن بشير عن المغيرة الضبي عن إبراهيم النَّخَعي عن شُريح أن عمر بن الخطاب كتب إليه في رجل طلّق امرأته ثلاثاً و هو مريض: أنْ وَرِّثها ما دامت في عدّتها، فإذا انقضت العدة فلا ميراث لها. وهو قول أبي حنيفة رحمه الله تعالى والعامة من فقهائنا.

Muḥammad said: "They inherit from him as long as they are in their *ᶜiddah,* but if their *ᶜiddah* comes to an end before he dies they have no inheritance. That is similar to what Hushaym ibn Bashīr mentioned of al-Mughīrah aḍ-Ḍabbī from Ibrāhīm an-Nakhaᶜī from Shurayḥ that ᶜUmar ibn al-Khaṭṭāb wrote to him concerning a man who had divorced his wife three times while he was [terminally] ill, 'Make her an heir as long as she is in her *ᶜiddah,* but when her *ᶜiddah* comes to an end [before he dies] she has no inheritance,' and that is the verdict of Abū Ḥanīfah and our *fuqahā'* in general."

١٣ باب المرأة تطلّق أو يموت عنها زوجها وهي حامل

13. A Woman who is Divorced or whose Husband Dies while She is Pregnant

٥٧٦ أخبرنا مالك، أخبرنا الزهري، أنّ ابنَ عمر سُئل عن امرأة يُتَوَفّى عنها زوجها؟ قال: إذا وضعت

فقد حلّت ، قال رجل من الأنصار كان عنده : إن عمر بن الخطاب قال : لو وضعت ما في بطنها وهو
على سريره لم يُدْفَن بعدُ حلّت .

576. Mālik informed us: "Az-Zuhrī informed us that Ibn ʿUmar was asked about a woman whose husband died and he said, 'If she gives birth then she is permitted [to remarry].' An Anṣārī man who was with him said, 'ʿUmar ibn al-Khaṭṭāb said, "Even if she gave birth to what was in her womb while he was on his bed not yet buried she would definitely be permitted [to marry]."'"

قال محمد : وبهذا نأخذ . وهو قول أبي حنيفة والعامة من فقهائنا .

Muḥammad said: "We adhere to this, and it is the verdict of Abū Ḥanīfah and our *fuqahāʾ* in general."

٥٧٧ أخبرنا مالك، أخبرنا نافع، عن ابن عمر قال : إذا وضعتْ ما في بطنها حلّت .

577. Mālik informed us: "Nāfiʿ informed us that Ibn ʿUmar said, 'When she delivers what is in her womb she is permitted [to marry].'"

قال محمد : وبهذا نأخذ في الطلاق والموت جميعاً، تنقضي عدّتها بالولادة . وهو قول أبي حنيفة رحمه الله تعالى .

Muḥammad said: "We adhere to this with respect to both divorce and death. Her *ʿiddah* comes to an end when she gives birth, and that is the verdict of Abū Ḥanīfah."

١٤ باب الإيلاء
14. A Husband's Vow to Abstain from Intercourse (*īlā*)

٥٧٨ أخبرنا مالك، أخبرنا الزهري، عن سعيد بن المسيّب قال : إذا آلى الرجلُ من امرأته ، ثم فَاء قبل
أن تمضي أربعة أشهر فهي امرأته لم يذهب من طلاقها شيء ، فإن مضت الأربعة الأشهر قبل أن يفيء
فهي تطليقة وهو أَمْلَكُ بالرجعة ما لم تنقض عدّتُها . قال : وكان مروان يقضي بذلك .

578. Mālik informed us: "Az-Zuhrī informed us that Saʿīd ibn al-Musayyab said, 'If a man vows to abstain from intercourse with his wife, but then later returns before four months have passed then she is [still] his wife and he has not used up any of her divorces. If the four months have passed before he returns then she is divorced, but he still has the right to return to her as long as her *ʿiddah* has not expired.' He said, 'Marwān used to give judgement based on that.'"

٥٧٩ أخبرنا مالك، أخبرنا نافع ، عن ابن عمر قال : أيُّما رجل آلى من امرأته فإذا مضت الأربعة
الأشهر وُقِفَ حتى يطلِّق أو يفيء، ولا يقع عليها طلاق وإن مضت الأربعة الأشهر حتى يُوقَفَ .

579. Mālik informed us: "Nāfiʿ informed us that ʿAbdullāh ibn ʿUmar said, 'If a man vows to abstain from intercourse with his wife, then when the four months have passed he is made to deliberate until he divorces her or returns to her. Divorce does not come about for her even if four months have passed until he has been made to deliberate [over his decision].'"

قال محمد: بلغنا عن عمر بن الخطاب وعثمان بن عفان وعبد الله بن مسعود وزيد بن ثابت أنهم قالوا: إذا آلى الرجل من امرأته فمضت أربعة أشهر قبل أن يفيء فقد بانت بتطليقة بائنة وهو خاطب من الخُطّاب وكانوا لا يَرَوْنَ أن يُوْقَفَ بعد الأربعة. وقال ابن عباس في تفسير هذه الآية: ﴿للذين يُؤْلُون من نسائهم تربُّصُ أربعة أشهر فإن فاؤوا فإن الله غفور رحيم وإن عزموا الطلاق فإن الله سميع عليم﴾، قال: الفيء الجماع في الأربعة الأشهر، وعزيمة الطلاق انقضاء الأربعة الأشهر، فإذا مضت بانت بتطليقة ولا يوقَف بعدها. وكان عبد الله بن عباس أعلم بتفسير القرآن من غيره. وهو قول أبي حنيفة والعامة من فقهائنا.

Muḥammad said: "It has reached us that ᶜUmar ibn al-Khaṭṭāb, ᶜUthmān ibn ᶜAffān, ᶜAbdullāh ibn Masᶜūd and Zayd ibn Thābit said, 'When a man vows to abstain from intercourse with his wife and four months pass before he returns to her then she is divorced with a final divorce such that he becomes one among her suitors [if he wishes],' and it was not their view that he is not made to deliberate after the four months. Ibn ᶜAbbās said in commentary on this *āyah*, 'Those who swear to abstain from sexual relations with their wives can wait for a period of up to four months. If they then retract their oath, Allah is Ever-Forgiving, Most Merciful. If they are determined to divorce, Allah is All-Hearing, All-Knowing,'[38] he said, '"Retracting their oath" is sexual intercourse within the four months, and "determination to divorce" is the termination of the four months, so when they are over she is clearly divorced [such that he has no right to return her], and he is not made to deliberate after that.' ᶜAbdullāh ibn ᶜAbbās had more knowledge of the interpretation of the Qur'ān than others. That is also the position of Abū Ḥanīfah and of our *fuqahā'* in general."

١٥ باب الرجل يطلّق امرأته ثلاثاً قبل أن يدخل بها

15. A Man who Divorces his Wife three times before He has Consummated the Marriage

٥٨٠ أخبرنا مالك، أخبرنا الزهريّ، عن محمد بن عبد الرحمن بن ثَوبان، عن محمد بن إياس بن بُكير قال: طلّق رجلٌ امرأته ثلاثاً قبل أن يدْخل بها ثم بدا له أن ينكحها فجاءَ يَستفتي، قال: فذهبت معه، فسأل أبا هريرة وابن عباس فقالا: لا يَنْكحها حتى تنكحَ زوجاً غيره، فقال: إنما كان طلاقي إياها واحدة. قال ابن عباس: أَرْسَلْتَ مِنْ يدك ما كان لك من فضْل.

580. Mālik informed us: "Az-Zuhrī informed us from Muḥammad ibn ᶜAbd ar-Raḥmān ibn Thawbān that Muḥammad ibn Iyās ibn al-Bukayr said, 'A man divorced his wife three times before consummating the marriage, and then it occurred to him to remarry her, and so he came seeking a judgement.' He said, 'I went along with him, and he asked Abū Hurayrah and Ibn ᶜAbbās who both said, "He may not remarry her until she has married a husband other than him." He said, "My divorce of her was only a single

one." Ibn ᶜAbbās said, "You let go from your hand whatever bounty you had.'"

قال محمدٌ: وبهذا نأخذُ. وهو قول أبي حنيفة والعامة من فقهائنا لأنه طلّقها ثلاثاً جميعاً، فوقعن عليها جميعاً معاً ولو فرقهن وقعت الأولى خاصة لأنها بانت بها قبل أن يتكلم ولا عدة عليها فتقع عليها الثانية والثالثة ما دامت في العدّة.

Muḥammad said: "We adhere to this, and it is the verdict of Abū Ḥanīfah and our *fuqahāʾ* in general, because he divorced her in three divorces at one time and so they happened to her together, all at once. If he had separated them, then the first one in particular would have come in to effect because she would have been clearly divorced from him [without his right to return][39] before he pronounced the second divorce and she would have had no *ᶜiddah*.[40] The second and third [divorces] come about as long as she is in her *ᶜiddah*."

١٦ باب المرأة يطلّقها زوجُها فتتزوّجُ رجلاً فيطلّقُ قبل الدخول

16. A Woman whose Husband Divorces her and She then Marries a Man who Divorces her before Consummating the Marriage

٥٨١ أخبرنا مالك، أخبرنا المِسْور بن رفاعة القُرَظي، عن الزَّبير بن عبد الرحمن بن الزَّبير: أن رفاعة بن سِمْوَال طلّق امرأتَه تميمةَ بنتَ وهب في عهد رسولِ الله صلّى الله عليه وسلّم ثلاثاً، فنكحها عبد الرحمَن بن الزبير، فأعرض عنها، فلم يستطع أن يمسَّها، ففارقها ولم يمسَّها، فأراد رفاعة أن ينكحها، وهو زوجها الأول الذي طلّقها، فذكر ذلك لرسول الله صلّى الله عليه وسلّم، فنهاه عن تزويجها، وقال: لا تحلُّ لك حتى تذوقَ العُسَيْلةَ.

581. Mālik informed us: "Al-Miswar ibn Rifāᶜah al-Quraẓī informed us from az-Zubayr ibn ᶜAbd ar-Raḥmān ibn az-Zabīr that Rifāᶜah ibn Simwāl divorced his wife Tamīmah bint Wahb during the epoch of the Messenger of Allah ﷺ and then ᶜAbd ar-Raḥmān ibn az-Zabīr married her but turned away from her in aversion and was unable to have intercourse with her, and so he divorced her and had not had sexual intercourse with her. Rifāᶜah wanted to marry her, and he was her previous husband who had divorced her, and so he mentioned that to the Messenger of Allah ﷺ but he forbade him to marry her and said, 'She is not permissible to you until she tastes the sweetness [of intercourse].'"

قال محمدٌ: وبهذا نأخذُ، وهو قولُ أبي حنيفةَ والعامةِ من فقهائنا لأن الثاني لم يجامعها فلا يحلُّ أن ترجع إلى الأول حتى يجامعها الثاني.

Muḥammad said: "We adhere to this, and it is the verdict of Abū Ḥanīfah and our *fuqahāʾ* in general, because the latter husband did not have sexual intercourse with her so she is not permitted to return to the former until the latter has intercourse with her."

١٧ باب المرأة تسافر قبل انقضاء عدتها

17. A Woman Travelling before the Expiry of her ᶜ*Iddah*

٥٨٢ أخبرنا مالك، حدثنا حُمَيْدُ بن قيس المكي الأعرج، عن عمرو بن شعيب، عن سعيد بن المسيِّب: أن عمر بن الخطاب كان يردُّ المتوفَّى عنهنَّ أزواجهن من البَيْداء يمنعهنَّ الحج .

582. Mālik informed us: "Ḥumayd ibn Qays al-Aᶜraj al-Makkī narrated to us from ᶜAmr ibn Shuᶜayb from Saᶜīd ibn al-Musayyab that ᶜUmar ibn al-Khaṭṭāb used to reject women from Baydāʾ whose husbands had died, preventing them from fulfilling the Ḥajj."

قال محمد: وبهذا نأخذ، وهو قولُ أبي حنيفة والعامة من فقهائنا لا ينبغي لامرأة أن تسافرَ في عدَّتِها حتى تنقضي من طلاق كانت أو موت.

Muḥammad said: "We adhere to this, and it is the verdict of Abū Ḥanīfah and our *fuqahāʾ* in general. A woman ought not to travel during her ᶜ*iddah* until the ᶜ*iddah* has come to an end, whether it is from divorce or death [of her husband]."

١٨ باب المتعة

18. *Mutᶜah* (temporary marriage)

٥٨٣ أخبرنا مالك، أخبرنا الزهري، عن عبد الله والحسن ابنَيْ محمد بن علي عن أبيهما عن علي بن أبي طالب جدّهما: أنه قال لابن عباس: نهى رسول الله صلّى الله عليه وسلّم عن مُتْعَة النساء يومَ خَيْبَر وعن أكل لحوم الحُمْرِ الإنسيَّة.

583. Mālik informed us: "Az-Zuhrī informed us from ᶜAbdullāh and al-Ḥasan the two sons of Muḥammad ibn ᶜAlī from their father that their grandfather ᶜAlī ﷺ said to Ibn ᶜAbbās, 'The Messenger of Allah ﷺ forbade temporary marriage with women on the day of Khaybar, and [he forbade] the flesh of domestic donkeys.'"

٥٨٤ أخبرنا مالك، أخبرنا الزهري، عن عروة بن الزبير: أن خَوْلة بنت حكيم دخلَتْ على عمر بن الخطاب، فقالت: إنَّ ربيعة بن أميَّة استمتع بامرأةٍ مولَّدةٍ فحملت منه، فخرج عمر فَزِعاً يجرُّ رداءه، فقال: هذه المُتعَة لو كنتُ تقدَّمتُ فيها لرجمتُ.

584. Mālik informed us: "Az-Zuhrī informed us from ᶜUrwah ibn az-Zubayr that Khawlah bint Ḥakīm went to see ᶜUmar ibn al-Khaṭṭāb and said to him, 'Rabīᶜah ibn Umayyah contracted a temporary marriage with a woman who was born and brought up among the Arabs [*muwalladah*] and she became pregnant by him.' ᶜUmar went out in dismay dragging his lower garment, saying, 'This temporary marriage, if I had been the first to come upon it I would have stoned.'"

قال محمد: المُتْعَة مكروهةٌ ، فلا ينبغي، فقد نهى عنها رسول الله صلّى الله عليه وسلّم فيما جاء في غير حديث ولا اثنين، وقول عمر: لو كنت تقدمتُ فيها لرجمتُ إنما نضعه من عمر على التهديد ، وهذا قول أبي حنيفة والعامة من فقهائنا.

Muḥammad said: "Temporary marriage is disapproved and it ought not to be done,[41] and the Messenger of Allah ﷺ forbade it in that which has been narrated in more than one or two *ḥadīth*. The saying of ᶜUmar, '...if I had been the first to come upon it I would have stoned,' we only regard it as ᶜUmar's threatening with punishment in order to frighten. This is also the verdict of Abū Ḥanīfah and our *fuqahāʾ* in general."

١٩ باب الرجل تكون عند امرأتان فيُؤثِرُ إحداهما على الأخرى

19. A Man who Has two Wives and who Shows Preference to One over the Other

٥٨٥ أخبرنا مالك، أخبرنا ابن شهاب، عن رافع بن خَديج : أنه تزوَّج ابنة محمد بن سَلَمة، فكانت تحته، فتزوّج عليها امرأة شابَّة فآثر الشابَّة عليها، فناشَدَتْه الطلاق فطلَّقها واحدة، ثم أمهلها حتى إذا كادت تحل ارتجعها، ثم عاد، فآثر الشابَّة، فناشدته الطلاق، فطلَّقها واحدة، ثم أمهلها حتى كادت أن تحلَّ ارتجعها، ثم عاد فآثر الشابَّة، فناشدته الطلاق، فقال: ما شئت إنما بقيتْ واحدة، فإن شئت استقررت على ما ترين من الأَثَرَة وإن شئت طلقتك، قالت: بل أستقِر على الأثرة فأمسكها على ذلك، ولم يَرَ رافعٌ أن عليه في ذلك إثماً حين رَضيت أن تستقر على الأثرة.

585. Mālik informed us: "Ibn Shihāb informed us that Rāfiᶜ ibn Khadīj married a daughter of Muḥammad ibn Maslamah and that she was still with him when he married a young wife and showed preference to the young wife over her. She pleaded with him to divorce her and he divorced her once and then he gave her time until she was almost free from her *ᶜiddah* then returned to her. Later he again showed preference to the young wife over her, so she pleaded with him to divorce her and her divorced her once, then gave her time until she was almost free from her *ᶜiddah* then returned to her. Later he again showed preference to the young wife over her, so she pleaded with him to divorce her. He said to her, 'Whatever you wish. There is only one [divorce] remaining to you. If you wish you can remain in spite of what you see of the preference [shown to the younger wife], and if you wish I will divorce you.' She said, 'No, I would rather remain in spite of the preference.'"

قال محمد: لا بأس بذلك إذا رضيت به المرأة ولها أن ترجع عنه إذا بدا لها. وهو قول أبي حنيفة والعامة من فقهائنا.

Muḥammad said: "There is no harm in that if the woman is contented with that, and she has the right to relinquish him if it seems the right thing to do. That is also the position of Abū Ḥanīfah and of our *fuqahāʾ* in general."

٢٠ باب اللِّعان

20. *Liᶜān*[42]

٥٨٦ أخبرنا مالك، أخبرنا نافع، عن ابن عمر: أن رجلاً لاعَنَ امرأته في زمان رسول الله صلّى الله عليه وسلّم فانتفى من ولدها، ففرّق رسول الله صلّى الله عليه وسلّم بينهما، وألحق الولد بالمرأة.

586. Mālik informed us: "Nāfiᶜ informed us from Ibn ᶜUmar that a man

engaged in *li^cān* with his wife during the time of the Messenger of Allah ﷺ and disowned her child. The Messenger of Allah ﷺ separated them and gave the parentage of the child to the woman."

قال محمد: وبهذا نأخذ. إذا نفى الرجل ولد امرأته ولاعَنَ فُرِّق بينهما، ولزم الولد أمَّه. وهو قول أبي حنيفة والعامة من فقهائنا رحمهم الله تعالى.

Muḥammad said: "We adhere to this. If the man disowns his wife's child and engages in *li^cān,* then they are separated, and the child stays with the mother. That is the position of Abū Ḥanīfah and of our *fuqahā'* in general."

٢١ باب متعة الطلاق

21. Maintenance in Divorce

٥٨٧ أخبرنا مالك، حدثنا نافع، عن ابن عمر قال: لكل مطلَّقة مُتْعة إلاّ التي تطلق وقد فُرِض لها صَدَاق ولم تُمَسّ فحسبُها نصفُ ما فُرِض لها.

587. Mālik informed us: "Nāfi^c narrated to us that Ibn ^cUmar said, 'Every divorced woman has the divorce settlement except for one who is divorced and he had fixed a dowry for her but had not consummated the marriage. Then her portion is a half of what he had fixed for her.'"

قال محمد: وبهذا نأخذ. وليست المتعة التي يُجبر عليها صاحبها إلاّ متعة واحدة، هي متعة الذي يطلّق امرأته قبل أن يدخل بها، ولم يَفرض لها، فهذه لها المتعة واجبة، يؤخذ بها في القضاء، وأدنى المتعة لباسها في بيتها: الدرع والملحَفة والخِمار. وهو قولُ أبي حنيفة والعامة من فقهائنا رحمهم الله.

Muḥammad said: "We adhere to this. There is only one divorce settlement which her ex-husband is compelled to give, which is the divorce settlement for a wife whom he divorced before consummating the marriage without fixing a dowry for her. For this one the divorce settlement is obligatory, and it is taken from him by judgement. The least of her divorce settlement is her clothing in her house: a long shift, her outer wrap and her head-covering. That is the position of Abū Ḥanīfah and of our *fuqahā'* in general, may Allah have mercy on them."

٢٢ باب ما يكره للمرأة من الزينة في العدة

22. What Adornment is Disapproved of for a Woman in her *^cIddah*

٥٨٨ أخبرنا مالك، أخبرنا نافع، أن صفيَّة بنت أبي عبيد اشتكت عينيها وهي حادّ على عبد الله بعد وفاته، فلم تكتحل حتى كادت عيناها أن ترمَصَا.

588. Mālik informed us: "Nāfi^c informed us that Ṣafiyyah bint Abī ^cUbayd's eyes suffered from a complaint while she was refraining from adornment because of the death of her husband ^cAbdullāh, and so she did not use kohl until her eyes had a dried white secretion in the corners of the eyes."

قال محمد : وبهذا نأخذ . لا ينبغي أن تكتحل بكحل الزينة ولا تدّهن ولا تتطيَّب، فأما الذُّرُور
ونحوه فلا بأس به، لأن هذا ليس بزينة . وهو قول أبي حنيفة والعامة من فقهائنا .

Muḥammad said, "We adhere to this. It is not fitting for her to apply cosmetic kohl nor to oil or perfume herself, but as for medicaments sprinkled in the eyes, etc., there is no harm in that, because this is not for cosmetic purposes. That is the position of Abū Ḥanīfah and of our *fuqahāʾ* in general."

٥٨٩ أخبرنا مالك، حدثنا نافع، عن صفيّة بنت أبي عُبيد، عن حفصة أو عائشة أو عنهما جميعاً:
أن رسول الله صلّى الله عليه وسلّم قال : لا يحلُّ لامرأة تؤمن بالله واليوم الآخر أن تُحِدَّ على مَيِّت فوق
ثلاث ليال إلاَّ على زوج .

589. Mālik informed us: "Nāfiʿ narrated to us from Ṣafiyyah bint Abī ʿUbayd from Ḥafṣah from ʿĀʾishah or from both of them that the Messenger of Allah ﷺ said, 'It is not ḥalāl for a woman who has imān in Allah and the Last Day to abstain from adornment in mourning for a death for more than three nights except for the husband.'"

قال محمد : وبهذا نأخذ . ينبغي للمرأة أن تُحِدَّ على زوجها حتى تنقضي عدّتها، ولا تتطيَّب ولا
تدّهن لزينة، ولا تكتحل لزينة، حتى تنقضي عدتها، وهو قول أبي حنيفة والعامة من فقهائنا .

Muḥammad said, "We adhere to this. A woman ought to abstain from adornment for her husband until her *ʿiddah* has expired, and she should not perfume herself nor oil herself for adornment, nor should she apply kohl for adornment until her *ʿiddah* expires. That is the position of Abū Ḥanīfah and of our *fuqahāʾ* in general."

٢٣ باب المرأة تنتقل من منزلها قبل انقضاء عدَّتها من موت أو طلاق

23. A Woman Moving from her House before the Expiry of an *ʿIddah* Arising from Death or Divorce

٥٩٠ أخبرنا مالك، أخبرني يحيى بن سعيد، عن القاسم بن محمد وسليمان بن يسار أنه سمعهما
يذكران أن يحيى بن سعيد بن العاص طلّق بنت عبد الرحمن بن الحَكَم البتَّةَ، فانتقلها عبدُ
الرحمن، فأرسلتْ عائشةُ إلى مروان وهو أمير المدينة : اتَّق الله واردُدْ المرأةَ إلى بيتها، فقال مروان في
حديث سليمان: إنَّ عبد الرحمن غلبني ، وقال في حديث القاسم: أوَما بَلَغَكَ شأنُ فاطمة بنت
قيس؟ قالت عائشة: لا يضرك أن لا تذكر حديث فاطمة، قال مروان: إن كان بكِ الشَّرُّ فَحَسْبُكِ ما
بين هذين من الشرِّ .

590. Mālik informed us: "Yaḥyā ibn Saʿīd informed me that he heard both al-Qāsim ibn Muḥammad and Sulaymān ibn Yasār mentioning that Yaḥyā ibn Saʿīd ibn al-ʿĀṣ divorced the daughter of ʿAbd ar-Raḥmān ibn al-Ḥakam irrevocably and so ʿAbd ar-Raḥmān made her move house. ʿĀʾishah sent a message to Marwān who was then Amīr of Madīnah, 'Have taqwā of Allah and return the woman to her house.' Marwān said, in the *ḥadīth* of Sulaymān, 'ʿAbd ar-Raḥmān overcame me,' and in the *ḥadīth* of al-Qāsim, 'Has the

business of Fāṭimah bint Qays not reached you?' ᶜĀʾishah said, 'It would do you no harm not to mention the *ḥadīth* of Fāṭimah.' Marwān said, 'If it is evil to you, then the evil between these two is sufficient evil for you.'"

قال محمد: وبهذا نأخذ. لا ينبغي للمرأة أن تنتقل من منزلها الذي طلّقها فيه زوجُها طلاقاً بائناً أو غيره، أو مات عنها فيه حتى تنقضي عدّتها. وهو قول أبي حنيفة والعامة من فقهائنا.

Muḥammad said: "We adhere to this. A woman ought not to move from her dwelling in which her husband divorced her with a divorce in which there is no return except through a new proposal, or other type of divorce, or in which her husband died, until her *ᶜiddah* has expired. That is the position of Abū Ḥanīfah and of our *fuqahāʾ* in general."

٥٩١ أخبرنا مالك، أخبرنا نافع، أن ابنة سعيد بن زيد بن نفيل طُلِّقت البتّة، فانتقلت، فأنكر ذلك عليها ابن عمر.

591. Mālik informed us: "Nāfiᶜ informed us that a daughter of Saᶜīd ibn Zayd ibn Nufayl was divorced irrevocably and she moved house. Ibn ᶜUmar objected to her behaviour."

٥٩٢ أخبرنا مالك، أخبرنا سعد بن إسحاق بن كعب بن عُجْرة، عن عمته زينب ابنة كعب بن عجرة، أن الفُرَيْعة بنت مالك بن سنان وهي أخت أبي سعيد الخُدريّ أخبرته: أنها أتت رسولَ الله ﷺ تسأله أن ترجع إلى أهلها في بني خُدرة، فإن زوجي خرج في طلب أَعْبُد له أَبَقُوا حتى إذا كان بطرف القَدُّوم أدركهم، فقتلوه، فقالت: فسألتُ رسول الله صلّى الله عليه وسلّم أنْ يأذنَ لي أن أرجع إلى أهلي في بني خُدرة فإن زوجي لم يتركني في مسكن يملكه ولا نفقة فقال: نعم. فخرجتُ حتى إذا كنت بالحجرة دعاني أو أمر من دعاني، فدُعيتُ له، فقال: كيف قلت؟ فرددتُ عليه القصة التي ذكرتُ له، فقال: امكثي في بيتك حتى يبلُغَ الكتاب أجلَه، قالت: فاعتددتُ فيه أربعة أشهر وعشراً، قالت: فلما كان أمر عثمان أرسل إليّ فسألني عن ذلك فأخبرته بذلك فاتّبعه وقضى به.

592. Mālik informed us: "Saᶜīd ibn Isḥāq ibn Kaᶜb ibn ᶜUjrah informed us from his paternal aunt Zaynab bint Kaᶜb ibn ᶜUjrah that al-Furayᶜah bint Mālik ibn Sinān, who was the sister of Abū Saᶜīd al-Khudrī, told him that she came to the Messenger of Allah ﷺ to ask him to be allowed to return to her family among Banī Khudrah, 'because my husband had gone out to look for some slaves of his who had fled, then when he was on the track leading to al-Qaddūm[43] he caught up with them and they killed him.' She said, 'So I asked the Messenger of Allah ﷺ to give me permission to return to my family among Banī Khudrah, because my husband did not leave me any house which he owned nor any maintenance. He said, "Yes," so I went. When I was in the courtyard he called me or told someone to call me, and I was summoned to him. He said, "What did you say?"' She said, 'I repeated to him the story I had mentioned to him, and he said to me, "Stay in your house until the appointed period reaches its term."' She said, 'I performed the *ᶜiddah* in it for four months and ten [days]. Then later in the amirate of

ᶜUthmān he sent for me and asked me about it and I told him about it, and he followed it and gave judgement by it.'"

٥٩٣ أخبرنا مالك، أخبرنا يحيى بن سعيد، عن ابن المسيّب: أنه سئل عن المرأة يطلّقها زوجها وهي في بيت بكَراء، على مَنِ الكرَاء؟ قال: على زوجها، قالوا: فإنْ لم يكن عند زوجها؟ قال: فعليها، قالوا: فإن لم يكُن عندها؟ قال: فعلى الأمير.

593. Mālik informed us: "Yaḥyā ibn Saᶜīd informed us from Ibn al-Musayyab that he was asked about a woman whose husband divorces her and she is in a rented house, 'Who is responsible for the rent?' He answered, 'Her husband.' They asked, 'What if her husband hasn't got it?' He answered, 'Then it is her responsibility.' They asked, 'What if she doesn't have it?' He answered, 'Then it is the responsibility of the Amīr.'"[44]

٥٩٤ أخبرنا مالك، أخبرنا نافع: أنّ ابن عمر طلّق امرأته في مسكن حفصة زوج النبي صلّى الله عليه وسلّم، وكان طريقه في حجرتها، فكان يسلك الطريق الأخرى من أدبار البيوت إلى المسجد، كراهة أن يستأذن عليها حتى راجعها.

594. Mālik informed us: "Nāfiᶜ informed us that Ibn ᶜUmar divorced his wife in the residence of Ḥafṣah[45] the wife of the Prophet ﷺ and his route [to the mosque][46] passed through her chamber, and so he would take another route behind the houses to the mosque, because he disliked to have to ask her permission [to pass through],[47] until he took her back."

قال محمد: وبهذا نأخذ، لا ينبغي للمرأة أن تنتقل من منزلها الذي طلّقها فيه زوجُها، إن كان الطلاقُ بائناً أو غيرَ بائن، أو مات عنها فيه حتى تنقضي عِدّتُها.

وهو قول أبي حنيفة والعامة من فقهائنا.

Muḥammad said, "We adhere to this. A woman ought not to move from the house in which her husband divorced her – whether or not the divorce is one in which the husband has the right to return to her in the ᶜiddah – or [the house] in which she was when her husband died until her *ᶜiddah* is completed. That is the position of Abū Ḥanīfah and of our *fuqahā᾿* in general."

٢٤ باب عدّة أمّ الولد

24. The *ᶜIddah* of a Slavewoman who is Mother of her Owner's Child (*Umm Walad*)

٥٩٥ أخبرنا مالك، حدثنا نافع، عن ابن عمر: أنه كان يقول: عدّة أمِّ الولد إذا تُوفي عنها سيّدُها حيضة.

595. Mālik informed us: "Nāfiᶜ narrated to us that Ibn ᶜUmar used to say, 'The *ᶜiddah* of a slavewoman who is mother of her owner's child (*umm walad*) and whose master dies, is one menstrual period.'"

٥٩٦ أخبرنا مالك، أخبرني الحسن بن عُمارة، عن الحكم بن عُيَيْنة، عن يحيى بن الجزّار، عن عليّ بن أبي طالب كرم الله وجهه أنه قال: عدّة أم الولد ثلاث حيض.

596. Muḥammad said: "Al-Ḥasan ibn ʿUmārah informed me from al-Ḥakam ibn ʿUyaynah from Yaḥyā ibn al-Jazzār from ʿAlī ibn Abī Ṭālib, may Allah ennoble his face, that he said, "The *ʿiddah* of the slavewoman who is mother of her owner's child is three menstrual periods."

٥٩٧ أخبرنا مالك، عن ثور بن يزيد، عن رجاء بن حَيْوَة، أن عمرو بن العاص سئل عن عدّة أم الولد؟ فقال: لا تُلبِسُوا علينا في ديننا إنْ تكُ أمةً فإنّ عدّتها عدة حُرّة.

597. Mālik informed us from Thawr ibn Yazīd from Rajāʾ ibn Ḥaywah that ʿAmr ibn al-ʿĀṣ was asked about the *ʿiddah* of the slavewoman who is mother of her owner's child and he said, "Do not make confusion in our dīn; if she is a slave woman her *ʿiddah* is the same as a free woman's *ʿiddah*."

قال محمد: وبهذا نأخذ وهو قول أبي حنيفة وإبراهيم النَّخَعي والعامة من فقهائنا.

Muḥammad said: "We adhere to this, and it is the verdict of Abū Ḥanīfah, Ibrāhīm an-Nakhaʿī and our *fuqahāʾ* in general."

٢٥ باب الخَلِيّة والبريّة وما يشبه الطلاق

25. 'Quittance' and 'Freedom' and whatever Resembles Divorce

٥٩٨ أخبرنا مالك، أخبرنا نافع، عن عبد الله بن عمر أنه كان يقول: الخَلِيّة والبَرِيّة ثلاث تطليقات كل واحدة منهما.

598. Mālik informed us: "Nāfiʿ informed us that ʿAbdullāh ibn ʿUmar used to say, 'Quittance[48] and freedom[49] [count as] three divorces, each of them.'"

٥٩٩ أخبرنا مالك، أخبرنا يحيى بن سعيد، عن القاسم بن محمد قال: كان رجلٌ تحته وليدة فقال لأهلها: شأنَكم بها؟ قال القاسم: فرأى الناس أنها تطليقة.

599. Mālik informed us: "Yaḥyā ibn Saʿīd informed us that al-Qāsim ibn Muḥammad said, 'There was a man who was married to a slavewoman and he said to her family, "She is your business."' Al-Qāsim said, 'People held the view that it was a divorce.'"

قال محمد: إذا نوى الرجل بالخَلِيّة وبالبريّة ثلاث تطليقات فهي ثلاث تطليقات وإذا أراد بها واحدة فهي واحدة بائن، دخل بامرأته أو لم يدخل. وهو قول أبي حنيفة والعامة من فقهائنا.

Muḥammad said: "If the man intends by 'quittance' and 'freedom' three divorces then it is three divorces. If he intends one divorce then it is one final divorce[50], whether or not he consummated the marriage."

٢٦ باب الرجل يُولَد له فيغلب عليه الشَّبَه

26. A Man to whom a Child is Born but who is Overcome by Doubt and Suspicion [as to its paternity]

٦٠٠ أخبرنا مالك، أخبرنا ابن شهاب، عن سعيد بن المسيب، عن أبي هريرة: أنّ رجلاً من أهل البادية أتى رسولَ الله صلّى الله عليه وسلّم، فقال: إنّ امرأتي ولدت غلاماً أسود، فقال رسول الله صلّى

الله عليه وسلّم: هل لك من إبل؟ قال : نعم، قال : ما ألوانُها؟ قال : حُمْر ، قال : فهل فيها من أوراق ؟ قال: نعم، قال : فيما كان ذلك؟ قال : أُراه نزعه عِرْقٌ يا رسول الله، قال : فلعل ابنَك نزعه عرق .

600. Mālik informed us: "Ibn Shihāb informed us from Saʿīd ibn al-Musayyab from Abū Hurayrah that a man from the country came to the Messenger of Allah ﷺ and said, 'My wife gave birth to a black child.' The Messenger of Allah ﷺ asked, 'Have you any camels?' He answered, 'Yes.' He asked, 'What colours are they?' He said, 'Red.' He asked, 'Are any of them tawny brown[51]?' He said, 'Yes.' He said, 'So why would that happen?'[52] He answered, 'I would think that a hereditary trait affected him, Messenger of Allah.' He said, 'It is likely that a hereditary trait affected your son.'"

قال محمد : لا ينبغي للرجل أن ينتفي من ولده بهذا ونحوه .

Muḥammad said: "A man ought not disown his child because of this and the like of it."

٢٧ بابُ المرأةِ تُسْلِمُ قَبْلَ زوجِهَا
27. A Woman Accepting Islam before her Husband

٦٠١ أخبرنا مالك، أخبرنا ابن شهاب : أنّ أمَّ حكيم بنت الحارث بن هشام كانت تحت عكرمة بن أبي جهل فأسلمت يوم الفتح ، وخرج عكرمة هارباً من الإسلام حتى قدم اليمن، فارتحلت أمُّ حكيم حتى قدمت فَدَعَتْه إلى الإسلام فأسلم، فقدم على النبي صلّى الله عليه وسلّم، فلما رآه النبي صلّى الله عليه وسلّم وثب إليه فرحاً وما عليه رداؤه حتى بايعه .

601. Mālik informed us: "Ibn Shihāb informed us that Umm Ḥakīm bint al-Ḥārith ibn Hishām was married to ʿIkrimah ibn Abī Jahl and that she accepted Islam on the Day of the Opening [of Makkah to Islam]. ʿIkrimah left, fleeing from Islam until he reached the Yemen. Umm Ḥakīm travelled until she reached him, and then called him to Islam and he accepted. He came to the Prophet ﷺ. When the Prophet ﷺ saw him he stood up for him hastily, overjoyed, without his over-garment, until he had pledged allegiance to him."

قال محمد : إذا أسلمت المرأة وزوجها كافر في دار الإسلام لم يفرّق بينهما حتى يُعرض على الزوج الإسلام، فإن أسلم فهي امرأته وإنْ أبى أن يُسلم فُرّق بينهما وكانت فرقتهما تطليقةً بائنة . وهو قول أبي حنيفة وإبراهيم النّخَعِي .

Muḥammad said: "If a woman accepts Islam while her husband is a kāfir in the Dār al-Islām they are not divorced until her husband is offered Islam. If he accepts Islam, then she is his wife. If he refuses to accept Islam, they are separated and their separation is a final divorce.[53] That is the verdict of Abū Ḥanīfah and Ibrāhīm an-Nakhaʿī."

٢٨ باب انقضاء الحيض

28. The Termination of the Menstrual Period

٦٠٢ أخبرنا مالك، أخبرنا ابن شهاب، عن عُروة بن الزبير، عن عائشة قالت: انتقلَتْ حفصةُ بنت عبد الرحمن بن أبي بكر حين دخلت في الدَّم من الحيضة الثالثة، فذكرتُ ذلك لعَمْرة بنت عبد الرحمن، فقالَتْ: صَدَقَ عروةُ، وقد جادلَها فيه ناسٌ، وقالوا: إن الله عزَّ وجلّ يقول: ﴿ثلاثة قروء﴾، فقالت: صدَقْتُم، وتدرون ما الأقراء؟ إنما الأقراءُ الأطهار.

602. Mālik informed us: "Ibn Shihāb informed us from ᶜUrwah ibn az-Zubayr that ᶜĀʾishah said, 'Ḥafṣah bint ᶜAbd ar-Raḥmān ibn Abī Bakr moved home when she began to bleed from her third menstrual period.' I [Ibn Shihāb] mentioned that to ᶜAmrah bint ᶜAbd ar-Raḥmān and she said, 'ᶜUrwah has told the truth, and some people argued with her [ᶜĀʾishah] about it. They said, "Allah ﷻ says, 'Three *qurūʾ*.'" She [ᶜĀʾishah] said, "You are right. And do you know what *qurūʾ* are? *Qurūʾ* are only periods of purity."'"

٦٠٣ أخبرنا مالك، أخبرنا ابن شهاب، عن أبي بكر بن عبد الرحمن بن الحارث بن هشام أنه كان يقول مثل ذلك.

603. Mālik informed us: "Ibn Shihāb informed us that Abū Bakr ibn ᶜAbd ar-Raḥmān ibn al-Ḥārith ibn Hishām used to say the same as that."

٦٠٤ أخبرنا مالك، أخبرنا نافع وزيد بن أسلم عن سليمان بن يسار أن رجلاً من أهل الشام يقال له الأحوص طلّق امرأته، ثم مات حين دخلت في الدم من الحيضة الثالثة، فقالت: أنا وارثته، وقال بنوه: لا ترثينه، فاختصموا إلى معاوية بن أبي سفيان فسأل معاوية فَضالة بن عُبيد وناساً من أهل الشام، فلم يجد عندهم علماً فيه، فكتب إلى زيد بن ثابت فكتب إليه زيد بن ثابت أنها إذا دخلت في الدم من الحيضة الثالثة فإنها لا ترثه ولا يرثها، وقد برأت منه وبرئ منها.

604. Mālik informed us: "Nāfiᶜ and Zayd ibn Aslam informed us from Sulaymān ibn Yasār that a man from the people of Shām who was called al-Aḥwaṣ divorced his wife and then died when she had commenced bleeding from the third menstrual period. She said, 'I am his heir.' His sons said, 'She does not inherit from him.' They took the dispute to Muᶜāwiyah ibn Abī Sufyān, and Muᶜāwiyah asked Faḍālah ibn ᶜUbayd and other people from Shām, but could find no one among them who had any knowledge about it. He wrote to Zayd ibn Thābit and Zayd ibn Thābit wrote back to him that when she began to bleed from the third menstrual period she did not inherit from him and he did not inherit from her, and that she was free from him and he was free from her."

٦٠٥ أخبرنا مالك، أخبرنا نافع مولى ابن عمر، عن عبد الله بن عمر مثل ذلك.

605. Mālik informed us: "Nāfiᶜ the *mawlā* of Ibn ᶜUmar informed us from ᶜAbdullāh ibn ᶜUmar the like of that."

قال محمد: انقضاء العدَّة عندنا الطهارة من الدم من الحيضة الثالثة إذا اغتسلت منها.

Muḥammad said, "The termination of the *ᶜiddah* according to us is becoming free from the bleeding of the third menstrual period, when she has performed *ghusl* from it."

٦٠٦ أخبرنا أبو حنيفة، عن حماد ، عن إبراهيم: أنَّ رجلاً امرأته تطليقة يملك الرجعة ثم تركها حتى انقطع دمها من الحيضة الثالثة ودخلت مُغْتَسَلَها وأدنت ماءها، فأتاها فقال لها: قد راجعتك، فسألت عمر بن الخطاب عن ذلك وعنده عبد الله بن مسعود، فقال عمر: قل فيها برأيك ، فقال: أُراه يا أمير المؤمنين أحق برجعتها ما لم تغتسل من حيضتها الثالثة، فقال : عمر رضي الله عنه: وأنا أرى ذلك، ثم قال عمر لعبد الله بن مسعود: كُنَيْفٌ مُلئ علماً.

606. Abū Ḥanīfah informed us from Ḥammād from Ibrāhīm that a man divorced his wife with one divorce in which he retained the right to take her back, and then he left her until the bleeding ceased from her third menstrual period and she had entered the place where she performed *ghusl* and had water close to her [with which to wash]. Then he came to her and said to her, "I take you back [to me in marriage]." She asked ʿUmar ibn al-Khaṭṭāb about that while ʿAbdullāh ibn Masʿūd was with him. ʿUmar said, "State your view about it." He said, "I think that he, Amīr al-Muʾminīn, still has the right to take her back as long as she has not performed *ghusl* from her third menstrual period." ʿUmar said ﷺ "I also think that." Then ʿUmar said to ʿAbdullāh ibn Masʿūd, "[You are] a satchel full of knowledge."

٦٠٧ أخبرنا سفيان بن عيينة، عن ابن شهاب، عن سعيد بن المسيّب قال : قال علي بن أبي طالب رضي الله عنه: هو أحق بها حتى تغتسل من حيضتها الثالثة.

607. Sufyān ibn ʿUyaynah informed us from Ibn Shihāb that Saʿīd ibn al-Musayyab said, "ʿAlī ibn Abī Ṭālib ﷺ said, 'He still has the right to her until she performs the *ghusl* from her third menstrual period.'"

٦٠٨ أخبرنا عيسى بن أبي عيسى الخيّاط المديني ، عن الشّعبي، عن ثلاثة عشر من أصحاب رسول الله صلى الله عليه وسلم كلهم قالوا: الرجل أحق بامرأته حتى تغتسل من حيضتها الثالثة. قال عيسى: وسمعت سعيد بن المسيَّب يقول : الرجل أحقُّ بامرأته حتى تغتسلَ من حيضتها الثالثة.

608. ʿĪsā ibn Abī ʿĪsā al-Khayyāṭ al-Madīnī informed us from ash-Shaʿbī from thirteen of the Companions of the Messenger of Allah ﷺ all of whom said, "A man still has the right to his wife until she performs the *ghusl* after her third menstrual period." ʿĪsā said, "I heard Saʿīd ibn al-Musayyab saying, 'A man retains the right to his wife until she performs the *ghusl* from the third menstrual period.'"

قال محمد: وبهذا نأخذ. وهو قول أبي حنيفة والعامة من فقهائنا.

Muḥammad said: "We adhere to this, and it is the verdict of Abū Ḥanīfah and our *fuqahāʾ* in general."

٢ باب المرأة يطلّقها زوجها طلاقاً يملك الرجعة فتحيض حيضة أو حيضتين ثم ترتفع حيضتها

29. A Woman whose Husband Divorces her with a Divorce in which He Retains the Right to Take her back after which She has one or two Menstrual Periods and then her Period Ceases

٦٠٩ أخبرنا مالك، أخبرنا يحيى بن سعيد، عن محمد بن يحيى بن حبان: أنّه كان عند جَدّه امرأتان هاشمية وأنصارية فطلّق الأنصارية و هي تُرضع، وكانت لا تحيض وهي تُرضع فمرَّ بها قريب من سنة، ثم هلك زوجها حبّان عند رأس السنة، أو قريب من ذلك لم تحض، فقالت: أنَا أَرِثُه ما لم أحض، فاختصموا إلى عثمان بن عفان رضي الله عنه فقضى لها بالميراث فلامت الهاشمية عثمان فقال: هذا عملُ ابنِ عمِّك هو أشار علينا بذلك، يعني علي بن أبي طالب كرَّم الله وجهه.

609. Mālik informed us: "Yaḥyā ibn Saᶜīd informed us from Muḥammad ibn Yaḥyā ibn Ḥabbān that his grandfather had two wives, one of whom was from [the tribe of] Hāshim and the other from the Anṣār. He divorced the one from the Anṣār while she was breast-feeding, so she did not have a menstrual period while she was breast-feeding. Almost a year passed, and then her husband Ḥabbān died at the end of the year or near to that and she had not had a menstrual period. She said, 'I inherit from him as long as I have not had a menstrual period.' They took the dispute to ᶜUthmān ibn ᶜAffān ﷺ and he passed judgement in her favour that she should inherit. The wife from Banī Hāshim blamed ᶜUthmān. He said [to her], 'This is the practice of your cousin [the son of your paternal uncle]; he counselled us to do that,' meaning, ᶜAlī ibn Abī Ṭālib, may Allah ennoble his face."

٦١٠ أخبرنا مالك، أخبرنا يزيد بن عبد الله بن قُسَيط ويحيى بن سعيد، عن سعيد بن المسيب أنه قال: قال عمر بن الخطاب رضي الله عنه: أيّما امرأة طُلِّقت فحاضت حيضة أو حيضتين ثم رُفِعَت حيضتها فإنها تنتظر تسعة أشهر فإن استبان بها حَمْلٌ فذلك وإلاّ اعتدَّت بعد التسعة ثلاثة أشهر ثم حلّت.

610. Mālik informed us: "Yazīd ibn ᶜAbdullāh ibn Qusayṭ and Yaḥyā ibn Saᶜīd informed us that Saᶜīd ibn al-Musayyab said, 'ᶜUmar ibn al-Khaṭṭāb ﷺ said, "If a woman is divorced and she has one or two menstrual periods and then her period ceases, she must wait for nine months. If it is clear that she is pregnant, then that is that. If not, she must perform an *ᶜiddah* of three months after the nine [months] and then she is permitted [to marry].""'

٦١١ قال محمد: أخبرنا أبو حنيفة، عن حماد عن إبراهيم: أن علقمة بن قيس طَلَّقَ امرأته طلاقاً يملك الرجعة فحاضت حيضة أو حيضتين، ثم ارتفع حيضها عنها ثمانية عشر شهراً، ثم ماتت فسأل علقمةُ عبدَ الله بن مسعود عن ذلك، فقال: هذه امرأة حبس اللّهُ عليك ميراثها فَكُله.

611. Muḥammad said: "Abū Ḥanīfah informed us from Ḥammād from Ibrāhīm that ᶜAlqamah ibn Qays divorced his wife with a divorce in which he retained the right of return and then she had one or two menstrual periods, and then

her period ceased for eighteen months. Later she died. ʿAlqamah asked ʿAbdullāh ibn Masʿūd about it, and he said, 'This is a woman whose inheritance[54] Allah has retained for you, so use [lit: eat] it.'"

٦١٢ أخبرنا عيسى بن أبي عيسى الخياط، عن الشعبي : أن علقمةَ بن قيس سأل ابن عمر عن ذلك فأمره بأكل ميراثها.

612. ʿĪsā ibn Abī ʿĪsā al-Khayyāṭ informed us from ash-Shaʿbī that ʿAlqamah ibn Qays asked Ibn ʿUmar about it and he told him to make use of [eat] her inheritance.

قال محمدٌ: فهذا أكثر من تسعة أشهر وثلاثة أشهر بعدها، فبهذا نأخذُ. وهو قولُ أبي حنيفة والعامة من فقهائنا، لأن العدة في كتاب الله عزَّ وجلَّ على أربعة أوجه لا خامس لها : للحامل حتى تضع، والتي لم تبلغ الحيضة ثلاثة أشهر، والتي قد يئست من المحيض ثلاثة أشهر، والتي تحيض ثلاث حيض، فهذا الذي ذكرتُم ليس بعدَّة الحائض ولا غيرها.

Muḥammad said: "This is more than nine months and [another] three months after that. We adhere to this, and it is the verdict of Abū Ḥanīfah and our *fuqahāʾ* in general, because the *ʿiddah* in the Book of Allah ﷻ has four aspects and there is no fifth; for the pregnant woman it is until she gives birth, for someone who has not yet attained to having a menstrual period it is three months, for someone who has passed the age of having menstrual periods it is three months, and for someone who has her period it is three menstrual periods. This which you mention is neither the *ʿiddah* of someone who has her menstrual period nor any other [kind]."

٣٠ باب عدة المستحاضة

30. The *ʿIddah* of the Woman whose Menstrual Bleeding Continues uninterruptedly beyond its ordinary Time [*Mustaḥāḍah*]

٦١٣ أخبرنا مالك، أخبرنا ابن شهاب : أن سعيد بن المسيّب قال: عدّة المستحاضة سنة.

613. Mālik informed us: "Ibn Shihāb informed us that Saʿīd ibn al-Musayyab said, 'The *ʿiddah* of the woman whose menstrual bleeding continues uninterruptedly beyond its ordinary time [*mustaḥāḍah*] is a year.'"

قال محمدٌ: المعروف عندنا أن عدَّتها على أقرائها التي كانت تجلس فيما مضى، وكذلك قال إبراهيم النخعي وغيره من الفقهاء، وبه نأخذ. وهو قول أبي حنيفة والعامة من فقهائنا، ألا ترى أنها تترك الصلاة أيام أقرائها التي كانت تجلس لأنها فيهنَّ حائض؟ فكذلك تعتدُّ بهن، فإذا مضت ثلاثة قروء منهنَّ بانت إن كان ذلك أقلَّ من سنة أو أكثر.

Muḥammad said: "What is well known with us is that her *ʿiddah* is according to her menstrual periods which she would previously have sat through. That is what Ibrāhīm an-Nakhaʿī and others of our *fuqahāʾ* said, and we adhere to it. It is the verdict of Abū Ḥanīfah and our *fuqahāʾ* in general. Do you not see that she leaves out the prayer for the days during which she used to have to abstain from the prayer because of her menstruation?[55] Similarly, she reckons her ᶜ*iddah* in terms of them [the normal menstrual periods] and when three menstrual periods are past then she is clearly divorced, whether that is less than a year or more."

٣١ باب الرَّضاع

31. Breast-feeding

٦١٤ أخبرنا مالك، أخبرنا نافع: أن عبد الله بن عمر كان يقول: لا رضاعة إلاَّ لمن أُرضِعَ في الصِّغَر .

614. Mālik informed us: "Nāfiᶜ informed us that ᶜAbdullāh ibn ᶜUmar used to say, 'There is no [relationship established by] breast-feeding except for someone who was breast-fed in childhood.'"

٦١٥ أخبرنا مالك، أخبرنا عبد الله بن أبي بكر ، عن عَمرة بنت عبد الرحمن، عن عائشة : أن رسول الله صلى الله عليه وسلم كان عندها، وإنها سمعت رجلاً يستأذن في بيت حفصة، قالت عائشة: فقلتُ : يا رسول الله، هذا رجل يستأذن في بيتك ، قال رسول الله صلى الله عليه وسلم: أُراه فلاناً لعمٍّ لحفصة من الرضاعة، قالت عائشة: يا رسول الله لو كان عمِّي فلان من الرضاعة حيّاً دخل عليَّ؟ قال : نعم .

615. Mālik informed us: "ᶜAbdullāh ibn Abī Bakr informed us from ᶜAmrah bint ᶜAbd ar-Raḥmān from ᶜĀʾishah that the Messenger of Allah ﷺ was with her and she heard a man seeking permission to enter Ḥafṣah's house. 'I said, "Messenger of Allah, this is a man who is seeking permission to enter your house." The Messenger of Allah ﷺ said, "I think it is so-and-so," a paternal uncle of Ḥafṣah's through breast-feeding.' ᶜĀʾishah said, 'Messenger of Allah, if my paternal uncle, so-and-so, through breast-feeding were alive, would he be able to come and visit me?' He said, 'Yes.'"

٦١٦ أخبرنا مالك، أخبرنا عبد الله بن دينار، عن سليمان بن يسار، عن عائشة: أن رسول الله صلى الله عليه وسلم قال: يحرِّم من الرضاعة ما يُحرِّم من الولادة .

616. Mālik informed us: "ᶜAbdullāh ibn Dīnār informed us from Sulaymān ibn Yasār from ᶜĀʾishah that the Messenger of Allah ﷺ said, 'That which is made *ḥarām* by lineage, is made *ḥarām* by breast-feeding.'"

٦١٧ أخبرنا مالك، أخبرنا عبد الرحمن بن القاسم، عن أبيه ، عن عائشة أنَّه كان يَدخُلُ عليها من أرضعته أخواتُها وبناتُ أخيها، ولا يدخل عليها من أرضعته نساء إخواتها.

617. Mālik informed us: "ᶜAbd ar-Raḥmān ibn al-Qāsim informed us from his father from ᶜĀʾishah that those whom her sisters and her sisters' daughters had breast-fed used to visit her, but that those whom her brothers' wives had breast-fed would not visit her."

٦١٨ أخبرنا مالك، أخبرني الزهري، عن عمرو بن الشَّريد : أن ابن عباس سُئل عن رجل كانت له امرأتان ، فأرضعت إحداهما غلاماً، والأخرى جارية، فسُئل هل يتزوج الغلام الجارية؟ قال: لا، اللّقاح واحد .

618. Mālik informed us: "Az-Zuhrī informed me from ᶜAmr ibn ash-Sharīk that Ibn ᶜAbbās was asked about a man who had two wives, one of whom breast-fed a boy and the other of whom breast-fed a girl. He was asked whether the boy could marry the girl, and he said, 'No. The husband[56] is the same.'"

٦١٩ أخبرنا مالك ، أخبرنا إبراهيم بن عُقبة : أنه سأل سعيد بن المسيَّب عن الرضاعة؟ فقال : ما كان في الحَولين وإن كانت مصَّة واحدة فهي تحرِّم وما كان بعد الحولين فإنما طعام يأكله .

619. Mālik informed us: "Ibrāhīm ibn ᶜUqbah informed us that he asked Saᶜīd ibn al-Musayyab about breast-feeding and he said, 'What occurs in the [first] two years, even if it is one suck, makes [marriage] *ḥarām*. Whatever happens after the two years is only nourishment which he takes.'"

٦٢٠ أخبرنا مالك، أخبرنا إبراهيم بن عقبة : أنه سأل عن عُروة بن الزبير فقال له مثل ما قال سعيد بن المسيَّب . (من أن ما كان في الحولين يحرم وما لا فلا .)

620. Mālik informed us: "Ibrāhīm ibn ᶜUqbah informed us that he asked ᶜUrwah ibn az-Zubayr and he said something similar to what Saᶜīd ibn al-Musayyab had said."

٦٢١ أخبرنا مالك، أخبرنا ثَور بن زيد : أن ابن عباس كان يقول: ما كان في الحولين وإن كانت مصَّة واحدة فهي تحرِّم.

621. Mālik informed us: "Thawr ibn Zayd informed us that Ibn ᶜAbbās used to say, 'Whatever occurred during the [first] two years, even if it was a single suck, makes [marriage] *ḥarām*.'"

٦٢٢ أخبرنا مالك، أخبرنا نافع مولى عبد الله بن عمر، أن سالم بن عبد الله أخبره: أن عائشة أم المؤمنين رضي الله عنها أرسلت به وهو يُرضَعُ إلى أختها أُمِّ كُلثوم بنت أبي بكر، فقالت: أرضعيه عشر رضعات حتى يدخل عليَّ، فأرضعتني أُم كُلثوم بنت أبي بكر ثلاث رضعات، ثم مَرِضَت، فلم ترضعني غير ثلاث مرار ، فلم أكن أدخل على عائشة من أجل أنَّ أمَّ كلثوم لم تُتمَّ لي عشر رضعات .

622. Mālik informed us: "Nāfiᶜ, the *mawlā* of ᶜAbdullāh ibn ᶜUmar, informed us that Sālim ibn ᶜAbdullāh informed him that ᶜĀ᾽ishah the Mother of the Mu᾽minūn ﷺ sent him, during the time he was breast-feeding, to her sister Umm Kulthūm bint Abī Bakr and she said, 'Breast-feed him ten times so that he can come to me [as an adult and learn].' So Umm Kulthūm bint Abī Bakr breast-fed me three times, and then she became ill, and thus only breast-fed me three times, and so I could not visit ᶜĀ᾽ishah[57] because Umm Kulthūm never completed ten breast-feedings for me."

٦٢٣ أخبرنا مالك، أخبرنا نافع، عن صفيَّة ابنة أبي عُبيد : أنها أخبرته أن حفصة أرسلت بعاصم بن عبد الله بن سعد إلى فاطمة بنت عمر ترضعه عشر رضعات ليدخل عليها، ففعلت ، فكان يَدخل عليها وهو يوم أرضعته صغير يُرضَع .

623. Mālik informed us: "Nāfiᶜ informed us that Ṣafiyyah the daughter of Abū ᶜUbayd had informed him that Ḥafṣah sent ᶜĀṣim ibn ᶜAbdullāh ibn

Saᶜd to Fāṭimah bint ᶜUmar [her sister] to breast-feed him ten times in order that [as an adult] he could come to visit her, and she did so. So he would visit her, and at the time she breast-fed him he was a child who was being breast-fed."

٦٢٤ أخبرنا مالك، أخبرنا عبد الله بن أبي بكر، عن عَمرة، عن عائشة قالت : كان فيما أنزل الله تعالى من القرآن: عشر رضعات معلومات يُحرِّمنَ، ثم نُسخن بخمس معلومات، فتُوفي رسول الله صلى الله عليه وسلم وهنَّ مما يُقرأ من القرآن.

624. Mālik informed us: "ᶜAbdullāh ibn Abī Bakr informed us from ᶜAmrah that ᶜĀ'ishah said, 'There was in that which Allah, exalted is He, revealed of the Qur'ān, "Ten known sucklings make [marriage] *ḥarām,*" and then later it was abrogated with "Five known sucklings", and then the Messenger of Allah ﷺ died and it was a part of what was recited of the Qur'ān.'"[58]

٦٢٥ أخبرنا مالك، أخبرنا عبد الله بن دينار، قال: جاء رجل إلى عبد الله بن عمر، وأنا معه عند دار القضاء، يسأله عن رضاعة الكبير، فقال عبد الله بن عمر: جاء رجل إلى عمر بن الخطاب، فقال: كانت لي وليدة فكنت أصيبها ، فعمدَت امرأتي إليها، فأرضعتها، فدخلت عليها ، فقالت امرأتي: دونك : والله قد أرضعتها، قال عمر رضي الله عنه : أوجِعهَا وائتِ جاريتَك فإنما الرضاعة رضاعة الصغير.

625. Mālik informed us: "ᶜAbdullāh ibn Dīnār informed us, 'A man came to ᶜAbdullāh ibn ᶜUmar while I was with him at the Dār al-Qaḍā'[59] asking him about the breast-feeding of an adult, and ᶜAbdullāh ibn ᶜUmar said, "A man came to ᶜUmar ibn al-Khaṭṭāb and said, 'I had a slave-woman and I used to have sexual intercourse with her. My wife went deliberately to her and suckled her, then when I went to her my wife said, "Beware! I have breast-fed her."' ᶜUmar said ﷺ 'Beat her, and go [and have sexual intercourse] with your slave-woman, because the breast-feeding [that makes marriage *ḥarām*] is only the breast-feeding of a child.'"'"

٦٢٦ أخبرنا مالك، أخبرنا ابن شهاب، وسئل عن رضاعة الكبير؟ فقال: أخبرني عُروة بن الزبير أن أبا حُذيفة بن عُتبة بن ربيعة كان من أصحاب رسول الله صلى الله عليه وسلم شهد بدراً وكان تَبَنَّى سالماً الذي يُقال له مولى أبي حُذيفة كما كان تبنَّى رسولُ الله زيدَ بن حارثة، فأنكح أبو حذيفة سالماً وهو يرى أنه ابنه أنكحه ابنة أخيه فاطمة بنت الوليد بن عتبة بن ربيعة، وهي من المهاجرات الأُوَل وهي يومئذ من أفضل أيَامَى قريش، فلما أنزل الله تعالى في زيد ما أنزل:﴿ادعُوهُم لآبائهم هو أقسط عند الله﴾ ردّ كل أحد تُبُنِّي إلى أبيه، فإن لم يكن يُعلم أبوه رُدَّ إلى مواليه.

فجاءَت سَهلة بنت سُهَيل امرأة أبي حذيفة وهي من بني عامر بن لُؤَيٍّ إلى رسول الله صلى الله عليه وسلم فيما بلغنا ، فقالت: كنا نُرى سالماً ولداً، وكان يدخل عليّ وأنا فُضل وليس لنا إلا بيت واحدٌ، فما ترى في شأنه؟ فقال لها رسول الله صلى الله عليه وسلم: فيما بلغنا أرضعيه خمس رضعات، فتحرم بلبنك أو بلبنها، وكانت تراه ابناً من الرضاعة، فأخذت بذلك عائشة فيمن تحبُّ أن يدخلَ عليها من الرجال، فكانت تأمر أم كلثوم وبنات أخيها يُرضعن من أحبَبنَ أن يدخل عليها، وأبى سائر أزواج النبي صلى الله عليه وسلم أن يدخل عليهم بتلك الرضاعة أحدٌ من الناس، وقلن لعائشة:

والله ما نرى الذي أمَرَ به رسول الله صلى الله عليه وسلم سهلة بنت سهيل إلا رخصةً لها في رضاعة سالم وحده من رسول الله صلى الله عليه وسلم، لا يدخل علينا بهذه الرضاعة أحد.
فعلى هذا كان رأي أزواجِ النبي صلى الله عليه وسلم في رضاعة الكبير.

626. Mālik informed us: "Ibn Shihāb informed us – he was asked about the breast-feeding of an adult – and he said, "ᶜUrwah ibn az-Zubayr informed me that Abū Ḥudhayfah ibn ᶜUtbah ibn Rabīᶜah was one of the Companions of the Messenger of Allah ﷺ who was present at Badr. He had adopted as his son Sālim, the one known as the *mawlā* of Abū Ḥudhayfah, just as the Messenger of Allah ﷺ had adopted Zayd ibn Ḥārithah as his son. Then Abū Ḥudhayfah, considering Sālim his son, married him to his brother's daughter Fāṭimah bint al-Walīd ibn ᶜUtbah ibn Rabīᶜah who was one of the first woman emigrants, and at that time one of the leading unmarried women of Quraysh. When Allah, exalted is He, revealed, "Call them after their fathers. That is closer to justice in Allah's sight," (Sūrat al-Ahzab: 5) then each person who had been adopted was traced back to his father, and if the father wasn't known then he was traced back to his *mawlās*. Then Sahlah bint Suhayl the wife of Abū Ḥudhayfah came – and she was from Banī ᶜĀmir ibn Lu᾿ayy – to the Messenger of Allah ﷺ according to that which has reached us. She said, "We used to look on Sālim as a son, and he would come in to see me while I was uncovered, and we have only one room. What do you think about his situation?" The Messenger of Allah ﷺ said to her, according to what has reached us, "Suckle him five times[60] so that you will make him an unmarriageable male relative (*maḥram*) by your milk," (or he became an unmarriageable male relative because of her milk). She used to think of him as a son through suckling. So ᶜĀ᾿ishah took the [same] position with respect to those men she wanted to come and visit her [to learn the dīn]. She used to tell Umm Kulthūm and the daughters of her brother [ᶜAbd ar-Raḥmān ibn Abī Bakr] to suckle whomever she wanted to come and visit her. All the other wives of the Prophet ﷺ refused that anyone should visit them by this suckling. They said to ᶜĀ᾿ishah, "By Allah! we think that what the Messenger of Allah ﷺ told Sahlah bint Suhayl to do was only a concession from the Messenger of Allah ﷺ for her concerning the suckling of Sālim alone. No one will [be allowed to] come to visit us by this type of suckling." That was the view of the wives of the Prophet ﷺ concerning the suckling of an adult.'"

٦٢٧ أخبرنا مالك، أخبرنا يحيى بن سعيد، عن سعيد بن المسيَّب: أنه سمعه يقول: لا رضاعة إلا في المهد، ولا رضاعة إلا ما أنبت اللحم والدم.

627. Mālik informed us: "Yaḥyā ibn Saᶜīd informed us from Saᶜīd ibn al-Musayyab that he heard him saying, 'There is only breast-feeding [for children]

in the cradle, and it is only breast-feeding if it nourishes and gives growth to flesh and blood."[61]

قال محمد: لا يُحرم الرضاع إلا ما كان في الحولين، فما كان فيها من الرضاع وإن كان مصَّةً واحدة فهي تُحَرِّم كما قال عبد الله بن عباس وسعيد بن المسيب وعروة بن الزبير، وما كان بعد الحولين لم يُحَرِّم شيئاً لأن الله عزَّ وجل قال: ﴿والوالدات يُرْضِعن أولادَهن حولين كاملين لمن أراد أن يتم الرضاعة﴾ فتمام الرضاعة الحولان، فلا رضاعة بعد تمامهما تُحَرِّم شيئاً.

وكان أبو حنيفة رحمه الله يحتاط بستة أشهر بعد الحولين، فيقول: يُحَرِّم ما كان في الحولين وبعدهما إلى تمام ستة أشهر، وذلك ثلاثون شهراً، ولا يُحَرِّم ما كان بعد ذلك. ونحن لا نرى أنه يُحَرِّم، ونرى أنه لا يُحَرِّم ما كان بعد الحولين. وأما لبن الفحل فإنّا نراه يُحَرِّم، ونرى أنه يحرم من الرضاع ما يحرم من النسب، فالأخ من الرضاعة من الأب تحرم عليه أخته من الرضاعة من الأب وإن كانت الأمّان مختلفتين إذا كان لبنهما من رجل واحد، كما قال ابن عباس: اللَّقاح واحد. فبهذا نأخذ. وهو قول أبي حنيفة رحمه الله.

Muḥammad said: "Breast-feeding only makes someone an unmarriageable male relative (*maḥram*) if it happens in the [first] two years. Whatever [the amount of] breast-feeding that takes place, even if it is only one suck, it establishes the relationship of being an unmarriageable male relative, as ʿAbdullāh Ibn ʿAbbās, Saʿīd ibn al-Musayyab and ʿUrwah ibn az-Zubayr said. Whatever happens after the two years does not make anything *ḥarām*, because Allah ﷻ says, 'Mothers should nurse their children for two full years – those who wish to complete the full term of nursing.' (Sūrat al-Baqarah: 231). So the completion of the nursing and breast-feeding is two years, and there is no breast-feeding after its expiry which establishes the relationship of being an unmarriageable male relative. Abū Ḥanīfah, may Allah have mercy on him, used to allow for a precautionary period of six months after the two years, saying, 'Whatever happens in the two years establishes the relationship of being an unmarriageable male relative and after them up to six months, and that is thirty months, but anything after that does not in any way establish the relationship of being an unmarriageable male relative.' But we do not think that it establishes the relationship of being an unmarriageable male relative, and we think that nothing beyond the two years establishes the relationship of being an unmarriageable male relative. As for any milk from any wife of a man, we maintain that it establishes the relationship of being an unmarriageable male relative, and we maintain that the relationship of being an unmarriageable male relative is established by breast-feeding just as it is by lineage, so that the brother from breast-feeding [from any wife] of a father is an unmarriageable male relative to his sister by breast-feeding [from any wife] of the same father, even if there were two different mothers, since their milks relate back to one man, as Ibn ʿAbbās said, 'The husband is the same.' This we adhere to and it is the verdict of Abū Ḥanīfah, may Allah have mercy on him."

كتاب الضَحايا وما يُجْزِئ منها

8. SACRIFICES AND WHAT OF THEM IS SUFFICIENT

٦٢٨ أخبرنا مالك، أخبرنا نافع: أن عبد الله بن عمر كان يقول في الضحايا والبُدْن الثَّنيّ فما فوقه.

628. Mālik informed us: "Nāfi[c] informed us that [c]Abdullāh ibn [c]Umar used to say concerning sacrifices and sacrificial animals that they should be what are termed *thanī*[62] and older."

٦٢٩ أخبرنا مالك أخبرنا نافع، عن ابن عمر: أنه كان ينهى عما لم تُسِنّ من الضحايا والبدن وعن التي نُقِصَ من خلْقها.

629. Mālik informed us: "Nāfi[c] informed us that Ibn [c]Umar used to forbid sacrificial animals that were too young and those which had some physical defect."

٦٣٠ أخبرنا مالك، أخبرنا نافع، عن عبد الله بن عمر: أنه ضَحّى مرة بالمدينة فأمرني أن أشتري له كَبْشاً فحيلاً أقرنَ ثم أذْبحَه له يومَ الأضحى في مصلّى الناس ففعلت، ثم حُمِل إليه، فحلق رأسه حين ذُبِح كَبشه وكان مريضاً لم يشهَد العيد مع الناس، قال نافع: وكان عبد الله بن عمر يقول: ليس حلاَقُ الرأس بواجبٍ على من ضَحَّى إذا لم يَحُجَّ وَقَدْ فَعَله عبد الله بن عمر.

630. Mālik informed us: "Nāfi[c] informed us that, 'Once [c]Abdullāh ibn [c]Umar sacrificed in Madīnah and he told me to buy a properly formed,[63] horned ram and then to sacrifice it for him on the day of *al-Aḍḥā* at the place where people prayed the *[c]Īd* outside the city [*muṣallā*], and so I did so. Then it was carried to him, and he shaved his head when his ram was sacrificed. He was ill at that time and was not present at the *[c]Īd* with people. [c]Abdullāh ibn [c]Umar used to say, "Shaving the head is not obligatory on the person who sacrifices," but [c]Abdullāh ibn [c]Umar did do it.'"

قال محمد: وبهذا كله نأخذ إلاّ في خصلةٍ واحدة، الجَذَع من الضأن إذا كان عظيماً أجزأ، في الهدي والأضحية، بذلك جاءت الآثار: الخَصيّ من الأضحية يُجزئ مما يجزئ منه الفحل. وأما الحلاق فنقول فيه بقول عبد الله بن عمر: إنه ليس بواجب على من لم يحجّ في يوم النحر. وهو قول أبي حنيفة والعامة من فقهائنا.

Muḥammad said: "We adhere to all of this except in one respect; the six month old sheep, if it is large, is sufficient as a *hady* offering or a sacrifice. Traditions are narrated about that. The castrated animal is sufficient for that for which the un-castrated animal is sufficient. As for shaving the head, we give the verdict which ᶜAbdullāh ibn ᶜUmar gave, that it is not obligatory on the Day of Sacrifice for someone who is not doing the Ḥajj, and that is the verdict of Abū Ḥanīfah and of our *fuqahā᾽* in general."

٦٣١ أخبرنا مالك، أخبرنا نافع، أن عبد الله بن عمر لم يكن يضحي عما في بطن المرأة.

631. Mālik informed us: "Nāfiᶜ informed us that ᶜAbdullāh ibn ᶜUmar did not sacrifice for children in the womb."

قال محمد: وبهذا نأخذ لا يضحى عما في بطن المرأة.

Muḥammad said: "We adhere to this; one does not sacrifice for the child in the womb."

١ باب ما يُكره من الضَّحَايَا

1. What Sacrifices are Disapproved

٦٣٢ أخبرنا مالك، أخبرنا عمرو بن الحارث، أن عُبيد بن فَيْرُوز أخبره أن البراء بن عازب سأل رسول الله صلى الله عليه وسلم: ماذا يُتَّقَّى من الضحايا؟ فأشار بيده، وقال: أربع وكان البراءُ بن عازب يشير بيده ويقول: يدي أقصر من يده وهي العَرْجاء البيِّن ظَلْعُها، والعوراء البيِّن عورها، والمريضة البيِّن مرضها، العَجْفاءُ التي لا تُنْقِي.

632. Mālik informed us: "ᶜAmr ibn al-Ḥārith informed us that ᶜUbayd ibn Fayrūz informed him that al-Barā᾽ ibn ᶜĀzib asked the Messenger of Allah ﷺ about what sacrificial animals ought to be avoided, and he indicated with his hand and said, 'Four,' – al-Barā᾽ ibn ᶜĀzib used to indicate with his hand and say, 'My hand is shorter than his hand,' – 'and they are the lame animal whose lameness is evident, an animal that is clearly one-eyed, an animal that is clearly sick, and a lean, emaciated animal which has no marrow [or fat].'"

قال محمد: وبهذا نأخذ. فأما العرجاءُ فإذا مَشَتْ على رِجلها فهي تجزئ وإن كانت لا تمشي لم تجزئ، وأما العوراء فإن كان بقي من البصر الأكثر من نصف البصر أجزأت، وإنْ ذهب النصف فصاعداً لم تجزئ، وأما المريضة التي فَسَدَتْ لمرضها والعجفاءُ التي لا تُنْقي فإنهما لا يجزئان.

Muḥammad said: "We adhere to this. As for the lame animal, if it walks on its feet then it is acceptable, but if it is not able to walk it is not acceptable. As for the one-eyed animal, if more than half of its sight remains it is acceptable, but if a half or more of its sight has gone then it is not acceptable. As for the sick creature which is significantly altered because of its sickness and the emaciated animal which has no marrow [or fat], then neither of them are acceptable."

٢ باب لحوم الأضاحي

2. The Meat of Sacrifices

٦٣٣ أخبرنا مالك، أخبرنا عبد الله بن أبي بكر، عن عبد الله بن واقد، أن عبد الله بن عمر أخبره: أنَّ رسولَ الله صلى الله عليه وسلم نهى عن أكل لحوم الضحايا بعد ثلاث.

قال عبد الله بن أبي بكر فذكرتُ ذلك لعَمْرة بنت عبد الرحمن فقالت: صدق ، سمعتُ عائشة أمّ المؤمنين تقول: دفَّ ناسٌ من أهل البادية حضرةَ الأضحى في زمان رسول الله صلى الله عليه وسلم، فقال: ادَّخروا الثلث وتصدَّقوا بما بقي، فلما كان بعد ذلك قيل : يا رسول الله، لقد كان الناس ينتفعون في ضحاياهم، يُجْملُوْن منها الوَدَك ويتَّخذون منها الأسْقيَةَ ، قال رسول الله صلى الله عليه وسلم: وما ذاك ؟ كما قال َقالوا: نَهَيْتَ عن إمساك لحوم الأضاحي بَعد ثلاث؟ فقال رسول الله صلى الله عليه وسلم: إنما نهيتكم من أجل الدافَّة التي كانت دفَّت حضرَةَ الأضحى، فكلوا وتصدَّقوا وادَّخروا.

633. Mālik informed us: "ᶜAbdullāh ibn Abī Bakr[64] informed us from ᶜAbdullāh ibn Wāqid[65] that ᶜAbdullāh ibn ᶜUmar informed him that the Messenger of Allah ﷺ prohibited eating the meat of the sacrificial animals after three days. ᶜAbdullāh ibn Abī Bakr said, 'So I mentioned that to ᶜAmrah bint ᶜAbd ar-Raḥmān and she said, "He told the truth. I heard ᶜĀʾishah the Mother of the Muʾminūn saying, 'Some people from the country came at the time of the sacrifices during the life of the Messenger of Allah ﷺ and he said, "Store up a third,[66] and give the rest away as *ṣadaqah*."' Then after that[67] someone said, "People used to take benefit from their sacrifices; they collected the fat from them, and took the skins of young sheep and goats to use for water carrying." The Messenger of Allah ﷺ said, "What is [preventing them from doing] that?" or however it was that he spoke. They answered, "[Didn't] you forbid the retention of the meat of sacrificial animals after three [days]?" The Messenger of Allah ﷺ said, "I only forbade you because of the company of people who came at the time of the sacrifices[68]. So eat, give as *ṣadaqah* and put [some] in storage."'""

٦٣٤ أخبرنا مالك، أخبرنا أبو الزبير المكيّ، عن جابر بن عبد الله أنه أخبره : أنَّ رسول الله صلى الله عليه وسلم نهى عن أكل لحوم الضحايا بعد ثلاث. ثم قال بعد ذلك: كلوا وتزوَّدوا وادَّخروا .

634. Mālik informed us: "Abu'z-Zubayr al-Makkī informed us that Jābir ibn ᶜAbdullāh informed him that the Messenger of Allah ﷺ forbade eating the meat of the sacrificial animals after three days. Then afterwards he said, 'Eat, take for travelling provisions, and put aside in storage [if you wish].'"

قال محمد: وبهذا نأخذ. لا بأس بالادِّخار بعد ثلاث والتزوُّد، وقد رخَّص في ذلك رسول الله صلى الله عليه وسلم بعد أن كان نهى عنه، فقوله الآخِرُ ناسخٌ للأوَّل، فلا بأس بالادِّخار والتزوُّد من ذلك. وهو قول أبي حنيفة والعامة من فقهائنا.

Muḥammad said: "We adhere to this. There is no harm in storing up for more than three days and taking some for travelling provisions, since the Messenger of Allah ﷺ gave a concession for that after having prohibited it, so that his later statement abrogates his earlier one. There is no harm in storing it and taking travelling provision from it, and that is the verdict of Abū Ḥanīfah and of our *fuqahāʾ* in general."

٦٣٥ أخبرنا مالك، أخبرنا أبو الزبير المكيّ، أن جابر بن عبد الله أخبره: أنّ رسول الله صلى الله عليه وسلم كان ينهى عن أكل لحوم الضحايا بعد ثلاث ثم قال بعد ذلك: كلوا وادَّخروا وتصدَّقوا.
635. Mālik informed us: "Abu'z-Zubayr al-Makkī informed us that Jābir ibn ᶜAbdullāh informed him that the Messenger of Allah ﷺ had forbidden eating the meat of the sacrificial animals after three days, but then later after that he said, 'Eat, put in storage and give as *ṣadaqah*.'"

قال محمد: وبهذا نأخذ. لا بأس بأن يأكل الرجل من أضحيته ويدَّخر ويتصدَّق، وما نُحبُّ له أن يتصدَّق بأقلَّ من الثُّلُث وإن تصدَّق بأقل من ذلك جاز.
Muḥammad said: "We adhere to this. There is no harm in a man eating from his sacrifice, storing it and giving it as *ṣadaqah*. We don't like him to give less than a third as *ṣadaqah*, but if he gives less than that as *ṣadaqah* it is acceptable."

٣ باب الرجل يذبح أضحيته قبل أن يغدوَ يوم الأضحى

3. A Man Slaughtering his Sacrificial Animal before Going to the the Place where People Pray the ᶜĪd outside the City [*Muṣallā*] on the Day of Sacrifice

٦٣٦ أخبرنا مالك، أخبرني يحيى بن سعيد، عن عبّاد بن تميم: أن عُوَيْمر بن أَشقَر ذبح أضحيته قبل أن يغدوَ يوم الأضحى، وأنّه ذَكَرَ ذلك لرسول الله ﷺ فأمره أن يعود بأضحيةٍ أخرى.
636. Mālik informed us: "Yaḥyā ibn Saᶜīd informed me from ᶜAbbād ibn Tamīm that ᶜUwaymir ibn Ashqar slaughtered his sacrifice before going [to the *muṣallā*] on the Day of Sacrifice and that he mentioned this to the Messenger of Allah ﷺ and he told him to repeat it with another sacrifice."

قال محمد: وبهذا نأخذ. إذا كان الرجل في مصرٍ يُصَلَّى العيدُ فيه، فذبح قبل أن يصلّي الإمام فإنما هي شاةُ لحم، ولا يجزئ من الأضحية، ومن لم يكن في مصرٍ وكان في بادية أو نحوها من القرى النائية عن المصر فإذا ذبح حين يطلع الفجر وحين تطلع الشمس أجزأه. وهو قول أبي حنيفة رحمه الله.
Muḥammad said: "We adhere to this. If a man is in a city in which he is praying the ᶜĪd, and he sacrifices before the *imām* prays, then it is only a ewe for meat, and it does not discharge [the duty of] the sacrifice. Someone who is not in a city but is in the countryside or somewhere similar such as villages remote from major cities,[69] then if he sacrifices when *Fajr* appears and when the sun rises, it discharges his duty, and that is the verdict of Abū Ḥanīfah, may Allah have mercy on him."

٤ باب ما يُجْزِئ من الضحايا عن أكثر من واحد

4. What Sacrifices are Acceptable from more than one Person

٦٣٧ أخبرنا مالك، أخبرنا عُمارة بن صَيّاد، أنّ عطاء بن يسار، أخبره أن أبا أيوب صاحب رسول

الله صلى الله عليه وسلم أخبره قال: كنا نُضحِّي بالشاة الواحدة يذبحها الرجل عنه وعن أهل بيته، ثم تباهى الناس بعد ذلك، فصارت مباهاة .

637. Mālik informed us: "ᶜUmārah ibn Ṣayyād informed us that ᶜAṭāᵓ ibn Yasār informed him that Abū Ayyūb the Companion of the Messenger of Allah ﷺ informed him, 'We used to sacrifice one ewe which a man would sacrifice for himself and on behalf of his immediate family, and then people began to compete with each other after that so that it became a matter of boastful competition.'"

قال محمد : كان الرجل يكون محتاجاً فيذبح الشاة الواحدة يُضَحِّي بها عن نفسه، فيأكل ويُطعم أهله، فأما شاةٌ واحدة تُذبح عن اثنين أو ثلاثة أضحية فهذا لا يجزئ، ولا يجوز شاة إلا عن الواحد . وهو قول أبي حنيفة والعامة من فقهائنا .

Muḥammad said: "A man could be in need and so sacrifice a single ewe as a sacrifice on his own behalf, and then eat from it and feed his family. As for a single ewe being slaughtered as a sacrifice on behalf of two or three people, this does not discharge the duty, and a sheep is only acceptable on behalf of a single person, and that is the verdict of Abū Ḥanīfah and of our *fuqahāᵓ* in general."

٦٣٨ أخبرنا مالك، أخبرنا أبو الزبير المكيّ، عن جابر بن عبد الله قال : نحرنا مع رسول الله صلى الله عليه وسلم بالحُدَيْبية البَدَنة عن سبعة والبقرة عن سبعة .

638. Mālik informed us: "Abu'z-Zubayr al-Makkī informed us that Jābir ibn ᶜAbdullāh said, 'We sacrificed along with the Messenger of Allah ﷺ at al-Ḥudaybiyah, a single camel on behalf of seven people or a single cow on behalf of seven people.'"

قال محمد : وبهذا نأخذ . البدنة والبقرة تُجزئ عن سبعة في الأضحية والهدي متفرقين كانوا أو مجتمعين من أهل بيت واحد أو غيره . وهو قول أبي حنيفة والعامة من فقهائنا رحمهم الله .

Muḥammad said: "We adhere to this. A camel and a cow are each sufficient for seven people as a sacrifice or *hady* offering, whether or not the people are separate or together, or from one single family unit, and that is the verdict of Abū Ḥanīfah and of our *fuqahāᵓ* in general, may Allah have mercy on them."

٥ باب الذبائح

5. Slaughtering Animals

٦٣٩ أخبرنا مالك، أخبرنا زيد بن أسلم، عن عطاء بن يسار : أن رجلاً كان يرعى لَقْحةً له بأُحُد ، فجاءها الموتُ فذكّاها بشِظَاظ ، فسأل رسول الله صلى الله عليه وسلم عن أكلها، فقال: لا بأس بها كلوها .

639. Mālik informed us: "Zayd ibn Aslam informed us from ᶜAṭāᵓ ibn Yasār that a man used to graze a milch camel of his on Uḥud. It was about to die and so he slaughtered it with a sharpened wooden stake. He asked the

Messenger of Allah ﷺ about eating it and he answered, 'There is no harm in it. Eat it.'"

٦٤٠ أخبرنا مالك، أخبرنا نافع، عن رجل من الأنصار، أنّ معاذ بن سعد أو سعد بن معاذ أخبره: أن جارية لكعب بن مالك كانت ترعى غنماً له بسَلْع فأصيبت منها شاة، فأدركتها ، ثم ذبحتها بحجر، فسُئل رسول الله صلى الله عليه وسلم عن ذلك فقال: لا بأس بها كلوها .

640. Mālik informed us: "Nāfiʿ informed us from a man of the Anṣār that Muʿādh ibn Saʿd or Saʿd ibn Muʿādh informed him that a slave girl of Kaʿb ibn Mālik used to graze his sheep and goats on Salʿ[70], and one of the sheep was on the point of death, and she managed to reach it and she slaughtered it with a stone. The Messenger of Allah ﷺ was asked about that and he said, 'There is no harm in it. Eat it.'"

قال محمـد : وبهـذا نأخـذ كل شيء أفرى الأوداج وأنهر الدم فذبحت به فلا بأس بذلك إلا السنّ والظفر والعظم، فإنه مكروه أن تُذبح بشيء منه . وهو قول أبي حنيفة والعامة من فقهائنا.

Muḥammad said: "We adhere to this. Everything whose jugular veins have been cut so that its blood flows and so that it perishes as a result of it, then there is no harm in it, except for the use of teeth, claws and bones, because it is disapproved to slaughter with any of these, and that is the verdict of Abū Ḥanīfah and of our *fuqahāʾ* in general."

٦٤١ أخبرنا مالك، أخبرنا يحيى بن سعيد، عن سعيد بن المسيّب أنه كان يقول : ما ذُبح به إذا بَضَّع فلا بأس به إذا اضطُررت إليه .

641. Mālik informed us: "Yaḥyā ibn Saʿīd informed us that Saʿīd ibn al-Musayyab used to say, 'Whatever is slaughtered, if it is cut[71] there is no harm in it if you are forced by necessity to do it.'"

قال محمـد : وبهـذا نأخـذ . لا بأس بذلك كلّه على ما فسّرتُ لك، وإن ذبح بسن أو ظفر منزوعين فأفرى الأوداج وأنهر الدم أُكل أيضاً . وذلك مكروه، فإن كانا منزوعين فإنما قتلها قتلاً فهي ميتة لا تؤكل . وهو قولُ أبي حنيفة رحمه الله تعالى .

Muḥammad said: "We adhere to this. There is no harm in any of that according to what I have explained to you. Even if it is slaughtered by a tooth or a claw which has been extracted and then the jugular veins are cut and the blood caused to flow, then it is also allowed to be eaten, but it is disapproved of. If the two [the tooth or claw] are not removed then it is just that he killed the animal and it is carrion and not to be eaten, and that is the verdict of Abū Ḥanīfah, may Allah have mercy on him."

٦ باب الصيد وما يُكره أكله من السباع وغيرها

6. Hunting and what Animals of Prey it is Disapproved of to Eat

٦٤٢ أخبرنا مالك، أخبرنا ابن شهاب، عن أبي إدريس الخَوْلاني ، عن أبي ثعلبة الخُشَني: أن رسول الله صلى الله عليه وسلم نهى عن أكل كلّ ذي ناب من السباع .

642. Mālik informed us: "Ibn Shihāb informed us from Abū Idrīs al-Khawlānī from Abū Thaᶜlabah al-Khushanī that the Messenger of Allah ﷺ forbade eating those animals of prey that have fangs."

٦٤٣ أخبرنا مالك، حدّثنا إسماعيل بن أبي حكيم، عن عَبِيْدَة بن سفيان الحضرمي ، عن أبي هريرة، عن رسول الله صلى الله عليه وسلم أنه قال: أكْلُ كل ذي ناب من السباع حرام.

643. Mālik informed us: "Ismāᶜīl ibn Abī Ḥakīm narrated to us from ᶜAbīdah ibn Sufyān al-Ḥaḍramī from Abū Hurayrah that the Messenger of Allah ﷺ said, "Eating any of the animals of prey that have fangs is ḥarām."

قال محمد: وبهذا نأخذ. يُكره أكل كلِّ ذي ناب من السِّبَاع وكُلِّ ذي مخْلب من الطير، ويُكره من الطير أيضاً ما يأكل الجِيَفَ مما له مِخْلب أو ليس له مخلب. وهو قول أبي حنيفة والعامة من فقهائنا وإبراهيم النخعي.

Muḥammad said: "We adhere to this. It is abhorrent[72] to eat any animal of prey which possesses fangs, and any bird which has talons. Also, birds which eat carrion whether or not they have talons are abhorrent, and that is the verdict of Abū Ḥanīfah and of our *fuqahā'* in general and Ibrāhīm an-Nakhaᶜī."

٧ باب أكل الضَّبّ

7. Eating Large Lizards[73]

٦٤٤ أخبرنا مالك، أخبرنا ابن شهاب، عن أبي أمامة بن سهل بن حنيف، عن عبد الله بن عباس، عن خالد بن الوليد بن المغيرة: أنه دخل مع رسول الله صلى الله عليه وسلم بيتَ ميمونة زوجِ النبي صلى الله عليه وسلم، فأُتي بضَبّ مَحْنُوذ فأهوى إليه رسول الله صلى الله عليه وسلم يده، فقال بعض النسوة اللاتي كنّ في بيت ميمونة: أخبِرُوا رسولَ الله صلى الله عليه وسلم بما يريد أن يأكل منه، فقلن: هو ضبّ، فرفع يدَه، فقلت: أحرام هو؟ قال: لا، ولكنه لم يكن بأرض قومي، فأجِدُني أعافُه. قال: فاجترَرْتُه فأكلتُ ورسول الله صلى الله عليه وسلم ينظُرُ.

644. Mālik informed us: "Ibn Shihāb informed us from Abū Umāmah ibn Sahl ibn Ḥunayf from ᶜAbdullāh ibn ᶜAbbās that Khālid ibn al-Walīd ibn al-Mughīrah entered the house of Maymūnah the wife of the Prophet ﷺ, along with the Messenger of Allah ﷺ. He was brought a roasted[species of] large lizard and the Messenger of Allah ﷺ stretched his hand towards it. Then some of the women who were in Maymūnah's house said, 'Tell the Messenger of Allah ﷺ what it is that he intends to eat,' and so they [the women] said, 'It is a lizard,' and then he lifted his hand away. I asked, 'Is it *ḥarām*?" and he answered, 'No, but it was not in my people's land, and so I feel repugnance for it.'" He said, "I pulled it [towards me] and ate, while the Messenger of Allah ﷺ looked on."[74]

٦٤٥ أخبرنا مالك، أخبرنا عبد الله بن دينار، عن عبد الله بن عمر أنّه قال: نادى رجل رسولَ الله صلى الله عليه وسلم، فقال: يا رسول الله، كيف ترى في أكل الضبّ؟ قال: لستُ بآكله ولامُحَرِّمه.

645. Mālik informed us: "ᶜAbdullāh ibn Dīnār informed us that ᶜAbdullāh

ibn ʿUmar said, 'A man called out to the Messenger of Allah ﷺ saying, "What is your view on eating lizard?" He answered, "I don't eat it, but I have not made it *ḥarām*."'"

قال محمد: قد جاء في أكله اختلاف، فأمّا نحن فلا نرى أن يؤكل.

Muḥammad said: "There is reported some disagreement about whether it can be eaten, but as for us we do not think that it should be eaten."

٦٤٦ أخبرنا أبو حنيفة، عن حمّاد، عن إبراهيم النَّخَعي، عن عائشة: أنّه أُهْدِيَ لها ضَبّ، فأتاها رسول الله صلى الله عليه وسلم فسألته عن أكله فنهاها عنه، فجاءت سائلة فأرادت أن تُطْعِمَها إيّاه، فقال لها رسول الله صلى الله عليه وسلم: أتُطْعِمِينَها ممّا لا تُأكلين؟

646. Abū Ḥanīfah informed us from Ḥammād from Ibrāhīm an-Nakhaʿī that ʿĀʾishah was given a gift of a large lizard. The Messenger of Allah ﷺ came to her and so she asked him about eating it. He forbade her to eat it. A beggar came and she [ʿĀʾishah] wanted to give it to her to eat, and so the Messenger of Allah ﷺ said, "Would you feed her with that which you would not want to eat?"

٦٤٧ أخبرنا عبد الجبّار، عن ابن عبّاس الهمدانيّ، عن عزيز بن مَرْثَد، عن الحارث، عن علي بن أبي طالب كرم الله وجهه: أنه نهى عن أكل الضبّ والضَّبُع.

647. ʿAbd al-Jabbār al-Hamdānī informed us from Ibn ʿAbbās al-Hamdānī from ʿAzīz ibn Marthad from al-Ḥārith that ʿAlī ibn Abī Ṭālib, may Allah ennoble his face, forbade the eating of the lizard and of the hyena.

قال محمدٌ: فتركه أحبّ إلينا. وهو قول أبي حنيفة رحمه الله تعالى.

Muḥammad said: "Leaving it is preferrable to us, and it is the verdict of Abū Ḥanīfah, may Allah, exalted is He, show him mercy."

٨ باب ما لَفَظَه البحرُ من السَّمَك الطّافي وغيره
8. Floating Fish which the Sea casts up, etc.

٦٤٨ أخبرنا مالك، حدثنا نافع، أن ابن عبد الرحمن بن أبي هريرة سأل عبد الله بنَ عمر عمّا لفظه البحر؟ فنهاه عنه، ثم انقلب فدعا بمصحف فقرأ: ﴿أُحِلَّ لَكُمْ صَيْدُ الْبَحْرِ وَطَعَامُهُ﴾، قال نافع: فأرسلني إليه أنْ ليس به بأس فَكُلْه.

648. Mālik informed us: "Nāfiʿ narrated to us that ʿAbd ar-Raḥmān ibn Abī Hurayrah asked ʿAbdullāh ibn ʿUmar about that which the sea casts up, and he forbade him it. Then he [ʿAbdullāh] went back [to his house] and called for a copy of the Qurʾān and recited, 'Anything you catch in the sea is *ḥalāl* for you, and all food from it,' (Sūrat al-Māʾidah: 96)." Nāfiʿ said, "Then he sent me to him as a messenger [to say], 'There is no harm in it, so eat it.'"

قال محمد: وبقول ابن عمر الآخر نأخذ. لا بأس بما لفظه البحر وبما حَسَر عنه الماءُ إنّما يُكره من ذلك الطّافي. وهو قول أبي حنيفة والعامة من فقهائنا رحمهم الله.

Muḥammad said: "This latter verdict of Ibn ʿUmar we adhere to. There is no harm in that which the sea casts up or from which the water recedes thus uncovering it. All that is disapproved of that is what is floating [because it is already dead]. And that is the verdict of Abū Ḥanīfah and of our *fuqahā*ʾ in general, may Allah have mercy on them."

٩ باب السمك يموت في الماء

9. Fish which Die in the Water

٦٤٩ أخبرنا مالك، أخبرنا زيد بن أسلم، عن سعيد الجاريّ بن الجار قال: سألتُ ابنَ عمر عن الحِيْتَان يقتُل بعضُها بعضاً، ويموت صَرَداً وفي أصل ابن الصوّاف: ويموت برداً قال: ليس به بأس. قال: وكان عبد الله بن عمرو بن العاص يقول مثل ذلك.

649. Mālik informed us: "Zayd ibn Aslam informed us that Saʿīd al-Jārī ibn al-Jār said, "I asked ʿUmar about fish which have killed each other or which die from cold (*ṣarad*)," – and in the original of Ibn aṣ-Ṣawwāf – "which die from cold (*bard*)." He said, 'There is no harm in it.'" He said, "ʿAbdullāh ibn ʿAmr ibn al-ʿĀṣ used to say the same as that."

قال محمد: وبهذا نأخذ. إذا ماتت الحيتْان من حَرّ أو برد أو قتلِ بعضها بعضاً فلا بأس بأكلها، فأما إذا ماتت مِيْتَةَ نفسها فَطَفَتْ فهذا يُكْرَه من السمك، فأما سوى ذلك فلا بأس به.

Muḥammad said: "We adhere to this. When fish die from heat or cold or from fighting each other, then there is no harm in eating them. However, if it dies itself of natural causes and then floats to the surface, it is disapproved of to eat this fish. Apart from that case, there is no harm in it."

١٠ باب ذكاةُ الجنين ذكاةُ أمه

10. The Slaughter of the Mother being the Slaughter of the Foetus

٦٥٠ أخبرنا مالك، أخبرنا نافع، أنّ عبد الله بن عمر كان يقول: إذا نُحرت النَّاقةُ فَذَكاةُ ما في بَطْنِهَا ذَكَاتُهَا إذا كانَ قد تمّ خَلْقُه ونَبَت شعره فإذا خرج من بطنها ذُبح حتى يَخرجَ الدمُ من جوفه.

650. Mālik informed us: "Nāfiʿ informed us that ʿAbdullāh ibn ʿUmar used to say, 'When the she-camel is slaughtered then the slaughter of that which is in her womb is [already accomplished by] her slaughter if it is completely formed and its hair has grown. When it emerges from her womb it is slaughtered so that the blood comes out of it.'"[75]

٦٥١ أخبرنا مالك، أخبرنا يزيد بن عبد الله بن قُسَيْط، عن سعيد بن المسيَّب أنه كان يقول: ذكاةُ ما كان في بطن الذبيحة ذكاةُ أمه إذا كان قد نبت شعرُه وتمّ خَلْقه.

651. Mālik informed us: "Yazīd ibn ʿAbdullāh ibn Qusayṭ informed us that Saʿīd ibn al-Musayyab used to say, 'The slaughter of that which is in the womb of the slaughtered animal consists in the slaughter of its mother as long as its hair has grown and it is completely formed.'"

قال محمد: وبهذا نأخذ إذا تَمَّ خَلقه، فذكاته في ذكاة أمّه فلا بأس بأكله. فأما أبو حنيفة فكان يَكره أكلَه حتى يخرجَ حيّاً فيُذكّى، وكان يَرْوي عن حماد عن إبراهيم أنّه قال: لا تكون ذكاةُ نس ذكاة نَفْسَيْن.

Muḥammad said: "This we adhere to if it is completely formed, so that its slaughter consists in the slaughter of its mother and there is no harm in eating it. As for Abū Ḥanīfah, he used to disapprove of eating it unless it emerged alive and was subsequently slaughtered. He used to narrate from Ḥammād from Ibrāhīm that he said, 'The slaughter of one being cannot become the slaughter of two beings.'"

١١ باب أكل الجراد

11. Eating Locusts

٦٥٢ أخبرنا مالك، حدّثنا عبد الله بن دينار، عن عبد الله بن عمر، عن عمر بن الخطّاب رضي الله عنه أنه سئل عن الجراد؟ فقال: وَددتُ أنّ عندي قَفْعَةً من جراد فآكل منه.

652. Mālik informed us: "ᶜAbdullāh ibn Dīnār narrated to us from ᶜAbdullāh ibn ᶜUmar that ᶜUmar ibn al-Khaṭṭāb ﷺ was asked about locusts, and he said, 'I wish I had a basket of locusts so that I could eat from it.'"

قال محمد: وبهذا نأخذُ. فجراد ذُكّي كلّه لا بأس بأكله إن أُخِذَ حيّاً أو ميتاً، وهو ذكيّ على كل حال. وهو قول أبي حنيفة والعامة من فقهائنا.

Muḥammad said: "We adhere to this. The locust is regarded as slaughtered, all of it, and there is no harm in eating it, whether it is taken alive or dead. It is regarded as [having the status of] being slaughtered whatever its condition, and that is the verdict of Abū Ḥanīfah and of our *fuqahāʾ* in general."

١٢ باب ذبائح نصارى العرب

12. Animals Slaughtered by Arab Christians

٦٥٣ أخبرنا مالك، أخبرنا ثور بن زيد الدِّيلي، عن عبد الله بن عباس، أنه سئل عن ذبائح نصارى العرب؟ فقال: لا بأس بها، وتلا هذه الآية ﴿ومن يتولّهم منكم فإنه منهم﴾.

653. Mālik informed us: "Thawr ibn Zayd ad-Dīlī informed us that ᶜAbdullāh ibn ᶜAbbās was asked about the slaughtered animals of Arab christians and he said, 'There is no harm in it,' and then he recited this *āyah*, 'Any of you who takes them as friends is one of them.' (Sūrat al-Māʾidah: 51)"

قال محمد: وبهذا نأخذ. وهو قول أبي حنيفة والعامة.

Muḥammad said: "We adhere to this, and it is the verdict of Abū Ḥanīfah and our *fuqahāʾ* in general."

١٣ باب ما قَتَل الحجر

13. That which has been Killed with a Stone

٦٥٤ أخبرنا مالك، أخبرنا نافع قال: رميْتُ طائرين بحجر وأنا بالجُرُف، فأصبتُهما، فأما أحدهما فمات، فطرحه عبد الله بن عمر، وأما الآخر فذهب عبد الله يذكّيه بقَدُوم فمات قبل أن يذكّيه فطرحه أيضاً.

654. Mālik informed us: "Nāfiᶜinformed us, 'I threw a stone at two birds when I was at Juruf and hit them. One of them died, and ᶜAbdullāh ibn ᶜUmar threw it away. As for the other, ᶜAbdullāh went to slaughter it with an adz,[76] but it died before he could slaughter it and so he threw it away as well."

قال محمد: وبهذا نأخذ. ما رُمي به الطير، فقُتل به قبل أن تُدْرَك ذكاتُه لم يؤكل، إلا أن يخرق أو يُبَضّع فإذا خرق وبضّع فلا بأس بأكله وهو قول أبي حنيفة والعامة من فقهائنا.

Muḥammad said: "We adhere to this. Those birds which have had something thrown at them and which are killed by it before they can be taken and slaughtered, are not to be eaten, unless it is pierced or cut into pieces. If it is pierced or cut into pieces there is no harm in eating it, and that is the verdict of Abū Ḥanīfah and of our *fuqahāʾ* in general."

١٤ باب الشاة وغير ذلك تُذَكّى قبل أن تموت

14. The Ewe or Goat and the like of it which are Slaughtered before they can Die [of natural causes]

٦٥٥ أخبرنا مالك، أخبرنا يحيى بن سعيد، عن أبي مُرَّةَ أنّه سأل أبا هريرة عن شاةٍ ذبحها فتحرّك بعضُها؟ فأمره بأكلها، ثُمَّ سأل زيد ابن ثابت فقال: إنّ الميتة لتتحرك، ونهاه.

655. Mālik informed us: "Yaḥyā ibn Saᶜīd informed us that Abū Murrah asked Abū Hurayrah about a ewe which he slaughtered [when he was afraid that it was dying or dead], a part of which had moved, and he told him to eat it. Then later he asked Zayd ibn Thābit and he said, 'That which has died of natural causes can move,' and he forbade him to eat it."

قال محمد: إذا تحرّكتْ تحرّكاً: أكبرُ الرأي فيه و، الظنُّ أنها حيّة أُكلت، وإذا كان تحرُّكها شبيهاً بالاختلاج، وأكبر الرأي والظن في ذلك أنها ميتة لم تؤكل.

Muḥammad said: "If it moves significantly the dominant view and opinion on it is that it is alive [i.e. before its slaughter], but that if its movement is like a quivering, then the dominant view and opinion about that is that it is an animal that has died of natural causes and it should not be eaten."

١٥ باب الرجل يشتري اللحمَ فلا يدري أذَكِيٌّ هو أم غير ذَكِيّ

15. A Man who Buys Meat not Knowing whether it has been Slaughtered [according to the *Sunnah*] or not

٦٥٦ أخبرنا مالك، أخبرنا هشام بن عروة، عن أبيه أنّه قال سُئِل رسول الله صلى الله عليه وسلم فقيل : يا رسول الله إنّ ناساً من أهل البادية يأتون بلُحْمان فلا ندري هل سَمَّوْا عليها أم لا؟ قال فقال: رسول الله صلى الله عليه وسلم: سَمُّوا الله عليها، ثم كُلوها. قال : وذلك في أول الإسلام .

656. Mālik informed us: "Hishām ibn ʿUrwah informed us that his father said, 'The Messenger of Allah ﷺ was asked, "Messenger of Allah, people from the country come here with meat and we do not know whether they mentioned the name [of Allah] over it or not." The Messenger of Allah ﷺ said, "Say the name of Allah over it and then eat it."'" He [Mālik] said, "And that was in the beginning of Islam."

قال محمد : وبهذا نأخذ . وهو قول أبي حنيفة إذا كان الذي يأتي بها مسلماً أو من أهل الكتاب ، فإن أتى بذلك مجوسي ، وذكر أن مسلماً ذبحه أو رجلاً من أهل الكتاب لم يُصدَّق ولم يُؤْكَلْ بقوله .

Muḥammad said: "We adhere to this, and it is the verdict of Abū Ḥanīfah if the person who brings it is a Muslim or one of the People of the Book. If a Majūsī[77] brings it and he mentions that a Muslim slaughtered it or a man from the People of the Book, he is not to be believed and it is not to be eaten in reliance on his statement."

١٦ باب صيد الكلب المعلَّم

16. The Catch of Trained Hunting Dogs

٦٥٧ أخبرنا مالك، أخبرنا نافع، أن عبد الله بن عمر كان يقول : في الكلب المعلَّم: كُلْ ما أمْسَكَ عليك، وإن قَتَلَ أو لم يَقْتُلْ.

657. Mālik informed us: "Nāfiʿ informed us that ʿAbdullāh ibn ʿUmar used to say concerning trained hunting dogs, 'Eat whatever it catches for you, whether it kills it or does not kill it.'"

قال محمد : وبهذا نأخذ . كل ما قُتل وما لم يُقتل إذا ذكَّيْتَه ما لم يأكل منه، فإنْ أكل فلا تأكل فإنما أمسكه على نفسه . وكذلك بلغنا عن ابن عباس رضي الله تعالى عنه . وهو قولُ أبي حنيفة والعامة من فقهائنا رحمهم الله .

Muḥammad said: "We adhere to this. Whatever is killed [by it], or whatever survives and you then slaughter it, as long as it has not eaten from it. If it eats from it, then do not eat it because it only caught it for itself. Similarly, it has reached us from Ibn ʿAbbās ﷺ and it is the verdict of Abū Ḥanīfah and our *fuqahā᾿* in general, may Allah have mercy on them."

١٧ باب العقيقة

17. ᶜAqīqah

٦٥٨ أخبرنا مالك، حدّثنا زيد بن أسلم، عن رجل من بني ضَمْرة عن أبيه أنّ النبيّ صلى الله عليه وسلم سُئِل عن العقيقة؟ قال: لا أحبّ العقوق، فكأنه إنما كره الاسم، وقال: من وُلد له ولدٌ فأَحَبَّ أن يَنْسُكَ عن ولده فليفعل.

658. Mālik informed us: "Zayd ibn Aslam narrated to us from a man from Banī Ḍamrah from his father that the Prophet ﷺ was asked about the ᶜaqīqah and he answered, 'I do not like disobedience (ᶜ*uqūq*),' as if he did not like the name. He said, 'Whoever has a child born to him and who wants to sacrifice for his child then let him do so.'"

٦٥٩ أخبرنا مالك، أخبرنا نافع عن عبد الله بن عمر أنه لم يكن يسأله أحد من أهله عقيقة إلا أعطاه إياه، وكان يعقّ عن ولده بشاة شاة عن الذكر والأنثى.

659. Mālik informed us: "Nāfiᶜ informed us concerning ᶜAbdullāh ibn ᶜUmar that if any of his family used to ask him for an ᶜ*aqīqah* he would give it to him. He would give a ewe as ᶜ*aqīqah* for his child, whether it was male or female."

٦٦٠ أخبرنا مالك، أخبرنا جعفر بن محمد بن علي، عن أبيه أنّه قال: وزنَتْ فاطمةُ بنت رسول الله ﷺ شعر حسن وحسين رضي الله عنهما وزينب وأمّ كُلثوم فتصدقتْ بوزن ذلك فضّة.

660. Mālik informed us: "Jaᶜfar ibn Muḥammad ibn ᶜAlī informed us that his father said, 'Fāṭimah the daughter of the Messenger of Allah ﷺ weighed the hair of Ḥasan and Ḥusayn ﷺ and that of Zaynab and Umm Kulthūm and gave the weight of that in silver as a *ṣadaqah*.'"

٦٦١ أخبرنا مالك، أخبرني ربيعة بن أبي عبد الرحمن، عن محمد بن علي بن حسين أنّه قال: وزنتْ فاطمة بنت رسول الله صلى الله عليه وسلم شعر حسن وحسين فتصدقتْ بوزنه فضّة.

661. Mālik informed us: "Rabīᶜah ibn ᶜAbd ar-Raḥmān informed me that Muḥammad ibn ᶜAlī ibn Ḥusayn said, 'Fāṭimah the daughter of the Messenger of Allah ﷺ weighed the hair of Ḥasan and Ḥusayn and gave its weight in silver as *ṣadaqah*.'"

قال محمدٌ: أما العقيقة فبلغنا أنها كانت في الجاهلية وقد فُعلت في أول الإسلام ثم نَسَخَ الأَضحى كلَّ ذبح كان قبله ونَسَخَ صومُ شهر رمضان كلَّ صوم كان قبله، ونَسَخَ غُسلُ الجنابة كلَّ غُسل كان قبله، ونَسَخَت الزكاةُ كل صدقة كان قبلها. كذلك بَلَغَنا.

Muḥammad said: "As for the ᶜ*aqīqah*, it has reached us that it used to be done in the *Jāhiliyyah* and was also done in the beginning of Islam, but that later the *Aḍḥā* [sacrifice of the Ḥajj] abrogated every sacrifice that had been before it, and fasting the month of Ramaḍān abrogated every fast which there had been before it, and the *ghusl* after sexual activity abrogates every *ghusl* which used to be done before it, and *zakāh* abrogates every *ṣadaqah* that was done before it. That is how it has reached us."

كتاب الدِّيات

9. COMPENSATION FOR KILLING AND INJURY

٦٦٢ أخبرنا مالك، أخبرنا عبد الله بن أبي بكر أن أباه أخبره عن الكتاب الذي كان رسول الله صلى الله عليه و سلم كَتَبَه لعمرو بن حزم في العُقُول ؛ فكتب أنَّ في النفس مائةً من الإبل، وفي الأنف إذا أُوعِيَتْ جَدْعاً مائةً من الإبل، وفي الجائفة ثلث النفس، وفي المأمومة مثلها، وفي العين خمسين، وفي اليد خمسين، وفي الرِّجْل خمسين، وفي كل إصبع مما هنالك عشر من الإبل، وفي السنّ خمس من الإبل، وفي المُوضحة خمس من الإبل.

662. Mālik informed us: "ᶜAbdullāh ibn Abī Bakr informed us that his father informed him concerning that which the Messenger of Allah ﷺ wrote for ᶜAmr ibn Ḥazm on compensation for bloodshed. He wrote that for a life taken [the payment] is a hundred camels, for a nose – if it is entirely amputated – one hundred camels, for a penetrating wound that reaches the vital organs a third of [the compensation] for the taking of a life and similarly for a wound that penetrates to the brain, for an eye fifty camels, for a hand fifty, for a leg or foot fifty, for each finger or toe ten camels, for teeth five camels, and for a wound that lays bare the bone five camels."

قال محمد: وبهذا كلّه نأخذ، وهو قولُ أبي حنيفة والعامة من فقهائنا.

Muḥammad said: "We adhere to this, all of it, and it is the verdict of Abū Ḥanīfah and our *fuqahā*ʾ in general."

١ باب الدية في الشَّفَتَيْن

1. Section on Compensation for the Lips

٦٦٣ أخبرنا مالك، أخبرنا ابن شهاب، عن سعيد بن المسيِّب أنَّه قال: في الشفتين الدية، فإذا قُطِعَت السفلى، ففيها ثلث الدية.

663. Mālik informed us: "Ibn Shihāb informed us that Saᶜīd ibn al-Musayyab said, 'For the two lips there is a [full] compensation [of one hundred camels]. Then if the lower one [alone] is cut off, there is a third of the [total] compensation for it.'"

قال محمدٌ: ولَسْنا نأخذ بهذا، الشفتان سواء، في كلّ واحدة منهما نصف الدية، ألا ترى أن الخنصر والإبهام سواء ومنفعتهما مختلفة. وهذا قول إبراهيم النخعي وأبي حنيفة والعامة من فقهائنا.

Muḥammad said: "We do not adhere to this. The lips are the same, and for each of them there is a half of the [full] compensation payment [of one hundred camels]. Do you not see that the little finger and the thumb and the largest toe are equal whereas they have different uses and benefits? This is also the verdict of Ibrāhīm an-Nakhaᶜī, Abū Ḥanīfah and our *fuqahā*ᵓ in general."

٢ باب دية العمد

2. Compensation for intentionally [Killing Someone]

٦٦٤ أخبرنا مالك، أخبرنا ابن شهاب، قال: مضت السُّنَّةُ أن العاقلة لا تحمل شيئاً من دِيَة العَمْد إلاَّ أن تشاء.

664. Mālik informed us: "Ibn Shihāb informed us, 'The *Sunnah* has previously been that the male relatives [who would ordinarily help to pay] bear none of the compensation paid for intentional killing unless they want to.'"

قال محمد: وبهذا نأخذ.

Muḥammad said: "We adhere to this."

٦٦٥ أخبرنا عبد الرحمن بن أبي الزِّناد، عن أبيه، عن عبيد الله بن عبد الله بن عُتبة بن مسعود، عن ابن عباس قال: لا تَعقِل العاقلة عمداً، ولا صلحاً، ولا اعترافاً ولا ما جنى المملوك.

665. ᶜAbd ar-Raḥmān ibn Abi'z-Zinād informed us from his father from ᶜUbaydullāh ibn ᶜAbdullāh ibn ᶜUtbah ibn Masᶜūd that Ibn ᶜAbbās said, "The male relatives do not bear [the cost of compensation] for intentional killing, nor [that incurred because of a] covenant, nor [that incurred because of] a confession, nor that which a slave has incurred."

قال محمد وبهذا نأخذ وهو قولُ أبي حنيفة والعامة من فقهائنا.

Muḥammad said: "We adhere to this, and it is the verdict of Abū Ḥanīfah and our *fuqahā*ᵓ in general."

٣ باب دية الخطأ

3. Compensation for Manslaughter [accidental killing]

٦٦٦ أخبرنا مالك، أخبرنا ابن شهاب عن سليمان بن يسار أنه كان يقول: في دية الخطأ عشرون بنتَ مخاض، وعشرون بنتَ لَبون، وعشرون ابنَ لبون، وعشرون حقَّة، وعشرون جَذَعة.

666. Mālik informed us: "Ibn Shihāb informed us that Sulaymān ibn Yasār used to say, 'The compensation for manslaughter [accidental killing, lit.: by mistake] is twenty she-camels just beginning their second year, twenty she-camels just beginning their third year, twenty he-camels just beginning their third year, twenty she-camels just beginning their fourth year, and twenty she-camels just beginning their fifth year."

قال محمدٌ: ولسنا نأخذُ بهذا، ولكنّا نأخذُ بقول عبد الله بن مسعود. وقد رواه ابن مسعود عن النبي صلى الله عليه وسلم أنه قال: دية الخطأ أخماس، عشرون بنت مخاض، وعشرون ابن مخاض، وعشرون بنت لبون، وعشرون حقّة وعشرون جَذَعة أخماس، وإنما خَالَفنا سُليمان بن يسار في الذكور فجعلها من بني اللبون، وجعلها عبد الله بن مسعود من بني مخاض، وهو قولُ أبي حنيفة مثل قول ابن مسعود.

Muḥammad said: "This is not the verdict we adhere to, but we adhere to the verdict of ᶜAbdullāh ibn Masᶜūd. Ibn Masᶜūd narrated that the Prophet ﷺ said, 'The compensatory payment for manslaughter [accidental killing] is in fifths: twenty she-camels just beginning their second year, twenty he-camels just beginning their second year, twenty she-camels just beginning their third year, twenty she-camels just beginning their fourth year, and twenty she-camels just beginning their fifth year, [these] are the fifths.' We only disagree with Sulaymān ibn Yasār concerning the males which he regarded as being in those beginning their third year, and which ᶜAbdullāh ibn Masᶜūd regarded as those beginning their second year, and that is the verdict of Abū Ḥanīfah just as it is the verdict of Ibn Masᶜūd."

٤ باب دية الأسنان

4. Compensation for Teeth

٦٦٧ أخبرنا مالك، أخبرنا داود بن الحُصين أن أبا غَطَفَان أخبره أن مروان بن الحكم أرسله إلى ابن عباس يسأله ما في الضِّرْس؟ فقال: إن فيه خمساً من الإبل، قال: فردَّني مروان إلى ابن عباس، فقال: فلِمَ تجعل مقدّم الفم مثل الأضراس؟ قال: فقال ابن عباس: لولا أنك لا تعتبر إلاّ بالأصابع عَقْلها سَواءٌ.

667. Mālik informed us: "Dāwūd ibn al-Ḥuṣayn informed us that Abū Ghaṭafān informed him that Marwān ibn al-Ḥakam sent him as a messenger to Ibn ᶜAbbās to ask him what [the compensation payment was] for a molar tooth. He answered, 'For it there are [to be paid] five camels.' Marwān sent me back to Ibn ᶜAbbās to ask, 'Why do you regard the [teeth at the] front of the mouth the same as the molar teeth?' Ibn ᶜAbbās answered, 'If only you were to reckon it according to the fingers; their compensation payments is the same[78].'"

قال محمد: وبقول ابن عباس نأخذُ، عقل الأسنان سواءٌ، وعقل الأصابع سواء، في كل إصبع عشر من الدية وفي كل سنّ نصف عشر من الدية، وهو قول أبي حنيفة والعامة من فقهائنا.

Muḥammad said: "We adhere to the verdict of Ibn ᶜAbbās: the compensation for each tooth is the same, and the compensation for each finger is the same. For each finger there is a tenth of the compensation,[79] and for each tooth there is half of a tenth of the compensation,[80] and that is the verdict of Abū Ḥanīfah and of our *fuqahā᾽* in general."

٥ باب أَرش السنِّ السوداء والعين القائمة

5. Compensation for a blackened Tooth and for an Eye which Remains [but is blinded]

٦٦٨ أخبرنا مالك، أخبرنا يحيى بن سعيد، أن سعيد بن المسيّب كان يقول: إذا أصيبت السنّ فاسودّت ففيها عَقْلها تامّاً.

668. Mālik informed us: "Yaḥyā ibn Saᶜīd informed us that Saᶜīd ibn al-Musayyab used to say, 'If a tooth is struck and it turns black, then the complete compensation [for a tooth] must be paid for it.'"

قال محمدٌ: وبهذا نأخذ، إذا أصيبت السنّ فاسودّت أو احمرّت أو اخضرّت، فقد تم عقلها وهو قول أبي حنيفة.

Muḥammad said: "We adhere to this. If a tooth is struck and it turns black, red or green then the complete compensation must be paid for it, and that is the verdict of Abū Ḥanīfah."

٦٦٩ أخبرنا مالك، أخبرنا يحيى بن سعيد، عن سليمان بن يسار أن زيد بن ثابت كان يقول: في العين القائمة إذا فُقئت مائة دينار.

669. Mālik informed us: "Yaḥyā ibn Saᶜīd informed us from Sulaymān ibn Yasār that Zayd ibn Thābit used to say, 'For the eye which remains but is blinded, a hundred dīnārs [must be paid].'"

قال محمدٌ: ليس عندنا فيها أرش معلوم، ففيها حكومة عدل، فإن بلغت الحكومة مائة دينار أو أكثر من ذلك، كانت الحكومة فيها، وإنما نضع هذا من زيد بن ثابت لأنه حكم بذلك.

Muḥammad said: "We have no known compensation for it and there has to be a just ruling made. If the ruling reaches a hundred dīnārs or more than that, then that is the ruling for it. We only implement this from Zayd ibn Thābit because he passed that judgement."

٦ باب النَّفَر يجتمعون على قتل واحد

6. A Group of Men Gathering to Kill one Man

٦٧٠ أخبرنا مالك، أخبرنا يحيى بن سعيد، عن سعيد بن المسيّب: أن عمر بن الخطاب قتل نفراً خمسة أو سبعة برجل قَتَلوه قَتْل غيلة وقال: لو تمالأ عليه أهل صنعاء قتلتهم به.

670. Mālik informed us: "Yaḥyā ibn Saᶜīd informed us from Saᶜīd ibn al-Musayyab that ᶜUmar ibn al-Khaṭṭāb killed a group of men – five or seven – for one man whom they had killed treacherously, and he said, 'Even if the people of Ṣanāᶜ had conspired against him, I would have killed them [all in retaliation] for him.'"

قال محمد: وبهذا نأخذ، إنْ قَتل سبعة أو أكثر من ذلك رجلاً عمداً قَتْلَ غيلة أو غير غيلة ضربوه بأسيافهم حتى قتَلوه قُتلُوْا به كلُّهم، وهو قولُ أبي حنيفة والعامَّة من فقهائنا رحمهم الله.

Muḥammad said: "We adhere to this. If seven or more than that deliberately kill a man, whether by treachery or not, striking him with their swords until they kill him, then all of them are killed [in retaliation] for him, and that is the verdict of Abū Ḥanīfah and of our *fuqahā᾿* in general, may Allah have mercy on them."

٧ باب الرجل يرث من دية امرأته والمرأة ترث من دية زوجها

7. A Man Inheriting the Compensation Payments of his Wife and the Wife Inheriting the Compensation Payments of her Husband

٦٧١ أخبرنا مالك، أخبرنا ابن شهاب أن عمر بن الخطاب نَشَدَ الناس بمنىً: من كان عنده علم في الدية أن يخبرني به، فقام الضحّاك بن سفيان، فقال: كتب إليَّ رسولُ الله صلى الله عليه وسلم في أَشْيَم الضِّبابي أن ورِّث امرأته من دِيَته، فقال عمر: ادْخُل الخِباءَ حتى آتيَك، فلما نزل أخبره الضحّاك بن سفيان بذلك، فقضى به عمر بن الخطاب.

671. Mālik informed us: "Ibn Shihāb informed us that ᶜUmar ibn al-Khaṭṭāb demanded to know of people at Minā, 'Whoever has knowledge of compensation should tell me about it.' Aḍ-Ḍaḥḥāk ibn Sufyān stood up and said, 'The Messenger of Allah ﷺ wrote to me about Ashyam aḍ-Ḍibābī, "Let his wife inherit from his compensation payment."' ᶜUmar said, 'Enter the tent [and wait] until I come to you.' When ᶜUmar came in, aḍ-Ḍaḥḥāk bin Sufyān informed him about it, and ᶜUmar ibn al-Khaṭṭāb passed judgement on that basis."

قال محمد: وبهذا نأخذ، لكل وارث في الدية والدّم نصيبٌ، امرأةً كان الوارث أو زوجاً أو غير ذلك. وهو قول أبي حنيفة والعامة من فقهائنا.

Muḥammad said: "We adhere to this. Each heir has a portion in the compensation and the right to retaliation [for premeditated murder], whether the heir is a woman, a husband or anyone else. This is the verdict of Abū Ḥanīfah and our *fuqahā᾿* in general."

٨ باب الجروح وما فيها من الأرش

8. Wounds and their Compensation

٦٧٢ أخبرنا مالك، أخبرنا يحيى بن سعيد، عن سعيد بن المسيّب، قال: في كل نافذة، في عضو من الأعضاء ثلث عقل ذلك العضو.

672. Mālik informed us: "Yaḥyā ibn Saᶜīd informed us that Saᶜīd ibn al-Musayyab said, 'For every piercing stab wound in any of the limbs there is [to be paid] a third of the compensation for [the total destruction or amputation of] that limb.'"

قال محمد: في ذلك أيضاً حكومة عدل، وهو قول أبي حنيفة والعامة من فقهائنا.

Muḥammad said: "For that also the judgement of just person must be rendered[81], and that is the verdict of Abū Ḥanīfah and of our *fuqahā᾿* in general."

٩ باب دية الجنين

9. The Compensation for a Foetus

٦٧٣ أخبرنا مالك، أخبرنا ابن شهاب، عن سعيد بن المسيّب: أن رسول الله قضى في الجنين يُقْتَلُ في بطن أمه بغُرَّة عبد أو وليدة، فقال الذي قضى عليه: كيف أغْرَمُ مَنْ لاَ شَرِبَ وَلاَ أَكَلَ، وَلاَ نَطَقَ، وَلاَ اسْتَهَلَّ، وَمِثْلُ ذَلِكَ يُطَلُّ، قال: فقال رسول الله ﷺ إنما هذا من أخوان الكُهَّان.

673. Mālik informed us: "Ibn Shihāb informed us from Sa^cīd ibn al-Musayyab that the Messenger of Allah ﷺ gave a judgement concerning the foetus that is killed in its mother's womb [that there should be paid in compensation] a fair-complexioned male or female slave. The one against whom he passed judgement asked, 'How can I pay for one who has neither drunk nor eaten, has neither spoken nor cried out, and the like of whom is of no account [in not having to be paid compensation for]?'[82]" He [Sa^cīd ibn al-Musayyab] said, "The Messenger of Allah ﷺ said, 'This is one of the brotherhood of the soothsayers.'"

٦٧٤ أخبرنا مالك، أخبرنا ابن شهاب، عن أبي سلمة بن عبد الرحمن، عن أبي هريرة: أن امرأتين من هُذَيْل استَبَّتَا في زمان رسول الله صلى الله عليه وسلم فَرَمَتْ إحداهما الأُخرى، فَطَرَحَتْ جنينها، فقضى فيه رسول الله صلى الله عليه وسلم بغرّة عبد أو وليدة.

674. Mālik informed us: "Ibn Shihāb informed us from Abū Salamah ibn ^cAbd ar-Raḥmān from Abū Hurayrah that two women of Hudhayl laid curses on each other during the life of the Messenger of Allah ﷺ and one of them threw [a projectile] at the other, who miscarried her baby. The Messenger of Allah ﷺ passed the judgement that there should be [paid in compensation] for him a fair-complexioned male or female slave."

قال محمد: وبهذا نأخذ، إذا ضُرِب بطن المرأة الحرّة فألقت جنيناً ميّتاً، ففيه غُرَّةُ عبدٍ أو أمة أو خمسون ديناراً أو خمس مائة درهم نصف عُشر الدية فإن كان من أهل الإبل أخذ منه خمسٌ من الإبل وإن كان من أهل الغنم أخذ منه مائة من الشاة نصف عُشر الدية.

Muḥammad said: "We adhere to this. If the womb of a free woman is struck and she delivers a still-born child, then there should be [paid in compensation] for it a fair-complexioned male or female slave, or fifty dīnārs or five hundred dirhams, which is a twentieth part of the complete compensation [for homicide]. If he is an owner of camels, then five camels are taken from him. If he is an owner of sheep, then a hundred ewes are taken from him [each of which are] a twentieth part of the [complete] compensation payment."

١٠ باب الموضحة في الوجه والرأس

10. Facial and Cranial Wounds which Lay bare the Bone

٦٧٥ أخبرنا مالك، أخبرنا يحيى بن سعيد، عن سليمان بن يسار أنه قال في الموضحة في الوجه: إن لم تُعبْ الوجهَ مثل ما في المُوضحة في الرأس.

675. Mālik informed us: "Yaḥyā ibn Sa^cīd informed us that Sulaymān ibn

Yasār said about a facial wound which lays bare the bone, 'If it does not scar the face then it is the like of [the compensation for] a cranial wound which lays bare the bone.'"

قال محمد: الموضحة في الوجه والرأس سواء، في كل واحدة نصف عشر الدية، وهو قول إبراهيم النَّخَعي وأبي حنيفة والعامة من فقهائنا.

Muḥammad said: "Facial and cranial wounds which lay bare the bone are the same. For each of them there is [to be paid] a twentieth of the [full] compensation, and that is the verdict of Abū Ḥanīfah and of our *fuqahāʾ* in general."

١١ باب البئر جُبار

11. [Death or Injury Caused by] a Well is to be Unretaliated and Uncompensated for

٦٧٦ أخبرنا مالك، حدّثنا ابن شهاب، عن سعيد بن المسيّب، وعن أبي سلمة بن عبد الرحمن، عن أبي هريرة أن رسول الله صلى اللّه عليه وسلم قال: جَرْحُ العجماء جُبار، والبئر جُبار، والمعدن جُبار، وفي الركاز الخمس.

676. Mālik informed us: "Ibn Shihāb narrated to us from Saʿīd ibn al-Musayyab and from Abū Salamah ibn ʿAbd ar-Raḥmān from Abū Hurayrah that the Messenger of Allah ﷺ said, "The wound [caused by] an escaped animal [*ʿujmāʾ*] is uncompensated and unretaliated [*jubār*], and [death or injury caused by] a well is unretaliated and uncompensated, and [death or injury caused by] a mine is unretaliated and uncompensated, and on minerals [*rikāz*][83] there is a fifth [due in *zakāh*]."

قال محمدٌ: وبهذا نأخذ. والجبار الهَدَرُ، والعجماء الدابة المنفلتة تجرحُ الإنسان أو تعقره، والبئر والمعدن، الرجلُ يستأجر الرجلَ يحفر له بئراً ومعدناً، فيسقط عليه، فيقتله فذلك هدرٌ. وفي الركاز الخمس، و الركاز ما استخرج من المعدن من ذهب أو فضّة أو رَصَاص أو نحاس أو حديد أو زيبق، ففيه الخمس وهو قول أبي حنيفة والعامة من فقهائنا.

Muḥammad said: "We adhere to this. And The meaning of jubār is [the same as the meaning of] hadar [both meaning of no account or unretaliated and uncompensated]. ʿUjmāʾ means a beast which has got loose and which injures or wounds a man. The [reference to a] well and the mine is that a man employs another man to dig a well or a mine for him, but it collapses on top of him and kills him. That is unretaliated and uncompensated. On rikāz there [must be paid] a fifth, and rikāz is that which is brought out of the mines such as gold, silver, lead, copper, iron or mercury, on which there is [to be paid] a fifth, and that is the verdict of Abū Ḥanīfah and of our *fuqahāʾ* in general."

٦٧٧ أخبرنا مالك، حدثنا ابن شهاب، عن حازم بن سَعيد بن مُحيِّصَة: أنّ ناقةً للبراء بن عازب

دخلت حائطاً لرجلٍ فأفسدَتْ فيه ، فقضى رسول الله صلى الله عليه وسلم أن على أهل الحائط حفظَها بالنهار، وأنّ ما أفسدت المواشي بالليل فالضمان على أهلها .

677. Mālik informed us: "Ibn Shihāb narrated to us from Ḥāzim ibn Saᶜīd ibn Muḥayyiṣah that a she-camel of al-Barā᾿ ibn ᶜĀzib entered a walled garden of a man and created chaos in it. The Messenger of Allah ﷺ gave the judgement that the owners of the walled garden must protect it during the day, and that whatever livestock ruin at night then their owners are liable for it."

١٢ باب من قَتَل خطأً ولم تُعرف له عاقلة

12. Someone who Kills accidentally and whose Relatives Responsible for Paying the Compensation payments are unknown

٦٧٨ أخبرنا مالك، أخبرني أبو الزِّناد أن سليمان بن يسار أخبره أن سائبة كان أعتقه بعضُ الحُجّاج ، فكان يَلْعَبُ مع ابن رجل من بني عابد ، فقتل السائبةُ ابنَ العابدي، فجاء العابديُّ أبو المقتول إلى عمر بن الخطاب، فطلب دية ابنه، فأبى عُمَر أن يَدِيَه، وقال: ليس له مولىً، فقال العابديُّ له : أرأيت لو أنَّ ابْني قَتَلَه ؟ قال: إذَنْ تُخْرِجُوا دِيَتَه، قال العَابديُّ : هو إذَنْ كالأَرْقَم إنْ يُتْرَكْ يَلْقَمْ وإن يُقْتَلْ يَنْقَمْ.

678. Mālik informed us: "Abu'z-Zinād informed us that Sulaymān ibn Yasār informed him that one of the people on Ḥajj had freed a slave and that he [the freed slave] had been playing with the son of a man from Banī ᶜĀbid, and the freed slave had killed the son of the ᶜĀbidī man. The ᶜĀbidī who was the father of the person who had been killed had come to ᶜUmar ibn al-Khaṭṭāb and demanded the compensation payment for his son, but ᶜUmar had refused to pay a compensation payment. He said, 'He has no *mawlā*.'[84] The ᶜĀbidī man asked, 'What do you think would be the case if my son had killed him?' He answered, 'Then you all would have to pay his compensation payment.' The ᶜĀbidī man said, 'Then he is like the black and white Arqam snake which if it is left alone will devour you and if it is killed will take revenge.[85]'"

قال محمدٌ: وبهذا نأخذُ، لا نرى أنَّ عمر أَبْطل ديتَه عن القاتل ولا نراه أبطل ذلك لأن له عاقلة، ولكن عمر لم يعرفها فيجعل الدية على العاقلة، ولو أن عمر لم يرَ له مولىً، ولا أنَّ له عاقلة لجَعَلَ دية من قُتلَ في ماله أو على بيت المال ، ولكنه رأى له عاقلةً ولم يعرفهم لأن بعضِ الحُجَّاج أعتَقَه ولم يُعْرَفْ المُعْتَقُ ولا عاقلته فأبطل ذلك عمر حتى يُعْرَفَ ، ولو كان لا يرى له عاقلةً لجعل ذلك عليه في ماله أو على المسلمين في بيت مالهم.

Muḥammad said: "We adhere to this. We do not think that ᶜUmar invalidated the compensation payment from the killer and we do not think that he invalidated that, because he did have a group of people responsible for paying his compensatory payment, but ᶜUmar did not know who they were so that he could place the responsibility for the compensation payment on them. If it had been that ᶜUmar did not think he had a *mawlā* nor that he had a body of people responsible for his compensation payment, then he would have regarded the compensation for the victim as due on that person's wealth or due on the *bayt al-māl*. However, he regarded him as having a body of people responsible for his compensation payment but he did not know who they were since someone on Ḥajj had freed him but it was not known who the person was nor who the body of people were who were responsible for the compensation payment. So ᶜUmar invalidated it until such time as they should be discovered. If he had not regarded him as having a body of people who were responsible for his compensation payment, then he would have made him personally responsible to pay it from his personal property or he would have made it the responsibility of the Muslims to pay from the *bayt al-māl*."

١٣ باب القسامة

13. The [Oath Known as] *Qasāmah*

٦٧٩ أخبرنا مالك، أخبرنا ابن شهاب، عن سليمان بن يسار وعراك بن مالك الغفاري أنهما حدَّثاه أن رجلاً من بني سعد بن ليث أجرى فرساً فوطِئ على إصبع رجل من بني جُهَينة فَنَزَف منها الدم فمات ، فقال عمر بن الخطاب للذين ادُّعي عليهم: أتَحْلفُون خمسين يميناً ما مات منها؟ فأبَوا وتحرَّجوا من الأَيْمان، فقال للآخرين : احلفُوا أنتم، فأَبَوْا فقَضي بشطر الدية على السعديِّين.

679. Mālik informed us: "Ibn Shihāb informed us that both Sulaymān ibn Yasār and ᶜIrāk ibn Mālik al-Ghifārī narrated to him that a man of Banī Saᶜd ibn Layth galloped his horse and it trod on the toe of a man from Banī Juhaynah. Blood flowed copiously from it and he died. ᶜUmar ibn al-Khaṭṭāb said to the ones against whom the claim was made, 'Do you swear fifty oaths that he did not die because of it?' But they refused [to swear] and shunned it as a wrong act, so he said to the others, 'Then you swear,' but they also refused. So he gave the judgement that a half of the compensation was due from the people of Banī Saᶜd."[86]

٦٨٠ أخبرنا مالك، حدَّثنا أبو ليلى بن عبد الله بن عبد الرحمن، عن سهل بن أبي حثمة، أنه أخبره رجال من كبراء قومه أن عبدَ الله بن سهل ومُحَيِّصة خرجا إلى خيبر من جهد أصابهما، فأُتي مُحيّصة فَأُخْبِر أن عبد الله بن سهل قد قُتل، وطُرِح في فقير أو عين، فأتى يهودَ، فقال : أنتم قتلتموه؟ فقالوا : والله ما قتلناه، ثم أقبل حتى قدم على قومه، فذكر ذلك لهم ثم أقبل هو وحُوَيّصة ، وهو أخوه أكبر منه وعبد الرحمن بن سهل فذهب ليتكلم، وهو الذي كان بخيبر، فقال له رسول الله صلى الله عليه وسلم: كبِّر كبِّر، يريد السنّ فتكلم حُوَيِّصَةُ، ثم تكلم مُحَيِّصَة، فقال رسول الله صلى الله عليه وسلم: إما أن يدُوا صاحبكم وإما أن يُؤْذَنُوا بحرب، فكتب إليهم رسول الله صلى الله عليه وسلم في ذلك فكتبوا له: إنّا والله ما قتلناه، فقال رسول الله صلى الله عليه وسلم لحويصة ومحيصة وعبد الرحمن : تَحْلِفُون وتَستَحِقُّون دمَ صاحبكم، قالوا : لا ، قال : فتحلف لكم يهود،

قالوا: لا، ليسوا بمسلمين. فَوَدَاه رسول الله صلى الله عليه وسلم من عنده ، فبعث إليهم بمائة ناقة حتى أُدخلت عليهم الدار . قال سهل بن أبي حثمة: لقد ركضتني منها ناقةٌ حمراء.

680. Mālik informed us: "Abū Laylā ibn ᶜAbdullāh ibn ᶜAbd ar-Raḥmān narrated to us that Sahl ibn Abī Ḥathmah narrated to him that some notable men of his people had informed him that ᶜAbdullāh ibn Sahl and Muḥayyiṣah went to Khaybar because of some distressing circumstances which afflicted them. Muḥayyiṣah was brought and told that ᶜAbdullāh ibn Sahl had been killed and flung down a well or a spring. So he went to the jews and asked, 'Did you kill him?' and they said, 'By Allah! we did not kill him.' Then he turned away and went to his people and mentioned that to them. He and Ḥuwayyiṣah – his elder brother – came forward as well as ᶜAbd ar-Raḥmān ibn Sahl and he [Muḥayyiṣah] began to speak, as he was the one who had been at Khaybar. The Messenger of Allah ﷺ said to him, 'The greater, the greater,' meaning in age, and so Ḥuwayyiṣah spoke and then Muḥayyiṣah spoke. The Messenger of Allah ﷺ said, 'Either they will pay the compensation for your companion or they will have war declared against them.' The Messenger of Allah ﷺ wrote to them about it and they wrote back to him, 'We, by Allah! did not kill him.' The Messenger of Allah ﷺ said to Ḥuwayyiṣah, Muḥayyiṣah and ᶜAbd ar-Raḥmān, 'You must take an oath and then you may receive what is due to you for the death of your companion.' They said, 'No.'[87] He said, 'So then the jews will swear an oath to you [that they did not kill him].' They said, 'No, they are not Muslims.' So the Messenger of Allah ﷺ paid the compensation himself[88] and he sent them one hundred she-camels [so many that they] entered into their house. Sahl ibn Abī Ḥathmah said, 'One red camel from among them kicked me.'"

قال محمد : إنما قال لهم رسولُ الله صلى الله عليه وسلم : أتَحْلِفُون وتستحقون دمَ صاحبكم، يعني بالدية ليس بالقَوَد، وإنما يدل على ذلك: أنه إنما أراد الدية دون القَود قوله في أول الحديث إما أن تَدُوا صاحبَكم، وإما أن تؤذَنوا بحرب. فهذا يدل على آخر الحديث ، وهو قوله: تحلفون وتستحقون دمَ صاحبكم، لأنَّ الدم قد يُستَحَقُّ بالدِّية كما يُستَحَقُّ بالقَوَد، لأنَّ النبي صلى الله عليه وسلم لم يقل لهم : تحلفون وتستحقون دم من ادَّعَيْتُم فيكون هذا على القود، وإنما قال لهم : تحلفون وتستحقون دم صاحبكم فإنما عَنَى به تستحقون دم صاحبكم بالدية، لأن أول الحديث يدل على ذلك وهو قوله: إما أن تَدُوا صاحبكم، وإما أن تُؤْذَنُوا بحرب، وقد قال عمر بن الخطاب: القَسامةُ توجب العَقْل ، ولا تُشيْطُ الدم في أحاديث كثيرة، فبهذا نأخذ وهو قولُ أبي حنيفة والعامة من فقهائنا.

Muḥammad said: "The Messenger of Allah ﷺ only said to them, 'Will you take an oath and receive what is due to you for the death of your companion?'[89] meaning a compensation payment and not the execution of the killer. What shows that he only meant compensation rather than the execution of the killer are his words at the beginning of the *ḥadīth,* 'Either you [jews] will pay the compensation for your companion or you will have war declared against you.'[90] This indicates the end of the *ḥadīth* which is his saying, 'You must take an oath and then you may receive what is due to you for the death of your companion,' because the taking of a life or inflicting an injury requires compensation just as it can require retaliation, because the Prophet ﷺ did not say to them, 'Swear an oath and claim as your right to the life of the one whom you claim [committed the murder],' which would be so in the case of retaliatory killing, but he only said to them, 'You must take an oath and then you may receive what is due to you for the death of your companion,' by which he simply meant 'you may receive what is due to you for the death of your companion by way of compensation,' because the beginning of the *ḥadīth* show that, i.e. his words, 'Either you [jews] will pay the compensation for your companion or you will have war declared against you.' ʿUmar ibn al-Khaṭṭāb said, 'The [oath of] *qasāmah* necessarily requires compensation and it does not [lead to] shedding of blood [as is shown] in many *aḥādīth*.' We adhere to this and it is the verdict of Abū Ḥanīfah and of our *fuqahāʾ* in general."

كتاب الحدود في السرقة

10. THE *ḤUDŪD* LIMITS WITH RESPECT TO THEFT

١ باب العبد يسرق من مولاه

1. A Slave who Steals from his Master

٦٨١ أخبرنا مالك، حدثنا الزهري، عن السائب بن يزيد أن عبد الله بن عمرو الحضرمي جاء إلى عمر بن الخطاب رضي الله عنه بعبد له، فقال: اقطع هذا فإنه سرق، فقال: وماذا سرق؟ فقال: سرق مرآة لامرأتي ثمنها ستون درهماً، قال عمر: أرسله ليس عليه قطع، خادمكم سرق متاعكم.

681. Mālik informed us: "Az-Zuhrī narrated to us from as-Sāʾib ibn Yazīd that ʿAbdullāh ibn ʿAmr al-Ḥaḍramī brought a slave of his to ʿUmar ibn al-Khaṭṭāb ﷺ and said, 'Cut off [the hand of] this one, because he stole.' He asked, 'What did he steal?' He answered, 'He stole a mirror of my wife's whose value is sixty dirhams.' ʿUmar said, 'Let him go. He is not liable to have [his hand] cut off. Your servant stole your goods.'"

قال محمد: وبهذا نأخذ. أيّما رجل له عبد سرق من ذي رحم محرم منه أو من مولاه أو من امرأة مولاه أو من زوج مولاته فلا قطع عليه في ما يسرق وكيف يكون عليه القطع فيما سرق من أخته أو أخيه أو عمّته أو خالته، وهو لو كان محتاجاً زَمِناً أو صغيراً أو كانت محتاجة أُجبر على نفقتهم فكان لهم في ماله نصيب، فكيف يقطع من سَرق ممن له في ماله نصيب؟! وهذا كله قول أبي حنيفة والعامة من فقهائنا.

Muḥammad said: "We adhere to this. If a man's slave steals from someone related [to the slave] to whom he is an unmarriageable male relative (*maḥram*), or from his master or from his master's wife or from his mistress's husband then he is not liable to the penalty of cutting off [the hand] for what he stole. How could he be liable to amputation [of the hand] for what he stole from his sister or his brother, or from his paternal or maternal aunts, whereas if he was in dire straits, chronically ill or a minor, or conversely if they were in dire straits, then he would be compelled to spend upon them for their needs and they would thus have a right to a portion of his wealth,[91] and so how could someone who stole from someone part of whose wealth he owns, have his hand cut off? All of this is the verdict of Abū Ḥanīfah and of our *fuqahāʾ* in general."

٢ باب من سرق ثمراً أو غير ذلك مما لم يُحْرَزْ

2. Someone who Steals Fruit or other Things which are Left Unguarded

٦٨٢ أخبرنا مالك، حدّثنا عبد الله بن عبد الرحمن بن أبي حسين أن رسول الله صلى الله عليه وسلم قال: لا قطع في ثمر معلّق ، ولا في حريسة جَبَل ، فإذا آواه المُرَاحُ أو الجَرِيْنُ فالقطع في ما بلغ ثمن المِجَنّ .

682. Mālik informed us: "ᶜAbdullāh ibn ᶜAbd ar-Raḥmān ibn Abī Ḥusayn narrated that the Messenger of Allah ﷺ said, 'There is to be no cutting off [of the hand] for fruit which is attached [to the trees], nor for things [sheep and goats] stolen from the mountain [at night], but when they [sheep and goats] are collected in their enclosure [at night] and [the fruits] are collected in their area for drying, then amputation is for whatever amounts to the value of a shield.'"

قال محمد: وبهذا نأخذ. من سَرَق ثمراً في رأس النخل أو شاةً في المرعى فلا قطع عليه، فإذا أُتيَ بالثمر الجرينَ أو البيت وأُتي بالغنم المُرَاحَ، وكان لها من يَحْفَظُها، فجاء سارق سرق من ذلك شيئاً يساوي ثمن المِجَنِّ، ففيه القطعُ، والمجنّ كان يساوي يومئذٍ عَشَرَةَ دراهم، ولا يقطع في أقلّ من ذلك. وهو قولَ أبي حنيفة والعامة منَ فقهائنا رحمهم الله.

Muḥammad said: "We adhere to this. Someone who steals fruits from the top of a tree or sheep from their pasturage is not liable to amputation. But if the fruits are brought to their drying floor or to the house, and sheep and goats are brought to their enclosure and there is someone there to guard them, and then a thief comes and steals anything from it whose value amounts to that of a shield, then he is liable to amputation [of the hand]. A shield at that time used to be worth ten dirhams, and there was no amputation for less than that. And That is the verdict of Abū Ḥanīfah and of our *fuqahāʾ* in general, may Allah have mercy on them."

٦٨٣ أخبرنا مالك، أخبرنا يحيى بن سعيد، عن محمد بن يحيى بن حَبّان أنّ غلاماً سرق وَدِيّاً من حائط رجل، فَغَرَسه في حائط سيّده، فخَرَج صاحبُ الوَدِيّ يلتمس وَدِيَّه فوجده، فاستعدى عليه مروانَ بنَ الحكم، فسجنَه وأراد قطعَ يده، فانطلق سيِّدُ العبد إلى رافع بنَ خَديج ، فسأله فأخبره أنه سمع رسولَ الله صلى الله عليه وسلم يقول : لا قطع في ثمرٍ ولا كَثَرٍ. والكَثَر الجُمّار.

قال الرجل : إن مروان أخذ غلامي وهو يريد قطعَ يده، فأنا أحبّ أن تمشي إليه فتخبره بالذي سمعت من رسول الله صلى الله عليه وسلم، فمشى معه حتى أتى مروان، فقال له رافع: أخذتَ غلامَ هذا؟ فقال : نعم، قال: فما أنت صانع قال: : أريد قطع يده، قال : فإني سمعت رسول الله صلى الله عليه وسلم يقول: لا قطع في ثمر ولا كَثَر، فأمر مروان بالعبد فأُرسل .

683. Mālik informed us: "Yaḥyā ibn Saᶜīd informed us from Muḥammad ibn Yaḥyā ibn Ḥabbān that a slave stole a small shoot or branch from a palm tree [intended for replanting] from a man's walled garden and planted it in his owner's walled garden. The owner of the shoot went out looking for his shoot and found it. He demanded of Marwān ibn al-Ḥakam that he should

have him brought before him, and so he imprisoned him and wanted to cut his hand off. The slave's owner went off to Rāfi^c ibn Khadīj and asked him, and he told him that he had heard the Messenger of Allah ﷺ saying, 'There is to be no amputation for fruit or for spadices.' The spadix is the heart or pith of the palm tree. The man said, 'Marwān took my slave and wants to cut his hand off, and so I want you to go and inform him of what you heard from the Messenger of Allah ﷺ.' So he walked with him until he reached Marwān, and Rāfi^c said to him, 'You took this man's slave?' He replied, 'Yes.' He asked him, 'Then what are you going to do?' He answered, 'I mean to cut off his hand.' He said, 'I heard the Messenger of Allah ﷺ saying, "There is no amputation for fruits nor for spadices."' So Marwān ordered that the slave be set free."

قال محمدٌ: وبهذا نأخذ. لا قطع في ثمر معلَّقٍ في شجر ولا في كَثَر والكَثَر الجُمَّار ولا في وَدِيّ ولا في شجر. وهو قول أبي حنيفة رحمه الله.

Muḥammad said: "We adhere to this. There is no amputation for fruits still attached to the tree nor for the spadix – and the spadix is the pith or heart of the palm tree – nor for a shoot or branch intended for replanting nor for a tree, and that is the verdict of Abū Ḥanīfah, may Allah have mercy on him."

٣ باب الرجل يُسرَق منه الشيء يجب فيه القطع فيهبه السارقَ بعد ما يرفعه إلى الإمام

3. A Man from whom Something is Stolen for which the Amputation [of the hand] is Required, but He Gives it as a Gift to the Thief after He had Raised the Matter to the *Imām*

٦٨٤ أخبرنا مالك، حدَّثنا الزهري، عن صفوان بن عبد الله بن أمية: قال: قيل لصفوان بن أمية: إنه مَنْ لم يُهاجر هلك، فدعا براحلته، فركبها حتى قَدِم على رسول الله صلى الله عليه وسلم، فقال: إنه قد قيل لي: إنه من لم يهاجر هلك، فقال له رسول الله صلى الله عليه وسلم: ارجعْ أبا وهب إلى أباطح مكة، فنام صفوان في المسجد متوسداً رداءَهُ فجاءه سارق فأخذ رداءَه، فأخذَ السارق فأتى به رسولَ الله صلى الله عليه وسلم فأمر رسول الله صلى الله عليه وسلم بالسارق أنْ تُقطعَ يده، فقال صفوان: يا رسول الله إني لم أُرِدْ هذا، هو عليه صدقة، فقال رسول الله صلى الله عليه وسلم: فهلاَّ قبل أن تأتيني به.

684. Mālik informed us: "Az-Zuhrī narrated to us that Ṣafwān ibn ^cAbdullāh ibn Umayyah said, 'Someone said to Ṣafwān ibn Umayyah that anyone who did not emigrate would perish, and so he called for his mount and rode it until he came to the Messenger of Allah ﷺ. He said, "Someone said to me, 'Whoever does not emigrate will perish.'" The Messenger of Allah ﷺ said to him, "Return, Abū Wahb, to the valleys of Makkah." So Ṣafwān slept in the mosque using his large outer garment as a pillow, and then a thief came and

took the garment. He caught the thief and took him to the Messenger of Allah ﷺ and the Messenger of Allah ﷺ ordered that the thief should have his hand cut off. Ṣafwān said, "Messenger of Allah, I didn't mean this. It is a *ṣadaqah* for him." The Messenger of Allah ﷺ said, "If only you had done it before bringing him to me."'"

قال محمد : إذا رُفع السارق إلى الإمام أو القاذف ، فوهب صاحبُ الحدِّ حدَّه لم يَنْبَغِ للإمام أن يعطِّل الحدّ، ولكنه يُمْضِيْه . وهو قولُ أبي حنيفة والعامة من فقهائنا .

Muḥammad said: "When the thief is brought before the *imām* or the slanderer [is brought before him], and the one who has the right to have the punishment for contravening the limit [*ḥadd*] applied relinquishes his [right to apply the] *ḥadd*, it is not correct for the *imām* not to apply the *ḥadd*, but he must carry it out. That is the verdict of Abū Ḥanīfah and of our *fuqahā᾽* in general."

٤ باب ما يجب فيه القطع

4. That for which Amputation is Required

٦٨٥ أخبرنا مالك، أخبرنا نافع مولى عبد الله بن عمر، عن ابن عمر : أن النبي صلى الله عليه وسلم قَطَع في مِجَنّ قيمته ثلاثة دراهم .

685. Mālik informed us: "Nāfi[c], the *mawlā* of [c]Abdullāh ibn [c]Umar, informed us from Ibn [c]Umar that the Prophet ﷺ cut off [the hand of a thief] for a shield whose value was three dirhams."

٦٨٦ أخبرنا مالك، أخبرنا عبد الله بن أبي بكر ، عن عَمْرة بنت عبد الرحمن : أنّ عائشةَ زوجَ النبيِّ صلى الله عليه وسلم خرجت إلى مكة، ومعها مولاتان لها ومعها غلام لبني عبد الله بن أبي بكر الصديق، وأنه بُعثَ مع تَيْنِك المرأتين ببُرد مَراجل قد خيطت عليه خرقةُ خضراء، قالت : فأخذ الغلام البُرد ففتق عنه فاستخرجه، وجعل مكانه لِبْداً أو فَرْوة، وخاط عليه .
فلمّا قدمنا المدينة دفعنا ذلك البُرد إلى أهله ، فلما فتقوا عنه وجدوا ذلك اللبْدَ ولم يجدوا البرد، فكلّموا المرأتين فكلمتا عائشة رضي الله عنها أو كتبتا إليها واتهمتا العبد، فسُئل عن ذلك، فاعترف فأمرت به عائشة فقُطعت يده .
وقالت عائشة: القطع في ربع دينار فصاعداً .

686. Mālik informed us: "[c]Abdullāh ibn Abī Bakr informed us from [c]Amrah bint [c]Abd ar-Raḥmān that [c]Ā᾽ishah the wife of the Prophet ﷺ went to Makkah along with two female *mawlās* and a male slave belonging to the children of [c]Abdullāh ibn Abī Bakr aṣ-Ṣiddīq and that there was sent with these two women a striped Yemeni outer garment like a cloak which had been stitched up in a green cloth. She [[c]Amrah] said, 'The slave took the garment and unstitched it [the green cloth] and removed it. He put some felt or skin in place of it and restitched it. When we reached Madīnah we gave that garment over to its owners. When they unstitched it they found the felt but they did not find the garment. They spoke to the two women who spoke to [c]Ā᾽ishah

ﷺ or they wrote to her, and they suspected the slave. He was asked about that and he confessed. ᶜĀ'ishah gave an order and his hand was cut off. ᶜĀ'ishah said, "Amputation is for a quarter of a dīnār or more.''"

٦٨٧ أخبرنا مالك، أخبرنا عبد الله بن أبي بكر، عن أبيه، عن عَمْرَةَ ابنة عبد الرحمن: أنَّ سارقاً سرق في عهد عثمان أُتْرُجَّةً فأمر بها عثمان أن تُقَوَّمَ فقُوِّمَتْ بثلاثة دراهم من صَرْف اثني عَشَرَ درهماً بدينار، فقطع عثمانُ يدَه.

687. Mālik informed us: "ᶜAbdullāh ibn Abī Bakr informed us from his father[92] from ᶜAmrah bint ᶜAbd ar-Raḥmān that a thief at the time of ᶜUthmān stole a citron. ᶜUthmān ordered that its price be evaluated and it was valued at three dirhams at the exchange rate of twelve dirhams to the dīnār, and so ᶜUthmān cut off his hand."

قال محمد: قد اختلف الناس فيما يُقطع فيه اليد: فقال أهل المدينة: ربع دينار ورَوَوْا هذه الأحاديث، وقال العراق: لا تُقطع اليد في أقلّ من عشرة دراهم، وَرَوَوْا ذلك عن النبي صلى الله عليه وسلم، وعن عمر، وعن عثمان، وعن علي، وعن عبد الله بن مسعود، وعن غير واحد. فإذا جاء الاختلاف في الحدود أُخِذَ فيها بالثِّقة، وهو قول أبي حنيفة والعامة من فقهائنا.

Muḥammad said: "People differ about that for which the hand must be cut off. The people of Madīnah say a quarter of a dīnār, and they narrate these *aḥādīth*. The people of ᶜIrāq say that the hand is not to be cut off for less than ten dirhams, and they narrate that from the Prophet ﷺ and from ᶜUmar, ᶜUthmān, ᶜAlī, ᶜAbdullāh ibn Masᶜūd and from others. When there is some disagreement about the punishments for contravention of the limits [*ḥudūd*], then the verdict is based on what is sure and trustworthy,[93] and that is the verdict of Abū Ḥanīfah and of our *fuqahā'* in general."

٥ باب السارق يسرق و قد قُطعت يدُه أو يده ورجلُه

5. A Thief who Steals and who has already had a Hand or a Hand and a Foot cut off

٦٨٨ أخبرنا مالك، أخبرنا عبد الرحمن بن القاسم، عن أبيه: أن رجلاً من أهل اليمن أقطعَ اليد والرِّجْل قَدِمَ، فنزل على أبي بكر الصِّدِّيق رضي الله عنه وشكا إليه أنَّ عامل اليمن ظلمه قال: فكان يصلِّي من الليل، فيقول أبو بكر: وأبيك ما لَيْلُكَ بليلِ سارق. ثم افتقدوا حُلِيّاً لأسماء بنت عُمَيْس امرأةِ أبي بكر، فجعل يطوف معهم، ويقول اللهم عليك بمن بيَّتَ أهلَ هذا البَيت الصالح، فوجدوه عند صائغ زعم أن الأقطع جاءه به، فاعترف به الأقطع وأشْهِدَ عليه. فأمر به أبو بكر، فقُطعت يدُه اليسرى، قال أبو بكر: والله لدُعاؤه على نفسه أشدُّ عندي عليه من سَرِقَته.

688. Mālik informed us: "ᶜAbd ar-Raḥmān ibn al-Qāsim informed us from his father[94] that a man of the people of the Yemen whose hand and foot had been cut off arrived [in Madīnah] and stayed with Abū Bakr aṣ-Ṣiddīq ﷺ. He complained to him that the governor of the Yemen had done him an injustice. He said, 'He used to pray at night, and Abū Bakr would say, "By your father!

your night is not the night of a thief." Later they missed a silver ornament of Asmā' bint ʿUmays the wife of Abū Bakr, and he went around with them saying, "O Allah! You are responsible for whoever acted at night against this good family." Then they found it in the possession of a goldsmith who claimed that the maimed man had brought it, and the maimed man confessed to it or someone witnessed against him. Abū Bakr gave the command that his left hand should be cut off. Abū Bakr said, "By Allah! his supplication against himself is definitely more serious in my view than is his theft.""'

قال محمد : قال ابن شهاب الزهريّ : يُروى ذلك عن عائشة أنّها قالت : إنما كان الذي سَرَق حُليّ أسماءَ أقطع اليد اليمنى ، فقطع أبو بكر رجله اليسرى، وكانت تُنكر أن يكون أقطع اليد والرجل، وكان ابنُ شهاب أعلمَ من غيره بهذا ونحوه من أهل بلاده وقد بَلَغنا عن عمر بن الخطاب وعن عليّ بن أبي طالب أنّهما لم يزيدا في القطع على قطع اليمنى أو الرجل اليسرى، فإن أُتي به بعد ذلك لم يقطعاه وضمّناه . وهو قول أبي حنيفة والعامة من فقهائنا رحمهم الله .

Muḥammad said: "Ibn Shihāb az-Zuhrī said, 'It is narrated from ʿĀ'ishah that she said, "The one who stole Asmā's ornament was only missing his right hand, and Abū Bakr cut off his left foot," and she used to deny that he had originally had his hand and foot cut off.' Ibn Shihāb had more knowledge than other people of his city about this and the like of it. It has reached us that ʿUmar ibn al-Khaṭṭāb and ʿAlī ibn Abī Ṭālib never exceeded the amputation of the right [hand] or the left foot, and if he was brought [before them] after that they would not amputate but would make him accountable[95], and that is the verdict of Abū Ḥanīfah and of our *fuqahā'* in general, may Allah have mercy on them."

٦ باب العبد يأبِقُ ثم يسرق

6. The Slave who Flees and then Steals

٦٨٩ أخبرنا مالك، أخبرنا نافع: أنّ عبداً لعبد الله بن عمر سرق وهو آبق، فبعث به ابن عمر إلى سعيد بن العاص ليقطع يده، فأبى سعيد أن يقطع يده، قال: لا تُقْطَعُ يدُ الآبق إذا سرق، فقال له عبد الله بن عمر: أفي كتاب الله وجدت هذا: إن العبد الآبق لا تقطع يده؟ فأمر به ابن عمر فَقُطِعَتْ يدُه.

689. Mālik informed us: "Nāfiʿ informed us that a slave belonging to ʿAbdullāh ibn ʿUmar stole while he was fleeing, and so Ibn ʿUmar sent him to Saʿīd ibn al-ʿĀṣ to cut off his hand, but Saʿīd refused to cut off his hand. He said, 'The hand of a runaway slave is not cut off if he steals.' ʿAbdullāh ibn ʿUmar said to him, 'Was it in the Book of Allah that you found this: "The runaway slave does not have his hand cut off"?' Ibn ʿUmar gave the order and his hand was cut off."

قال محمد : تُقطع يد الآبق وغير الآبق إذا سرق ولكن لا ينبغي أن يقطع السارق أحدٌ إلا الإمام الذي يحكم ، لأنه حدٌ لا يقوم به إلا الإمام أو من ولاّه الإمام ذلك وهو قول أبي حنيفة رحمه الله .

Muḥammad said: "The hand of the runaway slave and someone who is not a runaway is cut off if he steals, however no one ought to cut off the hand of a thief except for the governing *imām*, because it is a punishment for transgressing the limit [*ḥadd*] which only the *imām* or someone he appoints may undertake, and that is the verdict of Abū Ḥanīfah, may Allah have mercy on him."

٧ باب المختلس

7. Someone who Snatches

٦٩٠ أخبرنا مالك، أخبرنا ابن شهاب : أن رجلاً اختلس شيئاً في زمن مروان بن الحكم، فأراد مروان قطعَ يده، فدخل عليه زيد بن ثابت فأخبره أنه لا قطع عليه.

690. Mālik informed us: "Ibn Shihāb informed us that a man snatched something during the time of Marwān ibn al-Ḥakam and Marwān wanted to cut off his hand. Zayd ibn Thābit came to him and informed him that he was not liable to amputation."[96]

قال محمد : وبهذا نأخذ. لا قطع في المختلس . وهو قول أبي حنيفة رحمه الله تعالى.

Muḥammad said, "We adhere to this. There is no amputation for someone who snatches things. It is also the verdict of Abū Ḥanīfah, may Allah, exalted is He, show him mercy."

أبواب الحُدودِ في الزنـاء

11. THE *ḤUDŪD* LIMITS WITH RESPECT TO ADULTERY

١ باب الرجم

1. Stoning

٦٩١ أخبرنا مالك، أخبرنا ابن شهاب، عن عبيد الله بن عبد الله بن عتبة، عن عبد الله بن عباس : أنّه سمع عمر بن الخطاب يقول : الرجم في كتاب الله تعالى حقّ على من زنى إذا أُحْصن من الرجال والنساء، إذا قامت عليه البّينة أو كان الحَبْل أو الاعتراف .

691. Mālik informed us: "Ibn Shihāb informed us from ᶜUbaydullāh bin ᶜAbdullāh ibn ᶜUtbah that ᶜAbdullāh ibn ᶜAbbās heard ᶜUmar ibn al-Khaṭṭāb saying, 'Stoning in the Book of Allah, exalted is He, is compulsory for someone who commits adultery if they are or have been married whether men or women and if clear evidence is established against them or pregnancy ensues or there is a confession.'"

٦٩٢ أخبرنا مالك، حدَّثنا يحيى بن سعيد أنّه سمع سعيد بن المسيِّب يقول: لما صَدَرَ عمر بن الخطاب من منى أناخ بالأبطح ثم كَوَّمَ كَوْمة من بطحاء ثم طرح عليه ثوبه، ثم استلقى ومدَّ يديه إلى السماء، فقال: اللّهم كبِرَتْ سِنّي، وضَعُفَتْ قوّتي، وانتشرتْ رعيَّتي، فاقبضني إليك غير مضيِّع ولا مُفْرِط .

ثم قدمَ المدينة ، فخطب الناسَ فقال: أيها الناس، قد سُنَّتْ لكم السُّنَن، وفُرِضت لكم الفرائض، وتُرِكْتُمْ على الواضحة وصَفَّقَ بإحدى يديه على الأُخرى إلاّ أن لا تضلّوا بالناس يميناً وشمالاً، ثم إياكَم أن تَهلكوا عن آية الرجم، أن يقول قائل: لا نجد حدّين في كتاب الله، فقد رَجَم رسول الله صلى الله عليه وسلم ورجمنا ، وإني والذي نفسي بيده لولا أن يقول الناس زاد عمر بن الخطاب في كتاب الله لكتبتُها : الشيخ والشيخة إذا زَنَيا فارجموهما البتَّة ، فإنا قد قرأناها . قال سعيد بن المسيّب: فما انسلخ ذو الحجَّة حتى قُتل عمر .

692. Mālik informed us: "Yaḥyā ibn Saᶜīd narrated to us that he heard Saᶜīd ibn al-Musayyab saying, 'When ᶜUmar ibn al-Khaṭṭāb left Minā [returning from the Ḥajj] he made his camel lie down on its breast at Abṭaḥ[97], and then he gathered a pile of small stones and cast his cloak over them. He dropped to the ground and extended his hands to the sky and said, 'O Allah, I have become old and my strength has waned. My flock have spread wide, so take me back to You without [me] omitting anything or adding anything.' Then

he came to Madīnah and delivered the *khuṭbah* to people saying, '*sunnah*s have been laid down for you, and obligations imposed and you have been left upon the clear [path],' – and he struck one hand on the other – 'unless you stray with people to the right and the left. Moreover, beware of perishing because of [neglecting] the *āyah* of stoning, such that someone could say, "We do not find two punishments for transgressing the limits [*ḥadd*] in the Book of Allah," because the Messenger of Allah ﷺ stoned and we have stoned. And I, by the One in Whose hand is my self! If it were not that people would say, "ᶜUmar ibn al-Khaṭṭāb added something to the Book of Allah," I would have written it: "The mature[98] man and the mature woman, if they commit adultery stone them without exception," because we have recited it.' Saᶜīd ibn al-Musayyab said, 'Dhu'l-Ḥijjah had not ended before ᶜUmar was killed.'"

٦٩٣ أخبرنا مالك، أخبرنا نافع، عن عبد الله بن عمر: أن اليهود جاؤوا إلى النبي صلى الله عليه وسلم وأخبروه أن رجلاً منهم وامرأة زَنَيَا، فقال لهم رسولُ الله صلى الله عليه وسلم: ما تجدون في التوراة في شأن الرجم؟ فقالوا: نفضحهما ويُجْلَدَان، فقال لهم عبد الله بن سلام: كذبتم إن فيها الرجم، فأَتَوْا بالتوراة، فنشروها، فجعل أحدهم يده على آية الرجم، ثم قرأ ما قبلها وما بعدها، فقال عبد الله بن سلام: ارفع يدك، فرفع يده، فإذا فيها آية الرجم، فقال: صدقت يا محمد، فيها آية الرجم، فأمر بهما رسول الله صلى الله عليه وسلم فرُجما. قال ابن عمر: فرأيت الرجل يجنأ على المرأة يقيها الحجارة.

693. Mālik informed us: "Nāfiᶜ informed us from ᶜAbdullāh ibn ᶜUmar that the jews came to the Prophet ﷺ and told him that one of their men and a woman had committed adultery. The Messenger of Allah ﷺ asked them, 'What do you find in the *Tawrāh* concerning stoning?' They answered, 'We find in it that we have to humiliate them and that they are to be lashed.' ᶜAbdullāh ibn Salām said to them, 'You lie! Stoning is in it.' So they brought the *Tawrāh* and opened it, and one of them put his hand over the *āyah* of stoning and then recited what preceded it and what followed it. ᶜAbdullāh ibn Salām said, 'Lift your hand,' and he lifted his hand and there was the *āyah* of stoning in it. He [the jew] said, 'You have told the truth, Muḥammad. The *āyah* of stoning is in it.' The Messenger of Allah ﷺ gave the command and they were stoned. Ibn ᶜUmar said, 'I saw the man lean over her to protect her from the stones.'"

قال محمد: وبهذا كله نأخذ، أيّما رجلٍ حرٍّ مسلمٍ زنى بامرأة و قد تزوّج بامرأة قبلَ ذلك حرَّةً مسلمةً وجامعها ففيه الرجم، وهذا هو المُحْصَنُ فإن كان لم يُجامعها إنما تزوَّجها ولم يدخُل بها أو كانت تحته أمة يهودية أو نصرانية لم يكن بها مُحْصَناً، ولم يُرجَمْ وضُرِبَ مائة. وهذا هو قولُ أبي حنيفة رحمه الله والعامَّة من فقهائنا.

Muḥammad said: "We adhere to all of this. If a free Muslim man commits adultery with a woman, and he had previously been married to a free Muslim woman, and had had sexual intercourse with her,[99] then he must be stoned. And this person is [what is called] the muḥṣan. If he had not had sexual intercourse with her [his wife] but had only married her without consummating the marriage, or if he had owned a jewish or christian slave-woman, then he is not considered muḥṣan by that, and he is not stoned [for adultery] but he is struck one hundred times [with a lash]. And That is the verdict of Abū Ḥanīfah, may Allah have mercy on him, and of our *fuqahā᾽* in general."

٢ باب الإِقرار بالزناء

2. Admission of Adultery

٦٩٤ أخبرنا مالك، أخبرنا ابن شهاب، عن عبيد الله بن عبد الله بن عتبة، عن أبي هريرة وزيد بن خالد الجهني: أنَّهما أخبراه أن رجلين اختصما إِلى رسول الله ﷺ فقال أحدهما : يا نبيَّ الله اقضِ بيننا بكتاب الله، وقال الآخر وهو أَفْقَهُهُمَا أجلٍ يا رسولَ الله، فاقض بيننا بكتاب الله وائذن لي في أن أتكلَّم ، قال تكلَّمْ، قال : إِنَّ ابني كان عَسيفاً على هذا يعني أجيراً فزنى بامرأته . فأَخْبَرُوني أنَّ على ابني جلدَ مائةٍ، فافتديتُ منه بمائة شاة وجاريةٍ لي، ثم إِنيّ سألت أهل العلم فأخبروني إِنما على ابني جلدَ مائة وتغريبَ عام، وإِنما الرجم على امرأته ، فقال رسول الله صلى الله عليه وسلم: أما والذي نفسي بيده لأَقْضيَنَّ بينكم بكتاب الله تعالى : أمَّا غَنَمك وجاريتك فردٌّ عليك. وجَلَد ابنه مائة وغَرَّبَه عاماً، وأمر أُنَيْساً الأسلمي أن يأتي امرأة الآخر، فإِن اعترقَتْ رَجَمَهَا ، فاعترفَتْ فَرَجَمَهَا .

694. Mālik informed us: "Ibn Shihāb informed us from ᶜUbaydullāh ibn ᶜAbdullāh ibn ᶜUtbah that Abū Hurayrah and Zayd ibn Khālid al-Juhanī informed him that two men took a dispute to the Messenger of Allah ﷺ and one of them said, 'Messenger of Allah, judge between us by the Book of Allah!' The other said – and he was the more discerning of the two – 'Yes, Messenger of Allah, judge between us by the Book of Allah, and give me permission to speak.' He said, 'Speak.' He said, 'My son was a hireling for this one' – meaning an employee – 'and he committed fornication with his wife. They informed me that my son should be flogged one hundred times, and so I ransomed him with one hundred sheep and a female slave of mine. Then later I asked the people of knowledge and they informed me that my son must be flogged one hundred times and exiled for a year, and that there was only stoning for his wife.[100]' The Messenger of Allah ﷺ said, 'By the One in Whose hand is my self! I will judge between you by the Book of Allah, exalted is He. As for your sheep and your female slave, they are to be returned to you,' and he flogged his son one hundred times and exiled him for a year. He told Unays al-Aslamī to go to the other man's wife and if she confessed to stone her. She confessed and so he stoned her."

٦٩٥ أخبرنا مالك، أخبرنا يعقوب بن زيد، عن أبيه زيد بن طلحة، عن عبد الله بن أبي مُلَيْكة أنه أخبره: أن امرأةً أتت النبي صلى الله عليه وسلم فأخبرته أنها زنت وهي حاملٌ، فقال لها رسول الله صلى الله عليه وسلم: اذهبي حتى تَرضَعي، فلما وضعَتْ أتته، فقال لها: اذهبي حتى تُرضعي، فلما أرضَعَتْ أتته فقال لها: اذهبي حتى تَسْتَوْدِعيْه فاستودَعَتْه، ثم جاءته فأمر بها فأُقيم عليها الحدّ .

695. Mālik informed us: "Ya^c^qūb ibn Zayd informed us from his father Zayd ibn Ṭalḥah that ^c^Abdullāh ibn Abī Mulaykah informed him that a woman came to the Prophet ﷺ and told him that she had committed adultery. She was pregnant. The Messenger of Allah ﷺ said to her, 'Go away until you have delivered [the baby].' When she delivered the baby, she came back to him, and he said to her, 'Go away until you have completed the suckling.' When she had completed the suckling, she returned and he said to her, 'Go and entrust him to someone's safekeeping.' She went and entrusted him to someone's safekeeping, and then returned to him, and he gave the order and the punishment for transgressing the limit [ḥadd] was executed on her."

٦٩٦ أخبرنا مالك، أخبرنا ابن شهاب : أنَّ رجلاً اعترف بالزنى على نفسه على عهد رسول الله صلى الله عليه وسلم، وشهد على نفسه أربع شهادات فأمر به فحُدَّ . قال ابن شهاب : فمِنْ أجْلِ ذلك يُؤخذ المرء باعترافه على نفسه.

696. Mālik informed us: "Ibn Shihāb informed us that a man confessed to adultery in the time of the Messenger of Allah ﷺ and he witnessed against himself four times, and so he gave the command and he was subjected to the punishment for transgressing the limit [*ḥadd*]. Ibn Shihāb said, 'For that reason a man is punished on the basis of his own confession.'"

٦٩٧ أخبرنا مالك، حدّثنا زيد بن أسلم : أنّ رجلاً اعترف على نفسه بالزناء على عهد رسول الله صلى الله عليه وسلم، فدعا رسول الله صلى الله عليه وسلم بسَوْط فأتي بسَوْط مكسور، فقال: فوق هذا، فأُتيَ بسوط جديد لم تُقْطَعْ ثَمَرَته، فقال: بين هذين، فأُتيَ بسوطٍ قد رُكّب به فَلاَنَ، فأمر به فجُلدَ ، ثم قال: أيّها النَّاسُ قد آن لكم أن تنتهوا عن حدود الله، فمن أصابه من هذه القاذوراتَ شيئاً فليستتر بستر الله، فإنه من يُبْدِ لَنَا صفحتَه نُقِمْ عليه كتابَ الله عزّ وجلّ.

697. Mālik informed us: "Zayd ibn Aslam narrated to us that a man confessed to fornication in the time of the Messenger of Allah ﷺ and the Messenger of Allah ﷺ called for a whip. Someone brought a broken whip, and he said, 'More than this.'[101] Someone brought him a new whip the knots on the end of which had not been cut[102] and so he said, 'In between these two.' Someone brought him a whip which had been used on mounts and which had softened, and so he gave the command and he was whipped. Then he said, 'People, the time has come for you to keep within the limits of Allah. Whomever any of these foul things befalls, then let him veil himself with the veil of Allah,[103] because whoever makes his deed public to us, we will enact against him the [the punishment for transgressing the limit of] the Book of Allah ﷻ.'"

٦٩٨ أخبرنا مالك، أخبرنا نافع، أنّ صفيّةَ بنتَ أبي عُبَيد حدّثته عن أبي بكر الصدّيق رضي الله تعالى عنه: أنَّ رجلاً وقع على جارية بكْرٍ، فأَحْبَلها ، ثم اعترف على نفسه أنه زنى ولم يكن أُحْصِن ، فأمر به أبو بكر الصديق، فجُلِدَ الحدَّ ثم نُفيَ إلى فَدَك .

698. Mālik informed us: "Nāfi[c] informed us that Ṣafiyyah bint Abī ᶜUbayd told him from Abū Bakr aṣ-Ṣiddīq ﷺ that a man fell upon a virgin slavegirl and made her pregnant, and then he confessed that he had committed fornication and that he was not *muḥṣan*. Abū Bakr aṣ-Ṣiddīq gave the order and he was lashed with the punishment for transgressing the limit [*ḥadd*] and then exiled to Fadak."

٦٩٩ أخبرنا مالك، حدّثني يحيى بن سعيد قال: سمعت سعيد بن المسيّب يقول: إن رجلاً من أسلمَ أتى أبا بكر، فقال: إنّ الآخرَ قد زنى، قال أبو بكر: هل ذكرت هذا لأحد غيري؟ قال: لا، قال أبو بكر: تُبْ إلى الله عزّ وجلّ، واستتر بستر الله، فإن الله يقبل التوبة عن عبادة.

قال سعيد : فلم تقَرّ به نَفْسُه حتى أتى عمر بن الخطاب، فقال له كما قال لأبي بكر، فقال له عمر كما قال أبو بكر.

قال سعيد: فلم تقَرّ به نفسه حتى أتى النبي صلى الله عليه وسلم، فقال له : الآخرُ قد زنى، قال سعيد : فأعرض عنه النبي صلى الله عليه وسلم قال: فقال له ذلك مراراً، كلُّ ذلك يُعرض عنه حتى إذا أَكْثَرَ عَلَيه، بَعَث إلى أهله، فقال: أَيَشْتَكي؟ أَبه جِنَّةٌ ؟ قالوا : يارسول الله، إنّه لصحيح . قال : أبِكْرٌ أَمْ ثَيِّب قال: ثيبٌ. فأمر به فرُجِمَ.

699. Mālik informed us: "Yaḥyā ibn Saᶜīd narrated to me. He said, 'I heard Saᶜīd ibn al-Musayyab saying, "A man of Aslam came to Abū Bakr and said, 'This miserable wretch [before you] has committed adultery.' Abū Bakr asked him, 'Have you mentioned this to anyone but me?' He replied, 'No.' Abū Bakr said, 'Turn in *tawbah* to Allah ﷻ and allow yourself to be veiled by the veil of Allah, because Allah accepts *tawbah* from His slaves.'" Saᶜīd said, "His conscience would not rest easy with that until he had gone to ᶜUmar ibn al-Khaṭṭāb, and he said to him the like of what he had said to Abū Bakr. ᶜUmar spoke to him just as Abū Bakr had." Saᶜīd said, "His conscience would not rest easy with it until he had gone to the Prophet ﷺ and said to him, 'This miserable wretch has committed adultery.'" Saᶜīd said, "The Prophet ﷺ turned away from him." He said, "So he said it to him repeatedly, each time he [the Prophet, ﷺ] turning away from him, until when he had done it too many times [four times], he sent to his family asking, 'Does he complain of [possession by] a jinn?' They answered, 'Messenger of Allah, he is sound and healthy.' He asked, 'Is he a virgin or is he or has he been married[104]?' They said, 'Married,' and so he gave the command and he was stoned."'"

٧٠٠ أخبرنا مالك، أخبرنا يحيى بن سعيد أنه بلغه : أنّ رسول الله صلى الله عليه وسلم قال لرجل من أسلم يُدعَى هَزَّالاً : يا هَزَّال لو سَتَرْتَه بردائك لكان خيراً لك، قال يحيى : فحدَّثتُ بهذا الحديث في مجلس فيه يزيدُ بن نُعيم بن هزّال، فقال: هَزَّالٌ جدّي، والحديث صحيحٌ حقٌّ .

700. Mālik informed us: "Yaḥyā ibn Saᶜīd informed us that it had reached him that the Messenger of Allah ﷺ said to a man of Aslam called Hazzāl, 'Hazzāl, if only you had veiled him with your cloak it would have been better for you.' Yaḥyā said, 'So I narrated this *ḥadīth* in an assembly in which Yazīd ibn Nuᶜaym ibn Hazzāl was present and he said, "Hazzāl is my paternal grandfather, and the *ḥadīth* is sound and true."'"

قال محمد : وبهذا كله نأخذ . ولا يُحَدُّ الرجلُ باعترافه بالزنى حتى يُقِرَّ أربع مرات في أربع مجالس مختلفة ، وكذلك جاءت السُّنَّة : لا يُؤْخَذ الرجل باعترافه على نفسه بالزنى حتى يُقِرَّ أربع مرّاتٍ وهو قول أبي حنيفة والعامة من فقهائنا . وإن أقرّ أربع مرّات ثم رجع قُبِلَ رجوعُه وخُلِّيَ سبيلُه .

Muḥammad said: "We adhere to all of this. A man is not punished with the punishment for transgressing the limit [ḥadd] because of his confession of adultery until he confirms it four times in four different gatherings, and this is how the Sunnah is stated: A man is not taken to task for his confession against himself that he committed to having committed adultery until he confirms it four times. and That is the verdict of Abū Ḥanīfah and of our *fuqahā'* in general. If he affirms it four times and then retracts it, his retraction is to be accepted and the way [to this] is left open to him."

٣ باب الاستكراه في الزناء

3. Rape

٧٠١ أخبرنا مالك، حدّثنا نافع : أن عبداً كان يقوم على رقيق الخُمس، وأنه استَكره جاريةً من ذلك الرقيق، فوقع بها، فجلده عمر بن الخطّاب، ونفاه ، ولم يجلد الوليدة من أجل أنه استكرهها .

701. Mālik informed us: "Nāfiᶜ narrated to us that a slave used to watch over the slaves of the fifth [portion of the spoils of battle that are the due of the Amīr], and that he coerced a female slave from that group of slaves and had sexual intercourse with her. So ᶜUmar ibn al-Khaṭṭāb lashed him and sent him into exile, but he did not lash the woman, because she had been raped."

٧٠٢ أخبرنا مالك، حدّثنا ابن شهاب : أن عبد الملك بن مروان قضى في امرأةٍ أُصيبت مستكرهة بصَدَاقها على من فعل ذلك .

702. Mālik informed us: "Ibn Shihāb narrated to us that ᶜAbd al-Mālik ibn Marwān gave judgement concerning a woman who had been raped that she was due her dowry[105] from the one who had done that."

قال محمد : إذا استُكْرِهَتْ المرأة فلا حدّ عليها، وعلى من استكرهها الحدّ، فإذا وجب عليه الحدّ بطل الصداق، ولا يجب الحدّ والصداق في جماع واحد، فإن دُرِئَ عنه الحدُّ بشبهة وجب عليه الصداق، وهو قول أبي حنيفة وإبراهيم النخعي والعامة من فقهائنا .

Muḥammad said: "If a woman is raped, there is no punishment for transgressing the limit [*ḥadd*] against her, but there is a punishment for transgressing the limit against the one who raped her. If the punishment for transgressing the limit is due against him then there is no [payment of the value of the] dowry. The punishment for transgressing the limit and the dowry cannot both be required for one act of intercourse. If the punishment for transgressing the limit is averted from him because of [something which causes] doubt then the dowry is required [of him], and that is the verdict of Abū Ḥanīfah, Ibrāhīm an-Nakhaʿī and our *fuqahā᾽* in general."

٤ باب حد المماليك في الزناء والسكر

4. The Punishment for Transgressing the Limit [*ḥadd*] for Slaves who Commit Adultery or Become Intoxicated

٧٠٣ أخبرنا مالك، حدَّثنا يحيى بن سعيد، أن سليمان بن يسار أخبره، عن عبد الله بن عيّاش بن أبي ربيعة المخزومي قال : أمرني عمر بن الخطاب في فِتْيَةٍ من قريش، فجلدنا ولائدَ من ولائد الإمارة خمسين خمسين في الزناء .

703. Mālik informed us: "Yaḥyā ibn Saʿīd narrated to us that Sulaymān ibn Yasār informed him that ʿAbdullāh ibn ʿAyyāsh ibn Abī Rabīʿah al-Makhzūmī said, 'ʿUmar ibn al-Khaṭṭāb ordered me [to go] with some young men of Quraysh [as witnesses] and we lashed some of the slave-women of the amirate with fifty lashes each for fornication.'"

٧٠٤ أخبرنا مالك، أخبرنا ابن شهاب ، عن عبيد الله بن عبد الله بن عتبة، عن أبي هريرة، وعن زيد بن خالد الجُهني: أنَّ النبي صلى الله عليه وسلم سُئِل عن الأمة، إذا زنت ولم تُحْصَن ؟ فقال : إذا زنت فاجلدوها ، ثم إذا زنت فاجلدوها، ثم إذا زنت فاجلدوها، ثم بيعوها ولو بضَفير . قال ابن شهاب: لا أدري أ بعد الثالثة أو الرابعة. والضفير : الحبل.

704. Mālik informed us: "Ibn Shihāb informed us from ʿUbaydullāh ibn ʿAbdullāh ibn ʿUtbah from Abū Hurayrah and from Zayd ibn Khālid al-Juhanī that the Prophet ﷺ was asked about the slave-woman who fornicated but was not *muḥṣan,* and he answered, 'If she fornicates then lash her, then if she fornicates [again] lash her, then if she fornicates [again] lash her, then sell her even if only for a rope plaited from [goat's] hair [*ḍafīr*].' Ibn Shihāb said, 'I do not know if it was after the third or the fourth [that she should be sold].' And a *ḍafīr* is a rope."

قال محمد : وبهذا نأخذ. يُجلد المملوك والمملوكة في حد الزنا نصف حدّ الحرَّة خمسين جلدة، وكذلك القذف وشرب الخمر والسكر . وهو قولُ أبي حنيفة والعامة من فقهائنا.

Muḥammad said: "We adhere to this. The male or female slave receives fifty lashes for contravention of the limits [ḥadd] of fornication which is half of the penalty for transgressing the limit imposed on the free person, fifty lashes. It is similar for sexual slander and for drinking wine and for intoxication. and That is the verdict of Abū Ḥanīfah and of our *fuqahā᾽* in general."

٧٠٥ أخبرنا مالك، أخبرنا أبو الزناد، عن عمر بن عبد العزيز : أنَّه جلد عبداً في فرية ثمانين . قال

أبو زناد: فسألتُ عبدَ الله بن عامر بن ربيعة، فقال: أدركتُ عثمان بن عفان والخلفاء هَلُمْ جَرّاً، فما رأيت أحداً ضرب عبداً في فِرْيَة أكثر من أربعين.

705. Mālik informed us: "Abu'z-Zinād informed us that ᶜUmar ibn ᶜAbd al-ᶜAzīz lashed a slave with eighty lashes for slandererous allegations[106]. Abu'z-Zinād said, 'So I asked ᶜAbdullāh ibn ᶜĀmir ibn Rabīᶜah and he said, "I came upon ᶜUthmān ibn ᶜAffān and the *khulafā'* after them [until the time of ᶜUmar ibn ᶜAbd al-ᶜAzīz] and I never saw anyone lashing a slave for slander with more than forty lashes."'"

قال محمد: وبهذا نأخذ، لا يُضرب العبد في الفِرْية إلاّ أربعين جلدة نصف حدّ الحرّ. وهو قول أبي حنيفة والعامة من فقهائنا.

Muḥammad said: "We adhere to this. The slave is not lashed for slander with more than forty lashes, a half of the punishment for transgressing the limit due to a free person. And That is the verdict of Abū Ḥanīfah and of our *fuqahā'* in general."

٧٠٦ أخبرنا مالك، حدَّثنا ابن شهاب و سُئل عن حدّ العبد في الخمر؟ فقال: بلغنا أنَّ عليه نصف حدّ الحُرّ، وأنَّ علياً وعُمَر وعثمان وابن عامر رضي الله عنهم جلدوا عبيدهم نصف حدّ الحُرّ في الخمر.

706. Mālik informed us: "Ibn Shihāb narrated to us that when he was asked about the lashes given to a slave for [drinking] wine, he said, 'It has reached us that he is due a half of the punishment for transgressing the limit for a free person, and that ᶜAlī, ᶜUmar, ᶜUthmān and Ibn ᶜĀmir ﷺ lashed their slaves with a half of the punishment for transgressing the limit due to a free person in the case of wine.'"

قال محمد: وبهذا كله نأخذ. الحدّ في الخمر والسكر ثمانون، وحدّ العبد في ذلك أربعون. وهو قول أبي حنيفة والعامة من فقهائنا.

Muḥammad said: "We adhere to this. The punishment for transgressing the limit for wine and intoxication is eighty [lashes], and the punishment for transgressing the limit for the slave in that case is forty, and that is the verdict of Abū Ḥanīfah and of our *fuqahā'* in general."

٥ باب الحدّ في التعريض

5. The Punishment for Transgressing the Limit [*ḥadd*] for Sexual Innuendo [hinting at Adultery]

٧٠٧ أخبرنا مالك، أخبرنا أبو الرجال محمد بن عبد الرحمن، عن أمِّه عَمْرة بنت عبد الرحمن: أن رجلين في زمان عمر استبّا ، فقال أحدهما: ما أبي بزانٍ ولا أمي بزانية، فاستشار في ذلك عمر بن الخطاب، فقال قائل: مَدَح أباه وأمه ، وقال آخرون: وقد كان لأبيه وأمه مدح سوى هذا، نرى أن تجلده الحدّ ثمانين.

707. Mālik informed us: "Abu'r-Rijāl Muḥammad ibn ᶜAbd ar-Raḥmān

informed us from his mother ᶜAmrah bint ᶜAbd ar-Raḥmān that two men at the time of ᶜUmar cursed each other. One of them said, 'My father is not an adulterer and my mother is not an adulteress.' They asked ᶜUmar ibn al-Khattāb's advice about that, and someone said, 'He praised his father and his mother.' Others said, 'There could certainly have been some other praise for his father and mother. We think that he should be lashed with the punishment for transgressing the limit [*ḥadd*],' and so ᶜUmar gave him eighty lashes as a punishment for transgressing the limit."[107]

قال محمد: قد اختَلف في هذا على عمر بن الخطاب أصحابُ النبي صلى الله عليه وسلم، فقال بعضهم: لا نرى عليه حداً، مدح أباه وأمه، فأخذنا بقول من درأ الحدّ منهم وممن درأ الحدّ وقال: ليس في التعريض جلد عليٌّ بنُ أبي طالب رضي الله عنه، وبهذا نأخذ. وهو قول أبي حنيفة والعامة من فقهائنا.

Muḥammad said: "The Companions of the Prophet ﷺ disagreed with ᶜUmar about this, and one of them said, 'We do not think that he should be punished with the punishment for transgressing the limit. He praised his father and his mother.' So we adhere to the verdict of the one who averted the punishment for transgressing the limit from him. One of those who averted the punishment for transgressing the limit and who said, 'There is no punishment for transgressing the limit for slanderous innuendo,' was ᶜAlī ibn Abī Ṭālib ﷺ and we adhere to this, and it is the verdict of Abū Ḥanīfah and of our *fuqahā᾽* in general."

٦ باب الحدّ في الشرب

6. The Punishment for Transgressing the Limit [*ḥadd*] for Drinking [Alcohol]

٧٠٨ أخبرنا مالك، أخبرنا ابن شهاب، أن السائب بن يزيد أخبره قال: خرج علينا عمر بن الخطاب، فقال: إني وجدتُ من فلان ريح شراب، فسألته، فزعم أنه شرب طِلاء، وأنا سائل عنه فإن كان يُسكر جلدته الحدّ، فجلده الحدّ.

708. Mālik informed us: "Ibn Shihāb informed us that as-Sā᾽ib ibn Yazīd informed him, 'ᶜUmar ibn al-Khaṭṭāb came out to us and said, "I caught from so-and-so the smell of wine and I asked him [about it] and so he claimed that he had drunk a cooked fruit juice. I am going to make enquiries about it [the drink], and if it is one that intoxicates, I will have him lashed with the punishment for transgressing the limit," and he had him lashed with the punishment for transgressing the limit.'"

٧٠٩ أخبرنا مالك، أخبرنا ثور بن زيد الدِّيْلي: أن عمر بن الخطاب استشار في الخمر يشربها الرجل، فقال عليّ بن أبي طالب: أرى أن تضربه ثمانين، فإنه إذا شربها سَكِر، وإذا سَكِر هذى، وإذا هذى افترى. أو كما قال. فجَلَد عمر في الخمر ثمانين.

709. Mālik informed us: "Thawr ibn Zayd ad-Dīlī informed us that ᶜUmar ibn al-Khaṭṭāb took counsel concerning the wine which a man drank, and ᶜAlī ibn Abī Ṭālib said, "I think you should lash him eighty times, because when he drinks he becomes intoxicated, and when intoxicated he raves, and when he raves he fabricates lies [and slanders]," or as he said [or words to that effect].[108] So ᶜUmar gave eighty lashes for wine.'"[109]

٧ باب شرب البِتْعِ و الغُبَيْرَاء وغير ذلك

7. Drinking *bitᶜ*[110] and *ghubayrā*ʾ[111] etc.

٧١٠ أخبرنا مالك، أخبرنا ابن شهاب، عن أبي سلمة بن عبد الرحمن، عن عائشة قالت : سُئل رسول الله صلى الله عليه وسلم عن البِتْع ؟ فقال: كل شراب أَسْكَرَ فهو حرام .

710. Mālik informed us: "Ibn Shihāb informed us from Abū Salamah ibn ᶜAbd ar-Raḥmān that ᶜĀʾishah said, 'The Messenger of Allah ﷺ was asked about *bitᶜ* and he said, "Every drink which intoxicates is *ḥarām*."'"

٧١١ أخبرنا مالك، أخبرنا زيد بن أسلم، عن عطاء بن يسار: أن النبيّ صلى الله عليه وسلم سئل عن الغُبَيْراء ؟ فقال: لا خير فيها، ونهى عنها. فسألت زيداً ما الغُبَيْراء؟ فقال: السُكُرْكَة .

711. Mālik informed us: "Zayd ibn Aslam informed us from ᶜAṭāʾ ibn Yasār that the Prophet ﷺ was asked about *ghubayrā*ʾ and he said, 'There is no good in it,' and he forbade it. So I asked Zayd, 'What is *ghubayrā*ʾ?' And he said, '*As-sukrukah*.[112]'"

٨ باب تحريم الخمر و ما يُكره من الأشربة

8. The Prohibition of Wine and those Drinks which are Disapproved

٧١٢ أخبرنا مالك، أخبرنا زيد بن أسلم، عن أبي وَعْلة المصري، أنه سُئل ابن عباس عمّا يُعصرَ من العنب، فقال ابن عباس: أهدى رجل لرسول الله صلى الله عليه وسلم راوية خمرٍ، فقال له النبي صلى الله عليه وسلم: هل علمتَ أنّ الله عزّ وجلّ حرّمها ؟ قال: لا ، فسارَّه إنسان إلى جنبه، فقال له النبي صلى الله عليه وسلم: بِمَ ساررتَه ؟ قال: أمرته ببيعها، فقال: إن الذي حرَّم شربها حرَّم بيعها. قال : ففتح المزادتين حتى ذهب ما فيهما.

712. Mālik informed us: "Zayd ibn Aslam informed us from Abū Waᶜlah al-Miṣrī that Ibn ᶜAbbās was asked about those grapes which were squeezed, and Ibn ᶜAbbās said, 'A man gave a present of a leathern water-bag full of wine to the Messenger of Allah ﷺ and so the Prophet ﷺ asked him, "Have you [not] learnt that Allah ﷻ has forbidden it?" He answered, "No." So another man beside him whispered to him, and then the Prophet ﷺ asked him, "What did you whisper to him?" He answered, "I told him to sell it." He said, "The One Who forbids its consumption forbids its sale."' He said, 'He opened the two leathern water bags until what was in them was gone.'"

٧١٣ أخبرنا مالك، أخبرنا نافع، عن ابن عمر: أنَّ رجلاً من أهل العراق قال لعبد الله بن عمر: إنَّا نبتاع من ثمر النخل والعنب والقصب ، فَنعصره خمراً فنبيعه ؟ فقال له عبد الله بن عمر: إني أُشْهِدُ الله عليكم وملائكتَه ومن سمع من الجنِّ والإنس أني لا آمركم أن تبتاعوها ، فلا تبتاعوها ، ولا تعصروها، ولا تسقوها، فإنها رِجْسٌ من عمل الشيطان .

713. Mālik informed us: "Nāfiʿ informed us from Ibn ʿUmar that a man of the people of ʿIrāq said to ʿAbdullāh ibn ʿUmar that, 'We buy of the fruit of the date-palm, vines and sugar-cane and press them as wine and then sell them.' ʿAbdullāh ibn ʿUmar said to him, 'I call Allah to witness against you and His angels and whoever of the jinn and of human beings who hears that I do not tell you to purchase[113] it [the original purchase in order to make the wine] so do not purchase it, and do not press it and do not give it to drink, because it is "filth from the handiwork of shayṭān"[114].'"

قال محمد: وبهذا نأخذ. ما كرهنا شُربَه من الأشربة الخمر والسكر ونحو ذلك فلا خير في بيعه ولا أكل ثمن.

Muḥammad said: "We adhere to this. Those drinks, wine and other intoxicants and the like, we disapprove of,[115] therefore there is good neither in selling them nor in the money received."

٧١٤ أخبرنا مالك، أخبرنا نافع، عن ابن عمر قال: قال رسول الله صلى الله عليه وسلم: من شرب الخمر في الدنيا، ثم لم يَتُبْ منها حُرِمَها في الآخرة فلم يُسْقَها.

714. Mālik informed us: "Nāfiʿ informed us that Ibn ʿUmar said, 'The Messenger of Allah ﷺ said, "Whoever drinks wine in the world and then does not later turn in *tawbah* from it will be forbidden [the wine of] the next life [*ākhirah*] and will not be given it to drink."'"

٧١٥ أخبرنا مالك، أخبرنا إسحاق بن عبد الله بن أبي طلحة الأنصَاريّ، عن أنس بن مالك أنه قال: كنتُ أَسْقِي أبا عبيدة بن الجرّاح وأبا طلحة الأنصاري وأبيّ بن كعب شراباً من فَضِيْخ وتمر، فأتاهم آت، فقال: إن الخمر قد حُرِّمت، فقال أبو طلحة: يا أنس ، قم إلى هذه الجرار، فاكسرها فقمتُ إلى مِهْرَاس لنا فضربتُها بأسفله حتى تَكَسَّرَتْ .

715. Mālik informed us: "Isḥāq ibn ʿAbdullāh ibn Abī Ṭalḥah al-Anṣārī informed us that Anas ibn Mālik said, 'I used to serve Abū ʿUbaydah ibn al-Jarrāḥ, Abū Ṭalḥah al-Anṣārī and Ubayy ibn Kaʿb a drink of faḍīkh [an intoxicating drink prepared from unripe fresh dates steeped without cooking] and dried dates. Someone came to them and said, 'Wine has been declared *ḥarām*.' Abū Ṭalḥah said, 'Anas, go over to those ceramic jars and break them.' So I stood up and went and got our quern-stone[116] and struck them at their base until they broke.'"

قال محمد: النقيع عندنا مكروه . ولا ينبغي أن يُشرب من البُسْرْ والزبيب والتمر جميعاً.
وهو قول أبي حنيفة رحمه الله إذا كان شديداً يُسْكِر.

Muḥammad said: "According to us, the fermented infusion of raisins is abhorrent. An infusion of unripe fresh dates, raisins and dried dates together ought not to be drunk. That is the verdict of Abū Ḥanīfah, may Allah have mercy on him, if it is strong and intoxicates."

٩ باب الخليطين

9. Mixtures[117]

٧١٦ أخبرنا مالك، أخبرنا الثقة عندي، عن بكير بن عبد الله بن الأشجّ، عن عبد الرحمن بن حُبَاب الأسلمي، عن أبي قتادة الأنصاري: أنّ النبي صلى الله عليه وسلم نهى عن شرب التمر والزبيب جميعاً، والزَّهْو و الرُّطَب جميعاً.

716. Mālik informed us: "Someone who is trustworthy in my view informed us from Bukayr ibn ʿAbdullāh ibn al-Ashajj from ʿAbd ar-Raḥmān ibn Ḥubāb al-Aslamī from Abū Qatādah al-Anṣārī that the Prophet ﷺ forbade the drinking of [an infusion of] dried dates and raisins together, and [an infusion of] dates that are beginning to ripen and of fresh ripe dates together."

٧١٧ أخبرنا مالك، أخبرنا زيد بن أسلم، عن عطاء بن يسار: أن النبي صلى الله عليه وسلم نهى أن ينبذ البسر والتمر جميعاً، والتمر والزبيب جميعاً.

717. Mālik informed us: "Zayd ibn Aslam informed us from ʿAṭāʾ ibn Yasār that the Prophet ﷺ forbade that an infusion should be made of steeped unripe and dried dates together, or of steeped dried dates and raisins together."

١٠ باب نبيذ الدُّبَّاء والمُزَفَّت

10. *Nabīdh* Prepared in Gourds and Jars Coated with Pitch[118]

٧١٨ أخبرنا مالك، أخبرنا نافع، عن ابن عمر: أنَّ النبي صلى الله عليه وسلم خطب في بعض مغازيه. قال ابن عمر: فأقْبَلْتُ نحوَه فانصرف قبل أن أبلُغَه فقلت: ما قال؟ قالوا نهى أن يُنْبَذَ في الدُّبَّاء والمزفَّت.

718. Mālik informed us: "Nāfiʿ informed us from Ibn ʿUmar that the Prophet ﷺ delivered an address during one of his expeditions. Ibn ʿUmar said, 'I turned to go towards him but he finished before I reached him, so I asked, "What did he say?" They said, "He forbade the preparation of *nabīdh* in gourds and jars coated with pitch."'"

٧١٩ أخبرنا مالك أخبرنا العلاء بن عبد الرحمن عن أبيه أن النبي صلى الله عليه وسلم نهى أن ينبذ في الدباء والمزفت.

719. Mālik informed us: "Al-ʿAlāʾ ibn ʿAbd ar-Raḥmān informed us from his father that the Prophet, ﷺ forbade the preparation of *nabīdh* in gourds and vessels smeared with pitch."

١١ باب نبيذ الطِّلاء

11. *Nabīdh* Concentrated by Cooking [until two-thirds has gone]

٧٢٠ أخبرنا مالك، أخبرنا داود بن الحصين، عن واقد بن عمرو بن سعد بن معاذ، عن محمود بن لبيد الأنصاري، عن عمر بن الخطاب حين قَدِم الشام: شكى إليه أهل الشام وباءَ الأرض أو ثقلها، وقالوا: لا يصلح لنا إلاَّ هذا الشراب قال: اشربوا العسلِ، قالوا: لا يصلحنا العسل. قال له رجل من أهل الأرض: هل لك أن أجعل لك من هذا الشراب شيئاً لا يسكر، قال: نعم.

فطبخوه حتى ذهب ثلثاه، وبقي ثلثه، فأتَوْا به إلى عمر بن الخطاب، فأدخل أصبعه فيه، ثم رفع يده فتبعه يتمطط، فقال: هذا الطِّلاء مثلُ طلاء الإبل، فأمرهم أن يشربوه.

فقال عبادة بن الصامت: أحللتَها والله، قال: كَلّا والله ما أحللتُها، اللهم إني لا أُحل لهم شيئاً حرَّمته عليهم، ولا أُحرِّم عليهم شيئاً أحللته لهم.

720. Mālik informed us: "Dāwūd ibn al-Ḥuṣayn informed us from Wāqid ibn ᶜAmr ibn Saᶜd ibn Muᶜādh from Maḥmūd ibn Labīd al-Anṣārī that when ᶜUmar ibn al-Khaṭṭāb arrived in Shām the people of Shām complained to him of the pestilences of the land and its [water's] heaviness. They said, 'Nothing is effective for us except for this drink [an intoxicating *nabīdh*].' He said, 'Drink honey.' They said, 'Honey is not effective for us.' One of the men of the land asked him, 'Shall I make something for you from this drink that does not intoxicate?' He answered, 'Yes.' So they cooked it until two-thirds of it had gone, and one-third remained. They brought it to ᶜUmar ibn al-Khaṭṭāb, and he put his finger in it, then lifted his hand up and it followed [attached to his hand] in a viscous glutinous manner. He said, 'This is a tar like the tar [used for] camels,' and he told them to drink it. ᶜUbādah ibn aṣ-Ṣāmit said, 'You have declared it *ḥalāl*, by Allah!' He said, 'Certainly not, by Allah! I have not declared it *ḥalāl*. O Allah, I do not declare anything *ḥalāl* for them which You have made *ḥarām* for them, and I do not make anything *ḥarām* for them which You have made *ḥalāl*.'"

قال محمد: وبهذا نأخذ. لا بأس بشرب الطلاء الذي قد ذهب ثلثاه وبقي ثلثه، وهو لا يُسكر، فأما كلُّ معتَّق يُسكر فلا خير فيه.

Muḥammad said: "We adhere to this. There is no harm in drinking *nabīdh* which has been concentrated by cooking until two-thirds of it has gone and of which one-third remains, and which does not intoxicate. But as for any aged [drink] which intoxicates, there is no good in it."

كتاب الفرائض

12. THE OBLIGATORY PORTIONS OF INHERITANCE

٧٢١ أخبرنا مالك، أخبرنا ابن شهاب، عن قَبيصة بن ذُؤيب: أنّ عمر بن الخطاب رضي الله عنه فَرَضَ للجَدّ الذي يَفْرِضُ له الناس اليوم.

721. Mālik informed us: "Ibn Shihāb informed us from Qabīṣah ibn Dhu'ayb that ʿUmar ibn al-Khaṭṭāb ﷺ assigned the obligatory portion to a grandfather which people assign to him today."

قال محمد: وبهذا نأخذ في الجَدّ. وهو قول زيد بن ثابت وبه يقول العامة. وأما أبو حنيفة، فإنه كان يأخذ في الجَدّ بقول أبي بكر الصديق وعبد الله بن عباس رضي الله عنهم، فلا يورِّث الإخوة معه شيئاً.

Muḥammad said: "We adhere to this with respect to a grandfather, and it is the verdict of Zayd ibn Thābit, and people in general give this verdict. As for Abū Ḥanīfah, with respect to the grandfather, he used to adhere to the verdict of Abū Bakr aṣ-Ṣiddīq and ʿAbdullāh ibn ʿAbbās and so he would not assign any portion of the inheritance to siblings along with him."

٧٢٢ أخبرنا مالك، أخبرنا ابن شهاب، عن عثمان بن إسحاق بن خَرَشَة، عن قبيصة بن ذُؤيب أنه قال: جاءت الجَدّة إلى أبي بكر تسأله ميراثها، فقال: مالَكِ في كتاب الله من شيء، وما عَلِمْنا لكِ في سُنّة رسول الله صلى الله عليه وسلم شيئاً، فارجعي حتى أسألَ الناس، قال: فسأل الناس، فقال المغيرة بن شعبة: حضرتُ رسولَ الله صلى الله عليه وسلم أعطاها السُّدس، فقال: هل معك غيرُك؟ فقال محمد بن مسلمة: فقال مثل ذلك. فأنفذه لها أبو بكر، ثم جاءت الجَدّة الآخرى إلى عمر بن الخطاب تسأله ميراثها، فقال: مَالَكِ في كتاب الله من شيء وما كان القضاء الذي قُضي به إلاّ لغَيْركِ وما أنا بزائد في الفرائض من شيء ولكن هو ذلك السّدس، فإن اجتمعتما فيه فهو بينكما وأيّتكما خَلَتْ به فهو لها.

722. Mālik informed us: "Ibn Shihāb informed us from ʿUthmān ibn Isḥāq ibn Kharashah that Qabīṣah ibn Dhu'ayb said, 'A grandmother[119] came to Abū Bakr aṣ-Ṣiddīq asking him for her portion of the inheritance, and so he said to her, "There is nothing for you in the Book of Allah, and we know of nothing for you in the *Sunnah* of the Messenger of Allah ﷺ. So go away until I have asked people."' He said, 'He asked people, and al-Mughīrah ibn Shuʿbah said, "I was present when the Messenger of Allah ﷺ assigned to her a sixth." So he [Abū Bakr aṣ-Ṣiddīq] asked, "Is there anyone else with you

[who can affirm this narration]?" He said, "Muḥammad ibn Maslamah," and he said the like of that and so Abū Bakr executed that for her. Later, the other grandmother[120] came to ᶜUmar ibn al-Khaṭṭāb asking him for her portion of the inheritance, and he said, "There is nothing for you in the Book of Allah, and that judgement which was passed was for someone other than you [the maternal grandmother], and I do not intend to add anything to the fixed portions of inheritance, but it is that sixth. If both of you coincide then it is to be divided between you, and if either of you remains alone, then it is for her."'"

قال محمد: وبهذا نأخذ. إذا اجتمعت الجدّتان أُمّ الأم، وأُمّ الأب فالسدس بينهما وإن خلت به إحداهما فهو لها، ولا ترث معها جَدّة فوقها. وهو قول أبي حنيفة والعامة من فقهائنا رحمهم الله.

Muḥammad said: "We adhere to this. When both grandmothers are present, the mother's mother and the father's mother, then the sixth is to be divided between them. If only one of them remains then it is for her, and no other grandmother [such as the great grandmother] inherits along with her. That is the verdict of Abū Ḥanīfah and of our *fuqahā᾽* in general, may Allah have mercy on them."

١ باب ميراث العمة

1. The Inheritance of the Paternal Aunt

٧٢٣ أخبرنا مالك، أخبرنا محمد بن أبي بكر بن عمرو بن حزم: أنه كان يسمع أباه كثيراً يقول: كان عمر بن الخطاب يقول: عجباً للعمّة تُورَث ولا ترث.

723. Mālik informed us: "Muḥammad ibn Abī Bakr [ibn Muḥammad] ibn ᶜAmr ibn Ḥazm informed us that he often used to hear his father saying, "ᶜUmar ibn al-Khaṭṭāb used to say, "It is astonishing that the paternal aunt is inherited from but she does not inherit."'"

قال محمدٌ: إنما يعني عمر هذا فيما نرى أنها تُرث لأن ابن الأخ ذو سهم، ولا ترث لأنها ليست بذات سهم، ونحن نروي عن عمر بن الخطاب وعلي بن أبي طالب وعبد الله ابن مسعود، أنهم قالوا في العمة والخالة إذا لم يكن ذو سهم ولا عصبة: فللخالة الثلث، وللعمة الثلثان. وحديث يرويه أهل المدينة لا يستطعون ردّه أن ثابت بن الدَّحْداح مات ولا وارث له، فأعطى رسولُ الله صلى الله عليه وسلم أبا لُبَابَة بن عبد المنذر، وكان ابن أخته، ميراثه. وكان ابن شهاب يُوَرِّث العمّةَ والخالة وذوي القربات بقربتهم، وكان من أفقه أهل المدينة وأعلمهم بالرواية.

Muḥammad said: "In our view ᶜUmar only meant by this that she is inherited from because the son of her brother has a fixed portion [of her estate], but she does not inherit because she is not one of those with a fixed portion [in her brother's son's estate]. We narrate from ᶜUmar ibn al-Khaṭṭāb, ᶜAlī ibn Abī Ṭālib and ᶜAbdullāh ibn Masᶜūd that they said concerning the paternal aunt and the maternal aunt, in the case where there remains none of those [relatives] who are due fixed portions of the inheritance, nor male relatives [who would inherit in the absence of those who are due fixed portions], that the maternal aunt receives a third and the paternal aunt two thirds. They are unable to refute the *ḥadīth* which the people of Madīnah narrate that Thābit bin ad-Daḥdāḥ died without any to inherit from him, and so the Messenger of Allah ﷺ gave Abū Lubābah ibn ᶜAbd al-Mundhir, who was the son of his sister, his estate. Ibn Shihāb used to assign a portion of the inheritance to the paternal and maternal aunts and close relatives because of their relationship, and he was one of the most knowledgeable in *fiqh* of the people of Madīnah and the most knowledgeable of them concerning narration [of *aḥādīth*]."

٧٢٤ أخبرنا مالك، أخبرنا محمد بن أبي بكر، عن عبد الرحمن بن حنظلة بن عَجْلان الزُّرَقي أنه أخبره، عن مولًى لقريش كان قديماً يقال له ابن مِرْس قال: كنت جالساً عند عمر بن الخطاب، فلمّا صلّى صلاة الظهر قال: يا يرفأ هَلُمَّ ذلك الكتابَ لكتاب كان كتبه في شأن العمّة يُسأل عنه ويستخبر الله هل لها من شيء؟ فأتى به يرفأ، ثم دعا بتَوْرٍ فيه ماءٌ أو قدحٍ، فمَحَا ذلك الكتابَ فيه، ثم قال: لو رضيكِ الله أقرّكِ، لو رضيكِ الله أقرّكِ.

724. Mālik informed us: "Muḥammad ibn Abī Bakr informed us that ᶜAbd ar-Raḥmān ibn Ḥanẓalah ibn ᶜAjlān az-Zuraqī informed him from an old *mawlā* of Quraysh called Ibn Mirs who said, 'I was sitting with ᶜUmar ibn al-Khaṭṭāb, and when he prayed the prayer of *Ẓuhr* he said, "Yarfāʾ, bring that letter," – a letter which he had written with respect to the matter of the [inheritance of the] paternal aunt; it was asked about and he sought to know from Allah whether she has anything. So Yarfāʾ brought it. Then he called for a vessel with some water or a drinking bowl, and erased the letter in it. Then he said, "If Allah were content with [something for] you, He would have confirmed you[121], if Allah were content with [something for] you, He would have confirmed you."'"

٢ باب النبي صلى الله عليه وسلم هل يورث ؟

2. Whether the Prophet ﷺ was to be Inherited from

٧٢٥ أخبرنا مالك، أخبرنا أبو الزِّناد، عن الأعرج، عن أبي هريرة أن رسول الله صلى الله عليه وسلم قال: لا تَقْسِم ورثتي ديناراً، ما تركتُ بعد نفقة نسائي ومؤونة عاملي فهو صدقة.

725. Mālik informed us: "Abu'z-Zinād informed us from al-Aᶜraj from Abū Hurayrah that the Messenger of Allah ﷺ said, 'My estate is not measured into dīnārs. That which I have left, after the maintenance of my wives and the means of subsistence for my agent[122], then it is *ṣadaqah*.'"

٧٢٦ أخبرنا مالك، حدّثنا ابن شهاب، عن عروة بن الزبير، عن عائشة زوج النبي صلى الله عليه وسلم: أن نساء النبيِّ صلى الله عليه وسلم حين مات رسول الله صلى الله عليه وسلم أردْن أن يبعثن عثمان بن عفان إلى أبي بكر يسألن ميراثَهُنَّ من رسول الله صلى الله عليه وسلم، فقالت لهن عائشة:

أليس قد قال رسولُ الله صلى الله عليه وسلم: لا نُورَث ، ما تركنا صدقةٌ.

726. Mālik informed us: "Ibn Shihāb narrated to us from ʿUrwah ibn az-Zubayr from ʿĀʾishah the wife of the Prophet ﷺ that the wives of the Prophet ﷺ when the Messenger of Allah ﷺ died wanted to send ʿUthmān ibn ʿAffān to Abū Bakr; they were asking for their inheritance from the Messenger of Allah ﷺ. ʿĀʾishah said to them, 'Did the Messenger of Allah ﷺ not say, "We[123] are not inherited from; that which we leave is *ṣadaqah*"?'"

٣ باب لا يرث المسلم الكافر

3. A Muslim does not Inherit from a *Kāfir*

٧٢٧ أخبرنا مالك، أخبرنا ابن شهاب، عن عليّ بن حسين بن علي بن أبي طالب، عن عمر بن عثمان بن عفان، عن أسامة بن زيد أن رسول الله صلى الله عليه وسلم قال: لا يرث المسلمُ الكافر.

727. Mālik informed us: "Ibn Shihāb informed us from ʿAlī ibn Ḥusayn ibn ʿAlī ibn Abī Ṭālib from ʿUmar ibn ʿUthmān ibn ʿAffān from Usāmah ibn Zayd that the Messenger of Allah ﷺ said, 'The Muslim must not inherit from a *kāfir*.'"[124]

قال محمد: وبهذا نأخذُ . لا يورث المسلم الكافر ولا الكافر المسلم. والكفر ملّة واحدة، يتواثون به، وإن اختلفت مللهم ، يرث اليهوديُّ النصراني والنصرانيُّ اليهودي، وهو قول أبي حنيفة والعامة من فقهائنا .

Muḥammad said: "We adhere to this. The Muslim does not leave inheritance to the *kāfir*, nor the *kāfir* to the Muslim. *Kufr* is one religion by which they inherit from each other even if their religions are different. The jew inherits from the christian and the christian from the jew. That is the verdict of Abū Ḥanīfah and of our *fuqahāʾ* in general."

٧٢٨ أخبرنا مالك، عن ابن شهاب، عن علي بن حسين قال: وَرِثَ أبا طالب عقيلٌ وطالب، ولم يَرِثْه علي.

728. Mālik informed us from Ibn Shihāb that ʿAlī ibn Ḥusayn said, "ʿAqīl[125] and Ṭālib[126] inherited from Abū Ṭālib but ʿAlī[127] did not inherit from him."

٤ باب ميراث الولاء

4. The Inheritance of Freed Slaves

٧٢٩ أخبرنا مالك، حدّثنا عبد الله بن أبي بكر بن محمد بن عمرو بن حزم، أن عبد الملك بن أبي بكر بن عبد الرحمن بن الحارث بن هشام أخبره أن أباه أخبره: أن العاص بن هشام هلك وترك بنين له ثلاثة: ابنين لأمّ ورجلاً لعلّة، فهلك أحد الابنين اللذين هما لأم، وترك مالاً وموالي، فورثه أخوه لأمه وأبيه، وورث ماله وولاء مواليه، ثم هلك أخوه وترك ابنه وأخاه لأبيه، فقال ابنه: قد أحرزتُ ما كان أبي أحْرَزَ من المال وولاءَ الموالي، وقال أخوه: ليس كله لك، إنما أحرزتَ المال، فأما ولاء الموالي فلا، أرأيت لو هلك أخي اليوم ألستُ أرثه أنا؟ فاختصما إلى عثمان بن عفان فقضى لأخيه بولاء الموالي.

729. Mālik informed us: "ᶜAbdullāh ibn Abī Bakr ibn Muḥammad ibn ᶜAmr ibn Ḥazm narrated to us that ᶜAbd al-Mālik ibn Abī Bakr ibn ᶜAbd ar-Raḥmān ibn al-Ḥārith ibn Hishām informed him that his father informed him that al-ᶜĀṣ ibn Hishām perished[128] leaving three sons: two sons of [one] mother and a son from a co-wife. One of the two sons of the first mother perished leaving property and *mawlās,* and so his brother by the same mother and father inherited from him, and he inherited his property and the relationship of *walā'* [including their inheritance] of his *mawlās*. Then that brother died leaving his son and his paternal brother [from his mother's co-wife]. His son said, 'I take that which my father had taken of wealth and the *walā'* of the *mawlās*.' His brother said, 'It is not all yours. You only take the wealth. As for the *walā'* of the *mawlās,* then no. Don't you see that if my brother had died today, wouldn't I have succeeded him?' They took their dispute to ᶜUthmān ibn ᶜAffān and he passed judgement in favour of his brother [that he took] the *walā'* of the *mawlās*."

قال محمد : وبهذا نأخذ. الولاء للأخ من الأب دون بني الأخ من الأب والأم، وهو قول أبي حنيفة رحمه الله.

Muḥammad said: "We adhere to this. The *walā'* is for the paternal brother rather than for the children of the brother from the same father and mother, and that is the verdict of Abū Ḥanīfah, may Allah have mercy on him."

٧٣٠ أخبرنا مالك، أخبرنا عبد الله بن أبي بكر أن أباه أخبره : أنه كان جالساً عند أبان بن عثمان، فاختصم إليه نفر من جُهَيْنة ونفر من بني الحارث بن الخزرج وكانت امرأة من جهَيْنة عند رجل من بني الحارث بن الخزرج، يقال له إبراهيم بن كُليب ، فماتت فورثها ابنها وزوجها، وتركت مالاً وموالي، ثم مات ابنها، فقال وَرَثَتُه : لنا ولاء الموالي، وقد كان ابنها أحرزه ، وقال الجهنيّون : ليس كذلك، إنما هو موالي صاحبتنا، فإذا مات ولدها، فلنا ولاؤهم ونحن نرثهم، فقضى أبان بن عثمان للجهنيّين بولاء الموالي.

730. Mālik informed us: "ᶜAbdullāh ibn Abī Bakr informed us that his father informed him that he was sitting with Abān ibn ᶜAffān when a party from Juhaynah and a party from Banī al-Ḥārith ibn al-Khazraj picked a dispute to him. There was a woman from Juhaynah married to a man from Banī al-Ḥārith ibn al-Khazraj who was called Ibrāhīm ibn Kulayb. She died and so her son and her husband inherited from her. She left property and *mawlās*. Then her son died. Her heirs said, 'We have the *walā'* of the *mawlās*,' which her son had already taken it. The people of Juhaynah said, 'It is not like that. They are only the *mawlās* of our woman. When her son died, we have their *walā'* and we inherit from them.' Abān ibn ᶜAffān gave the judgement that the people of Juhaynah had the *walā'* of the *mawlās*."

قال محمد : وبهذا أيضاً نأخذ. إذا انقرض ولدها الذكور رجع الولاء وميراث من مات بعد ذلك من مواليها إلى عَصبتها. وهو قول أبي حنيفة والعامة من فقهائنا.

Muḥammad said: "This also we adhere to. If her male child dies, then the *walā᾿* and inheritance of whoever dies after that of her *mawlās* returns to her relatives [outside the group who have fixed shares in the inheritance]. That is the verdict of Abū Ḥanīfah and of our *fuqahā᾿* in general."

٧٣١ أخبرنا مالك، أخبرني مخبر عن سعيد بن المسيِّب: أنه سُئِل عن عبدٍ له ولدٌ من امرأة حُرَّةٍ لمن ولاؤهم ؟ قال: إن مات أبوهم وهو عبدٌ لم يُعتَقْ، فولاؤهم لموالي أمّهم.

731. Mālik informed us: "An informant informed me that Sa῾īd ibn al-Musayyab was asked about a slave who had a child by a free woman, 'Who has their *walā᾿*?' He answered, 'If their father has died while he was a slave and had not been freed, then their *walā᾿* belongs to their mother's heirs.'"

قال محمد: وبهذا نأخذ. وإن أعتق أبوهم قبل أن يموت جَرّ ولاءهم، فصار ولايتهم لموالي أبيهم. وهو قول أبي حنيفة والعمة من فقهائنا رحمهم الله.

Muḥammad said: "We adhere to this. If their father was freed before his death, that attracts their *walā᾿*, and it goes to their father's heirs. That is the verdict of Abū Ḥanīfah and of our *fuqahā᾿* in general, may Allah have mercy on them."

٥ باب ميراث الحميل

5. The Inheritance of the Child Carried by a Woman [into Dār al-Islām]

٧٣٢ أخبرنا مالك، أخبرنا بكير بن عبد الله بن الأشج، عن سعيد بن المسيب قال: أبى عمر بن الخطاب أن يُوَرِّثَ أحداً من الأعاجم إلاّ ما وُلد في العرب.

732. Mālik informed us: "Bukayr ibn ῾Abdullāh ibn al-Ashajj informed us that Sa῾īd ibn al-Musayyab said, '῾Umar ibn al-Khaṭṭāb refused to make any of the non-Arabs inherit [from each other][129] except for those born among the Arabs [since their lineages were sure].'"

قال محمد: وبهذا نأخذ. لا يورَث الحميل الذي يُسبى وتُسبى معه امرأة، فتقول هو ولدي، أو تقول هو أخي، أو يقول هي أختي، ولا نسب من الأنساب يورث إلاّ ببيِّنة إلاّ الوالد والولد، فإنه إذا ادَّعى الوالد أنه ابنه، وصدَّقه فهو ابنه، ولا يحتاج في هذا إلى بيِّنة إلاّ أن يكون الولد عبداً فيكذبه مولاه بذلك، فلا يكون ابن الأب ما دام عبداً حتى يصدقه المولى، والمرأة إذا ادعت الولد وشهدت امرأة حرة مسلمة على أنها ولدته، وهو يصدقها، وهو حرّ، فهو ابنها. وهو قول أبي حنيفة والعامة من فقهائنا رحمهم الله.

Muḥammad said: "We adhere to this. The child who has been captured and carried into Dār al-Islām and a woman captured along with him, is not made an heir, if she says, 'He is my boy,' or 'He is my brother,' or he says, 'She is my sister.' No [claim of] lineage is allowed to inherit except by clear evidence and corroborative testimony apart from the [case of the] father and child, because if the father claims that he is his son and he [the son] affirms it then he is [regarded as] his son. This does not need corroborative testimony or evidence, except in the case where the child is a slave and his owner denies it, in which case he will not be [regarded as] the son of the father as long as he is a slave, until the owner confirms it. When a woman claims a child and a free Muslim woman testifies that she did give birth to him, and the child affirms it and he is a free person, then he is [regarded as] her son. That is the verdict of Abū Ḥanīfah and of our *fuqahā'* in general, may Allah have mercy on them."

٦ فصل الوصية

6. The Bequest

٧٣٣ أخبرنا مالك، أخبرنا نافع، عن عبد الله بن عمر: أنَّ رسول الله صلى الله عليه وسلم قال: ما حقّ امرئ مسلم له شيءٌ يُوصي فيه يبيت ليلتين إلاّ و وصيَّته عنده مكتوبةٌ.

733. Mālik informed us: "Nāfi^c informed us from ^cAbdullāh ibn ^cUmar that the Messenger of Allah ﷺ said, 'It is not right for a Muslim man who has something to bequeath to spend two nights unless his bequest is with him written down.'"

قال محمد: وبهذا نأخذُ. هذا حسن جميل.

Muḥammad said, "We adhere to this. This is good and approved."

٧ باب الرجل يوصي عند موته بثلث ماله

7. A Man who Makes a Bequest of a Third of his Wealth on his Deathbed

٧٣٤ أخبرنا مالك، حدَّثنا عبد الله بن أبي بكر بن حزم أن أباه أخبره أن عمرو بن سليم الزُّرَقي أخبره أنه قيل لعمر بن الخطاب: إنَّ ههنا غلاماً يَفَاعاً من غسَّان ووارثُه بالشام، وله مال، وليس هنا إلاَّ ابنة عمّ له، فقال عمر: مُروه، فليوص لها فأوصى لهابمال يقال له بئر جُشَم. قال عمرو بن سُلَيْم: فبعتُ ذلك المالَ بثلاثين ألفاً بعد ذلك، وابنةُ عمِّه التي أوصى لها هي أمُّ عمرو بن سُليم.

734. Mālik informed us: "^cAbdullāh ibn Abī Bakr ibn Ḥazm narrated to us that his father informed him that ^cAmr ibn Sulaym az-Zuraqī informed him that someone said to ^cUmar ibn al-Khaṭṭāb, 'There is an adolescent boy here from Ghassān who has not reached puberty and his heir is in Shām, and he has some property. There is no one here but his paternal uncle's daughter.' ^cUmar said, 'Order him to leave her a bequest.' So he left her a bequest called the Well of Jusham. ^cAmr ibn Sulaym said, 'I sold that property for thirty thousand later on.' In fact, the daughter of his paternal uncle to whom he made bequest is the mother of ^cAmr ibn Sulaym."

٧٣٥ أخبرنا مالك، أخبرنا ابن شهاب، عن عامر ابن سعد بن أبي وقّاص، عن سعد بن أبي وقاص أنه قال: جاءني رسول الله صلى الله عليه وسلم عامَ حَجّة الوَداع يعودني من وجعٍ اشتدّ بي، فقلتُ: يا رسول الله، بلغ مني الوجع ما ترى، وأنا ذو مال ولا يرثني إلا ابنةٌ لي، أ فأتصدق بثلثي مالي؟ قال:

لا، قال: فبالشطر؟ قال: لا، قال: فبالثلث؟ ثم قال رسول الله صلى الله عليه وسلم: الثلثَ، والثلث كثير، أو كبير، إنّك إن تَذَرَ ورثتك أغنياء خيرٌ من أن تَذَرَهم عَالةً يتكفَّفُون الناسَ وإنك لن تُنْفقَ نفقة تبتغي بها وجه الله تعالى إلا أُجرْتَ بها حتى ما تجعلُ في في امرأتك، قال: قلت يا رسول الله، أُخلَّفُ بعد أصحابي؟ قال: إنك لن تُخَلَّفَ فتعملَ عملاً صالحًا تبتغي به وجه الله تعالى إلا ازددت به درجةً ورفعة، ولعلك أن تُخَلَّفَ حتى ينتفعَ بك أقوامٌ، ويُضَرَّ بك آخرون. اللّهم امض لأصحابي هجرتَهم ولا تردَّهم على أعقابهم، لكن البائس سعد بن خولة. يرثي له رسول الله صلى الله عليه وسلم أنْ ماتَ بمكةَ.

735. Mālik informed us: "Ibn Shihāb informed us from ᶜĀmir ibn Saᶜd ibn Abī Waqqāṣ that Saᶜd ibn Abī Waqqāṣ said, 'The Messenger of Allah ﷺ came to me in the year of the Farewell Ḥajj visiting me because of a severe pain I had. I said, "Messenger of Allah, the pain has become very severe as you see. I have some property and no one inherits from me but a daughter of mine. Should I give two thirds of my property as *ṣadaqah*?" He said, "No."' He asked, 'Then a half?' He said, 'No.' He asked, 'Then a third?' He answered, 'A third, and a third is a great deal,' or 'large'. That you leave your heirs self-sufficient is better than leaving them needy begging from people. You will not incur any expenditure seeking by it the face of Allah, exalted is He, but that you will be rewarded for it, even to the extent of that which you put in your wife's mouth.' He said, 'I asked, "Messenger of Allah, shall I be left behind [in Makkah] after my companions [have returned to Madīnah]?" He said, "If you are left behind and you do right actions by which you seek the face of Allah, exalted is He, you will always be increased by it in rank and honour. Perhaps you will be left behind [having a long life] until some peoples benefit from you and others are harmed by you. O Allah, complete their *hijrahs* for my companions and do not turn them back on their heels, but the unfortunate one was Saᶜd ibn Khawlah." The Messenger of Allah ﷺ was distressed for him because he had died in Makkah.'"

قال محمد: الوصايا جائزة في ثُلُث مال الميت بعد قضاء دَيْنه، وليس له أن يُوصي بأكثرَ منه، فإنْ أوصى بأكثر من ذلك فأجازَتْه الورثة بعد موته فهو جائز، وليس لهم أن يرجعوا بعد إجازتهم، وإن ردّوا رَجَع ذلك إلى الثلث لأن النبي صلى الله عليه وسلم قال: الثلث والثلث كثير، فلا يجوز لأحد وصية بأكثر من الثلث إلا أن يجيز الورثة. وهو قول أبي حنيفة والعامة من فقهائنا، رحمهم الله تعالى.

Muḥammad said: "Bequests of one third of one's property are permissible after discharge of one's debts. It is not permissible to bequeath more than that. If someone bequeaths more than that and the heirs allow it after his death, then it is acceptable, but they cannot change their minds after having allowed it. If [on the other hand] they reject it, then it returns to the third because the Prophet ﷺ said, 'A third, and a third is a great deal.' So it is not permitted for anyone to bequeath more than a third unless the heirs allow it. That is the verdict of Abū Ḥanīfah and of our *fuqahā'* in general, may Allah, exalted is He, show them mercy."

كتاب الأَيْمان والنذور وأدنى ما يجزئ في كفارة اليمين

13. OATHS AND VOWS AND THE LEAST THING THAT DISCHARGES THE EXPIATION OF AN OATH

٧٣٦ أخبرنا مالك، أخبرنا نافع: أن ابن عمر كان يُكفِّر عن يمينه بإطعام عَشَرَة مساكين، لكل إنسان مدٌّ من حنطلة، وكان يُعتق الجوار إذا وكّد في اليمين.

736. Mālik informed us: "Nāfi^c informed us that Ibn ^cUmar used to expiate an oath by feeding ten poor people, for each person a *mudd*[130] of wheat. He would free women slaves if he had stressed the oath."

٧٣٧ أخبرنا مالك، حدثنا يحيى بن سعيد، عن سلمان بن يسار قال: أدركتُ الناس وهم إذا أعطَوْا المساكين في كفارة اليمين أعْطَوْا مُدّاً من حنظلة بالمدّ الأصغر ورأوا أن ذلك يجزئُ عنهم.

737. Mālik informed us: "Yaḥyā ibn Sa^cīd narrated to us that Sulaymān ibn Yasār said, 'I used to come across the people,[131] and, when they gave to the poor people for the expiation of an oath, they used to give a *mudd* of wheat, the smaller *mudd*,[132] and they were of the view that that discharged it for them.'"

٧٣٨ أخبرنا مالك، أخبرنا نافع أن عبد الله بن عمر قال: من حلف بيمين فوكّدها ثم حنث، فعليه عتْقُ رقبة أو كسوة عَشَرَة مساكين، ومن حلف بيمين ولم يؤكّدها فحنث، فعليه إطعام عشرة مَساكين، لكل مسكين مدٌّ من حنطة، فمن لم يجد فصيام ثلاثة أيام.

738. Mālik informed us: "Nāfi^c informed us that ^cAbdullāh ibn ^cUmar said, 'Whoever swears an oath stressing it, and then later breaks his oath, must free a slave or clothe ten poor people. Whoever swears an oath without stressing it and then later breaks it, must feed ten poor people giving each poor person a *mudd* of wheat. Whoever does not have that, let him fast three days.'"

قال محمد: إطعام عَشَرَة مساكين غَدَاءً وعَشَاءً أو نصف صاع من حنطة أو صاع من تمر أو شعير.

Muḥammad said: "Feeding ten poor people morning and evening, or a half of a *ṣā^c*[133] of wheat, or a *ṣā^c* of dates or barley."

٧٣٩ قال محمد: أخبرنا سلاّم بن سُلَيْم الحنفي، عن أبي إسحاق السَّبيعي، عن يَرْفأ مولى عمر بن الخطاب رضي الله عنه قال: قال عمر بن الخطاب: يا يرفأ إني أنزلت مالَ الله منّي بمنزلة مال اليتيم إن

احتجتُ أخذتُ منه، فإذا أيْسَرْتُ رددْتُه وإن استَغْنَيْتُ استَعْفَفْتُ ، وإني قد وُلِّيت من أمر المسلمين أمراً عظيماً، فإذا أنتَ سمعتَني أحلفُ على يمين، فلم أمضها فأطعم عني عشرة مساكين خمسة أَصْوُع بُرٍّ بين كل مسكينين صاع .

739. Muḥammad said: "Sallām ibn Sulaym al-Ḥanafī[134] informed us from Abū Isḥāq as-Sabīᶜī from Yarfāʾ the *mawlā* of ᶜUmar ibn al-Khaṭṭāb ﷺ that he said, 'Yarfāʾ, I regard the property of Allah in respect to me in the same position as the orphan's property: if I am in need then I take some of it, but when I am in ample circumstances, then I repay it. [Otherwise] if I am in no need [of it] then I abstain from it. I have been put in charge of the tremendous affair of the Muslims, so if you hear me swear an oath which I do not discharge, then feed ten poor people on my behalf with ten *ṣāᶜ* of wheat, [dividing] a *ṣāᶜ* of wheat between each two poor people.'"

٧٤٠ أخبرنا يونس بن أبي إسحاق، حدّثنا أبو إسحاق، عن يسار بن نُمَيْر ، عن يرفاء غلام عمر بن الخطاب أن عمر قال له: إنّ عليّ أمراً من أمر الناس جسيماً فإذا رأيتني قد حلفتُ على شيء فأطعم عني عشرة مساكين، كل مسكين نصف صاع من بُرّ .

740. Yūnus ibn Abī Isḥāq informed us: "Abū Isḥāq narrated to us from Yasār ibn Numayr from Yarfāʾ the slave of ᶜUmar ibn al-Khaṭṭāb that ᶜUmar said to him, 'It is the weighty matter of the people's for which I am responsible, so whenever you see me having sworn an oath to do something [which I fail to do], then feed ten poor people on my behalf, each poor person receiving half of a *ṣāᶜ* of wheat."

٧٤١ أخبرنا سفيان بن عيينة، عن منصور بن المعتمر، عن شقيق بن سلمة، عن يسار بن نمير: أن عمر بن الخطاب أمر أن يُكَفِّرَ عن يمينه بنصف صاعٍ لكل مسكين.

741. Sufyān ibn ᶜUyaynah informed us from Manṣūr ibn al-Muᶜtamir from Shaqīq ibn Salamah from Yasār ibn Numayr that ᶜUmar ibn al-Khaṭṭāb ordered that he should expiate his oath [which he had failed to fulfil] with half of a *ṣāᶜ* for each poor person."

٧٤٢ أخبرنا سفيان بن عُيَينة، عن عبد الكريم ، عن مجاهد قال : في كل شيء من الكفّارات فيه إطعام المساكين نصفُ صاعٍ لكل مسكين.

742. Sufyān ibn ᶜUyaynah informed us from ᶜAbd al-Karīm that Mujāhid said, "For every type of expiation, in which there is to be the feeding of the poor people, there is to be half of a *ṣāᶜ* for each poor person."

٢ باب الرجل يحلف بالمشي إلى بيت الله

2. A Man who Swears an Oath to Walk to the House of Allah

٧٤٣ أخبرنا مالك، أخبرنا عبد الله بن أبي بكر، عن عمّته أنها حدَّثَتْه عن جدّته : أنها كانت جعلتْ عليها مشياً إلى مسجد قباء فماتت، ولم تَقْضه، فأفتى ابن عباس ابنتها أن تَمْشيَ عنها .

743. Mālik informed us: "ᶜAbdullāh ibn Abī Bakr informed me from his

paternal aunt that she narrated to him that his grandmother had imposed upon herself to walk to the mosque of Qubā᾽, but that she died without doing that. Ibn ᶜAbbās gave the judgement to her daughter that she should walk in her place."

٧٤٤ أخبرنا مالك، حدثنا عبد الله بن أبي حبيبة، قال: قلت لرجل وأنا حديث السّن ، ليس على الرجل يقول: عليّ المشي إلى بيت الله ولا يُسَمِّي نذراً شيءٌ؟ فقال الرجل: هل لك إلى أنْ أُعْطيكَ هذا الجرْو لجرو قثّاءٍ في يده، وتقول: عليّ مشي إلى بيت الله تعالى؟ فقلتُ نعم، فقلتُه، فمكَثتُ حيناً حتى عقلتُ ، فقيل لي : إنّ عليك مشياً. فجئتُ سعيد بن المسيّب فسألته عن ذلك فقال : عليك مشيٌ.
فمشيت.

744. Mālik informed us: "ᶜAbdullāh ibn Abī Ḥabībah narrated to us saying, 'I said to a man when I was young, "There is nothing binding on a man who says, 'I must walk to the House of Allah,' without calling it a vow." The man said, "Would you like me to give you this little thing," referring to a small cucumber in his hand, "if you to say, 'I undertake to walk to the House of Allah, exalted is He'?" So I answered, "Yes." I said it and then I remained some time passed until I came of age and someone said to me, "You have to walk." I went to Saᶜīd ibn al-Musayyab and asked him about it and he said, "You must walk," and so I walked.'"

قال محمد: وبهذا نأخذ. من جعل عليه المشي إلى بيت الله لزمه المشيُ إن جعله نذراً أو غير نذر. وهو قول أبي حنيفة والعامة من فقهائنا رحمهم الله تعالى.

Muḥammad said: "We adhere to this. Whoever makes an undertaking to walk to the House of Allah is obliged to walk, whether he makes it a vow or not, and that is the verdict of Abū Ḥanīfah and of our *fuqahā᾽* in general, may Allah, exalted is He, show them mercy."

٣ باب من جَعَل على نفسه المشي ثم عجز

3. Someone who Undertakes to Walk but then is Incapable

٧٤٥ أخبرنا مالك،عن عروة بن أُذَيْنَة أنّه قال : خرجتُ مع جَدَّةٍ لي عليها مشْيٌ إلى بيت الله حتى إذا كنا ببعض الطريق عجزتْ فأرسلت مولى لها إلى عبد الله بن عمر ليسأله، وخرجتُ مع المَوْلى، فسأله : فقال عبد الله بن عمر: مُرها فلتركب ثم لتمشِ من حيث عجَزْت.

745. Mālik informed us that ᶜUrwah ibn Udhaynah said, "I went with one of my grandmothers who was obliged to walk to the House of Allah until, when she had gone a part of the way, she became unable [to walk any further]. She sent one of her *mawlās* to ᶜAbdullāh ibn ᶜUmar to ask him and I went with the *mawlā* and he asked him. ᶜAbdullāh ibn ᶜUmar answered, 'Tell her to mount, and then she must walk [when capable] from the point where she grew incapable.'"

قال محمد: قد قال هذا قوم. وأحبُّ إلينا من هذا القول ما روي عن علي بن أبي طالب رضي الله عنه.

Muḥammad said: "Some people say this. What is preferable to us of these statements is that which is narrated from ᶜAlī ibn Abī Ṭālib ﷺ."

٧٤٦ أخبرنا شُعبة بن الحَجَّاج، عن الحكم بن عُتبة، عن إبراهيم النخعي، عن علي بن أبي طالب كرَّم الله وجهه، أنَّه قال: من نذر أنْ يحجَّ ماشياً، ثم عَجز فليَرْكَبْ ولْيَحُجَّ ولينحر بَدَنَة. وجاء عنه في حديث آخر: ويُهْدِي هدياً. فبهذا نأخُذُ، يكون الهَدي مكان المشي. وهو قول أبي حنيفة والعامة من فقهائنا.

746. Shuᶜbah ibn al-Ḥajjāj informed us from al-Ḥakam ibn ᶜUtbah from Ibrāhīm an-Nakhaᶜī that ᶜAlī ibn Abī Ṭālib, may Allah honour his face, said, "Whoever vows that he will perform the Ḥajj walking and then becomes incapable, let him mount, perform the Ḥajj and sacrifice a sacrificial animal[135]." It has also been narrated from him in another ḥadīth, "...let him make a *hady* offering[136]." [Muḥammad said] "We adhere to this. The offering is in place of the walking, and that is the verdict of Abū Ḥanīfah and of our *fuqahā*ᵓ in general."

٧٤٧ أخبرنا مالك، أخبرنا يحيى بن سعيد قال: كان عَلَيّ مشْيٌ، فأصابتني خاصرةٌ، فركبت حتى أتيت مكة فسألتُ عطاءَ بن أبي رباح وغيره، فقالوا: عليك هدي، فلما قدمتُ المدينة سألت فأمروني أن أمشي من حيث عجزت مرة أخرى، فمشيت.

747. Mālik informed us: "Yaḥyā ibn Saᶜīd informed us, 'I was obliged to walk, but I was afflicted by [a pain in] the side [perhaps in the kidneys]. I mounted to get to Makkah and then asked ᶜAṭāᵓ ibn Abī Rabāḥ and others. They said, "You must make an offering." Then when I came to Madīnah, they told me to walk, from that point where I had become incapable of walking, on another occasion, and so I walked.'"

قال محمدٌ: وبقول عطاء نأخذ. يركب وعليه هدي لركوبه وليس عليه أن يعود.

Muḥammad said: "The verdict of ᶜAṭāᵓ is the one we adhere to. He should mount and he must make an offering because of his having mounted, but he does not have to repeat [the Ḥajj]."

٤ باب الاستثناء في اليمين

4. Making an Exception in an Oath

٧٤٨ أخبرنا مالك، حدَّثنا نافع أن عبد الله بن عمر قال: من قال: والله، ثم قال: إن شاء الله، ثم لم يفعل الذي عليه لم يحنث.

748. Mālik informed us: "Nāfiᶜ narrated to us that ᶜAbdullāh ibn ᶜUmar said, 'Whoever says, "By Allah!" and then adds, "*inshaᵓAllāh*," and then does not do that which he swore to do has not failed to fulfil his oath.'"

قال محمد: وبهذا نأخذ. إذا قال: إن شاء الله ووصلها بيمينه فلا شيء عليه. وهو قول أبي حنيفة.

Muḥammad said: "We adhere to this. If he says *insha᾿Allāh,* and joins it [immediately] to his oath,[137] then there is nothing against him. That is the verdict of Abū Ḥanīfah."

٥ باب الرجل يموت وعليه نذر

5. A Man who Dies with a Vow [unfulfilled]

٧٤٩ أخبرنا مالك، حدثنا ابن شهاب، عن عبيد الله بن عبد الله بن عتبة بن مسعود، عن عبد الله بن عباس: أن سعد بن عُبادة استفتى رسولَ الله صلى الله عليه وسلم فقال: إن أُمِّي ماتت وعليها نذر لم تَقْضه، قال: اقضه عنها.

749. Mālik informed us: "Ibn Shihāb narrated to us from ᶜUbaydullāh ibn ᶜAbdullāh ibn ᶜUtbah ibn Masᶜūd from ᶜAbdullāh ibn ᶜAbbās that Saᶜd ibn ᶜUbādah sought a fatwā from the Messenger of Allah ﷺ saying, 'My mother died with a vow which she had not fulfilled,' and he said, 'Fulfil it for her.'"

قال محمد: ما كان من نذر أو صدقة أو حج قضاها عنها أجزأ ذلك إن شاء الله تعالى: وهو قول أبي حنيفة والعامة من فقهائنا رحمهم الله تعالى.

Muḥammad said, "Whatever vow, *ṣadaqah* or Ḥajj he discharges on her behalf will suffice [her], *inshā᾿Allāh,* exalted is He. That is the verdict of Abū Ḥanīfah and of our *fuqahā᾿* in general, may Allah, exalted is He, show them mercy."

٦ باب من حلف أو نذر في معصية

6. Someone who Swears an Oath or Vows to do an Act of Disobedience

٧٥٠ أخبرنا مالك، حدَّثنا طلحة بن عبد الملك، عن القاسم بن محمد، عن عائشة زوج النبي صلى الله عليه وسلم: أن النبي صلى الله عليه وسلم قال: من نذر أن يُطيع الله فليطعه، ومن نذر أن يعصيه فلا يعصه.

750. Mālik informed us: "Ṭalḥah ibn ᶜAbd al-Mālik narrated to us from al-Qāsim ibn Muḥammad from ᶜĀ᾿ishah the wife of the Prophet ﷺ that the Prophet ﷺ said, 'Whoever vows to obey Allah, then let him obey Him. Whoever vows to disobey Him, then let him not disobey Him.'"

قال محمد: وبهذا نأخذ. من نذر نذراً في معصية ولم يسمِّ فليُطع الله وليكَفِّر عن يمينه. وهو قولُ أبي حنيفة.

Muḥammad said: "We adhere to this. Whoever makes a vow to do an act of disobedience without naming it, then let him obey Allah and make expiation for his oath. That is the verdict of Abū Ḥanīfah."

٧٥١ أخبرنا مالك، أخبرني يحيى بن سعيد، قال: سمعت القاسم بن محمد يقول: أتت امرأة إلى ابن عباس فقالت: إنّي نذرت أن أنحر ابني، فقال: لا تنحري ابنَك، وكفِّري عن يمينك، فقال شيخ عند ابن عباس جالس: كيف يكون في هذا كفارة؟ قال ابن عباس: أرأيتَ أن الله تعالى قال: (والذين يظاهرون من نسائهم) ثم جعل فيه من الكفارة ما قد رأيت؟

751. Mālik informed us: "Yaḥyā ibn Saᶜīd informed me, 'I heard al-Qāsim

ibn Muḥammad saying, "A woman came to Ibn ᶜAbbās and said, 'I have vowed to slaughter my son.' He said, 'Do not slaughter your son, and make expiation for your oath.' A *shaykh* who was sitting with Ibn ᶜAbbās asked, 'How can there be an expiation for this?' Ibn ᶜAbbās answered, 'Don't you see that Allah, exalted is He, says, "Those who divorce their wives..." (Sūrat al-Mujādilah: 3) and then He appoints for it that expiation which you know?'""

قال محمد: وبقول ابن عباس نأخذ. وهذا مما وصفتُ لك أنه من حلف أو نذر نذراً في معصية، فلا يعصينَّ، وليُكَفِّرَنَّ، عن يمين.

Muḥammad said: "The verdict of Ibn ᶜAbbās is the one we adhere to. This is what I have described to you, that whoever swears an oath or vows to perform an act of disobedience, then he must not do the act of disobedience and must make expiation for his oath."

٧٥٢ أخبرنا مالك، أخبرنا ابن سهيل بن أبي صالح، عن أبيه عن أبي هريرة أنَّ رسول الله صلى الله عليه وسلم قال: من حلف على يمين فرأى غيرها خيراً منها فليُكَفِّرٍ عن يمينه وليفعل.

752. Mālik informed us: "Ibn Suhayl ibn Abī Ṣāliḥ informed us from his father from Abū Hurayrah that the Messenger of Allah ﷺ said, 'Whoever swears an oath, and then sees that something other than it is better than it, let him expiate his oath and let him do [it][138].'"

قال محمدٌ: وبهذا نأخذ وهو قولُ أبي حنيفة رحمه الله تعالى.

Muḥammad said: "We adhere to this, and it is the verdict of Abū Ḥanīfah, may Allah have mercy on him."

٧ باب من حلف بغير الله

7. Someone who Swears an Oath by other than Allah

٧٥٣ أخبرنا مالك، أخبرنا نافع، عن عبد الله بن عمر: أنَّ رسول الله صلى الله عليه وسلم سمع عمر بن الخطاب، وهو يقول: ولا وأبي، فقال رسول الله صلى الله عليه وسلم: إن الله ينهاكم أن تحلفوا بآبائكم، فمن كان حالفاً فليحلف بالله ثم ليبرر أو ليصمُتْ.

753. Mālik informed us: "Nāfiᶜ informed me from ᶜAbdullāh ibn ᶜUmar that the Messenger of Allah ﷺ heard ᶜUmar ibn al-Khaṭṭāb while he was saying, 'No! by my father!' So the Messenger of Allah ﷺ said, 'Allah forbids [you] swearing oaths by your fathers. Whoever would swear an oath then let him swear by Allah, and then let him be true [to his oath] or be silent.'"

قال محمد: وبهذا نأخذ. لا ينبغي لأحد أن يحلف بأبيه، فمن كان حالفاً فليحلف بالله ثمَّ ليبرُرْ أو ليَصْمُتْ.

Muḥammad said: "We adhere to this. No one ought to swear an oath by his father. Whoever would swear an oath, then let him swear by Allah and then let him be true [to his oath] or let him be silent."

٨ باب الرجل يقول: مَالُه في رِتَاجِ الْكَعْبَة

8. A Man Saying that his Wealth is [devoted] to the Door of the Kaʿbah[139]

٧٥٤ أخبرنا مالك، أخبرني أيّوب بن موسى من ولْد سعيد بن العاص، عن منصور بن عبد الرحمن الحَجَبيّ، عن أبيه ، عن عائشة زوج النبي صلى الله عليه وسلم أنها قالت فيمن قال: مالي في رِتَاج الكعبة يُكَفَّرُ ذلك بما يُكَفَّرُ اليمين .

754. Mālik informed us: "Ayyūb ibn Mūsā informed me from his father from the children of Saʿīd ibn al-ʿĀṣ from Manṣūr ibn ʿAbd ar-Raḥmān al-Ḥajabī from his father that ʿĀʾishah, the wife of the Prophet 鷺, said concerning someone who said, 'My property is [devoted] to the door of the Kaʿbah,' that, 'it is expiated by that which would expiate an oath.'"

قال محمد: قد بَلَغنا هذا عن عائشة رضي الله عنها. وأحبُّ إلينا أن يفيَ بما جعل على نفسه، فيتصدّق بذلك ويُمسك ما يقُوّتُه ، فإذا أفاد مالاً تصدّق بمثل ما كان أمسك . وهو قولُ أبي حنيفة والعامّة من فقهائنا.

Muḥammad said: "This has reached us from ʿĀʾishah 鷺. What is preferable to us is that he should fulfil that which he has imposed on himself and give that away as *ṣadaqah* retaining that which will sustain and nourish him [so as not to impoverish himself totally]. Then when he obtains [more] property he should give *ṣadaqah* the like of that which he retained. That is the verdict of Abū Ḥanīfah and of our *fuqahāʾ* in general."

٩ باب اللَّغْو مِن الأَيْمان

9. Inadvertent Statements in Oaths[140]

٧٥٥ أخبرنا مالك، أخبرنا هشام بن عروة، عن أبيه، عن عائشة رضي الله عنها أنها قالت: لغو اليمين: قول الإنسان : لا والله، وبلى والله .

755. Mālik informed us: "Hishām ibn ʿUrwah informed us from his father that ʿĀʾishah 鷺 said, 'An inadvertent statement in an oath is a person's saying, "No, by Allah!" and "Of course, by Allah!"'"

قال محمد: وبهذا نأخذ . اللغو ما حلف عليه الرجل، وهو يرى أنه حقٌّ، فاستَبَان له بعد أنه على غير ذلك، فهذا من اللغو عندنا.

Muḥammad said, "We adhere to this. An inadvertent statement is that which a man swears believing it to be right, but then later it becomes clear that it is not. This is an inadvertent statement according to us."

كتاب البُيوع في التجارات والسَّلَم

14. SALES: TRADING AND DEFERRED SALES

١ باب بيع العرايا

1. The Sale of Rights to the Produce of a Date-palm (*ᶜariyyah*)

٧٥٦ أخبرنا مالك، حدّثنا نافع، عن عبد الله بن عمر، عن زيد بن ثابت: أن رسول الله صلى الله عليه وسلم رخّص لصاحب العَرِيَّة أن يبيعَها بخرصها.

756. Mālik informed us: "Nāfiᶜ narrated to us from ᶜAbdullāh ibn ᶜUmar from Zayd ibn Thābit that the Messenger of Allah ﷺ made a concession for the person granted rights to the produce of a date-palm (*ᶜariyyah*)[141] to exchange this for an estimated amount [of its yield]."

٧٥٧ أخبرنا مالك، أخبرنا داود بن الحصين أن أبا سفيان مولى ابن أبي أحمد أخبره، عن أبي هريرة: أنّ رسول الله صلى الله عليه وسلم رخَّص في بيع العرايا فيما دون خمسة أوسق أو في خمسة أوسق. شكَّ داود لا يدري أقال خمسة أو فيما دون خمسة؟

757. Mālik informed us: "Dāwūd ibn al-Ḥuṣayn informed us that Abū Sufyān the *mawlā* of Ibn Abī Aḥmad informed him from Abū Hurayrah that the Messenger of Allah ﷺ granted a concession concerning the sale of the right to the produce of a date-palm (*ᶜariyyah*) in respect of that which is less than five *wasqs*[142] or equal to five *wasqs*. Dāwūd was in doubt and did not know whether he said five or less than five."

قال محمد: وبهذا نأخذ. وذكر مالك بن أنس أن العرية إنما تكون أن الرجل يكون له النخل، فيُطْعِمُ الرجلَ منها ثمرة نخلة أو نخلتين يلقُطُها لعياله، ثم يثقُل عليه دخولُه حائطَه، فيسأله أن يتجاوزَ له عنها على أن يعطيه بمكيلتها تمراً عند صرام النخل، فهذا كلُّه لا بأس به عندنا، لأن التمرَ كلَّه كان للأول وهو يعطي منه ما شاء فإن شاء سلَّم له تمر النخل وإن شاء أعطاها بمكيلتها من التمر، لأن هذا لا يُجعل بيعاً، ولو جُعل بيعاً ما حلَّ تمر بتمر إلى أجل.

Muḥammad said: "We adhere to this. Mālik ibn Anas mentioned that an *ᶜariyyah* is simply that a man has date palms and allows another man to eat from the fruit of one or two palms or for the man to take from them for his dependants. Later it becomes burdensome for him to go to the walled garden, and so he asks to be allowed to avoid that and to receive instead an equivalent measure of some dried dates at the season of harvesting the date palms. There is no harm in all of this according to us, because all of the dried dates belonged to the former [the owner] and he gives of it whatever he wishes. If he wishes, he can give him the dates of the date palm, and if he wishes he can give him an equivalent measure of dried dates, because this is not regarded as a sale. If it were a sale, then it would not be permissible to sell dates for other dates at a later date."

٢ باب ما يُكره من بيع الثمار قبل أن يَبدُوَ صلاحها

2. That which is Disapproved of in the Sale of Fruits[143] before they are Usable[144]

٧٥٨ أخبرنا مالك، حدَّثنا نافع، عن عبد الله بن عمر: أنَّ رسول الله صلى الله عليه وسلم نهى عن بيع الثمار حتى يبدوَ صلاحُها. نهى البائع والمشتري.

758. Mālik informed us: "Nāfi[c] narrated to us from [c]Abdullāh ibn [c]Umar that the Messenger of Allah ﷺ forbade the sale of fruits before they are usable. He forbade both the seller and the purchaser."

٧٥٩ أخبرنا مالك، أخبرنا أبو الرجال محمد بن عبد الرحمن، عن أمّه عَمْرة: أن رسول الله صلى الله عليه وسلم نهى عن بيع الثمار حتى ينجوَ من العاهة.

759. Mālik informed us: "Abu'r-Rijāl Muḥammad ibn [c]Abd ar-Raḥmān narrated to us from his mother [c]Amrah that the Messenger of Allah ﷺ forbade the sale of fruit until it was safe from the blight."

قال محمد: لا ينبغي أن يُباع شيء من الثمار على أن يُترك في النخل حتى يبلغَ، إلاَّ أن يحمَرَّ أو يصفَرَّ أو يبلغَ بعضُه، فإذا كان كذلك فلا بأس ببيعه على أن يُترك حتى يبلغَ، فإذا لم يحمرّ أو يصفرّ أو كان أخضر أو كان كُفَرَّى فلا خير في شرائه على أن يُترك حتى يبلغ. ولا بأس بشرائه على أن يُقطع و يُباع. وكذلك بلغنا عن الحسن البصري أنَّه قال: لا بأس ببيع الكُفَرَّى على أن يُقطع، فبهذا نأخذ.

Muḥammad said: "Nothing of fruit should be sold on the basis of it being left on the date palm until it should ripen unless it has reddened or yellowed and some of it has ripened. When it is like that then there is no harm in selling it on the basis that it should be left until it ripens. If it has not reddened or yellowed or if it is green or is a spathe, then in that case there is no good in selling it on the basis that it should be left until it ripens. There is no harm in selling it on the basis that it should be cut down and sold. Similarly, it has reached us that al-Ḥasan al-Baṣrī said, 'There is no harm in the sale of the spathe on the basis that it should be cut,' and we adhere to this."

٧٦٠ أخبرنا مالك، أخبرنا أبو الزِّناد، عن خارجة بن زيد بن ثابت، عن زيد بن ثابت: أنه كان لا يبيع ثمارَه حتى يطلع الثُرَيَّا يعني بيع النخل.

760. Mālik informed us: "Abu'z-Zinād informed us from Khārijah ibn Zayd ibn Thābit that Zayd ibn Thābit would not sell his fruit until the Pleaides rose, referring to the sale of his date palms [fruit]."

٣ باب الرجل يبيعُ بعضَ الثمرَ ويستثني بعضه

3. A Man Selling some Fruit and Excluding some [from the Sale]

٧٦١ أخبرنا مالك، أخبرنا عبد الله بن أبي بكر، عن أبيه: أنّ محمد بن عمرو بن حزم باع حائطاً له يقال له الأفْراق بأربعة آلاف درهم، واستثنى منه بثماني مائة درهم تمراً.

761. Mālik informed us: "ᶜAbdullāh ibn Abī Bakr informed us from his father that Muḥammad ibn ᶜAmr ibn Ḥazm sold a walled garden of his called al-Afrāq for four thousand dirhams, excluding from the sale eight hundred dirhams worth of dates."

٧٦٢ أخبرنا مالك، أخبرنا أبو الرِّجال، عن أمّه عَمْرة بنت عبد الرحمن: أنّها كانت تبيع ثمارها، وتستثني منها.

762. Mālik informed us: "Abu'r-Rijāl informed us from his mother ᶜAmrah bint ᶜAbd ar-Raḥmān that she used to sell her fruit and exclude some of it from the sale."

٧٦٣ أخبرنا مالك، أخبرنا ربيعة بن عبد الرحمن، عن القاسم بن محمد: أنّه كان يبيع ويستثني منها.

763. Mālik informed us: "Rabīᶜah ibn ᶜAbd ar-Raḥmān informed us that al-Qāsim ibn Muḥammad used to sell and exclude some of it."

قال محمد: وبهذا نأخذ. لا بأس بأن يبيع الرجل ثمره، ويستثني بعضَه إذا استثنى شيئاً من جملته ربعاً أو خمساً أو سدساً.

Muḥammad said: "We adhere to this. There is no harm in a man selling his fruit and excluding some of it, if he excludes something [specific] from the whole [sale], a quarter or a fifth or a sixth."

٤ باب ما يُكره من بيع التمر بالرطب

4. What is Disapproved of in the Sale of Dried Dates for Fresh Dates

٧٦٤ أخبرنا مالك، أخبرنا عبد الله بن يزيد مولى الأسود بن سفيان، أنّ زيداً أبا عيَّاش مولى لبني زهرة، أخبره أنّه سأل سعد بن أبي وقاص عمّن اشترى البيضاء بالسُّلت؟ فقال له سعد: أيُّهما أفضل؟ قال: البيضاء، قال: فنهاني عنه، وقال: سمعتُ رسول الله صلى الله عليه وسلم سُئل عمّنْ اشترى التمر بالرطب؟ فقال: أ ينقص الرُّطَبُ إذا يبس؟ قالوا: نعم، فنهى عنه.

764. Mālik informed us: "ᶜAbdullāh ibn Yazīd the *mawlā* of al-Aswad ibn Sufyān informed us that Zayd Abū ᶜAyyāsh the *mawlā* of Banī Zuhrah informed him that he asked Saᶜd ibn Abī Waqqāṣ about someone who bought ordinary barley with another variety of barley, so Saᶜd asked him, 'Which of the two are better?' He answered, 'The ordinary barley.'" He [Zayd] said, "He forbade me to do that and he said, 'I heard the Messenger of Allah ﷺ being asked about someone who bought dried dates with fresh dates and he asked, "Does the fresh date shrink when it dries?" He answered, "Yes," and so he forbade it.'"

قال محمد : وبهذا نأخذ . لا خير في أن يشتري الرجل قَفيز رطب بقفيزٍ من تمرٍ، يداً بيد ، لأن الرُّطَب يَنْقُصُ إذا جفّ فيصير أقلّ من قفيز، فلذلك فسد البيعَ فيه .

Muḥammad said: "We adhere to this. There is no good in a man buying a measure of twelve *ṣā*ᶜ of fresh dates with a similar measure of dried dates, hand to hand, because the fresh dates shrink when they dry and so become less than a measure of twelve *ṣā*ᶜ. It is for that reason the sale is corrupt."

٥ باب ما لم يُقبض من الطعام وغيره

5. Foods and Other Things that are not Taken Possession of

٧٦٥ أخبرنا مالك، أخبرنا نافع: أن حكيم بن حزم ابتاع طعاماً أمر به عمر بن الخطاب للناس، فباع حكيم الطعامَ قبل أن يستوفيَه ، فسمع بذلك عمر بن الخطاب رضي الله عنه فردّ عليه ، وقال: لا تبع طعاماً ابتعتَه حتى تستوفيَه.

765. Mālik informed us: "Nāfiᶜ informed us that Ḥakīm ibn Ḥizām bought food for people, which ᶜUmar ibn al-Khaṭṭāb ordered him to. Then Ḥakīm sold the food before he had taken possession of it. ᶜUmar ibn al-Khaṭṭāb ﷺ heard about that and rejected his sale. He said, 'Do not sell food which you have bought until you take possession of it.'"

٧٦٦ أخبرنا مالك، حدّثنا نافع، عن عبد الله بن عمر: أنّ رسول الله صلى الله عليه وسلم قال: من ابتاع طعاماً فلا يبعه حتى يَقْبضَه.

766. Mālik informed us: "Nāfiᶜ narrated to us from ᶜAbdullāh ibn ᶜUmar that the Messenger of Allah ﷺ said, 'Whoever buys food, let him not sell it until he takes possession of it.'"

قال محمد: وبهذا نأخذ. وكذلك كلُّ شيء بيْع من طعام أو غيره فلا ينبغي أن يبيعَه الذي اشتراه حتى يقبضه، وكذلك قال عبد الله بن عباس، قال: أما الذي نهى عنه رسول الله فهو الطعام أنْ يُباع حتى يُقْبَض.

وقال ابن عباس: ولا أحسب كل شيء إلا مثل ذلك. فبقول ابن عباس نأخذ، الأشياء كلها مثل الطعام، لا ينبغي أن يبيع المشتري شيئاً اشتراه حتى يقبضه، وكذلك قول أبي حنيفة رحمه الله إلا أنه رخّص في الدُّور والعَقَار والأرضين التي لا تُحوّل أنْ تُباع قبل أنْ تُقبض، أما نحن فلا نُجيز شيئاً من ذلك حتى يُقبض.

Muḥammad said: "We adhere to this. And similarly with everything which is sold of food or other things; the one who buys it ought not to sell it until he takes possession of it. That was also what ᶜAbdullāh ibn ᶜAmr said, 'As for what the Messenger of Allah ﷺ forbade, it is that food be sold before it is taken possession of.' Ibn ᶜAbbās said, 'I actually think that everything is like that.'[145] So, we adhere to the verdict that Ibn ᶜAbbās took - all things are like food; the purchaser ought not to sell anything he has bought until he takes possession of it. The verdict of Abū Ḥanīfah, may Allah have mercy on him, was similar, except that he allowed a concession in cases of houses, properties and lands which have not been substantially altered, that they may be sold before they are taken possession of. As for us, we do not regard as valid anything of that before they are taken possession of."

٧٦٧ أخبرنا مالك، حدثنا نافع، عن عبد الله بن عمر أنه قال : كنا نبتاع الطعام في زمان رسول الله ﷺ ، فبعث علينا مَنْ يأمرنا بانتقاله من المكان الذي نبتاعه فيه إلى مكان سواه قبل أنْ نبيعَه.

767. Mālik informed us: "Nāfi[c] narrated to us that [c]Abdullāh ibn [c]Umar said, 'We used to buy food at the time of the Messenger of Allah ﷺ and he sent someone to us to order us to transport it from the place in which we had bought it to another place before selling it.'"

قال محمد : إنما كان يُراد بهذا القبض لئلا يبيعَ شيئاً من ذلك حتى يقبضَه فلا ينبغي أن يبيع شيئاً اشتراه رجلٌ حتى يقبضه.

Muḥammad said: "What was meant by this was only taking possession so that none of it should be sold until taken possession of. A man ought not to sell anything he bought until he takes possession of it."

٦ باب الرجل يبيع المتاع أو غيره نسيئة ثم يقول: انْقُدْني وأضعُ عنك

6. A Man who Sells Goods or Something else on Deferred Terms and then says, "Pay me cash and I will lower the price."

٧٦٨ أخبرنا مالك، أخبرنا أبو الزِّناد ، عن بُسْر بن سعيد، عن أبي صالح بن عبيد مولى السَّفَّاح أنه أخبره: أنه باع بَزّاً من أهل دار نَخْلَة إلى أجل، ثم أرادوا الخروج إلى كوفة فسألوه أنْ يَنْقُدُوه، ويَضَعَ عنهم، فسأل زيدَ بن ثابت، فقال: لا آمرك أنْ تأكُلَ ذلك ولا تُوْكِلَه.

768. Mālik informed us: "Abu'z-Zinād informed us from Busr ibn Sa[c]īd that Abū Ṣāliḥ ibn [c]Ubayd the *mawlā* of as-Saffāḥ informed him that he sold garments called bazz to the people of Dār an-Nakhlah [in Madīnah] to be paid for later at a specific date. Then they wanted to leave to go to Kūfa, and so they asked to be able to pay him in cash and that he would reduce the price for them. He asked Zayd ibn Thābit about that and he said, 'I advise you not to consume that nor that you give it to someone else to consume.'"

قال محمد : وبهذا نأخذ . من وَجَبَ له دَيْن على إنسان إلى أجل، فسأل أن يَضَعَ عنه، ويُعَجِّل له ما بقي لم ينبغِ ذلك لأنه يعجِّل قليلاً بكثير دَيْناً، فكأنّه يبيع قليلاً نقداً بكثير دَيْناً. وهو قول عمر بن الخطاب وزيد بن ثابت وعبد الله بن عمر ، وهو قول أبي حنيفة .

Muḥammad said: "We adhere to this. Someone who owes a debt to someone at a specific time, and then asks him to reduce the amount in exchange forhastening the [time of the payment of] what remains, then that ought not to be done, because he would bring forward the payment of a little in place of a large debt. It is as if he is selling a little in cash for a large debt. That is the verdict of [c]Umar ibn al-Khaṭṭāb, Zayd ibn Thābit and [c]Abdullāh ibn [c]Umar, and it is the verdict of Abū Ḥanīfah."

٧ باب الرجل يشتري الشعير بالحنطة

7. A Man Buying Barley with Wheat

٧٦٩ أخبرنا مالك، حدَّثنا نافع: أنَّ سليمان بن يسار أخبره: أن عبد الرحمن بن الأسود بن عبد يغوث فنيَ عَلَفُ دابَّته فقال لغلامه: خذ من حنطة أهلك فاشترِ به شعيراً ولا تأخذ إلاَّ مثلاً بمثل.

769. Mālik informed us: "Nāfiᶜ narrated to us that Sulaymān ibn Yasār informed him that ᶜAbd ar-Raḥmān ibn al-Aswad ibn ᶜAbd Yaghūth ran out of fodder for his mount and so he said to his slave, 'Take some of your family's wheat and buy barley with it, but only take like for like.[146]'"

قال محمد: ولسنا نرى بأساً بأن يشتري الرجل قفيزين من شعير بقفيز من حنطة يداً بيد. والحديث المعروف في ذلك عن عبادة بن الصامت أنه قال: قال رسول الله صلى الله عليه وسلم: الذهب بالذهب مثلاً بمثل. والفضة بالفضة مثلاً بمثل، والحنطة بالحنطة مثلاً بمثل، والشعير بالشعير مثلاً بمثل. ولا بأس بأن يأخذ الذهب بالفضة والفضة أكثر، ولا بأس بأن يأخذ الحنطة بالشعير والشعير أكثر يداً بيد، في ذلك أحاديث كثيرة معروفة. وهو قولُ أبي حنيفة والعامة من فقهائنا.

Muḥammad said: "We see no harm in a man buying a measure of barley with a [similar] measure of wheat, hand to hand. The well-known *ḥadīth* on that from ᶜUbādah ibn aṣ-Ṣāmit is that he said, 'The Messenger of Allah ﷺ said, "Gold for gold, like for like. Silver for silver, like for like. Wheat for wheat, like for like, and barley for barley, like for like."' There is no harm in taking gold for silver and extra silver, nor is there any harm in taking wheat for barley and extra barley, hand to hand. There are many well known *aḥādīth* concerning that. That is the verdict of Abū Ḥanīfah and of our *fuqahā᾽* in general."

٨ باب الرجل يبيع الطعام نسيئة ثم يشتري بذلك الثمن شيئاً آخر

8. A Man who Sells Food on Credit the Payment for which is Deferred to a Certain Period, and then later He Buys Something else with the Price

٧٧٠ أخبرنا مالكٌ، حدَّثنا أبو الزِّناد، أن سعيد بن المسيِّب وسليمان بن يسار: كانا يَكْرهان أن يبيع الرجلُ طعاماً إلى أجل بذهب، ثم يشتري بذلك الذهب تمراً قبل أن يقبضها.

770. Mālik informed us: "Abu'z-Zinād narrated to us that Saᶜīd ibn al-Musayyab and Sulaymān ibn Yasār used to dislike a man selling food on delayed terms for gold [to be paid later], and then buying dates with that gold before taking possession of it [the gold]."

قال محمد: ونحن لا نرى بأساً أن يشتري بها تمراً قبل أن يقبضها إذا كان التمر بعينه، ولم يكن دَيْناً. وقد ذُكر هذا القول لسعيد بن جبير فلم يَره شيئاً وقال: لا بأس به. وهو قولُ أبي حنيفة والعامة من فقهائنا.

Muḥammad said: "We do not see any harm in him buying dates with it before taking possession of it if the dates are actual dates and not a debt.

This verdict is mentioned as being that of Saʿīd ibn Jubayr and that he did not see it as anything [harmful], and that he said, 'There is no harm in it.' That is the verdict of Abū Ḥanīfah and of our *fuqahāʾ* in general."

٩ باب ما يُكره من النَّجَش وتلقِّي السِّلَع

9. What is Disapproved of Bidding up the Price [*an-najash*] and Forestalling[147]

٧٧١ أخبرنا مالك، أخبرنا نافع عن عبد الله بن عمر: أن رسول الله صلى الله عليه وسلم نهى عن تلقِّي السلع حتى تهبط الأسواق، ونهى عن النَّجَش.

771. Mālik informed us: "Nāfiʿ informed us from ʿAbdullāh ibn ʿUmar that the Messenger of Allah ﷺ forbade going out to meet goods before they have reached the markets, and he forbade bidding up the price."

قال محمد: وبهذا نأخذ. كل ذلك مكروه، فأمّا النَّجش فالرجل يحضر فيزيد في الثمن ويعطي فيه ما لا يريد أن يشتري به ليُسمع بذلك غيره فيشتري على سَوْمه، فهذا لا ينبغي.

وأما تلقِّي السلع فكل أرض كان ذلك يضرّ بأهلها فليس ينبغي أن يُفعل ذلك بها، فإذا كثرت الأشياء بها حتى صار ذلك لا يضر بأهلها فلا بأس بذلك إن شاء الله تعالى.

Muḥammad said: "We adhere to this. All of it is disliked. As for bidding up the price [*an-najash*], it is that a man attends [the sale] and increases the price offered, and offers for it something which he has no intention of paying for it, so that someone else will overhear that and buy it at his price, and this is not acceptable. As for forestalling,[148] it ought not to be done in any land in which it would harm its people. When things multiply there until it becomes such that it will do no harm to its people, then there is no harm in it, *inshāʾAllāh*, exalted is He."

١٠ باب الرجل يُسلِم فيما يُكال

10. A Man Paying an Advance for Measured Goods

٧٧٢ أخبرنا مالك، حدَّثنا نافع: أن عبد الله بن عمر كان يقول: لا بأس بأنْ يبتاعَ الرجلُ طعاماً إلى أجل معلوم بسعر معلوم إن كان لصاحبه طعام أو لم يكن، ما لم يكن في زَرْع لم يَبْدُ صلاحُها أو في تمر لم يَبْدُ صَلاحُها، فإنَّ رسول الله صلى الله عليه وسلم نهى عن بيع الثمار وعن شرائها حتى يبدوَ صلاحُها.

772. Mālik informed us: "Nāfiʿ narrated to us that ʿAbdullāh ibn ʿUmar used to say, 'There is no harm in a man buying food on known delayed terms for a known price whether or not his fellow [the seller] has the food, as long as it is not for crops which have not ripened or dates which have not ripened, because the Messenger of Allah ﷺ forbade selling fruit or buying it before it is ripe.'"

قال محمد: هذا عندنا لا بأس به. وهو السَّلَم يُسلم الرجل في طعام إلى أجل معلوم بكيل معلوم من صنف معلوم، ولا خير في أن يشترط ذلك من زرع معلوم أو من نخل معلوم. وهو قول أبي حنيفة رحمه الله تعالى.

Muḥammad said: "In this, according to us, there is no harm. It is an advance which a man pays for food to be delivered at a specified time in a specified measure and of a specified variety. There is no good in his stipulating that it be from specific crops or from specific date palms. That is the verdict of Abū Ḥanīfah, may Allah, exalted is He, show him mercy."

١١ باب بيع البراءة

11. Sale with a Declaration of Freedom from Liability

٧٧٣ أخبرنا مالك حدَّثنا يحيى بن سعيد، عن سالم بن عبد الله بن عمر: أنه باع غلاماً له بثمان مائة درهم بالبراءة. وقال الذي ابتاع العبدَ لعبد الله بن عمر: بالعبد داء لم تُسَمِّه لي، فاختصما إلى عثمان بن عفان، فقال الرجل: باعني عبداً وبه داء، فقال ابن عمر: بعتُه بالبراءة، فقضى عثمان على ابن عمر، أن يحلف بالله: لقد باعه وما به داء يعلمه، فأبى عبد الله بن عمر أن يحلف، فارتجع الغلام فصحَّ عنده العبد، فباعه عبد الله بن عمر بعد ذلك بألف وخمس مائة درهم.

773. Mālik informed us: "Yaḥyā ibn Saᶜīd narrated to us that Sālim ibn ᶜAbdullāh ibn ᶜUmar sold a slave of his for eight hundred dirhams without liability [for any defects]. The one who bought the slave said to ᶜAbdullāh ibn ᶜUmar, 'The slave has an illness you did not tell me about.' They took the dispute to ᶜUthmān ibn ᶜAffān. The man said, 'He sold me a slave, but he had an illness.' Ibn ᶜUmar said, 'I sold him without any liability [for defects].' ᶜUthmān gave judgement against Ibn ᶜUmar that he must swear an oath by Allah that he had definitely sold him and that he had no illness of which he knew, but ᶜAbdullāh ibn ᶜUmar refused to swear an oath. The slave was returned to him and grew healthy again with him, so ᶜAbdullāh ibn ᶜUmar sold him after that for one thousand five hundred dirhams."

قال محمد: بَلَغَنا عن زيد بن ثابت أنه قال: من باع غلاماً بالبراءة فهو بريْ من كل عيب، وكذلك باع عبد الله بن عمر بالبراءة ورآها براءةً جائزة. فبقول زيد بن ثابت وعبد الله بن عمر نأخذ من باع غلاماً أو شيئاً، وتبرأَّ من كل عيب، ورضي بذلك المشتري وقبضه على ذلك فهو بريء من كل عيب علمه أو لم يعلمه لأن المشتري قد برَّأه من ذلك. فأما أهل المدينة قالوا: يبرأُ البائع من كل عيب لم يعلمه، فأما ما علمه وكتمه فإنه لا يبرأ منه، وقالوا: إذا باعه بيع المبرات برئ من كل عيب علمه أو لم يعلمه، إذا قال: بعتك بيعَ المبرات، فالذي يقول أتبرأ من كل عيب، وبيَّن ذلك أحرى أن يبرأ لما اشترط من هذا، وهو قولُ أبي حنيفة وقولنا والعامة.

Muḥammad said: "It has reached us that Zayd ibn Thābit said, 'Whoever sells a slave without any liability, then he has no liability for any defect, and that was the way that ᶜAbdullāh ibn ᶜUmar sold without any liability, and he thought that it was a permissible declaration of freedom from liability.' So we adhere to the verdict of Zayd ibn Thābit and ʿAbdullāh ibn ʿUmar; whoever sells a slave or anything, and declares himself free of liability for any defects, and the purchaser is contented with that and takes possession of it on that basis, then he [the seller] is not liable for any defects, neither those he knows of nor those he does not know of, because the purchaser gave him freedom from liability for that. As for the people of Madīnah, they said, 'The one who sells may declare himself free of liability for every defect which he does not know about. As for that which he knows about and conceals, then he may not declare himself free of liability for that.' They also said, 'If he sells with the sale of universal freedom from liability, then he is not liable for any defect, neither those he knows about, nor those he does not know about, if he says, "I sell to you with the sale of universal freedom from liability," then what he is saying is, "I am free of liability for every defect," and he makes that very clear, then it is more fitting that he is free of liability for what he has stipulated of that. That is the verdict of Abū Ḥanīfah, our verdict and [the verdict] of [our *fuqahāʾ*] in general."

١٢ باب بيع الغرر

12. Uncertain [*gharar*] Sales

٧٧٤ أخبرنا مالك، أخبرنا أبو حازم بن دينار، عن سعيد بن المسيّب : أن رسول الله صلى الله عليه وسلم نهى عن بيع الغَرَر.

774. Mālik informed us: "Abū Ḥāzim ibn Dīnār informed us from Saʿīd ibn al-Musayyab that the Messenger of Allah ﷺ forbade uncertain sales."

قال محمد : وبهذا كله نأخذ . بَيْع الغَرَر كلُّه فاسد . وهو قول أبي حنيفة والعامة .

Muḥammad said: "We adhere to this. Sales with uncertainty in them are all invalid, and that is the verdict of Abū Ḥanīfah and of [our *fuqahāʾ*] in general."

٧٧٥ أخبرنا مالك، أخبرنا ابن شهاب، عن سعيد بن المسيّب أنه كان يقول : لا ربا في الحيوان ، وإنما نُهي عن الحيوان عن ثلاث: عن المضامين والملاقيح ، وحَبَل الحَبَلَة. والمضامين ما في بطون إناث الإبل، والملاقيح ما في ظهور الجمال .

775. Mālik informed us: "Ibn Shihāb informed us that Saʿīd ibn al-Musayyab used to say, 'There is no usury in [the sale of] animals, but there are three things with respect to animals which are prohibited: the *maḍāmin,* the *malāqīḥ* and the offspring of the foetus.' The *maḍāmin* are those [foetuses] which are in the womb of female camels, the *malāqīḥ* are those offspring which are [potentially] in the backs of male camels."

٧٧٦ أخبرنا مالك أخبرنا نافع ، عن عبد الله بن عمر : أنّ رسول الله صلى الله عليه وسلم نهى عن بيع حَبَل الحَبَلَة . وكان بيعاً يبتاعه الجاهلية يبيع أحدُهم الجَزُور إلى أن تُنْتَجَ الناقة ، ثم تُنتَجُ التي في بطنها .

776. Mālik informed us: "Nāfiᶜinformed us from ᶜAbdullāh ibn ᶜUmar that the Messenger of Allah ﷺ forbade selling the offspring of the foetus, which was a sale performed in the *Jāhiliyyah* in which someone would sell a female camel [deferring payment] until [the time] the female camel gave birth and then that which was in its womb gave birth."

قال محمد: وهذه البيوع كلُّها مكروهة، ولا ينبغي لأنّها غَرَر عندنا، وقد نهى رسول الله صلى الله عليه وسلم عن بيعِ الغَرَر.

Muḥammad said: "All of these types of sale are disliked and ought not to be done because they are uncertain according to us, and the Messenger of Allah ﷺ has forbidden the sale with uncertainty."

١٣ باب بيع المزابنة

13. The Sale known as *Muzābanah*

٧٧٧ أخبرنا مالك، حدّثنا نافع، عن عبد الله بن عمر: أنّ رسول الله صلى الله عليه وسلم نهى عن بيع المزابنة. والمزابنة بيع الثَّمر بالتَّمْر وبيع العنب بالزبيب كَيْلاً.

777. Mālik informed us: "Nāfiᶜ narrated to us from ᶜAbdullāh ibn ᶜUmar that the Messenger of Allah ﷺ forbade the sale known as muzābanah, and muzābanah is to sell fresh fruit for dried dates and to sell grapes for raisins by measure."

٧٧٨ أخبرنا مالك، أخبرنا ابن شهاب، عن سعيد بن المسيّب: أنّ رسول الله صلى الله عليه وسلم نهى عن بيع المزابنة، والمحاقلة. والمزابنة اشتراء الثمر بالتمر، والمحاقلة اشتراء الزرع بالحنطة، واستكراء الأرض بالحنطة. قال ابن شهاب: سألت عن كرائها بالذهب والورق، فقال: لا بأس به.

778. Mālik informed us: "Ibn Shihāb informed us from Saᶜīd ibn al-Musayyab that the Messenger of Allah ﷺ forbade the sales [known as] *muzābanah* and *muḥāqalah. Muzābanah* is to buy fresh dates with dried dates, and *muḥāqalah* is to buy crops with wheat, and to rent land with wheat. Ibn Shihāb said, 'I asked about renting it [land] with gold and silver and he said, "There is no harm in it."'"

٧٧٩ أخبرنا مالك، حدّثنا داود بن الحُصَين، أنّ أبا سفيان مولى ابن أحمد أخبره أنّه سمع أبا سعيد الخدري يقول: نهى رسول الله صلى الله عليه وسلم عن المزابنة والمحاقلة. والمزابنة اشتراء الثمر في رؤوس النخل بالتمر، والمحاقلة كراء الأرض.

779. Mālik informed us: "Dāwūd ibn al-Ḥuṣayn narrated to us that Abū Sufyān the *mawlā* of Ibn Aḥmad informed him that he heard Abū Saᶜīd al-Khudrī saying, 'The Messenger of Allah ﷺ forbade *muzābanah* and *muḥāqalah*, and *muzābanah* is to purchase fruit still in the tops of the trees with dried dates, and *muḥāqalah* is renting land.'"

قال محمد: المزابنة عندنا اشتراء الثمر في رؤوس النخل بالتَّمْر كيلاً لا يُدرى التمرُ الذي أعطى أكثر أو أقل، والزبيب بالعنب لا يُدرى أيهما أكثر، والمحاقلة اشتراء الحَبّ في السنبل بالحنطة كيلاً لا يُدرى أيهما أكثر وهذا كله مكروه ولا ينبغي مباشرته. وهو قول أبي حنيفة والعامة وقولنا.

Muḥammad said: "According to us, *muzābanah* is to purchase fresh dates still at the top of the date-palms with dried dates by measure, when it is not known whether the dried dates which he gives are more numerous or fewer, and [paying] raisins for grapes not knowing which of them is in greater quantity. *Muḥāqalah* is to buy grain which is still in the ear with wheat by measure not knowing which of them is more numerous. All of this is disapproved of and ought not to be undertaken. That is the verdict of Abū Ḥanīfah and of us and of [our *fuqahā'*] in general."

١٤ باب شراء الحيوان باللحم

14. Buying Animals with Meat

٧٨٠ أخبرنا مالك، أخبرنا أبو الزِّناد ، عن سعيد بن المسيّب قال : نُهي عن بيع الحيوان باللحم. قال : قلتُ لسعيد بن المسيّب : أرأيتَ رجلاً اشترى شارفاً بعشر شياه أو قال شاة فقال سعيد بن المسيّب: إن كان اشتراها لينحرها فلا خيرَ في ذلك. قال أبو الزناد : وكان مَنْ أدركتُ من الناس يَنْهَوْن عن بيع الحيوان باللحم، وكان يُكْتَبُ في عُهُود العمّال في زمان أبانَ وهشام يُنْهَوْن عن ذلك .

780. Mālik informed us: "Abu'z-Zinād informed us that Sa'īd ibn al-Musayyab said, 'It is forbidden to sell animals [in exchange] for meat.' He [Abu'z-Zinād] said, 'I said to Sa'īd ibn al-Musayyab, "What do you think about a man who buys an aged she-camel with ten ewes?" or he said, "ewe?" Sa'īd ibn al-Musayyab answered, "If he bought it to slaughter it, then there is no good in that."' Abu'z-Zinād said, 'Those people I came upon [of the Followers] used to forbid selling animals [in exchange] for meat. It used to be written in the injunctions [register of rulings] of the governors at the time of Abān [ibn 'Uthmān ibn 'Affān] and Hishām [ibn Ismā'īl al-Makhzūmī] that, "They are forbidden to do that."'"

٧٨١ أخبرنا مالك، أخبرنا داود بن الحُصين، أنّه سمع سعيد بن المسيّب يقول : وكان من مَيْسر أهل الجاهلية بَيْعُ اللّحم بالشاة والشاتين.

781. Mālik informed us: "Dāwūd ibn al-Ḥuṣayn informed us that he heard Sa'īd ibn al-Musayyab saying, 'A part of the gambling of the people of *Jāhiliyyah* was the barter of meat for a sheep or two sheep.'"

٧٨٢ أخبرنا مالك، أخبرنا زيد بن أسلم، عن سعيد بن المسيّب أنه بلغه : أن رسول الله صلى الله عليه وسلم نهى عن بيع الحيوان باللحم.

782. Mālik informed us: "Zayd ibn Aslam informed us from Sa'īd ibn al-Musayyab that it reached him that the Messenger of Allah ﷺ forbade selling live animals for meat."

قال محمد : وبهذا نأخذ. من باع لحماً من لحم الغنم بشاة حيّة لا يُدى اللحمُ أكثر أو ما في الشاة أكثر فالبيع فاسد مكروهٌ لا ينبغي. وهذا مثل المزابنة والمحاقلة، وكذلك بيع الزيتون بالزيت ودُهن السِّمْسِم بالسِّمْسِم.

Muḥammad said: "We adhere to this. Whoever barters the meat of sheep and goats for a live sheep, and it is not known whether the meat is more or what is on the sheep is more, then the sale is corrupt and disapproved, and it ought not to be done. This is like *muzābanah* and *muḥāqalah*. Similarly, bartering olives for oil, and sesame oil for sesame seeds [is not allowed]."

١٥ باب الرجل يُساوِمُ الرجلَ بالشيء فيزيد عليه أحد

15. A Man Bargaining with another Man for Something, and then Someone else Offers him more

٧٨٣ أخبرنا مالك، حدّثنا نافع، عن عبد الله بن عمر: أنّ رسول الله صلى الله عليه وسلم قال: لا يبع بعضكم على بعض.

783. Mālik informed us: "Nāfi[c] narrated to us from [c]Abdullāh ibn [c]Umar that the Messenger of Allah ﷺ said, 'Do not bid against each other.'"

قال محمد: وبهذا نأخذ. لا ينبغي إذا ساوم الرجلُ الرجلَ بالشيء أن يزيد عليه غيرُه فيه حتى يشتري أو يَدَعَ.

Muḥammad said: "We adhere to this. When a man is bargaining with another for something, then someone else ought not to offer more for it so that he buys it or leaves it [so that the other person buys it at an inflated price]."

١٦ باب ما يوجب البيع بين البائع والمشتري

16. That which Makes the Exchange between the Seller and Buyer Obligatory

٧٨٤ أخبرنا مالك، أخبرنا نافع، عن عبد الله بن عمر: أن رسول الله صلى الله عليه وسلم قال: المتبايعان كلٌّ واحد منهما بالخيار على صاحبه ما لم يتفرَّقا، إلاَّ بيعَ الخيار.

784. Mālik informed us: "Nāfi[c] informed us from [c]Abdullāh ibn [c]Umar that the Messenger of Allah ﷺ said, 'Each of the two parties to a sale still has the option [to accept or reject] from his companion as long as they have not separated except in the case of the sale with an option [to revoke the sale].'"

قال محمد: وبهذا نأخذ، وتفسيره عندنا على ما بلغنا عن إبراهيم النَّخَعي أنه قال: المتبايعان بالخيار ما لم يتفرقا، قال: ما لم يتفرقا عن منطق البيع إذا قال البائع: قد بعتُك فله أن يرجع ما لم يقل الآخرُ: قد اشتريت، فإذا قال المشتري: قد اشتريتُ بكذا وكذا فله أن يرجع ما لم يقل البائع قد بعت. وهو قول أبي حنيفة والعامة من فقهائنا.

Muḥammad said: "We adhere to this. Its explanation according to us and according to what has reached us from Ibrāhīm an-Nakha[c]ī is that he said, 'The two parties to the sale still have the option as long as they have not separated.' He said, 'As long as they have not separated from discussing the terms of the sale. When the one who is selling says, "I have sold it to you," then he has the right to retract it as long as the other has not said, "I have bought it." When the purchaser says, "I will buy it for such and such," then he has the right to retract it as long as the seller has not said, "I have sold it [to you].''' And that is the verdict of Abū Ḥanīfah and of our *fuqahāʾ* in general."

١٧ باب الاختلاف في البيع بين البائع والمشتري

17. The Difference of Opinion Concerning the Sale between the Seller and Purchaser

٧٨٥ أخبرنا مالك، أنه بلغه أنَّ ابنَ مسعود كان يحدِّث أنَّ رسول الله صلى الله عليه وسلم قال: أيُّما بَيِّعان تبايعا، فالقولُ قولُ البائع أو يترادّان.

785. Mālik informed us that it had reached him that Ibn Masᶜūd used to narrate that the Messenger of Allah ﷺ said, "Whichever two parties buy and sell to each other, then the [decisive] word is that of the seller or else they both annul [the sale]."

قال محمد: وبهذا نأخذ. إذا اختلفا في الثمن تحالفا وترادّا البيع وهو قولُ أبي حنيفة والعامة من فقهائنا إذا كان المبيع قائماً بعينه، فإنْ كان المشتري قد استهلكه، فالقول ما قال المشتري في الثمن في قول أبي حنيفة، وأما في قولنا فيتحالفان ويترادّان القيمة.

Muḥammad said: "We adhere to this. If they disagree concerning the price, then they must both swear oaths and then they both annul the sale if the object of sale still exists, and that is the verdict of Abū Ḥanīfah and of our *fuqahāʾ* in general. If the buyer has already consumed it, then the position taken is that which the buyer says concerning the price according to the verdict of Abū Ḥanīfah. As for our verdict, it is that they both must swear oaths and then they return the price [of the object consumed]."

١٨ باب الرجل يبيع المتاع بنسيئة فيفلس المبتاع

18. A Man who Sells Goods for Deferred Payment and then later the Purchaser Becomes Bankrupt

٧٨٦ أخبرنا مالك، أخبرنا ابن شهاب، عن ابي بكر بن عبد الرحمن بن الحارث بن هشام أن رسول الله صلى الله عليه وسلم قال أيُّما رجلٍ باع متاعاً، فأفلس الذي ابتاعه ولم يقبض الذي باعه من ثمنه شيئاً فوجده بعينه فهو أحقُّ به، وإنْ مات المشتري فصاحب المتاع فيه أُسوةٌ للغُرماء.

786. Mālik informed us: "Ibn Shihāb informed us from Abū Bakr ibn ᶜAbd ar-Raḥmān ibn al-Ḥārith ibn Hishām that the Messenger of Allah ﷺ said, 'Whoever sells goods and then the purchaser becomes bankrupt before the seller has received anything of its price, but he finds [the goods] themselves, then he has the greater right to them. If the purchaser dies, then the owner of the goods is in the same position with respect to them as other creditors.'"

قال محمدٌ: إذا مات وقد قبضه فصاحبه فيه أُسوةٌ للغرماء، وإن كان لم يقبض المشتري فهو أحقٌّ به من بقية الغُرماء حتى يستوفيَ حقه، وكذلك إن أفلس المشتري ولم يقبض ما يشتري، فالبائع أحقٌّ بما باع حتى يستوفي حقّه.

Muḥammad said: "If he [the buyer] dies and he had taken possession of them, then his companion [the seller] is in the same position as the other creditors with respect to them [the goods]. If the buyer had not taken possession of them, then he [the seller] has more right to them than other creditors until he has received in full what is due to him by right. Similarly, if the buyer becomes bankrupt without having taken possession of what he had bought, then the seller has the greater right to that which he sold so that he can take what is due to him in full."

١٩ باب الرجل يشتري الشيء أو يبيعه فيُغْبَنُ فيه أو يُسَعِّر على المسلمين

19. A Man Buying or Selling Something in which He is Tricked and Price Regulation for the Muslims

٧٨٧ أخبرنا مالك، أخبرنا عبد الله بن دينار، عن عبد الله بن عمر: أن رجلاً ذكر لرسول الله صلى الله عليه وسلم أنه يُخْدَعُ في البيع، فقال له رسول الله صلى الله عليه وسلم: من بايعتَه فقل: لا خِلابَةَ. فكان الرجل إذا باع فقال: لا خِلابَةَ.

787. Mālik informed us: "ᶜAbdullāh ibn Dīnār informed us from ᶜAbdullāh ibn ᶜUmar that a man mentioned to the Messenger of Allah ﷺ that he was [often] deceived in buying and selling. The Messenger of Allah ﷺ said to him, 'Whoever you trade with then say, "No trickery!"' So when the man sold he would say, 'No trickery!'"

قال محمد: نُرى أن هذا كان لذلك الرجل خاصّة.

Muḥammad said: "We are of the view that this was for that man in particular."

٧٨٨ أخبرنا مالك، أخبرنا يونس بن يوسف، عن سعيد بن المسيّب: أنّ عمر بن الخطّاب مرّ على حاطب بن أبي بَلْتَعَةَ وهو يبيع زبيباً له بالسوق فقال له عمر: إمّا أن تزيدَ في السعر، وإما أن ترفع من سوقنا.

788. Mālik informed us: "Yūnus ibn Yūsuf informed us from Saᶜīd ibn al-Musayyab that ᶜUmar ibn al-Khaṭṭāb passed by Ḥāṭib ibn Abī Baltaᶜah when he was selling his raisins in the market place, and ᶜUmar said to him, 'Either raise the price,[149] or get out of our market.'"

قال محمدٌ: وبهذا نأخذ. لا ينبغي أن يُسَعَّر على المسلمين، فيُقال لهم: بِيْعُوا كذا وكذا بكذا وكذا، ويُجْبَرُوا على ذلك. وهو قول أبي حنيفة والعامة من فقهائنا.

Muḥammad said: "We adhere to this. The price ought not to be fixed for the Muslims, so that it is said to them, 'Sell such and such for such and such,' so that they are compelled to do that. That is the verdict of Abū Ḥanīfah and of our *fuqahā᾿* in general."

٢٠ باب الاشتراط في البيع وما يُفْسده

20. Stipulating Conditions in a Sale which Invalidate it

٧٨٩ أخبرنا مالك، أخبرنا الزهري، عن عبيد الله بن عبد الله بن عُتْبَة بن عبد الله بن مسعود: اشترى من امرأته الثَّقَفيَّة جاريةً واشترطَتْ عليه أنك إن بعْتها فهي لي بالثمن الذي تبيعُها به، فاستفتى في ذلك عمر بنَ الخطّاب، فقال: لا تَقْرَبْها وفيها شرطٌ لأحد.

789. Mālik informed us: "Az-Zuhrī informed us from ᶜUbaydullāh ibn ᶜAbdullāh ibn ᶜUtbah ibn ᶜAbdullāh ibn Masᶜūd that [ᶜAbdullāh ibn Masᶜūd] bought a slave girl from his wife of the tribe of Thaqīf, and she laid the condition on him that, 'If you sell her, then she is mine for the price for which you sell her.' He asked ᶜUmar ibn al-Khaṭṭāb for a judgement on that and he said, 'Do not approach her while anyone else has a condition pertaining to her.'"

قال محمد: وبهذا نأخذ. كلُ شرط اشتَرط البائع على المشتري، أو المشتري على البائع ليس من شروط البيع، وفيه منفعةٌ للبائع أو المشتري، فالبيع فاسد. وهو قول أبي حنيفة رحمه الله.

Muḥammad said: "We adhere to this. Every condition which the seller places on the buyer or which the buyer places on the seller, and which is not one of the [ordinary] conditions of sale, and in which there is some benefit for the seller or the buyer, then the sale is invalid. That is the verdict of Abū Ḥanīfah, may Allah have mercy on him."

٧٩٠ أخبرنا مالك، أخبرنا نافع، عن عبد الله بن عمر أنّه كان يقول: لا يطأ الرجل وليدةً إلا وليدَته، إن شاء باعها، وإن شاء وهبها، وإن شاء صنع بها ما شاء.

790. Mālik informed us: "Nāfiᶜ informed us that ᶜAbdullāh ibn ᶜUmar used to say, 'A man may only have sexual intercourse with a slave woman who is his slave woman whom if he wishes he may sell and if he wishes he may give away and if he wishes he may do with whatever he wishes.[150]'"

قال محمد: وبهذا نأخذ. وهذا تفسير: أنّ العبدَ لا ينبغي أن يَتَسرَّى، لأنه إن وهب لم يَجز هبته، كما يجوز هبة الحُرّ، فهذا معنى قول عبد الله بن عمر. وهو قول أبي حنيفة والعامة من فقهائنا.

Muḥammad said: "We adhere to this. This is the explanation of the fact that a slave ought not to own slave-girls because if he were to give her away, his gift would not be valid in the same sense as the gift of a free man is valid. This is the meaning of the saying of ᶜAbdullāh ibn ᶜUmar, and that is the verdict of Abū Ḥanīfah and of our *fuqahā'* in general."

٢١ باب من باع نخلاً مؤبَّراً أو عبداً، وله مال

21. Someone Selling Date-palms which have been Fecundated[151] and a Slave who has Property

٧٩١ أخبرنا مالك، أخبرنا نافع عن عبد الله بن عمر: أن رسولَ الله صلى الله عليه وسلم قال: من باع نخلاً قد أُبِّرتْ، فثمرتُها للبائع إلا أن يشترطها المبتاع.

791. Mālik informed us:"Nāfiᶜ informed us from ᶜAbdullāh ibn ᶜUmar that

the Messenger of Allah ﷺ said, 'Whoever sells date-palms which have been fecundated, then their fruit belongs to the seller unless the buyer stipulates them [as his].'"

٧٩٢ أخبرنا مالك، أخبرنا نافع، عن عبد الله بن عمر : أخبرنا مالك،، عمر بن الخطاب قال: من باع عبداً وله مال ، فماله للبائع إلا أن يشترطه المبتاع.

792. Mālik informed us: "Nāfiᶜ informed us from ᶜAbdullāh ibn ᶜUmar that ᶜUmar ibn al-Khaṭṭāb said, 'Whoever sells a slave who has property, then his property belongs to the seller unless the buyer stipulates it [as his].'"

قال محمد: وبهذا نأخذ، وهو قول أبي حنيفة.

Muḥammad said, "We adhere to this, and it is the verdict of Abū Ḥanīfah."

٢٢ باب الرجل يشتري الجارية ولها زوج أو تُهدى إليه

22. A Man Purchasing or Receiving as a Gift a Slave-girl who Has a Husband

٧٩٣ أخبرنا مالك، أخبرنا الزهري، عن أبي سلمة بن عبد الرحمن: أنّ عبد الرحمن بن عوف اشترى من عاصم بن عدي جارية، فوجدها ذات زوج فردّها .

793. Mālik informed us: "Az-Zuhrī informed us from Abū Salamah ibn ᶜAbd ar-Raḥmān that ᶜAbd ar-Raḥmān ibn ᶜAwf bought a slave-girl from ᶜĀṣim ibn ᶜAdī, but found her to have a husband and so he returned her."

قال محمد: وبهذا نأخذ. لا يكون بيعُها طلاقَها ، فإذا كانت ذات زوج فهذا عيب تُرَدُّ به. وهو قول أبي حنيفة والعامة من فقهائنا.

Muḥammad said: "We adhere to this. Her purchase is not [equivalent to] her divorce. Thus if she has a husband this is a defect in her for which she may be returned. That is the verdict of Abū Ḥanīfah and of our *fuqahāʾ* in general."

٧٩٤ أخبرنا مالك، أخبرنا ابن شهاب: أن عبد الله بن عامر أهدى لعثمان بن عفان جاريةً من البصرة ولها زوج، فقال عثمان: لن أَقْرَبَهَا حتى يفارقَها زوجُها، فأَرْضَى ابنُ عامر زوجَها ففارقها .

794. Mālik informed us: "Ibn Shihāb informed us that ᶜAbdullāh ibn ᶜĀmir gave ᶜUthmān ibn ᶜAffān a slave-girl from Baṣra who had a husband. ᶜUthmān said, 'I will not go near her until her husband separates from her.' Ibn ᶜĀmir gave her husband that which made him contented and he separated from her."

٢٣ باب عُهْدة الثلاث والسَّنَة

23. The Liability Agreements of Three [days] and of a Year

٧٩٥ أخبرنا مالك، أخبرنا عبد الله بن أبي بكر؟، قال: سمعت أبانَ بن عثمان وهشام بن إسماعيل يُعلّمان الناس عُهدةَ الثلاث والسَّنَة، يخطبان به على المنبر.

795. Mālik informed us: "ᶜAbdullāh ibn Abī Bakr informed us saying, 'I heard Abān ibn ᶜUthmān and Hishām ibn Ismāᶜīl teaching people about the

liability agreements of three days and of a year, about which they delivered *khuṭbahs* from the *minbar*.'"

قال محمد: لسنا نعرف عهدة الثلاث، ولا عهدة السنَة إلا أن يشترط الرجلُ خيارَ ثلاثة أيام، أو خيارَ سَنَةٍ فيكون ذلك على ما اشترط، وأما في قول أبي حَنيفة فلا يجوز الخيار إلا ثلاثة أيام.

Muḥammad said: "We do not recognise the liability agreement of three days, nor the liability agreement of a year unless the man stipulates his option of returning [the goods] in three days or his option of returning [the goods] in a year, so that in that case it will be according to what he stipulates. As for the verdict of Abū Ḥanīfah, it is that only the option of returning [the goods] in three days is valid."

٢٤ باب بيع الولاء

24. The Sale of the Relationship of *Walā*ʾ[152]

٧٩٦ أخبرنا مالك، أخبرنا عبد الله بن دينار، عن عبد الله بن عمر: أن رسول الله صلى الله عليه وسلم نهى عن بيع الولاء وهبته.

796. Mālik informed us: "ʿAbdullāh ibn Dīnār informed us from ʿAbdullāh ibn ʿUmar that the Messenger of Allah ﷺ forbade the sale of the relationship of *walā*ʾ and giving it away as a gift."

قال محمد: وبهذا نأخذ. لا يجوز بيع الولاء، ولا هبته، وهو قول أبي حنيفة، والعامَّة من فقهائنا.

Muḥammad said: "We adhere to this. It is not permitted to sell the relationship of *walā*ʾ, nor to give it away, and that is the verdict of Abū Ḥanīfah and of our *fuqahā*ʾ in general."

٧٩٧ أخبرنا مالك، أخبرنا نافع، عن عبد الله بن عمر، عن عائشة زوج النبي صلى الله عليه وسلم: أرادت أن تشتري وليدة فتُعتقها، فقال أهلها: نبيعك على أن ولاءها لنا، فذكرت ذلك لرسول الله صلى الله عليه وسلم، فقال: لا يمنعك ذلك، فإنما الولاءُ لمن أعتق.

797. Mālik informed us: "Nāfiʿ informed us from ʿAbdullāh ibn ʿUmar that ʿĀʾishah, the wife of the Prophet ﷺ, wanted to buy a female slave and set her free. Her owners said, 'We will sell her on condition that her *walā*ʾ belongs to us.' She mentioned that to the Messenger of Allah ﷺ and he said, 'Don't let that prevent you, because the *walā*ʾ only belongs to the person who sets free.'"

قال محمد: وبهذا نأخذ. الولاء لمن أعتق، لا يتحوَّل عنه، وهو كالنسب. وهو قول أبي حنيفة والعامة من فقهائنا.

Muḥammad said: "We adhere to this. The *walā*ʾ belongs to the person who sets free, and it may not be transferred from him, so it is just like a blood-relationship. That is the verdict of Abū Ḥanīfah and of our *fuqahā*ʾ in general."

٢٥ باب بيع أمهات الأولاد

25. The Sale of Slave Women who have Children by their Owners

٧٩٨ أخبرنا مالك، أخبرنا نافع، عن عبد الله بن عمر، قال : قال عمر بن الخطّاب: أيُّما وليدةٍ ولدت من سيِّدها فإنَّه لا يبيعها ولا يهبها ولا يُورِّثها ، وهو يستمتع منها فإذا مات فهي حُرَّة.

798. Mālik informed us: "Nāfi[c] informed us that [c]Abdullāh ibn [c]Umar said, "[c]Umar ibn al-Khaṭṭāb said, 'If a slave woman gives birth to a child by her owner, then he may not sell her, give her away nor leave her to be inherited. He has his enjoyment of her, and when he dies she is free."

قال محمد: وبهذا نأخذ. وهو قول أبي حنيفة والعامة من فقهائنا.

Muḥammad said: "We adhere to this, and that is the verdict of Abū Ḥanīfah and of our *fuqahā᾿* in general."

٢٦ باب بيع الحيوان بالحيوان نسيئة ونقداً

26. The Sale of Animals in Exchange for Animals on Deferred Terms or Paid for [on the spot]

٧٩٩ أخبرنا مالك، أخبرنا صالح بن كَيْسان، أن الحسن بن محمد بن عليّ، أخبره أنَّ عليّ بن أبي طالب باع جَمَلاً له يُدعى عُصَيْفيراً بعشرين بعيراً إلى أجل.

799. Mālik informed us: "Ṣāliḥ ibn Kaysān informed us that al-Ḥasan ibn Muḥammad ibn [c]Alī informed him that [c]Alī ibn Abī Ṭālib sold a camel of his called [c]Uṣayfir for twenty camels on deferred terms."

٨٠٠ أخبرنا مالك، أخبرنا نافع: أن عبد الله بن عمر اشترى راحلة بأربعة أبْعِرَة مضمونة عليه، يُوفِّيها إياه بالرَّبَذة.

800. Mālik informed us: "Nāfi[c] informed us that [c]Abdullāh ibn [c]Umar bought a riding camel with four camels which he guaranteed to pay in full to him at ar-Rabadhah."

قال محمد: بلغنا عن عليّ بن أبي طالب خلاف هذا.

Muḥammad said: "Something different to this has reached us from [c]Alī ibn Abī Ṭālib."

٨٠١ أخبرنا ابن أبي ذُؤَيْب ، عن يزيد بن عبد الله بن قُسَيْط، عن أبي حسن البزّار ، عن رجلٍ من أصحاب رسول الله صلى الله عليه وسلم عن عليّ بن أبي طالب كرم الله وجهه: أنه نهى عن بيع البعير بالبعيرين إلى أجل، والشاة بالشاتين إلى أجل. وبلغنا عن النبي صلى الله عليه وسلم: نهى عن بيع الحيوان بالحيوان نسيئة، فبهذا نأخذ. وهو قول أبي حنيفة والعامَّة من فقهائنا.

801. Ibn Abī Dhu᾿ayb informed us from Yazīd ibn [c]Abdullāh ibn Qusayṭ from Abu'l-Ḥasan al-Bazzār from a man of the Companions of the Messenger of Allah ﷺ that [c]Alī ibn Abī Ṭālib, may Allah ennoble his face, forbade selling one camel for two camels on deferred terms, or a sheep for two sheep on deferred terms. It has reached us that the Prophet ﷺ forbade selling animals

for animals on deferred terms, and we adhere to this, and that is the verdict of Abū Ḥanīfah and of our *fuqahā*ʾ in general."

٢٧ باب الشّركة في البيع

27. Partnership in Trade

٨٠٢ أخبرنا مالك، أخبرنا العلاء بن عبد الرحمن بن يعقوب، أن أباه أخبره قال: أخبرني أبي قال: كنت أبيع البزّ في زمان عمر بن الخطّاب، وإنّ عمر قال: لا يبيعُه في سوقنا أعجميّ، فإنهم لم يفقهوا في الدين، ولم يقيموا في الميزان والمكيال.
قال يعقوب: فذهبت إلى عثمان بن عفان، فقلت له: هل لك في غنيمة باردة؟ قال: ما هي؟ قلت: بزّ، قد علمتُ مكانه، يبيعه صاحبه برُخص، لا يستطيع بيعه، أشتريه لك ثم أبيعُه لك، قال: نعم، فذهبت فصفقت بالبز، ثم جئتُ به، فطرحتُ في دار عثمان، فلما رجع عثمان فرأى العُكُومْ في داره، قال: ما هذا؟ قالوا: بزّ جاء به يعقوب، قال: ادعوه لي، فجئتُ، فقال: ما هذا؟ قلتُ: هذا الذي قلتُ لك، قال: أَنظَرْتَه؟ قلتُ: كفيتُك ولكن رابَه حَرَسُ عمر، قال: نعم، فذهب عثمان إلى حرس عمر، فقال: إن يعقوب يبيع بَزّيْ فلا تمنعوه، قالوا: نعم، جئت بالبزّ السوقَ، فلم ألبث حتى جعلتُ ثمنه في مِزْوَدٍ وذهبت به إلى عثمان وبالذي اشتريتُ البزّ منه فقلت: عُدَّ الذي لك فاعتَدَّه وبقي مال كثير، قال: فقلت لعثمان: هذا لك، أما إني لم أَظْلِمْ به أحداً، قال: جزاك الله خيراً، وفرح بذلك، قال: فقلت: أما إني قد علمتُ مكان بيعها مثلها أو أفضل، قال: وعائدٌ أنت؟ قال: قلت: نعم، إن شئتَ، قال: قد شئتُ، قال: فقلتُ: فإني باغٍ خيراً فأشركني، قال: نعم بيني وبينك.

802. Mālik informed us: "Al-ᶜAlāʾ ibn ᶜAbd ar-Raḥmān ibn Yaᶜqūb informed us that his father informed him saying, 'My father said to me and he said, "I used to sell garments at the time of ᶜUmar ibn al-Khaṭṭāb, and ᶜUmar said, 'Do not let a non-Arab sell in our market because they have not come to have fiqh-understanding in the dīn, and they are not straight in weights and measures.'" Yaᶜqūb said, "So I went to ᶜUthmān ibn ᶜAffān and asked him, 'Do you want some spoils acquired without fatigue [easy profits]?' He asked, 'What is it?' I answered, 'Garments. I know where they are. Their owner is selling them cheaply and can hardly manage to sell them. I will buy them for you and then I will sell for you.' He said, 'Yes.' So I went and struck a deal for the garments. Then I came back to him and cast them into ᶜUthmān's house. When ᶜUthmān came back and saw the bundles in his house, he asked, 'What is this?' They answered, 'Garments which Yaᶜqūb brought.' He said, 'Call him for me.' I came and he said, 'What is this?' I answered, 'This is what I told you about.' He asked, 'Have you looked at it?' I answered, 'I stood in for you.' However, he was put into doubt because of ᶜUmar's watchmen [who were preventing non-Arabs selling in the market]. He said, 'Yes.' ᶜUthmān went to ᶜUmar's watchmen and said, 'Yaᶜqūb is selling my garments, so do not stop him.' They said, 'Yes.' I brought the garments to the market, and it was not very long before I put the takings in my provision satchel and

took it to ʿUthmān taking also the person from whom I had bought the garments. I said, 'Count what is yours,' and he did so and there remained a great deal of money." He said, "So I said to ʿUthmān, 'This is for you. As for me, I have not wronged anyone by it.' He said, 'May Allah reward you with the best!' and he rejoiced in that." He said, "I said, 'I have learnt of the place where it is sold, the like of it or better.' He said, 'Do you want to do it again?'" He said, "I said, 'Yes, if you want.' He said, 'I do.'" He said, "I said, 'Then, I desire what is best, so make me a partner.' He said, 'Yes, it is between me and you.'""

قال محمد: وبهذا نأخذ، لا بأس بأن يشترك الرجلان في الشراء بالنسيئة، وإنْ لم يكن لواحد منهم رأس مال، على أنَّ الربح بينهما، والوضيعة على ذلك، قال: وإن وَلِي الشراء والبيع أحدُهما دون صاحبه، ولا يفضل واحد منهما صاحبَه في الربح، فإن ذلك لا يجوز أن يأكل أحدهما ربح ما ضمن صاحبه. وهو قول أبي حنيفة والعامة من فقهائنا.

Muḥammad said: "We adhere to this. There is no harm in two men being partners in buying [goods] to be paid for later, if one of them does not have capital, on the basis that the profit is to be shared between them, and the loss is on the same basis." He said, "And if one of them apart from his companion undertakes the buying and selling, and there is no extra profit for either of them over the other, because it is not permitted for one of them to consume the profit to which his companion is entitled. That is the verdict of Abū Ḥanīfah and of our *fuqahāʾ* in general."

٢٨ باب القضاء

28. Judgement

٨٠٣ أخبرنا مالك، أخبرنا مالك، ابن شهاب، عن الأعرج، عن أبي هريرة، أن رسول الله صلى الله عليه وسلم قال: لا يَمنع أحدُكُم جارَه أن يَغْرِزَ خَشَبَةً في جداره، قال: ثم قال أبو هريرة: ما لي أراكم عنها معرضين؟ والله لأَرْمِيَنَّ بها بين أكتافكم.

803. Mālik informed us: "Ibn Shihāb informed us from al-Aʿraj from Abū Hurayrah that the Messenger of Allah ﷺ said, 'Let none of you prevent his neighbour from fixing a timber in his wall.'" He said, "Then Abū Hurayrah said, 'How is it that I see you averse to it? By Allah, I will cast it between your shoulder-blades!'"

قال محمد: هذا عندنا على وجه التوسُّع من الناس بعضهم على بعض، وحُسْن الخُلُق، فأما في الحكم فلا يُجْبَرون على ذلك. بلغنا أن شُريحاً اختُصِم إليه في ذلك، فقال للذي وضع الخشبة: ارفَعْ رِجْلَك عن مطيَّة أخيك. فهذا الحكم في ذلك، والتوسُّع أفضل.

Muḥammad said: "This, according to us, is by way of kind generosity of people towards each other, and good character. As for the legal position, they are not to be compelled to do it. It has reached us that a dispute was taken to

Shurayḥ on that issue, and that he said to the one who had fixed the timber, 'Lift your foot from your brother's riding camel [i.e. remove the timber], because this is the judgement with respect to that, but kind generosity is better.'"

٢٩ باب الهبة والصدقة

29. Gifts and *Ṣadaqah*

٨٠٤ أخبرنا مالك، أخبرنا داود بن الحُصين، عن أبي غَطَفَان بن طريف المُرّي ، عن مروان بن الحكم، أنه قال: قال عمر بن الخطّاب رضي الله تعالى عنه : مَن وهب هبةً لصلةِ رحم، أو على وجه صدقة، فإنه لا يرجع فيها، ومن وهب هبةً يرى أنَّه إنما أراد بها الثواب ، فهو علَى هبته، يرجع فيها إن لم يرضَ منها .

804. Mālik informed us: "Dāwūd ibn al-Ḥuṣayn informed us from Abū Ghaṭafān ibn Ṭarīf al-Murrī that Marwān ibn al-Ḥakam said, 'ᶜUmar ibn al-Khaṭṭāb ﷺ said, "Whoever gives a gift in order to strengthen a tie of kinship or by way of *ṣadaqah,* then he must not seek to have it returned. Whoever gives a gift thinking that he only means to obtain recompense by it then it is according to his gift, and he may have it returned if he is not pleased with it [the recompense].'"

قال محمد : وبهذا نأخذ . من وهب هبةً لذي رحم محرم، أو على وجه صدقة، فقبضها الموهوب له، فليس للواهب أن يرجع فيها، ومن وهب هبة لغير ذي رحم محرم، وقبضها، فله أن يرجع فيها إن لم يُثَبْ منها، أو يُزَدْ خيراً في يده ، أو يخرج من مِلْكه إلى ملك غيره. وهو قول أبي حنيفة والعامة من فقهائنا.

Muḥammad said: "We adhere to this. Whoever gives a gift to someone who is an unmarriageable male relative (*maḥram*), or as a *ṣadaqah,* and the person who has been given it takes possession of it, the one who has given it may not seek to have it returned. Whoever gives a gift to someone other than an unmarriageable male relative, and that person takes possession of it, he may seek to have it returned if he is not recompensed for it or given possession of something better, or it is transferred from his possession [the one given the gift] to someone else's possession. That is the verdict of Abū Ḥanīfah and of our *fuqahāʾ* in general."

٣٠ باب النُّحلَى

30. Presents

٨٠٥ أخبرنا مالك، أخبرنا ابن شهاب، عن حُميد بن عبد الرحمن بن عوف، وعن محمد بن النُعمان بن بَشير، يُحدِّثانه عن النعمان بن بشير قال: إنَّ أباه أتى به إلى رسول الله صلى الله عليه وسلم فقال : إني نَحَلْتُ ابني هذا غلاماً كان لي، فقال رسول الله صلى الله عليه وسلم : أَكُلَّ وَلَدِكَ نحلته مثل هذا؟ قال: لا، قال: فَأَرْجِعْه .

805. Mālik informed us: "Ibn Shihāb informed us from Ḥumayd ibn ᶜAbd ar-Raḥmān ibn ᶜAwf and from Muḥammad ibn an-Nuᶜmān ibn Bashīr who both narrated that an-Nuᶜmān ibn Bashīr said that his father brought him to the Messenger of Allah ﷺ and said, 'I have given a present to this son of mine of a slave I had.' The Messenger of Allah ﷺ asked, 'Have you given every child a present the like of this?' He answered, 'No.' He said, 'Then take him back.'"

٨٠٦ أخبرنا مالك، أخبرنا ابنِ شهاب، عن عروة، عن عائشة رضي الله عنها أنها قالت: إن أبا بكر كان نَحَلَها جُذاذ عشرين وسقاً من ماله بالعالية ، فلما حضرته الوفاة، قال: والله يا بُنَيَّةَ ما من الناس أحبُّ إليَّ غنىً بعدي منك، ولا أعزُّ عليَّ فقراً منك، وإني كنت نَحَلْتُك من مالي جُذاذ عشرين وسقاً فلو كنت جَذَذْتيْه ، واحتَزْتيه كان لك، فإنما هو اليوم مال وارث ، وإنما هو أخوك وأختاك، فاقسموه على كتاب الله عزَّ وجلّ، قالت: يا أبت ، واللّه لو كان كذا وكذا لتركته ، إنما هي أسماء، فمن الأخرى؟ قال: ذو بطن بنت خارجة أُراها جاريةً، فوَلَدَتْ جارية.

806. Mālik informed us: "Ibn Shihāb informed us from ᶜUrwah that ᶜĀ⁾ishah رضي الله عنها said that Abū Bakr had given her a present of twenty *wasq* loads of clippings from his property [of date-palms] at ᶜĀliyyah. When death was near, he said, 'By Allah! my dear daughter, there is no one whom I would prefer to see self-sufficiently independent after me than you. Nor is there anyone whose being in need is more distressing to me than yours. I had given you a present from my property of twenty wasq-loads of clippings. If you had clipped them and taken possession of them they would have been yours, but today they are the property of [my] heirs, which is your brother and two sisters, so divide them up according to the Book of Allah ﷻ.' She said, 'Father, by Allah! even if it had been such-and-such, I would definitely have left it. [However] there is only Asmā⁾, so who is the other [sister]?' He answered, 'The one in the womb of Bint Khārijah whom I think is a girl.' She gave birth to a girl."

٨٠٧ أخبرنا مالك، أخبرنا ابن شهاب، عن عروة بنِ الزُّبير، عن عبد الرحمن بن عبدٍ القاريِّ أنَّ عمر بن الخطاب قال: ما بالُ رجالٍ يَنْحَلُون أبناءَهم نُحْلاً ، ثم يُمسكونها ، قال : فإن ماتَ ابنُ أحدهم قال: مالي بيدي ولم أعطه أحداً، وإن مات هو قال: هو لابني ، قد كنت أعطيته إياه. من نحل نحلة لم يَحُزْها الذي نُحِلَها حتى تكون إن مات لورثته فهي باطل.

807. Mālik informed us: "Ibn Shihāb informed us from ᶜUrwah ibn az-Zubayr from ᶜAbd ar-Raḥmān ibn ᶜAbdin al-Qāriyy [from the tribe of Qārah] that ᶜUmar ibn al-Khaṭṭāb said, 'What is wrong with men who give their sons presents and then later retract them?' He said, 'Then if one of his sons dies he says, "My property is in my hand, and I did not give it to anyone," but if he himself is dying, he says, "It is my son's, I had given it to him." Whoever gives a present, of which the one who is given it does not take possession until such time that if [the owner] dies it goes to his heirs, then it is invalid.'"

٨٠٨ أخبرنا مالك، عن ابن شهاب، عن سعيد بن المسيّب، أن عثمان بن عفان قال: من نحل ولداً له صغيراً لم يبلغ أن يحوز نُحْلة فأعلن بها، وأشهد عليها، فهي جائزة، وإنَّ وَلِيَّها أبوه.

808. Mālik informed us from Ibn Shihāb from Sa^cīd ibn al-Musayyab that ^cUthmān ibn ^cAffān said, "Whoever gives a present to a small son of his who has not reached [the age] to take possession of the present, but makes it public and has it witnesses to it, then that is valid, and the one who is in charge of it is his father."

قال محمد: وبهذا كلّه نأخذ. ينبغي للرجل أن يسوّي بين ولده في النُحْلة، ولا يُفَضِّلُ بعضهم على بعضٍ، فمن نَحَل نُحْلة ولداً أو غيره، فلم يقبضها الذي نُحِلَها حتى مات الناحل و المنحول فهي مردودة على الناحل، وعلى ورثته ولا تجوز للمنحول حتى يقبضها، إلاّ الولد الصغير، فإن قبض والده له قَبْضٌ، فإذا أعلنها وأَشْهد بها فهي جائزة لولده، ولا سبيل للوالد إلى الرجعة فيها، ولا إلى اغتصابها بعد أن أشهد عليها. وهو قولُ أبي حنيفة والعامة من فقهائنا.

Muḥammad said: "We adhere to all of this. A man ought to treat his children equally in giving presents, and not prefer some over others. Someone who gives a present to a child or to someone else, and the one given the present does not take possession of it until the one who gives the present or the one given the present dies, then it is to be returned to the one who gave the present and to the heirs. It is not valid for the one given the present until he takes possession of it, except in the case of the small child, because if his father takes possession of it for him and if he makes it public and has it witnessed then it is valid for the father, and the father has no way to renege on it, nor any way to take it by force after he had it witnessed. That is the verdict of Abū Ḥanīfah and of our *fuqahā*ʾ in general."

٣١ باب العُمْرى والسُّكْنى

31. Granting a Dwelling to Someone for their Lifespan [*^cumrā*] and Granting the Use of a Dwelling to Someone for their Lifespan [*suknā*]

٨٠٩ أخبرنا مالك، أخبرنا ابن شهاب، عن أبي سلمة بن عبد الرحمن، عن جابر بن عبد الله أنَّ رسول الله صلى الله عليه وسلم قال: أيّما رجل أُعمر عُمرى له ولِعَقِبه فإنَّها للذي يُعطاها لا ترجع إلى الذي أعطاها، لأنه أعطى عطاءً وقعت الموارث فيه.

809. Mālik informed us: "Ibn Shihāb informed us from Abū Salamah ibn ^cAbd ar-Raḥmān from Jābir ibn ^cAbdullāh that the Messenger of Allah ﷺ said, 'If a man is given a dwelling for his lifespan and that of his posterity, then it belongs to the one who was given it and does not return to the one who gave it, because he gave a gift in which the shares of inheritance are calculated.'"

٨١٠ أخبرنا مالك، أخبرنا نافع: أنَّ ابن عمر وَرَّث حفصة دارها، وكانت حفصة قد أسكنت بنت زيد بن الخطّاب ما عاشت، فلما تُوفيت بنت زيد بن الخطاب قبض عبد الله بن عمر المسكن، ورأى أنه له.

810. Mālik informed us: "Nāfiʿ informed us that Ibn ʿUmar had inherited Ḥafṣah's house. Ḥafṣah had let Bint Zayd ibn al-Khaṭṭāb dwell in it as long as she lived. When Bint Zayd ibn al-Khaṭṭāb died, then ʿAbdullāh ibn ʿUmar took possession of the house, and he reckoned that it was his."

قال محمد: وبهذا نأخذ. العمرى هبة فمن أعمر شيئاً فهو له، والسكنى له عارية ترجع إلى الذي أسكنها، وإلى وارثه من بعده. وهو قول أبي حنيفة والعامة من فقهائنا، والعمرى إن قال هي له ولعقبه أو لم يقل ولعقبه فهو سواء .

Muḥammad said: "We adhere to this. Giving something for the duration of someone's life [*ʿumrā*] is a gift. So if someone gives something for the duration of someone's life then it is his. Granting the use of a dwelling for someone's lifetime [*suknā*] is granting the use of it but not its ownership [*ʿariyyah*], so that it returns to the one who granted its residence and to his heirs after him. That is the verdict of Abū Ḥanīfah and of our *fuqahāʾ* in general. As to the *ʿumrā* whether he says it is for him and his descendants, or does not say that it is for his descendants, it is the same."

كتاب الصرّف، وأبواب الرِّبا

15. MONEY CHANGING AND USURY

٨١١ أخبرنا مالك، أخبرنا نافع عن عبد الله، أن عمر بن الخطاب رضي الله عنه قال: لا تبيعوا الوَرق بالذهب، أحدُهما غائبٌ والآخر ناجزٌ، فإن استنظرك إلى أنْ يَلجَ بيتَه فلا تُنْظِرْه. إنّي أخاف عليكم الرَّماءَ، والرَّماء هو الربا.

811. Mālik informed us: "Nāfi[c] informed us from [c]Abdullāh that [c]Umar ibn al-Khaṭṭāb said, 'Do not sell silver for gold, one of them being absent and the other present as cash. And if he asks you to wait until he enters his house, then do not wait for him. I am afraid of *ramā'* [an added increment] for you,' and *ramā'* is usury."

٨١٢ أخبرنا مالك، أخبرنا عبد الله بن دينار، عن عبد الله بن عمر قال: قال عمر بن الخطاب: لا تبيعوا الذّهب بالذّهب إلا مثلاً بمثْل، ولا تبيعوا الوَرق بالوَرق إلا مثلاً بمثل، ولا تبيعوا الذهب بالوَرق أحدهما غائب والآخر ناجزٌ، وإن استنظرك حتى يَلجَ بيتَه فلا تُنظر، إني أخاف عليكم الرِّبا.

812. Mālik informed us: "[c]Abdullāh ibn Dīnār informed us that [c]Abdullāh ibn [c]Umar said, '[c]Umar ibn al-Khaṭṭāb said, "Do not sell gold for gold except like for like. Do not sell silver for silver except like for like. Do not sell gold for silver, one of them being absent and the other to hand. If he asks you to wait until he enters his house, do not wait. I fear usury for you."'"

٨١٣ أخبرنا مالك، حدّثنا نافع ؟، عن أبي سعيد الخُدْري، أن رسول الله صلى الله عليه وسلم قال: لا تبيعوا الذهب بالذهب إلا مثْلاً بمثْل، ولا تُشفُّوا بعضَها على بعض، ولا تبيعوا الوَرِق بالوَرِق إلا مثلاً بمثل، ولا تُشفُّوا بعضَها على بعضٍ، ولا تبيعوا منها شيئاً غائباً بناجز.

813. Mālik informed us: "Nāfi[c] narrated to us from Abū Sa[c]īd al-Khudrī that the Messenger of Allah ﷺ said, 'Do not sell gold for gold except like for like, and do not give a little increase in some of it over its countervalue. Do not sell silver for silver except like for like, and do not give a little increase in some of it over its countervalue. Do not sell some of it which is absent for something ready to hand.'"

٨١٤ أخبرنا مالك، حدّثنا موسى بن أبي تميم، عن سعيد بن يسار، عن أبي هريرة أن رسول الله صلى الله عليه وسلم قال: الدينار بالدينار والدرهم بالدرهم لا فضل بينهما.

814. Mālik informed us: "Mūsā ibn Abī Tamīm narrated to us from Sa[c]īd ibn Yasār from Abū Hurayrah that the Messenger of Allah ﷺ said, 'Dīnār for dīnār, and dirham for dirham with no excess between the two of them.'"

٨١٥ أخبرنا مالك، أخبرنا ابن شهاب، عن مالك بن أوس ابن الحَدَثان، أنّه أخبره: أنّه التمس صَرْفاً

بمائة دينار، وقال: فدعاني طلحة بن عبيد الله، فقال: فتراوَضْنا حتى اصطَرَف مني، فأخذ طلحةُ الذهبَ يُقَلِّبُها في يده، ثم قال: حتى يأتيَني خازني من الغابة، وعمرُ بن الخطاب يسمع كلامه، فقال: لا، والله لا تفارقه حتى تأخُذَ منه، ثم قال: قال رسول الله صلى الله عليه وسلم: الذهب بالفضّة رباً إلا هآءَ وهآءَ، والتمرُ بالتمر رباً إلا هآءَ وهآءَ، والشعير بالشعير رباً إلا هآءَ وهآءَ.

815. Mālik informed us: "Ibn Shihāb informed us that Mālik ibn Aws ibn al-Ḥadathān informed him that he was looking for change for one hundred dīnārs, and he said, 'Ṭalḥah ibn ᶜUbaydullāh called me.' He said, 'We negotiated until he procured [the dīnārs] from me.' So Ṭalḥah took the gold and turned it around in his hand, and then he said, '[Wait] until my treasurer comes to me from al-Ghābah,' while ᶜUmar ibn al-Khaṭṭāb was listening to his words, and he [ᶜUmar] said, 'No! By Allah! do not separate from him until you take [the change] from him.' Then he said, 'The Messenger of Allah ﷺ said, "Gold for silver is usury except 'Take this!' and 'Take this!' [in immediate exchange], and dates for dates are usury except 'Take this!' and 'Take this!', and barley for barley is usury except 'Take this!' and 'Take this!'"'"

٨١٦ أخبرنا مالك، أخبرنا زيد بن أسلم، عن عطاء بن يسار، أو عن سليمان بن يسار: أنه أخبره أن معاوية بن أبي سفيان باع سقايةً من ورقٍ أو ذهبٍ بأكثرَ من وزنها، فقال له أبو الدرداء: سمعتُ رسول الله صلى الله عليه وسلم ينهى عن مثلِ هذا إلا مثلاً بمثل، قال له معاوية: ما نرى به بأساً، فقال له أبو الدرداء: من يعذرُني من معاوية، أُخْبِرُهُ عن رسول الله صلى الله عليه وسلم ويُخبرني عن رأيه، لا أُساكِنْكَ بأرضٍ أنتَ بها، قال: فقدم أبو الدرداء على عمر بن الخطّاب فأخبره، فكتب إلى معاوية أن لا يبيع ذلك إلاّ مثلاً بمثل، أو وزناً بوزن.

816. Mālik informed us: "Zayd ibn Aslam informed us that ᶜAṭā᾽ ibn Yasār or Sulaymān ibn Yasār informed him that 'Muᶜāwiyah ibn Abī Sufyān sold a drinking cup made from silver or gold for more than its weight, and so Abu'd-Dardā᾽ said to him, "I heard the Messenger of Allah ﷺ forbade the like of this unless it was like for like." So Muᶜāwiyah said to him, "We see no harm in it." Abu'd-Dardā᾽ said to him, "Who will relieve me of Muᶜāwiyah? I tell him something from the Messenger of Allah ﷺ and he tells me his own opinion! I will not live in the same land in which you are!"' He said, 'So Abu'd-Dardā᾽ went to ᶜUmar ibn al-Khaṭṭāb [in Madīnah] and told him, and he [ᶜUmar] wrote to Muᶜāwiyah that he should not sell that except like for like, or weight for weight.'"

٨١٧ أخبرنا مالك، أخبرنا يزيد بن عبد الله بن قُسَيْط الليثي: أنه رأى سعيد بن المسيّب يُراطِلُ الذهب بالذهب، قال: فَيُفَرِّغُ الذهب في كفّة الميزان، ويُفَرِّغُ الآخر الذهبَ في كِفَّته الأخرى، قالَ: ثم يرفع الميزان، فإذا اعتدل لسان الميزان؟، أخَذَ وأعطى صاحبَه.

817. Mālik informed us: "Yazīd ibn ᶜAbdullāh ibn Qusayṭ al-Laythī informed us that he saw Saᶜīd ibn al-Musayyab weighing out gold against gold. He

would put the gold in the pan of the scales, and the other person would put his gold in the other pan. He said, 'Then he would lift the scales, and when the tongue of the scales was in the middle [because the two pans were level and equal], he would take [the other's gold] and give [his gold] to his companion.'"

قال محمد : وبهذا كله نأخذ على ما جاءت الآثار، وهو قولُ أبي حنيفة والعامّة من فقهائنا .

Muḥammad said: "We adhere to all of this in accordance with the traditions that have been narrated, and that is the verdict of Abū Ḥanīfah and of our *fuqahā'* in general."

١ باب الربا فيما يُكال أو يُوزَن

1. Usury that Occurs on Measured and Weighed Things

٨١٨ أخبرنا مالك، أخبرنا أبو الزِّناد، أنه سمع سعيد بن المسيّب يقول : لا ربا إلا في ذهب أو فضّةٍ أو ما يُكال أو يُوزن مما يُوكل أو يُشرب .

818. Mālik informed us: "Abu'z-Zinād informed us that he heard Sa'īd ibn al-Musayyab saying, 'There is no usury except in gold and silver, and in that which is measured and weighed of those things which are eaten and drunk.'"

قال محمد : إذا كان ما يُكال من صنف واحد، أو كان ما يوزن من صنفٍ واحدٍ ، فهو مكروه أيضاً، إلا مثلاً بمثل، يداً بيدٍ، بمنزلة الذي يؤكل ويُشرب وهو قول إبراهيم النخعي وأبي حنيفة والعامة من فقهائنا .

Muḥammad said: "If that which is measured is from one specie, or if that which is weighed is from one specie, then it is also disapproved, unless it is like for like, hand to hand, as is the situation with that which is eaten and drunk. That is the verdict of Ibrāhīm an-Nakha'ī, and Abū Ḥanīfah and our *fuqahā'* in general."

٨١٩ أخبرنا مالك، أخبرنا زيد بن أسلم، عن عطاء بن يسار قال : قال رسول الله صلى الله عليه وسلم: التمر بالتمر مثلاً بمثل، فقيل: يا رسول الله إن عاملك على خيبر وهو رجل من بني عدي من الأنصار يأخذ الصاع بالصاعين ، قال: ادعوه لي ، فدُعِيَ له، فقال رسول الله صلى الله عليه وسلم: لا تأخذ الصاعَ بالصاعين، فقال: يا رسول الله، لا يُعطوني الجَنِيبَ بالجَمع إلا صاعاً بصاعين، قال رسول الله صلى الله عليه وسلم: بع الجَمْع بالدراهم واشتر بالدراهم جنيباً .

819. Mālik informed us: "Zayd ibn Aslam informed us that 'Aṭā' ibn Yasār said, 'The Messenger of Allah ﷺ said, 'Dates for dates are like for like.' Someone said, 'Your agent in charge of Khaybar' – and he was a man from Banī 'Adī of the Anṣār – 'takes a *ṣā'* for two *ṣā'*.' He said, 'Call him to me,' and so he was called for. The Messenger of Allah ﷺ said, 'Do not take a *ṣā'* for two *ṣā'*.' He said, 'Messenger of Allah, they will not give me good quality dates for poor quality dates except one *ṣā'* for two *ṣā'*.' He said, 'Sell the poor quality dates for dirhams and with the dirhams buy good quality dates.'"

٨٢٠ أخبرنا مالك، أخبرنا عبد المجيد بن سُهَيْل والزهري، عن سعيد بن المسيّب، عن أبي سعيد الخُدري وعن أبي هريرة : انّ رسول الله صلى الله عليه وسلم استعمل رجلاً على خيبر، فجاء بتمر جنيب ، فقال له رسول الله صلى الله عليه وسلم أكُلّ تمر خيبر هكذا؟ قال: لا، والله يا رسول الله، ولكن الصاع من هذا بالصاعين ، والصاعين بالثلاثة ، فقال رسول الله صلى الله عليه وسلم: فلا تفعل، بعْ تمرك بالدراهم، ثم اشترِ بالدراهم جَنيباً، وقال في الميزان مثل ذلك .

820. Mālik informed us: "ᶜAbd al-Majīd ibn Suhayl and az-Zuhrī informed us from Saᶜīd ibn al-Musayyab from Abū Saᶜīd al-Khudrī and from Abū Hurayrah that the Messenger of Allah ﷺ put a man in charge of Khaybar. He brought some good quality dates, and so the Messenger of Allah ﷺ asked him, 'Are all of the dates of Khaybar like this?' He said, 'No, by Allah! Messenger of Allah. But a *ṣāᶜ* of this is [exchanged] for two *ṣāᶜ*, and two *ṣāᶜ* for three.' The Messenger of Allah ﷺ said, 'Then do not do so. Sell your dates for dirhams, and then later buy the good quality dates with the dirhams,' and he said with respect to things which are weighed the like of that."

قال محمد: وبهذا كله نأخذ. وهو قول أبي حنيفة والعامة من فقهائنا.

Muḥammad said: "We adhere to all of this, and it is the verdict of Abū Ḥanīfah and of our *fuqahā᾽* in general."

٨٢١ أخبرنا مالك، عن رجل : أنه سأل سعيد بن المسيّب، عن رجل يشتري طعاماً من الجار بدينارٍ ونصف درهم، أخبرنا مالك، أ يعطيه ديناراً أو نصف درهم طعاماً؟ قال: لا، ولكن يعطيه ديناراً ودرهماً، ويَرُدُّ عليه البائع نصف درهم طعاماً.

821. Mālik informed us from a man who asked Saᶜīd ibn al-Musayyab about a man who buys food at [the market of] al-Jār for a dīnār and a half of a dirham, "Should he give him a dīnār or a half of a dirham in the form of food?" He said, "No, but rather he should give him a dīnār and a dirham, and return to the seller a half a dirham's worth of food[153]."

قال محمدٌ: هذا الوجه أحبُّ إلينا، والوجه الآخر يجوز أيضاً إذا لم يُعطه من الطعام الذي اشترى أقلَّ مما يصيب نصف الدرهم منه في البيع الأول، فإن أعطاه منه أقلّ مما يصيب نصف الدرهم منه في البيع الأول، لم يجز ، وهو قولُ أبي حنيفة والعامة من فقهائنا.

Muḥammad said: "This way is preferable to us. The other way is also permissible, when he does not give him less than that of the food he bought which would equal half a dirham in the first sale. If he gives him less than that of it which would equal half a dirham in the first sale, it is not valid. That is the verdict of Abū Ḥanīfah and of our *fuqahā᾽* in general."

٢ باب الرجل يكون له العطايا أو الدَّيْن على الرجل فيبيعه قبل أن يَقْبِضَه

2. A Man who is Due a Stipend or is Owed a Debt by a Man and who Sells it before Receiving it

٨٢٢ أخبرنا مالك، أخبرنا يحيى بن سعيد : أنه سمع جميل المؤذِّن يقول لسعيد بن المسيّب : إنّي

رجلٌ أشتري هذه الأَرزاقَ التي يُعطيها الناس بالجار فأبتَاعُ منها ما شاء الله، ثم أريد أن أبيع الطعام المضمون عليَّ إلى ذلك الأجل، فقال له سعيد: أتريد أن توفّيهم من تلك الأرزاق التي ابتعتَ ؟ قال: نعم. فنهاه عن ذلك.

822. Mālik informed us: "Yaḥyā ibn Saᶜīd informed us that he heard Jamīl the *muᵓadhdhin* saying to Saᶜīd ibn al-Musayyab, 'I am a man who buys these provisions which people are given at al-Jār, and I buy of them what Allah wills [with deferred payment]. Then later I wish to sell the food which I have guaranteed [to pay for] at that later date.' Saᶜīd asked him, 'Do you mean to fulfil [your payments] to them [the owners from whom the provisions were bought] with the [proceeds of the sale of the] provisions which you bought?' He said, 'Yes,' and so he forbade him doing that."

قال محمد: لا ينبغي للرجل إذا كان له دَيْنٌ أن يبيعه حتى يستوفيَه لأنّه غَرَر فلا يُدْرى أيخرج أم لا يخرج. وهو قولُ أبي حنيفة رحمه الله.

Muḥammad said: "A man ought not, if he is owed a debt, to sell it until he takes it in full because it is an uncertain transaction (gharar), and he is not sure whether it will be paid or not. And That is the verdict of Abū Ḥanīfah, may Allah have mercy on him."

٨٢٣ أخبرنا مالك، أخبرنا موسى بن مَيْسرة: أنّه سمع رجلاً يسأل سعيد بن المسيّب فقال: إنّي رجل أبيع الدَّيْن، وذكر له شيئاً من ذلك، فقال له ابن المسيّب: لا تبع إلاّ ما آوَيْتَ إلى رحلك.

823. Mālik informed us: "Mūsā ibn Maysarah informed us that he heard a man asking Saᶜīd ibn al-Musayyab saying, 'I am a man who sells debts,' and he mentioned to him something about that. Saᶜīd ibn al-Musayyab said to him, 'Only sell what you have lodged in your dwelling [i.e. taken possession of].'"

قال محمد: وبه نأخذ. لا ينبغي للرجل أن يبيع ديناً له على إنسان إلاّ من الذي هو عليه لأن بيع الدين غررٌ لا يُدْرى أيخرج منه أم لا. وهو قول أبي حنيفة رحمه الله.

Muḥammad said: "We adhere to this. A man ought not to sell a debt he is owed by a person unless it is to that [same] person, because sale of a debt is an uncertain transaction about which it is not sure whether it will be paid or not. That is the verdict of Abū Ḥanīfah, may Allah have mercy on him."

٣ باب الرجل يكون عليه الدَّيْن فيقضي أفضل مما أخذه

3. A Man who Owes a Debt and who Repays with more than that which He Took

٨٢٤ أخبرنا مالك، أخبرنا حُميد بن قيس المكيّ، عن مجاهد قال: اسْتَسْلَفَ عبد الله بن عمر من رجل دراهم، ثم قضى خيراً منها، فقال الرجل: هذه خير من دَراهمي التي أسلفتك، قال ابن عمر: قد علمتُ ولكن نفسي بذلك طيّبة.

824. Mālik informed us: "Ḥumayd ibn Qays al-Makkī informed us that Mujāhid said, 'ᶜAbdullāh ibn ᶜUmar took a loan of some dirhams from a man, and then

he repaid it with more than that. The man said, "This is more than the dirhams which I lent you." Ibn ᶜUmar said, "I know, but I am contented with that.""'

٨٢٥ أخبرنا مالك، أخبرنا زيد بن أسلم، عن عطاء بن يسار، عن أبي رافع : أن رسول صلى الله عليه وسلم استسلف من رجلٍ بَكْراً فَقَدِمَتْ عليه إبل من صدقة فأمر أبا رافع أن يقضيَ الرجلَ بَكْرَه، فرجع إليه أبو رافع، فقال : لم أجد فيها إلاّ جملاً رَبَاعياً خيّاراً ، فقال : أعطه إياه، فإن خيار الناس أحسنُهم قضاءً.

825. Mālik informed us: "Zayd ibn Aslam informed us from ᶜAṭā᾽ ibn Yasār from Abū Rāfiᶜ that the Messenger of Allah ﷺ took a young camel as a loan from a man to be paid for later. Then the camels of the *ṣadaqah* (*zakāh*) came to him, and he told Abū Rāfiᶜ to pay the man for his young camel. Abū Rāfiᶜ came back to him and said, 'I can only find a choice four year old camel among them.' He said, 'Give it to him, because the best of people are those who are best in repayment.'"

قال محمد : وبقول ابن عمر نأخُذُ. لا بأسَ بذلك إذا كان من غير شَرْطَ اشتُرِطَ عليه. وهو قولُ أبي حنيفة رحمه الله.

Muḥammad said: "And we adhere to the verdict of Ibn ᶜUmar. There is no harm in that if it is not from a stipulation which he laid as a condition on him. That is the verdict of Abū Ḥanīfah, may Allah have mercy on him."

٨٢٦ أخبرنا مالك، أخبرنا نافع، عن ابن عمر قال: من اسلف سلفاً فلا يَشْتَرِط إلاّ قضاءَه .

826. Mālik informed us: "Nāfiᶜ informed us that Ibn ᶜUmar said, 'Whoever gives a loan must not stipulate anything but its repayment.'"

قال محمد : وبهذا نأخذ. لا ينبغي له أن يَشترط افضل منه ولا يشترط عليه أحسن منه، فإن الشرط في هذا لا ينبغي. وهو قولُ أبي حنيفة والعامة من فقهائنا.

Muḥammad said, "We adhere to this. He ought not to stipulate more than it, nor does he stipulate better than it, because stipulations ought not to be made in this, and that is the verdict of Abū Ḥanīfah and of our *fuqahā᾽* in general."

٤ باب ما يُكره من قطع الدراهم والدنانير

4. What is Disapproved of in Clipping Dirhams and Dīnārs

٨٢٧ أخبرنا مالك، أخبرنا يحيى بن سعيد، عن سعيد بن المسيّب أنّه قال : قطع الوَرِق والذهب من الفساد في الأرض.

827. Mālik informed us: "Yaḥyā ibn Saᶜīd informed us that Saᶜīd ibn al-Musayyab said, 'Clipping silver [dirhams] and gold [dīnārs] is a part of working corruption in the land.'"

قال محمد : لا ينبغي قطع الدراهم والدنانير لغير منفعة.

Muḥammad said: "Dirhams and dīnārs ought not to be clipped without any benefit."

٥ باب المعاملة والمزارعة في النخل والأرض

5. Transactions and Cropsharing Agreements in Date-palms and Land

٨٢٨ أخبرنا مالك، أخبرنا ربيعة بن أبي عبد الرحمن، أن حنظلة الأنصاري أخبره أنَّه سأل رافع بن خَديج عن كِراء المزارع فقال: قد نُهي عنه ، قال حنظلة: فقلتُ لرافع: بالذهب والورق؟ قال رافع: لا بأس بكرائها بالذهب والورق.

828. Mālik informed us: "Rabī^c^ah ibn Abī ^c^Abd ar-Raḥmān informed us that Ḥanẓalah al-Anṣārī informed him that he asked Rāfi^c^ ibn Khadīj about renting arable land, and he said, 'It has been forbidden.' Ḥanẓalah said, 'I said to Rāfi^c^, "With gold and silver?" Rāfi^c^ said, "There is no harm in renting it with gold and silver."'"

قال محمد: وبهذا نأخذ. لا بأس بكرائها بالذهب والورق بالحنطة كيلاً معلوماً وضرباً معلوماً ما لم يُشْتَرط ذلك مما يخرج منها، فإن اشْتُرط مما يخرج منها كيلاً معلوماً فلا خير فيه ، وهو قول أبي حنيفة والعامة من فقهائنا. وقد سُئل عن كِرائها سعيد بن جبير بالحنطة كيلاً معلوماً فرخَّص في ذلك فقال: هل ذلك إلاّ مثل البيت يُكْرَى.

Muḥammad said: "We adhere to this. There is no harm in renting it with gold and silver, and with wheat of a known measure and of a specific variety as long as that is not stipulated to be from what is produced by it [the land]. If it is stipulated to be from what is produced from it and of known measure then there is no good in it, and that is the verdict of Abū Ḥanīfah and of our *fuqahā*ʾ in general. Sa^c^īd ibn Jubayr was asked about renting it with wheat of a known measure and he gave a concessionary ruling allowing that saying, 'Is that anything other than like renting a house?'"

٨٢٩ أخبرنا مالك، أخبرنا ابن شهاب، عن سعيد بن المسيّب: أنَّ رسول الله صلى الله عليه وسلم حين فتح خيبر، قال لليهود: أُقِرُّكُمْ ما أَقَرّكم الله على أنَّ الثمرَ بيننا وبينكم، قال: وكان رسول الله صلى الله عليه وسلم يبعث عبدَ الله بن رَواحة، فيخرص بينه وبينهم.
ثم يقول: إن شئتم فلكم، وإن شئتم فلي، قال: فكانوا يأخذونه.

829. Mālik informed us: "Ibn Shihāb informed us from Sa^c^īd ibn al-Musayyab that the Messenger of Allah ﷺ at the time of the Opening of Khaybar [to Islam] said to the jews, 'I confirm you as long as Allah confirms you, on the basis that the fruits are between us and you.' He said, 'The Messenger of Allah ﷺ used to send ^c^Abdullāh ibn Rawāḥah to assess [the date harvest] between him and them, and then he would say, "If you wish it is yours, and if you wish it is mine."' He said, 'And so they used to take it.'"

٨٣٠ أخبرنا مالك، أخبرنا ابن شهاب، عن سليمان بن يسار: أنّ رسول الله صلى الله عليه وسلم كان يبعث عبد الله بن رواحة فيخرُص بينه وبين اليهود، قال: فجمعوا حُلِيّاً من حُلِيّ نسائهم، فقالوا: هذا لك، وخفِّف عنّا، وتجاوَزْ في القِسْمة، فقال: يا معشر اليهود، والله إنكم لَمِنْ أبغضِ خلق الله إليّ، وما ذاك بحاملي أن أحيفَ عليكم، أما الذي عرضتم من الرَّشوة فإنها سُحْتٌ وإنّا لا نأكلها، قالوا: بهذا قامت السموات والأرض.

830. Mālik informed us: "Ibn Shihāb informed us from Sulaymān ibn Yasār that the Messenger of Allah ﷺ used to send ᶜAbdullāh ibn Rawāḥah to make the assessment [of the division of the harvest] between him and the jews. He said, 'So they collected some of their womenfolk's jewellery and said, "This is for you; go easy on us and don't be too exact in the division." He answered, "Assembly of jews, by Allah! You are some of the most hateful of Allah's creation to me, but that will not lead me to be unjust to you. As for that which you have offered as a bribe, it is abominable and we do not accept it." They said, "By this the heavens and the earth stand."'"

قال محمد: وبهذا نأخذ. لا بأس بمعاملة النخل على الشَّطْر، والثلث، والربع، وبمزارعة الأرض البيضاء على الشطر، والثلث، والربع، وكان أبو حنيفة يَكره ذلك ويَذكر أن ذلك هو المخابرة التي نهى عنها رسول الله صلى الله عليه وسلم.

Muḥammad said: "We adhere to this. There is no harm in contracting someone to work with date-palms for a half, a third or a quarter [of the crop], or in contracting someone to work in growing crops on uncultivated land for a half, a third or a quarter [of the crop], but Abū Ḥanīfah used to disapprove of it and he would mention that it is the hiring of somone to work the land for a share of the crop [*mukhābarah*] which the Messenger of Allah ﷺ forbade."

٦ باب إحياء الأرض بإذن الإمام أو بغير إذنه

6. Reviving [Waste] Land by Permission of the *Imām* [*Sulṭān*] or without his Permission

٨٣١ أخبرنا مالك، أخبرنا هشام بن عروة، عن أبيه قال: قال النبي صلى الله عليه وسلم: من أحيى أرضاً ميّتة فهي له، وليس لعرقٍ ظالم حقّ.

831. Mālik informed us: "Hishām ibn ᶜUrwah informed us that his father said, 'The Prophet ﷺ said, "Whoever revives dead land, then it is his, and the unjustly [planted] root has no right."'"

٨٣٢ أخبرنا مالك، عن ابن شهاب، عن سالم بن عبد الله، عن عبد الله بن عمر، عن عمر بن الخطاب رضي الله عنه قال: من أحيى أرضاً ميتةً فهي له.

832. Mālik informed us: "Ibn Shihāb informed us from Sālim ibn ᶜAbdullāh from ᶜAbdullāh ibn ᶜUmar that ᶜUmar ibn al-Khaṭṭāb ؓ said, 'Whoever revives dead land, then it is his.'"

قال محمد: وبهذا نأخذ. من أحيى أرضاً ميتة بإذن الإمام أو بغير إذنه فهي له، فأما أبو حنيفة فقال: لا يكون له إلاّ أن يجعلها له الإمام، قال: وينبغي للإمام إذا أحياها أنْ يجعلَها له وإن لم يفعل لم تكن له.

Muḥammad said: "We adhere to this. Whoever revives dead land by permission of the *imām* or without his permission, then it is his. As for Abū Ḥanīfah, he said, 'It is not his unless the *imām* gives it to him. The *imām* ought, if he revives it, to give it to him, but if he does not do so, then it is not his.'"

٧ باب الصلح في الشِرْب وقسمة الماء

7. Conciliatory Agreements on Shares of Water and on Apportioning Water

٨٣٣ أخبرنا مالك، أخبرنا عبد الله بن أبي بكر أنَّ رسولَ الله صلى الله عليه وسلم قال في سبيل مَهْزُورٍ ومُذَيْنب: يُمسك حتى يبلغ الكعبين، ثم يُرْسِلُ الأعلى على الأسفل.

833. Mālik informed us:"ᶜAbdullāh ibn Abī Bakr informed us that the Messenger of Allah ﷺ said about the flood channels of Mahzūr and Mudhaynib, 'Dam them until it reaches the ankles and then release the higher [to flow] over the lower.'"[154]

قال محمد: وبه نأخذ، لأنه كان كذلك الصلح بينهم: لكل قوم ما اصطلحُوا وأسلموا عليه من عيونهم وسيولهم وأنهارهم وشِرْبهم.

Muḥammad said: "We adhere to this, because that was the agreement between them. Every people have what they are agreed upon together and accept respecting their springs, floodwaters, rivers and shares of water resources."

٨٣٤ أخبرنا مالك، أخبرنا عمرو بن يحيى، عن أبيه أنَّ الضحَّاك بن خليفة ساق خَلِيْجاً له حتى النهر الصغير من العُرَيْض، فأراد أن يمرَّ به في أرض لمحمد بن مسلمة، فأبى محمد بن مسلمة، فقال الضحاك: لِمَ تمنعني وهو لك منفعةٌ تشرب به أولاً وآخراً، ولا يضرُّك، فأبى، فكلَّم فيه عمرَ بن الخطّاب رضي الله تعالى عنه، فدعا محمدَ بنَ مَسْلمة فأمره أن يُخَلِّي سبيلَه فأبى، فقال عمرُ: لِمَ تمنع أخاك ما ينفعه وهو لك نافع تشرب به أولاً وآخراً ولا يضرُّك؟ قال محمد: لا والله، فقال عمر: واللّه ليمُرَّنَّ به ولو على بطنك. فأمره عمر أن يُجْرِيَه.

834. Mālik informed us: "ᶜAmr ibn Yaḥyā informed us from his father that aḍ-Ḍaḥḥāk ibn Khalīfah drove a small tributary stream of his, even a small river, from al-'Urayd [a valley in Madīnah]. He wanted to pass it through land of Muḥammad ibn Maslamah, but Muḥammad ibn Maslamah refused. So aḍ-Ḍaḥḥāk said, 'Why do you prevent me, when it will be of benefit to you and you can drink from it first and last, and it will not harm you?' But he continued to refuse, so he spoke about it to ᶜUmar ibn al-Khaṭṭāb ﷺ. He called Muḥammad ibn Maslamah and told him to make the way open for him, but he refused. ᶜUmar said, 'Why do you refuse your brother something which will benefit him, and which is also useful to you from which you can drink first and last, and which will not harm you?' Muḥammad said, 'No, by Allah!' ᶜUmar said, 'By Allah! he will pass through with it, even if it has to be over your belly,' and ᶜUmar told him to let it flow through."

٨٣٥ أخبرنا مالك، أخبرنا عمرو بن يحيى المازني، عن أبيه: أنَّه كان في حائط جدِّه رَبِيْعٌ لعبد الرحمن بن عوف، فأراد عبد الرحمن أن يحوِّله إلى ناحية من الحائط هي أرفق لعبد الرحمن وأقرب

إلى أرضه ، فمنعه صاحب الحائط، فكلَّم عبدُ الرحمن عمرَ بن الخطاب رضي الله عنه فقض لعبد الرحمن بتحويله .

835. Mālik informed us: "ᶜAmr ibn Yaḥyā al-Māzinī informed us from his father that there was a small stream belonging to ᶜAbd ar-Raḥmān ibn ᶜAwf in his father's walled garden. ᶜAbd ar-Raḥmān wanted to move it to a section of the garden easier for ᶜAbd ar-Raḥmān and nearer to his land, but the owner of the garden refused him permission. So ᶜAbd ar-Raḥmān spoke to ᶜUmar ibn al-Khaṭṭāb ﷺ and he gave judgement in favour of ᶜAbd ar-Raḥmān moving it."

٨٣٦ أخبرنا مالك، أخبرنا أبو الرِّجال، عن عَمْرة بنت عبد الرحمن أنَّ رسولَ الله صلى الله عليه وسلم قال: لا يُمْنَع نَقْعُ بئر.

836. Mālik informed us: "Abu'r-Rijāl informed us from ᶜAmrah bint ᶜAbd ar-Raḥmān that the Messenger of Allah ﷺ said, 'The surplus of [the water of] a well is not [to be] refused.'"

قال محمد: وبهذا نأخذ. أيُّما رجلٍ كانت له بئر فليس له أن يمنع الناس منها أن يستقوا منها لشفاههم وإبلهم وغنمهم، وأما لزرعهم ونخلهم فله أن يمنع ذلك. وهو قول أبي حنيفة والعامة من فقهائنا .

Muḥammad said: "We adhere to this. If a man has a well, he does not have the right to refuse people to draw water from it for their own lips and for their camels and their sheep. As for their crops and date palms, then he may refuse that, and that is the verdict of Abū Ḥanīfah and of our *fuqahā᾽* in general."

٨ باب الرجل يُعْتِق نصيباً له من مملوك أو يُسَيِّبُ سائبةً أو يُوصي بعتق

8. A Man Freeing his Portion of [the Ownership of] a Slave, or Freeing a Slave such that there is no *Walā᾽* Relationship [*Sā᾽ibah*], or Leaving a Testament to Free a Slave

٨٣٧ أخبرنا مالك، أخبرنا هشام بن عُروة، عن ابيه : أن أبا بكر سَيَّبَ سائبةً .

837. Mālik informed us: "Hishām ibn ᶜUrwah informed us from his father that Abū Bakr freed a slave in such a way that there was no *walā᾽* relationship."

قال محمد: قال رسول الله ﷺ في الحديث المشهور: "الولاء لمن أعتق"، وقال عبد الله بن مسعود: لا سائبةَ في الإسلام ، ولو استقام أن يُعتق الرجلُ سائبة فلا يكون لمن أعتقه ولاؤه لاستقام لمن طَلَبَ من عائشةَ أن تُعْتِق، ويكون الولاءُ لغيرها، فقد طَلَبَ ذلك منها، فقال رسول الله ﷺ: "الولاء لمن أعتق"، وإذا استقامَ أن لا يكون لمن أعتق ولاء استقام أن يُسْتَثْنَى عنه الولاء فيكون لغيره، واستقام أن يهب الولاء ويبيعه، وقد نهى رسول الله صلى الله عليه وسلم عن بيع الولاء وهبته. والولاء عندنا بمنزلة النسب وهو لمن أعتق إن أعتق سائبة أو غيرها. وهو قول أبي حنيفة والعامة من فقهائنا.

Muḥammad said: "The Messenger of Allah ﷺ said in the famous ḥadīth, 'The *walā᾽* belongs to the one who sets free.' ᶜAbdullāh ibn Masᶜūd said, 'There is no setting free without the relationship of *walāʾ* in Islam.' If it was right for a man to set a slave free in such a way that he does not get his *walāʾ* relationship, then it would be right for the one who asked ʿĀʾishah to set him free and for his *walāʾ* to go to someone other than her, because he asked that of her, and the Messenger of Allah ﷺ said, 'The *walāʾ* belongs to the one who sets free.' If it were right that there should be no *walāʾ* for the one who set free, then it would be right for him to be excluded from the *walāʾ* and for it to go to someone else, and it would be acceptable for someone to give it away or sell it, and yet the Messenger of Allah ﷺ forbade selling the *walāʾ* and giving it away. *Walāʾ*, according to us, is of the same order as kinship, and it belongs to the one who sets free, whether he sets someone free as a *sāʾibah* or otherwise. That is the verdict of Abū Ḥanīfah and of our *fuqahāʾ* in general."

٨٣٨ أخبرنا مالك، أخبرنا نافع، عن ابن عمر أن رسول الله صلى الله عليه وسلم قال: من أعتق شِرْكاً له في عبد وكان له من المال ما يبلغُ ثمنَ العبد، قُوِّم قيمةَ العَدْل، ثم أُعطِيَ شركاؤه حِصَصَهم وعَتَقَ عليه العبدُ، وإلاَّ فقد عَتَقَ منه ما أُعتِقَ.

838. Mālik informed us: "Nāfiʿ informed us from Ibn ʿUmar that the Messenger of Allah ﷺ said, 'Whoever sets free a share he has of a slave, and he has enough wealth to reach the price of the slave, then he [the slave] is evaluated at a moderate price, his partners are given their portions, and the slave becomes free at his expense [and he has the *walāʾ*]. Otherwise that much of him which he set free becomes free.'"

قال محمد: وبهذا نأخذُ من أعتق شِقْصاً في مملوك فهو حرّ كلُّه، فإن كان الذي أعتَقَ موسراً ضمن حصة شريكه من العبد، وإن كان مَعسراً سعى العبدُ لشركائه في حصصهم. وكذلك بلغنا عن النبي صلى الله عليه وسلم. وقال أبو حنيفة: يُعْتَق عليه بقدر ما أعتق، والشركاء بالخيار: إن شاؤا أعتقوا كما أعتق، وإن شاؤا ضَمَّنُوه إن كان موسراً، وإن شاؤا استَسْعَوْا العبدَ في حصصهم، فإن استسعوا أو اعتقوا كان الولاء بينهم على قدر حصصهم، وإن ضَمَّنُوا المعتق كان الولاءُ كله له، ورجع على العبد بما ضُمّن واستسعاه به.

Muḥammad said: "We adhere to this. Someone who sets free a portion of a slave then all of him is set free. If the one who sets free has some wealth then he must be liable for his partner's share of the slave. If he has no wealth, then the slave must exert himself to gain his partners their shares. Similarly, it has reached us from the Prophet ﷺ. Abū Ḥanīfah said, 'He is freed at his expense to the degree that he has freed him, and the partners have the choice: if they wish they may set him free as he has set him free; if they wish they can hold him liable if he is a person of some wealth; and if they wish they can require the slave to work to gain them their shares. If they demand that he work or they set him free, then the *walāʾ* is shared between them according to the measure of their shares. If they require the [original shareholder] who set him free to be liable [for the whole price] then the entire *walāʾ* is his, and he claims from the slave that for which he has been made liable and asks him to work for it."

٨٣٩ أخبرنا مالك، حدَّثنا نافع: أن عبد الله بن عمر أعتق ولد زنى وأمَّه .

839. Mālik informed us: "Nāfiᶜ narrated to us that ᶜAbdullāh ibn ᶜUmar set free an illegitimate child and its mother."

قال محمد: لا بأس بذلك. وهو حسنٌ جميل، بلغنا عن ابن عباسٍ أنه سُئل عن عبدين: أحدهما لبَغيَّةٍ والآخر لرِشْدَة: أيُّهُمَا يُعْتَق؟ قال: أغلاهما ثمناً بدينارٍ. فهكذا نقول. وهو قول أبي حنيفة والعامة من فقهائنا.

Muḥammad said; "There is no harm in that, and it is good and fine. It has reached us that Ibn ᶜAbbās was asked about two slaves, one of which was [the child] of an adulteress and the other of a right-acting woman, as to which of them should be freed? He said, 'The more expensive of them in dīnārs.' That is our verdict, and it is the verdict of Abū Ḥanīfah and of our *fuqahāʾ* in general."

٨٤٠ أخبرنا مالك، أخبرنا يحيى بن سعيد قال: تُوفِّي عبد الرحمن بن أبي بكر في نومٍ نامَه، فأعتقت عائشة رقاباً كثيرة.

840. Mālik informed us: "Yaḥyā ibn Saᶜīd informed us, 'ᶜAbd ar-Raḥmān ibn Abī Bakr died in his sleep, and ᶜĀʾishah set many slaves free.'"

قال محمد: وبهذا نأخذ. لا بأس أن يُعْتَق عن الميت، فإنْ كان أوصى بذلك كان الولاء له، وإن كان لم يُوصِ كان الولاء لمن أعتق، ويلحقه الأجر إن شاء الله تعالى.

Muḥammad said: "We adhere to this. There is no harm in setting slaves free on behalf of the dead. If he [the deceased] had stipulated that in his will, then the *walāʾ* is his. If he had not stipulated that in his will, then the *walāʾ* belongs to the person who sets free, and the reward is for him [the deceased], *inshāʾAllāh*, exalted is He."

٩ باب بيع المدبَّر

9. Selling a Slave who is to be Set Free on the Death of his Master [*Mudabbar*]

٨٤١ أخبرنا مالك، أخبرنا أبو الرِّجال، محمد بن عبد الرحمن، عن أمِّه عَمْرَة بنت عبد الرحمن: أن عائشة زوج النبي صلى الله عليه وسلم كانت أعتقت جارية لها عن دُبُرٍ منها، ثم إن عائشة رضي الله عنها بعد ذلك اشتكت ما شاء الله أن تشتكي، ثم إنه دخل عليها رجلٌ سِنْدي، فقال لها: أنت مَطبُوبَةٌ، فقالت له عائشة: ويلَك، من طَبَّني؟ قال: امرأة منْ نَعْتها كذا وكَذا، فوَصَفها، وقال: إنَّ في حَجْرها الآن صبيّاً قد بال، فقالت عائشة: ادعوا لي فلَانةَ جَاريةً كانت تخدُمها، فوجدوها في بيت جيران لهم في حَجْرها صبيٌّ، قالت: الآن حتى أغسل بول هذا الصبيّ، فغسلته ثم جاءت، فقالت لها عائشة: أسحرتني؟ قالت: نعم، قالت: لِمَ؟ قالت: أحببت العتقَ، قالت: فوالله لا تَعْتَقِيْنَ أبداً. ثم أمرت عائشة ابن أختها أن يبيعَها منَ الأعراب ممن يسيء ملَكَتها، قالت: ثم ابتَعْ

لي بثمنها رَقَبَةً ثم أعتقها، فقالت عمرة: فلبثَتْ عائشة رضي الله عنها ما شاء الله من الزمان، ثم إنها رَأَتْ في المنام أن اغتسلي من آبار ثلاثة يَمُدُّ بعضُها بعضاً فإنك تُشْفَيْنَ .
فدخل على عائشة إسماعيلُ بنُ أبي بكر وعبد الرحمن بن سعد بن زُرَارة، فذكرت أُمُّ عائشة الذي رأت ، فانطلقا إلى قَنَاة ، فوجدا آباراً ثلاثة يَمدُّ بعضُها بعضاً، فاستَقَوْا من كل بئر منها ثلاث شُجُبٍ حتى مَلؤوا الشُّجُب من جميعها، ثم أتَوْا بذلك الماء إلى عائشة، فاغتسلت فيه فشُفِيَتْ.

841. Mālik informed us: "Abu'r-Rijāl Muḥammad ibn ᶜAbd ar-Raḥmān informed us from his mother ᶜAmrah bint ᶜAbd ar-Raḥmān that ᶜĀʾishah the wife of the Prophet ﷺ had arranged to set a female slave of hers free after her death. Then later ᶜĀʾishah ؓ after that, complained of that which Allah willed that she suffer. Then a man from Sind came to her and said, 'You have had a spell put on you.' ᶜĀʾishah said to him, 'Woe to you! Who has put a spell on me?' He said, 'A woman whose description is such-and-such,' and he described her, and he said, 'In her lap right now there is an infant who has urinated.' ᶜĀʾishah said, 'Call so-and-so to me,' who was a slave woman who used to serve her. They found her in one of their neighbours' houses with an infant in her lap. She said, 'Right away, when I have washed off this infant's urine,' and she washed it and then came. ᶜĀʾishah asked her, 'Did you place a spell on me?' She answered, 'Yes.' She asked, 'Why?' She answered, 'I wanted to be set free.' She said, 'Then by Allah! You will never be set free!' ᶜĀʾishah told her sister's son to sell her to someone among the desert Arabs who treated his slaves badly. She said, 'Then with her price buy me a female slave and set her free.' ᶜAmrah said, 'Then ᶜĀʾishah ؓ remained [ill] as long as Allah willed, and then she saw in a dream, "Wash yourself from three wells which replenish each other, for then you will be healed." Ismāᶜīl ibn Abī Bakr and ᶜAbd ar-Raḥmān ibn Saᶜd ibn Zurārah visited ᶜĀʾishah and ᶜĀ'ishah's mother mentioned what she had seen. They went off to a channel and found three wells which replenished each other, and drew out of each well three water skins until they had filled the water-skins from all of them. Then they brought that water to ᶜĀʾishah and she washed herself and was healed.'"

قال محمد: أما نحن فلا نرى أن يُبَاع المدبَّر، وهو قول زيد بن ثابت، وعبد الله بن عُمَر، وبه نأخذ. وهو قول أبي حنيفة والعامّة من فقهائنا.

Muḥammad said: "As for us, we do not think that the slave who is to be set free on the death of his master [*mudabbar*] may be sold, and that is the verdict of Zayd ibn Thābit and ᶜAbdullāh ibn ᶜUmar, and we adhere to it. That is the verdict of Abū Ḥanīfah and of our *fuqahāʾ* in general."

٨٤٢ أخبرنا مالك، أخبرنا يحيى بن سعيد، أنه سمع سعيد بن المسيّب يقول: من أعتق وليدةً عن دُبُرٍ منه، فإنَّ له أنْ يطأها وان يزوِّجها، وليس له أن يبيعها ولا أن يهبها، وولدها بمنزلتها.

842. Mālik informed us: "Yaḥyā ibn Saᶜīd informed us that he heard Saᶜīd

ibn al-Musayyab saying, 'Whoever arranges for a female slave to be set free after his death [as a *mudabbarah*], may have sexual intercourse with her and may marry her, but he may not sell or give her away. Her child is in the same situation as her.'"

قال محمد : وبه نأخذ . وهو قول أبي حنيفة والعامة من فقهائنا .

Muḥammad said: "We adhere to this, and that is the verdict of Abū Ḥanīfah and of our *fuqahā᾽* in general."

١٠ باب الدعوى والشهادات وادّعاء النَّسَب

10. Claims and Testimonies, and Claiming Kinship [and Paternity]

٨٤٣ أخبرنا مالك، أخبرنا الزهري، عن عروة بن الزبير، عن عائشة رضي الله عنها قالت: كان عُتْبَة بن أبي وقّاص عَهِدَ إلى أخيه سعد بن أبي وقاص أنّ ابن وَليدة زَمْعَةَ منِّي فاقْبِضْه إليك، قالت: فلما كان عام الفتح أخَذه سعدٌ، وقال: ابن أخي قد كان عهد إليّ أخي فيه، فقام إِيه عبدُ بن زَمعة، فقال: أخي وابن وليدة أبي وُلد على فراشه، فتساوقا إلى رسول الله صلى الله عليه وسلم، فقال سعد: يا رسول الله، ابن أخي قد كان عَهِدَ إليّ فيه أخي عُتْبَة، وقال عبد بن زَمْعة: أخي ابنُ وليدة أبي، وُلدَ على فراشه، فقال رسول الله صلى الله عليه وسلم: هو لك يا عبد بن زَمْعة، ثم قال: الولد للفراش والعاهر الحَجَر، ثم قال لسودة بنت زَمْعة: احتجبي منه لما رأى من شَبَهِه بعُتْبة، فما رآها حتى لقي الله عزّ وجلّ .

843. Mālik informed us: "Az-Zuhrī informed us from ᶜUrwah ibn az-Zubayr that ᶜĀ᾽ishah ﵂ said, ''Utbah ibn Abī Waqqāṣ [on his deathbed] had charged his brother Saᶜd ibn Abī Waqqāṣ that, "The son of Zamᶜah's slave woman is mine, so take him to you."' She said, 'Then in the year of the Opening [of Makkah to Islam] Saᶜd took him, and he said, "My brother's son with whom he charged me." ᶜAbd ibn Zamᶜah stood up to him and said, "He is my brother, and the son of my father's slave woman and he was born on his [my father's] bed." They dragged each other to the Messenger of Allah ﷺ. Saᶜd said, "Messenger of Allah, he is my brother's son with whom my brother ᶜUtbah charged me." ᶜAbd ibn Zamᶜah said, "He is my brother, and the son of my father's slave woman, and he was born on his bed." So the Messenger of Allah ﷺ said, "He is yours, ᶜAbd ibn Zamᶜah." Then he said, "The child belongs to the bed [on which he was born], and for the adulterer there is stoning." Then he said to Sawdah bint Zamᶜah, "Veil yourself from him," because of the resemblance he saw in him to ᶜUtbah. He never saw her again until he met Allah ﷻ.'"

قال محمد : وبهذا نأخذ . الولد للفراش وللعاهر الحجر. وهو قول أبي حنيفة والعامة من فقهائنا .

Muḥammad said: "We adhere to this. The child belongs to the bed [on which he is born], and for the adulterer there is stoning, and that is the verdict of Abū Ḥanīfah and of our *fuqahā᾽* in general."

١١ باب اليمين مع الشاهد

11. An Oath along with a Witness

٨٤٤ أخبرنا مالك، أخبرنا جعفر بن محمد، عن أبيه: أن النبي صلى الله عليه وسلم قضى باليمين مع الشاهد.

844. Mālik informed us: "Ja^cfar ibn Muḥammad informed us from his father that the Prophet ﷺ gave judgement on the basis of an oath accompanied by a witness."

قال محمد: وبلغنا عن النبي صلى الله عليه وسلم خلافُ ذلك، وقال: ذكر ذلك ابن أبي ذئب عن ابن شهاب الزهري، قال: سَأَلْتُه عن اليمين مع الشاهد فقال: بدعة، وأول من قضي بها معاوية، وكان ابن شهاب أعلم عند أهل الحديث بالمدينة من غيره، وكذلك ابن جريج أيضاً، عن عطاء بن أبي رَبَاح قال: إنه قال: كان القضاء الأول لا يُقبل إلا شاهدان، فأول من قضى باليمين مع الشاهد عبدُ الملك بن مروان.

Muḥammad said: "Something different from that has reached us from the Prophet ﷺ." He said, "Ibn Abī Dhi'b mentioned that from Ibn Shihāb az-Zuhrī saying, 'I asked him about an oath along with a witness and he said, "An innovation [*bid^cah*], and the first to pass judgement on that basis was Mu^cāwiyah."' Ibn Shihāb was more knowledgeable than others according to the people of *ḥadīth* in Madīnah. Similarly, there was also Ibn Jurayj from ^cAṭā' ibn Abī Rabāḥ. He [Ibn Jurayj] said, 'He [^cAṭā' ibn Abī Rabāḥ] said, "At first judgement was only acceptable with two witnesses, and the first to pass judgement on the basis of an oath with a witness was ^cAbd al-Mālik ibn Marwān.'"

١٢ باب استحلاف الخصوم

12. Demanding Oaths from Disputants

٨٤٥ أخبرنا مالك، أخبرنا داود بن الحُصَين، أنه سمع أبا غَطَفان بن طَرِيْف المُرّي يقول: اختصم زيد بن ثابت وابنُ مُطيع في دار إلى مروانَ بن الحكم، فقضى على زيد بن ثابت باليمين على المنبر، فقال له زيد: أحْلفُ له مكاني، فقال له مروان: لا والله إلا عند مقاطع الحقوق، قال: فجعل زيد يحلف أن حقَّه لحقٌّ، وأبى أن يحلف عند المنبر، فجعل مروان يعجب من ذلك.

845. Mālik informed us: "Dāwūd ibn al-Ḥuṣayn informed us that he heard Abū Ghaṭafān ibn Ṭarīf al-Murrī saying, 'Zayd ibn Thābit and Ibn Muṭī^c took a dispute to Marwān ibn al-Ḥakam, and he gave judgement against Zayd ibn Thābit that he must swear an oath on the *minbar* [of the Prophet, ﷺ]. Zayd said to him, "I will swear an oath to it right here in my place." Marwān said to him, "No, by Allah! only at the place of deciding rights."' He said, 'Zayd began to assert that his claim was true and he refused to take an oath upon the *minbar*. Marwān became amazed at that.'"

قال محمد: وبقول زيد بن ثابت نأخذ وحيثما حلف الرجل فهو جائز، ولو رأى زيد بن ثابت أن ذلك يلزمه ما أبى أن يعطي الحق الذي عليه، ولكنه كره أن يُعْطي ما ليس عليه، فهو أحقُّ أن يُؤْخَذُ بقوله وفعله ممن استحلفه.

Muḥammad said: "We adhere to the verdict of Zayd ibn Thābit. Wherever the man takes an oath it is acceptable. If Zayd ibn Thābit thought that that was necessary for him he would not have refused to concede to the claim against him. However, he disliked to give what was not due from him. He has the stronger claim that his verdict and action be adhered to than does the one who required him to swear the oath."

١٣ باب الرَّهْن

13. The Pledge of a Pawn as Security

٨٤٦ أخبرنا مالك، أخبرنا ابن شهاب، عن سعيد بن المسيّب أنّ رسول الله صلى الله عليه وسلم قال: لا يُغْلَقُ الرَّهْن.

846. Mālik informed us: "Ibn Shihāb informed us from Saᶜīd ibn al-Musayyab that the Messenger of Allah ﷺ said, 'The pledge given as security is not forfeited.'"

قال محمد: وبهذا نأخذ. وتفسير قوله: "لا يُغلق الرهن"، أن الرجل كان يرهن الرهن عند الرجل، فيقول له: إن جئتُك بمالك إلى كذا وكذا، وإلا فالرهن لك بمالك، قال رسولُ الله صلى الله عليه وسلم: لا يُغْلَقُ الرهن، ولا يكون للمرتهن بماله. وكذلك نقول. وهو قول أبي حنيفة. وكذلك فسّره مالك بن أنس.

Muḥammad said: "We adhere to this. The explanation of his saying, 'The pledge given as security is not forfeited,' is that a man pledged an item with a man and said to him, 'If I bring you your money at such and such a time [then well and good], but if not then the pledge is yours for your money.' The Messenger of Allah ﷺ said, 'The pledge given as security is not forfeited,' and it does not belong to the one who advanced the money against the pledge in exchange for his money, and that is our verdict, and the verdict of Abū Ḥanīfah. Mālik ibn Anas explained it similarly."

١٤ باب الرجل يكون عنده الشهادة

14. A Man who Has some Testimony to Offer

٨٤٧ أخبرنا مالك، أخبرنا عبد الله بن أبي بكر، أن أباه أخبره عن عبد الله بن عمرو بن عثمان، أنّ عبد الرحمن بن أبي عمرة الأنصاري أخبره، أن زيد بن خالد الجُهَيني أخبره أن رسول الله ﷺ قال: ألا أخبركم بخير الشهداء؟ الذي يأتي بالشهادة، أو يُخْبِرُ بالشهادة قبل أن يُسألَها.

848. Mālik informed us: "ᶜAbdullāh ibn Abī Bakr informed us that his father informed him from ᶜAbdullāh ibn ᶜAmr ibn ᶜUthmān that ᶜAbd ar-Raḥmān

ibn Abī ᶜAmrah al-Anṣārī informed him that Zayd ibn Khālid al-Juhanī informed him that the Messenger of Allah ﷺ said, 'Shall I not tell you who is the best witness? The one who brings his testimony or tells of his testimony before he is asked for it.'"

قال محمد: وبهذا نأخذ. من كانت عنده شهادة لإنسان لا يعلم ذلك الإنسان بها، فليُخْبِرْه بشهادته، وإنْ لم يَسأَلْها إياه.

Muḥammad said: "We adhere to this. Whoever has some testimony in favour of a person about which that person does not know, then let him tell him his testimony, even if he does not ask him about it."

كتاب اللُّقَطة

16. LOST PROPERTY

٨٤٨ أخبرنا مالك، أخبرنا ابن شهاب الزهري : أنّ ضَوَالَّ الإبل كانت في زمن عمر رضي الله عنه إبلاً مرسلة تَنَاتَجُ لا يَمَسّها أحد، حتى إذا كان من زمن عثمان بن عفان أمر بمعرفتها وتعريفها، ثم تُباع فإذا جاء صاحبُها أُعطي ثمنَها .

848. Mālik informed us: "Ibn Shihāb az-Zuhrī informed us that the stray camels at the time of ʿUmar ibn al-Khaṭṭāb ﷺ used to be let free to roam, giving birth without anyone touching them. Then when it was the time of ʿUthmān ibn ʿAffān, he ordered that they should be identified and announced publicly, and later they were sold. Then if their owner came he was given their price."

قال محمد : كلا الوجهين حسنٌ. إن شاء الإمام تركها حتى يجيء أهلها، فإن خاف عليها الضَّيْعة أو لم يجد من يرعا ها فباعها، ووقَّف ثمنها حتى يأتي أربابها فلا بأس بذلك .

Muḥammad said: "Both methods are good. If the *imām* wants he may leave them until their people come. If he is afraid that they will be lost or perish, or he cannot find someone to pasture them and so sells them and keeps back the price until their owners come, then there is no harm in that."

٨٤٩ أخبرنا مالك، أخبرنا نافع: أن رجلاً وجد لُقَطة ، فجاء إلى ابن عمر، فقال : إنّي وجدت لُقَطَةً، فما تأمرني فيها؟ قال ابن عمر: عرّفها ، قال : قد فعلتُ، قال : زد، قال: قد فعلتُ، قال: لا آمرك أنْ تأكُلَها، لو شئتَ لم تأخُذْها .

849. Mālik informed us: "Nāfiʿ informed us that a man found some lost property, and came to Ibn ʿUmar saying, 'I have found some lost property. What do you advise me to do about it?' Ibn ʿUmar said, 'Make it known.' He said, 'I have done that.' He said, 'More.' He said, 'I have done that.' He said, 'I do not advise you to consume it. If you had wished, you would not have taken it [but left it where it was].'"

٨٥٠ أخبرنا مالك، أخبرنا يحيى بن سعيد، أنه قال : سمعت سليمان بن يسار يحدّث أن ثابت بن ضحَّاك الأنصاري حَدَّثَه : أنه وجد بعيراً بالحَرّة فعَرَّفه، ثم ذكر ذلك لعمر بن الخطاب رضي الله عنه، فأمره أنْ يُعرِّفَه، قال ثابت لعمر: قد شَغَلَني عنه ضَيْعَتي ، فقال له عمر: أرْسِلْه حيث وَجَدْتَه .

850. Mālik informed us: "Yaḥyā ibn Saʿīd informed us, 'I heard Sulaymān ibn Yasār narrating that Thābit ibn Ḍaḥḥāk al-Anṣārī narrated to him that he had found a camel at al-Ḥarrah and had made it known. Then he mentioned that to ʿUmar ibn al-Khaṭṭāb ﷺ and he told him to make it publicly known.

Thābit said to ʿUmar, "My property occupies me from doing that." ʿUmar said, "Let it go where you found it."'"

قال محمد: وبه نَأخُذُ. من التقط لُقطة تساوي عشرة دراهم فصاعداً عرّفها حولاً، فإن عُرفت وإلا تصدّق بها، فإن كان محتاجاً أكَلَها، فإن جاء صاحبها خَيّره بين الأجر وبين أن يَغْرمها له، وإن كان قيمتها أقلّ من عشرة دراهم عرّفها على قدر ما يرى أياماً، ثم صنع بها كما صنع بالأولى، وكان الحكم فيها إذا جاء صاحبها كالحكم في الأولى، وإن ردّها في الموضع الذي وجدها فيه برئ منها، ولم يكن عليه في ذلك ضمان.

Muḥammad said: "We adhere to this. Someone who finds lost property equal in value to ten dirhams or more must make it known for a year. Then if it is recognised [he must give it to the person], and if not he should give it away as ṣadaqah, but if he is in need he may consume it. Then if its owner comes he may give him the choice between recompense or being liable to him for it. If its value is less than ten dirhams, then he makes it known as he thinks fit for some days, and then he may do with it as he would do with the former. The judgement concerning it if its owner comes is the same as the judgement on the former. If he returns it to the place in which he found it, then he is free of responsibility for it and he is not liable for it."

٨٥١ أخبرنا مالك حدّثنا يحيى بن سعيد، عن سعيد بن المسيّب قال: قال عمر بن الخطاب رضي الله عنه وهو مسند ظهره إلى الكعبة: من أخذ ضَالّة فهو ضالّ.

851. Mālik informed us: "Yaḥyā ibn Saʿīd narrated to us that Saʿīd ibn al-Musayyab said, 'ʿUmar ibn al-Khaṭṭāb ؈ said while supporting his back against the Kaʿbah, "Whoever takes a stray is astray."'"

قال محمد. وبهذا نَأخُذ. وإنما يعني بذلك من أخذها ليَذهب بها، فأما من اخذها ليردّها أو ليعرّفها فلا بأس به.

Muḥammad said: "We adhere to this. He only meant by that someone who takes it in order to go off with it. As for someone who takes it in order to return it or to make it known, then there is no harm in that."

ا باب الشفعة

1. Pre-emption

٨٥٢ أخبرنا مالك، أخبرنا محمد بن عُمارة، أخبرني أبو بكر بن محمد بن عمرو بن حَزْم أن عثمان بن عفان رضي الله تعالى عنه قال: إذا وقعت الحدود في أرض فلا شُفعة فيها، ولا شفعة في بئر ولا في فحل نخل.

852. Mālik informed us: "Muḥammad ibn ʿUmārah informed us, 'Abū Bakr ibn Muḥammad ibn ʿAmr ibn Ḥazm informed me that ʿUthmān ibn ʿAffān ؈ said, "When the boundaries have been set up in land, then there is no pre-emption in it, nor is there pre-emption in a well or in male date-palms."'"

٨٥٣ أخبرنا مالك، أخبرنا ابن شهاب، عن أبي سلمة بن عبد الرحمن : أن رسول الله صلى الله عليه وسلم قضى بالشفعة فيما لم يُقسم، فإذا وقعت الحدود فلا شفعة فيه.

853. Mālik informed us: "Ibn Shihāb informed us from Abū Salamah ibn ᶜAbd ar-Raḥmān that the Messenger of Allah ﷺ passed judgement in favour of pre-emption in that [land and property] which had not been divided, and that when the boundaries have been set then there is no pre-emption."

قال محمد : قد جاءت في هذا أحاديث مختلفة، فالشريك أحقُّ بالشفعة من الجار، والجار أحقُّ من غيره، بلغنا ذلك عن النبي صلى الله عليه وسلم.

Muḥammad said: "Concerning this there have come contradictory *ḥadīth*. The partner has more right to pre-emption than does the neighbour, and the neighbour has more right than anyone else. That has reached us from the Prophet ﷺ."

٨٥٤ أخبرنا عبد الله بن عبد الرحمن بن يَعْلى الثقفي، أخبرني عَمْرو بن الشّريد، عن أبيه الشّريد بن سُوَيد قال: قال رسول الله صلى الله عليه وسلم: الجار أحقُّ بصَقَبه.

854. ᶜAbdullāh ibn ᶜAbd ar-Raḥmān ibn Yaᶜlā ath-Thaqafī informed us, "ᶜAmr ibn ash-Sharīd informed me that his father ash-Sharīd ibn Suwayd said, 'The Messenger of Allah ﷺ said, "The neighbour has more right to pre-emption."'"

وبهذا نأخذ. وهو قول أبي حنيفة والعامّة من فقهائنا.

"We adhere to this, and that is the verdict of Abū Ḥanīfah and of our *fuqahāʾ* in general."

٢ باب المكاتَب

2. The Slave who Writes a Contract to Buy his Freedom [*Mukātab*]

٨٥٥ أخبرنا مالك، أخبرنا نافع، عن ابن عمر أنّه كان يقول : المكاتب عبد ما بقي عليه من مكاتبته شيء.

855. Mālik informed us: "Nāfiᶜ informed us that Ibn ᶜUmar used to say, 'The slave who writes a contract to buy his freedom [*mukātab*] is a slave as long as there remains anything of his contract [still to pay].'"

قال محمد : وبهذا نأخذ. وهو قول أبي حنيفة، وهو بمنزلة العَبْد في شهادته وحدوده وجميع أمره، إلا أنه لا سبيل لمولاه على ماله ما دام مكاتباً.

Muḥammad said: "We adhere to this. That is the verdict of Abū Ḥanīfah. He is in the position of a slave with respect to his testimony, the punishments for contravention of the limits [*ḥudūd*] and all of his affair, except that there is no way for his owner to have access to his wealth as long as he is a *mukātab*."

٨٥٦ أخبرنا مالك، أخبرنا حميد بن قيس المكي : أن مكاتباً لابن المتوكل هلك بمكة وترك عليه بقية من مكاتبته، وديون الناس، وترك ابنة ، فأشكل على عامل مكة القضاء في ذلك، فكتب إلى

عبد الملك بن مروان يسأله عن ذلك، فكتب إليه عبد الملك أن أبدأ بديون الناس فاقْضِها، ثم اقض ما بقي عليه مكاتبته، ثم اقسم ما بقي من ماله بين ابنته ومواليه.

856. Mālik informed us: "Ḥumayd ibn Qays al-Makkī informed us that a slave who wrote a contract to buy his freedom [*mukātab*] from Ibn al-Mutawakkil died in Makkah leaving the remains of his contract for purchasing his freedom unpaid, [and leaving] debts to people, and he left a daughter. Passing judgement on that was difficult for the governor of Makkah and so he wrote to ᶜAbd al-Mālik ibn Marwān asking him about it. ᶜAbd al-Mālik ibn Marwān wrote to him, 'Begin with people's debts and pay them. Then pay what remains of his contract for purchasing his freedom. Then divide what remains of his property between his daughter and his previous owners.'"

قال محمد: وبهذا نأخذ وهو قول أبي حنيفة والعامة من فقهائنا إنه إذا مات بُدِئ بدُيُونِ النّاس ثم بمكاتبته، ثم ما بقي كان ميراثاً لورثته الأحرار مَن كانوا.

Muḥammad said: "We adhere to this. It is the verdict of Abū Ḥanīfah and of our *fuqahā*ᵓ in general that when he dies, one must begin with people's debts, then the contract for purchasing his freedom [must be paid], and then whatever remains of his property is inheritance for his free heirs whoever they are."

٨٥٧ أخبرنا مالك، أخبرنا الثقة عندي: أن عروة بن الزبير وسليمان بن يسار سئلا عن رجل كاتبَ على نفسه وعلى وَلَده ثم هلك المكاتب وترك بنين، أيسعَوْن في مكاتبة أبيهم أم هم عبيد؟ فقال: بل يَسْعَون في كتابة أبيهم، ولا يوضع عنهم لموت أبيهم شيء.

857. Mālik informed us: "Someone who is trustworthy in my view informed me that ᶜUrwah ibn az-Zubayr and Sulaymān ibn Yasār were asked about a man who wrote a contract to free himself and his child and then died leaving children, 'Should they work to fulfil the contract their father made or are they slaves?' He answered, 'On the contrary, they must work to fulfil the contract to purchase their freedom which their father made, and nothing of that is reduced for them because of the death of their father.'"

قال محمد: وبهذا نأخذ. وهو قول أبي حنيفة فإذا أدَّوْا عَتقوا جميعاً.

Muḥammad said: "We adhere to this and it is the verdict of Abū Ḥanīfah that if they fulfil it, they are all free."

٨٥٨ أخبرنامالك أخبرنا مخبرٌ أن أمَّ سلمة زوج النبي ﷺ كانت تقاطع مُكَاتَبِيْها بالذهب والوَرِق. والله تعالى أعلم.

858. Mālik informed us: "An informant informed me that Umm Salamah the wife of the Prophet ﷺ used to make a settlement with her slaves who wrote contracts to buy their freedom for gold and silver." And Allah, exalted is He, knows best.

٣ باب السَّبَق في الخيل

3. Racing Horses

٨٥٩ أخبرنا مالك، أخبرنا يحيى بن سعيد قال : سمعت سعيد بن المسيّب يقول : ليس برهانِ الخيل بأس، إذا أدخلوا فيها محلّلاً إن سَبَق أخَذَ السَّبَقَ ، وإن سُبق لم يكن عليه شيء .

859. Mālik informed us: "Yaḥyā ibn Saʿīd informed us, 'I heard Saʿīd ibn al-Musayyab saying, "In placing stakes on horses there is no harm if a third party [who places no stake] enters who renders the contract *ḥalāl* [*muḥallil*], and who if he wins takes the prize, but if beaten owes nothing."'"

قال محمد : وبهذا نأخذ . إنما يكره من هذا أن يضيع كل واحد منهما سَبَقاً ، فإن سبق أحدُهما أخذ السَّبَقَيْنِ جميعاً، فيكون هذا كالمبايعة ، فأما إذا كان السَّبق من أحدهما أو كانوا ثلاثة والسَّبق من اثنين منهم، والثالث ليس منه سبق، إن سَبَق أخَذَ وإن لم يسبقْ لم يَغْرَمْه ، فهذا لا بأس به أيضاً . وهو المحلِّل . الذي قال سعيد بن المسيّب .

Muḥammad said: "We adhere to this. All that is disapproved of is that both of them place a stake, and then if one of the two wins he takes both the stakes, because this would be like gambling. As for the case where one of them places the stake, or where they are three and the stake is placed by two of them, but the third has no stake and if he [the third person] wins, then he takes [the stake], but if he does not win he does not owe it, then there is no harm in this. That is the third person who renders the affair *ḥalāl* [*muḥallil*] about whom Saʿīd ibn al-Musayyab spoke."

٨٦٠ أخبرنا مالك، أخبرنا ابن شهاب، أنه سمع سعيد بن المسيّب يقول : إنّ القَصْواءَ ناقة النبي صلى الله عليه وسلم كانت تَسْبق كلما وقعت في سَبَاق ، فوقعت يوماً في إبل، فسُبقت ، فكانت على المسلمين كآبة أن سُبِقَتْ، فقال رسول الله صلى الله عليه وسلم : إنّ الناس إذا رفعوا شيئاً، أو أرادوا رَفْعَ شيء وَضَعَه اللّهُ .

860. Mālik informed us: "Ibn Shihāb informed us that he heard Saʿīd ibn al-Musayyab saying, 'Whenever Qaṣwā᾿, the she-camel of the Prophet ﷺ, entered a race she used to win. Then one day she entered a race with camels and was beaten, and it was distressing for the Muslims that she should have been beaten. The Messenger of Allah ﷺ said, "Whenever people raise something up or wish to raise something up, Allah lowers it."'"

قال محمد : وبهذا نأخُذُ . لا بأس بالسَّبْقِ في النَصْلِ والحافر والخُفِّ .

Muḥammad said: "We adhere to this. There is no harm in competing in archery and spear throwing, racing horses, mules and donkeys, and camels."

أبواب السِّيَر

17. MODES OF CONDUCT

٨٦١ أخبرنا مالك، أخبرنا يحيى بن سعيد، أنه بلغه، عن ابن عباس رضي الله عنه أنه قال: ما ظهر الغُلول في قوم قطّ إلاَّ ألقي في قلوبهم الرعْب، ولا فشا الزنى في قوم قطّ إلاَّ كَثُر فيهم الموت، ولا نَقَصَ قومٌ المكيال والميزان إلاَّ قُطِع عليهم الرزقُ، ولا حَكَم قومٌ بغير الحقِّ إلاَّ فشا فيهم الدمُ، ولا خَتَرَ قوم بالعهد إلاَّ سُلِّط عليهم العدوّ.

861. Mālik informed us: "Yaḥyā ibn Saᶜīd informed us that it reached him that Ibn ᶜAbbās ﷺ said, 'If taking something without right from the spoils ever becomes widespread among a people then terror [of the enemy] is cast into their hearts. If fornication ever becomes widespread among a people, then there is a great deal of death among them. If a people ever give short measure and light weight then provision is cut off from them. If a people ever rule by anything other than the truth, then [the spilling of] blood becomes widespread among them. If a people are ever unfaithful to their contracts, then the enemy is given power over them.'"

٨٦٢ أخبرنا مالك، أخبرنا نافع، عن ابن عمر: أن رسول الله صلى الله عليه وسلم بعث سريَّةً قِبَلَ نجد، فغنموا إبلاً كثيرة، فكان سُهمانُهم اثنَيْ عَشَر بعيراً، ونُفِّلوا بعيراً بعيراً.

862. Mālik informed us: "Nāfiᶜ informed us from Ibn ᶜUmar that the Messenger of Allah ﷺ sent a raiding party towards Najd and they gained many camels as spoils, so that the portion of each of them was twelve camels, and they were given camel after camel as extras."

قال محمد: كان النَّفل لرسول الله صلى الله عليه وسلم يُنَفِّل من الخُمُس أهلَ الحاجة، وقد قال الله تعالى: (قُل الأنفالُ للّه والرسول)، فأما اليوم فلا نَفَلَ بعد إحراز الغنيمة إلاَّ من الخُمُس لمحتاج.

Muḥammad said: "The extra ones belonged to the Messenger of Allah ﷺ and he gave extras from the fifth to those who were needy. Allah, exalted is He, said, 'Say: 'Booty [*al-anfāl*] belongs to Allah and the Messenger.' As for today, there are to be no extras after receiving the spoils except from the fifth for a needy one."

١ باب الرجل يعطي الشيء في سبيل الله

1. A Man Giving Something [to a warrior] in the Way of Allah

٨٦٣ أخبرنا مالك، أخبرنا يحيى بن سعيد عن سعيد بن المسيّب: أنه سُئِل عن رجل يُعطي الشيء في سبيل الله، قال: فإذا بلغ رأسَ مَغزاته فَهو له.

863. Mālik informed us: "Yaḥyā ibn Sa'īd informed us that Sa'īd ibn al-Musayyab was asked about a man who is given something in the Way of Allah. He answered, 'Then when he reaches the place intended by his expedition, it is his.'"

قال محمد: هذا قول سعيد بن المسيّب، وقال ابن عمر: إذا بلغ وادي القُرى فَهو له، وقال أبو حنيفة وغيره من فقهائنا: إذا دفعه إليه صاحبه فهو له.

Muḥammad said: "This was the verdict of Sa'īd ibn al-Musayyab. Ibn 'Umar said, 'When he reaches Wādī al-Qurā it is his.' Abū Ḥanīfah and others of our *fuqahā'* said, 'When the owner of it pays it to him, it is his.'"

٢ باب إثم الخوارج وما في لزوم الجماعة من الفضل

2. The Wrongdoing of the Khawārij, and what there is Concerning the Merit of Clinging to the United Body of Muslims [*Jamā'ah*]

٨٦٤ أخبرنا مالك، أخبرنا يحيى بن سعيد، عن محمد بن إبراهيم، عن أبي سَلَمة بن عبد الرحمن: أنه سَمِعَ أبا سعيد الخُدْري يقول: سمعت رسول الله صلى الله عليه وسلم يقول: يخرج فيكم قوم تُحقِّرُون صلاتَكم مع صلاتهم، وأعمالَكم مع أعمالهم، يقرؤون القرآنَ لا يجاوزُ حَنَاجرَهم، يمرُقون من الدِّين مروقَ السَّهمِ من الرمِّية، تنظر في النصل فلا ترى شيئاً، تنظر في القِدْح فلا ترى شيئاً، تنظر في الرِّيش فلا ترى شيئاً، وتَتَمارى في الفُوق.

864. Mālik informed us: "Yaḥyā ibn Sa'īd informed us from Muḥammad ibn Ibrāhīm from Abū Salamah ibn 'Abd ar-Raḥmān that he heard Abū Sa'īd al-Khudrī saying, 'I heard the Messenger of Allah ﷺ saying, "A people will emerge among you, in contrast to whose prayer you will despise your prayer, in contrast to whose actions [you will despise] your actions, and they will recite the Qur'ān but it will not pass their throats. They will go out of the *dīn* just like the passage of an arrow through the game; you look at the arrow head and you see nothing, you look at the shaft and you see nothing, you look at the feathers and you see nothing, and you have doubts about the notch."'"

قال محمد: وبهذا نأخذُ. لا خَيْرَ في الخروج، ولا ينبغي إلاّ لزوم الجماعة.

Muḥammad said: "We adhere to this. There is no good in departing [from obedience to the Amīr and from the united body of the Muslims], and one must simply hold firm to the united body of the Muslims [*jamā'ah*]."

٨٦٥ أخبرنا مالك، أخبرنا نافع، عن ابن عمر: أن رسول الله صلى الله عليه وسلم قال: من حمل علينا السلاح فليس منا.

865. Mālik informed us: "Nāfi' informed us from Ibn 'Umar that the Messenger of Allah ﷺ said, 'Whoever bears weapons against us is not one of us.'"

قال محمد: من حمل السلاح على المسلمين فاعترضهم به لقتلهم، فمن قتله فلا شيء عليه، لأنه أحلَّ دمَه باعتراض الناسِ بسيفه.

Muḥammad said: "If someone bears weapons against the Muslims and advances against them with them [the weapons] in order to kill them, and if someone else kills him there is nothing [of retaliation or compensatory payments] against him, because he made his own blood permissible by advancing against people with his sword."

٨٦٦ أخبرنا مالك، أخبرنا يحيى بن سعيد، أنه سمع سعيد بن المسيّب يقول: ألا أخبركم أو أُحَدِّثُكم أو أُحَدِّثُكم بخيرٍ من كثير من الصلاة والصدقة؟ قالوا: بلى، قال: إصلاحُ ذاتِ البين، وإياكم والبِغْضَةَ فإنما هي الحالقة.

866. Mālik informed us: "Yaḥyā ibn Saᶜīd informed us that he heard Saᶜīd ibn al-Musayyab saying, 'Shall I not inform you or narrate to you of that which is better than a great deal of prayer and *ṣadaqah*?' They answered, 'Yes, of course!' He said, 'Putting things right [between people]. Also, beware of hatred, because it is the razor [which shaves away the *dīn* and good actions]'"

٣ باب قتل النساء

3. Killing Women

٨٦٧ أخبرنا مالك، أخبرنا نافع، عن ابن عمر: أنَّ رسول الله صلى الله عليه وسلم رأى في بعض مغازيه امرأةً مقتولة، فأنكر ذلك، ونهى عن قتل النساء والصبيان.

867. Mālik informed us: "Nāfiᶜ informed us from Ibn ᶜUmar that during one of his expeditions the Messenger of Allah ﷺ saw a woman who had been killed, and he repudiated it and forbade the killing of women and children."

قال محمد: وبهذا نأخذ. لا ينبغي أن يُقتلَ في شيء من المغازي امرأةٌ ولا شيخٌ فانٍ، إلاّ أنْ تُقاتِلَ المرأة فتُقتل.

Muḥammad said: "We adhere to this. In none of the expeditions should a woman or a decrepit old man be killed unless the woman is fighting, in which case she may be killed."

٤ باب المرتد

4. Apostates

٨٦٨ أخبرنا مالك، أخبرنا عبد الرحمن بن محمد بن عبدٍ القاريٌّ، عن أبيه، قال: قدم رجل على عمر بن الخطّاب رضي الله عنه من قِبَل أبي موسى، فسأله عن الناس، فأخبره ثم قال: هل عندكم من مُغْرِبَة خبر؟ قال: نعم، رجل كفر بعد إسلامه، فقال: ماذا فعلتم به؟ قال: قرّبناه فضربنا عنقه، قال عمر رضي الله عنه: فهلاّ طبقتم عليه بيتاً ثلاثاً وأطعمتموه كلَّ يومٍ رغيفاً، فاستبتموه لعله يتوب ويرجع إلى أمر الله، اللّهم إني لم آمُر، ولم أحْضُر، ولم أرْضَ إذ بلغني.

868. Mālik informed us: "ᶜAbd ar-Raḥmān ibn Muḥammad ibn ᶜAbdin al-Qāriyy informed us that his father said, 'A man came to ᶜUmar ibn al-Khaṭṭāb

ﷺ from Abū Mūsā. He [ᶜUmar] asked him about people and he told him. Then he asked, "Have you any unusual news?" He answered, "Yes, a man became a *kāfir* after his Islam." He asked, "What did you do with him?" He said, "We drew him near and struck off his head." ᶜUmar ﷺ said, "Why did you not imprison him in a house for three [days] and feed him every day a loaf of bread, and encourage him to turn in *tawbah*, so that he might repent and return to the command of Allah? O Allah, I did not command it, I wasn't present, and I wasn't pleased with it when it reached me."'"

قال محمد: إن شاء الإمام أخر المرتدّ ثلاثاً إن طَمِعَ في توبته، أو سأله عن ذلك المرتدُّ، وإن لم يطمع في ذلك ولم يسأله المرتد فقتله فلا بأس بذلك.

Muḥammad said: "If the *imām* wishes he can give a respite of three days to the apostate if he hopes that he will turn in *tawbah* or if the apostate has asked him for that. If there is no hope and the apostate has not asked him for that and he kills him, then there is no harm in that."

٥ باب ما يُكره من لُبْس الحرير والدِّيباج

5. What is Disapproved of in Wearing Silk and Brocade

٨٦٩ أخبرنا مالك، أخبرنا نافع، عن ابن عمر، أن عمر بن الخطاب رضي الله عنه قال لرسول الله ﷺ ورأى حُلّةً سِيَراء تُباع عند باب المسجد، فقال: يارسول الله لو اشتريتَ هذه الحُلّةَ فلبستَها يوم الجمعة وللوفود إذا قدموا عليك؟ قال: إنما يَلْبَس هذه من لا خلاقَ له في الآخرة. ثم جاء رسول الله صلى الله عليه وسلم منها حُلَلٌ فأعطى عمر منها حُلّة، فقال: يا رسول الله، كَسوتَنيْها وقد قُلتَ في حُلّة عُطارِدٍ ما قلت؟ قال: إني لم أكْسُكَها لتَلْبَسها فكساها عمر أخاً له من أمِّه مشركاً بمكة.

869. Mālik informed us: "Nāfiᶜ informed us from Ibn ᶜUmar that ᶜUmar ibn al-Khaṭṭāb ﷺ said to the Messenger of Allah, ﷺ when he saw a set of garments of silk being sold at the door to the mosque, 'Messenger of Allah, if only you would buy this set of garments and wear it on the day of Jumuᶜah and for the delegations when they come to you.' He said, 'The only one who wears this is the one who has no portion in the next life [*ākhirah*].' Then some of the garments came to the Messenger of Allah ﷺ and he gave ᶜUmar one of them. He said, 'Messenger of Allah, you have given it to me to wear and yet you said about ᶜUṭayrid's robe that which you said!' He said, 'I did not give it to you for you to wear it.' So ᶜUmar gave it to a brother of his from his mother in Makkah who was one of those who associated partners with Allah."

قال محمد: لا ينبغي للرجل المسلم أن يلبس الحرير والديباج والذهب، كل ذلك مكروه للذكور من الصغار والكبار، و لا بأسَ به للإناثَ لو لا بأس به أيضاً بالهديّة إلى المشرك المحارب، ما لم يُهْدَ إليه سلاحٌ أو درع. هو قول أبي حنيفة والعامة من فقهائنا.

Muḥammad said: "A Muslim man ought not to wear silk, brocade and gold. All of that is disapproved for males whether young or adults, but there is no harm in it for women, and there is also no harm in it as a gift to one of those who associate partners with Allah with whom one is at war, as long as a weapon or a coat of mail is not given to him. That is the verdict of Abū Ḥanīfah and of our *fuqahā'* in general."

٦ باب ما يُكره من التختّم بالذهب

6. What is Disapproved of in Wearing a Gold Signet-ring[155]

٨٧٠ أخبرنا مالك، أخبرنا عبد الله بن دينار، عن ابن عمر قال: اتخذ رسول الله صلى الله عليه وسلم خاتَماً من ذهب، فقام رسول الله صلى الله عليه وسلم فقال: إني كنتُ أَلْبَس هذا الخاتم، فنبذه، وقال: والله لا أَلْبَسُه أبداً، قال: فنبذ الناس خواتيمهم.

870. Mālik informed us: "ᶜAbdullāh ibn Dīnār informed us that Ibn ᶜUmar said, 'The Messenger of Allah ﷺ took a signet-ring made of gold. Then the Messenger of Allah ﷺ stood and said, "I had worn this signet-ring," and he cast it away and said, "By Allah! I will never wear it [again]!"' He said, 'Then people cast away their signet-rings [of gold].'"

قال محمد: وبهذا نأخذ. لا ينبغي للرجل أن يتختَّم بذهب ولا حديد ولا صُفْر ولا يتختم إلاّ بالفضّة. فأما النساء فلا بأس بتختُّم الذهب لهُنَّ.

Muḥammad said: "We adhere to this. A man ought not to wear a signet-ring of gold, nor iron nor copper, and he should only take a signet-ring of silver. As for women there is no harm in them wearing signet-rings of gold."

٧ باب الرجل يُمرّ على ماشية الرجل فيحتلبُها بغير إذنه

7. A Man Coming Across the Livestock of a Man and Milking it without his Permission

٨٧١ أخبرنا مالك، أخبرنا نافع، عن ابن عمر أنَّ رسول الله صلى الله عليه وسلم قال: لا يحتلبَنَّ أحدُكم ماشية امرئ بغير إذنه، أيُحبّ أحدُكم أن تُؤتى مَشْرَبته فتُكسَر خزانتُه فينتقل طعامه؟ فإنما تَخْزُن لهم ضُروعُ مواشيهم أطعمتَهم، فلا يحلبَنَّ أحدٌ ماشية امرئ بغير إذنه.

871. Mālik informed us: "Nāfiᶜ informed us from Ibn ᶜUmar that the Messenger of Allah ﷺ said, 'Let none of you milk a man's livestock without his permission. Would any of you like someone to come into his upper chamber, break [into] his cupboard and remove his food? The udders of their livestock are the stores of their food, so let no one milk a man's livestock without his permission.'"

قال محمد: وبهذا نأخذُ. لا ينبغي لرجل مرَّ على ماشية رجل أن يحلب منها شيئاً بغير أمر أهلها، وكذلك إن مرَّ على حائط له فيه نخل أو شجر فيه ثمر فلا يأخُذَنَّ من ذلك شيئاً، ولا يأكلُه إلاّ بإذن أهله إلاّ أن يُضْطَرَّ إلى ذلك، فيأكل ويشرب ويغرم ذلك لأهله. وهو قول أبي حنيفة رحمه الله.

Muḥammad said: "We adhere to this. A man who passes another man's livestock ought not to milk anything from it without the express instruction of the owners. It is similar if he passes an orchard of his in which there are date palms or fruit-bearing trees; he must not take anything from it, nor should he eat any of it without the permission of its people unless he is forced by dire necessity to do so, then he should eat and drink and consider it a debt to be repaid to its people. That is the verdict of Abū Ḥanīfah, may Allah have mercy on him."

٨ باب نزول أهل الذمة مكة والمدينة وما يُكره من ذلك.
8. The Alighting of the People of the Dhimmah in Makkah and Madīnah, and what is Disapproved of in it

٨٧٢ أخبرنا مالك، أخبرنا نافع، عن ابن عمر: أن عمر رضي الله عنه ضَرَبَ للنصارى واليهود والمجوس بالمدينة إقامة ثلاث ليال يَتَسوَّقُون ويقضُون حوائجهم، ولم يكن أحدٌ منهم يقيم بعد ذلك.

872. Mālik informed us: "Nāfiʿ informed us from Ibn ʿUmar that ʿUmar ☼ specified that the christians, jews and Majus should be allowed residence in Madīnah for three nights to traffic in the market and deal with their needs. None of them were allowed to reside after that."

قال محمد: إن مكة والمدينة وما حَولهما من جزيرة العرب، وقد بلغنا عن النبي صلى الله عليه وسلم أنه لا يبقى دينان في جزيرة العرب. فأخرج عمر رضي الله تعالى عنه من لم يكن مسلماً من جزيرة العرب لهذا الحديث.

Muḥammad said: "Makkah and Madīnah and their entire surroundings are part of the Arabian peninsula, and it has reached us from the Prophet ☼ that two *dīns* are not to remain in the Arabian peninsula. So ʿUmar ☼ expelled whoever was not a Muslim from the Arabian peninsula because of this *ḥadīth*."

٨٧٣ أخبرنا مالك، أخبرنا إسماعيل بن حكيم، عن عمر بن العزيز قال: بلغني أن النبي صلى الله عليه وسلم قال: لا يبقيَن دينان بجزيرة العرب.

873. Mālik informed us: "Ismāʿīl ibn Ḥakīm informed us that ʿUmar ibn ʿAbd al-ʿAzīz said, 'It has reached me that the Prophet ☼ said, "Two *dīns* must not remain in the Arabian peninsula."'"

قال محمد: قد فعل ذلك عمر بن الخطاب ☼، فأخرج اليهود والنصارى من جزيرة العرب.

Muḥammad said: "ʿUmar ibn al-Khaṭṭāb ☼ did that, and he expelled the jews and christians from the Arabian peninsula."

٩ باب الرجل يُقيم الرجلَ من مجلسه ليجلس فيه وما يُكره من ذلك.
9. A Man Making a Man Get up from his Seat in order for him to Sit there and what is Disapproved of in that

٨٧٤ أخبرنا مالك، أخبرنا نافع، عن ابن عمر رضي الله عنهما: أن رسول الله صلى الله عليه وسلم كان يقول: لا يُقيم أحدُكم الرجلَ من مجلسه فيجلس فيه.

874. Mālik informed us: "Nāfiʿ informed us from Ibn ʿUmar ☼ that the

Messenger of Allah ﷺ used to say, 'Let none of you make a man get up from his seat and then sit in it.'"

قال محمد : وبهذا نأخذُ . لا ينبغي للرجل المسلم أن يصنع هذا بأخيه ويقيمه من مجلسه، ثم يجلس فيه .

Muḥammad said: "We adhere to this. A Muslim man ought not to treat his brother in this way making him get up from his seat, and then sitting in it."

١٠ باب الرُّقَى

10. An Amulet or Incantation Recited over a Sick Person as a Cure [*Ruqyah*]

٨٧٥ أخبرنا مالك، أخبرنا يحيى بن سعيد، أخبرتني عَمْرَة : أن أبا بكر دخل على عائشة رضي الله عنهما وهي تشتكي ، ويهودية تَرْقيها، فقال: ارقيها بكتاب الله .

875. Mālik informed us: "Yaḥyā ibn Saᶜīd informed us, 'ᶜAmrah informed me that Abū Bakr visited ᶜĀʾishah, may Allah be pleased with them both, when she had a complaint, while a jewess was treating her with an amulet or incantation recited over the sick to effect a cure [*ruqyah*] and he said, "Treat her with the Book of Allah."'"

قال محمد : وبهذا نأخذ . لا بأسَ بالرُّقى بما كان في القرآن، وما كان من ذكر الله، فأما ما كان لا يعرف من كلام فلا ينبغي أن يُرقَى به .

Muḥammad said: "We adhere to this. There is no harm in using that which is in the Qurʾān as an incantation or amulet [to effect a cure in a sick person] or using whatever there is of *dhikr* of Allah. As for speech which is not well known to be right, then one ought not to use it as an incantation or amulet."

٨٧٦ أخبرنا مالك، أخبرنا يحيى بن سعيد ، أن سليمان بن يَسار أخبره، أن عروة بن الزبير أخبره : أن رسول الله صلى الله عليه وسلم دخل بيت أم سلمة وفي البيت صبيٌّ يبكي ، فذكروا أنَّ به العينَ ، فقال له رسول الله صلى الله عليه وسلم: أفلا تستَرقُون له من العين؟

876. Mālik informed us: "Yaḥyā ibn Saᶜīd informed us that Sulaymān ibn Yasār informed him that ᶜUrwah ibn az-Zubayr informed him that the Messenger of Allah ﷺ entered the room of Umm Salamah and in her room there was a small child crying. They mentioned that he had been affected by 'the eye'. The Messenger of Allah ﷺ said to them, 'But do you not seek to treat him [with a *ruqyah* and cure him of] "the eye"?'"

قال محمد : وبه نأخذ . لا نرى بالرقية بأساً إذا كانت من ذكر الله تعالى .

Muḥammad said: "We adhere to this. We do not think that there is any harm in amulets or incantations recited over the sick in order to effect a cure [*ruqyah*] if they are from *dhikr* of Allah, exalted is He."

٨٧٧ أخبرنا مالك، أخبرنا يزيد بن خُصَيفة: أن عمر بن عبد الله بن كعب السَّلَمي، أخبره أن نافع بن جبير بن مُطْعم أخبره، عن عثمان بن أبي العاص: أنه أتى رسول الله ﷺ ، قال عثمان: وبي وَجَع

حتى كاد يُهْلِكُني قال: فقال رسول الله ﷺ : امسحه بيمينك سبعَ مراتٍ وقل: أعوذ بعزَّة الله وقدرته من شرِّ ما أجِد، ففعلتُ ذلك، فأذهب الله ما كان بي فلم أزل بعدُ آمرُ به أهلي وغيرهم.

877. Mālik informed us: "Yazīd ibn Khusayfah informed us that ᶜUmar ibn ᶜAbdullāh ibn Kaᶜb as-Salami informed him that Nāfiᶜ ibn Jubayr ibn Muṭᶜim informed him that ᶜUthmān ibn Abi'l-ᶜĀṣ went to the Messenger of Allah ﷺ. ᶜUthmān said, 'And I had a pain which came close to killing me.' He said, 'The Messenger of Allah ﷺ said, "Wipe it with your right hand seven times, and say, 'I seek refuge with the might of Allah and His power from the evil of what I experience.'" So I did that and Allah drove what I was experiencing away from me. I always tell my family and others to do it.'"

١١ باب ما يُسْتَحَبُّ من الفأل والاسم الحسن

11. What Good Omens and Good Names are Approved of

٨٧٨ أخبرنا مالك، أخبرنا يحيى بن سعيد ، أن النبي صلى الله عليه وسلم قال للَقْحَة عنده: من يحلب هذه الناقة؟ فقام رجلٌ فقال له: ما اسمك؟ فقال له مُرَّة ، قال : اجلس، ثم قال: من يحلب هذه الناقة؟ فقام رجلٌ فقال له: ما اسمك؟ قال: حربٌ قال : اجلس، ثم قال: من يحلب هذه الناقة؟ فقام آخر فقال: ما اسمك؟ قال: يَعيش قال: احلب.

878. Mālik informed us: "Yaḥyā ibn Saᶜīd informed us that the Prophet ﷺ said about a milch camel he had, 'Who will milk this she-camel?' So a man stood and he asked him, 'What is your name?' and he answered, 'Murrah – bitterness.' He said, 'Sit down.' Then he said, 'Who will milk this she-camel?' So a man stood, and he asked him, 'What is your name?' and he answered, 'Ḥarb – war.' He said, 'Sit down.' Then he said, 'Who will milk this she-camel?' So another stood, and he asked him, 'What is your name?' and he said,'Yaᶜīsh – he lives,' and he said, 'Milk!'"

١٢ باب الشرب قائماً

12. Drinking while Standing

٨٧٩ أخبرنا مالك، أخبرنا ابن شهاب، أنَّ عائشة زوج النبي صلى الله عليه وسلم وسعد بن أبي وقّاص كانا لا يَرَيَان بشُرْب الإنسان وهو قائم بأساً .

879. Mālik informed us: "Ibn Shihāb informed us that ᶜĀ᾿ishah the wife of the Prophet ﷺ and Saᶜd ibn Abī Waqqāṣ used to think that there was no harm in a man drinking while standing."

٨٨٠ أخبرنا مالك، أخبرني مُخْبِرٌ: أن عمر بن الخطّاب وعثمان بن عفّان وعلي بن أبي طالب رضي الله تعالى عنهم كانوا يشربون قياماً.

880. Mālik informed us: "An informant informed me that ᶜUmar ibn al-Khaṭṭāb, ᶜUthmān ibn ᶜAffān and ᶜAlī ibn Abī Ṭālib ﷺ used to drink while standing."

قال محمد: وبهذا نأخذ. لا نرى بالشرب قائماً بأساً. وهو قول أبي حنيفة والعامة من فقهائنا.

Muḥammad said: "We adhere to this. We see no harm in drinking while standing, and that is the verdict of Abū Ḥanīfah and of our *fuqahā*ʾ in general."[156]

١٣ باب الشرب في آنية الفضّة

13. Drinking from a Silver Vessel

٨٨١ أخبرنا مالك، أخبرنا نافع، عن زيد بن عبد الله بن عمر، عن عبد الله بن عبد الرحمن بن أبي بكر الصدّيق رضي الله عنه، عن أمّ سلمة زوج النبي صلى الله عليه وسلم أنّ النبي صلى الله عليه وسلم قال: إنّ الذي يشرب في آنية الفضة إنما يُجَرْجِرُ في بطنه نار جهنّم.

881. Mālik informed us: "Nāfiᶜ informed us from Zayd ibn ᶜAbdullāh ibn ᶜUmar from ᶜAbdullāh ibn ᶜAbd ar-Raḥmān ibn Abī Bakr aṣ-Ṣiddīq ﷺ from Umm Salamah the wife of the Prophet ﷺ that the Prophet ﷺ said, 'The one who drinks from a silver vessel is only pouring the Fire of Jahannam into his belly.'"

قال محمد: وبهذا نأخذ. يُكره الشربُ في آنية الفضّة والذهب ولا نرى بذلك بأساً في الإناء المفضّض. وهو قول أبي حنيفة والعامة من فقهائنا.

Muḥammad said: "We adhere to this. Drinking from a vessel made of silver or gold is abhorrent[157], but we see no harm in a silver-plated vessel, and that is the verdict of Abū Ḥanīfah and of our *fuqahā*ʾ in general."

١٤ باب الشرب والأكل باليمين

14. Eating and Drinking with the Right Hand

٨٨٢ أخبرنا مالك، أخبرنا ابن شهاب، عن أبي بكر بن عُبَيْد الله، عن عبد الله بن عمر أن رسول الله صلى الله عليه وسلم قال: إذا أكل أحدكم فليأكُل بيمينه، وليشرب بيمينه، فإنّ الشيطان يأكل بشماله ويشرب بشماله.

882. Mālik informed us: "Ibn Shihāb informed us from Abū Bakr ibn ᶜUbaydullāh from ᶜAbdullāh ibn ᶜUmar that the Messenger of Allah ﷺ said, 'When any of you eat, then let him eat with his right hand and let him drink with his right hand, because the shayṭān eats with his left hand and drinks with his left hand.'"

قال محمد: وبه نأخذ. لا ينبغي أن يأكل بشماله ولا يشرب بشماله إلاّ من علّة.

Muḥammad said, "We adhere to this. One ought not to eat with one's left hand or drink with one's left hand unless there is good cause."

١٥ باب الرجل يشرب ثم يناول مَنْ عَنْ يَمينِه

15. A Man Drinking and then passing it to Someone on his Right Hand

٨٨٣ أخبرنا مالك، أخبرنا ابن شهاب، عن أنس بن مالك: أن رسول الله صلى الله عليه وسلم أُتي

بلَبن قد شِيْب بماء، وعن يمينه أعرابي، وعن يساره أبو بكر الصديق رضي الله عته، فشرب ثم أعطى الأعرابي، ثم قال: الأيمن فالأيمن.

883. Mālik informed us: "Ibn Shihāb informed us from Anas ibn Mālik that the Messenger of Allah ﷺ was given milk which had been mixed with water, and to his right there was a bedouin and to his left Abū Bakr aṣ-Ṣiddīq ؓ. He drank and then he gave it to the bedouin, and then said, 'The right and then the right.'"

قال محمد: وبه نأخذ.

Muḥammad said, "We adhere to this."

٨٨٤ أخبرنا مالك، أخبرنا أبو حازم، عن سهل بن سعد الساعدي: أن النبي ﷺ أُتي بشراب فشرب منه، وعن يمينه غلام وعن يساره أشياخ فقال للغلام: أتأذن لي في أن أُعْطِيَه هؤلاء؟ فقال: لا والله لا أوثر بنصيبي منك أحداً، قال: فَتَلَّه رسول الله صلى الله عليه وسلم في يده.

884. Mālik informed us: "Abū Ḥāzim informed us from Sahl ibn Saʿd as-Sāʾidī that the Prophet ﷺ was brought a drink from which he drank, and to his right there was a boy and to his left some old men. He asked the boy, 'Will you permit me to give it to them?' He answered, 'No, by Allah! I will not give preference over my portion from you to anyone!'" He said, "So the Messenger of Allah ﷺ placed it in his hand."

١٦ | باب فَضْل إجابة الدعوة
16. The Merit in Accepting Invitations

٨٨٥ أخبرنا مالك، أخبرنا نافع، عن ابن عمر: أن رسول الله ﷺ قال: إذا دُعي أحدُكم إلى وليمة فليأتها.

885. Mālik informed us: "Nāfiʿ informed us from Ibn ʿUmar that the Messenger of Allah ﷺ said, 'When any of you are invited to a wedding feast then let him go to it!'"

٨٨٦ أخبرنا مالك، حدَّثنا ابن شهاب، عن الأعرج، عن أبي هريرة ؓ: أنه كان يقول: بئس الطعام طعامُ الوليمة يُدعى لها الأغنياءُ ويُترك المساكين، ومن لم يأت الدعوةَ فقد عصى اللَّهَ ورسوله.

886. Mālik informed us: "Ibn Shihāb narrated to us from al-Aʿraj that Abū Hurayrah ؓ used to say, 'How bad is the food of a wedding feast to which the wealthy are invited and from which the poor[158] are left out. Whoever does not come when invited has disobeyed Allah and His Messenger.'"

٨٨٧ أخبرنا مالك، أخبرنا إسحاق بن عبد الله بن أبي طلحة، عن أنس بن مالك رضي الله عنه قال: سمعتُه يقول: إن خيّاطاً دعا رسولَ الله صلى الله عليه وسلم إلى طعام صَنَعَه، قال أنس: فذهبتُ مع رسول الله صلى الله عليه وسلم إلى ذلك الطعام، فقرَّب إلى رسول الله صلى الله عليه وسلم خبزاً من شعير ومَرَقاً فيه دُبَّاء، قال أنس: فرأيت رسول الله صلى الله عليه وسلم يَتَتَبَّعُ الدُّبَّاء من حول القَصْعة، فلم أزل أُحبُّ الدُّبَّاء منذ يومئذ.

887. Mālik informed us: "Isḥāq ibn ʿAbdullāh ibn Abī Ṭalḥah informed us

from Anas ibn Mālik ﷺ. He [ᶜAbdullāh ibn Abī Ṭalḥah] said, 'I heard him [Anas] saying, "A tailor invited the Messenger of Allah ﷺ to some food which he had made." Anas said, "So I went with the Messenger of Allah ﷺ to that meal, and he set barley bread and a broth in which were gourds near to the Messenger of Allah ﷺ." Anas said, "I said the Messenger of Allah ﷺ seeking out the gourds from all around the platter, and so I have continued to love gourds from that day."'"

٨٨٨ أخبرنا مالك، أخبرنا إسحاق بن عبد الله بن أبي طلحة، قال : سمعت أنس بن مالك رضي الله عنه يقول: قال أبو طلحة لأُمّ سليم: لقد سمعتُ صوت رسول الله ﷺ ضعيفاً أعرف فيه الجوع فهل عندكِ من شيء ؟ قالت: نعم، فأخْرَجَتْ أقراصاً من شعير، ثم أخذَتْ خماراً لها ثم لَفَّتْ الخُبزَ ببعضه ، ثم دسّته تحت يديّ وردّتني ببعضه؟، ثم أرسلَتْني إلى رسول الله صلى الله عليه وسلم، فذهبتُ به ، فوجدتُ رسول الله صلى الله عليه وسلم جالساً في المسجد ومعه الناس، فقمت عليهم ، فقال لي رسول الله صلى الله عليه وسلم: أ أرسَلك أبو طلحة؟ قلتُ : نعم، قال: فقال: بطعام ؟ فقلتُ: نعم، فقال رسول الله صلى الله عليه وسلم لمن معه : قوموا ، قال: فانطلقتُ بين يديهم، ثم رجعت إلى أبي طلحة، فأخبرتُه ، فقال أبو طلحة : يا أمَّ سُليم قد جاء رسولُ الله صلى الله عليه وسلم بالناس ، وليس عندنا من الطعام ما نُطْعمُهم ، كيف نصنع؟ فقالت: الله ورسوله أعلم ، قال: فانطلق أبو طلحة حتى لقي رسول الله صلى الله عليه وسلم، فأقبل هو ورسول الله صلى الله عليه وسلم حتى دخلا ، فقال رسول الله صلى الله عليه وسلم : هَلُمّي يا أمَّ سليم ما عندك، فجاءت بذلك الخبز، قال: فأمر به رسول الله صلى الله عليه وسلم فَفُتّ ، وعَصَرت أم سليم عُكّةً لها ، فآدَمَتْه ، ثم قال رسول الله صلى الله عليه وسلم فيه ما شاء الله أن يقول، ثم قال: ائذن لعشرة ، فأذن لهم فأكلوا حتى شبعوا، ثم خرجوا ، ثم قال: ائذن لعشرة، فأذن لهم، فأكلوا حتى شبعوا، ثم خرجوا، ثم قال : ائذن لعشرة، فأذن لهم، فأكلوا حتى شبعوا، ثم خرجوا، ثم قال: ائذن لعشرة، فأذن لهم، فأكلوا حتى شبعوا، ثم خرجوا، ثم قال: ائذن لعشرة، حتى أكل القوم كلُّهم، وشبعوا وهم سبعون أو ثمانون رجلاً .

888. Mālik informed us:"Isḥāq ibn ᶜAbdullāh ibn Abī Ṭalḥah informed us, 'I heard Anas ibn Mālik ﷺ saying, "Abū Ṭalḥah said to Umm Sulaym, 'I heard the voice of the Messenger of Allah ﷺ sounding weak, and I recognised hunger in it; so do you have anything?' She answered, 'Yes,' and brought out round flat loaves of barley bread. Then she took a scarf of hers and wrapped the bread in part of it, and stuck it under my arm, and wrapped some of it around my upper part [as a protection from the sun] and sent me to the Messenger of Allah ﷺ. I went off with it and found the Messenger of Allah ﷺ seated in the mosque along with some people. I [went and] stood among them, and the Messenger of Allah ﷺ asked me, 'Has Abū Ṭalḥah sent you?' I answered, 'Yes.' He asked, 'Food?' I answered, 'Yes.' The Messenger of Allah ﷺ said to those with him, 'Stand up.'" He [Anas] said, "I went before them and returned to Abū Ṭalḥah and told him. Abū Ṭalḥah said, 'Umm Sulaym, the Messenger of Allah ﷺ has come with people, and we do not have any food to feed them. What will we do?' She answered,

'Allah and His Messenger know best.'" He [Anas] said, "Abū Ṭalḥah went out to meet the Messenger of Allah ﷺ and he and the Messenger of Allah ﷺ returned and entered [the house]. The Messenger of Allah ﷺ said, 'Bring whatever you have, Umm Sulaym,' and she brought that bread." He [Anas] said, "The Messenger of Allah ﷺ gave the instruction and it was broken into pieces, and Umm Sulaym squeezed out a leather vessel [containing some fat] and used that as a condiment for it [the bread]. Then the Messenger of Allah ﷺ said over it what Allah willed that he say [in supplication and blessing] and then said, 'Let in ten,' and he let them in and they ate until they were full and went out. Then he said, 'Let in ten [more],' and he let them in and they ate until they were full and went out. Then he said, 'Let in ten [more],' and he let them in and they ate until they were full and went out. Then he said, 'Let in ten [more],' and he let them in and they ate until they were full and went out. Then he said, 'Let in ten [more],' until all of the people had eaten and were full, and there were seventy or eighty men."'"

قال محمد: وبهذا نأخذ. ينبغي للرجل أن يُجيب الدعوة العامة، ولا يتخلّف عنها إلا لعلّة، فأما الدعوة الخاصّة فإن شاء أجاب وإن شاء لم يُجب.

Muḥammad said: "We adhere to this. A man ought to respond to open invitations and not stay away from them unless because of some reasonable excuse. As for specific invitations, if he wishes he may accept them and if he wishes he need not accept them."

٨٨٩ أخبرنا مالك، أخبرنا أبو الزناد، عن الأعرج، عن أبي هريرة، قال: قال رسول الله صلى الله عليه وسلم: طعام الاثنين كافٍ للثلاثة وطعام الثلاثة كافٍ للأربعة.

889. Mālik informed us: "Abu'z-Zinād informed us from al-Aᶜraj that Abū Hurayrah said, 'The Messenger of Allah ﷺ said, "The food of two is sufficient for three, and the food of three is sufficient for four."'"

١٧ باب فضل المدينة

17. The Superiority of Madīnah

٨٩٠ أخبرنا مالك، أخبرنا محمد بن المنكدر، عن جابر بن عبد الله: أن أعرابياً بايع رسولَ الله صلى الله عليه وسلم على الإسلام، ثم أصابه وَعَك بالمدينة، فجاء إلى رسول الله صلى الله عليه وسلم فقال: أقلني بيعتي، فأبى، ثم جاء فقال: أقلني بيعتي، فأبى، ثم جاء فقال: أقلني بيعتي؟، فأبى، فخرج الأعرابي، فقال رسول الله صلى الله عليه وسلم: إن المدينة كالكير، تنفي خَبَثها وتَنْصع طيبها.

890. Mālik informed us: "Muḥammad ibn al-Munkadir informed us from Jābir ibn ᶜAbdullāh that a bedouin pledged allegiance to the Messenger of Allah ﷺ on the basis of Islam. Then the fever [endemic to] Madīnah struck him, and he came to the Messenger of Allah ﷺ and said, 'Release me from my pledge of allegiance,' but he refused. Then again he came and said,

'Release me from my pledge of allegiance,' but he refused. Then again he came and said, 'Release me from my pledge of allegiance,' but he refused. The bedouin went out, and the Messenger of Allah ﷺ said, 'Madīnah is like the blacksmith's bellows [or his furnace]; it removes its impurities and purifies its good [parts].'"

١٨ باب اقتناء الكلب

18. Training Dogs

٨٩١ أخبرنا مالك، أخبرنا يزيد بن خُصيفَة، أن السائب بن يزيد أخبره، أنّه سمع سفيان بن أبي زهير وهو رجلٌ من شَنُوءَة، وهو من أصحاب رسول الله صلى الله عليه وسلم يحدّث أناساً معه، وهو عند باب المسجد، قال: سمعت رسول الله صلى الله عليه وسلم يقول: من اقتنى كلباً لا يُغني به زرعاً ولا ضرعاً نُقص من عمله كل يوم قيراط. قال: قلت: أنت سمعتَ هذا من رسول الله صلى الله عليه وسلم؟ قال: إيْ وربِّ الكعبة وربِّ هذا المسجد.

891. Mālik informed us: "Yazīd ibn Khusayfah informed us that as-Sā'ib ibn Yazīd informed him that he had heard Sufyān ibn Abī Zuhayr – and he was a man of Shanū'ah and one of the Companions of the Messenger of Allah ﷺ – narrating to some people with him while he was at the door of the mosque, saying, 'I heard the Messenger of Allah ﷺ saying, "Whoever has a dog that is not for the purpose of guarding crops or cattle will be lessened by a great mountain worth of [the reward for] his action every day." He [as-Sā'ib] said, 'I asked, "Did you hear this from the Messenger of Allah, ﷺ?" He answered, "Yes, by the Lord of the Kaᶜbah! By the Lord of this mosque!"'"

قال محمدٌ: يُكره اقتناء الكلب لغير منفعة، فأما كلب الزرع أو الضرع أو الصيد أو الحرس فلا بأس به.

Muḥammad said: "It is disliked to keep a dog without some benefit, but as for dogs used for [guarding] crops and cattle, or for hunting or for guarding property, then there is no harm in it."

٨٩٢ أخبرنا مالك، عن عبد الملك بن مَيْسَرة، عن إبراهيم النَّخَعي قال: رخّص رسول الله صلى الله عليه وسلم لأهل البيت القاصي في الكلب يتخذونه.

892. Mālik informed us from ᶜAbdullāh ibn Maysarah that Ibrāhīm an-Nakhaᶜī said, "The Messenger of Allah ﷺ made a concession for people living in remote houses making use of dogs."

قال محمد: فهذا للحرَس.

Muḥammad said: "This is for guarding."

٨٩٣ أخبرنا مالك، أخبرنا عبد الله بن دينار، عن عبد الله بن عمر، قال: من اقتنى كلباً إلاّ كلبَ ماشية أو ضارياً نُقص من عمله كلّ يوم قيراطان.

893. Mālik informed us: "ᶜAbdullāh ibn Dīnār informed us that ᶜAbdullāh ibn ᶜUmar said, 'Whoever takes a dog – unless it is a dog for cattle or a

trained hunting dog – will be lessened in [the reward for] his action every day by two great mountains worth.'"

١٩ باب ما يُكره من الكذب وسوء الظن والتجسُّس والنميمة

19. The Abhorrence of Lying, Bad Opinion, Spying and Carrying Tales

٨٩٤ أخبرنا مالك، أخبرنا صفوان بن سليم، عن عطاء بن يسار: أن رسول الله صلى الله عليه وسلم سأله رجل فقال: يا رسول الله أَكْذبُ امرأتي؟ قال رسول الله صلى الله عليه وسلم: لا خير في الكذب، فقال يا رسول الله: أعدُها وَأقولُ، قال رسول الله صلى الله عليه وسلم: لا جُناح عليك.

894. Mālik informed us: "Ṣafwān ibn Sulaym informed us from ʿAṭāʾ ibn Yasār that the Messenger of Allah ﷺ was asked by a man who said, 'Messenger of Allah, may I lie to my wife?' The Messenger of Allah ﷺ answered, 'There is no good in lying.' So he asked, 'May I promise her and say [that I will do such and such for her]?' The Messenger of Allah ﷺ said, 'There is no wrong against you.'"

قال محمد: وبهذا نأخذ. لا خير في الكذب في جدّ ولا هزل، فإن وسعَ الكذب في شيء ففي خَصْلة واحدة أن ترفَعَ عن نفسك أو عن أخيك مظلمة، فهذا نرجوا أن لا يكون به بأس.

Muḥammad said: "We adhere to this. There is no good in lying whether in seriousness or jest. If lying is permissible for any reason it is only for one thing: that you should remove some injustice or oppression from yourself or from your brother. In this, we hope there will be no harm."

٨٩٥ أخبرنا مالك، أخبرنا أبو زناد، عن الأعرج، عن أبي هريرة: أن رسول الله ﷺ قال: إيّاكم والظنَّ، فإن الظنَّ أكذب الحديث، ولا تجسَّسُوا ولا تنافسوا ولا تحاسدوا ولا تباغضوا ولا تدابروا، وكونوا عبادَ الله إخواناً.

895. Mālik informed us: "Abu'z-Zinād informed us from al-Aʿraj from Abū Hurayrah that the Messenger of Allah ﷺ said, 'Beware of suspicion[159], because suspicion is the most mendacious form of speech. Also do not pry or spy, do not compete with each other, do not envy each other, do not hate each other, and be slaves of Allah as brothers."

٨٩٦ أخبرنا مالك، أخبرنا أبو زناد، عن الأعرج، عن أبي هريرة، عن رسول الله صلى الله عليه وسلم أنه قال: من شرّ الناس ذو الوجهين الذي يأتي هؤلاء بوجه وهؤلاء بوجه.

896. Mālik informed us: "Abu'z-Zinād informed us from al-Aʿraj from Abū Hurayrah that the Messenger of Allah ﷺ said, 'One of the worst of people is the two-faced person who comes to these with one face and comes to those with [another] face.'"

٢٠ باب الاستعفاف عن المسألة والصدقة

20. Restraining Oneself from Asking, and *Ṣadaqah*

٨٩٧ أخبرنا مالك، أخبرنا ابن شهاب، عن عطاء بن يزيد الليثي، عن أبي سعيد الخُدري: أنّ ناساً

من الأنصار سألوا رسول الله صلى الله عليه وسلم فأعطاهم، ثم سألوه فأعطاهم، ثم سألوه فأعطاهم، حتى أنفَدَ ما عنده، فقال: ما يكنْ عندي من خير فلن أدَّخرَه عنكم، من يستعفَّ يُعِفَّه اللهُ، ومن يستَغْنِ يُغنه الله، ومن يَتَصَبَّرْ يُصَبِّرْه الله، وما أعطي أحدٌ عطاءً هو خيرٌ، وأوسعُ من الصبر.

897. Mālik informed us: "Ibn Shihāb informed us from ʿAṭāʾ ibn Yazīd al-Laythī from Abū Saʿīd al-Khudrī that some people of the Anṣār asked from the Messenger of Allah ﷺ and so he gave to them. Then later they asked from him and so he gave to them. Then later they asked from him and so he gave to them until he had exhausted what he had, and then he said, 'Whatever good I have, I will never hoard it from you. Whoever restrains himself, then Allah will give him self-restraint, and whoever seeks to be independent, then Allah will give him independence. Whoever seeks to be steadfast, Allah will make him steadfast, and no one has been given a gift which is better and vaster than steadfastness.'"

٨٩٨ أخبرنا مالك، أخبرنا عبد الله بن أبي بكر، أن أباه أخبره: أن رسول الله صلى الله عليه وسلم استعمل رجلاً من بني عبد الأَشْهل على الصدقة، فلما قدم سأله أبْعِرَةً من الصدقة، قال: فغضب رسول الله صلى الله عليه وسلم حتى عُرِف الغضبُ في وجهه، وكان مما يُعْرَفُ به الغضبُ في وجهه أن يَحْمَرَّ عيناه، ثم قال: الرجل يسألني ما لا يصلح لي ولا له، فإن منعتُه كرهتُ المنعَ، وإن أعطيتُه أعطيته ما لا يصلح لي ولا له، فقال الرجل: لا أسألك منها شيئاً أبداً.

898. Mālik informed us: "ʿAbdullāh ibn Abī Bakr informed us that his father informed him that 'The Messenger of Allah ﷺ put a man of Banī ʿAbdin al-Ashhal in charge of the *ṣadaqah* [*zakāh*]. When he came he asked him for camels from the *ṣadaqah*.' He said, 'So the Messenger of Allah ﷺ became so angry that the anger could be seen in his face, and one way that anger could be seen in his face was that his eyes reddened. Then he said, "The man asks me for something that is not right for me nor for him. If I refuse him, I detest to refuse, but if I give him, I will give him that which is not right for me nor for him." The man said, "I will never [again] ask you for anything of it."'"

قال محمد: لا ينبغي أن يُعطى من الصدقة غنياً. وإنما نَرَى أن النبي صلى الله عليه وسلم قال ذلك، لأنّ الرجل كان غنياً، ولو كان فقيراً لأعطاه منها.

Muḥammad said: "A wealthy man ought not to be given anything from the *ṣadaqah* [*zakāh*]. We only think that the Prophet only ﷺ said that because the man was wealthy, and that if he had been needy he would have given him something from it."

٢١ باب الرجل يكتب إلى الرجل يبدأ به

21. A Man Writing to Another Man and Beginning with the Other

٨٩٩ أخبرنا مالك، أخبرنا عبد الله بن دينار، عن عبد الله بن عمر رضي الله عنه: أنه كتب إلى أمير المؤمنين عبد الملك يُبايعه فكتب: بسم الله الرحمن الرحيم، أما بعد، لعبد الله عبد الملك أمير

المؤمنين من عبد الله بن عمر، سلامٌ عليك ، فإني أحمَد إليك الله الذي لا إله إلاَّ هو وأُقِرُّ لك بالسمع والطاعة على سُنَّة الله ، وسُنَّة رسول الله صلى الله عليه وسلم فيما استطعت .

899. Mālik informed us: "ᶜAbdullāh ibn Dīnār informed us that ᶜAbdullāh ibn ᶜUmar ﷺ wrote to the Amīr al-Mu᾽minīn ᶜAbd al-Mālik to pledge allegiance to him, and he wrote, 'In the name of Allah, the All-Merciful, the Most Merciful. To the slave of Allah, ᶜAbd al-Mālik ibn Marwān from ᶜAbdullāh ibn ᶜUmar, peace be upon you. I praise before you Allah the One, that there is no god but Him, and I confirm to you [my] hearing and obedience according to the Sunnah of Allah and the Sunnah of the Messenger of Allah ﷺ as much as I am able.'"

قال محمد : لا بأس إذا كتب الرجل إلى صاحبه أن يبدأ بصاحبه قبل نفسه .

Muḥammad said: "There is no harm when a man writes to his correspondent if he begins with his correspondent before himself."

٩٠٠ عن عبد الرحمن بن أبي الزِّناد، عن أبيه، عن خارجة بن زيد بن ثابت : أنه كتب إلى معاوية : بسم الله الرحمن الرحيم، لعبد الله معاوية أمير المؤمنين، من زيد بن ثابت . ولا بأس بأن يبدأ الرجل بصاحبه قبل نفسه في الكتاب .

900. From ᶜAbd ar-Raḥmān ibn Abi'z-Zinād from his father from Khārijah ibn Zayd there is that Zayd ibn Thābit wrote to Muᶜāwiyah, "In the name of Allah, the All-Merciful, the Most Merciful. To the slave of Allah, Muᶜāwiyah Amīr al-Mu᾽minīn from Zayd ibn Thābit."

[Muḥammad said] "There is no harm if a man starts with his correspondent before himself in writing."

٢٢ باب الاستئذان

22. Seeking Permission [to Enter a Room or Dwelling]

٩٠١ أخبرنا مالك، أخبرنا صفوان بن سُليم، عن عطاء بن يسار : أن رسول الله صلى الله عليه وسلم سأله رجلٌ، فقال : يا رسول الله أستأذنُ على أمّي؟ قال : نعم، قال الرجل : إني معها في البيت، قال : استأذن عليها، قال : إني أخدمُها، قال رسول الله صلى الله عليه وسلم : أتُحبُّ أن تراها عريانة؟ قال : لا، قال : فاستَأذنْ عليها .

901. Mālik informed us: "Ṣafwān ibn Sulaym informed us from ᶜAṭā᾽ ibn Yasār that a man asked the Messenger of Allah ﷺ saying, 'Messenger of Allah, should I seek permission [to enter where] my mother [is]?' He answered, 'Yes.' The man said, 'I am with her in the house.' He said, 'Seek permission [to enter where] she is.' He said, 'I serve her.' The Messenger of Allah ﷺ said, 'Do you want to see her naked?' He answered, 'No.' He said, 'So seek permission [to enter where] she is.'"

قال محمد : وبهذا نأخذ . الاستئذان حَسَن ، وينبغي أن يستأذن الرجل على كل من يَحْرُم عليه النظر إلى عورته ونحوها .

Muḥammad said: "We adhere to this. A man ought to seek permission [to enter wherever anyone is] for whose private parts and the like it is *ḥarām* for him to see."

٢٣ باب التصاوير والجَرَس وما يُكره منها

23. The Abhorrence of Figures or Images[160] and Bells

٩٠٢ أخبرنا مالك، أخبرنا نافع، عن سالم بن عبد الله، عن الجرّاح مولى أُم حَبيبة عن أُمّ حبيبة : أن رسول الله صلى الله عليه وسلم قال: العِيْرُ التي فيها جَرَس لا تصحبها الملائكة .

902. Mālik informed us: "Nāfi^c informed us from Sālim ibn ^cAbdullāh from al-Jarrāḥ the *mawlā* of Umm Ḥabībah from Umm Ḥabībah that the Messenger of Allah ﷺ said, 'The caravan in which there is a bell is not accompanied by the angels.'"

قال محمد : وإنما رُوي ذلك في الحرب لأنه يُنْذَر به العدوُّ.

Muḥammad said: "That is only related with respect to war, because the enemy is given warning by it."

٩٠٣ أخبرنا مالك، أخبرنا أبو النضر مولى عمر بن عبد الله بن عبيد الله، عن عبد الله بن عتبه بن مسعود: أنه دخل على أبي طلحة الأنصاري يَعُوده ، فوجد عنده سهلَ بنَ حُنَيف ، فدعا أبو طلحة إنساناً يَنزع نَمَطاً تحته، فقال سهل بن حنيف: لِمَ تنزعُه ؟ قال: لأنَّ فيه تصاوير، وقد قال رسول الله فيها ما قد علمتَ . قال: سهل : أوَلَم يقل إلاَّ ما كان رَقْماً في ثوبٍ؟ قال: بلَى ، ولكنه أطيب لنفسي.

903. Mālik informed us: "Abu'n-Naḍr the *mawlā* of ^cUmar ibn ^cAbdullāh ibn ^cUbaydullāh informed us that ^cAbdullāh ibn ^cUtbah ibn Mas^cūd went in to see Abū Ṭalḥah al-Anṣārī in order to visit him while sick, and he found Sahl ibn Ḥunayf there with him. Abū Ṭalḥah called for someone to remove a coverlet from under him. Sahl ibn Ḥunayf asked, 'Why are you removing it?' He answered, 'Because of the images on it, about which the Messenger of Allah ﷺ said that which you know.' Sahl asked, 'Did he not say, "...except for what is decoration on a garment"?' He answered, 'Yes of course, but it is more pleasing to me [to remove it].'"

قال محمد: وبهذا نأخذ. ما كان فيه من تصاوير من بساط يُبْسَط أو فراش يُفرَش أو وِسادة فلا بأس بذلك. إنما يُكره من ذلك في الستر وما يُنصب نَصْباً. وهو قولُ أبي حنيفة والعامة من فقهائنا.

Muḥammad said: "We adhere to this. Those images which are on a carpet that is spread out, or bedding that is laid out or pillows, then there is no harm in that. The only thing [of this kind] that is disapproved of is curtains and things that are set up or stood up. That is the verdict of Abū Ḥanīfah and of our *fuqahā^ɔ* in general."

٢٤ باب اللَّعِب بالنَّرْد

24. Playing Backgammon

٩٠٤ أخبرنا مالك، عن موسى بن مَيْسرة، عن سعيد بن أبي هند، عن أبي موسى الأشعري : أن رسول الله صلى الله عليه وسلم قال: من لَعِبَ بالنَّرد فقد عصى الله ورسولَه .

904. Mālik informed us from Mūsā ibn Maysarah from Saᶜīd ibn Abī Hind from Abū Mūsā al-Ashᶜarī that the Messenger of Allah ﷺ said, "Whoever plays backgammon has disobeyed Allah and His Messenger."

قال محمد: لا خير باللعب كلِّها من النَّرْد والشِّطْرَنج وغير ذلك.

Muḥammad said: "There is no good in any game, whether backgammon, chess or whatever."

٢٥ باب النظر إلى اللعب

25. Watching People at Play

٩٠٥ أخبرنا مالك، أخبرنا أبو النَّضْر، أنه أخبره من سمع عائشة تقول : سمعت صوتَ أناس يلعبون من الحَبَش وغيرهم يومَ عاشوراء، قالت: فقال رسول الله صلى الله عليه وسلم: أتُحِبِّين أن تري لَعِبَهم؟ قالت: قلت : نعم، قالت : فأرسل إليهم رسول الله صلى الله عليه وسلم فجاؤوا ، وقام رسول الله صلى الله عليه وسلم بين الناس فوضع كفَّه على الباب، ومَدَّ يده ، ووضعتُ ذَقني على يده، فجعلوا يلعبون وأنا أنظر ، قالت: فجعل رسول الله صلى الله عليه وسلم يقول : حسبك ، قالت: وأسكتُ مرتين أو ثلاثاً، ثم قال لي: حسبُكِ، قلت: نعم. فأشار إليهم فانصرفوا.

905. Mālik informed us: "Abu'n-Naḍr informed us that someone informed him that he had heard ᶜĀ᾽ishah saying, 'I heard the voice of some Abyssinian people and others playing on the Day of ᶜĀshūrā᾽.' She said, 'So the Messenger of Allah ﷺ said, "Would you like to see their playing?"' She said, 'I said, "Yes."' She said, 'The Messenger of Allah ﷺ sent for them and they came, and the Messenger of Allah ﷺ stood among the people and leant his shoulder on the door, and stretched out his hand, and then I put my chin on his hand, and they began to play while I watched.' She said, 'The Messenger of Allah ﷺ began to say, "Is that enough for you?"' She said, 'I was silent twice or three times, and then he said to me, "Is that enough for you?" and I said, "Yes." He made a sign to them and they went away.'"

٢٦ باب المرأة تصل شعرها بشعر غيرها

26. A Woman Lengthening her Hair with Someone else's Hair

٩٠٦ أخبرنا مالك، أخبرنا ابن شهاب، عن حُميد بن عبد الرحمن: أنه سمع معاوية بن أبي سفيان عام حَجَّ وهو على المنبر يقول: يا أهلَ المدينة أين علماؤكم؟ وتناول قُصَّةً من شعرٍ، كانت في يد حَرَسيّ سمعت رسول الله ﷺ ينهي عن مثل هذا، ويقول : إنما هلكت بنو إسرائيل حين اتخذ هذه نساؤهم.

906. Mālik informed us: "Ibn Shihāb informed us from Ḥumayd ibn ᶜAbd ar-Raḥmān that he heard Muᶜāwiyah ibn Abī Sufyān, the year he performed Ḥajj, on the *minbar* saying, 'People of Madīnah! Where are your people of knowledge?' – and he was holding in his hand a lock of hair (i.e. a hairpiece) which had been in a guard's hand – 'I heard the Messenger of Allah ﷺ forbidding the like of this, saying, "The Children of Isrāʾīl only perished when their women took to this."'"

قال محمد : وبهذا نأخذ . يُكره للمرأة أن تصل شعراً إلى شعرها أو تتخذ قُصَّة شعر، ولا بأس بالوصل في الرأس إذا كان صوفاً . فأما الشعر من شعور الناس فلا ينبغي . وهو قول أبي حنيفة والعامّة من فقهائنا رحمهم الله تعالى .

Muḥammad said: "We adhere to this. It is disapproved of for a woman to interlock some other hair with her hair or wear a hairpiece. There is no harm in a hair extension made of wool, but as for any human hair, it ought not to be done. That is the verdict of Abū Ḥanīfah and of our *fuqahāʾ* in general, may Allah, exalted is He, show them mercy."

٢٧ باب الشفاعة

27. Intercession

٩٠٧ أخبرنا مالك، حدّثنا ابن شهاب، عن أبي سلمة بن عبد الرحمن، عن أبي هريرة أن رسول الله ﷺ قال: لكلِّ نبيٍّ دعوة ، فأريد إن شاء الله أن أختبئ دعوتي شفاعةً لأُمّتي يومَ القيمة .

907. Mālik informed us: "Ibn Shihāb narrated to us from Abū Salamah ibn ᶜAbd ar-Raḥmān from Abū Hurayrah that the Messenger of Allah ﷺ said, 'Every prophet had a supplication, and I want, *inshāʾAllāh*, to save my supplication as intercession for my community on the Day of Rising.'"

٢٨ باب الطيب للرجل

28. Perfume for Men

٩٠٨ أخبرنا مالك، أخبرنا يحيى بن سعيد : أن عمر بن الخطاب كان يتطيّب بالمسك المُفَتَّت اليابس .

908. Mālik informed us: "Yaḥyā ibn Saᶜīd informed us that ᶜUmar ibn al-Khaṭṭāb used to perfume himself with crushed dry musk."

قال محمد : وبهذا نأخذ . لا بأسَ بالمسك للحيّ وللميّت أن يتطيّب . وهو قول أبي حنيفة والعامة رحمهم الله تعالى .

Muḥammad said: "We adhere to this. There is no harm in the living or the dead being perfumed and that is the verdict of Abū Ḥanīfah and of [our *fuqahāʾ*] in general, may Allah, exalted is He, have mercy on them."

٢٩ باب الدعاء
29. Supplication

٩٠٩ أخبرنا مالك، أخبرنا إسحاق بن عبد الله بن أبي طلحة، عن أنس بن مالك، قال: دعا رسولُ الله صلى الله عليه وسلم على الذين قَتلوا أصحاب بئر معونة ثلاثين غداةً، يدعو على رِعْلٍ وذَكْوان وعُصَيَّة: عصت الله ورسولَه. قال أنس: نزل في الذين قُتلوا ببئر مَعُونَة قرآنٌ قرأناه حتى نُسخ: بلِّغوا قومنا أنَّا قد لَقينا ربَّنا ورضي الله عنا ورضينا عنه.

909. Mālik informed us: "Isḥāq ibn ʿAbdullāh ibn Abī Ṭalḥah informed us that Anas ibn Mālik said, 'The Messenger of Allah ﷺ supplicated for thirty mornings against the people who killed the people of Bi'r Maʿūnah, supplicating against [the tribes of] Riʿl, Dhakwān and ʿUṣayyah, "They have disobeyed [*ʿaṣat*] Allah and His Messenger."' Anas said, 'Some Qur'ān was revealed about those who were killed at Bi'r Maʿūnah which we used to recite until it [its recitation] was abrogated, "Convey to our people that we have met our Lord, and Allah is pleased with us and we are pleased with Him."'"

٣٠ باب ردّ السلام
30. Returning the Greeting of Peace

٩١٠ أخبرنا مالك، أخبرنا أبو جعفر القاري، قال: كنت مع بن عمر، فكان يسلِّم عليه، فيقول: السلام عليكم، فيقول مثلَ ما يُقال له.

910. Mālik informed us: "Abū Jaʿfar al-Qārī informed us, 'I was with Ibn ʿUmar and people would greet him saying, "Peace be upon you," and he would say the like of what had been said to him.'"

قال محمد: هذا لا بأس به. وإن زاد الرحمة والبركة فهو أفضل.

Muḥammad: "There is no harm in this, and if one adds 'mercy' and 'blessing' [by saying 'and the mercy of Allah and His blessing'] it is better."

٩١١ أخبرنا مالك، أخبرنا إسحاق بن عبد الله بن أبي طلحة، أن الطفيل بن أُبَيّ بن كعب أخبره: أنه كان يأتي عبد الله بن عمر، فيغدُوْ معه إلى السوق، قال: وإذا غَدَوْنا إلى السوق لم يمرّ عبد الله بن عمر على سقّاطٍ، ولا صاحب بيعٍ، ولا مسكين، ولا أحدٍ إلاّ سلّم عليه.

قال الطفيلُ بن أُبَيّ بن كعب: فجئت عبد الله بن عمر يوماً فاستتبعني إلى السوق، قال: فقلت ما تصنع في السوق؟ ولا تقف على البيّع، ولا تسأل عن السلع، ولا تساوم بها، ولا تجلس في مجلس السوق، اجلس بنا ههنا نتحدّث، فقال عبد الله بن عمر: يا أبا بطن وكان الطفيل ذا بطن إنما نَغْدُوْ لأجل السلام، نسلّم على من لَقينا.

911. Mālik informed us: "Isḥāq ibn ʿAbdullāh ibn Abī Ṭalḥah informed us that aṭ-Ṭufayl ibn Ubayy ibn Kaʿb informed him that he used to visit ʿAbdullāh ibn ʿUmar and go out with him early in the morning to the market. He said, 'When we went early in the morning to the market ʿAbdullāh ibn ʿUmar did not pass by a seller of cheap goods or any trader or any poor person or any

person at all but that he greeted him.' At-Tufayl ibn Ubayy ibn Kaᶜb said, 'I went to ᶜAbdullāh ibn ᶜUmar one day and he asked me to follow him to the market.' He said, 'I asked, "What are you doing in the market, when you are not engaged in trading, and you are not asking about goods and you don't ask about their prices, and [when] you are not sitting in the gatherings in the market? Sit with us here and let us talk."' ᶜAbdullāh ibn ᶜUmar said, 'O big-bellied man!' Because aṭ-Ṭufayl had a [large] belly, 'We only go because of the [greeting of] peace. We greet whomever we meet.'"

٩١٢ أخبرنا مالك، أخبرنا عبد الله بن دينار، عن عبد الله بن عمر قال: قال رسول الله صلى الله عليه وسلم: إن اليهود إذا سلّم عليكم أحدهم فإنما يقول: السام عليكم، فقولوا: عليك.

912. Mālik informed us: "ᶜAbdullāh ibn Dīnār informed us that ᶜAbdullāh ibn ᶜUmar said, 'The Messenger of Allah ﷺ said, "Whenever any of the jews greets you they only say, 'As-sāmu ᶜalaykum – death upon you,' so say, 'ᶜAlayka – upon you.'"'"

٩١٣ أخبرنا مالك، أخبرنا أبو نعيم وهب بن كَيْسان، عن محمد بن عمرو بن عطاء، قال: كنت جالساً عند عبد الله بن عباس، فدخل عليه رجل يماني فقال: السلام عليكم ورحمة الله وبركاته، ثم زاد شيئاً مع ذلك أيضاً قال ابن عباس رضي الله عنهما: من هذا؟ وهو يومئذ قد ذهب بصره قالوا: هذا اليماني الذي يَغْشاك، فعرّفوه إياه حتى عرفه، قال ابن عباس: إن السلام انتهى إلى البركة.

913. Mālik informed us: "Abū Nuᶜaym Wahb ibn Kaysān informed us that Muḥammad ibn ᶜAmr ibn ᶜAṭāʾ said, 'I was sitting with ᶜAbdullāh ibn ᶜAbbās and a Yemeni man came to see him, and he said, "As-salāmu ᶜalaykum wa raḥmatu'llāhi wa barakātuh – peace be upon you and the mercy of Allah and His blessings," and then he added something along with that also. Ibn ᶜAbbās ؓ said, "Who is this?" and his sight had left him at that time. They answered, "It is this Yemeni who comes regularly to visit you," and they described him to him until he recognised him. Ibn ᶜAbbās said, "[The greeting of] peace finishes with the blessing."'"

قال محمد: وبهذا نأخذ. إذا قال السلام عليكم ورحمة الله وبركاته فليكفف، فإن اتباع السُّنَّة أفضل.

Muḥammad said: "We adhere to this. If someone says, 'As-salāmu ᶜalaykum wa raḥmatu'llāhi wa barakātuh – peace be upon you and the mercy of Allah and His blessings,' then let him refrain from more than that, because following the *Sunnah* is better."

٣١ باب الدعاء

31. Supplication

٩١٤ أخبرنا مالك، أخبرنا عبد الله بن دينار، وقال: رآني ابن عمر وأنا أدعو فَأُشير بأصبعيّ أصبع من كلّ يدٍ فَنَهاني.

914. Mālik informed us: "ᶜAbdullāh ibn Dīnār informed us, 'Ibn ᶜUmar saw me while I was supplicating and I was pointing with my fingers, a finger from each hand, and he forbade me.'"

قال محمد: وبقول ابن عمر نأخذُ. ينبغي أن يُشير بأصبعٍ واحدة . وهو قولُ أبي حنيفة رحمه الله.

Muḥammad said: "The verdict of Ibn ᶜUmar is the one we adhere to. One ought to point with one finger [in the *tashahhud*]. That is the verdict of Abū Ḥanīfah, may Allah have mercy on him."

٩١٥ أخبرنا مالك، أخبرنا يحيى بن سعيد، أنه سمع سعيد بن المسيّب يقول: إن الرجل ليُرفَع بدعاءِ وَلَده من بَعده. وقال بيده فرفَعَها إلى السماء.

915. Mālik informed us: "Yaḥyā ibn Saᶜīd informed us that he heard Saᶜīd ibn al-Musayyab saying, 'A man will be raised [in degree] by the supplication of his son after him,' and he indicated with his hand and raised it up towards the sky."

٣٢ باب الرجل يهجر أخاه

32. A Man Forsaking and Shunning his Brother

٩١٦ أخبرنا مالك، أخبرنا ابن شهاب، عن عطاء بن يزيد، عن أبي أيوب الأنصاري صاحب رسول الله صلى الله عليه وسلم قال: لا يحلّ لمسلم أن يهجر أخاه فوق ثلاث ليالٍ، يلتقيان، فيُعرض هذا ويُعرض هذا، وخيرهم الذي يبدأ بالسلام.

916. Mālik informed us: "Ibn Shihāb informed us from ᶜAṭāʾ ibn Yazīd that Abū Ayyūb al-Anṣārī the companion of the Messenger of Allah ﷺ said, 'It is not permitted for a Muslim to shun his brother for more than three nights, they both meeting and this one turning away and that one turning away. The best of them is the one who initiates the greeting of peace.'"

قال محمد: وبهذا نأخذ. لا ينبغي الهجرة بين المسلمين.

Muḥammad said: "We adhere to this. Muslims ought not to shun each other."

٣٣ باب الخصومة في الدِّين والرجل يشهد على الرجل بالكفر

33. Arguing about the *Dīn*, and a Man Bearing witness to the *Kufr* of another Man

٩١٧ أخبرنا مالك، أخبرنا يحيى بن سعيد، أن عمر بن عزيز قال: من جَعَل دينه غَرَضاً للخصومات أكثر التنقُّل.

917. Mālik informed us: "Yaḥyā ibn Saᶜīd informed us that ᶜUmar ibn ᶜAbd al-ᶜAzīz said, 'Whoever makes his *dīn* a target of disputes repeatedly changes position.'"

قال محمد: وبهذا نأخذ. لا ينبغي الخصومات في الدين.

Muḥammad said: "We adhere to this. One ought not to dispute about the *dīn*."

٩١٨ أخبرنا مالك، أخبرنا عبد الله بن دينار، عن ابن عمر قال: قال رسول الله صلى الله عليه وسلم: أيُّما امرئ قال لأخيه: كافر، فقد باء بها أحدهما.

918. Mālik informed us: "ᶜAbdullāh ibn Dīnār informed us that Ibn ᶜUmar said, 'The Messenger of Allah ﷺ said, "Whenever a man says to his brother, '*Kāfir*!' then it proves true of one or the other of them."'"

قال محمد: لا ينبغي لأحد من أهل الإسلام أن يشهد على رجل من أهل الإِسلام بذنب أذنبه بكفرٍ، وإنْ عَظُم جُرمه، وهو قول أبي حنيفة والعامة من فقهائنا.

Muḥammad said: "None of the people of Islam ought to witness against another man of the people of Islam because of a wrong action which he has done that he is thus a *kāfir*, even if his crime is very great. That is the verdict of Abū Ḥanīfah and of our *fuqahā*ᵓ in general."

٣٤ باب ما يُكره من أكل الثوم

34. The Disapproval of Eating Garlic

٩١٩ أخبرنا مالك، أخبرنا ابن شهاب، عن سعيد بن المسيّب: أن النبي صلى الله عليه وسلم قال: من أكل من هذه الشجرة وفي رواية: الخبيثة فلا يقربنَّ مسجدَنا، يُؤذينا بريح الثُّوم.

919. Mālik informed us: "Ibn Shihāb informed us from Saᶜīd ibn al-Musayyab that the Prophet ﷺ said, 'Whoever eats from this shrub,' – and in one version 'malodorous [shrub]' – 'then let him not approach our mosque, disturbing us with the smell of the garlic.'"

قال محمد: إنما كُرِه ذلك لريحه، فإذا أمَتَّه طَبْخاً فلا بأس به. وهو قول أبي حنيفة والعامة رحمهم الله تعالى.

Muḥammad said: "It is only disapproved of because of its smell, so that when you extinguish it by cooking, then there is no harm. That is the verdict of Abū Ḥanīfah and of [our *fuqahā*ᵓ] in general, may Allah, exalted is He, show them mercy."

٣٥ باب الرؤيا

35. Dreams

٩٢٠ أخبرنا مالك، أخبرنا يحيى بن سعيد، قال: سمعت أبا سلمة يقول: سمعتُ أبا قتادة يقول: سمعتُ رسول الله صلى الله عليه وسلم يقول: الرؤيا من الله والحُلْم من الشيطان، فإذا رأى أحدكم الشيء يكرهه فلينفُثْ عن يساره ثلاث مرات إذا استيقظ، وليتعوَّذ من شرِّها فإنها لن تضرّه إن شاء الله تعالى.

920. Mālik informed us: "Yaḥyā ibn Saᶜīd informed us, 'I heard Abū Salamah saying, "I heard Abū Qatādah saying, 'I heard the Messenger of Allah ﷺ saying, "The good dream [*ru*ᵓ*yā*][161] is from Allah and the confused dream [*ḥulm*] is from shayṭān. When any of you sees something he dislikes [in a

dream] let him spit lightly to his left three times when he wakes up and seek refuge from its evil, because then it will not harm him, *inshā'Allāh,* exalted is He."''''

٣٦ باب جامع الحديث

36. Miscellaneous *Ḥadīth*

٩٢١ أخبرنا مالك، أخبرنا يحيى بن سعيد، عن مُحمد بن حَبَّان، عن يحيى، عن محمد بن يحيى بن حَبَّان، عن عبد الرحمن الأعرج، عن أبي هريرة رضي الله تعالى عنه قال: نهى رسول الله صلى الله عليه وسلم عن بيعتين، عن لِبْستين، وعن صلاتين، وعن صوم يومين، فأما البيعتان: المنابذةُ والملامسة، وأما اللبستان: فاشتمال الصمَّاء والاحتباء بثوب واحد كاشفاً عن فرجه، وأما الصلاتان: فالصلاة بعد العصر حتى تغرب الشمس والصلاة بعد الصبح حتى تطلع الشمس، وأما الصيامان فصيام يوم الأضحى ويوم الفطر.

921. Mālik informed us: "Yaḥyā ibn Sa῾īd informed us from Muḥammad ibn Ḥabbān from Yaḥyā from Muḥammad ibn Yaḥyā ibn Ḥabbān from ῾Abd ar-Raḥmān al-A῾raj that Abū Hurayrah ﷺ said, 'The Messenger of Allah ﷺ forbade two sales, two forms of dressing, two prayers and fasting two days. As to the two sales, they are *munābadhah* – where the two parties throw the items to be exchanged to each other without verification of their quality, thus concluding the sale – and *mulāmasah* – where a party buys a sealed package without examination of the contents. As for the two types of dressing, they are *ishtimāl aṣ-ṣammā᾿*[162] and *al-iḥtibā᾿*[163] in a single garment which exposes one's private parts. As for the two prayers, they are [non-obligatory] prayers after *῾Asr* until the setting of the sun, and [non-obligatory] prayers after the morning prayer until the rising of the sun. As for the two fasts, they are fasting on the day of *al-Aḍḥā* and the day of *al-Fiṭr*.'"

قال محمد: وبهذا كله نأخذ. وهو قول أبي حنيفة رحمه الله.

Muḥammad said: "All of this we adhere to, and it is the verdict of Abū Ḥanīfah, may Allah have mercy on him."

٩٢٢ أخبرنا مالك، أخبرني مُخْبِرٌ: أنَّ ابن عمر قال وهو يُوصي رجلاً: لا تَعْتَرِض فيما لا يعنيك، واعتزل عدوّك، واحذر خليلك إلاَّ الأمين، ولا أمين إلاَّ من خشي الله، ولا تصحب فاجراً كي تتعلّم من فجوره، ولا تُفش إليه سرَّك، واستشر في أمرك الذين يَخْشَوْنَ الله عزَّ وجل.

922. Mālik informed us: "An informant informed me that Ibn ῾Umar said – while counselling a man – 'Do not turn to what does not concern you, and keep your distance from your enemy, and beware of your close friend, apart from the trustworthy one and there is none who is trustworthy except for someone who fears Allah. Do not keep the company of a wicked person in case you learn his wickedness and do not share a secret with him. Take counsel in your affair with those who fear Allah ﷻ.'"

٩٢٣ أخبرنا مالك، أخبرنا أبو الزُّبير المكيّ، عن جابر بن عبد الله: أن رسول الله صلى الله عليه وسلم نهى أن يأكلِ الرجل بشماله، ويمشي في نعل واحدة، وأن يشتمل الصَّمَّاء أو يحتبي في ثوب واحد، كاشفاً عن فرجه.

923. Mālik informed us: "Abu'z-Zubayr al-Makkī informed us from Jābir ibn ᶜAbdullāh that the Messenger of Allah ﷺ forbade a man eating with his left hand, walking with a single sandal, or dressing in *ishtimāl aṣ-ṣammā*ᵓ[158] or *al-iḥtibā*ᵓ[159] in a single garment which exposes one's private parts."

قال محمد: يُكره للرجل أن يأكل بشماله، وأن يشتمل الصمَّاء، واشتمال الصمَّاء أن يشتمل وعليه ثوب، فيشتمل به فتنكشف عورته من الناحية التي تُرفع من ثوبه، وكذلك الاحتباءُ في الثوب الواحد.

Muḥammad said: "It is disapproved of for a man to eat with his left hand or to dress in *ishtimāl aṣ-ṣammā*ᵓ[158] and *ishtimāl aṣ-ṣammā*ᵓ is to envelop oneself in a single robe in which one envelops oneself, and so expose one's private parts on the side from which one raises one's robe. *Iḥtibā*ᵓ[159] in a single garment is similar."

٣٧ باب الزهد والتواضع

37. Doing without and Humbling Oneself

٩٢٤ أخبرنا مالك، أخبرنا عبد الله بن دينار، أن ابن عمر أخبره: أن رسول الله صلى الله عليه وسلم كان يأتي قُبَاءَ راكباً وماشياً.

924. Mālik informed us: "ᶜAbdullāh ibn Dīnār informed us that Ibn ᶜUmar informed him that the Messenger of Allah ﷺ used to come to Qubāᵓ mounted and walking."

٩٢٥ أخبرنا مالك، أخبرنا إسحاق بن عبد الله بن أبي طلحة: أن أنس بن مالك حدَّثه هذه الأحاديث الأربعة، قال أنس: رأيت عمر بن الخطاب وهو يومئذ أمير المؤمنين قد رَقَّع بين كتفيه برقاعٍ ثلاث، لَبَّد بعضَها فوق بعض، وقال أنس: وقد رأيتُ يُطْرَحُ له صاعُ تمرٍ فيأكله حتى يأكلِ حَشَفَه، قال أنس: وسمعت عمر بن الخطاب رضي الله عنه يوماً، و خرجت معه حتى دخل حائطاً، فسمعته يقول: و بيني وبينه جدار وهو في جوف الحائط: عُمر بن الخطاب أمير المؤمنين بخٍ بخْ والله يا ابن الخطاب لتتَّقِيَنَّ الله أو ليُعذِّبنَّك، قال أنس: وسمعت عمر بن الخطاب وسلَّم عليه رجل، فردَّ عليه السلام، ثم سألَ عمر الرجلَ: كيف أنت؟ قال الرجل: أحمَد الله إليك، قال عمر رضي الله عنه: هذه أردتُ منك.

925. Mālik informed us: "Isḥāq ibn ᶜAbdullāh ibn Abī Ṭalḥah informed us that Anas ibn Mālik narrated to him these four *aḥādīth*. Anas said, 'I saw ᶜUmar ibn al-Khaṭṭāb, and he at that time was the Amīr al-Muᵓminīn, and he had patched [his garment] between his shoulders with three patches stuck one on top of the other.' Anas said, 'I saw a *sa*ᶜ of dates being put before him and he ate them, even the poor quality dates and dry ones.' Anas said, 'I heard ᶜUmar ibn al-Khaṭṭāb ؓ once, when I had gone out with him

and he entered an orchard, and I heard him saying while there was a wall between me and him and he was inside the orchard, "ᶜUmar ibn al-Khaṭṭāb Amīr al-Mu'minīn, wonderful! wonderful! Ibn al-Khaṭṭāb, you must fear Allah or He will punish you."' Anas said, 'I heard ᶜUmar ibn al-Khaṭṭāb when a man greeted him and he returned the greeting, and then ᶜUmar asked the man, "How are you?" and the man said, "I praise Allah to you." ᶜUmar ﷺ said, "This I wanted from you."'"

٩٢٦ أخبرنا مالك، أخبرنا هشام بن عروة، عن أبيه قال: قالت عائشة: كان عمر بن الخطاب يبعث إلينا بأحظّائنا من الأكارع والرؤوس.

926. Mālik informed us: "Hishām ibn ᶜUrwah informed us that his father said, 'ᶜĀ'ishah said, "ᶜUmar ibn al-Khaṭṭāb used to send us our portions of sheep's trotters and heads."'"

٩٢٧ أخبرنا مالك، أخبرني يحيى بن سعيد، أنه سمع القاسم. يقول: سمعت أسلم مولى عمر بن الخطاب رضي الله تعالى عنه يقول: خرجت مع عمر بن الخطاب وهو يريد الشام، حتى إذا دنا من الشام أناخ عمر، وذهب لحاجة، قال أسلم: فطرحت فَرْوَتي بين شقَّي رَحْلي، فلما فرغ عمر عَمَدَ إلى بعيري فركبه على الفروة وركب أسلم بعيرَه، فخرجا يسيران حتى لقيهما أهل الأرض، يتلقَّوْن عمر، قال أسلم: فلما دنَوْا منا أشَرْتُ لهم إلى عمر، فجعلوا يتحدثون بينهم، قال عمر: تطمَحُ أبصارُهم إلى مراكب مَن لا خلاق لهم، يريد مراكب العجم.

927. Mālik informed us: "Yaḥyā ibn Saᶜīd informed me that he heard al-Qāsim saying, 'I heard Aslam the *mawlā* of ᶜUmar ibn al-Khaṭṭāb ﷺ saying, "I went out with ᶜUmar ibn al-Khaṭṭāb when he intended to go to Shām. When he was near Shām ᶜUmar made his mount sit and went off to relieve himself." Aslam said, "I cast my garment between the two sides of my saddle. When ᶜUmar had finished he deliberately went to my camel and mounted it on top of my garment," and Aslam rode on his [ᶜUmar's camel]. They continued travelling until the people of the land [Shām] met them coming out to receive ᶜUmar. Aslam said, "When they drew near I pointed them to ᶜUmar, and they began discussing among themselves. ᶜUmar said, 'Their eyes hoped to see the mounts of those who have no portions [in the next life [*ākhirah*]],'" meaning the mounts of [the *kāfir* kings of] the non-Arabs [such as the Roman and Persian kings].'"

٩٢٨ أخبرنا مالك، أخبرنا يحيى بن سعيد، قال: كان عمر بن الخطاب يأكل خبزاً مفتوتاً بسمن، فدعا رجلاً من أهل البادية فجعل يأكل ويتّبعُ باللقمة وَضَرَ الصحفة، فقال له عمر: كأنك مُقْفِرٌ، قال: والله ما رأيت سمناً ولا رأيت أكلاً به منذ كذا وكذا، فقال عمر رضي الله عنه: لا آكل السمن حتى يُحيِي الناسُ من أول ما أُحْيَوا.

928. Mālik informed us: "Yaḥyā ibn Saᶜīd informed us, 'ᶜUmar ibn al-Khaṭṭāb used to eat broken bread with clarified butter. He invited a man from the countryside, and he began to eat using the pieces of bread to wipe up the grease on the platter. ᶜUmar said to him, "It is as if you are in need." He said,

"By Allah! I have not seen clarified butter nor have I seen any food with it since such-and-such [a time]." ᶜUmar ﷺ said, "I will not eat clarified butter until people are given [a pleasant] life as they were first given life [with the return of rain and thus crops, etc.]"'"

٣٨ باب الحبّ في الله

38. Love for the Sake of Allah

٩٢٩ أخبرنا مالك، أخبرنا إسحاق بن عبد الله بن أبي طلحة، عن أنس بن مالك : أن أعرابياً أتى رسول الله صلى الله عليه وسلم فقال: يا رسول الله متى الساعة ؟ قال : وما أعددْتَ لها؟ قال: لا شيء ، والله إني لقليل الصيام والصلاة وإني لأحبُّ الله ورسوله، قال : إنك مع من أحببتَ.

929. Mālik informed us: "Isḥāq ibn ᶜAbdullāh ibn Abī Ṭalḥah informed us from Anas ibn Mālik that a bedouin came to the Messenger of Allah ﷺ and asked, 'Messenger of Allah, when is the Hour?' He said, 'What have you prepared for it?' He answered, 'Nothing. By Allah! I have little fasting and prayer, and I love Allah and His Messenger.' He said, 'You are with whomever you love.'"[164]

٣٩ باب فضل المعروف والصدقة

39. The Merit of Good Treatment and *Ṣadaqah*

٩٣٠ أخبرنا مالك، أخبرنا أبو الزِّناد ، عن الأعرج، عن أبي هريرة، قال: قال رسول الله ﷺ : ليس المسكين بالطَّوّاف الذي يطوف على الناس، تردُّه اللقمةُ واللقمتان، والتمرة والتمرتان، قالوا : فما المسكين يا رسول الله؟ قال: الذي ما عنده ما يُغْنيه ولا يُفطَن له فيُتصدَّق عليه ، ولا يقوم فيسأل الناس .

930. Mālik informed us: "Abu'z-Zinād informed us from al-Aᶜraj that Abū Hurayrah said, 'The Messenger of Allah ﷺ said, "The bereft person is not the one who continually goes around people and who is satisfied by a morsel or two, or a date or two." They asked, "Then who is the bereft person, Messenger of Allah?" He answered, "The person who does not have enough to suffice him, but he is not noticed and so is not given *ṣadaqah,* and he does not get up and ask people."'"

قال محمد: هذا أحقُّ بالعطية، وأيهما أعطيتَه زكاتك أجزاك ذلك. وهو قول أبي حنيفة والعامة من فقهائنا.

Muḥammad said: "This one has more right to be given something, but whichever of the two you give your *zakāh to,* that will be accepted of you, and that is the verdict of Abū Ḥanīfah and of our *fuqahā'* in general."

٩٣١ أخبرنا مالك، أخبرنا زيد بن أسلم، عن معاذ بن عمرو بن سعيد، عن معاذ؟، عن جدّته: أن رضي الله عنه صلى الله عليه وسلم قال: يا نساء المؤمنات ، لا تحقِرَنّ إحداكن لجارتها ولو كُراع شاة مُحرق.

931. Mālik informed us: "Zayd ibn Aslam informed us from Muᶜādh ibn ᶜAmr ibn Saᶜīd from Muᶜādh[165] from his paternal grandmother that the Messenger of Allah ﷺ said, 'Believing [*mu᾽mināt*] women! Let none of you despise [to give to or receive a gift from] her female neighbour even if it is only a roasted sheep's trotter.'"

٩٣٢ أخبرنا مالك، أخبرنا زيد بن أسلم، عن أبي بُجَيْد الأنصاري ثم الحارثي، عن جدّته: أن رسول الله صلى الله عليه وسلم قال: ردّوا المسكين ولو بظِلْفٍ مُحرقٍ.

932. Mālik informed us: "Zayd ibn Aslam informed us from Abū Bujayd al-Anṣārī and, moreover, al-Ḥārithī from his paternal grandmother that the Messenger of Allah ﷺ said, 'Give to the poor person even if only a roasted trotter [of a cow, sheep or goat].'"

٩٣٣ أخبرنا مالك، أخبرنا سُمَيّ عن أبي صالح السمّان، عن أبي هريرة، عن رسول الله صلى الله عليه وسلم: بينما رجل يمشي بطريق فاشتدّ عليه العطش فوجد بئراً فنزل فيها، فشرب ثم خرج، فإذا كلب يلهث يأكل الثرى من العطش فقال: لقد بلغ هذا الكلب من العطش مثل الذي بلغ بي، فنزل البئر فملأ خُفّه ثم أمسك الخفَّ بفيه حتى رَقِيَ فسقي الكلب، فشكر الله له فغفر له، قالوا: يا رسول الله، وإنّ لنا في البهائم لأجراً؟ قالَ: في كل ذَات كَبِد رطبة أجر.

933. Mālik informed us: "Sumayy informed us from Abū Ṣāliḥ as-Sammān from Abū Hurayrah from the Messenger of Allah ﷺ 'While a man was walking on the road he became terribly thirsty and then he found a well, and so he climbed down into it and drank. Then he came out and found a dog panting, eating the soil from thirst. So he said, "This dog is as thirsty as I was," and so he climbed down into the well and filled his leathern sock, held it tight in his mouth until he had climbed out and gave the dog to drink. Allah accepted his action and forgave him.' They asked, 'Messenger of Allah, do we have a reward for beasts?' He answered, 'For every moist [living] thing possessing a liver there is a reward.'"

٤٠ باب حق الجار

40. The Neighbour's Rights

٩٣٤ أخبرنا مالك، أخبرنا يحيى بن سعيد، أخبرني أبو بكر بن محمد بن عمرو بن حزم، أن عَمْرة حدّثته: أنها سمعت عائشة تقول: سمعت رسول الله صلى الله عليه وسلم يقول: ما زال جبرئيل يُوصيني بالجار حتى ظننتُ لَيُوَرِّثَنّه.

934. Mālik informed us: "Yaḥyā ibn Saᶜīd informed us, 'Abū Bakr ibn Muḥammad ibn ᶜAmr ibn Ḥazm informed me that ᶜAmrah narrated to him that she heard ᶜĀ᾽ishah saying, "I heard the Messenger of Allah ﷺ saying, 'Jibril continued to advise me about the neighbour so much that I thought that he would make him an heir.'"'"

٤١ باب اكتتاب العلم

41. Recording Knowledge

٩٣٥ أخبرنا مالك أخبرنا يحيى بن سعيد أن عمر بن عبد العزيز كتب إلى أبي بكر بن عمرو بن حزم: أن انظر ما كان من حديث رسول الله صلى الله عليه وسلم أو سنته أو حديث عمر أو نحو هذا فاكتبه لي فإني قد خفت دروس العلم وذهاب العلماء.

935. Mālik informed us: "Yaḥyā ibn Saᶜīd informed us that ᶜUmar ibn ᶜAbd al-ᶜAzīz wrote to Abū Bakr ibn ᶜAmr ibn Ḥazm: 'Look and see what there is of the *ḥadīth* of the Messenger of Allah ﷺ or his *Sunnah,* or *ḥadīth* of ᶜUmar or the like of this and write it to me, because I am afraid of the obliteration of knowledge and the departure of the people of knowledge.'"

قال محمد: وبهذا نأخذ ولا نرى بكتابة العلم بأسا وهو قول أبي حنيفة رحمه الله.

Muḥammad said: "We adhere to this. We see no harm in writing knowledge down, and that is the verdict of Abū Ḥanīfah, may Allah have mercy on him."

٤٢ باب الخضاب

42. Dyeing Hair

٩٣٦ أخبرنا مالك، أخبرنا يحيى بن سعيد، أخبرنا محمد بن إبراهيم، عن أبي سلمة ابن عبد الرحمن، أن عبد الرحمن بن الأسود بن عبد يغوث كان جليساً لنا، وكان أبيض اللحية والرأس، فغدا عليهم ذات يوم، وقد حمّرها، فقال له القوم: هذا أحسن، فقال: إن أمّي عائشة زوج النبي صلى الله عليه وسلم أرسلت إليّ البارحة جاريتَها نُخَيْلَةَ فأقسمَتْ عليّ لأصبغنّ، فأخبرتني أن أبا بكر رضي الله عنه كان يصبغ.

936. Mālik informed us: "Yaḥyā ibn Saᶜīd informed us, 'Muḥammad ibn Ibrāhīm informed us from Abū Salamah ibn ᶜAbd ar-Raḥmān that, "ᶜAbd ar-Raḥmān ibn al-Aswad ibn ᶜAbd Yaghūth was sitting with us, and he had a white beard and head. One day He came to them one morning and he had reddened it. People said to him, 'This is better.' He said, 'My mother ᶜĀʾishah the wife of the Prophet ﷺ sent her servant-girl Nukhaylah as a messenger to me yesterday adjuring me to dye it, and she informed me that Abū Bakr ؓ used to dye [his hair and beard].'""'

قال محمد: لا نرى بالخضاب بالوَسَمة والحنّاء والصُّفْرة بأساً، وإن تركه أبيض فلا بأس بذلك، كلُّ ذلك حسن.

Muḥammad said: "We do not think that in dyeing [the hair and beard] with indigo, henna and yellow [apart from Saffron] there is any harm, and if someone leaves it white, there is no harm in that. All of that is good."

٤٣ باب الولي يستقرض من مال اليتيم

43. A Guardian Investing the Property of an Orphan

٩٣٧ أخبرنا مالك، أخبرنا يحيى بن سعيد قال: سمعت القاسم بن محمد يقول: جاء رجل إلى ابن عباس ﷺ فقال له: إن لي يتيماً وله إبل فأشرب من لبن إبله؟ قال له ابن عباس: إن كنتَ تبغي ضالَّة إبله، وتَهْنَأ جَرْبَاها وتليط حوضها، وتسقيها يوم وِرْدها فاشرب غير مضر بنَسْلٍ، ولا ناهك في حَلَب.

937. Mālik informed us: "Yaḥyā ibn Saᶜīd informed us, 'I heard al-Qāsim ibn Muḥammad saying, "A man came to Ibn ᶜAbbās, ﷺ and said to him, 'I have an orphan and he owns some camels, so may I drink from his camels' milk?' Ibn ᶜAbbās said to him, 'If you search for his stray camels, smear them with pitch against mange, plaster and repair their watering troughs, give them to drink on the day they come to drink, then you may drink but without harming the [camels'] progeny nor consuming the milk completely.'"'"

قال محمد: بلغنا أن عمر بن الخطاب رضي الله عنه ذكر والي اليتيم، فقال: إن استغنى استعفَّ، وإن افتقر أكل بالمعروف قرضاً. بلغنا عن سعيد بن جبير فسرَّ هذه الآية (ومن كان غنيّاً فلْيَسْتَعْفِفْ ومَن كان فقيراً ليأكل بالمَعْرُوف) قال: قرضاً.

Muḥammad said: "It has reached us[166] that ᶜUmar ibn al-Khaṭṭāb ﷺ mentioned the guardian of an orphan and he said, 'If he is independently wealthy he should abstain, but if he is in need he may eat [from the orphans' property] considering it as a loan.' It has reached us that Saᶜīd ibn Jubayr explained this *āyah*, 'Those who are wealthy should abstain from it altogether. Those who are poor should use it sensibly and correctly,' (Sūrat an-Nisa: 6) and he said, 'As a loan.'"

٩٣٨ أخبرنا سفيان الثوري، عن أبي إسحاق، عن صلَة بن زُفَر: أن رجلاً أتى عبد الله بن مسعود رضي الله عنه فقال: أوصني إلى يتيم، فقال: لا تشتَرِيَنّ من ماله شيئاً ولا تستقرض من ماله شيئاً.

والاستعفاف عن ماله عندنا أفضل. وهو قول أبي حنيفة والعامَّة من فقهائنا.

938. Sufyān ath-Thawrī informed us from Abī Isḥāq from Ṣilah ibn Zufar that a man came to ᶜAbdullāh ibn Masᶜūd ﷺ and said, "Give me counsel about the orphan," and he said, "Do not buy anything with his property, and do not take a loan of anything from his property."

[Muḥammad said:] "Abstaining from his property is preferable to us, and that is the verdict of Abū Ḥanīfah and of our *fuqahā᾽* in general."

٤٤ باب الرجل ينظر إلى عورة الرجل.

44. A Man Looking at the Private Parts of another Man

٩٣٩ أخبرنا مالك، أخبرنا يحيى بن سعيد، قال: سمعت عبد الله بن عامر يقول: بينا أنا أغتسل ويتيم كان في حَجْر أبي، يَصُبُّ أحدنا على صاحبه إذ طلع علينا عامر ونحن كذلك، فقال: ينظر بعضكم إلى عورة بعض؟ والله إني كنت لأحسبكم خيراً منّا. قلت: قوم وُلِدوا في الإسلام لم يُولَدوا في شيء من الجاهلية، والله لأظنّكم الخَلْفَ.

939. Mālik informed us: "Yaḥyā ibn Sa^c^īd informed us, 'I heard ^c^Abdullāh ibn ^c^Āmir saying, "While I was doing *ghusl*, and an orphan was in the care of my father, one of us pouring the water for the other, ^c^Āmir came upon us while we were like that. He said, 'Are you looking at each other's private parts? By Allah! I had thought you better than us. I said [to myself], "A people who were born in Islam and were not born into anything of the *Jāhiliyyah*. By Allah! I think you are the [evil generation] which is coming.[167]"'"'"

قال محمد : لا ينبغي للرجل أن ينظر إلى عورة أخيه المسلم إلاّ من ضرورة لمداواة ونحوه .

Muḥammad said: "A man ought not to look at the private parts of his brother Muslim unless because of some overriding necessity such as for medical treatment and the like."

٤٥ باب النفخ في الشُّرْب

45. Blowing into a Drink

٩٤٠ أخبرنا مالك، أخبرنا أيوب بن حبيب مولى سعد بن أبي وقّاص، عن أبي المثنى الجهني قال: كنت عند مَرْوان بن الحكم فدخل أبو سعيد الخُدري على مروان، فقال له مروان : أسمعتَ من رسول الله صلى الله عليه وسلم أنه نهى عن النفخ في الشراب؟ قال: نعم ، فقال له رجل: يا رسول الله، إني لا أرْوَى من نَفَس واحد، قال: فأبِنْ القَدَحَ عن فيك ثم تنفَّس، قال : فإني أرى القذاة فيه، قال: فأهرِقْها .

940. Mālik informed us: "Ayyūb ibn Ḥabīb the *mawlā* of Sa^c^īd ibn Abī Waqqāṣ informed us that Abu'l-Muthannā al-Juhanī said, 'I was with Marwān ibn al-Ḥakam when Abū Sa^c^īd al-Khudrī came in to see Marwān. Marwān asked him, "Have you heard that the Messenger of Allah ﷺ forbade blowing into a drink?" He answered, "Yes. A man said to him, 'Messenger of Allah, I am not quenched in one breath.' He said, 'Take the vessel away from your mouth and then take a breath.' He said, '[What if] I see some bits [of dirt] in it?' He answered, 'Tip it out.'"'"

٤٦ باب ما يُكْرَهُ من مصافحة النساء

46. The Disapproval of Shaking Hands with Women

٩٤١ أخبرنا مالك، أخبرنا محمد بن المنكدر، عن أُمَيْمَة بنت رُقَيْقَة أنها قالت : أتيتُ رسول الله صلى الله عليه وسلم في نسوة تُبَايعُه فقلنا: يا رسول الله، نُبايُعك على أن لا نُشرك بالله شيئاً ، ولا نسرق، ولا نزني، ولا نقتل أولادنا، ولا نأتي ببهتان نَفْتريه بين أيدينا وأرجلنا، ولا نعصيك في معروف ، قال رسول الله صلى الله عليه وسلم: فيما استطعتُنَّ ، وأطقْتُنَّ، قلنا : الله ورسوله أرحم بنا منَّا بأنفسنا، هَلُمَّ نُبايعك يا رسول الله صلى الله عليه وسلم، قال : إنِّي لا أُصافحُ النساءَ ، إنما قولي لمائة امرأة كقولي لامرأة واحدة، أو مثل قولي لامرأة واحدة .

941. Mālik informed us: "Muḥammad ibn al-Munkadir informed us that Umaymah bint Ruqayqah said, 'I came to the Messenger of Allah ﷺ among some women who were pledging allegiance to him, and we said, "Messenger of Allah, we pledge allegiance to you that we will not associate anything with Allah as a partner, we will not steal, we will not commit adultery, we will not kill our children, we will not give a false ascription of paternity, and we will not disobey you in respect of what is right." The Messenger of Allah ﷺ said, "As much as you are able and have the capacity for." We said, "Allah and His Messenger are more merciful to us than we are to ourselves. Come let us pledge allegiance to you, Messenger of Allah." He said, "I do not shake hands with women. My word to a hundred women is as my word to a single woman," or "like my word to a single woman."'"

٤٧ باب فضائل أصحاب رسول الله صلى الله عليه وسلم

47. The Merits of the Companions of the Messenger of Allah ﷺ

٩٤٢ أخبرنا مالك، أخبرنا يحيى بن سعيد، أنه سمع سعيد بن المسيّب يقول: سمعت سعد بن أبي وقّاص يقول: لقد جَمَعَ لي رسول الله صلى الله عليه وسلم أَبَوَيْه يوم أُحُد.

942. Mālik informed us: "Yaḥyā ibn Saʿīd informed us that he heard Saʿīd ibn al-Musayyab saying, 'I heard Saʿd ibn Abī Waqqāṣ saying, "The Messenger of Allah ﷺ united together his parents [in the oath, 'may my mother and father be your ransom'] for me on the day of Uḥud."'"

٩٤٣ أخبرنا مالك، أخبرنا عبد الله بن دينار، قال: قال ابن عمر رضي الله عنهما: بعث رسول الله صلى الله عليه وسلم بَعْثاً فأمَّر عليهم أسامة بن زيد، فطعن الناس في إِمْرَته، فقام رسول الله صلى الله عليه وسلم، وقال: إنْ تطعنوا في إِمْرَته فقد كنتم تطعنون في إِمْرَة أبيه من قبلُ، وأيْمُ الله إنْ كان لخَليقاً للإمْرة، وإنْ كان لَمِنْ أحبّ الناس إليّ من بعده.

943. Mālik informed us: "ʿAbdullāh ibn Dīnār informed us, 'ʿAbdullāh ibn ʿUmar ﷺ said, "The Messenger of Allah ﷺ sent out an expedition and he made Usāmah ibn Zayd their Amīr, but people spoke disparagingly about his being given the command. The Messenger of Allah ﷺ stood and said, 'If you speak disparagingly about his being given the command, you also spoke disparagingly about the command of his father before him. By Allah! He is certainly worthy of command, and he is certainly one of the most beloved people to me after him [his father].'"'"

٩٤٤ أخبرنا مالك، عن أبي النضر مولى عمر بن عبد الله بن معْمَر، عن عُبَيد يعني ابن حنين، عن أبي سعيد الخُدري: أن رسول الله صلى الله عليه وسلم جلس على المنبر فقال: إن عبداً خيَّره الله تعالى بين أن يُؤْتيَه من زهرة الدنيا ما شاء، وبين ما عنده، فاختار العبد ما عنده، فبكى أبو بكر رضي الله عنه، وقال: فَدَيْناك بآبائنا وأمهاتنا، قال: فعجبنا له، وقال الناس: انظروا إلى هذا الشيخ يُخبر رسول الله صلى الله عليه وسلم بخبر عبدٍ خيّره الله تعالى، وهو يقول: فديناك بآبائنا وأمهاتنا.

فكان رسول الله صلى الله عليه وسلم هو المُخَيَّر ، وكان أبو بكر رضي الله عنه أعلَمنا به . وقال رسول الله صلى الله عليه وسلم: إن أمنَّ الناس عليّ في صحبته وماله أبو بكر، ولو كنت متَّخذاً خليلاً لاتَّخذتُ أبا بكر خليلاً ولكن أخوة الإسلام، ولا يُبْقَيَنَّ في المسجد خَوخة إلاّ خوخة أبي بكر.

944. Mālik informed us from Abu'n-Naḍr the *mawlā* of ᶜUmar ibn ᶜAbdullāh ibn Muᶜammar from ᶜUbayd, meaning Ibn Ḥunayn, from Abū Saᶜīd al-Khudrī that the Messenger of Allah ﷺ sat on the *minbar* and said, "A slave has been given the choice by Allah, exalted is He, between Him giving him whatever he wants of the blossom of the world and between that which is with Him, and the slave has chosen what is with Him," and so Abū Bakr ﷺ wept and said, "We would ransom you with our fathers and our mothers." He [Abū Saᶜīd al-Khudrī] said, "We were amazed at him, and people said, 'Look at this shaykh whom the Messenger of Allah ﷺ informs about a slave whom Allah, exalted is He, has given a choice and he says, "We would ransom you with our fathers and our mothers"!' And the Messenger of Allah ﷺ was the one who had been given the choice, and Abū Bakr ﷺ was the most knowledgeable of us about it. The Messenger of Allah ﷺ said, 'The most generous of people towards me in his companionship and with his property has been Abū Bakr, and if I were to take an intimate friend I would have taken Abū Bakr as an intimate friend, but it is the brotherhood of Islam. Let none of the small doors into the mosque remain except that of Abū Bakr.'"

٩٤٥ أخبرنا مالك، أخبرنا ابن شهاب، عن إسماعيل بن محمد بن ثابت الأنصاري، أن ثابت بن قيس بن شَمَّاس الأنصاري، قال: يا رسول الله، لقد خَشيْتُ أن أكونَ قد هلكتُ قال: لِمَ ؟ قال: نهانا الله أن نُحبَّ أن نُحْمَدَ بما لم نَفْعَلْ، وأنا امرؤ أُحبّ الحمدَ ، ونهانا عن الخُيَلاء ، وأنا امرؤ أحبُّ الجمالَ ، ونهانا الله أن نرفعَ أصواتَنا فوق صوتكَ، وأنا رجلٌ جَهيرُ الصوت، فقال رسول الله صلى الله عليه وسلم: يا ثابت، أما تَرْضَى أن تعيش حَميداً ، وتُقْتَلَ شهيداً ، وتَدْخُلَ الجَنَّةَ .

945. Mālik informed us: "Ibn Shihāb informed us from Ismāᶜīl ibn Muḥammad ibn Thābit al-Anṣārī that Thābit ibn Qays ibn Shammas al-Anṣārī said, 'Messenger of Allah, I am afraid that I have perished!' He asked, 'Why?' He said, 'Allah forbids us loving to be praised for that which we have not done, and I am a man who loves praise. He forbids us to be vain and I am a man who loves beauty. Allah forbids us raising our voices over your voice and I am a man who has a loud voice.' The Messenger of Allah ﷺ said, 'Thābit, are you not content that while you live you are praised, that you will die as a *shahīd* and that you will enter the Garden?'"

٤٨ باب صفة النبي صلى الله عليه وسلم

48. The Description of the Prophet ﷺ

٩٤٦ أخبرنا مالك، أخبرنا ربيعة، عن أبي عبد الرحمن، أنه سمع أنس بن مالك يقول: كان رسول

الله صلى الله عليه وسلم: ليس بالطويل بالبائن ، ولا بالقصير، ولا بالأبيض الأمهق، وليس بالآدم، وليس بالجَعْد القَطَط، ولا بالسَّبط، بعثه الله على رأس أربعين سنة ، فأقام بمكة عشر سنين ، وبالمدينة عشر سنين، وتوفاه الله على رأس ستين سنة وليس في رأسه ولحيته عشرون شعرة بيضاء.

946. Mālik informed us: "Rabīʿah informed us that Abū ʿAbd ar-Raḥmān heard Anas ibn Mālik saying, 'The Messenger of Allah ﷺ was not excessively tall, nor was he short, and he was not curly haired, nor lank haired. Allah sent him at the beginning of [his] fortieth year, and he stayed in Makkah for ten years [after that] and in Madīnah for ten years. Allah took him back at the beginning of [his] sixtieth year, while there was not yet in his hair and beard twenty white hairs.'"[168]

٤٩ باب قبر النبي صلى الله عليه وسلم وما يُستحب من ذلك

49. The Grave of the Prophet ﷺ and what is Desirable with Respect to it

٩٤٧ أخبرنا مالك، أخبرنا عبد الله بن دينار، أن ابن عمر: كان إذا أراد سفراً ، أو قدم من سفر جاء قبر النبي صلى الله عليه وسلم فصلى عليه، ودعا ثم انصرف.

947. Mālik informed us: "ʿAbdullāh ibn Dīnār informed us that Ibn ʿUmar used – when he wanted to travel or returned from a journey – to come to the grave of the Prophet ﷺ and ask for blessings for him, make supplication and then leave."

قال محمد: هكذا ينبغي أن يفعله إذا قدم المدينة يأتي قبر النبي صلى الله عليه وسلم.

Muḥammad said: "That is what to be done, that when one comes to Madīnah one should visit the grave of the Prophet ﷺ."

٥٠ باب فضل الحياء

50. The Merit of Modesty

٩٤٨ أخبرنا مالك، عن ابن شهاب، عن علي بن حسين، يرفعه إلى النبي صلى الله عليه وسلم، قال: من حُسْن إسلام المرأ تركه ما لا يعنيه .

948. Mālik informed us from Ibn Shihāb from ʿAlī ibn Ḥusayn who attributed it to the Prophet ﷺ that he said "A part of the excellence of a man's Islam is his leaving what does not concern him."

قال محمد: هكذا ينبغي للمرء المسلم أن يكون تاركاً لما لا يعنيه.

Muḥammad said: "A Muslim man ought to abandon what does not concern him."

٩٤٩ أخبرنا مالك، أخبرنا سلمة بن صفوان الزرقي، عن يزيد بن طلحة الركاني، أن النبي صلى الله عليه وسلم قال: إنّ لكل دين خُلُقاً ، وخُلُق الإسلام الحياء.

949. Mālik informed us: "Salamah ibn Ṣafwān az-Zuraqī informed us from Yazīd ibn Ṭalḥah ar-Rukani that the Prophet ﷺ said, 'Every *dīn* has a natural disposition, and the natural disposition of Islam is modesty.'"

٩٥٠ أخبرنا مالك، أخبرنا مُخْبِرٌ، عن سالم بن عبد الله، عن ابن عمر: أن النبي صلى الله عليه وسلم مرّ على رجل يعظ أخاه في الحَياء، فقال رسول الله صلى الله عليه وسلم: دَعْه فإن الحياء من الإيمان.

950. Mālik informed us: "An informant informed us from Sālim ibn ᶜAbdullāh from Ibn ᶜUmar that the Prophet ﷺ passed a man who was admonishing his brother because of his modesty, and the Messenger of Allah ﷺ said, 'Leave him alone, because modesty is a part of *imān*.'"

٥١ باب حقّ الزوج على المرأة

51. The Husband's Right over his Wife

٩٥١ أخبرنا مالك، أخبرنا يحيى بن سعيد، أخبرني بَشير بن يسار، أن حُصَين بن مِحْصَن أخبره: أن عَمَّةً له أتت رسول الله ﷺ، وأنها زعمت أنه قال لها: أذات زوجٍ أنتِ؟ فقالت: نعم، فزعمت أنه قال لها: كيف أنتِ له؟ فقالت: ما آلوه إلا ما عجزْتُ عنه، قال: فانظري أين أنتِ منه، فإنما هو جنّتُك أو نارُك.

951. Mālik informed us: "Yaḥyā ibn Saᶜīd informed us, 'Bashīr ibn Yasār informed me that Ḥuṣayn ibn Miḥṣan informed him that a paternal aunt of his came to the Messenger of Allah ﷺ and that she claimed that he asked her, "Do you have a husband?" She answered, "Yes." Then she claimed that he asked her, "How are you towards him?" and that she said, "I only fall short in what I am incapable of doing." He said, "Then look to how you are in relation to him, because he is either your heaven or your hell."'"

٥٢ باب حقّ الضيافة

52. The Duty of Hospitality

٩٥٢ أخبرنا مالك، أخبرنا سعيد المَقْبُري، عن أبي شُرَيح الكعبي: أن رسول الله صلى الله عليه وسلم قال: من كان يؤمن بالله واليوم الآخر فَلْيُكْرِم ضيفه، جائزته يومٌ ولَيلة، والضيافة ثلاثة أيام، فما كان بعد ذلك فهو صدقة، ولا يحلّ له أن يَثْوي عنده حتى يُحرجَه.

952. Mālik informed us: "Saᶜīd al-Maqburī informed us from Abū Shurayḥ al-Kaᶜbī that the Messenger of Allah ﷺ said, 'Whoever believes in Allah and the Last Day then let him honour his guest generously. Going to one's utmost in being generous to him is for a day and a night, and [ordinary] hospitality is three days, and whatever comes after that is a *ṣadaqah*. It is not *ḥalāl* for him to reside with him so much that he causes him hardship.'"

٥٣ باب تشميت العاطس

53. Asking for Mercy for Someone who Sneezes

٩٥٣ أخبرنا مالك، أخبرنا عبد الله بن أبي بكر بن عمرو بن حزم، عن أبيه: أن رسول الله صلى الله

عليه وسلم قال: إن عَطَس فشمِّتْه ، ثم إن عطس فشمّته، ثم إن عطس فشمّته ثم إن عطس فقل له: إنك مضنوكٌ . قال عبد الله بن أبي بكر: لا أدري أبعد الثالثة أو الرابعة.

953. Mālik informed us: "ᶜAbdullāh ibn Abī Bakr ibn ᶜAmr ibn Ḥazm informed us from his father that the Messenger of Allah ﷺ said, 'If he sneezes, then ask for mercy for him. Then if he sneezes [again], ask for mercy for him. Then if he sneezes [again] say to him, "You have a cold."' ᶜAbdullāh ibn Abī Bakr said, 'I don't know if it is after the third or the fourth.'"

قال محمد: إذا عَطَس فشمِّتْه، ثم إن عطس فشمِّتْه، فإن لم تشمّته حتى يعطس مرتين أو ثلاثاً أجزاك أن تشمّته مرة واحدة.

Muḥammad said: "If he sneezes then ask for mercy for him, and if he sneezes again, then ask for mercy for him. If you don't ask for mercy for him until he sneezes twice or three times, it is enough that you ask for mercy for him once."

٥٤ باب الفرار من الطاعون

54. Fleeing from the Plague

٩٥٤ أخبرنا مالك، أخبرنا محمد بن المنكدر، أن عامر بن سعد بن أبي وقّاص أخبره، أن أسامة بن زيد أخبره: أن رسول الله صلى الله عليه وسلم قال: إن هذا الطاعون رِجْزٌ أُرْسِل على مَنْ كان قبلكم، أو أُرْسِل على بني إسرائيل شك ابن المنكدر في أيّهما قال فإذا سمعتم به بأرض فلا تدخلوا عليه وإن وقع في أرض فلا تخرجوا فراراً منه .

954. Mālik informed us: "Muḥammad ibn al-Munkadir informed us that ᶜĀmir ibn Saᶜd ibn Abī Waqqāṣ informed him that Usāmah ibn Zayd informed him that the Messenger of Allah ﷺ said, 'This plague is a punishment that was sent against those who were before you,' or 'it was sent against Banī Isrā᾽īl,' – Ibn al-Munkadir was unsure which of the two of them he said – 'so if you hear of it in a land then do not enter where it is, and if it happens in a land [where you are] do not leave it in flight from it.'"

قال محمد: هذا حديث معروف قد رُوي عن غير واحد ، فلا بأس إذا وقع بأرض أن لا يدخلها اجتناباً له.

Muḥammad said: "This is a well known *ḥadīth* which more than one person has narrated, so when it happens in a land, there is no harm in not entering it in order to avoid it."

٥٥ باب الغِيبة والبُهْتان

55. Backbiting and Slander

٩٥٥ أخبرنا مالك، أخبرنا الوليد بن عبد الله بن صيّاد، أن المطّلب بن عبد الله بن حَنْطَب المخزوميّ: أخبره أن رجلاً سأل رسول الله صلى الله عليه وسلم، ما الغيبة ؟ قال رسول الله صلى الله عليه وسلم:

أنْ تَذْكُرَ من المرء ما يكره أن يسمع، قال : يا رسول الله، وإن كان حقّاً ؟ قال رسول الله صلى الله عليه وسلم: إذا قلتَ باطلاً فذلك البهتان .

955. Mālik informed us: "Al-Walid ibn ᶜAbdullāh ibn Ṣayyād informed us that al-Muṭṭalib ibn ᶜAbdullāh ibn Ḥanṭab al-Makhzūmī informed him that a man asked the Messenger of Allah ﷺ 'What is backbiting?' The Messenger of Allah ﷺ said, 'That you mention about a man that which he would dislike to hear.' He asked, 'Messenger of Allah, even if it is true?' The Messenger of Allah ﷺ said, 'If you spoke falsely then that would be slander.'"

قال محمد : وبهذا نأخذ . لا ينبغي أن يذكر لأخيه المسلم الزَّلَّةَ تكون منه مما يَكْرَه، فأما صاحب الهوى المُتَعَالِنُ بهواه المتعرِّف به، والفاسق المتعالن بفسقه فلا بأس ، أن تذكر هذين بفعلهما . فإذا ذكرتَ من المسلم ما ليس فيه فهو البهتان، وهو الكذب .

Muḥammad said: "We adhere to this. One ought not to mention about one's brother Muslim some slip he has made which he dislikes. As for the person of erroneous opinions (*hawā*) who openly displays his erroneous views and seeks to be well known for them, or the depraved person who is open about his depravity, then there is no harm in mentioning these two and their actions. If you mention something about a Muslim which is not true then that is slander, which means it is a lie."

٥٦ باب النوادر

56. Unusual Matters

٩٥٦ أخبرنا مالك، أخبرنا أبو الزبير المكيّ، عن جابر بن عبد الله : أن رسول الله صلى الله عليه وسلم قال: أَغْلِقُوا الباب ، وأَوْكُوا السِّقاء، وأكفئوا الإِناء أو خمِّروا الإِناء وأطفئوا المصباح، فإن الشيطان لا يفتح غَلَقاً، ولا يَحُلّ وِكاءً، ولا يكشف إناءً، وإن الفُوَيْسِقَةَ تَضْرِم على الناس بيتَهم .

956. Mālik informed us: "Abu'z-Zubayr al-Makkī informed us from Jābir ibn ᶜAbdullāh that the Messenger of Allah ﷺ said, 'Lock the door, tie up the water-skin, turn the drinking vessel upside down – or cover the drinking vessel – and extinguish the lamp, because shayṭān cannot open what is locked, nor can he untie what is tied, and he cannot uncover the vessel. Also vermin [the rat and the mouse] set fire to people's houses [by tipping over lamps and candles].'"

٩٥٧ أخبرنا مالك، أخبرنا أبو الزِّناد، عن الأعرج، عن أبي هريرة قال : قال رسول الله صلى الله عليه وسلم: المسلم يأكل في مِعى والكافر يأكل في سبعة أمعاء .

957. Mālik informed us: "Abu'z-Zinād informed us from al-Aᶜraj that Abū Hurayrah said, 'The Messenger of Allah ﷺ said, "The Muslim eats in one intestine but the *kāfir* eats in seven intestines."'"

٩٥٨ أخبرنا مالك، أخبرنا صفوان بن سُلَيم يرفعه إلى رسول الله صلى الله عليه وسلم، أنه قال: الساعي على الأَرْمَلَةِ والمسكين، كالذي يجاهد في سبيل الله أو كالذي يصوم النهار ويقومُ الليل .

958. Mālik informed us: "Ṣafwān ibn Sulaym informed us, ascribing it to the Messenger of Allah ﷺ, that he said, 'The person who exerts himself on behalf of widows and the poor is like someone who fights in the way of Allah, or like someone who fasts during the day and stands in prayer at night.'"

٩٥٩ أخبرنا مالك، أخبرني ثور بن زيد الدّيلي، عن أبي الغيث مولى أبي مطيع، عن أبي هريرة، عن رسول الله صلى الله عليه وسلم مثلَ ذلك.

959. Mālik informed us: "Thawr ibn Zayd ad-Dīlī informed me from Abu'l-Ghayth the *mawlā* of Abū Muṭīᶜ from Abū Hurayrah from the Messenger of Allah ﷺ the like of that [*ḥadīth*]."

٩٦٠ أخبرنا مالك، أخبرنا محمد بن عبد الله بن صَعْصعة، أنه سمع سعيدَ بن يَسَار أبا الحُباب يقول: سمعت أبا هريرة يقول: قال رسول الله صلى الله عليه وسلم: من يُريد الله به خيراً يُصبْ منه.

960. Mālik informed us: "Muḥammad ibn ᶜAbdullāh ibn Ṣaᶜṣaᶜah informed us that he heard Saᶜīd ibn Yasār Abu'l-Ḥubāb saying, 'I heard Abū Hurayrah saying, "The Messenger of Allah ﷺ said, 'Whomever Allah wills good, He afflicts him [with illnesses and trials].'"'"

٩٦١ أخبرنا مالك، أخبرنا ابن شهاب، عن سالم وحمزة ابنَيْ عبد الله بن عمر، عن ابن عمر: أنّ رسول الله صلى الله عليه وسلم قال: إن الشؤم في المرأة والدار والفرس.

961. Mālik informed us: "Ibn Shihāb informed us from Sālim and Ḥamzah, the two sons of ᶜAbdullāh ibn ᶜUmar from Ibn ᶜUmar that the Messenger of Allah ﷺ said, 'Misfortune is in a woman, a house and a horse.'"[169]

قال محمد: إنما بلغنا أن النبي صلى الله عليه وسلم قال: إنْ كان الشؤم في شيء ففي الدار والمرأة والفرس.

Muḥammad said: "It has only reached us that the Prophet ﷺ said, 'If there is misfortune in anything, it is in a house, a woman and a horse.'"

٩٦٢ أخبرنا مالك، أخبرنا عبد الله بن دينار، قال: كنت مع عبد الله بن دينار، قال: كنت مع عبد الله بن عمر بالسوق عند دار خالد بن عقبة، فجاء رجل يريد أن يُناجيَه، وليس معه أحدٌ غيري وغير الرجل الذي يريد أن يُناجيَه، فدعا عبد الله بن عمر رجلاً آخر حتى كنّا أربعة قال: فقال لي وللرجل الذي دعا: استرخيا شيئاً فإني سمعتُ رسول الله صلى الله عليه وسلم يقول: لا يتناجى اثنان دون واحد.

962. Mālik informed us: "ᶜAbdullāh ibn Dīnār informed us, 'I was with ᶜAbdullāh ibn ᶜUmar in the market at the house of Khālid ibn ᶜUqbah, and a man came meaning to speak to him in confidence, but there was no one else with him but me and the man who wanted to speak to him in confidence. ᶜAbdullāh ibn ᶜUmar called another man so that we would be four [people].'" He [ᶜAbdullāh ibn Dīnār] said, "He [Ibn ᶜUmar] said to me and to the man he had called, 'Withdraw a little, because I heard the Messenger of Allah ﷺ saying, "Let not two [people] talk confidentially [meaning to] exclude others."'"

٩٦٣ أخبرنا مالك، أخبرنا عبد الله بن دينار، عن ابن عمر: أن رسول الله صلى الله عليه وسلم قال: إن من الشجر شجرةً لا يسقط ورقُها، وإنها مَثَلُ المسلم فحدِّثوني ما هي؟ قال عبد الله بن عمر: فوقع الناس في شجر البوادي، فوقع في نفسي أنها النخلة، قال: فاستحييتُ، فقالوا: حَدِّثْنا يا رسول الله ما هي؟ قال: النخلة، قال عبد الله: فحدَّثتُ عمر بن الخطاب بالذي وقع في نفسي من ذلك، فقال عمر: والله لأن تكون قُلْتَها أحبُّ إليَّ من أن يكون لي كذا وكذا.

963. Mālik informed us: "ᶜAbdullāh ibn Dīnār informed us from Ibn ᶜUmar that the Messenger of Allah ﷺ said, 'Of trees there is one whose leaves do not fall, and it is like the Muslim, so tell me what it is.' ᶜAbdullāh ibn ᶜUmar said, 'People fell into discussing the trees of the countryside, but it occurred to me that it was the date-palm.' He said, 'But I was shy, and they said, "Tell us, Messenger of Allah, what it is." He said, "It is the date-palm."' ᶜAbdullāh said, 'I told ᶜUmar ibn al-Khaṭṭāb about what had occurred to me, and ᶜUmar said, "By Allah! If you had said it, it would have been more beloved to me than that I should have such-and-such."'"

٩٦٤ أخبرنا مالك، أخبرنا عبد الله بن دينار، قال: قال ابن عمر: قال رسول الله صلى الله عليه وسلم: غفار غفر الله لها، وأسلم: سالمها الله وعُصَيَّةُ: عصت الله ورسولَه.

964. Mālik informed us: "ᶜAbdullāh ibn Dīnār informed us, 'Ibn ᶜUmar said, "The Messenger of Allah ﷺ said [about the following three tribes], 'Ghifār, may Allah forgive (*ghafara*) them; Aslam, may Allah make them at peace (*sālama*); and ᶜUṣayyah have disobeyed (*ᶜaṣat*) Allah and His Messenger.'"'"

٩٦٥ أخبرنا مالك، أخبرنا عبد الله بن دينار، عن ابن عمر، قال: كنا حين نبايع رسول الله صلى الله عليه وسلم على السمع والطاعة يقول لنا: فيما استطعتم.

965. Mālik informed us: "ᶜAbdullāh ibn Dīnār informed us that Ibn ᶜUmar said, 'When we used to pledge allegiance to the Messenger of Allah ﷺ to hear and obey, he would say to us, "In that which you are able."'"

٩٦٦ أخبرنا مالك، أخبرنا عبد الله بن دينار، عن ابن عمر قال: قال رسول الله صلى الله عليه وسلم لأصحاب الحِجْر: لا تَدْخلوا على هؤلاء القوم المعذَّبين إلاَّ أن تكونوا باكين فإن لم تكونوا باكين فلا تدخلوا عليهم أنْ يصيبكم مثلَ ما أصابهم.

966. Mālik informed us: "ᶜAbdullāh ibn Dīnār informed us that Ibn ᶜUmar said, 'The Messenger of Allah ﷺ said about the people of Ḥijr,[170] "Do not go amongst these people who have been punished unless you are weeping. Then if you are not weeping, do not go amongst them in case the like of what happened to them should happen to you."'"

٩٦٧ أخبرنا مالك، أخبرنا عبد الله بن عبد الرحمن بن معمر، عن أبي مُحَيريز قال: أدركتُ ناساً من أصحاب رسول الله صلى الله عليه وسلم يقولون: منْ أشراط الساعة المعلومة المعروفة أن ترى الرجل يدخل البيت لا يشُكُّ من رآه أن يدخله لسوء غيرَ أن الجُدُر تُواريه.

967. Mālik informed us: "ᶜAbdullāh ibn ᶜAbd ar-Raḥmān ibn Muᶜammar informed us from Abū Muḥayrīz that he said, 'I came across people who

were Companions of the Messenger of Allah ﷺ who said, "One of the well known and well recognised signs of the Hour is that a man will be seen entering a house, no one who sees him doubting that he enters it for evil, except that the walls veil him.'""

٩٦٨ أخبرنا مالك، أخبرني عمّي أبو سهيل قال: سمعتُ أبي يقول: ما اعرف شيئاً مما كان الناس عليه إلاّ النداء بالصلاة.

968. Mālik informed us: "My paternal uncle Abū Suhayl informed me, 'I heard my father saying, "I do not recognise anything of that which people [the Companions] used to do except for the call to prayer.'""

٩٦٩ أخبرنا مالك، أخبرني مُخْبِرٌ: أن رسول الله صلى الله عليه وسلم قال: إني أُنَسىَّ لأَسُنَّ.

969. Mālik informed us: "An informant informed me that the Messenger of Allah ﷺ said, 'I am made to forget so that I can set the *Sunnah* [for cases of forgetfulness].'"

٩٧٠ أخبرنا مالك، بن أنس، أخبرنا ابن شهاب الزهري، عن عبادة بن تميم، عن عمه عتبة: أنه رأى رسول الله صلى الله عليه وسلم مستلقياً في المسجد، واضعاً إحدى يديه على الأخرى.

970. Mālik ibn Anas informed us: "Ibn Shihāb az-Zuhrī informed us from ᶜUbādah ibn Tamīm that his paternal uncle ᶜUtbah saw the Messenger of Allah ﷺ lying down upon his back in the mosque with one hand placed on the other."

٩٧١ أخبرنا مالك، أخبرنا ابن شهاب: أن عمر بن الخطاب، وعثمان بن عفان رضي الله تعالى عنهما كانا يفعلان ذلك.

971. Mālik informed us: "Ibn Shihāb informed us that ᶜUmar ibn al-Khaṭṭāb and ᶜUthmān ibn ᶜAffān ؓ both used to do that."

قال محمد: لا نرى بهذا بأساً. وهو قول أبي حنيفة رحمه الله.

Muḥammad said: "We see no harm in this, and it is the verdict of Abū Ḥanīfah, may Allah have mercy on him."

٩٧٢ أخبرنا مالك، أخبرنا يحيى بن سعيد قال: قيل لعائشة رضي الله عنها: لو دُفِنْتِ معهم قال: قالت: إني إذاً لأَنا المبتدئة بعملي.

972. Mālik informed us: "Yaḥyā ibn Saᶜīd said to us and he said, 'Someone said to ᶜĀ'ishah ؓ "If only you were to be buried along with them [the Prophet ﷺ Abū Bakr and ᶜUmar ؓ]!" She answered, "Then my own deeds would start all over again.'"'"[171]

٩٧٣ أخبرنا مالك قال: قال سلمة لعمر بن عبد الله: ما شأن عثمان بن عفان لم يُدْفن معهم؟ فسكت ثم أعاد عليه قال: إن الناس كانوا يومئذ متشاغلين.

973. Mālik informed us: saying, "Salamah said to ᶜUmar ibn ᶜAbdullāh, 'What was it with ᶜUthmān ibn ᶜAffān that he was not buried with them?' But he was silent until he asked him again and then he said, 'People at that time were [too] busy with each other.'"

٩٧٤ أخبرنا مالك، أخبرنا زيد بن أسلم، عن عطاء بن يسار : أن النبي صلى الله عليه وسلم قال : من وُقِيَ شَرَّ اثنين وَلَجَ الجنَّة وأعاد ذلك ثلاث مرات مَنْ وُقِيَ شَرَّ اثنين ولج الجنة ما بين لَحْيَيْه وما بين رجليه .

974. Mālik informed us: "Zayd ibn Aslam informed us from ʿAṭāʾ ibn Yasār that the Prophet ﷺ said, 'Whoever is protected from the evil of two things will enter the Garden,' and he repeated it three times, 'whoever is protected from the evil of two things will enter the Garden: that which is between his jaws and that which is between his legs.'"

٩٧٥ أخبرنا مالك قال: بلغني أن عيسى بن مريم عليه السلام كان يقول : لا تُكثروا الكلام بغير ذكر الله، فتقسُوَ قلوبُكم فإن القلب القاسي بعيد من الله تعالى ولكن لا تعلمون ولا تنظروا في ذنوب الناس كأنكم أرباب وانظروا فيها كأنكم عبيد، فإنما الناس مُبتَلًى ومُعافًى فارحموا أهل البلاء واحمدوا الله تعالى على العافية .

975. Mālik informed us: saying, "It has reached me that ʿĪsā ibn Maryam ﷺ used to say, 'Do not speak a lot without remembrance of Allah so that your hearts become hard, because a hard heart is far from Allah, exalted is He, but you do not know. Do not look at people's wrong actions as if you were lords but look at them as if you were slaves,[172] because people are only tested [with wrong actions] or granted safety [from such trials]. Have mercy on those who are tested and praise Allah, exalted is He, for being granted safety.'"

٩٧٦ أخبرنا مالك، حدثني سمّي مولى أبي بكر، عن أبي صالح السمّان، عن أبي هريرة : أن رسول الله صلى الله عليه وسلم قال: السفر قطعة من العذاب، يمنع أحدكم نومَه وطعامَه وشرابه، فإذا قضى أحدُكم نَهمته من وجهه فَلْيُعَجِّلْ إلى أهله .

976. Mālik informed us: "Sumayy the *mawlā* of Abū Bakr narrated to me from Abū Ṣāliḥ as-Sammān from Abū Hurayrah that the Messenger of Allah ﷺ said, 'Travel is a portion of the torment; it prevents any of you from sleeping, eating and drinking. So when any of you have finished with what you needed to do, then let him hasten to your family.'"

٩٧٧ أخبرنا مالك، أخبرنا يحيى بن سعيد، عن سالم بن عبد الله قال: قال عمر بن الخطاب رضي الله عنه: لو علمتُ أن أحداً أقوى على هذا الأمر منّي لكان أنْ أُقدَّم فيُضرب عنقي أهونُ عليَّ ، فمن وَلِيَ هذا الأمر بعدي فليعلم أن سيردّه عنه القريبُ والبعيدُ، وأيم الله إن كنتُ لأقاتل الناس عن نفسي .

977. Mālik informed us: "Yaḥyā ibn Saʿīd informed us that Sālim ibn ʿAbdullāh said, 'ʿUmar ibn al-Khaṭṭāb ﷺ said, "If I had known that anyone else had more strength for this affair than me, it would have been easier for me to be brought forward and have my head struck off. So whoever takes charge of this matter [the *khilāfah*] after me should know that both those who are near and those who are remote will reject it of him. By Allah, I had to fight people in defence of myself[173]."'"

٩٧٨ أخبرنا مالك، أخبرني مُخْبِرٌ، عن أبي الدرداء رضي الله تعالى عنه، قال: كان الناس وَرَقاً لا شوك فيه، وهم اليوم شوك لا ورق فيه، إن تركتَهم لم يتركوك وإن نقدتَهم نقدوك.

978. Mālik informed us: "An informant informed me that Abu'd-Dardā' ﷺ said, 'People used to be leaves without thorns, but today they are thorns without leaves. If you leave them alone, they will not leave you alone, and if you criticise them they will criticise you.'"

٩٧٩ أخبرنا مالك، أخبرنا يحيى بن سعيد أنه سمع سعيد بن المسيّب يقول: كان إبراهيم عليه السلام أول الناس ضيَّف الضيف، وأول الناس اختتن، وأول الناس قصَّ شاربه، وأول الناس رأى الشيب، فقال: يا رب ما هذا؟ فقال الله تعالى: وقار يا إبراهيم، قال: ربِّ زدني وقاراً.

979. Mālik informed us: "Yaḥyā ibn Sa'īd informed us that he heard Sa'īd ibn al-Musayyab saying, 'Ibrāhīm ﷺ was the first person to give hospitality to the guest, the first person to circumcise himself, the first person to trim the moustache, and the first person who saw gray hairs. So he said, "My Lord! what is this?" And Allah, exalted is He, answered, "Dignity, Ibrāhīm." He said, "Lord, increase me in dignity."'"

٩٨٠ أخبرنا مالك، أخبرنا يحيى بن سعيد، أنه سمع سعيد بن المسيّب يحدثه عن أنس أنه قال: قال رسول الله صلى الله عليه وسلم: كأني أنظر إلى موسى عليه السلام يهبط من ثنيَّة هَرْشي ماشياً، عليه ثوب أسود.

980. Mālik informed us: "Yaḥyā ibn Sa'īd informed us that he heard Sa'īd ibn al-Musayyab narrating to him that Anas said, 'The Messenger of Allah ﷺ said, "It is as if I were looking at Mūsā ﷺ descending from Thaniyyah Harshī [between Makkah and Madīnah] walking, wearing a black robe."'"

٩٨١ أخبرنا مالك، أخبرنا يحيى بن سعيد، أنه سمع أنس بن مالك يقول: دعا رسول الله صلى الله عليه وسلم الأنصار ليُقطع لهم بالبَحرين، فقالوا: لا والله إلاّ أن تُقْطِع لإخواننا من قريش مثلها، مرتين أو ثلاثاً، فقال: إنكم سترون بعدي أَثَرَة فاصبروا حتى تلقَوْني.

981. Mālik informed us: "Yaḥyā ibn Sa'īd informed us that he heard Anas ibn Mālik saying, 'The Messenger of Allah ﷺ called the Anṣār to grant them the income from certain parts of Baḥrayn, and they said, "No, by Allah! Not unless you grant our brothers of Quraysh the like of it," two or three times. So he said, "After me, you will see [people] taking things exclusively for themselves and sharing them with no one else, so be steadfast until you meet me."'"

٩٨٢ أخبرنا مالك، أخبرنا يحيى بن سعيد، أخبرني محمد بن إبراهيم التيمي، قال: سمعت علقمة بن أبي وقاص يقول: سمعت عمر بن الخطاب يقول: سمعت رسول الله صلى الله عليه وسلم يقول: إنما الأعمال بالنية، وإنما لامرئٍ ما نوى، فمن كانت هجرتُه إلى الله ورسوله فهجرته إلى الله ورسوله، ومن كانت هجرته إلى دنيا يُصيبُها أو امرأة يتزوَّجُها فهجرتُه إلى ما هاجر إليه.

982. Mālik informed us: "Yaḥyā ibn Sa'īd informed us, 'Muḥammad ibn Ibrāhīm at-Taymī informed me, "I heard 'Alqamah ibn Abī Waqqāṣ saying,

'I heard ᶜUmar ibn al-Khaṭṭāb saying, "I heard the Messenger of Allah ﷺ saying, 'Actions are only by intentions, and for every man there is that which he intends. So whoever's emigration is to Allah and His Messenger then his emigration is to Allah and His Messenger, but whoever's emigration is to some worldly gain which he can acquire or a woman he will marry then his emigration is to that for which he emigrated.'"'"

٥٧ باب الفأرة تقع في السَّمْن

57. A Mouse Falling into Clarified Butter

٩٨٣ أخبرنا مالك، أخبرنا ابن شهاب، عن عُبيد الله بن عتبة، عن عبد الله بن عباس : أن النبي صلى الله عليه وسلم سُئل عن فأرة وقعت في سمن فماتتْ؟ قال: خذوها وما حولها من السَّمْن فاطرحوه.

983. Mālik informed us: "Ibn Shihāb informed us from ᶜUbaydullāh ibn ᶜUtbah from ᶜAbdullāh ibn ᶜAbbās that the Prophet ﷺ was asked about a mouse which fell into clarified butter and died, and so he answered, 'Take it and what surrounds it of clarified butter and throw it away.'"

قال محمد: وبهذا نأخذ. إذا كان السمن جامداً أُخذت الفأرةُ وما حولها من السمن فرُميَ به، وأُكل ما سوى ذلك، وإن كان ذائباً لا يُؤكل منه شيء، واسْتُصبحَ به. وهو قول أبي حنيفة والعامة من فقهائنا.

Muḥammad said: "We adhere to this. If the clarified butter is solid then the mouse and what surrounds it of clarified butter are taken and thrown away, and the rest of it may be eaten, but if it is liquid then none of it should be eaten, but it can be used for lighting lamps. That is the verdict of Abū Ḥanīfah and of our *fuqahā*ᵓ in general."

٥٨ باب دباغ الميتة

58. Tanning [the Skins of] Carrion[174]

٩٨٤ أخبرنا مالك، حدَّثنا زيد بن أسلم، عن أبي وَعلة المصري، عن عبد الله بن عباس: أن رسول الله صلى الله عليه وسلم قال: إذا دُبغ الإهَاب فقد طهُر.

984. Mālik informed us: "Zayd ibn Aslam narrated to us from Abū Waᶜlah al-Miṣrī [the Egyptian] from ᶜAbdullāh ibn ᶜAbbās that the Messenger of Allah ﷺ said, 'When the skin is tanned it becomes pure.'"

٩٨٥ أخبرنا مالك، أخبرنا يزيد بن عبد الله بن قُسيط ، عن محمد بن عبد الرحمن بن ثَوْبان، عن أمّه ، عن عائشة زوج النبي ﷺ : أن رسول الله ﷺ أمر أن يُستمتع بجلود الميتة إذا دُبغت.

985. Mālik informed us: "Yazīd ibn ᶜAbdullāh ibn Qusayṭ informed us from Muḥammad ibn ᶜAbd ar-Raḥmān ibn Thawbān from his mother from ᶜĀᵓishah, the wife of the Prophet ﷺ, that the Messenger of Allah ﷺ ordered that the skins of carrion should be made use of if they have been tanned."

٩٨٦ أخبرنا مالك، أخبرنا ابن شهاب، عن عبيد الله بن عبد الله، قال : مرَّ رسول الله صلى الله عليه وسلم بشاة كان أعطاها مولى لميمونة زوج النبي صلى الله عليه وسلم ميتة فقال رسول الله صلى الله عليه وسلم: هلاّ انتفعتم بجلدها، قالوا: يا رسول الله إنها ميتة، قال : إنما حُرِّم أكلها .

986. Mālik informed us: "Ibn Shihāb informed us that ᶜUbaydullāh ibn ᶜAbdullāh said, 'The Messenger of Allah ﷺ passed by a sheep which a *mawlā* of Maymūnah the wife of the Prophet ﷺ had given, but it was dead. The Messenger of Allah ﷺ said, "Why do you not make use of its skin?" They said, "Messenger of Allah, it is carrion!" He said, "It is only eating it that is *ḥarām*."'"

قال محمد : وبهذا نأخذ . إذا دبغ إهاب الميتة فقد طهر، وهو ذكاته ولا بأس بالانتفاع به، ولا بأس ببيعه . وهو قول أبي حنيفة والعامة من فقهائنا رحمهم الله .

Muḥammad said: "We adhere to this. When the skin of carrion is tanned it becomes pure, and that is [in place of] its sacrifice, and there is no harm in making use of it, and there is no harm in selling it. That is the verdict of Abū Ḥanīfah and of our *fuqahā'* in general, may Allah have mercy on them."

٥٩ باب كَسْب الحَجّام

59. The Earnings of a Cupper

٩٨٧ أخبرنا مالك، حدثنا حُميد الطويل، عن أنس بن مالك قال : حَجم أبو طَيْبة رسولَ الله صلى الله عليه وسلم فأعطاه صاعاً من تمر وأمر أهله أن يُخَفِّفُوا عنه من خَرَاجه .

987. Mālik informed us: "Ḥumayd aṭ-Ṭawīl narrated to us that Anas ibn Mālik said, 'Abū Taybah cupped the Messenger of Allah ﷺ and he gave him a *ṣāᶜ* of dates and told his people [his owners] to lighten the burden of his daily payments.'"

قال محمد : وبهذا نأخذ . لا بأس أن يُعطى الحجّام أجراً على حجامته . وهو قول أبي حنيفة .

Muḥammad said: "We adhere to this. There is no harm in the cupper being paid a wage for his cupping. That is the verdict of Abū Ḥanīfah."

٩٨٨ أخبرنا مالك، أخبرنا نافع، عن ابن عمر قال: المملوك وماله لسيّده ولا يصلُح للمملوك أن يُنفق من ماله شيئاً بغير إذن سيّده إلاّ أنْ يأكُلَ أو يَكْتَسيَ أو ينفق بالمعروف .

988. Mālik informed us: "Nāfiᶜ informed us that Ibn ᶜUmar said, 'The slave and his property belong to his master, and it is not permissible for the slave to spend any of his property without the permission of his master except for food, clothing or ordinary everyday expenditure [*maᶜrūf*].'"

قال محمد : وبهذا نأخذ . وهو قول أبي حنيفة إلا أنّه يرخّص له في الطعام الذي يوكّل أن يُطْعِمَ منه، وفي عارية الدابّة ونحوها . فأما هبة درهم ودينار أو كسوة ثوب فلا . وهو قول أبي حنيفة رحمه الله .

Muḥammad said: "We adhere to this, and it is the verdict of Abū Ḥanīfah except in the case where he grants him concessions with respect to the food he is entrusted with to feed [others] from it, or the loan of a beast of burden and the like. But as for giving away a dirham or a dīnār or clothing someone in a robe, then no. That is the verdict of Abū Ḥanīfah, may Allah have mercy on him."

٩٨٩ أخبرنا مالك، عن زيد بن أسلم، عن أبيه قال : كنت لعمر بن الخطاب تسعُ صحاف يبعث بها إلى أزواج النبي صلى الله عليه وسلم، إذا كانت الطُّرفَةُ أو الفاكهةُ أو القَسْم، وكان يبعث بآخرهن صفحة إلى حفصة ، فإن كان قلة أو نقصان كان بها.

989. Mālik informed us from Zayd ibn Aslam that his father said, "ʿUmar ibn al-Khaṭṭāb used to have nine large platters which he would send to the wives of the Prophet ﷺ if there was a gift [of some food] or fruits or a portion [of meat and others things]. He used to send as the last of them a platter to Ḥafṣah [his daughter], and if there was only a little or a smaller [portion], it would be in hers."

٩٩٠ أخبرنا مالك، أخبرنا يحيى بن سعيد، أنه سمع سعيد بن المسيّب يقول : وقعت الفتنة يعني فتنة عثمان فلم يبق من أهل بدر أحد، ثم وقعت فتنة الحَرَّة فلم يبق من أصحاب الحديبية أحد، فإن وقعت الثالثة لم يبقَ بالناس طباخٌ .

990. Mālik informed us: "Yaḥyā ibn Saʿīd informed us that he heard Saʿīd ibn al-Musayyab saying, 'The civil disturbances and sedition [*fitnah*] happened' – meaning the disturbances around ʿUthmān – 'and none of the people of Badr remained. Then the civil disturbances and sedition of al-Ḥarrah happened and none of the Companions of al-Ḥudaybiyyah remained. If a third happens then no intelligence will remain among people.'"

٩٩١ أخبرنا مالك، أخبرنا عبد الله بن دينار، عن ابن عمر، عن رسول الله صلى الله عليه وسلم قال: كلُّكُم راعٍ وكلُّكم مسؤولٌ عن رَعِتَّته ، فالأمير الذي على الناس راعٍ عليهم، وهو مسؤول عنهم ، والرجل راعٍ على أهله وهو مسؤول عنهم، وامرأةُ الرجلِ راعيةٌ على مال زوجها، وهي مسؤولة عنه ، وعبد الرجلِ راعٍ على مال سيّده وهو مسؤول عنه ، فكلُّكُمْ راعٍ وكُلُّكُمْ مسؤولٌ عن رعيّته .

991. Mālik informed us: "ʿAbdullāh ibn Dīnār informed us from Ibn ʿUmar that the Messenger of Allah ﷺ said, 'Each one of you is a shepherd and each one of you is answerable for his flock. The Amīr who is over people is a shepherd over them and he is answerable for them. A man is a shepherd over his family and he is answerable for them. A man's wife is a shepherdess of her husband's property and wealth, and she is answerable for it. A man's slave is a shepherd over his master's property and wealth and he is answerable for it. Each of you is a shepherd and each of you is answerable for his flock.'"

٩٩٢ أخبرنا حدّثنا عبد الله بن دينار، عن ابن عمر، قال: قال رسول الله صلى الله عليه وسلم: إن الغادر يقوم يوم القيمة يُنصب له لواءٌ، فيقال هذه غُدرة فلان.

992. Mālik informed us: "ʿAbdullāh ibn Dīnār narrated to us that Ibn ʿUmar said, 'The Messenger of Allah ﷺ said, "The treacherous person will rise on the Day of Rising and a flag will be set up for him and it will be said, 'This is the treachery of so-and-so.'"'"

٩٩٣ أخبرنا مالك، أخبرنا نافع، عن ابن عمر، أن رسول الله صلى الله عليه وسلم قال: الخيل في نواصيها الخير إلى يوم القيمة.

993. Mālik informed us: "Nāfi' informed us from Ibn 'Umar that the Messenger of Allah ﷺ said, 'Horses; in their forelocks there is good until the Day of Rising.'"

٩٩٤ أخبرنا مالك، أخبرنا عبد الله بن دينار، عن ابن عمر: أنه رآه يبول قائماً.

994. Mālik informed us: "'Abdullāh ibn Dīnār informed us that he saw Ibn 'Umar urinating standing."

قال محمد: لا بأس بذلك، والبول جالساً أفضل.

Muḥammad said: "There is no harm in that, but urinating sitting is better."

٩٩٥ أخبرنا مالك، عن أبي الزناد، عن الأعرج، عن أبي هريرة: أن رسول الله صلى الله عليه وسلم قال: ذروني ما تركتكم فإنما هلك من كان قبلكم بسؤالهم واختلافهم على أنبيائهم فما نهيتُكم عنه فاجتنبوه.

995. Mālik informed us from Abu'z-Zinād from al-A'raj from Abū Hurayrah that the Messenger of Allah ﷺ said, "Leave me alone as long as I leave you, because those before you only perished because of their questioning and their disagreeing with their prophets. Whatever I forbid you, then avoid it."

٩٩٦ أخبرنا مالك، حدّثنا أبو الزنّاد، عن الأعرج، عن ابي هريرة قال: قال رسول الله صلى الله عليه وسلم: أرأيت ابنَ أبي قُحافة نزع ذَنوباً أو ذَنوبين، في نَزْعه ضعف والله يغفر له، ثم قام عمر بن الخطّاب، فاستحالت غَرْباً، فلم أرَ عبقريّاً من الناس ينزع نَزْعه، حتى ضرب الناس بعَطَن.

996. Mālik informed us: "Abu'z-Zinād narrated to us from al-A'raj that Abū Hurayrah said, 'The Messenger of Allah ﷺ said, "I saw [in a vision] the son of Abū Quḥāfah [Abū Bakr] drawing a leather bucket or two [of water from a well] and in his drawing there was some weakness, and Allah will forgive him. Then 'Umar ibn al-Khaṭṭāb stood and it was transformed into a large leather bucket, and I have never seen a chief of the people drawing water as he did, so that people lay down around the well [their thirsts satisfied]."'"

٦٠ باب التفسير

60. *Tafsīr*

٩٩٧ أخبرنا مالك، أخبرنا داود بن الحُصَين، عن أبي يربوع المخزومي، أنه سمع زيد بن ثابت يقول: الصلاة الوُسطى صلاة الظهر.

997. Mālik informed us: "Dāwūd ibn al-Ḥuṣayn informed us that Abū Yarbū' al-Makhzūmī heard Zayd ibn Thābit saying, 'The middle prayer[175] is the prayer of *Ẓuhr*.'"

٩٩٨ أخبرنا مالك، أخبرنا زيد بن أسلم، عن عمرو بن رافع، أنه قال: كنت أكتب مصحفاً لحفصة زوج النبي صلى الله عليه وسلم قالت: إذا بلغتَ هذه الآية فآذنّي، فلما بلغتُها آذَنْتها فقالت: حافظوا على الصلوات والصلاة الوسطى، وصلاة العصر وقوموا للّه قانتين.

998. Mālik informed us: "Zayd ibn Aslam informed us that ᶜAmr ibn Rāfiᶜ said, 'I was writing a copy of the Qurʾān for Ḥafṣah the wife of the Prophet ﷺ and she said, "When you reach this *āyah* [mentioning the midmost prayer] then tell me." So when I reached it I told her and she said, "Safeguard the *ṣalāh* – especially the middle one and the afternoon prayer. Stand in obedience to Allah."'"

٩٩٩ أخبرنا مالك، أخبرنا زيد بن أسلم، عن القَعْقَاع بن حكيم، عن أبي يونس مولى عائشة، قال: أَمَرَتْني أن أكتب لها مصحفاً، قالت: إذا بلغتَ هذه الآية فآذنّي (حافظوا على الصلوات والصلاة الوسطى)، فلما بلغتها آذنَتْها وأمَلَّتْ عليّ: (حافظوا على الصلَوات والصلاة الوسطى وصلاة العصر وقوموا للّه قانتين ، سمعتها من رسول الله صلى الله عليه وسلم.

999. Mālik informed us: "Zayd ibn Aslam informed us from al-Qaᶜqāᶜ ibn Ḥakīm that Abū Yūnus the *mawlā* of ᶜĀʾishah said, 'She told me to write a copy of the Qurʾān for her, and she said, "When you reach this *āyah* then tell me, 'Safeguard the *ṣalāh* – especially the middle one.'" When I reached it I told her and she dictated to me, "'Safeguard the *ṣalāh* – especially the middle one and the afternoon prayer. Stand in obedience to Allah.' I heard it from the Messenger of Allah ﷺ."'"

١٠٠٠ أخبرنا مالك، أخبرنا عمارة بن صياد، أنه سمع سعيد بن المسيّب يقول في الباقيات الصالحات: قول العبد: سبحان الله والحمد لله ولا إله إلاّ الله والله أكبر ولا حول ولا قوة إلاّ بالله العلي العظيم.

1000. Mālik informed us: "ᶜUmārah ibn Ṣayyād informed us that he heard Saᶜīd ibn al-Musayyab saying concerning the 'right actions which are lasting' (Sūrat al-Kahf: 45) [that they are] the slave's saying, '*Subḥāna'llāh* – Glory be to Allah, *al-ḥamdu lillāh* – praise belongs to Allah, *lā ilāha illa'llāh* – There is no god but Allah, *Allāhu akbar* – Allah is greater, *wa lā ḥawla wa lā quwwata illā billāhi'l-ᶜaliyyi'l-ᶜaẓīm* – there is no power and no strength but by Allah, the Exalted, the Vast.'"

١٠٠١ أخبرنا مالك، أخبرنا ابن شهاب وسئل عن المحصَنات من النساء، قال: سمعت سعيد بن المسيّب يقول: هنّ ذوات الأزواج. ويرجع ذلك إلى أن الله حرم الزنا.

1001. Mālik informed us: "Ibn Shihāb informed us that he was asked about the '*muḥṣanāt* of women' (Sūrat an-Nisa: 24) and he said, 'I heard Saᶜīd ibn al-Musayyab saying, "They are those having husbands, and that refers to the fact that Allah has forbidden adultery."'"

١٠٠٢ أخبرنا مالك، أخبرنا محمد بن أبي بكر بن عمر بن حزم أن أباه أخبره، عن عمرة بنت عبد الرحمن، عن عائشة زوج النبي صلى الله عليه وسلم، أنها قالت: ما رأيتُ مثلَ ما رغبت هذه الأمة عنه، من هذه الآية: (وإِنْ طَائفَتَان منَ الْمُؤْمنينْ اقتتلوا فَأصْلحُواْ بينهما، فإن بغتْ إحداهما على الأخرى فقاتلوا التي تبغي حتى تفيء إلى أمر الله فإن فاءت فأصلحوا بينهما.

1002. Mālik informed us: "Muḥammad ibn Abī Bakr ibn ᶜUmar ibn Ḥazm informed us that his father informed him from ᶜAmrah bint ᶜAbd ar-Raḥmān that ᶜĀ᾽ishah the wife of the Prophet ﷺ said, 'I have not seen anything the like of which this *ummah* turns away from more than this *āyah*, "If two parties of the *mu᾽minūn* fight, make peace between them; but if one of them attacks the other unjustly, fight the attackers until they revert to Allah's command. If they revert, make peace between them…"'" (Sūrat al-Ḥujurāt: 9)

١٠٠٣ أخبرنا مالك، أخبرنا يحيى بن سعيد، عن سعيد بن المسيّب في قول الله عزَّ وجلَّ: ﴿الزاني لا ينكح إلاَّ زانيةً أو مشركة والزانية لا ينكحها إلاَّ زانٍ أو مشرك﴾، قال: وسمعته يقول: إنها نُسخت هذه الآية بالتي بعدها ثم قرأ: ﴿وأنكحوا الأيامى منكم والصالحين من عبادكم وإمائكم﴾.

1003. Mālik informed us: "Yaḥyā ibn Saᶜīd informed us from Saᶜīd ibn al-Musayyab concerning His saying ﷻ, 'A man who has fornicated may only marry a woman who has fornicated or a woman of those who associate partners with Allah [*mushrikūn*]. A woman who has fornicated may only marry a man who has fornicated or a man of those who associate partners with Allah [*mushrikūn*],' (Sūrat an-Nur: 3) that 'this *āyah* is abrogated by the one after,' and then he recited, 'Marry off those among you who are unmarried and those of your slaves and slavegirls who are right-acting (*ṣāliḥūn*).' (Sūrat an-Nur: 32)."

قال محمد: وبهذا نأخذ. وهو قول أبي حنيفة والعامة من فقهائنا لا بأس بتزوّج المرأة، وإن كانت قد فجرت، وإن يتزوجها من لم يفجُرْ.

Muḥammad said: "We adhere to this, and it is the verdict of Abū Ḥanīfah and of our *fuqahā᾽* in general. There is no harm in a woman marrying if she has fornicated, even if the person who marries her has not fornicated."

١٠٠٤ أخبرنا مالك، أخبرنا عبد الرحمن بن القاسم، عن أبيه، أنه كان يقول في قول الله عزَّ وجل: ﴿ولا جُنَاح عليكم فيما عرَّضتم به من خطبة النساء أو أكْنَنْتُم في أنفسكم﴾، قال: أن تقول للمرأة وهي في عدَّتها من وفاة زوجها: إنك عليَّ كريمة وإني فيك لراغب، وإن الله سائق إليك رزقاً، ونحو هذا من القول.

1004. Mālik informed us: "ᶜAbd ar-Raḥmān ibn al-Qāsim informed us that his father used to speak concerning the saying of Allah ﷻ 'Nor is there anything wrong in any allusion to marriage you make to a woman, nor for any you keep to yourself' (Sūrat al-Baqarah: 233) and he said, 'It is that you say to a woman while she is in her *ᶜiddah* after the death of her husband, "I honour you highly, and Allah drives provision towards you," and such-like statements.'"

١٠٠٥ أخبرنا مالك، حدثنا نافع، عن ابن عمر، قال: دُلُوك الشَّمس مَيْلها.

1005. Mālik informed us: "Nāfiᶜ narrated to us from Ibn ᶜUmar that he said, 'The "*dulūk* of the sun" (Sūrat al-Isrā᾽: 78) is its decline.'"

١٠٠٦ أخبرنا مالك، حدثنا داود بن الحصين، عن ابن عباس قال: كان يقول: دُلوك الشمس مَيْلها وغسق الليل اجتماع الليل وظُلْمته.

1006. Mālik informed us: "Dāwūd ibn al-Ḥuṣayn narrated to us that Ibn ᶜAbbās used to say, 'The "*dulūk* of the sun" is its decline and the *ghasaq* of the night (Sūrat al-Isrāᵓ: 78) is the night's growing darker.'"

قال محمد: هذا قول ابن عمر وابن عباس، وقال عبد الله بن مسعود: دُلوكها غروبها، وكلٌّ حَسَن.

Muḥammad said: "This is the verdict of Ibn ᶜUmar and Ibn ᶜAbbās. ᶜAbdullāh ibn Masᶜūd said, 'Its *dulūk* is its setting,' and each of them is good."

١٠٠٧ أخبرنا مالك، حدثنا عبد الله بن دينار، أن عبد الله بن عمر أخبره: أن رسول الله صلى الله عليه وسلم قال: إنما أجَلُكم فيما خلا من الأمم، كما بين صلاة العصر إلى مغرب الشمس؟، وإنما مَثَلُكم وَمَثَلُ اليهود والنصارى كرجل استعمل عُمّالاً فقال: من يعمل لي إلى نصف النهار على قيراط قيراط؟ قال: فعملت اليهود، ثم قال: من يعمل لي من نصف النهار إلى العصر على قيراط قيراط؟ فعملت النصارى على قيراط قيراط، ثم قال: من يعمل لي من الصلاة العصر إلى المغرب الشمس على قيراطين قيراطين، ألا فأنتم الذين يَعملون من صلاة العصر إلى مغرب الشمس على قيراطين قيراطين، قال: فغضب اليهود والنصارى، وقالوا: نحن أكثر عملاً وأقلّ عطاءً، قال: هل ظلمتكم من حقكم شيئاً؟ قالوا: لا، قال: فإنه فضلي أُعطيه من شئت.

1007. Mālik informed us: "ᶜAbdullāh ibn Dīnār narrated to us that ᶜAbdullāh ibn ᶜUmar informed him that the Messenger of Allah ﷺ said, 'Your term in comparison to the nations which have passed away is like [the time] between the afternoon prayer until the sunset. The simile of you and of the jews and the christians is that of a man who employed workers and he said, "Who will work for me up to the middle of the day for a great mountain's worth [*qīrāṭ*] each?" and so the jews worked. Then he said, "Who will work for me from the middle of the day up until the afternoon for a great mountain's worth each?" and the christians worked for a great mountain's worth each. Then he said, "Who will work for me from the afternoon until sunset for two great mountains' worth each?" Certainly, you are the ones who are working from the afternoon until sunset for two great mountains' worth each.' He said, 'The jews and the christians became angry and said, "We worked more and received less!" He said, "Have I wronged you in anything of your due?" They answered, "No." He said, "Then it is My overflowing favour which I give to whomever I wish."'"

قال محمد: هذا الحديث يدل على أن تأخير العصر أفضل من تعجيلها، ألا ترى أنه جعل ما بين الظهر إلى العصر أكثر مما بين العصر إلى المغرب في هذا الحديث، ومن عجّل العصر كان ما بين الظهر إلى العصر أقلّ مما بين العصر إلى المغرب، فهذا يدل على تأخير العصر، وتأخير العصر أفضل من تعجيلها، ما دامت الشمس بيضاءَ نقيّة لم تُخالطها صُفْرةٌ. وهو قول أبي حنيفة رحمه الله والعامة من فقهائنا رحمهم الله تعالى.

Muḥammad said: "This ḥadīth shows that delaying the afternoon prayer is better than performing it early. Do you not see that he regarded [the time] between the midday and the afternoon as more than [the time] between afternoon and sunset in this *ḥadīth*? Whoever performs the afternoon prayer early then [the time] between midday up until afternoon is less than that between afternoon and sunset. This shows that one should delay the afternoon prayer, and that delaying the afternoon prayer is better than performing it early, as long as the sun is pure white and unmixed with yellow. That is the verdict of Abū Ḥanīfah and of our *fuqahāʾ* in general, may Allah have mercy on them."

18. NOTES FOR THE *MUWAṬṬAʾ*

[1] *Janābah* covers all situations in which a man or a woman become in need of a *ghusl* because of sexual intercourse or voluntary and involuntary ejaculation.

[2] Cupping is a form of medical treatment which is to be found in disparate societies and cultures including China, Japan and Arabia, and was widely used in Europe until comparatively recently. It consisted traditionally in using some burning material (today vacuum producing equipment) to create greatly reduced pressure in cups placed on parts of the body, often back, neck, head, and limbs. The Chinese and Japanese use it along the acupuncture meridians.

[3] *Ḍuḥā* is the optional set of *rakʿahs* performed after the sun has risen until just before midday.

[4] An emission.

[5] i.e. the woman's emission is the cause of the child sometimes resembling her.

[6] Wāʾil came from the Ḥaḍramawt to Madīnah for a short period, whereas Ibn Masʿūd❀ had a lifelong companionship with the Messenger of Allah ❀.

[7] Umm al-Qurʾān is the "Core of the Qurʾān" i.e. the Fātiḥah.

[8] Shaykh ʿAbd al-Ḥayy says about *at-taḥiyyāt*, "Some explain it as the Kingdom, some as endless existence [*baqāʾ*] and some as the greeting [*as-salām*]."

[9] *Zākiyāt* are right actions according to Ibn Ḥabīb.

[10] *Aṣ-ṣalawātu lillāh.* Qāḍī Abu'l-Walīd said, "It means that it is not correct that anything other than Allah should be intended by them [prayers]." Ar-Rāfiʿī said, "It means mercy belongs to Allah for His slaves."

[11] *Tawashshuḥ* is to wear a cloth as do those in *iḥrām* passing it under the right armpit and over the left shoulder thus securing it.

[12] Shaykh ʿAbd al-Ḥayy appends a note that this is connected to the *ʿiqāl* with which the camel is hobbled, but that is another narration of the ḥadīth. However, in this narration mention is made of the camel whose halter has been loosened to give it ease [*muʿallaqah*].

[13] This is the view of Imām Muḥammad. The dominant view in the Ḥanafī madhhab is different.

[14] *Ṣawm al-wiṣāl* – uninterrupted fasting – was special to the Messenger of Allah ❀ and it is not something for his ummah to practise.

[15] Also commonly referred to as *Ḥajj tamattuʿ*.

[16] *Iḥrām* means accepting, or taking upon oneself, or recognising the inviolability of inviolable things.

[17] Tamattuʿ.

[18] In the *Muwaṭṭaʾ* of Yaḥyā it is, "Mālik from Dāwūd ibn al-Ḥusayn that Abū Ghaṭafān ibn Ṭarīf al-Murrī informed him that his father…"

[19] Sūrat al-Baqarah: 195)

[20] A *mudd* is loosely defined as the volumetric measure that can be contained in two cupped hands. However, in Madīnah it had a specific definition.

[21] The *kiswah* is the cloth covering the Kaʿbah.

[22] as remuneration for the work of slaughtering.

[23] However, in this instance he is liable to sacrifice a small animal, i.e. a sheep or a goat.

[24] Al-Muḥaṣṣab is located in the northern suburb of Makkah currently known as Maᶜabidah.

[25] *Mighfar* is a protective covering of chain mail worn under a cap or helmet.

[26] Saffron, which was commonly used for marriages.

[27] The dowry is the right of the woman in the marriage and does not belong to the parents and so the women here are deprived of their rights.

[28] Sulṭān: this covers the ruler or the *qāḍī.*

[29] A slave woman who had borne a child to her owner.

[30] A variant reading of Sūrat aṭ-Ṭalāq: 1 which ordinarily reads, "O Prophet! When any of you divorce women, divorce them during their period of purity (*ᶜiddah*)."

[31] Ad-Daraj is a place in Madīnah.

[32] *Mawlā.* The *walāʾ* of a tribe is a form of alliance whereas the other use of *mawlā* refers to the freed slave and his relationship to his former owner.

[33] *Bāʾinah* divorce is final and the husband has no right to take his wife back within her *ᶜiddah.* He may however propose to her again if he wishes.

[34] The expiation [*kaffārah*] for *ẓihār* is to free a slave, fast two consecutive months or feed sixty poor people.

[35] If the first husband had divorced her twice, then if he divorces her again in the second marriage, it is the final divorce.

[36] And he can return to her in the *ᶜiddah.*

[37] Then consummates the marriage and is subsequently divorced.

[38] (Sūrat al-Baqarah: 224-5)

[39] This is the case with the divorce of a virgin. A single divorce is a clear divorce without an *ᶜiddah,* since the *ᶜiddah* period is instituted to see if there are any children.

[40] But presumably he would have been one of her suitors if he had so wished.

[41] Mālik and others took the position that it is *ḥarām.*

[42] *Liᶜān* is the process outlined in Sūrat an-Nur 6-9: "Those who make an accusation against their wives and have no witnesses except themselves, such people should testify four times by Allah that they are telling the truth and a fifth time that Allah's curse will be upon them if they are lying. And the punishment is removed from her if she testifies four times by Allah that he is lying and a fifth time that Allah's anger will be upon her if he is telling the truth."

[43] A place six miles from Madīnah.

[44] From the property in the *bayt al-māl.*

[45] His sister.

[46] He used to go to the mosque through Ḥafṣah's chamber which adjoined the mosque.

[47] Because she passed her *ᶜiddah* in the house of Ḥafṣah, where she had been divorced.

[48] The statement, "I am quit of you."

[49] The statement, "I am free of you."

[50] In which he must propose to her and marry her again in order to be re-united.

[51] *Awrāq* is possibly a sandy grey.

[52] Why would a camel of one colour give birth to a camel of another colour?

[53] In which he would have to accept Islam, then propose to her and marry her again in order to be re-united.

[54] i.e. the property she left.

[55] i.e. the *mustaḥāḍah* reckons the normal length of her menstrual period and then does the prayer outside of those days even though she is still bleeding.

[56] Literally, 'the impregnator'. It means since the husband of the two women who breastfed the children is one person that they become related as half-siblings.

[57] Without her wearing *ḥijāb* and having the company of a *maḥram* male.

[58] The recitation of the latter *āyah* was abrogated around the time of the death of the Messenger of Allah ﷺ but not everyone knew of its abrogation.

[59] A house which had once belonged to Sayyidunā ʿUmar.

[60] Supporting narrations say that she did not suckle directly but that she gave him some of her milk to drink.

[61] i.e. before the child receives nourishment of solid food.

[62] Camels which are five or more years old, cattle which are two or more years old, and sheep and goats which are one or more years old.

[63] Possibly meaning not castrated.

[64] Ibn Muḥammad ibn ʿAmr ibn Ḥazm.

[65] ʿAbdullāh ibn Wāqid ibn ʿAbdullāh ibn ʿUmar al-ʿUmarī al-Madanī. Ibn Ḥibbān regarded him as trustworthy. Aṣ-Ṣuyūṭī said that he died in 119 AH.

[66] For two more days.

[67] The next year.

[68] So that the Muslims would share with these travellers rather than storing up the meat for themselves.

[69] Such that there is no ʿĪd prayer performed there.

[70] A mountain near Madīnah.

[71] There is a difference of interpretation as to whether he refers merely to cutting the animal or cutting the jugular veins.

[72] Muḥammad uses the word *makrūh* but here in the sense *ḥarām*.

[73] The species of lizard referred to is large somewhat akin in size to the iguana of South America.

[74] Khālid ؓ was making clear that it is *ḥalāl* since the Messenger of Allah ﷺ did not object to him eating it.

[75] i.e. it is slaughtered to remove the blood, but not to render it *ḥalāl* since that has been achieved in the slaughter of the she-camel.

[76] A carpenter's tool like an axe for cutting away the surface of the wood.

[77] A zoroastrian. The category covers some other religions who are not technically People of the Book.

[78] Although the benefits of each finger are different.

[79] i.e. ten camels.

[80] i.e. five camels.

[81] Meaning that there is no known *sharīʿah* source on it, and it is up to the *qāḍī* to render a just judgement by his own exertion of the intellect to arrive at a judgement [*ijtihād*]. Mālik held the view that there was no widely accepted view on that in Madīnah.

[82] His question was in rhyming prose.

[83] *Rikāz* has the meaning of those minerals that are taken out of the earth without great effort on the part of the person so doing, e.g. in open-cast mining. The *zakāh* is one fifth.

[84] Because the man on Ḥajj who had freed him was unknown and untraceable.

[85] It was regarded as a misfortune to kill such a snake since it was believed that the jinn took revenge for its death or perhaps that it was a jinn which itself took revenge for its death.

[86] The judgement is an unusual one which is not the ordinary basis for judgement since it is regarded that ʿUmar ✿ awarded half of the compensatory payment as an extraordinary measure due to the unusual mode of death. The ordinary judgement would have been either that there was no compensatory payment due or that a full compensatory payment was due.

[87] Because they had not witnessed his murder.

[88] From the *zakāh*.

[89] In this wording it is in the form of a question and differs from the version above.

[90] The wording differs from that narrated above. Here the jews are addressed directly whereas in the text of the ḥadīth they are referred to in the third person.

[91] And conversely he would have a right upon some portion of their wealth.

[92] Abū Bakr ibn Muḥammad ibn ʿAmr ibn Ḥazm

[93] Meaning that both the people of Madīnah and ʿIrāq would agree that the punishment for contravention of the limits [*ḥadd*] is applied for a theft of ten dirhams, but differ about a theft of lesser value.

[94] His father was al-Qāsim ibn Muḥammad ibn Abī Bakr aṣ-Ṣiddīq

[95] By taking from him a surety of property or money.

[96] As opposed to someone who goes to where another person has deliberately put his goods believing them to be in security and steals something.

[97] A valley between Minā and Makkah known as al-Muḥaṣṣab.

[98] Shaykh and Shaykhah mean people who are *muḥṣān* i.e. are or have been married.

[99] i.e. he has consummated the marriage.

[100] Because she was *muḥṣānah* but the young man was not *muḥṣān*.

[101] The whip was old and broken and would not have caused pain.

[102] Meaning that it had not been used very much and so had not softened.

[103] Allah's veil is if no others know about the deed.

[104] The Arabic word *thayyib* means someone who either is married or has been married and who has consummated the marriage.

[105] i.e. the dowry of someone of her standing.

[106] Slander here means allegations of adultery.

[107] The digital copy of the text lacks the last sentence which is to be found in the printed copy.

[108] An expression denoting some doubt in the narrator as to the exact words.

[109] Thus it was not a punishment for contravention of the limits [*ḥadd*] imposed by the Qurʾān nor by the Prophet ✿.

[110] *Al-bitʿ* is an intoxicant made from honey which the people of the Yemen used to drink.

[111] An intoxicant made from either sorghum, maize or rice.

[112] An Ethiopian name for the same drink.

[113] In Yaḥyā ibn Yaḥyā's version of the *Muwaṭṭa'* it is, "I do not tell you to sell it."

[114] Sūrat al-Mā'idah: 90.

[115] Meaning "consider *ḥarām*".

[116] The hollowed-out stone used for grinding grain into flour, etc. It was also used for *wuḍū'*.

[117] This denotes an infusion of raisins and an infusion of dried dates mixed together and cooked after that, and left until it ferments and becomes strong.

[118] Prohibited since these vessels concentrated the alcohol content more than other vessels.

[119] Thought to have been the maternal grandmother

[120] Thought to have been the paternal grandmother.

[121] He would have confirmed a portion for the maternal aunt with a specific mention in an *āyah*.

[122] Mullā ᶜAlī al-Qārī said, "What is meant by it is the khalīfah after him."

[123] i.e. meaning "We Prophets are not inherited from."

[124] "'Nor [may] a *kāfir* [inherit from] a Muslim,' is the completion of the ḥadīth from all the other companions of az-Zuhrī, but Mālik shortened it," said Ibn ᶜAbd al-Barr.

[125] He was a *kāfir* at the time of the death of Abū Ṭālib and became a Muslim at the time of Ḥudaybiyyah. Some say his Islam was delayed until the Opening of Makkah [to Islam] and that he emigrated at the beginning of 8 AH.

[126] Ṭālib died as a *kāfir* before Badr.

[127] ᶜAlī and Jaᶜfar were Muslims at that time and so did not inherit.

[128] He died, being killed on the day of Badr as a kāfir.

[129] Explained by Shaykh ᶜAbd al-Ḥayy al-Laknawī, may Allah have mercy on him, to mean that he would not make them inheritors on the basis of their claims but only on the basis of clear testimony and evidence, since at that time they were foreign and unknown as opposed to the situation that pertained among the Arabs where the lineages and genealogies were all known.

[130] The mudd is the two cupped hands full. See footnote 19.

[131] The Companions and the greatest of the Followers.

[132] Known as the *mudd* of the Prophet ﷺ.

[133] The *ṣāᶜ* is four *mudds.*

[134] Ḥanafī from the tribe of Bani Ḥanīfah.

[135] A camel or a cow.

[136] A sheep, however the former is preferrable.

[137] He does not leave a gap and say it after some time.

[138] Perhaps meaning, "do the better matter".

[139] i.e. devoted to the upkeep, service and maintenance of the Kaᶜbah.

[140] "Allah will not take you to task for inadvertent statements in your oaths, but He will take you to task for the intention your hearts have made." (Sūrat al-Baqarah: 223)

[141] The *ᶜariyyah* is a date-palm which is granted to a poor person for him to take its dates. In view of his poverty it is permitted him to sell the dates on the tree for other dates

already harvested, a practice which is not ordinarily permitted.

[142] The *wasq* is a measure equivalent to sixty *ṣā*ᶜ.

[143] Fruits of trees, e.g. olives, etc.

[144] i.e. fitting for consumption by humans and as fodder for animals.

[145] Narrated by al-Bukhārī and others.

[146] Equal measures.

[147] The practice of going out to meet goods before they reach the market, which also in the Middle Ages in Europe was also considered impermissible.

[148] This prophetic prohibition has particular significance for our age in which monopolistic concerns completely prevent access to the purchase of goods by any but themselves and thus form cartels that fix prices.

[149] Shaykh ᶜAbd al-Ḥayy said, "i.e. that you sell for the same price as the people of the market sell." Note that monopoly capitalism is based to a large extent on undercutting, a practice which is here forbidden.

[150] Such as setting her free, writing a contract for her to purchase her freedom, leaving a bequest in his will that she be freed, etc.

[151] Date-palms yield imperfect crops of dates if the cultivators do not fecundate the females with the spadix of the males.

[152] *Walā᾽* is the relationship that adheres on the setting free of a slave, such that the one who sets the slave free is an heir of the slave.

[153] A half dirham did not exist as a coin.

[154] The person who owns the higher walled garden which the water first reaches, allows all the water to come into his garden until it reaches the ankles of someone standing in it, and then he closes the entrance to his garden so that the water proceeds further down to the lower garden.

[155] *Khātam* intrinsically carries the sense of something which is used to seal documents, and is thus a signet-ring

[156] This is permissible although the approved and preferable way is to sit and drink, as is conveyed in numerous traditions to this effect.

[157] *Makrūh* in the usage of Imām Muḥammad can convey a much stronger sense than later scholars gave to it, and I have rendered it here as 'abhorrent'.

[158] *Miskīn* is often taken to denote those who have no property and no income, whereas *faqīr* can denote someone who has both property and income but not enough income to meet expenditure.

[159] The dominant sense of *ẓann* is 'opinion', but then here it means 'suspicion' or to hold a 'bad opinion' of someone.

[160] *Taṣwīr* contains the sense of a sculpted form and of an image.

[161] *Ru᾽yā* being from the root of the verb 'to see' has also the sense of 'vision'.

[162] *Ishtimāl aṣ-ṣammā᾽* is wearing only a garment made of a single piece of cloth without openings for the hands to emerge so that when the wearer brings out his hands from beneath the garment he exposes his private parts.

[163] *Al-iḥtibā᾽* is wearing only a single garment and sitting in a crouching position in such a way that the shins are upright and the legs are kept together either with a cloth or with the hands, which posture allows for the exposing of the private parts.

[164] Another wording in another ḥadīth is "A man is with whomever he loves," which can also mean also that someone will keep the company of whomever he loves.

18. Notes for the *Muwaṭṭa᾽*

[165] The correct *isnād* is that in the *Muwaṭṭa᾽* of Yaḥyā, "Mālik from Zayd ibn Aslam al-ᶜAdawī from ᶜAmr ibn Saᶜd ibn Muᶜādh from his grandmother."

[166] Narrated by ᶜAbd ar-Razzāq, Ibn Saᶜd, Saᶜīd ibn Manṣūr, Ibn Abī Shaybah, ᶜAbd ibn Ḥumayd, Ibn Abi'd-Dunyā, Ibn Jarīr, Ibn al-Mundhir, an-Naḥḥās in his *Nāsikh*, al-Bayhaqī in his *Sunan*.

[167] Probably a reference to Sūrah Maryam: 59 "An evil generation succeeded them who neglected the *ṣalāh* and followed their appetites."

[168] The idea here is an approximation of years and not specifics as it is known that he lived to sixty-three years of age, spending thirteen years in Makkah after the revelation of the Qur'ān and ten in Madīnah .

[169] The more commonly known and fuller ḥadīth is in the *Muwaṭṭa᾽* of Yaḥyā that "Mālik related to me from Abū Ḥāzim ibn Dīnār from Sahl ibn Saᶜd as-Sāᶜidī that the Messenger of Allah ﷺ said, 'If it exists, it is in a horse, a woman, and a house,' meaning ill luck."

[170] The people of Ḥijr are mentioned in Qur᾽ān. They disobeyed their prophet and were destroyed.

[171] Shaykh ᶜAbd al-Ḥayy said, "i.e. then I would begin afresh my actions in the future and my action in the past would be voided," meaning, "If I were to do that my actions would be voided," as if she said it out of humility and courtesy.

[172] The *Muwaṭṭa᾽* of Yaḥyā has, "Do not look at people's wrong actions as if you were lords, but look at your own wrong actions as if you were slaves."

[173] Shaykh ᶜAbd al-Ḥayy said, "i.e. 'I had to fight people in particular and in general in order to defend myself until no one opposed me in my dīn, my *dunyā*, and my honour,' as al-Qārī mentioned."

[174] Carrion are animals not slaughtered according to the sharīᶜah but not including pigs whose skins never become *ḥalāl*.

[175] "Safeguard the *ṣalāh* – especially the middle one." Sūrat al-Baqarah: 238

INTRODUCTION TO THE *RIJĀL*

Shaykh Niᶜmatu'llāh al-Aᶜẓamī

The Sunnah of the Prophet ﷺ, that is, his noble ḥadīth, his sayings, his actions, and his affirmations, enjoyed from the very beginning the good fortune of complete and meticulous care, and of being acted upon by the noble Companions and the outstanding Followers. As a result, it was completely safeguarded and transmitted in minute detail in confirmation of the words of Allah, Exalted is He:

> It is We Who have sent down the Reminder
> and We Who will preserve it.
> (Sūrat al-Ḥijr: 9)

A part of the preservation of the Reminder and the Noble Book, is the preservation of the Sunnah, because the Sunnah explains it [the Book] and lends specific content to its judgements and its objectives. He said ﷺ:

> And We have sent down the Reminder to you
> so that you can make clear to mankind
> what has been sent down to them
> (Sūrat an-Naḥl: 44)

The Position of Madīnah in the Sunnah

Every city which gave way to Islam and in which the Muslims became settled had its portion of knowledge which differed from the others, sometimes a little but sometimes a great deal, according to the number of the Companions who came to it and resided there. The portion of the Abode of the Prophetic Emigration, Madīnah al-Munawwarah, was the fullest portion because of the abundance of Companions there, since it, (and Makkah al-Mukarramah after its surrender to Islam) was the first Dār al-Islām and the place for which the Muslims' hearts longed.

The Sunnah thrived there from whence it overflowed and spread throughout the lands of Islam and it was inherited by people, generation from generation, tribe from tribe. The number of *fuqahāʾ* and ḥadīth scholars multiplied extensively, for it has been transmitted that Mālik said, "I showed this book of mine to seventy of the *fuqahāʾ* of Madīnah." When Mālik was growing up the Sunnah had already begun the process of being recorded and compiled.

Madīnah's Precedence in the Recording of the Sunnah

The Sunnah was recorded in Madīnah al-Munawwarah before all of the other great capital cities. Imām Muḥammad ibn Shihāb az-Zuhrī (died 124 AH) of Madīnah, the shaykh of Mālik, set down his compositions there, as did another of his shaykhs the Madīnan, Mūsā ibn ʿUqbah (died 114 AH), and the Madīnan, Muḥammad ibn Isḥāq al-Muṭṭalibī (died 151 AH), and Ibn Abī Dhiʾb Muḥammad ibn ʿAbd ar-Raḥmān (died 198 AH) of Madīnah.

During the lives of these men and after them other imāms of the ḥadīth and the Sunnah composed works in Makkah al-Mukarramah, Kūfa, Baṣra, and Khurāsān, but the leading place in recording the Sunnah belongs to the notable people of knowledge of Madīnah al-Munawwarah.

Imām Mālik's composition of the *Muwaṭṭaʾ*

Imām Mālik's composition of the *Muwaṭṭaʾ* is numbered among the books (the Ten Books) which record the Sunnah in Madīnah and elsewhere, and is the first in terms of compiling it according to categories of fiqh.

The people of knowledge mention that Imām Mālik's composition of the *Muwaṭṭaʾ* came about as the result of the suggestion of the Abbasid khalīfah Abū Jaʿfar al-Manṣūr made during one of his Ḥajj journeys. Al-Manṣūr invited him to visit him and Abū Jaʿfar honoured him and made him sit beside him, asking him many questions. His [Mālik's] manner, knowledge, intellect, the penetration of his thinking and the soundness of his responses pleased him and he recognised his station in knowledge, in the dīn, and as an imām of the Muslims.

The noted scholar and historian Qāḍī Imām Ibn Khaldūn said in his *Muqaddimah*:

> Abū Jaᶜfar had a rank in knowledge and in the dīn before the khilāfah and after it. It was he who said to Mālik while indicating to him to compose the *Muwaṭṭa*ʾ, "Abū ᶜAbdullāh, no one remains on the face of the earth more knowledgeable than me or you, but the khilāfah has occupied me. You must compose a book for people by which they will benefit. In it you should avoid the concessions (*rukhṣah*) that Ibn ᶜAbbās grants, the severities of Ibn ᶜUmar, and the unusual and singular positions (*shādhdh*) that Ibn Masᶜūd takes. Arrange it and make it accessible (*waṭṭi*ʾ)[1] for people." Mālik said, "By Allah! He taught me composition on that day."

Imām Mālik composed the *Muwaṭṭa*ʾ according to the method which Abū Jaᶜfar al-Manṣūr had indicated. He compiled the choicest of the ḥadīth and the traditions narrated among the People of Madīnah. He gathered the body of practices (*ᶜamal*) which was transmitted by large numbers of one generation to large numbers of the next generation (*tawātur*), avoiding the concessions granted by Ibn ᶜAbbās, the severities of Ibn ᶜUmar and the singular and unusual positions adopted by Ibn Masᶜūd. He confined himself to narrating only from the shaykhs of the People of Madīnah except for six people: Abū'z-Zubayr from Makkah, Ibrāhīm ibnAbī ᶜAblah from Shām, ᶜAbd al-Karīm ibn Mālik from al-Jazīrah (north-west ᶜIrāq), ᶜAṭāʾ ibn ᶜAbdullāh from Khurāsān, Ḥumayd aṭ-Ṭawīl and Ayyūb as-Sakhtiyānī from Baṣra. He completed the work during the khilāfah of al-Mahdī.

Thus was completed the composition of this book the *Muwaṭṭa*ʾ in which Imām Mālik collected the ḥadīth of the Messenger of Allah ﷺ, the judgements of the Companions and the Followers, and the view which he considered the consensus of the People of Madīnah, from which he never departed. So he collected together the ḥadīth in the widest sense and whatever was connected to them of the traditions of the first generation because they were the main point of reference for practical rulings.

The number of ḥadīth and traditions narrated in the *Muwaṭṭa*ʾ

Al-Abhurī Abū Bakr said, "The sum total of what is in the *Muwaṭṭa*ʾ of traditions from the Prophet ﷺ, and from the Companions and the Followers is one thousand, seven hundred and twenty ḥadīth, of which those with a chain of transmission are six hundred, those which are *mursal* ḥadīth [ascribed directly to the Prophet ﷺ without mentioning the Companion or Companions from whom it was heard] are two hundred and twenty-two, and those which are *mawqūf* [statements made without ascribing them to the Prophet ﷺ] are six hundred and thirteen. Of the rulings of the Followers there are two hundred and eighty-five."

The particular merits of the *Muwaṭṭa'*

The *Muwaṭṭa'* has very many particular merits by which it is distinguished from the other books of ḥadīth. I shall mention them here briefly.

First, that it is the composition of an Imām who was a faqīh and a scholar of ḥadīth, a leading *mujtahid* (one who could exert his intellect to arrive at a judgement) whose judgement is followed and to whose imāmate in fiqh and in ḥadīth the imāms of his own age and subsequent ages testifed without there being any dispute.

Second, the Imām of the Imāms, the faqīh, ḥadīth scholar and mujtahid Imām ash-Shāfiʿī, bore witness to the *Muwaṭṭa'*, and he is sufficient for you. He said:

> There is not on the surface of the earth a book which is more *ṣaḥīḥ* after the Book of Allah than the book of Mālik.

Third, that it is one of the compositions from the middle of the second century of the hijrah, so that it precedes everything and is preceded by nothing else since it is the first book in its category, and whatever precedes has superiority. He was the Imām who laid down the path for the composition of works on ḥadīth according to categories of fiqh, and all the trustworthy ones after him modelled themselves on him, such as ʿAbdullāh ibn al-Mubārak, al-Bukhārī, Muslim, Saʿīd ibn Manṣūr, Abū Dāwūd, at-Tirmidhī, an-Nasā'ī, Ibn Mājah and others.

A brief biographical note on Imām Mālik the author of the *Muwaṭṭa'*

He was Mālik ibn Anas ibn Mālik al-Aṣbaḥī al-Ḥimyarī of Madīnah, Abū ʿAbdullāh, the Imām of the Abode of the Hijrah, one of the four Imāms. He was born and died in Madīnah. He was firm in his dīn, remote from the rulers and kings. He was denounced to Jaᶜfar, the uncle of al-Manṣūr al-ᶜAbbāsī who had him flogged, which dislocated his shoulder. Ar-Rashīd sent for him to come and narrate ḥadīth to him and he said, "Amīr al-Muʾminīn, one comes to knowledge, it does not come to one. It is visited, it does not visit." So ar-Rashīd went to his house and leaned against the wall.[2] Mālik said, "Amīr al-Muʾminīn, a part of honouring the Messenger of Allah ﷺ is honouring knowledge," and so he went and sat down before him.

His prestige reached the furthest extent, so that the people of the cities and the provinces narrated ḥadīth in his name, and his *fatwās* were widely published and remembered in Egypt, Shām and all the lands of the West. In Andalus he was the Imām along with whom no other imām was mentioned. He had influence in Madīnah which equalled that of the authorities who governed it.

Allah marked Mālik out with a quality which clung to him, i.e. awe. The rulers were in awe of him, and they would feel humbled in his presence. The awe they had of him reached a point such as kings and amirs did not attain, so he was held in awe even though he had no [formal] authority.

Mālik was held in high esteem during his lifetime, and was honoured by people until he died in 179 AH.

The *Muwaṭṭaʾ* of Imām Muḥammad

Ḥāfiẓ Muḥammad ibn ᶜAbdullāh ad-Dimashqī, better known as Ibn Nāṣir ad-Dīn, found the number of narrators of the *Muwaṭṭaʾ* resulted in eighty-three narrations, the most famous of which in this age among the people of the East, is that of Muḥammad ibn al-Ḥasan ash-Shaybānī, and among the people of the West, that of Yaḥyā al-Laythī.

The former is distinguished by its explanations of that which the people of ᶜIrāq adhered to of the recorded ḥadīth of the Ḥijāz in the *Muwaṭṭaʾ*, and that which they did not adhere to because of other proofs which Muḥammad derives in his *Muwaṭṭaʾ*. It is very useful for those who wish to compare the views of the people of Madīnah with those of the people of ᶜIrāq, and it explains the proofs of the two groups.

The latter is distinguished along with the other narrations of the *Muwaṭṭaʾ* (apart from that of Imām Muḥammad) by the fact that it contains a record of the *ᶜamal*, that is, the practice of the People of Madīnah, and the explanations of Mālik comprising something like three thousand cases organised into categories of fiqh.[3]

One of the merits of the the *Muwaṭṭaʾ* of Imām Muḥammad is that its narrator, Imām Muḥammad ibn al-Ḥasan ash-Shaybānī, is a faqīh, a major ḥadīth scholar and one who is followed in his own right, and to whose imāmate in fiqh, ḥadīth and Arabic language others have borne witness. He stayed close to his shaykh Mālik for three years, and heard the book from him in his own words so that he was filled up and was quenched. He drank, and he drank in large draughts from his understanding, knowledge and narration, applying to it his extraordinary capacity for intellectual penetration, his all round intelligence, and the giftedness of his faculty for discernment.

Another merit of it is that Imām Muḥammad ibn al-Ḥasan ash-Shaybānī was the pupil of the two Imāms, Imām Abū Ḥanīfah and Abū Yūsuf. He was the shaykh of Imām ash-Shāfiʿī, and he skilfully narrated from his own shaykh, Mālik. After narrating the ḥadīth of a chapter, he added to it an explanation of his *madhhab* on the issue, whether in agreement or in disagreement, and an explanation of the *madhhab* of his shaykh, Imām Abū Ḥanīfah, whether in agreement or disagreement, and sometimes an explanation of the *madhhab* of his shaykh, Imām Mālik, and sometimes also the *madhhab* of our *fuqahāʾ* in general. Because of the great number of ḥadīth which he narrates in it from people other than Mālik, and because of the great extent of his own intellectual exertions in arriving at judgements and his own fiqh which he includes in it, and the fiqh of Imām Abū Ḥanīfah and others, in almost every single chapter, and the *madhhabs* of some of the Companions in some of the chapters, then this book became famous as the *Muwaṭṭaʾ Imām Muḥammad.*

It is not strange that the *Muwaṭṭaʾ* of Muḥammad is not simply a book which he narrated literally as the narrator had heard it from the author without adding anything extra, or making any commentary on it, or corrections. On the contrary, it is a book in which there is the fiqh of Imām Muḥammad, the fiqh of his shaykh, Imām Abū Ḥanīfah and the fiqh of our Ḥanafī people in general who preceded Imām Muḥammad. There are also the *madhhabs* of some of the Companions, and some discussion of the positions that Mālik and others took.

It is a record of the fiqh of the people of ḥadīth, of exertion of the intellect to arrive at judgements (*ijtihād*) and of theoretical understanding (*raʾy*) of the Ḥijāz and ʿIrāq, along with a comparison of these *madhhabs* and theoretical understandings as they apply to cases. This is an extremely precious additional merit for whoever grasps and recognises its value. So it is not strange that the *Muwaṭṭa'* should be ascribed to Imām Muḥammad because it is narrated from him and because he added many ḥadīth and added a great deal of knowledge to it with respect to the fiqh of ḥadīth, the rulings of each chapter and the comparison of different intellectual efforts to arrive at judgements.

As for the number of ḥadīth ascribed directly to the Prophet ﷺ and traditions which stop short at Companions and those who came after them which are in the *Muwaṭṭa'* of Imām Muḥammad, whether with or without chains of transmission, they are in total one thousand, one hundred and eighty, of which those which are transmitted by way of Mālik are one thousand and five, and those which are transmitted through others one hundred and seventy-five, and those which are transmitted from Abū Ḥanīfah thirteen, those from Abū Yūsuf four, and the rest from other people.

A small biographical fragment on Imām Muḥammad the narrator of the *Muwaṭṭa'*

He was Muḥammad ibn al-Ḥasan ibn Farqad ash-Shaybānī, one of the *mawlās*[4] of [the tribe of] Shayban. He was Abū ʿAbdullāh, an imām in fiqh and in the science of the principles of fiqh. It was he who spread the knowledge of Imām Abū Ḥanīfah. He was originally from the village of Ḥarsatā in al-Ghūṭah, the fertile oasis to the south of Damascus. He was born in Wāsiṭ in 131 AH and grew up in Kūfa. He listened to Imām Abū Ḥanīfah whose *madhhab* became dominant in his thinking and for which he was known. Then he moved to Baghdād and ar-Rashīd appointed him *qāḍī* of ar-Riqqah.

Ash-Shāfiʿī said, "Urged to say that the Qur'ān was revealed in the language of Muḥammad ibn al-Ḥasan, I would say so, because of the purity of his language."

Ḥāfiẓ adh-Dhahabī said, "He succeeded to the leadership in fiqh in ʿIrāq after Abū Yūsuf, and imāms learnt their fiqh from him. He made compilations, and he was one of the sharpest intellects in the world. He was appointed chief *qāḍī* by ar-Rashīd and he attained unsurpassed rank, prestige and following. Ash-Shāfiʿī considered him a definitive proof in ḥadīth, and it is related of him that he was prodigiously endowed with an incisive mind, a complete intellect, pre-eminent authority and a great capacity for recitation."

So this is a small glimpse of biographical material on Imām Muḥammad ibn al-Ḥasan who narrated the *Muwaṭṭa'* from Imām Mālik, and may He reward them both with the best reward in their support of knowledge, the dīn and of the Muslims.

At-Taᶜlīq al-mumajjad – the commentary on the *Muwaṭṭa'* of Imām Muḥammad

A large group of the earlier and later scholars have written commentaries on the *Muwaṭṭa'* of Yaḥyā, but only three scholars have written commentaries on the *Muwaṭṭa'* of Imām Muḥammad: Bīrizādah, ᶜAlī al-Qārī and Shaykh ᶜAbd al-Ḥayy al-Laknawī.

There is no doubt that the book *at-Taᶜlīq al-mumajjad ᶜalā Muwaṭṭa' Muḥammad* is a tremendous book and a magnificent commentary from Imām ᶜAbd al-Ḥayy al-Laknawī. He began its composition towards the end of 1292 AH at the age of twenty-seven, but he was interrupted by travels, various accidental occurrences and things that kept him occupied, so that he completed his composition in Shaᶜbān 1295.

It shows an astonishing talent and a remarkable ability that a young man who was Indian both in abode and linguistically should scale the heights of the *Muwaṭṭa'* at the age which he did. He included in it the most splendid and radiant of his knowledge and the highest of his cognisance of the noble ḥadīth and its sciences, Ḥanafī fiqh, the other *madhhabs* and every other science which is connected to it, even if in the least way. This book is like a matchless pearl and one of the most precious jewels of knowledge.

The reader who studies it will find merits within it by which Imām al-Laknawī is distinguished, and will be astonished at the strength of his talent and his mastery of precise and accurate determination, accuracy and thoroughness, his discussion of the relative positions of the madhhabs and different views, distinguishing which of them are weightier or weaker, his independence, impartiality and fairness, without misrepresenting the texts and without losing direction.

Similarly the reader will find him mentioning the biographical details of the narrators who occur in the chains of transmission, their states and what is relevant to their standing as trustworthy or weak narrators, but without partiality due to *madhhab* affiliation, so that the status of the ḥadīth becomes completely clear in terms of its soundness or weakness.

Shaykh Niᶜmatu'llāh al-Aᶜẓamī
Scholar of Ḥadīth, Dār al-ᶜUlūm Deoband

NOTES TO THE INTRODUCTION TO THE RIJĀL

[1] His command *waṭṭi*ʾ comprises the senses of facilitating, making something easy and accessible, and smoothing a path, and it is from this that one meaning of the name *Muwaṭṭa*ʾ derives: The Smoothed and Levelled Path Made Easy for People.

[2] In some accounts, ar-Rashīd sat down on a small raised seat on which Imām Mālik ordinarily sat in order to teach.

[3] See *The Origins of Islamic Law* by Yasin Dutton, pp.22-26.

[4] *Mawlās* by alliance and not by being freed from slavery.

THE SCIENCE OF THE INVALIDATION (*JARḤ*) AND AUTHENTICATION (*TA^cDĪL*) OF ḤADĪTH AND ITS ROLE IN THEIR PROTECTION AND PRESERVATION

Shaykh Ashraf ^cAlī Simsiti pur Bihar under the supervision of *Shaykh Ni^cmatu'llāh al-A^cẓamī*

The Obligation to Obey the Sunnah and the Obligation to Propagate it

Know that after the Book (of Allah), the prophetic Sunnah is second in rank as a proof and as an obligation which must be acted upon and followed. He, may praise of Him be clearly manifest and may His name be exalted, has said: "And We have sent down the Reminder to you so that you can make clear to mankind what has been sent down to them", (Sūrat an-Naḥl – The Bee: 44). The protection of the Sunnah is thus also a protecting of the Book, that is, a protection of its laws. Allah has taken upon Himself to protect His Book saying: "It is We Who have sent down the Reminder and We Who will preserve it", (Sūrat al-Ḥijr: 9).

Given also that [Allah's] promise to preserve the Book [necessarily] includes protection of the Sunnah, so Allah has created men to protect the Sunnah from the machinations of the schemers, the intrigues of the liars and the distortions of the deviators. And He, glorious is He and exalted, commanded the mu'minūn to follow the Messenger ﷺ and to keep firmly to the upright guidance saying: "Whatever the Messenger gives you, you should accept and whatever he forbids you, you should forego", (Sūrat al-Ḥashr – the Gathering: 7).

The Messenger ﷺ conveyed the message, ensured that people listened to it, commanded that it be conveyed to others and that others listen to it, saying: "Convey [the Message] from me even it is a single *āyah*"; and "May Allah help the man who has heard something from us and who then conveys it as he had heard it. And it may well be that the transmitter is more attentive and retains it better than the one who listens", (at-Tirmidhī transmitted it); and "Whoever passes on a ḥadīth from me believing it to be false, then he will [be reckoned] among the liars". However, what [had been commanded] would never have come to be had not the Islamic sharīᶜah been protected (with all that it contains with respect to [Allah's] promises and threats, His warning and giving of good news, the commanding to the good and the forbidding of evil).

Furthermore, had the biographies of the men who committed all this to memory and the status and circumstances of the imāms who transmitted these [biographies] not been preserved, the sharīᶜah might have been adulterated by other [laws], as happened to that of the jews and christians through the addition of the sayings of their rabbis and priests. Thus, no excuse can ever be accepted after this from anyone who rejects any part of the firmly established Sunnah. For this reason, the Muslims attached such importance to the transmission of the Sunnah and travelled [so widely] in order to obtain this Sunnah during the time of the companions and during the time after it up to the last period of narration at the end of the third century.

The Necessity of the Science of Verification (*Naqd*)

As it is impossible for everyone to be present at every event there is no conceivable way for those who are absent to gain knowledge of them except by way of oral or written transmission. Likewise, it is not possible for those born after these events to have knowledge of them except by way of narration from those before them. Moreover, given that the ḥadīth are reports, we are under an obligation to examine the status of the narrator from whom we heard the narration, as to whether his narration may be relied upon or not, and then to examine the status of the person from whom this man had narrated, and so on until [an examination of all] the intermediary [narrators in the chain of narration] is complete.

We must ascertain whether the first narrator was actually present at the event or not and whether he was capable of understanding it and remembering it by heart; and then we must examine the subject-matter which has been narrated to see whether it accords with the rank and circumstances of the man to whom it is ascribed and to see whether what happened could have happened at that time.

Existence of the Science of Verification (*Naqd*) and Meticulous Scrutiny (*Tadqīq*) at the Time of the Messenger ﷺ

The Companions were endowed by Allah with the capacity to take upon themselves the burden of trust and to transmit the sharīcah to the people, and their integrity (*cadālah*) is well established by virtue of the integrity accorded to them by Allah, by His declaration of their purity and by His selecting them [above others]. The integrity of none of them need be affirmed by any human being after Allah's affirmation of their integrity. On the other hand, if no mention had been made by Allah and His Messenger about them, then it would have been necessary to establish absolute certainty as to their integrity with respect to the status and circumstances associated with them, namely, the hijrah, jihād, their championing of Islam, their striving and expending of their wealth, their [extended] family of forebears and descendants, their giving mutual advice and admonishment regarding the dīn, the strength of their imān and their degree of certainty.

The Companions ﷺ did not lie to others and did not lie to each other. It is related from Ḥumayd who said: "We were with Anas ibn Mālik ﷺ when he said: 'By Allah, not everything which we relate to you from the Messenger of Allah ﷺ have we heard from him [directly], but [there was no danger because] we did not lie to each other.'" (Related from aṭ-Ṭabarānī in *al-Kabīr*, and his narrators are ranked as absolutely correct (*ṣaḥīḥ*)).

Thus, on account of the general level of truthfulness and the widespread degree of trustworthiness among them they hardly needed to mention the chain of narration (*isnād*) and they did not need to scrutinise meticulously [what was narrated]. Indeed, the matter was left up to the narrator himself – if he wanted to have the chain of transmission (*isnād*) attributed to himself he attributed it to himself, and if he wanted to leave it out then he left it out.

However, making mistakes is part of the natural disposition of man (*fiṭrah*). A person may make a mistake through forgetfulness or he may make a deliberate mistake. Either way the result is the same with regard to the veracity or falsehood of the ḥadīth. For this reason, research and scrutiny into the ḥadīth of the Messenger of Allah ﷺ began while he was alive, albeit on a very restricted scale. There are many examples which prove this, one of which being the occasion when cAlī ﷺ came with the animals of the Prophet ﷺ to be sacrificed in Makkah (*budun*) and he found Fāṭimah with those who had left their special state of *iḥrām* and who had returned to the normal, everyday state (after completing the rites of Ḥajj) wearing a coloured dress and kohl on her eyes. When he censured her for this she replied: "My father commanded me to do this!" [The narrator] said: "and ᶜAlī ﷺ used to say in ᶜIrāq: 'So I went to the Messenger of Allah ﷺ to object to Fāṭimah's behaviour and to seek a formal legal judgement (*fatwā*) from the Messenger of Allah ﷺ regarding what she had transmitted from him. So I informed him that I had objected to this in her and he replied: "She told the truth, she told the truth!"'" (this has been narrated by Muslim in the long ḥadīth of Jābir in the 'Book of Ḥajj').

In the light of this ḥadīth and others, we can affirm that the sciences of verification, research and meticulous scrutiny began during his time ﷺ albeit in a very restricted way.

Development of the Science of Verification after the Death of the Prophet

After the death of the Prophet ﷺ came the turn of Abū Bakr and ᶜUmar ﷺ and the science of verification developed more vigorously with regard to its exactness (*taḥqīq*) and documentation (*tawthīq*).

It is related from Qābiṣah ibn Dhu᾽ayb that he said: "A grandmother came to Abū Bakr ﷺ asking him for her inheritance and he replied: 'There is nothing [prescribed] in the Book of Allah [for you], and there is also nothing [prescribed] in the Sunnah of the Messenger of Allah ﷺ – come back [later so that I have time] to ask people (i.e. the companions who know).' So he asked about the matter and al-Mughīrah ibn Shuᶜbah replied: 'I was with the Messenger of Allah ﷺ when he gave [the grandmother] a sixth.' Abū Bakr said: 'Was there anyone else with you?' Then Muḥammad ibn Maslamah said the same as what al-Mughīrah had said. So Abū Bakr gave it to her." (This is related by Mālik, Aḥmad and at-Tirmidhī, Abū Dāwūd and Ibn Mājah).

This does not mean that Abū Bakr did not accept any ḥadīth unless it was narrated by two people, as we invariably find that Abū Bakr did not ask for another ḥadīth from someone who related a ḥadīth to him from the Prophet ﷺ except in the case of the text regarding the grandmother. It was as if he wanted to instruct the Companions by the careful procedure of confirmation (*tathabbut*) of this ḥadīth. This is similar to the request for a second narrator on behalf of ᶜUmar ibn al-Khattāb ﷺ from Abū Mūsā al-Ashᶜarī ﷺ with regard to the issue of 'seeking permission' (*isti᾽dhān*). That ᶜUmar ibn al-Khattāb wanted to instruct others in the careful procedure of checking of a ḥadīth is proved by his saying to Abū Mūsā al-Ashᶜarī: "I do not have any doubts as to your [trustworthiness] but the ḥadīth is attributed to the Prophet [himself] ﷺ [and we must be certain]." And in another narration it reads: "I [just] wanted to check [it]."

So, if this was the case with respect to al-Mughīrah ibn Shuᶜbah and Abū Mūsā al-Ashᶜarī – who were both from amongst the most illustrious of the Companions – then it follows that there is all the more reason to check those below them (in rank) from amongst the Companions and the Followers (*Tābiᶜūn*), and it is all the more appropriate and proper to pay careful attention to the transmission of the ḥadīth.

It was for this reason that adh-Dhahabī said of Abū Bakr: "He was the first to take precautions regarding the acceptance of reports (*akhbār*)."

Al-Ḥākim has said: "The first person to guard against [the transmission of] lies from the Messenger of Allah ﷺ was Abū Bakr ؓ then ᶜUmar Ibn al-Khattāb who extended the discussion regarding this science. A number of the Companions, during his time and after it, undertook the meticulous verification of ḥadīth, like ᶜAlī, the Mother of the Muʾminūn, ᶜĀʾishah, Ibn ᶜAbbās and others, and they established other principles for the verification of ḥadīth – like comparing the ḥadīth to the Qurʾān and comparing the ḥadīth to a *ṣaḥīḥ* ḥadīth known to be safe [from any corruption] (*maḥfūẓ*)."

So, despite their acknowledgment that the narrator of the ḥadīth was truthful and trustworthy, and despite their knowledge that the narrators of the ḥadīth did not lie when transmitting from the Messenger, ﷺ we observe how they sometimes impute a mistake to the narrator, [or charge that] he has forgotten something, or misheard, because the [ḥadīth in question] conflicted with the Qurʾān.

Moreover, ᶜUmar ibn al-Khattāb said to Fāṭimah ؓ [not the daughter of the Messenger of Allah ﷺ] on the occasion of the well-known incident she was involved in: "We do not abandon the Book of our Lord or the Sunnah of our Prophet ﷺ merely for the sake of what a woman has said, for we do not know [with certainty] whether she has indeed remembered [all the ḥadīth] or forgotten [part of it] – she has a right to lodging and a basic allowance. Allah, Exalted is He, has said: 'Do not evict them from their homes, nor should they leave, unless they commit an outright indecency' (Sūrat aṭ-Ṭalāq – Divorce: 1)".

There is also Sayyidah ᶜĀʾishah ؓ when she heard from ᶜUmar that he had related from the Messenger of Allah ﷺ that the dead person is tormented by the wailing [and lamenting] of his family. She said: "May Allah have mercy on ᶜUmar! No, by Allah! the Messenger of Allah ﷺ did not relate that

Allah torments the Mu᾽min by someone wailing [over his death] but rather he said: 'Allah increases the torment of the kāfir by the wailing of his family.'" ᶜĀ᾽ishah continued: "and may the Qur᾽ān be enough for you: 'No burden-bearer can bear another's burden.'" (Sūrat al-Anᶜām – Livestock: 164).

Likewise, when the words of Ibn ᶜUmar were mentioned to her ﵂: "The dead person is tormented by the wailing of his family" she said: "May Allah have mercy on Abū ᶜAbd ar-Raḥmān! He heard something but did not remember it [correctly]"; and in another narration: "Allah will surely forgive Abū ᶜAbd ar-Raḥmān as he did not lie but rather [merely] forgot and made a mistake"; and in another narration: "You will surely relate from me from people who neither lie or were lied to but the hearing [of those who transmitted] will be at fault". (This is related by Muslim in the 'Book of Burial' – *Kitāb al-Janā᾽iz*).

The Beginning of Falsification (*waḍᶜ*) of Ḥadīth and Care and Concern (*ihtimām*) for the Isnād

So the Companions ﵃ were confident of the overall level of truthfulness and trustworthiness amongst themselves, and they did not have any concern about the chain of transmission (*isnād*) during the time of the Messenger ﷺ or during most of the time of the four rightly-guided khulafā᾽ until near to half way through the first century when the *fitnah* (i.e. political strife and unrest) occurred with the killing of our master, ᶜUthmān in AH 35, when political ambitions stirred in the hearts of certain people and a certain lack in the accuracy and transmission could be noted.

Adh-Dhahabī said: "There was hardly anyone [who was considered] of little authority (*daᶜīf*) during the first century in which the Companions and the outstanding Followers died out – except isolated individuals (*al-wāḥid baᶜd al-wāḥid*). However, when the second century began they were to be found amongst the later circles of the Followers." He has also said: "As for the Followers among them, there were hardly any amongst them who lied deliberately, although there were some who made mistakes and were prone to erroneous conjecture. Moreover, those who rarely made mistakes and who when they transmitted, transmitted what was in all probability true, and those who made several mistakes but who were considered nevertheless as being among the [true] 'vessels' of knowledge were also excused. However, the ḥadīth of those whose mistakes were excessive and who were characterised by excessive isolation were not taken as proof. This hardly occurred in the first generation of Followers although it existed amongst the minor figures from among the Followers and those [who came] after them."

As for the companions of the Followers, like Mālik and al-Awzāᶜī and others of similar type, they were considered as belonging to the above mentioned ranks although there were others of their time who deliberately told lies or who often made mistakes.

So at this point the ᶜulamāʾ took great care regarding the careful procedure of confirmation and documentation of reports and enquired about the chain of transmission (*isnād*). Imām Muslim narrates in the beginning of his *Ṣaḥīḥ* from the illustrious Follower Muḥammad ibn Sīrīn, may Allah have mercy on him, that they did not use to ask about the chain of transmission (*isnād*) but when the *fitnah* occurred they would say: "Name your men for us!" and so they would examine the people of the Sunnah and accept their ḥadīth and they would examine the people of innovation and reject their ḥadīth.

And so the [first recorded] date of enquiring about the *isnād* began in this age, and the [first] research into the person who had cited (*qāʾil*) the ḥadīth, and into whether he was free of faults, was the latter half of the first century.

This science of verification relied on:

1. Comparing the narrated report (*khabar*) to a report guaranteed safe from corruption (*maḥfūẓ*), from a well known Companion acquainted with the matter in question such that whatever accorded with the well known, *maḥfūẓ* report was accepted, and whatever contradicted the well known *maḥfūẓ* report, was rejected. Imām Muslim narrated at the beginning of his *Ṣaḥīḥ* from Ibn Abī Mulaykah that the latter said: "I wrote to Ibn ᶜAbbās [requesting] that he write to me and that he be concise in what he said to me (or in another interpretation, recorded in an-Nawawi's *sharḥ*: and that he not disclose the sayings of the people of *fitnah*) and he replied: '[You are] a sincere young man, and I too select the matters [which I choose to narrate to someone], and I do not disclose [everything] to him.'"

He [then] said: "And he demanded this of me, so he began to write things from him and pass other things over saying: 'By Allah, had he demanded this of me he would have been going astray.'"

2. Becoming acquainted with the situation of the narrator and his status regarding integrity, accuracy in memorisation or recording, and his veracity or exaggeration (*tazayyud*). The Imām and Follower, Muḥammad ibn Sīrīn said: "They did not use to ask about the chain of transmission (*isnād*) but

when the *fitnah* occurred they would say: 'Name your men for us!' and so they would examine those who were the people of the Sunnah and take from them and examine those who were the people of innovation and reject their ḥadīth."

3. The question as to the *isnād* as mentioned above, is close (in meaning) to the words of the Imām Ibn Sīrīn, and this comparison between the narrated report and a *maḥfūẓ* report is known in the science of terminology as 'verification of the text' (*naqd al-matn*); and the ascertaining of the state of the narrator, that is, as to his sincerity or exaggeration, is what is known as the 'verification of the *isnād*' (*naqd al-isnād*). On this basis, it is possible to say with certainty and absolute conviction that the science of research into the narrator, what is narrated (the text) and the *isnād*, came into being in the latter half of the first century of the Hijrah.

Thus, Abū Bakr ﷺ was the first to ensure against lies [being transmitted] from the Messenger of Allah ﷺ and he was the first who took precautions regarding the acceptance of reports. Then ᶜUmar and ᶜAlī were the first to extend the discussion regarding this science, and a number of the Companions practised this science of verification during the life of ᶜUmar and after his death, like for example, the Mother of the Mu᾽minūn ᶜĀ᾽ishah and others.

The Verification (of Ḥadīth) in the School of Madīnah

Ibn Ḥibbān said: "Then a group of the people of Madīnah from amongst the leading figures (*sādāt*) of the Followers took up the way [of teaching and transmission] of ᶜUmar and ᶜAlī, adopted their Sunnah and followed their guidance regarding their practice of caution with respect to narrations – these included:

1. Saᶜīd ibn al-Musayyab (d. 94AH)
2. Al-Qāsim ibn Muḥammad ibn Abū Bakr (d.104)
3. Sālim ibn ᶜAbdullāh ibn ᶜUmar (d.104)
4. ᶜAlī ibn al-Ḥusayn ibn ᶜAlī (d.93)
5. Abū Salmā ibn ᶜAbd ar-Raḥmān ibn ᶜAwf (d.94)
6. ᶜUbaydullāh ibn ᶜAbdullāh ibn ᶜUtbah (94)
7. Khārijah ibn Zayd ibn Thābit (d.100)
8. ᶜUrwah ibn az-Zubayr ibn al-ᶜAwwām (d.94)
9. Abū Bakr ibn ᶜAbd ar-Raḥmān ibn al-Ḥārith ibn Hishām (d.94)

10. Sulaymān ibn Yasār (d. after 100)

The following acquired mastery from the above and distinguished themselves in this science in Madīnah:

1. Az-Zuhrī (d.124)
2. Yaḥyā ibn Sa^cīd al-Anṣārī (d.144)
3. Hishām ibn ^cUrwah (d.146)
4. Sa^cīd ibn Ibrāhīm

They all belonged to a group from the people of Madīnah. However, the most vigilant and careful amongst them and the one with the greatest memorisation of ḥadīth, the one who was most constant in his journeying to find ḥadīth and the one with the greatest enthusiasm and striving (*himmah*) was az-Zuhrī, may Allah have mercy on him.

The (Science of) Verification in ^cIrāq

The ḥadīth of the Messenger of Allah ﷺ spread with the Islamic conquest, and a large number of these ḥadīth were to be found in ^cIrāq. For this reason another school of verification arose in ^cIrāq alongside that of Madīnah.

At-Tirmidhī said: "We find that more than one of the Imāms of the Followers spoke about these men of ḥadīth, they included:

1. Al-Ḥasan al-Baṣrī (d.110AH)
2. Tāwūs (d-104)
3. Sa^cīd ibn Jubayr (d.94)
4. Ibrāhīm an-Nakha^cī (d.96)
5. ^cĀmir ash-Sha^cbī (d.105)

"Some of the other leading figures may be added to these Imāms, such as:

6. Ibn Sīrīn (d.110)"

Ibn Rajab mentions that Ibn Sīrīn was the first to subject the men of ḥadīth to critical verification and to discriminate the trustworthy from the rest.

Yaᶜqūb ibn Shaybah said: "I said to Yaḥyā ibn Maᶜīn: 'Do you know of any one of the Followers who subjected the men of ḥadīth to critical verification as much as Ibn Sīrīn did?' and he indicated (with a motion) of his head: 'No!'" Yaᶜqūb said: "I heard ᶜAlī ibn al-Madīnī say: 'He would inspect the ḥadīth and research into the chain of transmission (*isnād*), and we do not know anyone who preceded Muḥammad ibn Sīrīn [in this science].'"

In reality, it is not possible to ascertain with absolute certainty who was the first to speak regarding the men of ḥadīth and who endeavoured to investigate the chain of transmission (*isnād*). If Ibn al-Madīnī, may Allah have mercy on him, considered Ibn Sīrīn to be the first to discuss the men of ḥadīth scientifically, then we find difficulty in agreeing with this view as there were *ᶜulamā᾽* in Madīnah who carried out investigation of the chains of transmission (*isnād*) and research into the ḥadīth who were older and who often disposed of a wider knowledge than Ibn Sīrīn.

If, however, we restrict the words of Ibn al-Madīnī to the region of ᶜIrāq alone, then they would be inaccurate, as among the men who practised this science of verification was ash-Shaᶜbī (19-103AH) who was born before Ibn Sīrīn and also died before him (33-110AH); and likewise al-Ḥasan al-Baṣrī (21-110AH). Moreover, even if Saᶜīd ibn Jubayr (46-95AH) and Ibrāhīm an-Nakhaᶜī (47-96AH) were both born later than him, they died before him. For this reason, (their) mentioning that Ibn Sīrīn was the first is perhaps rather in the sense of 'foremost', that is, with regard to the depth of his discussion, not with respect to establishing primacy in an absolute manner.

Then after them came:

1. Ayyūb as-Sakhtiyānī (d.131)
2. Ibn ᶜAwn (d.150)

Extension of the Discussion of those Versed in the Science of Verification and the Spreading of this Science to Other Areas

There is no doubt that travel in search of knowledge during the life of the Prophet ﷺ and the journeys of the Companions after his death for the sake of ḥadīth of the Messenger of Allah ﷺ was a well known and widespread phenomenon; and likewise, the travels of the Followers. However, the science of the men of transmission did not develop in any significant way and was not practised among the *ᶜulamā᾽* and the men of verification until half way into the second century of the Hijrah. This was because those who succeeded the first generation did not harbour weaknesses. Indeed, most of those who succeeded the Companions were trustworthy and truthful.

Then there appeared individuals who lacked the capacity to transmit correctly and whose veracity was subject to discussion, like al-Ḥārith al-Aᶜwar, ᶜĀṣim ibn Khamra and the like. There were also amongst them a number of leading figures of the people of innovation from the Khawārij, Shīᶜah and the Qadariyyah, from whom we ask Allah for protection, like ᶜAbd ar-Raḥmān ibn Muljam, Mukhtār ath-Thaqafī al-Kadhdhāb (The Liar), and Saᶜīd al-Juhaynī.

Commitment to the *dīn* and acts of *taqwā* were stronger in that (earlier) age than in the one which followed. Moreover, political differences were only just beginning and the motives for any falsification of ḥadīth were of a restricted nature with respect to the period immediately following the first generation. However, falsification increased during the second and third century, although in the main it had to do with events which occurred in the first half of the first century hijrī.

A number of imāms of the science of verification and great *muḥaddithūn* distinguished themselves through their knowledge of the rank and circumstances of the men of ḥadīth and their ability to verify them. A vast subject matter developed regarding knowledge of the men of ḥadīth as travelling for knowledge became a necessary prerequisite for ḥadīth. One collected information from among all the experts of verification and the *muḥaddithūn* after the time of the Followers, that is, in the majority of cases, from all centres of knowledge in the Islamic world at that time. Only rarely did one restrict the gathering of knowledge to the particular area [of a narrator]. Thus the discussions of these experts of verification was not restricted to the men of one particular region alone but rather encompassed all of the narrators in general. Indeed, during this period there existed numerous other schools of the science of verification in various Islamic regions.

For this reason Ibn Ḥibbān said: "Then a group of imāms and *fuqahā*ᵓ from amongst the Muslims took from them this ḥadīth methodology, this procedure for discriminating the [trustworthy] men [from the rest], this way of preserving the sunnahs and of identifying those [transmitters] of little authority. Among [the trustworthy] are:

1. Sufyān ibn Saᶜīd ath-Thawrī (al-Kufa) (d.162)
2. Mālik ibn Anas (Madīnah) (d.179)

3. Shuʿbah ibn al-Ḥajjāj (central region) (d.160)
4. ʿAbd ar-Raḥmān ibn ʿAmr al-Awzāʿī (Beirut) (d.156)
5. Ḥammād ibn Salamah (Baṣra) (d.176)
6. Al-Layth ibn Saʿd (Egypt) (d.175)
7. Ḥammād ibn Zayd (Makkah) (d.179)
8. Sufyān ibn ʿUyaynah (Makkah) (d.198)

There is also a group of others with the above mentioned. However, the most exacting of them with regard to verification of the sunnahs and the most persistent in this – so much so that they made it their only activity and did not occupy themselves with anything else – were three in number: Mālik, ath-Thawrī and Shuʿbah (*al-Majrūḥīn*, p.40)." Ibn Ḥibbān said in *ath-Thiqāt* (The Trustworthy Narrators): "Shuʿbah was the first to investigate the matter of the *muḥaddithūn* and the subject of the narrators of little authority (*ḍuʿafā'*) and those omitted (*matrūkūn*) from consideration in ʿIrāq. [This investigation was so respected that] it became an exemplary knowledge and so the people of ʿIrāq then imitated his example after this, describing him as the first to broaden the scope of invalidation and authentication." (Book of the Trustworthy Narrators: 3/438)

One notices from this list that the experts in the science of verification (*nuqqād*) came from a variety of countries, some from ʿIrāq, some from Shām (Greater Syria), the Ḥijāz or Egypt and that this verification was not restricted to Madīnah, Kūfa and Baṣra, as was the case before. Ibn Ḥibbān said: "Then a group took up this science from them after their generation, namely the recording of ḥadīth, discrimination of the trustworthy men from the unreliable, investigation of those of little authority and research into the means of narration, these included:

1. ʿAbdullāh ibn al-Mubārak (d.181)
2. Yaḥyā ibn Saʿīd al-Qaṭṭān (d.198)
3. Wakīʿ ibn al-Jarrāḥ (d.197)
4. ʿAbd ar-Raḥmān ibn Fahdī (d.198)
5. Muḥammad ibn Idrīs ash-Shāfiʿī (d.204)

"There was a group associated with them. However, the most strict in their examination of the matter of the *muḥaddithūn* and the most prone to reject those of little authority or those usually omitted as unreliable – to the extent that they made it into a special art of theirs and did not transmit it to others despite their holding to the dīn, their extreme scrupulousness and their legal understanding of the Sunnah – were two men: Yaḥyā ibn Saᶜīd al-Qaṭṭān and ᶜAbd ar-Raḥmān ibn Fahdī," (*al-Majrūḥīn* 1/52).

Yaḥyā ibn Saᶜīd completed his studies in this art at the hand of Shuᶜbah ibn al-Ḥajjāj. Ibn Ḥibbān said: "Then a group took up from them the method of testing ḥadīth and the verification of the men with regard to the reports. To this end they journeyed to the large cities to collect the sunnahs; they carried out an investigation of the towns and the various outlying regions and discovered the weak points regarding those usually omitted from consideration and the failings of those of little authority; they explained the particularities of the status and circumstances of the trustworthy, those guilty of forgery or falsification, the acceptable imāms and those to be omitted from consideration. [So respected was their method] that they came to be imitated with regard to the reports, and the later imāms of instruction took up their way and method regarding the narrations, these included:

1. Aḥmad ibn Ḥanbal (d.240)
2. Yaḥyā ibn Maᶜīn (d.233)
3. ᶜAlī ibn al-Madīnī (d.234)
4. Abū Bakr ibn Abī Shaybah (d.235)
5. Isḥāq ibn Ibrāhīm al-Ḥanẓalī (d.238)
6. ᶜUbaydullāh ibn ᶜUmar al-Qawārīrī (d.235)
7. Zuhayr ibn Ḥarb Abū Khaythamah (d.234)

A group of their companions was associated with them. However, among the most scrupulous regarding the dīn, the most assiduous in their research of those to be omitted from consideration and those who held the most tenaciously and persistently to this art were Aḥmad ibn Ḥanbal, Yaḥyā ibn Maᶜīn and ᶜAlī ibn al-Madīnī, may Allah have mercy on them," (*al-Majrūḥīn*: 1/54).

"Then another group took up from them, these included:

1. Muḥammad ibn Yaḥyā adh-Dhahlī (d.258)
2. ᶜUbaydullāh ibn ᶜAbd ar-Raḥmān ad-Dārimī (d.255)
3. Abū Zurᶜah ar-Rāzī (d.263)
4. Muḥammad ibn Ismāᶜīl al-Bukhārī (d.256)
5. Muslim ibn al-Ḥajjāj (d.161)
6. Abū Dāwūd as-Sijistānī (d.275)

"There was also a group associated with them who applied themselves assiduously to the recollection (of ḥadīth), who made a great many written records, who outstripped all others in their journeying for knowledge and who were persistent in maintaining the Sunnah and memorisation, composing works of ḥadīth and intense study – to such an extent that those who came after them from amongst our shaykhs adopted this practice (*madhhab*) and this method (*maslak*). [Such was their exemplary imitation] that if one of them were asked as to the number of letters (*aḥruf*) in the [texts of the ḥadīth describing the] sunnahs, then he would be able to enumerate them for each and every sunnah; and if a [letter] *alif* or a *waw* had been added to them, he would exclude it because of his own desire [to narrate the text in a grammatically correct fashion], but then would also record it leaving the [extra letter in] out of [sheer] respect for [anything transmitted of] the dīn," (*al-Majrūḥīn*: 57/1).

Let us pause a moment to consider the matter of the history of verification of ḥadīth as these last two generations represent the culmination of this science. Some of their writings on verification are still extant. As for those who lived before these two generations, their discussion is to be found dispersed in the books of invalidation and authentication. However, we do not know of any book from these two generations which is solely devoted to 'invalidation and authentication' and which remains extant to this day, even though there are authoritative reference works which indicate that there were a number of specialists in the science of verification who composed works on the subject of invalidation and authentication. Let us mention as examples:

1. Shuᶜbah ibn al-Ḥajjāj (d.160)
2. ᶜAbdullāh ibn al-Bakī (d.) who [wrote] a book on history most likely [composed] in the mode of the book of 'Major History' (*at-Tārīkh al-kabīr*) of al-Bukhārī or according to the manner of the 'Minor History' (*at-Tārīkh aṣ-ṣaghīr*)
3. Al-Layth ibn Saᶜd (d.175) who [wrote] a book of history
4. ᶜAbd ar-Raḥmān ibn Mahdī (d.198)
5. Yaḥyā ibn al-Qaṭṭān (d. 198)
6. Abū Dāwūd aṭ-Ṭayālisī (d.204) who was followed by a number of shaykhs.

The Science of Invalidation and Authentication

Imām al-Bayhaqī said in the introduction to his book *Dalāʾil an-Nubuwwah* (The Proofs of Prophethood): "Whoever examines the diligence of the people of memorisation, the science of the status and circumstances of the narrators, and which reports are acceptable and which unacceptable, then he will realise that they spared no effort in this, to the extent that the son would find fault with his father if he came across something in his [method] which obliged him to reject his report, and the father would invalidate the [report of his] son, the brother [would censure the reports of his] brother and no one feared the blame of people, so great was their awe of Allah. Moreover, no one witheld his [censure of invalid reports] out of fear for any trouble he might cause to relatives, nor for the sake of any gift of money – and there are many stories about them in this respect.

"They dealt with the narrator himself, his narrations, his shaykhs, his [level of] memorisation, his forgetfulness, his accuracy, his being prone to confuse narrations or *isnāds,* his weakness of intellect or authority, his strength, his delivery of the reports, his youth, his old age, his being resident or travelling at the time of narration, and all the other matters which are connected with the business of narration, to the extent that they would mention very fine and subtle merits or trifling blemishes. They would mention too [whether the narrator was] a beginner or a qualified jurist and they would compare between the narrators to ascertain which was the best at memorisation, the most accurate, the first to report and the one who kept the closest company of the shaykhs and imāms of narration; [they would mention] those who preceded the narrator in question and those who came afterwards, those who kept the company [of his teachers] for a long time and those who did so for only a short time. In this way they endeavoured to the best of their ability to represent the narrator in the best possible light; they were able to reveal his attributes and explain his method – and they were extraordinary experts in this!"

They were so extraordinary that the German savant Dr. Sprenger (despite his vehement opposition to Islam) said in his introduction in English to the book *al-Iṣābah fī tamyīz aṣ-ṣaḥābah* (The Correct Method of Discriminating Between the Companions) by Ḥāfiẓ ibn Ḥajar, (published in Calcutta, India, 1853-1863): "There has never been a people or nation in former times, just as there does not exist now amongst contemporary peoples or nations, people who had such a mastery of the tremendous science of men's names (and biographies) like that possessed by the Muslims, a science which dealt with the status and circumstances of five hundred thousand men and their activity (in the realm of transmission)."

Even if these words are exaggerated with regard to the number cited by the above mentioned doctor, there is no doubt that this art which the Muslim ummah alone practised played a substantial role in maintaining the strength of the dīn and the clarity of the law – out of their jealous concern to guard their dīn from ruin they safeguarded and accurately recorded everything, both of major and minor importance.

This resulted in the total removal of the falsifiers (of ḥadīth), of the deceivers and liars, of those of little authority, and of the negligent. By these means – and whatever was closely associated with the above mentioned method – the pure Sunnah was preserved from any intrusion of spurious material, and praise belongs to Allah, may He be exalted.

Thus, [the task of] those who teach this science to their fellow men in this age of ours – and the ages before it and after it – has been facilitated; [the task of] giving a fair and measured judgement on the ḥadīth or its narrator on the basis of what these earlier generations had recorded for us from the narrators [is facilitated] to the extent of their capacity to master this science of ḥadīth of which the first generations had an absolute mastery, and into which they had a penetrating insight, for no one comes close to emulating them and no one of any eminence or nobility would seek to find fault in them.

This (verification) of the men of ḥadīth became afterwards one of the various sciences of ḥadīth in its own right. It was called the 'science of invalidation and authorisation'. Men of extraordinary talent distinguished themselves in this science as did a number of quite brilliant scholars, beginning from the time of the noble Companions and those who followed them with utmost correctness and uprightness, and ending with the Ḥāfiẓs adh-Dhahabī, al-ʿIraqī and Ibn Ḥajar.

The Beginning of Written Records of the Science of Invalidation and Authentication

The experts of ḥadīth used to relate orally the sayings of those versed in the science of the men, just as they would relate the ḥadīth. The first to collect the sayings on this subject was Yaḥyā ibn Saʿīd al-Qaṭṭān. Adh-Dhahabī said in the introduction to *Mīzān al-iᶜtidāl* (The Balanced Scales): "The first to collect the sayings on this subject was the Imām Yaḥyā ibn Saᶜīd al-Qaṭṭān."

Then the *muḥaddithūn* took up the method of testing and selecting the men with regard to the reports, and clarified the rank and circumstances of the 'trustworthy', the 'fraudulent' and those 'omitted (altogether)'. [They became so adept in this science] that a group of them came to be imitated in the science of traditions, namely, Aḥmad ibn Ḥanbal, Yaḥyā ibn Maᶜīn, ᶜAlī ibn al-Madīnī, Abū Bakr ibn Abī Shaybah, Isḥāq ibn Ibrāhīm al-Ḥanẓalī (better known as Ibn Rahwayh), Zuhayr ibn Ḥarb, Abū Khaythamah and a group of their associates. However, the most scrupulous amongst them, those most assiduous in their research into those to be omitted, and those most persevering in this art, were Aḥmad ibn Ḥanbal, Yaḥyā ibn Maᶜīn and ᶜAlī ibn al-Madīnī. No writer on the subject of 'invalidation and authentication' would omit mention of Yaḥyā ibn Maᶜīn, ᶜAlī ibn al-Madīnī or Aḥmad ibn Ḥanbal.

Ibn Rajab said: "Ibn Maᶜīn disliked having the sayings about invalidation and authentication written down and I believe he himself did not write anything down on the subject. Rather, his companions asked him questions on the matter and they wrote down what he said, these included ᶜAbbās ad-Dawrī, Ibrāhīm ibn al-Junayd, Maṣr ibn Muḥammad, Mufaḍḍal al-Ghallabī, ᶜUthmān ibn Saᶜīd ad-Dārimī, Yazīd ibn al-Haythamah and others" (Ibn Rajab).

Ibn Maᶜīn was one of the strictest regarding invalidation – and how many of the trustworthy were declared invalid by ibn Maᶜīn! The 'two Shaykhs' (Muslim and al-Bukhārī) and others, however, transmitted from them and even the strict among them did not accept his [standard of] invalidation at all.

Adh-Dhahabī said in his treatise entitled, 'Enumeration of Those Whom One May Rely Upon Regarding Invalidation and Authentication': "A group of them are zealous in their invalidation and cautious in their authentication, disparaging the narrator for two or three mistakes. In this way they reduce the weight of the ḥadīth in question. Thus, if they do deem someone trustworthy, then take a tight grasp of his words and hold firmly [to the conviction] that he has been deemed trustworthy; but if they deem a man to be of little authority, then examine whether others agree with his being deemed of little authority. If they do, and this [judgement] does not run counter to any of the perspicacious men of this science, then he is surely of little authority; and if anyone has deemed him trustworthy, then what they have said regarding him is not accepted – except with an [added] explanation.

"Thus, it is not enough that Ibn Maʿīn says that he is of little authority without explaining the reason for his weakness, if others have deemed him trustworthy. With regard to such cases, one should refrain from assessing the ḥadīth as *ṣaḥīḥ* (i.e. correct without a doubt); rather [it should be assessed as being] closer in rank to a *ḥasan* ḥadīth (i.e. good but not of the infallibility of the *ṣaḥīḥ*). Ibn Maʿīn, Abū Ḥātim and al-Jūzajānī are [well known for being] zealous in their censure (*mutaᶜannitūn*).

"However, as for Aḥmad ibn Ḥanbal, one of his writings is entitled, *al-ᶜIlal wa-maᶜrifat ar-rijāl* (The Defects and Knowledge of the Men). It is a narration of his son ᶜAbdullāh and is not ordered according to any specific basis but rather is a collection of the statements of Aḥmad regarding the invalidation of the [trustworthiness of the] men of ḥadīth and a description of who they are, including for example, mention of the cognomen (*kunyā*) by which they were known, their fellow men and companions, the date of their death and the times they travelled; news of any afflictions or hardships they endured, and other information connected to their lives and their physical and moral character. Included too is mention that they had or had not heard [ḥadīth directly] from one of their shaykhs and other information connected to the verification or invalidation of the chain of transmission (*isnād*) of the ḥadīth of the man in question."

As for ᶜAlī ibn al-Madīnī, he was a philosopher and a doctor of this science – a doctor capable of diagnosing an unsound ḥadīth. He was also a spokesman for the group of ḥadīth experts and the first to initiate the setting down in writing of the principles of ḥadīth terminology and the recording of some of its issues – which he arranged by collecting a single subject in one or various parts.

ᶜAlī ibn al-Madīnī is reckoned a moderate among the experts of verification (*nuqqād*) as he said: "Yaḥyā ibn Saʿīd and ᶜAbd ar-Raḥmān ibn Mahdī agreed to omit a man; I also did not relate the ḥadīth from him; if they differed with each other I took the saying of ᶜAbd ar-Raḥmān as he was the most moderate of them, while there was a severity [to be observed] in Yaḥyā." This is an indication that ᶜAlī ibn al-Madīnī did not consider himself a person of excessive severity.

A Definition of the Science of Invalidation and Authentication

This science is concerned with research – by means of a special vocabulary – as to the potential invalidation or authentication of narrators, and as to the rank and status assigned to these terms (*Kashf aẓ–Ẓunūn* 'The Removal of

Uncertainties'). The etymological meaning of the word *jarḥ* (invalidation) is 'to wound the body with a sword or the like' and is used to refer to someone's fault or failing; its meaning, as a particular term of this science, refers to the assessment by the expert in memorisation and the science of verification (*al-ḥāfidh an-nāqid*) of the narrator leading to a rejection of his narration or its being deemed to be of little authority.

The Various Kinds of Books of Invalidation and Authentication

In their biographies of the men of ḥadīth, the *ᶜulamāʾ* have composed innumerable books on invalidation and authentication. One may classify these compositions in three ways:

1. The kind which deals with those of little authority (*ḍuᶜafāʾ*) only, like the 'Minor'– and 'Major works regarding those of little authority' (*aḍ–Ḍuᶜafāʾ aṣ-ṣaghīr* and *al-kabīr*) of al-Bukhārī; *aḍ–Ḍuᶜafāʾ* of Abū Ḥātim ar-Rāzī, of Ibn al-Jārūd, of Ibn Khuzaymah, of Abū Jaᶜfar Muḥammad ibn ᶜAmr al-ᶜAqilī, of Shahīn al-Wāᶜiẓ, of Ibn Shahīn al-Baghdādī, of Ḥakīm al-Kabīr, of Abū Nuᶜaym al-Aṣbahānī and of al-Khaṭīb al-Baghdādī; *aḍ–Ḍuᶜafāʾ wa'l-kadhdhābūn wa'l-matrūkūn min aṣḥāb al-ḥadīth* (Those of Little Authority, the Liars and Those to be Omitted amongst the Experts of Ḥadīth) by ᶜUthmān Saᶜīd ibn ᶜAmr al-Barādhaᶜī; *aḍ–Ḍuᶜafāʾ wa'l-matrūkūn* (Those of Little Authority and Those to be Omitted) by an-Nasāʾī and al-Dāraquṭnī; *al-Kāmil fī ḍuᶜafāʾ ar-rijāl* (The 'Completion' Regarding the Men of Weak Authority) by al-Jurjānī; *Kitāb al-majrūḥīn* (The Book of Those Deemed Invalid) by Ibn Ḥibbān as-Sabtī; and *al-Madkhal ilā maᶜrifat al-iklīl* (Introduction to the Crowning Science) by Ḥakīm an-Naysābūrī.

2. Writings which deal only with the trustworthy narrators like *ath-Thiqāt wa'l-muthabbitūn* (The Reliable and the Trustworthy) by Ibn al-Madīnī who was the first to compose something on the trustworthy; *ath-Thiqāt* by Ibn Ḥibbān; *Tārīkh asmāʾ ath-thiqāt fa-man naqala ᶜanhum al-ᶜilm* (A Directory of the Names of the Trustworthy and Those who Transmitted Knowledge from Them) by Ibn Shahīn al-Wāᶜiẓ; *al-Madkhal ilā aṣ-Ṣaḥīḥayn* (An Introduction to the Two Ṣaḥīḥs) by Abū ᶜAbdullāh al-Ḥākim.

3. Writings which combine the trustworthy and those of little authority like *at-Tārīkh* (The Historical Directory) by Imām al-Layth ibn Saᶜd, ᶜAbdullāh ibn al-Mubārak, al-Faḍl ibn Dakīn, ᶜAlī ibn al-Madīnī and Abū Bakr ibn Abī Shaybah; and by al-Bukhārī, the 'Major' 'Minor' and 'Middle' [versions of

at-Tārīkh]; *aṭ-Ṭabaqāt al-kubrā* (The Major Directory of the Various Generations of Narrators) of Ibn Sa'd; *Ma'rifat ar-rijāl* (Science of the Men) and *at-Tārīkh wa'l-'ilal* (A Directory of the Men of Ḥadīth and Their Failings) both by Yaḥyā ibn Ma'īn; *al-'Ilal wa'r-rijāl* (The Failings and the Men of the Science of Ḥadīth) of Aḥmad ibn Ḥanbal; *Kitāb al-jarḥ wa't-ta'dīl* (The Book of Invalidation and Authentication) by Abū Ḥātim ar-Rāzī.

Writings on the Men of Ḥadīth Mentioned in the Six Books and Other Works

The writings which are mentioned above regarding knowledge of the men of the science of ḥadīth deal with the narrators of ḥadīth in a general way without restricting themselves to the men of one particular book.

There are also other writings in which the authors were concerned only with biographies of narrators in particular books; they did not turn their attention to any other narrators. These books are distinguished from others by the fact that they encompass the biographies of all the narrators in those particular books, and this makes it easier for the researcher who wants information about narrators in particular books. This work of research began in the fourth century of the Hijrah, and the first book to be composed on this science was the book *at-Ta'rīf bi-rijāl al-Muwaṭṭa'* (Identification of the Men of the *Muwaṭṭa'*) by Abū Zakariyyā Yaḥyā ibn Zakariyyā al-Qurṭubī (d.255).

At the same time, some authors began to combine [identification of] the men of al-Bukhārī and Muslim into one work; but there was no attempt to combine the men of other than these two works during this period. It may well be that the reliance of the *'ulamā'* (in general) on the two *Ṣaḥīḥs* and the fact that the men in them both are all trustworthy was what led the *'ulamā'* of ḥadīth to combine the men of these two works. The first person to compose such a work was Abu'l-Ḥasan 'Alī ibn 'Umar ad-Dāraquṭnī (d.385). As for the works which combine the men of the 'Four Sunnahs', the 'Five Books' or the 'Six Books', they appeared soon after this when Abū Bakr Aḥmad ibn Muḥammad al-Barqānī (d.425) composed a book containing the names of the Shaykhs of al-Bukhārī, Muslim, Abū Dāwūd, at-Tirmidhī and an-Nasā'ī [as mentioned] in their works about the Companions and Followers who preceded these Shaykhs.

Then the *'ulamā'* wrote a number of books in which they combined the biographies of the people mentioned in the 'Six Books'.

The [work entitled] *al-Kamāl* ('Completion') and the Concern of the *ᶜUlamāʾ* with it

The most famous of these books is *al-Kamāl fi asmāʾ ar-rijāl* (The Completion of the Directory of Names of the Men) by al-Ḥāfiẓ ᶜAbd al-Ghanī al-Muqaddisī al-Jamāʾilī (d. 600). This book remained the foundation for a great number of works which refined it, improved it or added to it throughout the following three centuries. Thus, it was revised by al-Ḥāfiẓ Abū Ḥajjāj Yūsuf ibn az-Zakī al-Mazzī (d.742) in his book *Tahdhīb al-kamāl* (A Revision of the 'Completion') which became the most important work on the subject. For this reason a group of *ᶜulamāʾ* occupied themselves with this work, abridging or revising it. Ḥāfiẓ adh-Dhahabī (d.748) summarised it in his book *al-Kāshif ᶜan rijāl al-kutub as-sittah* (Disclosure of the Men of the Six Books); and adh-Dhahabī also revised it in his work *Tahdhīb at-tahdhīb* (A Revision of the Revision) adding some of the [narrators] who had died [and who were missing from] the *Tahdhīb al-kamāl;* then Mughlaṭāʾī added an appendix to adh-Dhahabī in his book *Ikmāl tahdhīb al-kamāl* (The Completion of the Revision of the 'Completion').

Here are the names of the *ᶜulamāʾ* who revised the book *al-Kamāl fi asmāʾ ar-rijāl* or who emended or summarised it, with the names of their works arranged chronologically:

1. *Tahdhīb al-kamāl* by al-Mazzī (d.742)
2. *Tahdhīb at-tahdhīb* by adh-Dhahabī (d.748)
3. *al-Kāshif* also by adh-Dhahabī
4. *Tahdhīb at-tahdhīb* by al-Ḥāfiẓ ibn Ḥajar al-ᶜAsqalānī (d.852)
5. *Taqrīb at-tahdhīb* also by al-Ḥāfiẓ ibn Ḥajar al-ᶜAsqalānī
6. *Khulāṣah tahdhīb tahdhīb al-Kamāl* by al-Khazrajī (d.924)

Tahdhīb at-tahdhīb

Ḥāfiẓ ibn Ḥajar al-ᶜAsqalānī revised the *Tahdhīb al-kamāl* in his well-known work *Tahdhīb at-tahdhīb,* improving and rearranging it. Here is the method of his summary *Tahdhīb al-kamāl*:

1. He summarised, in particular, the principles of invalidation and authentication to facilitate study;

2. He omitted the lengthy writing-down of ḥadīth which al-Mazzī had recorded together with their complete chains of transmission (*isnād*) reaching back to the first narrator; this [omission] amounts to about a third of the original length of the book;

3. He omitted many of the shaykhs and students in the biography in question restricting himself to the most well known among them and to those noted for the most memorisation – if the narrator had described them at unusual length;

4. He did not usually omit anything in the short bibliographies;

5. He did not list alphabetically the shaykhs and students in the person's biography but rather arranged them according to age, memorisation, chain of transmission (*isnād*), age, kinship and other factors;

6. He omitted excessive discussion during some of the biographies as this would not have given any additional indication of [the level of a person's] trustworthiness or invalidation;

7. He added statements of those expert in the science of 'invalidation and deeming trustworthy' from other sources to the biographies;

8. He often omitted any difference of opinion as to the [precise date of] death of a man unless it was of clear benefit;

9. He added [other] biographies which he considered fulfilled his exacting standards;

10. He added statements to some biographies which did not exist in the original but he prefaced them with the words, 'I said';

11. He kept to the abbreviations used by al-Mazzī although he omitted three of them (*mīm-qāf, sīn-yā, ṣād*);

12. He omitted the three divisions mentioned by al-Mazzī at the beginning of the book.

In short, the book *Tahdhīb at-tahdhīb* of Ḥāfiẓ ibn Ḥajar is a very valuable, carefully written book of great benefit. The Ḥāfiẓ clearly exerted himself to the utmost; he summarised what was fitting to be summarised and he added what was missing from the original when this addition was needed. He wrote carefully, revised and refined, and by means of his wide-ranging acquaintance with this science he was able to seek assistance from a number of other works for his book, whose composition is of a most satisfactory and pleasing style.

Taqrīb at-tahdhīb (Access to the *Tahdhīb*)

The Ḥāfiẓ Ibn Ḥajar made a summary of his *Tahdhīb at-tahdhīb* reducing it to about a sixth of its size. He entitled it *Taqrīb at-tahdhīb*. In the introduction he mentions that the impetus for writing this book came from some of his brothers who had requested that he abstract just the names of the people whose biographies figure in *Tahdhīb at-tahdhīb*. He regarded his response to their request as something which would correspond to his overall goal and be of further benefit.

The Ḥāfiẓ used the following method in his book:

1. He mentions all the biographies which are in *Tahdhīb at-tahdhīb;*

2. He uses the same abbreviations as he used in *Tahdhīb at-tahdhīb* itself except that he changes the abbreviations of the 'Four sunnahs' if they were collected [in one work];

3. He mentions the various ranks of narrators in the introduction classifying them into twelve kinds, and he uses the terminology of invalidation and authentication for each biography;

4. He mentions in the introduction of the book the various generations of the narrators' biographies, also arranging them into twelve ranks;

5. He adds a section at the end of the book related to the description of the women about whom there were doubts [as to the validity of their transmission];

6. [Finally,] the Ḥāfiẓ's judgement of every one of them is based on the most correct of what has been said of the person in question, on the most equitable description [of his character] and in the most concise terms – so much so that the biography is usually not more than one line long but includes the name of the man, that of his father and his grandfather, and the family relationship, lineage, surname and cognomen for which he is most known. He records any variations in the spelling of his names; he also records any particularity the person is noted for regarding the science of invalidation and authentication; then he includes a description of the period of each narrator such that it acts as a substitute for any information omitted with regard to his shaykhs and to those who then narrated from him.

الرِّجَال
THE NARRATORS

Shaykh ᶜAbd al-Ḥayy al-Laknawī

A

"A man" [ḥadīth 821]. There is in the *Muwaṭṭaʾ* of Yaḥyā and its commentary, "Mālik from Muḥammad ibn ᶜAbdullāh ibn Abī Maryam al-Khuzāᶜī." Abū Ḥātim said, "A right-acting Madīnan shaykh," and Ibn Ḥibbān mentioned him in *ath-Thiqāt* as the one who asked Saᶜīd ibn al-Musayyab, and so by that the unknown man is made known.

"A narrator who is trustworthy to me" [ḥadīth 716]. Az-Zurqānī said, "Some say that it was Makhramah ibn Bukayr or Ibn Luhayᶜah, because al-Walīd ibn Muslim narrated it from ᶜAbdullāh ibn Luhayᶜah."

Abān ibn ᶜUthmān ibn ᶜAffān, Abū ᶜAbdullāh the Madīnan, [son of] the Amīr al-Muʾminīn the third of the Khulafāʾ who took the right way, was a Follower who had many narrations and who was a trustworthy narrator. He died in 105 AH.ᶜAbbād ibn al-ᶜAwwām. Adh-Dhahabī said in *Tadhkirat al-ḥuffāẓ*, "ᶜAbbād ibn al-ᶜAwwām the imām and scholar of ḥadīth Abū Sahl al-Wāsiṭī. Abū Dāwūd and others regarded him as a trustworthy narrator. Ibn Saᶜd said, 'He was one of the noble men in every respect.' He had become a shīᶜah and ar-Rashīd imprisoned him for a time and then later released him, and so he resided in Baghdād. There is disagreement about the date of his death after 180 AH and some say three, five, six and seven years after that. There is agreement about using him as a decisive proof." (Abridged)

ᶜAbbād ibn Tamīm ibn Ghaziyyah al-Māzinī. He narrated from his father, who was a Companion, and from his paternal uncle ᶜAbdullāh ibn Zayd al-Māzinī. An-Nasāʾī and others declared him a trustworthy narrator, as as-Suyūṭī said.

ᶜAbbād ibn Ziyād was a *mawlā* of al-Mughīrah ibn Shuᶜbah and not one of his children as narrated.

ᶜAbd al-ᶜAzīz ibn Ḥakīm. Ibn Ḥibbān mentioned him among the trustworthy narrators of the Followers, where he said, "ᶜAbd al-ᶜAzīz ibn Ḥakīm al-Ḥaḍramī whose kunyā was Abū Yaḥyā. He narrated from Ibn ᶜUmar and is counted among the people of Kūfa. From him narrated ath-Thawrī and Isrāʾīl. He died after 130 AH. He is the one who is usually called

Ibn Abī Ḥakīm." In *Mīzān al-iʿtidāl* is to be found that Ibn Maʿīn said he was a trustworthy narrator, but that Abū Ḥātim said, "He is not strong."

ʿAbd al-Jabbār [ḥadīth 647]. ʿAbd al-Jabbār ibn ʿAbbās al-Hamdānī [rather than ʿAbd al-Jabbār *from* Ibn ʿAbbās al-Hamdānī, in the view of ʿAbd al-Ḥayy al-Laknawī]. He said in *Tahdhīb at-tahdhīb,* "ʿAbd al-Jabbār ibn al-ʿAbbās ash-Shibāmī al-Hamdānī the Kūfan. Shibām is a mountain in the Yemen. He narrated from Abū Isḥāq as-Sabīʿī, ʿAdī ibn Thābit, Salamah ibn Kuhayl, Qays ibn Wahb, ʿAwn, ʿUthmān ibn al-Mughīrah ath-Thaqafī, ʿUrayb ibn Marthad al-Mashriqī and a number of others, and from him narrated Ibn al-Mubārak, Ismāʿīl ibn Muḥammad ibn Juḥādah, Muslim ibn Qutaybah, Ibrāhīm ibn Yūsuf ibn Abī Isḥāq as-Sabīʿī, Abū Aḥmad az-Zubayrī, al-Ḥasan ibn Ṣāliḥ, Wakīʿ and others. ʿAbdullāh ibn Aḥmad [ibn Ḥanbal] said from his father, 'I hope that there is no harm in him, and he used to be a Shīʿah.' Ibn Maʿīn and Abū Dāwūd said, 'There is no harm in him.' Abū Ḥātim said he was a trustworthy narrator. Al-Bazzār said, 'His ḥadīth are straight.' Al-ʿIjlī said, 'A little right-acting person (*ṣuwayliḥ*) in whom there is no harm.'" (Abridged)

There is in *Ansāb as-Samʿānī* after mention that ash-Shibāmī derives from Shibām a land in the Yemen, "The person who is well known with respect to it is ʿAbd al-Jabbār ibn ʿAbbās ash-Shibāmī al-Hamdānī one of the people of Kūfa. He narrated from ʿAwn ibn Abī Juḥayfah and ʿAṭā' ibn as-Sā'ib, and from him narrated Ibn Abī Zā'idah and the Kūfans. He was in the main a Shīʿah."

ʿAbd al-Karīm ibn Abi'l-Mukhāriq. Two [narrators] are called ʿAbd al-Karīm, the first of whom is a trustworthy narrator about whom there is agreement, and from whom al-Bukhārī and Muslim narrated, and he is Ibn Mālik al-Jazarī and his kunyā was Abū Saʿd. The second was Ibn Abi'l-Mukhāriq whose kunyā was Abū Umayyah, and he is to be abandoned, as found in *al-Qawl al-musaddad fi'dh-dhibb ʿan musnad Aḥmad* by Ḥāfiẓ Ibn Ḥajar al-ʿAsqalānī. He said in *at-Tamhīd,* "He is weak, about which the people of ḥadīth are unanimous. He was a teacher in a Qur'ān school, of a good way of life, and his way of living deceived Mālik [about his qualities as a narrator of ḥadīth], for he was not one of the people of his town so that he could know him. He died in 126 AH or 127 AH. As-Suyūṭī said in *Mirqāt aṣ-ṣuʿūd,* 'It is not sound in that which ʿAbd al-Karīm ibn Abi'l-Mukhāriq alone narrates to judge that he fabricated, because Mālik narrated from him, and it is well known that it was his habit only to narrate from those he regarded as trustworthy narrators even if others discovered what necessarily required taking a critical view of him.'" The name of Ibn Abi'l-Mukhāriq is said to have been Qays but some say Ṭāriq.

ʿAbd al-Karīm al-Jazarī was ʿAbd al-Karīm ibn Mālik al-Jazarī Abū Saʿīd al-Ḥarrānī and he was one of those who were firmly established and one whom the imāms regarded as a trustworthy narrator. Ibn Maʿīn said that he was a firmly established trustworthy narrator. Ibn Saʿd said, "He was a trustworthy narrator who had many ḥadīth." He died in 127 AH. He is not the same as ʿAbd al-Karīm ibn Abi'l-Mukhāriq Abū Umayyah the Baṣran about whom there is disagreement, but they are often confused for each other, as found in *Muqaddimah Fatḥ al-bārī* by Ḥāfiẓ ibn Ḥajar and others. Al-Jazarī is ascribed to the Jazīrah (island or peninsula) of Ibn ʿUmar which was a place built up and populated by a man well known as Ibn ʿUmar who is not ʿAbdullāh ibn ʿUmar the Companion. Ibn al-Athīr al-Jazarī, the author of *an-Nihāyah fī gharīb al-ḥadīth* and *Jāmiʿ al-uṣūl,* is also ascribed to him. As-Suyūṭī said in *Lubb al-lubāb fī taḥrīr al-ansāb,* "Al-Jazarī is ascribed to a number of lands: Mawṣil, Sanjār, Ḥarrān, ar-Rahā, ar-Riqqah, Raʾs ʿAyn, Āmid, Diyārbakr and the island of Ibn ʿUmar." In the *Jāmiʿ al-uṣūl,* "The ascription is to the island, which is the land between the Euphrates and the Tigris among which are Diyārbakr and Rabīʿah."

ʿAbd al-Majīd ibn Suhayl and az-Zuhrī [ḥadīth 820]. This is how it is found in many copies of this book, and similarly in a copy upon which is the commentary of al-Qārī. Apparently it shows that Mālik had two shaykhs for this narration who both narrated from Ibn al-Musayyab, first, ʿAbd al-Majīd, and second, az-Zuhrī. However, it seems that the "and" which precedes az-Zuhrī is a mistake of the copyist and that really it is a descriptive name for ʿAbd al-Majīd himself [that he was from Banī Zuhrah], and that he alone is the shaykh of Mālik in this narration. There is disagreement about his name, and some say ʿAbd al-Majīd as in this book, and some say ʿAbd al-Ḥamīd which is incorrect. In the *Muwaṭṭaʾ* of Yaḥyā and its commentary by az-Zurqānī there is, "'Mālik from ʿAbd al-Ḥamīd,' which is how Yaḥyā, Ibn Nāfiʿ and Ibn Yūsuf narrated it. The dominant majority of the narrators of the *Muwaṭṭaʾ* say ʿAbd al-Majīd, and it is the one which is well known, and this is how al-Bukhārī and al-ʿUqaylī mention it, and it is the correct position and the truth about which there is no doubt. The former [ʿAbd al-Ḥamīd] is a mistake, as Abū ʿUmar [Ibn ʿAbd al-Barr] said, "Ibn Suhayl is the husband of Thurayyā bint ʿAbdullāh ibn ʿAbd ar-Raḥmān ibn ʿAwf az-Zuhrī and he is a trustworthy narrator who may be adduced as a proof. He has only this single *marfūʿ* ḥadīth in the *Muwaṭṭaʾ* narrated from Ibn al-Musayyab." In *Isʿāf al-mubaṭṭaʾ*

of as-Suyūṭī, "ᶜAbd al-Majīd ibn Suhayl ibn ᶜAbd ar-Raḥmān ibn ᶜAwf az-Zuhrī Abū Muḥammad the Madīnan who narrated from his paternal uncle Abū Salamah, Saᶜīd ibn al-Musayyab, and Abū Ṣāliḥ Dhakwān, and from whom Mālik, ad-Darāwardī and others narrated. An-Nasā᾽ī and Ibn Maᶜīn declared him to be a trustworthy narrator." There is the like of that in *at-Taqrīb, al-Kāshif* and elsewhere.

ᶜAbd al-Mālik ibn Abī Bakr is ᶜAbd al-Mālik ibn Abī Bakr ibn ᶜAbd ar-Raḥmān ibn al-Ḥārith ibn Hishām of Makhzūm, the Madīnan. He was a trustworthy narrator, and died in the khilāfah of Hishām, as is in *Taqrīb at-tahdhīb.*

ᶜAbd al-Mālik ibn Marwān was one of the *khulafā᾽* of Banī Umayyah. He was the son of Marwān ibn al-Ḥakam ibn Abi'l-ᶜĀṣ, and he was the first person in Islam to be called ᶜAbd al-Mālik. In his khilāfah there took place events which are mentioned in *Mir᾽āt al-jinān* by al-Yāfiᶜī and elsewhere. His death, according to what is in *Ḥayāt al-ḥayawān,* was in 76 AH.

ᶜAbd al-Mālik ibn Maysarah (this spelling is from *al-Mughnī* and *Tahdhīb at-tahdhīb*) al-Hilālī Abū Zayd al-ᶜĀmirī the Kūfan. He narrated from Ibn ᶜUmar, Abu'ṭ-Ṭufayl, Ṭāwūs, Saᶜīd ibn Jubayr and others. Shuᶜbah, Misᶜar and Manṣūr narrated from him. Ibn Maᶜīn, an-Nasā᾽ī and al-ᶜIjlī said that he was a trustworthy narrator. Al-Bukhārī mentioned him as one of those who died in the second decade of the second century. He is not the same as ᶜAbd al-Mālik ibn Abī Sulaymān Maysarah, the Kūfan.

ᶜAbd ar-Raḥmān al-Ḥuraqī – by ascription to Ḥuraqah, a clan of Hamdān, but some say of Juhaynah, which is the correct position. Ibn Ḥibbān mentioned him in *ath-Thiqāt,* as found in *at-Taqrīb* and *al-Ansāb.*

ᶜAbd ar-Raḥmān ibn ᶜAbd, al-Qāriyy – by ascription to Qārah a sub-clan of Khuzaymah ibn Mudrikah said az-Zurqānī – was the appointee of ᶜUmar in charge of the *bayt al-māl.* Al-ᶜIjlī mentions him as one of the trustworthy narrators among the Followers. Al-Wāqidī said different things about him, sometimes saying that he was a Companion, and sometimes that he was a Follower. He died in 88 AH. That is what Ibn Ḥajar said.

ᶜAbd ar-Raḥmān ibn ᶜAbdullāh, al-Masᶜūdī by ascription to Masᶜūd the father of ᶜAbdullāh ibn Masᶜūd. A large group of his descendants have become famous with this name [al-Masᶜūdī] as as-Samᶜānī mentions, of them ᶜAbd ar-Raḥmān ibn ᶜAbdullāh ibn Masᶜūd al-Hudhalī the Kūfan who narrated from his father, and from ᶜAlī, al-Ashᶜath ibn Qays and Masrūq, and from whom narrated his two sons al-Qāsim and Maᶜn, Sammāk ibn Ḥarb, Abū

Isḥāq as-Sabīʿī and others. Yaʿqūb ibn Shaybah said, "He was a trustworthy narrator with few ḥadīth." He died in 79 AH.

ʿAbd ar-Raḥmān ibn ʿAbdullāh ibn ʿUtbah ibn ʿAbdullāh ibn Masʿūd, the Kūfan, al-Masʿūdī (mentioned in ḥadīth 116). This is how he is mentioned in his ascription in *Tahdhīb at-tahdhīb* and *Tadhkirat al-ḥuffāẓ*. What is in *at-Taqrīb* and *al-Ansāb* is, "ʿAbd ar-Raḥmān ibn ʿAbdullāh ibn ʿUtbah ibn Masʿūd narrated from Abū Isḥāq as-Sabīʿī, Abū Isḥāq ash-Shaybānī, al-Qāsim ibn ʿAbd ar-Raḥmān al-Masʿūdī, ʿAlī ibn al-Aqmar, ʿAwn ibn ʿAbdullāh ibn ʿUtbah ibn Masʿūd and others. From him narrated the two Sufyāns, Shuʿbah, Jaʿfar ibn ʿAwn, ʿAbdullāh ibn al-Mubārak and others. Ibn Maʿīn, Ibn al-Madīnī, Aḥmad and others declared him a trustworthy narrator. He became confused at the end of his life, and died in 120 AH."

ʿAbd ar-Raḥmān ibn ʿAbdullāh ibn Abī Ṣaʿṣaʿah al-Anṣārī al-Māzinī, whom an-Nasāʾī and Abū Ḥātim regarded as a trustworthy narrator. He died during the khilāfah of Manṣūr as found in *Isʿāf al-mubaṭṭaʾ* of as-Suyūṭī.

ʿAbd ar-Raḥmān ibn Abī ʿAmrah al-Anṣārī. In the narration of Yaḥyā [ḥadīth 847] is from Abū ʿAmrah al-Anṣārī. Ibn ʿAbd al-Barr said, "In this way Yaḥyā, Ibn al-Qāsim, Abū Musʿab, and Musʿab az-Zubayrī narrated it. Al-Qaʿnabī, Maʿn and Yaḥyā ibn Bukayr said that it was from Ibn Abī ʿAmrah. Similarly, Ibn Wahb and ʿAbd ar-Razzāq narrating from Mālik named him ʿAbd ar-Raḥmān and thus removed the problem, for this is the correct position, and this ʿAbd ar-Raḥmān is one of the best of the Followers, as found in *Sharḥ az-Zurqānī* .

ʿAbd ar-Raḥmān ibn Abī Bakr aṣ-Ṣiddīq ʿAbdullāh ibn Abī Quḥāfah ʿUthmān. He was ʿĀʾishah's full brother, their mother being Umm Rumān. He accepted Islam in the period of calm after al-Ḥudaybiyyah, and his name had been ʿAbd al-Kaʿbah, so the Messenger of Allah ﷺ named him ʿAbd ar-Raḥmān. He has good merits. It is unknown among the Companions four people each of whom was the son of the one before him and each of whom was a Companion of the Prophet ﷺ and accepted Islam except for Abū Quḥāfah, his son Abū Bakr, his son this ʿAbd ar-Raḥmān and his son Abū ʿAtīq Muḥammad. He had lived in Madīnah, and he refused to pledge allegiance to Yazīd when Muʿāwiyah sought it. Muʿāwiyah sent him one hundred thousand dirhams but he returned them and said, "I will not sell my dīn in exchange for my world." He went to Makkah and died suddenly in a place whose name is Ḥabashī, ten miles from Makkah, and then he was carried there and buried in al-Maʿlā. That was in 53 AH according to the majority, but some say 55 AH or 52 AH, as found in *Asad al-ghābah fī maᶜrifat aṣ-ṣaḥābah* by Ibn al-Athīr al-Jazarī.

ᶜAbd ar-Raḥmān ibn Abī Hurayrah. Al-Qārī said, "This ᶜAbd ar-Raḥmān has only this ḥadīth [ḥadīth 648 in which he is mentioned as Ibn ᶜAbd ar-Raḥmān ibn Abī Hurayrah] in the *Muwaṭṭa᾽*." Ibn Ḥibbān mentioned him in *ath-Thiqāt.*

ᶜAbd ar-Raḥmān ibn Abī Laylā was mujtahid of the generation of the Followers and one of the trustworthy narrators of the ḥadīth scholars.

ᶜAbd ar-Raḥmān ibn Abī Saᶜīd al-Khudrī was a trustworthy narrator from whom Muslim and the other four [at-Tirmidhī, an-Nasā᾽ī, Ibn Mājah and Abū Dāwūd] narrated. He died in 112 AH as az-Zurqānī said.

ᶜAbd ar-Raḥmān ibn Abi'z-Zinād. He was utterly truthful, a faqīh and Madīnan. His memory changed when he came to Baghdād. He died in 74 AH, as found in *at-Taqrīb*. His father was Abu'z-Zinād ᶜAbdullāh ibn Dhakwān.

ᶜAbd ar-Raḥmān ibn Aflaḥ. He is thus to be found in many copies, and in the copy in the *Sharḥ al-Qārī*. In the *Muwaṭṭa᾽ Mālik* in the version of Yaḥyā,[ḥadīth 548] is "from Abu'n-Naḍr the *mawlā* of ᶜUmar ibn ᶜUbaydullāh from Ibn Abī Aflaḥ the *mawlā* of Abū Ayyūb al-Anṣārī from an Umm Walad of Abū Ayyūb..." Its commentator az-Zurqānī said, "He is ᶜUmar ibn Kathīr ibn Aflaḥ the Madīnan and a trustworthy narrator." What Ibn Ḥajar said in *Taqrīb at-tahdhīb* agrees with him, "ᶜUmar ibn Kathīr ibn Aflaḥ the Madīnan the *mawlā* of Abū Ayyūb was a trustworthy narrator." As-Suyūṭī said in *Isᶜāf al-mubaṭṭa᾽*, "ᶜUmar ibn Kathīr ibn Aflaḥ the Madīnan the *mawlā* of Abū Ayyūb narrated from Ibn ᶜUmar, Kaᶜb, Nāfiᶜ, and many others, and from him narrated Ibn ᶜAwn, Yaḥyā al-Anṣārī, and others. An-Nasā᾽ī regarded him as a trustworthy narrator."

ᶜAbd ar-Raḥmān ibn al-Aswad. He was one of those born in the time of the Messenger of Allah ﷺ and it is said that he was a Companion. His father was one of those who mocked the Messenger of Allah ﷺ. That is what Ibn Ḥibbān said in *Kitāb ath-thiqāt*. Ibn al-Athīr al-Jazarī said in *Asad al-ghābah*, "ᶜAbd ar-Raḥmān ibn al-Aswad ibn ᶜAbd Yaghūth ibn Wahb ibn ᶜAbd Manāf ibn Zuhrah al-Qurashī az-Zuhrī had great standing among people. He was the son of the maternal uncle of the Prophet ﷺ. He reached the time of the Prophet ﷺ but it is not authentically established that he saw him or kept his company. Sulaymān ibn Yasār and Marwān and others narrated from him.

ᶜAbd ar-Raḥmān ibn ᶜAwf. One of the ten given the good news of the Garden. He died in 32 AH.

ᶜAbd ar-Raḥmān ibn Ḥanẓalah ibn ᶜAjlān az-Zuraqī, by ascription to Banī Zurayq a clan of the Anṣār. As-Samᶜānī mentioned him. Ibn al-Athīr said in *Jāmiᶜ al-uṣūl*, "ᶜAbd ar-Raḥmān ibn Ḥanẓalah az-Zuraqī related from a *mawlā* of Quraysh called Ibn Mirs.

ᶜAbd ar-Raḥmān ibn Ḥubāb al-Aslamī al-Anṣārī, the Madīnan. Ibn Ḥibbān regarded him as a trustworthy narrator, as found in *at-Taqrīb* and *Isᶜāf al-mubaṭṭaʾ* of as-Suyūṭī.

ᶜAbd ar-Raḥmān ibn al-Mujabbar ibn ᶜAbd ar-Raḥmān ibn ᶜUmar ibn al-Khattāb. There is in *Sharḥ* al-*Muwaṭṭa* by az-Zurqānī, "ᶜAbd ar-Raḥmān ibn al-Mujabbar, of Quraysh, al-ᶜAdawī narrated from his father and from Sālim. His son Muḥammad and Mālik and others narrated from him. Al-Fallās and others regarded him as a trustworthy narrator." Ibn Mākūlā said, "It is unknown in narration to have ᶜAbd ar-Raḥmān ibn ᶜAbd ar-Raḥmān ibn ᶜAbd ar-Raḥmān, three times in one name, except for this one, because the name of al-Mujabbar was ᶜAbd ar-Raḥmān and his father was ᶜAbd ar-Raḥmān al-Aṣghar."

ᶜAbd ar-Raḥmān ibn al-Qāsim ibn Muḥammad ibn Abī Bakr aṣ-Ṣiddīq, the Madīnan, faqīh. Aḥmad and more than one other person regarded him as a trustworthy narrator. He died in Shām in 126 AH. That is how it is found in *Isᶜāf al-mubaṭṭaʾ* of as-Suyūṭī.

ᶜAbd ar-Raḥmān ibn ᶜUthmān ibn ᶜUbaydullāh at-Taymī, the Madīnan, was one of the Companions. He was killed along with Ibn az-Zubayr. His son ᶜUthmān, one of the fifth, is trustworthy. That is how it is found in *at-Taqrīb.*

ᶜAbd ar-Raḥmān ibn Muḥammad ibn ᶜAbdin al-Qāriyy is ᶜAbd ar-Raḥmān ibn Muḥammad ibn ᶜĀʾishah ibn ᶜAbdin as found in the Muwaṭṭaʾ of Yaḥyā, and his ascription of al-Qāriyy is to Qārah a clan of the Arabs. He was one of the People of Madīnah and ᶜUmar's appointee to take care of the *bayt al-māl.* He was a trustworthy narrator from whom ᶜUrwah, Ḥumayd ibn ᶜAbd ar-Raḥmān, and his two sons Ibrāhīm and Muḥammad narrated. He died in 88 AH, as as-Samᶜānī and his father mentioned. He said in *at-Taqrīb,* "Muḥammad ibn ᶜAbdullāh ibn ᶜAbd ar-Raḥmān ibn ᶜAbdin al-Qāriyy the Madīnan is acceptable."[1]

ᶜAbd ar-Raḥmān ibn Sahl ibn Zayd ibn Kaᶜb ibn ᶜĀmir ibn ᶜAdī al-Anṣārī was present at Badr, Uḥud, al-Khandaq and all of the major events, and during his khilāfah ᶜUmar appointed him his governor over Baṣra.

ᶜAbd ar-Raḥmān ibn Yaᶜqūb al-Juhanī al-Madanī. An-Nasā'ī said, "There is no harm in him. His son was al-ᶜAlā' Abū Shibl, the utterly truthful Madīnan, as found in *al-Isᶜāf* and *at-Taqrīb*.

ᶜAbd ar-Raḥmān ibn Yazīd ibn Jāriyah al-Anṣārī is Abū Muḥammad the Madīnan whom Ibn Ḥibbān mentioned among the trustworthy narrators of the Followers. It is said that he was born in the lifetime of the Prophet ﷺ, and he died in 93 AH. He witnessed the Farewell Khutbah.

ᶜAbd ar-Raḥmān ibn Yazīd ibn Qays an-Nakhaᶜī – by ascription to Nakhaᶜ, a tribe – Abū Bakr the Kūfan who narrated from his brother al-Aswad ibn Yazīd, his uncle ᶜAlqamah ibn Qays, Ḥudhayfah, Ibn Masᶜūd, Abū Mūsā, ᶜĀ'ishah and others, and from whom narrated his son Muḥammad, Ibrāhīm an-Nakhaᶜī, Abū Isḥāq as-Sabīᶜī, Manṣūr and others. Ibn Saᶜd, Ibn Maᶜīn, al-ᶜIjlī and ad-Dāraquṭnī said that he was a trustworthy narrator. He died in 73 AH, but some say 83 AH. So it is stated in *Tahdhīb at-tahdhīb*.

ᶜAbd ar-Raḥmān al-Madanī. He saw [the Prophet ﷺ] and was one of the major trustworthy narrators of the Followers. He died in 43 AH, as az-Zurqānī mentioned.

ᶜAbdullāh ibn ᶜAbd ar-Raḥmān ibn Abī Ṣaᶜṣaᶜah, the father of ᶜAbd ar-Raḥmān, was a Follower and a trustworthy narrator, as az-Zurqānī said. An-Nasā'ī declared him a trustworthy narrator, as found in *al-Isᶜāf*.

ᶜAbdullāh ibn ᶜAbd ar-Raḥmān ibn Muᶜammar was Abū Ṭawālah the qāḍī of Madīnah on behalf of ᶜUmar ibn ᶜAbd al-ᶜAzīz. He was a trustworthy narrator and died in 134 AH, as found in *at-Taqrīb*.

ᶜAbdullāh ibn ᶜAbd ar-Raḥmān ibn Yaᶜlā ath-Thaqafī. He said in *at-Taqrīb*, "ᶜAbdullāh ibn ᶜAbd ar-Raḥmān ibn Yaᶜlā ibn Kaᶜb, of Ṭā'if, Abū Yaᶜlā ath-Thaqafī was utterly truthful."

ᶜAbdullāh ibn ᶜAbdullāh ibn ᶜUmar ibn al-Khattāb of Quraysh al-ᶜAdawī Abū ᶜAbd ar-Raḥmān, the Madīnan. He was a Follower who was unanimously agreed to be a trustworthy narrator. He was his father's executor. He died in Madīnah in 105 AH. All of the group of [six ḥadīth collectors] narrated from him apart from Ibn Mājah. That is how it is stated in *Ḍiyā' as-sārī*. In many versions of this book he is [mistakenly mentioned as] ᶜUbaydullāh ibn ᶜAbdullāh.

ᶜAbdullāh ibn ᶜAbdullāh ibn Jābir ibn ᶜAtīk was an Anṣārī Madīnan Follower. Ibn Maᶜīn, Abū Ḥātim and an-Nasā'ī regarded him as a trustworthy narrator, as found in *Isᶜāf al-mubaṭṭa'* of as-Suyūṭī.

ᶜAbdullāh ibn ᶜĀmir ibn Rabīᶜah ibn ᶜĀmir ibn Mālik ibn Rabīᶜah ibn Ḥujayr ibn Salāmān ibn Mālik ibn Rabīᶜah ibn Rufaydah ibn ᶜAnz ibn Wā'il ibn Qāsiṭ al-ᶜAnzī – there is a difference of views about his ascription – Abū Muḥammad. The Prophet ﷺ died when he was four or five years old, and he had a brother older than him called ᶜAbdullāh, and the older brother died as a *shahīd* on the day of Ṭāʾif. The younger [brother] died in 85 AH, but some say 70 AH. Their father was ᶜĀmir and he was an ally of Banī ᶜAdī ibn Kaᶜb, and so for that reason he was called al-ᶜAdawī. He made both hijrahs and was present at Badr and the events after it, and he died in 32 AH but some say 33 AH, or 35 AH. That is how it is stated in *Jāmiᶜ al-uṣūl* by Ibn al-Athīr al-Jazarī.

ᶜAbdullāh ibn ᶜĀmir. Az-Zurqānī said, "He is Ibn ᶜĀmir ibn Kurayz ibn Ḥabīb ibn ᶜAbd Shams ibn ᶜAbd Manāf of Quraysh. He was born in the lifetime of the Prophet ﷺ, and he was brought to him and he spat lightly upon him." Ibn Ḥibbān said, "He was a Companion, and his maternal uncle's son ᶜUthmān ibn ᶜAffān appointed him governor of Baṣra in 29 AH, and he opened Khurāsān and Kirmān to Islam. He died in Madīnah in 57 AH or 58 AH. His father was a Companion of those who accepted Islam at the Opening [of Makkah to Islam]."

ᶜAbdullāh ibn ᶜAmr ibn ᶜUthmān al-Umawī who was given the honorific name of al-Miṭrāf. He was a noble trustworthy narrator of the Followers and died in Egypt in 96 AH.

ᶜAbdullāh ibn ᶜAmr is Abū ᶜAbd ar-Raḥmān or Abū Muḥammad ᶜAbdullāh ibn ᶜAmr ibn al-ᶜĀṣ ibn Wāʾil ibn Hishām as-Sahmī. There were only eleven years between him and his father and he accepted Islam before his father. He strove and exerted himself in acts of worship and had abundant knowledge and was one of the greatest of the Companions. He died in either 63, 65, 68, 73, or 77 AH in either Makkah, Ṭāʾif, Cairo or Palestine. That is how it is stated in *Tahdhīb at-tahdhīb* and elsewhere.

ᶜAbdullāh ibn ᶜAyyāsh ibn Abī Rabīᶜah – whose name [Abū Rabīᶜah] was ᶜAmr ibn al-Mughīrah ibn ᶜAbdullāh ibn ᶜUmar ibn Makhzūm of Quraysh and Makhzūm, and he was a Companion and son of a Companion. He was born in Abyssinia. He memorised from the Prophet ﷺ, but he did not narrate from him, but he narrated from ᶜUmar and others. His father was one of the early Muslims, as az-Zurqānī said.

ᶜAbdullāh ibn Abī Bakr ibn Muḥammad ibn ᶜAmr ibn Ḥazm al-Anṣārī, the Madīnan, the qāḍī of Madīnah who died in 135 AH, as az-Zurqānī mentioned. His father was Abū Bakr ibn Muḥammad ibn ᶜAmr ibn Ḥazm al-Anṣārī.

ᶜAbdullāh ibn Abī Ḥabībah the Madīnan and the *mawlā* of az-Zubayr ibn al-ᶜAwwām who narrated from Abū Umāmah ibn Sahl ibn Ḥunayf and from ᶜUthmān. Al-Bukhārī mentioned him [narrating] from Ibn Mahdī, and Bukayr ibn al-Ashajj, Mālik, and Abū Ḥanīfah in his *Musnad* narrated from him, "I heard Abu'd-Dardā᾿ ..." and he mentioned the ḥadīth on the merit of someone saying lā ilāha illa'llāh – There is no god but Allah. Ibn al-Ḥidhā᾿ said, "He is one of the men about whom it is sufficient to know that Mālik narrated from them," as found in *Sharḥ az-Zurqānī* .

ᶜAbdullāh ibn Abī Mulaykah. It is said that his name [Abū Mulaykah's] was Zuhayr at-Taymī, the Madīnan, a trustworthy narrator of the Followers. He died in 117 AH, as az-Zurqānī said.

ᶜAbdullāh ibn al-Faḍl. Az-Zurqānī said, "A trustworthy narrator, and one of the narrators of all of them [the major ḥadīth collectors]. He was a lesser Follower of the same generation as az-Zuhrī." As-Suyūṭī said, "An-Nasā᾿ī, Abū Ḥātim and Ibn Maᶜīn regarded him as a trustworthy narrator."

ᶜAbdullāh ibn Ḥunayn was a Follower and trustworthy narrator who died during the amirate [khilāfah] of Yazīd. The group [of major ḥadīth narrators] narrated from him, as az-Zurqānī mentioned.

ᶜAbdullāh ibn az-Zubayr. He was Abū Ḥabīb but some say Abū Bakr ᶜAbdullāh ibn az-Zubayr (az-Zubayr was one of the ten given the good news [of the Garden]) ibn al-ᶜAwwām al-Asadī. He was born in the first year of the Hijrah and the Messenger of Allah ﷺ supplicated for him and asked for blessings for him. He fasted and prayed a great deal, and he was pledged allegiance as khalīfah in 64 AH at the end of the epoch of Yazīd ibn Muᶜāwiyah, and the people of Ḥijāz, Yemen, ᶜIrāq and Khurāsān united in obedience to him. Al-Ḥajjāj, the governor on behalf of ᶜAbd al-Mālik ibn Marwān killed him in 72 AH. One of the things he did was to rebuild the Kaᶜbah according to the foundations of Ibrāhīm, upon him and upon our Prophet blessings and peace, as found in *Jāmiᶜ al-uṣūl* and elsewhere.

ᶜAbdullāh ibn Kaᶜb (the *mawlā* of ᶜUthmān ibn ᶜAffān) al-Ḥimyarī, the Madīnan. He was utterly truthful. Muslim and an-Nasā᾿ī narrated from him, as az-Zurqānī said.

ᶜAbdullāh ibn Masᶜūd. When Ibn Masᶜūd is used unqualifiedly it refers to ᶜAbdullāh ibn Masᶜūd ibn Ghāfil ibn Ḥabīb al-Hudhalī Abū ᶜAbd ar-Raḥmān, one of the first of the forerunners, and one of the great people of knowledge of the Companions. ᶜUmar put him in charge of Kūfa. He died in 32 AH or in the year after in Madīnah, as stated in *at-Taqrīb*. He was the keeper of his sandals and his toothstick ﷺ. He emigrated to Ethiopia and was present at

Badr and the battles after it. He was appointed qāḍī of Kūfa during the khilāfah of ᶜUmar up until the middle of the khilāfah of ᶜUthmān, and then moved to Madīnah where he died in 32 AH as stated in *Asmāʾ rijāl al-mishkāh.*

ᶜAbdullāh ibn Muḥammad ibn ᶜAlī ibn Abī Ṭālib Abū Hāshim, the Madīnan. Ibn Saᶜd and an-Nasāʾī regarded him as a trustworthy narrator. He died in 98 AH, as found in *Isᶜāf al-mubaṭṭaʾ* of as-Suyūṭī.

ᶜAbdullāh ibn Muḥammad ibn ᶜAlī ibn Abī Ṭālib al-Hāshimī, the Madīnan. Al-ᶜIjlī, Ibn Saᶜd and an-Nasāʾī regarded him as a trustworthy narrator. He died in 98 AH. See also his brother al-Ḥasan.

ᶜAbdullāh ibn Muḥammad ibn Abī Bakr aṣ-Ṣiddīq was the brother of al-Qāsim ibn Muḥammad and one of the trustworthy narrators of the Followers. He was killed at al-Ḥarrah in 63 AH.

ᶜAbdullāh ibn Qays ibn Makhramah. Al-ᶜAskarī said, "He saw the Prophet ﷺ." Ibn Abī Khaythamah, al-Baghawī and Ibn Shahīn mentioned him among the Companions. Al-Bukhārī and Ibn Abī Ḥātim mentioned him as one of the great Followers and that his father was a Companion. So it is found in the *Sharḥ az-Zurqānī.*

ᶜAbdullāh ibn Rāfiᶜ. Ibn Ḥajar said, "ᶜAbdullāh ibn Rāfiᶜ al-Makhzūmī Abū Rāfiᶜ the Madīnan was the *mawlā* of Umm Salamah, and he was trustworthy."

ᶜAbdullāh ibn Sahl. He and his brother ᶜAbd ar-Raḥmān [see his entry] who began to speak in the presence of the Prophet ﷺ telling the story of the killing of ᶜAbdullāh, and so the Messenger of Allah ﷺ said to him, "The elder! The elder!" [They] are two sons of Sahl ibn Zayd ibn Kaᶜb ibn ᶜĀmir ibn ᶜAdī al-Anṣārī. As for ᶜAbdullāh he was killed at Khaybar, and it was because of him that the *qasāmah* oath was taken. These two were the two sons of the brother of Ḥuwayyiṣah and Muḥayyiṣah the two sons of Masᶜūd ibn Kaᶜb ibn ᶜĀmir ibn ᶜAdī al-Ḥārithī al-Khazrajī.

ᶜAbdullāh ibn Shaddād is Abu'l-Walīd al-Laythī the Madīnan ᶜAbdullāh ibn Shaddād. Some say his name was Usāmah and Shaddād and his honorific name was Ibn al-Hād, and his name was ᶜAmr and that his honorific name was al-Hādī. Some say his name was Usāmah ibn ᶜAmr ibn ᶜAbdullāh ibn Jābir ibn Bishr. Shaddād narrated from the Prophet ﷺ and he was a Companion. Ibn Saᶜd mentions him as one of those present at al-Khandaq. He had resided in Madīnah but moved to Kūfa. His son ᶜAbdullāh narrated from his father and from Ibn Masᶜūd, Ibn ᶜAbbās, Ibn ᶜUmar, his maternal aunt Asmāʾ bint ᶜUmays the wife of Abū Bakr aṣ-Ṣiddīq, his mother's maternal aunt Maymūnah the Umm al-Muʾminin, ᶜĀʾishah, Umm Salamah and others.

From him a large number narrated. Al-ʿIjlī and al-Khaṭīb said, "He was one of the great Followers and one of their trustworthy narrators." Abū Zurʿah, an-Nasā'ī and Ibn Saʿd said he was a trustworthy narrator. Ibn ʿAbd al-Barr said in *al-Istīʿāb* that he was born in the time of the Messenger of Allah ﷺ. Al-Maymūnī said, "Aḥmad was asked as to whether he had heard anything from the Prophet ﷺ and he said he had not." He died in 81 AH, but some say 82 AH. That is how it is in *Tahdhīb at-tahdhīb.*

ʿAbdullāh ibn Thābit is from Aws, but it is sometimes said that he was from Ẓufr. He died during the life of the Prophet ﷺ. Al-Wāqidī and Ibn al-Kalbī said that he was ʿAbdullāh ibn ʿAbdullāh and that both he and his father were Companions. Al-Kalbī said, "He ﷺ buried him in his shirt, and the father lived until the khilāfah of ʿUmar," as az-Zurqānī mentioned.

ʿAbdullāh ibn ʿUmar ibn Ḥafṣ ibn ʿĀṣim ibn ʿUmar ibn al-Khattāb Abū ʿAbd ar-Raḥmān al-ʿUmarī, the Madīnan whom a group of people regard as weak, including Ibn al-Madīnī, Yaḥyā ibn Saʿīd and others. Aḥmad, Ibn Maʿīn and Yaʿqūb ibn Shaybah regarded him as a trustworthy narrator. He died in Madīnah in 171 AH, as found in *Tahdhīb at-tahdhīb.* I have gone to some lengths in discussing his trustworthiness and that he may be used in proof in my treatise *al-Kalām al-mabrūr fi radd al-qawl al-manṣūr* and in my treatise *as-Saʿy al-mashkūr fi'r-radd ʿala'l-madhhab al-ma'thūr,* both of which examine the case of visiting the tomb of the Prophet ﷺ.

ʿAbdullāh ibn ʿUmar ibn al-Khattāb ibn Nufayl of Quraysh Abū ʿAbd ar-Raḥmān. He became a Muslim early on while young and emigrated with his father. He took part in al-Khandaq and all of the battles. The Messenger of Allah ﷺ called him the "Right-acting Slave – al-ʿAbd aṣ-Ṣāliḥ". He has numerous virtues. He died in 73 AH, but some say 74 AH. It is thus in the *Tahdhīb at-tahdhīb* by the Ḥāfiẓ ibn Ḥajar. When one says "Ibn ʿUmar" one means ʿAbdullāh ibn ʿUmar ibn al-Khattāb even though ʿUmar also had others sons, just as when one says Ibn ʿAbbās, Ibn Masʿūd, Ibn az-Zubayr without any qualification one means the one with the name ʿAbdullāh. His biography is expanded upon in *Tadhkirat al-ḥuffāẓ* by adh-Dhahabī and by others. It is stated in *Isʿāf al-mubaṭṭa'*, "ʿAbdullāh ibn ʿUmar ibn al-Khattāb, of Quraysh, al-ʿAdawī Abū ʿAbd ar-Raḥmān the Makkan. He became a Muslim very early on along with his father while he was a youth, and indeed on the contrary, it is narrated that he was the first child to be born in Islam. He was regarded too young [to fight] on the day of Uḥud, but he was present at al-Khandaq and the events after it. The Prophet ﷺ said about him, 'He is a right-acting man.' His sons narrated from him: Sālim, Ḥamzah, ᶜAbdullāh, Bilāl, ᶜUbaydullāh, ᶜUmar, and Zayd, and his grandson Muḥammad ibn Zayd, and Abū Bakr ibn ᶜUbayd, his *mawlā* Nāfiᶜ, Zayd ibn Aslam, ᶜAṭāʾ and a great number of other people. The number of ḥadīth ascribed to him according to Baqī ibn Mukhallad is one thousand six hundred and thirty ḥadīth. He died in 73 AH, but some say 74 AH."

ᶜAbdullāh ibn ᶜUtbah ibn Masᶜūd al-Hudhalī, father of ᶜUbaydullāh ibn ᶜAbdullāh ibn ᶜUtbah [ḥadīth 177] the nephew of ᶜAbdullāh ibn Masᶜūd whom a large number regarded as a trustworthy narrator and who is one of the great Followers. He died after 70 AH as is mentioned in *at-Taqrīb* and elsewhere.

ᶜAbdullāh ibn Wāqid ibn ᶜAbdullāh ibn ᶜUmar al-ᶜUmarī, the Madīnan. Ibn Ḥibbān regarded him as a trustworthy narrator. He died in 119 AH, as as-Suyūṭī said.

ᶜAbdullāh ibn Yazīd al-Anṣārī al-Khatmī was ᶜAbdullāh ibn Yazīd ibn Zayd ibn Ḥuṣayn al-Anṣārī al-Khaṭmī – by ascription to Banī Khaṭmah, a tribe of the Anṣār. He was a minor Companion, as is mentioned by al-ᶜAynī and others.

ᶜAbdullāh ibn Yazīd – the *mawlā* of al-Aswad ibn Sufyān – al-Makhzūmī al-Maqburī. Aḥmad and Yaḥyā regarded him as a trustworthy narrator. He died in 148 AH, as is mentioned in *al-Isᶜāf*.

ᶜAbdullāh ibn Zayd ibn ᶜĀṣim ibn Kaᶜb al-Anṣārī al-Māzinī, the famous Companion. He narrated the description of wuḍūʾ and other things, and he became a shahīd at al-Ḥarrah in 63 AH as found in *Taqrīb at-tahdhīb*.

ᶜAbdullāh ibn Zayd ibn ᶜĀṣim. He is the grandfather of ᶜAmr ibn Yaḥyā. The author of the book *Tahdhīb al-kamāl* said in introduction to ᶜAmr ibn Yaḥyā ibn ᶜAmmārah that he was the son of the daughter of ᶜAbdullāh ibn Zayd ibn ᶜĀṣim and that is not the case. It is thus in *Tahdhīb at-tahdhīb* of the Ḥāfiẓ Ibn Ḥajar. ᶜAbdullāh ibn Zayd ibn ᶜĀṣim is not the ᶜAbdullāh ibn Zayd ibn ᶜAbd Rabbihī who narrated the ḥadīth on the *adhān*, and whoever says they are the same is deluded. As-Suyūṭī mentions that this ᶜAbdullāh al-Māzinī died in 63 AH.

ᶜAbdullāh aṣ-Ṣunābiḥī. This is how the dominant majority of narrators say [ḥadīth 182]. Muṭarrif and Isḥāq ibn ᶜĪsā aṭ-Ṭabāᶜ said it was Abū ᶜAbdullāh aṣ-Ṣunābiḥī and Ibn ᶜAbd al-Barr said, "That is correct. He is ᶜAbd ar-Raḥmān ibn 'Usaylah one of the Followers and a trustworthy narrator. It is also narrated as... 'I heard the Messenger of Allah ﷺ ...' and that is a mistake because aṣ-Ṣunābiḥī did not meet him. Ḥāfiẓ said in *al-Iṣābah*, 'The apparent meaning of it is that ᶜAbdullāh aṣ-Ṣunābiḥī does not exist, about which there are views, for Yaḥyā ibn Maᶜīn said, "ᶜAbdullāh aṣ-Ṣunābiḥī from whom the Madīnans narrate [in a way] which makes it seem as if he was a Companion." Ibn as-Sakkan said, "It is said that he was a Companion." The narrations of Muṭarrif and aṭ-Ṭabāᶜ from Mālik are contrary to the common view, but Mālik was not alone in that, for on the contrary, Ḥafṣ ibn Maysarah followed him in that, narrating from Zayd ibn Aslam from ᶜAṭā᾿ from ᶜAbdullāh aṣ-Ṣunābiḥī, "I heard the Messenger of Allah ﷺ ..." and similarly Zuhayr ibn Muḥammad according to Ibn Mandah, and similarly Muḥammad ibn Jaᶜfar ibn Abī Kathīr and Khārijah ibn Musᶜab, the four narrating from Zayd with it [the rest of the ḥadīth]. Ad-Dāraquṭnī narrated it by way of Ismāᶜīl ibn al-Ḥārith and Ibn Mandah by way of Ismāᶜīl aṣ-Ṣā᾿igh from Mālik from Zayd with it [the rest of the ḥadīth], declaring clearly that he [ᶜAbdullāh aṣ-Ṣunābiḥī] had heard it [from the Messenger of Allah ﷺ], as az-Zurqānī mentioned.

ᶜAbīdah ibn Sufyān al-Ḥaḍramī was a trustworthy narrator and was regarded as such by an-Nasā᾿ī and al-ᶜIjlī, as found in *al-Isᶜāf*.

Abū ᶜAbd ar-Raḥmān [ḥadīth 571]. Ibn ᶜAbd al-Barr said, "There is disagreement about the name of Abū ᶜAbd ar-Raḥmān the shaykh of az-Zuhrī. Some say Sulaymān ibn Yasār, but that is unlikely since he is too important for his name to be concealed, or to be alluded to by his *kunyā.* Some said Abu'z-Zinād, which is even more unlikely because he did not narrate from Zayd ibn Thābit, he did not see him, and Ibn Shihāb did not narrate from him [in turn]. Some say that he was Ṭāwūs, which is more likely to be correct. He would only have concealed his name because Ṭāwūs used to impugn Banī Umayyah and would supplicate against them in his assemblies, but Ibn Shihāb would go to see them and accept their grants. He was asked one time while in the assembly of Hishām, 'Do you narrate from Ṭāwūs?' and he answered the questioner, 'If you had seen Ṭāwūs, you would know that he does not lie,' but he did not answer him as to whether or not he narrated from him. All of this is an indication that Abū ᶜAbd ar-Raḥmān in this ḥadīth [571] is Ṭāwūs."

Abu'l-ᶜĀṣ ibn ar-Rabīᶜ. There is a disagreement about his name. Some said it was Laqīṭ, Mahsham, Hashīm, Muhayshim, but the majority believe it was the first named. He accepted Islam and the Messenger of Allah ﷺ returned Zaynab to him. He died in 12 AH, as found in *al-Istīᶜāb.*

Abu'l-ᶜAwwām al-Baṣrī. Ibn Ḥajar said in *at-Taqrīb,* "ᶜAbd al-ᶜAzīz ibn ar-Rubayyiᶜ al-Bāhilī Abu'l-ᶜAwwām the Baṣran is a trustworthy narrator of the seventh generation. It is stated in *Tahdhīb at-tahdhīb,* 'ᶜAbd al-ᶜAzīz ibn ar-Rubayyiᶜ al-Bāhilī Abu'l-ᶜAwwām the Baṣran narrated from Abu'z-Zubayr the Makkan and ᶜAṭā'. From him narrated ath-Thawrī, an-Naḍr ibn Shumayl, Wakīᶜ, and Rawḥ ibn ᶜUbādah.' Ibn Maᶜīn said, 'Trustworthy.' Ibn Ḥibbān mentioned him in *ath-Thiqāt*." Some of the leading people of our age think that the Abu'l-ᶜAwwām al-Baṣrī mentioned in this narration is ᶜImrān ibn Dawar Abu'l-ᶜAwwām al-Qaṭṭān al-Baṣrī. He said in *Tahdhīb at-tahdhīb* in his biographical notice about him, "He narrated from Qatādah, Muḥammad ibn Sīrīn, Abū Isḥāq ash-Shaybānī and Ḥumayd aṭ-Ṭawīl. From him narrated Ibn Mahdī, Abū Dāwūd aṭ-Ṭayālisī, Abū ᶜAlī al-Ḥanafī and others. ᶜAbdullāh said narrating from his father Aḥmad, "I hope that his ḥadīth are right." Ibn Ḥibbān mentioned him among the trustworthy narrators. Al-Bukhārī said, "Utterly truthful, [but] he imagined [some things]." Al-ᶜIjlī said, "A Baṣran who is trustworthy." (Abridged)

Abū Ayyūb al-Anṣārī's name was Khālid ibn Zayd ibn Kulayb ibn Thaᶜlabah ibn ᶜAbd ibn ᶜAwf ibn Ghanam ibn Mālik ibn an-Najjār. He was present at Badr, Uḥud, al-Khandaq and all the rest of the events with the Messenger of Allah ﷺ and he died in Constantinople in the land of the Byzantines in 50 AH, and it is also said in 51 AH in the amirate of Muᶜāwiyah, as found in *al-Istīᶜāb*.

Abu'l-Baddāḥ ibn ᶜĀṣim ibn ᶜAdī. We have not come across his name and his kunyā is his name. Al-Wāqidī said, "Abu'l-Baddāḥ was an honorific name by which he became generally known, and his kunyā was Abū ᶜAmr." Ibn al-Madīnī and Ibn Ḥibbān said the same. Some said that his kunyā was Abū Bakr, and some said his name was ᶜAdī. He was one of the trustworthy narrators of the Followers. He died in 117 AH but some say 110 AH.

Abū Bakr ibn ᶜAbd ar-Raḥmān. It is said that his name was Muḥammad and it is said that it was Abū Bakr and that his kunyā was Abū ᶜAbd ar-Raḥmān, but the correct position is that his kunyā and his name were one and the same, and he was blind. Al-ᶜIjlī and others regarded him as a trustworthy narrator. He died in 93 AH. So it is to be found in *Isᶜāf al-mubaṭṭa'* of as-Suyūṭī.

Abū Bakr ibn ᶜAbdullāh an-Nahshalī by ascription to Banī Nahshal, a tribe. As-Samᶜānī mentioned him in *al-Ansāb*. In *al-Kāshif* and *at-Taqrīb* it is stated, "Abū Bakr ibn ᶜAbdullāh an-Nahshalī the Kūfan. It is said that his name was ᶜAbdullāh ibn Qaṭṭāf or Ibn Abī Qaṭṭāf. Some say it was Wahb and some say Muᶜāwiyah. He was utterly truthful and a trustworthy narrator. He died in 166 AH." It is probable that it is him.

Abū Bakr ibn Muḥammad ibn ᶜAmr ibn Ḥazm al-Anṣārī, the qāḍī of Madīnah.

Abū Bakr ibn Sulaymān ibn Abī Ḥathmah was a trustworthy narrator who was knowledgeable in genealogies, but whose own name is not known. Abū Ḥathmah was ᶜAbdullāh ibn Ḥudhayfah al-ᶜAdawī and he was Madīnan, as is found in *at-Taqrīb*.

Abū Bakr ibn ᶜUbaydullāh ibn ᶜAbdullāh ibn ᶜUmar ibn al-Khattāb. On this the narrators of the *Muwaṭṭa᾿* are unanimously agreed except for Yaḥyā who said Abū Bakr ibn ᶜAbdullāh ibn ᶜAbdullāh ibn ᶜUmar, but that is a mistake, as Ibn ᶜAbd al-Barr said. Az-Zurqānī said, "This Abū Bakr was a Follower who was a trustworthy narrator and who died after 130 AH. His father ᶜUbaydullāh was the full brother of Sālim ibn ᶜAbdullāh." Ibn ᶜAbd al-Barr said about the narration of Yaḥyā ibn Bukayr, "In this narration there is an extra piece which is that it is from his father from Ibn ᶜUmar, but none of the other followers of Mālik agreed with him on that. It is not unknown that Abū Bakr should narrate from his grandfather."

Abū Bakr ibn ᶜUmar according to most of the narrators of the *Muwaṭṭa᾿* and correctly according to Yaḥyā but according to others Ibn ᶜAmr, as Ibn ᶜAbd al-Barr said, and he said, "He is Abū Bakr ibn ᶜUmar ibn ᶜAbd ar-Raḥmān ibn ᶜAbdullāh ibn ᶜUmar ibn al-Khattāb, whose name we have not come across. He was of Quraysh, al-ᶜAdawī and Madīnan and one of the trustworthy narrators." There is only this single ḥadīth [208] ascribed to him in the *Muwaṭṭa᾿* and in the two *ṣaḥīḥ* books, as stated in the *Sharḥ az-Zurqānī* .

Abū Bakr aṣ-Ṣiddīq is Abū Bakr ᶜAbdullāh ibn ᶜUthmān Abū Quḥāfah ibn ᶜĀmir ibn ᶜAmr ibn Kaᶜb who had the honorific surname of al-'Atiq. He was the close friend of the Prophet ﷺ in the cave, who was present with him at all the major events and battles, and he was the first man to accept Islam. He has noted noble qualities. He died in 13 AH. So it is to be found in *Asmā᾿ rijāl al-mishkāh.*

Abū Bakrah Nufayᶜ ibn al-Ḥārith ath-Thaqafī as stated in *Jāmiᶜ al-uṣūl* by Ibn al-Athīr al-Jazarī. In *al-Istīᶜāb* his name is Nufayᶜ ibn Masrūḥ, and it has been said Nufayᶜ ibn al-Ḥārith ibn Kaldah. He came out on the day of Ṭā᾿if to the Messenger of Allah ﷺ and accepted Islam along with the slaves of Ṭā᾿if, and the Messenger of Allah ﷺ set him free, and so he is counted among his mawlās. He died in Baṣra in 51 AH or 52 AH.

Abū Bujayd al-Anṣārī and then al-Ḥārithī and in another copy he is Ibn Bujayd which agrees with that which is in the *Muwaṭṭa*ᵓ of Yaḥyā and elsewhere. He is al-Ḥārithī by ascription to Banī Ḥārithah a clan of Khazraj of the Anṣār. His grandmother was Umm Bujayd.

Abu'd-Dardāᵓ ᶜUwaymir ibn ᶜĀmir, but some say ᶜĀmir, of Banī Kaᶜb ibn al-Khazraj al-Anṣārī al-Khazrajī. There is considerable disagreement on his name and lineage, and he is most known by his kunyā, and ad-Dardāᵓ was his daughter. He was a faqīh and an ᶜālim, and was present at those battles after Uḥud. He resided in Shām and died in Damascus in 32 AH, but some say 31 AH, and some say 34 AH. So it is to be found in the book *Jāmiᶜ al-uṣūl.*

Abū Ghaṭafān. See Ghaṭafān.

Abu'l-Ghayth the *mawlā* of Abū Muṭīᶜ. He mentions in *Tahdhīb at-tahdhīb* and *at-Taqrīb* that he was the *mawlā* of Ibn Muṭīᶜ and that the name of Abu'l-Ghayth was Sālim the Madīnan, whom Ibn Ḥibbān mentions in *ath-Thiqāt,* and whom Ibn Saᶜd and Ibn Maᶜīn regarded as a trustworthy narrator.

Abū Ḥamzah [ḥadīth 265]. There are many Kūfans called Abū Ḥamzah mentioned in *Tahdhīb at-tahdhīb* and *al-Kāshif* and other books, some of whom are trustworthy narrators and some of whom are weak, and I do not know who the one mentioned here is.

Abu'l-Ḥasan Mūsā ibn Abī ᶜĀᵓishah. Al-Qārī said in *Sanad al-anām sharḥ Musnad* al-*Imām,* "He was one of the great Followers." There is in *Taqrīb at-tahdhīb,* "Mūsā ibn Abī ᶜĀᵓishah al-Hamdānī – their *mawlā* – Abu'l-Ḥasan the Kūfan was a trustworthy narrator and a worshipper." In *al-Kāshif* it is stated, "Mūsā ibn Abī ᶜĀᵓishah al-Hamdānī the Kūfan [narrated] from Saᶜīd ibn Jubayr and ᶜAbdullāh ibn Shaddād. From him narrated Shuᶜbah, Jarīr and ᶜUbaydah. When he was seen, Allah was remembered."

Abu'l-Ḥasan al-Bazzār is ascribed to the sale of seeds of herbs and leguminous plants, as as-Samᶜānī mentioned. Ibn Ḥibbān said in *Thiqāt at-tābiᶜīn,* "Abu'l-Ḥasan al-Bazzār narrated from ᶜAlī, '[The sale of] animals for animals is not allowable on deferred terms.' Abu'l-ᶜUmays narrated from him."

Abū Ḥāzim is Salamah ibn Dīnār al-Aᶜraj the person who did without the [the things of this] world (zāhid). He was a trustworthy narrator who narrated a great many ḥadīth, and he used to tell stories in the mosque of Madīnah. He died after 140 AH, as found in *Isᶜāf al-mubaṭṭa*ᵓ of as-Suyūṭī.

Abū Ḥudhayfah ibn ᶜUtbah ibn Rabīᶜah ibn ᶜAbd Shams ibn ᶜAbd Manāf of Quraysh. His name was Hāshim, but some say Hushm. He was one of the eminent Companions. He emigrated on both emigrations, was present at Badr, Uḥud, al-Khandaq, al-Ḥudaybiyyah and all of the battles, and he was killed as a shahīd on the day of al-Yamāmah at the time of Abū Bakr ﷺ. His wife was Sahlat bint Sahl ibn ᶜAmr and she was of Quraysh and ᶜĀmir. She bore Abū Ḥudhayfah Muḥammad ibn Abī Ḥudhayfah, and to Shamākh ibn Saᶜīd she bore Bukayr ibn Shamākh, and to ᶜAbd ar-Raḥmān ibn ᶜAwf she bore Sālim ibn ᶜAbd ar-Raḥmān, as found in *al-Istīᶜāb*.

Abū Ḥumayd as-Sāʾidī's name was al-Mundhir ibn Saᶜd ibn al-Mundhir, or ibn Mālik. It is said that his name was ᶜAbd ar-Raḥmān or ᶜAmr. He was present at Uḥud and the events after it, and he lived until the beginning of 60 AH, as az-Zurqānī mentioned.

Abū Hurayrah. He is the Ḥāfiẓ of the Companions. There are many disagreements as to his name and his father's name, the weightiest of which according to the majority is ᶜAbd ar-Raḥmān ibn Sakhr. He died in 59 AH, but some say one or two years before that. (*Taqrīb at-tahdhīb*).

Abū Idrīs al-Khawlānī. His name is ᶜĀʾidhu'llāh ibn ᶜAmr al-Qārī, the devout worshipper whose father was a Companion. He was born in the prophetic epoch and is trustworthy and a decisive proof. He died in 80 AH. As stated by As-Suyūṭī and others.

Abū Isḥāq as-Sabīᶜī is ᶜAmr ibn ᶜAbdullāh ibn ᶜUbayd, and some say ᶜAlī, as-Sabīᶜī by ascription to Sabīᶜ a tribe from Hamdān, he was Kūfan. He was born two years before the end of ᶜUthmān's khilāfah, and he narrated from ᶜAlī ibn Abī Ṭālib and al-Mughīrah ibn Shuᶜbah – he did see them but he never heard directly from them – and from Sulaymān ibn Ṣurd, Zayd ibn Arqam, al-Barāʾ ibn ᶜĀzib, Jābir ibn Samurah, an-Nuᶜmān ibn Bashīr, al-Aswad ibn Yazīd an-Nakhaᶜī and his brother ᶜAbd ar-Raḥmān ibn Yazīd and his son ᶜAbd ar-Raḥmān ibn al-Aswad, Saᶜīd ibn Jubayr, al-Ḥārith al-Aᶜwar and others. His son Yūnus, his grandson Isrāʾīl ibn Yūnus and his other grandson Yūsuf ibn Isḥāq, as well as Qatādah, Sulaymān at-Taymī, Misᶜar, ath-Thawrī, Sufyān ibn ᶜUyaynah and others narrated ḥadīth from him. Aḥmad, Ibn Maᶜīn, an-Nasāʾī, al-ᶜIjlī and Abū Ḥātim said he was a trustworthy narrator, and he has many virtues which are set out in detail in *Tahdhīb at-tahdhīb*. His death was in 128 AH, 129 AH, 126 AH or 127 AH, more than one person said. As-Samᶜānī said in *Kitāb al-Ansāb* when mentioning as-Sabīᶜī "... In Kūfa there is a place well known as as-Sabīᶜ because this tribe came to reside there. One of the people of knowledge who is ascribed to this place is Abū Isḥāq as-Sabīᶜī whose name is ᶜAmr ibn ᶜAbdullāh ibn ᶜAlī ibn Aḥmad as-Sabīᶜī al-Hamdānī who was born in 29 AH during the khilāfah of ᶜUthmān, and who saw ʿAlī, Usāmah, Ibn ʿAbbās, al-Barāʾ ibn ʿĀzib, Zayd ibn al-Arqam, Abū Juḥayfah and Ibn Abī Awfā. Those who narrated from him were al-Aʿmash, ath-Thawrī and Manṣūr. He died in 127 AH. His son was Yūnus ibn Abī Isḥāq."

Abū Isḥāq ash-Shaybānī by ascription to Shaybān a tribe of Bakr ibn Wāʾil, which as-Samʿānī mentioned in *al-Ansāb.* He is Sulaymān ibn Abī Sulaymān Abū Isḥāq ash-Shaybānī, their *mawlā,* the Kūfan,, who narrated from ʿAbdullāh ibn Abī Awfā, Zirr ibn Hubaysh, Abū Bardah ibn Abī Mūsā, ʿAbdullāh ibn Shaddād ibn al-Hād, ʿAbd al-ʿAzīz ibn Rafīʿ, ʿIkrimah, Ibrāhīm an-Nakhaʿī and others. From him narrated his son Isḥāq, Abū Isḥāq as-Sabīʿī, Ibrāhīm ibn Ṭahmān, Ibn ʿUyaynah and others. Ibn Maʿīn said, "A trustworthy narrator who is a decisive argument." Ibn Abī Ḥātim said, "Utterly truthful, his ḥadīth are good." Al-ʿIjlī said, "He was a trustworthy narrator and one of the major companions of ash-Shaʿbī." Yaḥyā ibn Bakīr said, "He died in 129 AH." Ibn Numayr said, "He died in 139 AH, and his father's name was Fayrūz, and it is said, 'Khāqān,' and some said, 'Mihrān.'" So it is stated in *Tahdhīb at-tahdhīb.*

Abū Jaʿfar Muḥammad ibn ʿAlī ibn al-Ḥusayn ibn ʿAlī ibn Abī Ṭālib, and he is well known as al-Bāqir which he was named because he enlarged his knowledges and sciences a great deal, i.e. he expanded them and deepened them. He heard his father Zayn al-ʿĀbidīn and Jābir ibn ʿAbdullāh, and from him narrated his son Jaʿfar aṣ-Ṣādiq and others. He was born in 56 AH and died in Madīnah in 117 AH, as al-Qārī mentioned in *Sanad al-anām sharḥ Musnad* al-*Imām.*

Abū Jaʿfar al-Qārīʾ. His name was Yazīd ibn al-Qaʿqāʿ and he was Madīnan from Makhzūm, but some have said Jundub ibn Fayrūz, and others that it was Fayrūz. He was a trustworthy narrator. He died in 127 AH, but some have said in 130 AH. Az-Zurqānī.

Abū Jahm whose name was ʿĀmir, but some say ʿUbayd, son of Ḥudhayfah the Companion from Quraysh of those who accepted Islam at the Opening [of Makkah to Islam]. He was one of the shaykhs of Quraysh, and his house was in Balāṭ a place in Madīnah between the mosque and the market. That is what az-Zurqānī said.

Abū Juhaym is ʿAbdullāh ibn Juhaym al-Anṣārī from whom Busr ibn Saʿīd the *mawlā* of the Ḥaḍramis narrated, from the Messenger of Allah ﷺ concerning the one who passes in front of someone praying. Mālik narrated it from Abu'n-Naḍr the *mawlā* of ʿUmar ibn ʿUbaydullāh from Busr from Abū Juhaym, without giving his name, because he is more famous by his kunyā. It is said that he was the son of Ubayy ibn Kaᶜb's sister, but I have not come across his lineage among the Anṣār. That is how it is found in *al-Istīᶜāb fī aḥwāl al-aṣḥāb* by Ibn ᶜAbd al-Barr, may Allah have mercy on him.

Abū Kudaynah Yaḥyā ibn al-Muhallab. That is how al-Fattanī spelt it in *al-Mughnī*. He said in *at-Taqrīb*, "Yaḥyā ibn al-Muhallab Abū Kudaynah al-Bajalī the Kūfan is a trustworthy narrator who is utterly truthful and of the most reliable of the Followers."

Abū Laylā was ibn ᶜAbdullāh ibn ᶜAbd ar-Raḥmān ibn Sahl al-Anṣārī, but some said that his name was ᶜAbdullāh. He was a younger Follower who was a trustworthy narrator, as found in *Sharḥ* al-*Muwaṭṭa'* by az-Zurqānī. In *Isᶜāf al-mubaṭṭa'* by as-Suyūṭī it is stated that, "He was Abū Laylā ibn ᶜAbdullāh ibn ᶜAbd ar-Raḥmān ibn Sahl al-Anṣārī, the Madīnan. Ibn Saᶜd said his name was ᶜAbdullāh ibn Sahl ibn ᶜAbd ar-Raḥmān and that is how he is ascribed in chains of transmission." In *Taqrīb at-tahdhīb* it is stated that, "He is Abū Laylā ibn ᶜAbdullāh ibn ᶜAbd ar-Raḥmān ibn Sahl al-Anṣārī the Madīnan, but some say that his name was ᶜAbdullāh. He is a trustworthy narrator." Al-Qārī was mistaken when he thought that this Abū Laylā was ᶜAbd ar-Raḥmān ibn Abī Laylā the Kūfan, who was famous as Ibn Abī Laylā, or his father.

Abū Māᶜiz ᶜAbdullāh ibn Sufyān was one of the notables of the Followers.

Abū Maᶜshar's name was Najīḥ ibn ᶜAbd ar-Raḥmān as-Sindī, a *mawlā* of Banī Hāshim who was best known by his kunyā. It is said that his name was ᶜAbd ar-Raḥmān ibn al-Walīd ibn Hilāl in whom there was weakness. At-Tirmidhī said, "He is discussed with respect to his memory." Aḥmad said, "Utterly truthful, but he does not establish the chain of transmission." Ibn ᶜAdī said, "His ḥadīth are written even though he is weak," as found in *al-Kāshif* and *at-Taqrīb* and *Qānūn al-Mawḍūᶜāt.*

Abū Muᶜāwiyah al-Makfūf i.e. the one whose sight is prevented, meaning he was blind. He is Muḥammad ibn Khāzim aḍ-Ḍarīr the Kūfan who became blind when he was young. He was a trustworthy narrator and the person with the best memory for the ḥadīth of al-Aᶜmash, but he makes mistakes in other people's ḥadīth. He narrated from al-Aᶜmash and Sufyān, and from him narrated Aḥmad, Isḥāq and Ibn Maᶜīn. He died in 195 AH as is mentioned in *al-Kāshif* and *at-Taqrīb.*

Abū Muḥayrīz. In one copy it is Ibn Muḥayrīz, but he is Abū Muḥayrīz ᶜAbdullāh ibn Muḥayrīz ibn Janādah the Makkan from the clan of Abū Maḥdhūrah in whose care he was an orphan. He narrated from Abū

Maḥdhūrah, Abū Saᶜīd al-Khudrī, Muᶜāwiyah, ᶜUbādah ibn aṣ-Ṣāmit, Umm ad-Dardā' and others. He was a Follower and a trustworthy narrator and one of the best of the Muslims, as found in *Tahdhīb at-tahdhīb.*

Abū Murrah. His name was Yazīd, but some say ᶜAbd ar-Raḥmān. He was Madīnan and a trustworthy narrator of those from whom everyone narrated as az-Zurqānī mentioned. The Ḥāfiẓ said, "He was the *mawlā* of Umm Hāniʾ in reality, but he was ascribed to being a *mawlā* of ᶜAqīl metaphorically because of the least social mixing because he was her brother or because he used to hold to the company of ᶜAqīl a lot."

Abu'l-Muthannā. Adh-Dhahabī said in *al-Kunā*, "Abu'l-Muthannā al-Juhanī [narrated] from Saᶜd and Abū Saᶜīd, and from him [narrated] Ayyūb and Muḥammad ibn Abī Yaḥyā. He was a trustworthy narrator." Ibn ᶜAbd al-Barr said, "I didn't come across his name."

Abu'n-Naḍr the *mawlā* of ᶜUmar ibn ᶜAbdullāh ibn ᶜUbaydullāh [ḥadīth 903] was Sālim ibn Abī Umayyah. However, Abu'n-Naḍr was the *mawlā* of ᶜUmar ibn ᶜUbayd ibn Muᶜammar at-Taymī not of ᶜUmar ibn ᶜAbdullāh ibn ᶜUbaydullāh which is very probably a mistake of a copyist. In some copies of this book is found, "Abu'n-Naḍr the *mawlā* of ᶜUmar ibn ᶜUbaydullāh informed us from ᶜUbaydullāh ibn ᶜAbdullāh ibn ᶜUtbah ibn Masᶜūd ..." and this is *ṣaḥīḥ*. Sālim Abu'n-Naḍr the Madīnan narrated from Anas and as-Sāʾib ibn Yazīd. From him narrated Mālik, al-Layth and the two Sufyāns. Aḥmad and others regarded him as a trustworthy narrator. He died in 129 AH. That is how it is found in *Isᶜāf al-mubaṭṭaʾ* of as-Suyūṭī. Az-Zurqānī mentioned him as Sālim ibn Abī Umayyah who was a Follower and a trustworthy narrator.

Abū Qays ᶜAbd ar-Raḥmān ibn Tharwān al-Awdī because of his relationship to Awd a tribe of Madhḥij. So it is stated in *al-Ansāb*. In *al-Kāshif* of adh-Dhahabī, "ᶜAbd ar-Raḥmān ibn Tharwān Abū Qays al-Awdī [narrated] from Shurayḥ. Shuᶜbah and ath-Thawrī narrated from him. He is trustworthy." It is stated in *at-Taqrīb*, "ᶜAbd ar-Raḥmān ibn Tharwān Abū Qays al-Awdī the Kūfan. He is utterly truthful. He died in 120 AH."

Abū Rāfiᶜ was the *mawlā* of the Messenger of Allah ﷺ. He was first of all the slave of al-ᶜAbbās who gave him to the Messenger of Allah ﷺ who set him free. His name is most reliably recorded as Aslam the Copt, but some have said Ibrāhīm, Thābit, Hurmuz, Sinān, Ṣāliḥ, Yasār, ᶜAbd ar-Raḥmān, Yazīd or Quzmān. He died during the khilāfah of ᶜUthmān but some say during the khilāfah of ᶜAlī which is the correct view. This is as Ibn ᶜAbd al-Barr mentioned in *al-Istīᶜāb.*

Abu'r-Rijāl is Muḥammad ibn ᶜAbd ar-Raḥmān ibn ᶜAbdullāh ibn Ḥārithah ibn an-Nuᶜmān al-Anṣārī. He heard Anas ibn Mālik and his mother, and from him narrated ath-Thawrī and Mālik. He was one of the greatest of the trustworthy narrators. His mother, ᶜAmrah bint ᶜAbd ar-Raḥmān ibn Asᶜad ibn Zurārah, was in ᶜĀ'ishah's lap who brought her up, and from whom she narrated a great deal, and she is one of the famous women of the Followers. Her son, Muḥammad, was given the kunyā Abu'r-Rijāl because he had ten male children, as Ibn al-Athīr and others mentioned.

Abu's-Sā'ib. The Ḥāfiẓ said, "It is said that his name was ᶜAbdullāh ibn as-Sā'ib al-Anṣārī the Madīnan. He was a trustworthy narrator from whom Muslim narrates as well as the Four, and al-Bukhārī in the section on recitation. He was the *mawlā* of Hishām ibn Zuhrah, but it is also said the *mawlā* of ᶜAbdullāh ibn Hishām ibn Zuhrah and it is said the *mawlā* of Banī Zuhrah.

Abū Saᶜīd al-Khudrī whose name was Saᶜd ibn Mālik ibn Sinān ibn ᶜUbayd ibn Thaᶜlabah al-Anṣārī al-Khudrī. Khudrah and Khudārah are two small tribes of the Anṣār. He was one of the Ḥāfiẓs who memorised a great deal, and one of the eminent men of intellect. He died in 74 AH. That is how it is found in *al-Istīᶜāb*. He was present at every event after Uḥud, and died in Madīnah in 63, 64, or 65 AH, and some say 74 AH. That is how it is found in *Jāmiᶜ al-uṣūl.* He is al-Khudrī by ascription to Khudrah who is al-Abjar ibn ᶜAwf ibn al-Ḥārith ibn al-Khazraj. Banū Khudrah are a tribe of the Khazrajī Anṣār and are ascribed to Khudrah. That is how it is found in *al-Ansāb* of as-Sama'ni and *Jāmiᶜ al-uṣūl*.

Abū Salamah ibn ᶜAbd ar-Raḥmān ibn ᶜAwf az-Zuhrī. It is said that his name was ᶜAbdullāh, but some say Ismāᶜīl, and others say that his name was his kunyā. Ibn Saᶜd and others regarded him as a trustworthy narrator. He died in Madīnah in 94 AH. That is how it is found in *Isᶜāf al-mubaṭṭa'* of as-Suyūṭī.

Abū Ṣāliḥ Dhakwān as-Sammāk az-Zayyāt, the Madīnan. Aḥmad said, "He was a trustworthy narrator, the best of people." Ibn al-Madīnī said, "A trustworthy narrator, firmly established." He died in Madīnah in 101 AH, as found in *Isᶜāf al-mubaṭṭa'* of as-Suyūṭī. He was the father of Suhayl ibn Abī Ṣāliḥ, and he was a right-acting trustworthy narrator whose ḥadīth are used as proofs." Abū Dāwūd said, "I asked Ibn Maᶜīn, 'Who was the firmly established one in narrating from Abū Hurayrah?' He answered, 'Ibn al-Musayyab, Abū Ṣāliḥ, Ibn Sīrīn and al-Aᶜraj.'" He died in 101 AH as is in *Tahdhīb at-tahdhīb.*

Abū Ṣāliḥ ibn ᶜUbayd the *mawlā* of as-Saffāḥ – as-Saffāḥ was the honorific name of the first of the *khulafā'* of Banī al-ᶜAbbās who was ᶜAbdullāh ibn Muḥammad ibn ᶜAlī ibn ᶜAbdullāh ibn al-ᶜAbbās, as we found it expressed in a copy on which al-Qārī had written a commentary. In the *Muwaṭṭa'* of Yaḥyā it is stated, "Mālik from Abu'z-Zinād from Busr ibn Saᶜīd from ᶜUbayd ibn Abī Ṣāliḥ the *mawlā* of as-Saffāḥ..." It is stated in *Jāmiᶜ al-uṣūl,* "Abū Ṣāliḥ ᶜUbayd ibn Abī Ṣāliḥ the *mawlā* of as-Saffāḥ was a Follower who narrated from Zayd ibn Thābit and from whom Busr ibn Saᶜīd narrated." In the *Kitāb ath-Thiqāt* by Ibn Ḥibbān it is stated, "ᶜUbayd ibn Khuzāᶜah is counted as one of the People of Madīnah. He narrated from Zayd ibn Thābit, and Busr ibn Saᶜīd narrated from him."

Abū Shurayḥ al-Kaᶜbī – by ascription to Kaᶜb ibn ᶜAmr a clan of of Khuzāᶜah. His name was Khuwaylid ibn ᶜAmr according to that which is best known, or ᶜAmr ibn Khuwaylid, or Hāni', or Kaᶜb ibn ᶜAmr, or ᶜAbd ar-Raḥmān. He accepted Islam before the Opening [of Makkah to Islam], and he died in Madīnah in 68 AH, as found in *al-Istīᶜāb* and elsewhere.

Abū Sufyān *mawlā* of Ibn Abī Aḥmad. His name was Wahb says ad-Dāraquṭnī. Others said his name was Quzmān. Ibn Saᶜd said, "He was a trustworthy narrator with few ḥadīth of whom six are narrated." That is how it is found in *Sharḥ az-Zurqānī* and *at-Taqrīb.*

Abū Suhayl ibn Mālik the paternal uncle of Mālik ibn Anas. His name was Nāfiᶜ. Aḥmad, Abū Ḥātim and an-Nasā'ī regarded him as a trustworthy narrator. So it is found in *Isᶜāf al-mubaṭṭa'* of as-Suyūṭī. His father [ḥadīth 135] was Mālik ibn Abī ᶜĀmir, the grandfather of Imām Mālik and one of the trustworthy narrators of the Followers.

Abū Ṭalḥah al-Anṣārī is the husband of Anas' mother Umm Sulaym, and whose name was Zayd ibn Sahl ibn al-Aswad ibn Ḥarām an-Najjārī al-Khazrajī al-Anṣārī, and he is well known by his kunyā. He was one of the great Companions who was present at the pledge of allegiance at al-ᶜAqabah, Badr and the events thereafter. He died in 31 AH, 34 AH, or even 51 AH, as found in *at-Taqrīb.* The Prophet ﷺ said to him that his voice in the army was better than a hundred men. His wife Umm Sulaym bore him a child who died in infancy, and then later ᶜAbdullāh ibn Abī Ṭalḥah in whom they were blessed, and who in turn is the father of Isḥāq. His brothers were ten in number from each of whom knowledge was taken, as Ibn ᶜAbd al-Barr mentioned in *al-Istīᶜāb.*

Abū Thaᶜlabah al-Khushanī is Jurhum but some say Jurthūm ibn Nāshib, and some say Ibn Nāshim, and others say his name was ᶜAmr ibn Jurthūm and even other names. He was one of those who "pledged allegiance under the tree" and the Messenger of Allah ﷺ sent him to his people and they accepted Islam. He resided in Shām and died in the time of Muʿāwiyah, but some say in the time of ʿAbd al-Mālik in 75 AH, as found in *al-Istīʿāb*. His ascription to Khushayn is to the tribe of Quḍāʿah, as as-Samʿānī mentioned.

Abū ʿUbayd the *mawlā* of ʿAbd ar-Raḥmān (the Companion, and nephew of ʿAbd ar-Raḥmān ibn ʿAwf). His name was Saʿd ibn ʿUbayd az-Zuhrī and he was a major Follower found in the main books of ḥadīth, as az-Zurqānī said.

Abū ʿUbaydah is ibn ʿAbdullāh ibn Masʿūd, and he is well known by his kunyā, and the most famous thing is that he has no name other than it, but some say that his name was ʿĀmir. He was a Kūfan and a trustworthy narrator, one of the great Followers, and he narrated from his father, and from him narrated Isḥāq as-Sabīʿī and ʿAmr ibn Murrah. The weightiest view is that it is not sound that he heard from his father. He died in 180 AH, as found in *at-Taqrīb* and *Jāmiʿ al-uṣūl*.

Abū ʿUbaydah ibn al-Jarrāḥ was ʿĀmir ibn ʿAbdullāh al-Fihrī the 'trusted one' (*Amīn*) of this community [ummah]. ʿUmar appointed him amīr over Shām.

Abū Umāmah is counted among the Companions because he saw [the Prophet ﷺ], but he did not hear him. His name was Asʿad, but it is also said that it was Saʿd. He died in 100 AH. His father was Sahl ibn Ḥunayf the famous Companion who was one of the people of Badr, as az-Zurqānī mentioned.

Abū Wāʾil is Shaqīq ibn Salamah al-Asadī, the Kūfan. Adh-Dhahabī said in *Tadhkirat al-ḥuffāẓ*, "*Mukhḍaram* [someone half of whose life was lived in the Jāhiliyyah and half in Islam], magnificent. He narrated from ʿUmar, ʿUthmān, ʿAlī, Ibn Masʿūd, ʿĀʾishah and a large body of others. From him narrated al-Aʿmash, Manṣūr and Ḥuṣayn. It is said that he accepted Islam during the lifetime of the Prophet ﷺ. An-Nakhaʿī said, 'I reckon Abū Wāʾil as one of those by whom we are defended.' He died in 82 AH."

Abū Waʿlah. So it is to be found in many copies, but he is Ibn Waʿlah as in the *Muwaṭṭaʾ* of Yaḥyā. In the narration of Ibn Wahb it is, "from Mālik from Zayd from ʿAbd ar-Raḥmān ibn Waʿlah as-Sabāʾī one of the people of Egypt." In the *Jāmiʿ al-uṣūl* it is stated, "Ibn Waʿlah is ʿAbd ar-Raḥmān ibn Waʿlah as-Sabāʾī a Follower." As-Samʿānī said in *al-Ansāb*, "As-Sabāʾī is by ascription Sabā who is Sabaʾ ibn Yashḥab ibn Yuʿrab ibn Qaḥṭān, and they are a group who ascribe themselves to him most of whom are from Egypt."

Then later he said, "One of them was ᶜAbd ar-Raḥmān ibn Usmayfaᶜ ibn Waᶜlah who narrated from Ibn ᶜUmar and Ibn ᶜAbbās. He was a noble person in Egypt." In *Isᶜāf al-mubaṭṭa'* of as-Suyūṭī, "An-Nasā'ī, Ibn Maᶜīn and al-ᶜIjlī regarded him as a trustworthy narrator."

Abū Wāqid al-Laythī from the tribe of Layth ibn Bakr ibn ᶜAbd Manāt ibn ᶜAlī ibn Kinānah ibn Khuzaymah ibn Ilyās ibn Muḍar. There is disagreement about his name, and some say al-Ḥārith ibn ᶜAwf, some say al-Ḥārith ibn Mālik ibn Usayd ibn Jābir ibn ᶜAtūdah ibn ᶜAbd Manāt ibn Sajᶜ ibn ᶜĀmir ibn Layth. Some say he was present at Badr with the Messenger of Allah ﷺ and that he had become a Muslim early on, and some say that he was one of the those who accepted Islam at the the Opening [of Makkah to Islam], but the former is more sound. He died in Makkah in 68 AH as found in *al-Istīᶜāb.*

Abū Yarbūᶜ al-Makhzūmī, and in a copy Ibn Yarbūᶜ which accords with what is in the *Muwaṭṭa'* of Yaḥyā, and he is ᶜAbd ar-Raḥmān ibn Saᶜīd ibn Yarbūᶜ al-Makhzūmī Abū Muḥammad, the Madīnan who is ascribed to his grandfather, and who is one of the trustworthy narrators of the Followers. He is mentioned in *at-Taqrīb.*

Abū Yūnus the *mawlā* of ᶜĀ'ishah [ḥadīth 349]. Ibn Ḥibbān regarded him as a trustworthy narrator, as as-Suyūṭī said. [Ḥadīth 999] Az-Zurqānī said that he was one of the trustworthy narrators of the Followers. His name is not known.

Abū Ẓabyān. ᶜAbd al-Ghanī and Ibn Mākūlā gave the exact spelling. Al-Ḥāzimī said, "Most of the people of ḥadīth and language [spell it thus] Ẓabyān. His name was Ḥuṣayn ibn Jundub ibn ᶜAmr ibn al-Ḥārith ibn Waḥshī ibn Mālik ibn Rabīᶜah al-Janbī al-Madhḥijī by ascription to the tribe of Madhḥij of the people of Kūfa. He is a famous Follower who heard from ᶜAlī, ᶜAmmār and Usāmah ibn Zayd. From him narrated his son Qābūs and al-Aᶜmash. He died in Kūfa in 90 AH. That is how Ibn al-Athīr al-Jazarī mentioned it in *Jāmiᶜ al-uṣūl.* There is in *Tahdhīb at-tahdhīb,* 'He narrated from ᶜUmar, ᶜAlī, Ibn Masᶜūd, Salman, Usāmah ibn Zayd, ᶜAmmār, Ḥudhayfah, Abū Mūsā, Ibn ᶜAbbās, Ibn ᶜUmar and ᶜĀ'ishah, and of the Followers from ᶜAlqamah, Abū ᶜUbaydah ibn ᶜAbdullāh Ibn Masᶜūd, Muḥammad ibn Saᶜd ibn Abī Waqqāṣ and others. From him narrated his son Qābūs, Abū Isḥāq as-Sabīᶜī, Salamah ibn Kuhayl, al-Aᶜmash, and Sammāk ibn Ḥarb. Ibn Maᶜīn, al-ᶜIjlī, Abū Zurᶜah, an-Nasā'ī and ad-Dāraquṭnī said he was trustworthy, and Ibn Ḥibbān mentioned him in *ath-Thiqāt.* Ad-Dāraquṭnī was asked, "Did Abū Ẓabyān meet ᶜUmar and ᶜAlī?" He answered, "Yes." Ibn Abī ᶜĀṣim said he died in 89 AH. Ibn Saᶜd and others said he died in 90 AH, and others have said other dates.'"

Abu'z-Zinād is ᶜAbdullāh ibn Dhakwān, and Abu'z-Zinād is his cognomen, but it used to annoy him because of the meanings associated closely with the Fire (*zinād* is a steel for striking fire), however, he has become famous as such because of the excellence of his intelligence. Al-Bukhārī said, "The soundest of the chains of transmission of Abū Hurayrah is: Abu'z-Zinād from al-Aᶜraj from him." Al-Wāqidī said, "He died in 130 AH," and as-Suyūṭī and others say the same.

Abu'z-Zubayr Muḥammad ibn Muslim ibn Tadrus the Makkan, the *mawlā* of Ḥakīm ibn Ḥizām, one of the Followers of Makkah. He heard Jābir, ᶜĀʾishah, Ibn ᶜAbbās, Ibn ᶜUmar and others. Mālik narrated from him, the two Sufyāns, Ayyūb as-Sakhtiyānī, Ibn Jurayj, Shuᶜbah, ath-Thawrī, and others. He was a ḥāfiẓ who was a trustworthy narrator. He died in 128 AH. That is how it is found in *Jāmiᶜ al-uṣūl* and *al-Kāshif.* He narrated from Jābir, Ibn ᶜUmar, Ibn ᶜAbbās, Ibn az-Zubayr and ᶜĀʾishah, and from him narrated Mālik, Abū Ḥanīfah, Shuᶜbah and the two Sufyāns. Ibn al-Madīnī, Ibn Maᶜīn and an-Nasāʾī regarded him as a trustworthy narrator. He died in 128 AH, as found in *Isᶜāf al-mubaṭṭaʾ* of as-Suyūṭī.

ᶜAfīf ibn ᶜAmr ibn al-Musayyab as-Sahmī. I read in the handwriting of adh-Dhahabī, "It is not known who he was, i.e. ᶜAfīf ibn ᶜAmr. Ibn Ḥibbān mentions him in *ath-Thiqāt,* and an-Nasāʾī said he was a trustworthy narrator. That is how it is found in the *Tahdhīb at-tahdhīb* of Ibn Ḥajar.

Aḥmad [ḥadīth 159].[2]

ᶜĀʾishah bint Abī Bakr aṣ-Ṣiddīq the wife of the Prophet ﷺ and the most beloved of his wives to him. Her mother was Umm Rumān bint ᶜĀmir ibn ᶜUwaymir ibn ᶜAbd Shams. He married her when she was a girl of six or seven, two years before the Hijrah according to Abū ᶜUbaydah. Others said it was three years before the Hijrah. He took up residence with her in Madīnah when she was nine. Az-Zuhri said, "If ᶜĀʾishah's knowledge were to be gathered together with the knowledge of all of the wives of the Messenger of Allah ﷺ and the knowledge of all women, the knowledge of ᶜĀʾishah would be superior." That is how it is found in *al-Istīᶜāb* of Ibn ᶜAbd al-Barr. Abu'ḍ-Ḍuḥā said that Masrūq said, "I saw the major Companions of the Prophet ﷺ asking her about the shares of inheritance." ᶜAṭāʾ said, "ᶜĀʾishah was the person with the most fiqh and the most knowledgeable of people." She died in 57 AH, but some say 58 AH, on the 17th of Ramaḍān. That is how it is found in *al-Istīᶜāb fī aḥwāl al-aṣḥāb* by Ibn ᶜAbd al-Barr.

ᶜĀʾishah bint Qudāmah ibn Maẓᶜūn was of Quraysh and Jumaḥ. She was a Companion as was her mother Rīṭah bint Sufyān who was one of those who pledged allegiance [at al-ᶜAqabah], as found in *al-Istīᶜāb*.

ᶜĀʾishah bint Ṭalḥah of Quraysh. She was extremely beautiful. A trustworthy narrator from whom the six have narrated as az-Zurqānī mentioned.

ᶜAlāʾ (or al-ᶜAlāʾ) ibn ᶜAbd ar-Raḥmān ibn Yaᶜqūb. His name was Abū Shibl. He was a Madīnan and utterly truthful as stated in *al-Isᶜāf* and *at-Taqrīb*. He was the *mawlā* of al-Ḥuraqah, a tribe of Hamdān as Ibn Ḥibbān said or from Juhaynah as ad-Dāraquṭnī said, which is correct, as stated in *Ansāb as-Samᶜānī*. He died in 132 AH. Ibn Ḥibbān mentioned him in *ath-Thiqāt* as found in *at-Taqrīb* and *al-Ansāb*.

Al-ᶜAlāʾ ibn al-Ḥārith. Al-ᶜAlāʾ ibn al-ᶜAlāʾ ibn al-Ḥārith ibn ᶜAbd al-Wārith al-Ḥaḍramī Abū Wahb or Abū Muḥammad of Damascus. He narrated from Makḥūl, az-Zuhrī and ᶜAmr ibn Shuᶜayb. From him narrated al-Awzāᶜī, ᶜAbd ar-Raḥmān ibn Thābit ibn Thawbān and others. Ibn Maᶜīn, Ibn al-Madīnī and Abū Dāwūd said he was a trustworthy narrator. Abū Ḥātim said, "He was one of the best of the companions of Makḥūl." Duḥaym said, "He has priority over the companions of Makḥūl, and he is a trustworthy narrator who died in 136 AH." That is how it is found in *Tahdhīb at-tahdhīb*.

ᶜAlī ibn ᶜAbd ar-Raḥmān al-Muᶜāwī. Abū Zurᶜah and an-Nasāʾī regarded him as a trustworthy narrator as as-Suyūṭī said. He was called al-Muᶜāwī by ascription to Banī Muᶜāwiyah a part of the Anṣār. He was a Madīnan Follower who was a trustworthy narrator, and from whom Muslim and Abū Dāwūd narrated, as az-Zurqānī said.

ᶜAlī ibn Abī Ṭālib ᶜAbd Manāf ibn ᶜAbd al-Muṭṭalib of Quraysh al-Hāshimī the son of the paternal uncle of the Messenger of Allah ﷺ and the husband of the daughter of the Messenger of Allah ﷺ. He grew up with the Prophet ﷺ and prayed with him as the first of people [to do so]. He was present at all the battles and expeditions apart from Tabūk [for which we was left in charge of Madīnah]. He has many merits, and was killed as a shahīd on the night of the Jumuᶜah thirteen days before the end of Ramaḍān in 40 AH in Kūfa, as found in *Asad al-ghābah* and *Isᶜāf al-mubaṭṭaʾ* of as-Suyūṭī, by which we know that the narration of Ibrāhīm an-Nakhaᶜī from him was *mursal* because he did not live at that time.

ᶜAlī ibn Ḥusayn ibn ᶜAlī ibn Abī Ṭālib who is Zayn al-ᶜĀbidīn the son of Sayyid ash-Shuhadāʾ al-Ḥusayn.

ᶜAlqamah ibn Qays ibn ᶜAbdullāh ibn Mālik ibn ᶜAlqamah Abū Shabil an-Nakhaᶜī, the Kūfan paternal uncle of al-Aswad an-Nakhaᶜī. He was born during the lifetime of the Messenger of Allah ﷺ and narrated from ᶜUmar, ᶜUthmān, ᶜAlī, Saᶜd, Ḥudhayfah, Abu'd-Dardā', Ibn Masᶜūd, Abū Mūsā, Khālid ibn al-Walīd, Salamah ibn Yazīd al-Juᶜfī, ᶜĀ'ishah and others. From him narrated his brother's son ᶜAbd ar-Raḥmān ibn Yazīd ibn Qays an-Nakhaᶜī, his sister's son Ibrāhīm ibn Yazīd an-Nakhaᶜī, Ibrāhīm ibn Suwayd an-Nakhaᶜī, ᶜĀmir ash-Shaᶜbī, Abū Wā'il Shaqīq ibn Salamah, Abū Isḥāq as-Sabīᶜī and others. Ibn al-Madīnī said, "The people who knew ᶜAbdullāh ibn Masᶜūd best were ᶜAlqamah, al-Aswad, ᶜUbaydah and al-Ḥārith." Ibn Maᶜīn, Shuᶜbah, Ibn Sīrīn and others said he was a trustworthy narrator and praised him. He is one of the most significant companions of Ibn Masᶜūd. He died in 161 AH, but some say 162, 163, 165, 172 and even after that.

ᶜAlqamah ibn Wā'il ibn Ḥujr al-Ḥaḍramī al-Kindī the Kūfan narrated from his father, al-Mughīrah ibn Shuᶜbah and Ṭāriq ibn Suwayd. From him narrated his brother ᶜAbd al-Jabbār, his nephew Saᶜīd, ᶜAmr ibn Murrah, Sammāk ibn Ḥarb and others. Ibn Ḥibbān mentioned him in *ath-Thiqāt*. Ibn Saᶜd said, "He was a trustworthy narrator with few ḥadīth." Al-ᶜAskarī quoted Ibn Maᶜīn as saying, "ᶜAlqamah narrating from his father is a *mursal* ḥadīth." So it is stated in *Tahdhīb at-tahdhīb*.

ᶜAlqamah [ḥadīth 26]. Al-Qārī said in his Sharḥ, "He is ᶜAlqamah ibn Abī ᶜAlqamah [see ḥadīth 85] Bilāl the *mawlā* of ᶜĀ'ishah the mother of the mu'minūn, and he narrated from Anas ibn Mālik and from his own mother. Mālik ibn Anas and others narrated from him." He is a Madīnan. There are other men known as ᶜAlqamah from among the scholars of Kūfa, one of whom may be one of Imām Muhammad's narrators for one of his narrations. (See ᶜAlqamah ibn Qays, and see p. 222 of at-Taᶜlīq al-mumajjad, from Dār al-Qalam of Damascus, for a detailed discussion). His mother [ḥadīth 390] was the freed slave [mawlāh] of ᶜĀ'ishah ؓ [see Marjānah].

Amāmah bint Zaynab is Amāmah bint Abi'l-ᶜĀṣ ibn ar-Rabīᶜ ibn ᶜAbd al-ᶜUzzā ibn ᶜAbd Shams ibn Manāf. Her mother was Zaynab the daughter of the Messenger of Allah ﷺ. She was born in the time of the Messenger of Allah ﷺ and he used to love her, and probably carried her on his neck in the prayer. ᶜAlī ibn Abī Ṭālib married her after Fāṭimah. When ᶜAlī was killed, al-Mughīrah ibn Nawfal ibn al-Ḥārith ibn ᶜAbd al-Muṭṭalib married her to whom she bore Yaḥyā, and then she died while married to him. Some said that she did not give birth neither while married to ᶜAlī nor to al-Mughīrah, and that Zaynab has no posterity, as stated in *al-Istīᶜāb*.

Al-Aᶜmash is derived from al-ᶜAmash which is expressive of weaksightedness and the fact that tears used to stream from his eyes because of an illness. The person who is famous with this name is Sulaymān ibn Mihrān al-Asadī al-Kāhilī – their *mawlā* – Abū Muḥammad the Kūfan whose origin was in Ṭabaristān, but who was born in Kūfa. He narrated from Anas, but it is not established that he heard from him directly, and from Ibn Abī Awfā, Abū Wāʾil, Qays ibn Abī Ḥāzim, ash-Shaᶜbī, an-Nakhaᶜī and others. From him narrated Abū Isḥāq as-Sabīᶜī, Shuᶜbah, the two Sufyāns and others. Ibn Maᶜīn said he was a trustworthy narrator. An-Nasāʾī said he was a firm trustworthy narrator. Ibn ᶜAmmār said, "There is not among the narrators of ḥadīth anyone more firm than al-Aᶜmash, and Manṣūr is also firm except that al-Aᶜmash had more knowledge than he did about the chain of transmission." He died in 147 AH, but some say 146 AH, and there is a lengthy biographical notice on him in *Tahdhīb at-tahdhīb.*

ᶜĀmir ash-Shaᶜbī is ᶜĀmir Sharāḥīl ash-Shaᶜbī, by ascription to Shaᶜb a sub-clan of Hamdān, he was Kūfan, and he was one of the great Followers. He was a faqīh, poet and he narrated from one hundred and fifty Companions. He died in 104 AH, and some say in 109 AH as is mentioned by as-Samᶜānī. He mentioned in *Tahdhīb at-tahdhīb,* "Makḥūl said, 'I have never seen anyone more discerning (*afqah,* lit. with more fiqh) than him.' Ibn ᶜUyaynah said, 'The people after the Companions were ash-Shaᶜbī in his time and ath-Thawrī in his time.' Ibn Maᶜīn said, 'When ash-Shaᶜbī narrates a ḥadīth from a man whom he names, then he is a trustworthy narrator.' He and Abū Zurᶜah said that he was a trustworthy narrator. Ibn Ḥibbān mentioned him in *ath-Thiqāt.* Al-ᶜIjlī said, 'Ash-Shaᶜbī could hardly relate a *mursal* ḥadīth that was not *ṣaḥīḥ.*' Abū Dāwūd said, 'The *mursal* ḥadīth of ash-Shaᶜbī are preferable to me than the *mursal* ḥadīth of an-Nakhaᶜī.'" (Abridged)

ᶜĀmir ibn Saᶜd ibn Abī Waqqāṣ az-Zuhrī, the Madīnan. Ibn Ḥibbān regarded him as a trustworthy narrator. He died in 96 AH, but some say in 103 AH, as stated in *Isᶜāf al-mubaṭṭaʾ*.

ᶜAmmār ibn Yāsir is Abu'l-Yaqẓān ᶜAmmār ibn Yāsir ibn ᶜĀmir ibn Mālik ibn Kinānah. He accepted Islam and emigrated [both] to Abyssinia and Madīnah. He was present at Badr and all the battles. The Messenger of Allah ﷺ said to him, "The rebellious party will kill you," and he was killed at Ṣiffīn while with ᶜAlī ؓ. The people with Muᶜāwiyah killed him in 37 AH. That is how it is found in *Jāmiᶜ al-uṣūl* by Ibn al-Athīr al-Jazarī.

ᶜAmr ibn al-Ḥārith ibn Yaᶜqūb ibn ᶜAbdullāh al-Anṣārī – he was their *mawlā* – Abū Umayyah, the Egyptian. Ibn Maᶜīn, an-Nasāʾī and many others regarded him as a trustworthy narrator. He died in 148 AH, but some say 149 AH, as stated in *al-Isᶜāf*.

ᶜAmr ibn ash-Sharīd ath-Thaqafī aṭ-Ṭā᾿ifī Abu'l-Walīd of Ṭā᾿if was one of the trustworthy narrators of the Followers, as az-Zurqānī and others said.

ᶜAmr ibn ᶜUbaydullāh al-Anṣārī whom Ibn Ḥibbān mentioned in the book *ath-Thiqāt* in which he named his father as ᶜUbayd. He said, "He was from Banī al-Ḥārith ibn al-Khazraj of the people of Madīnah. He narrated from Ibn ᶜAbbās and from him narrated Mālik ibn Anas and Sulaymān ibn Bilāl."

ᶜAmr ibn al-ᶜĀṣ ibn Wā᾿il as-Sahmī the Companion. He became a Muslim in the year of al-Ḥudaybiyyah, and was made the amīr of Egypt twice. He died there around 40 AH, and some say after 50 AH. That is how az-Zurqānī mentioned it in his *Sharḥ* al-*Muwaṭṭa*. ᶜAmr ibn al-ᶜĀṣ accepted Islam at the hands of an-Najāshī (the Negus) before accompanying the Prophet ﷺ and so a riddle was made of him when it was said, "He was a Companion who narrated many ḥadīth and who accepted Islam at the hands of a Follower."

ᶜAmr ibn Ḥazm ibn Zayd ibn Lawdhān al-Anṣārī was present at al-Khandaq and the events after that. He was the governor for the Messenger of Allah ﷺ in Najrān. He died after 50 AH, as az-Zurqānī said. He was Abū Muḥammad, but some say Abu'ḍ-Ḍāḥik, ᶜAmr ibn Ḥazm ibn Zayd ibn Lawdhān ibn ᶜAmr ibn ᶜAbd ᶜAwf ibn Ghanam ibn Mālik ibn an-Najjār al-Anṣārī al-Khazrajī an-Najjārī the Madīnan. The first event at which he was present with the Messenger of Allah ﷺ was al-Khandaq, and the Messenger of Allah ﷺ appointed him as the governor of Najrān in the Yemen, and he sent along with him a writing in which there were the obligatory shares of inheritances and the Sunnahs, the amounts paid in zakāh, retaliations and compensatory payments due for damages done and wounds inflicted, and compensatory payments due for homicide. This writing of his is famous. Abū Dāwūd, an-Nasā᾿ī and others narrated it in separate bits, and the most complete narration of it is by an-Nasā᾿ī in the chapter on compensatory payments for homicides and injuries. He died in Madīnah in 51 AH or 53 AH or 54 AH according to the different views, as found in *Tahdhīb an-Nawawī.*

ᶜAmr ibn Ḥusayn was a trustworthy narrator. Muslim and at-Tirmidhī narrated from him, and he was ᶜAmr ibn Ḥusayn ibn ᶜAbdullāh al-Jumaḥī – their *mawlā* – Abū Qudāmah, the Makkan, as found in *at-Taqrīb*.

ᶜAmr ibn Muḥammad ibn Zayd. So it is given in some copies and in some authentic copies it is given as ᶜUmar ibn Muḥammad ibn Zayd who is ᶜUmar ibn Muḥammad ibn Zayd ibn ᶜAbdullāh ibn ᶜUmar ibn al-Khattāb al-ᶜAdawī, the Madīnan who resided in ᶜAsqalān, and who narrated from his father and grandfather Zayd, and from his father's paternal uncle Sālim, and Zayd ibn

Aslam, Nāfiʿ and others. From him narrated Shuʿbah, Mālik, the two Sufyāns and Ibn al-Mubārak. Ibn Saʿd said, "He was a trustworthy narrator with few ḥadīth." ʿAbdullāh ibn Aḥmad said [narrating] from his father, "A shaykh who is a trustworthy narrator, and in whom there is no harm." Ḥanbal said [narrating] from Aḥmad, "A trustworthy narrator." Ibn Maʿīn, al-ʿIjlī, Abū Dāwūd and Abū Ḥātim said the same. Most of his residence was in Shām and then he went to Baghdād and then Kūfa, where they learnt from him. He died after his brother Abū Bakr, and Abū Bakr died after the uprising of Muḥammad ibn ʿAbdullāh ibn Ḥasan which occurred in 145 AH. So it is found in the *Tahdhīb at-tahdhīb.*

ʿAmr ibn Murrah [ḥadīth 107] is Abū ʿAbdullāh ʿAmr ibn Murrah ibn ʿAbdullāh ibn Ṭāriq ibn al-Ḥārith ibn Salamah ibn Kaʿb ibn Wāʾil ibn Jamal ibn Kinānah ibn Nājiyah ibn Murād al-Jamalī al-Murādī, the blind Kūfan. He narrated from ʿAbdullāh ibn Abī Awfā, Abū Wāʾil, Saʿīd ibn al-Musayyab, ʿAbd ar-Raḥmān ibn Abī Laylā, ʿAmr ibn Maymūn al-Awdī, Saʿīd ibn Jubayr, Musʿab ibn Saʿd, an-Nakhaʿī and others. From him narrated his son ʿAbdullāh, Abū Isḥāq as-Sabīʿī, al-Aʿmash, Manṣūr, Ḥuṣayn ibn ʿAbd ar-Raḥmān, ath-Thawrī, Shuʿbah and others. Ibn Maʿīn said that he was a trustworthy narrator. Abū Ḥātim said that he was utterly truthful and a trustworthy narrator. Shuʿbah said, "He had the most knowledge among them. I have not seen anyone of the people of ḥadīth who did not conceal gaps in his chains of transmission (*tadlīs*) except for Ibn ʿAwn, ʿAmr ibn Murrah and Misʿar. There was no one in Kūfa more beloved to me than him nor was there anyone better." Ibn Ḥibbān mentioned him in the book *ath-Thiqāt* and he said, "He was one of the Murjiʾah[3]." He died in 116 AH. Ibn Numayr and Yaʿqūb ibn Sufyān regarded him as a trustworthy narrator. So it is found in the *Tahdhīb at-tahdhīb*, *al-Kāshif* and *Tadhkirat al-ḥuffāẓ*. Al-Qārī wrongly considered him a Companion.

ʿAmr ibn Rāfiʿ al-ʿAdawī – he was their *mawlā* – and he is acceptable. He mentions him in *at-Taqrīb.*

ʿAmr ibn Shuʿayb ibn Muḥammad ibn ʿAbdullāh ibn ʿAmr ibn al-ʿĀṣ of Quraysh. It very often occurs in the books of ḥadīth that we find "ʿAmr ibn Shuʿayb from his father from his grandfather…" Ibn al-Qaṭṭān said, "When trustworthy narrators transmit from him then he is a trustworthy narrator whom one may use in proof." Al-Bukhārī said, "I saw Aḥmad ibn Ḥanbal, ʿAlī ibn al-Madīnī, Isḥāq ibn Rāhwayh and people in general of our companions using the ḥadīth of ʿAmr ibn Shuʿayb from his father from his grandfather in proof. None of the Muslims abandon him." He died in 118 AH, as found in *Isʿāf al-mubaṭṭa'* of as-Suyūṭī.

ʿAmr ibn Sulaym az-Zuraqī, by ascription to Banī Zurayq, ibn ʿAbd Ḥārithah, a clan of the Anṣār, as as-Samʿānī mentioned.

ʿAmr ibn ʿUbaydullāh al-Anṣārī. Ibn Ḥibbān mentioned him in *Kitāb ath-Thiqāt* but he called his father ʿUbayd, and he said, "He was from Banī al-Ḥārith ibn al-Khazraj of the people of Madīnah. He narrated from Ibn ʿAbbās and from him Mālik ibn Anas and Sulaymān ibn Bilāl narrated."

ʿAmrah bint ʿAbd ar-Raḥmān ibn Saʿd ibn Zurārah was in the room of ʿĀ'ishah who brought her up, and she narrated many ḥadīth from her and from others. A large number narrated from her among them Yaḥyā ibn Saʿīd al-Anṣārī, his son Abu'r-Rijāl Muḥammad ibn ʿAbd ar-Raḥmān ibn Ḥārithah and Abū Bakr ibn Muḥammad ibn ʿAmr ibn Ḥazm. She died in 103 AH and is one of the famous female Followers. That was what Ibn al-Athīr al-Jazarī said in *Jāmiʿ al-uṣūl.* She died before the end of the first century or just after as as-Suyūṭī mentioned.

ʿAmrah bint Ḥazm was the paternal aunt of the grandfather of ʿAbdullāh ibn Abī Bakr and so she was called his paternal aunt metaphorically speaking. She was a companion of old from whom Jābir the Companion narrated.

Anas ibn Mālik was the servant of the Messenger of Allah ﷺ and he served him for ten years. The Messenger of Allah ﷺ supplicated for him saying, "O Allah increase him in wealth and in children, and enter him into the Garden." He died in 102 AH, but some say 92 AH, having passed one hundred years in age. So it is found in *Isʿāf al-mubaṭṭa' bi rijal* al-*Muwaṭṭa'* of as-Suyūṭī.

Anas ibn Sīrīn is Abū Mūsā Anas the son of Sīrīn al-Anṣārī, the Madīnan, the *mawlā* of Anas, and he is the brother of Muḥammad ibn Sīrīn. He narrated from his master, Ibn ʿAbbās, Ibn ʿUmar and a large group. From him narrated Shuʿbah and the two Ḥammāds. Ibn Maʿīn declared him to be a trustworthy narrator as well as an-Nasā'ī, Abū Ḥātim, Ibn Saʿd and Al-ʿIjlī. He died in 118 AH, but it is also said 125 AH. So it is found in *Tahdhīb at-tahdhīb.*

ʿAqīl ibn Abī Ṭālib ibn ʿAbd al-Muṭṭalib ibn Hishām of Quraysh whose kunyā was Abū Yazīd. We have narrated that the Prophet ﷺ said to him, "Abū Yazīd, I love you with two loves: a love because of your kinship to me, and a love because of what I know of my uncle's love for you." ʿAqīl went to Baṣra and then Kūfa, and then later he went to Shām. He died in the time of Muʿāwiyah. That is in *al-Istīʿāb.*

Al-Aᶜraj. As-Samᶜānī said in *al-Ansāb,* "Al-Aᶜraj... is because of an ascription to *al-ᶜaraj* – natural lameness. The one who is well known by this name is Abū Ḥāzim ᶜAbd ar-Raḥmān ibn Hurmuz ibn Kaysān al-Aᶜraj the *mawlā* of Muḥammad ibn Rabīᶜah ibn al-Ḥārith ibn ᶜAbd al-Muṭṭalib who narrated from Abū Hurayrah and from whom az-Zuhrī and Abu'z-Zinād narrated in turn."

Arqam ibn Shuraḥbīl. His names are as al-Fattanī spelt them out. He said in *Tahdhīb at-tahdhīb,* "Arqam ibn Shuraḥbīl the Kūfan al-Awdī narrated from Ibn ᶜAbbās and Ibn Masᶜūd. From him narrated Abū Isḥāq and his brother Hudhayl ibn Shuraḥbīl. Abū Zurᶜah said he is trustworthy, and Aḥmad ibn Ḥanbal used his ḥadīth as definitive proofs. Ibn ᶜAbd al-Barr said, 'It is a *ṣaḥīḥ* ḥadīth and Arqam is a tremendous trustworthy narrator.' Al-ᶜUqaylī transmitted with a sound chain of transmission from Abū Isḥāq as-Sabīᶜī that he said, 'Hudhayl and Arqam were two sons of Shuraḥbīl one of the best companions of Ibn Masᶜūd.'" (Abridged)

Asīd was the father of Khālid ibn Asīd and of his brother ᶜAttāb ibn Asīd whom the Messenger of Allah ﷺ apppointed governor of Makkah in the year of the Opening [of Makkah to Islam].

ᶜĀṣim ibn ᶜAdī ibn al-Jadd ibn al-ᶜIjlān ibn Ḥārithah al-Quḍāᶜī al-Anṣārī was one of the Companions who was present at Uḥud and other events. He lived for 125 years, as found in *Sharḥ az-Zurqānī* .

ᶜĀṣim ibn Kulayb ibn Shihāb ibn al-Majnūn al-Jarmī, the Kūfan. He narrated from his father, Abū Buraydah, ᶜAlqamah ibn Wāʾil ibn Ḥujr and others. From him narrated Shuᶜbah, the two Sufyāns and others. An-Nasāʾī regarded him as a trustworthy narrator and Ibn Maᶜīn. Abū Dāwūd said, "He was one of the best of the people of Kūfa." Ibn Ḥibbān mentioned him among the trustworthy narrators, and he gave the date of his death as 137 AH. His father Kulayb ibn Shihāb was a trustworthy narrator. So it is stated in *Tahdhīb at-tahdhīb* and *al-Kāshif.* In *al-Ansāb* of as-Samᶜānī it is stated, "Al-Jarmī by ascription to Jarm a Yemeni tribe from whom of the Companions there was Shihāb ibn al-Majnūn al-Jarmī, the grandfather of ᶜĀṣim ibn Kulayb."

Aslam the father of Zayd ibn Aslam was a *mawlā* of ᶜUmar and a trustworthy narrator who had lived half of his life in the Jāhiliyyah and half of it in Islam. He died in 87 AH. So it is found in *Isᶜāf al-mubaṭṭaʾ* of as-Suyūṭī and other works.

Asmāʾ bint ᶜUmays was the sister of Maymūnah the wife of the Prophet ﷺ and of Umm al-Faḍl the wife of al-ᶜAbbās, and she was the sister of their sisters by the same mother who were nine in number, and some say ten. Asmāʾ was one of the emigrants to the land of the Ethiopians along with her husband Jaᶜfar ibn Abī Ṭālib to whom she bore Muḥammad, ᶜAbdullāh and ᶜAwn. Then she emigrated to Madīnah. When Jaᶜfar was killed Abū Bakr aṣ-Ṣiddīq married her and she bore him Muḥammad. When he died, ᶜAlī married her and she bore him Yaḥyā, as found in *al-Istīᶜāb.*

Al-Aswad ibn Yazīd ibn Qays an-Nakhaᶜī by ascription to the tribe of Nakhaᶜ in Kūfa. He narrated from Abū Bakr, ᶜUmar, Ḥudhayfah, Bilāl, ᶜĀʾishah, Abū Maḥdhūrah, Abū Mūsā and Ibn Masᶜūd and was a faqīh who did without the [things of this] world and who was the one of his companions who issued fatwās. Abū Isḥāq as-Sabīᶜī, Ibrāhīm an-Nakhaᶜī – his sister's son – Abū Bardah ibn Abī Mūsā and a group narrated from him. Aḥmad, Yaḥyā, Ibn Saᶜd and al-ᶜIjlī regarded him as a trustworthy narrator. He died in Kūfa in 75 AH, but some say 74 AH, says Ibn Abī Shaybah. So it is found in *Tahdhīb at-tahdhīb.*

ᶜAṭāʾ [ḥadīth 264] is either Ibn Abī Rabāḥ, the Makkan or Ibn Yasār the Madīnan, and in some editions it is found as, "ᶜAṭāʾ ibn Yasār…".

ᶜAṭāʾ ibn Abī Rabāḥ Aslam Abū Muḥammad of Quraysh, the Makkan. He narrated from ᶜĀʾishah, Ibn ᶜAbbās, Abū Hurayrah and others. Al-Awzāᶜī, Ibn Jurayj, Abū Ḥanīfah, al-Layth and others narrated from him. He is trustworthy, a faqīh, of high standing. He died in 114 AH according to the well known position. So it is found in adh-Dhahabi's *al-Kāshif* and Ibn Hajar's *at-*Taqrīb.

ᶜAṭāʾ ibn Yasār Abū Muḥammad al-Hilālī the Madīnan, the *mawlā* of Maymūnah the mother of the muʾminūn. He was an eminent trustworthy narrator who was given to worship of Allah and who delivered admonitory discourses. He was one of the Followers, and he died in 94 AH, but some say after that. That is how it is found in *at-Taqrīb.* ᶜAṭāʾ ibn Yasār al-Hilālī Abū Muḥammad the Madīnan narrated from Ibn Masᶜūd, Zayd and Ibn ᶜUmar. From him narrated Abū Ḥudhayfah, Zayd ibn Aslam and others. Ibn Maᶜīn, Abū Zurᶜah, an-Nasāʾī and others regarded him as a trustworthy narrator. He died in 94 AH, but some say 103 AH. That is how it is found in *Isᶜāf al-mubaṭṭaʾ* of as-Suyūṭī. He was the brother of Sulaymān, ᶜAbdullāh and ᶜAbd al-Mālik who were all mawlās of Maymūnah the mother of the muʾminūn who wrote contracts with all of them that they could purchase their freedom, and all of them took knowledge from her, but ᶜAṭāʾ was the one with the most ḥadīth. All of them were trustworthy narrators, as az-Zurqānī mentioned.

ᶜAṭāᵓ ibn Yazīd al-Laythī the Madīnan was one of the trustworthy narrators of the Followers. He died in 105 or 107 AH. His father's name was Yazīd. That is how it is found in *Isᶜāf al-mubaṭṭaᵓ* of as-Suyūṭī and *at-Taqrīb*. In some copies it is given as Zayd.

ᶜAṭāᵓ al-Khurāsānī is ᶜAṭāᵓ ibn Abī Muslim Maysarah, and some say ᶜAbdullāh al-Khurāsānī Abū ᶜUthmān the *mawlā* of al-Muhallab ibn Abī Ṣufrah according to the most well known position, but some say a *mawlā* of Hudhayl. He was originally from the city of Balkh in Khurāsān, and he resided in Shām. He was born in 50 AH, and he was an eminent person knowledgeable in the Qurᵓān and an ᶜālim whom Ibn Maᶜīn regarded as a trustworthy narrator. He died in 135 AH. Al-Bukhārī recorded him among the weak narrators because of the narration of al-Qāsim ibn ᶜĀṣim ibn al-Musayyab that he called him [ᶜAṭāᵓ] a liar, but Ibn ᶜAbd al-Barr refuted that because the narration of someone such as al-Qāsim cannot be used against the likes of ᶜAṭāᵓ, who was one of the eminent people of knowledge, as az-Zurqānī mentioned.

ᶜAtīk ibn al-Ḥārith ibn ᶜAtīk is acceptable he said in *at-Taqrīb*.

Ayyūb ibn Abī Tamīmah Kaysān as-Sakhtiyānī Abū Bakr the Baṣran. He was called as-Sakhtiyānī by ascription to the sale of *sakhtiyān,* which are sheepskins, which Ayyūb used to sell and from which he gained this ascription, as is mentioned in *Ansāb as-Samᶜānī* and its abridgement by Ibn al-Athīr known as *al-Lubāb.* As for what as-Suyūṭī said in his abridgement *Lubb al-Lubāb* that it was spelt as *sikhtiyān,* then ᶜAbdullāh ibn Sālim the Baṣran and Makkan has previously written about drawing attention to that. Ayyūb saw Anas and narrated from ᶜAṭāᵓ, ᶜIkrimah, ᶜAmr ibn Dīnār, al-Qāsim ibn Muḥammad, ᶜAbd ar-Raḥmān ibn al-Qāsim and others. From him narrated Shuᶜbah, the two Ḥammāds, the two Sufyāns, Mālik, Ibn ᶜUlayyah and others. Ibn Saᶜd said, "He was a trustworthy narrator who was firmly established in ḥadīth, was comprehensive, with great knowledge, and he was a decisive proof and a just witness." Abū Ḥātim said, "He was a trustworthy narrator, and one does not ask about the like of him." ᶜAlī said, "The most firmly established in [narrating] from Nāfiᶜ are Ayyūb, ᶜUbaydullāh and Mālik." The trustworthy narrators have said a great deal in praise of him as he explained at length in *Tahdhīb al-kamāl* and *Tahdhīb at-tahdhīb* and *Tadhkirat al-ḥuffāẓ*. He died in 131 AH.

Ayyūb ibn Ḥabīb the *mawlā* of Saᶜd ibn Abī Waqqāṣ. Adh-Dhahabī said in *al-Kāshif*, "Ayyūb ibn Ḥabīb the Madīnan [narrated] from Abu'l-Muthannā, and from him narrated Mālik and Fulayḥ. An-Nasā'ī regarded him as a trustworthy narrator."

Ayyūb ibn ᶜUtbah Abū Yaḥyā the qāḍī of al-Yamāmah from Banī Qays ibn Thaᶜlabah. There is disagreement as to whether he is trustworthy or weak. Ibn Ḥajar said in *Tahdhīb at-tahdhīb*, "He narrated from Yaḥyā ibn Abī Kathīr, ᶜAṭā', Qays ibn Ṭalq al-Ḥanafī and a large body of people. Those who narrated from him included Abū Dāwūd aṭ-Ṭayālisī, Aswad ibn ᶜĀmir, Muḥammad ibn al-Ḥasan, Aḥmad ibn Yūnus and others. Ḥanbal said, narrating from Aḥmad, 'Weak.' He said in another place, 'Trustworthy except for the fact that he does not get the ḥadīth of Yaḥyā ibn Abī Kathīr straight.' Ad-Dūrī said, narrating from Ibn Maᶜīn, 'Abū Kāmil said, "He is not anything."' Ibn al-Madīnī, al-Jūzajānī, ᶜAmr ibn ᶜAlī and Muslim said, 'Weak,' and ᶜAmr added, 'He had a bad memory, although he was a truthful person.' Al-ᶜIjlī said, 'His ḥadīth are [to be] written down, but he is not strong.' Al-Bukhārī said, 'According to them he is flabby.' (Abridged)" Ayyūb's shaykh was Qays ibn Ṭalq, one of the Followers, an utterly truthful man. His father was Ṭalq ibn ᶜAlī ibn al-Mundhir, al-Ḥanafī by relationship to the tribe of Banū Ḥanīfah, Abū ᶜAlī al-Yamāmī and is reckoned among the Companions. Ibn Ḥajar mentioned him in *Taqrīb at-tahdhīb*, as did others.

ᶜAzīz ibn Marthad. He mentioned in *Ansāb as-Samᶜānī* after mention of al-Mashriqī by ascription to Mashriq a clan of Hamdān, "The person who is best known with this ascription is ᶜUrayb ibn Marthad al-Mashriqī al-Hamdānī who narrated statements from the Followers which stop short at them [*maqṭūᶜ*], and from whom narrated ᶜAbd al-Jabbār ibn al-ᶜAbbās ash-Shibāmī." (Abridged) From this it is known that the name of the shaykh of ᶜAbd al-Jabbār was ᶜUrayb and not ᶜAzīz.

B

Al-Barāʾ ibn ʿĀzib ibn al-Ḥārith ibn ʿAdī al-Anṣārī of Aws. The first encounter at which he was present was the Trench (al-Khandaq). He went to reside in Kūfa where he died at the time of Musʿab ibn az-Zubayr in 72 AH as stated in *Jāmiʿ al-uṣūl.*

Al-Barāʾ ibn Qays. Ibn Ḥibbān said in Thiqāt at-tābiʿīn, "Al-Barāʾ ibn Qays Abū Kabshah, the Kūfan, is counted as one of the people of Kūfa, and he narrated from Ḥudhayfah and Saʿd, and other people narrated from him.

Bashīr ibn Saʿd Abu'n-Nuʿmān ibn Thaʿlabah al-Anṣārī al-Khazrajī. He was a major Companion who was present at Badr, and he was the father of an-Nuʿmān ibn Bashīr. He became a shahīd at ʿAyn at-Tamr, as az-Zurqānī mentioned.

Bashīr ibn Yasār al-Ḥārithī the Madīnan. Ibn Maʿīn declared him a trustworthy narrator. Ibn Saʿd said, "He was an old shaykh who had reached most of the Companions of the Messenger of Allah ﷺ, but who had few ḥadīth."

Bilāl ibn al-Ḥārith ibn ʿĀṣim ibn Saʿīd ibn Qurrah ibn Khalādah ibn Thaʿlabah Abū ʿAbd ar-Raḥmān al-Muznī. He came to the Prophet ﷺ in the deputation from Muzaynah in 5 AH, and he carried the banner for Muzaynah on the day of the the Opening [of Makkah to Islam]. Later he lived in Baṣra, and he died in 60 AH in the last days of Muʿāwiyah ؓ as stated in *Asad al-ghābah fī maʿrifat aṣ-ṣaḥābah* by ʿIzz ad-Dīn ibn Muḥammad who is better known as Ibn al-Athīr al-Jazarī.

Bilāl ibn Rabāḥ, the Ethiopian, the muʾadhdhin whose mother was Ḥamāmah. He became a Muslim and emigrated early on. He was the *mawlā* of Abū Bakr ؓ and he was present at Badr and all of the major battles and military expeditions. He died in Damascus in 17 or 18 AH, but some say 20 AH, or even 21 AH when he was just over sixty years old. Some say he died in Madīnah, but that is wrong. That is how it is found in *al-Iṣābah* and other works such as the *Tahdhīb* of an-Nawawī.

Bishr [ḥadīth 159]. So this chain of transmission appears in some copies, but in others it is Bisr, and in some Muḥammad ibn Bishr. Until now, I have not been able to find out who he is, or who his shaykh Aḥmad is so that I could find out from the books on the narrators whether or not they are trustworthy, and perhaps Allah will graciously bestow that knowledge on me later.[4]

Bukayr ibn ʿAbdullāh ibn al-Ashajj [ḥadīth 160]. So this name appears in numerous copies, but in the *Muwaṭṭaʾ* of Yaḥyā it is narrated as "from Mālik from someone he regarded as a trustworthy narrator", who was al-Layth ibn Saᶜd, as ad-Dāraquṭnī mentioned. Manṣūr ibn Salamah said, "This is one of those Mālik narrated from al-Layth as Ibn ᶜAbd al-Barr mentioned. Most of what is in the books of Mālik from Bukayr, then his companions say that he took it from the books of Bukayr which he had taken from Makhramah his son and investigated. However, this does not apply here, as az-Zurqānī mentioned. Bukayr was a trustworthy narrator from whom the six narrated. He died in 120 AH or after, said az-Zurqānī .

Bukayr ibn ᶜĀmir was Abū Ismāᶜīl Bukayr – the diminutive form – ibn ᶜĀmir al-Bajalī, the Kūfan about whom there is disagreement. He narrated from Qays ibn Abī Ḥāzim, Abū Zurᶜah ibn ᶜAmr ibn Jarīr and others. From him narrated ath-Thawrī, Wakīᶜ and others. Aḥmad once said, "His ḥadīth are fine, there is no harm in him," but another time [he said], "He is not strong." An-Nasāʾī regarded him as weak, as did Abū Zurᶜah and Ibn Maᶜīn. Ibn ᶜAdī said, "He was not given much to narration, and his narrations are few, but I have not found any texts of his which are to be rejected, and he is one of those whose ḥadīth are written down." Ibn Saᶜd and al-Ḥākim said that he was a trustworthy narrator, and Ibn Ḥibbān mentions him in *ath-Thiqāt*. That is how it is found in *Tahdhīb at-tahdhīb*.

Bushayr ibn Yasār al-Ḥārithī al-Anṣārī, their *mawlā,* the Madīnan. Ibn Maᶜīn said that he was a trustworthy narrator. Ibn Saᶜd said, "He was a great shaykh and a faqīh who lived to meet most of the Companions, but he narrated few ḥadīth." An-Nasāʾī said he was a trustworthy narrator. So it is found in *Tahdhīb at-tahdhīb*.

Busr ibn Miḥjan was an utterly truthful Follower as is said in *at-Taqrīb*. Aṭ-Ṭaḥāwī mentioned from Abū Dāwūd al-Barnasī from Aḥmad ibn Ṣāliḥ al-Miṣrī that he said, "I asked a large number as to who was his [Miḥjan's] son of the group of men around him and no two of them differed in saying that he was Bishr, as ath-Thawrī said." Abū ᶜUmar said, "Mālik said Busr and ath-Thawrī said Bishr, but most people take the position that Mālik took." That is how it is found in *al-Istīᶜāb fī aḥwāl al-aṣḥāb* by Ibn ᶜAbd al-Barr. For his father see Miḥjan ad-Dīlī.

Busr ibn Saᶜīd was a Madīnan worshipper and a trustworthy narrator who was a ḥāfiẓ, and a narrator whom everyone used, said az-Zurqānī .

D

Aḍ-Ḍaḥḥāk ibn Khalīfah ibn Thaʿlabah al-Anṣārī al-Ashhalī. He was present at the engagement of Banī an-Naḍīr and there are no narrations from him. He was suspected of being a hypocrite, then later he turned in tawbah and became right acting, as is in *al-Iṣābah* and elsewhere.

Aḍ-Ḍaḥḥāk ibn Qays ibn Khālid ibn Wahb al-Fihrī Abū Anīs the well known amīr was a Companion, and he was killed in the events of Marj Rāhiṭ in 64 AH as az-Zurqānī and others said.

Aḍ-Ḍaḥḥāk ibn Sufyān ibn ʿAwf ibn Kaʿb ibn Abī Bakr ibn Kilāb ibn Rabīʿah al-Kilābī al-ʿĀmirī aḍ-Ḍibābī, by ascription to Ḍibāb ibn ʿĀmir ibn Ṣaʿṣaʿah and also to a place in Kūfa, but however as aḍ-Ḍabābī it is by ascription to Ḍabāb a clan of Banī al-Ḥārith and of Quraysh. He is counted as one of the people of Madīnah. He had resided in Najd and the Prophet ﷺ appointed him as ruler over those of his people who accepted Islam. He was one of the bravest of the Companions, as Ibn al-Athīr mentioned in Jāmiʿ al-uṣūl.

Ḍamrah ibn Saʿīd ibn Abī Ḥannah ʿAmr ibn Ghaziyah al-Anṣārī al-Māzinī by ascription to Māzin ibn an-Najjār a tribe of the Anṣār. He narrated from Abū Saʿīd, Anas and a number of others, and from him narrated Mālik, Ibn ʿUyaynah and they regarded him as a trustworthy narrator, as stated in *al-Kāshif* by adh-Dhahabī. His father Saʿīd was Ibn Abī Ḥannah. Ibn Maʿīn, an-Nasāʾī, Abū Ḥātim and Al-ʿIjlī said he was a trustworthy narrator. Ibn Ḥibbān mentioned him in *ath-Thiqāt*. So it is found in *Tahdhīb at-tahdhīb.*

The daughter of Zayd ibn Thābit. They mention that Zayd had the following daughters: Ḥasanah, ʿAmrah, Umm Kulthūm and others, but I have only seen narations from Umm Kulthūm the wife of Sālim ibn ʿAbdullāh ibn ʿUmar.

Dāwūd ibn al-Ḥuṣayn. Ibn Maʿīn regarded him as a trustworthy narrator. He died in 135 AH, as stated in *al-Isʿāf*.

Dāwūd ibn Qays al-Farrāʾ – by ascription to the sale and sewing of furs as is mentioned by as-Samʿānī. Abū Sulaymān Dāwūd ibn Qays al-Farrāʾ ad-Dabbāgh the Madīnan who narrated from as-Sāʾib ibn Yazīd, Zayd ibn Aslam, Nāfiʿ the *mawlā* of Ibn ʿUmar, Nāfiʿ ibn Jubayr ibn Muṭʿim and others. From him narrated the two Sufyāns, Ibn al-Mubārak, Yaḥyā al-Qaṭṭān, Wakīʿ and others. Ash-Shāfiʿī, Aḥmad Ibn Maʿīn, Abū Zurʿah, Abū Ḥātim, an-Nasāʾī, as-Sājī, Ibn al-Madīnī and others regarded him as a trustworthy narrator, and the author of *at-Tahdhīb* and *Tahdhīb at-tahdhīb* mentioned their expressions. He died in the khilāfah (*wilāyah*) of Abū Jaʿfar.

Dāwūd ibn Sa'd ibn Qays [ḥadīth 128]. So it appears in some copies and in some other copies it is given as Dāwūd ibn Qays who is probably the aforementioned Dāwūd ibn Qays al-Farrā', the Madīnan.

Dhu'l-Yadayn – "Two Hands". Ibn Ḥajar said, "Most take the position that his name was al-Khirbāq relying upon what occurred in the ḥadīth of 'Imrān ibn Ḥuṣayn according to Muslim whose wording is, 'A man stood up to him, said to be al-Khirbāq in whose hands there was length...' This is what those do who unite together the ḥadīth of Abū Hurayrah with the ḥadīth of 'Imrān, which is the weightiest in my view, even though Ibn Khuzaymah and those who follow him inclined to regard them as separate [ḥadīth about different men]. What made them do that was the difference that occurs in the development [of the ḥadīth], because in the ḥadīth of Abū Hurayrah there is that the salām was after two [*rak'ahs*] and in the ḥadīth of 'Imrān that it was after three."

F

Al-Faḍl ibn ᶜAbbās was the brother of ᶜAbdullāh ibn ᶜAbbās the son of the maternal uncle of the Messenger of Allah ﷺ. He had many merits, and he was present at Ḥunayn and the Farewell Ḥajj. He went to Shām after the death of the Prophet ﷺ, and died in the precincts of Jordan in the plague of ᶜAmawās in 18 AH, but some say in 15 AH and other things, as Ibn al-Athīr said.

Al-Faḍl ibn Ghazwān as is found in a number of authentic copies, but what is in Tahdhīb at-tahdhīb and at-Taqrīb and al-Kāshif is that he was al-Fuḍayl – with the diminutive – ibn Ghazwān Ibn Jarīr aḍ-Ḍabbī – their *mawlā* – Abu'l-Faḍl the Kūfan, who narrated from Sālim, Nāfiᶜ, ᶜIkrimah and others, and from whom narrated his son Muḥammad, ath-Thawrī, Ibn al-Mubārak, Wakīᶜ and others. Ibn Ḥibbān mentioned him in *ath-Thiqāt* and Aḥmad, Ibn Maᶜīn, Yaᶜqūb ibn Sufyān and others regarded him as a trustworthy narrator. He was killed after 140 AH.

Father of Muḥammad ibn ᶜAbdullāh ibn ᶜAbd ar-Raḥmān ibn Abī Ṣaᶜṣaᶜah was ᶜAbdullāh ibn ᶜAbd ar-Raḥmān ibn Abī Ṣaᶜṣaᶜah. An-Nasāʾī regarded him as a trustworthy narrator, as found in *Isᶜāf al-mubaṭṭaʾ* of as-Suyūṭī.

Father of Saᶜīd al-Maqburī. His name was Kaysān ibn Saᶜīd al-Maqburī, the Madīnan, Abū Saᶜīd the *mawlā* of Umm Sharīk. He was a firmly established trustworthy narrator and he died in 100 AH. His son Saᶜīd al-Maqburī was a Madīnan and a trustworthy narrator, and he died around 120 AH, or a little before or after that, as found in *at-Taqrīb.*

Father of ᶜUbaydullāh ibn ᶜAbdullāh ibn ᶜUtbah [ḥadīth 177] see ᶜAbdullāh ibn ᶜUtbah ibn Masᶜūd al-Hudhalī.

Al-Furayᶜah bint Mālik ibn Sinān. Ibn ᶜAbd al-Barr said in *al-Istīᶜāb*, "Al-Furayᶜah bint Mālik ibn Sinān was the sister of Abū Saᶜīd al-Khudrī. She is called al-Fāriᶜah. She was present at the Pledge of Allegiance of Riḍwān. Her mother was Ḥabībah bint ᶜAbdullāh ibn Salūl, and Zaynab bint Kaᶜb ibn ᶜUjrah narrated her ḥadīth respecting the residence granted to the widow, which most of the *fuqahāʾ* of the different lands use.

G

Ghaṭafān ibn Ṭarīf is mentioned in present editions, but in the *Muwaṭṭa'* of Yaḥyā it is mentioned that it is "from Mālik from Dāwūd ibn al-Ḥuṣayn that Abū Ghaṭafān ibn Ṭarīf al-Murrī informed him that his father..." Abū Ghaṭafān's name was Sa'd and he was a Follower who was a trustworthy narrator. His father Ṭarīf was also one of the Followers, and his ascription – al-Murrī – is to Murr which is a tribe, as as-Sam'ānī mentioned.

The grandmother [ḥadīth 179] of Isḥāq ibn 'Abdullāh ibn Abī Ṭalḥah see Umm Sulaym.

H

Habbār ibn al-Aswad ibn al-Muṭṭalib ibn Asad ibn ᶜAbd al-ᶜUzzā of Quraysh the famous Companion who accepted Islam after the Opening [of Makkah to Islam], and who made good his Islam, as Ibn al-Athīr mentioned in *Asad al-ghābah fī maᶜrifat aṣ-ṣaḥābah.*

Ḥabīb. He said in *Tahdhīb at-tahdhīb,* "Ḥabīb ibn ᶜUbayd ar-Raḥabī Abū Ḥafṣ al-Ḥimṣī narrated from al-ᶜIrbāḍ ibn Sāriyah, al-Miqdām ibn Maᶜdīkarib, Jubayr ibn Nufayr, Bilāl ibn Abi'd-Dardāʾ and others. From him narrated Jarīr ibn ᶜUthmān, Thawr ibn Yazīd, and Muᶜāwiyah ibn Ṣāliḥ. An-Nasāʾī said that he was a trustworthy narrator. He said, "And Ḥabīb ibn ᶜUbayd said, 'I managed to meet seventy men of the Companions.'" Al-ᶜIjlī said that he was a trustworthy narrator, and Ibn Ḥibbān mentioned him among the trustworthy narrators." (Abridged)

Ḥafṣah bint ᶜUmar ibn al-Khattāb whom the Messenger of Allah ﷺ married in 3 AH according to most of them but Abū ᶜUbaydah said in 2 AH. She died in 41 AH, but some say in 39 AH. So it is found in *al-Isᶜāf.*

Al-Ḥajjāj ibn ᶜAmr ibn Ghaziyyah al-Anṣārī al-Māzinī, the Madīnan, was a Companion. He was present at Ṣiffīn along with ᶜAlī ﷺ, as found in *Sharḥ az-Zurqānī.*

Al-Ḥakam ibn ᶜUyaynah. He is thus recorded in the present copies, but the correct position according to *Mushtabih an-nisbah, Tahdhīb at-tahdhīb,* and its *Taqrīb* and elsewhere is that he was al-Ḥakam ibn ᶜUtaybah Abū Muḥammad al-Kindī – their *mawlā* – the Kūfan who narrated from a large number of Companions and Followers. Ibn ᶜUyaynah, Ibn Mahdī, Aḥmad, Yaḥyā ibn Saᶜīd, al-ᶜIjlī, Ibn Saᶜd and others regarded him as a trustworthy narrator. Al-Bukhārī said in *at-Tārīkh al-kabīr,* "Al-Qaṭṭān said, 'Shuᶜbah said, "Al-Ḥakam [narrating] from Mujāhid is [from a] writing unless he said, 'I heard...'"'" Ibn Ḥibbān said in *ath-Thiqāt,* "He used to omit mentioning gaps in his chains of transmission (*tadlīs*)." He died in 113 AH, 114 AH or a year after that.

Ḥakīm ibn Ḥizām ibn Khuwaylid ibn Asad ibn ᶜAbd al-ᶜUzzā of Quraysh and Asad. He was the son of the brother of Khadījah, the mother of the believers (Umm al-Muʾminīn). He accepted Islam on the day of the Opening [of Makkah to Islam] and became a Companion when he was 74 years old. He lived up until 54 AH or after.

Ḥammād ibn Abī Sulaymān Muslim al-Ashᶜarī Abū Ismāᶜīl, the Kūfan, the faqīh. Muᶜammar said, "I have seen no one more discerning in fiqh than these: az-Zuhrī, Ḥammād and Qatādah." Ibn Maᶜīn said, "Ḥammād is trustworthy." Abū Ḥātim said, "Utterly truthful." Al-ᶜIjlī said, "From Kūfa and trustworthy, he was the most discerning in fiqh of Ibrāhīm's companions." An-Nasā᾽ī, "Trustworthy, except for the fact that he was one of the Murji᾽ah." He died in 120 AH, but some say 119 AH. So it is found in *Tahdhīb at-tahdhīb*.

Al-Ḥārith ibn ᶜAbdullāh al-Aᶜwar al-Hamdānī, the Kūfan, who narrated from ᶜAlī, Ibn Masᶜūd and Zayd ibn Thābit, and from whom narrated ash-Shaᶜbī, Abū Isḥāq as-Sabīᶜī, ᶜAṭā᾽ ibn Abī Rabāḥ and a large group. Ash-Shaᶜbī declared him a liar according to what Muslim narrated in the *Muqaddimat aṣ-ṣaḥīḥ*, as did Abū Isḥāq, ᶜAlī ibn al-Madīnī and others. Yaḥyā ibn Maᶜīn declared him to be a trustworthy narrator, and Ibn Ḥibbān said that, "He was in the main a Shīᶜah, who was weak in ḥadīth." He died in 65 AH. Aḥmad ibn Ṣāliḥ al-Miṣrī said, "Al-Ḥārith al-Aᶜwar was a trustworthy narrator. How excellent was his memory and how good is that which he narrates from ᶜAlī!" and he praised him. Someone said to him, "But ash-Shaᶜbī said, 'He used to lie'!" He answered, "He did not lie about ḥadīth but he only used to lie in his personal opinions (*ra᾽y*)." Adh-Dhahabī said, "An-Nasā᾽ī, along with his stubborn insistence about narrators [that they be impeccable] has used him in proof even though the dominant majority regard him as weak and yet transmit his ḥadīth in the different chapter headings, and this ash-Shaᶜbī calls him a liar and then he later transmits from him! The apparent meaning is that he lies in his citations but not in ḥadīth," as it is stated in *Tahdhīb at-tahdhīb*.

Al-Ḥārith ibn Abī Dhubāb is al-Ḥārith ibn ᶜAbd ar-Raḥmān ibn ᶜAbdullāh ibn Saᶜd, but some say al-Mughīrah ibn Abī Dhubāb ad-Dawsī, the Madīnan. He narrated from his father, his paternal uncle, Saᶜīd ibn al-Musayyab, Mujāhid and others. From him narrated Ibn Jurayj, Ismāᶜīl ibn Umayyah and others. Abū Zurᶜah said, "There is no harm in him." Ibn Ḥibbān mentioned him among the trustworthy narrators, and he said, "He was one of those who by the use of skill renders things sound (*mutqin*)." He died in 126 AH. So it is found in *Tahdhīb at-tahdhīb*.

Al-Ḥasan al-Baṣrī is one of the greatest of the Followers and he is al-Ḥasan ibn Abi'l-Ḥasan Yasār. His mother was a mawlāh of Umm Salamah, and he was born two years before the end of the khilāfah of ᶜUmar. He moved from Madīnah to Baṣra upon the murder of ᶜUthmān. He narrated from a large group of the Companions, and a large group of the Followers narrated from him. He was an imām and a trustworthy narrator, possessing knowledge, doing-without (*zuhd*), scrupulousness (*wara*ᶜ) and worship. He died in Rajab 110 AH. That is how it is found in *Jāmi*ᶜ *al-uṣūl*, and there is a very long biography of him in *Tahdhīb at-tahdhīb* and elsewhere.

Al-Ḥasan ibn Muḥammad ibn ᶜAlī ibn Abī Ṭālib al-Hāshimī, the Madīnan, was one of the eminent people of the people of the House (Ahl al-Bayt), and one of the most knowledgeable people on differences of opinion. Al-ᶜIjlī regarded him as a trustworthy narrator. Ad-Dāraquṭnī said, "His ḥadīth are *ṣaḥīḥ*." He died in 95 AH, but some say 101 AH.

Al-Ḥasan ibn ᶜUmārah al-Bajalī, the Kūfan Abū Muḥammad, the qāḍī of Baghdād. He narrated from az-Zuhrī, al-Ḥakam ibn ᶜUtaybah, Abū Isḥāq as-Sabīᶜī and others, and from him narrated the two Sufyāns and many others. ᶜĪsā ibn Yūnus regarded him as a trustworthy narrator, and he said that he was a right-acting shaykh, but many were critical of him as a narrator, among them an-Nasāʾī, Ibn Maᶜīn, Ibn al-Madīnī, Aḥmad, Shuᶜbah, ad-Dāraquṭnī, as-Sājī, al-Jūzajānī and others, saying that he is to be abandoned (*matrūk*), or dropped, or he may not be used as a proof, or his ḥadīth are rejected, and the like of that. An-Naḍr said he narrated from Shuᶜbah, "Al-Ḥasan ibn ᶜUmārah transmitted me ḥadīth from al-Ḥakam which had no [genuine] source." He died in 153 AH, as stated in *Tahdhīb at-tahdhīb* and elsewhere.

Ḥāṭib ibn Abī Baltaᶜah ᶜAmr ibn ᶜUmayr al-Lakhmī the sworn ally of Banī Asad. He was present at Badr, and died in 30 AH, as az-Zurqānī said.

Hazzāl ibn Dhiʾāb ibn Yazīd ibn Kulayb al-Aslamī was the one who had a slave girl with whom Māᶜiz had intercourse, and so Hazzāl said to him, "Go to the Messenger of Allah ﷺ and tell him, so that perhaps some Qurʾān might be revealed." So he went to him and what happened happened, and so the Prophet ﷺ said to him, "Hazzāl! If only you had veiled him with your robe!" i.e. if only you had not urged him to divulge the secret it would have been better. His son was Nuᶜaym ibn Hazzāl, about whom some said that he was a Companion and others said not, and whose son Yazīd was a Follower who was a trustworthy narrator, as Ibn al-Athīr mentioned in *Asad al-ghābah fī maᶜrifat aṣ-ṣaḥābah* and *Jāmi*ᶜ *al-uṣūl*.

Hishām ibn Ismāᶜīl ibn Hishām ibn al-Walīd ibn al-Mughīrah al-Makhzūmī. He was governor of Madīnah on behalf of ᶜAbd al-Mālik ibn Marwān, and Ibn Ḥibbān mentioned him in the *Kitāb ath-thiqāt*.

Hishām ibn ᶜUrwah ibn az-Zubayr ibn al-ᶜAwwām al-Asadī, the Madīnan, narrated from his father and his uncle ᶜAbdullāh ibn az-Zubayr. From him narrated Mālik, Abū Ḥanīfah and Shuʿbah. Abū Ḥātim and others regarded him as a trustworthy narrator. He died in 145 AH. So it is found in *Isʿāf al-mubaṭṭaʾ* of as-Suyūṭī.

Ḥizām ibn Saʿīd ibn Muḥayyiṣah is mentioned by Shaykh ʿAbd al-Ḥayy as "Ḥizām ibn Saʿīd. Thus I have seen it in numerous copies of this book, but what is in *Jāmiʿ al-uṣūl* by al-Jazarī, the *Taqrīb* of Ibn Ḥajar and the *Isʿāf* of as-Suyūṭī was that he was Ḥarām ibn Saʿd, but some say Ḥarām ibn Sāʿidah ibn Muḥayyiṣah the Anṣārī and Madīnan Follower who was a trustworthy narrator, but who narrated few ḥadīth. He died in 113 AH in Madīnah.

Ḥudhayfah ibn al-Yamān. Al-Yamān's name was Ḥisl, but it is also said al-Ḥusayl – its diminutive – ibn Jābir ibn ʿAmr ibn Rabīʿah al-ʿAbsī the confederate of Banī ʿAbd al-Ashhal of the Anṣār. His father was given the honorific cognomen of al-Yamān because he spilt some blood among his people and fled to Madīnah where he became a confederate of the Anṣār who were from the Yemen. Ḥudhayfah and his father accepted Islam and were both present at Uḥud and al-Yamān was killed in the battle of Uḥud, the Muslims killing him by mistake. Ḥudhayfah gave them [his right to retaliation or compensation for] his blood. Ḥudhayfah was the companion of the secret of the Messenger of Allah ﷺ and has numerous virtues. He died in Madāʾin in 36 AH. So it is found in *Tahdhīb al-asmāʾ waʾl-lughāt* by an-Nawawī.

Ḥumaydah bint ʿUbayd ibn Rafāʿah. Yaḥyā alone among the narrators of the *Muwaṭṭaʾ* said that she was called Ḥamīdah. Yaḥyā said that she was the daughter of Abū ʿUbaydah ibn Farwah but that was a mistake of his. The rest of the narrators of the *Muwaṭṭaʾ* said she was the daughter of ʿUbayd ibn Rafāʿah, except for Zayd ibn al-Ḥubāb who said, from Mālik, "The daughter of ʿUbayd ibn Rāfiʿ." But the correct position is that [her father was] Rafāʿah ibn Rāfiʿ al-Anṣārī, as Ibn ʿAbd al-Barr said. Ibn Mandah took the position that neither she nor her maternal aunt Kabshah were known to have narrated anything other than this ḥadīth, and that thus the single ḥadīth [ḥadīth 90] in the *Muwaṭṭaʾ* from them was not sound, but al-ʿAynī said, "Ḥumaydah has another ḥadīth on responding to the person who sneezes which Abū Dāwūd narrated, and a third one narrated by Abū Nuʿaym. Isḥāq ibn ʿAbdullāh narrated from her and he is a trustworthy narrator."

Ḥumayd ibn ʿAbd ar-Raḥmān was Abū ʿAbd ar-Raḥmān and a Madīnan. Al-ʿIjlī and others regarded him as a trustworthy narrator. He died in 95 AH, but some say in 105 AH, as found in *Isʿāf al-mubaṭṭaʾ* of as-Suyūṭī. Az-Zurqānī said that he was Ḥumayd ibn ʿAbd ar-Raḥmān az-Zuhrī and a Madīnan. He was a trustworthy narrator and one of the major Followers. Yaḥyā ibn Yaḥyā al-Laythī added in his transmission of the *Muwaṭṭa*ʾ that he was the son of ʿAbd ar-Raḥmān ibn ʿAwf.

Ḥumayd ibn Mālik ibn al-Khaytham. This is how we found it expressed in some copies upon which the commentary of al-Qārī is based and he spelt al-Khaytham thus. Ibn Ḥajar in *at-Taqrīb* spelt it as a diminutive when he said, "Ḥumayd ibn Mālik ibn Khuthaym, and it is said that Mālik was his grandfather and the name of his father was ʿAbdullāh. He was a trustworthy narrator." He mentioned in *Tahdhīb at-tahdhīb* about its spelling something different when he said in his biographical note about him, "Ibn Saʿd said, 'He was from the old generation and had few ḥadīth.' Ibn Ḥibbān mentioned him in *ath-Thiqāt,* and al-Bukhārī mentioned his grandfather in *at-Tārīkh* where he spelt his name among those who narrated from him as al-Khutam. In the narration of Ibn al-Qāsim of al-*Muwaṭṭa*ʾ they spelt it like that but with a 'tha' as Khutham, and Muslim spelt it like that but as al-Khuttam. They spelt it in *al-Aḥkām* by Ismāʿīl al-Qadi as al-Khuththam." (Abridged) Ibn al-Athīr spelt it in *an-Nihāyah* as it is spelt in *at-Taqrīb.*

Ḥumayd ibn Qays was Abū Ṣafwān al-Aʿraj al-Qārīʾ. There was no harm in him, and he was one of the narrators of whom everybody availed. He died in 130 AH, but some say after that, as az-Zurqānī mentioned.

Ḥumayd aṭ-Ṭawīl was Ḥumayd ibn Abī Ḥumayd Abū ʿUbaydah, the Baṣran aṭ-Ṭawīl. He narrated from Anas, al-Ḥasan and ʿIkrimah, and from him narrated Mālik, Shuʿbah, the two Ḥammāds, the two Sufyāns and many others. Ibn Maʿīn and Abū Ḥātim declared him to be a trustworthy narrator. He died in 143 AH as found in *Isʿāf al-mubaṭṭa*ʾ of as-Suyūṭī.

Al-Ḥuraqah are a tribe from Hamdān, Ibn Ḥibbān said, or from Juhaynah as ad-Dāraquṭnī said and that is the sound position. That is how it is found in *Ansāb as-Samʿānī.*

Ḥuṣayn ibn ʿAbd ar-Raḥmān as-Sulamī, the Kūfan, Abu'l-Hudhayl, son of the paternal uncle of Manṣūr ibn al-Muʿtamir. He narrated from Jābir ibn Samurah, ʿAmārah ibn Ruwaybah, Ibn Abī Laylā and Abū Wāʾil. From him narrated Shuʿbah, Abū ʿAwānah and others. He was a trustworthy narrator and a decisive proof and a ḥāfiẓ with short chains of transmission. Aḥmad said, "Ḥuṣayn is a trustworthy narrator who is to be relied upon, and he is one of the great ones of the people of ḥadīth." He lived for 93 years and died in 136 AH. So it is found in *Tadhkirat al-ḥuffāẓ.*

Ḥuṣayn ibn Ibrāhīm [ḥadīth 263]. So it is found in the present copy, and I have not come across his condition in *Tahdhīb at-tahdhīb, Taqrīb at-tahdhīb, al-Kāshif, Jāmiᶜ al-uṣūl, Mīzān al-iᶜtidāl* and others. Previously I came across in my research into the subject of raising the hands [in prayer] a narration from Abū Yūsuf Yaᶜqūb ibn Ibrāhīm from Ḥuṣayn ibn ᶜAbd ar-Raḥmān, where it transpired that he was one of his higher shaykhs, and so perhaps it is him. In the book *al-Ḥujjaj* it is: Ḥuṣayn from Ibrāhīm, so it seems that specifically al-Ḥuṣayn is the former and Ibrāhīm is an-Nakhaᶜī.

Ḥuṣayn ibn Miḥṣan. Ibn Ḥibbān mentions him in *Thiqāt at-tābiᶜīn.* Ibn as-Sakan said, "It is said that he was a Companion except that his narration is from his paternal aunt and he has no narrations from the Messenger of Allah ﷺ," as stated in *Tahdhīb at-tahdhīb* and *Taqrīb at-tahdhīb.*

Hushaym ibn Bashīr. He said in *at-Taqrīb* "Hushaym in the diminutive form, ibn Bashīr ibn al-Qāsim ibn Dīnār as-Sulamī Abū Muᶜawiyah ibn Abī Ḥāzim of Wāsiṭ was a trustworthy narrator and firmly established [but] used to conceal ommissions in his *isnāds* [by *tadlīs*] and narrate *mursal* ḥadīth a great deal. He was Ḥanafī[5] and died in 183 AH.

I

Ibn ᶜAbbās is ᶜAbdullāh ibn ᶜAbbās ibn ᶜAbd al-Muṭṭalib al-Hāshimī, the son of the paternal uncle of the Messenger of Allah ﷺ who is known as the Learned Man and the Ocean, because of the great amount of his knowledge. He has very famous merits which are mentioned in the books about the Companions such as *Asad al-ghābah,* the *al-Iṣābah* and others. He died in Ṭāʾif in 68 AH, but some say 69 AH, and others 70 AH. That is mentioned in *at-Tahdhīb.* Al-ᶜAynī said in *al-Bināyah sharḥ al-Hidāyah* in the book on the Ḥajj concerning the investigation on the stopping at Muzdalifah, "When one uses 'Ibn ᶜAbbās' unqualifiedly one only means ᶜAbdullāh ibn ᶜAbbās." He also mentioned in *al-Bināyah* in the book *al-Ḥaẓr wa'l-ibāḥah* that ḥadīth scholars use as their technical terms when they mention ᶜAbdullāh that they mean ᶜAbdullāh ibn Masᶜūd even if others are included apparently [in that designation]. Similarly they say Ibn ᶜUmar meaning ᶜAbdullāh ibn ᶜUmar even though ᶜUmar had other sons apart from ᶜAbdullāh." ᶜAlī al-Qārī the Makkan said in *Jamᶜ al-wasāʾil bi sharḥ ash-shamāʾil,* i.e. [the commentary on] the *Shamāʾil* of at-Tirmidhī, "The technical usage of ḥadīth scholars is that if ᶜAlī is used unqualifiedly at the end of the [list of] names [in an isnād] then it is ᶜAlī ibn Abī Ṭālib, and that if ᶜAbdullāh is used unqualifiedly then it is ᶜAbdullāh ibn Masᶜūd, and that where al-Ḥasan is used without qualification it is al-Ḥasan al-Baṣrī. It is similar with the unqualified use of Abū Bakr, ᶜUmar and ᶜUthmān." Al-Qārī also said in his book *al-Athmār al-janiyyah fī ṭabaqāt al-ḥanafiyyah,* "When Ibn ᶜAbbās is used unqualifiedly only ᶜAbdullāh is meant. Similarly, when Ibn ᶜUmar and Ibn az-Zubayr are used without qualification. As for when ᶜAbdullāh is used without qualification then it is ᶜAbdullāh ibn Masᶜūd in the technical usage of the people of knowledge among the fuqahāʾ and the scholars of ḥadīth." This ought to be memorised because it is useful.

Ibn ᶜAbd ar-Raḥmān ibn Abī Hurayrah [ḥadīth 648]. See ᶜAbd ar-Raḥmān ibn Abī Hurayrah.

Ibn Abī Aḥmad was ᶜAbdullāh ibn Abī Aḥmad Jahsh of Quraysh al-Asadī. A large number mention him as one of the trustworthy narrators of the Followers. That is what az-Zurqānī said.

Ibn Abī Dhiʾb is Muḥammad ibn ᶜAbd ar-Raḥmān ibn al-Mughīrah ibn Abī Dhiʾb, the Madīnan, who narrated from ᶜIkrimah, Nāfiᶜ and a large number of others, and from whom narrated Muᶜammar, Ibn al-Mubārak and Yaḥyā al-Qaṭṭān, as adh-Dhahabī mentioned in *al-Kāshif.*

Ibn Abī Mulaykah is ᶜAbdullāh ibn ᶜUbaydullāh ibn ᶜAbdullāh ibn Abī Mulaykah whose name was Zuhayr at-Taymī. He was a trustworthy narrator and a faqīh. He died in 117 AH, as az-Zurqānī said.

Ibn Abī Qatādah was ᶜAbdullāh ibn Abī Qatādah, the Madīnan, and he was a trustworthy narrator and one of the Followers. He died in 95 AH. Ibn Saᶜd said, "Thābit ibn Abī Qatādah married her [Kabshah] and she bore him children." In the narration of Ibn al-Mubārak there is that Mālik said she [Kabshah] was the wife of Abū Qatādah but Ibn ᶜAbd al-Barr said that this was his mistake and that she was married to his son. Az-Zurqānī said so.

Ibn Buḥaynah from the name of his mother by which [kunyā] he became known. He is ᶜAbdullāh ibn Mālik ibn al-Qashab al-Azdī and is one of the great ones of the Companions. He died after 50 AH. So it is found in *at-Taqrīb* and elsewhere.

Ibn Jurayj is ᶜAbd al-Mālik ibn ᶜAbd al-ᶜAzīz Ibn Jurayj al-Umawī, their *mawlā*, the Makkan, the faqīh. He was an eminent, trustworthy narrator. He died in 150 AH or after. So it is found in *at-Taqrīb* and *al-Kāshif*.

Ibn Masᶜūd. See ᶜAbdullāh ibn Masᶜūd.

Ibn Mirs. It is spelt thus in *al-Mughnī* and he said, "He was a *mawlā* of Qurasyh."

Ibn Muᶜammar ibn ᶜUthmān ibn ᶜAmr ibn Saᶜd ibn Taym of Quraysh was one of the notables of Quraysh and one of their nobles. He died in Damascus in 82 AH. His grandfather was Muᶜammar the Companion, the son of the paternal uncle of Abū Quḥāfah the father of Abū Bakr aṣ-Ṣiddīq, az-Zurqānī said.

Ibn Shihāb az-Zuhrī. Az-Zuhri denotes his relationship to Zuhrah ibn Kilāb ibn Murrah ibn Kaᶜb ibn Lu᾽ayy. So it is stated in *al-Ansāb*. An-Nawawī said in *Tahdhīb al-asmā᾽ wa'l-lughāt*: "Muḥammad ibn Muslim ibn ᶜUbaydullāh ibn ᶜAbdullāh Ibn Shihāb ibn ᶜAbdullāh ibn al-Ḥārith ibn Zuhrah ibn Kilāb ibn Murrah ibn Kaᶜb ibn Lu᾽ayy Abū Bakr of Quraysh az-Zuhrī the Madīnan. He lived in Shām and was at Aylah. Sometimes they say, "az-Zuhrī" and sometimes "Ibn Shihāb" ascribing him to his grandfather's grandfather. He was a minor Follower [in that he didn't meet as many of the Companions as major Followers had], and he heard from Anas, Sahl ibn Saᶜd, as-Sā᾽ib ibn Yazīd, Abū Umāmah and Abu'ṭ-Ṭufayl. A great number of the major Followers and their Followers narrated from him. We narrate that al-Layth ibn Saᶜd said, 'I have never seen an ᶜālim more comprehensive than Ibn Shihāb, nor one who was more knowledgeable than him.' Ash-Shāfiᶜī said, 'If it had not been for az-Zuhrī the Sunnahs would have left Madīnah.' He died in Ramaḍān of 124 AH, and was buried in a town on the outskirts of Shām called Shaghab." (Abridged)

Ibn Sīrīn. His name was Muḥammad. An-Nawawī mentioned in *at-Tahdhīb* that his father – Sīrīn – was the *mawlā* of Anas ibn Mālik, and that he had six children: Muḥammad, Maᶜbad, Anas, Yaḥyā, Ḥafṣah and Karīmah, all of whom are trustworthy narrators and among the eminent Followers. Most often when Ibn Sīrīn is used unqualifiedly it refers to this Muḥammad Abū Bakr, the Baṣran, and imām in tafsīr, interpretation of dreams, ḥadīth and fiqh. He heard from Ibn ᶜUmar, Abū Hurayrah, Ibn az-Zubayr and others, but he did not hear from Ibn ᶜAbbās, so that his ḥadīth from him are *mursal*. The imāms praised him a great deal. He died in Baṣra in 110 AH.

Ibn Suhayl ibn Abī Ṣāliḥ. See Suhayl ibn Abī Ṣāliḥ.

Ibn Ukaymah [the diminutive of Akmah]. His name was ᶜUmārah but it is also said it was ᶜAmmār and some say ᶜAmr and some say ᶜĀmir al-Laythī Abu'l-Walīd, the Madīnan. He was a trustworthy narrator and died in 101 AH. That was what az-Zurqānī said.

Ibn Umm Maktūm's name was ᶜAmr, but some say Ḥuṣayn. The Prophet ﷺ named him ᶜAbdullāh. He accepted Islam of old and was present at the battle of Qādisiyyah [15 AH/636 CE] in the khilāfah of ᶜUmar where he was shahīd. The best known thing about his father's name is that he was Qays ibn Zāʾidah, and that his mother's name was ᶜĀtikah from Makhzūm. One of them claimed that he was born blind and that his mother was given her kunyā because of him [Umm Maktūm – mother of the blind one] because of the concealing of the light of his sight, as az-Zurqānī mentioned.

Ibn az-Zubayr [ḥadīth 118] see Abu'z-Zubayr.

Ibrāhīm ibn ᶜAbdullāh ibn Hunay al-Hāshimī – he was their *mawlā* – was a Follower who was Madīnan. Ibn Saᶜd said, "He was a trustworthy narrator who narrated a great many ḥadīth and from whom all narrated." He died after the first century as az-Zurqānī mentioned.

Ibrāhīm ibn Muḥammad is Ibrāhīm ibn Muḥammad ibn Abī Yaḥyā whose name is Samᶜān al-Aslamī Abū Isḥāq, the Madīnan, about whom there is disagreement as to whether he is trustworthy or weak. He said in *Tahdhīb al-kamāl* and *Tahdhīb at-tahdhīb*, "He narrated from az-Zuhrī, Yaḥyā ibn Saᶜīd al-Anṣārī, Ṣāliḥ the *mawlā* of at-Tawʾamah (the twin), Muḥammad ibn al-Munkadir and others. From him narrated ath-Thawrī, ash-Shāfiᶜī, and Abū Nuᶜaym. Abū Ṭālib said narrating from Aḥmad, 'His ḥadīth are not to be written. He used to narrate rejected ḥadīth without any source.' Ash-Shāfiᶜī said, 'Trustworthy in ḥadīth.' Ibn ᶜAdī said, 'I asked Aḥmad ibn Muḥammad ibn Saʿīd,' – meaning Ibn ʿAqdah – "Do you know anyone who spoke well about Ibrāhīm other than ash-Shāfiʿī?" He said, "Yes. Aḥmad ibn Yaḥyā narrated to us, 'I heard Hamdān ibn al-Aṣbahānī. I asked, "Do you base your dīn on the ḥadīth of Ibrāhīm?" He said, "Yes."'" Then Aḥmad ibn Muḥammad ibn Saʿīd said to me, "I examined the ḥadīth of Ibrāhīm a great deal and he is not someone whose ḥadīth are rejected."' Ibn ʿAdī said, 'And this is what he said as he said it. And I have also examined his ḥadīth a great deal and I do not find among them any which are rejected, except from shaykhs who interpret, and he is among those whose ḥadīth are to be recorded. He has a *Muwaṭṭaʾ* which is a number of sizes larger than the *Muwaṭṭaʾ* of Mālik. He died in 184 AH, but some say 191 AH.'"

Ibrāhīm ibn ʿUqbah. He said in *al-Isʿāf*, "Aḥmad, Yaḥyā and an-Nasāʾī regarded him as a trustworthy narrator." ʿUqbah was Madīnan.

Ibrāhīm ibn Yazīd al-Umawī al-Khūzī, the Makkan and *mawlā* of ʿUmar ibn ʿAbd al-ʿAzīz. He narrated from Ṭāwūs, ʿAṭāʾ, Abu'z-Zubayr and others, and from him narrated Wakīʿ, ʿAbd ar-Razzāq, and ath-Thawrī. Ibn Maʿīn said, "He is not a trustworthy narrator, and he is nothing." Abū Zurʿah, Abū Ḥātim and Ibn Numayr regarded him as weak. Abū Zurʿah and Abū Ḥātim said, "His ḥadīth are rejected." Al-Bukhārī said, "They were silent [in narrating] from him," and ad-Dūlābī said, "meaning that they abandoned him." An-Nasāʾī said, "Abandoned." Ibn ʿAdī said, "He is numbered among those whose ḥadīth are written down even if he is considered weak." He died in 151 AH, as stated in *Tahdhīb al-kamāl*.

Ibrāhīm an-Nakhaʿī is by ascription to Nakhaʿ a tribe of the Arabs which settled in Kūfa from where their fame spread. Ibn Mākūlā said, "From this tribe are ʿAlqamah, al-Aswad and Ibrāhīm. So it is found in the *Ansāb* of as-Samʿānī." He mentioned in *Tahdhīb at-tahdhīb*, "Ibrāhīm ibn Yazīd ibn Qays ibn al-Aswad ibn ʿAmr Abū ʿImrān an-Nakhaʿī the Kūfan, the muftī of the people of Kūfa who was a right-acting man and a faqīh." Al-Aʿmash said, "He was good in ḥadīth." Ash-Shaʿbī said, "He left after him no one more knowledgeable than himself." Abū Saʿīd al-ʿAlāʾī said, "He very often used *mursal* ḥadīth [which he ascribed directly to the Prophet ﷺ without mentioning the Companion or Companions from whom he heard them] and a body of the imāms regard his *mursal* ḥadīth as sound." Al-Aʿmash said, "I said to Ibrāhīm, 'Give me something from Ibn Masʿūd with a chain of transmission.' He said, 'If I narrate you something from a man from ʿAbdullāh that is what I heard. If I say, "ʿAbdullāh said..." then it is from more than one person.'" Abū Ḥātim said, "an-Nakhaʿī did not meet any of the

Companions except for ᶜĀʾishah, but he did not hear anything from her, and he reached Anas but he did not hear anything from him." He was born in 55 AH and died in 96 AH.

An informant [ḥadīth 880]. In the *Muwaṭṭaʾ* of Yaḥyā is found, "...Mālik that it had reached him that ᶜUmar ..." Its commentator said, "Those things about which Mālik said they 'reached' him are *ṣaḥīḥ*, as Ibn ᶜUyaynah said."

ᶜIrāk ibn Mālik. As-Suyūṭī said in *Isᶜāf al-mubaṭṭaʾ*, "ᶜIrāk ibn Mālik al-Ghifārī, by ascription to the tribe of Banī Ghifār, the Madīnan narrated from Ibn ᶜAbbās, Abū Hurayrah, Ibn ᶜUmar, ᶜĀʾishah and a large group of people, and from him narrated Sulaymān ibn Yasār, Khaytham and ᶜAbdullāh the two sons of ᶜIrāk. Abū Zurᶜah and Abū Ḥātim regarded him as a trustworthy narrator. He died in Madīnah in the khilāfah of Yazīd ibn ᶜAbd al-Mālik." This spelling – ᶜIrāk – is what Ibn Ḥajar used in *at-Taqrīb*, Ibn al-Athīr in *Jāmiᶜ al-uṣūl*, and al-Fattanī in *al-Mughnī* and others.

ᶜĪsā ibn Abī ᶜĪsā al-Khayyāṭ al-Madīnī. Adh-Dhahabī said in *al-Kāshif*, "ᶜĪsā ibn Abī ᶜĪsā al-Khayyāṭ narrated from his father and from ash-Shaᶜbī and a number of others, and from him narrated Wakīᶜ, Ibn Abī Fudayk and a number of others. They declared him weak. He is a Kūfan who resided in Madīnah. He was a tailor and then seller of wheat. He died in 151 AH." There is in *at-Taqrīb*, "ᶜĪsā ibn Abī ᶜĪsā al-Ḥannāṭ al-Ghifārī Abū Mūsā al-Madīnī whose origin was in Kūfa. His father's name was Maysarah. He is called al-Khayyāṭ – the tailor – and al-Ḥannāṭ – the seller of wheat – and he had dealt with the three trades [the third was selling a type of leaf as camel fodder]. He is abandoned [as a narrator], of the sixth generation. He died in 51 AH, but some say before that."

ᶜĪsā ibn Ṭalḥah ibn ᶜUbaydullāh was an eminent trustworthy narrator. He died in 100 AH, and his father was one of the Ten [promised the Garden], as al-Ḥāfiẓ said.

Isḥāq ibn ᶜAbdullāh ibn Abī Ṭalḥah. As-Suyūṭī said, "Abū Zurᶜah, Abū Ḥātim and an-Nasāʾī regarded him as trustworthy. Ibn Maᶜīn said, "Trustworthy and a decisive argument." He died in 134 AH. [His grandfather Abū Ṭalḥah] was Zayd ibn Sahl.

Isḥāq ibn Rāshid was Abū Sulaymān Isḥāq ibn Rāshid al-Ḥarrānī, but some say ar-Raqī , the *mawlā* of Banī Umayyah, but some say the *mawlā* of ᶜUmar. He narrated from az-Zuhrī, ᶜAbdullāh ibn Ḥasan ibn al-Ḥasan ibn ᶜAlī, Muḥammad ibn ᶜAlī Zayn al-ᶜĀbidīn Abū Jaᶜfar al-Bāqir and others, and from him narrated a whole group. Ibn Ḥibbān and Ibn Shahīn mentioned him among the trustworthy narrators, and an-Nasā᾿ī, Ibn Ma῾īn and Abū Ḥātim regarded him as a trustworthy narrator, as found in *Tahdhīb at-tahdhīb* and other books.

Ismā῾īl ibn Abī Khālid al-Aḥmasī, their *mawlā,* the Kūfan, by ascription to al-Aḥmas a party of Bajlah who resided in Kūfa, as as-Sam῾ānī mentioned. He narrated from his father, Abū Juḥayfah, ῾Abdullāh ibn Abī Awfā, Qays ibn Abī Ḥāzim – from whom he narrated a great deal – and others. From him narrated Shu῾bah, the two Sufyāns, Ibn al-Mubārak, Yaḥyā al-Qaṭṭān and others. Ibn Ma῾īn, Ibn Mahdī and an-Nasā᾿ī said that he was a trustworthy narrator. Al-῾Ijlī said, "A trustworthy Kūfan Follower." Abū Ḥātim said, "I do not give precedence over him to any other of ash-Sha῾bī's companions, and he is a trustworthy narrator. He died in 126 AH." So it is stated in *Tahdhīb at-tahdhīb.*

Ismā῾īl ibn ῾Ayyāsh al-῾Anbasī Abū ῾Utbah al-Ḥimṣī. Ya῾qūb ibn Sufyān said, "Some people spoke about him [negatively] but he is a trustworthy narrator, a just man, the most knowledgeable of people of the ḥadīth of the people of Shām. The most that they said was he narrated unusual things [perhaps in the sense of unusual ḥadīth (*gharā᾿ib*) having a single narrator at some stage of the chain of transmission] from the trustworthy narrators of Madīnah and Makkah." Yazīd ibn Hārūn said, "I have not seen anyone who memorised more than Ismā῾īl ibn ῾Ayyāsh, I do not know, perhaps not even Sufyān ath-Thawrī." ῾Uthmān ad-Dārimī said, "I hope that there should be no harm in him." Muḥammad ibn ῾Uthmān ibn Abī Shaybah narrated from Yaḥyā ibn Ma῾īn, "A trustworthy narrator in that which he narrates from the people of Shām. As for his narrations from the people of Ḥijāz, his book was lost and he became mixed up in his memorisation from them. He died in 181 AH, but some say 182 AH." So it is found in *Tahdhīb at-tahdhīb.*

Ismā῾īl ibn Ḥakīm [ḥadīth 873] was Ismā῾īl ibn Abī Ḥakīm of Quraysh. Ibn Ma῾īn and an-Nasā᾿ī regarded him as a trustworthy narrator. He died in 130 AH, as az-Zurqānī mentioned.

Ismā῾īl ibn Ibrāhīm [ḥadīth 263]. In *Tahdhīb at-tahdhīb* and *al-Mīzān,* he mentioned many with this name and lineage some of whom were trustworthy narrators and some of whom were weak. Apparently the person mentioned here is Ismā῾īl ibn Ibrāhīm ibn Muhājir al-Bajalī and an-Nakha῾ī the Kūfan whom al-Bukhārī and an-Nasā᾿ī regarded as weak. Abū Ḥātim said, "He is not strong, but his ḥadīth are to be written. He narrated from his father, Ismā῾īl ibn Abī Khālid and others, and from him narrated Ibn Numayr, Wakī῾, Ṭalq ibn Ghanām, Abū ῾Alī al-Ḥanafī and others."

Ismāᶜīl ibn Ibrāhīm ibn Muqsim al-Asadī – their *mawlā* – Abū Bishr, the Baṣran, who is best known as Ibn ᶜUlayyah a dimunitive from his mother's name, but some say his maternal grandmother. He used to dislike being called that to such an extent that he used to say, "Whoever calls me that is backbiting me." He narrated from ᶜAbd al-ᶜAzīz ibn Suhayb, Ḥumayd aṭ-Ṭawīl, Ayyūb, Ibn ᶜAwn and others. From him narrated Shuᶜbah, Ibn Jurayj and others. Ibn Saᶜd, an-Nasāʾī and others declared him to be a trustworthy narrator. He died in 193 AH. He has a long biographical note comprising high praise in *Tahdhīb at-tahdhīb* and elsewhere.

Ismāᶜīl ibn Muḥammad ibn Saᶜd Abū Muḥammad, the Madīnan, is trustworthy and a decisive proof and one of the Followers. He died in 134 AH. He was the grandson of Saᶜd ibn Abī Waqqāṣ. The five narrated from him. So it is found in *Taqrīb at-tahdhīb.*

Ismāᶜīl ibn Muḥammad ibn Thābit ibn Qays ibn Shammās al-Anṣārī, the Madīnan. Ibn Ḥibbān mentioned him in *Thiqat at-Tabi'in*.

Isrāʾīl ibn Yūnus is Abū Yūsuf Isrāʾīl ibn Yūnus ibn Abī Isḥāq as-Sabīᶜī al-Hamdānī, the Kūfan. He narrated from his grandfather whom we have mentioned before, Ziyād ibn ᶜAlāqah, ᶜĀṣim al-Aḥwāl and others. From him narrated ᶜAbd ar-Razzāq, Wakīᶜ and a large group. Aḥmad said, "He was a shaykh who was a trustworthy narrator." Abū Ḥātim said, "A trustworthy narrator who was utterly truthful." Al-ᶜIjlī regarded him as a trustworthy narrator as did Yaᶜqūb ibn Shaybah, Abū Dāwūd, an-Nasāʾī and others. He died in 162 AH or 165 AH or 161 AH according to the different sayings. So it is found in *Tahdhīb at-tahdhīb.*

J

Jābir ibn ᶜAbdullāh, Abū ᶜAbdullāh but some say Abū ᶜAbd ar-Raḥmān and even Abū Muḥammad. He went on expeditions with the Prophet ﷺ nineteen times but he was not present at Badr. He died in Madīnah, but some say Makkah, in 78 AH, and others say 79 AH and even 74 AH. So it is stated in *Isᶜāf al-mubaṭṭa'* of as-Suyūṭī. Jābir is Abū ᶜAbdullāh Jābir ibn ᶜAbdullāh ibn ᶜAmr ibn Ḥarām ibn ᶜAmr ibn Sawād ibn Salamah al-Anṣārī, one of the most famous of the Companions. He was present at Badr – according to what is said – and what came after it. His father was one of the twelve leading men [to pledge allegiance at al-ᶜAqabah]. Jābir became blind at the end of his life, and he died in Madīnah in 74 AH, but some say 77 or 78 AH, and he was the last of the Companions to die in Madīnah. So it is found in *Jāmiᶜ al-uṣūl.*

Jābir ibn ᶜAbdullāh al-Ḥarāmī – by ascription to Ḥarām ibn Kaᶜb al-Anṣārī [ḥadīth 454]. He was the grandfather[6] of Jābir ibn ᶜAbdullāh, as as-Samᶜānī mentioned.

Jābir ibn ᶜAtīk was a major Companion. He died in 61 AH, as az-Zurqānī mentioned.

Jābir al-Juᶜfī is someone about whom there is discussion, and even if some critics regard him as a trustworthy narrator, the dominant majority – among them Abū Ḥanīfah – criticise him strongly and abandon him. As-Samᶜānī mentions in *al-Ansāb* after mentioning that, "Al-Juᶜfī (by ascription to a tribe of Kūfa, Juᶜfī ibn Saᶜd of Mudhḥij) is Abū Yazīd Jābir al-Juᶜfī one of the people of Kūfa who narrates from ᶜAṭā' and ash-Shaᶜbī, and from whom narrates ath-Thawrī and Shuᶜbah. He died in 128 AH and he was a Sabaite and one of the companions of ᶜAbdullāh ibn Saba'.[7] He used to say, 'ᶜAlī ﷺ will return to the world.' Yaḥyā ibn Maᶜīn said, 'He was a liar who believed in returning to the present state of existence after death.'" He mentioned in *Tahdhīb at-tahdhīb,* "Jābir ibn Yazīd ibn al-Ḥārith Abū ᶜAbdullāh al-Juᶜfī is said to be Abū Yazīd the Kūfan. He narrated from Abu'ṭ-Ṭufayl, Abu'ḍ-Ḍuḥā, ᶜIkrimah, ᶜAṭā', Ṭāwūs and a large group. From him narrated Shuᶜbah, ath-Thawrī, Isrā'īl, al-Ḥasan ibn Ḥayy, Sharīk, Misᶜar and others. Ibn ᶜUlayyah said [narrating] from Shuᶜbah, 'Jābir was utterly truthful in ḥadīth.' Wakīᶜ said, 'Whatever you are in doubt about, do not doubt that Jābir was a trustworthy narrator.' Ath-Thawri said to Shuᶜbah, 'If you talk disparagingly about Jābir, I will talk about you.' Ibn Maᶜīn said, 'He was a liar.' Once he said, 'His ḥadīth are not to be written.' Yaḥyā ibn Saᶜīd said [narrating] from Ismāᶜīl ibn Abī Khālid that ash-Shaᶜbī said to Jābir, 'You will not die until you have lied against the Messenger of Allah ﷺ.' Ismāᶜīl said, 'Days and nights had not passed before he was suspected of lying.' Someone said to Zāʾidah, 'Why do you not narrate from Ibn Abī Laylā, Jābir al-Juᶜfī and al-Kalbī?' He said, 'As for al-Juᶜfī, by Allah! he was a liar who believed in returning to this existence after death.' Abū Yaḥyā al-Ḥimmānī said [narrating from Abū Ḥanīfah, 'I have never met among those I have met anyone more given to lying than al-Juᶜfī. I never brought him any of my views but that he brought me a tradition about it claiming that he had thirty thousand ḥadīth which he had not made public.' Aḥmad said, 'Yaḥyā al-Qaṭṭān and ᶜAbd ar-Raḥmān ibn Mahdī abandoned him.' An-Nasāʾī said, 'His ḥadīth are abandoned,' and he once said, 'He is not a trustworthy narrator; his ḥadīth are not to be written.' Al-Ḥākim said, 'His ḥadīth are gone.' Ibn ᶜAdī said, 'He has good ḥadīth, but he is closer to being weak than to being truthful.' Ayyūb, Layth ibn Abī Sālim and al-Jūzajānī said he was a liar, and similarly Ibn ᶜUyaynah, Aḥmad and Saᶜīd ibn Jubayr." (Abridged)

Jaᶜfar ibn Muḥammad is the Imām Abū ᶜAbdullāh Jaᶜfar aṣ-Ṣādiq al-Hāshimī, Madīnan, ibn Muḥammad – who was well known as al-Bāqir – ibn ᶜAlī – who was well known as Zayn al-ᶜĀbidīn – ibn Ḥusayn ibn ᶜAlī ibn Abī Ṭālib. He was one of the chiefs of the Ahl al-Bayt and one of the devoted worshippers of the Followers of the Followers. He was born in 80 AH in Madīnah and died there in 148 AH. He narrated from his father and from ᶜAṭāʾ, ᶜUrwah and a large group of people, and from him narrated Mālik, Abū Ḥanīfah, Yaḥyā ibn Saᶜīd al-Anṣārī, Shuᶜbah, the two Sufyāns and others. Ibn Maᶜīn said that he was a trusted and trustworthy narrator. Abū Ḥātim said, "He was a trustworthy narrator, the like of whom is not to be asked about," as stated in *Isᶜāf al-mubaṭṭaʾ* of as-Suyūṭī. His father was Muḥammad al-Bāqir.

Jamīl al-Muʾadhdhin was Jamīl ibn ᶜAbd ar-Raḥmān al-Mu'adhdhin, the Madīnan. His mother was one of the children of Saᶜd al-Qarẓ. He heard from Saᶜīd ibn al-Musayyab and ᶜUmar ibn ᶜAbd al-ᶜAzīz, and Mālik narrated from him through Yaḥyā ibn Saᶜīd and directly without intermediary, as az-Zurqānī said.

Jarīr ibn ᶜUthmān. As-Samᶜānī mentioned him in *al-Ansāb* in relation to ar-Raḥabī – by ascription to Raḥabah a clan of Ḥimyar, and he said, "One of those related to him is Abū ᶜUthmān Jarīr ibn ᶜUthmān ibn Jabr ibn Aḥmar ibn Asᶜad ar-Raḥabī al-Ḥimṣī, he is called Abū ᶜAwn. He listened to ᶜAbdullāh ibn Busr the Companion, Rashīd ibn Saᶜd, ᶜAbd ar-Raḥmān ibn Maysarah and others. From him narrated Baqiyyah, Ismāᶜīl ibn ᶜAyyāsh, ᶜĪsā ibn Yūnus,

Muᶜādh ibn Muᶜādh al-ᶜAnbarī, al-Ḥakam ibn Nāfiᶜ and a large group apart from them. He was a reliable trustworthy narrator. Al-ᶜIjlī said, 'Jarīr from Shām is a trustworthy narrator. It is quoted of him that he used to abuse ᶜAlī ibn Abī Ṭālib, and it is also quoted of him that he renounced that position. He was born in 80 AH, and died in 163 AH.'" (Abridged)

Al-Jarrāḥ the *mawlā* of Umm Ḥabībah. As-Suyūṭī said in *Isᶜāf al-mubaṭṭaʾ* that his honorific was Abu'l-Jarrāḥ. He narrated from his former owner Umm Ḥabībah. ᶜUthmān, Sālim and others narrated from him. Ibn Ḥibbān declared him a trustworthy narrator. It is also said that his name was az-Zubayr.

Jubayr ibn Muṭᶜim ibn ᶜAdī ibn Nawfal ibn ᶜAbd Manāf was a Companion who accepted Islam on the day of the Opening [of Makkah to Islam]. He died in 58 AH or 59 AH, as az-Zurqānī mentioned.

Jumhān the *mawlā* of the tribe of Aslam [ḥadīth 562]. He was a Madīnan of the old generation and acceptable, as Ibn Ḥajar said in *Taqrīb at-tahdhīb*. In *Tahdhīb at-tahdhīb* it is stated that he was Jumhān Abu'l-ᶜAlāʾ, but some say Abū Yaᶜlā, the *mawlā* of the tribe of Aslam, who is counted as one of the Madīnans. He narrated from ᶜUthmān, Saᶜd, Abū Hurayrah and Umm Bakrah al-Aslamiyyah. From him narrated ᶜUrwah and ᶜUmar ibn Nabīh. Muslim mentioned him in the first generation of the people of Madīnah, and Ibn Ḥibbān mentioned him in *ath-Thiqāt*. ᶜAlī ibn al-Madīnī said, "He was my mother's grandfather, who was one of those taken prisoner as far as I know." (Abridged.) Al-Qārī mistakenly spelt his name Jamhān.

K

Kaʿb al-Aḥbār. See Kaʿb ibn Qāniʿ.

Kaʿb ibn Qāniʿ Abū Isḥāq al-Ḥimyarī is one of the great Followers, better known as Kaʿb al-Aḥbār who was one of the Muslims from the People of the Book. Muʿāwiyah said, "He is the most truthful of those who narrate from the Book." He died in 32 AH in Ḥimṣ, as stated in *Isʿāf al-mubaṭṭaʾ* of as-Suyūṭī.

Kaʿb ibn ʿUjrah ibn Umayyah ibn ʿAdī al-Anṣārī who went to reside in Kūfa and who died in Madāʾin 51 AH or later. Ibn ʿUmar, Ibn ʿAbbās and others narrated from him and of the Followers, Ibn Abī Laylā, Abū Wāʾil and others. Ibn al-Athīr said, "He was with the Messenger of Allah ﷺ at al-Ḥudaybiyyah in iḥrām, and the Messenger of Allah ﷺ saw him with lice falling from his head on to his face, and so he asked him, "Do your vermin bother you?" He answered, "Yes." So he told him to shave [his head], and Allah revealed about it his saying, "If any of you are ill or have a head injury," (Sūrat al-Baqarah: 195) meaning "do not shave your heads in the state of iḥrām unless you are compelled to do so by a sickness or an affliction of the head such as vermin or a headache."

Kabshah bint Kaʿb ibn Mālik al-Anṣārīyyah the wife of Ibn Abī Qatādah and the maternal aunt of Ḥumaydah. It is said that she was a Companion. Ibn Ḥibbān regarded her as a trustworthy narrator and said she was a Companion.

Kathīr ibn aṣ-Ṣalt al-Kindī was a major Madīnan Follower, who was born during the lifetime of the Messenger of Allah ﷺ. Those who regard him as a Companion make a mistake, as az-Zurqānī said.

Kaysān ibn Saʿīd al-Maqburī, the Madīnan was Abū Saʿīd, the father of Saʿīd al-Maqburī. He was the *mawlā* of Umm Sharīk and a trustworthy narrator who was firmly established. He died in 100 AH as stated in *at-Taqrīb*.

Khālid ibn ʿAbdullāh. Apparently it is Khālid ibn ʿAbdullāh ibn ʿAbd ar-Raḥmān ibn Yazīd aṭ-Ṭaḥḥān Abuʾl-Haytham al-Wāsiṭī who narrated from Ismāʿīl ibn Abī Khālid, Ḥumayd aṭ-Ṭawīl, Sulaymān at-Taymī, Abū Isḥāq ash-Shaybānī and others, and from whom Wakīʿ, Ibn Mahdī, Yaḥyā al-Qaṭṭān and others narrated. Ibn Saʿd, Abū Zurʿah, an-Nasāʾī, Abū Ḥātim and at-Tirmidhī regarded him as a trustworthy narrator. He died in 179 AH. So it is found in *Tahdhīb al-kamāl* by al-Mizzī.

Khālid ibn Asīd. Hishām ibn al-Kalbī said, "He accepted Islam on the day of the Opening [of Makkah to Islam], and he resided in Makkah. He was one of those "whose hearts were reconciled [to Islam]." Ibn Durayd said, "He was a carpenter." It is said that he was lost on the day of al-Yamāmah, but it is said that he died before that, as az-Zurqānī said.

Khālid ibn ᶜUqbah ibn Abī Muᶜayṭ of Quraysh and [Banī] Umayyah. He was a Companion from those who accepted Islam at the Opening [of Makkah to Islam], and his home was at the marketplace of Madīnah. Az-Zurqānī mentions him.

Khālid ibn al-Walīd ibn al-Mughīrah was the son of the maternal aunt of Ibn ᶜAbbās, and he was Abū Sufyān of Makhzūm. He accepted Islam after Ḥudaybiyyah and before the Opening [of Makkah to Islam], and was present at the battle of Muʾtah. He died in Ḥimṣ in 21 AH, but some say in Madīnah, as stated in *Isᶜāf al-mubaṭṭaʾ* of as-Suyūṭī.

Khallād ibn as-Sāʾib al-Anṣārī of Banī al-Ḥārith ibn al-Khazraj was a Follower who was a trustworthy narrator. Those who assert that he was a Companion are mistaken, as az-Zurqānī mentioned. His father was as-Sāʾib ibn Khallād (see his entry).

Khansāʾ bint Khidhām. Ibn ᶜAbd al-Barr said in *al-Istīᶜāb*, "Khansāʾ bint Khidhām ibn Wadīᶜah al-Anṣārī of Aws. Her father married her off against her will and the Messenger of Allah ﷺ overturned her marriage. The ḥadīth differ as to her condition at that time. In Mālik's narration from ᶜAbd ar-Raḥmān ibn al-Qāsim from his father from ᶜAbd ar-Raḥmān and Mujammiᶜ from her, there is that she was someone who had already been married (*thayyib*). Ibn al-Mubārak mentioned from ath-Thawrī from ᶜAbd ar-Raḥmān ibn al-Qāsim from ᶜAbdullāh ibn Yazīd ibn Wadīᶜah from Khansāʾ, that she was at the time a virgin. Mālik's transmission is the correct one. Muḥammad ibn Isḥāq narrated from Ḥajāj ibn as-Sāʾib from his father from his grandmother Khansāʾ that he said, 'She was at that time unmarried and her father married her to a man from Banī ᶜAwf but then she was proposed to by Abū Lubābah ibn ᶜAbd al-Mundhir and her case was raised before the Messenger of Allah ﷺ and he ordered that she be allowed to have her desire, and so she married Abū Lubābah."

Khārijah ibn Zayd ibn Thābit was one of the 'seven *fuqahāʾ*' of Madīnah and one of the greatest of the trustworthy narrators. He died in 99 AH, but some say 100 AH, as Ibn Ḥibbān said. He was the maternal uncle of Saᶜīd as az-Zurqānī said.

Khidhām. Khidām is thus spelt in *al-Fatḥ* and *at-Taqrīb*. Some say that it is Khidhām ibn Wadīᶜah, but others say Ibn Khālid. He was one of the eminent Companions, as az-Zurqānī said, and the father of Khansāʾ.

Kurayb the *mawlā* of Ibn ᶜAbbās is Ibn Abī Muslim Abū Rushd ibn al-Ḥijāzī whom an-Nasāʾī, Ibn Maᶜīn and Ibn Saᶜd regarded as a trustworthy narrator. He died in 98 AH as found in *Isᶜāf al-mubaṭṭa*ʾ of as-Suyūṭī.

L

Layth [ḥadīth 263] is ibn Abī Sulaym. Ḥāfiẓ ᶜAbd al-ᶜAẓīm al-Mundhirī said at the end of his book *at-Targhīb wa't-tarhīb*, "There is disagreement about him, and people have narrated from him, but Yaḥyā and an-Nasā᾽ī regarded him as weak, and Ibn Ḥibbān said, 'He became confused and mixed things up towards the end of his life.' Ad-Dāraquṭnī said, 'He was a man of Sunnah, and they only repudiate his joining together ᶜAṭā᾽, Ṭāwūs and Mujāhid, and nothing else.' Ibn Maᶜīn regarded him as a trustworthy narrator in one narration from him." I have gone to some lengths in writing about his biograpical details in my treatise on visiting the Prophet ﷺ *al-Kalām al-mabrūr fī radd al-qawl al-manṣūr wa radd al-madhhab al-ma᾽thūr* which is called *as-Saᶜy al-mashkūr* when some people of merit in our age held the opinion that his weakness reached the extent that he could not be used in proof.

M

Maḥmūd ibn Labīd al-Anṣārī al-Ashhalī of Banī ᶜAbd al-Ashhal was born during the life of the Prophet ﷺ and he narrated ḥadīth from the Prophet ﷺ. Muslim mentioned him in the second generation of the Followers *and he did not do anything nor is there known about him what he taught others* [sic][8]. He died in 96 AH. So it is found in *al-Istīᶜāb.*

Maḥmūd ibn Muḥammad al-Marwazī – by ascription to Marw and the 'z' is attached to the ascription to distinguish it from *al-marwī* a well known robe worn in ᶜIrāq – ascribed to a sub-section of Kūfa, as as-Samᶜānī said. I have not yet come across biographical material on him so that it can be known whether he is a trustworthy narrator or weak, may Allah graciously bestow the discovery of that upon me.

Makhramah ibn Sulaymān al-Wālibī al-Asadī the Madīnan whom Ibn Maᶜīn regarded as a trustworthy narrator. Al-Wāqidī said, "The Ḥarūriyyah (Khawārij) killed him in 130 AH at Qudayd, as stated in *Isᶜāf al-mubaṭṭa'* of as-Suyūṭī. He is al-Wālibī by ascription to Wālibah a sub-clan of Asad, as as-Samᶜānī mentioned.

Makḥūl is Abū ᶜAbdullāh al-Hudhalī the Damascene faqīh who narrated many *mursal* ḥadīth. He narrated from ᶜUbādah, Ubayy, ᶜĀ'ishah and the great Companions. Abū Ḥātim said, "I have not seen anyone with more fiqh than Makḥūl." There is a great deal of praise of him and mention that he is one of the trustworthy narrators from the critical scholars of ḥadīth as he expanded in some detail in *Tahdhīb at-tahdhīb,* and in *Tadhkirat al-ḥuffāẓ*. He died in 113 AH, but people say other dates as well.

Mālik ibn ᶜĀmir al-Anṣārī al-Aṣbaḥī was one of the major Followers and a trustworthy narrator. Everyone narrates from him. He died in 74 AH according to the correct position. He is the grandfather of Imām Mālik and the father of Abū Suhayl. As-Suyūṭī and others said likewise.

Mālik ibn Aws ibn al-Ḥadathān. Ibn al-Athīr said in *Jāmiᶜ al-uṣūl,* "Mālik ibn Aws ibn al-Ḥadathān ibn ᶜAwf ibn Rabīᶜah Abū Saᶜīd an-Naṣrī of Banī Naṣr ibn Muᶜāwiyah. There is disagreement as to whether or not he was a Companion, but his father was a Companion. Ibn ᶜAbd al-Barr said, 'Most people affirm that he was [a Companion].' Ibn Mandah said, 'It is not established.' He narrated from the ten given the good news [of the Garden] and others. He died in Madīnah in 92 AH."

Mālik ibn al-Ḥārith. Adh-Dhahabī said in *al-Kāshif*, "Mālik ibn al-Ḥārith as-Sulamī [narrated] from Abū Saᶜīd al-Khudrī and ᶜAlqamah an-Nakhaᶜī, and from him narrated Manṣūr and al-Aᶜmash. He was a trustworthy narrator, and he died in 194 AH."

Manṣūr ibn al-Muᶜtamir Abū ᶜAttāb as-Sulamī the Kūfan a firmly established trustworthy narrator. He died in 132 AH. From him narrated ath-Thawrī, Shuᶜbah, Sulaymān at-Taymī and others. So it is found in *Jāmiᶜ al-uṣūl* by Ibn al-Athīr al-Jazarī and *at-Taqrīb* of Ibn Ḥajar.

Marjānah. See "his mother".

Marwān ibn al-Ḥakam ibn Abi'l-ᶜĀṣ ibn Umayyah. It is said that he had seen [the Messenger of Allah ﷺ]. If that is established, still he does not rise above the rank of someone who is discussed critically. If not, ᶜUrwah ibn az-Zubayr said, "Marwān is not suspected in ḥadīth." Sahl ibn Saᶜd as-Sā᾽idī the Companion narrated depending upon his veracity. They only take revenge on him because he shot Ṭalḥah on the day of the Camel with an arrow and killed him. Later he drew his sword seeking the khilāfah until what happened, happened, as described in *Hady as-sārī: muqaddimah Fatḥ al-bārī* of Ḥāfiẓ Ibn Ḥajar.

The maternal aunt of ᶜAbdullāh ibn Abī Bakr. Az-Zurqānī said, "Ibn al-Ḥidhā᾽ said, 'She was ᶜAmrah bint Ḥazm the maternal aunt of the grandfather of ᶜAbdullāh ibn Abī Bakr, and it is said that she was his maternal aunt in a metaphorical sense.' Ḥāfiẓ followed that by saying, 'ᶜAmrah was an early Companion, from whom Jābir the Companion narrated, so that then the narration of ᶜAbdullāh from her is interrupted since he did not reach her. The most obvious thing is that what is meant is his actual maternal aunt who was Umm ᶜAmr or Umm Kulthūm.'" The original case must be to interpret it to refer to his actual aunt, and the person who claims that it is used metaphorically must explain the narration along with his claim which necessarily means that the chain of transmission is interrupted, whereas the source contradicts that.

Maymūnah bint al-Ḥārith al-Hilāliyyah whose name had been Barrah, and whom the Messenger of Allah ﷺ named Maymūnah. She died in Sarf in 51 AH, but some say 66 AH and others 63 AH. So it is found in *al-Istīᶜāb fī aḥwāl al-aṣḥāb* by Ibn ᶜAbd al-Barr.

"Men from the great ones of their people" [ḥadīth 680]. Ḥāfiẓ Ibn Ḥajar said in the *Muqaddimah Fatḥ al-bārī*, "They were Muḥayyiṣah and Ḥuwayyiṣah the two sons of Masᶜūd, and ᶜAbd ar-Raḥmān and ᶜAbdullāh the two sons of Sahl."

Miḥjan ad-Dīlī of Banī ad-Du'il ibn Bakr ibn ᶜAbd Manāf is counted as one of the people of Madīnah, from whom narrated his son Busr ibn Miḥjan, but it is also said Bishr ibn Miḥjan.Abū Nuᶜaym said, "The correct name is Busr." His tribe were Banī ad-Dīl according to al-Kisā'ī, Abu ᶜUbayd, Muḥammad ibn Ḥabīb and others, but [Banī] ad-Du'il who was Ibn Bakr ibn ᶜAbd Manāf ibn Kinān according to az-Zurqānī. Miḥjan ibn Abī Miḥjan ad-Dīlī was a Companion who had few ḥadīth, as az-Zurqānī said. The spelling of Miḥjan is as spelt out by al-Qārī.

Al-Miqdād ibn ᶜAmr ibn Thaᶜlabah al-Kindī is well known as Ibn al-Aswad. Al-Aswad ibn ᶜAbd Yaghūth adopted him as a son when he was small so that he became known by him [as Ibn al-Aswad]. He was present at Badr and all the other events. He died in 33 AH. That is found in *Isᶜāf al-mubaṭṭa'* of as-Suyūṭī.

Misᶜar ibn Kidām ibn Ẓahīr al-Hilālī Abū Salamah the Kūfan, an eminent, firmly established, trustworthy narrator. He died in 153 AH, but some say 155 AH. So it is found in *Taqrīb at-tahdhīb* and elsewhere.

Al-Miswar ibn Makhramah ibn Nawfal of Quraysh. Both he and his father were Companions, which he mentioned in *al-Iṣābah* and other books.

Al-Miswar ibn Rifāᶜah ibn Abī Mālik al-Quraẓī by ascription to Banī Qurayẓah a lesser Madīnan Follower who is acceptable. In the *Muwaṭṭa'* he has a single *marfūᶜ* ḥadīth, but in the six [collections] there is not a single ḥadīth from him. Ibn Ḥibbān regarded him as a trustworthy narrator. He died in 138 AH.

"His mother" [ḥadīth 390] the freed slave [*mawlāh*] of ᶜĀ'ishah ﷺ was Marjānah and she was the mawlāh of ᶜĀ'ishah and an accepted narrator. She was the mother of ᶜAlqamah [ḥadīth 26]. Ibn Ḥibbān regarded her as a trustworthy narrator, as stated in *al-Isᶜāf.*

Muᶜādh ibn ᶜAmr ibn Saᶜīd narrating from Muᶜādh from his grandmother [ḥadīth 931]. So it is found in many copies, but the correct chain of transmission is in the *Muwaṭṭa'* of Yaḥyā and its commentary, "Mālik from Zayd ibn Aslam al-ᶜAdawī from ᶜAmr ibn Saᶜd ibn Muᶜādh by ascription to his grandfather since he was ᶜAmr ibn Muᶜādh ibn Saᶜd ibn Muᶜādh al-Ashhalī the Madīnan, whose kunyā was Abū Muḥammad.

Muᶜādh ibn Jabal ibn ᶜAmr ibn Aws al-Anṣārī al-Khazrajī Abū ᶜAbd ar-Raḥmān, the Madīnan. He was present at al-ᶜAqabah, Badr and all of the major events, and he was one of the four Anṣār who collected the entire

Qur'ān in the life of the Prophet ﷺ. Jābir, Ibn ʿUmar, Ibn ʿAbbās, Abū Mūsā and a great number of others narrated from him. He died in the plague of ʿAmawās in 18 AH as stated in *al-Isʿāf.*

Muʿādh ibn Saʿd [ḥadīth 640]. There is a doubt in the ḥadīth as to whether it is Muʿādh ibn Saʿd or Saʿd ibn Muʿādh. Az-Zurqānī said, "Thus the doubt occurred, and Ibn Mandah and Abū Nuʿaym mention Muʿādh ibn Saʿd among the Companions. He said that in *al-Iṣābah.*"

Muʿāwiyah ibn Abī Sufyān was Muʿāwiyah ibn Sakhr ibn Ḥarb ibn Umayyah ibn ʿAbd Shams ibn ʿAbd Manāf of Quraysh and Banī Umayyah. He accepted Islam, he, his father, his brother Yazīd, and his mother Hind bint ʿUtbah ibn Rabīʿah ibn ʿAbd Shams, on the day of the Opening [of Makkah to Islam]. He was one of those "whose hearts were reconciled [*mu'allafah qulūbuhum*]", and he made good his Islam, and wrote [the revelation] for the Messenger of Allah ﷺ. When Yazīd his brother died, he [ʿUmar] appointed him as his [Yazīd's] successor to his governorship in Shām. When ʿUthmān was appointed khalīfah, he gathered all of Shām under his authority, and it continued like that until ʿUthmān was killed, and he remained alone in Shām and did not pledge allegiance to ʿAlī. The battle of Ṣiffīn took place between him and ʿAlī. All of that is examined in greater detail in *al-Kāmil fi't-tārīkh.* When ʿAlī was killed, al-Ḥasan [became khalīfah and after negotiations] surrended the amirate [khilāfah] to Muʿāwiyah. He died in the middle of Rajab in 60 AH, as stated in *Asad al-ghābah fi maʿrifat aṣ-ṣaḥābah* by Ibn al-Athīr al-Jazarī. [See also *Tārīkh al-khulafā'* published in English as *The History of the Khalifahs* by Jalal ad-Dīn as-Suyūṭī, Ta-Ha Publishing Ltd., and *Al-ʿAwāṣim min al-qawāṣim* published in English as *Defence Against Disaster* by Qāḍī Abū Bakr ibn al-ʿArabī, Madīnah Press].

Al-Mubārak ibn Faḍālah Abū Faḍālah – the *mawlā* of the family of al-Khattāb – al-ʿAdawī, the Baṣran. He was an utterly truthful person who sometimes omitted to mention gaps in his chains of transmission (*mudallis*). Abū Zurʿah said, "When he says, 'He narrated to us…' he is a trustworthy narrator." He narrated from al-Ḥasan al-Baṣrī and Bakr al-Muznī, and from him narrated Ibn al-Mubārak and others. He died in 166 AH according to the authentic position, as found in *at-Taqrīb* and *al-Kāshif.*

Al-Mughīrah aḍ-Ḍabbī was Ibn Miqsam aḍ-Ḍabbī by ascription to Ḍabbah a tribe – their mawlā – Abū Hishām, the blind Kūfan. He was a trustworthy narrator who was very exact except that he sometimes omitted to mention gaps in his chains of transmission (*tadlīs*). He narrated from an-Nakhaʿī, ash-Shaʿbī and Abū Wāʾil, and from him narrated Jarīr, Shuʿbah, Zāʾidah and others. He died in 136 AH according to the correct opinion, as found in *al-Kāshif* and *at-Taqrīb*.

Al-Mughīrah ibn Ḥakīm narrated from Abū Hurayrah and Ibn ʿUmar. From him narrated Nāfiʿ, Ibn Jurayj and Jarīr ibn Ḥāzim. He was a trustworthy narrator. So it is found in *al-Kāshif* by adh-Dhahabī.

Al-Mughīrah ibn Shuʿbah ibn Abī ʿĀmir ibn Masʿūd ibn Muʿtab ibn Mālik ibn Kaʿb ath-Thaqafī whose kunyā was Abū ʿAbdullāh or Abū ʿĪsā. He accepted Islam in the year of al-Khandaq and came as an emigrant [to Madīnah]. Some say that the first event he was present at was al-Khandaq. He died in 50 AH in Kūfa. So it is found in *al-Istīʿāb*.

Muḥammad [ḥadīth 159] is not Imām Muḥammad, but Abū ʿAlī aṣ-Ṣawwāf the pupil of Bishr ibn Mūsā al-Asadī. A later copyist gave this chain of transmission.

Muḥammad ibn Abān ibn Ṣāliḥ is one of those whom a large group of critical scholars regard as weak. It is stated in *Mīzān al-iʿtidāl* by adh-Dhahabī, "Muḥammad ibn Abān ibn Ṣāliḥ of Quraysh, said to be al-Juʿfī the Kūfan. He narrated from Zayd ibn Aslam and others. Abū Dāwūd and Ibn Maʿīn regarded him as weak. Al-Bukhārī said, 'He is not strong.' Someone said he was one of the Murjiʾah." It is stated in *Lisān al-mīzān* by al-Ḥāfiẓ Ibn Ḥajar, "An-Nasāʾī said, 'Muḥammad ibn Abān ibn Ṣāliḥ of Quraysh was Kūfan, and he is not a trustworthy narrator.' Ibn Ḥibbān said, 'Weak.' Aḥmad said, 'He was not of those who lie.' Ibn Abī Ḥātim said, 'I asked my father about him and he said, "He is not strong. His ḥadīth are to be written down, but he may not be used as a proof."' Al-Bukhārī said in *at-Tārīkh*, 'They say that his memory is not dependable.'"

Muḥammad al-Bāqir ibn ʿAlī – who [ʿAlī] was well known as Zayn al-ʿĀbidīn – ibn Ḥasan ibn ʿAlī ibn Abī Ṭālib. He was called al-Bāqir because of the vastness [*tabaqqur*] of his knowledge. He died in Madīnah in 118 AH, but some say 119 AH, as stated in *at-Taqrīb* and *Jāmiʿ al-uṣūl*

Muḥammad ibn ʿAbd ar-Raḥmān ibn Thawbān al-ʿĀmirī, the Madīnan whom an-Nasāʾī and ibn Saʿd regarded as a trustworthy narrator and about whom Abū Ḥātim said, "The like of him is not to be asked about," as stated in *al-Isʿāf*.

Muḥammad ibn ʿAbdullāh ibn ʿAbd ar-Raḥmān ibn Abī Ṣaʿṣaʿah was Abū ʿAbdullāh al-Anṣārī al-Māzinī and he was a trustworthy narrator. He died in 139 AH according to *Isʿāf al-mubaṭṭaʾ* of as-Suyūṭī. He is ascribed to his father, and his grandfather to his [father's] grandfather because he was ʿAbd ar-Raḥmān ibn ʿAbdullāh ibn Abī Ṣaʿṣaʿah.

Muḥammad ibn ʿAbdullāh ibn Nawfal ibn al-Ḥārith ibn ʿAbd al-Muṭṭalib. He was Hāshimī and a Madīnan and was acceptable, as az-Zurqānī said.

Muḥammad ibn Abī Bakr [ibn Muḥammad] ibn ʿAmr ibn Ḥazm. As-Suyūṭī said in *Isʿāf al-mubaṭṭaʾ*, "Muḥammad ibn Abī Bakr [ibn Muḥammad] ibn ʿAmr ibn Ḥazm al-Anṣārī the qāḍī of Madīnah. He narrated from his father Abī Bakr ibn Muḥammad ibn ʿAmr ibn Ḥazm and az-Zuhrī, and from him narrated Mālik and his own son ʿAbd ar-Raḥmān, Shuʿbah, and the two Sufyāns. He died in 132 AH.

Muḥammad ibn Abī Bakr aṣ-Ṣiddīq. His kunyā was Abu'l-Qāsim. After his father died, he grew up in the care of ʿAlī with whom he was present at the battles of the Camel and Ṣiffīn. He was one of the devotees of Quraysh but, however, he also aided in the killing of ʿUthmān [although he stepped back and repented before the actual blow and was not one of the murderers]. ʿUthmān had made him governor of Egypt, and he resided there until Muʿāwiyah sent the armies among whom were ʿAmr ibn al-ʿĀṣ and Muʿāwiyah ibn Khadīj. There was fighting and Muḥammad ibn Abī Bakr was defeated and was killed by Ibn Khadīj in Ṣafar 38 AH, as stated in *Tuḥfat al-muḥibbīn fī manāqib al-khulafāʾ ar-rāshidīn.*

Muḥammad ibn Abī Bakr ath-Thaqafī the Ḥijāzī. He was a trustworthy narrator, but he only has this single ḥadīth [386] from Anas, as az-Zurqānī mentioned

Muḥammad ibn ʿAlī ibn Abī Ṭālib al-Hāshimī the Madīnan was better known as Ibn al-Ḥanafiyah, and she [al-Ḥanafiyah] was Khawlah of Banī al-Yamāmah, the wife of ʿAlī ﷺ. Al-ʿIjlī and others regarded him as a trustworthy narrator. He died in 73 AH, as stated in *Isʿāf al-mubaṭṭaʾ* of as-Suyūṭī.

Muḥammad ibn ʿAmārah ibn ʿĀmir ibn ʿAmr ibn Ḥazm. Ibn Maʿīn regarded him as a trustworthy narrator, but Abū Ḥātim regarded him as less trustworthy, as as-Suyūṭī said.

Muḥammad ibn ʿAmr ibn ʿAṭāʾ ibn ʿAbbās ibn ʿAlqamah al-ʿĀmirī of Quraysh and a Madīnan, was one of the trustworthy narrators of the Followers. He narrated from Abū Ḥumayd, Abū Qatādah and Ibn ʿAbbās, as found in *Jāmiʿ al-uṣūl.*

Muḥammad ibn ᶜAmr ibn Ḥalḥalah ad-Duʾalī is Madīnan and Ibn Maᶜīn and an-Nasāʾī regarded him as a trustworthy narrator, as is mentioned by as-Suyūṭī. He is ad-Duʾalī, but it is also mentioned in *at-Taqrīb* about him that he was ad-Dīlī, both of which are by ascription to a tribe.

Muḥammad ibn ᶜAmr ibn Ḥazm. Ibn Ḥibbān said in *ath-Thiqāt*, "His kunyā was Abū ᶜAbd al-Mālik. He was born in 10 AH during the life of the Prophet ﷺ. He died on the day of al-Ḥarrah in 63 AH. His son Abū Bakr and others narrated from him."

Muḥammad ibn Ibrāhīm ibn al-Ḥārith ibn Khālid at-Taymī Abū ᶜAbdullāh, the Madīnan. He was a trustworthy narrator. He died in 120 AH according to the most sound position, as found in *at-Taqrīb*. Ibn Maᶜīn, Abū Ḥātim, an-Nasāʾī and others regarded him as a trustworthy narrator. Aḥmad said, "There is something in his ḥadīth. He narrates things that are rejected [or unknown]." He died in 120 AH, and he narrates the ḥadīth, "Actions are only by intentions..." in the version of Muḥammad ibn al-Ḥasan. So it is found in *Isᶜāf al-mubaṭṭaʾ* of as-Suyūṭī.

Muḥammad ibn ᶜIjlān. Adh-Dhahabī said in *al-Kāshif*, "Muḥammad ibn ᶜIjlān the Madīnan, the right-acting faqīh [narrated] from his father, Anas and many others. From him narrated Shuᶜbah, Mālik, al-Qaṭṭān and many others. Aḥmad and Ibn Maᶜīn regarded him as a trustworthy narrator. Others said he had a bad memory. He died in 143 AH."

Muḥammad ibn Jubayr ibn Muṭᶜim was Abū Saᶜīd al-Qurashī an-Nawfalī. He was a trustworthy narrator and one from whom all transmited. He died at the end of the first century, as az-Zurqānī and others mention.

Muḥammad ibn al-Munkadir ibn ᶜAbdullāh ibn al-Hudayr at-Taymī the Madīnan, is an eminent trustworthy narrator. He died in 130 AH or after that. That is how it is in *at-Taqrīb*.

Muḥammad ibn ᶜUqbah the *mawlā* of az-Zubayr was the brother of Mūsā ibn ᶜUqbah, the Madīnan. He was a trustworthy narrator as stated in *at-Taqrīb*.

Muḥammad ibn Yaḥyā ibn Ḥabbān al-Anṣārī, the Madīnan. An-Nasāʾī, Ibn Maᶜīn and Abū Ḥātim regarded him as a trustworthy narrator. He died in Madīnah in 121 AH, as stated in *Isᶜāf al-mubaṭṭaʾ* of as-Suyūṭī. He was a Madīnan faqīh who was a trustworthy narrator. He said, "My grandfather Ḥabbān ibn Munqidh al-Anṣārī al-Māzinī, the Companion had...," as az-Zurqānī said.

Muḥammad ibn Zayd at-Taymī was a trustworthy narrator from whom Muslim and the four narrated, as az-Zurqānī mentioned. His mother [ḥadīth 164] was Umm Ḥarām. He said in *at-Taqrīb*, "It is said that her name was Āminah."

Muḥill aḍ-Ḍabbī. Al-Qārī said that it was Miḥill and was the name of a number of ḥadīth scholars. But this is not sufficient in this context. In *at-Taqrīb* there is, "Muḥill ibn Khalīfah aṭ-Ṭā᾽ī, the Kūfan, was a trustworthy narrator of the fourth generation, and Muḥill ibn Muḥriz aḍ-Ḍabbī, the Kūfan, in whom there is no harm, is of the sixth. He died in 153 AH." He makes clear that it is spelt 'Muḥill' ad-Ḍabbi, about which Muḥammad Tahir al-Fattanī declared clearly when he said in *al-Mughnī*, "Muḥill ibn Khalīfah is spelt thus – but some say 'Maḥill' – as is Muḥill ibn Muḥriz." Thus al-Qārī's mistake is clear, and the Creator knows best. In *al-Kāshif* of adh-Dhahabī there is, "Muḥill ibn Khalīfah aṭ-Ṭā᾽ī narrated from his grandfather ᶜAdī ibn Ḥātim and Abu's-Samḥ, and from him narrated Shuᶜbah and Saᶜd Abū Mujāhid. As for Muḥill ibn Muḥriz aḍ-Ḍabbī narrating from ash-Shaᶜbī , he was younger than him."

Mujabbar. See al-Mujabbar.

Al-Mujabbar. He is called al-Mujabbar [the one whose bone was set] because he fell and broke [a limb] and his bone was set. That is what Ibn ᶜAbd al-Barr said. It is stated in *Jāmiᶜ al-uṣūl*, "Al-Mujabbar ibn ᶜAbd ar-Raḥmān al-Aṣghar ibn ᶜUmar. It is said that his name was ᶜAbd ar-Raḥmān." There is in *Mushtabih an-nisbah* by al-Ḥāfiẓ ᶜAbd al-Ghanī, "Mujabbar. Al-Mujabbar ibn ᶜAbd ar-Raḥmān ibn ᶜUmar ibn al-Khattāb. Mālik narrated from his son ᶜAbd ar-Raḥmān." Az-Zubayr ibn Bakkār said, "He [the father] died while he was in the womb, and so when he was born Ḥafṣah called him after his father, and she said, 'Perhaps, Allah will put his affairs in a good state (*yajburuhu*).'" He said in *al-Istīᶜāb*, "ᶜUmar had three children all of whom were called ᶜAbd ar-Raḥmān, the oldest of whom was a Companion, the middle one of whom was given the kunyā Abū Shaḥmah and he was the one whom his father, ᶜUmar, flogged because of wine, and the third was the father of al-Mujabbar."

Mujāhid was Ibn Jabr Abū al-Ḥajjāj al-Makhzūmī – their *mawlā* – the Makkan, the Qur᾽ān teacher, commentator and ḥāfiẓ. He heard Saᶜd, ᶜĀ᾽ishah, Abū Hurayrah, and Ibn ᶜAbbās with whom he spent some time and to whom he recited the Qur᾽ān. Al-Aᶜmash, Manṣūr, Ibn ᶜAwn, Qatādah and others narrated from him. Qatādah said, "The most knowledgeable of those who remain concerning tafsīr is Mujāhid." Ibn Jurayj said, "That I should have heard from Mujāhid is more beloved to me than my family and my property." He was among the notable trustworthy narrators. So it is found in *Tadhkirat al-ḥuffāẓ* by adh-Dhahabī. He mentioned in *at-Taqrīb* and elsewhere that he died either one, two, three or four years after 100 AH.

Mujammiʿ ibn Yazīd ibn Jāriyah al-Anṣārī was one of the great Followers who died in 60 AH.

Mūsā ibn Abī Tamīm the Madīnan. Abū Ḥātim said, "He was a trustworthy narrator in whom there was no harm," as as-Suyūṭī mentioned. Az-Zurqānī said, "In the *Muwaṭṭaʾ* there is only this single *marfūʿ* ḥadīth [814] from him."

Mūsā ibn Maysarah ad-Dīlī, their *mawlā,* Abū ʿUrwah, the Madīnan, was a trustworthy narrator. Mālik used to praise him and describe him as being someone of merit. He died in 133 AH, said az-Zurqānī .

Mūsā ibn Saʿd ibn Zayd ibn Thābit. Adh-Dhahabī said in *al-Kāshif,* "Mūsā ibn Saʿd or Saʿīd [narrated] from Sālim and Rabīʿah ar-Raʾy. From him narrated ʿUmar ibn Muḥammad. He was regarded as a trustworthy narrator." In *at-Taqrīb,* "Mūsā ibn Saʿd or Saʿīd ibn Zayd ibn Thābit al-Anṣārī, the Madīnan, is acceptable."

Mūsā ibn ʿUqbah was a *mawlā* of the family of az-Zubayr, but it is said that he was a *mawlā* of Umm Khālid, the wife of az-Zubayr. He is a trustworthy narrator. He died in 141 AH, as stated in *al-Kāshif.*

Musʿab ibn Saʿd ibn Abī Waqqāṣ az-Zuhrī Abū Zurārah, the Madīnan, is trustworthy and he died in 103 AH. His father was Saʿd ibn Abī Waqqāṣ. So it is found in *Taqrīb at-tahdhīb.*

Muslim ibn Abī Maryam. Abū Dāwūd, an-Nasāʾī and Ibn Maʿīn regarded him as a trustworthy narrator. He died in the khilāfah of al-Manṣūr, as is mentioned in *al-Isʿāf.*

Al-Muṭṭalib ibn ʿAbdullāh ibn Ḥanṭab – which occurs in the Muwaṭṭaʾ of Yaḥyā as Ḥuwayṭab and is a mistake – and he is Abu'l-Ḥakam al-Muṭṭalib ibn ʿAbdullāh ibn Ḥanṭab ibn al-Ḥārith ibn ʿUbayd ibn ʿUmar ibn Makhzūm al-Makhzūmī of Quraysh and a Madīnan, one of the trustworthy narrators of the Followers, as found in *Jāmiʿ al-uṣūl.*

Al-Muṭṭalib ibn Abī Wadāʿah as-Sahmī. He was ʿAbdullāh as-Sahmī, a Companion who accepted Islam on the day of the Opening [of Makkah to Islam]. He resided in Madīnah where he died. His mother was Arwā bint al-Ḥārith ibn ʿAbd al-Muṭṭalib, and was the daughter of the paternal uncle of the Prophet ﷺ, as az-Zurqānī mentioned.

N

Nāfiʿ. Shaykh al-Islām adh-Dhahabī said in *Tadhkirat al-ḥuffāẓ*, "Nāfiʿ Abū ʿAbdullāh al-ʿAdawī, the Madīnan, narrated from his *mawlā*[9] Ibn ʿUmar, ʿĀʾishah, Abū Hurayrah, Umm Salamah, Rāfiʿ ibn Khadīj and a group of others. From him narrated Ayyūb, ʿUbaydullāh, Ibn Jurayj, al-Awzāʿī, Mālik, al-Layth and a large number of people. Al-Bukhārī and others said that the soundest chain of transmission is that of Mālik from Nāfiʿ from Ibn ʿUmar. Ibn Wahb said, 'Mālik narrated to me saying, "I used to go to Nāfiʿ while I was a boy young in years and he would narrate to me. He would sit after the morning prayer in the mosque and hardly anyone would come to him."' Ḥammād ibn Zayd and Muḥammad ibn Saʿd said, 'Nāfiʿ died in 117 AH.' Yaḥyā ibn Maʿīn said, 'Nāfiʿ was Daylamī.' Nāfiʿ said, 'I served Ibn ʿUmar for thirty years, and then Ibn ʿUmar was given thirty thousand dirhams for me and he said, "I fear that the dirhams will be a trial for me," and he set me free.'" (Abridged) It is stated in *Jāmiʿ al-uṣūl*, "Nāfiʿ ibn Sarjis, the *mawlā* of Ibn ʿUmar, was Daylamī and one of the great Madīnan Followers who were famous for ḥadīth. He was one of the trustworthy narrators about whose ḥadīth there is consensus and which are acted upon. The greater part of the ḥadīth of Ibn ʿUmar revolve around him. Mālik said, 'When I heard the ḥadīth of Nāfiʿ from Ibn ʿUmar I did not care whether I heard it from anyone else.' He died in 117 AH, but some say 120 AH." There is the like of that in *Isʿāf al-mubaṭṭaʾbi rijāl* al-*Muwaṭṭaʾ* of as-Suyūṭī because he said, "Nāfiʿ ibn Sarjis ad-Daylamī, the *mawlā* of Ibn ʿUmar, the Madīnan, narrated from his *mawlā* (Ibn ʿUmar) and from Rāfiʿ ibn Khadīj, Abū Hurayrah, ʿĀʾishah, Umm Salamah, and others. From him narrated his sons ʿAbdullāh, Abū Bakr, ʿUmar, and az-Zuhrī, Mūsā ibn ʿUqbah, Abū Ḥanīfah, Mālik, al-Layth and many others." What we know from *ath-Thiqāt* of Ibn Ḥibbān is that Nāfiʿ the *mawlā* of Ibn ʿUmar, was not Ibn Sarjis but someone else, because he said first of all under the letter *nun*, "Nāfiʿ the *mawlā* of Ibn ʿUmar. Ibn ʿUmar gained him [as spoils] in one battle. His kunyā was Abū ʿAbdullāh, but there is disagreement about his lineage and there is nothing sound about it in my view for me to mention. He narrated from Ibn ʿUmar, Abū Saʿīd, and many people narrated from him. He died in 117 AH." Then later he said, "Nāfiʿ ibn Sarjis al-Ḥijāzī the *mawlā* of Banī Sibāʿ whose kunyā is Abū Saʿīd. He narrated from Abū Wāqid al-Laythī. There narrated from him ʿAbdullāh ibn ʿUthmān ibn Khashīm." The author of *al-Mishkāh* mentioned in *Asmāʾ rijāl al-Mishkāh* concerning his lineage the like of what is said in *Jāmiʿ al-uṣūl*, [confusing Ibn Sarjis and the *mawlā* of Ibn ʿUmar] since he said, "Nāfiʿ ibn

Sarjis was Daylamī and one of the great Followers. He heard from Ibn ʿUmar and Abū Saʿīd. Many others narrated from him, among them Mālik and az-Zuhrī." He mentioned in *at-Taqrīb* and *at-Tahdhīb* and in *Tahdhīb at-tahdhīb* and *al-Kāshif,* "Nāfiʿ Abū ʿAbdullāh the Madīnan, the *mawlā* of Ibn ʿUmar, died in 117 AH," without mentioning his lineage.

Nāfiʿ ibn Jubayr ibn Muṭʿim. He was a trustworthy narrator from whom everyone narrated. He died in 99 AH, as az-Zurqānī mentioned.

Nāfiʿ the *mawlā* of Abū Qatādah is either Ibn ʿAbbās or Ibn ʿAyyāsh Abū Muḥammad al-Aqraʿ the Madīnan, and he is a trustworthy narrator, and in reality the *mawlā* of Abū Qatādah, as an-Nasāʾī and al-ʿIjlī mentioned. Ibn Ḥibbān said, "That is said about him because of his attachment to him [Abū Qatādah], and if not then he was the *mawlā* of ʿUqaylah bint Ṭalq of Ghifār," as is found in *Sharḥ az-Zurqānī* .

An-Najāshī was one of the chiefs of the Followers. He accepted Islam but did not emigrate. The Muslims emigrated to him in Abyssinia and he treated them well. The Prophet ﷺ sent ʿAmr ibn Umayyah to him with two letters, the first of which invited him to Islam, and the second of which asked him to marry Umm Ḥabībah to him. He took the letter and placed it upon his eyes and accepted Islam, and he married Umm Ḥabībah to him. ʿAmr ibn al-ʿĀṣ accepted Islam at his hands. That is how it is found in *Ḍiyāʾ as-sārī*. In *Sharḥ al-Qārī* it is stated, "An-Najāshī is a name of the ruler of the Ethiopians (Abyssinians) just as one says Chosroes and Caesar for the kings of Persia and Rome. His name was Aṣḥamah." The Prophet ﷺ informed of his death in Rajab of 9 AH.

Negus. See an-Najāshī.

Nuʿaym ibn ʿAbdullāh al-Mujmir, the *mawlā* of ʿUmar ibn al-Khattāb. He was Abū ʿAbdullāh, the Madīnan, whom Ibn Maʿīn, Abū Ḥātim and others regarded as a trustworthy narrator. Al-Mujmir is an attribute of Nuʿaym because he used to carry the incense burner [*mijmar*] in front of ʿUmar ﷺ when he went out to the prayer during Ramaḍān, as Ibn Ḥibbān said. Ibn Mākūlā said, "He used to fumigate the mosque with incense." He was a trustworthy narrator from the middlemost of the Followers, as found in *at-Taqrīb*. Nuʿaym spent twenty years close to Abū Hurayrah and narrated a great deal from him, as found in as-Samʿānī's *Ansāb.* In *Fatḥ al-bārī* it is stated, "Both he and his father ʿAbdullāh were described as that [*Mujmir*] because both of them used to fumigate the mosque of the Prophet ﷺ with incense. One of the people of knowledge claimed that his father was described as that literally, but he only metaphorically, but there are views about that."

Nuᶜaym ibn Hazzāl. It is said that he was a Companion, but others say not. His son was Yazīd, as Ibn al-Athīr mentioned in *Asad al-ghābah fī maᶜrifat aṣ-ṣaḥābah* and *Jāmiᶜ al-uṣūl.*

Nubayh ibn Wahb, the brother of ᶜAbd ad-Dār, was ibn Wahb ibn ᶜUthmān al-ᶜAbdarī, the brother of Banī ᶜAbd ad-Dār ibn Qusayy the tribe, i.e. he was one of them. He was one of the younger Followers. He died in 126 AH. His shaykh was ᶜUmar ibn ᶜUbaydullāh ibn Muᶜammar ibn ᶜUthmān ibn ᶜAmr ibn Kaᶜb al-Qurayshi, whose grandfather Muᶜammar was a Companion, but who was himself a Follower, as Ibn Ḥibbān mentioned in *ath-Thiqāt,* and as it is similarly found in *Sharḥ az-Zurqānī.* Nubayh ibn Wahb ibn ᶜUthmān ibn Abī Ṭalḥah al-Ḥajabī narrated from Abū Hurayrah, Muḥammad ibn al-Ḥanafiyah and Aban ibn ᶜUthmān. From him narrated his sons ᶜAbd al-Aᶜlā, ᶜAbd al-Jabbār, ᶜAbd al-ᶜAzīz as well as Ayyūb ibn Mūsā, Nāfiᶜ, Ibn Isḥāq and a large body of people. An-Nasā᾽ī and others regarded him as a trustworthy narrator as found in *al-Isᶜāf.*

Nukhaylah is the name of a servant girl of ᶜĀ᾽ishah, as az-Zurqānī said.

An-Nuᶜmān ibn Bashīr al-Anṣārī al-Khazrajī. Both he and his father were Companions. Later he went to live in Shām and then he was appointed amīr of Kūfa. Later he was killed at Ḥimṣ in 65 AH as az-Zurqānī and others said.

Q

Qabīṣah ibn Dhuʾayb ibn Ḥalḥalah al-Khuzāʿī, the Madīnan. He was born in the year of the Opening [of Makkah to Islam] and he narrated from ʿUthmān, Ibn ʿAwf, Ḥudhayfah, Yazīd ibn Thābit, ʿĀʾishah and Umm Salamah. Az-Zuhrī said, "He was one of the people of knowledge of this ummah." He died in Shām in 87 AH, as stated in *Isʿāf al-mubaṭṭaʾ* of as-Suyūṭī. Makḥūl said, "I saw no one more knowledgeable than him in Shām." *Jāmiʿ al-uṣūl.*

Qābūs. Ḥāfiẓ ibn Ḥajar said in *at-Taqrīb,* "Qābūs ibn Abī Ẓabyān al-Janbī, the Kūfan, who has in him some weakness." There is in *al-Ansāb* of as-Samʿānī, "Al-Janbī is by ascription to Janb a number of tribes, but some say to a tribe of Madhḥij, to whom Abū Ẓabyān al-Janbī is ascribed. His personal name is Ḥuṣayn ibn Jundub. He narrated from ʿAlī ﵁ and Ibn Masʿūd. His son was Qābūs ibn Abī Ẓabyān al-Janbī." (Abridged)

Al-Qaʿqaʿ ibn Ḥakīm. He was from Kinānah and was a Madīnan who was a trustworthy narrator. He mentioned him in *al-Kāshif.*

Al-Qāsim ibn Muḥammad ibn Abī Bakr aṣ-Ṣiddīq, the Madīnan. Ibn Saʿd said that he was an eminent trustworthy narrator, a scrupulous faqīh and ʿālim. He died in 106 AH according to the sound position. That is what as-Suyūṭī and others said.

Qatādah ibn Diʿāmah – as al-Fattanī spelt it in *al-Mughnī* – ibn Qatādah ibn ʿAzīz Abu'l-Khattāb as-Sadūsī the blind Baṣran Qurʾānic commentator – he was born blind. He narrated from Anas ﵁, ʿAbdullāh ibn Sarjis ﵁, Saʿīd ibn al-Musayyab and others, and from him narrated Misʿar, Abū ʿAwānah, Hishām ad-Dastawāʾī, Saʿīd ibn Abī ʿArūbah and others. Ibn Sīrīn said, "He had the greatest capacity for memorisation of people." Aḥmad said, "He was knowledgeable of the Qurʾānic commentary [*tafsīr*] and of the disagreements of the people of knowledge," and he described him as having powers of memory and knowledge of fiqh and he went to great lengths in his mention of him. He was one of the most magnificent of the trustworthy narrators, well versed in Arabic and the dialects, the history of the Arabs and their genealogies. He died in the plague in Wāsiṭ in 118 AH, but some say 117 AH. So it is found in the *Tadhkirat al-ḥuffāẓ* by adh-Dhahabī and there is a lengthy and comprehensive biographical note comprising people's praise of him in *Tahdhīb at-tahdhīb* and elsewhere.

Qays ibn Abī Ḥāzim is Abū ʿAbdullāh al-Bajalī, the Kūfan and major Follower. He emigrated to the Prophet ﷺ but missed being a Companion by a single night. He narrated from Abū Bakr, ʿUmar and others. From him narrated Bayān ibn Bishr, Ismāʿīl ibn Abī Khālid and a great number of other people, and they regarded him as a trustworthy narrator. It is said that he he united in himself to have narrated from the ten men promised [the Garden]. He died after or before 90 AH having exceeded a hundred years in age. So it is found in *at-Taqrīb* and *al-Kāshif*. Ibn al-Athīr mentioned in *Jāmiᶜ al-uṣūl* that he narrated from the ten given the good news [of the Garden] except for ᶜAbd ar-Raḥmān ibn ᶜAwf. Ibn ᶜUyaynah said, "There was not in Kūfa anyone who narrated more from the Companions of the Prophet ﷺ than Qays ibn Abī Ḥāzim." Abū Ḥāzim's name was Ḥuṣayn ibn ᶜAwn, but it is also said that it was ᶜAwf ibn al-Ḥārith, and some say ᶜAwf ibn al-Ḥārith of Banī Aslam ibn Aḥmas ibn al-Ghawth ibn Anmār al-Aḥmasī al-Bajalī.

Qays ibn ar-Rabīᶜ al-Asadī – by ascription to Asad. He was a trustworthy narrator whom Shuᶜbah and Sufyān regarded as such. It is narrated of Ibn ᶜUyaynah, "I have not seen in Kūfa anyone better in ḥadīth than him," but Wakīᶜ and others regarded him as weak in ḥadīth. Ibn ᶜAwn said, "The generality of his narrations are straight, and the right position respecting him is that of Shuᶜbah, and there is no harm in him." He died in 107 AH, and people have said other dates, as found in *Tahdhīb at-tahdhīb*.

Qudāmah ibn Maẓᶜūn ibn Ḥabīb ibn Wahb ibn Ḥudhāfah ibn Jumaḥ of Quraysh and Jumaḥ. He was the maternal uncle of ᶜAbdullāh and Ḥafṣah the son and daughter of ᶜUmar ibn al-Khattāb. He emigrated to Abyssinia with his two brothers ᶜUthmān ibn Maẓᶜūn and ᶜAbdullāh ibn Maẓᶜūn, and was then later present at Badr and the rest of the events. He died in 36 AH, as found in *al-Istīᶜāb*.

R

Rabīʿah ibn ʿAbdullāh ibn al-Hudayr at-Taymī, the Madīnan. He narrated from ʿUmar, Ṭalḥah, Abū Saʿīd al-Khudrī, and from him narrated his brother's two sons Muḥammad and Abū Bakr – both sons of al-Munkadir ibn ʿAbdullāh – and Ibn Abī Mulaykah. Ibn Ḥibbān mentioned him in *ath-Thiqāt*. Ibn Saʿd said, "He was born at the time of the Messenger of Allah ﷺ and he was a trustworthy narrator who narrated few ḥadīth." Al-ʿIjlī said, "A Madīnan Follower who was a trustworthy narrator. He died in 93 AH." So it is found in *Tahdhīb at-tahdhīb*.

Rabīʿah ar-Raʾy – the shaykh of Mālik – ibn Abī ʿAbd ar-Raḥmān Farrūkh at-Taymī Abū ʿUthmān, but some say Abū ʿAbd ar-Raḥmān, a pre-eminent Follower, one of the fuqahāʾ of Madīnah. He heard from Anas ibn Mālik and as-Sāʾib ibn Yazīd. Ath-Thawri and Mālik narrated from him. He was Madīnan, a faqīh and one of the notables. Aḥmad said he was a trustworthy narrator, and Yaʿqūb ibn Shaybah said that he was a firmly established trustworthy narrator. He died in 136 AH, as stated in *Isʿāf al-mubaṭṭaʾ* of as-Suyūṭī.

Ar-Rabīʿ ibn Ṣabīḥ as-Saʿdī al-Baṣrī was an utterly truthful man who had a bad memory. He was a devout worshipper and a mujāhid. Ar-Rāmahurmuzī said, "He was the first person in Baṣra to compile a book." He died in 160 AH. So it is found in *at-Taqrīb*. He mentioned in *Tahdhīb at-tahdhīb* that he narrated from al-Ḥasan al-Baṣrī, Ḥumayd aṭ-Ṭawīl, Yazīd ar-Raqāshī, Abu'z-Zubayr, Abū Ghālib and others. From him narrated ath-Thawrī, Ibn al-Mubārak, Wakīʿ and others. Al-ʿIjlī and Ibn ʿAdī said there is no harm in him.

Rāfiʿ ibn Khadīj was a well known Companion who was present at Uḥud and everything after it. He died at the beginning of 74 AH, as as-Suyūṭī mentioned.

Rajāʾ ibn Ḥaywah. He said in *at-Taqrīb*, "Rajāʾ ibn Ḥaywah al-Kindī al-Filisṭīnī was a trustworthy narrator and a faqīh. He died in 112 AH."

S

Aṣ-Ṣaᶜb ibn Jaththāmah ibn Qays ibn Rabīᶜah al-Laythī was one of the major Companions and he died during the khilāfah of ᶜUthmān according to the most correct view.

Ṣadaqah ibn Yasār. ᶜAbdullāh ibn Aḥmad said [narrating] from his father, "He is one of the trustworthy narrators." Ibn Maᶜīn said he was a trustworthy narrator, and Abū Ḥātim said that he was a right-acting person. Al-Ājurrī said [narrating] from Abū Dāwūd, "He was a trustworthy narrator." I asked, "One of the people of Makkah?" He said, "One of the people of al-Jazīrah who resided in Makkah." So it is found in *Tahdhīb at-tahdhīb.*

Saᶜd ibn Abī Waqqāṣ Mālik ibn Wahb ibn ᶜAbd Manāf ibn Zuhrah ibn Kilāb az-Zuhrī Abū Isḥāq was one of the ten who were promised the Garden, and whose merits are numerous and who was the last of the ten to die, dying, according to the most well know position, in 55 AH. So it is found in *Taqrīb at-tahdhīb.*

Saᶜd ibn Isḥāq ibn Kaᶜb ibn ᶜUjrah. As-Suyūṭī said in *al-Isᶜāf,* "Saᶜd ibn Isḥāq ibn Kaᶜb ibn ᶜUjrah al-Quḍāᶜī, the Madīnan was an ally of the Anṣār. Ibn Maᶜīn, an-Nasā᾿ī and others regarded him as a trustworthy narrator. He died after 140 AH. His aunt was Zaynab bint Kaᶜb, the wife of Abū Saᶜīd al-Khudrī, whom Ibn Ḥibbān regarded as a trustworthy narrator.

Ṣafiyyah is the Umm al-Mu᾿minin Ṣafiyyah bint Ḥuyayy ibn Akhṭab ibn Saᶜyah of the Children of Isrā᾿īl of the tribe of Hārūn ibn ᶜImrān the brother of Mūsā. Her husband, Kinānah, was killed in the battle of Khaybar when the Messenger of Allah ﷺ opened it [to Islam] in 7 AH. She fell among the captives and the Messenger of Allah ﷺ chose her for himself. She accepted Islam and he freed and married her. She[10] died in 52 AH, but some say other things, as Ibn al-Athīr mentioned.

Ṣafiyyah bint Abī ᶜUbayd the wife of ᶜAbdullāh ibn ᶜUmar whom he married in the lifetime of her father, and ᶜUmar gave her a dowry on his behalf of four hundred dirhams. She bore him Wāqid, Abū Bakr, Abū ᶜUbaydah, ᶜUbaydullāh, ᶜUmar, Ḥafṣah and Sawdah. Ibn Mandah said, "She reached [to meet] the Prophet ﷺ but did not hear anything from him." But ad-Dāraquṭnī rejected that. Al-ᶜIjlī and Ibn Ḥibbān mentioned her as one of the trustworthy narrators of the Followers. So says az-Zurqānī.

Ṣafwān ibn ᶜAbdullāh ibn Ṣafwān ibn Umayyah al-Jumaḥī, the Makkan who was one of the Followers. Al-ᶜIjlī said he was a trustworthy narrator.

His grandfather Ṣafwān was the man of the story [in ḥadīth 684]. He died during the days in which ᶜUthmān was killed, as stated in *Isᶜāf al-mubaṭṭa'* of as-Suyūṭī and in *at-Taqrīb*.

Ṣafwān ibn Umayyah was the grandfather of Ṣafwān ibn ᶜAbdullāh. He was ibn Umayyah ibn Khalf ibn Wahb ibn Qudāmah ibn Jumaḥ of Quraysh, the Companion, who was one of those whose hearts were reconciled to Islam.

Sahl ibn ᶜAbbās at-Tirmidhī by ascription to Tirmidh or Turmidh or Tarmidh, but the former is the well known [version], a city near to Balkh as as-Samᶜānī said. Adh-Dhahabī said in *Mīzān al-iᶜtidāl,* "Ad-Dāraquṭnī abandoned [narrating from] him, and he said, 'He is not a trustworthy narrator.'"

Sahl ibn Abī Ḥathmah is Abū ᶜAbd ar-Raḥmān, but some say Abū Yaḥyā, Sahl ibn Abī Ḥathmah al-Anṣārī, the Madīnan. The name of Abū Ḥathmah was ᶜAbdullāh, but some say ᶜĀmir, ibn Sāᶜidah ibn ᶜĀmir ibn ᶜAdī, a younger Companion who pledged allegiance under the tree [at al-Ḥudaybiyah] and who was present at all the battles except for Badr, as Ibn Abī Ḥātim said. Ibn al-Qaṭṭān said, "This is not correct." Ibn Ḥibbān, al-Wāqidī, Abū Jaᶜfar aṭ-Ṭabarī, Ibn as-Sakan, al-Ḥākim and others said that he was a boy of eight when the Prophet ﷺ died. Adh-Dhahabī mentioned that he died in the khilāfah of Muᶜāwiyah, as stated in *Tahdhīb at-tahdhīb, Taqrīb at-tahdhīb, Jāmiᶜ al-uṣūl* and elsewhere.

Sahl ibn Saᶜd as-Sā'idī – by ascription to Sāᶜidah ibn Kaᶜb ibn al-Khazraj, a tribe of the Anṣār which as-Suyūṭī mentions in *Lubb al-lubāb fi taḥrīr al-ansāb*. He was the last of the Companions to die in Madīnah. He died in 88 AH, but some say 91 AH, as stated in *Isᶜāf al-mubaṭṭa'* of as-Suyūṭī.

Saᶜīd ibn Abī ᶜArūbah – whose name was Mihrān [i.e. Abū ᶜArūbah's] – al-ᶜAdawī being a *mawlā* of Banī ᶜAdī ibn Yashkur, Abu'n-Naḍr, the Baṣran. Ibn Maᶜīn, an-Nasā'ī and Abū Zurᶜah said he was a trustworthy narrator, and Ibn Abī Khaythamah said, "The most firmly established of people in [narrating from] Qatādah were Saᶜīd ibn Abī ᶜArūbah and Hishām ad-Dastawā'ī." Abū Dāwūd aṭ-Ṭayālisī said, "He was the one who memorised most from among the companions of Qatādah." Abū Ḥātim said, "He was, before he confused things, a trustworthy narrator." Ibn Ḥibbān mentioned him in *ath-Thiqāt,* and he said that he died in 155 AH, and that he remained in a state wherein he mixed things up for five years. So it is found in *Tahdhīb at-tahdhīb*.

Saᶜīd – some say that he was Saᶜd – ibn ᶜAmr ibn Sulaym az-Zuraqī al-Anṣārī. Ibn Maᶜīn and Ibn Ḥibbān regarded him as a trustworthy narrator.

He died in 134 AH. Ibn ᶜAbd al-Barr said, "He has no other ḥadīth than this one [564] in the *Muwaṭṭaʾ*," as az-Zurqānī and al-Qārī said.

Saᶜīd ibn Hishām. So we find it in the copies we have. What is in *Tahdhīb al-kamāl* and its *Tahdhīb* and in its *Taqrīb* and its *Tadhhib* and in *al-Kāshif*, the *Jāmiᶜ al-uṣūl* and in the book *ath-Thiqāt* by Ibn Ḥibbān is that his name was Saᶜd ibn Hishām ibn ᶜĀmir al-Anṣārī, the Madīnan, the son of Anas' paternal uncle. He narrated from his father, ᶜĀʾishah, Ibn ᶜAbbās, Samurah, Anas and others, and from him narrated Zurārah and al-Ḥasan al-Baṣrī. An-Nasāʾī and Ibn Saᶜd declared him to be a trustworthy narrator. He became a shahīd at Mukrān, a place in India. So it is found in the book *al-Ḥujjaj.*

Saᶜīd ibn Jubayr is Abū ᶜAbdullāh the Kūfan and one of the noted imāms. When the people of Kūfa used to come to Ibn ᶜAbbās to ask for fatwās he would say, "Is Saᶜīd ibn Jubayr not among you?" Al-Ḥajjāj killed him in Shaᶜbān 95 AH, as stated in *Isᶜāf al-mubaṭṭaʾ* of as-Suyūṭī.

Saᶜīd ibn al-Musayyab is Abū Muḥammad al-Makhzūmī of Quraysh the Madīnan, and one of the chiefs of the Followers. Makḥūl said, "I went around the whole land but I didn't meet anyone more knowledgeable than Ibn al-Musayyab." He was born two years into the khilāfah of ᶜUmar and died in 93 AH. That is how the author of *al-Mishkāh* mentioned him in *Asmāʾ rijāl al-mishkāh.* He was the lord of the fuqahāʾ of the Followers. Qatādah said, "I saw no one more knowledgeable of the ḥalāl and the ḥarām than him." So it is found in *Isᶜāf al-mubaṭṭaʾ* of as-Suyūṭī.

Saᶜīd ibn Sulaymān ibn Zayd ibn Thābit. He was one of the narrators whom everyone used and one of the trustworthy narrators, as az-Zurqānī said.

Saᶜīd [207] is ibn Yasār, the Madīnan Follower who was a trustworthy narrator. He died in 117 AH, but some say a year before that. Everyone narrates from him as found in the *Sharḥ* of az-Zurqānī .

Saᶜīd al-Jārī ibn al-Jār. So it is found in many copies, and in the *Muwaṭṭaʾ* of Yaḥyā it is from Saᶜīd al-Jārī the *mawlā* of ᶜUmar ibn al-Khattāb. As-Samᶜānī mentioned about his name that it was Saᶜd without a *yā* [i.e. not Saᶜīd] when he said that al-Jārī is by ascription to al-Jār which is an area on the coast near to the Madīnah of the Prophet ﷺ, and the one ascribed to it is Saᶜd ibn Nawfal al-Jārī who was ᶜUmar's governor. He narrated from Abū Hurayrah and ᶜAbdullāh ibn ᶜUmar and from him narrated Zayd ibn Aslam." Ibn al-Athīr named him similarly in *Jāmiᶜ al-uṣūl.*

Saᶜīd al-Maqburī or al-Maqbarī. He used to reside near a graveyard [*maqbarah*] and was thus ascribed to it [in his name]. He mixed things up four years before his death, and Mālik and the like of him had heard from him before that, says az-Zurqānī . His name was Saʿīd ibn Abī Saʿīd Kaysān, the Madīnan. They agree that he is a trustworthy narrator. He died in 123 AH. So it is found in *Isʿāf al-mubaṭṭaʾ* of as-Suyūṭī. He was Saʿīd Abū Saʿīd, and he was a Madīnan who was a trustworthy narrator. He died at the end of the twenties [after the first century] or a little before it, as stated in *at-Taqrīb*. For his father [ḥadīth 310] see Kaysān ibn Saʿīd al-Maqburī.

Saʿīd ar-Raqāshī by ascription to Raqāsh the name of a woman who had so many children that they became a tribe, and she was the daughter of Sabīʿah ibn Qays ibn Thaʿlabah. As-Samʿānī and Ibn al-Athīr mentioned him. This Saʿīd is probably Saʿīd ibn ʿAbd ar-Raḥmān ar-Raqāshī whom adh-Dhahabī mentioned in *Mīzān al-iʿtidāl* and said, "Yaḥyā ibn al-Qaṭṭān regarded him as soft, but a group regard him as a trustworthy narrator. Ibn ʿAdī said, 'Ibn al-Qaṭṭān hesitated over him, but I see no harm in him.' It is narrated of Ibn Sīrīn that ʿUmar ibn al-Khattāb said, 'Have taqwā of Allah and have taqwā [be wary] of people.'" I myself [Shaykh ʿAbd al-Ḥayy] think that this is a mistake from the copyists, for I found this exact same narration in the Book of Ḥajj in which is, "Muḥammad [said], 'Ar-Rabīʿ ibn Ṣabīḥ al-Baṣrī informed us from Yazīd ar-Raqāshī [see his entry] from Anas and from al-Ḥasan al-Baṣrī both of whom ascribed it directly [to the Prophet ﷺ]...'"

Salamah ibn Ṣafwān ibn Salamah az-Zuraqī – by ascription to Banī Zurayq – was a trustworthy Madīnan narrator.

Ṣāliḥ ibn Abī Ṣāliḥ Nabhān al-Madīnī. He narrated from Ibn ʿAbbās, ʿĀʾishah, Abū Hurayrah and others. From him narrated Ibn Abī Dhiʾb, Ibn Jurayj, the two Sufyāns and others. Bishr ibn ʿUmar said, "I asked Mālik about him and he said, 'He is not trustworthy.'" Aḥmad ibn Ḥanbal said, "It is as if Mālik reached him when he became confused and mixed things up. Those who heard from him before that, then that [is acceptable]. The great ones of the people of Madīnah narrated from him and his ḥadīth are fine, and I know nothing bad about him." Aḥmad ibn Saʿīd ibn Abī Maryam said, "I heard Ibn Maʿīn saying, 'Ṣāliḥ the *mawlā* of at-Tawʾamah (the twin) is trustworthy and a decisive argument.' I said, 'Mālik gave up listening to him.' He answered, 'Mālik only reached him after he had aged and was in his dotage.'" Al-Jūzajānī said, "He changed later in life, but the ḥadīth of Ibn Abī Dhiʾb from him are acceptable because he listened to him of old, but ath-Thawrī listened to him after he had altered." Ibn ʿAdī said, "There is no harm in him, when the older ones narrate from him such as Ibn Abī Dhiʾb,

Ibn Jurayj and Ziyād ibn Saᶜd." Al-ᶜIjlī said, "A Follower who is trustworthy." He died in 125 AH. So it is found in *Tahdhīb at-tahdhīb*.

Ṣāliḥ ibn Kaysān. He was the Madīnan *mawlā* of Ghifār, whom Aḥmad and Ibn Maᶜīn regarded as a trustworthy narrator. He died after 140 AH, as stated in *al-Isᶜāf*.

Sālim Abu'n-Naḍr, the Madīnan. See him under Abu'n-Naḍr.

Sālim ibn ᶜAbdullāh Ibn ᶜUmar Abū ᶜAmr or Abū ᶜAbdullāh was Madīnan and a faqīh. Mālik said, "No one in his time more resembled those who had passed away of the right-acting people in terms of doing-without [*zuhd*] and merit, than he did." Aḥmad ibn Ḥanbal and Isḥāq ibn Rāhwayh said, "The soundest chain of transmission is Ibn Shihāb az-Zuhrī from Sālim from his father." Al-ᶜIjlī said, "A Madīnan Follower who was trustworthy, he died in 106 AH according to the soundest view." His father was ᶜAbdullāh ibn ᶜUmar ibn al-Khattāb.

Sallām ibn Sulaym al-Ḥanafī by ascription to the tribe of Banī Ḥanīfah. As-Samᶜānī said in *al-Ansāb*, "Ḥanafī by ascription to Banī Ḥanīfah, a people the majority of whom resided in al-Yamāmah and who had followed Musaylimah the Liar who claimed to be a prophet. Then later they accepted Islam in the time of Abū Bakr. It is well known that a large body of people are ascribed to them." It is found in *Tahdhīb at-tahdhīb*, "Sallām ibn Sulaym al-Ḥanafī their *mawlā* Abu'l-Aḥwaṣ the Kūfan narrated from Abū Isḥāq as-Sabīᶜī, Sammāk ibn Ḥarb, Ziyād ibn ᶜAlāqah, al-Aswad ibn Qays, Manṣūr and others. From him narrated Wakīᶜ, Ibn Mahdī, Abū Nuᶜaym, Saᶜīd ibn Manṣūr and others. Al-ᶜIjlī said, 'He was trustworthy, a person of the Sunnah and following.' Abū Zurᶜah and an-Nasā'ī said, 'Trustworthy.' Ibn Ḥibbān mentioned him in *ath-Thiqāt*. Al-Bukhārī said, 'ᶜAbdullāh ibn Abi'l-Aswad narrated to me saying, "He died in 79" meaning after the century [179 AH].'" (Abridged) It is stated in al-Fattanī's *Mughni*, "Sallām: everyone [with that name] is with a doubled [lam] except for ᶜAbdullāh ibn Salām [the Companion], and Abū ᶜAbdullāh Muḥammad ibn Salām the shaykh of al-Bukhārī, but a group of people spell it with a doubling [of the lam]. Apart from in the two *ṣaḥīḥ* books there are another three: Salām ibn Muḥammad, Muḥammad ibn ᶜAbd al-Wahhāb ibn Salām and Salām ibn Abi'l-Ḥaqīq." There is also in it, "Sulaym [with the letters sīn, lām, yā, mīm]: everyone [with that name] has it spelled with *ḍamm* ['u' on the first letter] except for Salīm ibn Ḥayyān." I saw in the *Sharḥ al-Qārī* that he explains the ascription of him being Ḥanafī as his saying, "He is ascribed to Abū Ḥanīfah, with omission of the extra letters [the yā and tā marbūṭah] as in the case of *al-faraḍi* [as an adjective from *farīḍah*]."And this is an obvious mistake, and it is thought that it originates from one of the transcribers of his book and not from him.

Shaqīq ibn Salamah ibn Wā'il, al-Asadī by ascription to Asad, the name of a number of tribes.

Ash-Sharīd ibn Suwayd ath-Thaqafī was a Companion who was present at the pledge of allegiance of Riḍwān.

Sharīk ibn ᶜAbdullāh ibn Abī Numayr, Abū ᶜAbdullāh, the Madīnan. Ibn Saᶜd and Abū Dāwūd regarded him as a trustworthy narrator. Ibn Maᶜīn and an-Nasā'ī said that there is no harm in him. Ibn ᶜAdī said, "When a trustworthy narrator narrates from him there is no harm in him. That is how it is in *Hady as-sārī* the introduction to *Fatḥ al-bārī* by al-Ḥāfiẓ Ibn Ḥajar. In Yaḥyā's copy it is Abū Namīr and the spelling is according to az-Zurqānī .

Shaykh Abū ᶜAlī [118] the author's shaykh. I [Shaykh ᶜAbd al-Ḥayy] have not yet come across biographical material on him [or Maḥmūd ibn Muḥammad al-Marwazī] so that it can be known whether they are trustworthy narrators or weak narrators, may Allah graciously bestow the discovery of that upon me.[11]

Ash-Shifā' was Bint ᶜAbdullāh ibn ᶜAbd Shams ibn Khālid of Quraysh al-ᶜAdawiyyah and one of the women who pledged allegiance. Aḥmad ibn Ṣāliḥ said, "Her name was Laylā but ash-Shifā' was used more often," as found in *al-Istiᶜāb.*

Shuᶜbah ibn al-Ḥajjāj ibn al-Ward al-ᶜItkī – their *mawlā* – Abū Bisṭām of Wāsiṭ and Baṣra. He was a trustworthy narrator and a thorough ḥāfiẓ. Ath-Thawrī used to say, "He is the Amīr al-Mu'minīn in ḥadīth." He died in 120 AH. His shaykh was al-Ḥakam ibn ᶜUtbah according to the copies of this book or ᶜUtaybah according to the Ḥāfiẓ in *at-Taqrīb* and he was a firmly established trustworthy narrator who was one of the greatest companions of an-Nakhaᶜī.

Shurayḥ is Ibn al-Ḥārith ibn Qays the qāḍī Abū Umayyah al-Kindī, the Kūfan. [ḥadīth 575]. It is said that it is Shurayḥ ibn Sharaḥbīl one of the trustworthy narrators of the eminent men who had lived in both the Jāhiliyyah and Islam. ᶜUmar made him the qāḍī of Kūfa and then later ᶜAlī. Then after him he withdrew from the post of qāḍī a year before his death in the time of al-Ḥajjāj. He lived for 120 years, and died in 78 AH, but some say 80 AH. Ibn Maᶜīn and others regarded him as a trustworthy narrator, as found in *Tadhkirat al-ḥuffāẓ* of adh-Dhahabī.

Ṣilah ibn Zufar was Abu'l-ᶜAlā᾽ al-ᶜAbsī the Kūfan who narrated from ᶜAmmār, Ḥudhayfah, Ibn Masᶜūd, ᶜAlī and Ibn ᶜAbbās, and from whom narrated Abū Wā᾽il, Abū Isḥāq as-Sabīᶜī, Ayyūb as-Sakhtiyānī and others. Al-Khaṭīb, Ibn Kharrāsh and Ibn Ḥibbān said that he was a trustworthy narrator, and similarly it is narrated of Ibn Maᶜīn, al-ᶜIjlī and Ibn Numayr. He died during the khilāfah of Musᶜab ibn az-Zubayr, as found in *Tahdhīb at-tahdhīb*.

A son of Saᶜd ibn Abī Waqqāṣ [ḥadīth 126]. Ibn ᶜAbd al-Barr said in *al-Istidhkār*, "This ḥadīth is interrupted and is not sound."

Sufyān ibn ᶜUyaynah is the ḥāfiẓ and Shaykh al-Islām, Abū Muḥammad Sufyān ibn Abī Zuhayr. Ibn al-Madīnī and Khalīfah said, "The name of his father was al-Fard, but some say it was Numayr ibn ᶜAbdullāh ibn Mālik, and he is called an-Numayrī because he was one of the children of an-Nimr ibn ᶜUthmān ibn Naṣr ibn Zahrān who came to reside in Madīnah, and he was a man from Azd, Shanū᾽ah ibn al-Ghawth ibn Nabt ibn Mālik ibn Zayd ibn Kahlān ibn Sabā᾽ the well known tribe, as az-Zurqānī mentioned.

Sufyān ibn ᶜUyaynah al-Hilālī, the Kūfan, the ḥadīth scholar of the Ḥaram in Makkah. He was born in 107 AH, and heard from az-Zuhrī, Zayd ibn Aslam, Manṣūr ibn al-Muᶜtamir and others. From him narrated al-Aᶜmash, Shuᶜbah, Ibn Jurayj, Ibn al-Mubārak, ash-Shāfiᶜī, Aḥmad, Yaḥyā ibn Maᶜīn, Isḥāq ibn Rāhwayh and innumerable others. Adh-Dhahabī said in *Tadhkirat al-ḥuffāẓ*, "He was an imām, a decisive proof, a ḥāfiẓ, with vast knowledge and a great rank. Ash-Shāfiᶜī said, 'If it had not been for Mālik and Sufyān the knowledge of the Ḥijāz would have gone.' Al-ᶜIjlī said, 'He was firmly established in ḥadīth.' Ibn Maᶜīn said, 'He was the most firmly established in [narrating from] ᶜAmr ibn Dīnār, and the imāms agree on using him as a decisive proof.' He performed the Ḥajj seventy times, and died in 198 AH." (Abridged)

Sufyān ath-Thawrī is Abū ᶜAbdullāh Sufyān ibn Saᶜīd ibn Masrūq ath-Thawrī, the Kūfan by ascription to Thawr – ibn ᶜAbd Manāt ibn Add ibn Ṭānijah, a tribe. He narrated from many people and in turn many narrated from him as al-Mizzī explained in detail in *Tahdhīb al-kamāl*. He mentioned in his biographical note that, "Shuᶜbah, Ibn ᶜUyaynah, Abū ᶜĀṣim and Ibn Maᶜīn all said that he was the Amīr al-Mu᾽minīn in ḥadīth. Ibn al-Mubārak said, 'I wrote down [ḥadīth] from one thousand one hundred shaykhs. I did not write down from anyone better than Sufyān.' Shuᶜbah said, 'Sufyān has a better memory than me.' Ibn Mahdī said, 'Wahb used to prefer Sufyān over Mālik for his memorisation.' Ad-Dūrī said, 'I saw that Yaḥyā ibn Maᶜīn did not prefer anyone over Sufyān in his age with respect to fiqh, ḥadīth, doing without or anything.' He was born in 97 AH, and died in Baṣra in 161 AH." (Abridged.)

Suhayl ibn Abī Ṣāliḥ. Ibn Suhayl ibn Abī Ṣāliḥ is how we find it in one of the copies, but in some others it is Suhayl ibn Abī Ṣāliḥ, and in two corrected copies it is Ibn Abī Ṣāliḥ, and this is the correct position which agrees with the narration of "Yaḥyā from Mālik from Suhayl ibn Abī Ṣāliḥ from his father…" Perhaps the "ibn" in addition to the name Suhayl in the first copy is one of the additions of the copyist, because this narration is from Suhayl ibn Abī Ṣāliḥ and not from his son nor is it to Suhayl ibn Abī Ṣāliḥ ibn Abī Ṣāliḥ. He is Suhayl ibn Abī Ṣāliḥ Abū Yazīd, the Madīnan whom Ibn Ḥibbān mentioned in *ath-Thiqāt*. Ibn Saᶜd said, "He was a trustworthy narrator who had many ḥadīth." Al-Ḥākim said, "One of the pillars of ḥadīth from whom Muslim narrated a great deal concerning fundamental principles and also as confirmatory material for other ḥadīth. Mālik narrated from him, and he [Mālik] is the judge concerning the shaykhs of Madīnah, the discriminatory person who can discriminate gold from false gold. Ibn Qāniᶜ dated his death as 138 AH. His father was Abū Ṣāliḥ Dhakwān as-Sammān az-Ziyat, the Madīnan.

Sulaymān ibn Abī Ḥathmah. Ibn Ḥibbān said, "He was a Companion and one of the eminent Muslims and their people of right action. ᶜUmar put him in charge of the market, and made people follow him as imām in the standing [in *tarāwīḥ*] in Ramaḍān, as az-Zurqānī mentioned."

Sulaymān ibn Yasār is one of the notables. An-Nasāʾī said, "He was one of the imāms." Abū Zurᶜah said, "An eminent and trusted trustworthy narrator." He died in 107 AH. So it is found in *Isᶜāf al-mubaṭṭaʾ* of as-Suyūṭī. Az-Zuhri said, "He was one of the ᶜulamāʾ." Az-Zuhri said, "He was a well trusted and trustworthy narrator. He died in 107 AH."

Summayy [ḥadīth 976] the *mawlā* of Abū Bakr ibn ᶜAbd ar-Raḥmān ibn al-Ḥārith ibn Hishām.

Suwayd ibn Nuᶜmān ibn Mālik ibn ᶜĀʾid ibn Majdaᶜah ibn Ḥashm ibn Ḥārithah al-Anṣārī al-Awsī. He was present at the [pledge of] Riḍwān, and some say at Uḥud and the events after it. He is counted as one of the people of Madīnah and his ḥadīth are counted as theirs. So it is found in *Jāmiᶜ al-uṣūl.*

T

At-Taw'amah is Bint Umayyah ibn Khalf the Madīnan, the sister of Rabīʿah ibn Umayyah ibn Khalf. She had a twin sister in the womb and so for that reason she is called at-Taw'amah (the twin), and Ṣāliḥ Nabhān al-Madīnī is ascribed to her. That is what Abū Saʿd as-Samʿānī said in the book *al-Ansāb*.

Ṭalḥah ibn ʿAbd al-Mālik al-Aylī. Abū Dāwūd, an-Nasā'ī and a group regarded him as a trustworthy narrator, as found in *Isʿāf al-mubaṭṭa'* of as-Suyūṭī.

Ṭalḥah ibn ʿAbdullāh ibn ʿAwf was the nephew of ʿAbd ar-Raḥmān ibn ʿAwf and he was a trustworthy narrator who narrated a great deal, and a faqīh and Follower. He died in 97 AH.

Ṭalḥah ibn ʿAmr ibn ʿUthmān al-Ḥaḍramī the Makkan is spoken about [critically]. He said in *Tahdhīb at-tahdhīb,* "He narrated from ʿAṭā' ibn Abī Rabāḥ, Muḥammad ibn ʿAmr ibn ʿAlqamah, Ibn az-Zubayr, Saʿīd ibn Jubayr and others. Those who narrated from him include Jarīr ibn Ḥāzim, ath-Thawrī, Abū Dāwūd aṭ-Ṭayālisī, Wakīʿ and others. Aḥmad said, 'Nothing, and his ḥadīth are to be abandoned.' Ibn Maʿīn said, 'He is nothing, weak.' Al-Jūzajānī said, 'Unacceptable in his ḥadīth, but Ibn ʿAdī narrated some of his ḥadīth.' He said, 'Trustworthy people narrated from him but in people in general of what he narrates he is not followed.' ʿAbd ar-Razzāq said, 'I heard Muʿammar saying, "I, Shuʿbah, ath-Thawrī and Ibn Jarīr gathered together and a shaykh came to us and dictated four thousand ḥadīth to us from memory, without making a mistake except in two places while we were looking at the book. The mistake was not from us nor from him, but it was only from a higher narrator. The man was Ṭalḥah ibn ʿAmr.'" (Abridged) This weakness does not harm him in the basic matter intended, because ʿIkrimah ibn ʿAmmār followed him in his narration from ʿAṭā', and Saʿīd ibn Jubayr followed ʿAṭā' in the narration of aṭ-Ṭaḥāwī.

Ṭalḥah ibn ʿUbaydullāh was one of the ten given the good news [of the Garden]. He was Ṭalḥah ibn ʿUbaydullāh ibn ʿUthmān ibn ʿAmr of Quraysh and Taym. He was one of the first forerunners who were present at Uḥud and everything after it. It is narrated of him that he said, "The Messenger of Allah ﷺ named me on the day of Uḥud, Ṭalḥah al-Khayr [the good], and on the day of Difficulty, Ṭalḥah al-Fayyāḍ [the overflowing], and on the day of Ḥunayn Ṭalḥah al-Jawwādd [the liberally generous]." He was a shahīd in the battle of the Camel in 36 AH, and has many virtues which Ibn al-Athīr mentioned in *Asad al-ghābah fi maʿrifat aṣ-ṣaḥābah.*

Ṭāwūs was Ibn Kaysān al-Yamānī, and some say that his name was Dhakwān and that Ṭāwūs (Peacock) was his honorific. He was a Follower who was a trustworthy narrator, and he died in 106 AH, but some say after that, as az-Zurqānī mentioned.

Thābit ibn Ḍaḥḥāk ibn Khalīfah al-Anṣārī al-Ashbīlī is the well known Companion. He died in 64 AH according to the correct position, as stated in *al-Iṣābah* and elsewhere.

Thābit ibn Qays ibn Shammās al-Anṣārī was one of the notables of the Anṣār who was present at Uḥud and those battles after it. He was the Imām Khaṭīb [who gave the khuṭbah] of the Anṣār, and was a shahīd on the Day of al-Yamāmah in 12 AH, as found in *Jāmi*ᶜ *al-uṣūl*.

Thaᶜlabah ibn Abī Mālik al-Quraẓī. There is disagreement as to whether or not he was a Companion. Ibn Maᶜīn said, "He saw [the Prophet ﷺ]." Ibn Saᶜd said, "His father – Abū Mālik whose name was ᶜAbdullāh ibn Sām – came from the Yemen and he was from [the tribe of] Kindah. He married a woman of Qurayẓah and was known as [al-Quraẓī because of] them," as az-Zurqānī mentioned.

Thawr ibn Yazīd ibn Ziyād al-Kilāᶜī – and it is said he was ar-Rajabī – Abū Khālid al-Ḥimṣī. He narrated from Makḥūl, Rajāʾ ibn Ḥaywah, ᶜAṭāʾ, ᶜIkrimah and others, and from him narrated the two Sufyāns, Mālik and others. Ibn Saᶜd, Aḥmad ibn Ṣāliḥ, Duḥaym, Yaḥyā ibn Saᶜīd, Wakīᶜ and others regarded him as a trustworthy narrator. He died in 55 AH, as found in *Tahdhīb at-tahdhīb*.

Thawr ibn Zayd ad-Dīlī – their *mawlā* – the Madīnan. Ibn Maᶜīn, Abū Zurᶜah and an-Nasāʾī regarded him as a trustworthy narrator. He died in 135 AH, as stated in *Isᶜāf al-mubaṭṭaʾ* of as-Suyūṭī.

Aṭ-Ṭufayl ibn Ubayy ibn Kaᶜb al-Anṣārī al-Khazrajī was one of the trustworthy narrators of the Followers. It is said that he was born in the time of the Prophet ﷺ, and that his ḥadīth are precious. His kunyā was Abū Baṭn as Ibn al-Athīr mentioned in *Jāmi*ᶜ *al-uṣūl*.

U

ᶜUbādah ibn aṣ-Ṣāmit is Abu'l-Walīd al-Anṣārī al-Khazrajī, one of the chiefs who was present at both of [the pledges of allegiances at] al-ᶜAqabah, and who was present at Badr, Uḥud, the pledge of allegiance called Riḍwān, and all of the major events and battles. He died in Shām in the khilāfah of Muᶜāwiyah, as stated in *al-Iṣābah* and elsewhere.

ᶜUbādah ibn Tamīm from his uncle ᶜUtbah. This is found in many copies [in ḥadīth 970], but what is in the *Muwaṭṭa᾿* of Yaḥyā is, "Mālik from ᶜAbbād ibn Tamīm al-Māzinī [see his entry] from his paternal uncle…" and this is how al-Bukhārī narrated it in the chapters on mosques, the chapters on clothing, and the chapters on seeking permission to enter, and Muslim in the chapters on clothing, Abū Dāwūd in [the chapters on] courtesy, at-Tirmidhī in seeking permission, and he said that it is good and *ṣaḥīḥ,* and an-Nasā᾿ī in *ṣalāh,* all of them by way of Mālik. At-Tirmidhī stated that the paternal uncle of ᶜAbbād ibn Tamīm al-Māzinī was ᶜAbdullāh ibn Zayd al-Māzinī [see his entry], as do the commentators of *Ṣaḥīḥ al-Bukhārī,* Ibn Ḥajar in *Fatḥ al-Bārī,* al-ᶜAynī in *ᶜUmdat al-qārī,* al-Kirmānī in *al-Kawākib ad-darārī,* and al-Qasṭallānīī in *Irshād as-sārī.* They also mention that ᶜAbbād is spelt thus, and ᶜAbdullāh ibn Zayd, his paternal uncle, is the brother of his mother's father, and we have previously mentioned both of them.

ᶜUbayd [in ḥadīth 28] is probably the father of Ḥabīb or someone else. There are in the book *Thiqāt at-tābiᶜīn* by Ibn Ḥibbān many Kūfans and people of Shām whose names were ᶜUbayd, but to this day I don't know specifically who he is, and perhaps Allah will uncover some new information for me. This [Ḥabīb narrating from ᶜUbayd] is what we have found in some copies but I do not think it is sound, and I think what is sound is that which is in some dependable copies, that it is from Ḥabīb ibn ᶜUbayd, so that the narrator from Abu'd-Dardā᾿ is Ḥabīb without any intermediary.

ᶜUbayd ibn Fayrūz. As-Suyūṭī mentions that he was Abu'ḍ-Ḍaḥḥāk, the Kūfan, whom an-Nasā᾿ī and Abū Ḥātim considered a trustworthy narrator. Ibn ᶜAbd al-Barr said, "The narrators from Mālik do not differ over this ḥadīth [632]. Only ᶜAmr narrates from Sulaymān ibn ᶜAbd ar-Raḥmān who narrates it from ᶜUbayd leaving out Mālik's mention of Sulaymān. The ḥadīth is unknown except from him, and no one other than him narrated it from ᶜUbayd, and ᶜUbayd himself is only known for this ḥadīth. A large group narrated from Sulaymān among whom were Shuᶜbah, al-Layth from ᶜAmr."

ᶜUbayd ibn Jurayj at-Taymī – their *mawlā* – the Madīnan, was one of the trustworthy narrators of the Followers, as al-Ḥāfiẓ ibn Ḥajar mentions.

ᶜUbaydullāh ibn ᶜAbdullāh ibn ᶜUmar was one of the notable Followers. He was a firmly established and trustworthy narrator. He died before his brother Sālim, as Ibn al-Athīr said.

ᶜUbaydullāh ibn ᶜAbdullāh ibn ᶜUtbah ibn Masᶜūd al-Hudhalī Abū ᶜAbdullāh, was one of the seven fuqahāʾ of Madīnah. He narrated from his father, Ibn ᶜAbbās, Ibn ᶜUmar and an-Nuᶜmān ibn Bashīr. From him narrated az-Zuhrī, Sālim Abu'n-Naḍr and a party of others. Abū Zurᶜah, al-ᶜIjlī and more than one regarded him as a trustworthy narrator. He died in 94 AH or 95 AH, but some say 98 AH. So it is found in *Isᶜāf al-mubaṭṭaʾ bi rijāl al-Muwaṭṭaʾ*.

ᶜUbaydullāh ibn ᶜUmar ibn Ḥafṣ ibn ᶜĀṣim ibn Amīr al-Muʾminīn ᶜUmar ibn al-Khattāb Abū ᶜUthmān al-ᶜUmarī al-ᶜAdawī, the Madīnan. He is one of the greatest of the trustworthy narrators. He narrated one ḥadīth from Umm Khālid bint Khālid the Companion and from al-Qāsim ibn Muḥammad ibn Abī Bakr aṣ-Ṣiddīq, Sālim ibn ᶜAbdullāh ibn ᶜUmar, ᶜAṭāʾ, Nāfiᶜ, al-Maqburī, az-Zuhrī and others. From him narrated Shuᶜbah, the two Sufyāns, Yaḥyā al-Qaṭṭān and others. An-Nasāʾī said he was a reliable trustworthy narrator. Abū Ḥātim said, "I asked Aḥmad about ᶜUbaydullāh, Mālik and Ayyūb, as to which of them was more firmly established in narrating from Nāfiᶜ, and he said, 'ᶜUbaydullāh is the one of them who memorised best and the most firmly established of them, and the one who narrated most.'" Aḥmad ibn Ṣāliḥ said, "ᶜUbaydullāh is preferrable to me to Mālik [in narrating] from Nāfiᶜ." He died in 147 AH in Madīnah. That is how adh-Dhahabī mentioned it in *Tadhkirat al-ḥuffāẓ*.

ᶜUbaydullāh al-Khawlānī was the foster son of Maymūnah and a trustworthy narrator. The two Shaykhs narrate from him as is mentioned by az-Zurqānī .

Ubayy ibn Kaᶜb ibn Qays al-Anṣārī an-Najjārī Abu'l-Mundhir. He was one of the eminent Companions and the chief of the Qurʾān reciters. He died in 29 AH or 32 AH, and people say other things [dates], as found in *at-Taqrīb.*

ᶜUmar ibn ᶜAbd al-ᶜAzīz was one of the Khulafāʾ ar-Rāshidūn. He was Abū Ḥafṣ ᶜUmar ibn ᶜAbd al-ᶜAzīz ibn Marwān ibn al-Ḥakam al-Umawī of Quraysh. He had such knowledge, doing without the [things of the] world (*zuhd*), taqwā, justice, abstinence, and good character, that there was no one like him in the days of his amirate. He was appointed khalīfah after Sulaymān ibn ᶜAbd al-Mālik ibn Marwān in 99 AH, and he died in 101 AH. He had numerous virtues, and is counted as one of the renewers of the dīn at the beginning of a century, as found in *Jāmiᶜ al-uṣūl*.

ᶜUmar ibn ᶜAbdullāh ibn Kaᶜb as-Salamī [ḥadīth 877]. So it appears in the copy on which al-Qārī and others wrote commentary but in the *Muwaṭṭa᾽* of Yaḥyā it is ᶜAmr. As-Suyūṭī said in *al-Isᶜāf,* "ᶜAmr ibn ᶜAbdullāh ibn Kaᶜb ibn Mālik al-Anṣārī as-Salamī narrated from Nāfiᶜ ibn Jubayr, and Yazīd ibn Khuṣayfah narrated from him. An-Nasā᾽ī regarded him as a trustworthy narrator."

ᶜUmar ibn Dharr al-Hamdānī. Dharr is spelt out thus by al-Fattanī in *al-Mughnī* and not Dhirr as al-Qārī mentioned. He was ibn ᶜAbdullāh ibn Zurārah al-Hamdānī by ascription to Hamdān a tribe which resided in Kūfa. As-Samᶜānī said, "One of the people of Kūfa. He narrated from ᶜAṭā᾽ and Mujāhid, and Wakīᶜ and the people of ᶜIrāq narrated from him. He died in 150 AH. Ibn Ḥibbān said he was one of the Murji᾽ah." It is stated in *at-Taqrīb,* "ᶜUmar ibn Dharr ibn ᶜAbdullāh ibn Zurārah al-Hamdānī al-Murhabī [the monastic], the Kūfan, Abū Dharr the trustworthy narrator who was accused of being one of the Murji᾽ah."

ᶜUmar ibn Ḥusayn was a trustworthy narrator from whom Muslim and at-Tirmidhī narrated. He was ᶜUmar ibn Ḥusayn ibn ᶜAbdullāh al-Jumaḥī – their *mawlā* – Abū Qudāmah al-Makkī, as stated in *at-Taqrīb.*

ᶜUmar ibn al-Khattāb is Abū Ḥafṣ ᶜUmar ibn al-Khattāb al-ᶜAdawī of Quraysh. He is one of "the ten" [promised the Garden], and one of the Khulafā᾽ ar-Rāshidūn. He was named al-Fārūq. He accepted Islam in the sixth year of prophethood, but some say the fifth year. Islam became public with his Islam. Ibn Masᶜūd said, "By Allah! I reckon that if the knowledge of ᶜUmar was put into one pan of the scales and the knowledge of all other people on the earth were to be put into another pan, the knowledge of ᶜUmar would be heavier." He has many merits, and was killed as a shahīd in Dhu'l-Ḥijjah 23 AH. From *Asmā᾽ rijāl al-mishkāh* by the author of the *Mishkāh.*

ᶜUmar ibn ᶜUthmān ibn ᶜAffān. Ibn ᶜAbd al-Barr said, "Thus Mālik said, but all the other companions of Ibn Shihāb say ᶜAmr ibn ᶜUthmān and Ibn Bukayr narrated it from Mālik with some doubt and said, 'From ᶜUmar ibn ᶜUthmān or ᶜAmr ibn ᶜUthmān.' Ibn al-Qāsim said about him, 'From ᶜAmr ibn ᶜUthmān.' But what is established from Mālik was that he was ᶜUmar, as Yaḥyā and all the other narrators narrated it. There is no disagreement that ᶜUthmān had a son called ᶜUmar and another called ᶜAmr, but the only disagreement is concerning whether this ḥadīth is from ᶜUmar or ᶜAmr. The companions of Ibn Shihāb apart from Mālik say that he is ᶜAmr ibn ᶜUthmān and Mālik says that he is ᶜUmar, and ash-Shāfiᶜī and Yaḥyā ibn Saᶜīd al-Qaṭṭān acquainted him with that and he refused to retract and said that he is ᶜUmar.

The truth is that Mālik is the one against whom others have to be measured in terms of memorisation and exact attention to detail, but no one is safe from making mistakes and the people of ḥadīth refuse anyone else in this chain of transmission than ᶜAmr." Al-ᶜIrāqī said, "It does not necessarily follow from the fact that Mālik alone among the trustworthy narrators narrates the name of this narrator thus, along with the fact that each of them is a trustworthy narrator, that the text [of the ḥadīth] should be rejected nor that it should be regarded as an extremely rare and divergent text, for on the contrary it is in any case sound, and the most extreme case is that this chain of transmission [of the ḥadīth] would be regarded as rejected or extremely rare and divergent because of trustworthy narrators' differing with Mālik about that."

ᶜUmārah ibn Ṣayyād was ᶜUmārah ibn ᶜAbdullāh ibn Ṣayyād al-Anṣārī Abū Ayyūb, the Madīnan, who was ascribed to his grandfather Ṣayyād. His father is the one about whom people said that he was the Dajjāl. Ibn Maᶜīn and an-Nasāʾī regarded him [ᶜUmārah] as a trustworthy narrator. He died after 130 AH, as stated in *Isᶜāf al-mubaṭṭaʾ* of as-Suyūṭī.

Umaymah bint Ruqayqah. Ruqayqah was the sister of Khadījah, the mother of the muʾminīn, bint Khuwaylid ibn Asad so that Khadījah was Umaymah's maternal aunt. Her father was Najād ibn ᶜAbdullāh ibn ᶜUmayr, but some say ᶜAbdullāh ibn Najād of Quraysh, as found in *al-Istīᶜāb* and elsewhere.

ᶜUmayr the *mawlā* of Ibn ᶜAbbās was Ibn ᶜAbdullāh al-Hilālī. An-Nasāʾī and Ibn Ḥibbān regarded him as a trustworthy narrator. He died in 104 AH, as stated in *al-Isᶜāf.*

ᶜUmayr ibn Saᶜd, but some say [ᶜUmayr ibn] Saᶜīd an-Nakhaᶜī aṣ-Ṣuhbānī by ascription to Ṣuhbān a clan of an-Nakhaᶜ. His kunyā was Abū Yaḥyā. He was a reliable and trustworthy narrator. He died in 107 AH but some say 115 AH. So it is found in *al-Ansāb* and *at-Taqrīb.*

Umm Bujayd is best known by her kunyā, and her name was Ḥawwāʾ bint Yazīd ibn as-Sakan.

Umm al-Faḍl was Lubābah bint al-Ḥārith al-Hilāliyyah, the sister of Maymūnah the mother of the muʾminūn, and the wife of al-ᶜAbbās ibn ᶜAbd al-Muṭṭalib. It is said that she was the first woman to accept Islam after Khadījah, as stated in *al-Istīᶜāb*.

Umm Ḥabībah the wife of the Prophet ﷺ and the daughter of Abū Sufyān. Her name was Ramlah, and there is no disagreement about that except from a few solitary individuals. She died in 44 AH, as stated in *Isᶜāf al-mubaṭṭaʾ* of as-Suyūṭī.

Umm Hāni' was the full sister [*shaqīqah*] of ᶜAlī, and their mother was Fāṭimah bint Asad, also the mother of Ṭālib, ᶜAqīl and Jaᶜfar. There is disagreement about her name, and some say Hind and some say Fākhitah. She was married to Hubayrah ibn Abī Wahb ibn ᶜAmr ibn ᶜĀ'idh ibn ᶜImrān ibn Makhzūm, and accepted Islam in the year of the Opening [of Makkah to Islam]. So it is found in *al-Istīᶜāb*.

Umm Kulthūm bint Abī Bakr was a Follower. Her father, Abū Bakr ﷺ died while she was yet unborn and she was born after his death. She narrated a ḥadīth as a *mursal* ḥadīth because of which Ibn Mandah and Ibn as-Sakan mentioned her among the Companions, but they made a mistake, as az-Zurqānī said.

Umm Qays is the sister of ᶜUkāshah. She became a Muslim very early on and emigrated to Madīnah. Her *mawlā*, ᶜAdī ibn Dīnār, narrated from her, as did Wābiṣah ibn Maᶜbad and others. So it is found in *al-Isᶜāf*. Az-Zurqānī said her name was Judhāmah, but some say it was Āminah.

Umm Salamah is Hind bint Abī Umayyah, whose name [Abū Umayyah's] was Ḥudhayfah ibn al-Mughīrah ibn ᶜAbdullāh. She was of Quraysh and [the clan] Makhzūm. The Messenger of Allah ﷺ married her right after the battle of Badr. She died in Shawwāl 62 AH as stated in *Isᶜāf al-mubaṭṭa'* of as-Suyūṭī. Before the Messenger of Allah ﷺ she was married to Abū Salamah ibn ᶜAbd to whom she bore ᶜUmar and Salamah, as mentioned in *al-Istīᶜāb*.

Umm Sulaym is Bint Milḥān ibn Khālid ibn Zayd ibn Ḥarām ibn Jundub of an-Najjār and the Anṣār. There is disagreement about her name and some said Sahlah, Rumaylah, Mulaykah, or al-Ghumayḍā'. She was married to Mālik ibn an-Naḍr the father of Anas ibn Mālik before Islam and she bore him Anas. When she accepted Islam, it was offered to her husband who grew enraged and died there and then. After him Abū Ṭalḥah al-Anṣārī married her to whom she bore ᶜAbdullāh ibn Abī Ṭalḥah. So it is found in *al-Istīᶜāb*. Mulaykah was the grandmother of Isḥāq ibn ᶜAbdullāh ibn Abī Ṭalḥah, Mālik says. The pronoun in "his grandmother" [ḥadīth 179] refers to Isḥāq and she was the mother of his father ᶜAbdullāh ibn Abī Ṭalḥah and is Umm Sulaym bint Milḥān wife of Abū Ṭalḥah al-Anṣārī. She was the mother of Anas ibn Mālik. She had been married to his father Mālik ibn an-Naḍr to whom she bore Anas ibn Mālik and al-Barā' ibn Mālik, and then later Abū Ṭalḥah married her, as Ibn ᶜAbd al-Barr said. Her name was Sahlah or Rumaylah, Rumaythah, Mulaykah, al-Ghumayḍā' or ar-Rumayṣā' (an eminent woman Companion who died during the khilāfah of ᶜUthmān, *Taqrīb at-tahdhīb* 2/622). She had been married to Mālik ibn Abi'n-Naḍr, the father of Anas, before Islam. When Allah brought Islam she accepted it along with her people, but when she offered it to her husband he grew enraged and died as a kāfir. Abū Ṭalḥah married her and she bore him a son who died in infancy, the aforementioned Abū ʿUmayr in the ḥadīth of an-Nughayr. Then she bore him ʿAbdullāh ibn Abī Ṭalḥah in whom he received blessing and who is the father of Isḥāq, who had ten brothers from each of whom knowledge was taken, as Ibn ʿAbd al-Barr mentioned in *al-Istiʿāb*. She was al-Ghumayṣāʾ, but some say ar-Rumayṣāʾ, Sahlah, Unayfā, Rumaythah, or Rumaylah. Her mother was Mulaykah bint Mālik, as found in *at-Tanwīr* (169 S). The Ḥāfiẓ said that she was Mulaykah.

Umm Sulaymān see ash-Shifāʾ.

An Umm Walad of Ibrāhīm ibn ʿAbd ar-Raḥmān ibn ʿAwf. The author of *al-Azhār* and *al-Ghawāmiḍ* transmitted that her name was Ḥamīdah. Az-Zurqānī said, "She was an acceptable but younger Follower." Ḥāfiẓ mentioned in *at-Taqrīb*, "Ḥamīdah [narrated] from Umm Salamah. It is said that she is the Umm Walad of Ibrāhīm. She is acceptable, of the fourth [generation]."

ʿUrwah ibn Udhaynah. [ʿUrwah's father's name] Udhaynah was an honorific and his name was Yaḥyā ibn Mālik ibn al-Ḥārith ibn ʿAmr al-Laythī. ʿUrwah was a poet of good love poetry. He was a trustworthy narrator, but he has only this one ḥadīth in the *Muwaṭṭaʾ*. His grandfather Mālik ibn al-Ḥārith has a narration from ʿAlī, as Ibn ʿAbd al-Barr and others mention.

ʿUrwah ibn az-Zubayr ibn al-ʿAwwām al-Asadī Abū ʿAbdullāh, the Madīnan. Ibn ʿUyaynah said, "There are three people who had the most knowledge of ʿĀʾishah's ḥadīth: al-Qāsim, ʿUrwah and ʿAmrah bint ʿAbd ar-Raḥmān." He narrated from his father and from his brother ʿAbdullāh, and from ʿAlī and his two sons, and ʿĀʾishah. From him narrated his sons ʿAbdullāh, Muḥammad, ʿUthmān and Hishām. He died in 94 AH. So it is found in *Isʿāf al-mubaṭṭaʾ* of as-Suyūṭī.

Usāmah the son of Zayd ibn Ḥārithah ibn Sharāḥīl al-Hāshimī the *mawlā* of the Messenger of Allah ﷺ. He had many virtues. The Prophet ﷺ said to ʿĀʾishah, "Love him because I love him," which at-Tirmidhī narrated. He appointed him the amīr of the army among whom were ʿUmar, and he himself tied the standard for him. He died in Madīnah or in the surrounding countryside of the villages in 54 AH, and some say other things, as an-Nawawī mentioned in *Tahdhīb al-asmāʾ waʾl-lughāt*

Usāmah ibn Zayd, the Madīnan. Adh-Dhahabī said in *Mīzān al-iʿtidāl*, "Usāmah ibn Zayd al-Laythī – their *mawlā* – the Madīnan, who [narrated] from Ṭāwūs and his generation. From him narrated Ibn Wahb, Zayd ibn al-Ḥubbāb, ᶜUbaydullāh ibn Mūsā. Aḥmad said, 'He is not anything,' upon which his son elaborated, saying, 'If you examine his ḥadīth, you will recognise things which are not acceptable.' Yaḥyā ibn Maᶜīn said he was a trustworthy narrator, but Yaḥyā al-Qaṭṭān used to regard him as weak. An-Nasā'ī said, 'He is not strong.' Ibn ᶜAdī said, 'There is no harm in him.' ᶜAbbās and Aḥmad ibn Abī Maryam narrated from Yaḥyā, 'A trustworthy narrator.' Ibn Abī Maryam added from him, 'A decisive proof.' Abū Ḥātim said, 'His ḥadīth are to be written down, but he is not to be used as a decisive proof.' He died in 153 AH." (Abridged) It is stated in *at-Taqrīb*, "He was an utterly truthful man who made mistakes." He has a long biographical note in *Tahdhīb at-tahdhīb*.

ᶜUthmān ibn Abi'l-ᶜĀṣ. The Prophet ﷺ appointed him as governor of Ṭā'if, and then later Abū Bakr and ᶜUmar both made him the amīr. He died in 51 AH, which is mentioned in *Asad al-ghābah fī maᶜrifat aṣ-ṣaḥābah* and elsewhere.

ᶜUthmān ibn ᶜAffān ibn Abi'l-ᶜĀṣ ibn Umayyah ibn ᶜAbd Shams ibn ᶜAbd Manāf al-Qurashī, Dhu'n-Nurayn – the Possessor of the Two Lights. He has a great quantity of virtues and was killed as a shahīd in Dhu'l-Ḥijjah 35 AH, as found in *at-Taqrīb* and *Jāmiᶜ al-uṣūl*. In *Isᶜāf al-mubaṭṭa'* of as-Suyūṭī it is said that he was killed on Jumuᶜah the 18th of Dhu'l-Ḥijjah 35 AH.

ᶜUthmān ibn Isḥāq ibn Kharashah was one of the Followers whom Ibn Maᶜīn regarded as a trustworthy narrator. He was of Quraysh and of [Banī] ᶜĀmir and a Madīnan, as mentioned in *at-Taqrīb*.

ᶜUwaymir ibn Ashqar ibn ᶜAwf al-Anṣārī. Some said he was Ibn Ashqar ibn ᶜAdī ibn Khansā' ibn Mabdhūl ibn ᶜAmr ibn Ghanam ibn Māzin ibn an-Najjār al-Anṣārī al-Māzinī. He was present at Badr, and ᶜAbbād ibn Tamīm al-Māzinī narrated from him as a *mursal* ḥadīth, as Ibn al-Athīr said in *Jāmiᶜ al-uṣūl*.

W

Wahb ibn Kaysān. He said in *al-Is^c^āf*, "Wahb ibn Kaysān of Quraysh their *mawlā*, Abū Nu^c^aym the Madīnan. An-Nasā^ʾ^ī and Ibn Sa^c^d regarded him as a trustworthy narrator. He died in 127 AH."

Wā^ʾ^il al-Ḥaḍramī by ascription to Ḥaḍramawt a land in the Yemen. Wā^ʾ^il ibn Ḥujr was a great king there. When news of the appearance of the Prophet ﷺ reached him he left his kingdom and set off to go to him. The Prophet ﷺ gave people the news of his arrival three days before he came, and when he came he drew him near to where he sat and said, "This is Wā^ʾ^il who has come to you from the land of the Yemen – a remote land – [and he has come] obediently without coercion desiring Allah and His Messenger. O Allah bless Wā^ʾ^il and his children." Then he granted him some land. He died during the amirate of Mu^c^āwiyah. His sons narrated from him: ^c^Alqamah and ^c^Abd al-Jabbār. So it is found in the *Ansāb as-Sam^c^ānī*. In the *Jāmi^c^ al-uṣūl* by Ibn al-Athīr it is stated, "Abū Hunaydah Wā^ʾ^il ibn Ḥujr ibn Rabī^c^ah ibn Wā^ʾ^il al-Ḥaḍramī was one of the princes and chiefs of Ḥaḍramawt and his father had been one of their kings. He came as a delegate to the Prophet ﷺ and accepted Islam, and he ﷺ gave people the news of his coming [beforehand]."

Al-Walīd ibn ^c^Abdullāh ibn Ṣayyād. He was the brother of ^c^Amārah ibn ^c^Abdullāh ibn Ṣayyād. Az-Zurqānī said, "Al-Bukhārī did not mention him in his *Tārīkh*, nor did Abū Ḥātim, and Ibn ^c^Abd al-Barr didn't write a biographical note for him, but Ibn Ḥibbān mentioned him in *ath-Thiqāt*, and Mālik's narration from him is sufficient evidence of his trustworthiness."

Wāqid ibn Sa^c^d ibn Mu^c^ādh al-Anṣārī was a trustworthy narrator from whom Muslim and the three transmitted. He died in 120 AH, as az-Zurqānī mentioned. Ibn ^c^Abd al-Barr said, "All the other narrators say 'from Wāqid ibn ^c^Amr ibn Sa^c^d ibn Mu^c^ādh.'"

Wāsi^c^ ibn Ḥabbān ibn Munqidh ibn ^c^Amr al-Anṣārī. Abū Zur^c^ah regarded him as a trustworthy narrator, as is in *Is^c^āf al-mubaṭṭa^ʾ^* of as-Suyūṭī.

The wife of ^c^Abdullāh ibn Mas^c^ūd from the tribe of Thaqīf [ḥadīth 789]. Her name was Zaynab bint ^c^Abdullāh ibn Mu^c^āwiyah ibn ^c^Attāb ibn al-As^c^ad ibn Ghāḍirah. She was a Companion who narrated from the Prophet ﷺ and from her husband. The son of her brother and Busr ibn Sa^c^īd narrated from her, as found in *al-Istī^c^āb* by Ibn ^c^Abd al-Barr.

Y

Yaḥyā ibn al-Jazzār [son of the butcher]. He said in *at-Taqrīb* and *al-Kāshif*, "Yaḥyā ibn al-Jazzār al-ᶜUranī, the Kūfan. It is said that the name of his father was Zabān. He narrated from ᶜAlī and ᶜĀʾishah, and from him narrated al-Ḥakam and al-Ḥasan al-ᶜUranī. He was a trustworthy narrator who was utterly truthful, but who was accused of being a fanatical Shīᶜah."

Yaḥyā ibn Muḥammad ibn Ṭaḥlāʾ was Madīnan from the tribe of Taym. He narrated from his father and ᶜUthmān. Mālik, ad-Darāwardī and others narrated from him. Ibn Ḥibbān mentions him among the trustworthy Followers. That is how az-Zurqānī mentions him. His father was ᶜAbd ar-Raḥmān ibn ᶜUthmān ibn ᶜUbaydullāh at-Taymī, the Madīnan, and he was one of the Companions. He was killed along with Ibn az-Zubayr. His son ᶜUthmān, who was of the fifth generation, is trustworthy. So it is found in *at-Taqrīb*.

Yaḥyā ibn Saᶜīd is the Shaykh al-Islām Abū Saᶜīd Yaḥyā ibn Saᶜīd ibn Qays ibn ᶜAmr al-Anṣārī, the Madīnan, the qāḍī of Madīnah. He narrated from Anas, ᶜAdī ibn Thābit, as-Sāʾib ibn Yazīd, Abū Umāmah, Saᶜīd ibn al-Musayyab, al-Qāsim ibn Muḥammad, ᶜAlī ibn al-Ḥusayn and others. From him narrated Abū Ḥanīfah, Shuᶜbah, Mālik, the two Sufyāns, the two Ḥammāds, Ibn al-Mubārak and a great number of other people. Ayyūb as-Sakhtiyānī said, "I left no one behind in Madīnah with more fiqh than him." Yaḥyā al-Qaṭṭān said, "He has precedence over az-Zuhrī." Abū Ḥātim said, "He is a trustworthy narrator, the equal of az-Zuhrī." Al-ᶜIjlī said, "An eminent faqīh and trustworthy narrator." He died in al-Hāshimiyyah in 143 AH. So it is found in *Tadhkirat al-ḥuffāẓ* by adh-Dhahabī. Ibn Saᶜd said, "He was a trustworthy narrator who had many ḥadīth, and he is a firmly established proof." He died in 143 AH. So it is found in *Isᶜāf al-mubaṭṭaʾ* of as-Suyūṭī.

Yaᶜqūb ibn Ibrāhīm is the Imām Abū Yūsuf the qāḍī and companion of Imām Abū Ḥanīfah. Adh-Dhahabī said in *Tadhkirat al-ḥuffāẓ*, "Qāḍī Abū Yūsuf, the faqīh of the ᶜIrāqis, Yaᶜqūb ibn Ibrāhīm al-Anṣārī, the Kūfan, was the companion of Abū Ḥanīfah. He heard Hishām ibn ᶜUrwah, Abū Isḥāq ash-Shaybānī, ᶜAṭāʾ ibn as-Sāʾib and people of their generation. From him narrated Muḥammad ibn al-Ḥasan the faqīh, Aḥmad ibn Ḥanbal, Bishr ibn al-Walīd and Yaḥyā ibn Maᶜīn. He grew up in the search for knowledge, but his father was a poor man and Abū Ḥanīfah paid frequent attention to him [probably maintaining him]. Al-Muznī said, 'Of all the people he is the one who most follows ḥadīth.' Yaḥyā ibn Maᶜīn said, 'There is no one among the people of theory (*raʾy*) who has more ḥadīth and is more firmly established than Abū Yūsuf.' Aḥmad said, 'He was fair and just in ḥadīth.' He died in Rabīc al-Ākhir 182 AH when he was 69 years old. There are many stories about him in knowledge and in leadership, and I have dedicated a volume to him and a volume to his companion Muḥammad ibn al-Ḥasan. His oldest shaykh was Ḥuṣayn ibn cAbd ar-Raḥmān." (Abridged). He has a long biographical note in *Ansāb as-Samcānī* which I have mentioned in the introduction to this commentary, just as I have also mentioned his biography in the *Muqaddimat al-Hidāyah* and in *an-Nāfic al-kabīr liman yuṭālicu al-jāmic aṣ-ṣaghīr* and in *al-Fawā'id al-bahiyyah fī tarājim al-ḥanafiyyah*.

Yacqūb ibn Zayd ibn Ṭalḥah of Quraysh and of Taym was an utterly truthful person and a Madīnan. His father Zayd [mistakenly written "Abū Zayd"] ibn Ṭalḥah was a minor Follower. Al-Ḥākim thought that he was a Companion, but it is not like that, as al-Ḥāfiẓ expanded upon in *al-Iṣābah.* His grandfather was cAbdullāh [an addition here is "ibn cUbaydullāh" which seems to be mistaken] ibn Abī Mulaykah, and it is said that his name [Abū Mulaykah's] was Zuhayr at-Taymī the Madīnan, a trustworthy narrator of the Followers. He died in 117 AH, as az-Zurqānī said.

Yacqūb the Madīnan and *mawlā* of al-Ḥuraqah is acceptable. His son was cAbd ar-Raḥmān al-Ḥuraqī – by ascription to Ḥuraqah, a clan of Hamdān, but some say of Juhaynah, which is the correct position. cAbd ar-Rahman's son was Abū Shibl al-cAlā' the *mawlā* of al-Ḥuruqah who died in 132 AH. Ibn Ḥibbān mentioned both of them in *ath-Thiqāt* as found in *at-Taqrīb* and *al-Ansāb.*

Yarfā' the door-keeper or chamberlain of cUmar had lived in the Jāhiliyyah, and he performed the Ḥajj with cUmar in the khilāfah of Abū Bakr. He is mentioned in the two *ṣaḥīḥ* books concerning the story of the quarrel between cAlī and cAbbās over the ṣadaqah of the Messenger of Allah ﷺ as az-Zurqānī said.

Yasār ibn Numayr. Al-Ḥāfiẓ said in *at-Taqrīb,* "Yasār ibn Numayr, the Madīnan, was the *mawlā* of cUmar ibn al-Khattāb. He was a trustworthy narrator and went to live in Kūfa."

Yazīd ibn cAbdullāh ibn Qusayṭ. He said in *at-Taqrīb,* "Yazīd ibn cAbdullāh ibn Qusayṭ ibn Usāmah al-Laythī Abū cAbdullāh, the Madīnan al-Acraj is a trustworthy narrator. He died in 122 AH."

Yazīd ibn cAbdullāh ibn Usāmah ibn al-Hād al-Laythī, the Madīnan. Ibn Macīn and an-Nasā'ī regarded him as a trustworthy narrator. He died in 139 AH, as found in *al-Iscāf*.

Yazīd ibn Jāriyah al-Anṣārī al-Awsī was the father of ᶜAbd ar-Raḥmān and Mujammiᶜ. Ibn Saᶜd mentions him as one of the Companions, and az-Zurqānī said the same. Ibn ᶜAbd al-Barr said in *al-Istīᶜāb,* "Yazīd ibn Ḥārithah (Ḥārithah and Jāriyah are identical if the letters are not marked with the diacriticals) al-Yarbūᶜī ibn ᶜĀmir ibn Mujammiᶜ ibn al-ᶜAṭāf, and he is Abū Mujammiᶜ."

Yazīd ibn Khuṣayfah was Yazīd ibn ᶜAbdullāh ibn Khuṣayfah ibn ᶜAbdullāh ibn Yazīd al-Kindī the Madīnan, and he was a trustworthy narrator from among the narrators used by everyone [of the major transmitters]. He is sometimes ascribed to his grandfather Khuṣayfah [as Ibn Khuṣayfah] as is mentioned in *at-Taqrīb* and others.

Yazīd ibn Nuᶜaym ibn Hazzāl was a minor Follower, as Ibn al-Athīr mentioned in *Asad al-ghābah fi maᶜrifat aṣ-ṣaḥābah* and *Jāmiᶜ al-uṣūl.*

Yazīd ibn Ṭalḥah ar-Rukānī – by ascription to Rukānah the father of Ṭalḥah – ibn ᶜAbd Yazīd ibn Hāshim. Ibn Ḥibbān mentioned this Yazīd in *Thiqāt at-tābiᶜīn* as found in *Sharḥ az-Zurqānī* .

Yazīd ibn Ziyād. Ibn Ḥajar said in *Taqrīb at-tahdhīb,* "Yazīd ibn Ziyād or ibn Abī Ziyād is probably ascribed to his grandfather [Ziyād], and is a *mawlā* of Banī Makhzūm and a Madīnan. He was trustworthy."

Yazīd ar-Raqāshī [ḥadīth 63 in which some have said that Saᶜīd ar-Raqāshī is a mistake for this Yazīd]. Adh-Dhahabī said in *al-Kāshif* in introducing him, "Yazīd ibn Abān ar-Raqāshī the worshipper narrated from Anas and al-Ḥasan, and from him narrated Ṣāliḥ al-Murrī and Ḥammād ibn Salamah, but he is weak." He mentioned in *Tahdhīb at-tahdhīb* in discussing ar-Rabīᶜ, "Yazīd ar-Raqāshī was one of his shaykhs," and in it there is no mention of [the name] Saᶜīd.

Yūnus ibn Abī Isḥāq as-Sabīᶜī. His kunyā was Abū Isrāʾīl and he narrated from his father Abū Isḥāq. He died in 159 AH. It is stated in *at-Taqrīb,* "Yūnus ibn Abī Isḥāq as-Sabīᶜī Abū Isrāʾīl the Kūfan was utterly truthful and made only a few mistakes. He died in 152 AH, according to the correct view."

Yūnus ibn Yūsuf ibn Ḥimās was one of the devotees of the People of Madīnah, and he was a trustworthy narrator. Ibn Ḥibbān said, "He is Yūsuf ibn Yūnus, and those who reverse the order [of these two names] have made a mistake," as mentioned in *at-Taqrīb*.

Z

Az-Zabīr ibn ᶜAbd ar-Raḥmān ibn az-Zabīr ibn Bāṭiyā al-Quraẓī, the Madīnan. The name in both cases is spelt Zabir according to all narrators of the *Muwaṭṭa*ᵓ except for Ibn Bakīr who narrated it as az-Zubayr in the first case and az-Zabīr in the second. Ibn ᶜAbd al-Barr said, "The correct position is that both are az-Zabīr, i.e. from Mālik." Ibn Ḥajar said in *al-Iṣābah,* "He is az-Zubayr as opposed to his grandfather who is az-Zabīr."

Zabrāᵓ, a mawlāh of Banī ᶜAdī ibn Kaᶜb. It is spelt thus according to Ibn al-Athīr.

Zayd Abū ᶜAyyāsh the *mawlā* of Banī Zuhrah. Abū Ḥanīfah regarded the ḥadīth [764] as defective because of him and he said, "It is based on Zayd Abū ᶜAyyāsh and he is unknown." Ibn Ḥazm said the same, but others replied that the ḥadīth is *ṣaḥīḥ* and that Zayd is not an unknown person. Az-Zurqānī said, "Zayd's kunyā was Abū ᶜAyyāsh and his father's name was ᶜAyyāsh and he was a Madīnan Follower who was utterly truthful. It is transmitted from Mālik that he was the *mawlā* of Saᶜd ibn Abī Waqqāṣ and some say that he was the *mawlā* of Banī Makhzūm." It is stated in the *Tahdhīb at-tahdhīb* by Ibn Ḥajar al-ᶜAsqalānī, "Zayd ibn ᶜAyyāsh Abū ᶜAyyāsh az-Zuraqī, but some say al-Makhzūmī. He narrated from Saᶜd, and from him narrated ᶜAbdullāh ibn Yazīd and ᶜImrān ibn Abī Unays. Ibn Ḥibbān mentioned him in *ath-Thiqāt,* and at-Tirmidhī, Ibn Khuzaymah and Ibn Ḥibbān declare the aforementioned ḥadīth [764] of his to be *ṣaḥīḥ*. Ad-Dāraquṭnī said he was a trustworthy narrator, and al-Ḥākim said in *al-Mustadrak,* 'This is a *ṣaḥīḥ* ḥadīth because of the unanimous agreement of the imāms of transmission on the imāmate of Mālik and that he is completely reliable in everything which he narrates since only the *ṣaḥīḥ* exists in his narrations, particularly as regards narration from the People of Madīnah. The two shaykhs did not narrate it since they feared the unknown character of Zayd.'" There is in *Fatḥ al-qadīr sharḥ al-Hidāyah,* "The author of *at-Tanqīḥ* said, 'There is no harm in Zayd ibn ᶜAyyāsh Abū ᶜAyyāsh az-Zuraqī, the Madīnan. Our shaykhs mention from Abū Ḥanīfah that he is unknown, but this aspersion is refuted by saying that he is a trustworthy narrator and that Mālik narrated from him in the *Muwaṭṭa*ᵓ, and that he did not narrate from an unknown person. Al-Mundhirī said, 'How could he be unknown when two trustworthy narrators have narrated from him: ᶜAbdullāh ibn Yazīd and ᶜImrān ibn Abī Unays? They are both people whom Muslim used as proofs in his *Ṣaḥīḥ* and the imāms of this field recognise it. Mālik narrated his ḥadīth even though he took extraordinary precautions about his narrators.' Ibn al-Jawzī said in *at-Taḥqīq,* 'Abū Ḥanīfah said that he was unknown, but even if he did not know him the imāms of transmission knew him.'" In *Ghāyat al-bayān sharḥ al-Hidāyah,* "They transmit the ascription of weakness to him from Abū Ḥanīfah, but that ascription of weakness is not correct according to the books of ḥadīth. Whoever claims that is duty bound to explain himself." In *al-Bināyah* by al-ʿAynī at the mention of the author of *al-Hidāyah* that Zayd ibn ʿAyyāsh is weak according to the transmitters it is stated, "This is not correct. On the contrary, he is a trustworthy narrator according to ḥadīth transmitters." In *at-Talkhīṣ al-ḥabīr,* "A group, among whom are aṭ-Ṭaḥāwī, aṭ-Ṭabarī, Ibn Ḥazm and ʿAbd al-Haqq, regard this ḥadīth as defective because of the unknown character of Zayd, but the answer is that ad-Dāraquṭnī said, 'He is a firmly established trustworthy narrator,' and al-Mundhir said, 'Two trustworthy narrators transmitted from him and Mālik relied upon him along with the fact that he took extraordinary precautions [about his narrators]. At-Tirmidhī and al-Ḥākim declared it to be *ṣaḥīḥ,* and he said, "I do not know anyone who cast aspersions on him."'" In general the accusation that he is unknown has been completely removed from Zayd, both the fact that he himself is unknown or that his character is unknown, both of them by specific statements by the critical scholars of ḥadīth.

Zayd ibn Aslam Abū Usāmah, but some say Abū ʿAbdullāh, was Zayd ibn Aslam al-ʿAdawī the Madīnan, the faqīh, who was the *mawlā* of Madīnah. Aḥmad, Abū Zurʿah, Abū Ḥātim, Muḥammad ibn Saʿd, an-Nasāʾī and Ibn Kharāsh said that he was a trustworthy narrator. Yaʿqūb ibn Shaybah said, "He was a trustworthy narrator of the people of fiqh and knowledge, and he had knowledge of commentary [of the Qurʾān]." He died in 136 AH, but some people say something else. So it is found in *Tahdhīb at-tahdhīb* and it is similar in *Isʿāf al-mubaṭṭaʾ* of as-Suyūṭī.

Zayd ibn Khālid al-Juhanī is Abū ʿAbd ar-Raḥmān the Madīnan, but some say Abū Ṭalḥah or Abū Zurʿah. He was the man responsible for the banner of Juhaynah on the day of the Opening [of Makkah to Islam]. He died in 78 AH in Madīnah, but some say 68 AH and others say 50 AH, in Egypt, but some say in Kūfa at the end of the khilāfah of Muʿāwiyah, as stated in *Isʿāf al-mubaṭṭaʾ* of as-Suyūṭī.

Zayd ibn Ṭalḥah was a minor Follower. Al-Ḥākim thought that he was a Companion, but it is not like that, as al-Ḥāfiẓ expanded upon in *al-Iṣābah.*

Zayd ibn Thābit. His honorific was Abū Saʿīd, but some say Abū Khārijah. He was an-Najjārī and Madīnan. He was the scribe of the revelation and one of those who collected all of the Qurʾān during the lifetime of the Messenger of Allah ﷺ. He died in 45 AH, but some say in 48 AH and others 51 AH, as found in *al-Isᶜāf*. He was one of those "firmly rooted in knowledge" [see Qurʾān, Sūrah Āl ᶜImrān: 7].

Zaynab was the eldest of the daughters of the Messenger of Allah ﷺ. She accepted Islam and emigrated when her husband refused to accept Islam. She died in the lifetime of the Messenger of Allah ﷺ in 8 AH, as mentioned in *al-Istīᶜāb*.

Zaynab bint Abī Salamah is the step-daughter of the Prophet ﷺ. Her mother was Umm Salamah, the mother of the believers, and her father was Abū Salamah ᶜAbdullāh ibn Asad al-Makhzūmī the Companion, as mentioned in *al-Istīᶜāb* and elsewhere.

Zaynab bint Kaᶜb ibn ᶜUjrah was the wife of Abū Saᶜīd al-Khudrī. Ibn Ḥibbān regarded her as a trustworthy narrator, as as-Suyūṭī said in *al-Isᶜāf*.

Az-Zuhrī. See Ibn Shihāb az-Zuhrī.

Zurārah – as he spelt it in *al-Mughnī* – Ibn Abī Awfā, and it is thus in some copies. However, in many of the edited copies it is Ibn Awfā. He mentioned in *at-Tahdhīb* and elsewhere that he was Zurārah ibn Awfā al-ᶜĀmirī Abū Ḥājib the Baṣran. An-Nasāʾī, Al-ᶜIjlī, Ibn Ḥibbān and others declared him a trustworthy narrator. He died in 93 AH according to what Ibn Saᶜd said, but others have said otherwise.

NOTES TO THE *RIJĀL*

[1] Shaykh Zakariyya expanded on this at some length in *al-Awjuz* 12/179 when he said, "And that which the author of *at-Taᶜlīq al-Mumajjad* mentions about his biographical notice confuses him with the biographical notice of his grandfather's brother, because the appointee of ᶜUmar died in 88 AH and is ᶜAbd ar-Raḥmān al-Qāriyy, and Imām Malik's birth took place after his death, so how could he narrate from him? On the contrary ᶜAbdullāh ibn ᶜAbdin al-Qāriyy is the brother of ᶜAbd ar-Raḥmān, and this ᶜAbd ar-Raḥmān had been ᶜUmar's appointee ﷺ and the grandfather of Yaᶜqūb ibn ᶜAbd ar-Raḥmān ibn Muḥammad ibn ᶜAbdullāh ibn ᶜAbdin al-Qāriyy, from whom Mālik narrated in the *Muwaṭṭa*ᵓ. Similarly, ᶜAbd ar-Raḥmān ibn Muḥammad is the one from whom Mālik narrated in this ḥadīth."

[2] Aḥmad ibn Mihrān an-Nasawī a companion of Imām Muḥammad who narrated the *Muwaṭṭa*ᵓtfrom him according to Dr Taqī ad-Dīn an-Nadwī.

[3] The *Murjiᵓah* are the dialectical opposite of the Khawārij. They are noted for taking a lax position on points of ᶜaqīdah on which the Khawārij were severe.

[4] He is Bishr ibn Mūsā al-Asadī according to Dr Taqī ad-Dīn an-Nadwī.

[5] It is not clear if he was of the Ḥanafī *madhhab* or from the tribe of Banī Ḥanīfah.

[6] If he was the grandfather, then he must have been the maternal grandfather, because his paternal grandfather was ᶜAmr ibn Ḥarām ibn ᶜAmr. The *Muwaṭṭa*ᵓ of Yaḥyā has simply Jābir ibn ᶜAbdullāh. He himself could have been named al-Ḥarāmī because of his great grandfather, and Allah knows best.

[7] ᶜAbdullāh ibn Sabaᵓ was a notorious extreme shīᶜah from a jewish background.

[8] I can make no sense of this passage: فلم يصنع شيأً ولا علم منه ما علم غيره

[9] Mawlā means the slave who has been set free. However, both the ex-owner and the ex-slave are the mawlā of each other. The walāᵓ relationship includes the ex-owner inheriting from his ex-slave, and his commitment to paying compensatory payments for injuries caused others or in cases of manslaughter.

[10] Text has mistakenly, "He died."

[11] This ḥadīth is not a narration of Muḥammad ibn al-Ḥasan and is not to be found in authentic copies.... It is a ḥadīth that is only to be found in a copy of Abū ᶜAlī aṣ-Ṣawwāf which has been entered into the text by mistake by some copyists. This Abū ᶜAlī is not a shaykh of the author's, but rather he is aṣ-Ṣawwāf, Muḥammad ibn Aḥmad ibn al-Ḥasan aṣ-Ṣawwāf who is a narrator from the fourth century whose shaykh was al-Marwazī whose biography is in *Tārīkh Baghdād* by al-Khaṭīb.

BIBLIOGRAPHY

Bewley, Abdalhaqq and Aisha, *The Noble Qur'an, a new rendering of its meanings in English,* Bookwork, Norwich UK. 1420 AH/1999CE. This has been used throughout in our translation of the *Muwaṭṭa*ʾ.

Bewley, Aisha, *A Glossary of Islamic Terms*. Ta-Ha, London, UK.

Dutton, Yasin, *The Origins of Islamic Law: The Qurʾān, the Muwaṭṭaʾ, and Madīnan ᶜAmal,* Curzon Press, Surrey, 1999.

Ibn al-Athīr, Imām Majd ad-Dīn, *an-Nihāyah fī gharīb al-ḥadīth wa'l-athar,* Cairo 1965. Text from http://www.muhaddith.org.

Ibn Saᶜd, *aṭ-Ṭabaqāt al-kubrā,* partially translated and published in English as *The Men of Madinah Vols. I & II,* and *The Women of Madinah,* by Aisha Bewley, Ta-Ha Publishing Ltd., London. 1995.

al-Laknawī, ᶜAbd al-Ḥayy, *at-Taᶜlīq al-mumajjad li Muwaṭṭaʾ al-Imām Muḥammad* edited by Dr. Taqī ad-Dīn an-Nadwī, Dār al-Qalam, Damascus, first edition 1413 AH/1991 CE. Use was also made of the text from http://www.muhaddith.org.

Lane, E.W., *Arabic-English Lexicon,* The Islamic Texts Society, Cambridge, England, 1984.

Mālik ibn Anas, Imām, *al-Muwaṭṭaʾ* in the narration of Yaḥyā ibn Yaḥyā al-Laythī. Translated by Aisha Bewley and Yacoub Johnson. Madinah Press, Norwich, 1982.

al-Mālikī al-Ḥasanī, Muḥammad ibn ᶜAlawī, *Anwār al-masālik ilā riwāyāt Muwaṭṭaʾ Mālik*. Doha, Qatar. Muḥarram 1400 AH.

as-Sufi, Shaykh Dr. Abdalqadir, *Root Islamic Education,* Madīnah Press.

as-Suyūṭī, Jalāl ad-Dīn, *Isᶜāf al-Mubaṭṭaʾ bi rijāl al-Muwaṭṭaʾ*, Dār Iḥyāʾ al-Kutub al-ᶜArabiyyah, Egypt.

Zakariyya, Shaykh Muḥammad, *Awjaz al-Masālik ilā Muwaṭṭāʾ Mālik.* Dār al Fikr, Beirut, Lebanon. 1980.

GLOSSARY OF TERMS

adhān	the call to prayer
ʿiddah	the period when the divorced or widowed woman waits before being eligible for remarriage.
fuqahāʾ	the people knowledgeable in fiqh.
ghusl	the complete washing of the body.
hady	the offering of a sacrificial animal in Makkah.
īlāʾ	a man's swearing an oath to abstain from sexual intercourse with his wife.
īmān	acceptance of, trust in and affirmation of Allah, His Messengers, His Books, His angels, the Last Day and that the Decree of good and evil is from Him.
iqāmah	the second call to prayer done in the mosque prior to the prayer.
isnād	the chain of transmission of a ḥadīth.
izār	the wrapper of material around the lower half of the body, as in the sarong.
janābah	being in the condition of needing a *ghusl* after sexual intercourse or a nocturnal emmission.
jihād	striving and fighting to see that the Word of Allah is uppermost.
jizyah	the tax paid by People of the Book who agree to live under Muslim governance.
junub	someone who is in a condition of *janābah*.
khuṭbah	an address, as that given on the day of Jumuʿah or an ʿĪd.
liʿān	the procedure outlined in Sūrat an-Nūr in which a couple one of whom accuses the other of adultery enter into a process involving laying curses on themselves if they are lying.
mawlā	a freed slave and also someone affiliated to a tribe.
maḥram	someone ineligible to marry a woman under any circumstances who may legitimately accompany her, e.g. a father, brother etc.

muʾadhdhin	the person who calls people to prayer with the *adhān.*
mudabbar	a slave who is to be set free on the death of his master.
mukātab	a slave who writes a contract to purchase his freedom.
muʾmin	a person who has *īmān.*
qiblah	the direction of Makkah faced in the prayer.
rakᶜah	a complete unit of prayer comprising standing reciting Qurʾān, bowing, standing again, and prostrating twice.
shahīd	literally a witness, i.e. someone who dies in the way of Allah.
shahādah	witnessing, and in particular both witnessing and bearing witness that there is no god but Allah and that Muḥammad is the Messenger of Allah ﷺ. Also dying in the way of Allah as a witness.
ṣadaqah	sometimes refers to *zakāh* and sometimes to optional extra acts of giving, and even sometimes to expiatory acts of generosity.
ṣalāh	the prayer.
tashahhud	the prayer repeated in the last seated part of the *ṣalāh.*
tayammum	the purification with dry earth preparatory for the prayer done in place of *wuḍūʾ* when the latter is not possible.
walāʾ	the relationship between the freed slave (*mawlā*) and his former master which includes the latter's inheritance from the former in case of his death.
wuḍūʾ	the washing done preparatory for the prayer or for reciting Qurʾān from a textual copy.

INDEXES

Guide to the Indexes

This edition of the *Muwaṭṭa'* of Imām Muḥammad ibn al-Ḥasan ash-Shaybāni contains three indexes. The Index of Introductions and the Science of Invalidation and Authentication is an index of the material contained in the introduction of Shaykh ʿAbd al-Ḥayy al-Laknawī, the introduction to the *Rijāl* and the section on the Science of the Invalidation and Authentication of Ḥadīth. The Index of the Verdicts and Practices of the Companions and Early Muslims gathers together ḥadīth that mention the verdicts, practices and sayings of the Companions and the verdicts of the early Muslims as cited by Imām Mālik and Imām Muḥammad ibn al-Ḥasan ash-Shaybānī. The General Index contains a detailed listing of the subjects and topics covered in the main body of the *Muwaṭṭa'*.

Ḥadīth Locators

Each ḥadīth is referenced with a ternary locator, of which the first part identifies the chapter containing the ḥadīth, the second part identifies the section number, and the final part identifies the ḥadīth itself. For example ḥadīth 1.43.165 refers to ḥadīth 165 in section 43 of chapter 1. Where a selection of ḥadīth refer to the same subject, ḥadīth ranges are used, for example the locator 1.43.165-7 refers to ḥadīths 165, 166 and 167 in section 43 of chapter 1.

Index of Introductions
and the Science of Invalidation and Authentication

T

U

V

W

Y

Z

Index of the Verdicts and Practices of the Companions and the Early Muslims

A

Abān ibn ʿAffān
  on liability agreements, 14.23.795
  position on the inheritance of freed slaves, 12.4.730
ʿAbd al-Mālik ibn Marwān
  letter from ʿAbdullāh ibn ʿUmar, 17.21.899
  on punishment for rape, 11.3.701
  on slaves with contracts to buy their freedom, 16.2.856
  use of oath along with witness, 15.11.844
ʿAbd ar-Raḥmān ibn ʿAwf
  divorce of wife during terminal illness of, 7.12.574
ʿAbd ar-Raḥmān ibn Abī Bakr, marriage of, 7.9.567
ʿAbd ar-Raḥmān ibn az-Zabīr, 7.16.581
ʿAbdullāh ibn ʿAbbās
  on the causes of calamities and misfortunes, 17.0.861
  on compensation for injuring the teeth, 9.4.667
  on divorce before consummation of marriage, 7.15.580
  on divorce by abstaining from intercourse, 7.14.579
  on the expiation of oaths, 13.2.743, 13.6.751
  on the greeting of *salām*, 17.30.913
  on the guardian using the orphan's property, 17.43.937
  on hunting game with dogs, 8.16.657
  on meat slaughtered by christians, 8.12.653
  night prayer of, 1.46.171
  position on making up missed fasts, 4.9.361
  position on selling goods before taking possession of them, 14.5.766
  position on the grandfather's share of inheritance, 12.0.721
  position on marriage while in *iḥrām*, 5.22.437
  position on verses of prostration in Surāt al-Ḥajj, 1.80.270
  position on washing hair while in *iḥrām*, 5.15.419
  practice of sufficing with *wuḍū'* before Jumuʿah on a cold day, 1.17.65
  sūrahs recited in the *Maghrib* prayer, 1.74.246
  tafsīr of verse on *dulūk* of sun, 17.60.1006
  talbiyah of, 5.4.390
  on touching the private parts, 1.5.14-15, 1.5.17
  on unmarriageability because of breast-feeding, 7.31.618, 7.31.621
  on which of two slaves to set free, 15.8.839
  on a woman remarrying her former husband, 7.8.565
  Witr prayer of, 1.77.256, 1.79.258, 1.79.263
ʿAbdullāh ibn ʿĀmir
  on looking at another's private parts, 17.44.939
  Witr prayer of, 1.77.253
  on *wuḍū'* after eating cooked food, 1.6.33

B

D

F

H

I

Y

Z

General Index of the Muwatta

A

B

C

D

E

F

G

H

I

J

K

L

zakāh on camels, 3.2.324
zakāh on cows, 3.10.339
See also animals; agriculture.
lizards, 8.7.644-7
locusts
killing and eating while in *iḥrām*, 5.24.444-5
permissibility of, 8.11.652
lost property
announcing, 16.0.849-50
stray camels, 16.0.848, 16.0.850-1
love of Allah and His Messenger, 17.38.929
lying, 17.19.894-6, 17.55.955

M

madhy. *See* prostatic fluid.
Madīnah
non-Muslims entering, prohibition on, 17.8.872-3
superiority of, 17.17.890
visiting the grave of the Prophet, 17.49.947
Maghrib prayer
combining with *ʿIshāʾ*, 1.59.202-5, 5.47.487-9
prohibition of repeating, 1.62.218-9
recitation of Ibn ʿUmar in, 1.37.134
recommended sūrahs for, 1.74.246-7
time of, 1.1.1, 17.60.1005-6
voluntary prayers after, 1.98.295
as Witr of daytime prayers, 1.75.249
Magians, taking *jizyah* from, 3.7.333
magic, spell cast against ʿĀʾishah, 15.9.841
maḥram. *See* unmarriageable relatives.
maintenance in divorce, 7.21.587. *See also* divorce
Makkah
departing from, 5.68.515-6
entering without *iḥrām*, 5.31.459
ghusl performing before entering, 5.37.471-2
non-Muslims entering, prohibition on, 17.8.872-3
opening [to Islam] of, 5.73.522
manslaughter, compensation for, 9.3.666
markets
greeting people in, 17.30.910-1
forestalling goods, prohibition of, 14.9.771
price regulation, 14.19.788
marriage
after having fornicated, 17.60.1003
betrothed woman, prohibition of proposing to, 6.4.527
consent of the bride, 6.5.528, 6.12.539-40
dowry (*See* under dowry)
husband's right over his wife, 17.51.951
in which man is impotent, 6.11.537-8
man with four wives marrying again, 6.6.529-30
prohibited by breast-feeding, 7.31.614-27
remarrying a former husband, 7.8.565
remarrying a former wife, 7.16.581
secret, invalidity of, 6.9.533
showing preference to one wife over the other, 7.19.585
shighār marriage, prohibition of, 6.8.532
spending equal amounts of time with each wife, 6.1.523
temporary, 7.18.583-4
wedding invitations, accepting, 17.16.885-6
while in *iḥrām*, 5.22.435-7
without a guardian, 6.13.541
witnesses required for valid, 6.9.533-4
a woman converting to Islam before husband, 7.27.601
woman in *ʿiddah*, making allusions to, 17.60.1004

N

O

P

Q

R

S

T

U

V

W

Y

Z